The
GREAT
BRITAIN
GUIDE

The ultimate getaway guide to all the best-loved areas of Britain

Publishing Manager: David Watchus
Managing Editor: Isla Love
Project Editor: Sheila Hawkins
Additional writing and introduction by Terry Marsh
Senior Designers: Kat Mead and Alison Fenton
Page Layout: Andrew Milne Design and Kat Mead
Picture Research: Alice Earle
Cartographic Editor: Jenny Wood of Skelley Cartographic Services
Cartographic Production: AA Mapping Services
Copy Editor: Marilynne Lanng
Proofreaders: Suzanne Juby and Marilynne Lanng
Image retouching and repro: Michael Moody
Print Buyer: Helen Brown
Index: Marie Lorimer

Produced by AA Publishing
© AA Media Limited 2007
Reprinted January and April 2010

Published by AA Publishing (a trading name of AA Media Limited, whose registered office is Fanum House, Basing View, Basingstoke, Hampshire RG21 4EA; registered number 06112600).

 This product includes mapping data licensed from the Ordnance Survey® with the permission of the Controller of Her Majesty's Stationery Office.
© Crown copyright 2010. All rights reserved. Licence number 100021153.

A04419

ISBN: 978-0-7495-6607-4
ISBN: 978-0-7495-6608-1 (SS)

A CIP catalogue record for this book is available from the British Library.

The contents of this book are believed to be correct at the time of printing. Nevertheless, the publishers cannot be held responsible for any errors or omissions or for changes in the details given in this book or for the consequences of any reliance on the information it provides. We have tried to ensure accuracy in this book, but things do change and we would be grateful if readers would advise us of any inaccuracies they may encounter. This does not affect your statutory rights.

We have taken all reasonable steps to ensure that the walks and cycle rides in this book are safe and achievable by people with a realistic level of fitness. However, all outdoor activities involve a degree of risk and the publishers accept no responsibility for any injuries caused to readers whilst following these walks and cycle rides. For advice on walking and cycling in safety, see the walking and cycling in safety pages. Some of the walks and cycle rides may appear in other AA books and publications.

Visit AA Publishing at theAA.com/shop

Colour reproduction by Keene Group, Andover
Printed in China by Leo Paper Group

Title page images:
Opposite Pooley Bridge Boathouse, Ullswater, Lake District
Previous Devil's Dyke, Fulking, West Sussex

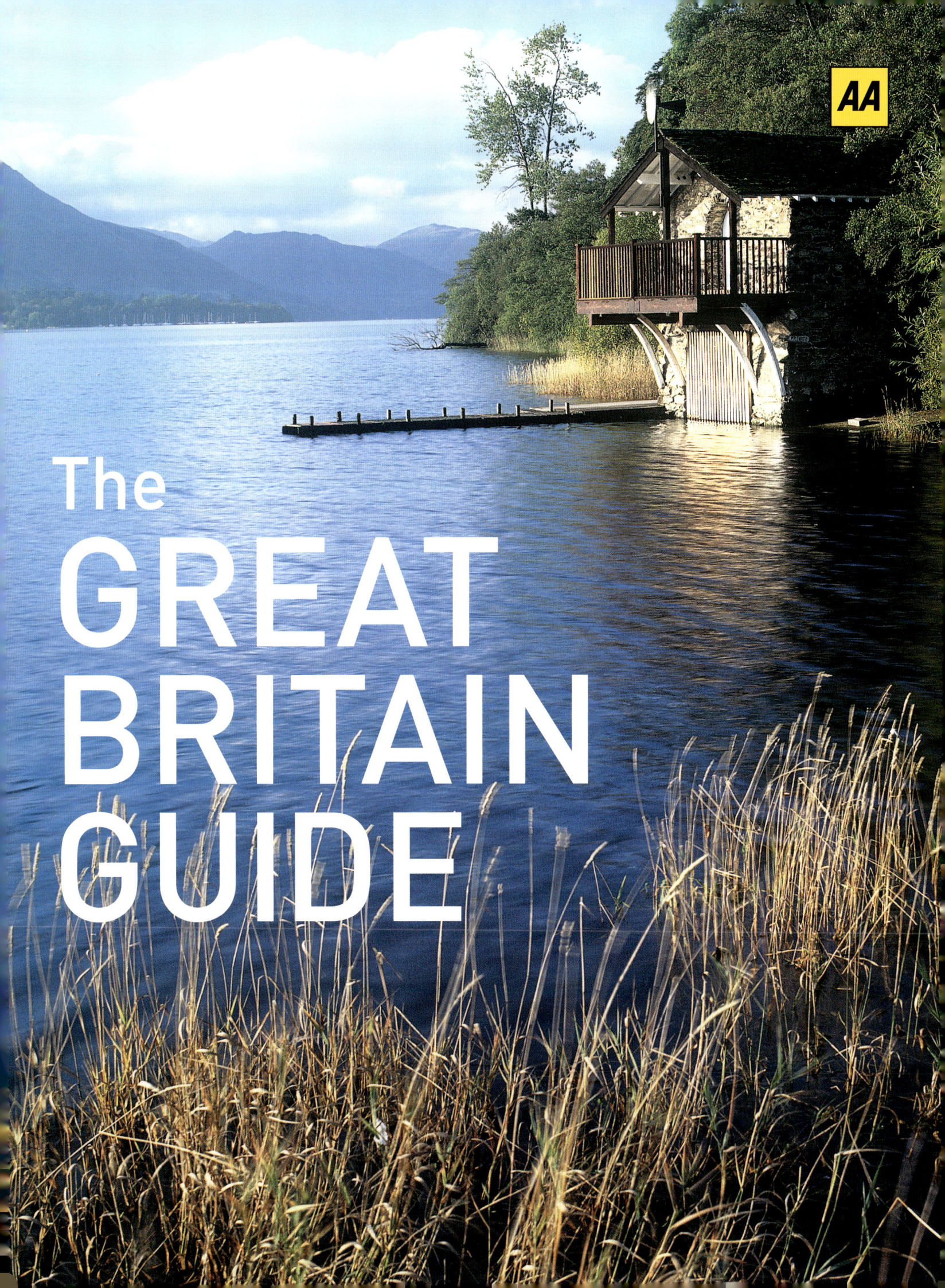

The

GREAT BRITAIN GUIDE

CONTENTS

URQUHART CASTLE ON LOCH NESS

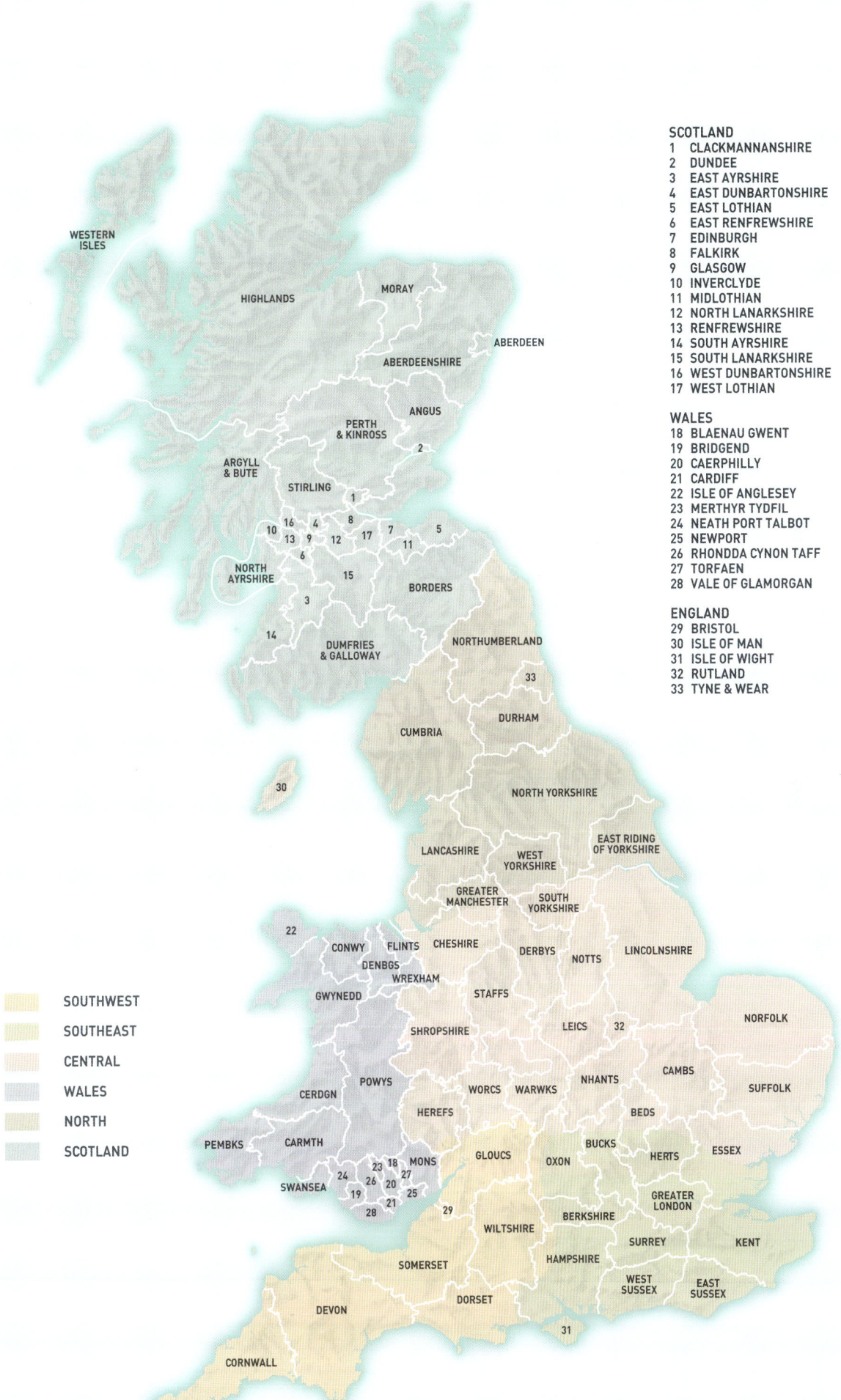

SCOTLAND
1 CLACKMANNANSHIRE
2 DUNDEE
3 EAST AYRSHIRE
4 EAST DUNBARTONSHIRE
5 EAST LOTHIAN
6 EAST RENFREWSHIRE
7 EDINBURGH
8 FALKIRK
9 GLASGOW
10 INVERCLYDE
11 MIDLOTHIAN
12 NORTH LANARKSHIRE
13 RENFREWSHIRE
14 SOUTH AYRSHIRE
15 SOUTH LANARKSHIRE
16 WEST DUNBARTONSHIRE
17 WEST LOTHIAN

WALES
18 BLAENAU GWENT
19 BRIDGEND
20 CAERPHILLY
21 CARDIFF
22 ISLE OF ANGLESEY
23 MERTHYR TYDFIL
24 NEATH PORT TALBOT
25 NEWPORT
26 RHONDDA CYNON TAFF
27 TORFAEN
28 VALE OF GLAMORGAN

ENGLAND
29 BRISTOL
30 ISLE OF MAN
31 ISLE OF WIGHT
32 RUTLAND
33 TYNE & WEAR

SOUTHWEST
SOUTHEAST
CENTRAL
WALES
NORTH
SCOTLAND

The Great Britain Guide

The abiding beauty of Britain is its astounding diversity and contrast, that and an ability to cram a huge amount into what is, comparatively, a small space. The whole country is not unlike a miniature work of art, in which the brush strokes detail its most minute aspects and set them against a rich background of history, tradition and heritage.

At one extreme, Britain – England, Scotland and Wales – has great swathes of largely uninhabited, sometimes bleak and barren, open moorland and rugged mountainous terrain where those with a yearning for adventure and the 'outdoor' life have long found a welcome niche. At the other end of the scale, the country has arguably the richest heritage of stunning architectural buildings and striking monuments in the world covering many periods from prehistoric to modern...twenty-three of which have been awarded World Heritage Site status.

This matchless historical pedigree spans centuries, and in itself is one of the country's finest and most precious assets. Britain today exists as a country for all ages and all interests, and responds both to leisurely appreciation of its buildings and culture, as well as far more involved exploration on foot, cycle, horseback, in a car and even on the flotilla of boats and barges that gently cruise the country's inland canals and quiet waterways.

The mantle of history lies across the whole country from the striking pomp and circumstance of glittering ceremonial to the localised celebrations that commemorate less widely known causes and events. Take almost any part of Britain at random, and you will discover some defining moment in the calendar of Man's cultural and social awakening that occurred there: Kent saw the building of Canterbury cathedral, seat of the Anglican church in Britain; Oxford, the so-called 'City of the dreaming spires', was the foundation of nationwide higher education provision that today has no equal, and not a few stunning buildings and museums. Cumbria boasts the superb stone circle at Castlerigg, an ancient monument that pre-dates other circles like Stonehenge and Avebury, and is the birthplace and home-base of one of Britain's leading poets of the 19th century, William Wordsworth. Shropshire, and the Iron Bridge gorge in particular, carved by the Severn, Britain's longest river, has long been regarded as the cradle of the industrial revolution; Warwickshire is the home of the bard, William Shakespeare, and Worcestershire the birthplace of the great British composer, Edward Elgar. Glasgow, surprisingly, was the unlikeliest of places from which Britain's renowned and prized tea shop tradition arose, while the great castle at Caernarfon in North Wales, long resounding to a note of discord between the English and the Welsh, is nevertheless the site of investiture of the Princes of Wales and one of the finest castles in Britain.

ROCKFORD COMMON

The natural beauty of Britain is equally unrivalled, a compact miscellany of landscapes rich and verdant, gentle and inspiring, rugged and wild, and none more so than the coast, tormented and constantly fashioned by the Irish and North seas. In places subdued by the trappings of Victorian seaside leisure ideology, elsewhere the coast of Britain is untamed and simply breathtaking, from Land's End to John o'Groats. To follow the coast, along many stretches defined as 'heritage coast' is to experience a constantly changing scene, from Norfolk and Suffolk, around the white cliffs of Dover – where at South Foreland lighthouse Marconi tested the first ship-to-shore radio – along the undulating coast of the South Downs, around the sea cliffs of Cornwall and Devon, and by way of the shores of Pembrokeshire, Ceredigion and Gwynedd, to the Lake District and the superb but infrequently visited west coast of southern Scotland.

Further north, the borders of Scotland reach out to remote rugged headlands like Ardnamurchan, the westernmost point of Britain, and like much of what lies beyond serves to underline the fact that the British mainland is an island among many islands. Mull, Skye, the Western Isles, Orkney and Shetland are all a part of Britain, but have evolved their own cultures and traditions that are colourful threads in a remarkable and ancient tapestry.

Britain actively conserves and protects its landscape heritage through the mechanism of fourteen National Parks. Forty smaller but no less vital areas have been designated as Areas of Outstanding Natural Beauty, an accolade that is not given lightly, and a description that means exactly what it says: the parks are beautiful, they are entirely natural and they are outstanding.

National Parks in contrast are not nationally owned, but rather parks for the nation, which are truly special places, each notably different from the others. The newest and smallest of them, created in 2005, features the former royal hunting ground of William the Conqueror, the New Forest. North of the border, the high tundra-like mountains and ancient pine woods of the Cairngorms were made a national park in 2003 only a year after the designation of the Loch Lomond National Park, a place of rolling lowland landscapes and high mountains with lochs and rivers, forests and woodlands.

The compactness of Britain brings another welcome dimension, that of ease of access. So well developed is Britain's air, road and rail infrastructure that there are few places that are not easily accessible, and those that remain are all the more rewarding for being just a little awkward to get to. Moreover, that accessibility continues throughout the year, and there are few parts of Britain that cannot be reached whatever the season.

Spring and autumn reveal natural Britain at its most colourful, the one with the burgeoning blues and greens of a ripening countryside, the other with the warm, golden hues that herald winter. Indeed winter snows may hinder exploration for a while, but such inconvenience is short-lived, and, in any case, adds a whole new quality to the year-round appreciation of a truly remarkable country.

The Great Britain Guide has everything you need for your visit, from walks and cycle rides to car tours complete with information along the way. There are details of the main annual events in each region and some great pubs and cosy tea rooms to stop at and enjoy the local fare. *The Great Britain Guide* will help you make the most of your trip.

WALKS & CYCLE RIDES

Each walk and cycle ride has a panel giving information for the walker and cyclist, including the distance, terrain, nature of the paths, and where to park your car.

WALKING

All of the walks are suitable for families, but less experienced family groups, especially those with younger children, should try the shorter walks. Route finding is usually straightforward, but the maps are for guidance only and we recommend that you always take the relevant Ordnance Survey map with you.

RISKS

Although each walk has been researched with a view to minimising any risks, no walk in the countryside can be considered to be completely free from risk. Walking in the outdoors will always require a degree of common sense and judgement to ensure that it is as safe as possible, especially for young children.

- Be particularly careful on cliff paths and in upland terrain, where the consequences of a slip can be serious.
- Remember to check tidal conditions before walking on the seashore.
- Some sections of route are by, or cross, busy roads. Remember traffic is a danger even on minor country lanes.
- Be careful around farmyard machinery and livestock.
- Be prepared for the consequences of changes in the weather and check the forecast before you set out.
- Ensure the whole family is properly equipped with suitable clothing and a good pair of boots or sturdy walking shoes.

- Take waterproof clothing with you and a torch if you are walking in the winter months.
- Remember the weather can change quickly at any time of the year, and in moorland and heathland areas, mist and fog can make route-finding much harder. In summer, take account of the heat and sun by wearing a hat, sunscreen and carrying enough water.
- You should carry a mobile phone, whistle and, if possible, a survival bag on walks away from centres of population. If you do have an accident requiring emergency services, make a note of your position as accurately as possible and dial 999.

CYCLING

In devising the cycle rides in this guide, every effort has been made to use designated cycle paths, or to link them with quiet country lanes and waymarked byways and bridleways. In a few cases, some fairly busy B-roads have been used to join up with quieter routes.

RULES OF THE ROAD

- Ride in single file on narrow and busy roads.
- Be alert, look and listen for traffic, especially on narrow lanes and blind bends. Be extra careful when descending steep hills, as loose gravel or a poor road surface can lead to an accident.
- In wet weather make sure that you keep an appropriate distance between you and other riders.
- Make sure you indicate your intentions clearly.
- Brush up on The Highway Code before venturing out onto the road.

OFF-ROAD SAFETY CODE OF CONDUCT

- Only ride where you know it is legal to do so. Cyclists are not allowed to cycle on public footpaths, marked in yellow. The only 'rights of way' open to cyclists are bridleways (blue markers) and unsurfaced tracks, known as byways, which are open to all traffic and waymarked in red.
- Canal towpaths: you need a permit to cycle on some stretches of towpath (www.waterscape.com). Remember that access paths can be steep and slippery so always push your bike under low bridges and by locks.
- Always yield to walkers and horses, giving adequate warning of your approach and dismount if necessary.
- Don't expect to cycle at high speeds.
- Keep to the main trail to avoid any unnecessary erosion to the area beside the trail and to prevent skidding, especially in wet weather conditions.
- Remember to follow the Country Code.

WALK & CYCLE RIDE MAP LEGEND

▪▪▪→	Route	▭	Built-up Area
❶	Route Waypoint	▭	Woodland Area
– – –	Adjoining Path	🚻	Toilet
☀	Viewpoint	P P	Car Park
•	Place of interest	⊞	Picnic Area
⌂	Steep Section	START	Cycle Start Point
⊞	Picnic Area		

PREPARING YOUR BICYCLE

Check the wheels, tyres, brakes and cables. Lubricate hubs, pedals, gear mechanisms and cables. Make sure you have a puncture repair kit, pump, a bell, a rear rack to carry useful panniers and a set of lights.

EQUIPMENT

- A cycling helmet provides essential protection.
- Make sure you are visible to other road users, by wearing light-coloured or luminous clothing in daylight and sashes or reflective strips in failing light and darkness.
- Take extra clothes with you, depending on the season, and a wind/waterproof jacket.
- Carry a basic tool kit, a pump, a strong lock and a simple first aid kit.
- Always carry enough water for your outing.
- Tell somebody of your planned route.

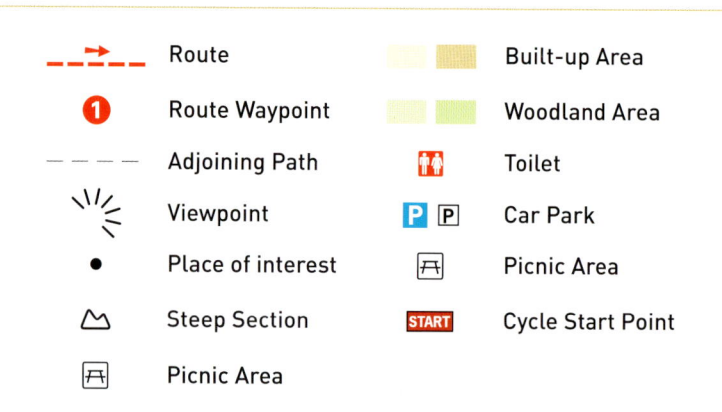

DITCHLING

Southwest England

Southwest England

The West country of Britain is a land of diverse terrain that stretches from the hills and vales of the Mendip Hills in the east to the tip of the Cornish peninsula that points west out to the big rollers of the Atlantic, not forgetting the flower-filled meadows of the Isles of Scilly, and the rugged moors of Dartmoor and Exmoor in between.

Parts of its coastline, stretching from Devon to Dorset, bears witness to prehistoric times with the fossil-strewn Jurassic coast, and there is evidence of ancient civilisations dotted all over the countryside. Inland, Somerset is famous for the delicious cider that has been produced here for hundreds of years and the Cotswolds complete with picture-postcard villages of pale stone-built cottages.

Cities, towns and villages of note include Exeter with its grand cathedral, and Plymouth famous for its noble seafaring history and architecture influenced by wealthy merchants, to St Ives threaded with a labyrinth of small cobbled streets and Selworthy in Somerset renowned for its many lovely thatched cottages set amid woodland.

Wherever you go in this part of the region you'll see marvellous contrasts in its beautiful and varied countryside, find fantastic beaches and resorts, and travel through market towns and tiny villages where West Country traditions are still upheld.

Cornwall

CLOCKWISE FROM TOP LEFT: NEWQUAY HARBOUR; WATERGATE; MULLION COVE; WHIPSIDDERY

BEDRUTHAN STEPS MAP REF 398 D6

Access to the beach at Bedruthan has been difficult over the years because of the crumbling nature of the cliffs, but the National Trust has built a secure stairway from the clifftop at Carnewas. The famous 'Steps' are the weathered rock stacks that stand in bold isolation amidst the sand. Bedruthan Steps are the result of sea erosion on the caves and arches in the friable slate cliffs. According to local legend, a mythical giant, Bedruthan, was reputed to use the stacks as stepping stones; but to nowhere in particular it seems. There is a National Trust shop and café on the clifftop in what was the office building of the old Carnewas iron mine. This is a delightful spot to indulge, as cream teas and other Cornish treats are the order of the day.

BODMIN MOOR MAP REF 398 E6

Cornwall's largest area of high moorland has been bisected by the A30, but the moor falls naturally into contrasting east and west sectors. The eastern side seems less wild and rugged than the undulating hills and rocky ridges of Brown Willy and Rough Tor to the west, while around the remote village of Minions it has all the raw beauty of wild country. The moor has been torn apart in places. The ragged, gaping hole of Cheesewring Quarry above Minions is the result of a moorland industry that was as vigorous as the copper mining

industry that left behind great engine houses like nearby Phoenix United Mine. Cheesewring's granite was used to build Devonport Dockyard, Birkenhead Docks and part of Copenhagen Harbour and was included in the materials used in the Thames Embankment and Westminster and Tower bridges. The quarry's name comes from the remarkable formation of layered granite that stands at its western edge, named after its similarity to a cider press used to squeeze the 'cheese' or juice from apples. It is formed by erosion of the weaker horizontal joints in the granite.

Close to the southwestern edge of the quarry is the reconstructed cave dwelling of Daniel Gumb, who was a stone-cutter in the 18th century. He built a much larger original cave dwelling here for himself and his family. Gumb was blessed with considerable intellectual gifts. He was known as 'the Mountain Philosopher' and was said to be well versed in astronomy and mathematics. Gumb's original cave was destroyed in the 1870s when Cheesewring Quarry was extended, but the roof of the present one is part of the original and has on its surface a carving of one of Euclid's theorems. Minions Heritage Centre, in a Cornish engine house, has displays on the history of the landscape from the Stone Age up until the present day.

Bodmin Moor is much older than its mining industry. Close to Minions village is a cluster of interesting early Bronze

Age (2500–1500 BC) monuments including the stone circles of the Hurlers and their adjacent standing stones. Craddock Moor to the west is peppered with burial mounds from the Bronze Age, hut circles of the Iron Age, and medieval field systems. North of Minions is Twelve Men's Moor and the rocky ridges of Kilmar Tor and Bearah Tor. Further north, a broad sweep of moorland runs through marshy ground to Fox Tor and then washes up against the asphalt boundary of the A30. To the west, the River Fowey flows from near Bolventor and Jamaica Inn, through a long, shallow valley. There are reservoirs with the characteristics of natural lakes at Colliford and Siblyback, and where the Fowey turns to the west at Draynes Bridge it pours through deep woods and moss-shrouded boulders at Golitha Falls. North of Minions, the moor drops suddenly into the deeply wooded valley of the River Lynher with peaceful hillside villages, such as North Hill.

BUDE MAP REF 398 E5

There are few more exhilarating beaches than Bude's Summerleaze when the sea rolls on to the sand in long, unbroken waves. The Bude Canal shaped much of the immediate hinterland of Bude Harbour and is now a popular attraction for boating, walking and watching wildlife. The canal was built in the early 19th century to carry calcium-rich sand to inland farms,

where it was used to enrich the soil. Bude Canal reached nearly to Launceston, but its full potential was never realised and its use declined by the middle of the 19th century. Much of the history of the canal is illustrated in the Bude-Stratton Museum at the Old Forge on the Lower Wharf.

Bude is a busy, friendly town – The Strand and Belle Vue are the main shopping streets. There is a good visitor centre in the car park near the harbour. A series of easily accessible and attractive beaches stretches north from Bude: Crooklets, Northcott Mouth and Sandy Mouth. The last two are almost covered at high tide. There are some pleasant walks along the coast path to the north where the clifftop area is level, cropped grassland. To the south of Bude, via a scenic road, is the vast expanse of Widemouth Bay.

Bude has few traditional buildings. The town evolved in the 19th century from a small fishing port through the grafting on of functional buildings, first for commerce, then for tourism. Just inland is Stratton. This medieval market town with a history that pre-dates Anglo-Saxon times was once the chief settlement of the area.

CADGWITH MAP REF 398 D8

Thatched and slate-roofed cottages crowd together at Cadgwith between encroaching hillsides and cliffs. A slim shingle beach runs to either side of a rocky promontory called the Todden. Cadgwith is best visited

CADGWITH

SHOWERY TOR, BODMIN MOOR

Visit
KIT HILL
The magnificent granite dome of Kit Hill rises to just over 1,000 feet (305m) above the town of Callington, about 4 miles (6.4km) northwest of Calstock. It stands in splendid isolation, as if torn between the granite masses of Bodmin Moor to the west and Dartmoor to the east. For centuries Kit Hill was quarried for stone and delved into for tin, copper, zinc, lead and even silver, but it is now a country park. The hill is crowned by an 80-foot (24m) chimney stack built in 1858 as part of the engine house of the Kithill Consols mine. There are several pathways around the hill, including both a waymarked walking trail and a pleasant heritage trail.

Activity
FALMOUTH AFLOAT
Various river and sea cruises are available from Falmouth's Prince of Wales Pier and from other boarding points around the estuary. Ferries leave for Flushing and St Mawes, and when the tide allows, there are cruises upriver to Malpas from where a five-minute bus ride connects with Truro. There are also trips along the coast and then up the Helford River; evening cruises on the Fal are another option, especially during the summer months, along with sea-angling trips from the Prince of Wales Pier.

Visit
LIZARD LAKES
Cornwall has few natural lakes of any size but there are some reservoirs. The Argal Waterpark is about 2 miles (3km) from Falmouth along the A394. The reservoir here is tree-fringed and peaceful, with much birdlife and paths skirting the shoreline. Coarse fishing is available all year and the fly-fishing season is from March to October. Stithians Lake is within easy reach of Falmouth and Helston along the A394. There is a car park on the east side of the lake near the dam and another situated at its north end.

Activity
OTTER SANCTUARY
The Tamar Otter Park and Wild Wood is in North Petherwin, which is reached by turning west off the B3254 at Langdon Cross, about 3 miles (4.8km) north of Launceston. Here, the Otter Trust's aim is to rehabilitate and breed otters for introduction to the wild. Dormice and several species of deer feature here also.

on foot; there is a car park on the high ground above the village, from where a path leads down to the village. Fishing boats still work from Cadgwith's beach where pilchards were once landed in vast quantities until the decline of the fishery in the early 20th century. Today Cadgwith's many fishermen use inkwell-shaped pots to catch lobster and crab, and gill nets to catch cod, pollack, monkfish and other species. The old buildings, known as cellers, where the pilchards were salted and pressed for oil, have been carefully converted for modern use.

The small building on the cliff to the north of the cove was a coastguard watch house that was built more than 100 years ago. The coast path to the south of Cadgwith (with the sea on your left) leads to the spectacular Devil's Frying-Pan, a huge gulf in the vegetated cliffs where a sea cave collapsed centuries ago leaving an arch of rock connecting both sides.

The rugged Lizard area is especially noted for the extensive variety and value of its plant life. Pink thrift, the powder-blue squill, cliff bluebells and kidney vetch grow in profusion here, but seemingly insignificant-looking plants may well be rare and vulnerable. Visitors are asked not to pick even the most prolific wild flowers and to take care while walking.

CRACKINGTON HAVEN MAP REF 398 E5
The mighty and dramatic bulwark of cliff at Crackington is best viewed from the southern approach. It seems to dwarf the cove and beach, its twisted and folded shale mellowed by swathes of grass and sedge. Crackington was a haven of sorts

during the 19th century, but it was a port in the most basic sense – small vessels simply ran on to the sand as the tide dropped to offload coal and to load slates.

The coast path from Crackington Haven leads north to Castle Point. Take a deep breath for the climb out of the cove. There are the remnants of Iron Age embankments at Castle Point. A mile or so further on is Dizzard Point where an old oak wood clings to the slopes.

FALMOUTH MAP REF 398 D8
Vessels of all types and sizes still bustle in and out of Falmouth harbour, lending excitement and atmosphere to one of the world's largest natural harbours. Falmouth developed as a port after Henry VIII built Pendennis and St Mawes castles, the guardians of the Fal Estuary. Both are built in the distinctive clover-leaf design and St Mawes is renowned as a fine example of military architecture. Visitors here can explore the dungeons, barrack rooms and cannon-lined castle walls.

During the late 17th century the port became a packet station, from where small, fast-sailing brigantines took mail to northwest Spain, and in later years as far as North America, the West Indies and South America. Gold and silver bullion was carried and the packets provided a passenger service. By the 1830s over 40 packets worked out of Falmouth. They were well-armed against privateers, French naval hostility and even Algerian pirates. The crews supplemented their meagre wages with smuggling and by carrying unofficial goods; tales of swashbuckling abound. The packet service

had transferred to Southampton by 1850 but Falmouth's position as a major port was secured by a vigorous pilchard fishery, the development of Falmouth docks and a thriving shipbuilding industry. Ship repair, bunkering, cargo handling and yacht-building industries still continue today.

Falmouth's rather straggling form gives it less unity than might be expected of a port, as the town follows the riverside through a chain of linking main streets, but this makes it intriguing to explore. It is centred on The Moor, once just a muddy creek and now emphatically urban, and it is here that you will find the Falmouth Art Gallery, well worth a visit, on the upper floor of the old Passmore Edwards Free Library. As well as changing exhibitions there are permanent displays of paintings including those of Henry Scott Tuke, the Victorian painter who spent his last years near Falmouth. From The Moor, Webber Street leads to the Prince of Wales Pier.

Some of Falmouth's many engaging features include the 111-step Jacob's Ladder that leads up from The Moor, and watch out for the recurring theme of Falmouth's 'Opes', the passageways, which run between the town's buildings.

The National Maritime Museum Cornwall, on Falmouth's busy waterfront, includes the delightful National Small Boat Collection of more than one hundred boats. There is also a unique tidal gallery with windows that reveal the rise and fall of the tide, and breathtaking views across Falmouth Harbour from the top of a 95-foot (29m) tower. Use the aptly-named Park & Float and sail over to the museum on a classic ferry.

FOWEY

FOWEY MAP REF 398 E7

Buildings crowd out Fowey's waterfront but there is a wonderful sense of unity within the jumble of narrow streets and there is access to the harbour and quay from various points. Fowey (pronounced 'Foy') was a major port from the earliest times. More than 700 seamen from the town and its surrounding parishes took part in the Siege of Calais in 1346 when the town supplied 47 vessels compared to London's 25. In return, Fowey was attacked and burnt by the French in 1380 and in 1467. It was the Port of Cornwall in every sense and its seamen earned the title 'the Fowey Gallants'. These outstanding sailors were known for their arrogance and contempt for the law, and their energies soon turned to lucrative piracy. When Edward IV took a grip on the

port, Fowey turned to equally lucrative, but honest, trade. China clay and the enterprise of the Treffry family brought prosperity, and today ocean-going ships pass upriver to Golant' quays from where clay is still exported.

Fowey draws you in from the long descent of Lostwithiel Street to Trafalgar Square, then on round the Town Quay and Webb Street. The buildings crowd in from all sides and even the dark-stoned Church of St Fimbarrus with its decorated tower seems to overhang.

The true face of Fowey is seen from the river or from Polruan on the opposite shore. Tall houses rise sheer from the waterfront, and when night falls in summer the boat-bobbing river is starred with lights. From the bottom of Lostwithiel Street, the Esplanade leads southwest

to Readymoney Cove, where a small sandy beach lies below tree-shrouded St Catherine's Point. St Catherine's Castle crowns the Point; built between 1538 and 1542 as part of the chain of defences set up along the coast by Henry VIII in response to hostility from France and the Holy Roman Empire. The castle can be reached up steep steps from the beach or by a leisurely track.

Driving through Fowey should be avoided at the busiest times. The main car park at the entrance to the town is signed from the A3082. You will find a good mix of shops lining the bustling streets, along with fine galleries, craft and antique shops. Fowey's pubs are full of a sea-going atmosphere and there are several good restaurants. The museum is in the town hall at Trafalgar Square and the Tourist Information Centre is at the far end of Fore Street.

Overlooking the town is Place, the historic home of the Treffry family (not open to the public). The original 15th-century house was rebuilt in Regency Gothic style during the 19th century and it is certainly a delightfully eccentric building. Impressive, tree-shrouded Golant lies 1.5 miles (2.4km) north of Fowey and is reached from the B3269. In this charming village the small but absorbing Church of St Sampson commemorates one of Cornwall's great Celtic saints.

GORRAN HAVEN MAP REF 398 D7

Gorran Haven lies just south of Mevagissey at the seaward end of a shallow valley. A labyrinth of narrow, steep lanes and passageways climbs from the harbour and an intriguing little chapel built on solid rock dates from the 15th century. South of Gorran Haven, the mighty Dodman Point thrusts its bull's head into the seaway. The Dodman, as it is commonly known, is 373 feet (114m) high. The Iron-Age earthworks that enclose the seaward area of the Dodman are more than 2,000 feet (609m) long and 20 feet (6m) high.

GRIBBIN HEAD MAP REF 398 E7

Southwest of Fowey, Gribbin Head (National Trust) shoulders out the western sea, preventing it from having too much influence on sheltered Fowey. The headland, always referred to by locals as The Gribbin, is crowned with a bizarre monolith – the 84-ft (25m) Daymark tower painted in barber-shop red and white. The Daymark was erected in 1832 in order to distinguish The Gribbin from St Anthony's Head at the entrance to Falmouth Bay. The two headlands look similar from the seaward approach and sailors regularly mistook The Gribbin for St Anthony's Head, with catastrophic results when

they sailed blindly into the shallows of St Austell Bay instead of the safer, deep waters of Falmouth Bay.

Inland of The Gribbin is Menabilly, where author Daphne du Maurier made her home and drew on her surroundings for inspiration for a number of her novels. In the eastern shelter of The Gribbin is Polridmouth Cove, with adjoining beaches and an ornamental lake.

The Gribbin can be reached on foot from a car park at Menabilly Barton, a mile (1.6km) inland. To the west, the tiny Polkerris faces into St Austell Bay. There is a car park halfway down the tree-shaded approach, from where it is just a short walk to the pleasant beach.

HELFORD MAP REF 398 D8

There is irresistible romance attached to Helford and its tree-shrouded river and creeks. The price is that the area can become uncomfortably busy during popular holiday periods. Lovely though the village is, the dense nature of this serene landscape rewards those who explore further than Helford itself. The countryside is more tame, compared with the extremes of the coast, and though access along the riverbank is limited in places, there are a number of fine walks to be enjoyed from Helford.

To the west lies Frenchman's Creek, romanticised by both authors Sir Arthur Quiller-Couch and Daphne du Maurier and still enchanting today, even when the falling tide reveals a plain of mud. A path leads east from Helford to the coast at Dennis Head and to St Anthony and Gillan, with great views over to Falmouth. These quiet places are best visited on foot as parking spaces are difficult to find.

A seasonal passenger ferry from Helford sails to Helford Passage on the north bank, from where the National Trust's Glendurgan Garden and the adjacent Trebah Garden can be visited. Glendurgan is one of the great subtropical gardens of the South West, situated on the banks of the Helford River near Mawnan Smith. Hydrangeas, camellias and rhododendrons flourish amidst lovely woodland and there is an engaging maze. Trebah Garden has, among its attractions, a fine water garden. The smaller garden at Penjerrick, just over a mile (1.6km) north of Mawnan Smith, is where Chilean firebushes, magnolias, with their delicate blooms, and azaleas flourish.

ISLES OF SCILLY MAP REF 398 A8

The Isles of Scilly are famously known as the 'Fortunate Islands' or the 'Sunshine Islands'. These ancient islands deserve the superlatives, though their beauty and uniqueness require no exaggeration.

The hundred or so islands and islets that make up the archipelago lie just 28 miles (45km) west-southwest of Land's End as the crow flies. Only five islands are inhabited – St Agnes, Bryher, St Mary's, St Martin's, and Tresco – and together they offer a rare combination of seascapes, golden beaches and crystal-clear sea, with quiet green corners inland.

Bryher lies amidst the northwestern group of islands that include Tresco. It is 1.5 miles (2.4km) long and barely half a mile (0.8km) across at its widest point. Bryher faces Tresco across the narrow channel of New Grimsby Sound and island life is focused on the beaches that fringe the Sound. Here boats draw up at a granite quay, or at the jetty, built as one of Anneka Rice's famous television 'challenges' to extend landing times on Bryher and now known as 'Annequay'.

Just over 1 mile (1.6km) wide, is the island of St Agnes. This island has a special atmosphere of serenity. It is the most southerly of the group and is separated from St Mary's by the deep water channel of St Mary's Sound. The Turk's Head Inn and the Post Office are at the hub of the community. To the east the main island is linked by a narrow sandbar to the smaller tidal 'island' of Gugh and off its western shore is the protected bird island of Annet. Further out to sea, beyond Annet lie the dramatic Western Rocks – reefs that end at the Bishop Rock Lighthouse.

The most northerly island in the group, St Martin's is 2 miles (3.2km) in length and just over half a mile (800m) wide. Landing on St Martin's can be adventurous at certain states of the tide, when walking the plank to reach the sandy shore from launches is necessary. Walking here is exhilarating, though the lure of magnificent beaches such as Great Bay on St Martin's northern shore tends to distract.

St Mary's is the largest of the Isles of Scilly. Its main settlement of Hugh Town is the marine metropolis of the islands, and it is from Hugh Town Quay that the passenger launches leave for the exciting sea-trips that are an essential part of holidaying on Scilly. There are beaches on the north and south side of Hugh Town, the southern bay of Porth Cressa being particularly delightful. A footpath follows the coastline for a 9-mile (14.4km) circuit, passing several well-preserved prehistoric sites on the way. Early flower growing developed in Scilly from the late 1860s. Daffodils and narcissi are still exported from the islands, but the trade has declined in recent years.

Attractive Tresco lies at the sheltered heart of the islands. It is much more of a show-place than the rest of Scilly, a private domain where there is an atmosphere of carefully regulated life and of gentle pace. The exquisite subtropical gardens surrounding Tresco Abbey House are the main focus of the island. A priory to St Nicholas was established by Benedictine monks during the 12th century; the scant ruins which remain are now incorporated into the Abbey Gardens, where examples of Burmese Honeysuckle, Australian Scarlet Bottle-brush, gigantic ice plants, Aloes, Dracaenas, Mimosa, and a host of other exotics line the terraced pathways. Tresco has a heliport from where connections can be made to Penzance. Dogs must be kept on leads on Tresco.

KYNANCE COVE MAP REF 398 C8

Victorian visitors first visited Kynance with their painting kits and sketch books and the cove was visited by a poet, Tennyson, and a prince, Albert. Kynance satisfied perfectly the romantic ideal of the picturesque in Nature. The whole of the beach is awash at high tide and emerges fresh and shining as each day dawns. Huge gnarled monoliths of serpentine rock that rise up from the beach create a beautiful seascape. One of the largest of these is Asparagus Island, with Steeple Rock and the Sugar Loaf lying between it and the mainland. For some, part of the charm of Kynance lies in its unexpectedness, hidden as it is below the flatness of the Lizard Peninsula.

The cove and the cliff land to the east are in the care of the National Trust, which has provided a car park above Kynance and a viewpoint for visitors with disabilities. Descent to the cove is steep, and the return is quite strenuous. Care should be taken if swimming off the cove – the tide comes in rapidly and the currents close to shore are dangerous.

The Kynance area is of great biological importance. Rare species grow in the area including sedges and tiny liverworts. Spiders, moths and even a rare European woodlouse are also found here. The mild climate and a maritime environment partly explain the diversity of the local wildlife.

KYNANCE COVE

LANHYDROCK MAP REF 398 E7

Magnificent Lanhydrock lies about 2.5 miles (4km) north of Lostwithiel via the B3268, or can be reached from Bodmin via the A30. It is approached along an avenue of stately beech trees, which leads through the beautiful parkland. On first sight the house gives every impression of being wholly Tudor. In fact, all that remains of the original house, built between 1630 and 1642 for wealthy Truro merchant Sir Richard Robartes, is the gatehouse, entrance porch and north wing. The east wing was removed, and the rest fell victim to a terrible fire in 1881, but the house was rebuilt to match the surviving part. The interiors are very grand, notably the Long Gallery, and there are lavish furnishings throughout the house. Of all the 50 rooms that are open, visitors tend to find the 'below stairs' sections of most interest, including the kitchen, larders, bakehouse, dairy, cellars and servants' quarters.

Lanhydrock is surrounded by beautiful grounds, with some pleasant rides and paths to stroll along. Adjoining the house are formal gardens with clipped yews and bronze urns, while the higher garden is famed for its lovely magnolias and magnificent rhododendron blooms.

LISKEARD MAP REF 398 E7

With Bodmin Moor to the north, and Looe to the south, Liskeard makes an ideal choice as a holiday centre. Liskeard was a Coinage town from medieval times and Coinage endowed the town with a status and prosperity that encouraged other business; copper mining during the 19th century further increased the town's wealth. When mining declined Liskeard continued to thrive as the important focus point of road and rail communications throughout east Cornwall and is still the northern terminus of the branch railway that connects with Looe.

Today Liskeard's attractive townscape reflects its prosperous history. The streets, quite narrow in places, are flanked by tall buildings. Fine individual examples include the notable Victorian Webb's Hotel, hip-roofed and stolid, which overlooks the Parade, whilst the Guildhall's Italianate tower dominates Market Street. In Well Lane, off Market Street, is the ancient Pipe Well; unfortunately, the water is now considered unfit to drink and the well is gated. Liskeard's Church of St Martin, the second largest church in Cornwall after St Petroc's at Bodmin, suffered some heavy-handed Victorian restoration and is rather dull because of it. Liskeard is a busy shopping centre, in keeping with its commercial traditions. On market days, the country comes to town bringing a refreshing bustle to the streets.

LIZARD PENINSULA MAP REF 398 D8

The Lizard Downs are rich in ancient artefacts that date from a time when early man found reasonable grazing on this area's poorly drained soil. The serpentine soil also supports a remarkable variety of rare plants. The Lizard's mild climate encourages these plants but the main reason for the area's unique botanical nature is that the Lizard was joined to the European land mass thousands of years ago, when these plants spread effortlessly and flourished on what are now the peninsula's coastal fringes.

There are subtle distinctions between species and a specialist's knowledge is required to identify many of the plants. But everyone can recognise and enjoy the attractive Cornish Heath, Erica Vagans, a type of heather found in substantial quantities only on The Lizard. It has dark green leaves and spikes of small pink or lilac flowers. Closer to the clifftops, blue spring squill, the pink thrift and the sea campion contribute to a mosaic of wild flowers in spring and summer.

Lizard village is a convenient base from which to explore Lizard Point, the most southerly point in Britain, and its adjoining coastline. You can park at the Point, where there is an old lifeboat station that has long been superseded by the modern station at Kilcobben Cove situated to the northeast. The view seaward is exhilarating and the air can be mild even in midwinter, but when the tide is out, swathes of pungent smelling seaweed may dull the edge of the bracing sea air. Choughs returned to breed in Cornwall on Lizard Point in 2001 after an absence of more than 50 years and the RSPB operates a Chough Watchpoint in spring. The coast path leads west above high cliffs. To the east the path passes through a green, sheltered landscape above cliffs draped with the invasive Hottentot Fig, or mesembryanthemum.

The Lizard's position has long made it dangerous to seagoing vessels. For a mile (1.6km) seaward off Lizard Point the sea tumbles in frightening overfalls during stormy weather. To the northeast lies the promontory of Black Head and beyond here the deadly Manacles Reef.

The Lizard Lighthouse dominates the coast to the east. A warning light was first established here in 1612. Today's powerful light flashes every three seconds and can be seen in clear weather from up to 29 miles (46.7km) away. The fog signal is delivered by siren every 60 seconds.

About 1.5 miles (2.4km) east of Lizard Point is Church Cove, and its attractive little church of Landewednack. The cove is reached on foot from the car park past thatched cottages. A short walk south

LIZARD POINT

along the coast path takes you straight to the remarkable cliffside site of the Lizard-Cadgwith lifeboat house.

LOOE MAP REF 398 E7

Tourism came early to Looe. It is said that the bathing machine came to Looe beach as early as 1800 when war with France sent the leisured classes to southwest England in search of a home-grown alternative to French resorts. But it was the arrival of the railway, that led to the growth of the tourism that sustains Looe today.

The old town of East Looe is a delight. There is something of a French style in its ordered layout and in the way that the tall buildings seem to accentuate the narrowness of streets and passageways. The houses are painted in a variety of colours. The old pilchard-curing cellars by the quay are built from unadorned stone and many of the cottages have an outside stone staircase indicating that the ground floors were used as pilchard processing cellars and net stores. There is an interesting museum of local history in the Old Guildhall in Higher Market Street. Looe is Cornwall's second largest fishing port and the fishing industry brings a maritime bustle to the harbour and quayside at East Looe. Looe's viewpoint, Banjo Pier, can be reached from the quay and the East Looe Bay beach adjoins it.

West Looe was always the smaller settlement. It has a lovely outlook across the harbour to East Looe and the older parts of the town around Fore Street and Princes Square have some pleasant features. There is a big car park on the west side of the river at Millpool where there is a Discovery Centre.

The delightful Kilminorth Woods are reached easily from the Millpool car park. Waymarked walks lead through a splendid oak wood and alongside the West Looe River. The woods and river are rich in plant, insect and bird life. These include herons, which nest in the trees on the opposite bank. Further information can be obtained at the Discovery Centre.

WALK 1

ALONG BUDE BAY

The windswept coastal grasslands of north Cornwall seem unlikely havens for plant life, but, around Bude, the cliff edges especially provide a unique refuge for wild flowers. This walk follows the flat cliff land north of Bude with an inland section on the return. Along the way you'll find numerous wild flowers that turn the cliff-top into a riot of colour in spring and early summer and butterflies. Look out for the meadow brown, probably Britain's commonest butterfly, the common blue, a small butterfly with an almost lilac tinge, and for the glamourous painted lady with its tawny-orange wings and black and white markings.

DISTANCE/TIME 5 miles (8km) 2h30 **MAP** OS 111 Bude, Boscastle & Tintagel and 126 Clovelly & Hartland **START** Crooklets Beach car park; grid ref: SS 204071 **TRACKS** Excellent throughout, grassy coast path, field paths and metalled lanes **THE PUB** The Inn on the Green, Flexbury. Tel: 01288 356013; www.innonthegreen.info

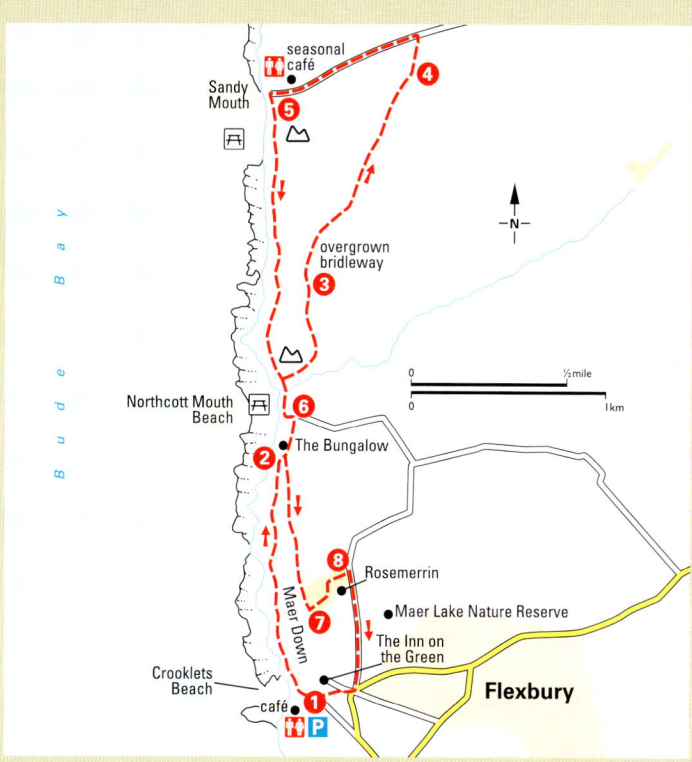

1 Go towards the beach, cross a bridge and head for some steps. Pass in front of beach huts, then turn left along a stony track which passes between walls. Go up some steps and onto the coast path, signed 'Maer Cliff'.

2 Go through a gate and along a track behind a white building, called Northcott House. Bear off to the left, by a signpost, and go down a path to the sea at Northcott Mouth beach. From here, bear right along a track that will take you back inland, past a group of houses on the left, and continue uphill to pass some more houses.

3 Where the track bends around to the right, leave it and keep straight ahead to reach a gate. Keep outside the left edge of the overgrown bridle path ahead.

4 When you reach a field gate, follow a track through some fields ahead. Keep left at a junction with another track, then continue to the T-junction that connects with a public road. Turn left here and walk down the road, taking care, to Sandy Mouth.

5 Pass the National Trust information kiosk and descend towards the beach, then go left and uphill and follow the coast path back to Northcott Mouth beach, and a red lifeguard hut that you passed earlier.

6 Follow the roadside path just past the lifeguard hut and retrace your steps to the white bungalow you passed earlier. Go along the track behind the building and then keep straight ahead along a broad track along the edge of three fields.

7 At a field corner by a footpath sign go through the open gateway ahead then turn left and follow the field edge into a hedged-in path. Continue ahead between trees to a lane by a house at Rosemerrin. Continue to reach a road.

8 Turn right along the road, with Maer Lake Nature Reserve down to your left. Cross over at a junction with Maer Down Road, take a left trun , and then turn right, passing The Inn on the Green, and you can make your way to your car at the car park.

WALK 2

AROUND CADGWITH

This wandering route between coast and countryside leads inland to the sleepy village of Ruan from where a narrow lane leads down to the Poltesco Valley. From Carleon Cove the coast path is followed pleasantly to the tiny fishing village of Cadgwith. Beyond the village the coast path leads to the Devil's Frying Pan, a vast gulf in the cliffs caused by the collapse of a large section of coast. From here the path closely follows the edge of the steep cliffs before turning inland to the Church of the Holy Cross at Grade. Beyond the church is the ancient St Ruan's Well and the road back to the start of this ramble.

DISTANCE/TIME 4.5 miles (7.2km) 2h **MAP** OS Explorer 103 The Lizard **START** Cadgwith car park, about 350 yards (320m) from Cadgwith. Busy in summer; grid ref: SW 719146 **TRACKS** Very good, coast path occasionally rocky in places, field paths **THE PUB** The Cadgwith Cove Inn, Cadgwith Cove. Tel: 01326 290513; www.cadgwithcoveinn.com

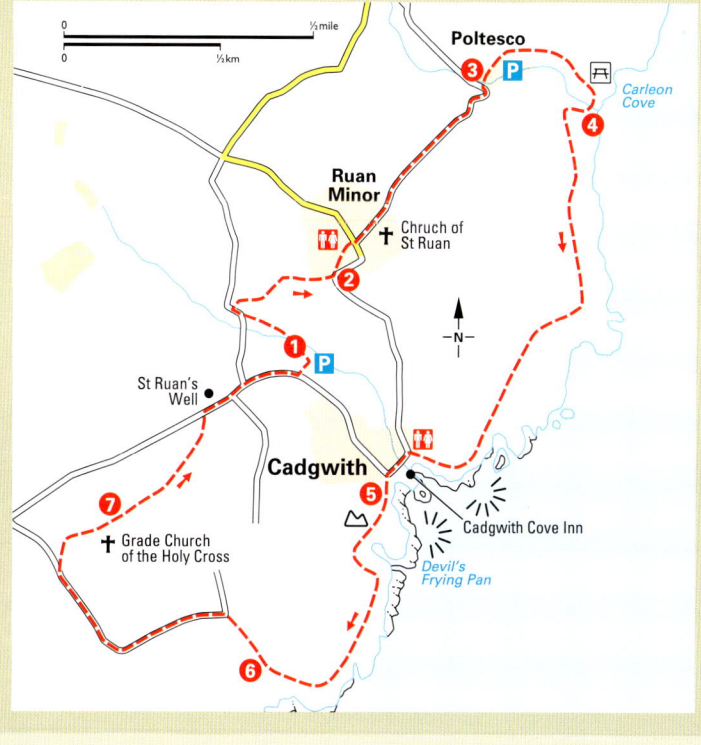

1 Go left along a grassy rise below the car park, to reach a stile. Go across a field and then branch right through a gate to join a wooded path. Turn right at a lane, cross over a bridge then, on the corner by the postbox, go up the track ahead. Turn right at an unsigned junction and continue to the main road at Ruan Minor.

2 Go left and then, just after you pass the shop, turn left again down a surfaced path. Rejoin the main road by a thatched cottage. Cross diagonally right, then go down a lane past the Church of St Ruan.

3 Just after passing an old mill and then a bridge, go right at a T-junction to reach the car park at Poltesco. From the far end of the car park follow a track, signposted 'Carleon Cove'. Go right at a junction.

4 Turn left at a T-junction just above the cove and again turn left where the path branches in about 0.25 mile (400m). Continue along the cliff-edge path to Cadgwith.

5 Follow a narrow path, signposted 'Coast Path'. When you get to a house gateway, go left and up a surfaced path, signposted 'Devil's Frying Pan'. Once you reach an open area turn left, then continue past Townplace Cottage, and finally cross over a meadow to reach the Devil's Frying Pan itself. Continue to walk along the coast path for a further 0.5 mile (800m).

6 At a junction, just past a chalet studio, follow a path inland to reach a T-junction with a rough track. Turn left and, when you get to a public lane, go left again. You will reach the entrance to Grade church after about 1 mile (1.6km). Continue through the gate to the church.

7 Follow the field edge to walk behind the church and then cross over the next field to eventually reach a lane. St Ruan's Well is opposite diagonally left. Turn right and continue on for 200yds (183m), then branch off right between some stone pillars to return to the car park at Cadgwith.

A COASTAL ROUTE FROM CRACKINGTON HAVEN

Crackington Haven has given its name to a geological phenomenon, the Crackington Formation, a fractured shale that has been shaped into contorted forms. Along the open cliff south from Crackington the remarkable geology unfolds. Looking back from Bray's Point, you see the contortions in the high cliff face of Pencarrow Point on the north side. Soon the path leads above Tremoutha Haven and up to the cliff edge beyond the headland of Cambeak. A short distance further on you arrive above Strangles Beach, where again you look back to such fantastic features as Northern Door. The second part of the walk turns inland and descends into East Wood and the peaceful Trevigue Valley, much of which is a nature reserve.

1 From the Crackington Haven car park entrance go left to cross a bridge, and then turn right at a telephone kiosk. Follow a broad track round to the left, continue between a signpost and an old wooden seat, then go through a kissing gate to get onto the coastal path. On reaching a fork in the path continue to follow the coast path right, signed 'Cambeak'.

2 Cross over a footbridge then, when you get to a fork of several paths, follow the white arrow left and take the path up a sheltered valley on the inland side of the steep hill. From here continue walking straight ahead and along the cliff path.

3 Where a stretch of low inland cliffs begins, at another junction of paths and a marker post, follow the route towards the left side (signed 'Trevigue') following the path until you eventually reach a road by a National Trust sign for The Strangles.

4 Go left, walking past the farm entrance to Trevigue, then, in just a few paces, turn right to walk down a drive by the Trevigue sign. Then bear off to the left to walk across the grass and go through a gate by a signpost.

5 Proceed to walk directly down the field, keeping to the left of a telegraph pole, to reach a stile. Continue downhill to the edge of a wood. Go down a tree-shaded path to a junction of paths in a shady dell by the river.

6 Turn sharp left at the junction of paths to follow the signpost towards 'Haven', and then continue ahead on the obvious path down to reach the wooded river valley.

7 Cross over a footbridge, and then turn left at a junction with a track. Cross over another footbridge and go straight ahead to reach a gate by some houses. Follow a track and then a lane to the main road. Turn left to reach the car park and the start of the walk.

DISTANCE/TIME 3.5 miles (5.7km) 1h45 **MAP** OS Explorer 111 Bude, Boscastle & Tintagel **START** Crackington Haven car park or Burden Trust car park, along B3263 to Wainhouse; grid ref: SX 145968 **TRACKS** Good coastal footpath and woodland tracks, 9 stiles **THE PUB** The Coombe Barton Inn, Crackington Haven Tel: 01840 230345; www.combebartoninn

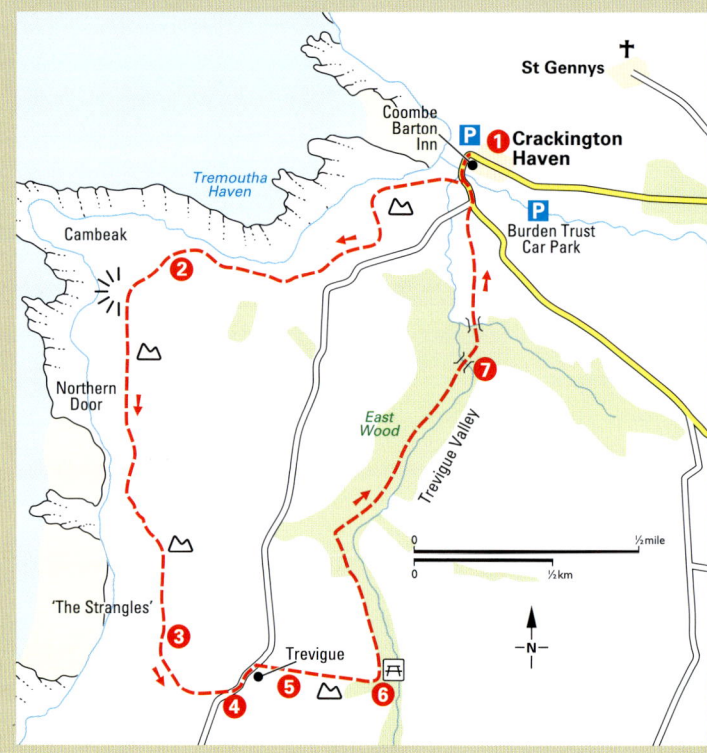

FROM FOWEY TO POLKERRIS

Explore the coast and countryside near Fowey – also known as Daphne du Maurier country. The walk starts from Readymoney Cove and follows inland lanes and tracks and then the coastal path, where a minor roller-coaster hike takes you to St Catherine's Point. There is then a steep descent back to to Readymoney Cove.

1 From the bottom end of the car park walk down St Catherine's Parade, then turn right towards the inlet of Readymoney Cove. Continue to the end of the road, above the beach, and follow the initially rocky Love Lane uphill on the Saints Way. Carry on past the first junction, ignoring the options by a National Trust sign for 'Covington Woods'.

2 Turn left at the next junction and climb up some wooden steps to reach Allday's Fields. Follow the right-hand field edge. At a field gap follow a grassy track ahead, crossing a stile by a gate to reach a lane end at Coombe Farm. Proceed to follow the lane ahead.

3 At a road, turn right and continue until you reach Lankelly Farm. Go past a junction on the right and then follow Prickly Post Lane for a few paces. Turn off left onto a gravel drive, then keep left and continue along a narrow fenced-in path.

4 Follow the path to the right of a house at Trenant, then cross over the tarmac drive and the wall stile ahead. Keep ahead, alongside the field edge, then steeply descend to a footbridge and a stile in a field below Tregaminion Farm. Walk up the field to reach a gate, continue ahead between buildings

and then turn right, then left, to reach a T-junction with a road by the entrance gate to the lovely little church of Tregaminion.

5 Turn right and then in 100yds (91m) go left into a field. When you reach a junction on the edge of some woods, take the right-hand branch that zig-zags down to the beach, cove and Rashleigh Inn at Polkerris.

6 Retrace your steps up the zig-zag path and walk back to the church. Continue along the road to a car park, then stay on the surfaced road, signposted 'Menabilly Farm'. Continue when the surfaced road becomes a track and then a path, which descends to Polridmouth Cove. Turn left along the coast path.

7 Continue to follow the coast path, signposted 'Lankelly Cliff'. At open ground, follow the seaward field edge. Go steeply into, and then out of, Coombe Haven (take care here). Enter Covington Wood and then keep left at the immediate junction.

8 Turn right at a junction to reach St Catherine's Castle. Return along the path and descend the steps at the first junction on the right, to reach Readymoney Beach. Return to your car via St Catherine's Parade.

DISTANCE/TIME 5 miles (8km); 3h **MAP** OS Explorer 107 St Austell & Liskeard **START** Readymoney Cove car park; grid ref: SX 118511 **TRACKS** Field paths, rough lanes and coastal footpath; 8 stiles **THE PUB** The Rashleigh Inn, Polkerris. Tel: 01726 813991

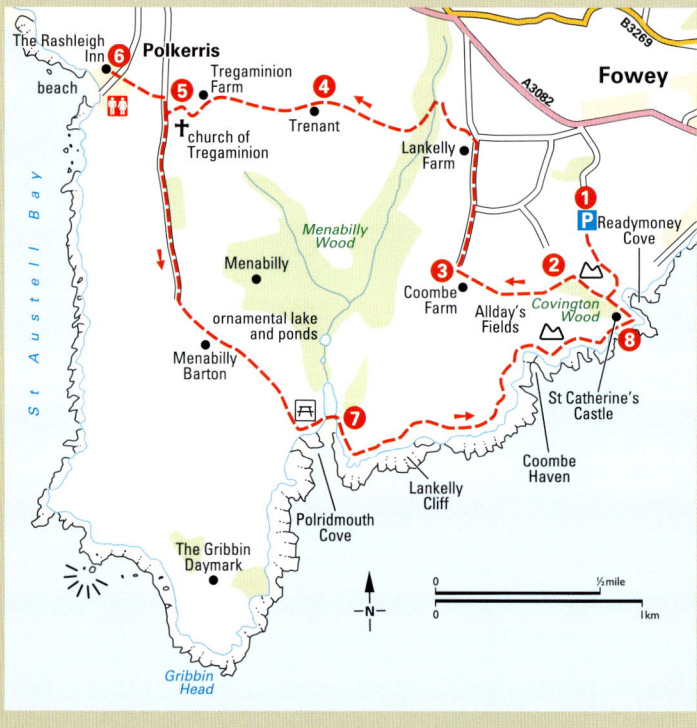

MARAZION MAP REF 398 C8

Marazion is a town first and foremost. It was the main trading port of Mount's Bay until Penzance developed its own markets and port during the 16th century. But Marazion has remained as distinctive as its lovely name, which derives, rather plainly, from the Cornish word for market. There is an informative little museum at the town hall in Market Square, antique and craft shops to browse and pleasant pubs, restaurants and cafés.

Marazion Beach offers safe bathing and is a glorious suntrap. It offers good windsurfing especially during spring and autumn, when conditions are breezy. A few miles east lies Prussia Cove, a secluded rocky inlet of great charm reached most rewardingly by a pleasant 2-mile (3.2km) walk along the coast path.

The great complement to Marazion is the castellated Isle of St Michael's Mount (cared for by the National Trust), the most romantic offshore island in Britain and a matching image to Mont St Michel off the Normandy coast. The Mount was dedicated to St Michael after claims of miraculous sightings of the saint by 5th-century fishermen. Even today shafts of celestial light seem drawn to St Michael's Mount although a view of angels is perhaps less likely. In its day the Mount has been a monastery, a prison, and a castle-under-siege. The Mount is defined as a part-time island by successive high tides during which it may be reached by a pleasant boat trip. At low tide the approach is on foot along a fine cobbled causeway.

MEVAGISSEY MAP REF 398 D7

Mevagissey tucks into the land and guards itself within the folded arms of its inner and outer harbours. It is one of Cornwall's most popular resorts, a fishing village whose simple charm attracts tourists in their thousands. It became a leading pilchard fishing port in Tudor times and continued as such into the 21st century. For many years it supplied the navy with pilchards, which became known as Mevagissey Ducks. Today there is still a fishing fleet based here but, as modern fishermen, one that is far more diverse. Like most Cornish fishing villages Mevagissey has great character, especially in the old part of the village that lies between the Fountain Inn and the Battery on the eastern side of the harbour. The refurbished aquarium at the old lifeboat house on the South Quay gives an insight into life in deeper waters (the profits go to the upkeep and improvement of Mevagissey harbour). There is a little museum of local history on the East Quay and, engagingly for this sea-going town, there is a model railway museum in Meadow Street.

ST MICHAEL'S MOUNT

Heligan was once a lost garden, but now has been well and truly found. It lies northwest of Mevagissey and can be reached from the B3273 St Austell road. Restored Victorian features include lakes and ponds, an Italian Garden, an extensive valley garden with a splendid collection of tree ferns, and huge productive gardens and extensive fruit houses.

MORWENSTOW & COOMBE
MAP REF 398 E5

The delightful parish of Morwenstow lies at the northern extreme of Cornwall in the narrow corridor of land that the infant Tamar River withholds from its Devon neighbour. Its coast is awesome, yet unexpected, when approached across fields that end without much warning at the edge of 300-foot (91.5m) cliffs. This is the land of the famous Culm Measures, great twisted slabs of shale that rise from remote boulder beaches that are ribbed with fins of sea-washed rock.

Its natural beauty apart, Morwenstow owes much of its fame to the reputation of the Victorian parson, eccentric and poet, Robert Stephen Hawker, who was vicar at the Church of St Morwenna for many years. The church has good Norman features and is beautifully situated among trees in a shallow combe that leads towards the sea. The interior of the church is pleasantly melancholic, especially at dusk, when there is a wonderful feeling of isolation. Make sure you visit Morwenstow with time to spare as the pretty land around the church, and the stretch of cliffs to the west, is owned and conserved by the National Trust and worth a visit.

Southwards from Morwenstow is Coombe hamlet, set in a wooded valley that is eaqually as peaceful. The river reaches the sea at Duckpool where the pebble beach has built up to dam a small pool of fresh water. Just north of Coombe, the coast path passes just above Lower Sharpnose Point, where spectacular natural piers of rock jut out into the sea like the massive walls of ruined temples.

Inland the large satellite dishes of the Cleave Camp Satellite Station seem alien amidst such raw natural beauty, and dominate the view for miles around.

The Eden Project

Built in a china clay pit approaching the end of its working life, in the heart of Cornwall's clay mining country, the Eden Project is the story of man's dependence on plants, connecting plants, people and places. Dominated by the futuristic-looking biome structures, which have the appearance of giant-sized bubble wrap, the Project is much more than just a green theme park. Sure, it's all about plants, but it's a story told in a very special and unique way. Eden is a living demonstration of regeneration and aims to reconnect people with their environments locally and globally. This is not a place that pretends to have all the answers, but one that prefers people to explore their world with a fresh eye.

Life on Earth after all depends on the survival of the plants that surround us – each day of our lives, we use plants from every continent, often without realising it. To help explain the importance of plants, the Eden Project offers a cathartic passageway into a fascinating interactive world of plants and people, a living drama, one that explores our global garden inheritance, displaying plants as you may never have seen them before.

The vision of the first horticultural directors of Eden, Philip McMillan Browse and Peter Thoday, was to re-create the major elements of the world's flora, and to integrate a particular focus on the relationship people have with plants...and that doesn't just mean talking to them! The fact that the site chosen for Eden was a clay pit is itself a key element in the overall story. Gardeners everywhere will realise that it is a mere bagatelle, just a few days' work, to build a garden many tens of thousands of square metres in size that portrays the diverse and rich flora of the world – well almost – but quite another to do so in the soil-less crater prone to flooding that was Bodelva. On the plus side, the site was south facing and sheltered.

The project opened to the public in March 2001 and three months later had already welcomed its millionth visitor. What makes the Eden Project so special is that it successfully combines ecology, horticulture, science, art and architecture. It provides

an informative and enjoyable experience, while simultaneously promoting ways of maintaining a sustainable future in terms of human global dependence on plants and trees. The exhibits include over one hundred thousand plants representing five thousand species from many of the climate zones of the world.

The site is huge, and you cannot visit Eden without being stunned by the sheer magnitude of it all. The incredible biome structures are the biggest conservatories in the world, and are split into a 'Humid Tropics Biome' and a 'Warm Temperate Mediterranean Biome'. Another world record reflects the 230 miles (389km) of free-standing scaffolding poles used during construction of the humid tropics biome, which today contains thousands of plant species. The bubbles are made of inflated hexagonal transparent 'plastic' windows, and flimsy as they may seem each hexagon is tough enough to take the weight of an entire rugby team.

The Humid Tropics Biome is 240 metres long, 110 metres wide and 50 metres high, easily tall enough to accommodate trees from the tropical rainforests; in fact, they tell you, this is the largest rain forest in captivity! The biome contains more than 1,000 plant species at an air temperature between 18° and 35°C; waterfalls and mist sprays help to keep the air moist.

In the Humid Tropics Biome, you experience the sights, smells and sheer scale of the rainforest, typical of the Oceanic Islands, Malaysia, West Africa and tropical South America, but without the many and varied rainforest inhabitants that can make you very poorly, or dead. Rainforests have up to 60 inches of rain in a year, but in the tropical biome the soil is kept moist by a soil irrigation system.

In this beautifully controlled environment there are insects, butterflies and some lizards. Here, too, you can find plants like palms and bananas, rubber trees, rice, coffee, sugar, pineapples, bamboo, and lilies.

BELOW LEFT Lemon trees are among the many tropical fruits that thrive in the perfect growing conditions created in the Temperate Biome.

BELOW MIDDLE The King Protea (Protea cyanaroides), is found on moist sandstone slopes throughout the Cape Peninsular in South Africa.

RIGHT Originating from Sumatra, Indonesia, the 'Corpse plant' (*Amorphallus Titanum*) is the biggest flower in the world – and the smelliest when it blooms! Its yellow spike is wrapped in a single leaf and when the plant prepares for pollination, the spike heats up and gives off a putrid smell which attracts insects.

BOTTOM & OPPOSITE An alliance of the faith and the fortunes of two construction company giants, Sir Alfred and Robert McAlpine, enabled the 18-month creation of The Eden Project and its spectacular domes. The latest addition to the site is 'The Core', a £15 million education centre that was designed using nature's growth pattern, and elements of a tree, as inspiration.

The air in the Warm Temperate Biome is a little cooler, and maintained between 15° and 25°C (77°F) in the summer and a minimum of 10°C (50°F) in the winter. Warm temperate zones include the Mediterranean regions, parts of California and South Africa, South-West Australia and Chile, where plants thrive on drought and poor thin soils. Summers are hot and dry, whereas winters are cool and wet. Plants in the Warm Temperate Biome include tobaccos, grape vines, cotton, varieties of olives and luscious Mediterranean fruits and peppers.

Within the unique experience of Eden, you encounter stories that demonstrate the ways in which man uses plants for food and medicine, and even for construction and entertainment. It also covers how plants affect the air we breathe and a whole lot more, and provides information on the relationship between plants and the development of our diverse global cultures.

Eden offers a glimpse, too, into the future, explaining the use of plants in new designs and technologies. For everyone there is a chance to be involved, to feel, taste and use plants on themed tours and in a wide range of workshops.

But it's not only just plants and more plants. Eden has been voted the UK's best rock music venue and the arts generally are integral to how the Eden project gets its message across. In fact, the whole site is liberally dotted with thought-provoking artworks and installations. Eden's in-house creative team encourages world-renowned theatre companies to use Eden as a venue and you can see plays as well as rock and pop concerts and even go clubbing.

The Eden project is continuously developing and will probably never be completely finished. 'The Edge', one of the next big constructions, is part of the evolution of Eden, having its roots in an ambition to have a biome that focuses on desert regions. It will concentrate on the challenges of water use and water security, energy use and energy security and the climate change brought about by these.

In a nutshell Eden is about man's delicate but often complex relationship with plants and is a showcase for questions and some, but not all, of the answers. Eden is about education and communication of the principal environmental issues of the day, all presented in an engaging, accessible, hands-on, and sometimes humorous way.

MOUSEHOLE MAP REF 398 C8

'Mouz'l', as it should be pronounced, is a fishing village of strong character, though the days are long gone when its harbour was crammed with pilchard-fishing boats. The name derives from obscure roots. Its old Cornish name is Porth Enys, meaning 'the landing place by the island'. The small island offshore from Mousehole is called St Clement's after a hermit who is said to have maintained a warning light.

Tempting alleyways and passages wriggle between sturdy cottages in Mousehole and the harbourside Ship Inn rounds things off with a flourish. The far end of Mousehole's tiny harbour has a splendid inner wall of irregular granite blocks, a perfect subject for imaginative photography. There are some shops, cafés and restaurants. Mousehole was not built for the motor car and is best explored on foot – there is a car park by the harbour and another on the outside of the village on the road from Newlyn.

A steep hill takes you inland from Mousehole to the village of Paul where the Church of St Pol de Leon has some impressive features. These include a memorial to the Mousehole crew of the local lifeboat, the *Solomon Browne*. They died heroically near Lamorna during an appalling storm in December 1981 after repeated attempts to save the eight people aboard the wrecked cargo vessel *Union Star*. The road out of Mousehole to the west leads up the steep Raginnis Hill. Part way up is the famous Mousehole Bird Hospital, a refuge for countless injured birds many of which are the victims of oil pollution. The recovery cages often contain several very vocal birds.

MULLION MAP REF 398 C8

Mullion is a large village a short distance inland from the harbour at Mullion Cove. There is a lovely sense of anticipation on first approaching Mullion and the village lives up to expectations – a bustling place with an excellent variety of shops, art and craft galleries and some good pubs. The Church of St Melanus has a remarkable collection of wooden bench-ends depicting characters, including a jester and a monk. Mullion Cove is fascinating and dramatic in winter high seas. Big cliffs and sea stacks, gold-leafed with yellow lichen, enclose the narrow inlet and its substantial piers. Offshore lies the bulky mass of Mullion Island, flickering with seabirds.

The coast to the south is pleasantly remote, especially around Predannack Head and Vellan Head, with delightful coast walks to either side of the cove. Just to the north of Mullion is Polurrian Cove where there is a large sandy beach and further north again is the popular Poldhu Cove with its sandy dunes.

NARE HEAD MAP REF 398 D7

Nare Head is the focus of a beautiful stretch of coastline that borders the little parishes of Gerrans, Veryan and St Michael Caerhays, between the Roseland Peninsula and Dodman Point. The easiest approach to the area is along the A3078 then on an unclassified road that leads to the village of Veryan, noted for its unique and elegant church and for its remarkable thatched round houses. The Church of St Symphorian is impressive, with a dark tower of mottled stone. There are a number of beaches along the shores of Gerrans Bay and Veryan Bay. The best beaches are at Pendower and Carne where there is good parking and access to Nare Head. To the east is the quiet little village of Portloe, which has a small car park at its eastern end. Further east again is a beach at Porthluney below Caerhays Castle. The castle is a picturesque, 19th-century replacement for an older building, which has a fine woodland garden.

NEWQUAY MAP REF 398 D7

Newquay is geared unashamedly to its splendid beaches, of course, and in places there seem to be more hotels and guest houses than breathing space. But there is still a strong sense of the 'old' Newquay. Sea-angling trips are available; a good way of appreciating the marine environment and the sea-going traditions of this Cornish town.

The town is lively. The beaches and broad, busy streets with shops, pubs and clubs make Newquay the epitome of bright and breezy holiday-making. Yet there are quiet corners in flower-filled

MOUSEHOLE

NEWQUAY

parks and gardens. Attractions include a zoo and fun pools and a swimming pool at the Water World in Trenance Leisure Park off Edgcumbe Avenue.

The Elizabethan manor house of Trerice (National Trust) lies just 3 miles (4.8km) southeast of Newquay. It is an exquisite building. The Elizabethan gardens have long since disappeared but the Trust has laid out the south side of the old garden with fruit trees in a classic 17th-century pattern. There is a restaurant in the Barn and a hayloft has a collection of interesting antique lawnmowers.

PADSTOW MAP REF 398 D6

Padstow is a likeable, good-natured town in a fine position on the Camel Estuary. Its maritime history is a noble one, though it was often tragic. The shifting sand bar across the mouth of the estuary, the Doom Bar, is extremely dangerous at certain states of the tide and in heavy seas. Records show that over 300 vessels were wrecked here between 1760 and 1920. At low tide, a vast expanse of sand sweeps away from Padstow, shading to gold towards the sea and to honey-coloured mud towards the inner estuary and Little Petherick Creek. Padstow's busy harbour has been modernised, but in keeping with

traditional style. The buildings that cluster around it have great variety, and the maze of streets and narrow passageways behind it are pleasantly cool on sunny mornings. Padstow was a busy trading port from the earliest times, and Welsh and Irish saints of the Dark Ages landed here. St Petroc arrived from Wales in the 6th century and stayed for 30 years, founding a monastery, which thrived until 981 when it was destroyed by marauding Vikings. The present Church of St Petroc is pleasantly sombre within its shaded churchyard. The route of the old railway line, closed in 1967, is now the Camel Trail, a walking and cycle route. North of Padstow is Stepper Point, the fine headland at the entrance to the estuary.

The Saints' Way, 'Forth an Syns' in Cornish, is a 28-mile (45km) route from Padstow to Fowey. It is a delightful route that can be walked in two days and is best started at the Church of St Petroc.

PENZANCE MAP REF 398 C8

Penzance has a sunny, friendly character gained from its south-facing position on the most sheltered part of Mount's Bay and from the bustle of its many attractive streets. It has the only promenade in Cornwall and it is a rather lengthy one,

with wonderful views. The open-air, art deco Jubilee Swimming Pool rounds off the harbour end of the promenade. Penzance harbour is small but has a busy atmosphere and a mix of vessels from fishing boats to visiting yachts; the passenger boat to the Isles of Scilly leaves from the outer pier.

A pleasant approach to the harbour, from the busy Market Place, is down the diverting Chapel Street where there are antique and craft shops, pubs and eating houses. Penzance's attractive main street, Market Jew Street, is enhanced further by a raised granite terrace. There are shops of all kinds here, and in the pedestrianised Causewayhead that leads inland from Market Place. Towards the sea, and to either side of Morrab Road, are Morrab Gardens and Penlee Park; the former is a lovely ornamental garden, while the latter houses the Penlee House Gallery and Museum. The gallery stages excellent temporary exhibitions, often of work by the 19th- and early 20th-century Newlyn-based painters, such as Stanhope and Elizabeth Forbes, Walter Langley and 'Lamorna' Birch, who lived in the area from 1880 to 1940. The museum has good displays of local archaeology, social and local history, and the environment.

To the west, Penzance merges with Newlyn, the major fishing port in the southwest. Newlyn harbour is full of life and colour. Scores of fishing boats of all types and sizes work from here in spite of the increasing difficulties of the modern international industry. The large fish market bustles with activity in the early morning as boats land a remarkable variety of fish. Parking at Newlyn is difficult, and most visitors find that a walk along Penzance's spacious promenade and on along the seafront to Newlyn is a pleasant alternative, which can be combined with a visit to the Newlyn Art Gallery along the way.

Just outside Penzance is the National Trust's Trengwainton Garden, a superb complex of five walled gardens set amid mature woodland, which is at its best during the spring and early summer months. Trengwainton Garden can be reached via Heamoor, or from Tremethick Cross on the St Just road.

Penzance has a summer festival called Golowan that lasts for ten days in mid-June and involves numerous cultural events and entertainment. It culminates in Mazey Day when the streets of Penzance are closed to traffic and the main street, Market Jew Street, hosts a street fair.

PORTHCURNO BAY

PORTHCURNO & MINACK THEATRE
MAP REF 398 C8

The pure, golden sand of Porthcurno's beaches and the crystal clear clarity of its sea supports Cornwall's claim to be an alternative to the Mediterranean. Under a blazing summer sun, the comparison is apt. Granite towers and pinnacles lie embedded in the steep vegetated slopes that encircle the bay and the superb sand lies deeply against the shoreline. Some of the adjoining beaches are covered at high tide but the main Porthcurno beach is always available, sparkling and luxurious.

For many years Porthcurno was the centre of international cable telegraphy. From here, undersea telegraph cables communicated with the rest of the world and, at one time, the Cable and Wireless Company ran a training college in the Porthcurno Valley. In 1994, the company donated Porthcurno beach and its adjacent cliff land to the National Trust, as the company had relocated its main training facilities to Coventry. There is a fascinating telegraph museum housed in underground chambers within the old Porthcurno college complex just inland from the large car park.

You are really spoiled for choice when you visit Porthcurno. The main beach is marvellously persuasive for wriggling the toes and to either side lie lovely coastal walks. Eastward is the famous Logan Rock, a vast monolith that once rocked at the touch of a finger but is less

responsive now, and westward is the well-known Minack Theatre, lovely Porth Chapel beach and the little Church of St Levan. St Levan can also be reached along the narrow road that climbs steeply uphill from Porthcurno. There is a car park by the church. All around Porthcurno Bay you will find sheltered coves, such as Penberth, and exquisite tidal beaches, and the eastern side is flanked by the magnificent headland of Treryn Dinas.

ROSELAND PENINSULA
MAP REF 398 D7

This beautiful peninsula seems quietly detached from mainstream Cornwall. Flanked on its eastern side by a craggy, rock-fringed coast curving north into Gerrans Bay, it is bordered on the west by the River Fal, with Mylor and Feock set opposite. The very tip of the Roseland Peninsula is pierced by the twisting Percuil River that cuts deeply inland to create even smaller peninsulas. The area is famous for St Mawes, St Mawes Castle and for the peaceful Church of St Just-in-Roseland. A pleasant alternative to the A3078 route out on to the peninsula, is to take the A39 southwards from Truro, the B3289, past Trelissick Gardens and then cross the Fal by the King Harry Ferry. Another approach is to take the passenger ferry from Falmouth to St Mawes.

St Just-in-Roseland is an exquisite place. The church stands on the banks of a small creek, its mellow stonework

embedded in a garden of shrubs and graceful trees that include palms as well as indigenous broad leaves.

On the promontory of land between Carrick Roads and the Percuil River stands St Mawes, deservedly popular and besieged with moored yachts in summer. On Castle Point to the west is Henry VIII's majestic St Mawes Castle, a quiet triumph of good Tudor design over function and renowned for its symmetry and decoration. The outer arm of the Roseland terminates at St Antony Head (one of the properties cared for by the National Trust on the peninsula) where there is a lighthouse and gun battery with an interesting history. On the east coast, further north, is Portscatho, open to the sea and with excellent sandy beaches nearby.

ST IVES MAP REF 398 C7

St Ives' rare character springs from its fishing traditions, its artistic inheritance, and its tourism industry. There is a clash of style amongst all three at times, but St Ives has survived such competing interests. Not only is the town the archetypal Cornish fishing port, it also has magnificent beaches of silken sand that offer both safe family bathing and surf to sing about. The town has aimed determinedly upmarket in recent years and has benefited greatly from the opening of the modern Tate St Ives in 1993. The gallery stands above Porthmeor Beach, its curves and crests are as white as the

waves below. The paintings on display are by leading artists of the St Ives School including Patrick Heron, Peter Lanyon and Terry Frost. It is a joy to find such paintings within the very landscape that inspired them. The view seaward from the gallery's roof terrace is worth crossing the world for. Before the Tate opened, the Barbara Hepworth Museum and Sculpture Garden was the most important artistic attraction here and still remains popular.

St Ives is a delight because of its narrow, canyon-like streets, ubiquitous granite cobbles, and clear, sea-mirrored light. The parish church of St Ia is one of the finest in Cornwall. St Ives harbour area, known locally as 'Downlong', is a maze of exquisite vernacular granite buildings where you catch satisfying glimpses of shady courtyards and passageways. And there are always those beaches to escape to: Porthminster to the south is sheltered and calm; Porthmeor to the north is a bit more lively and popular with the surfing crowd – through winter and summer.

There are several smaller beaches at the harbour and in the lee of the Island, (which is the breezy, green promontory that juts out to sea from a low-lying neck of land). The price of all this is potential overcrowding at the busiest holiday periods. Avoid dawdling through St Ives by car and be prepared for close-quarters humanity in the narrow Fore Street and along the busy harbour front. There is a useful park-and-ride scheme at Trenwith above the town and another at Lelant Station, southeast of the town, which uses a little branch line. Artistic ambience – and, at times, pretension – means that St Ives has numerous art galleries and craft shops. There is an excellent town museum at Wheal Dream, and most of the town's numerous restaurants, tea rooms and pubs are of quality and character.

TINTAGEL MAP REF 398 E6

Tintagel should not be missed, even if a visit is fleeting. The focus of this relentlessly 'themed' village is the ruined castle moulded to the blunt summit of 'the Island' of Tintagel Head and approached across a narrow neck of land. The castle is 13th century, but the romance of the site has attracted competing claims for its origins: Iron Age enclosure, Celtic monastery, Roman signal station and, of course, the court of King Arthur. The prominence of the Island suggests that it was used as a defensive site from the earliest times, face-on to the Atlantic.

Barras Nose to the north and Glebe Cliff to the south are in the care of the National Trust. It is tempting to say that the hinterland is in the care of the King Arthur industry, but Tintagel village offers much more than that. The wonderfully antiquated Old Post Office (National Trust) at the heart of the village is a delightful building. It is actually a small 14th-century manor house, with a central hall rising the full height of the building, and became a post office only in Victorian times. King Arthur's Great Halls in Fore Street is a remarkable token of dedication to a theme. The building was completed in the early 1930s and is devoted to Arthurian memorabilia and includes a collection of stained-glass windows.

TRURO MAP REF 398 D7

Truro's great cathedral catches the eye from all quarters. It rises from the heart of the city, its honey-coloured stone and lancet windows reflecting the sun, its great Gothic towers piercing the sky. There is no trace of the Norman castle that once stood at Truro, nor of the Dominican friary that stood near the low ground by the river, but the cathedral makes up for their loss.

Truro's fortunes rose and fell over the years, but by the late 18th century it had become the political and cultural centre of Georgian Cornwall. It was during the last years of the 18th century that such famous features as Boscawen Street and Lemon Street were built. Today Boscawen Street is a broad, cobbled space, entered at both ends from narrow thoroughfares.

The granite façade of the City Hall graces Boscawen Street, and Lemon Street survives as one of the finest examples of a late Georgian street in Britain, its houses perfectly aligned to either side of a broad avenue that climbs uphill.

There are hidden glories in Truro amid the modern developments. From the Moorfield car park, a lane leads to Victoria Square, but parallel and to its right is the elegant Georgian crescent of Walsingham Place. Throughout the heart of Truro, the lanes connecting the main streets are lined with attractive shops, cafés and restaurants. From the west end of Boscawen Street, King Street leads up to the pedestrianised area of High Cross in front of the cathedral. The stylish Assembly Rooms, with a façade of Bath stone, stands nearby.

Seen from its forecourt the cathedral seems crowded in by buildings, instead of being the dominating presence that commands the view from outside the city. But the west front and its soaring towers is exhilarating. The foundation stones of the cathedral were laid in 1880 and the western towers were finally dedicated in 1920. Truro's cathedral is thus a Victorian building. Its design is mainly Early English Gothic but with strong French influences that are seen in the great spires. The interior is glorious. It is vaulted throughout

and pillars and arches are in elegant proportion, the air light beneath the great roofs. There are beautiful individual features such as the exquisite baptistry. All that remains of the old parish church of St Mary's is incorporated into the south aisle. Those with an eye for ancient stonework may find the outer wall of the old church a reassuring contrast to the smooth planes of the Victorian cathedral.

Pydar Street runs northwards from the cathedral and serves as a pleasant pedestrian concourse. A short distance away is the stylish Crown Court, and just below here are the pleasant Victoria Gardens. Boscawen Park, by the Truro River, is reached along the road to Malpas. The Royal Cornwall Museum in River Street has an excellent collection of minerals and there are exhibitions covering archaeology and mining. The little art gallery has works by John Opie, the 18th-century portrait painter, who was born near St Agnes. Truro is an excellent shopping centre with numerous shops offering a great variety of quality goods.

ZENNOR MAP REF 398 C7

Storm-tumbled cliffs and wheeling gulls guard Penwith's wild, Atlantic shoreline. The sleepy village of Zennor with its rough tawny hills slope down towards the echoing sea cliffs. Between hills and

sea lies a narrow coastal plateau of small irregular fields whose Cornish 'hedges' of rough granite date from the Iron Age. Because of its antiquity this long-farmed landscape has earned Zennor protected status for ecological and archaeological reasons. Such vulnerability should be taken into account when visiting Zennor and its surrounding countryside. Below the car park is the Wayside Museum; it is crammed with exhibits about different ways of farming, mining, archaeology and folklore. Zennor's Church of St Senara stands proud over the village.

Zennor has an endearing myth of a mermaid. The mermaid was said to have seduced a local chorister into the deep, dark waters below the lofty Zennor Head. On quiet evenings, the smooth heads of seals bobbing in the sea perpetuate the legend and an attractive bench-end motif in the church encourages the tale.

Access to Zennor Head and to the coast path is on foot down a narrow lane that starts behind the Tinner's Arms. Zennor Head has a flat top, but its western flank is spectacular. Towering cliffs plunge into a narrow gulf, the sea crashes white against the shoreline far below. If you can tear yourself away from thoughts of mermaids, it is an invigorating 6-mile (9.6km) walk eastwards to St Ives along some of the most remote coastline in Cornwall.

ST IVES

HELFORD ESTUARY

The Helford River is enduringly popular with land-based visitors and leisure sailors alike, yet the area manages somehow to absorb it all. The pelt of trees that line the estuary and its creeks plays a great part of muffling this human racket so that you can enjoy this circuit of the peaceful tidal creeks.

DISTANCE/TIME 5 miles (8km) 3h **MAP** OS Explorer 103 The Lizard **START** Helford village car park (busy in summer); grid ref: SW 759261 **TRACKS** Good woodland paths and tracks, field paths, short section of quiet lane, 9 stiles **THE PUB** The Shipwright's Arms, Helford. Tel: 01326 231235

1 As you leave the car park, turn left along a path, signed 'Coast Path'. Go through a metal gate and then follow a sunken track. Go down steps, then turn right along a lane. At a steep right-hand bend, bear off ahead along a track. Pass behind a house and follow this permissive path through the approaching trees for about 1 mile (1.6km), and keep to the left at any junctions.

2 Leave the wooded area via a metal gate, then turn left along a field edge to a stone stile. Follow the bottom edge of the next two fields. Go through a field gap beside a white pole and a post with an orange triangle (these are navigation marks). Follow the field edge ahead. Go through a kissing gate, then follow the field edge (there's a seat and viewpoint on the left), to where it ends at the beginning of a wide track (to make the short circuit of Dennis Head, follow the track ahead until you get to a stile on the left).

3 To continue on the main route, turn sharply right at the start of the wide track and follow the left-hand field edge and then a path across the open field. Join a track behind a house, then go through a kissing gate and descend to St Anthony-in-Meneage Church. If you have time, visit the church as

it has some fine features, including a finely engraved 15th-century font. Follow the road alongside Gillan Creek.

4 Just past where the road curves round a bay, go up right through a gate by a public footpath sign. Follow a broad track through trees to houses at Roscaddon. Keep ahead along a track that leads to Manaccan at a T-junction opposite Manaccan church.

5 Go through the churchyard and on through the gate opposite to a road (the village shop is to the left). Keep ahead to a junction, the New Inn is down to the left, then go up right, past the school. Keep uphill, then turn left along Minster Meadow, go over a stile, and through fields to reach a road.

6 Go diagonally left to the stile opposite, go across a field, then turn left following signposts to reach woods. Follow the path ahead. At a junction keep straight ahead, go over a stile and reach a second junction.

7 Bear right and follow a broad track through trees. Continue ahead at a further junction to reach some buildings at Helford. Keep ahead on reaching a surfaced road and follow the road up to return to the car park.

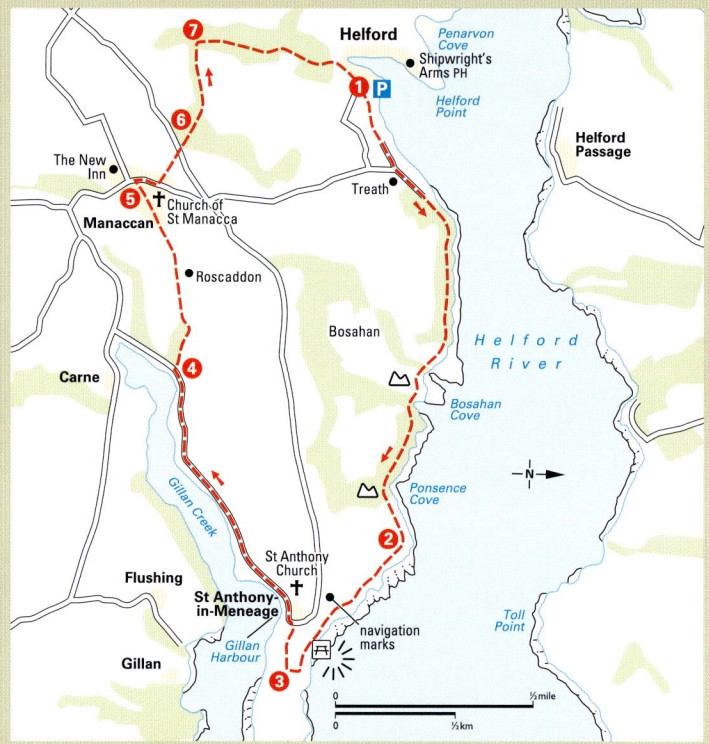

A COASTAL WALK NEAR ST IVES

This delightful walk starts from the maritime heart of St Ives and heads west along the glorious coastline. This is a very remote and wild part of the west Cornwall coast, a landscape of exquisite colours in spring and summer. Ancient field paths lead unswervingly back towards St Ives with a sequence of granite stiles recalling a very different world when folk travelled by foot out of necessity.

DISTANCE/TIME 3.25 miles (5.2km) 1h45 **MAP** OS Explorer 102 Land's End **START** Upper Trenwith car park, St Ives or Porthmeor Beach; grid ref: SW 522408 **TRACKS** Promenade, coastal path (can be quite rocky), field paths, 6 stiles **THE PUB** The Sloop Inn, St Ives. Tel: 01736 796584

1 Walk along the harbour front towards Smeaton's Pier. Just before the pier entrance, turn left to walk up Sea View Place. Once you reach where the road bends, keep going straight ahead into Wheal Dream. Turn right to walk past St Ives Museum, then continue along a walkway until you reach Porthgwidden Beach.

2 Cross the car park above the beach and climb up to the National Coastwatch lookout. Carry on climbing to the Chapel of St Nicholas on the headland via a path that runs behind the lookout, then follow a footway down to Porthmeor Beach. Go along the beach up to the car park.

3 Go up some steps found beside the public toilets, then turn right along a surfaced track past some bowling and putting greens. Continue straight ahead to enjoy the views at the rocky headlands of Carrick Du and Clodgy Point.

4 From the distinctive square-cut rock on Clodgy Point walk uphill and then pass through a low wall. Follow the path round to the right and across a wet area. In about 0.5 mile (800m) turn left at a junction.

5 Reach a T-junction with a track just past a National Trust sign, 'Hellesveor Cliff'. Turn left and head inland, following a hedged-in track, which is probably centuries-old. Such tracks gave access to the cliff, where animals were grazed and where the stone was gathered for building and furze for fuel.

6 Follow the path through the field and then across a stile. Go through a metal gate, pass a field gap and down a hedged-in path. Afterwards, cross a stile and pass between high hedges to reach a lane.

7 Turn right along the lane (Burthallan Lane) to a T-junction with the main road. Turn left and follow the road downhill to Porthmeor Beach and the car park.

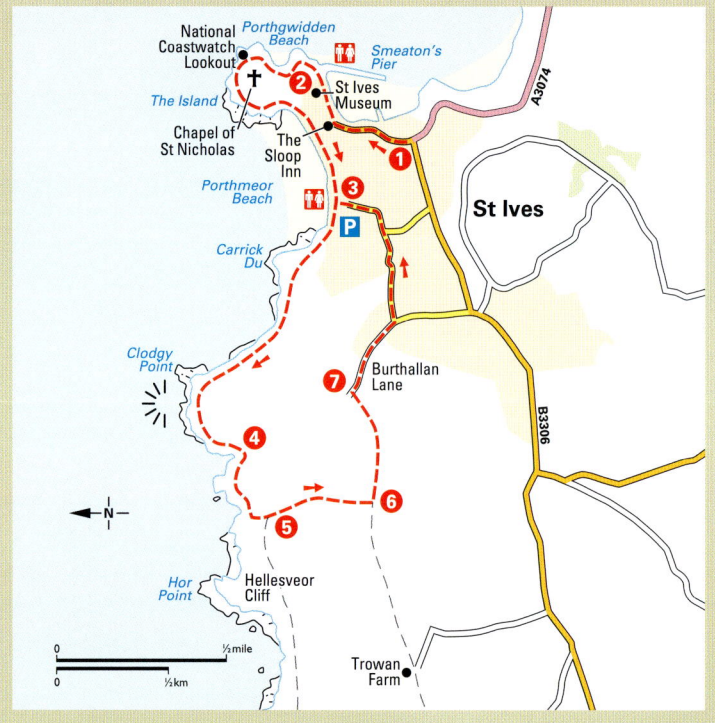

DISTANCE/TIME 10 miles (16.1km) 2h   **MAP** OS Explorer 106 Newquay & Padstow   **START** The Quarryman Inn, Edmonton; grid ref: SW 964727   **TRACKS** Well-surfaced former railway track

THE PUB The Quarryman Inn, Edmonton. Tel: 01208 816444   **CYCLE HIRE** Camel Trail Cycle Hire, Wadebridge. Tel: 01208 814104

DISTANCE/TIME 7 miles (11.3km) 1h30; including optional extension 10 miles (16.1km) 2h30

MAP OS Explorer 105 Falmouth & Mevagissey   **START** Pentewan Valley Cycle Hire; grid ref: SX 017473   **TRACKS** Mainly well-surfaced track, some woodland paths and a little roadwork

THE PUB The Ship Inn, Pentewan. Tel: 01726 842855; www.staustellbrewery.co.uk

THE CAMEL TRAIL – EDMONTON TO PADSTOW

Fabulous views, wonderful birdlife and unusual maritime plants make this section of the Camel Trail a delight at any time of year. If you want to keep away from the crowds, turn round on the edge of Padstow, or just dive in quickly for an ice cream.

1 The Quarryman Inn is a fascinating place. Behind the pub are two terraces of stone cottages, originally homes for workers at the quarries (Point 3); when these fell into disuse in the early 20th century the building became a TB isolation hospital. Today it is a very welcoming pub. From the car park turn right. At the crossroads turn left and enjoy a lovely downhill run, with increasingly good views over towards the River Camel and farmland beyond. The Camel was known as the Allen River until 1870, thought to derive from the Irish word 'alain', for beautiful: it's clear to see why. Pass through the hamlet at Tregunna and follow the lane over a bridge until you get to its end. Turn right down a narrow earthy path to reach the trail.

2 Turn right and follow the trail along the edge of the estuary. At low tide it's almost like cycling along the edge of a beach as the river is flanked by broad expanses of sand and the views are superb. The creeks and sandbanks attract wintering wildfowl – widgeon, goldeneye, long-tailed duck – as well as many divers and waders, spring and autumn migrants. En route, look out for curlew, oystercatcher, shelduck and little egret. One of the main reasons for constructing the railway was to transport sea sand, which is rich in lime, from the estuary to fertilise farmland away from the coast. Granite, slate, tin, iron and copper from mines on Bodmin Moor were exported.

3 A long cutting ends at the spoil heaps of the old slate quarries, with rounded, wooded Cant Hill opposite. The estuary is widening as it approaches the sea; there's a glimpse of Padstow ahead on the left bank. The mouth of the Camel Estuary is marred by the notorious Doom Bar, a shifting sandbank responsible for more than 300 shipwrecks from 1760 to 1920. If you're gently cycling along the Camel Trail on a sunny day it's difficult to imagine such disasters.

4 Continue past Pinkson Creek – you may see herons – and continue on to pass the parking area at Oldtown Cove. Once through the next cutting you'll get fantastic views towards Rock, on the other side of the estuary, with Brea Hill and Daymer Bay beyond, and out to the open sea. The trail bears away from the estuary through a cutting.

5 Cross the bridge over Little Petherick Creek. The Saints' Way, a 30-mile (48km) walking route, links Fowey on the south coast with Padstow's St Petroc's Church. It runs along the edge of the creek and past the obelisk (commemorating Queen Victoria's jubilee in 1887) on Dennis Hill, seen ahead. The creek is also an important habitat for little egret and a good range of wading birds.

6 Follow the trail past a lake on the left and then past houses on the edge of Padstow, with moored boats on the water on the right. Rock, opposite, is a popular sailing and watersports venue, and there's always masses to watch on the water. The trail ends at the quay and car park; you should dismount at this point to explore the town. Retrace your tracks along the Camel Trail to Edmonton.

THROUGH THE PENTEWAN VALLEY

A ride along the banks of the St Austell River, with an optional extension to the Lost Gardens of Heligan. This pleasant route follows the line of the old Pentewan railway along the tranquil St Austell river.

1 From the village car park return towards the B3273 and pass through the parking area for Pentewan Valley Cycle Hire. Go round a staggered barrier on to the trail, which emerges from shady woods on to the banks of the St Austell River.

2 Turn right and follow the trail along the riverbank.

3 Note the turn-off left across the river to the Lost Gardens of Heligan. Pass a small parking area into King's Wood (Woodland Trust), and follow the trail as signed left back on to the riverbank. Dip into woodland again, then bear right on to a lane.

4 Turn left; pass a small parking area to meet a tarmac lane on a bend. Bear right as signed. Turn left opposite 'Brooklea' and continue on a wooded path, with a caravan site left. The track bears left at Molingey – with London Apprentice across the river – then right to run along the right bank of the river again. Continue to follow this tarmac way as it bears right through fields, then left to reach the edge of the water treatment works. Turn left for 50yds (46m) to meet the B3273. Turn right to walk along the pavement.

5 Cross the lane to Tregorrick, and take the second lane on the right (Sawles Road – unsigned). Follow this lane to its end. For St Austell turn left uphill to cross the A390. To reach Pentewan either turn around here, or turn right and cycle steeply uphill through countryside. Drop to a T-junction and turn right, steeply downhill, through Tregorrick. At the B3273 turn left to return to Pentewan on the outward route.

6 Heligan extension: After passing Point 2, turn right to cross the river on the footbridge (dismount). At the B3273, turn left. Pass the touring park on the left, then turn right to cross the road as signed. Turn left, then continue on a track. Climb steadily uphill for 0.75 mile (1.2km), levelling off as the track passes beneath a road. Bear left to reach a fork. Keep left to meet the road; turn left for 0.5 mile (0.8km); Heligan on the left.

7 On leaving Heligan, turn right along the road. Cycle downhill, with great views over St Austell Bay. Turn left on the first narrow lane, steeply downhill. At the next minor road, turn left, even more steeply, to meet the B3273 opposite Pentewan Sands Holiday Park. Turn left towards the Esso garage, then right into Pentewan village.

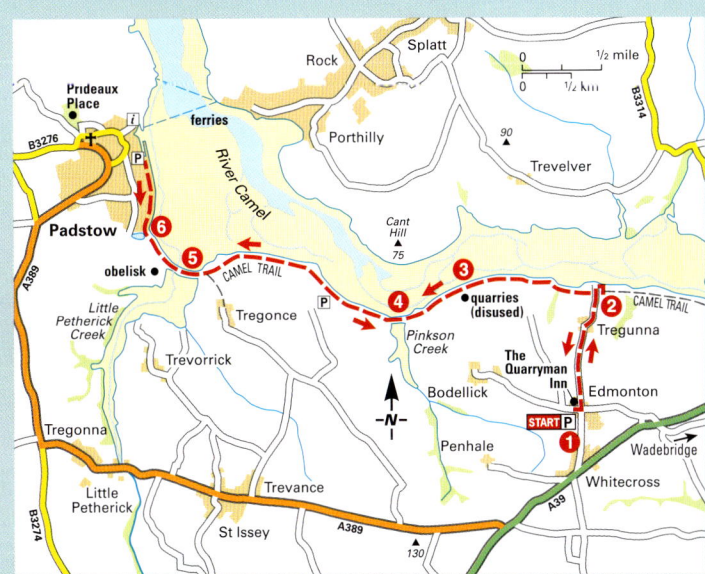

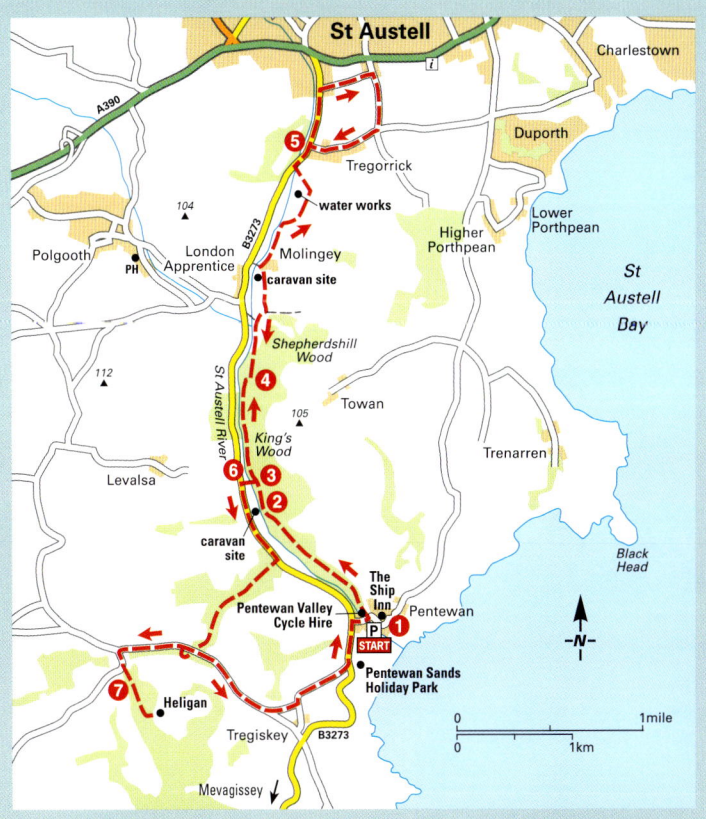

DISTANCE/TIME 5 miles (8km) 1h30 **MAP** OS Explorer 102 Land's End **START** The Godolphin Arms car park, Marazion; grid ref: SW 516306 **TRACKS** Short stretch of road, track generally level, rough and bumpy in places **THE PUB** The Godolphin Arms, Marazion. Tel: 01736 710202; www.godolphinarms.co.uk

DISTANCE/TIME 10 miles (16km) 2h **MAP** OS Explorer 104 Redruth & St Agnes **START** The beach car park, Portreath; grid ref: SW 654453 **TRACKS** Well-surfaced track, some road work **THE PUB** The Basset Arms, Portreath. Tel: 01209 842077; www.ccinns.co.uk

MARAZION TO PENZANCE

Enjoy an easy ride along one of south Cornwall's most beautiful bays. This level, easy, there-and-back route along the edge of Mount's Bay, with spectacular views over stunning St Michael's Mount, is an ideal option for families with young children. With just a short road stretch at the start and finish, the ride runs along the back of the huge expanse of sands that lie between Marazion and Penzance.

1 This ride is part of the First and Last Trail, the first stretch of the Cornish Way long-distance cycle route, which starts at Land's End and runs for 180 miles (288km) through the county. Marazion, where this ride starts, is Cornwall's oldest charter town, dating from 1257. Its unusual name comes from the Cornish 'marghas yow' – meaning 'Thursday market'. Marazion was the main trading port in Mount's Bay until Penzance overtook it in the 16th century. It's worth having a look around this attractive village before you set off. From the pub car park cycle uphill (away from the beach) on to West End. (The Godolphin Arms can be found by turning right.) Turn left along West End and cycle out of the village. There is a parking area on the left along much of this road, so look out for people opening their car doors suddenly. Marazion Marsh lies to the right.

2 Where the road bears right to cross the main Penzance to Exeter railway line, keep straight ahead through a parking area, with the Pizza Shack (and toilets behind) on the right. Take care cycling through the car park.

3 Keep ahead and leave the car park to the left of the old station (now the Station pub), to join a level track that runs along the back of the beach. Follow this track, passing public toilets on the right.

4 Take care where the track drops down to meet an entrance road to a beachside car park (there are warning notices 'Give way to traffic'). Pass through the parking area and continue along the track, with the railway close by on the right.

5 Go past the heliport, from which helicopters fly regularly to the Isles of Scilly, which lie more than 17 miles (28km) southwest of Land's End (day trips are available). Pleasant views open up ahead towards Penzance.

6 On approaching the station the track narrows into a concrete walkway and becomes busier, so look out for pedestrians. Follow the track into the car park by Penzance railway and bus station, with the Tourist Information Centre to the right. There's lots to see in Penzance, which developed as an important pilchard-fishing centre in medieval times. The arrival of the Great Western Railway in Victorian times gave the town another boost and it is now the main centre in the area known as Penwith (the far western part of Cornwall). The pretty harbour is full of interest, and it is from here that the RMV *Scillonian* makes regular sailings to the lovely Isles of Scilly. When you've had your fill of this busy little harbour, relocate the Tourist Information Office, where you should turn round and return to Marazion. The First and Last Trail actually runs along the road to Newlyn, but the extended route is pretty busy in terms of traffic and therefore is not recommended for families with young children.

PORTREATH TRAMROAD

This ride ambles into the heart of old industrial Cornwall, following a trail that crosses the county for 11 miles (17.5km) to Devoran on Restronguet Creek.

1 From the car park turn left, pass the Portreath Arms Hotel then bear left along Sunny Vale Road. As it bears right, bear left on to the tramway. Go through woodland, over the access road to a reservoir, through more woodland then fields, until you reach a white cottage on the left. Go along a lane to a minor road. Cross the road at Cambrose.

2 Turn left along the pavement and follow the road past Elm Farm. After 500yds (457m), turn right on a lane to a T-junction at Lower Forge. Cross the road and keep ahead until the next T-junction to go back on to the tramway. Follow this to North Downs (1.75 miles/2.8km); turn left to a road. Turn right on the pavement to the roundabout.

3 Turn left across the road and follow the pavement. Cycle uphill, pass another small roundabout and a café on the left. At the top of the hill turn right to cross the A30.

4 Over the bridge turn left down a rough track. Bear left at Boscawen Farm and follow the track past Boscawen Mine. Pass Wheal Busy chapel left, to a lane junction. Keep ahead; 109yds (100m) on, turn right down a bridleway, then right on a track at the bottom. Go downhill, keep ahead, cross a lane, then go uphill. Bear left to meet a road.

5 Cross over and follow a track through a parking area and downhill past Killifreth Mine's Hawke's Shaft pumping house. Enter Unity Woods; keep left at the fork and follow the bumpy track downhill to a junction.

6 Turn right, rejoining the tramway. Follow the track out of the woods, with a road (B3298) left. Cross the road and continue to the left of the road. At the junction, turn left along the pavement. After 109yds (100m) turn right to cross the road, passing to the right of the Fox and Hounds pub. At the next road turn left and pass under the railway bridge. At the T-junction by the Crossroads Motel, cross the A30 and rejoin the outward route.

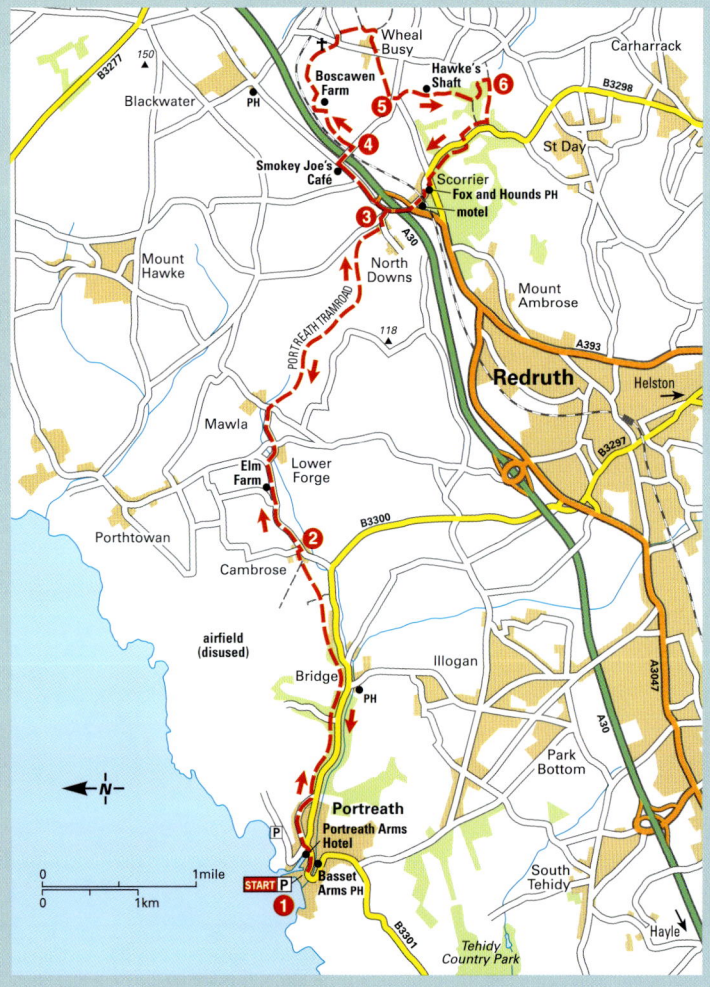

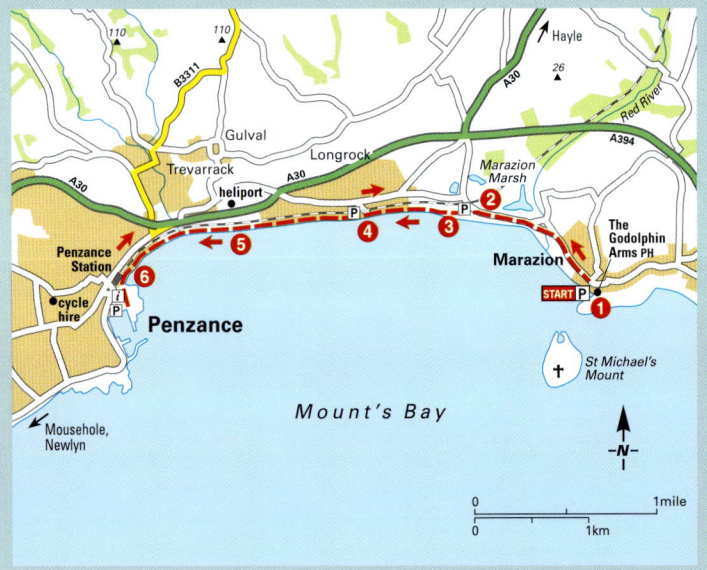

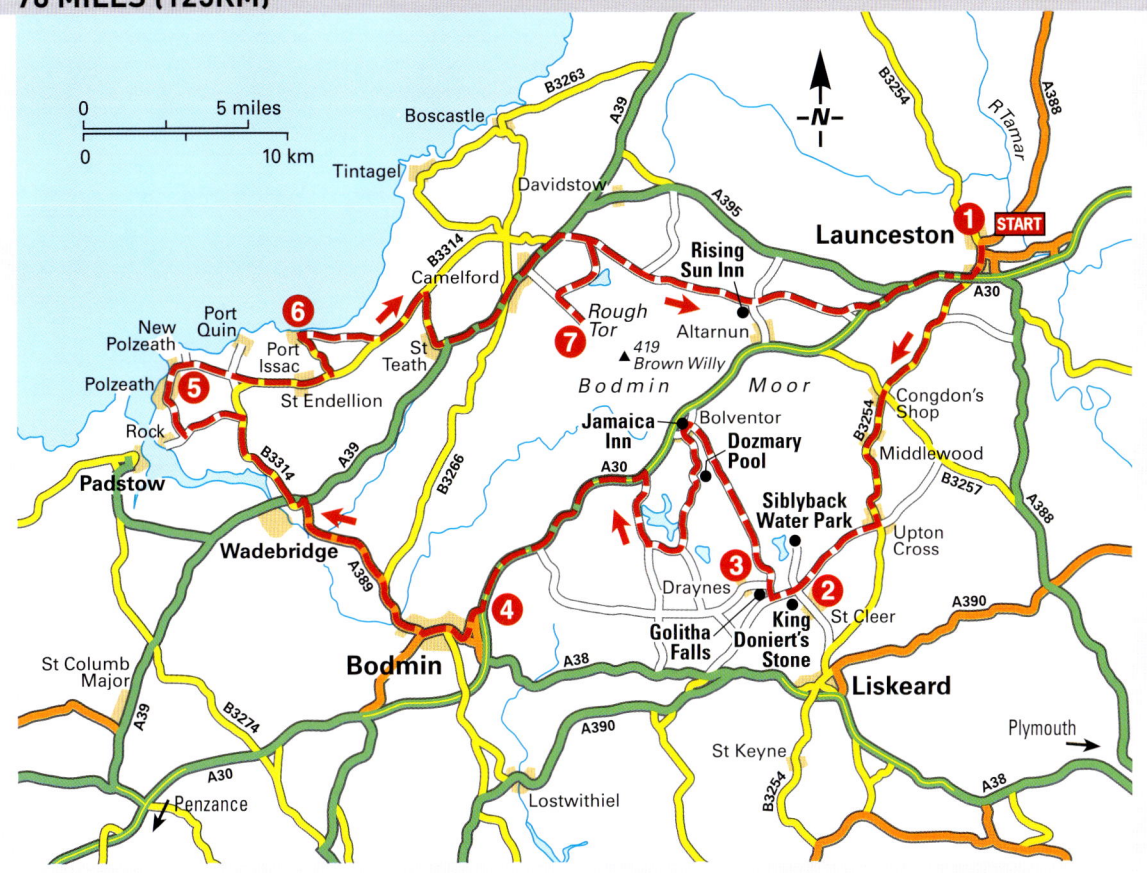

BODMIN MOOR & THE NORTH COAST

This drive takes in the wildest and loveliest parts of Bodmin Moor, with a visit to the north coast by way of contrast. The Minions area is dominated by ruined mine engine houses, Cheesewring Quarry, and by the rounded bulk of Caradon Hill, while the fine granite ridge of Rough Tor (pronounced 'Row Tor') dominates the western side of Bodmin Moor. The moorland slopes have numerous remains of Bronze Age circles and prehistoric field boundaries.

Route Directions

Start at Launceston, once a Norman fortified town and now home to fine architecture and interesting little streets.

1 Leave Launceston on the A388 (A30) signed 'Bodmin'. Go under the A30 then, at a roundabout, take the third exit, signed 'South Petherwin B3254'. Pass through South Petherwin and keep on the B3254 to a crossroads with the B3257 at Congdon's Shop (there's a war memorial opposite). Keep ahead for 5 miles (8km), passing through Middlewood and Darleyford, to a crossroads at Upton Cross. Turn right on to an unclassified road, signed 'Minions, Siblyback Lake'. Pass through Minions. Keep ahead at the next junction, signed 'St Cleer', passing a road on the right to Siblyback Watersports Centre.

Siblyback Watersports Centre on Siblyback Lake is a great place to go windsurfing, kayaking, canoeing, sailing, rafting, rowing, power boating or even angling. The centre offers tuition with fully qualified instructors for all levels of ability and the prices are pretty reasonable.

2 Continue on the main route, passing King Doniert's Stone on the left (parking). At the next junction, turn right, signed 'Draynes, Golitha Falls'. After 300yds (274m), a left turn over a bridge leads to a convenient car park (toilets). From here, it is only a short walk to the spectacular Golitha Falls, a National Nature Reserve.

3 Continue to Bolventor. Just before a junction is Daphne du Maurier's Smugglers at Jamaica Inn Centre. At the junction turn left to Jamaica Inn, then left opposite the Inn, signed 'Dozmary Pool'. In 1.5 miles (2.4km) pass Dozmary Pool and around the edge of Colliford Lake (park at Colliford Dam). At a junction turn right, signed 'Bodmin'. Continue to the A30. Turn left, to 'Bodmin'.

If you can, take a brief detour to Dozmary Pool, it said to be the final resting place of King Arthur's legendary sword Excalibur.

4 After 7 miles (11.2km), bear left on to the A389, signed 'Bodmin'. Keep ahead for Bodmin, ignoring left-hand routes, then turn right at a junction, signed 'Bodmin

A389'. At a mini-roundabout, go right and along Pool Street and on through Bodmin following signs for Wadebridge, A389. At a junction, turn right by a clock tower, signed 'Wadebridge' and continue on the A389 for 6 miles (9.6km). At a roundabout take the first exit signed 'Rock, Polzeath'. Turn right at the next roundabout on to the B3314, signed 'Rock, Polzeath'. Cross the Trewornan Bridge, then after 2 miles (3.2km) turn left, signed 'Rock, Trebetherick'. Continue for 2 miles (3.2km), then opposite a garage turn right into Trewint Lane, signed 'Trebetherick, Polzeath'. In 0.75 miles (1km), turn left at the next junction, signed 'Trebetherick, Polzeath'. Pass through Trebetherick and descend steeply into Polzeath, then ascend even more steeply.

If you are a surfer, you might like to make a detour to the surfing beaches of Polzeath, where wet-suited surfers gather year-round.

5 In 1.25 miles (2km) pass a turn-off to New Polzeath. Pass a left turn to Portquin, then keep left off the bend, signed 'St Endellion, Port Isaac'. Soon join the B3314 and go left. Continue through St Endellion, then turn left on to the B3267, signed 'Port Isaac'. Go through the upper part of Port Isaac (park here to visit the village – toilets).

Attractive little Port Isaac is really popular with visitors and, because the car is sidelined, can truly claim to be 'unspoilt'. The houses are tightly crowded together with only narrow

passageways, called 'drangs', between them. You'll have to breathe in to get through the narrowest passageway, Squeeze Belly Alley.

6 Leave Port Isaac and then descend steeply to Portgaverne. Ascend steeply, then continue to the B3314. Turn left, signed 'Delabole', and continue for 1.75 miles (2.8km) to a junction with the B3267. Turn right, signed 'St Teath'. Keep ahead through St Teath, signed 'Camelford'. Descend steeply to a T-junction with the A39 and turn left, signed 'Bude, Camelford'. Go through Camelford and continue along the A39 for 2 miles (3.2km), then turn right, signed 'Roughtor, Altarnun, Crowdy Reservoir'. After a mile (1.6km) turn right, signed 'Crowdy Reservoir', and follow the road (a one-time air strip), passing Crowdy Reservoir. At a crossroads, turn left, and soon after you reach a car park below the impressive granite ridge of Rough Tor.

This is a chance to stretch your legs. Leaving the car park you can take one of several paths towards the top of the Tor. You should come prepared for a muddy walk in wet weather.

7 Return to the crossroads, turn right, pass Crowdy Reservoir again, then, at a junction, turn right signed 'Altarnun'. Continue for about 5 miles (8km) to pass the Rising Sun Inn. Keep left and continue ahead, ignoring all side roads. After 3.5 miles (5.6km) pass Polyphant and reach the A30. Turn left and return to Launceston.

HELFORD RIVER & THE LIZARD

An absorbing drive past some lovely lakes and on through the popular Helford River area with its quiet tidal creeks to The Lizard, Britain's most southerly point. The south side of the Helford Estuary is a delightful landscape of wood-fringed creeks and inlets. Helford is worth a diversion from the main route of the tour, although access is down narrow lanes and driving can become quite restricted especially during busy holiday periods.

Route Directions

The tour starts in Helston, a pleasant market town which was once a port (until the silting of the River Cober landlocked the town).

1 Leave Helston on the B3297, signed 'Redruth'. After 6 miles (9.6km), having passed via Wendron and the access to Poldark Mine, turn right on to an unclassified road, signed 'Carnmenellis'. After 2 miles (3.2km), at a T-junction turn left, signed 'Stithians'. Continue ahead, with Stithians Reservoir situated on the right.

The reservoir is a good place for watersports and has superior birdlife so remember to take your binoculars with you.

2 Pass the Golden Lion Inn and continue across a causeway. At the next junction turn right, signed 'Stithians', and continue through Goonlaze. (Note: access road to Stithians dam and car park, just after Goonlaze.) Continue to drive through Stithians (toilets just past the church), then, on the other side of the village at a crossroads, go straight across and down Tregonning Road, signed for 'Mabe'. Follow a very narrow lane for 1.25 miles (2km) then take a right turning at a T-junction, signed 'Longdowns'. In 0.75 miles (1.2km), just after you pass a quarry, go left at a T-junction. Soon you will reach the A394. Turn left here, signed 'Falmouth'. Only a short distance up ahead, and just past a garage, branch right. Reach Mabe Burnthouse and, at a junction at the village centre, bear right, signed 'Mawnan' and 'Constantine'. Keep left at the next junction, signed 'Mawnan Smith'.

A short distance further on, a side road branches right down to the Argal Water Park. There is a car parking area here and some lovely waterside walks.

3 On the main route, follow signs for Mawnan Smith. Go directly over a crossroads, signed 'Mawnan Smith and Helford Passage' and continue for approximately 2 miles (3.2km) to reach Mawnan Smith, a pleasant village within lovely surroundings. Keep right by the Red Lion Inn, signed 'Budock Vean', and then follow the signs for Helford Passage and Constantine. Carry on, passing Glendurgan Garden, a delightful woodland valley garden of 40 acres (16ha), then pass the equally fine Trebah Gardens.

The gardens are filled with subtropical plants in an area covering more than 25 acres (10ha) with plenty to amuse children of all ages and to interest adults. Careful planting has ensured colour year-round.

4 Follow signs for Porth Navas and Constantine along a winding and often narrow lane (with passing places). Pass through Porth Navas and follow the signs for Constantine. When you reach a T-junction, go left through Constantine. On the far side of the village ignore the first left turn signed 'Vicarage Terrace, Gweek' and take the next left turn signed 'Gweek'. Pass through Brill and turn left at the next junction signed 'Gweek'. Go through Gweek. (Just past the Gweek Inn and before a bridge, a road to the left, called 'Meneth', leads to the National Seal Sanctuary.)

Gweek, just beyond Culdrose, is the home of the National Seal Sanctuary, Europe's largest rescue centre for seals. Injured seal pups are diligently cared for at the hospital and returned to the sea when they are fit and healthy. Those that are too badly disabled are given a new home at the sanctuary.

5 Go left by a thatched house, signed 'Mawgan' and 'St Keverne'. Continue through a wooded area and, at a roundabout, go left, signed 'Mawgan'. Drive carefully through Mawgan, keeping left at a junction, signed 'Manaccan and Helford', pass Mawgan church and then follow signs for Manaccan and Helford along a narrow and winding road with some steep inclines and sharp bends. Pass through St Martin and reach Newtown-in-St Martin. The main route goes right at a junction, just past the Prince of Wales pub. (For a diversion to Helford, keep past this junction to reach a junction with a road leading left signed 'Manaccan, Helford'.) On the main route, continue onwards until you get to a junction with the B3293. Here, turn left, signed 'St Keverne'. Continue on and pass the Goonhilly Satellite Earth Station.

Goonhilly is a complex of giant communication antennas and claims to be the world's largest and oldest satellite station.

6 A few hundred yards beyond the Earth Station turn right, signed 'Cadgwith and Kennack Sands', and follow along this

arrow-straight road to reach Kuggar. At a junction, turn right signed 'The Lizard'. At the next crossroads go forward, signed 'St Ruan and Cadgwith'. Continue through the village of St Ruan and after about half a mile (0.8km) pass a side road leading left. (300yds/274m down this side road is a large car park for Cadgwith.) On the main route keep ahead, and continue following signs for The Lizard. At a junction with the A3083, turn left for Lizard Point (toilets). Return along the A3083 to Helston, passing Culdrose Naval Air Base on the way back to Helford.

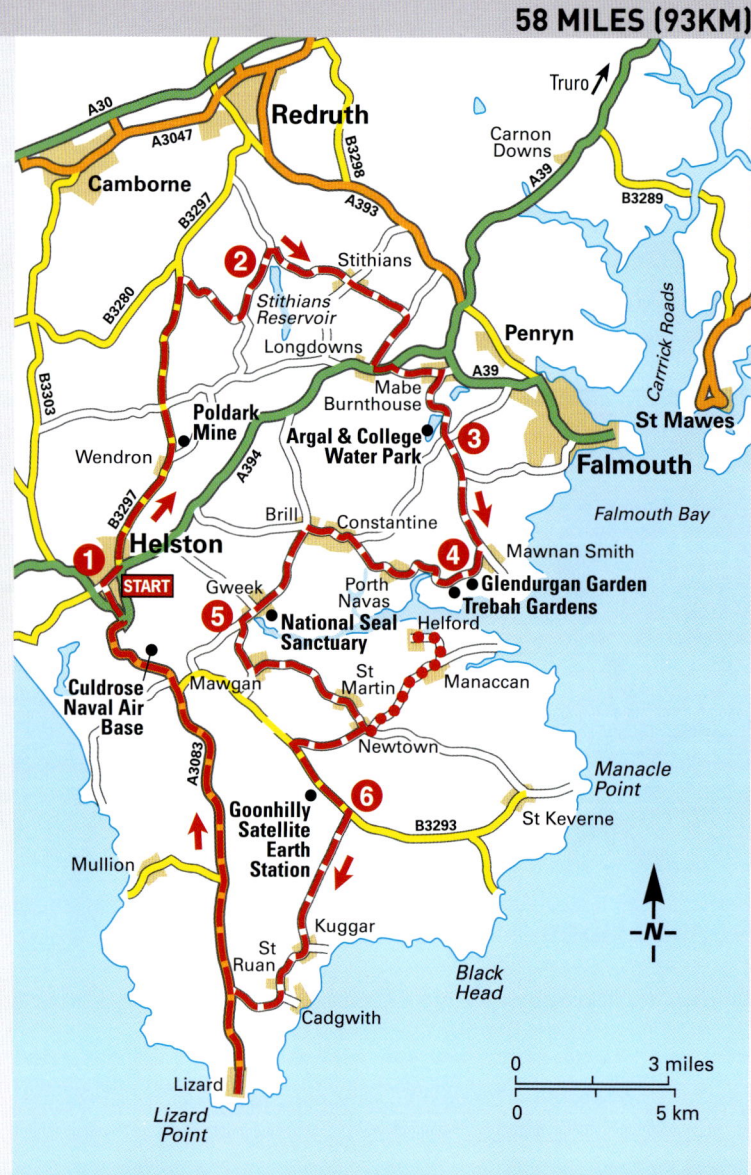

Devon

CLOCKWISE FROM TOP LEFT: PEBBLES AT BUDLEIGH SALTERTON; TORQUAY; GREAT WESTERN CANAL AT TIVERTON; STATUE OF RICHARD HOOKER AT EXETER CATHEDRAL; DAWLISH WARREN BEACH; SURFING AT SAUNTON SANDS

BRIXHAM

BARNSTAPLE MAP REF 398 F4

Barnstaple has attractive little alleyways, quiet corners and some fine buildings. These include the covered Pannier Market, built in the mid-19th century, where traditional markets as well as craft and antiques markets are held. Part of the same development is Butcher's Row, built to house 33 butchers' shops, though it has now been infiltrated by greengrocers, fishmongers and delicatessens.

One of the most historic sites in Barnstaple is the huge mound created by the Normans as a vantage point for their castle (only fragments of the original wall remain). But Barnstaple's history goes back further; records show that it was already the commercial centre for north Devon when it was first granted a charter in AD 930. It continued to prosper, becoming a major port for trade with America, and the ornate Queen Anne's Building down by the river dates from that era. Extensively renovated, it is now open to the public and contains the excellent Barnstaple Heritage Centre, portraying the history of the town with interactive displays and 'face-to-face' speaking models of figures from the town's past. These include the Elizabethan town clerk

Adam Wyatt, whose book *Lost Chronicle* is on sale in the Heritage Centre shop, and Mistress Grace Beaple, who, during the Civil War, sheltered Prince Charles (later Charles II). There are also reconstructions of the interior of a merchant's ship, a Civil War trench and scenes from earlier eras.

Near the bridge the Museum of North Devon has lively and imaginative exhibits, including a room which takes visitors into an underwater world, complete with sound effects, with giant turtles and large fish mounted on a realistic marine background. The display of north Devon pottery is spectacular and, of course, Tarka the Otter is never very far away (the Tarka Trail passes through the town).

North of the town are the famous Marwood Hill Gardens, which occupy about 12 acres (5ha) of a sheltered valley. Pathways lead down between the hillside trees and shrubs to a series of ponds, inhabited by some enormous koi carp.

BEER MAP REF 399 H6

The lovely little fishing village of Beer occupies one of the most sheltered positions along this coast and its fishermen gained a reputation for hardy seamanship because they could put to

sea when others were kept at home by the pounding waves. Beer is known also for having the most westerly chalk cliffs in England, contrasting vividly with the deep red cliffs nearby and the lush green of the surrounding countryside. It was once home to a fine lace-making industry, established here by refugees from the Netherlands, and the quality of the work rivalled the more famous Honiton lace.

The Beer Quarry Caves offer a totally different experience, with an hour-long tour of these man-made caverns that extend for a quarter of a mile (400m) in each direction. The Romans worked these quarries nearly 2,000 years ago, and the vast caverns with vaulted roofs connected with natural stone pillars were hewn by hand over the intervening centuries. The Cretaceous limestone quarried at Beer was highly prized by stonemasons. Soft and easy to carve when it first comes out of the ground, it hardens when it is exposed to the elements; examples of the carved stone can be seen in Exeter Cathedral.

BRANSCOMBE MAP REF 399 H6

Branscombe is gorgeous. It stretches along one of the prettiest combes on the south coast, with picture-book thatched

cottages – complete with roses all around the door – lovely inns and an ancient church. St Winifred's dates back to just after the Norman Conquest and its tower contains a priest's room, from the time when the priest lived in the church.

Until 1987, the village bakery was the last traditional bakery in use in the county. Along with the old forge, Manor Mill and some farms and cottages have now been preserved by the National Trust and visitors can see the large faggot-fired oven, the great dough bins and traditional baking equipment in the baking room.

The drive from the village to the beach is along a narrow lane that goes steeply up and then down again to the sheltered bay. Much of the land to either side, including farmland and foreshore in places, is in the care of the National Trust and there are lovely walks, including one from the village. The shingle beach has rock pools at low tide and is good for swimming.

BRIXHAM MAP REF 399 G7

The least commercialised part of Torbay, Brixham is home to a pretty harbour surrounded by some fine old buildings and a handful of pretty colour-washed cottages. Here the fish and chip shops, inexpensive cafés and other typical seaside outlets seem to try to blend in with their traditional surroundings. This is very much a seafaring community, as evidenced by the replica of Francis Drake's ship the *Golden Hind* in the harbour (open to the public) and the aquarium and trawling exhibition on the dockside. Fishing continues today but only on a small scale. The Brixham Museum, New Road, traces the ebb and flow of the town's maritime fortunes over nine centuries of seafaring; you can get right up to date by visiting the nearby marina.

There are some fine beaches – St Mary's Bay is large and sandy, but the rest are small shingle or pebble shores and are relatively peaceful and undeveloped. Just to the east of the town lies Berry Head Country Park, a splendid nature reserve, ideal for walking and for enjoying the views from the headland. The remains of a huge Napoleonic fort can also be visited here.

BUDLEIGH SALTERTON

MAP REF 399 H6

Budleigh Salterton became a resort in the wake of royal visits to nearby Sidmouth in Georgian and Victorian times, but it was – and remains – a quiet place, free of much of the bustle and amusements often associated with seaside holidays. It occupies a position on the west side of the Otter estuary (it was originally called Ottermouth), where one of the main industries used to be salt-panning, hence the 'Salterton' part of the name.

The beach at Otterhead (the mouth of the River Otter) is all pebbles, which shelve quite steeply into the sea, but swimming is safe enough in calm weather. If you prefer sand on your beach, walk westwards along the coast path to Littleham Cove, which is small and sheltered from the elements.

Many fine old buildings remain in the town, including Fairlynch in Fore Street, now a small but interesting museum that has displays on local history, the natural history of the River Otter and the Budleigh Salterton Railway, as well as a beautiful display of Devon lace and a fine costume collection. The Grade II listed building itself is of interest, being one of only a handful of thatched museums in the country, with many original features.

A little way inland is Otterton, a particularly pretty village made more so by its many thatched cottages. The watermill is the last working mill on the River Otter and you can see it in operation – milling takes place about three days a week. There are various displays on milling, as well as a craft shop, a gallery, a Devon food shop and a restaurant, plus live music on some evenings.

BURGH ISLAND   MAP REF 398 F7

One of the many curiosities of Devon, Burgh Island is a tiny rock covering just 28 acres (11ha) and can be seen clearly from the headland at Bigbury-on-Sea. Until the mid-19th century Burgh Island was a prosperous pilchard-fishing community. A lookout was stationed here and when the great shoals of pilchards were spotted he would shout out – hence the name.

Burgh Island is in fact only an island at high tide. At other times you can walk or drive – 'England 282 metres', says the sign! The most novel way to arrive, however, is at high tide, aboard the extraordinary Burgh Island sea tractor, which, with its passenger compartment raised high above the waves, can safely cross in up to 7 feet (2m) of water.

CLOVELLY   MAP REF 398 E5

Of all Devon's pretty villages, this is surely the most famous and the most visited – which can make it too crowded for comfort at the height of the season. You need real stamina to visit Clovelly. Its single cobbled street has an alarming gradient which drops some 400 feet (122m) over the course of half a mile, and traffic is banned, so visitors have to park at the top of the hill and explore on foot. Two things you should be aware of: first, because of the steep cobbles, wear sensible footwear; second, visitors enter the village through the visitor centre and pay an admission fee. But if all this strikes you as commercialised, don't be put off, because Clovelly is well worth it. As if the narrow cobbled street weren't picturesque enough, the colour-washed 16th-century cottages that cluster along its slopes are decked with flowers and shrubs, and at the bottom is the lovely little harbour.

If you find walking back up the street a trial, spare a thought for those who live here – everything, from food to fuel and furniture, has to be carried down this street, or lowered on sleds. For those who may be weak of leg and short of breath, there is a Land Rover service from Easter to October to the car park by a back route. On the way to Clovelly along the A39 near Bucks Mills is Hobby Drive. It was constructed as a hobby (hence the name) in the 19th century by a wealthy local landowner. It is closed to traffic now, but offers a 3-mile (4.8km) walk through wooded slopes above the coastline.

BUDLEIGH SALTERTON

DARTMOUTH MAP REF 399 G7

The ancient town and deep-water port of Dartmouth enjoys an unrivalled setting at the mouth of the picturesque River Dart, with steep green hills to either side and a busy, colourful estuary. The Embankment is a lovely uncluttered promenade, free of tourist trappings, and the attractive houses of Kingswear, many built for Dartmouth's wealthy merchants and sea captains, dot the far bank. Neither major road nor railway link has ever reached Dartmouth and this has undoubtedly helped the centre of town – a tiny web of criss-crossing cobbled streets and narrow alleyways – to retain its atmosphere and to protect it from the onslaught of modern traffic that blights many coastal towns.

In the very centre is the Boatfloat, a charming inner harbour only accessible to small craft. In the tourist information office, on the corner of the car park, is Thomas Newcomen's Atmospheric Steam Engine, invented in 1712, which is claimed to be the first ever successful steam engine. Also just off the Boatfloat, on Duke Street, is the 17th-century Butterwalk, a four-storey arcaded house decorated with wood carvings, its three upper floors supported by 11 granite pillars. It now houses shops and the delightful small Dartmouth Museum, with a whole flotilla of model ships and original 17th-century plaster and panelling. Further along Duke Street is the old cobbled market square

and building, erected in 1829, now home to various permanent shops but still the site of the weekly market.

Two buildings that have survived from the 14th century are the Cherub pub, Dartmouth's oldest building (1380) and Agincourt House. The prettiest part of town, however, is the charming cobbled quayside of Bayard's Cove. The Pilgrim Fathers put into this cove in 1620 en route to the New World and around five centuries earlier the Crusaders departed from here. You can explore the shell of a fortress, which was built in 1510 to protect the entrance to the harbour. Near the mouth of the river is Dartmouth Castle (English Heritage), a small fortification built in 1481 to stop sea raids on the town.

DAWLISH MAP REF 399 G6

This pleasantly old-fashioned seaside resort, once the haunt of authors, is famous for its landscaped gardens, known as the Lawn. These stretch back from the front, flanked by two peaceful streams which are home to black swans. Around here you'll find some fine Regency, Georgian and Victorian buildings, and there is a small local museum on Barton Terrace. One curious feature is that the mainline train runs alongside the beach. As many nostalgic local photographs confirm, this was a stirring sight in the days of steam and for most people it was the only way to get to the seaside.

EXETER MAP REF 399 G6

Exeter has just about everything you could wish for in a city. It has magnificent old buildings, fascinating places to visit, a lively arts programme and a new area with shops and restaurants, Princesshay, as well as a few surprises. Where else, for instance, can you explore the tunnels of a medieval water supply?

At its heart is the spectacular cathedral, which rises up from spacious lawns. The earliest part, the two great towers, dates from 1110, but most of the building is of the 14th century, including the beautiful west front, with its carved figures of apostles, prophets and soldiers. Inside the cathedral, the first thing that catches your eye is the roof of the central aisle. Dating from 1369, it is the longest unbroken Gothic vault in the world and can be studied using the magnifying mirrors provided.

The choir, with its magnificent oak carving, is in the centre of the cathedral. The bishop's throne, dating from 1312, is undoubtedly the finest in the country, and the 49 canopied stalls, dating from the 19th century, reflect its style. The cathedral has magnificently decorated tombs and monuments, delightful features among the carvings and peaceful little chapels, where there is no need to hurry.

One of the city's other major attractions is the revitalised historic quayside, where it is easy to imagine the wool-trading

vessels moored up alongside the quay. Here you can discover 2,000 years of Exeter's history in the Quay House Visitor Centre, where lively displays explain the history and development of the area. Then take your time to browse around a few of the antiques and craft shops.

Before extensive bombing in World War II changed the city, it was essentially medieval, and a number of old timbered buildings still exist, particularly along West Street and Stepcote Hill. Exeter's Guildhall has been used as the meeting place of the council since 1330 and visitors can see its remarkable timber roof and the collection of portraits, guild crests and civic silver.

The remains of St Nicholas's Priory, off Fore Street, date back to 1070. On the special 'Living History' days 17th-century daily life is recreated. A most impressive reminder of Victorian Exeter exists in the extensive Royal Albert Memorial Museum, built in flamboyant Gothic style and housing rich collections.

EXMOUTH MAP REF 399 G6

There was a medieval settlement and port here at the mouth of the River Exe, but because of the tendency to silting at this eastern side of the river, Exmouth eventually could not compete as a port with Topsham or Exeter. The docks built at the western end of the Esplanade in the mid-19th century have been developed and now feature a smart marina and modern

DARTMOUTH

Visit

DAWLISH WARREN NATURE RESERVE

More than 450 plant species are protected at this 500-acre (200ha) nature reserve, including a number of orchids and the famous Warren crocus, only found here. A large hide looks out over the estuary, where sanderling, oystercatchers and terns can be seen. In midwinter the estuary is host to Brent geese and a flock of wintering avocets. There is a visitor centre where guided walks start from.

housing complex, the latter enjoying superb sea views. As a resort, Exmouth began to develop at the end of the 18th century and today it is a popular spot, with long sandy beaches where there are rock pools to explore at half-tide.

Approximately 2 miles (3.2km) north is A La Ronde (National Trust), a 16-sided thatched house that was built in 1796 for spinster cousins Jane and Mary Parminter. Both the house and its contents are the result of their Grand Tour of Europe, and the interiors mirror their particular eccentricities. The rooms are arranged around an octagonal hall, and the Shell Gallery is decorated with shells, feathers and other natural materials.

GREAT TORRINGTON MAP REF 398 F5

This is a delightful little town with a great deal to see and do. Turn off the through-road going into the town centre and you will discover the heart of the place – a charming square that is most people's idea of what a real town centre should be. There is a lovely old inn, which has Civil War connections, a fine town hall and a market hall, and just around the corner from the square the Plough Arts Centre has a lively programme of jazz, theatre, film and stand-up comedy.

Great Torrington is set high on a hill overlooking lush agricultural land. On three sides it is bordered by common land, preserved by an Act of Parliament, and below it flows the wide River Torridge. The Dartington Crystal factory was established in the town in the 1960s, when Swedish craftsmen were brought here to train a local workforce in the difficult art of glass-blowing. The company rapidly expanded, exporting its fine crystal all over the world, but its operation here is very much geared to the large number of visitors it receives. The factory tours are fascinating, and walkways enable visitors to look down over the teams of craftsmen and witness their glass-blowing skills. Every stage in the production, from furnace

to packing case, can be seen. There is a very good video introduction and a display of glassware in the entrance hall, as well as the opportunity to buy from a range of glassware in the showroom.

Just south of the town on the B3220 Exeter road, Rosemoor Gardens have long been famous and are continuing to expand and develop new areas of cultivation. The original 8 acres (3.2ha) were created by Lady Anne Barry to surround her home, but in 1988 she gave them, along with a further 32 acres (13ha) of land, to the Royal Horticultural Society, which has wasted no time in making full use of the golden opportunity provided. A National Garden has been thoughtfully created here, and the previously uncultivated land has been planted with a number of gardens.

There are two rose gardens, wonderful herbaceous borders, a lovely herb garden and potager, colour-themed gardens, an extensive stream and bog garden centred on an ornamental lake, a cottage garden and a foliage garden. Fruit and vegetable cultivation is featured and exciting new developments are always under way. There is a good visitor centre with a restaurant and shop, and plants for sale.

HARTLAND POINT MAP REF 398 E5

To many people, Hartland Point is more dramatic than Land's End. It looks out over one of the most treacherous stretches of water in Britain, with strong currents and huge jagged rocks. Even on the calmest of days, the waters swirl menacingly around the headland. Just to the east is lovely, unspoilt Shipload Bay (National Trust), practically inaccessible since the steps leading to the beach were damaged. Hartland Quay is 3 miles (4.8km) in the other direction, accessible by road.

The village of Hartland, inland, is pleasant, but its parish church at nearby Stoke is a real treasure, its size out of all proportion to the local community. Also nearby, you'll find Hartland Abbey, an 18th-century Gothic-style mansion.

HONITON MAP REF 399 H5

This town is easy to explore because just about everything is in the High Street, a charming wide thoroughfare lined with Georgian buildings. Its unity of style is due to a series of fires during the 18th century, which destroyed much of the original town that had stood here since about 1200. The straightness of its main street is due to the fact that the town was originally built astride an old Roman road. High Street is one of those streets that just begs you to get out of your car and wander up and down for a while, to browse around the variety of little shops, many of them selling antiques, and explore the courtyards and alleyways that run off at right angles. The old Pannier Market has been converted into an attractive little parade of shops.

Of course, what Honiton is most famous for is lace, and there is a wonderful collection in the Allhallows Museum, housed in Honiton's oldest building, a 13th-century chapel beside St Paul's Church. The museum also has lace-making demonstrations and displays which relate to the town's pottery and clock-making industries.

LUNDY MAP REF 398 E4

Lundy has an enormous variety of things to see and do. It is reached by boat, the MS *Oldenburg*, from either Bideford or Ilfracombe, and the trip takes 2 hours. There is also a year-round helicopter service available.

Just over 3 miles (4.8km) long and about half a mile (800m) across at its widest point, Lundy has steep granite cliffs rising to over 400 feet (122m) and the land varies from rough grazing in the north to fertile farm land in the south. Although once famous for its successful breeding colony of puffins, numbers fell significantly. Thankfully, after a gap of several years and conservation work by the RSPB, puffins bred again on Lundy in 2005. Visitors will see many other kinds of birds, as well as seals, basking

sharks, sika deer, Soay sheep, mountain goats and Lundy ponies. There is a great deal of evidence of the island's fascinating history to see also, including an ancient burial chamber and a cave that was used as a prison. You can also see the cannons which were fired in Georgian times as a fog warning and a chasm that opened up when tremors from the Lisbon earthquake in 1755 reached Lundy. The real hub of the island's social life is the Marisco Tavern, a friendly pub serving Lundy beer.

All of Lundy is beautiful, but the most spectacular views can be enjoyed from the west side. If wild plants are your particular interest, explore the eastern side, and if you are a climber there are more than 60 challenging rock faces which can be tackled; many are closed during the seabird breeding season (April to July).

OTTERY ST MARY MAP REF 399 H6

This pleasant little town lies on the River Otter and was the birthplace in 1772 of the poet Samuel Taylor Coleridge, whose father was vicar of St Mary's Church. The church may seem too grand for a sleepy little Devon town, and it certainly had more modest beginnings in the 13th century, but in 1340 Bishop John de Grandisson had it enlarged, with Exeter Cathedral much in his mind. The interior is rich in medieval craftsmanship and there is an ancient astronomical clock, which is still in working order.

Not far away from Ottery is Cadhay, a classic Tudor manor house which was enlarged and remodelled in Georgian style. It is an interesting house with a history of mixed fortunes – one minute a social honeypot, the next declining as the owners fell into debt after supporting the wrong side in the Civil War. In the 18th century a new owner raised its status once more, only for it to become a boarding house for agricultural workers in the 19th century. But in 1909 Cadhay was rescued and restored and is now a fascinating and charming place to visit.

PAIGNTON MAP REF 399 G7

Around a century ago Paignton was described as 'a neat and improving village and bathing place'. It remains a popular bathing place but is no longer a village, and, due to its amusement arcades, inexpensive cafés and discount stores, is often regarded as a poor relation to neighbouring Torquay. Paignton, however, is unabashed, and performs its role of provider of cheap holidays very effectively.

The beaches, some of the best in the Southwest, are the main draw, particularly Goodrington Sands, which has the region's largest water park. Although the town itself may appear devoid of high culture, there are historic houses to visit. Oldway Mansion, built by Isaac Singer (founder of the sewing-machine empire) in 1874, is now used as council offices, but the best rooms are open to the public. Just outside town is Compton Castle (National Trust), a fortified manor house built between 1340 and 1520 and home to the descendants of Sir Humphrey Gilbert, who colonised Newfoundland. Paignton Zoo, in 75 acres (30ha) a mile (1.6km) from the town, is one of the largest zoos in the country, with all the favourites – lions, tigers, elephants, rhinos, monkeys and giraffes. For many visitors the finest thing to come out of Paignton is the Paignton and Dartmouth Steam Railway, which steams along to Kingswear by the Dart estuary.

SALCOMBE MAP REF 399 G7

The blue saucer of Salcombe Bay, aflutter with white triangular sails, surrounded by the green hills of the South Hams and fringed by golden pocket-handkerchief beaches, is one of south Devon's finest sights. Salcombe is among the largest yachting centres in England and several old wharf houses are workshops for boat makers and marine engineers.

The tiny golden beach of North Sands is adjacent to the picturesque ruin of Salcombe Castle/Fort Charles, which was built in 1544 but was destroyed during the Civil War. Continue on to South Sands and Splat Cove or catch a ferry to one of the beaches on the other side of the bay.

About 1.5 miles (2.4km) southwest of Salcombe, at Sharpitor, is Overbecks Museum and Garden (National Trust), a charming Edwardian house which is largely dedicated to local maritime affairs. Overbecks' beautifully landscaped 6-acre (2.4ha) garden, set high above the estuary, is full of rare and exotic specimens which flourish in the area's mild micro-climate and is worth a visit for its views alone.

SAUNTON SANDS & BRAUNTON BURROWS MAP REF 399 F4

Saunton Sands is one of the best beaches in Devon, a 3-mile (4.8km) curve of golden sands backed by grassy dunes. Towards the northern end of the beach is a little car park with a small shop, toilets and a café. It is at this end that most visitors congregate, particularly surfers and those with young families. If you walk further on you will have a quieter beach experience, and an interrupted walk across the sand to the sea. Be warned, though, that the very southern end of the beach has treacherous sea currents which make swimming here very dangerous.

It is better to turn inland here and explore the Braunton Burrows. This incorporates one of the largest sand dune systems in Britain and is famous for its plant and animal life, receiving Biosphere status from UNESCO in 2002. Marram grass holds the sands in place, and where the ground has stabilised, other plants, such as stonecrop, viper's bugloss and evening primrose, carpet the ground with splashes of colour. In the damper areas there are the marsh varieties of marigolds, orchids and helleborines. Flocks of wading birds populate the estuary, migrating birds rest here and there is also a huge variety of moths and butterflies. The Ministry of Defence leases an area of the reserve for training; red warning flags are flown when exercises are in progress.

SIDMOUTH MAP REF 399 H6

This is a quiet and genteel resort, and has been since it was favoured by royal patronage in the early 19th century. Much of its architecture goes back to Regency days, with elegant wrought-iron balconies and white-painted façades, and colourful gardens and floral displays enhance the scene. One of these imposing Regency buildings, in Church Street, houses the Sid Vale Heritage Centre, with interesting collections and detailed information about local history; guided walks depart from here two mornings a week. Visitors with a scientific bent should check out the Norman Lockyer Observatory on Salcombe Hill, with its planetarium, library, radio and weather stations, and historic telescopes.

A complete transformation comes over (or overcomes) Sidmouth during the first week in August, when singers, dancers and musicians from all over the world descend on the town for its famous music festival. Organised events are staged at various venues around the town, not to mention the impromptu ones that occur whenever two or more performers find themselves in any previously peaceful pub, street corner, park or bit of beach. Sitting in the sun listening to some good live music is a bonus for some holidaymakers.

SLAPTON MAP REF 399 G7

Slapton Sands is an uncommercialised 2-mile (3.2km) long windswept shingle ridge, a favourite spot for walking. Slapton Ley, which is divided from the beach by the road, is a freshwater lake, famous for its wildfowl. This is a National Nature Reserve and a public hide, for birdwatching, is situated in the Torcross car park.

Slapton (0.5 mile/800m inland and not to be confused with Torcross, at the southernmost part of Slapton Sands) has a fine medieval church. The impressive tower to the north of the church is all that remains of the College of Chantry Priests, founded in 1373. North of Slapton Sands is sandy Blackpool Sands, perhaps the best beach in the South Hams.

START POINT MAP REF 399 G7

The dramatic southwesterly tip of the South Hams, Start Point has cliffs rising over 100 feet (30.5m) high. On the south side they are almost sheer and streaked by quartz veins which run through the dark rock. A lighthouse (tours available) warns shipping off the dangerous bank known as the Skerries. In Elizabethan times pirates were hung in chains here as a warning to other lawless seafarers.

From Start Point the coast path heads west along to Prawle Point, the most southern extremity of Devon. The latter, which can be lashed by the full fury of

the waves in stormy weather, has been chiselled and chipped into an almost vertical drop, plunging into the sea, beneath the coastguard lookout station.

TEIGNMOUTH MAP REF 399 G6

The red cliffs with a verdant fringe and the red-sand beaches of Teignmouth (which should be pronounced 'Tin-muth') create a distinctive Devon seafront; the picture complete with an old-fashioned pier.

The town became a fashionable holiday resort in the late 18th and early 19th centuries and if you look along Powderham Terrace or the Den, or just up above the fronts of the many cafés and tourist shops, you will see that it retains a good deal of its Georgian and early Victorian architecture. The Quays are full of character; this is the old harbour area, which has for centuries shipped huge quantities of Bovey ball clay and Dartmoor granite. A small fishing fleet also operates from here. You can learn more about the town's local and maritime history if you go to the museum in French Street.

A narrow bridge connects Teignmouth to pretty Shaldon village. There the houses, many of which date back to Georgian

times, are packed so closely together that the only sensible way of visiting the village is by ferry from Teignmouth, a service that dates back to Elizabethan times.

There's a fine church to see but the favourite attraction is the charming Shaldon Wildlife Trust. It is a breeding centre for rare and endangered species of small mammals, exotic birds and reptiles and because of its tiny size many of its inmates are very tame. Close by, the erroneously named 'Smuggler's tunnel' leads down to Shaldon's own beach, the Ness, backed by a bold red cliff. Looking out from the top of the cliff there are marvellous views of Teignmouth and across the Teign estuary.

TIVERTON MAP REF 399 G5

For a town to prosper these days, its proximity to the motorway network is of considerable importance. In times gone by it was the rivers that provided a lifeline. Tiverton, with its two rivers, the Grand Western Canal and the M5 just a short distance away, has always been advantaged and it remains a lively centre. Tiverton's appearance owes much to the prosperity of its textile and clothing

industries in the 16th and 17th centuries, when rich wool merchants endowed their town with such splendid buildings as St Peter's Church, Blundell's School, the fine Great House and three sets of almshouses. St George's Church, built in 1773, is thought to be one of the finest Georgian churches to be built in Devon.

Tiverton's history is documented in the town museum in St Andrew Street. It includes the Heathcoat Lace Gallery, an agricultural section, two waterwheels and a railway gallery. Tiverton's two rivers are the Exe and the Lowman (Tiverton means 'two-ford town'), and the former is overlooked by Tiverton Castle. Dating from 1106, all that remains of the original building is one circular tower.

North of Tiverton is Knightshayes Court (National Trust) which is well worth taking time out to visit. This ornate 19th-century mansion was built for Sir John Heathcoat-Amory. Designed by William Burges, it features rich Gothic-style decoration, painted ceilings and wall stencilling. The house is more than equally matched by the wonderful grounds that surround it, comprising pleasing formal gardens, woodland and ornamental shrubs.

SIDMOUTH

Visit
PREHISTORIC RESIDENTS

As far as we know, the earliest human occupation of the British Isles was around 400,000 years ago and Kents Cavern provides evidence to this effect. At Torquay a layer of conglomerate limestone revealed simple tools and signs of stone working from that date, as well as the earlier remains of animals such as sabre-toothed tigers and mammoths.

Visit
A FLAVOUR OF HISTORIC SHALDON

Every Wednesday during the summer months, Shaldon turns the clock back to 1785 with traders dressed in period costume, special craft stalls and evening entertainment.

Visit
TWO ANCIENT WATERING HOLES

Walk to the top of Fore Street in Totnes, then up into the Narrows, then left into Leechwell Street and you will reach the town's oldest pub, 17th-century Kingsbridge Inn. To the left, Leechwell Lane runs down to an ancient well with three granite troughs. This was once thought to have had medicinal properties.

TORQUAY MAP REF 399 G7

Torquay is south Devon at its most continental – a balmy climate, palm trees sparkling with coloured lights and millionaires' yachts basking in the marina. The large number of English-language students and foreign tourists adds an exotic chatter to the town. Yet this is also the capital of the English Riviera.

From humble beginnings as a fishing village, the town's resort career began during Napoleonic times, and during the height of the Victorian era its mild winters were attracting consumptives and fashionable visitors on doctors' orders. By 1850 it was proclaiming itself 'Queen of the Watering Holes' and today it is still a popular seaside resort.

The centre of town is the lively marina and harbour, including the copper-domed Edwardian Pavilion, which houses an excellent shopping centre. Eastwards the cliffs rise up to Daddy Hole Plain, a great chasm in the cliff where the plain meets the sea, and the views from here are superb. Continue east to the point at Hope's Nose for more sea panoramas.

The beaches, though not as broad and sandy as those to be found at neighbouring Paignton, are numerous and spread well apart, which helps to dissipate the summer crowds. The most attractive of the major beaches is Oddicombe, with its backdrop of steep sandstone cliffs topped by lush woodland. The descent is steep and a cliff railway runs down 720 feet (220m) to the shingle below.

The Oddicombe/Babbacombe area is also home to Torquay's best tourist attractions. Kents Cavern forms one of the most important prehistoric sites in Europe, where a half a mile (800m) guided tour takes you back through two million years of history. More cave finds can be seen at the Torquay Museum on Babbacombe Road. The museum has a wide range of galleries and some fascinating displays.

Another excellent wet-weather option, in the charming St Marychurch parish, is Bygones, a life-size re-creation of a Victorian street, illustrating shops and dwellings, including an ironmonger, grocer, sweet shop and apothecary. Visit the giant model railway and the 'Trench Experience' of World War I. A further option, and one of Torquay's main attractions is Babbacombe Model Village, an outstanding piece of design.

Next to the harbour is Torre Abbey, from where the town derives its name. Constructed in the 12th century, the abbey was dissolved and subsumed into a 16th-century mansion, itself remodelled in the Georgian period. It now holds the municipal art gallery and history collection. In the grounds are monastic ruins, the well-preserved abbey gatehouse, exotic gardens and a splendid 12th-century tithe barn, known as the Spanish Barn, since it was used in 1588 to hold around 400 Armada prisoners who had been captured by Sir Francis Drake.

About one mile (1.6km) west of the centre of town is the chocolate-box village of Cockington, a delightful crossroads gathering of thatched cottages with an old smithy, working waterwheel, village stocks and a mill pond. The grounds and gardens of 19th-century Cockington Court are open to the public and include a craft centre and gallery.

WATERSMEET MAP REF 399 G4

This renowned beauty spot, now in the care of the National Trust, can be reached on footpaths from Lynmouth or by car. Once at Watersmeet, the network of riverside paths expands to give walkers plenty of choice. The waters that meet here are the East Lyn River and Hoaroak Water, both of which take the form of a series of pools, with water tumbling from one to another over the rocks. The steep sides of the valley are heavily wooded, mostly sessile oak, with some beech and larch, with an undergrowth of ferns, mosses and an abundance of wild flowers. The National Trust has an information centre, shop and tea rooms at Watersmeet House.

TORQUAY

BICKLEIGH & THE EXE VALLEY

Leave the crowds behind at picturesque Bickleigh Bridge and explore the lovely Exe Valley along leafy country lanes and wild-flower strewn tracks. Bickleigh Castle on the banks of the River Exe is approached along a quiet lane, shaded by huge oak, ash and beech trees. Bickleigh Mill, the working watermill (Point 1), has craft shops and a restaurant.

DISTANCE/TIME 4.25 miles (6.8km) 2h   **MAP** OS Explorer 114 Exeter & the Exe Valley **START** Bickleigh Mill just off A396 at Bickleigh Bridge; grid ref: SX 939075   **TRACKS** Country lanes, some very narrow **THE PUB** The Fisherman's Cot, Bickleigh. Tel: 01884 855237

1 From the public parking area at the edge of Bickleigh Mill walk back, with care, to the A396 and cross the bridge. Turn left down the A3072, following the brown tourist sign for Bickleigh Castle. Take the first lane to your left, running along the edge of the flood plain on the Exe Valley Way (EVW). Bickleigh Castle will soon be found on the right at the edge of trees. Go straight on past Way Farm.

2 Just after the buildings of Way Farm turn right to leave the Exe Valley Way, roughly signposted 'Lee Cross & Perry Farm'. Take care, as this is a narrow lane, carrying busy traffic from local farms. Keep along the lane as it climbs steeply uphill and after 700yds (640m) brings you to the farm at Lee Cross.

3 Immediately after the house keep straight ahead along the road. Pass Perry Farm and continue until you reach a T-junction; turn left on to a green lane. Continue on this lane until you reach another T-junction. Turn right. The lane now levels off and the way forward becomes easier.

4 Where the green lane meets the tarmac lane turn left and proceed steeply downhill (EVW). The views over the River Exe, and to Silverton church beyond, are absolutely delightful. Follow the lane down until you see Tray Mill Farm on the right.

5 The way home is straight on along the lane, but it's worth doing a small detour to the river here. Turn right through the farmyard (no sign) and pass through a metal gate on to a concrete standing. Ahead you will be able to see a suspension bridge over the river; cross it and go straight on to reach the dismantled railway track. Do not turn left along the track, although it would take you back to your car, as this track is privately owned and has no public right of way.

6 The path goes straight on here to meet the A396. You can do that, turning left, then eventually right to walk through Bickleigh village back to the mill, but as it is such a busy road, you would be better advised to retrace your steps to Tray Mill Farm and take the quieter route back to Bickleigh Mill.

7 Back on the lane by Tray Mill Farm, turn right and continue straight along the lane, past Bickleigh Castle, turning right at the A3072, and then right again and over the bridge to return to your car.

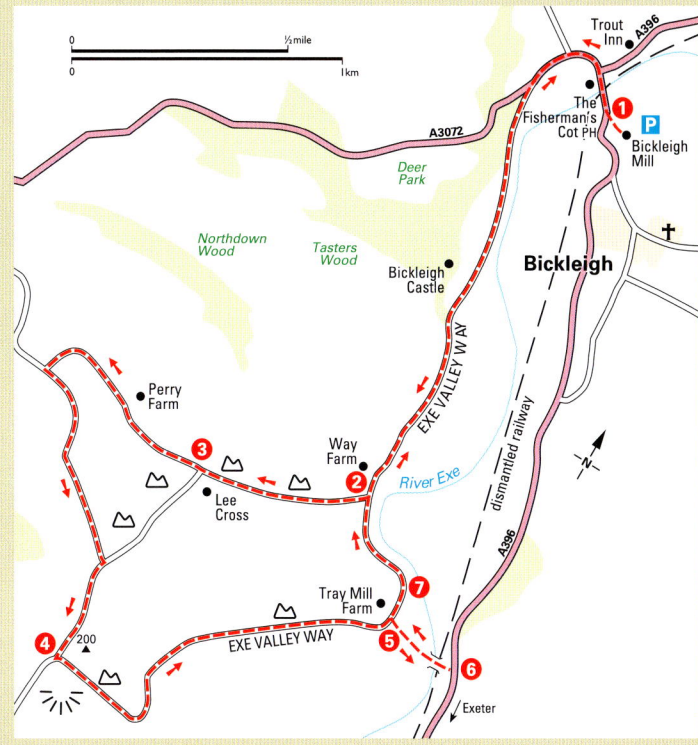

WALK 8

BIGBURY-ON-SEA & BURGH ISLAND

This short walk, initially inland through farmland, returns to Bigbury-on-Sea via the dramatic coastal path. Just off Bigbury beach, 307yds (282m) from shore, lies craggy Burgh Island, which can still be reached by giant sea tractor whenever the tide is in. When the tide is out, however, you can simply stroll across the sand.

DISTANCE/TIME 3 miles (4.8km) 1h45   **MAP** OS Explorer OL20 South Devon   **START** Huge car park at Bigbury-on-Sea; grid ref: SX 651442   **TRACKS** Fields, tracks (muddy in winter), coast path, 2 stiles **THE PUB** The Pilchard Inn, Burgh Island. Tel: 01548 810514

1 Leave the beach-side car park through the entrance. Follow the coast path signs right (for the low tide route to the seasonal ferry to Bantham), then left towards the road, and then left again up a grassy area. Turn left before the bungalow, then left (unmarked path) to reach the road. Turn right and then walk steeply uphill to Mount Folly Farm.

2 Turn left along a gravelly track (signed 'Ringmore'). At the top of the field there is a junction of paths; go through the gate, then through the metal gate ahead, keeping downhill by the hedge on your right. Walk downhill, passing through a kissing gate. Cross the farm track and walk up the field, to a stile, then descend steps into a lane.

3 Cross over, following signs for Ringmore, through the left of the two gates. Walk down into the next combe, keeping the hedgebank right. Cross the stream at the bottom on a concrete walkway and go over a stile. Ignore the path left, but go straight ahead, uphill, through a plantation and gate on to a narrow path between a fence and a hedge.

4 Pass through a kissing gate, then turn right. Next, turn immediately left uphill though a metal kissing gate to join a track

that leads on to Ringmore. Then turn right at the lane, and then left at the church to find the Journey's End pub.

5 From the pub turn right down the narrow lane which gives way to a footpath. It winds round to meet a tarmac lane. Turn left downhill. Walk straight on down the track (signed to 'Lower Manor Farm') and keep going down past the 'National Trust Ayrmer Cove' notice. After a small gate the track splits; keep left (unsigned) and straight on.

6 Turn left through a kissing gate and walk towards the cove on a grassy path above the combe (left). Pass through a gate and over two stiles to reach the beach.

7 Follow coast path signs ('Challaborough') left over a small footbridge, then climb uphill to the cliff top and views over Burgh Island. The cliffs are crumbly here – take care. The path is narrow, with a wire fence left, and leads to Challaborough.

8 Turn right along the beach road and follow the track that leads uphill along the coast towards Bigbury. Go straight on to meet the tarmac road, then right on a narrow gravel path to the car park.

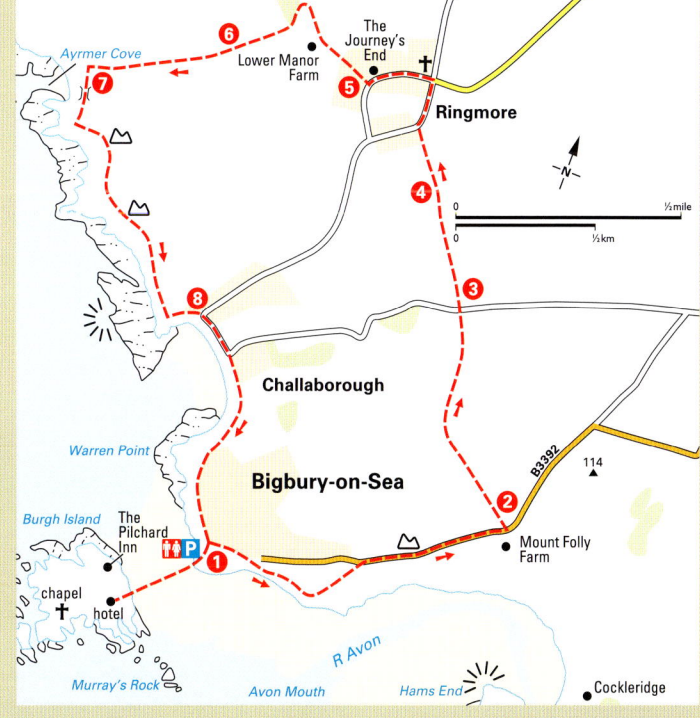

EAST PORTLEMOUTH TO LIMEBURY POINT

Follow this coastal stroll from the hamlet of East Portlemouth, which has some of the best views in the area. From Limebury Point you can see across the estuary to Overbecks (National Trust), an elegant Edwardian house in a magnificent setting above South Sands. A ferry connects East Portlemouth and Salcombe.

DISTANCE/TIME 4 miles (6.4km) 2h **MAP** OS Explorer OL20 South Devon **START** Near phone box in East Portlemouth or in small parking bay; grid ref: SX 746385 **TRACKS** Good coast path, field paths and tracks **THE PUB** The Victoria Inn, Salcombe. Tel 01548 842604; www.victoriainnsalcombe.co.uk

1 Walk through the parking area at East Portlemouth on a narrow tarmac footpath signposted 'Salcombe', which eventually gives way to steep steps.

2 When you reach the lane at the bottom of the steps, turn right if you want to visit the Venus Café or catch the ferry to Salcombe. Once you disembark the ferry in Salcombe, The Victoria Inn is on the main street and has commanding views of the Salcombe Estuary. Or, if you want to get on with the walk, turn left and follow along the lane as it tracks the edge of the estuary. This part is the official route of the coastal path and it passes some very exclusive residences in almost subtropical surroundings.

3 The lane leads to the pretty, sandy beach at Mill Bay. Follow the coast path signs for Gara Rock along the edge of a sycamore wood, with lovely views across the estuary, and glimpses of inviting little coves.

4 At Limebury Point you reach open cliff with great views to South Sands and Overbecks opposite and craggy Bolt Head. The coast path now veers eastwards below Portlemouth Down, which was divided into strip fields in the late 19th century.

5 The path along this stretch undulates steeply and is rocky in places. Keep going until you reach the bench and viewpoint over the beach at Rickham Sands. Just beyond this, as the coastal path continues right along the cliffs (there is reasonable access to the beach), take the left fork and then climb steeply up below the lookout to reach the wall in front of the Gara Rock Hotel.

6 Turn left to reach the hotel drive and walk straight on up the lane. After 100yds (91m) turn left through a gate in the hedge signposted 'Mill Bay'. Walk straight across the field (the roped-off area indicates a car park for the beach) with lovely views to Salcombe and Malborough church beyond. Go through a small copse, then a gate and across the farm track. Go through a gate.

7 This leads down a beautiful bridle path, running downhill beneath ancient pollarded lime trees, with a grassy combe to the right. The path passes the car park to Mill Bay.

8 Turn right along the lane. To avoid the steps, look for a footpath sign pointing right, up a steep path, to regain East Portlemouth and your car; if not, go along the lane and retrace your steps up the steep tarmac path.

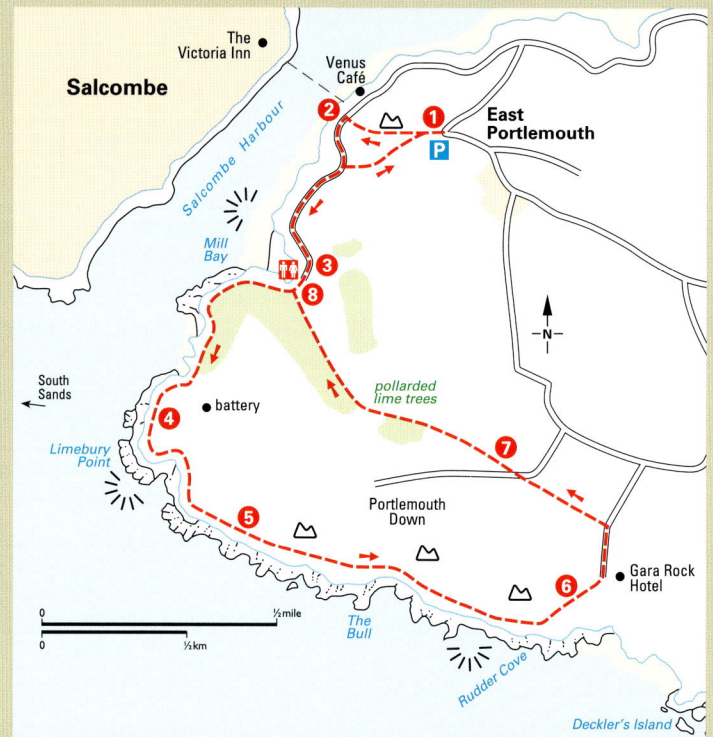

ALONG CLIFFS TO DARTMOUTH CASTLE

This is an easy round walk along the cliffs to Blackstone Point and Dartmouth Castle – and a ferry ride to the pub. Cared for by English Heritage, 15th-century Dartmouth Castle, which occupies a fine position at the mouth of the Dart, was built to protect the homes and warehouses of the town's merchants.

DISTANCE/TIME 3 miles (4.8km) 2h **MAP** OS Explorer OL20 South Devon **START** National Trust car park at Little Dartmouth; grid ref: SX 874491 **TRACKS** Easy coastal footpath and green lanes **THE PUB** The Royal Castle Hotel, Dartmouth. Tel 01803 833033; www.royalcastle.co.uk. Drive to Dartmouth or take the ferry from Stumpy Steps.

1 Go through the right-hand car park, following the signs 'Coast Path Dartmouth'. Continue through a kissing gate, keeping the hedge to your right. Walk through the next field, and then continue on through a gate to join with the coast path.

2 Turn left; there are lovely views here west to Start Point and east towards the Day Beacon above Kingswear. The coast path runs a little inland from the cliff edge, but you can always continue straight ahead to walk above Warren Point for sea views (a plaque here reveals that this land was given to the National Trust in 1970 by the Devon Federation of Women's Institutes).

3 Continue left to pass above Western Combe Cove (with steps down to the sea) and then Combe Point (take care as it's a long drop to the sea from here).

4 Rejoin the coast path through an open gateway in a wall and follow it above Shinglehill Cove. The path turns inland, passes through a gate, becomes narrow and a little overgrown, and twists along the back of Willow Cove. It passes through a wooded section (with a field on the left) and then climbs around the back of Compass Cove.

Keep going to pass through a gate. Continue left to reach a wooden footpath post, then turn sharp right, down the valley to the cliff edge. Follow the path on, through a gate near Blackstone Point.

5 Leave the path right to clamber down on to the rocks here. Retrace your steps and continue on the coast path as it turns inland along the side of the estuary and runs through deciduous woodland.

6 The path meets a surfaced lane opposite Compass Cottage; go right on to the lane and then right again steeply downhill, keeping the wall to your left. At the turning space go right down steps to the castle and café.

7 Retrace your route up the steps to the tarmac lane at Point 6, then go left to pass Compass Cottage, and then straight on up the steep lane (following signs for 'Little Dartmouth') and through a kissing gate on to National Trust land.

8 The path runs along the top of a field and through a five-bar gate on to a green lane. Go through a gate and the farmyard at Little Dartmouth and then continue ahead along a tarmac lane to the car park.

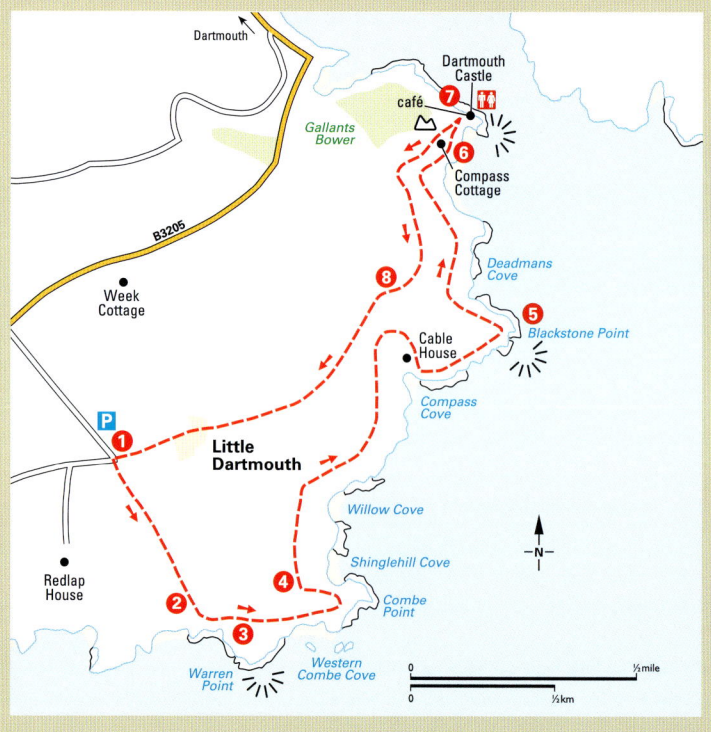

DISTANCE/TIME 11 miles (17.6km) 2h15 **MAP** OS Explorer 128 Taunton & Blackdown Hills and 114 Exeter & the Exe Valley **START** Sampford Peverell; grid ref: ST 030142 **TRACKS** Canalside path, most gritty **CYCLE HIRE** Abbotshood Cycle Hire, Halberton. Tel: 01884 820728 **THE PUB** Globe Inn, Sampford Peverell. Tel: 01884 821214; www.globe-inn.com

ALONG THE GRAND WESTERN CANAL TO TIVERTON

This peaceful ride along the banks of the old Grand Western Canal passes through the Grand Western Canal Country Park and the beautiful countryside of mid-Devon before finally reaching the centre of Tiverton. The canal provides ideal wildlife habitats and it's a wonderful place for wild flowers and butterflies, too.

1 From the back of the car park, pass the tennis court (left), bear left round a gate and uphill to the towpath (don't go too fast or you might easily overshoot!). Construction of the canal began in 1810, part of a scheme to link the English and Bristol Channels via Exeter and Bristol, but only the Tiverton and Taunton stretch was completed, in 1814. Competition from the railways eventually forced the closure of the canal, although this section was still being used to transport limestone from quarries in the area around Westleigh to Tiverton as late as 1924.

2 Turn left along the towpath, passing The Globe Inn. Pass under Sampford Peverell bridge (best to dismount) and continue along a short stretch of quiet lane. Where that bears left, keep ahead along the canalside and you will find yourself immediately out in the countryside, with good views of the wooded Blackdown Hills to the left – you may well feel as if you're miles away from anywhere. Pass under Battens Bridge, then Rock Bridge. The next bridge is constructed from metal. These – look out for them along the route – were originally wooden swing bridges, which allowed the passage of barges and linked farmers' land where it was split by the canal.

3 Continue cycling along an embanked stretch to pass under the Greenway Bridge (car park) and then Sellake Bridge. Note how the canal takes a wide sweep to the left; this is known as the Swan's Neck, and was necessary to avoid the village of Halberton.

4 Next stop is Tiverton Road Bridge (car park and picnic area), where you may see canoes and kayaks. There was once a stone-crushing yard here; the journey from a quarry 8 miles (12.9km) away at Whipcott took 2.5 hours, with two horses pulling three 10-ton barges. Note milestone III on the left; it's only 3 miles (4.8km) further to the basin at Tiverton. Keep on to Crownhill Bridge, once known as Change Path. Horses had to change to the right bank here; you do the same by crossing the bridge and turning left.

5 Cross the brick aqueduct of the Bristol and Exeter Railway line, built in 1847; the Tiverton branch closed to passenger traffic in 1964. Three more bridges bring you to neat hedges and bungalows marking the edge of Tiverton. Tidcombe Bridge (look out for milestone I) marks another loop, made necessary by the Bishop of Exeter's refusal to allow the canal within 100yds (91m) of his home, grand Tidcombe Hall, nearby.

6 Built in 1842, Tiverton Canal Basin makes an excellent focus for this ride. You can buy refreshments en route at the thatched 16th-century Canal Tearooms, below the basin or from the floating Barge Canal shop. Look out too for the old lime kilns to the right. Until the late 19th century limestone was burnt here to produce fertiliser. Farmers are said to have travelled up to 30 miles (48km) each way by horse and cart to collect it. To return to the start point at Sampford Peverell, simply retrace your steps back along the canal towpath to the car park.

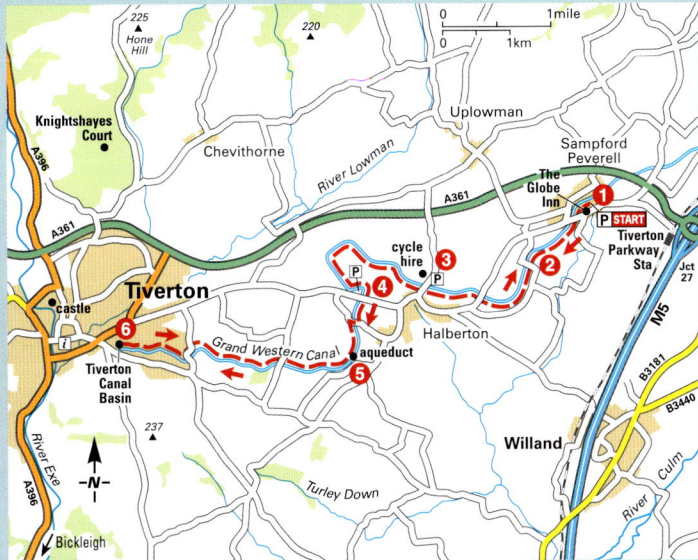

DISTANCE/TIME 12 miles (19.3km) 2h15 **MAP** OS Explorer 114 Exeter & the Exe Valley and 110 Torquay & Dawlish **START** The Quay, Exeter; grid ref: SX 920920 **TRACKS** Mainly well-surfaced path **THE PUB** Turf Hotel, Exminster. Tel: 01392 833128; www.turfpub.net

EXETER SHIP CANAL

Follow the banks of the historic Exeter Ship Canal from the city's hub: the old quayside. The route runs through a lovely stretch of 'inner city' countryside before striking south along the canal through nature reserves and marshes to reach the Turf hotel, situated on the Exe estuary.

1 From Saddles & Paddles cross the quay to the riverside. Turn right and cycle upstream to Cricklepit Bridge (built in 1905). From here turn right over the bridge and right again on the other side. Cycle along the riverside walkway and keep ahead to cycle between the river on the left and canal basin (originally called The New Cut) on the right. Pass Trew's Weir, and the Port Royal on the opposite bank, to reach the canal.

2 Turn left over the canal; turn right along the tarmac way between the canal and the flood prevention 'trough'. Where the path forks, keep left. Look for yellow flag iris and purple loosestrife below left. Pass playing fields on the right bearing right at the end to reach the canal by a small car park (right).

3 Do not cross the canal; turn left on a tarmac cycle track that parallels the canal. The track bears away from the canal to pass to the left of the Double Locks pub, built in 1702. Continue to a fork just before the A379, passing the Double Locks Wetlands on the left, a managed area of reedbeds, a haven for wild flowers, birds and insects.

4 Take the right fork; cross the A379 at the traffic lights (note the swing bridge over the canal). On the other side, the track becomes (initially) narrower and tougher. Pass a small parking area (right) then cycle under the M5; from now on you're out in peaceful countryside. The Exe Estuary silted up during the 14th century, and the canal – the earliest working ship canal in England – was started around 1564, linking Exeter to Trenchard's Sluice (which entered the river by the M5 viaduct). The canal was extended to Topsham (a port since Roman times, seen across the canal and river to the left) in 1676. In the early 19th century – under the engineer James Green – it reached the Turf Lock. Its fortunes deteriorated after Brunel's railway reached Exeter in 1844, and then Exmouth (on the east side of the estuary) in 1861.

5 Arrive at the basin at the Turf Lock where the canal reaches the Exe estuary and you have lovely views ahead towards the sea. The building housing The turf Hotel was built around the same time, and probably accommodated visiting boat crews. Horse-drawn barges then transported goods up the canal to Exeter.

6 Cycle back to Exeter. Exminster Marshes (this side) and Bowling Green marshes (on the other side of the estuary) are RSPB reserves, so keep an eye out for birdlife. It is also an important place for migrant birds.

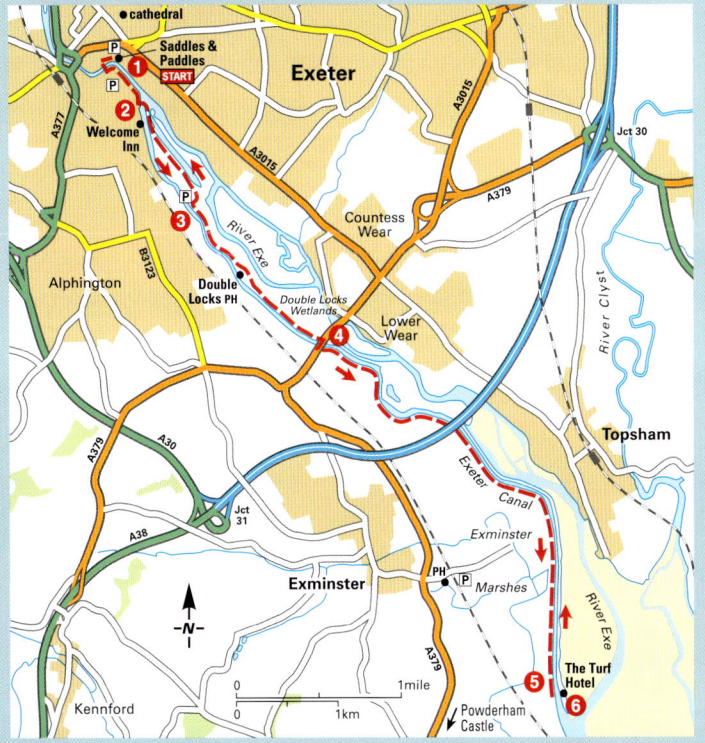

DISTANCE/TIME 11 miles (17.7km) 1h30 MAP OS Explorer 139 Bideford, Ilfracombe & Barnstaple START Braunton car park (contributions); grid ref: SS 486365 TRACKS Level tarmac and gritty former railway track THE PUB The Williams Arms, Wrafton. Tel: 01271 812360; www.williams-arms.co.uk

DISTANCE/TIME 11 miles (17.7km) 2h30 MAP OS Explorer 126 Clovelly & Hartland START Car park on Great Torrington Common; grid ref: SS 485193 TRACKS Level former railway track, now smooth tarmac CYCLE HIRE Torridge Cycle Hire, Tel: 01805 622633; Bideford Cycle Hire, Tel: 01237 4241123 THE PUB The Puffing Billy, Great Torrington. Tel: 01805 623050

BRAUNTON TO BARNSTAPLE

Visiting Barnstaple by car at the height of the tourist season can be something of a trial as this north Devon market town can get pretty choked by traffic. So what better way to get into the heart of Barnstaple than by cycling from Braunton via the Tarka Trail along the edge of the Taw estuary.

1 The car park marks the site of the old Braunton railway station, closed in 1965. Bear left and leave the car park by the police station (right). Bear right on to Station Road and cycle down it, passing the cycle hire on the left. Turn right into Station Close and then immediately left down a tarmac way. At the end cross the lane; keep ahead through black bollards to cross another lane, with a roundabout right.

2 Follow signs left to pick up the old railway line. Pass a wetland conservation area (left) and a barrier to cross a lane (fences mark the boundary of RAF Chivenor).

3 (Note: For The Williams Arms turn left here; at the end of the lane cross the A361 with care; the pub is on the other side.) Cycle on to reach a roundabout at the entrance to RAF Chivenor. Cross the road by the roundabout and continue into a wooded section.

4 Emerge suddenly from woodland on to the Taw Estuary, with far-reaching views. Listen for the oystercatcher's piping call, and watch out for curlew, easily identified by its curving bill. In winter thousands of migrant birds feed on the broad sandbanks here. Pass castellated Heanton Court on the left, a refuge for Royalists in the Civil War. Continue cycling along the banks of the Taw and eventually pass the football club.

5 Cross arched Yeo Bridge, a swing bridge over a tributary of the Taw, and pass the Civic Centre on the left (cyclists and pedestrians seperate here). Bear left away from the river to meet the road. Turn right along the cycle path past old Barnstaple Town Station on the right (the railway reached the south side of the river in 1854, and this side in the early 1870s). Bear right as signed, then carry on left along the quay (take note: there is no wall along the edge; cycle with care).

6 Continue on to pass Barnstaple Heritage Centre (left), with its elaborate statue of Queen Anne. The Riverside Café (with cycle racks) lies a few yards along on the left, just before Barnstaple's Long Bridge over the Taw (there has been a bridge here since the 13th century). There is evidence of a settlement at Barnstaple from early Saxon times; trade via the Taw was vital to the town's prosperity for centuries. Queen Anne's Walk marks the site of the Great and Little Quays, once bustling with ocean-going ships.

GREAT TORRINGTON TO BIDEFORD

This ride, part of the Tarka Trail, from Great Torrington to Bideford, along the broad banks of the River Torridge, is one of three options, and can easily be linked to the route from Instow to Barnstaple.

1 Turn right along the A386 and descend to pick up the Tarka Trail on the right before Rolle Bridge. The trail runs between The Puffing Billy – the old station building – and cycle hire found in the goods yard opposite. Turn left along the trail to pass the pub and garden (cycle racks) located on the left.

2 Pause at the next river crossing to look at Beam Weir; as you cross the river for the third time look left towards Beam Aqueduct. Part of the railway utilised the bed of the former Rolle canal, involved in a scheme to link with the Bude Canal, in north Cornwall; only a 6-mile (9.7km) section was completed, in 1827. Pass a picnic area left, and continue between the A386 and the Torridge (right).

3 Where the Torridge takes a wide loop east cycle through Landcross Tunnel (lit), then through a cutting by Landcross Bridge. Now with the River Yeo on the left, cycle on to meet the old iron railway bridge over the Torridge.

4 The whole feel of the route changes here: the river is wide and slow, with large expanses of saltmarsh and reedbed. The bridge overlooks the Pool of the Six Herons (mentioned in the novel Tarka) – look out for herons, lapwing, redshank and curlew. Saltmarsh plants (specially adapted to seawater inundations) and reedbeds protect the river banks from erosion, and the mudflats support millions of invertebrates, food for wading birds. Limestone was shipped in from South Wales for burning in the limekiln left of the bridge; local woodland supplied timber for charcoal.

5 Continue along the right bank of the Torridge, with good views of Bideford, a significant port in medieval times, but today a busy market town and working port. Its 24-arched stone bridge recalls the town's early prosperity – it is said that each arch was funded by a local parish, and the size of the arch reflects their respective wealth!

6 Turn-around is old Bideford Stayion – 220.5 miles (355km) from Waterloo! The Tarka Trail goes on to Instow. Refreshments are available from the railway Carriage Visitor Centre. If you have time, after the ride, look around historical Great Torrington.

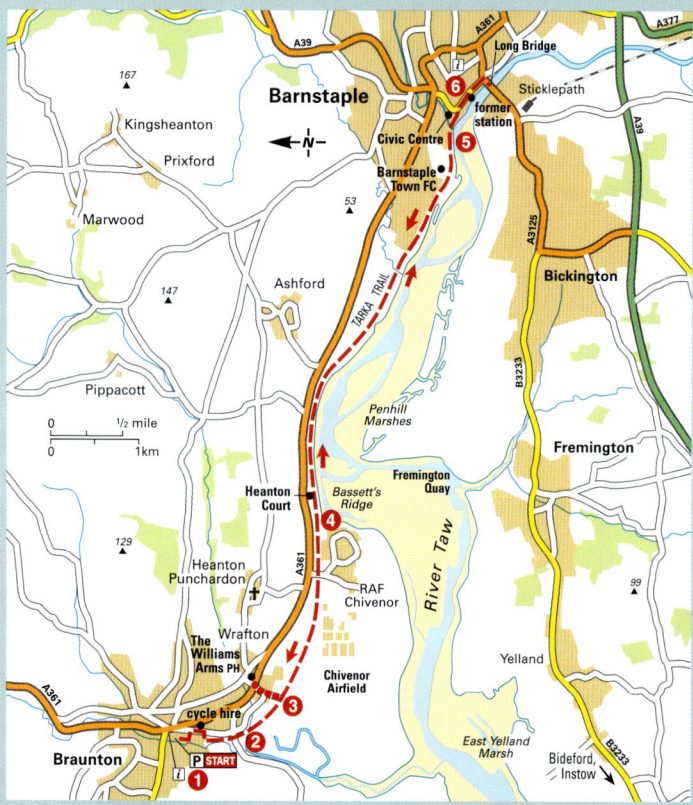

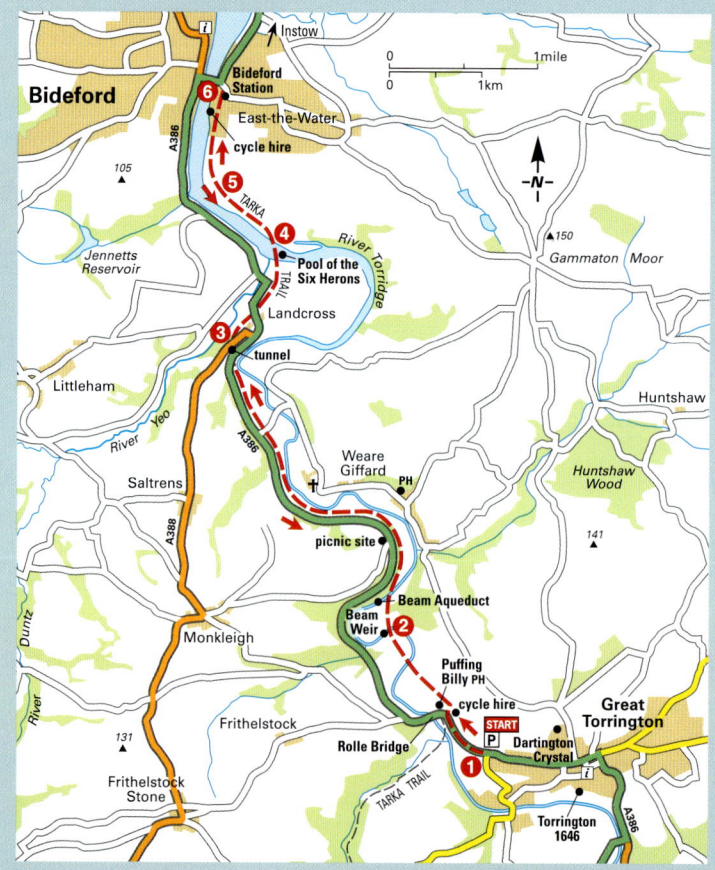

Dartmoor
& Tamar Valley

CLOCKWISE FROM TOP LEFT: CLIMBING ON HAYTOR, DARTMOOR; OKEHAMPTON CASTLE; DARTMOOR PONIES; BUCKLAND IN THE MOOR

DARTMOOR & TAMAR VALLEY

BOVEY TRACEY MAP REF 399 G6

Bovey Tracey is a market town which bills itself as the Gateway to Dartmoor, because of its location at the busy southeastern corner of the moor. It is definitely worth a stop to explore the woodland and riverside walks of the Parke Estate (National Trust), half a mile (800m) west of the town. Parke is also the headquarters of the Dartmoor National Park Authority.

Back in the centre of Bovey Tracey is the beautifully restored Riverside Mill building – never actually used as a mill. It was built in 1850 as stables and the waterwheel simply scooped water from the river to a cistern used by the stables and adjacent house. It now houses a showcase for the members of the Devon Guild of Craftsmen, who produce some of the finest contemporary arts and crafts in the country, including jewellery, textiles, prints, ceramics and furniture.

Nearby is the Teign Valley Glass and House of Marbles centre, a shop in the former Bovey Tracey Pottery buildings selling marbles and glassware, games and toys. This is a major wet-weather attraction but the real interest is in the free demonstrations of glass-blowing. Three museums on the site explain the history of the Bovey potteries.

Near Bovey Tracey there are a number of tors – naturally formed granite rock towers, often weathered into strange shapes by the forces of erosion. Huge Haytor Rocks are the most accessible; the 30-feet (9m) high Bowerman's Nose is the most curiously shaped, resembling a face when looked at in profile. According to one legend, it is a local man who defied the injunction to rest on the Sabbath, went out hunting and was turned to stone; another story in local folklore has it that he disturbed a coven of local witches, who subsequently petrified him and his hounds (Hound Tor). Nearby lies the Hound Tor Deserted Medieval Village, the scant remains of dwellings, stables and grain stores of farmsteads abandoned at the time of the Black Death in the 14th century.

BUCKLAND IN THE MOOR
MAP REF 399 G6

Athough, you may not know it, you have probably already seen Buckland in the Moor. Its thatched cottages, nestling on the edge of the moor – it is the perfect English rural retreat – has starred on countless calendars, a thousand jigsaws and biscuit tins by the score.

Another building in Buckland in the Moor that deserves the time for a visit is the interesting 15th-century church – however, not because it is an outstanding example of Early English architecture (parts of it date back to the 12th century), or because of its fine Norman font (most visitors don't even see its superb screen). The big attraction of the church is its clock face, on which the numerals have been replaced by the twelve letters M Y D E A R M O T H E R – a superb example of English sentimentality in a perfect setting.

DARTMEET MAP REF 398 F6

Dartmoor's two principal rivers are the East Dart and the West Dart. Dartmeet, not surprisingly, is where they come together and is a popular beauty spot with a characteristic Dartmoor clapper bridge spanning the river. Like many such places in the area, Dartmeet can get very busy in the high season, but a short walk – going north along the river is a good bet – will soon take you through the valley where you can enjoy spectacular scenery away from the crowds.

HAYTOR & FOX TOR
MAP REFS 399 G6 & 398 F6

Dartmoor is dotted with huge lumps of granite known as tors and Haytor is a particularly stunning example, situated close to the Devon village of Haytor Vale, and can be spotted on the skyline from as far away as Exeter. Haytor attracts many visitors and is a popular spot for walkers and hikers throughout the year. Rising to 1,500 feet (457m), Haytor stands on the eastern edge of Dartmoor, from where there are far-reaching views out to the coastline and the beautiful surrounding countryside. You can also enjoy views of the Teign estuary from its formidable summit. Although not a difficult climb, the summit is a popular challenge for climbers, and especially with schoolchildren.

Fox Tor is a much more modest beauty spot but the surrounding swampland was the inspiration behind a location in the well-known novel, *The Hound of the Baskervilles* by Sir Arthur Conan Doyle.

IVYBRIDGE MAP REF 398 F7

This small, often overlooked town on the River Erme most probably takes its name from the picturesque 13th-century humpbacked bridge which still spans the river today. There's nothing of great interest in the town but a walk north along the river is recommended. At Longtimbers Wood (a few minutes away) you will see some impressive granite pillars – all that remains of the viaduct that Brunel built in 1848 for the Great Western Railway.

Northwest of Ivybridge at Sparkwell is the popular Dartmoor Wildlife Park and Falconry Centre. This entertaining zoo park, set in beautifully landscaped countryside, features birds of prey, lions, tigers, seals, bison and bears among its collection of around 150 species.

OKEHAMPTON MAP REF 398 F6

Okehampton is the main town of north Dartmoor, with a range of shops for locals as well as for tourists, including a quaint Victorian covered arcade. Its main street, Fore Street, is dominated by the fine 14th-century tower of the Chapel of St James. At the opposite end of this street, tucked away in a charming cobbled courtyard adjacent to the White Hart Inn, is the excellent Museum of Dartmoor Life.

This is housed in an early 19th-century mill complete with a working waterwheel and is bristling with a range of weird and wonderful old objects relating to Dartmoor crafts and industries.

A short walk from the centre are the ruins of Okehampton Castle (English Heritage), the largest castle in Devon. Some parts of the castle date back to Norman times, though most of what remains today was built in the early 14th century by Hugh Courtenay, the Earl of Devon. Following the execution of the Earl in 1538 the castle was destroyed by Henry VIII. Today just enough remains to give a good idea of what it must have looked like. An entertaining personal stereo tour guides visitors around the buildings, at the same time outlining a supposed day in the life of the lady of the castle in medieval times. The setting, high on a hill overlooking the river and the beautiful woodlands which were once used as a royal deer park, is majestic.

PLYMOUTH MAP REF 398 F7

Plymouth's seafaring legacy is legendary. The port was naturally blessed with one of Europe's finest deep-water anchorages and, with the patronage of Sir Francis Drake and Sir John Hawkins, established its supremacy in the 16th century. It was, of course, from here in 1588 that Drake sailed to crush the Armada. In 1620 a more peaceable crew, the Pilgrim Fathers, set off from Plymouth aboard the *Mayflower* to make a new life in North America and lay the foundation for New England. In later years Captain Cooke launched his voyages of discovery from here, while in the 19th century hundreds of colonists and convicts set sail to Australia from Plymouth. Recent history has not been so kind – the city was devastated during World War II and the city centre has been completely rebuilt, but much of the old harbour area survived.

Start your visit on the grassy Hoe (the word 'hoe' means 'high place' or 'hill') for a marvellous view over Plymouth Sound and its busy shipping lanes. Smeaton's Tower, the archetypal and unmissable red-and-white lighthouse in the middle of the Hoe, was built in 1759 and once stood out on the treacherous Eddystone Rocks, 14 miles (22.5km) out to sea. It was replaced in 1882 by a bigger lighthouse and was reassembled here. Climb to the top for panoramic views. Just below the lighthouse is the Dome, which through high-tech audiovisual displays and hands-on exhibits gives an informative and yet entertaining interpretation of Plymouth's history. You can even scan the shipping on the Sound using satellite technology.

Next to the Hoe is the Royal Citadel, a powerful star-shaped fortress built between 1666 and 1675. It is now home to a commando regiment but guided tours in summer (tickets available from the Dome) show the most interesting buildings, including the Royal Chapel of St Katherine (rebuilt in 1845). Just below the Citadel you'll find the National Marine Aquarium, with displays in vast tanks.

Keep walking down the hill and you will reach the Barbican, Plymouth's old harbour area. Several pleasure trips set off from here, the most popular being a one-hour tour around the dockyards. The oldest part of the Barbican is New Street, a cobbled street built in 1581, lined with timber-framed and jettied houses, including the atmospheric Elizabethan House, a rare surviving Tudor house which once belonged to a local sea captain. Also on New Street is a charming small Elizabethan garden. On Barbican Quay you will find the new and exciting Mayflower Centre, where you can learn all about the history of the Barbican and experience the amazing story of the Pilgrim Fathers and the journey of the *Mayflower*.

DARTMEET

Visit
THE GREAT BARN

The architectural highlight of the Buckland Abbey estate is the fine 14th-century Great Barn. It has a superb arch-braced roof, measures 159 feet (48m) long by 32 feet (10m) wide and, to the ridge, 60 feet (18m) high, thus making it one of the largest barns in the country.

Visit
BUCKLAND'S TEN COMMANDMENTS

Just to the east of Buckland in the Mooris Buckland Beacon, the West Country's answer to Mount Sinai, you will find a version of the Ten Commandments carved in 1928, on a granite block, to mark Parliament's rejection of the proposed new Book of Common Prayer.

Visit
DARTMOOR PONIES

At the Dartmoor Pony Heritage Centre at Brimpts Farm, near Dartmeet, you can get a close look at this delightful native breed. The centre was set up by the DPH Trust in 2006 to educate visitors on the history and heritage of the native Dartmoor Pony.

In the modern centre of town, just a short walk north, some old buildings survived the wartime bombing. On Finewell Street is the Prysten House (also known as Yogges House – visit by appointment only), a merchant's home and the oldest (1498) dwelling in the city, built around three sides of a galleried courtyard. Nearby is the Merchant's House, a classic four-storey Elizabethan building now housing a lively museum and a fully stocked apothecary's shop. The City Museum and Art Gallery has an outstanding collection of fine and decorative arts and holds temporary exhibitions throughout the year.

PRINCETOWN MAP REF 398 F6

Princetown is Dartmoor at its bleakest, greyest and grimmest. No wonder, then, that this spot was chosen for Dartmoor Prison. It was built in 1806 to house French prisoners captured during the Napoleonic Wars, and between 1812 and 1814 it confined Americans taken during the War of Independence. Conditions were grim and overcrowded and around 1,000 Frenchmen and Americans died here from jail fever. From 1816 to 1850 the prison stood empty, until it was revived for criminal offenders. Displays at the Prison Heritage Centre, which is housed in converted prison stables, give a fascinating history of Dartmoor Prison.

At 1,400 feet (427m) above sea level, Princetown claims to be the highest town in England (though in fact it is very little more than a village). However, its altitude makes it the natural centre of the 'High Moorland' and there is a good Dartmoor National Park visitor centre and information point in the restored early 19th-century Old Duchy Hotel.

TAVISTOCK MAP REF 398 F6

Tavistock today is little more than a pleasant market town but it was once home to the most powerful abbey in southwest England. Parts of the Benedictine structure still stand, the abbey gateway has been incorporated into the town hall and opposite its infirmary dining hall is now a chapel. Betsey Grimbal's Tower, the abbey's west gatehouse, stands next to the Bedford Hotel and part of the cloisters is retained in the yard of the handsome 15th-century Church of St Eustace.

The town's second great period of wealth came in the 13th century with tin mining, when Tavistock became the largest of Devon's four stannary towns. By the time the supply of tin had been exhausted in the 17th century, a thriving cloth trade was prospering in Tavistock and then along came the great 'copper rush' of the mid- to late 19th century when a rich lode was discovered locally. As boom turned to bust

Tavistock's population dropped from 9,000 to 6,000 and the market town readjusted to its original role. Today Tavistock's famous Victorian covered Pannier Market is rarely free of stalls, with different goods sold on different days.

Tavistock's most famous son is Francis Drake, who was born in 1542 at Crowndale Farm just south of the town. There's nothing to see there, but there is a fine statue at the end of Plymouth Road in the town centre. This is the original (cast in 1883) of the famous one on Plymouth Hoe, which is a copy.

WIDECOMBE IN THE MOOR
MAP REF 399 G6

This picturesque Dartmoor village, set among rolling green hills, surrounded by high granite-strewn ridges, really does attract thousands of visitors in summer and at peak times its natural charm can be somewhat overwhelmed. However, despite the pubs, tea rooms and tourist paraphernalia, little has changed here over the centuries. The famous fair is still celebrated on the second Tuesday in September, but its remit has grown from the simple horse-trading fair it once was to accommodate the coachloads who now descend upon it. The impressive spire of the local Church of St Pancras, 'the Cathedral of the Moors', is a landmark

for miles. The church was built in the 14th century and enlarged over the course of the subsequent two hundred years. It is more than 100 feet (30.5m) in length, and its most notable feature is its fine roof bosses. Look out for the interesting and unusual sign of the three rabbits. Ironically this docile emblem, linked to alchemy, was adopted by the tin miners. A less docile crowd you could never wish to meet; Sir Walter Raleigh, in his capacity as Warden of the Stannaries (tin mines), described them as 'the roughest and most mutinous men in England'.

The adjacent Church House, owned by the National Trust, dates back to 1537, when it was a brewhouse. The Church House was also a rest house for outlying farming families who had a very long distance to travel to Widecombe for services. The house later became almshouses, then it became a school and it now serves as the village hall. It also hosts the village's monthly market. The adjacent Sexton's Cottage is now a National Trust and Dartmoor information centre and shop. If you want to drink in the real atmosphere of Widecombe the pleasant main village pub, the Old Inn, dates back to the 14th century, but it has been much altered and is often packed with visitors. Walk a little way past and you'll find the ancient Rugglestone Inn.

WIDECOMBE IN THE MOOR

AROUND BRENT TOR

This is a steady climb up to the 13th-century Church of St Michael de Rupe at Brent Tor. Lying just inside the large national park boundary, the strange natural formation of Brent Tor is a remnant of the mass of lava that furiously poured out on to the seabed here over 300 million years ago, when the area was just a shallow sea. This extraordinary landmark provides the perfect focus for an exploration of this quiet corner of west Devon.

1 Walk straight ahead from your car towards Brent Tor, which positively invites you to visit it. Where the lane veers right turn, instead, left along an unfenced lane (dead end and weak bridge signs). Go gently downhill and over a cattle grid. The tarmac lane becomes a gravelly track and passes Blacknor Park (left), to cross the old railway line.

2 The stony track runs steeply uphill, then levels off and runs into a green lane. At the following T-junction of tracks take a left turn to pass South Brentor Farm and a lane (right), and then continue to walk straight on slightly uphill – under some beech trees – to pass 'Hillside' on the left.

3 Just past two cottages on the left the lane bends sharp left. Turn right through a metal gate following the bridleway marker along the bottom of the field, keeping the hedge left. Brent Tor is above to the right. Pass through double metal gates to meet the Tavistock to Lydford road – take care, there is fast traffic on this road.

4 Turn right for the car park, toilets and information board for Brent Tor on the left.

5 Turn right and take the steep path up to the church then retrace your steps to the road; turn right past Brentor Inn on the left.

6 At two white cottages, turn right down a tarmac lane signposted 'Brentor and Mary Tavy'. The lane runs downhill, with the moor rising up behind the village ahead. This western edge of the moor is very different from the eastern side, where there is usually a long drive in along wooded river valleys.

7 At the edge of the houses go straight on, keeping the old chapel right, until you reach the 1914–18 war memorial. Turn right slightly downhill to pass the phone box, church and village hall. Follow the lane as it veers right to cross the old railway line. You can see the old station, complete with its platform canopy, below you to the right.

8 Go over the cattle grid and up the lane. At the right-hand bend, cut left diagonally over the edge of Gibbet Hill on an indistinct grassy track. The lane goes back to the car, but this route is more pleasant. At the crest of the hill you will see the route back to your car on the lane below to the right.

DISTANCE/TIME 4 miles (6.4km) 2h **MAP** OS Explorer 112 Launceston & Holsworthy **START** Lay-by past cattlegrid outside Mary Tavy on moorland road to North Brentor village; grid ref: SX 495800 **TRACKS** Tracks and green lanes, open fields and lanes **THE PUB** The Brentor Inn, North Brentor. Tel: 01822 811001

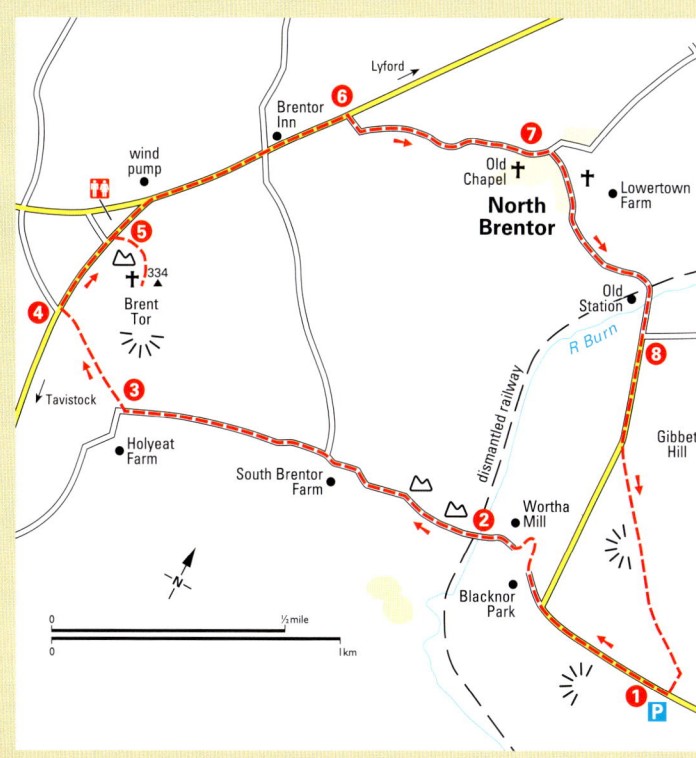

WALK 12

BRIDFORD & THE TEIGN VALLEY

A lovely walk in springtime, when you can enjoy the sight of many tiny wild daffodils covering the river banks of the Teign.

1 From the car park, cross the road, following the signs to the youth hostel. Turn right up the concrete track, then left. At the youth hostel turn right and follow signs for Heltor Farm. The steep path leads you uphill through delightful oak, then beech woodland. At a fork in the paths turn left and go up over some wooden steps by the gate into a field.

2 Follow wooden footpath posts up the field. Go through a metal gate, then between granite gateposts; Heltor Rock on the right. Pass signs for Lower Heltor Farm. Before a metal gate on to a green lane, turn left through a gate and follow footpath signs through woodland. (With a dog, walk on the right of way around the farmhouse.)

3 Follow the signs down wooden steps, across ponds and through a gate. Turn left up the tarmac lane.

4 At the top of the lane turn left following signs for Bridford. After 200yds (183m) turn left over a stile up the fenced permissive path to Heltor for lovely views. Retrace your steps to the road and turn left.

5 When the lane bends left, then right, to reach the edge of Bridford. Turn right down a steep lane signed 'Parish Hall and Church'. Follow the path round the churchyard, down steps and right to find The Bridford Inn.

6 Turn left from the pub and take the road through the village. Take Neadon Lane on the right. Just past where a bridleway joins (from the left) the lane dips to the right, downhill; take the left fork ahead to pass Westbirch Farm. Take the path up to the left, beside the field behind the farm. Take the stile and cross the field, keeping the wire fence to your right. Continue up the right-hand edge of the next field to a stile in the top corner. Then cross over a tumbledown granite wall and carry straight on through an area of prickly gorse bushes, heading towards a footpath signpost. Cross a stile by some beech trees.

7 Continue along the top of the field and down a green lane towards Lower Lowton Farm. At a wooden gate turn right along the permissive bridleway to avoid the farm. At the next T-junction turn right, towards Steps Bridge, then through a small wooden gate. Continue down the deeply banked green lane until you reach a gate on to a surfaced lane.

8 Turn left through the middle gate, signed 'Byway to Steps Bridge'. When you reach the edge of Bridford Wood turn right, following the footpath signposts. The path is fairly narrow and quite steep. Go left, then right, to cross a sandy track. The path then runs to the left, now high above the river, to Steps Bridge, where it meets the road opposite the café. Turn left here to return to your car.

DISTANCE/TIME 5 miles (8km) 2h45 **MAP** OS Explorer 110 Torquay & Dawlish **START** Free car park at Steps Bridge; grid ref: SX 804883 **TRACKS** Woodland paths, open fields and country lanes, 7 stiles **THE PUB** The Bridford Inn, Bridford. Tel: 01647 252436

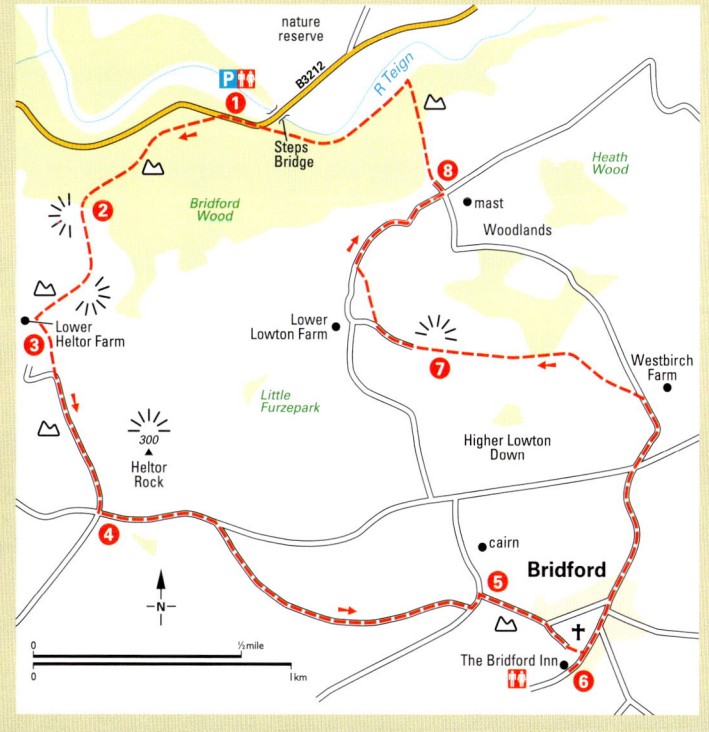

WOODS AROUND LUSTLEIGH

This is a relatively gentle route and will take you through pretty Lustleigh Cleave, via Wreyland's old thatched farmhouses. It also runs through unspoilt Lustleigh – a charming (some would even say perfect) Devon village. The walk then heads steeply back uphill. For much of the walk you pass through Woodland Trust-managed Bovey Valley Woodlands, where you will see ancient trees and a rich variety of plantlife. You will also meander along a delightful stretch of the picturesque east bank of the River Bovey. However, there are some steep ascents and descents on rough paths and lanes in some areas of the walk that are not suitable for very young children.

DISTANCE/TIME 4 miles (6.4km) 2h **MAP** OS Explorer OL28 Dartmoor **START** By side of lane at Hammerslake; grid ref: SX 774815 **TRACKS** Tracks through woodland, over fields and along some steep, narrow country lanes **THE PUB** Cleave Inn, Lustleigh. Tel: 01647 277223

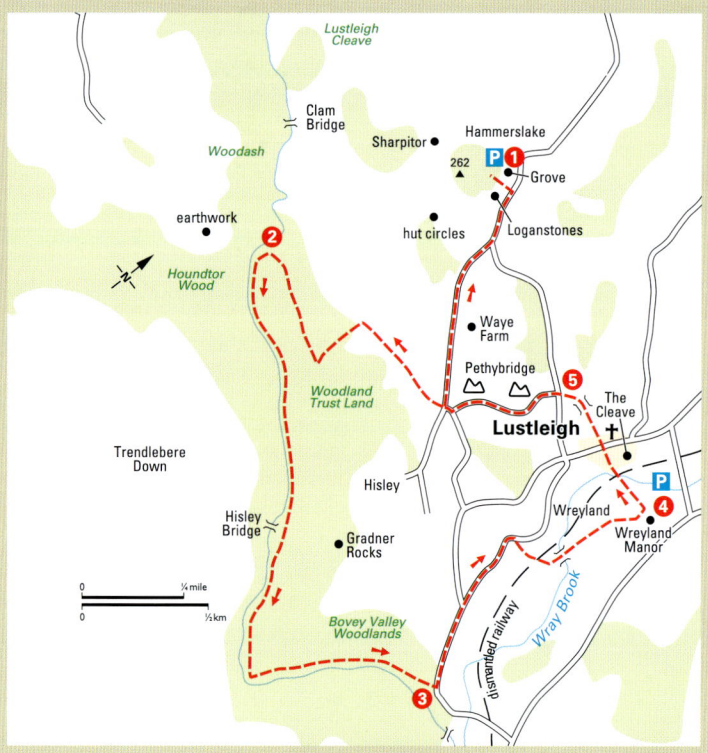

1 Walk along the lane in the direction of Lustleigh. Pass Waye Farm and shortly after turn right up a stony track signed 'Lustleigh Cleave'. Pass through Heaven's Gate and proceed downhill into the valley. Turn left through a gate into Woodland Trust land. Follow the grassy paths to a track at the bottom of the hill.

2 Turn left through conifers, past the ivy-covered ruins of Boveycombe Farm, to reach a fork. Go right towards the old packhorse bridge at Hisley. Don't cross over; turn left and follow the river bank into the Bovey Valley Woodlands. Keep along the river bank, then pass through a gate and across the field to join a lane at a metal gate.

3 Turn left uphill and take the first lane you come to on the right. Soon take the footpath signed 'Wreyland' right. Keep right, following the path to cross the bridge over Wray Brook. Go left (look to the left and you will see

the old railway viaduct) and follow the signs along the field edge, then continue through a gate into Wreyland.

4 Turn left to pass Wreyland Manor and its cricket pitch and then enter Lustleigh by the green, the oldest part, with its stone cross erected in memory of Henry Tudor, parish rector 1888–1904. Turn left at the church and go straight ahead between the dairy and post office into the Town Orchard. Carry on past the May Day rock to the end of the orchard and cross the leat on a wooden bridge. Go through the gate and, at the next junction of paths, drop down right to see the magical granite 'footbridge'.

5 Retrace your steps to the junction and go straight over to join the lane. Turn left, then first right to zig-zag very steeply up a lane to reach Pethybridge, between two thatched cottages. Turn left, then right at the top. Walk past Waye Farm and return to your car.

DARTMOOR'S HIGHEST TOWN

At 14,000 feet (4,268m) above sea level, Princetown is the highest town on Dartmoor, its name derived from 'Prince's town' from the early 19th century, when the then Prince of Wales decreed that a prison be built on the moor to hold prisoners captured in the Napoleonic Wars. The area is famous for its ghost sightings and features prominently in the folklore and many legends.

DISTANCE/TIME 7 miles (11.3km) 3h **MAP** OS Explorer OL28 Dartmoor **START** Main car park in Princetown, grid ref: SX 588735 **TRACKS** Tracks, leat-side paths and moorland **THE PUB** The Plume of Feathers, Princetown. Tel: 01822 890240

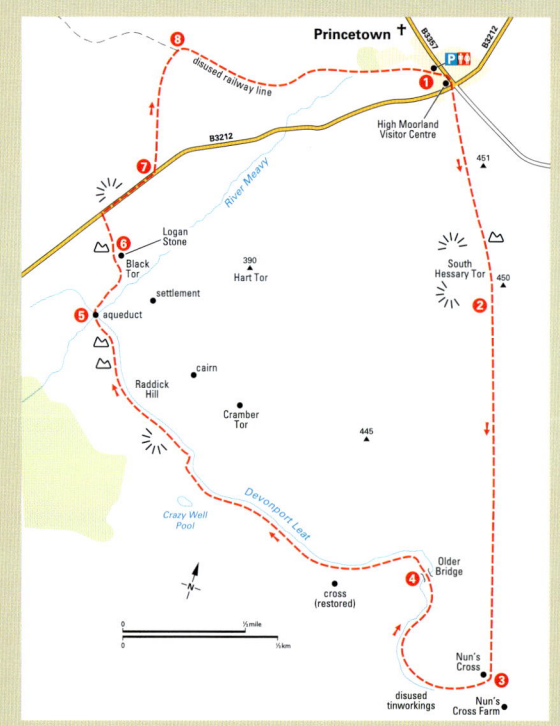

1 Leave the car park past the toilet block; turn right to pass High Moorland Visitor Centre. Cross the road and follow the lane between two pubs and their car parks behind. After a while a small gate leads to a track which ascends to South Hessary Tor (views to Plymouth Sound ahead; prison behind).

2 Follow the track as it drops gently, passing some boundary stones. It crosses two other tracks (look left for view of Devonport Leat) before dropping to Nun's Cross. Nun's Cross Farm (c1870) is on the left.

3 Turn 90 degrees to the right at a crossroads to go over a bumpy area of disused tin workings to find the end of a tunnel where the leat emerges (near remains of cottage under beech and three hawthorn trees). Walk along the right of the bank of the leat.

4 Where the leat bends north cross it on the Older Bridge (granite slabs); walk along the left bank (Burrator reservoir on the left). Follow the leat. There are various crossing places; cross back to the right bank before descending to Meavy Valley. The leat picks up speed as it rushes downhill here; take care, the path is steep and rocky.

5 River Meavy is crossed via an aqueduct and the leat turns left. Take the grassy path on the right leading uphill away from the river (the tin workings in the valley are worth exploration). The path passes through a tumbledown wall; after this, turn left and climb up to Black Tor.

6 Go straight on past Logan Stone (balanced so it can be rocked on its base), and on across open moorland to the road (here there are lovely views of Brentor, Swelltor Quarries and the disused railway line ahead). Turn right when you get to the road.

7 Shortly, opposite the blocked off parking place, turn left and cross the grass, aiming for the mast on North Hessary Tor (boggy in places, but passable).

8 At the railway track turn right and walk back to the edge of town. Where the path splits, keep left and go through a small gate to a tarmac road. Pass the Devon Fire & Rescue Service building to reach the car park on the right.

DISTANCE/TIME 5 miles (8km) 1h45 **MAP** OS Explorer OL28 Dartmoor **START** Princetown car park (contributions); grid ref: SX 588735 **TRACKS** Rocky former railway track and one particularly steep and rough section **CYCLE HIRE** Runnage Farm, Postbridge (plus camping barn). Tel: 01822 880222 **THE PUB** Dartmoor Inn, near Princetown. Tel: 01822 820221

DISTANCE/TIME 7 miles (11.3km) 2h **MAP** OS Explorer OL20 South Devon **START** Steamer Quay (or Longmarsh) car park; grid ref: SX 809596 **TRACKS** Country house drive, rough woodland path, tarmac lane **THE PUB** Durant Arms, Ashprington. Tel: 01726 842855; www.thedurantarms.com

THE PRINCETOWN RAILWAY

There's a long history of granite quarrying on wild Dartmoor. It began around 1820 at Haytor Quarry and (in direct competition) at Swelltor and Foggintor. The old quarry workings are now flooded and provide a pleasant and peaceful picnic spot. This is a tough ride through the landscape of Dartmoor, along the old route of the Princetown to Yelverton railway.

1 Turn left out of the car park along a stretch of rough road. Just past the fire station (left) bear left as signed (disused railway/Tyrwhitt Trail) on a narrow fenced path, which then bears right. Go through the gate. The path then widens into a gritty track and passes a coniferous plantation (right).

2 Suddenly you're out in the open on a long embankment, looking towards the forests around Burrator Reservoir ahead right, below Sheeps Tor and Sharpitor (right). Continue along the contours of the hill – it's quite rough – and as you progress look ahead left to the railway winding its way towards Ingra Tor. This is the old Plymouth and Dartmoor railway line, the brainchild of Sir Thomas Tyrwhitt, who was a friend of and private secretary to the Prince Regent. Originally a tramway with horse-drawn wagons, it opened in 1823. The line was part of Tyrwhitt's plans to exploit the area's natural resources (granite), while at the same time enabling materials such as coal and lime to be brought to Princetown more easily. The Princetown Railway Company (a subsidiary of the Great Western Railway) took it over in 1881; it reopened as a steam railway in 1883, but was not profitable and closed in 1956. However, it makes a great cycle track.

3 Reach the edge of Foggintor Quarry (right), with Swelltor Quarry on the hill ahead; a track crosses the trail. The site of King Tor Halt (1928), from where a siding led to Foggintor, is nearby. Keep straight ahead, almost immediately taking the left fork (the track becomes grassier). Look right towards the spoil heaps of Foggintor Quarry. Follow the track on – look left towards Merrivale Quarry (Dartmoor Inn is just out of sight below) – and try to spot the Bronze Age Merrivale stone rows. Follow the track as it bears left round the hill (below King's Tor Quarry), to enjoy views right over Vixen Tor, almost 1,050ft (317m) high, home to one of the moor's most evil folklore characters, the witch Vixana. Pass through a cutting – there is another branch also that joins right – and keep cycling on to another fork.

4 Keep right along the lower track; views change again, with the wooded Walkham Valley below right and – on a good day – the sparkling waters of Plymouth Sound in the distance. About 50yds (46m) beyond the fork look left to see a pile of dressed stone on the upper track: 12 granite corbels, cut in 1903 for work on London Bridge, but excess to requirements. Pass the spoil heaps of Swelltor Quarry; the track is now fenced on the right, with views ahead to the bridge en route for Ingra Tor.

5 Where the track starts to curve sharp right, turn left opposite an old gate. Push your bike up a rough, rocky track to regain the outward route near Foggintor Quarry.

6 Turn right and make your way bumpily back to Princetown. The building of the infamous prison in 1806, originally for French prisoners from the Napoleonic Wars, was also down to Thomas Tyrwhitt. Since 1850 it has been a civilian establishment.

ALONG THE DART VALLEY TRAIL

The ideal escape route from the hustle and bustle of Totnes – which can get very busy in holiday times – to the peaceful, beautiful valley of the River Dart. The ride undulates through parkland and meadows of the Sharpham Estate overlooking the meandering Dart, before a tough climb through woodland. The lovely village of Ashprington, and the Durant Arms, provide a great focus.

1 From the car park follow the road back towards Totnes. Turn left on to Seymour Road, then left over Totnes Bridge (built to replace a smaller one in 1838, and a toll bridge until 1881) – the lowest crossing point of the Dart – to reach the roundabout at the bottom of Fore Street. Turn left along the Plains, at one time an area of tidal marsh; the old riverside warehouses have now been converted into stylish accommodation. Keep ahead along New Walk to reach the Steam Packet Inn on the left.

2 As the road bends sharp left turn right up narrow tarmac Moat Hill. After about 20yds (18m) turn left as signed 'Ashprington', on a gritty, fenced track, gently uphill.

3 At the end bear right then left on to the old driveway to Sharpham House, initially walled. Pass out into the open briefly – look back for good views over the river at Totnes – then back into woodland. Continue uphill to cross a cattle grid in woodland. There follows a lovely downhill run through parkland, with fantastic views ahead left over reedbeds fringing the river. The drive runs uphill into woodland again and passes into the Sharpham Estate via a gate. Continue through two more gates and back into parkland – watch out for cowpats beneath your wheels and cows in front of you! A long downhill run, with Pinhay Plantation right, leads towards the river. Eventually, pass through a gate and out on to a track to reach a signpost.

4 Turn right along a narrow gritty track that runs uphill away from the river. Follow this as it bears left with the hedge and continues uphill. Pass over a cattle grid, at which point cyclists are asked to dismount. Continue up the rough, rooty track – Leafy Lane – through Lower Gribble Plantation – it's quite a slog. Pass through a staggered barrier; the track levels off and reaches a lane, with the entrance to Sharpham House left. Sharpham House was built in the late 18th century – replacing an Elizabethan building – for Captain Philemon Pownall of HMS *Favourite*, funded by prize money from the capture of a Spanish treasure ship. His grandson later lost Sharpham when he gambled away the family fortune. Situated on the warm south-facing slopes above the Dart, the estate now hosts a working vineyard and cheese dairy, and a shop and café.

5 Turn right along the narrow – but quiet lane – for 0.5mile (800m). A pleasant downhill run ends in the centre of Ashprington. The Durant Arms, an inn since 1725 and renamed in honour of the Durant family of Sharpham, is on the left.

6 To return to Totnes, it is possible to follow a different route along the undulating country lanes. To do this, turn right at the war memorial in Ashprington and follow the lane to Ashprington Cross. Turn right and follow that lane all the way back to meet Moat Hill and turn right for New Walk. However, as Devon lanes are usually narrow and twisty, with high hedges and poor visibility, it is safer to return via the outward route you cycled out on.

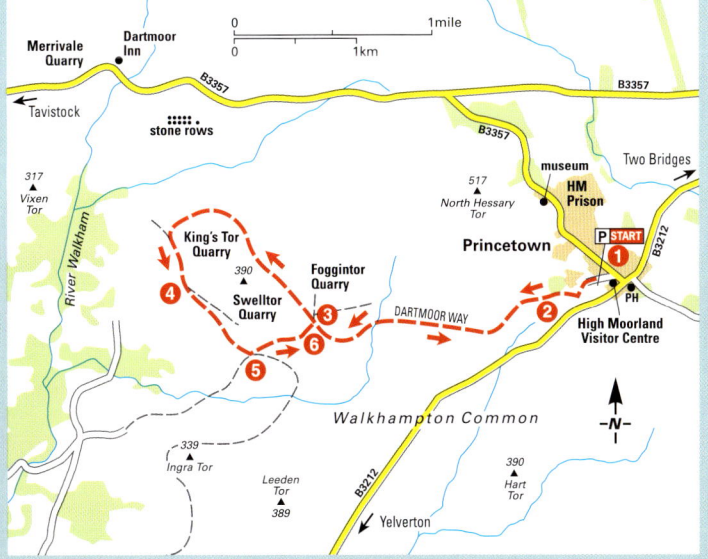

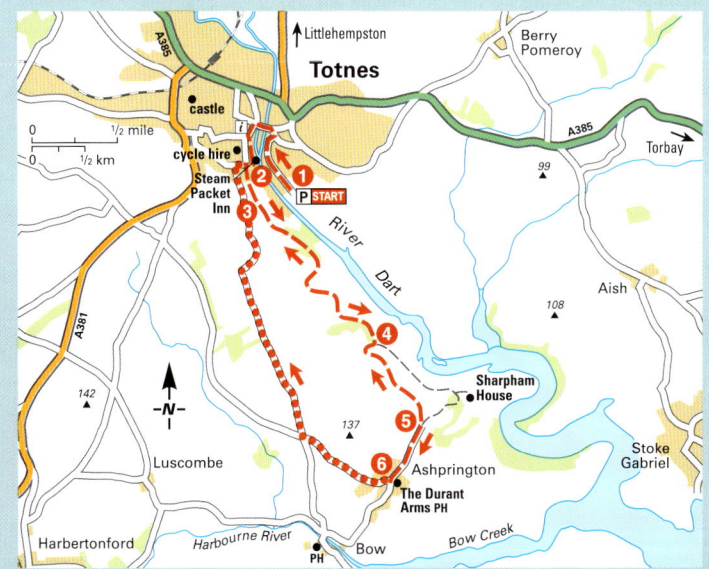

DARTMOOR & THE TAMAR VALLEY

This drive skirts the northwestern edge of Dartmoor before climbing on to its most spectacular, granite-dotted open moorland. From the most southerly point of the drive, the return is through the beautiful countryside of the Tamar Valley. The drive begins in Okehampton, which has an attractive wide main street, flanked by some fine old buildings. Just off the main street is a cobbled courtyard housing a Victorian tea room, a tourist information centre and the Museum of Dartmoor Life. The impressive ruins of Okehampton Castle are on the southwestern edge of the town.

Route Directions

1 From the traffic lights in the town centre take the B3260, signposted 'Tavistock'. In 3 miles (4.8km) cross a road bridge and turn right on to the A30, signposted 'Launceston'. In 1 mile (1.6km) take the A386, signed 'Tavistock' and 'Plymouth', and continue for 9 miles (14.4km) to Mary Tavy.

Mary Tavy, a peaceful village now, was once famous for its tin- and copper-mining industry. The preserved remains of Wheal Betsy engine house are passed just before reaching the village.

2 Continue for 3.75 miles (6km), making sure you make the most of the fine views of Dartmoor on the left, to reach Tavistock.

Tavistock is one of four stannary towns around the moor and is essentially a product of 19th-century prosperity. It still has a thriving covered market (the town was granted a market charter in 1105) and bustling main street and is one of the most attractive 'working' towns in the county.

3 Just before reaching the town centre, make a left turn on to the B3357, which is signposted 'Princetown'. The road soon climbs on to open moorland with huge outcrops of granite all around, including Coxtor on the left.

4 In 6.5 miles (10.5km) turn right, signed 'Princetown', and continue for 1 mile (1.6km) to Princetown, with sombre views down over the prison to the left. Pass the Dartmoor Prison Museum and the excellent High Moorland Visitor Centre, then turn right at a roundabout on to the B3212, which is signed 'Yelverton, Plymouth', a road which has some of the most spectacular views on the moor. In 6.25 miles (10km) reach a roundabout and take the first exit on to the A386, signposted 'Plymouth'. In half a mile (800m) turn right, signposted 'Crapstone, Buckland Monachorum, Milton Combe', with brown tourist signs to The Garden House and Buckland Abbey. In 1.25 miles (2km) detour left to visit Buckland Abbey.

Leave enough time to visit this splendid former monastic foundation which later became the home of Sir Francis Drake.

5 Continue on the main route, passing The Garden House in half a mile (800m) on the right. In another half mile (800m) turn left, signposted 'Milton Combe' and 'Bere Alston'. After a further half mile (800m) turn right, signposted 'Bere Alston', descending through a delightful wooded valley to cross the River Tavy at a picturesque stone bridge, following signs for 'Bere Alston'. Ascend a 1-in-5 (20%) hill and in 2 miles (3.2km) turn right, signed 'Gulworthy' and 'Tavistock'. In another 2.5 miles (4km) detour left for a mile (1.6km) to visit Morwellham Quay.

This once thriving copper mine and port has been accurately renovated and carefully restored to form a splendid open-air museum, staffed by craftsmen and other workers in period costume.

6 On the main route continue for 1.5 miles (2.4km) to meet the A390. Keep ahead over the roundabout, signed 'Chipshop', 'Lamerton' and 'Milton Abbot'. In 4.75 miles (7.6km) cross the B3362, then in 1.25 miles (2km) turn right, signposted 'Brentor'. In a further mile (1.6km) continue straight on at crossroads, signed 'Brentor'. In 1.5 miles (2.4km) reach the car park for Brent Tor Church on the right.

Perched atop a high grassy mound with great rocks strewn all around, the church has panoramic views from all sides.

7 Shortly after the car park, turn left signed 'Brentor' and 'Lydford'. In about 3 miles (4.8km) you will pass the first entrance to Lydford Gorge on the left.

This beautiful wooded gorge, owned by the National Trust, has a 3.5-mile (5.6km) walk with a waterfall at one end and the spectacular Devil's Cauldron at the other.

8 Continue for 1.5 miles (2.4km) to reach Lydford Castle, a great square stone keep which dates from 1195. In 0.75 miles (1.2km) turn left on to the A386, signposted 'Okehampton'. In 5.75 miles (9.2km) turn right on to the A30, signed 'Okehampton' and 'Exeter'. In half a mile (800m) turn left, signed 'Okehampton', and follow the B3260 for 2.5 miles (4km) back to the town centre.

Exmoor & the Quantocks

CLOCKWISE FROM TOP: PORLOCK VILLAGE; DUNKERY BEACON; EXMOOR NATIONAL PARK; THE QUANTOCKS; CROWCOMBE

BRENDON HILLS MAP REF 399 G4

The Brendon Hills form an elongated ridge located to the east of the main part of Exmoor. Unlike the uplands of Exmoor and the Quantocks, the Brendon Hills are characterised by extensive cultivation. For centuries the Hills were mined for minerals, mainly ironstone, an activity that reached its zenith during the 19th century when a railway was built to take the ore to Watchet and onward to Ebbw Vale for smelting. The mines were eventually worked out by the turn of the century. A miners' chapel remains at Beulah, along with ruins of cottages and the steep mineral railway incline that steadfastly served the mines.

These lovely hills merge into the eastern side of Exmoor, and are within Exmoor National Park. The highest point is Lype Hill at 1,388 feet (422m). The terrain is broken by a series of streams and rivers running roughly southwards to meet Wimbleball Lake or River Haddeo.

CULBONE MAP REF 399 G4

Culbone village, originally a centre for charcoal burners and once supporting a colony of lepers, is today renowned for its little church, only accessible by a long walk. Reputedly the smallest in England, although St Olaf's in Wasdale in the Lake District would justifiably have something to say about that, Culbone's church has a chancel merely 13'6" x 10' (4m x 3m), and a nave 21'6" x 12'4" (6.4m x 3.6m). This diminutive place of worship has an overall length of just 35 feet. Dedicated to St Beuno and, set in a small clearing, it seats a congregation of about 30 people in some companiable and intimate degree of discomfort, and nestles in an endearing valley about 3 miles (5km) from Porlock. The church has Saxon parts, and there are numerous legends surrounding its history. To get there you trace the delicate fretwork of a green English woodland, with glimpses of the sea far below through a break in the foliage. Luxuriant ferns grow on the hillside along which the path is etched. Except for a rustle of leaves and a whisper of wind blown up from the sea, you can walk along here in reflective silence, far removed from the world below.

The nearby Culbone Stone is an early medieval standing stone which is about one metre high, which was discovered in 1940. The stone lies in woodland close to the parish boundary, and has an incised wheeled cross, suggesting that it dates originally from the 7th to the 9th century.

Samuel Taylor Coleridge, one of the 'Lake Poets', knew Somerset and Culbone well. On one visit he followed a zigzag path from Porlock Weir to Culbone, passing through ancient woodland that 'abounded in wild deer, foxes, badgers and martin cats'. Whortleberries made a carpet beneath the trees, and the sound of the waves breaking below and distant views across to Wales filled him with 'pleasure and astonishment'. For Coleridge, Culbone was one of Somerset's holy places. If anyone ever needs time to be alone with their thoughts, Culbone is the place to come.

DUNKERY BEACON MAP REF 399 G4

At 1,702 feet (519m), Dunkery Beacon is the highest hill on Exmoor, and also the highest point in Somerset. The shortest route of ascent goes from Dunkery Gate, a brief haul of 0.6 miles (1km) and height gain of 433 feet (132m). With little to interrupt the view, those from the summit include the Bristol and English Channel coastlines, the Brecon Beacons, Bodmin Moor, Dartmoor, as well as the Severn Bridges. It is claimed you can see Cleeve Hill, 86 miles (138km) away in Gloucestershire. But from the top of Dunkery Beacon the horizon is 55 miles (88.5km) away, making this unlikely.

The hill is a lush carpet of heather, and in summer a richly deep purple. For the botanist, the Beacon area and adjacent woodland make this a fascinating place; ling and bell heather grow in abundance, along with gorse, sessile oak, ash, rowan, hazel, bracken, mosses, lichens and ferns, as well as whitebeam. This is a good spot, too, to see robust Exmoor ponies and shy red deer, birds of many varieties including dippers, snipe, skylarks and kestrels, while the nearby Horner Woods often yield redstart, pied flycatchers, wood and willow warblers, chiffchaff and lesser spotted woodpeckers. Horner Woods are also the home to 14 of the 16 UK bat species, which include the very elusive barbastelle and Bechstein bats. There are now thought to be only about 1,000 Exmoor ponies remaining in the world, which, if true, means they are rarer than the Giant Panda. About 150 live on the upland expanses of Exmoor.

PORLOCK BAY

CROWCOMBE, QUANTOCKS

The area around Dunkery Beacon is scattered with several Bronze Age burial mounds at or near the summit, notably Rowbarrows, Kit Barrows, Joaney How and Robin How. The beacon was the site of a former fire beacon, and is still used occasionally for celebratory bonfires.

DUNSTER MAP REF 399 G4

On the eastern edge of Exmoor and actually in Somerset, Dunster is one of the most picturesque medieval villages in Devon, complete with a huge Norman castle that dominates the entire area. Now in the care of the National Trust, Dunster Castle was substantially altered in the early 17th century and further work was carried out in 1868, but its core medieval character was preserved to a large extent. The oak-panelled halls have magnificent ceilings and there are many reminders of the Luttrell family, who called this home for some 600 years until 1950.

The village is one of the loveliest in Britain, its medieval character perfectly preserved. The main street of pretty little shops and tea rooms sits cosily between two high wooded hills, one topped by the castle, and is distinguished by the octagonal Yarn Market, a relic of its days as an important wool centre.

EXFORD MAP REF 399 G4

This tiny village, reputedly the smallest on Exmoor, is sometimes referred to as the capital of Exmoor. It has a small green draped around a medieval stone bridge. As the name suggests, Exford sits on the River Exe and has been the site of a ford or bridge for hundreds of years. The small village has a couple of traditional inns set around the green and its Crown Hotel is one of the best known hostelries in Exmoor. The church of St Salvyn stands to the east of the village, and has a fine wooden screen and a 16th-century tower.

PORLOCK MAP REF 399 G4

Nestled quaintly in the embrace of the Exmoor hills, there has been a village on the existing site since ancient times. Indeed, there is evidence of a Stone Age settlement on the land nearby. Today's coastal village edges on to a saltmarsh nature reserve, created in the late 20th century by the breach of some low-lying land. This area has protected status.

Porlock is a traditional, attractive Exmoor village, with everything a working community could need in the way of services and shopping, as well as pubs, restaurants and hotels that appeal to visitors and locals.

Always popular, Porlock was a favourite of the 18th-century poet Coleridge (who actually lived a short distance away at Nether Stowey), and part of a walk from the Quantocks to Exmoor is named after him. Another of the Romantic poets fond of Porlock was William Wordsworth.

Insight
HUNTING THE EARL

If you are in Combe Martin over the Spring Bank Holiday, you will witness the Hunting of the Earl of Rone, a ceremony with its roots in pagan times but which has been adapted over time to incorporate some other historical events. The original Hobby Horse procession is now preceded by a chase through the woods in pursuit of the 'Earl', who is then placed on a donkey backwards and led in the main procession to the beach, where he is then dumped into the sea.

Insight
LORNA DOONE

The combes and heathery moorland around Malmsmead and Oare are the setting for R. D. Blackmore's story of the tragic heroine Lorna Doone and her lawless family. It is based on the exploits of a real-life family of Scottish outlaws who came to Exmoor, failed at farming and turned instead to a life of crime.

THE QUANTOCKS MAP REF 399 H4

Running in a gently curving line northwest to southeast from near Watchet on the Bristol Channel to the northern reaches of Taunton, the Quantock Hills form a wide spread of rolling heather moorland, brackeny hills and wooded combes. Designated in 1956 as the first of England's Areas of Outstanding Natural Beauty (AONB), the whole region is hugely popular for walking, and rightly so. With narrow lanes and homogeneous hamlets huddled in hollows this is a classically English landscape, much admired by Wordsworth and Coleridge, both of whom lived here. Because of the special nature of the Quantocks, much of it is covered by a designation of Site of Special Scientific Interest (SSSI) for the geologically interesting coastline to the maritime heathlands on the northern hills. There are archaeological remains on the higher parts of the hills, notably Bronze Age barrow mounds and an Iron Age hill fort. The hills are famous for their views which reputedly embrace nine counties.

For so small an area, the landscape shows great variety, its heights offering a remarkable air of solitude and wildness. Underlying rocks range from the ominously named Hangman Grits on the tops, to the undulating shales and distinctive red sandstone of the West Country. Eastward, long broad valleys form an enclosed landscape of copses and hedgerows that spill away towards the Somerset Levels.

The heathland and sessile oak woodlands of the AONB are nationally important wildlife habitats, and native red deer still roam here. Much of southern Britain's heathland has vanished or survives as fragments, making the AONB's extensive heaths particularly valuable.

SELWORTHY MAP REF 399 G4

On first impression, the thatched, cream-coloured stone cottages that flank the hill rising to the 15th-century church in Selworthy seem completely in harmony, part of the rural landscape. But, unlike neighbouring villages, Selworthy was substantially rebuilt in 1828 by Sir Thomas Acland of Killerton, a philanthropist who sought to provide homes for the pensioners on his Holnicote Estate. The houses, today in National Trust ownership but privately tenanted, are built using traditional materials and designs to produce what is an intentionally old-fashioned village, a modest variation on the vernacular architecture with typically tall chimneys and deep thatched eaves. The church sits at the top of the village and provides a lovely view over a rash of thatched roofs and tidy cottage gardens across the Vale of Porlock to the heathery heights of Dunkery Beacon.

The wider Holnicote Estate covers a large part of Exmoor National Park including the high tors of Dunkery and Selworthy Beacons. Selworthy is just one of the villages within the estate, which also embraces Allerford, Bossington, Horner and Luccombe, in addition to 4 miles (7km) of coastline between Porlock Bay and Minehead, where the South West Coast Path begins. There are over 100 miles (160km) of footpaths through the fields, dense woods, moors and pretty villages of the estate.

TARR STEPS MAP REF 399 G4

The Tarr Steps are an ancient bridge between Withypool and Dulverton over the River Barle, just where Little River joins the main valley. The bridge is an especially fine 'clapper bridge', hundreds of years old, and consists of 15 large, unmortared slabs, or 'stepping stones', resting on each other, and each weighing around 2 tons. The actual age of the bridge is still unknown, but it has clearly been restored over the years. Tarr Steps is a scheduled ancient monument but, although once thought to be prehistoric, it is now accepted as of mediaeval origin.

The River Barle is particularly attractive and joins the Exe south of Dulverton, and both the river and Tarr Steps are popular tourist attractions. The river and valley woodlands are Sites of Special Scientific Interest, and are rich in wildlife.

The term 'clapper' bridge is thought to derive from the Latin *claperius*, meaning pile of stones. The surrounding woodland is a National Nature Reserve that mainly consists of oak woodland with ash, hazel and sycamore, and beech in some of the drier areas. The woodland is however, particularly important for moss species, liverwort and lichen, while springtime brings a blanket of bluebells.

WILLS NECK MAP REF 399 H4

Wills Neck, the highest point of the Quantock Hills, is a heather-covered dome rising to 1260 feet (384 metres). Not surprisingly, the views from the top are absolutely amazing, with the entire Quantocks seen end-on in both directions, of course. To the northeast the Bristol Channel spreads across the distant horizon, with the town of Bridgwater in view away to the east. The Mendips, Wells and Glastonbury Tor can also be seen, and, on the clearest of days, even the Severn Bridges spanning the Bristol Channel, and linking England with Wales.

TARR STEPS

EXMOOR & THE NORTH COAST'S WOODED COMBES

This tour takes in the beautiful wooded valleys of the coast, the rolling pastures of its hinterland and the wild open moorland of western Exmoor, before visiting the beauty spot of Watersmeet. The early part of the drive is on steep, narrow roads with hairpin bends. It is slow going and you'll need to take care, but the scenery is well worth the time it takes.

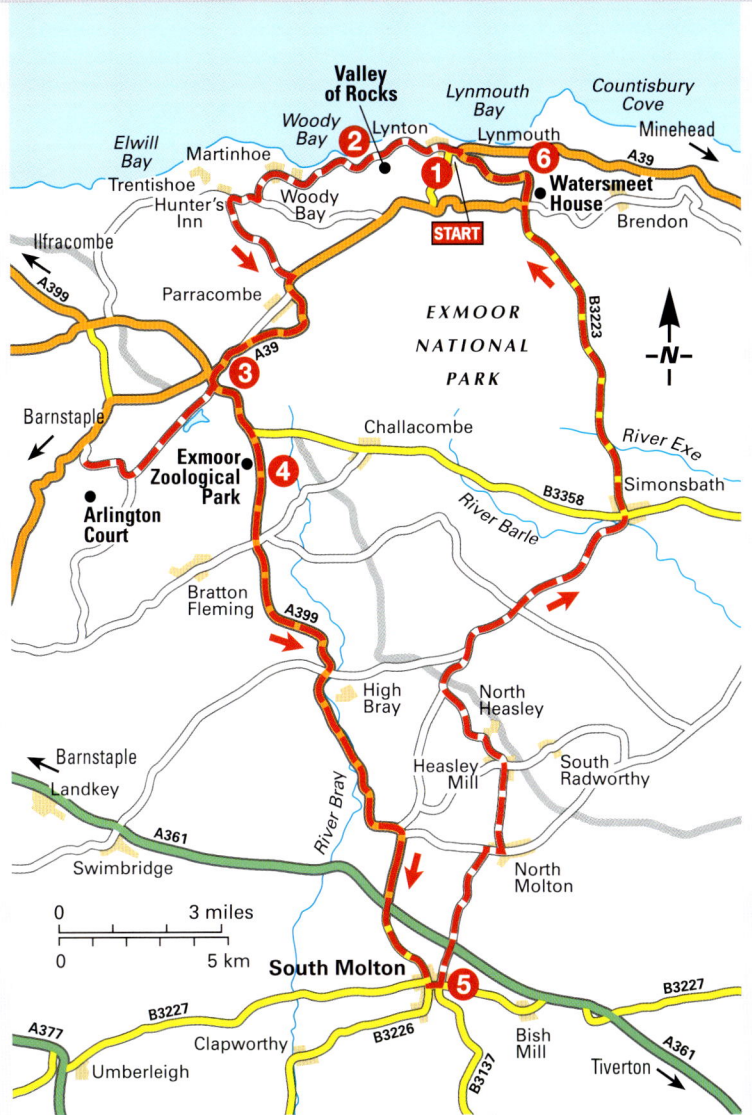

Route Directions

1 Set out with Lynton town hall and tourist information office on your right, and follow signs for the Valley of Rocks, which you will reach shortly after leaving the town.

This beautiful dry valley has huge, fascinating sandstone rock formations created by freeze-thaw action during the ice age, and is populated by wild goats. From the road there are glimpses of the sea and a walk here will be even more rewarding. There is a picnic area on the left at the start of the valley and a large parking area, the last until the end of the valley, on the right.

2 The road passes into the pretty Lee Valley Estate and continues past Lee Abbey Christian Community, where a small toll is payable. Follow the narrow road downhill, then uphill as it turns away from the coast, winding its way through steep, wooded combes, for 0.75 mile (1.2km). At the next junction keep straight ahead, signposted 'Woody Bay'. Pass the Woody Bay Hotel and later a National Trust car park on the left, then in a mile (1.6km) at a T-junction turn right. In another mile (1.6km) – having passed through Martinhoe, and just past a telephone box – take the right fork downhill, signed 'Hunter's Inn, Heddons Mouth, Trentishoe'. Turn left at Hunter's Inn up a narrow lane. In 2.25 miles (3.6km) meet the A39 and turn right, signposted 'Barnstaple'. After 3.25 miles (5.2km) turn left on to the A399 at Blackmoor Gate, signposted 'South Molton'. Turn right instead at Blackmoor Gate if you want to visit Arlington Court: turn right, then left, signed 'Barnstaple', and continue for 3.25 miles (5.2km) before turning right, signposted 'Arlington Court'.

This charming house (National Trust) dates from 1822 and contains some fascinating collections and beautiful architectural details, such as the impressive Victorian staircase which has natural light from three stained-glass windows.

3 On the main route, continue with hilly agricultural land on both sides of the road. In another 2.25 miles (3.6km) detour right to visit the lovely Exmoor Zoological Park.

The zoo specialises in small exotic animals. You can see wolves, Arctic foxes, lemurs, gibbons and even cheetah.

4 Return to the A399 and turn right. In 10 miles (16km) at a roundabout, take the 2nd exit, signposted 'South Molton' and continue for 1.5 miles (2.4km) into the town.

South Molton, where you can see some particularly elegant Georgian buildings dotted along the main street, still enjoys a position very much at the heart of the surrounding farming community.

5 From the main street in South Molton, pass the market hall and museum, and the health centre on the right and turn left into Station Road, signposted 'North Molton', with lovely views as you leave the town. In just under a mile (1.6km), meet the A361 and turn right, then immediately left, still signposted 'North Molton', and continue for 2.25 miles (3.6km) into the village. Just as you pass a petrol station on the left, turn left, following the signs for 'Heasley Mill' and 'Simonsbath', turning left again at the square. After travelling for 1 mile (1.6km) bear left, signposted 'North Heasley' and 'Simonsbath'. In half a mile (800m) at a crossroads continue forward, signposted 'Simonsbath' and then after 1.75 miles (2.8km) turn right at a T-junction, signposted 'Simonsbath' and 'Exford' to climb steadily on to Exmoor. In 5.25 miles (8.4km) turn left on to the B3223, signposted 'Lynton'. In 6 miles (9.7km) turn right on to the A39, which is signposted 'Lynmouth and Watersmeet'.

Watersmeet is one of the county's premier beauty spots. The confluence of the East Lyn River and Hoaroak Water and set in a beautiful, deep, wooded valley, with a wonderful network of footpaths, it also has that all-important National Trust tea room.

6 Continue down the wooded valley to return to Lynmouth, attractively set around the pretty river valley and tiny harbour, and Lynton, looking out from the cliff top. The two towns are linked by the famous cliff railway.

WIMBLEBALL LAKE WOODLAND WATER

Natural and artificial landscapes merge beautifully on this route through peaceful wooded valleys, heathland and across the Wimbleball Dam. The reservoir here was created in the 1970s and covers an area of nearly 380 acres (157ha). The water is a hive of activity year round, popular with every type of watersports enthusiast as well as ornithologists curious to see the many birds it attracts.

DISTANCE/TIME 6 miles (9.7km) 3h **MAP** OS Outdoor Leisure 9 Exmoor **START** Frogwell Lodge car park, Haddon Hill; grid ref: SS 969285 **TRACKS** Rough descent, long climb, easy track between, 1 stile **THE PUB** The Rock Inn, Waterrow. Tel: 01984 623293

1 Leave the car park by a small gate to the left of the toilets. Turn right to cross a tarred track; head downhill on a path through gorse, grass and heather until you reach an area of open birch woods which give rise to easier going. If you lose the path, just keep heading downhill. Above the reservoir is a stony track.

2 Turn left. The track emerges on to open grassland and then starts rising to the left. Look for a stile down on the right, into woodland. Cross; turn left on the path that emerges near Wimbleball Dam. A side-trip to the dam gives wonderful views of Hartford Bottom, below.

3 Return along the dam and turn right into a tarmac lane ('Bury 2.5'). At the bottom keep ahead on a concrete path ('Bridleway'). With the bridge ahead, bear left on to a grass track ('Bridleway to Bury') which leads to a ford; watch for a footbridge on the right. Cross, then take the track between the houses; finally turn left into Hartford.

4 Turn left ('Bury 2') on a track, passing through woods beside River Haddeo. The track is now stony to the village of Bury.

5 Turn left to Packhorse Bridge situated beside the road's ford. Ignore the riverside track on the left, then continue for 180yds (165m). Once you have walked thus far, turn left at the bridleway sign. From here, pass between houses to a sign for Haddon Hill, and the sunken track which climbs steeply; the lovely stream at the bottom flows over orange bedrock. At the top of Haddon Hill, the track then continues between high hedges, before turning left to follow a short climb up to Haddon Farm.

6 Pass to the left of the farm's buildings, out on to an access track. After approximately 0.25 mile (400m) you will reach a corner of a wood. After a short stretch a stile above leads into a wood. Ignore the pointing signpost but instead bear to the left to go up the left-hand side of a clump of a wood to a gate on to open hillside. Continue up alongside the wood to the top corner.

7 From here take the track bearing left to eventually cross the crest of a hill. Then, turn right, on to the wide track which runs up to the top of Haddon Hill and the trig point. Enjoy the views and then continue downhill to the car park where you started.

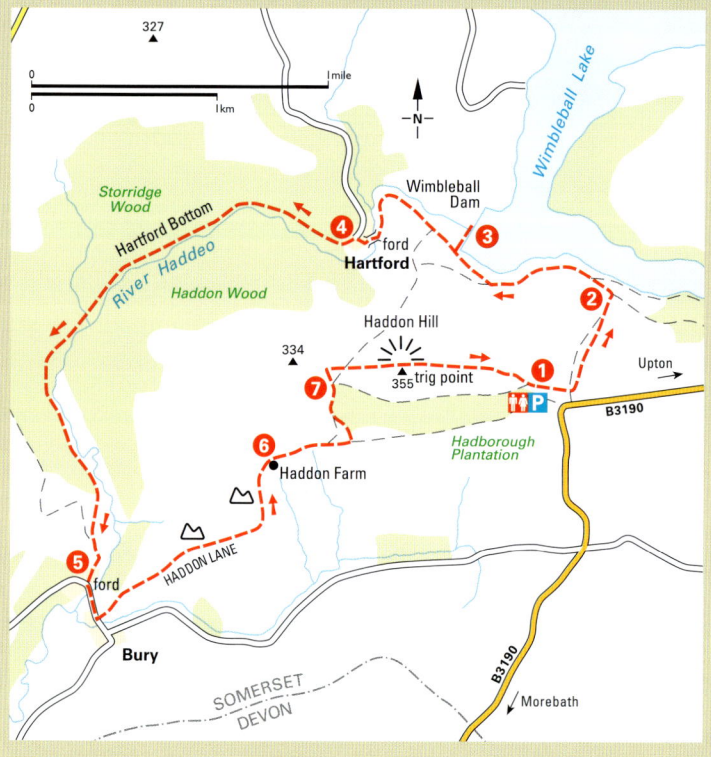

TARR STEPS BRONZE AGE TRACKWAYS

On this walk you will be able to visit one of the world's 'oldest' bridges, just south of Withypool. This ancient stone causeway spans the River Barle, as part of an ancient track that meanders through woodland, and draws crowds year on year. Known as a prehistoric 'clapper bridge' the stones are thought to date back to 1000 BC and probably weigh upwards of 5 tons.

DISTANCE/TIME 5.25 miles (8.4km) 2h30 **MAP** OS Outdoor Leisure 9 Exmoor **START** Car park just over .25 mile (400m) east of Tarr Steps (parking at Tarr Steps for disabled drivers only); grid ref: SS 872323 **TRACKS** Riverside paths and field tracks, some open moor, no stiles **THE PUB** The Crown Hotel, Exford. Tel: 01643 831554; www.crownhotelexmoor.co.uk

1 Leave the bottom of the car park by a footpath on the left-hand side ('Scenic Path'). This leads down to the left of a road to Little River, crossing 2 footbridges to Tarr Steps, over the River Barle, ahead.

2 Cross the Steps, turning upstream at the far side ('Circular Walk'). Follow the river bank path past a wire footbridge. After 0.75 mile (1.2km) cross a side-stream on some stepping stones, where you will then reach a footbridge over the river.

3 Cross the footbridge, and then continue upstream (river is now on your left). After 0.75 mile (1.2km) the path crosses a wooden footbridge, then divides at a signpost.

4 Turn right, uphill ('Winsford Hill'). A wide path goes up through woods with a stream on the right. Where it meets a track turn briefly right to ford a stream; continue uphill on a narrower signed path. At a low bank with beech trees turn right to a gate; follow the foot of a field to a tarred lane. Go up to the cattle grid on to open moor. Bear right here on to a faint track heading up between some gorse bushes. After 250yds (229m) you will reach a 4-way signpost.

5 Turn right (signed 'Knaplock') and take a path that leads downwards to reach the hedge tucked into the corner. Follow the hedge for a short while, then take the path that slants gradually up and into the moor. After approximately 170yds (155m) you will see a sign that points back down towards moor-foot banking. The beech bank crosses straight ahead: aim for the lower end, where a soft track leads straight forward, with the occasional blue-paint spot. After about 0.25 mile (400m) the track then turns downhill, and afterwards turns back towards the left (here the going under foot becomes firmer as it reaches Knaplock Farm).

6 Once you reach the farm buildings turn downhill (signed for 'Tarr Steps'), and on to a muddy farm track. Where this track turns off into a field, continue walking straight ahead on a stony track, called Watery Lane. After an initial descent this becomes a smooth path down to the River Barle. Turn left here and walk downstream. When the path rises above the river, look for a fork on the right (signed 'Footpath'). This rejoins the river to pass through an open field. Here, cross the road and turn left to go up a scenic path to return to your car.

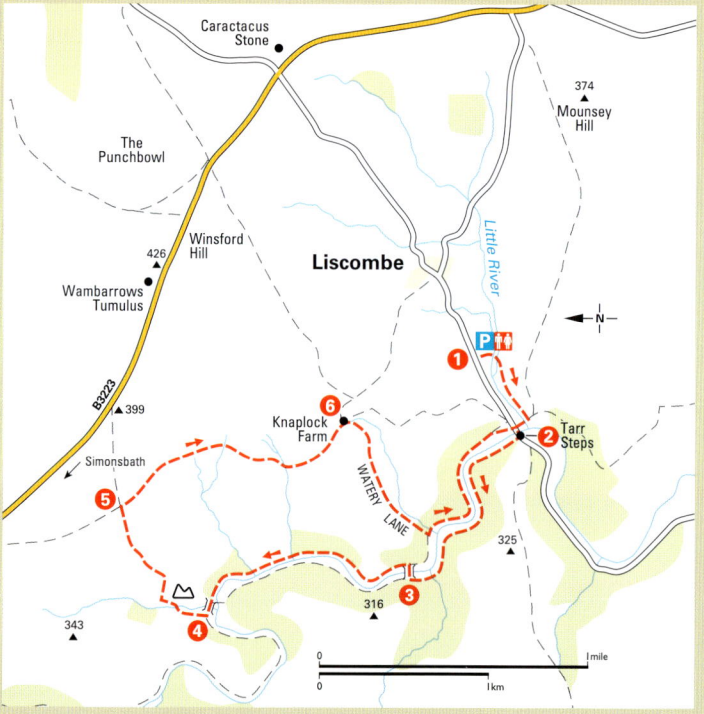

PORLOCK WILDWOOD & SEA VIEWS

A stiff climb through the wildwood for a sudden sea view. Set as it is in the vale of the hills of Exmoor on three of its four sides, Porlock is undeniably pretty and the coastline seems to add that finishing touch. The landscape has inspired many poets to write romantic verse, including Wordsworth and Coleridge – in fact Coleridge was supposed to have been stopped mid-flow by a 'person from Porlock', whilst he was penning his work 'Kubla Khan'.

DISTANCE/TIME 6 miles (9.7km) 3h15 **MAP** OS Outdoor Leisure 9 Exmoor **START** Porlock central car park, grid reference: SS 885468 **TRACKS**: Initial stiff climb then smooth, well-marked paths, no stiles **THE PUB** The Ship Inn, Porlock. Tel: 01643 862507; www.shipinnporlock.co.uk

1 From the car park follow signs for the public library and then turn left. Before the church turn right (Parsons Street). Once you get to the parking area (with toilets), a bridleway sign for Hawkcombe points upstream towards a footbridge.

2 The path climbs through bamboo and laurel foliage, to join the bridleway from below, and tracks up through a wood, passing below a wall with a bench. At the top of a low wall the paths divide.

3 Turn left, still climbing; immediately bear right on to a sunken path. Emerge from this path at a white house ('Halsecombe House'), then keep ahead to a field gate marked with a blue spot. Follow the left edge of the field, pass to the left-hand of two gates, leading back into some woodland. Take the bridleway ahead (with occasional blue waymarkers). The track becomes a terraced path, running near to the top edge of a wood for about 1 mile (1.6km) to reach the track.

4 Turn left down the track, then turn right into a narrow path ('Whitstone Post'), which runs through bracken and heather into the head of Hawk Combe. As the path enters a hawthorn thicket, bear right to a road signpost at Whitstone Post.

5 Cross the main A39 into a parking area; turn right on to a wide path. After 110yds (100m) turn left on a track. Where it turns left, turn right into a smaller track. Go through gorse and heather (from here there are superb views over Porlock Bay), then rejoin the A39 at a cattle grid.

6 Turn left, then right into a track (bridleway to Porlock). Cross two cattle grids to Point 4 of the upward route. Keep on the track for 125yds (114m); turn left to a terraced path which runs downhill, to a wider path. Turn right and continue down to a stream.

7 The path runs downstream. On reaching some houses it becomes a tarred lane and descends through a wood. At a high wall on the right a sign points to a footbridge. Over this, the path ascends through woods. Bear left on a path ('No Horses') and descend to join the street at a parking area. Turn left to cross the stream; finally turn right into Mill Lane and Porlock.

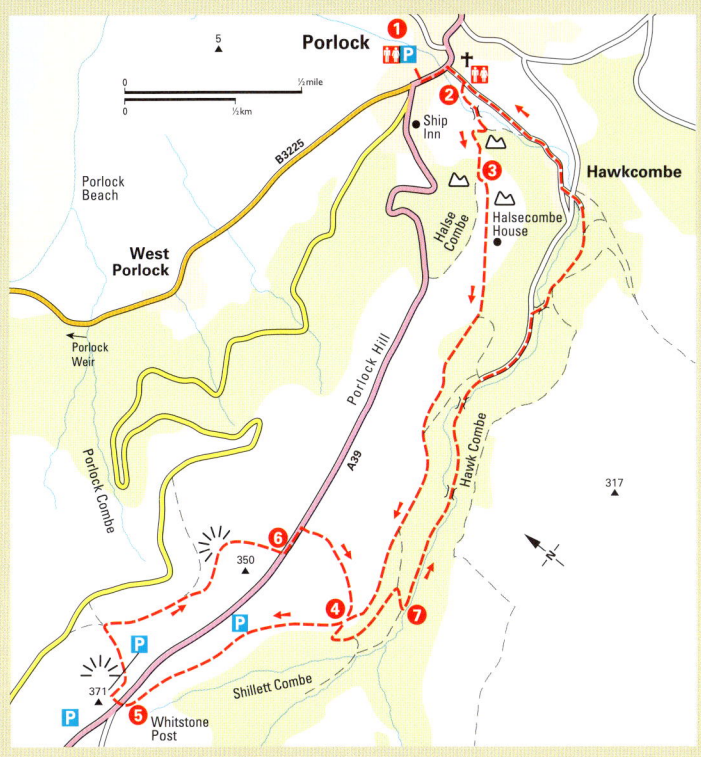

WALK 18

ALONG THE QUANTOCK COASTLINE

This stimulating walk overlooking the coastline takes in Tudor villages, breezy cliffs, industrial remnants and interesting geology underfoot. Places of interest that are also en route include the oil retort house which is near to the beach at Kilve, and was built during the time when oil was extracted from the shale there.

DITANCE/TIME 3 miles (4.8km) 1h45 **MAP** OS Explorer 140 Quantock Hills & Bridgwater **START** Pay-and-display car park at the end of Sea Lane; grid ref: ST 144442 **TRACKS** Tracks, field paths, and grassy cliff top, 7 stiles **THE PUB** The Hood Arms, Kilve. Tel: 01278 741477

1 From the car park head back along the lane to a ruined chantry. Turn into the churchyard through the lychgate. Pass to the left of the church and continue until you get to a kissing gate.

2 Take the signposted track that crosses the field to a gate with a stile; bear right to another gate with a stile and pass along the foot of East Wood. (At the far end, a stile allows wandering into the wood, April to August only.) Ignoring the stile on the left, keep ahead to a field gate with a stile and a track that crosses a stream.

3 The track bends left past the gardens and ponds of East Quantoxhead to a tarred lane. Turn right, head towards Tudor Court House, but before a gateway bear left into the car park. Pass through the gateway to a tarred path beyond two more kissing gates. In an open field the path bears right to eventually reach St Mary's Church.

4 Return to the 1st kissing gate but don't go through it; instead bear right to the field gate, and cross a field beyond to get to a lane. Turn right and, where the lane bends left, keep ahead on to a green track. At the top, turn right at the 'Permissive path' notice.

5 Follow the field edges down to a cliff top, and turn right. The cliff top path leads on to a stile before reaching a sharp dip, with the ruined limekiln standing opposite. The limekiln was constructed around 1770 and was used to process the limestone brought to the area from Wales. Most of the rest of Somerset is limestone, but it was easier at that time to bring it by sea across the Bristol Channel than to transport it around the county to other towns on land.

6 Turn round at the head of the dip, and then trace your steps back left to the cliff top. Here an iron ladder descends to the foreshore: you can see alternating layers of blue-grey lias here (a type of limestone) as well as grey shale. Interesting fossils can be found here also, but a note of warning: the cliffs are unstable – hard hats are now standard wear for geologists working here. Alternatively, if you have a suitably trained dog and the right sort of spear, you could even pursue the traditional and old sport of 'glatting' – a former popular pastime of hunting for conger eels in rock pools. From here continue along the wide cliff-top path until you reach a tarred path that then bears right, crossing a stream and leads you back into the car park on Sea Lane.

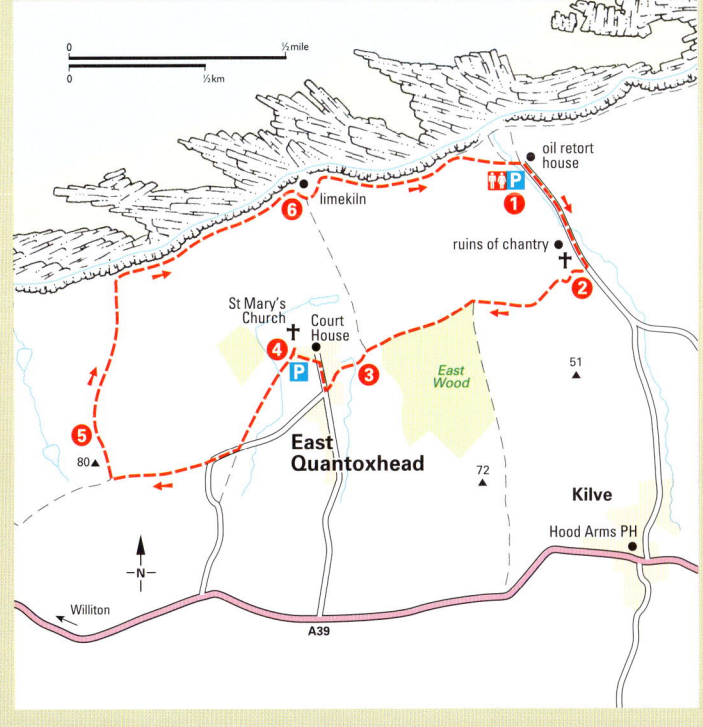

Somerset & the Mendips

CLOCKWISE FROM TOP: CHEDDAR GORGE; WELLS CATHEDRAL; GLASTONBURY TOR

AXBRIDGE MAP REF 399 J4

The early inhabitants of the area around Axbridge were almost certainly the Romans, who are known to have mined lead on the top of the Mendips. Earlier still, prehistoric man fashioned draughty homes from the local caves, and his primitive flint tools have been found scattered widely across the slopes of the hills of the surrounding area.

But the documented history of Axbridge can be traced only to the time of King Alfred (849–899), ruler of the West Saxons, when it served as part of the Saxons' defence system for Wessex against the Vikings. Axbridge appears in the Domesday survey of 1086 as Alse Bruge, meaning 'the ash tree bridge', and was part of the royal manor of Cheddar.

The town was granted a Royal Charter in 1202, when King John sold most of the royal manor of Cheddar to the Bishop of Bath and Wells. As an important centre for cloth manufacture and trade, Axbridge flourished and developed during the Tudor period, and this was reflected in its early royal charters allowing it to hold markets and fairs, and to then become a royal borough. For a period of time, Axbridge even boasted its own mint and coinage bearing the town's own symbol, that of the Lamb and Flag.

Later, the town's importance waned, leading to stagnation, and the need to preserve many of the historic buildings in the town centre. These include King John's Hunting Lodge, a misleadingly named three-storey, 15th-century timber-framed house situated on the corner of the market place, jettied over the street in a double overhang, and by its date clearly much too late for King John (1199–1216). This historical house is now used as a small museum of local history.

Axbridge is a very old borough and sent members to parliament in the reigns of Edward I (1272–1307) and Edward III (1327–77), but it was a costly privilege, and so the burgesses prayed to be excused. As a result, Axbridge ceased to have a voice in the legislature.

BURRINGTON COMBE

MAP REF 399 J4

Burrington Combe is a carboniferous limestone gorge near the village of Burrington, on the north side of Beacon Batch in the Mendip Hills. 'Combe' or 'coombe' is a word of Celtic origin that occurs in several forms throughout different parts of Britain, and denotes a steep-sided valley or hollow. The gorge contains the entrances to many of the caves of the Mendip Hills, including Aveline's Hole and Goatchurch Cavern.

Apparently, Augustus Montague Toplady (1740–78), an Anglican vicar, was inspired to compose the poem 'Rock of Ages' while evading a thunderstorm by sheltering below a rock in the combe. The alleged rock remains a prominent and frequently visited feature situated on the opposite side of the road from the car park.

Archaeological excavation of early cemeteries, notably at Aveline's Hole (a Mesolithic burial vault, thought to be the earliest scientifically dated cemetery in Britain), has revealed evidence of human occupation of the combe and its caves from Bronze Age times. The human bone fragments unearthed in the cemetery, came from about 21 individuals, and are thought to be more than 10,000 years old, coincidental with the end of the last Ice Age when the present period of warm climate was beginning. Moreover, a further recent study has revealed a series of inscribed crosses on the wall of Aveline's Hole, in a style comparable with others discovered from Northern France, Germany and Denmark, giving, scientists now believe, a wider context for the finds of the period, and a rare suggestion of what may have been a basic means of communication used in those times. In recognition of its biological and geological interest, a large area within and around the combe became a Site of Special Scientific Interest in 1952.

CHEDDAR MAP REF 399 J4

Distinguished for its deep limestone gorge, Cheddar is unique. The gorge is no mere stripling, but Britain's largest gorge. The Cheddar Yeo in Gough's Cave is Britain's biggest underground river, and the Gorge Cliffs the highest inland limestone cliffs. Quite a tally for so compact an area.

Not surprisingly, the Cheddar Gorge is a Site of Special Scientific Interest, mainly because of the interesting calcareous grassland, limestone buttresses and horseshoe bats that find the caves much to their liking. Pairs of Peregrines nest on the cliff face and an efficient Ground Force team of Soay sheep keep the scrubland mown.

Gough's Cave is an internationally famous archeological site because of finds some 12–13,000 years old, and Britain's oldest complete skeleton a mere 9,000 years old. The cave lies within the Mendip Hills Area of Outstanding Natural Beauty. The village of Cheddar has a long history, and was an important Roman and Saxon centre. As early as 1130, the Gorge was claimed as one of the 'Four Wonders of England', but historically, Cheddar's wealth came from farming and making the eponymous cheese. Legend has it that cheese was a chance discovery after a milkmaid left a pail of milk in the nearby caves, returning later to find that the milk had turned into a tasty substance, and so Cheddar cheese was born. Would that it were so simple.

Certainly cheese making was well established more than 800 years ago. Henry II (1154-89) declared Cheddar cheese to be the best in Britain, and the

Court financial records show that in 1170 the king bought 10,240lb (xxkg) of Cheddar at a cost of a farthing per pound.

As elsewhere in Britain, popular tourism began with the arrival of the railway, in this case the Cheddar Valley Railway, which opened in 1869–70, providing workers from surrounding towns with the opportunity to make the most of bank holidays by visiting other towns in the area. The railway was popularly known as the Strawberry Line, because it passed close by the strawberry-growing fields that adorned the southwest-facing slopes on the Cheddar side of the valley. Until the Beeching Axe fell on British rail lines in 1965, 'Strawberry Special' trains carried the fruit across the country.

EBBOR GORGE MAP REF 399 J4

The Ebbor Gorge National Nature Reserve is a largely wooded site on the southern escarpment of the Mendip Hills. It forms part of the Mendip Woodlands Special Area of Conservation. The scarp is split by two valleys: Ebbor Gorge, a dry limestone gorge, and Hope Wood valley, which has a stream. There are two geologically important caves on the site with deposits that include bones of Ice Age mammals.

While the bulk of the reserve is comprised of ash and maple woodland, a number of woodland glades and areas of limestone grassland appear.

Hope Wood valley, which is quite humid, is ideal for ferns and fungi, and over 250 species of mosses, liverworts and lichens have been recorded at the site. Areas of coppice have also been cut in order to improve the reserve for woodland butterflies, particularly the rare white letter hairstreak, making this one of the most fascinating areas in the region for those interested in natural history.

GLASTONBURY MAP REF 399 J4

What is it about the town of Glastonbury and its Tor that excites so much fervour, anguish and passion?

In the past, Glastonbury Tor and surrounding land was an island joined to dry land by a narrow peninsular, but surrounded by marshes. In Neolithic times, transitory people inhabited lake villages near the island, which from the earliest days appears to have been treated as a sacred place.

From the shadows of pre-history come legends of this Isle of Avalon, a place of the dead, a sacred burial ground. Although primarily thought of in connection with King Arthur, Christians believe that the first British church was erected here (at the behest of Joseph of Arimathea) about 30 years after the death of Jesus, to shelter the Holy Grail. Legend also claims that

CHEDDAR GORGE

Visit
WILLOWS AND WETLANDS VISITOR CENTRE

The Somerset Levels are renowned for their excellent reed-growing conditions and expert weavers have been coming to this area for their materials for years. As well as the specialist raw material, the reeds are also processed and used to make charcoal for use by artists. The reeds are harvested in the spring each year and the processing of the willows can be seen at the Willows and Wetlands Visitor Centre in Stoke St Gregory.

Insight
FLYING VISITORS

The Somerset Levels and the surrounding moors are an important habitat for small mammals, plants, insects and birds. Waterfowl come here throughout the winter and it is also an important breeding area for wading birds, such as lapwing and redshanks. Indeed the lapwing population here is being carefully monitored because its numbers are still in decline, despite recent efforts to create a perfect breeding habitat. You may also be lucky enough to spot some birds of prey such as kestrels and barn owls.

Joseph had earlier visited Glastonbury along with Jesus as a child. The English poet, William Blake believed this story, and wrote the poem that became the words to the most patriotic of English songs, 'Jerusalem'. Later spin-doctoring of the various storylines contends that Joseph of Arimathea himself came to Britain and became the first bishop of Christianity.

Today, Avalon is commonly associated with present-day Glastonbury, and there is undoubtedly something other-worldly about the place. King Arthur and Guinevere are said to lie buried here, and it was home to medieval saints. This numinous hill, preternaturally cloaked in mystery, legend, beliefs and half-beliefs, dominates the surrounding countryside, and, more prosaically, provides outstanding views over Somerset, Dorset and Wiltshire. At the summit, excavation has exposed plans of two superimposed churches of which only a 15th-century tower remains. Of course, everyone knows that Glastonbury Tor is home to Gwyn ap Nudd, King of the Fairies, who kindly allows it to be managed by the National Trust. It is an agreeable walk up the Tor, especially if you want to distance yourself from the brew of rival faiths fermenting in the town.

In the Middle Ages, when the great Benedictine abbey was founded here, the region was described as England's 'holyest earthe'; many feel that nothing has changed. In spite of all the attention, Glastonbury is a bustling and energetic small town, a place with rich traditions, a cosmopolitan community with an eye to the future. It nestles against a backdrop of soft, green, rolling hills, and has been a pilgrimage place for many for thousands of years, and continues to be so.

Today the town, a unique, atmospheric community, also hosts the world-renowned Glastonbury Festival – the music festival being the number one event of the year for some – pilgrimages, musical events, a carnival, several conferences and other events. People visit from the world over, searching for something – inner peace, spiritual enlightenment, the meaning of life – and producing a mixture of locals and incomers in which threads of paganism and mysticism are woven together with those of Christianity.

PRIDDY MAP REF 399 J4

High on the plateau-like landscape of the Mendip Hills, southeast of Cheddar, Priddy village is built around a large green that is used each summer in August for a traditional sheep fair. It is thought that the fair was moved from Bath in the 14th century because of the plague, although there appear to be records of a sheep fair in Priddy earlier than this.

Each year, in February, Priddy holds a folk festival, claimed to be the friendliest folk festival in Britain. Quite what the criteria for 'friendliness' are is not clear.

The Mendip Hills Area of Outstanding Natural Beauty was designated in 1972 and enfolds the western and central area of the Mendip Hills range which reaches from Bleadon in the west to Chewton Mendip in the east. The soft, undulating Carboniferous limestone plateau is the main feature of the area which today is predominantly pastoral and criss-crossed by drystone walls largely dating from the 18th-century enclosure laws.

The Mendip Hills have a rich archaeological heritage, from Mesolithic cave deposits to historic World War II military features. The landscape appears to have had ritual importance in Neolithic times, with mortuary enclosures such as Ashen Hill barrow cemeteries and the enigmatic Priddy Circles.

The four Priddy Circles, huge circular formations crossing a number of field boundaries, have been interpreted as henge monuments created for ritual purposes. Their form is different from other known henge monuments, however, and their function is unknown. They appear to have been in some way linked to some of the other ritual monuments nearby, like the Priddy Nine Barrows.

GLASTONBURY

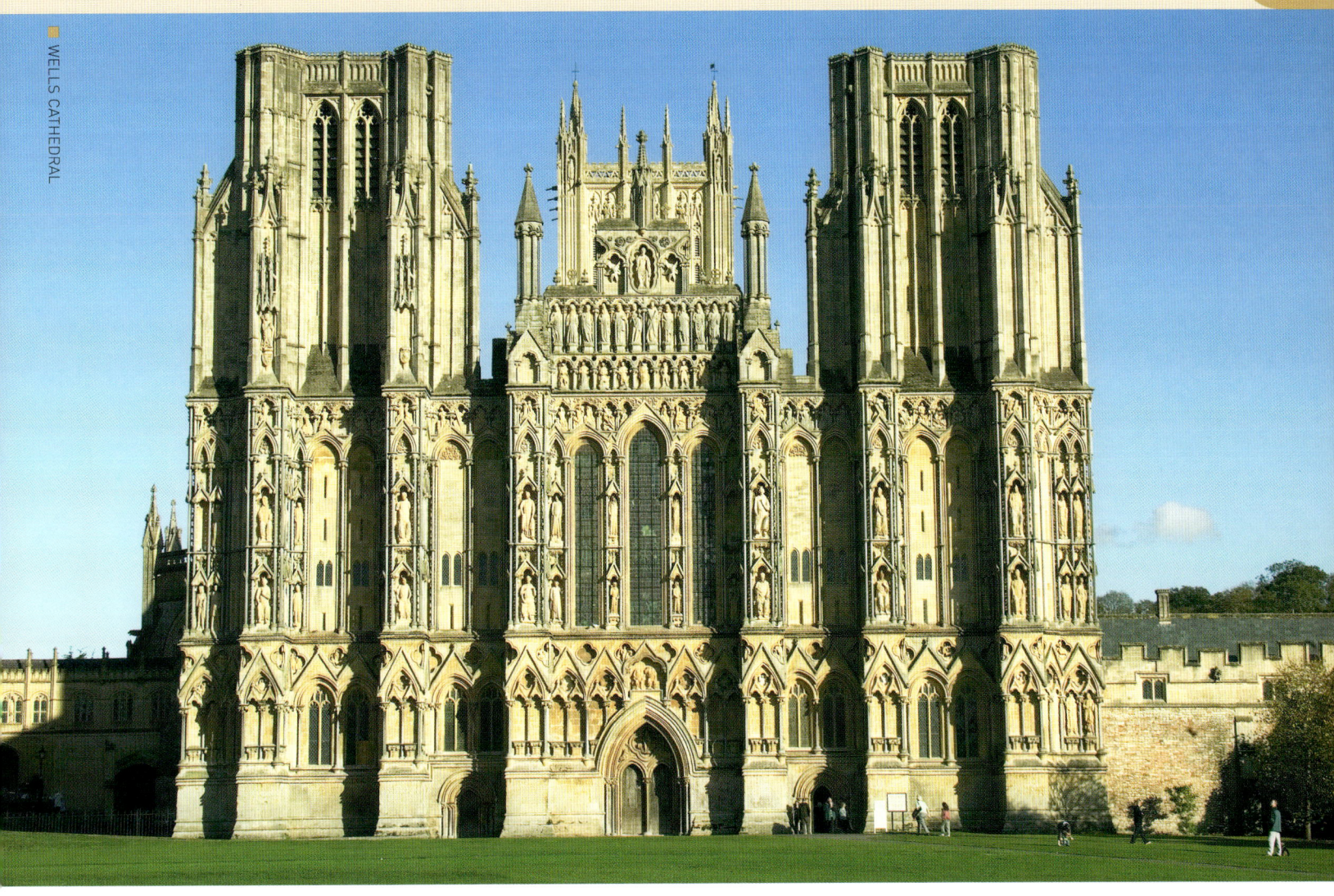

WELLS CATHEDRAL

SHEPTON MALLET MAP REF 399 J4
The small, mainly stone-built, town of Shepton Mallet has interest way beyond its size. Rich in history, in the centre of town is an elaborate market cross dating from the 1500s, and the town has England's oldest prison, first used in 1610, and still in use having had a chequered history and seen a number of prisoners executed. The prison is a Grade II listed building, one of its finer points probably not appreciated by the inmates. During World War II, many national treasures, such as the Domesday Book, were kept safe here.

Archaeologists uncovered a significant number of Roman artefacts in the early 1990s at a site adjacent to the nearby Fosse Way, including a Chi-Rho amulet, held to be among the earliest evidence of Christianity in England.

Somerset is famous for cider, and Shepton Mallet is home to Europe's largest cider plant. This is where they produce Blackthorn Cider, Gaymer's Olde English cider and Babycham.

SOMERSET LEVELS MAP REF 399 J4
At the heart of gentle Somerset, lies an amorphous, beautiful and quite remarkable area known as the 'Levels and Moors', an area that has international significance as one of the most important wetlands certainly in Europe and quite possibly in the world.

All of the levels and moors in Somerset were submerged until about 6,500 years ago, when peat deposits began to form in the salt marsh, fens and raised bogs. To cross these wetlands and reach dry islands of rock in the valleys, prehistoric people constructed wooden tracks, the oldest of which, Sweet Track, is a raised walkway built nearly 6,000 years ago, and still existing today.

The Somerset Levels are a haven to migrating and resident birds. Part of the moors is drier agricultural land and part is made up of wetland nature reserves and wilder areas. Throughout history, water levels have risen and fallen and, in recent centuries, the Levels have been artificially drained. Mining of peat over the last century has left pools and lakes, favourable for water birds.

STREET MAP REF 399 J4
On the southwest edge of Glastonbury, the village of Street has a history dating to Roman times, but played second fiddle to Glastonbury until 1829 when the Clark brothers started their shoe factory and began a business that is today multinational. Clarks Shoes still have their headquarters in Street today; the original factory is now a show museum.

Clarks, like many other benevolent industrialists, built terraces of model homes for their workers, and provided the village with a civic hall, library, open-air swimming pool and theatre, which are all still in use today.

WELLS MAP REF 399 J4
England's smallest city is a real gem, with one of the finest cathedrals in Britain. History oozes from the buildings, and the market place seems to have buildings in almost every architectural style. Vicar's Close is said to be the most complete medieval street in Europe.

The Market Place provides a link between the cathedral, the Bishop's Palace and the High Street, and has numerous attractive shops. Market days (Wednesday and Saturday) see a thriving outdoor market with a variety of stalls.

Wells is the home town of athlete Mary Rand, who, on 14th October 1964 at the Olympic Games, with a leap of 22ft 2¼ins (6.76m), became the first woman athlete ever to jump over 22 feet (6.7m). With that gold medal she became the first British woman track and field athletics champion in Olympic history. The actual length of her jump is marked out in brass markers close to Penniless Porch, found just off the Market Place.

WOOKEY HOLE MAP REF 399 J4
Wookey Hole has been fashioned by the River Axe, creating the most fascinating underground scenery. The name 'Wookey' is thought to derive from the Old English *wocig*, meaning an animal trap. The village is principally known for its show caves, a paper mill and a museum.

A visit to Wookey Hole is ideal for all the family, and all ages, and tours take visitors through the history of man and caves, including legend and folklore, where the first cave dive was attempted, and the spot where the mythical Witch of Wookey was turned to stone.

Nearby Glencot Country House Hotel, a late Victorian mansion built in Grand Jacobean style, is a Grade II listed building dating from 1887. The attractive 18th-century Bubwith farmhouse is also a Grade II building, as is the town's attractive high street post office.

POLDEN HILLS: EDGE OF THE LEVELS

This walk takes you from Polden's edge down on to the Somerset Levels and back up again. The Polden Hills run parallel almost to the Mendip Hills and lying in between is an area of little-populated, marshy wetland along the coastline and inland an area of moor, called the Somerset Levels. The hill ridge has been a well-trodden route as it was once the line of a Roman road, and its western extremes can be traced as a Saxon route.

DISTANCE/TIME 4.5 miles (7.2km) 2h15 **MAP** OS Explorer 141 Cheddar Gorge **START** Car Park at Street Youth Hostel, just off B3151, another car park on south side of the road; grid ref: ST 480345 **TRACKS** Initially steep then easy tracks and paths, 3 stiles **THE PUB** Castlebrook Inn, Compton Dundon. Tel: 01458 443632

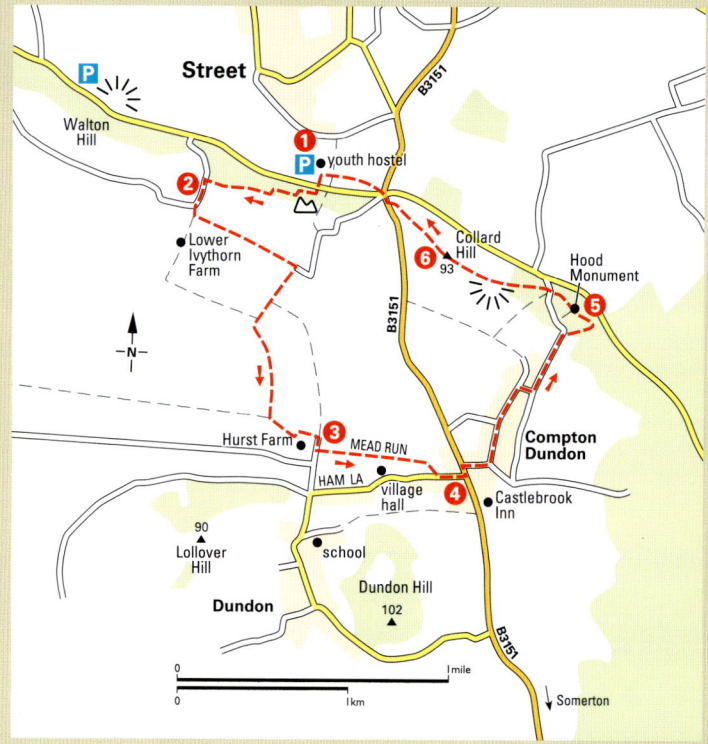

1 From the parking area on the youth hostel side, cross and turn right on to a woodland path. Shortly after, a smaller path descends on the left by some steps. At the foot of a wood, turn right; at the field corner go down a short way to the track which runs along the base of a wood to a lane.

2 Go down to Lower Ivythorn Farm entrance; then turn left into a track. After 0.5 mile (800m) this reaches the corner of an unsurfaced road; then turn right. After 0.5mile (400m) a track turns left into a field. Follow the edge, with a ditch and a fence on the left, to a gate. In the next field continue alongside a ditch to a corner. The former footbridge here is derelict. Take the gate on the left, then turn right on to a field track, passing left of Hurst Farm, to a tarred lane.

3 Turn right to a bridleway sign on the left. Follow a green track to Ham Lane. This leads to a crossroads of the B3151 in Compton Dundon (Castlebrook Inn to the right).

4 Cross the busy B3151 and pass between an ancient market cross (on the right) and a Victorian obelisk (to the left) into Compton Street. Once you reach the first junction keep to the left, towards Hood Monument above. As the street climbs, turn right and then turn left up the lane beyond. Where it reaches some woodland turn off through a waymarked gate (signed 'Reynolds Way'). A path slants up into a wood. Shortly before it arrives at the road, make a left turn along the top of an area of steep ground, in order to reach Hood Monument.

5 Continue walking down through the wood to a minor road, with the main road some 50yds (46m) away to the right. Ignore the path descending opposite but turn right for a few steps to a footpath sign and also to a kissing gate. The grass path heads on up to the crest of Collard Hill (here, there are wide views to the left).

6 From the summit go straight ahead down to a tile and the signposted crossroads of the B3151. Cross over both the roads. The ridge road is signposted for the youth hostel; the path is just to the right, crossing a glade into woodland. Keep to the right of the hummocky ground to reach the wood's edge; follow this path back to the car park.

EBBOR GORGE: COLERIDGE'S INSPIRATION

This sublime limestone gorge is thought to have inspired works by the founder of the Romantic movement Samuel Taylor Coleridge (1772–1834). This deep ravine, cutting into the limestone of the northern Mendips, contains huge caverns that were once home to an earlier group: the Stone Age hunter-gatherers.

DISTANCE/TIME 4.75 miles (7.7km) 2h30 **MAP** OS Explorer141 Cheddar Gorge **START** Lane above Wookey Hole (optional small fee); grid ref: ST 521484 **TRACKS** Small paths and field edges, with a rugged descent, 9 stiles **THE PUB** TheWookey Hole Inn, Wookey Hole. Tel: 01749 676677; www.wookeyholeinn.com

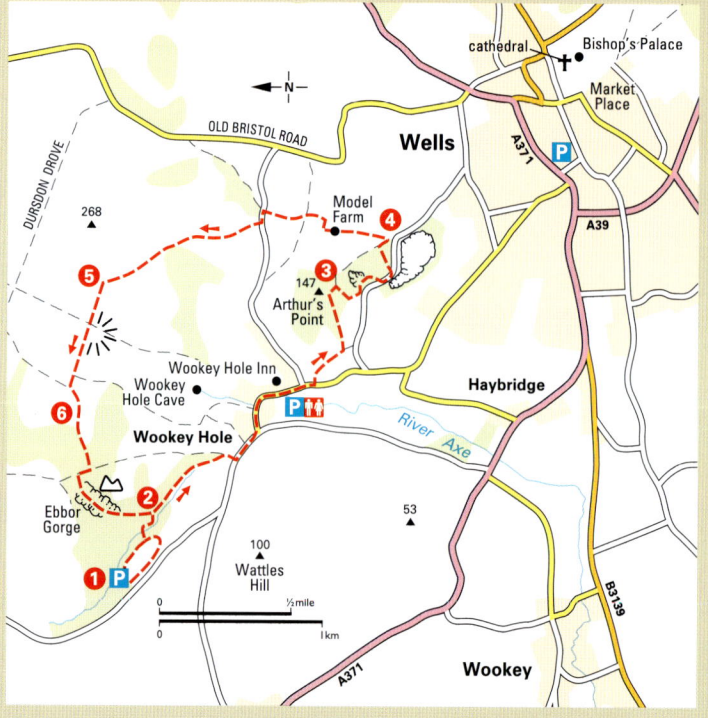

1 From the notice-board at the top end of the car park descend a stepped path. After the clearing, turn left ('The Gorge'). A wide path crosses a stream to another junction.

2 Turn right, away from the gorge; then follow the valley down to the road. Turn left, passing through the village of Wookey Hole. At the end of the village, the road bends to the right; go through a kissing gate on the left (to a 'West Mendip Way' waymarker post). After two more kissing gates turn left up a spur to a stile and you will eventually reach the top of Arthur's Point.

3 Bear to the right into some woods again. Beware: hidden in the brambles ahead is the top of a quarry crag; turn to the right, down to stile. Go down a field edge to a kissing gate; bear left between boulders back into the wood. After a sharp rise bear right, to join Lime Kiln Lane below, which bends left with a path on the left diverting through to the bottom of a wood. This emerges at the end of a short field track; follow this down to a footpath signpost.

4 Turn sharp left on a track that passes through Model Farm. Follow the track through the farm, turning right by some houses to continue to a track to Tynings Lane. Turn left to a signposted stile on your right. Go up here with the fence on the right, then bear left to a gate with a stile. Go straight up the next large field, aiming for a gateway with tractor ruts. The track leads up through a wood and a field to a gate. Slant upwards in the same direction to yet another gate next to a stile some 100yds (91m) below the field's top left corner.

5 The path then runs along the tops of three fields with a splendid view across the Levels to the left. With a stile on the right and a gate and a horse trough in front, turn downhill with the fence on the right; follow the fence along until you reach a stile which will lead you into Ebbor Gorge Nature Reserve.

6 The second gate takes you into a wood. At the junction with the red arrow and a sign ('Car Park') pointing forward, turn right into the valley and walk straight down – the path then narrows to a rocky gully. At the foot of the gorge turn right (signed 'Car Park'). You are now back at Point 2 of the outward walk. Here, you can cross the stream. Turn left at the T-junction with the wood edge and then veer back towards the right to the car park.

Dorset & the Purbecks

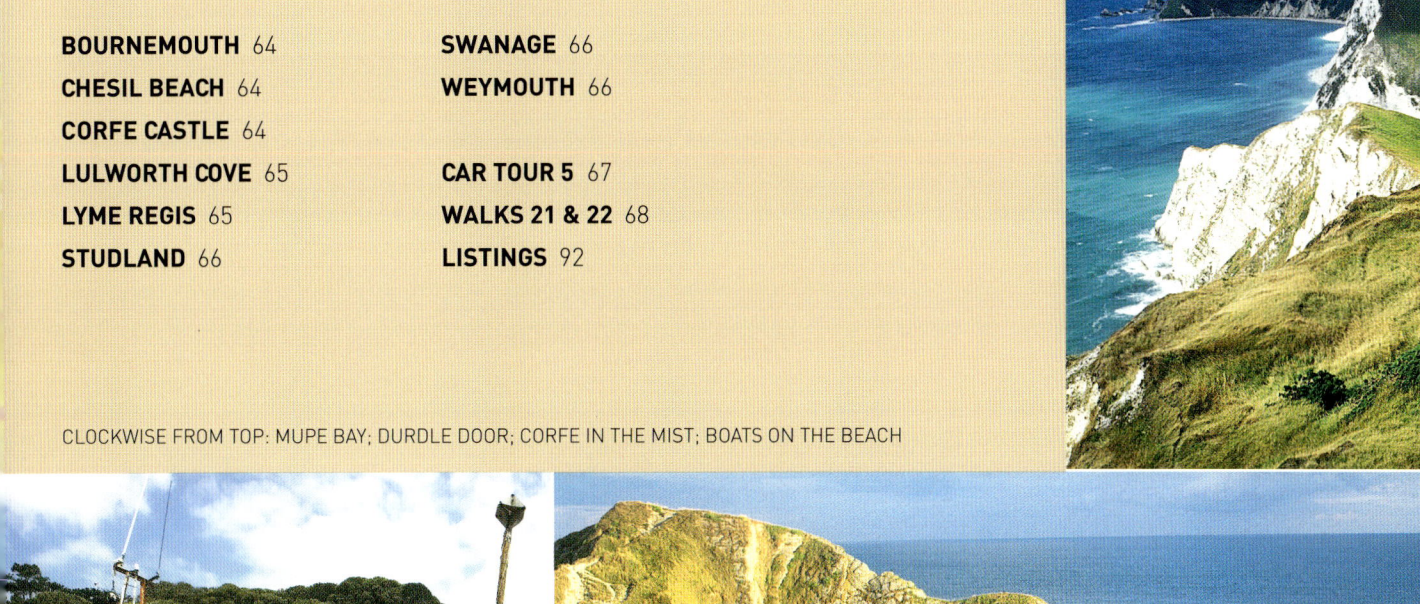

CLOCKWISE FROM TOP: MUPE BAY; DURDLE DOOR; CORFE IN THE MIST; BOATS ON THE BEACH

BOURNEMOUTH MAP REF 400 D7

Bournemouth is the queen of the south coast holiday resorts, with its 6 miles (9.6km) of fine golden sands, its pier complete with striped deck chairs and theatre for nostalgic summer shows (rebuilt several times), its orderly winter gardens, its palm-tree lined parks and compact town centre dedicated to serious shopping, as well as a vast hinterland of suburban sprawl.

Unlike its more serious neighbour, Poole, Bournemouth has never really been anything other than a resort. It was a small village in the early 19th century, at the time when many of the pine trees that now scent the air were first planted. Blessed with a mild climate, and a south-facing location in a sheltered cleft, the settlement boomed towards the end of the 19th century, and most of the town's central buildings date from this period, with Victorian buildings interspersed with some later art deco. New luxury blocks of offices and modern accommodation may have changed the skyline forever, but the town's heart has a comfortable, still old-fashioned feel that remains appealing to many holiday-makers.

The town centre is shaped around the Lower, Centre and Upper Gardens, a long, leafy park around the flowing Bourne stream, with magnificent island flowerbeds, scenic tethered balloon flights, an aviary, a mini-golf centre and various refreshment stops. Around the upper end and the Square cluster all the main shopping streets, with arcades leading off the largely pedestrianised Old Christchurch Road. The most appealing of these is the glazed 1866 Victorian Arcade housing well-known Dingles department store and designer outlets including Gucci and Karen Millen. Beales is Bournemouth's large independent department store. Opposite, is St Peter's Church, with Arts and Crafts wall paintings, a chapel dedicated to the Oxford Movement reformer John Keble, the grave of novelist Mary Shelley (and the heart of her brother) in the churchyard.

The lower end of the park runs past the Pavilion Theatre, under the main road and out on to the seafront, with the pier just ahead. Bournemouth's pier is a functional affair, reinforced with ugly concrete that has seen it survive when others along this coastline have been washed away.

Photographs at the far end show how it was partly demolished during World War II to prevent its use in a possible German invasion. Now it has a pier theatre and amusements, and great views back to the town, and the western beaches with their beach huts tucked under the sandy cliffs. A land train offers transport up and down the seafront. The twin domes near the pier entrance mark the aquarium, and the modern glazed building on the seafront is the IMAX cinema complex. Set behind this, on East Cliff, you will find the interestingly turreted Russell-Cotes Art Gallery and Museum, which is home to a collection of fine Victorian paintings and treasures from around the world.

CHESIL BEACH MAP REF 399 J6

This deep shingle strip runs for 18 miles (29km) east of Lyme Bay, from Burton Bradstock to Portland.

CORFE CASTLE MAP REF 400 C8

Corfe is the best-known village on the so-called Isle of Purbeck, and is packed with pubs, tea rooms and little shops that make it a magnet for summer visitors, especially keen walkers in the area.

The huge and toothy ruin of Corfe Castle seems to fill the gap in the wall of the Purbeck Hills with its presence. It has a grim history. In AD 978 a youthful King Edward (the Martyr) was murdered here by his stepmother; his body was buried without ceremony at Wareham, while his half-brother took the throne as Ethelred II (the Unready). However, stories of miracles soon resulted in the exhumation of Edward's body. The body was then transported to Shaftesbury, where an abbey grew up in his honour.

Around 1106 the big square Norman keep was built, to defend against raiders from the sea and to impress the local populace. King John used it as a lifelong prison for his niece Eleanor, a potential threat to his throne. Edward II, deposed by his wife, was imprisoned here briefly.

During the Civil War the castle's owner, Sir John Bankes, eventually sided with the king, leaving his spirited wife Mary, with a handful of women and just five men, to fight off a siege in 1642. History books state that the 500-strong Parliamentarian army stripped all the lead from the church roof to make their bullets, and stored their gunpowder and shot in the organ pipes,

CORFE CASTLE

but they failed to take the castle. After a second siege, the castle was betrayed in 1646 by one of its defenders, and after it was abandoned it was destroyed to prevent its use again.

South of Corfe, Worth Matravers is a picturesque village of lichen-encrusted grey cottages, complete with duck pond. Men from here have worked in the local quarries for centuries, and Purbeck marble (in fact a type of limestone) from this area was famously sent inland for the building of Salisbury Cathedral. The Square & Compass, an old fashioned pub with smoked beams and a big stone hearth, is a favourite with walkers. On the nearby cliffs stands 800-year-old St Adhelm's Chapel, a sturdy, buttressed brown cube, that has only one tiny little window. Near the coastguard station is a steel memorial to the brilliant work of radar developers here in 1940–42.

LULWORTH COVE   MAP REF 400 C8

Lulworth Cove is an almost perfectly circular bay in the rolling line of limestone cliffs that form Dorset's southern coast. It provides a safe anchorage for small fishing boats and pleasure craft, and a place of safe water for summer bathers. The wave-polished grey, black and red pebbles of the shingle beach, from wren's egg to ostrich egg in size, are reminiscent of childhood jars of pebble sweets. To the west, along the South West Coast Path, lie rolling, chalky downs and the landmark of Durdle Door, below the cliffs. To the east lie Worbarrow and Mupe bays.

The geology of the area is intriguing, and a visit to the Heritage Centre in the village will help you to identify the various rock formations. The oldest layer is the gleaming white Portland stone, much employed by Christopher Wren in his rebuilding of London. It is a finely grained oolite around 140 million years old, consisting of tightly compressed fossilised shells, and occasionally throws up giant flat-coiled ammonites, called a titanite, which may be seen incorporated decoratively into many house walls across Purbeck. Above this is a thick layer of Purbeck marble, a rich limestone where dinosaur, reptile and fish fossils are usually found. The soft layer above this consists of Wealden beds – a belt of colourful sedimentary clays, silts and sands that are unstable and prone to landslips when exposed. Crumbly white chalk overlays this, the remains of microscopic sea creatures and shells deposited over a long period of time when a deep sea covered much of Dorset, some 75 million years ago.

The Fossil Forest in the sea cliffs east of Lulworth Cove is an intriguing oddity, but don't go looking for stone trees. What you see are the stone rings where sediment has bubbled up around the tree-trunks that rotted away millions of years ago. Together with the fossilised soil discovered beneath the tree boles, they give an insight into Jurassic life here, 135 million years ago.

Lulworth Castle Park at nearby East Lulworth was an impressive hunting lodge, built four-square in 1608 with pepperpot towers. Unfortunately, it was gutted by fire in 1929, but it is now a handsome shell, but still only partly restored. Other attractions on the estate include an interesting circular chapel, an animal farm and an adventure playground for children, and summer jousting events.

Nearly 200 rescued and endangered apes and monkeys have found a new, welcoming home at Monkey World, a few miles north of the small village of Wool. The park has of 65 acres (26ha) of woodland, where the monkeys can recuperate in a safe environment that was built especially for them.

LYME REGIS   MAP REF 399 H6

The cliff exposures along the Dorset and East Devon coast provide an almost continuous sequence of Triassic, Jurassic and Cretaceous rock formations spanning the Mesozoic Era, and record 185 million years of Earth history. Here there is a range of internationally important fossil localities which have produced some well-preserved and diverse evidence of life during Mesozoic times.

This is why the Dorset coast holds World Heritage status, granted in 2001, and why Lyme Regis is perfectly placed to experience this geological antiquity. The town, a pretty seaside resort, features in John Fowles' classic novel *The French Lieutenant's Woman*, which is set in the town in the 19th century.

STUDLAND MAP REF 400 D7

The glorious sands in Studland Bay are justly famous, and attract over a million visitors a year, so it's worth getting up early to have them to yourself. You are unlikely to be alone for long, though.

As you progress up the beach, getting warmer, you can shed your clothes with impunity, for the upper stretch opens its arms to naturists – and even on a bright winter's morning you'll spot brave souls sunbathing naked in the shelter of the marram-covered dunes. Off shore, big, sleek motor boats let rip as they emerge from the constraints of Poole Harbour. Watch out, too, for the orange and blue of the Poole lifeboat on manoeuvres, and the yellow and black pilot boat nipping out to lead in the tankers. Jet-skiers zip around the more sedate sailing yachts, all dodging the small fishing boats. It's a perfect seaside harmony, complete with wheedling, soaring gulls.

Behind the beach lies the old rugged heath, part of the same nature reserve that is in the care of English Nature and the National Trust. They are currently working together on a programme of restoration, reclaiming heath that had become farmland, and clearing scrub and maintaining controlled grazing to prevent it all reverting to woodland. All six of Britain's reptiles – common lizard, sand lizard, smooth snake, adder, grass snake, slow worm – live on the heath.

SWANAGE MAP REF 400 D8

In the early 19th century Swanage was a small, bustling industrial port shipping stone from the 60 or more quarries in the area. A growing fashion for sea-bathing would in time change the focus of the town forever. The real changes to the face of Swanage came with the extraordinary collecting habit of a man called George Burt, who was a contractor with an eye for ornate architecture.

With his uncle John Mowlem, a local stonemason and philanthropist, Burt shipped marble from the old quarries of Purbeck up to London, where many old buildings were being knocked down to make way for new construction. He was reluctant to see such fine stonework discarded, so Burt salvaged large whole pieces, transported them back to Dorset as ballast, and re-erected them in his home town, giving Swanage an 'instant' architectural heritage.

The Town Hall is a prime example of Burt's influence. He had donated a reasonably plain and simple building to the town in 1872; but in 1883 he added a façade by Wren, which he had rescued from the Mercers' Hall in London's Cheapside. In a park near the pier you can see a grand archway removed from Hyde Park Corner, and three statues and some columns rescued from Billingsgate Market. There is also an absurd but rather elegant clock tower, removed from the south end of London Bridge in 1867, where it had been set as a memorial to the Duke of Wellington.

Durleston Castle is an original folly by Burt dating from 1887, designed from the start as a cliff-top restaurant on Durleston Head. Facts and figures from around the world are carved into enormous stone slabs set into the walls below. Burt added an unusual large, segmented stone globe of the world. It is grey and rather disappointing, but nevertheless in a beautiful spot where you can sit during the evening, watching the sunset fade the sea into the sky, with the lonely shape of the lighthouse at the end of the Needles winking from across the water.

At Studland Museum and Heritage Centre you can learn more about the area, including tales of smuggling and the actual development of Purbeck's stone-quarrying industry. And for a nominal fee, try the delights of Swanage's Victorian pier, which announces penny-in-the-slot machines and 'Wot the butler saw' – no seaside visit can be complete without it. The pier suffered in the past from neglect and threat of demolition, but is now undergoing restoration.

WEYMOUTH MAP REF 399 J6

Facing out into Portland Harbour, Weymouth is an ancient port, dating from medieval times, but given fashionable credentials after George III took to staying there in the 18th century, effectively making Weymouth one the first tourist destinations in Britain.

The attractive seafront esplanade overlooking the wide sandy bay is comprised almost exclusively of terraces constructed in the Georgian and Regency periods between 1770 and 1855.

During World War II, Weymouth played a key role in the D-Day landings in Normandy – a memorial on the esplanade records the events of 1944 and 1945.

STUDLAND

60 MILES (96KM)

POOLE & THE ISLE OF PURBECK

The Isle of Purbeck is the fascinating area to the west of Poole, a landlocked island of high hills and sea cliffs. The route entails a complete circuit of Poole Harbour, with a short ferry ride at the end. On the way you will see lovely villages and a deserted village, sheltered bays, a ruined castle, seaside resorts, a seaside pier and the long sandy beach of Studland.

Route Directions

Explore the quaint and busy quayside at Poole, with its shops, pubs and the Poole pottery factory outlet, then begin the drive.

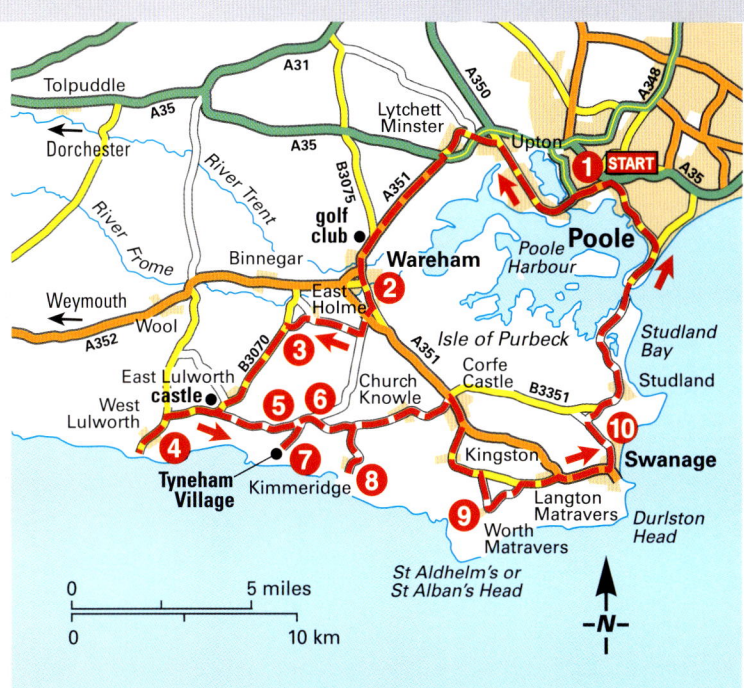

1 Leave Poole town centre and follow the signs for Hamworthy and Poole Bridge. Cross the bridge, by the Sunseeker boatyard, and continue towards Hamworthy and Rockley Park. After 2.5 miles (4km) pass under two railway bridges, with Upton Park signed to your left. Continue through Upton, and at the double roundabout by the clock tower turn left, signed 'Lytchett Minster'. Pass through Lytchett Minster. At the roundabout with the A35, go straight ahead, signed 'A351 Wareham'. Continue ahead across several roundabouts and through traffic lights, following signs to Wareham. Go straight on at the next roundabout, signed 'Corfe Castle', and bear left at the next roundabout, and follow signs for Wareham.

Make sure you stop off to explore the historic town of Wareham, which is on the banks of the River Frome.

2 In Wareham continue down the High Street, then cross the river. Continue to Stoborough and bear right, following signs for Creech. At the junction with the A351 turn left and immediately right, signed 'Creech, Steeple and Kimmeridge'. After this, turn right on to a minor road, looking for signs to East and West Lulworth.

The route passes through an area of farmland and open heath that is typical of the area, with pine forests, and parkland at East Holme. There is a stunning view of the long chalk ridge of the Purbeck Hills to your left.

3 After 2.5 miles (4km), turn left for East Lulworth. Look out for tanks crossing (this is the Lulworth army training area). Continue through the village of East Lulworth. At the T-junction turn left and continue through West Lulworth village to Lulworth Cove.

Park on the right, by the heritage centre, to explore beautiful Lulworth Cove and walk part of the South West Coast Path.

4 Retrace your route for 3 miles (5km) back up the hill and almost to the gates of Lulworth Castle. Turn right here, and take the next narrow turning right, signed 'Tyneham Village'.

This winding road rises along the back of the ridge and up to the crest, with superb views across the country inland.

5 After 4.5 miles (7km), you'll come across Whiteways Viewpoint on your right.

At the viewpoint you can enjoy views down over the coast and Kimmeridge Bay, and also right across to Poole Harbour.

6 Continue on the same road and to a turning circle on the left which marks the tight right turn down to Tyneham village. Follow the road down to the church.

Here you can explore the deserted Purbeck village of Tyneham, which was evacuated during World War 11 in 1943. It is now used by the Army as a firing range.

7 Go back up the road to the turning circle and turn right. Just before another viewpoint turn right towards Steeple and Kimmeridge. The narrow road descends sharply. Turn right, signed to Kimmeridge and the sea. The road crosses a valley and goes up a ridge before descending to pass by Smedmore House. Finally, it zig-zags down through Kimmeridge village. Note: a toll is payable if you want to continue down to the beach car park on Kimmeridge Bay.

The pebble beach here, with its long rock ledges and numerous rock pools, is popular with families and watersports enthusiasts. You can find people canoeing here at most times of the year.

8 Retrace your route back across the valley and turn right, signed 'Church Knowle and Corfe Castle'. After 1.5 miles (2.5km) pass through Church Knowle. Continue towards Corfe Castle and turn right to Swanage on the A351. Make your way through the centre of Corfe Castle village. On the other side of the village turn right, signed 'Langton Matravers'. Cross the Common. Follow the road left, and soon turn right, which is signed 'Worth Matravers'. Continue for a mile (1.6km), passing the quarry on your right. Park your car in the car park just above Worth Matravers.

Walk down the hill and bear right if you want to visit the duck pond and the church of St Nicholas in Worth Matravers.

9 Turn left at the Square and Compass pub, at the sign to Langton Matravers. Turn right at the main road and descend to Langton Matravers. At the junction with the A351 turn right and then follow signs for Swanage town centre and to the beach.

The traditional seaside resort of Swanage has a gently shelving sandy beach and a Victorian pier. In summer the beach is particularly crowded with families.

10 Leave Swanage on the coast road, signed 'Studland, Poole and Bournemouth' via toll ferry. After 3 miles (5km) turn right for Studland on the B3351. Continue to the ferry crossing Studland Heath.

The toll ferry crossing to Sandbanks takes about 10 minutes only, but expect to queue for some time in high season. Follow the B3369 coast road, past Compton Acres, back into the centre of Poole.

CORFE CASTLE CIRCUIT

This is a loop to Kingston from the ruins of Corfe Castle. The route takes in Corfe Common and part of the Purbeck Way incorporating downland, heath and village streets. The Common is crisscrossed by narrow bridlepaths and walkways.

DISTANCE/TIME 4.25 miles (6.8 km) 2h **MAP** OS Explorer OL 15 Purbeck & South Dorset **START** Corfe Castle village car park (fee); grid ref: SY 958818 **TRACKS** Village lanes, rocky lanes (slippery after rain), moorland tracks, grassy paths **THE PUB** The Greyhound Inn, The Square, Corfe Castle. Tel: 01929 480205

1 From the car park bear right then right again on to West Street. At the end, go straight over a cattle grid. Bear left on a path across the heath; look for Kingston church tower. Cross duckboards and go uphill, forking right by a tumulus, and then walk to the right of a stone block. Continue over the brow of the hill and then descend, in line with the church tower. The path gradually veers right and it leaves the Common by way of a kissing gate, stiles and footbridges.

2 Bear half-left across a field, and across the next, regaining the line of the tower. Go over a bridge and ascend a wooded path. Climb over a stile and continue up the left edge of a field. Maintain your direction after you cross the next stile. Go through a thick hedge and head straight across the next field (the flag pole on the church tower being the line) to a kissing gate and turn right up a track. On the ascent fork left, taking the path up through the woods.

3 At the top, turn left to the road and walk down through the village. At the junction by the Scott Arms turn right. After the converted church, go over a stile on the left and bear half-right, signposted to Afflington. Pass through a gate at the bottom corner of the field and continue along the left boundary of the next field to a stile in the corner. Shortly after, bear left through scrubland, then turn left on to a stony track. As the track bears right take the path left (Purbeck Way) over a stile and take the track left into a field.

4 Turn right, go through a gate and go right over a stile. Cross a narrow, wooded strip to a stile and turn left beside the woods. Climb over a further stile and proceed straight on, soon to bear left through a gate and around the left edge of a field. Turn left over another stile and over a footbridge, then continue over a further stile and turn sharp right. Cross a metalled drive, a stile, a causeway and then a bridge on to the Common.

5 Go straight on over Corfe Common towards the castle ruins. Bear left at a concrete marker, and proceed right to a gate. Cross the B3069, through a gate and straight on, later bearing right behind houses. Go through a kissing gate and follow the path towards the centre of Corfe. After it winds through some housing walk across fields leading into a playground. Turn left and then right into West Street to reach the square.

6 Turn left by the castle on the path below the walls. Go left up the road and left again by a gate and over a stile (by a sign to The Rings). Cross the fields via a series of gates to return to the car park in West Street.

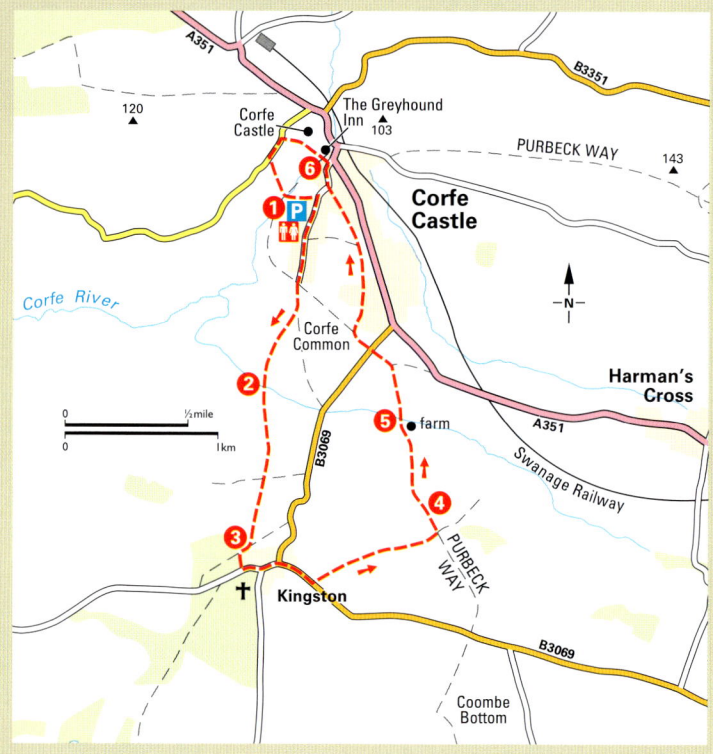

WALK 22

DURDLE DOOR & LULWORTH COVE

An exhilarating walk on a stunning stretch of coastline visiting Durdle Door, a spectacular natural rock arch in the sea, and Lulworth Cove some 2 miles (4km) along the coast, before turning inland and skirting the village of West Lulworth. The white chalk that breaks through the soil here underlies Dorset's famous downland and is seen in the exposed soft, eroded cliffs at White Nothe. West Lulworth is also the starting point for many who wish to go looking for fossils on Dorset's Jurassic Coast world heritage site.

DISTANCE/TIME 3.25 miles (5.3km) 2h **MAP** OS Explorer OL 15 Purbeck & South Dorset **START** Car park (fee) above Durdle Door, grid ref: SY 811804 **TRACKS** Stone path, grassy tracks, tarmac **THE PUB** The Castle Inn, West Lulworth. Tel: 01929 400311; www.thecastleinn-lulworthcove.co.uk

1 From the corner of the car park at Durdle Door Caravan Park take the path down to Durdle Door. Return the same way but before steeply ascending take the fork to the right, signed to Lulworth Cove. Follow the path along the coast a while and down to the cove (the Heritage Centre and Stair Hole are worth visiting).

2 Turn sharp left up some steps, signed to Bindon Hill. Walk through a wooded area to a stile, then turn sharp right to skirt the rim of the cove. Near to the top take the path left to Bindon Hill and on the brow, at a junction with a much wider path, turn right. Walk across ancient earthworks and by the entrance to Lulworth Army Ranges, then turn left down towards the village of West Lulworth. Cross a stile and bear half-left across a field, crossing the stile on the left just before the bottom.

3 Continue to walk along a fenced path at the back of the village. The path swings left up some steps (steps right lead down to the Main Street where you turn right for the Castle Inn), then along to an unmade road.

At the junction with Bindon Road turn left, and in 25yds (23m) turn right over a stile, signed to Lulworth Cove. In 10yds (9m) take the fork right through a gate and keep to the right edge of the field. At the waymarker, turn right and cross over a stile, signed 'Durdle Door'. From here, descend the fenced path down to the road.

4 Turn right, and in 50yds (46m) turn left to Durdle Door. Cross the stile and walk along the left-hand edge of a field. After the next stile ascend some steps through a small wooded area to a stile and turn right along a chalk path, signed 'Durdle Door Camp Site'. Ignore the parallel track, and continue across fields. After four stiles return to the corner of the car park.

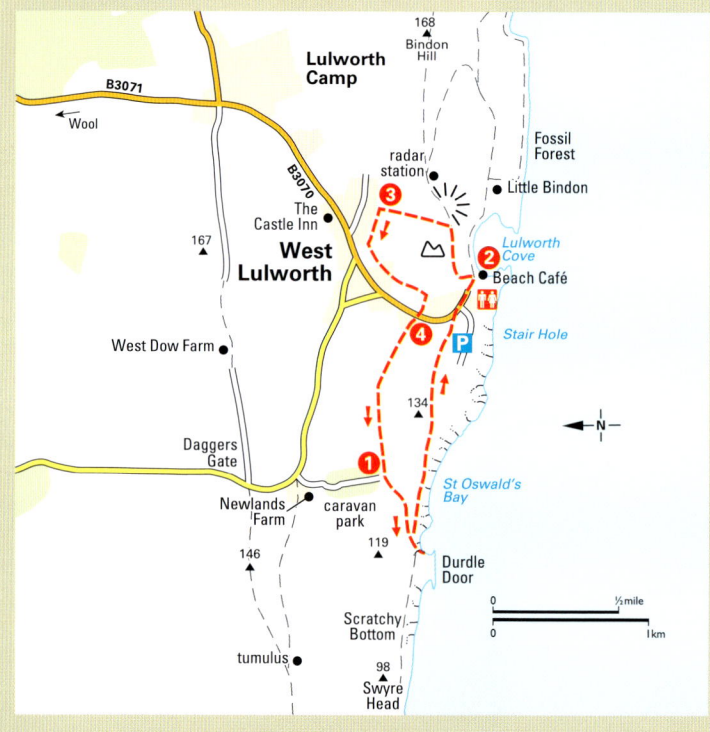

Salisbury & Plains

CLOCKWISE FROM TOP: STONEHENGE; SALISBURY CATHEDRAL; CATHEDRAL CLOSE; WILTON HOUSE

OLD SARUM MAP REF 400 D6

Old Sarum's history dates back to a time long before records were made, and the giant earthwork is founded on an Iron Age camp that covered around 56 acres (23ha). The earliest settlers were followed by Romans, Anglo-Saxons, Danes and Normans – William the Conqueror is said to have reviewed his troops here in 1070. A Norman castle and cathedral were erected, but water was scarce on this plain, and the military and ecclesiastical factions could not agree who should take precedence. Accordingly, in 1220 a new cathedral was planned to the south in nearby New Sarum – or Salisbury – using stones from the old one. It seems that the spirit went out of Old Sarum in more ways than one, as the castle fell into decay, and the town was gradually abandoned. There's not much left to see of this once-thriving settlement today, but for the excavated foundations of the old cathedral and fragments of the castle.

MARLBOROUGH DOWNS

MAP REF 400 D5

The Marlborough Downs are just one part of the North Wessex Downs Area of Outstanding Natural Beauty, although the name 'North Wessex' is not a traditional one, the area being better known by a series of overlapping local names, including the Marlborough Downs. Beyond the town of Marlborough, the Downs sweep in a wide semi-circle to the south around the headwaters of the River Kennet, and are extensively used for training race horses often providing an exciting spectacle on the Downs gallops.

Characteristically, the Downs form high, large-scale rolling chalk downland with a dramatic scarp on the northern edge and intensive arable farming, sparse woodland cover and few hedgerows.

ROMSEY MAP REF 400 E6

This small town on the River Test is dominated by its magnificent Abbey Church of 1120–70, a handsome Norman building with a low, square tower, massive walls, a splendid south doorway and an interior of beautifully carved Norman arches. It contains two remarkable Saxon stone carvings from earlier churches on the site, and its treasures include the Romsey Psalter (a 15th-century illuminated manuscript), and a monument to the noted economist Sir William Petty (1623–87), born in Romsey and a founder member of the Royal Society. Lord Mountbatten of Burma (1900–79), the one-time confidant to Prince Charles, is buried here in the abbey.

Romsey is an attractive place with many pleasing streets of Georgian and later houses. It centres on spacious Market Place, which has a statue in the middle of Lord Palmerston, the Victorian statesman who lived at nearby Broadlands.

SALISBURY MAP REF 400 D6

Salisbury feels comparatively spacious and regular – it was planned and built on a grid structure, beside the River Avon. Many old streets are named after the goods that were sold there – Fish Row, Butchers Row, and so on. Some have been pedestrianised, and highlights to look for include the 16th-century façade of Joiner's Hall on St Ann Street and the 18th-century Guildhall. The Poultry Cross in Silver Street dates to the 15th century.

Unusually, the Gothic cathedral was built in almost one go, the majority of it being completed by 1258, at a cost of around £27,000. The main exception is its soaring spire, 404 feet (123m) high, which was added in the 14th century and is the structure's most identifiable feature, painted most memorably by John Constable from across the water meadows in 1823. A climb up 332 steps and through the cathedral's roof spaces takes you to the top of the tower for far-reaching views over the city and around.

Salisbury cathedral's interior was drastically remodelled in the 18th century by James Wyatt, who 'decluttered' it by clearing screens and tombs and throwing out some of the old stained glass. Wyatt also covered over the 13th-century roof painting in the choir, but this was later restored. Nowadays, the most striking glass is the intense blue 'Prisoners of Conscience Window' in the Trinity Chapel.

Two of the cathedral's most prized possessions are the clock of 1386, the oldest in England, and an original copy of the Magna Carta, the 'great document' forced by rebellious barons on King John at Runnymede in 1215, to limit the monarch's more arbitrary powers. It's surprisingly small for such a significant document, about A3 size.

A stroll around the extensive cathedral close is essential, including gracious old houses such as the Old Deanery, and the King's House, now home to the interesting Salisbury and South Wiltshire Museum, which includes finds from Stonehenge, watercolours by Turner, history relating to Old Sarum, and the Warminster Jewel. Mompesson House is a gem in Queen Anne style, with notable plasterwork and a pretty walled garden, and played a starring role in the 1995 film of Jane Austen's *Sense and Sensibility*. The Wardrobe contains a military museum.

The 17th-century Palladian mansion of Wilton House, home of the Earl of Pembroke, lies west of the town, and is well worth a look for its famous Single and Double Cube Rooms and its elegant gardens. The house was also the most unlikely setting for the D-Day landings headquarters during World War II; much more recently, scenes from the movies *The Madness of King George*, *Mrs Brown* and the 2005 movie *Pride and Prejudice* were all filmed here.

Visit
CATHEDRAL CHOIR

There has been a choir at Salisbury Cathedral for around 800 years, and today the cathedral choir is famous for admitting girls as well as boys. In 1991, on the 900th anniversary of the founding of the boys' choir, the cathedral decided to found the girls' choir. Girls and boys as young as seven years old can now join the choir school. The children take part in regular school lessons alongside their twice-daily singing practices. You can go along to hear the choristers rehearsing at evensong during term time and at special services held throughout the year. You can find out about concerts at the cathedral at the website www.salisburycathedral.org.uk

SALISBURY CATHEDRAL

STOCKBRIDGE MAP REF 400 E6

Lying deep in the broad Test valley, and spanning that many-streamed river on an artificial causeway constructed in Roman times, Stockbridge consists of a gracious wide street lined with an attractive variety of little houses and shops, with open views eastwards to the hills. It feels as if it should be the main thoroughfare of a sizeable town, but it is not, and behind the elegant façades, the gift and antiques shops, the art galleries and the hotels are the broad water meadows of the River Test. Some of the river's streamlets, teeming with trout, flow under and alongside the main street.

The most prestigious of English angling clubs, The Houghton, has its headquarters at the Grosvenor Hotel, Stockbridge's most impressive building, with a great pillared porch that juts out into the street and a room above. The town was on a main drovers' route between Wales and Surrey and Kent, and sheep fairs were held here from Tudor times until the early 20th century.

Stockbridge Common Marsh is ancient land in the care of the National Trust, as is the open Stockbridge Down, where there is a large Bronze Age cemetery.

Northwest of Stockbridge, on the A343, is the Museum of Army Flying at Middle Wallop airfield, which celebrates the history of army aviation. Exhibits include an Argentine Huey helicopter, captured during the Falklands War, and there are hands-on games and activities.

STONEHENGE MAP REF 400 D6

There was a henge at Stonehenge around 5,000 years ago, but it was little more than a ditch and bank around an open space. About 4200BC, the Beaker People appeared and began building a double ring of stones inside the henge.

These 'bluestones' were brought several hundred miles from Preseli in South Wales. Transporting the stones was an impressive achievement; most weigh more than 4 tons, and were brought to Salisbury Plain by boat and sledge, a process that must have taken decades.

Impressive it may have been, but the stones were barely in position before they were demolished, and may even have been moved to another building site. Speculation among archaeologists is that there was a shift in the power balance of the area, and the Beaker People were ousted by a local revolt. A new circle was erected, this time using more easily obtainable 'Sarsen' stones from the Marlborough Downs, to form an inner horseshoe surrounded by a circle. This is today's famous circle.

But what is Stonehenge? Is it an astronomical observatory? A Druid temple, perhaps? The truth is, no-one knows. Current favourite is that Stonehenge was a form of multipurpose ceremonial centre, relating to fertility, death and rebirth.

WILTON MAP REF 400 D6

A small village of thatched cottages and a duck pond, Wilton is renowned for its windmill. The only working windmill in Wessex, the Wilton Mill was built in 1821 after construction of the Kennet and Avon canal, and was operational for 100 years, until the introduction of steam roller mills and fast production of cheap bread made it redundant. But in 1976, the mill was fully restored and is today managed by the Wilton Windmill Society.

Built as a traditional tower mill with a fantail to turn the cap, to ensure that the sails always point into the wind, the mill has four sails; it is fully operational, and produces stoneground wholemeal flour as a souvenir of your visit.

STONEHENGE

Cotswolds

CLOCKWISE FROM TOP: LAVENDER AT SNOWSHILL; GUITING POWER; IRIS AT HIDCOTE MANOR GARDEN; ULEY BURY; PITTVILLE PUMP ROOM

BLOCKLEY MAP REF 404 D7

This handsome village, situated along the fast-flowing Blockley Brook, is less well known than many of its neighbours but has a subtle appeal undoubtedly worthy of attention. Blockley was a silk town and by 1880, just before the failure of the industry in the area, the six mills here employed some 600 people. Many of the weavers' cottages remain, the older ones towards the village centre, the 19th-century silk workers' cottages terraced along the northern edge. One of the old mills can be seen beyond a pool near the church, while the village, with its pretty mill stream, is dotted with houses of varying ages and appeal. A beautiful garden, Mill Dene, has been created around one of the old mills.

BOURTON-ON-THE-WATER

MAP REF 400 D3

The busiest honeypot in the area is this attractive village, watered by the River Windrush, which flows proudly along the main street beneath a succession of five graceful footbridges, earning for Bourton the title 'the Venice of the Cotswolds'. A tourist mecca, and to be avoided if rural calm is what you yearn for, the village does have a lot to offer in the way of attractions. Birdland is a sanctuary for birds, with a remarkable collection of penguins in stream-side gardens. Here, there is also a model village (Bourton in miniature), a perfume factory, a motor museum, the Dragonfly Maze, and a model railway exhibition, all within walking distance of each other and of the main street. Just off the main street is Bourton's church, St Lawrence's, a mixture of elements, with a medieval chancel, Victorian nave and distinctive domed Georgian tower, complete with skull on the exterior, a salutary reminder of our mortality.

Bourton can be best appreciated in the evenings after the crowds have dispersed, when a walk around its back streets and along the meandering river is a very pleasant experience.

Just to the east of Bourton are a series of gravel pits which, now filled with water, have become sanctuaries for waterfowl and make a very pleasant walk by following the path across Station Road from the car park. West of Bourton is a group of interesting villages, Notgrove, Cold Aston, Turkdean and Hazleton, that are well worth a visit.

BURFORD MAP REF 400 D4

Just off the main Oxford road, Burford is all but invisible to passing motorists. Drive north from the roundabout, however, and almost immediately, from the brow of the ridge, Burford slips away before you in a cascade of handsome inns and charming cottages. The wide main street, lined with shops and pubs, passes the church to the right before crossing the Windrush on a medieval bridge of 1322, by the old mill.

Burford's prosperity over the centuries has depended on three factors – wool, quarrying and coaching. There were burgesses here in the 13th century and the town developed rapidly to become an important wool centre.

The nearby quarries at the Barringtons, Upton and especially Taynton produced some of the most notable stone in the Cotswolds. Much of that stone was used in the construction of some of England's finest buildings – Blenheim Palace, St Paul's Cathedral and various Oxford colleges. The Barringtons also produced the Strongs, a family of masons – Sir Thomas Strong was Christopher Wren's master mason in the construction of St Paul's Cathedral. Another eminent family of masons, the Kempsters, came from Upton and Burford.

A fillip for Burford came with the dawn of the coaching era from the 18th century, when the town was an important stop on the route to Oxford and London. This, however, came to an end with the railway, which happened to bypass Burford.

Burford is a delight to stroll about. While the High Street is the main thoroughfare, Sheep Street to the west, and Witney Street and Church Lane to the east, have much to offer. Along Sheep Street there are some fine inns – the Bay Tree Hotel and the Lamb Inn (the old brewery next door houses the Tourist Information Centre) – while Witney Street boasts perhaps the finest building in the town, the 17th-century Great House. From Witney Street, Guildenford leads to Church Lane where a row of almshouses (1457), are close to St John the Baptist church.

The 15th-century parish church is impressive. Among the chapels and monuments, perhaps the finest is the one erected in 1628 to Sir Lawrence Tanfield, Lord Chief Baron of the Exchequer to James I. Another fine memorial, to Edmund Harman, barber-surgeon to Henry VIII, includes the first representation in Britain of Amazonian Indians from the New World. On the rim of the font the autograph of a Leveller, one of 340 Roundhead mutineers kept here for three days during the Civil War, is inscribed: 'Anthony Sedley prisner 1649' (sic). From the High Street, near the bridge, Priory Lane takes you past the handsome building of the Elizabethan Priory, which is now home to a Benedictine Anglican community.

BURFORD

Back on the High Street, on the corner of Sheep Street, is the pillared Tolsey, a Tudor house where wool merchants used to meet and which now houses a museum of considerable interest. Further down is the wide arch of the old George Hotel where Charles I used to stay with Nell Gwynn and which later became an important coaching inn. Their son was created Earl of Burford.

Approximately 3 miles (4.8km) south of Burford are the Cotswold Wildlife Park and Gardens, set in the grounds of a delightful 19th-century mansion.

CASTLE COMBE MAP REF 399 K3

Generally considered one of the loveliest villages in the Cotswolds, Castle Combe is very popular and can get crowded. Parking is a problem here and visitors are asked to use the car park. The perfection of this pretty village means that it is also used by film producers.

Like many other Cotswold villages, Castle Combe's wealth came from the sheep and wool industry. Most of its houses here were weavers' houses, and it was allowed to hold a fair for trading sheep and wool. The 14th-century Market Cross, with the old water pump beside it, forms the centre of the village. The nearby Butter Cross was dismantled during the 19th century. A favourite view of the village is from the old weavers' cottages, across the bridge. The museum contains many items of local interest.

Outside the village is the motor-racing circuit, which continued to host national championship races until the 1990s. Motor-racing test-drives and other automotive events are still held here.

CHELTENHAM MAP REF 400 C3

Built against the base of the Cotswold escarpment, overlooked by Cleeve and Leckhampton Hills, Cheltenham is ideal for visiting not only the Cotswolds but also the Severn Vale, the Forest of Dean and the Wye Valley. It is also the scene for several festivals: a Folk Festival in February; the National Hunt Festival when the Gold Cup is run; Jazz in April; the June Science Festival; the Summer Cricket Festival in the grounds of the Boys' College and the Music Festival in July; and the ever popular Literature Festival in October.

Cheltenham is usually associated with the Regency period, when a market town of insignificance became a fashionable watering hole. The ensuing building boom has left a town of considerable elegance, of handsome, wide streets lined with Regency-style villas and terraces.

The town centre is fairly compact and can easily be explored on foot. The original town ran along the current High Street, now home to major chain stores and two shopping arcades. The Regency town spread southwards along the Promenade, one of the finest town thoroughfares in the country, today lined with elegant shops. The magnificent terrace at the northern end, built to accommodate those coming to take the waters, now houses the Municipal Offices and the Tourist Information Centre. In front is the Neptune Fountain and a statue to Edward Wilson, the Cheltenham botanist who accompanied Captain Scott on his ill-fated expedition to the South Pole. The Promenade continues to the imposing façade of the Queens Hotel, built on the site of the Imperial Well.

The road narrows between the shops here. It is worth walking along Queens Circus towards Fauconberg Street, on the right, a short way – on the right is Cheltenham Ladies' College, part of which conceals the original Royal Well; on the left is one of Cheltenham's loveliest streets, Montpellier Street, which is lined with interesting shops raised from the road behind wide pavements. A small alleyway on the left from Montpellier Street leads back towards the main road passing old Montpellier Arcade to the left. At the top of the road is the Rotunda, now a bank although originally the Montpellier Spa, its design was apparently based on the Pantheon in Rome. The well-preserved interior is well worth a look.

If you have the time there is plenty more Regency architecture to see and appreciate in the area close to Montpellier, notably in Lansdowne, which is just to the west of Montpellier. Heading southeast will take you to Suffolk Square, beyond which, along Suffolk Parade and Suffolk Road, are some antique and curio shops.

North of the High Street is Pittville and its showpiece, the Pittville Pump Rooms. The Pump Rooms constitute a magnificent architectural ensemble and were designed between 1825 and 1830 by a local man, John Forbes. They were to be the focal point of Joseph Pitt's Pittville Estate. His legacies are the Pump Rooms, Pittville Park with its lake surrounded by villas in an array of fantastic styles, Pittville Lawn, and Clarence Square and Wellington Square. In the Pump Rooms, which are often used for concerts and recitals, you can taste the waters or visit the museum on the upper floor.

Visit
DECORATIVE IRONWORK

Cheltenham is noted for its ironwork which decorates many of the early buildings of the town. Balconies of finely wrought iron adorn the elegant buildings, adding a continental atmosphere to the streets and squares. Particularly fine examples can be found along Oxford Parade, Royal Parade and Suffolk Square.

Visit
BIRDLAND

Birdland was established by the late Len Hill, who purchased two small islands in the South Atlantic. These islands, part of the Falkland Islands group, are inhabited by penguins and a considerable variety of other birds, some of which can be seen at Birdland, along with macaws, parrots and cockatoos, in varied habitats on the banks of the River Windrush at Bourton-on-the-Water. You can watch the penguins zipping through the water via the glass-sided pool.

Visit
CHELTENHAM RACECOURSE

A visit to the racecourse is a 'must' for anyone interested in watching the world's top chasers and hurdlers. The track is best known for the National Hunt Festival in March, the top three-day meeting of the season which features the Gold Cup and Champion Hurdle and attracts more than 50,000 spectators. The Hall of Fame tells the story of the history of the racecourse.

CHIPPING CAMPDEN MAP REF 403 J6

The loveliest village in the Cotswolds is a gilded masterpiece. The main street curves in a shallow arc lined with houses each grafted to the next but each with its own distinctive embellishments.

As the name suggests ('Chipping' means market), Chipping Campden was a market town, one of the most important of the medieval wool towns in the Cotswolds. The town then dozed for centuries until Edward Ashbee moved his Guild of Handicraft here from London in 1902. A few craftsmen continue their work today.

Campden's church, at the north end of the town, is perhaps the finest wool church in the Cotswolds, with a magnificent tower and a spacious interior that contains the largest brass, to William Grevel, that exists in the county. The Gainsborough Chapel houses the fine 17th-century marble tomb of Sir Baptist Hicks and his wife, who built the nearby stone almshouses in 1612, as well as Campden House, which was razed during the Civil War.

Among many fine houses in the village is Grevel House, on the High Street opposite Church Street. It once belonged to William Grevel, a wool merchant largely responsible for the church in its current form and who, it is supposed, was the original model for the merchant in Chaucer's *Canterbury Tales*.

Just off Leysbourne, which is the northern extension of the High Street, is the Ernest Wilson Memorial Garden, a charming little botanical enclave snug in the shadow of the church. The garden commemorates the eccentric plant collector who was born here in 1876. In the middle of the village, on stone pillars, is the 1627 Market Hall.

CHIPPING NORTON MAP REF 400 D3

This busy market town, the highest in Oxfordshire at 646 feet (197m), is distinguished at its outskirts by the large Victorian tweed mill, now converted to flats, that sits in a fold to the west of the town. The Bliss Tweed Mill, built in 1872 by the Lancashire architect George Woodhouse, closed in 1980 and is an unusual reminder, in the Cotswolds, of the Industrial Revolution; and yet there is something disconcertingly memorable about this example of the Victorian age.

The heart of Chipping Norton has to be the Market Square which is dominated by the 19th-century Town Hall, with its Tuscan-style portico. Opposite the Town Hall steps is the museum, which has displays on local history. Around the town you'll find a varied collection of shops, hotels and houses dating back to the 17th century, though most are 18th century.

From the square, the town slopes down Church Street past a row of almshouses dating back to 1640, towards St Mary's, a Perpendicular church containing some fine brasses and impressive tombs. Its most unusual feature is the hexagonal porch with a vaulted ceiling. Behind the church are the motte-and-bailey earthworks that show that the town was already of some importance in the Norman period.

CIRENCESTER MAP REF 400 D4

Now a busy market town, Cirencester was once the most important city in England after London, during the Roman occupation. Called Corinium Dubunnorum and founded as a military headquarters in AD 49, a number of important roads radiated from the city – the Fosse Way, Ermin Street and Akeman Street. The Saxons renamed Corinium 'Cirencester' (which from 'Coryn', means the 'top part', in reference to the River Churn, the highest source of the Thames; and 'Ceastre', which means 'fort') but practically destroyed the town, preferring instead to build smaller settlements outside the walls. Only in the Middle Ages did Cirencester regain something of its former glory when it became the premier of the Cotswold wool towns. Markets still take place each Monday and Friday.

The town is most easily explored on foot. There are a number of well-signposted car parks within easy reach of the city centre, while the market square is the most convenient place to begin discovery of the town. The 15th-century parish church, one of the largest in England, is the main feature. Its magnificent Perpendicular tower was built with the reward given by Henry IV to a group of local earls who foiled a rebellion. Its fine roof is illuminated by clerestory windows, while the east and west windows are filled with medieval stained glass. The best-known feature of the exterior, however, is the three-storeyed south porch, overlooking the market square, which was built by some of the abbots in the late 15th century as an office for the abbey and which became the Town Hall after the Dissolution. It was one of the finest in the country and was only returned to the church in the 18th century.

Opposite the church, the Tourist Information Centre is in the Victorian Corn Hall, on the Market Square, which also hosts a weekly market and has a permanent exhibition of local crafts. Cricklade Street, running south from the square, is the site of the Brewery Arts Centre, where craft studios are currently housed in the old brewery.

On Park Street, close to Cirencester Park, is Corinium Museum, which brings to life many aspects of local history and displays its various finds, including the mosaics that were made in the area from the Roman and later eras.

Close by is Thomas Street, the location of the 15th-century Weavers Hall almshouse (also known as St Thomas's Hospital) and also Coxwell Street, lined with merchants' houses. Farther north is Spitalgate Lane, with the arcade of the nave of St John's Hospital, and another group of almshouses. Due east from here is the mysterious-looking Spital Gate, all that remains of the old abbey. From here a walk through the Abbey Grounds, where the remnants of the Roman walls can be seen at the eastern boundary, will take you back to the town centre.

No visit to Cirencester would be complete without a glimpse, at the very least, of Cirencester Park, probably the finest example of geometric landscaping in the country. It is approached up Cecily Hill, one of the prettiest streets in Cirencester, which leads to the wrought-iron entrance gates. The park was the conception of the 1st Lord Bathurst in the early 18th century and the house (not open to the public), behind one of the largest yew hedges in the world, was built to his own design. The park was landscaped with the help of the poet Alexander Pope, among others, who has celebrated the construction of the park in verse. In fact there is a corner known as Pope's Seat near the polo ground.

It is an excellent place for walking (the grounds are privately owned but open to walkers and riders), especially along the Broad Ride, which stretches out from the entrance almost to Sapperton.

Apart from the wall in the Abbey Garden, the only other surviving Roman souvenir is the superb 2nd-century Roman Amphitheatre, which is one of the largest and best preserved in the country. It is found on Cotswold Avenue.

COLN VALLEY MAP REF 400 D4

The River Coln, a tributary of the Thames, is arguably the lovliest of the many rivers that ripple peacefully through the Cotswolds. It rises on the escarpment not far from Cheltenham then gently descends the slopes, passing through a number of pretty villages en route.

Withington has an unusually large church with a fine Norman doorway and a handsome wall monument to Sir John and Lady Howe of Compton Cassey. The 17th-century mansion of Compton Cassey is now a magnificent farmhouse, lying in splendid isolation in the middle of the valley, forcing the Yanworth road to curve around it. As you approach it you may see a rhinoceros in a field close by. If so it will be the product of the artist's gallery, Compton Cassey Gallery, which now occupies the house.

From here the river passes close to Chedworth Roman Villa and thence to Fossebridge, a steep point on the Roman Fosse Way where an ancient inn continues to attract passing customers. On the other side of the road the Coln furrows across the meadows of Coln St Dennis, a small, silent village built around a green, with a small Norman church. Look for the inscription to Joan Burton on the interior wall of the tower, as well as the Norman corbel stones that line the nave.

Further on is the pretty hamlet of Calcot and then almost immediately Coln Rogers with a church remarkable for its Saxon plan and Saxon window north of the chancel. At the old mill in Winson, where the road zigzags, there are charming gardens and towards the centre of the village you'll find some converted barns. The compact green is overlooked by a classical-looking manor house. After Winson come Ablington and Bibury.

Finally, before going on to Fairford and Lechlade, the Coln arrives at Coln St Aldwyns, where the green is shaded by a magnificent horse chestnut tree and the New Inn is a fine pub. A pretty churchyard surrounds the church, which has memorial windows commemorating John Keble, the 19th-century reformer, and his father. It is possible to walk along the Coln from here to Bibury.

THE GUITINGS MAP REF 400 D3

The valley running east of Winchcombe is sprinkled with some charming villages. There are two Guitings, for example – the intriguingly named Temple Guiting and Guiting Power. Temple Guiting takes its name from the Knights Templar who owned the manor from the 12th century, and is a pretty village among trees at the edge of the stream. Its church is an interesting mix of styles and, although there are fragmentary remains of the Norman construction, the tower, pulpit and windows are 18th century, with stained glass from the 16th century.

Guiting Power, a couple of miles to the south of Temple Guiting, is clustered around a small green, and is a perfect example of an English village.

The church to the south of the village, also once owned by the Knights Templar, has an exceptionally fine Norman south doorway, although the interior is rather uninspiring. The foundations of a Saxon chapel have been discovered just to the north of the existing church.

HIDCOTE MANOR GARDEN
MAP REF 404 D7

Four miles (6.4km) northeast of Chipping Campden, in the hamlet of Hidcote Bartrim, is the National Trust property of Hidcote Manor, famous above all for its series of scenic gardens that have transformed a 17th-century property of comparative mediocrity into an inspiration for modern gardeners.

The 11-acre (4.5ha) garden, a mix of formal design and seemingly haphazard planting, was created over the course of 40 years after Hidcote was purchased in 1907 by the great horticulturist Major Lawrence Johnston. In fact, there are a number of separate gardens, each created to a different design and producing different colours of flowers and shrubs. The effect is heightened by the use of walls and hedges of copper and green beech, box, holly, hornbeam and yew, which protect the plants, many of which are rare or unique, from the severe Cotswold winds. Within the hedges are the formal Bathing Pool Garden, the Fuchsia Garden, the White Garden as well as the Kitchen Garden and a less formal creation by a stream. In addition there are a beech avenue, a lime alley. and visitors can enjoy magnificent views of hill and vale.

Kiftsgate Court Gardens, near Hidcote Manor, are on a wooded slope from where there are views across the Oxfordshire wolds. The house is largely Victorian, while the gardens were created after World War I by Heather Muir. The terraced areas above the scarp are a paradise of colourful flower beds and shrubs, while the slope is covered in pines. The gardens are famous for a collection of roses, including *Rosa filipes* 'Kiftsgate', believed to be the largest rose in the United Kingdom at almost 60 feet (18.3m) high.

KELMSCOTT MAP REF 400 D4

Kelmscot is a small village, the fame of which is inseparable from the 19th-century poet and artist, William Morris. On the façade of a terrace of cottages on the main street, there he is in carved relief seated in the shade of a tree, knapsack and hat at his side. Kelmscott Manor, on the edge of the village, was his home from 1871 until his death in 1896. Morris is buried in the local churchyard in a grave, designed by Philip Webb and which was modelled on a Viking tomb.

Kelmscott Manor (limited public opening) was built in the late 16th century. Morris only rented it but it now contains a fine collection of items associated with the man and with his craft, most notably those comparatively simple, domestic artefacts that he strove to see reinvigorated through the Arts and Crafts Movement. It also contains some pictures by Rossetti and Burne-Jones. This village came to mean much to him, and he named his private printing press in London after it.

RIVER COLN

LECHLADE ON THAMES

MAP REF 400 D4

This is another town with the peculiar quality that derives more from its rivers, notably the Thames, than from the Cotswolds. In the Middle Ages the town was on the Salt Way but Lechlade is very much a river town. At the confluence of three rivers – the Coln, the Leach and the Thames – it was at Lechlade that stone quarried at Taynton was loaded on to wagons before setting out for London, to be used in the construction of St Paul's Cathedral. From 1789 the Thames was linked to the Severn via the Thames and Severn Canal (which started close to here) to the southeast at Inglesham, where the old round house, built for the canal lengthmen (who were responsible for the maintenance of certain lengths of the canal, hence the name), still stands.

Inevitably, wherever there are rivers there are bridges. Just south of the town, the A361 crosses the Thames with the old tollbridge, the 18th-century Halfpenny (or Ha'penny) Bridge; while to the east the A417 crosses the Thames by means of the 13th-century St John Bridge where a statue of Father Thames presides close to the Thames' highest lock and from where there is a fine view of the town.

Lechlade is built about its pretty Market Square, and its wool church. The square, and the streets that radiate from it – Burford Street, High Street and St John Street – are overlooked by a collection of fine 17th- to 19th-century buildings. The church, with its distinctive spire, dates from the late 15th century when it was built largely from the same quarries at Taynton that later provided the stone for St Paul's Cathedral. The church contains an east window from 1510 and the brass of wool merchant John Townsend, as well as a fine chancel roof.

The bustle of commercial river life has long gone from Lechlade, although pleasure craft still bring colour and movement to the canal and it is possible to hire small boats from the boatyard near the Ha'penny Bridge. The walk along the Thames, southwest from the Ha'penny Bridge, is very enjoyable and at Inglesham there is the pretty church of St John the Baptist, 30feet (100m) from the river, which was salvaged by William Morris.

Just to the southeast of Lechlade is Buscot Park, a handsome 18th-century house, with a well-known series of paintings by Burne-Jones in the saloon, and a trio of Rembrandts among many other works of art reflecting the taste of the 1st Lord Faringdon.

PAINSWICK MAP REF 400 C4

'The Queen of the Cotswolds' sits more or less at the point of transition from the northern to the southern Cotswolds. Perched regally at the edge of the steep slopes of the Painswick Valley, the town is a hive of activity about the network of lanes around the church.

Like other important towns in this part of the Cotswolds, Painswick's prosperity reached its peak in the 17th and 18th centuries when the stream below was harnessed to work the mills producing wool cloth. The water purity also meant that cloth dyeing became important. The character of the village depends considerably on the fine houses built by the wealthy wool merchants of the era.

But the most striking feature of Painswick is the graceful 17th-century spire of the church. The church itself is mainly 15th-century and contains some interesting monuments, although it is the churchyard for which Painswick is especially noted. There are two reasons for this. Interesting features include the colonnades of yew, which have graced the churchyard since 1792. There are said to be only 99, since the Devil always kills off the hundredth, and indeed, it is now impossible to count them with ease since some are intertwined with each other. The other distinction are table tombs from the 17th and 18th centuries, many of which were carved by a local mason, Joseph Bryan, and his two sons.

Stroll around the heart of the town and along Bisley Street, the original main street and the oldest part of the town. Here you will find the Little Fleece, now a National Trust bookshop in a largely 17th-century house that was built on to the 14th-century Fleece Inn.

Just outside the town, on the Gloucester road, is Painswick Rococo Garden, the landscaped 18th-century garden around Painswick House. It is utterly charming, particularly in early spring when snowdrops flower in abundance.

THE SLAUGHTERS MAP REF 400 D3

These two villages with unlikely names ('slaughter' means muddy, which they are no longer) are, like Bourton-on-the-Water, synonymous with the Cotswolds. Upper Slaughter, partly clustered around the fine 17th-century manor (now an hotel) and the 12th-century church, is the more pastoral of the two. Beyond the church (which contains a monument to F E Witts, 19th-century rector and lord of the manor, who wrote *Diary of a Cotswold Parson*) the scene is absurdly picturesque, with the forded River Eye bubbling in the shade of an oak tree below some wonderful stone cottages.

Lower Slaughter, about a half-mile (800m) walk away, is somewhat different in character. The River Eye is spanned by a number of flattish footbridges. The 19th-century corn mill, with its working waterwheel and steam chimney, has an interesting museum and has demonstrations to show the workings of a Victorian flour mill. Among its collection is one of only three unused millstones left in the country. There is an award-winning gift and craft shop and riverside tea room, and free tastings of their handmade organic ice-creams in the summer.

LOWER SLAUGHTER

SNOWSHILL MAP REF 403 J6

Pronounced (according to who you speak to), 'Snowzzle', or even 'Snozzle', this charming and comparatively remote village is famous, above all, for Snowshill Manor, an interesting National Trust property from the Tudor period that once belonged to the wealthy and eccentric sugar plantation owner, Charles Wade. An ardent collector of anything that was crafted, he filled the manor house with his finds, living, meanwhile, in the Priest's House set in the lovely terraced garden, but without any comforts or conveniences and sleeping in an old Tudor bed. The fame of Snowshill Manor spread, so that eminent people – John Buchan, John Betjeman, J B Priestley, and Queen Mary who apparently declared that the finest thing in the house was Charles Wade – were frequent visitors.

SOUTH CERNEY MAP REF 400 D4

South Cerney, which is 3 miles (4.8km) southeast of Cirencester, is situated on the banks of the River Churn, where you will find rows of attractive cottages along Silver Street and Church Lane. The church has a Norman south doorway above which are some sculptures reflecting Heaven and Hell, while within are the remains of a 12th-century crucifix, one of the earliest wood carvings in the country.

The old Thames and Severn Canal passes just to the north of the village and walks along the towpath are possible; but the village is best known, nowadays, for a series of flooded gravel pits that make up the Cotswold Water Park. Broadly speaking there are two sections, one between Cricklade and Kemble (where South Cerney is situated), the other between Fairford and Lechlade, which provide facilities for nature lovers, bird watchers and sportsmen alike. There are seven nature reserves and the wetlands attract millions of wildfowl, particularly in the winter. The various activities coexist happily on 140 lakes.

STANTON MAP REF 403 J6

Stanton has a fine collection of farmhouses and cottages, most of which were built during the 17th century, the golden period of Cotswold vernacular architecture. A village of quite ridiculous perfection, it seems almost to have been preserved in aspic; and indeed is regularly used as the backdrop for period films. It owes its peculiar 'frozen-in-time' quality to the man who bought much of the village before World War I, the architect Sir Philip Stott from Oldham in Lancashire.

Living in Stanton Court, he was determined to restore the village. This he did, introducing modern conveniences

in the process, but ensuring by means of a covenant, that the more unsightly features of the 20th century were not allowed to disfigure the village. A place to stroll around (making use of the car park around the corner of the Broadway road), the church, St Michael's, is delightful and well worth a visit. It has a handsomely slender spire, and a number of 12th-century features in the north arcade and also two pulpits, one 14th century, one Jacobean. It also has some 15th-century stained glass, which came from Hailes Abbey near Winchcombe. The village's fine pub, the Mount Inn, is at its far end in the shadow of Shenbarrow Hill, with its Iron Age earthworks and magnificent views.

STANWAY MAP REF 403 J6

No more, really, than a hamlet, Stanway is dominated by Stanway House and its quite beautiful gatehouse. Just off the B4077 Stow road, Stanway House is reached by passing the striking St George and Dragon, a bronze war memorial by Alexander Fisher on a plinth by Sir Philip Stott, 'saviour' of nearby Stanton.

For a long time the 17th-century gatehouse was thought to have been designed by Inigo Jones. This theory has been superseded by the belief that it is the work of Timothy Strong, the mason from the Barringtons whose family worked with Sir Christopher Wren on St Paul's Cathedral. The glow of the stone is breathtaking, particularly at sunset.

The house itself, a Jacobean building with medieval origins, has changed hands only once in more than 1,000 years and definitely warrants a visit. Still inhabited by the owner, Lord Niedpath, whose aristocratic presence is much in evidence, the house wears an attractive lived-in aspect; and although it contains many items of interest and value, some even unique, a less-fossilised atmosphere in a house is hard to imagine.

In the grounds there is a magnificent tithe barn, which was built about 1370. The old water gardens have been superbly restored and pride of place must go to the fountain, the tallest in Britain, which rises to over 300 feet (90m). The old brewhouse has been revived and the coppers are built over log fires, making this one of the few log-fired breweries in the country. Several beers are produced, the most popular is Stanny, available in many local pubs.

Situated next to the house is the church with a Jacobean pulpit. Near by is a delightful, thatched wooden cricket pavilion set on saddle stones, presented to the village by J M Barrie, author of children's classic, *Peter Pan*. Barrie, a keen cricketer, was a frequent visitor to Stanway in the early 20th century.

TEWKESBURY MAP REF 403 H6

Tewkesbury's considerable historical significance was largely governed by its location on the banks of the rivers Severn and Avon which were instrumental in the 16th-century cloth and mustard trade and the later flour trade. Its importance depended, too, on its medieval Benedictine monastery of which only the magnificent church remains. The monastery was built by the Norman, Robert Fitzhamon, who used the Severn to import stone from Normandy for its construction. After his death the 'Honour of Tewkesbury', as the patronage came to be known, passed on to an illegitimate son of Henry I and then to the de Clare family.

The abbey became one of the most powerful in the kingdom, owning large areas of sheep-grazing land and constructing many fine tithe barns in the process – some of these survive, for example, at Stanway. The abbey was dissolved In 1539 but Tewkesbury's citizens bought the church for the total sum of £483.

Because of its location close to two rivers which tend to flood, the town, unable to expand, folded in on itself. Throughout the 17th and 18th centuries this was achieved by building around narrow alleyways, several of which have survived (Machine Court, Fish Alley, Fryzier Alley) off the main streets – Barton Street, Church Street and High Street. There is a great deal more of Tewkesbury than at first appears; its half-timbered and brick houses present one of the country's finest historical ensembles.

However, the town is dominated by the Abbey Church of St Mary and the eye filled by its great 148-foot (45m) square Norman tower. Inside, one of the most striking features is the set of 14 Norman pillars which support the 14th-century roof. The choir is illuminated by some 14th-century stained-glass windows, while around it radiate six chapels containing monuments to the wealthy families that have influenced both the church and the town. The west front exterior is notable for its dramatic Norman arch, of almost unsurpassed grandeur.

There is a lot to enjoy in the town. A circular walk includes, in dry weather, a stroll across the Ham – an enormous meadow that separates the Mill Avon from the Severn and which invariably floods each winter – to the river.

Opposite the church is the handsome Bell Hotel. From here Mill Street leads you down to Abel Fletcher's Mill (Abbey Mill), so called because it is thought to have played a role in the Victorian novel, *John Halifax, Gentleman*, much of which is set in the fictional town of Nortonbury, which

was modelled on Tewkesbury. From here you can either walk along St Mary's Road, with its attractive timbered cottages, or cross the River Avon and strike out across the Severn Ham. Every year the grass of the Ham, which is owned by the town, is cut and auctioned off according to a local, centuries-old tradition.

At the Severn turn right to walk along by the weir and return across the meadow this side of the flour mills. You can cross the old mill bridge and then walk along the River Avon. At King John's Bridge recross the river and turn right into the High Street to the Cross, now a memorial but the site of the medieval High Cross that was razed by Puritans in 1650.

On your left, Barton Street will take you to the fascinating Tewkesbury Museum, located in a 17th-century building that also houses the Tourist Information Centre. The museum features a model of the Battle of Tewkesbury. Church Street, to your right, takes you past the distinctive Royal Hop Pole Hotel, which featured famously in Charles Dickens' novel *The Pickwick Papers*. Beyond this is a row of restored 15th-century cottages built by wealthy medieval merchants. One, known as the Merchant's House, is presented exactly as it would have looked in its heyday. Another, the John Moore Countryside Museum, takes its name from the local writer whose stories were based on Tewkesbury and the countryside and villages around nearby Bredon.

On the right, an alleyway leads down to the Old Baptist Chapel and Court. Although the actual building dates back to the 15th century, it became a chapel only in the 17th century.

ULEY MAP REF 399 K2

Uley is a large and pretty village of 18th-century houses scuttling down the hillside into a deep valley, which became prosperous through wool dyeing. There is still a functioning brewery, while the Crown is a fine pub. Uleybury overlooks the town – it is a classic site for a hillfort, being a flat 32-acre (13ha) plateau surrounded by steep slopes.

North of Uley, towards Frocester Hill, is Hetty Pegler's Tump – the unusual name comes from the 17th-century landowner's wife. This 180-foot (55m) Neolithic barrow, surrounded by a stone wall, has a long central chamber that can be entered, with some discomfort, by obtaining the key from a nearby cottage. It may be wise to take a torch. East of Uley, within reasonable striking distance by foot, is Owlpen Manor, a beautifully sited and picturesque 15th-century manor house, which has an intersting collection of Arts and Crafts furniture. Close by also is the 19th-century church and 18th-century mill.

About a mile (1.6km) east of Owlpen is a most tranquil garden at Kingscote called Matara. Both Eastern and Western ideas of garden design are blended to produce a very restful place.

WINCHCOMBE MAP REF 400 D3

The capital of the Saxon kingdom of Mercia, Winchcombe is a town of considerable interest, with several legacies of its past that deserve investigation. There was an important abbey here during the Middle Ages, but all that now remains is the wall on one side of Abbey Terrace (behind which is private property) and the abbey church, now Winchcombe parish church. The handsome church, built between 1465 and 1468, owes its present form to wealthy local woolmen. Of note here are the 40 or so gargoyles, the Winchcombe Worthies, on the exterior, said to represent unpopular monks, a sign of dissatisfaction with the abbey at the time.

Strung all along the main street are an assortment of interesting buildings (including the fine Jacobean old school on Abbey Terrace), as well as the Railway Museum and the Winchcombe Museum located in the town hall.

Sudeley Castle, Gardens and Exhibitions, entered down Vineyard Street, is superb. Little remains of the original medieval castle, but of the 15th-century reconstruction undertaken by Ralph Botelar, St Mary's Chapel, the ruined banqueting hall, the tithe barn and the Portmare Tower are extant.

WINDRUSH VALLEY MAP REF 400 D3

The Windrush rises at Taddington, near Snowshill, and wanders through many villages already mentioned. Beyond Bourton it widens as it approaches the Thames and continues through a number of villages to the north of the A40, on the borders of Gloucestershire and Oxfordshire. A pleasant walk, the Windrush Way goes from Winchcombe to Bourton-on-the-Water.

Sherborne, on a tributary of the Windrush, has been for centuries part of the Sherborne estate; before that the land was owned by the Abbots of Winchcombe, whose sheep were sheared on the banks of the river every summer. Sherborne House, allegedly haunted by its former owner, John 'Crump' Dutton, the Royalist hunchback, was rebuilt in the 19th century. It now belongs to the National Trust and, although it is not open to the public, there are waymarked walks through the woods and parkland. Lodge Park, an elaborate grandstand for deer-coursing in the 17th century, is open to the public.

The next village to the east is Windrush, with a church topped by a fine Perpendicular tower and a magnificent Norman south doorway surrounded by beakheads, bird-like grotesques of mysterious origin. Then come the Barringtons, first Little, then Great, once renowned for their stone quarries and the local families of masons, the Kempsters and the Strongs, who worked them. No evidence remains of the old subterranean quarries and Little Barrington is a quiet little village, its cottages very prettily clustered about its village green. The Fox Inn nearby, is by a bridge over the river, built by local master mason Thomas Strong, principal contractor of St Paul's and regarded by Christopher Wren as the leading builder of the day. Great Barrington, to the north, has a Norman church with some fine monuments by the well-known 18th-century sculptor Joseph Nollekens, while the country house and landscaped gardens of Barrington Park are to the east of it.

East of Great Barrington lies Taynton, another village that once supplied London and Oxford with its famous prime building stone, it was transported overland to Lechlade and thence by barge to London. Beyond it is Burford and then Widford church, the poignant remains of a once-thriving village that simply disappeared, probably as a result of the plague. The 13th-century church, built on the site of a Roman villa, stands on a raised mound overlooking the river, and is worth a look for its box pews, and the wall paintings that date from the 14th century.

A short way from Widford is Swinbrook, a village associated with the famous Mitford family, particularly five of Lord Redesdale's daughters – Nancy, Diana, Unity, Jessica and Deborah. Unity went on to become a close friend of Adolf Hitler, Diana married the British fascist leader, Sir Oswald Moseley, Deborah became the Duchess of Devonshire, while Nancy and Jessica became well-known writers. Nancy, Pamela, Diana and Unity are buried in the graveyard of the church, which contains the wonderful triple-decker monument to the Fettiplace family who once owned a mansion here.

WINDRUSH VALLEY

WALK 23

BLOCKLEY, BATSFORD & THE ARBORETUM

This walk starts in the unspoilt village of Blockley then passes through Batsford village at the gates of Batsford Park with its 90 species of magnolia, maples, cherry trees and conifers, stunning in autumn but colourful throughout the spring and summer too. The arboretum also has a falconry centre. Blockley is a pretty village that prospered in the 19th century and its fast-flowing stream, which once powered six silk mills, is now a delightful feature of the village.

DISTANCE/TIME 4.5 miles (7.2km) 2h15 **MAP** OS Explorer OL45 The Cotswolds **START** On the edge of the churchyard, just off the main street at Blockley; grid ref: SP 165349 **TRACKS** Lanes, tracks and fields, 5 stiles **THE PUB** The Crown Inn, Blockley. Tel: 01386 700245

1 Setting off with Blockley's church above you to the right, walk south along Lower Street, the B4479, past Lower Brook House. Just beyond this point turn left on to a lane signed to Pasture Farm. Follow it along and up the hill for approximately 0.25 mile (400m). As you approach a barn, bear off right to go behind it.

2 Follow the field edge up and along, leaving at the top corner on to a grassy drove that later widens into a neglected field. Continue on, walking beside the top boundary and eventually pass into a crop field. Carry on by the left-hand hedge, and continue in the same direction across the next field as its hedge curves down the slope.

3 Emerging on to a road, walk left down to a crossroads, there turning right into Batsford estate village. At a T-junction, Batsford church lies to the right, while the onward route is left, back to the main road and then on the right.

4 Leave after some 50yds (46m) along a contained footpath on the right and maintain your direction for 0.5 mile (800m) at the edge of successive fields, which are overlooked by Batsford House, set against a curtain of woodland to the west.

5 On reaching a field still bearing the ridges of medieval ploughing, turn right by a four-fingered waymark towards a house. Keep ahead across a drive (which leads to Batsford Arboretum) and follow a rising path to a stile below a wood. Joining a track just above, follow it up for 400yds (366m) to a waymark, there doubling back sharp right. Turn left in front of gates into the private park and continue by the estate wall. Cresting the hill you will meet a lane.

6 Cross to a track opposite, which drops beside a couple of fields. Finding a path in the bottom trees, follow it left through a gate. After 250yds (230m), mount a stile beside another gate on the right and descend the hill along the field edge towards Blockley. At the bottom, go over a stile on the right and continue down, crossing Park Farm's drive to a stile in the lower right corner. Keep at the edge of the next field and leave along a track out to a lane. Turn right back past Lower Brook House.

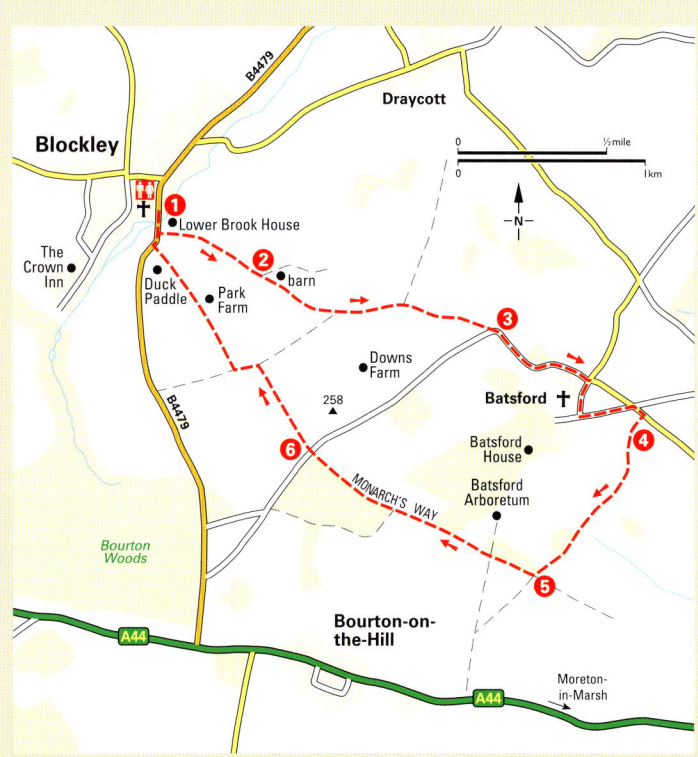

WALK 24

AROUND CUTSDEAN & FORD

A lovely walk through open countryside that was once the focus of England's most valued export, wool. Watch out for horses being exercised on 'The Gallops' along the way. Cutsdean today is a small, pretty village on the high wolds above the beginnings of the River Windrush. The origin of the village's name is uncertain: it might derive from 'cot', a sheep fold, and 'wolds', the hills where the sheep grazed; or the village might have been the seat of Cot, an Anglo-Saxon chief, in the 'wolds'.

DISTANCE/TIME 5.75 miles (9.3km) 2h45 **MAP** OS Explorer OL45 The Cotswolds **START** Cutsdean village or beside lane to the east; grid ref: SP 087302 (Cutsdean village centre) **TRACKS** Tracks, fields and lane, 5 stiles **THE PUB** The Plough Inn, Ford. Tel: 01386 584215; www.theploughinnatford.co.uk

1 Follow the uphill lane that heads east away from the village of Cutsdean for just over a mile (1.6km), until you eventually arrive at a crossroads.

2 Continue along the lane opposite, ignoring after 0.5 mile (800m) the turning off left that leads to Scarborough Farm. After a while, rising beyond a dip, the track eventually emerges out from the woodland into some open ground.

3 Keep walking ahead past a waymark to a lateral boundary a little further on and go through the right-hand one of the two openings before you. Continue at the field edge with a wall on your left for some 500yds (457m) to a waypost and then bear right across the field towards a plantation.

4 Pass through the trees, then as you emerge on the far side, double back sharp right to get on to a track beside them. Continue on for approximately a mile (1.6km) to Ford Hill Farm, leaving past the farmhouse along its drive to meet a road.

5 Opposite, the imposing gateway to Jackdaw's Castle heralds a long metalled drive beside 'The Gallops'.

6 Shortly after dropping past the stables, half hidden behind a banking over to the right, look for a waymark and sign directing you right across the training track. If the horses are running, heed well the warning notice. Continue downhill on your right, emerging at its end on to a road in front of The Plough Inn at Ford.

7 Walk down the hill, turning off right just before the river at the entrance of a drive. Over a stile before you, follow the top of a wooded bank beside paddocks behind the house, the path later curving left amongst the trees to reach a stile.

8 Turn half right along the field, crossing the head of a muddy stream to gain the left corner. Once over a stile, follow the field edge left, eventually passing the church to emerge in the village of Cutsdean. The lane along which the walk began lies to the right.

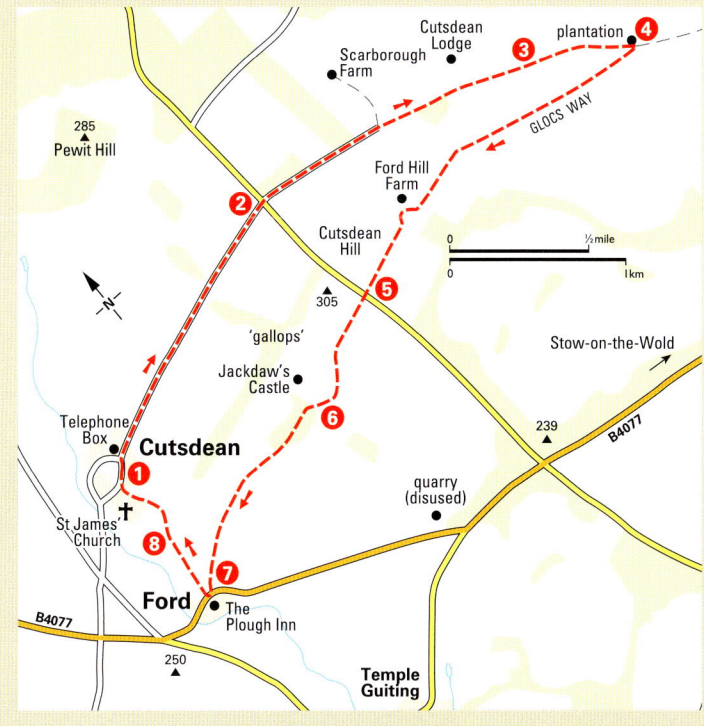

DISTANCE/TIME 20 miles (32.2km) 4h; shorter route 15 miles (24.1km) 3h MAP OS Explorer 155 Bristol & Bath and 156 Chippenham & Bradford-on-Avon START Bradford-on-Avon railway station (pay car park); grid ref: ST 825606 TRACKS Gravel towpath, some road THE PUB The George, Mill Lane, Bathampton. Tel: 01225 425079

DISTANCE/TIME 11.25 miles (26.9km) 2h30 MAP OS Explorer OL45 The Cotswolds START Coln St Aldwyns; grid ref: SP 145052 TRACKS Minor lanes THE PUB The Swan, Southrop. Tel: 01367 850205

FROM BRADFORD-ON-AVON ALONG THE KENNET & AVON CANAL

The Kennet and Avon Canal is ideal for cyclists and passes through picturesque countryside. You can turn around at the riverside pub at Bathampton although the locks you pass on the way into Bath are well worth seeing.

1 Leaving the station car park, turn right along the main road in the direction of Frome. Continue past a mini-roundabout to the Canal Tavern and Lock Inn Café. Go between them to join the towpath and follow it past Grange Farm with its massive 600-year-old tithe barn. The River Avon runs below to the right, containing Barton Farm Country Park's picnic and wildlife areas within the intervening spit of land. Beyond a gate, continue beside the canal to Avoncliff.

2 The canal now makes an abrupt turn across the Avon Valley, carried above both the river and railway on an imposing aqueduct. Do not cross, but at a sign to Dundas just before, drop steeply right towards the Cross Guns pub, then double back left underneath the bridge, climbing left to gain the opposite towpath. Tacked along the wooded valley, the waterway runs pleasantly on, harbouring an assortment of ducks, coots and moorhens. Turning a corner opposite Limpley Stoke, pass beneath a road bridge, then look out on the left for a glimpse of a viaduct taking the A36 across the Midford Brook valley.

3 Another sharp turn heralds the Dundas Aqueduct, beyond which is the last remnant of the Somerset Coal Canal. The track just before it leads to Brassknocker Basin, with a small exhibition. The route, however, continues ahead, signed 'Bath and Claverton', behind a maintenance building and a derrick and onto the opposite bank. About a mile (1.2km) further on, immediately beyond a bridge, a track drops across the railway to the river where there is a restored pump house (Claverton Pumping Station), built in 1813. There are views to Bathford and Batheaston as you pedal the final 1.75 miles (2.8km) to Bathampton and the pub.

4 To extend the ride, continue beside the canal, the eastern suburbs of Bath rising on the opposite side of the valley. Eventually the city comes into view. There are a couple of short tunnels to pass through at Sidney Gardens, where you should dismount. Between them, two ornate cast-iron bridges span the canal, which, together with the elaborate façade of the second tunnel beneath Cleveland House, were added to placate the owners of Sidney Park, as the cargo barges passed through their land.

5 Emerging below Cleveland House, the towpath doubles back on to the opposite bank, passes warehouses, now a marina, and rises to a road. Taking care, diagonally cross and drop back to the towpath, here negotiating steps. Beyond, the canal falls through a succession of locks, the path periodically rising to cross a couple of roads and a track before meeting the River Avon. To explore Bath, carry on a little further by the river to emerge on the road beside Churchill Bridge in the city centre. As the city is busy, it is perhaps preferable to secure your bikes while you wander around. The return is back the way you came, but remember you have to climb steps to the road at Bathwick Hill and dismount through the tunnels at Sidney Gardens, or you can return by train.

THE LEACH & COLN VALLEYS

Many Cotswold villages, content in their anonymity tucked away off the tourist trail, offer a quiet escape from hectic modern life and are attracting many new inhabitants from out of the cities. This pleasant ride meanders through villages such as these, crossing the gently rolling downs between the pretty Coln and Leach valleys. The route starts in the picturesque village of Coln St Aldwyns, with its ivy-clad cottages, which is pleasantly surrounded by pastureland and lies close to the hamlet of Hatherop.

1 The crossroads in the middle of Coln St Aldwyns is marked by a sturdy spreading chestnut tree. Begin the ride along the lane signed to Quenington and Fairford, which passes by The New Inn. On leaving the village, cycle over the River Coln and climb to a crossroads at the edge of Quenington village. Go left on to Fowlers Hill and then drop back into the valley, following the signs to Southrop and Lechlade as you bend past a junction to re-cross the River Coln. After a bit of a pull, the lane rises up over open downland and then follows the line of an ancient salt way for a little while. Pedal for a further 2.5 miles (4km), following signs for Southrop past some junctions, before losing height down to a 'Give Way' junction.

2 Go left, gaining height along a gentle fold in the rolling hillside. Stay with the main lane as it later turns to rise over the hill, winding down on the other side into Southrop. Carry on past the village hall and The Swan, the street slotted between high-kerbed pavements and now signed to Filkins.

3 After dropping away and crossing the second river that features on this journey, the Leach, turn off left to the villages of Fyfield and Eastleach. Keep cycling left again as the lane splits at Fyfield, following the gently rising valley all the way to Eastleach. There are two separately named halves to the village and the lane ends at a junction by the church in Eastleach Martin. Here, go left, and re-cross the Leach to enter the neighbouring parish, swinging left again beneath a massive willow tree, from which a track leads off to Eastleach Turville's church.

4 The main lane winds its way on past the village cross and then past a row of almshouses before it reaches a junction below The Victoria pub. Keep cycling straight ahead, the way signed 'Hatherop and Burford', climbing shortly to a second junction where you should go right in the direction of Burford and Westwell. Undulate onwards across open hills that are interspersed with sporadic clumps of copse. Stay to the left at successive turnings to curve above the higher reaches of the Leach valley. The signs you come across on this part of the route should now be directing you to the villages of Hatherop and Coln St Aldwyns.

5 For 1.25 miles (2km), the way follows the course of Akeman Street, a Roman road, passing a turn off signed to Dean Farm before breaking away from the line of the ancient thoroughfare into Hatherop village itself. When you reach a junction, take a right towards Coln St Aldwyns, winding down to leave the village past Hatherop School. From this point, it is then only a short ride back to the start point at Coln St Aldwyns.

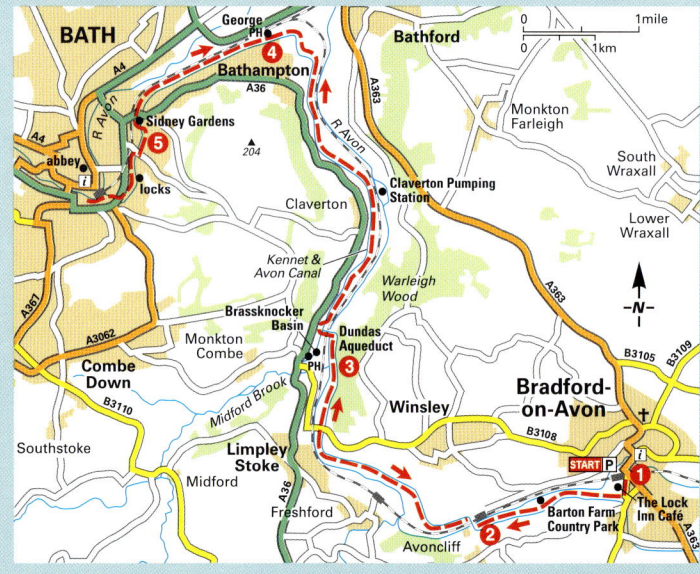

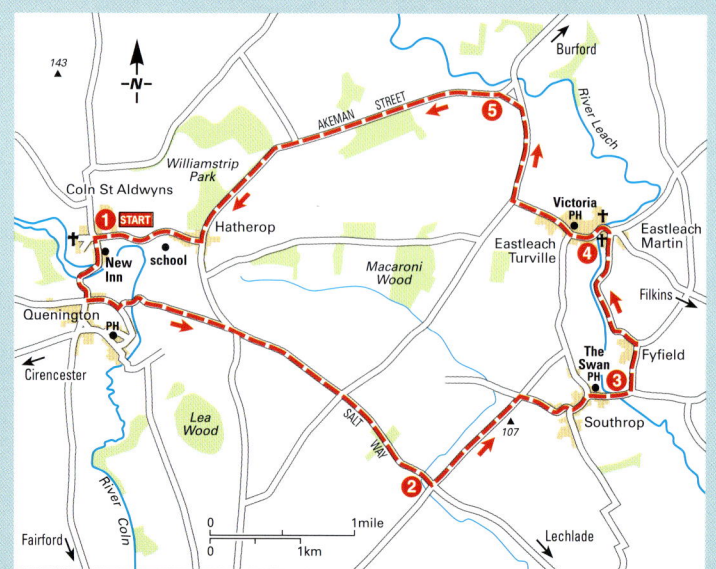

WALK 25

CORSHAM & CORSHAM PARK

This walk explores Corsham where 15th-century Flemish gabled cottages and baroque-pedimented 17th-century Hungerford Almshouses mix with larger Georgian residences. The walk continues through adjacent Corsham Park.

DISTANCE/TIME 4 miles (6.4km) 1h45 **MAP** OS Explorer 156 Chippenham & Bradford- on-Avon **START** Long-stay car park, Newlands Lane, Corsham; grid ref: ST 871704 **TRACKS** Field paths and country lanes, 10 stiles **THE PUB** The Flemish Weaver, Corsham. Tel: 01249 701929

1 Turn left out of the long-stay car park and then left again along Post Office Lane to reach the High Street. Turn left, and go past the tourist information centre and turn right into Church Street opposite The Flemish Weaver. Continue past the impressive entrance to Corsham Court and then enter St Bartholomew's churchyard.

2 Bear right across the churchyard, leaving through a gate and walk ahead to join the main path across Corsham Park. Turn left and walk along the south side of the park, passing Corsham Lake, to reach a stile and gate. Keep ahead to follow a fenced path beside a track to a kissing gate and then proceed across a field to a stile and lane.

3 Turn left, pass Park Farm, a splendid stone farmhouse on your left, and shortly take the waymarked footpath right along a drive to pass Rose and Unicorn House. At its end on the right, cross over a stile and follow the right-hand field edge to a stile, then bear half left to a stone stile in the field corner. Ignore the path arrowed to the right and head straight across the field to a further stile and metalled farm track.

4 Through a gap diagonally opposite, bear half left to a stone stile to the left of a cottage. Maintain the same direction across the next field and pass through a gap in the far left corner. Continue along the left-hand side of a field to a stile in the corner. Turn left along the lane for 0.5 mile (800m) to the A4.

5 Go through the gate in the wall on your left and walk along the centre of parkland pasture. Through a metal kissing gate, maintain your direction, gradually closing with the left boundary to reach another kissing gate on the edge of Mynte Wood. Follow the wide path to a further gate and bear half right to a stile.

6 Keep the same direction on a vague path across the parkland beyond, joining the far boundary and following it left to a kissing gate hidden in a thicket in the corner. Continue by the perimeter to a further gate in the next corner, where there are fine views right to Corsham Court. Follow the field edge as it bends right, but when it then curves right again, keep ahead to join the churchyard wall. Pass the stile over which you entered the park to another stile ahead.

7 Turn left down an avenue of trees to emerge on to Lacock Road, noting the stone almshouses opposite. Turn right, and then go right again along the High Street, which is pedestrianised. Turn left back along Post Office Lane to the car park.

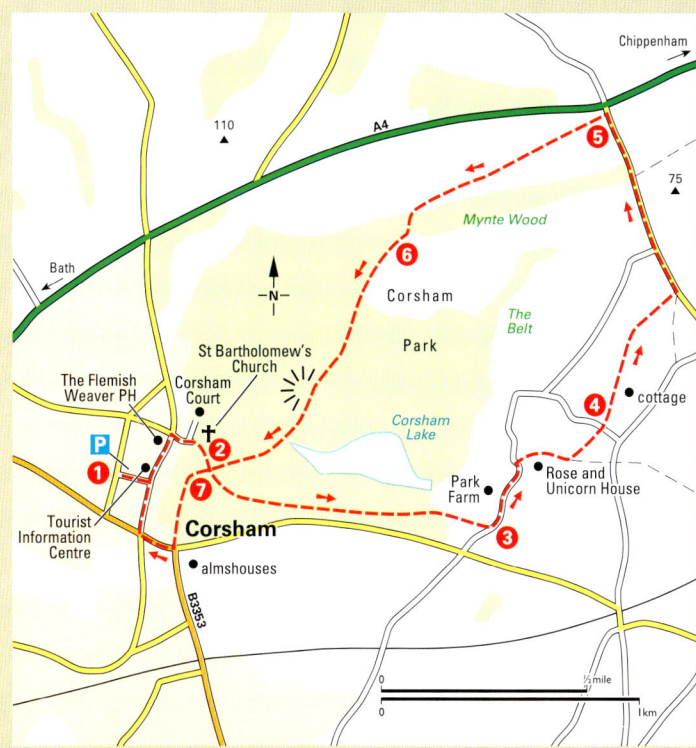

WALK 26

SEVERNSIDE AT ASHLEWORTH & HASFIELD

This is a fine walk along the banks of the River Severn, visiting a preserved tithe barn. The barn, and Ashleworth Court next to it, dates from the late 15th century.

DISTANCE/TIME 6.5 miles (10.5km) 2h45 **MAP** OS Explorer 179 Gloucester, Cheltenham & Stroud **START** Ashleworth Quay; limited parking on grass verges in the vicinity of the tithe barn; grid ref: SO 818251 **TRACKS** Tracks, fields, lanes and riverbank, 21 stiles **THE PUB** The Boat Inn, Ashleworth. Tel: 01452 700 272

1 From the tithe barn, walk along the lane towards the River Severn, passing The Boat Inn pub on your left-hand side.

2 Turn left to cross over a stile and follow the river bank. Follow it for just over 3 miles (4.8km). Views of Sandhurst Hill will come and go across the river, followed by sightings of The Red Lion pub, sadly also out of reach.

3 Eventually you will pass a house, Haw Farm. Immediately after it follow a track that swings away from the river and then pass several half-timbered houses. It becomes a lane and Haw Bridge appears before you.

4 Approaching the pub, where the lane splits, climb over a stile on the left into a field. Walk straight on, but then as the field opens up, bear half left to a gate in the far corner. Through it, go forward a few paces, turn right to cross a bridge and then continue straight on across two more fields.

5 Emerging on to a junction of lanes, cross to walk down the one opposite, signed Tirley Hill. After 30yds (27m), turn over a plank bridge and stile concealed in the hedge on the left. Cross the field, aiming for a gateway about half-way along the right-hand hedge. Maintain the same line in the next field, exiting through a gateway on to a lane.

6 Walk right and pass Great House Farm, staying with the lane as it later winds left up the hill. After passing two houses, cross left into a field. Head downhill to the far-right corner and rejoin the lane.

7 Turn left and continue into Hasfield, keeping left for Ashleworth. Hasfield Church is then signed off left opposite a telephone box, and if you go to have a look, return to the main lane. Carry on through the village, keeping left again at the next junction, still heading towards Ashleworth.

8 After 0.25 mile (400m), look for a waymarked track into a field on the right. Follow the perimeter track, but leave it over a stile on the left, after entering the second field. Continue parallel with the track in the adjacent enclosure. Keep forward past Colways Farm to a kissing gate on the right. Pass through and go left beside the hedge. In the next field, go diagonal to the far corner and, over a bridge there, bear half left across field. Over more stiles, cross a track and head towards a pylon, passing Stonebow Farm, lying over to the left. Carry on to a last stile and escape onto a lane. In the corner of the junction, diagonally left, return to the fields over yet another stile. Make for a gap in the far corner and keep ahead at the field edge, finally returning to the tithe barn.

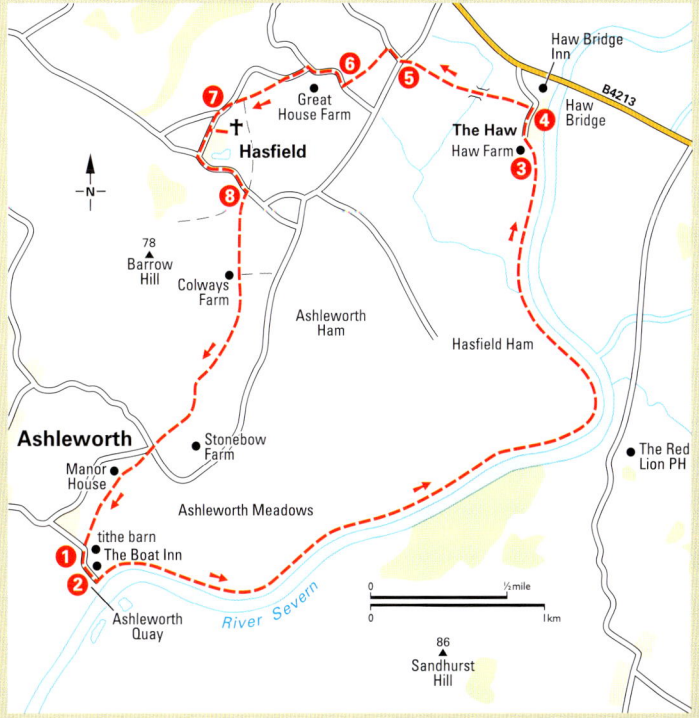

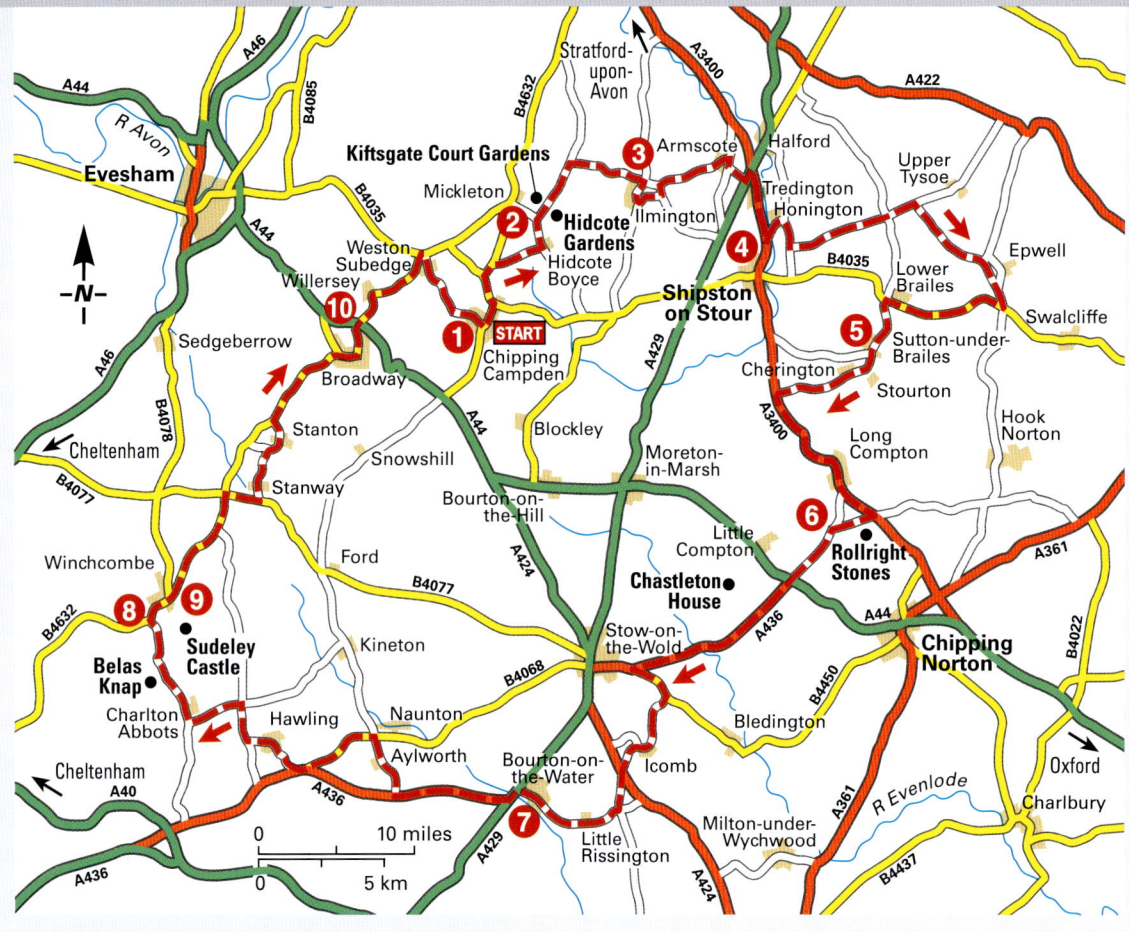

A TOUR OF THE NORTHERN COTSWOLDS

Starting from Chipping Campden, the finest of the Cotswold wool towns with a magnificent church and pretty houses, this superb circular car tour takes in many of the highlights of the northern Cotswolds as well as several worthy, though much less frequently visited, places in the area.

Route Directions

It's worth lingering for a while in Chipping Campden. For many, this town represents Cotswold charm at its best and it is possibly the one of the area's most attractive towns.

1 From the Market Hall on Chipping Campden's High Street head for Mickleton on the B4081, and turn right just after the end of the speed restrictions. Soon turn right again for Hidcote Boyce. At a crossroads turn left to Hidcote Bartrim, Mickleton and Hidcote Gardens. Follow signs for Hidcote Gardens and Kiftsgate Court Gardens.

Both Hidcote Gardens and Kiftsgate Court Gardens are well worth a visit.

2 Drive past Kiftsgate, signed for Quinton and Stratford, to reach a T-junction. Turn right and continue to Ilmington village which has a charming manor house and church.

3 Just after entering Ilmington turn right signed 'Chipping Campden', then left for Shipston, keeping left at the war memorial. Pass the Red Lion pub, continuing in the direction of Stratford. At the end of the

village turn right and drive to Armscote, where you pass the Fox and Goose, and turn right for Blackwell and Tredington. Soon, just after a thatched barn and a pond, turn left for Tredington. Continue to reach the A429 and turn left signed 'Stratford, Warwick'. At a roundabout take the third exit to join the A3400, signed 'Tredington, Oxford'.

In the porch floor of St John the Baptist Church in the village of Tredington are the fossilised remains of a prehistoric marine reptile similar to an ichthyosaurus.

4 After about a mile (1.6km) beyond Tredington turn left for Honington, through some pineapple-topped gates. Drive through Honington and then turn right at a junction for Barcheston. After a further 0.5 mile (800m) go left at a T-junction opposite farm buildings for St Dennis and Tysoe. Pass a crossroads for St Dennis Farm and continue for about a mile (1.6km) to reach another crossroads; go forward, signed 'Tysoe', and continue, to join another road at a corner. Turn right here and then fairly soon go left towards Compton Wynyates house, and Epwell. Follow the Epwell signs. Turn right

at a crossroads, and continue in the direction of Banbury and Sibfords. Continue to the B4035 and take a right turn, soon arriving at Lower Brailes. Drive past the George Hotel and then turn left, just after a school sign, into Sutton Lane for Stourton, Cherington and Long Compton.

The little village of unusually-named Sutton-under-Brailes has a pretty village green overlooked by cottages and houses.

5 Halfway through Sutton-under-Brailes turn left for Stourton, Cherington and Long Compton. Drive through Stourton, then Cherington and continue to follow signs for Long Compton until meeting the A3400. Turn left here and drive through Long Compton. Ignore the first sign for Little Rollright almost at the end of the village, but take the second turning, after about a mile (1.6km) on the right, for Little Rollright, to see the famous Rollright Stones.

These ancient standing stones consist of two stone circles and a monolith. They are believed to date from the Bronze Age.

6 Continue to the A44, turn right and then immediately left on to the A436, passing Chastleton House. Continue following signs for Stow then, after 4 miles (6.4km), turn left along the B4450 signed 'Bledington'. Keep going to cross a bridge and then immediately

turn right for Icomb. Turn right at Icomb war memorial and then left at a T-junction towards Little Rissington. Cross the A424 and continue for almost a mile (1.6km) to turn right at the crossroads. Drive through Little Rissington and then Bourton-on-the-Water.

7 Head for the A429, where you turn left. Soon fork right on to the A436 and after about 2 miles (3.2km), turn right for Aylworth. Continue through Aylworth to a crossroads, turning left on the B4068 towards Cheltenham. Join the A436 and then soon turn right following signs to Hawling and Winchcombe. Continue to Hawling and, some way past the church, turn right at a T-junction for Roel and Winchcombe. On reaching the crossroads at Roel turn left for Charlton Abbots. Continue for about 1.5 miles (2.4km) with some fine views along the way. Bypass Charlton Abbots and then at the next T-junction turn right for Winchcombe. Keep going towards Winchcombe, passing the Neolithic barrow Belas Knap, and Sudeley Castle down on the right.

There are good views from Belas Knap, one of the best-preserved Neolithic barrows in the UK. Sudeley Castle is also well worth a visit.

8 Eventually you come to the B4632 – turn right here to drive through Winchcombe, which was the capital of Saxon Mercia.

In Winchcombe look out for the Winchcombe Worthies, the carved gargoyles that embellish the façade of the little parish church.

9 Drive for 3 miles (4.8km) to a roundabout and take the 3rd exit on to the B4077, following signs for Stow. Continue for a mile (1.6km), then turn left at the war memorial for Stanton. Pass Stanway, then after about 1.5 miles (2.4km) turn right. Drive through Stanton, following signs to Broadway, to rejoin the B4632. Turn right here following the B4632 Stratford signs. Turn right, and then turn left through Broadway, continuing to follow the signs for the village centre.

Broadway's wide main street is lined with horse chestnut trees and a mixture of period houses and stone cottages.

10 In Broadway continue to the roundabout on the A44. Take the 2nd exit off the roundabout, still following the B4632 'Stratford' signs to Willersey. Drive through Willersey to a roundabout. Turn right here and continue towards Weston Subedge. Go through Weston Subedge and then turn right by the Seagrove Arms for Dover's Hill. Continue up Dover's Hill, with fine views, to a major crossroads, then go forward and down the hill to return to Chipping Campden and the start of the tour.

ALONG THE ROMANTIC ROAD

This drive, beginning and ending in the splendidly preserved Regency town of Cheltenham will take you through some delightful, but lesser-known areas of the Cotswolds as well as through pretty Burford and Cirencester. The route passes through some of the most beautiful villages in the Cotswolds, some of which, such as Bibury and Sheepscombe, inspired artists and authors alike.

Route Directions

Explore the heart of Cheltenham. This Regency town (it received the royal approval of George III) is renowed for its handsome terraces and its horse racing.

1 From Cheltenham take the A40 London road to pass through Charlton Kings, where author Lewis Carroll was inspired to write *Alice Through the Looking Glass*, and then pass by Dowdeswell Reservoir, the largest stretch of water in Gloucestershire. Shortly afterwards, turn right to Dowdeswell, to climb fairly steeply up the Cotswold escarpment. Follow this country lane, crossing three sets of crossroads, towards Withington. Go through the village, pass the Mill Inn and continue until a sign indicates Chedworth Villa and Yanworth. Follow a narrow country lane around the solitary manor farmhouse and gallery of Compton Cassey, until the road breaks off for the Roman villa.

The remains of Chedworth Villa, excavated in 1864, considered to be the finest in the country, are set in a pretty wooded combe. There are fine 4th-century mosaics, two bathhouses, a hypocaust (underfloor heating system) and a good museum.

2 After visiting the villa, pass through Yanworth village and head onwards for Northleach. Drive through the Market Place, turn right into the High Street and soon after make a left turn. At the next T-junction, turn right to go towards Farmington. Drive through Farmington village and then follow the lanes along the delightfully named Windrush Valley and its quiet villages of Sherborne (Sherborne House is said to be haunted) and Windrush. Turn right towards Little Barrington.

With its picture-postcard post office and large village green, Little Barrington is situated at the heart of stone-producing country and was once the home of Thomas Strong, who was the master mason for St Paul's Cathedral.

3 Pass through Little Barrington, continue to the A40 and turn left. Bypass Burford by continuing across a roundabout and then, after about a mile (1.6km), turn sharp left and then make a right turn for Widford and then for Swinbrook.

Swinbrook is a pretty village associated with the five Mitford sisters, two of whom are buried in the churchyard.

4 Leave Swinbrook and then fork left for Fulbrook. Proceed along a single-track road to a reach a junction with A361, turn left and left again at a mini-roundabout to cross a medieval bridge into Burford.

Burford, one of the loveliest of Cotswold villages, slopes down to the Windrush and has a plethora of shops, inns and delightful houses. The High Street runs down to a narrow three-arched bridge over the River Windrush. Take a leisurely stroll through the town and you'll stumble across a host of historic treasures – especially in the little side streets that run off the High Street. For example the Great House in Witney Street, built around 1690, and the Doll's House (1939). Situated just south of the town is the popular Cotswold Wildlife Park.

5 Drive up the main street to a roundabout on the A40 and go straight across on the A361 in the direction of Lechlade. Continue for 4 miles (6.4km) then bear left to Filkins.

Visit the nearby village of Filkins, home to the Swinford Museum, which depicts west Oxfordshire's fascinating rural heritage.

6 At the far end of the village, rejoin the A361 to Lechlade. From Lechlade bear right on the A417 towards Fairford.

Fairford is known for its large RAF base. The village church contains the finest set of medieval stained glass in England.

7 Cross over the river and turn right for Quenington and on to Coln St Aldwyns. Pass the New Inn on the right and, at the end of the village, go straight over the staggered crossroads, signed 'Bibury', and shortly turn left down Salt Way.

Bibury was famously described by artist and designer William Morris as 'the most beautiful village in the Cotswolds'.

8 From Bibury, take the B4425 and continue on, passing through Barnsley.

9 Continue to drive straight ahead until you reach one of the principal towns in the Cotswolds, Cirencester.

In Roman times, this town was second in importance only to London. You could easily spend a day here exploring the church, Corinium Museum and pleasant shops and cafés. Market days are Monday and Friday.

10 Take the A419 towards Stroud, looking for a small road on the right in the direction of Sapperton after driving for about 3 miles (4.8km). Follow this road to the Daneway pub, near the entrance to the Thames and Severn Canal Tunnel. From here take the road, on a corner on the left, which climbs up towards Bisley. To get there fork left, then right and follow the road through Waterlane until you come to a crossroads at a main road just outside Bisley. Cross carefully and go down to the main thoroughfare of this handsome village. Turn right, then left opposite the post office. Pass the Bear Inn and, at Stancombe Farm, turn right towards The Camp and Birdlip. Immediately after The Camp take the left turn at an electricity generator, in the direction of Sheepscombe.

11 Cross the B4070 then fork right for the village, passing the village hall and pub. Keep on this narrow road until you reach the A46, where you turn left for Painswick.

Known as the 'Queen of the Cotswolds', Painswick slopes down to Painswick Brook where you can see the old textile mills.

12 From Painswick, you return along the A46 heading towards Cheltenham. Continue through several miles of beech woodland, passing by Prinknash Abbey on the left, and Cooper's Hill on the right.

Cooper's Hill is the scene of the dangerous annual Whitsun cheese-rolling event, which probably dates from the 16th century.

13 Descend to the vale, and continue to drive, via a roundabout, through the village of Shurdington, back to Cheltenham.

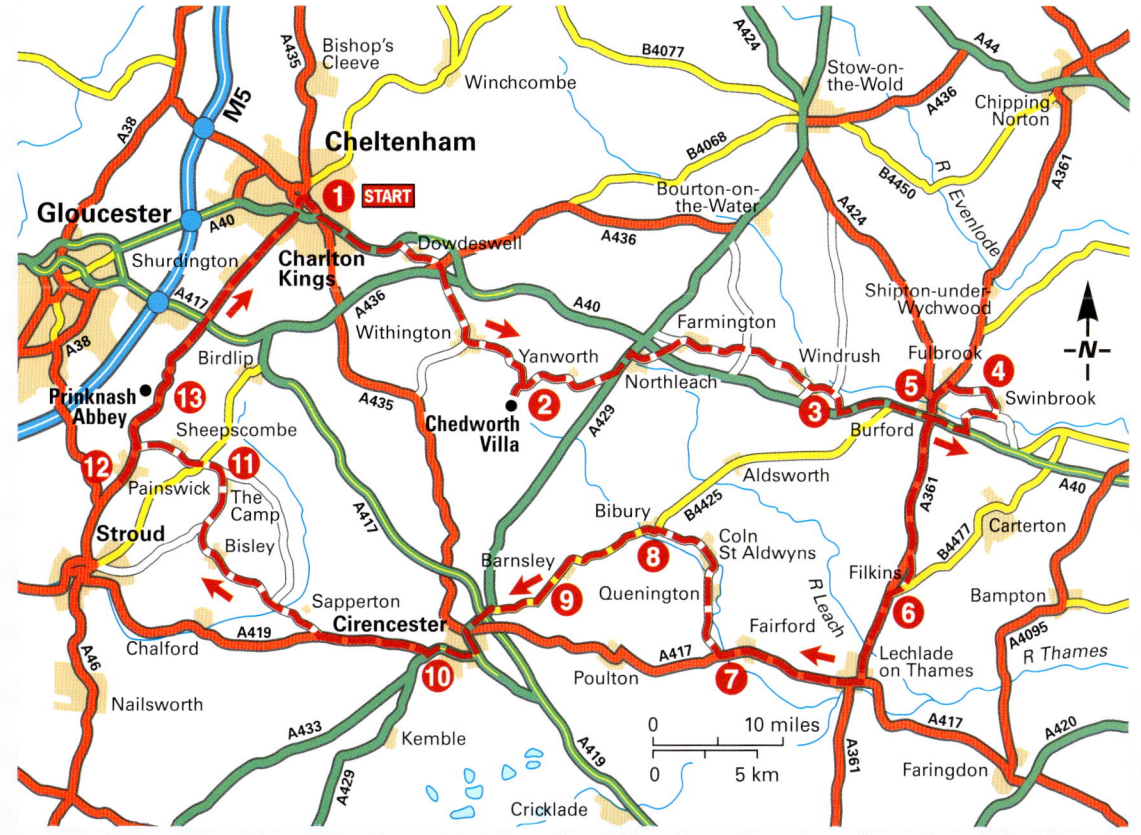

WALK 27

PAINSWICK & WASHPOOL VALLEY

This is an enjoyable walk from Painswick through the Washpool Valley.

1 Leave the car park right along the main street. Turn left into Gloucester Street, the B4073, keeping ahead. After 0.25 mile (400m), go right on to Golf Course Road, then bear left through a car park, and left on a track, signed 'Cotswold Way and Painswick Beacon'. Fork right on to a path continuing ahead across the golf course and a lane.

2 Pass left of a cemetery then cross a fairway to a wood. Carry on and join a quarry track to a lane. Go left, then right, climbing at the left edge of the golf course. Descending beyond Painswick Hill, take a path, then a track left to regain the B4073.

3 Turn right, then bear left along a path through trees. Emerge on to a lane bend, and go sharp left on a waymarked track. Keep ahead to Spoonbed Farm, pass the house to a gate and on to a field track. In the second field, by a large ash, cross into and continue in the next field. Over a stile in the corner, go through a plantation and past a power-cable post in the next field. Leave at the corner by Upper Holcombe Farm to a lane.

4 Turn left, pass Holcombe House and go to a sharp bend at Holcombe Farm. Leave on a track ahead. After it swings right, mount a stile by a gate on the left and follow the left boundary. In the next field go right to a stile in the hedge, then follow a path downhill. Over a bridge, take the right path. Climb to a field to continue up its left edge.

5 Emerging at the top corner, walk out to a track, and follow it left to Edge Farm. Approaching the yard gate, bear right to a gate. Cross a meadow to another gate, continuing at the edge of the next field to Parkhurst Farm. Keep ahead past cottages, joining a track to a lane. Turn up the hill. After 250yds (230m) opposite a house, go over a stile (left). Bear half-right across to another stile, where a path leads into Edge.

6 Turn left, then right, past the village hall to Edge Hill Farm. Before the farmhouse, go over a stile on the left. Go left to a second stile and follow the left hedge downfield. Across a bridge, climb ahead, over successive stiles, to a gate. Cross a track to a second gate and swing left, leaving the field corner on to Jenkin's Lane. A few paces left, bear off right on a track into a field. Keep ahead from field to field and a track finally leads you past houses to a lane by Wragg Castle Farm.

7 Walk down to the busy main road, crossing with care to Pincot Lane opposite. Follow it for 0.25 mile (400m) down to Painswick Stream and up the hill to a group of cottages. Over a stile on the left, strike out across a field, to Sheephouses. Leave along the main drive, then bear left where it forks. Through a gate on the right, cross the mill-pond dam and follow the stream then along a path to emerge on to a lane. Go left and keep ahead as it climbs for 0.33 mile (500m) back into Painswick.

DISTANCE/TIME 7.25 miles (11.7km) 3h45 **MAP** OS Explorer 179 Gloucester, Cheltenham & Stroud **START** Car park (pay and display) near library, just off main road, in Painswick; grid ref: SO 865095 **TRACKS** Fields and tracks, golf course and a green lane, 29 stiles

THE PUB The Falcon Inn, Painswick. Tel: 01452 814222; www.falconinn.com

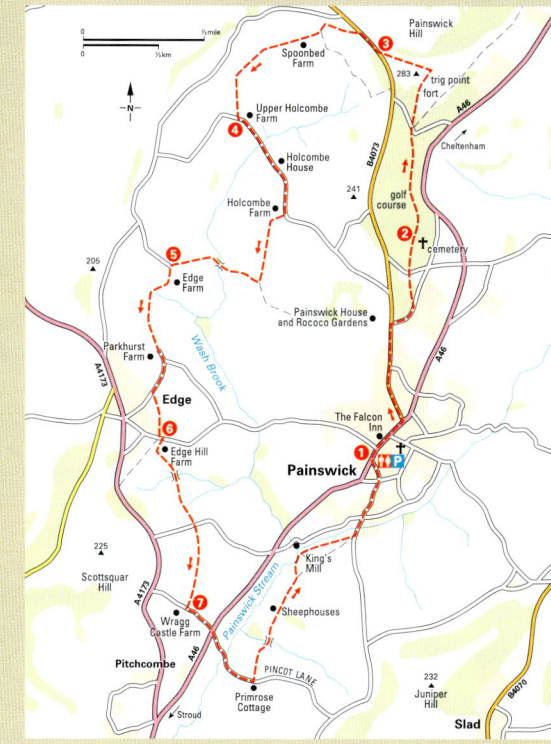

WALK 28

WINCHCOMBE & SUDELEY CASTLE

A rewarding walk above the thriving Cotswold village of Winchcombe with its fine 'wool church', financed through income from the medieval wool trade. Sudeley Castle chapel is the burial place of Henry VIII's sixth queen, Catherine Parr.

1 Leave the long-stay car park behind the library by a pedestrian access at its far-left corner and then turn right along Cowl Lane into the town centre. Turn left on to High Street and then go right in front of The White Hart Inn, Castle Street. Soon after crossing a bridge at the bottom, turn left beside Briar Cottage along a narrow alley to a field behind. Strike half right across a meadow, which still bears ridges and furrows, the remnants of medieval ploughing methods.

2 Emerging on to a lane, turn right. At the end of a high stone wall on your right, turn into a field on the left and stride out half right to a gap, about two-thirds of the way along the right-hand hedge. Over a bridge and stile, bear left to another stile by a gate. Maintain your diagonal course through a break in the middle of the right-hand hedge until you reach a protruding corner and then turn with the fence up the hill to a stile in the overgrown corner.

3 Now climbing more steeply up Dunn's Hill, strike a bee-line across the curve of the left-hand fence to a stile beside a gate at the top of the field. Carry on up by the fence and into the next field then bear half right to a stile in the top corner. Keep ahead over more stiles, until the fence on your left turns away.

4 At that point, swing right down the hill to a stile beside a gate, about half-way along the boundary. A field track leads past a small building protected within a fenced enclosure, marking St Kenelm's Well.

5 Passing into the next field, leave the track, bearing right to cross the field to a stile and gate, two-thirds of the way down the opposite hedge. Keep downhill, aiming left of Sudeley Hill Farm at the bottom to emerge at a road. Turn left and then go right along a lane that is signed to Sudeley Lodge Parks Farm.

6 Opposite a cottage, leave right on a footpath falling at the edge of a field. Over a stile, turn right and then left to remain within the field, but leave at the bottom corner. Go forward to a stile on the right and, guided by obvious waymarkers, walk half left, eventually joining a fence to pass Sudeley Castle, which is on the right.

7 Passing through two kissing gates into the park, go along a path to the main drive. Cross to a gate beyond the lawn opposite and bear half right over open grazing, later crossing another track to leave through a kissing gate in the farthest corner. Back in Castle Street, turn left and retrace your outward steps past The White Hart Inn to the car park.

DISTANCE/TIME 3.75 miles (6km) 2h **MAP** OS Explorer OL45 The Cotswolds **START** Long stay car park on Back Lane, Winchcombe; grid ref: SP 023284 **TRACKS** Fields and lanes, 13 stiles

THE PUB The White Hart Inn, Winchcombe. Tel: 01242 602 359

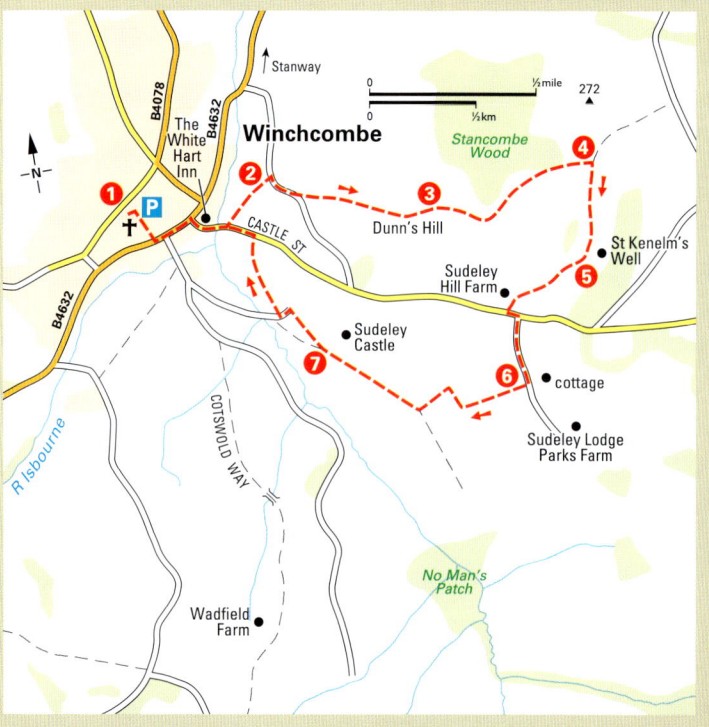

Forest of Dean

CLOCKWISE FROM RIGHT: RIVER WYE, SYMONDS YAT; BLUEBELLS IN THE FOREST OF DEAN

COLEFORD MAP REF 403 G7

The small market town of Coleford, one of the oldest existing communities in the Forest of Dean, lies some 4 miles (7km) east of the Welsh border, close to the Wye Valley. Coleford takes its name from one of the two rivers that merge in its centre, at what was once a busy fording point.

The town's buildings are mainly Georgian in appearance, although many of the façades cover much older buildings. The tang of coaching days lingers in the large arched entrance to 'The Angel' pub, while the free-standing Clock Tower was formerly attached to an attractive octagonal church, demolished when it was considered too small for the local population; only the tower was left intact. The town also has an interesting octagonal church which was built in 1821.

Today, the town's excellent location at the heart of the Forest, makes it hugely popular with canoeists, walkers and cyclists. Coleford is a thriving community and administrative centre of the Forest of Dean, one of the most distinctive areas of Britain. The beautiful region has a persuasive charm and character that is unique. The magnificent landscapes and stunning scenery have inspired artists, craftspeople, inventors, poets and playwrights alike. This ancient royal forest of oak and beech covers an area of about 26,000 acres (10,500ha) between the Severn and Wye. It became a National Forest Park in 1938. Forest residents (known as 'commoners') retain their ancient feudal rights of sheep pasturage and hold their Verderers' Court, something of a judicial anachronism, at Speech House in Coleford. It became the place one went to talk or to make a speech, hence the name. Today it is a hotel.

The town has a rich history, first recorded as Colevorde in 1275 when it was part of the royal hunting forest. It was in Coleford in the 1800s that the process of making steel was invented, at a furnace built by David Mushet senior.

GOODRICH MAP REF 403 G7

Sitting on a neck of land where the River Wye loops around wooded Coppet Hill, Goodrich is particularly famed for its castle, today a romantic ruin built in the 13th century to a square design, with large rounded towers at the corners.

Goodrich stands majestically on a wooded hill commanding the Wye at the point where it enters the valley of Symonds Yat. Work on the castle started in the late 11th century, by the English thegn, Godric, who gave it his name. Later, the splendid square keep which still forms the core you see today, was added, probably in the time of the Earl of Pembroke and Lord of Goodrich (1148–76).

During the Civil War, Goodrich was held by both sides. The Royalists eventually surrendered in 1646 when threatened with undermining and bombardment by a huge Parliamentarian mortar, the famous 'Roaring Meg', the only surviving Civil War mortar in Britain, now returned to the castle after more than 350 years.

LYDNEY MAP REF 399 J2

There are records of a community in this area and on this site since Roman times. Not surprising since its position is ideal for a market town to flourish in, being between the Forest of Dean and the wide River Severn. Nowadays the busy town covers an area just under 9 square miles (23sq km) and is bordered by the A48 road, which joins Gloucester to Chepstow, and is on the Gloucester to Cardiff rail route. The town is known also as the terminus of the Forest of Dean Railway, which runs between Lydney and Norchard.

The town also stretches to Lydney harbour and docks, which have been the subject of a regeneration scheme and are being restored to their former working glory. Built by the Romans, the harbour's importance grew as it was vital for transporting the iron ore being mined in the Forest of Dean. The town became a centre of trading and the harbour's ability to take sea-going ships made it ever more popular and useful. As a consequence of this, nearby Porlock canal was built to take the cargo further inland, providing an efficient way of moving iron ore and coal as the roads at that time were poor.

Lydney is also known for Lydney Park, situated just west of the town itself. which has some Roman ruins within the estate grounds. The house was originally the home of Sir William Wintour, who was Admiral to the Fleet during the reign of Queen Elizabeth I in 1588. Many of the ships that went to battle with the Spanish Armada were built at Lydney using timber felled from the nearby Forest of Dean.

The Roman remains at Lydney Park include a temple thought to be dedicated to a Celtic god, and the structure itself seems to resemble a shrine or maybe even a healing place.

SYMONDS YAT MAP REF 403 G7

The wonder with Symonds Yat Rock, an internationally renowned viewpoint and the site of an Iron Age hill fort, is that it simply doesn't crumble under the weight of the thousands of enthralled visitors that scramble over it each year. The cliffs are populated by peregrine falcon that soar above the Wye valley below, and the viewpoint is a perfect place from which to watch and photograph them. Elsewhere fallow deer are often glimpsed in the surrounding woodlands, usually in the early morning or dusk; badgers and foxes are plentiful, too. Otters have been spotted on stretches of the River Wye.

Peregrines have made thier homes in the limestone cliffs of Coldwell Rocks for two decades or more, and the many

TINTERN ABBEY

parts of South Wales, etc. relative chiefly to *Picturesque Beauty; made in the summer of the year 1770.* It was (and is) a classic book, and an inspiration to the country's early tourists.

Today you can enjoy the Wye Valley for its unrivalled scenery, which is at its best when the colours are lush green in spring or mellow red and gold in autumn. Today the valley and the area around Symonds Yat is a delight to be discovered on foot, by canoe or by bicycle.

TINTERN ABBEY MAP REF 399 J2

Founded by Walter de Clare, Lord of Chepstow, in 1131, Tintern Abbey is on the River Wye in Monmouthshire, only the second Cistercian foundation in Britain, and the first in Wales. The abbey almost entirely rebuilt and enlarged between 1220 and 1287, and the building finally completed, except for minor additions, in the early 14th century. The abbey was dissolved in 1537, and its property granted to the then Lord of Chepstow. Although the cruciform church is today without its roof (it was plundered for its lead very soon after the Dissolution) and the nave is damaged, many vital details of a style transitional from Early English to Decorated Gothic are preserved.

The remains of Tintern we see today, are a mish-mash of building endeavour spanning the 400-year period between 1136 and 1536. Little remains of the original buildings, and much of what was built later was demolished in 1537 during the Dissolution of the Monasteries, although a few sections of walling were embraced into later buildings. However, the two recessed cupboards on the east side of the cloisters date from this time.

Immortalised by William Wordsworth in his poem 'Tintern Abbey', this is one of the most spectacular ruins in Britain and not only inspired Wordsworth but more than one painting by Turner, and a poem by a less well-known contemporary of Wordsworth, Edmund Gardner. In his poem, more fully titled 'Lines composed a few miles above Tintern Abbey, on revisiting the banks of the Wye during a tour in July 13, 1798', Wordsworth perfectly sets the scene, one of

steep and lofty cliffs,
That on a wild secluded scene impress
Thoughts of more deep seclusion; and connect
The landscape with the quiet of the sky.

In time Tintern Abbey established two daughter houses, Kingswood in Gloucester (1139) and Tintern Parva, which is situated west of Wexford in the southeast of Ireland (1203). The Cistercians were clearly one of the most progressive and successful orders in both the 12th and 13th centuries.

crevices in the rock face are equally desirable nesting sites for ravens and jackdaws. Other birds of prey – goshawks and buzzards – are also often present. On a warm summer's evening, grass snakes and adders can sometimes be spotted basking in the sunlit clearings. Dragonflies and damselflies (including white-legged damselflies) frequent the banks of the River Wye, while the exquisite holly blue butterflies and

the hummingbird hawkmoth are often found around the viewing point. Not surprisingly, Symonds Yat Rock is a Site of Special Scientific Interest, and because of its European importance it has the status of a Special Area of Conservation, too. What underscores this important designation is the rare lime and yew woodland.

With so much natural interest, it is no wonder the Wye Valley is an Area of Outstanding Natural Beauty. In the

18th century the river was used to ferry goods from Chepstow to Hereford, an activity that generated a number of boat-building yards along the route. The Valley also became popular at this time, when poets, artists and well-to-do gentlemen of leisure came to follow the 'Wye Tour' a high priority in their pursuit of the picturesque. Cleric William Gilpin was among these, and in 1782 he published *Observations on the River Wye and several*

Bath

CLOCKWISE FROM RIGHT:
ROYAL CRESCENT; ROMAN BATHS

BATH MAP REF 399 K3

One of the most magnificent towns in Europe, Bath is known chiefly for its Roman baths and for its elegant Georgian architecture, the result of its fashionable re-emergence as a spa in the 18th century. Although not strictly speaking a Cotswold town, Bath is nonetheless inseparable from the area, not least because its buildings are made of Cotswold limestone. Archaeological evidence indicates that the first settlement here, Aquae Sulis, was Roman. Later, an important Saxon abbey was built here, and then later still, a Norman cathedral. The famous waters continued to be used, but it was not until the 17th century that the fashion for medicinal waters led to new building under the sponsorship of Master of Ceremonies, Richard 'Beau' Nash, architect John Wood and, later, City Surveyor, Thomas Baldwin.

The town is dramatically situated over the surrounding hills, presenting a magnificent aspect. There is a great deal to see in Bath but you can enjoy many of the highlights on foot. Since parking can be a problem, use the park-and-ride system. The bus from the Lansdown car park sets you down at Queen's Square, which is a good place to start walking.

The centre of Bath can be divided into four – the oldest part is the city centre around the abbey and baths, the Upper Town was built as the town expanded, while Kingsmead is the liveliest area at night. Bathwick and Widcombe are west of the Pulteney Bridge. The following walk takes in part of the first three areas; places not featured are described afterwards. Queen Square was John Wood's first important work and takes its name from Queen Caroline, consort of George II. The obelisk in the centre was built to honour the visit of the Prince and Princess of Wales in 1738. Wood's masterpiece, the Circus, begun in 1754, is at the top of Gay Street, which runs north along the east side of Queen Square and passes the Jane Austen Centre on the right. The Circus is a design of great originality, the façade of each of the three floors is framed in a series of columns, from bottom to top, Doric, Ionic and Corinthian.

From here it is a stroll west along Brock Street to another magnificent ensemble, the Royal Crescent, begun by John Wood's son in 1767. Number 1, which is open to the public, has been restored to look as it would have done some 200 years ago. A longer walk would take you further north to a number of other crescents, those of Somerset Place, Camden, Cavendish and Lansdown. Behind Lansdown Crescent is Beckford's Walk, replete with the splendid follies placed there by the eccentric millionaire William Beckford. Gravel Walk, opposite No 1 Royal Crescent, threads through parkland and shortly turns left, past the Georgian Garden, to Queen's

Parade Place. Turn left, then left again to re-enter Gay Street and then turn right into George Street and right again into Milsom Street. Continue into Burton Street as it becomes Union Street and turn left into Northumberland Place. Pass through this little alley of shops to the High Street and cross over to the Guildhall.

Beyond the Guildhall is the covered market. On the far side of the market is Grand Parade and the River Avon and to the left the magnificence of Pulteney Bridge, designed by Robert Adam in 1769. On the other side of the bridge is a marvellous vista down Great Pulteney Street towards the Holburne Museum and steps down to the riverside walk.

Turning right along Grand Parade will bring you to Orange Grove. Pass the east end of the abbey and continue down Terrace Walk. By the Huntsman Inn, turn right down North Parade Passage to Sally Lunn's House, built in 1622 and one of the oldest houses in Bath. Here Sally Lunn created her famous Bath buns and the original faggot oven and period kitchenware are still exhibited. Although it is still a coffee house, it is also a museum and the medieval and Roman excavations are the largest on show in Bath.

North Parade Passage emerges at Abbey Green. Turn right here for the abbey itself, the third to be built on this site. The first was built in the 8th century by Offa, King of Mercia. The 12th-century

Norman abbey fell into disrepair and was replaced by this smaller version. Inside, after passing a manned desk where 'voluntary' payment is expected, there is much to admire – its magnificent ceiling and windows, and array of plaques. The Heritage Vaults tell the story of the abbey and include some detailed Saxon and Norman stonework and a reconstruction of the Norman cathedral.

In the courtyard, a favourite place with buskers and other performers, the National Trust shop is in Marshall Wade's House, the oldest Palladian-style building in Bath. Opposite are the Roman baths, the best-preserved Roman religious spa from the ancient world. The remains of a temple can be seen here, as well as objects discovered in the area of the baths over the centuries. Next door are the elegant Pump Rooms, which are a great venue for a coffee, lunch or even a glass of the fairly unpleasant-tasting mineral water – and all can be taken accompanied by period music played by the Pump Rooms Trio. The atmosphere is extremely civilised.

From Abbey Church Yard turn left into Stall Street, then right along Bath Street to Cross Bath, a delightful example of Bath's former hot mineral water sources, housed in an 18th-century building and with the Thermae Bath Spa to the left. Beyond, on the right of Cross Bath, is the entrance to St John's Hospital, a medieval foundation, still offering sheltered housing.

Take the wide pavement further to the right of Cross Bath, turning left by Chandos Buildings, and continue past the back of the Hospital to the road and Westgate Buildings. Turn right until you reach Sawclose to the right. Before continuing up there have a look at Kingsmead Square on the left, where Rosewell House is a rare example of the baroque style in this Georgian city. Continue up Sawclose where the Theatre Royal, opened in 1805, is on the left. Next door is the former home of Beau Nash. Cross the road to enjoy a good view of the theatre and then turn right down Upper Borough Walls.

Along Upper Borough Walls are the remnants of the medieval city wall opposite the Royal National Hospital for Rheumatic Diseases. After the wall turn left down a narrow lane and then left into Trim Street, where General Wolfe's former residence is marked with a memorial plaque. Turn right through Trim Bridge arch to Queen Street and then left by the junction with Quiet Street into Wood Street, which will bring you back to Queen Square.

Bath has many unusual museum collections. In Upper Town the Assembly Rooms, on Bennett Street, were built to complement the Pump Room. In the basement you'll find the Museum of Costume, which covers the history of clothes from the 16th century to the present day. Close by, at Circus Lodge, is the Museum of East Asian Art covering 7,000 years of history to include exhibits of jade, bamboo and lacquer.

On the Paragon, in the Countess of Huntingdon's Chapel, you'll find the Building of Bath Museum, which shows how the city was created. Not far from the Assembly Rooms, in Julian Road, is the Museum of Bath at Work, which tells the story of the city's trades and industries.

The Victoria Art Gallery is on Bath Street. It has important paintings by British and European Masters, as well as fascinating scenes of early Bath life. There are also collections of porcelain, watches and other decorative items.

The Holburne Museum of Art, in a Palladian villa, is home to the city's finest collections, particularly silverware, porcelain, furniture and paintings. These treasures are displayed along with examples of 20th-century art and crafts. Among the interesting places in the area is Beckford's Tower, standing on the summit of Lansdown. It was built in 1825 to house part of William Beckford's art collection and now holds a museum devoted to his life. Two miles (3.2km) southeast of Bath, the American Museum at Claverton Manor, a fine 19th-century house, illustrates typical American life from the 17th to 19th centuries.

BATH SPA

CORNWALL

■ TOURIST INFORMATION

Bodmin
Shire Hall, Mount Folly. Tel: 01208 76616;
www.bodminlive.com

Bude
The Crescent Car Park.
Tel: 01288 354240; www.visitbude.info

Falmouth
11 Market Strand, Prince of Wales Pier.
Tel: 01326 312300

Fowey
The Ticket Shop, Post Office, 4 Custom
House Hill. Tel: 01726 833616

Isles of Scilly
Hugh Town, St Mary's. Tel: 01720 422536;
www.simplyscilly.co.uk

Liskeard
Foresters Hall, Pike Street.
Tel: 01579 349148; www.liskeard.gov.uk

Looe
The Guildhall, Fore St, East Looe.
Tel: 01503 262072

Mevagissey
St Georges Square. Tel: 01726 844857;
www.mevagissey-cornwall.co.uk

Newquay
Municipal Buildings, Marcus Hill.
Tel: 01637 854020; www.newquay.org.uk

Padstow
North Quay. Tel: 01841 533449

Penzance
Station Road. Tel: 01736 362207

St Ives
The Guildhall, Street-an-Pol.
Tel: 01736 796297

Truro
Municipal Buildings, Boscawen Street.
Tel: 01872 274555; www.truro.gov.uk

■ PLACES OF INTEREST

**Barbara Hepworth Museum
& Sculpture Garden**
Barnoon Hill, St Ives. Tel: 01736 796226;
www.tate.org.uk

Bude-Stratton Museum
Lower Wharf, Bude. Tel: 01288 353576

Eden Project
Bodelva, St Austell. Tel: 01726 811911;
www.edenproject.com

Falmouth Art Gallery
Municipal Buildings, The Moor.
Tel: 01326 313863;
www.falmouthartgallery.com. Free.

Fowey Museum
Town Hall, Trafalgar Square, Fowey.

King Arthur's Great Halls
Fore Street, Tintagel. Tel: 01840 770526;
www.kingarthursgreathall.com

Lost Gardens of Heligan
Pentewan, near Mevagissey.
Tel: 01726 845100; www.heligan.com

Marazion Town Museum
Town Hall, The Square.

Mevagissey Aquarium
South Quay. Tel: 01726 843305

Minack Theatre & Exhibition Centre
Porthcurno. Tel: 01736 810181;
www.minack.com

Minions Heritage Centre
Minions. Tel: 01579 362350

**Mousehole Wild Bird Hospital
& Sanctuary**
Raginnis Hill. Tel: 01736 731386;
www.mouseholebirdhospital.org.uk

National Maritime Museum Cornwall
Discovery Quay, Falmouth.
Tel: 01326 313388; www.nmmc.co.uk

Newlyn Art Gallery
New Road, Newlyn, Penzance.
Tel: 01736 363715;
www.newlynartgallery.co.uk

Old Guildhall Museum
Higher Market Street, East Looe.
Tel: 01503 263709

Pendennis Castle
Falmouth. Tel: 01326 316594

Porthcurno Telegraph Museum
Porthcurno. Tel: 01736 810966;
www.porthcurno.org.uk

St Ives Museum
Wheal Dream. Tel: 01736 796005

St Michael's Mount
Marazion. Tel: 01736 710265;
www.stmichaelsmount.co.uk

Southeast Cornwall Discovery Centre
Millpool, West Looe. Tel: 01503 262777

Tate St Ives
Porthmeor, St Ives. Tel: 01736 796226;
www.tate.org.uk

Tintagel Castle
Tel: 01840 770328

Trelissick Garden
Feock, near Truro. Tel: 01872 862090

Tresco, Isles of Scilly
Abbey Garden and Valhalla.
Tel: 01720 424105; www.tresco.co.uk

■ FOR CHILDREN

Newquay Zoo
Trenance Leisure Park, Newquay.
Tel: 01637 873342;
www.newquayzoo.org.uk

World of Model Railways
Meadow Street, Mevagissey.
Tel: 01726 842457;
www.model-railway.co.uk

■ SPORTS & ACTIVITIES
ANGLING

Coarse fishing
Argal Reservoir, Penryn, Falmouth.
Tel: 01837 871565
Porth Reservoir, near Newquay.
Tel: 01637 877959
South West Lakes Trust.
Tel: 01566 771930
Tamar Lakes Water Park, near Bude.
Permit required. Tel: 01409 211514

Fly fishing
East and West Looe rivers. Permits from
Looe sub Post Office. Tel: 01503 262110

Siblyback Watersports Centre.
Fishing permits available on site.
Tel: 01579 342366

Sea fishing
Day and half-day trips from Fowey, Looe
and Polruan. Shark-fishing from Looe.
Tel: 01503 264355;
www.looechandlery.co.uk
Mevagissey Shark & Angling Centre.
Tel: 01726 843430
National Boatmen's Association,
Newquay. Tel: 01637 876352
Various trips from Padstow harbour;
enquire locally.

BOAT TRIPS

Bude
Rowing boats and canoes for hire at
Bude Canal.

Falmouth
Prince of Wales Pier. Regular passenger
ferries to St Mawes and Flushing.
River cruises to Roseland Peninsula
and Truro.

Fowey
River cruises and motor boat hire.
Fowey Tourist Information Centre
has more details.

Looe
Sea cruises from harbour.

Padstow
Pleasure trips available from the harbour.

Isles of Scilly
Steamship Company. Day trips to
Isles of Scilly. Tel: 0845 710 5555;
www.ios-travel.co.uk

St Ives
Sea cruises from the harbour.

Truro
River trips from Town Quay or Malpas
to Falmouth. Enterprise Boats.
Tel: 01326 374241/ 313234;
www.enterprise-boats.co.uk

CYCLE HIRE

Bodmin
Bodmin Cycle Hire, Bodmin and Wenford
Railway station. Tel: 01208 73555

Bude
North Coast Cycles, 2 Summerleaze
Avenue. Tel: 01288 352974

Liskeard
Liskeard Cycles, Pig Meadow Lane.
Tel: 01579 347696

Looe
Looe Mountain Bike Hire.
Tel: 01503 263871

Mevagissey
Pentewan Valley Cycle Hire, 1 West End,
Pentewan. Tel: 01726 844242;
www.pentewanvalleycyclehire.co.uk

Mullion
Atlantic Forge. Tel: 01326 240294

Newquay
Cycle Revolution, 7 Beach Road.
Tel: 01637 872634

Padstow
Padstow Cycle Hire Ltd, South Quay.

Tel: 01841 533533;
www.padstowcyclehire.com

Penzance
The Cycle Centre, New Street.
Tel: 01736 351671
Pedals Bike Hire, Kiosk 17, Wharfside
Shopping Centre. Tel: 01730 360600

GOLF COURSES

Falmouth
Falmouth Golf Club, Swanpool Road.
Tel: 01326 311262;
www.falmouthgolfclub.com

Mullion
Mullion Golf Club, Cury.
Tel: 01326 240685;
www.mulliongolfclub.co.uk

■ ANNUAL EVENTS & CUSTOMS

'Gig racing' is still a popular sport in
Cornwall. Races are held throughout
the summer at venues such as Cadgwith
and Porthleven.

Bodmin
Riding and Heritage Day, Jul.

Bude
Jazz Festival, end of Aug.

Falmouth
Falmouth Regatta Week, Aug.
Various maritime events including
racing of Falmouth classic yachts
as well as dinghies.
www.falmouthweek.co.uk

Fowey
Daphne du Maurier Festival, May.
Fowey Regatta, Aug.

Isles of Scilly
Tresco Marathon, Apr.
Camel Rock Festival, Aug.
Gig racing throughout the summer from
St Mary's Quay.
World Gig Racing Championships
early May.

Liskeard
Carnival Week & Agricultural Show, Jun.

Looe
Carnival Week, Jul/Aug.

Mevagissey
Mevagissey Feast Week, Jun.

Mousehole
Sea, Salts & Sail Festival, Jul.

Newquay
Cornwall Gardens Festival, mid-Mar
to May.
Hot Air Balloon Festival, May.
British National Surf Championships, Jul.
RAF St Mawgan International Air Day,
early Aug.
Pro-Am Surf Championships, Aug.

Padstow
May Day Festival.

Penzance
Golowan Festival and Mazey Day, Jun;
www.golowan.co.uk

St Ives
St Ives Feast Day, early Feb.
St Ives Festival of Music, early Sep.

DEVON

■ TOURIST INFORMATION

Barnstaple
36 Boutport Street. Tel: 0845 458 2003;
www.staynorthdevon.co.uk

Brixham
The Old Market House, The Quay.
Tel: 01803 852861;
www.englishriviera.co.uk

Budleigh Salterton
Fore Street. Tel: 01395 445275;
www.visitbudleigh.com

Dartmouth
The Newcomen Engine House,
Mayor's Avenue. Tel: 01803 834224;
www.discoverdartmouth.org.uk

Dawlish
The Lawn. Tel: 01626 215665;
www.southdevon.org.uk

Exeter
Civic Centre, Paris Street.
Tel: 01392 265700; www.exeter.gov.uk

Exmouth
Alexandra Terrace. Tel: 01395 222299;
www.exmouthguide.co.uk

Honiton
Dowell Street East Car Park.
Tel: 01404 43716;
www.discoverdevon.com

Ottery St Mary
Tel: 01404 813964;
www.otterytourism.org.uk

Paignton
The Esplanade. Tel: 01803 558383;
www.paigntontic@torbay.gov.uk

Salcombe
Council Hall, Market Street.
Tel: 01548 843927;
www.salcombeinformation.co.uk

Sidmouth
Ham Lane. Tel: 01395 516441;
www.visitsidmouth.co.uk

Teignmouth
The Den. Tel: 01626 215666;
www.southdevon.org.uk

Tiverton
Phoenix Lane. Tel: 01884 255827;
www.middevon.gov.uk

Torquay
Vaughan Parade. Tel: 01803 296296;
www.englishriviera.co.uk

■ PLACES OF INTEREST

A La Ronde
Summer Lane, Exmouth.
Tel: 01395 265514;
www.nationaltrust.org.uk

Allhallows Museum
High Street, Honiton. Tel: 01404 44966;
www.honitonmuseum.co.uk

Barnstaple Heritage Centre
Queen Anne's Walk, The Strand.
Tel: 01271 373003

Beer Quarry Caves
Quarry Lane, Beer. Tel: 01297 680282;
www.beerquarrycaves.fsnet.co.uk

Brixham Museum
Brixham. Tel: 01803 856267;
www.brixhamheritage.org.uk

Cadhay
Ottery St Mary. Tel: 01404 812299;
www.cadhay.org.uk

Clovelly
Tel: 01237 431781; www.clovelly.co.uk

Cockington Country Park
Torquay. Tel: 01803 606035;
www.countryside-trust.org.uk

Dartington Crystal
Great Torrington. Tel: 01805 626244;
www.dartington.co.uk

Dartmouth Castle
Dartmouth. Tel: 01803 833588;
www.english-heritage.org.uk

Dartmouth Museum
6 Butterwalk, Dartmouth.
Tel: 01803 832923
www.english-heritage.org.uk

Exeter Cathedral
Cathedral Church of St Peter.
www.exeter-cathedral.org.uk

Fairlynch Museum
Budleigh Salterton. Tel: 01395 442666;
www.devonmuseums.net

Hartland Abbey & Gardens
Hartland. Tel: 01237 441264;
www.hartlandabbey.com

Hartland Quay Museum
Hartland. Tel: 01288 331353

Knightshayes Court
Bolham, near Tiverton.
Tel: 01884 254665
www.nationaltrust.org.uk

Marwood Hill Gardens
Barnstaple. Tel: 01271 342528;
www.marwoodhillgardens.co.uk

Museum of North Devon
The Square, Barnstaple.
Tel: 01271 346747
www.devonmuseums.net

Norman Lockyer Observatory
Salcombe Hill, Sidmouth.
Tel: 01395 579941; www.projects.ex.ac.uk

Oldway Mansion
Torquay Road, Paignton.
Tel: 01803 207933

Overbecks Museum & Garden
Sharpitor. Tel 01548 842893;
www.nationaltrust.org.uk

Paignton Zoo
Totnes Road, Paignton.
Tel: 01803 697500
www.paigntonzoo.org.uk

Paignton & Dartmouth Steam Railway
Torbay Road, Paignton. Tel: 01803 555872;
www.paignton-steamrailway.co.uk

Quay House Visitor Centre
Exeter. Tel: 01392 271611;
www.exeter.gov.uk

Rosemoor Gardens
Great Torrington. Tel: 01805 624067;

Royal Albert Memorial Museum
Queen Street, Exeter. Tel: 01392 265858;

www.exeter.gov.uk. Free.

Sid Vale Heritage Centre
Church Street, Sidmouth.
Tel: 01395 516139

Tiverton Castle
Tiverton. Tel: 01884 253200;
www.tivertoncastle.com

Torquay Museum
529 Babbacombe Road, Torquay.
Tel: 01803 293975;
www.devonmuseums.net

Torre Abbey Historic House & Gallery
The Kings Drive, Torquay.

Torrington Museum & Archive
Town Hall, The Square.
Tel: 01805 624324;
 www.devonmuseums.net

■ SPORTS & ACTIVITIES

ANGLING

Coarse fishing
Grand Western Canal, Tiverton. Day
and season tickets from tackle shops.

Fly fishing
Bellbrook Valley Trout Fishery, Oakford,
Tiverton. Tel: 01398 351292;
www.bellbrookfishery.co.uk.
Book in advance.

CYCLE HIRE

Barnstaple
Biketrail, Fremington Quay.
Tel: 01271 372586;
www.biketrail.co.uk

Exeter
Saddles & Paddles, King's Wharf,
The Quay. Tel: 01392 424241;
www.sadpad.com

Exmouth
Knobblies, 107 Exeter Road.
Tel: 01395 270182

Great Torrington
Torridge Cycle Hire, The Station.
Tel: 01805 622633

Honiton
Cycle Honiton, King Street.
Tel: 01404 47211

Sidmouth
Sidmouth Cycles, 110 High Street.
Tel: 01395 579786

Tiverton
Maynards Cycle Shop, 25 Gold Street.

Torquay
Simply The Bike, Belgrave Road.
Tel: 01803 200024;
www.simplythebike.co.uk

DARTMOOR & TAMAR VALLEY

■ TOURIST INFORMATION

Okehampton
White Hart Courtyard. Tel: 01837 53020;
www.okehamptondevon.co.uk

Tavistock
Town Hall Building, Bedford Square.
Tel: 01822 612938;
www.tavistock-devon.co.uk

OTHER INFORMATION

Bovey Tracey
Lower car park. Tel: 01626 832047;
www.boveytracey.gov.uk

Ivybridge
Global Travel.
Tel: 01752 867035

■ PLACES OF INTEREST

**Dartmoor Wildlife Park
& Falconry Centre**
Sparkwell. Tel: 01752 837645

Devon Guild of Craftsmen
Riverside Mill, Bovey Tracey.
Tel: 01626 832223; www.crafts.org.uk

Museum of Dartmoor Life
West Street, Okehampton.
Tel: 01837 52295; www.museumof
dartmoorlife.eclipse.co.uk

Okehampton Castle
Okehampton. Tel: 01837 52844;
www.english-heritage.org.uk

■ SPORTS & ACTIVITIES

ANGLING

Fly fishing
Drakelands, Hemerdon.
Tel: 01752 344691
Milemead Fisheries, Mill Hill, Tavistock.
Tel: 01822 610888;
www.milemead.fisheries.com

■ ANNUAL EVENTS & CUSTOMS

Okehampton
Okehampton Show, Aug and Carnival,
mid-Oct.

Tavistock
Goosey Fair, mid-Oct.

Widecombe in the Moor
Widecombe Fair 2nd Tue Sep.

EXMOOR

■ TOURIST INFORMATION

Porlock
Tel: 01643 863150

■ PLACES OF INTEREST

Doverhay Manor Museum
Porlock. Tel: 01643 862420

Dunster Castle
Tel: 01643 821314;
www.nationaltrust.org.uk

Dunster Watermill
Dunster. Tel: 01643 821759;
www.dunsterwatermill.co.uk

■ SPORTS & ACTIVITIES

COUNTRY PARKS & NATURE RESERVES

Dunster Forest
Tel: 01398 323665

SOMERSET LEVELS & MENDIPS

■ TOURIST INFORMATION

Cheddar
Tel: 01934 744071

Glastonbury
Tel: 01458 832954
Shepton Mallet
Tel: 01749 345258:
www.visitsomerset.co.uk

DORSET & THE PURBECKS
■ **TOURIST INFORMATION**
Bournemouth
Westover Road. Tel: 0845 051 1700;
www.bournemouth.co.uk
Swanage
The White House, Shore Road.
Tel: 01929 422885; www.swanage.gov.uk

■ **PLACES OF INTEREST**
Corfe Castle (NT)
Tel: 01929 481294
Lulworth Castle & Park
East Lulworth, Wareham.
Tel: 0845 450 1054; www.lulworth.com
Monkey World
Wool, near Wareham. Tel: 0800 456600;
www.monkeyworld.org

■ **SPORTS & ACTIVITIES**
CYCLE HIRE
Poole
First Floor, Dolphin Shopping Centre,
Poole. Tel: 01202 680123;
www.cycle-paths.co.uk
FISHING
Poole Sea Angling Centre
Rear of 5 High Street, Poole.
Tel: 01202 676597;
www.pooleseaanglingcentre.co.uk
WATERSPORTS
FC Watersports Academy
By Sandbanks Hotel, Sandbanks, Poole.
Tel: 01202 708283;
www.fcwatersports.co.uk
WALKING
Ghost Walks of Old Poole Town
Meet at Scaplen's Court Museum,
Sarum Street. Tel: 07977 969080

■ **ANNUAL EVENTS & CUSTOMS**
Bournemouth
Classic Cars on the Prom.
Sun from 4pm, mid-Apr to mid-Sep.
Carnival, first week Aug.
Tel: 0771 359 0629;
www.bournemouthcarnival.org.uk
Swanage
Regatta & Carnival Week, late Jul,
early Aug.
www.swanagecarnival.com

SALISBURY & THE PLAINS
■ **TOURIST INFORMATION**
Salisbury
Fish Row. Tel: 01722 334956

■ **PLACES OF INTEREST**
Mompesson House (NT)
Cathedral Close, Salisbury.

Tel: 01722 335659
Museum of Army Flying
Middle Wallop, Stockbridge
Tel: 01264 784421;
www.flying-museum.org.uk
Old Sarum (EH)
Castle Road, Salisbury. Tel: 01722 335398
Salisbury & South Wiltshire Museum
The King's House, 65 The Close,
Salisbury. Tel: 01722 332151;
www.salisburymuseum.org.uk
Salisbury Cathedral
Cathedral Close. Tel: 01722 555120;
www.salisburycathedral.org.uk
Wilton House
Wilton, Salisbury. Tel: 01722 746720;
www.wiltonhouse.co.uk

■ **SPORTS & ACTIVITIES**
CYCLE HIRE
Hayball Cyclesport
The Black Horse Chequer, Salisbury.
Tel: 01722 411378; www.hayball.co.uk

■ **ANNUAL EVENTS & CUSTOMS**
Salisbury
St George's Day. Street theatre, pageantry
and dragons, 23 Apr.
International Arts Festival.
A variety of art-related events to suit all
ages, mid-May to mid-Jun.

COTSWOLDS
■ **TOURIST INFORMATION**
Burford
The Brewery, Sheep Street.
Tel: 01993 823558
Cheltenham
Cheltenham Municipal Offices,
77 The Promenade. Tel: 01242 522878;
www.visitcheltenham.gov.uk
Chipping Campden
High Street. Tel: 01386 841206
Chipping Norton
The Guildhall, Goddards Lane.
Tel: 01608 644379
Cirencester
Market Place. Tel: 01285 654180
Painswick
The Library, Stroud Road.
Tel: 01452 813552
Tewkesbury
The Museum, 64 Barton Street.
Tel: 01684 295027;
www.tewkesburybc.gov.uk
Winchcombe
The Town Hall, High Street.
Tel: 01242 602925

■ **PLACES OF INTEREST**
Birdland
Rissington Road, Bourton-on-the-Water.
Tel: 01451 820480; www.birdland.co.uk
Chedworth Roman Villa
Yanworth, near Cheltenham
Tel: 01242 890256;

www.nationaltrust.org.uk
Chipping Norton Museum
High Street, Chipping Norton.
Tel: 01608 641712
**Cotswold Motoring Museum, Toy
Collection & Village Life Exhibition**
The Old Mill, Bourton-on-the-Water.
Tel: 01451 821255;
www.cotswold-motor-museum.com
Cotswold Perfumery
Bourton-on-the-Water.
Tel: 01451 820698;
www.cotswold-perfumery.co.uk
Cotswold Wildlife Park
Burford. Tel: 01993 823006;
www.cotswoldwildlifepark.co.uk
**Gloucestershire & Warwickshire
Railway**
Toddington Station, Winchcombe.
Tel: 01242 621405; www.gwsr.com
Hailes Abbey
Winchcombe. Tel: 01242 602398;
www.english-heritage.org.uk
John Moore Countryside Museum
41 Church Street, Tewkesbury.
Tel: 01684 297174;
www.gloster.demon.co.uk
Mill Dene Garden
Blockley. Tel: 01386 700457;
www.milldenegarden.co.uk
Model Village
Old New Inn, Main Street, Bourton-on-
the-Water. Tel: 01451 820467;
www.theoldnewinn.co.uk
Old Mill Museum
Mill Lane, Lower Slaughter.
Tel: 01451 820052;
www.oldmill-lowerslaughter.com
Owlpen Manor
Uley. Tel: 01453 860261;
www.owlpen.com
Pittville Pump Room & Museum
Pittville Park, Cheltenham.
Tel: 01242 523852. Free admission to
Pump Room.
Railway Museum
Gloucester Street, Winchcombe.
Tel: 01242 609305
Snowshill Manor
Tel: 01386 852410;
www.nationaltrust.org.uk
Stanway House
Tel: 01386 584469;
www.stanwayfountain.co.uk
Sudeley Castle
Winchcombe. Tel: 01242 602308;
www.sudeleycastle.co.uk
Tewkesbury Abbey
Church Street, Tewkesbury.
Tel: 01684 850959
Tewkesbury Museum
64 Barton Street, Tewkesbury.
Tel: 01684 292901;
www. tewkesburymuseum.org.uk
Winchcombe Folk & Police Museum
Old Town Hall, Winchcombe.

Tel: 01242 609151;
www.sunloch.demon.co.uk/museum.htm

■ **FOR CHILDREN**
Dragonfly Maze
Bourton-on-the-Water.
Tel: 01451 822251
■ **SPORTS & ACTIVITIES**
CYCLING
Cheltenham
Compass Holidays, 48 Shurdington Road.
Tel: 01242 250642

■ **ANNUAL EVENTS & CUSTOMS**
Burford
Dragon Procession, Jun.
Cheltenham
Folk Festival, Feb.
National Hunt, Prestbury Park, Mar.
Jazz Festival, Apr/May.
Science Festival, Jun.
International Festival of Music, Jul.
Chipping Campden
Dover's Hill Olympick Games and
Scuttlebrook Wake; Spring Bank Hol
www.olimpickgames.co.uk
Cirencester
Cotswold Country Fair, Jul.
Cooper's Hill
Cheese Rolling, Spring Bank
Holiday Mon.
Guiting
Guiting Power, Festival of Music
and Arts, Jul.
Painswick
Church Clypping Ceremony, late Sep.
Tewkesbury
Food Festival, May.
Medieval Fair, Jul.

BATH
■ **TOURIST INFORMATION**
Bath
Abbey Chambers, Abbey Churchyard.
Tel: 01225 477101;
www.visitbath.co.uk

■ **PLACES OF INTEREST**
Bath Abbey Heritage Vaults
Tel: 01225 422462
Jane Austen Centre
Gay Street, Bath. Tel: 01225 443000;
www.janeausten.co.uk
Number 1, Royal Crescent
Bath. Tel: 01225 428126
Roman Baths Museum
Stall Street, Bath. Tel: 01225 477785;
www.romanbaths.co.uk
Thermae Bath Spa
Hot Bath Street, Bath. Tel: 01225 331234;
www.thermaebathspa.com

■ **ANNUAL EVENTS & CUSTOMS**
Literature Festival, Feb or Mar.
Music Festival, May/Jun.
Mozartfest, Nov.

PUBS

CORNWALL

Bay View Inn
Widemouth Bay, Bude EX23 0AW
Tel: 01288 361273;
www.bayviewinn.co.uk
Savour a pint of Sharp's on the sun deck, absorb the view across the glorious sandy beach – just two reasons to visit this free house on Cornwall's north coast. Add a lively, candlelit bar, imaginative, freshly prepared food using locally sourced produce, and stylish bedrooms.

Cadgwith Cove Inn
Cadgwith, Ruan Minor, Helston
TR12 7JX. Tel: 01326 290513;
www.cadgwithcoveinn.com
An unspoilt hamlet of thatched cottages is the setting for this old-fashioned, bustling local. Crab sandwiches and a pint of Sharp's Doom Bar provide the perfect lunch, best enjoyed on the sunny terrace with views across the cove.

Shipwrights Arms
Helford, Helston TR12 6JX
Tel: 01326 231235
Stunningly located on the banks of the Helford Estuary, the narrow approach road is restricted to pedestrians only. This is a pretty thatched pub with a terraced garden and picnic benches on the water's edge. The bar is traditional, with rustic furnishings and plenty of nautical bits and pieces. Summer buffet lunches and evening barbecues draw the crowds.

Star Inn
Fore Street, St Just TR19 7LL
Tel: 01736 788767
St Just's oldest pub has a low-beamed bar, a polished slate floor, glowing coal fires and walls packed with mining and seafaring memorabilia. Pop in to experience the homely, unspoilt atmosphere and the St Austell beer.

Tinners Arms
Zennor, St Ives TR26 3BY
Tel: 01736 796927;
www.tinnersarms.com
A former tin miners' local, it is now an oasis for walkers tackling the St Ives to Zennor coastal walk. Two open fires warm the bar, filled with flagstones and pine tables, where you can rest and refuel on Sharp's ales and fresh fish.

DEVON

The Double Locks Hotel
Canal Banks, Exeter EX2 6LT
Tel: 01392 256947; www.youngs.co.uk
This no-nonsense pub, renowned for its good food, real ales and extensive garden, is great on a sunny day. In a cute lock-keeper's cottage on the banks of the Exeter Ship Canal, the pub is a popular choice for outdoor enthusiasts and families. The food here is reasonably priced, and has choices ranging from steak and ale pie to haddock fishcakes.

The Masons Arms
Branscombe EX12 3DJ
Tel: 01297 680300;
www.masonsarms.co.uk
This Grade II listed inn, originally a 1360 cider house, is in the pretty village of Branscombe. Food is a serious business here: where possible, all ingredients are grown or reared locally, with lobster and crab from Branscombe beach, so expect excellent restaurant-style meals.

The Mountpleasant Inn
Nomansland, Tiverton EX16 8NN
Tel: 01884 860271
A bustling, friendly, family-run pub that welcomes everyone, especially other families. Set in the heart of the county, this popular inn dates from the 18th century, when it began life as a simple ostler's house. Today there is an attractive restaurant in the former blacksmith's forge, which serves a variety of reasonably priced food.

Olde Churston Court Inn
Churston, Brixham TQ5 0JE
Tel: 01803 842186;
www.churstoncourt.co.uk
A visit to this huge Grade I listed inn is an extraordinary experience, as it used to be a Saxon manor and was once the haunt of sea captains and smugglers. Large, attractive inglenook fireplaces, flagstone floors, weaponry (and the odd suit of armour) fill every room. On the menu is fresh fish.

The Puffing Billy
Station Hill, Great Torrington EX38 8JD
Tel: 01805 623050
A pub with a difference, in a partially converted station on the old Barnstaple railway line, now the route of the Tarka Trail. The pub is full of railway memorabilia and has a small garden next to the track. The pub serves a wide range of food to suit most tastes and also sells locally brewed Cavalier ale.

The Tower Inn
Slapton, near Dartmouth TQ7 2PN
Tel: 01548 580216;
www.thetowerinn.com
A mile from Slapton Sands, this inn was built as cottages to house the men working on the Collegiate Chantry of St Mary. Expect church-pew seating, a lovely garden and a sophisticated menu.

DARTMOOR & TAMAR VALLEY

The Elephant's Nest Inn
Horndon, Mary Tavy, Tavistock
PL19 9NQ. Tel: 01822 810273
A pub since the mid-19th-century, the building dates back to the 16th century, when it was used to accommodate tin and copper miners. There's a beamed bar with an open fire, two dining rooms and a pretty garden. The interesting menu includes black spice lamb curry, turbot steak with chervil hollandaise, and the home-made, if unusually named, 'Elephant burger'.

EXMOOR

The Crown Hotel
Exford, Somerset TA24 7PP
Tel: 01643 831554/5;
www.crownhotelexmoor.co.uk
Set in the heart of the Exmoor National Park, this 17th-century coaching inn is thought to be the oldest working inn on the moor. It is especially popular for equine enthusiasts as it has plenty of stabling and is set in three acres of gardens and woodlands. There is an excellent bar menu available also.

DORSET & THE PURBECKS

The Bankes Arms Hotel
Watery Lane, Studland BH19 3AU
Tel: 01929 450225
Once the haunt of smugglers, this creeper-clad inn is renowned for its large menu of fresh fish and seafood, including fresh mussels, crab gratin and lobster dishes. There are meat options, too, such as lamb noisettes in mint, honey and orange sauce. Each year the pub hosts a beer festival, with around 60 real ales on tap accompanied by music, Morris dancing and stone carving in the garden.

The Castle Inn
Main Road, West Lulworth BH20 5RN
Tel: 01929 400311
This thatched and beamed atmospheric pub close to Lulworth Cove, is perfectly placed for walkers. There's an extensive tiered garden, which fills up quickly on summer days, and is especially popular with families. Dogs are permitted too. The menu includes some staples such as chicken, ham and mushroom pie, seafood stew, and fillet steak with oysters. And for something unusual, flambé dishes are cooked at your table. Beers include Ringwood Best.

SALISBURY & THE PLAINS

The Haunch of Venison
1–5 Minster Street, Salisbury SP1 1TB
Tel: 01722 411313
Craftsmen working on the cathedral spire were some of the early customers of this pub, dating back to 1320. A restaurant in summer serves treats such as pork with coriander and ginger.

The Mayfly
Testcombe, Stockbridge SO20 6AZ
Tel: 01264 860283
A firm favourite with fly-fishermen, this lovely old country pub, the Mayfly looks onto the fast-flowing River Test. A selection of hot and cold meats, quiches and pies is laid out buffet-style, along with a few hot daily specials. Beers include Ringwood Best and Wadworth 6X.

COTSWOLDS

Eight Bells
Church Street, Chipping Campden
GL55 6JG. Tel: 01386 840371;
www.eightbellsinn.co.uk
This is the oldest inn in Chipping Campden and is near the famous church. It has two cosy bars, a smart dining room and a very pleasant terrace at the back. They serve a good range of local food at lunchtime and in the evenings.

The Bell at Sapperton
Sapperton GL7 6LE
Tel: 01285 760761;
www.foodatthebell.co.uk
The 300-year-old Bell is elegant in an understated way – all stone walls and fresh flowers on scrubbed tables. Enjoy dishes such as home-made ravioli with Portland crab or braised pork in red wine and balsamic sherry inside or in the pretty garden or courtyard.

FOREST OF DEAN

The Saracens Head Inn
Symonds Yat HR96JL
Tel: 01600 890435;
www.saracensheadinn.co.uk
Formerly a cider mill, this riverside inn sits on the east bank of the Wye where the river flows through a picturesque gorge. At just over a mile from the Welsh border, the inn is in a great location for exploring this unspoiled area. Choose from dishes such as roast wood pigeon breast, seared yellow fin tuna, terrine of wild rabbit or poached smoked haddock.

BATH

The Old Green Tree
12 Green Street BA1 2JZ
Tel: 01225 448259
18th-century, three-roomed, oak-panelled pub, loved for its faded splendour, dim and atmospheric interior and a front room decorated with World War II Spitfire pictures. The menu includes soup and bangers and mash (which use probably the best sausages in Bath!).

TEA ROOMS
CORNWALL

Carnewas Tea Room and Garden
Bedruthan, St Eval, Wadebridge
PL27 7UW. Tel: 01637 860701
The dramatic coastline at Bedruthan is renowned for its cliff-top views. Take in the view with a cream tea or a plate of cakes from the National Trust tea room on the cliff top, which is housed in the office building of the Carnewas iron mine.

Charlotte's Tea House
Coinage Hall, 1 Boscawen Street, Truro
TR1 2QU. Tel: 01872 263706
This lovingly restored tea house is on the first floor of the Coinage Hall. Victorian uniforms, china cups and antiques add to the charm. The menu offers sandwiches and delicious set teas – cream teas with light, home-made scones and high teas with sandwiches and irresistible cakes.

Crumpets Tea Shop
1 Fore Street, Polruan, Fowey PL23 1PQ
Tel: 01726 870806
Just a five-minute boat trip across the estuary from Fowey, Crumpets is a traditional tea shop decked out in yellow and blue, with sea-related prints on the walls. Just the ticket for light lunches, home-cooked cakes or a delicious cream tea, served with home-made jam.

Polpeor Café
Lizard Point, The Lizard, TR12 7HJ
Tel: 01326 290939
At Britain's most southerly café, perched high on the cliffs on Lizard Point, you can watch waves crashing onto rocks and choughs wheeling around the cliffs while you tuck into a local crab salad and sandwiches or a traditional cream tea. On fine summer days, the suntrap terrace right on the cliff edge is the place to eat.

Rick Stein's Café
10 Middle Street, Padstow PL28 8AP
Tel: 01841 532700; www.rickstein.com
The most relaxed of Rick Stein's restaurants is a casual café-with-rooms decked out with a nautical theme. It's open all day, so call in for breakfast or an excellent cappuccino and peruse the papers, or arrive early for deliciously simple lunches and dinners – salt and pepper prawn, whole grilled mackerel with tomato and onion salad, or chickpea, parsley and salt cod stew.

Sarah's Crab Shop
Cadgwith Cove, Helston TR12 7JX
Tel: 01326 290539
Sarah is dedicated to fresh crab and you'll find her tiny shop-cum-café smack beside the beach and the boats that supply her with the crab that she sells from the shop window. Buy it by the pound or have it made into a memorable crab sandwich. She will also prepare you a delicious cream tea – savour both at tables by the beach.

DEVON

Canal Tea Room
Lime Kiln Cottage, Grand Western Canal, Tiverton EX16 4AQ. Tel: 01884 252291
Enjoy home-made cakes, scones and local ice cream at this lovely tea garden attached to a thatched cottage with a pond and covered seating. It's situated just below the basin of the Grand Western Canal.

The Cosy Teapot
13 Fore Street, Budleigh Salterton
EX9 6NH. Tel: 01395 444016
The cries of seagulls accompany you on a visit to this traditional, genteel tea shop just a few minutes' walk from the beach. Floral-patterned china, sumptuous cakes, a range of sandwiches and tasty lunches all add to the homely atmosphere. If you dare, try the Black Forest Cream Tea – cherry jam, clotted cream and a chocolate scone. Gluten-free options are also available.

Four & Twenty Blackbirds Tea Shoppe
43 Gold Street, Tiverton EX16 6QB
Tel: 01884 257055
Low beams, vases of flowers, and antique furniture create a homely atmosphere at this traditional tea shop near the clock tower. Choose from different 'teas': Maid's (apple tart), King's (cheese and chutney), Queen's (egg), Jenny Wren's (scones, jelly, ice cream) and Blackbird's (sandwiches and cake).

The Sea Shanty
Branscombe Beach EX12 3DP
Tel: 01297 690577
The thatched Sea Shanty is right on Branscombe's beach, and has been serving refreshments for more than 70 years. It's the ideal setting for a cream tea or a light lunch, with crab, lobster and fish straight off the beach. With a walled sun-trap courtyard, an open fire inside, tables by the beach and wonderful views, this is a perfect spot all year round.

Soar Mill Cove Hotel
Near Salcombe, Devon TQ7 3DS
Tel: 01548 561566
A single storey building of local stone and slate, the hotel overlooks the beach and cove without impacting on this area of outstanding natural beauty. Tea is served in the lounge, on the deck or out in the lovely garden.

Weavers Cottage
Cockington, Torquay TQ2 6XA
Tel: 01803 606991
This typical country cottage (think roses round the door, thatched roof and pink walls), tucked away in a tranquil wooded valley, was originally the home farm for the Cockington Estate. Enjoy a cream tea or slice of cake in the pretty courtyard.

DARTMOOR & TAMAR VALLEY

Brimpts Farm
Dartmeet, Dartmoor PL20 6FG
Tel: 01364 631450;
www.brimptsfarm.co.uk
Brimpts Farm has a spectacular setting above Dartmeet and overlooking Yar Tor. Their cream teas have been justly renowned since 1913; the menu includes dishes made from fresh local produce.

EXMOOR

Lewis's Tea Rooms, 13 The High Street, Dulverton TA22 9HB. Tel: 01398 323850
This instantly welcoming tea shop, on the southern fringes of Exmoor National Park, occupies a pair of 18th-century cottages. At either end fires blaze in the winter and, in summer, the flower-filled courtyard tempts visitors outside. When it comes to tea time, speciality loose-leaf teas and fat scones with strawberry jam and clotted cream are always winners.

SOMERSET & MENDIPS

Grosvenor Hotel
High Street, Stockbridge SO20 6EU
Tel: 01264 810606
Enjoy a cream tea, or toasted tea cakes with a choice of teas and coffees, in the comfort of this grand old fishing hotel, which juts into the High Street.

Lillie Langtry's
High Street, Stockbridge SO20 6HF
Tel: 01264 810954
This old building on the main street was once an inn frequented by actress Lillie Langtry. Today it is a homely tea room, serving crumpets dripping with butter and home-made jam, and scones with clotted cream from a neighbouring Jersey herd. Lunches can be served on the shady terrace by the stream.

DORSET & THE PURBECKS

The Tea Shop
11a Trinity Street, The Harbourside, Weymouth DT4 8TW. Tel: 01305 788052
The Tea Shop is well known for its scrumptious selection of cakes and tasty afternoon tea favourites; don't leave without trying the Dorset apple cake. Coeliac and diabetic dietary needs are catered to here. A selection of local produce is for sale also.

SALISBURY & THE PLAINS

The Polly Tea Rooms
8 St Thomas's Square, Salisbury
SP1 1BA. Tel: 01722 336037
Just a short walk from the cathedral, The Polly Tea Rooms is in the ideal location to stop for a break. In winter the cosy decor inside is very inviting and in summer the little tables outside provide the perfect place to watch the world go by whilst tucking into some of the delicious hand-made chocolates.

COTSWOLDS

Badgers Hall
High Street, Chipping Campden
GL55 6HB. Tel: 01386 840839;
www.badgershall.com
A true taste of the Cotswolds: the building is 15th-century, honey-coloured stone with exposed oak beams, mullioned windows and open fireplaces. Home-made cakes, scones and pastries are freshly baked on the premises using local produce. They also have charming bedrooms available.

Black Cat
High Street, Lechlade on Thames
Tel: 01367 252273
This extended snug tea room is in Lechlade's busy high street. The interior is simplicity itself with white painted walls and tableware. There is a range of more than forty teas to choose from.

Juri's Tearoom
High Street, Winchcombe GL54 5LJ
Tel: 01242 602469;
www.juris-tearoom.co.uk
On the High Street of this lovely village, Juri's traditional stone tea room is run by a Japanese family who are dedicated to maintaining high standards. Their freshly made cakes are first class. The patio garden and conservatory are delightful.

The Mad Hatter
Riverside, Bourton-on-the-Water
GL54 2BX. Tel: 01451 821508;
www.the-mad-hatter-tearoom.co.uk
This lovely 18th-century building beside the River Windrush is a treat to visit. Enjoy their cream teas, delicious home-made cakes and lovely garden.

BATH

Sally Lunn's
4 North Parade Passage, Bath
Tel: 01225 461634;
www.sallylunns.co.uk
The famous Sally Lunn Bun was originally baked in Georgian times and is still on offer in this historic tea shop in the oldest house in Bath. Come here for breakfast, lunch or a magnificent cream tea.

Southeast England

Southeast England

The gentle landscape of the southeast encompasses chalk downland ridges that stretch away to the west; deep beech woods that shelter herds of timid roe deer; towering white cliffs that form a stunning backdrop along the coast and myriad thatched cottages nestled around their village greens. The region includes The New Forest, an area well-known for its wildlife conservation projects and its unspoilt natural beauty. One of Britain's newest national parks, it is a haven for walkers and cyclists. Nearby is Winchester, the ancient capital of England, with its medieval cathedral and links with Jane Austen and the mythical King Arthur and his round table.

And within striking distance of all this is London, the country's capital and one of the most famous cityscapes in the world, where the cultural life encompasses world-class opera, theatre, cinema, street festivals, art exhibitions and much more. But here too, you'll find a number of beautiful parks that are like green oases amid the hustle and bustle of city life.

The New Forest

CLOCKWISE FROM TOP: BURLEY; BUCKLERS HARD LEADING TO THE BEAULIEU RIVER; NEW FOREST PONY, BEAULIEU

BEAULIEU MAP REF 400 E7

The pretty village of Beaulieu is now synonymous with the National Motor Museum, the private passion of the then Lord Montagu. His forefathers acquired the Beaulieu estate in Tudor times, with its Cistercian abbey founded in 1204.

The abbey was torn down as part of the Dissolution of the Monasteries countrywide, but the fine cloisters survived and now contain a re-created monastic garden; the refectory became the parish church; and the Domus, the lay brothers' apartments, now houses an exhibition about abbey life. The Tudor house created from the 14th-century gatehouse was reconstructed in the 19th century as the present Palace House, and today shows the domestic workings of a Victorian household. During World War II the estate became the top-secret training school for those involved in the Special Operations Executive (SOE), where agents prepared for operations behind enemy lines in occupied France and Europe, and this story is told in the Secret Army Exhibition.

Lord Montagu first opened this lovely Palace House to the public in 1952, and the brilliant motor museum is dedicated to the memory of his father. It was in fact John Montagu who had successfully petitioned parliament to abolish the 12mph (19kph) speed limit, among other notable achievements. Today there are more than 250 vintage beauties and stars of the car world to admire in this famous collection, ranging from world record breakers such as 'Bluebird' and 'Golden Arrow' to TV favourites including Mr Bean's green Mini, and James Bond's Lotus submarine car from the movie *The Spy Who Loved Me*. A trip on the 'Wheels' pod ride transports you through a century of motoring history, and you can explore the site on a replica 1912 bus or the high-level monorail. Look out for the special events and exhibitions that take place throughout the year.

BREAMORE MAP REF 400 D6

Breamore (pronounced 'Bremmer') is an unspoiled village in the northeast corner of the New Forest, with many attractive redbrick, thatched cottages grouped tranquilly around its village green. It's a scene jealously guarded from change, and even the village stocks still stand, opposite the Bat and Ball pub. Little St Mary's Church, which dates from about 1000, is one of the most interesting Saxon survivals in Hampshire. The 12th-century porch contains part of the Saxon rood screen, a fine piece of carving, though the figures have been damaged.

The redbrick Elizabethan manor house of Breamore, built on the hillside in 1583, was purchased by Queen Anne's physician, Sir Edward Hulse, in the 18th century, and is still a family home with collections of paintings, furniture, needlework and porcelain. The Great Hall has its original carved stone fireplace, and in the Victorian kitchen hangs gleaming copperware.

In the old farmyard the Countryside Museum has full-size replicas of the village shops that would have made the estate self-sufficient, including a wheelwright's, a blacksmith's and a brewery.

BROCKENHURST MAP REF 400 D7

Brockenhurst is a big, pleasant village set amid wooded countryside. On the northern outskirts are two of the largest and loveliest of the New Forest 'lawns', Butts Lawn and Balmer Lawn, the latter overlooked by an elegant hotel.

New Forest churches tend to stand aloof from their villages and ancient Brockenhurst's St Nicholas' church, hidden away to the east, is no exception. It is reputedly the oldest in the forest, and it was the only one recorded in the 1086 Domesday survey. The yew tree that almost smothers the building has a girth of more than 20 feet (6m), and is known to be more than 1,000 years old.

To the northwest of Brockenhurst the Rhinefield Ornamental Drive features coniferous trees, including very large redwoods. Forest walks on either side of the drive include a 'Tall Trees Walk'. Further on, Bolderwood Drive passes close to the ancient Knightwood Oak, and the deer sanctuary whose platforms offer a view of deer roaming in the forest.

BUCKLERS HARD MAP REF 400 E7

Two redbrick, terraced rows of Georgian houses face each other across a wide open space that slopes gently down to the Beaulieu River, on the Beaulieu estate. The area is kept free of cars and presents a peaceful rural scene. Yet Bucklers Hard, originally called Montagu Town, was the shipyard that built many of the men-of-war for Nelson's fleet, including his favourite ship, *Agamemnon*. The yard was busy, but overreached itself and folded in 1811. During World War II Bucklers Hard revived its shipbuilding tradition, and some parts of a Mulberry Harbour for the

D-Day landings were constructed here. In the Maritime Museum are models of the ships built here, and reconstructed cottage interiors offer an insight into the life of 18th-century shipyard workers.

Today, pleasure craft ride the tranquil waters of the Beaulieu River and, in summer, cruises set off from the quay. A riverside walk leads to Beaulieu village.

BURLEY MAP REF 400 D7

Burley is an excellent centre for walking, horse-riding and mountain biking. This attractive village is set high above the River Avon amid the bleak heathlands of the western New Forest, where ponies and cattle roam freely. Burley Beacon is the village's high point, reached by the gravel track from Pound Lane, and from it the view expands westwards over the Avon Valley. Even better is the view from Castle Hill, topped by an Iron Age camp, at nearby Burley Street. Red deer roam in the grounds of grand Burley Manor.

During the 1950s Burley had its own resident witch, called Sybil Leek, who dressed in black robes with a jackdaw perched on her shoulder. Despite her 'white' tendencies, local resentment caused her to flee to America. Since then the village has specialised in witchcraft shops as well as the usual range of antiques and souvenirs. A window in the

little church commemorates Constance Applebee, who died in 1981 at the ripe old age of 107. Burley is also home to New Forest Cider, a cider farm with a shop and an exhibition to show how it is made.

CHRISTCHURCH MAP REF 400 D7

This ancient town lies on the south coast where the rivers Stour and Avon pour into the bay. At the time of the Domesday survey there were only 21 houses here and it was named Twynham. The church was started later in the 11th century, and became an Augustinian priory around 1150. All that remains is the Priory Church, looming gold above the town, and worth exploring inside for its carvings. Look out for the Norman turret in the north transept, and the superb carving of the Salisbury Chantry. Nearby Place Mill, mentioned in the Domesday Book, was used for fulling (cleaning and thickening cloth) and corn grinding until 1808, and now has displays of old milling items, with an art and crafts gallery upstairs.

One of Christchurch town's most unusual sights is its surviving ducking stool, reached via a flagged alleyway beside the Olde George Inn – a wooden stool on the end of a pole which can be swung out into the chilly millstream, in a scolds' punishment revived with good humour in 1986. The town's Red House

Museum is a collection of local and natural history, housed in an appealing old Georgian house with a lovely garden.

Across the estuary, the pastel-coloured rows of beach huts on Mudeford's sandy peninsula are a cheerful throwback to childhood bucket-and-spade holidays of the early 20th century. This windswept peninsula has an archaeological record dating back 12,500 years, when Stone Age hunter-gatherers left a campsite on its seaward edge. Some 10,500 years later, Iron Age folk settled and built up a trading port on the inner shore, where Barn Field stands today. The great Double Dikes date from this period, built to shelter a village of timber-framed dwellings.

Barn Field has been untouched by farming since the Romans left in around AD 410 and its rare status is protected by conservationists. It's an area of low, acid grassland gripping onto thin soil, maintained by the salt-laden winds and the teeth of the rabbit population. Decimation of the rabbits by myxomatosis in the 1950s allowed gorse and bramble to take hold, but scrub clearance and controlled cattle grazing has done much to restore the original balance. Today it is an important site for ground-nesting birds such as the skylark and meadow pipit, and adorned with heath bedstraw, autumn hawkbit and harebell.

Activity
THE HAMPSHIRE AVON

The River Avon rises to the east of Devizes in Wiltshire and flows southwards for 48 miles (77km) to the English Channel at Christchurch. In its upper chalky reaches it is a noted clear trout stream, but where it flows through Hampshire past Breamore and Fordingbridge the acid soils of the New Forest change its nature and it becomes a river for coarse fishing. Below Ringwood it is renowned for salmon. The waymarked Avon Valley Path, opened in 1992, follows the river for 34 miles (54.5km) from Salisbury to Christchurch and the coast.

Insight
NEW FOREST PONIES

New Forest ponies may roam freely, but they are not strictly wild – they belong to the commoners. The Victorians 'improved' the hardy ponies that had grazed the forest for centuries, surviving on a diet of gorse, bracken and brambles, by inter-breeding them with Arab stallions – and now they mainly eat grass. Every autumn the ponies are rounded up for branding and marking, and several times a year ponies are sold at Beaulieu Road Station.

ELING MAP REF 400 E7

The Saxon village of Eling, on a little tidal creek off Southampton Water, was a shipbuilding village until the end of the 19th century. Before that it was a small port from where Henry I is said to have sailed to Normandy in 1130.

The creek, a sheltered little harbour for sailing craft, is crossed by a fast causeway with sluice gates to hold back the high tides and, in the little building on the northern shore, the power of Southampton Water's famous double tides is harnessed and used to produce wholemeal flour. Eling Tide Mill is the only surviving tide mill regularly milling pure stoneground flour. The Domesday Book of 1086 records a mill here. The manor of Eling was later part of the endowment to Winchester College in 1385 and even at this time the mill and causeway had long been a ruin, but it was not until 1415 that the Wardens and Fellows of the college sought to find a means of rebuilding and maintaining the mill and causeway. The solution was to let the mill to Thomas Midlyngton of Southampton for a term of 50 years at a fee of 13 shillings and 4 pence. In return he was required to restore the mill within two years and to maintain it, assisted by a grant of 20 marks (approximately £13.30p) and, as a charitable act "for the salvation of his soul", to rebuild and maintain the causeway "to last for a hundred years", although he was also granted the right to "remove sand and clay for his own convenience". The present building dates from the 18th century. It was restored in 1980 and milling demonstrations are given, depending on the tides. You can learn more about Eling and neighbouring Totton in the heritage centre by the mill.

The causeway across the creek at Eling carries the only remaining toll road in Hampshire, which records show has been in operation since at least 1418.

EMERY DOWN MAP REF 400 D7

Emery Down is a pretty little village, full of character, just outside Lyndhurst within the New Forest National Park.

The New Forest had a famous snakecatcher, Henry 'Brusher' Mills (1840-1905). He was born at Emery Down and lived in a charcoal burner's makeshift hut. In his time he is said to have caught 30,000 snakes and 3,500 adders, some of which he sold to zoos, but others were less fortunate – he made them into an ointment as a cure for rheumatism. The pub in which he used to drink at Brockenhurst is today called The Snakecatcher.

The artist Sven Berlin, one of the characters who made up the artistic community of St Ives, has been described as 'England's most important neglected artist'. He moved to the New Forest in a horse-drawn gypsy caravan in 1953 and painted a portfolio of paintings documenting the last days of the Forest gypsies. The celebrated English composer, Ralph Vaughan Williams, visited Berlin at his Emery Down home and collected songs from the gypsies.

EXBURY MAP REF 400 E7

This pleasant estate village nestling on the Beaulieu River is famed for the magnificent rhododendron gardens at Exbury House. They were the creation of banker Lionel de Rothschild, whose passion was gardening – and he gardened on a magnificent scale.

Rothschild started here in the 1920s, with 600 acres (243ha) of wooded slopes overlooking the river. He split the land into 250 acres (101ha) of gardens and 350 acres (142ha) of arboretum. He imported more than 1,000 varieties of rhododendron, then created 452 more by careful crossing. Today the gardens are run by his son, Edmund.

The mild climate of the Beaulieu River valley ensures a long flowering season, with absolutely breathtaking displays between April and June. Camellias, azaleas and magnolias contribute to the glory of an Exbury spring. Other gardens here include a daffodil meadow, rock garden, rose garden and water garden. A miniature steam railway offers a 20-minute tour of the Summer Lane Garden, leading to the American Garden. Dogs on a short lead are welcome.

FURZEY GARDENS MAP REF 400 D7

Designed by Hugh Dalrymple, Furzey Gardens was established in 1922 and has much to hold the attention of budding horticulturists. Deep in the middle of the New Forest in pretty Minstead, the informal gardens have a wonderful collection of rhododendrons and azaleas, that create an amazing display of colour when in full bloom. Other parts of the garden are given over to many varieties of heathers and an extensive range of winter and summer flowering shrubs, as well as a separate sensory garden. For walkers, there is a lake to amble round.

LYMINGTON MAP REF 400 D7

Lymington is a busy sailing town at the mouth of the Lymington River. It received its charter in 1200 and became a free port, flourishing as the closest mainland harbour to the Isle of Wight, to which ferries still run. In the Middle Ages Lymington rivalled Southampton as a major port – and the numerous creeks around here were much frequented by smugglers well into the 18th century. Today the tidal salt marshes stretch for 10 miles (16km), and are protected as a national nature reserve.

For many years the town's prosperity depended on the production of salt, but sadly this trade eventually died out and Lymington briefly became a fashionable bathing place. By the end of the 19th century it had developed as a sailing centre, and today the town has an excellent yacht basin and is the headquarters of two sailing clubs. There is boat building too and, as with many ports, it is famed for its inns – reputedly there were once 45.

The wide Georgian and Victorian High Street, which climbs the hill from the quay to the church, bursts into life on Saturdays when there is a vibrant 700-year-old market, with a great variety of stalls laid out along both sides of the street. Enjoy views from the hilltop back down across the river, then take a look at the Church of St Thomas, which looks 18th century, with its jaunty white cupola and galleried interior, but is actually medieval. The town's St Barbe Museum is dedicated to the history of the New Forest coast, including hands-on displays for children, while its art gallery offers an ever changing range of exhibitions of world-class artworks.

To the north of Lymington is lovely Spinners, a beautiful woodland garden cultivating rhododendrons, magnolias, Japanese maples and much more. To the south, on Hurst Spit, stands Hurst Castle, one of Henry VIII's defences against possible Spanish invasion with its characteristic sturdy design. It was part of the modern coastal artillery defences in both world wars and in use until 1956.

LYNDHURST MAP REF 400 D7

The 'Capital of the New Forest' is a fairly sizeable town, and is the only one within the historical confines of the forest. It was designated the New Forest's administrative centre in 1079 by William I, and it continues to be the seat of the ancient Court of Verderers formed to protect the rights of the commoners. The Court Room and the Forestry Commission offices are housed in the beautiful 17th-century Queen's House where the Verderers meet every two months. All New Forest animals are under their jurisdiction, while patrolling

FURZEY GARDENS

the forest is the remit of four 'Agisters' – a medieval word meaning 'collector'. The Forestry Commission manages the woodland of the New Forest.

Lyndhurst is a town of narrow streets leading off the main High Street, which snarls up with traffic during peak holiday times. It is full of tourist shops and eating places, with Victorian and Edwardian architecture to admire. The 1860 church, on the site of two earlier ones, dominates the High Street with its 160-foot (49m) spire. It contains windows by Burne-Jones and a fresco, *The Parable of the Virgins*, by Lord Leighton. In the village churchyard lies Mrs Hargreaves, who died in 1934. As the little Alice Liddell, she was the real inspiration for Lewis Caroll's Alice in Wonderland. The town is the home of the New Forest Visitor Centre and Museum.

Lyndhurst's central position makes it an ideal base for exploring the forest, which still presses up close to the town's boundaries. To the west of Lyndhurst sits the picturesque thatched hamlet of Swan Green, formerly the site of an important pony fair, and Emery Down, famed for its Portuguese fireplace, which stands alone in the open air. It was constructed of cobble stones on the site of a building that was occupied by Portuguese troops during World War I, and it serves as a memorial to them. The New Forest Reptile Centre, 2 miles (3.2km) south west of Lyndhurst, is a conservation and education facility dedicated to rare native species, where you can also explore the circular Reptile Trail. To the east Bolton's Bench car park is an excellent starting point for walks over White Moor Heath.

STONEY CROSS MAP REF 400 D7

Stoney Cross airfield was built late in 1942 on an area anciently occupied by man; there is still a megalithic Round Barrow, surrounded by a ditch, a short distance from the Janesmoor Pond carpark on the A31. The airfield made a significant contribution to World War II and was used by both the Royal Air Force and the United States Air Force. At one time the Ninth Air Force had 472 American personnel based there. Following the end of hostilities in Europe, Stoney Cross was used as a staging post for RAF transports flying to the Far East.

The airfield was closed in 1946 and for a period following the war, the airfield was abandoned and quickly became overgrown. In the 1960s the Forestry Commission created tree plantations and the site was developed to meet the needs of public recreation. Stoney Cross has now been returned to managed heathland and the facilities include fishing for under 17s and radio-controlled boating.

LYMINGTON

NO MOORING LANDING ONLY

NO MOORING

A FOREST WALK FROM FRITHAM

A walk from a hidden hamlet and the site of a former gunpowder factory, through woodland and open heathland. Look out for nests of wood ants beside the tracks, the mounds will be feverish with activity on dry warm days, and listen for the distinctive 'yaffle' of the green woodpecker, which feeds on the wood ants.

DISTANCE/TIME 6 miles (9.6km) 3h **MAP** OS Outdoor Leisure 22 New Forest **START** Forestry Commission car park beyond Royal Oak pub; grid ref: SU 230141 **TRACKS** Gravel forest tracks, heathland and woodland paths **THE PUB** The Royal Oak, Fritham. Tel: 02380 812606

1 Turn left out of the car park and head downhill along the road which eventually becomes gravelled and then passes Eyeworth Pond to the right. Continue past Eyeworth Cottage and Eyeworth Lodge, then take the footpath on the right beyond Oak Tree Cottage at the end of the track.

2 Bear off to the left and then, at a fork, keep left through the trees close to the field boundary. As the boundary swings further to the left, bear right along a track between tall coniferous and deciduous woods. At the T-junction by a large single fir, turn left along the grassy track. Now, cross a ford and then walk on up to a junction.

3 Turn right on to a gravel track and then, where it bears sharply to the right, keep ahead with the grassy track. Ascend into more open countryside and continue to climb along the meandering path, ignoring paths left and right, across the edge of Fritham Plain. The path bears right towards the trees to a track. Turn left, then right and enter Sloden Inclosure.

4 Walk through the Inclosure, then descend across open heathland towards a cottage. Cross a bridge and bear right and then, just before Holly Hatch Cottage, turn left through

a gate. At a fork, bear right along a grassy track and gently climb through Holly Hatch Inclosure to reach a gravel track.

5 Turn left, then after 400yds (366m), turn right at a major junction and shortly reach a gate on the woodland edge. Turn left, on to a wide track beside the wood, then keep left at a fork. The track soon becomes concrete and passes to the right of Cadmans Pool. Cross a metalled road and take a left turn along a grassy track to enter more woodland.

6 In 50yds (46m), turn right, the trees giving way to gorse and grassland. As the footpath becomes indistinct, maintain direction and soon bear left on to the gravel track. Continue to a gate and walk across some concrete, taking the path in the bottom right-hand corner leading into South Bentley Inclosure.

7 Walk down to a gate (No 75) and turn right. Cross a stream and head along an indistinct path, soon to bear half left through a copse to reach a larger stream. Walk along the right-hand bank and cross the bridge.

8 Continue ahead, the path passing a house and gate to become a gravelled drive. Keep to the drive until the junction by The Royal Oak pub. Turn back to the car park.

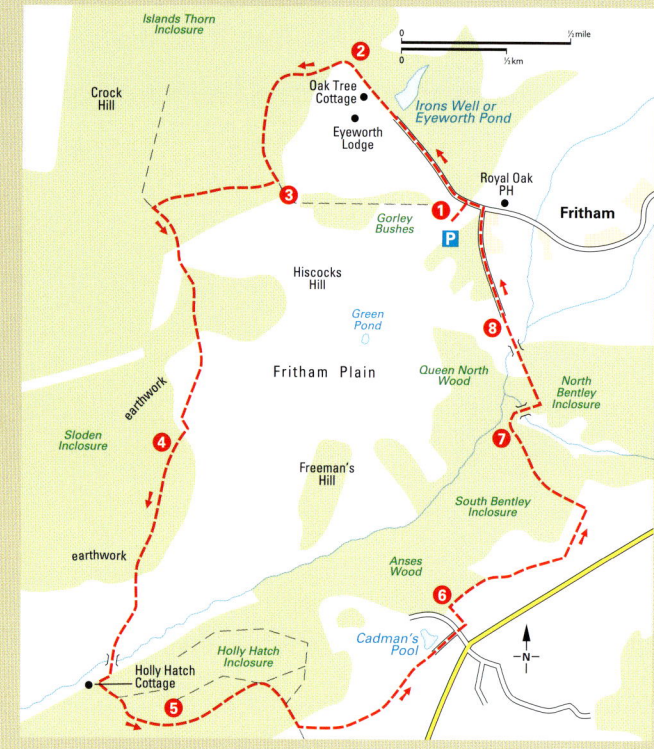

NEW FOREST TRAILS AROUND BANK

Ancient oaks, towering conifers and historic inclosures (managed woodland where young trees are protected from deer and ponies) are on the route. Soon after starting the longer walk you'll pass the most famous and probably the oldest tree in the forest, the Knightwood Oak, thought to be at least 350 years old.

DISTANCE/TIME 5 miles (8km) 3h **MAP** OS Outdoor Leisure 22 New Forest **START** Brock Hill Forestry Commission car park; grid ref: SU 266057 **TRACKS** Grass and gravel forest tracks, heathland paths, some roads **THE PUB** The Oak Inn, Pinkney Lane, Bank. Tel: 02380 282350

1 Take the gravel path at the top end of the car park (to the right of 'The Tall Trees Trail' sign), parallel with the road. In 100yds (91m) turn right and down to a gravel track. Cross over, then where it curves left, keep ahead to a gate and the A35. Cross, go through a gate and keep to the track, uphill to a junction. Turn right and then follow the path to a road. Cross into Knightwood Oak car park and follow the signs leading to the tree itself.

2 From the oak bear right down a wide ride. Go through a gate and keep to the path through open woodland and bear right towards the A35. Just before a gate and the A35 take the narrow path on the left. Cross a footbridge, turn left along the line of a drainage ditch and continue to a cottage. Turn left for the New Forest Reptile Centre.

3 Return past Holiday Hills Cottage. After 300yds (274m), at a barrier on the left, drop down to a path and follow it across a bridge.

4 Keep to the main path, and at the top of a rise fork right. In 25yds (23m) turn to the right, dropping and skirting left around cottages and Allum Green. Climb through trees to a crossing of paths and turn right. Soon, bear half right across a clearing and

footbridge. Continue through the woodland edge to a telegraph pole. Bear right for 50yds (46m), then left through a gate to the A35.

5 Turn left, then right across the road to a gate. Head to a garden boundary and right on a narrow path to a lane in Bank. Turn right, pass The Oak Inn and go through and up out of the hamlet. Before a sharp left-hand bend (by a cattle grid), bear right beside a barrier and continue on a wide path.

6 Go through the patch of trees and scrub to a fork on the edge of a clearing. Keep right on the path between an oak and a holly tree. Continue past a pretty cottage and along the drive to a metalled lane at Gritnam.

7 Turn left, and after 100yds (91m), before a bridge, turn right to a telegraph pole. Follow the path and go left along the track to the water treatment works. Keep left and continue into thicker woodland which soon becomes more open. Cross a footbridge and then turn left. After 25yds (23m) fork right.

8 Walk through Brinken Wood and cross to a bridge over Warwickslade Cutting. Bear right, go through a gate and sharp right at the gravel track. Swing left to the car park.

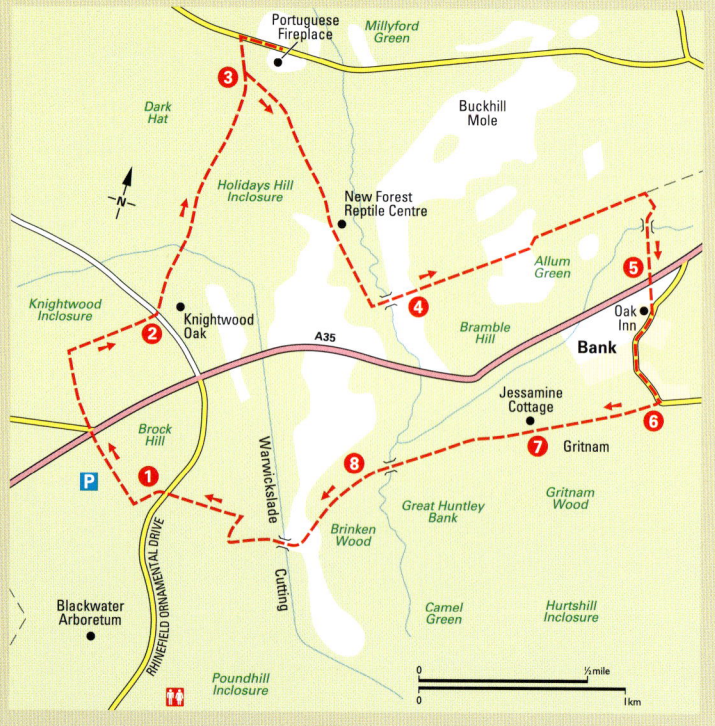

AROUND ROMAN ROCKBOURNE

Through fields and dense woodland, this walk discovers Rockbourne, which has one of Hampshire's prettiest village high streets and is home to one of the most interesting Roman villa complexes in the country. The walk continues to Whitsbury, where foundations of another Roman building lie over Iron Age settlements.

DISTANCE/TIME 4.5 miles (7.2km) 1h45 **MAP** OS Outdoor Leisure 22 New Forest or OS Explorer 130 Salisbury & Stonehenge **START** Rockbourne village hall car park; grid ref: SU 113184 **TRACKS** Field paths, woodland bridleways and tracks, 9 stiles **THE PUB** The Rose and Thistle, Rockbourne. Tel: 01725 518236

1 Turn left out of the car park and take the lane on your right towards Manor Farm. Turn right, signed to the church, and cross the gravel drive to a path to St Andrew's Church. Continue along the right-hand edge of the churchyard to a junction of paths. Keep straight on behind houses, ignoring two paths right, then cross a stile and turn immediately right through a gate.

2 Follow the field edge down to a junction of paths. Keep left to a gate and maintain direction across two stiles and along the field edge to a stile in the corner. Climb the stile immediately right and bear left along the edge of a meadow to a stile. Pass in front of a thatched cottage to a stile and track, opposite Marsh Farm.

3 Bear left, then right through a gate and keep to the left through pasture to another gate. Bear half-right to a gate in the corner and head along the field edge to a stile and lane. To visit the Roman Villa, turn right to get to a T-junction, and turn right, then left into the entrance. Retrace your steps.

4 Back at the lane, cross onto a track and then, along in a copse, at a junction of tracks, take the arrowed path left up a steep bank into a field. Keep to the left-hand edge

and head across a field to a track. Turn right, then left down and through the edge of some woodland. Pass a house to enter a lane.

5 Turn right, then left on a bridleway, and up through Radnall Wood. At a fork of paths, bear left (follow the blue arrow) and pass behind Whitsbury House to a lane. Turn left, then right on a track between properties to a lane. Turn right, then bear off right on the bridleway through Whitsbury Wood.

6 At a junction with a track, bear left and walk beside paddocks to a bungalow. Turn left along a track between paddocks towards Whitsbury church. Now turn left at the T-junction and shortly enter the churchyard. Go through the gate opposite the church door and descend to the lane.

7 Turn left for The Cartwheel Inn, or turn right, then turn left along a farm drive and keep ahead, bearing left, then right between paddocks, uphill to a gate. Turn turn left along the field edge and then head across the field where you will come to a track.

8 Turn right and follow the track left to a junction of a few tracks. Step over the stile opposite and head to Rockbourne church. Retrace steps back to the village hall.

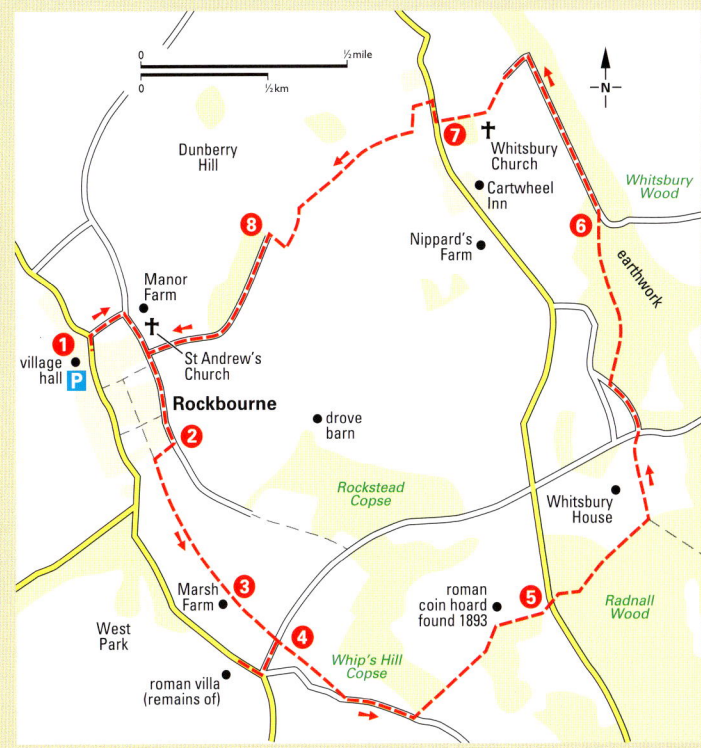

WALK 32

EXBURY – HAMPSHIRE'S GREAT GARDEN

Spectacular year-round displays await in the superb 200-acre (80ha) gardens. From brilliant spring and summer flowers to the wonderful autumnal displays of the maples. There is a steam railway ride through the gardens and exhibitions and events, including craft demonstrations.

DISTANCE/TIME 6 miles (9.7km) 3h **MAP** OS Outdoor Leisure 22 New Forest **START** Pay-and-display car parks at Lepe Country Park; grid ref: SZ 455985 **TRACKS** Fields, woodland and foreshore paths, some roads, 8 stiles **THE PUB** The Master Builders House Hotel, Bucklers Hard Tel: 01590 616253; www.themasterbuilders.co.uk

1 Walk west from the car park on the road. Keep left along the path and pass The Watch House. At the lighthouse, bear right to reach a lane, then turn left. As the road curves left, cross a stile on the right. Walk along the field edge, then bear left over a bridge.

2 Keep by a fence to a stile, then head straight across a field. Briefly pass by woodland and then follow the path to a stile near a telegraph pole. Cross the next stile and take the path leading to a stile on the woodland edge ahead. Continue on through the trees, bearing right beyond a footbridge, then right with a waymarker post to join a bridleway arrowed to the left.

3 Enter a field, then walk up the left-hand edge of the field, skirting East Hill Farm to a track. Where the track curves sharply left, turn right through a gate. Follow the path ahead and then enter a field and turn right. Follow the field edge to a T-junction. Turn left and head towards a stile and lane.

4 Turn right, going through a gate by a cattle grid; take the footpath left through a gate (by a cattle grid) to join the track to Gatewood Farm. Bear right at a fork and walk around the farm. Remain on the track for 0.75 mile

(1.2km) to a gate and a lane. Go straight across to visit Exbury Gardens. If you want refreshments, the gardens have a tea room.

5 On leaving the gardens, turn right along the road. Where the road bends left, keep ahead (signed 'Inchmery Lane'). Continue to a waymarked path and stile on the left.

6 Proceed across grassland into woodland, following a path right, through trees. At the crossing of paths, turn left through the woodland fringe. On leaving the trees, turn right along a field edge by woodland to a stile. Maintain your course, bearing right with a waymaker, and soon follow a path through scrub into woodland. Cross a footbridge and bear left, eventually reaching a lane.

7 Turn left and follow the lane to the shore. Proceed along the foreshore (follow the fingerpost) close to the high tide line and continue below Inchmery House. Pass Lepe House and rejoin the outward route. The final stretch along the foreshore may be impassable at high tide, so keep to the lane around Inchmery House, then, just before the road junction, turn right beside the barrier and head down to the foreshore to pick up the path past Lepe House.

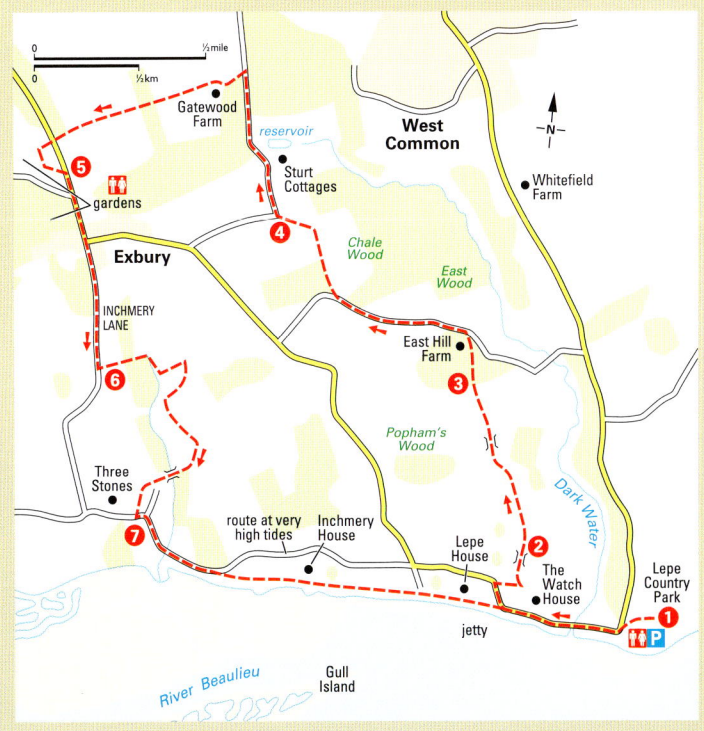

DISTANCE/TIME 6 miles (9.7km) 1h **MAP** OS Explorer OL22 New Forest **START** Public pay car park, Burley; grid ref: SU 211030 **TRACKS** Busy village centre, quiet lanes and an old railway route **THE PUB** The Queen's Head, Burley, Ringwood. Tel: 012425 403423

DISTANCE/TIME 7 miles (11.3km) 1h45 **MAP** OS Explorer OL22 New Forest **START** Spring Bushes car park, on the road that runs west from Emery Down, near Lyndhurst, just north of Ringwood; grid ref: SU 196107 **TRACKS** Gravelled forest tracks, two short sections on rural lanes **THE PUB** The High Corner Inn, Linwood. Tel: 01425 473973

A NEW FOREST LOOP FROM BURLEY

This route takes you through the heart of Burley, with its antiques shops, tea rooms and horse-drawn wagon rides, then joins the Castleman cycle trail where you can experience the surrounding heathland from a level stretch of old railway line. There are good opportunities for birdwatching on the route.

1 Turn right out of the car park, stop at the next road junction, and then continue straight ahead. Fork left at the war memorial into Pound Lane, which is signed to Bransgore. Cycle past the Forest Teahouse and cider shop, then follow the lane out over the heath until you get to Burbush Hill.

2 Fork left just before the old railway bridge, following the waymarked off-road cycle track through the Forestry Commission's car park and continue down on to the old railway line. The Castleman Trail sets out from a lovely sandy cutting, which is smothered with brilliant purple heather during late summer. Soon the old line emerges from the cutting on to a low embankment, where there are good views out over the boggy heath. You'll often see horse riders in the area and birdwatchers should look out for green woodpeckers, as well as for wetland birds like lapwings, curlews and redshanks, which nest on the heath in early summer. The trail then rises briefly to the broken brickwork of Greenberry Bridge, which survived the closure of the railway, only to be demolished in 1995 when it became unsafe. Continue forward to the low wooden barriers that guard the minor road crossing at Holmsley Passage, where you can still see sections of the original railway lines embedded in the road.

3 If you wish, you can shorten the ride by turning left here and returning to the start point. Otherwise, to complete the full route, cross the road and continue along the old railway line. The trail becomes much more shaded as it follows a perfectly straight line through an avenue of lovely oak trees. The track then crosses over two small bridges that herald the approach to Holmsley Station. Here, look out for the old brick platform situated over to your right before dismounting your bicycle at the wooden gate that marks the end of the cycle track.

4 Beyond the gate and across the road, the Old Station Tea Rooms are well worth a visit for morning coffee, lunch or a cream tea. There's a pleasant garden, as well as a gift shop where you can buy a souvenir of your visit to this unusual refreshment stop. Turn here and retrace your outward route to Holmsley Passage (Point 3). Turn right on to the quiet lane. Follow the lane up the hill and then stop at the 5-way junction.

5 Cross straight over towards Burley Lawn and zigzag left, then right, past The White Buck Inn and taking you into Bennetts Lane.

6 Bear left when you eventually reach the next junction leading into Beechwood Lane and keep cycling straight on through Lester Square until you finally reach a T-junction. Turn left here towards Burley, and continue cycling past the pretty little brick-built church of St John the Baptist for the final 400-yd (366m) cycle stretch that takes you back to the car park in Burley village.

A CIRCUIT AROUND LINWOOD

This ride offers a good chance of some peace and quiet, and the opportunity to see the New Forest at its best. You'll follow the waymarked Forestry Commission off-road cycle tracks deep into the heart of the Forest for the majority of the ride, with two short sections on tarred roads.

1 Turn right out of the car park and continue straight on, passing the end of the gravel track that leads up to The High Corner Inn.

2 At Woodford Bottom bear left at the wooden barrier on your right and pass the ford across the Dockens Water stream, also on your right. Keep to the waymarked cycle route as it closely follows the gravelled track that winds across the open heath, past a few scattered houses and the tree-capped mound of Black Barrow. A few smaller tracks lead off of the main track to the left and to the right, but the main gravelled trail is easy enough to follow. Keep cycling straight on as a similar track leads in from your left near the thatched Bogmyrtle Cottage, until you join a tarred lane. Almost at once the lane turns sharp left through a tiny ford and climbs gently up to the road junction located near to The Red Shoot Inn.

3 Turn left opposite the post-box, still following the waymarked cycle route, and continue to cycle uphill until the road levels off and swings round to the left at Amie's Corner. Fork right here, sticking with the waymarked cycle route as it eventually joins a gravelled forest track. The trail then dives into Milkham Inclosure through wooden gates situated beside an attractive whitewashed cottage, then the trail drops down a way to a bridge over the Linford Brook.

4 A few yards further on turn left at the numbered waymark post 5, then follow the track as it winds through open mixed woodland and then re-crosses the Linford Brook. Continue as the track bears right at the next waymark post, then right again in front of a pair of wooden gates where you enter an area of mainly coniferous woodland. Another pair of wooden gates punctuates your progress to the top of the hill, where further gates lead you out into the Forestry Commission's Milkham car park. Go through here, cross the car park, and stop at the road junction.

5 Turn left towards Linwood and follow the narrow tarred lane for 500yds (457m) until it bears away to the left. Fork right here on to the waymarked cycle trail that follows the gravel track towards Broomy Lodge and Holly Hatch. Here your route crosses the high heathland plateau of Broomy Plain. This is a good spot to see Dartford warblers, meadow pipits and stonechats, and you'll also enjoy good long views towards Cranborne Chase and the Wiltshire Downs. Bear right at the next fork and then follow the trail down into Holly Hatch Inclosure.

6 At the foot of the hill, numbered waymark post 3 stands at the forest crossroads. Turn left here, on to a lovely tree-shaded track with soft green verges that leads you through the oak woods. Two pairs of wooden gates mark your progress through the inclosure, and at length the oaks give way to conifers. Follow the waymarked trail until you rejoin your outward route at a low wooden barrier. Turn left here, and climb the short hill back to The High Corner Inn.

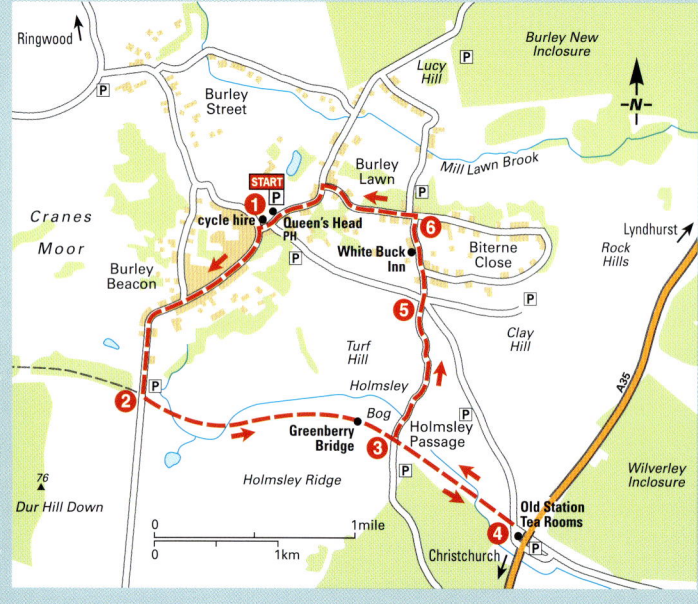

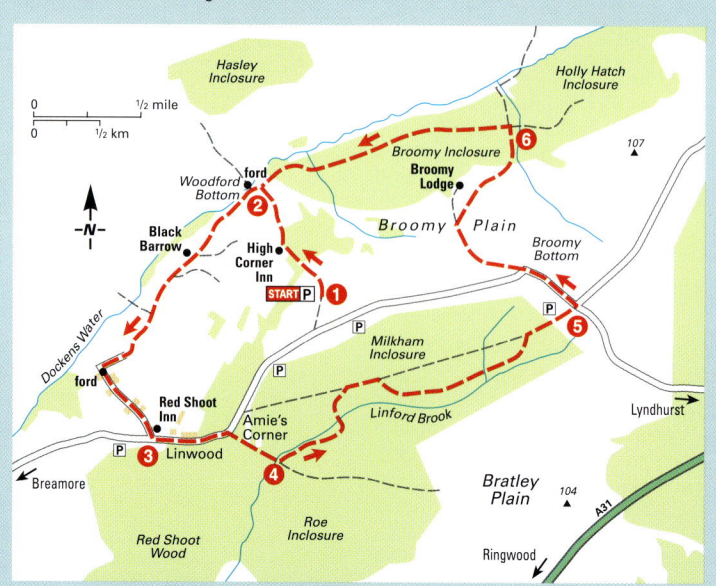

Isle of Wight

CLOCKWISE FROM TOP LEFT: SAILING BOATS AT COWES WEEK; ISLE OF WIGHT; ENTRANCE GATEHOUSE AT CARISBROOKE CASTLE; MEDUSA MOSAIC, BRADING ROMAN VILLA

COWES

BRADING MAP REF 400 E7

In Roman times Bembridge Down was an island and Brading faced it across a tidal channel. In about AD 300 the Romans built a villa here, one of the best in Britain with fabulous mosaics. A vineyard on the slopes near the villa continues a tradition of wine-making begun in Roman times. In 1338 an embankment was built at Yar Bridge, creating a harbour to connect Bembridge Down with the rest of the Isle of Wight. Brading was an important port, but the harbour here, too, experienced increased silting. It was reclaimed in 1878–80 and is now an area of marshy meadows, a breeding ground for birds.

'Brading the Experience' illustrates in waxworks the characters from 2,000 years of island history, alongside displays of wax animals, steam and vintage cars, and a carousel-themed café. Brading also has the Lilliput Museum of Antique Dolls and Toys. Morton Manor, rebuilt in 1680, has beautiful gardens and a small vineyard producing the island's best wines. The Church of St Mary, the Isle of Wight's oldest church, is believed to mark the spot where St Wilfred converted the island to Christianity, and a chapel contains the tombs of the Oglander family, important in affairs of the island for 800 years.

To the northwest, Nunwell House, seat of the Oglanders, is where Charles I spent his last night on the island.

CARISBROOKE MAP REF 400 E7

Carisbrooke, once the capital of the Isle of Wight, is inland above the Medina River to the west of the modern capital, Newport, and is overlooked by its impressive castle. The High Street is pleasant, and narrow Castle Street leads up from an old ford and a streamside footpath to get to the castle. St Mary's Church, with its lofty 15th-century tower, was the church of a priory dissolved as long ago as 1415.

Carisbrooke Castle is a big, well-preserved Norman fortress built high on an artificial mound. The oldest parts are the keep and the surviving sections of curtain walls, which were constructed in the 12th century and strengthened at the end of the 16th century. A head for heights is needed to walk the ramparts, but you will be rewarded with excellent views of the interior of the castle and the surrounding countryside. A very popular attraction is the well, 161 feet (49m) deep, with a 16th-century wheel to draw up the water in buckets. It is worked today by donkeys – learn more of this at the Donkey Centre. The castle also houses the Isle of Wight Museum.

COWES MAP REF 400 E7

Cowes, on the island's northern tip, is divided by the River Medina. On the west bank is the sailing capital of Britain, on the east is a residential and industrial area, where high-speed ships, flying boats and seaplanes were built during World War II, and the Hovercraft was developed. Beyond all this lies the peace of Osborne House, Queen Victoria's favourite residence.

West Cowes, home of the Royal Yacht Squadron, has an attractive winding High Street and a good array of shops. You can see ships and boats of all sorts from the Victoria Parade. The inaugural Cowes Regatta took place between naval vessels in 1776, and the yacht club was founded in 1815. In 1856 Cowes Castle became the Squadron's headquarters, and the 22 brass guns from the Royal Adelaide, King William IV's yacht, were positioned in front of the castle to start races and salute victorious yachts – as they still do. There have always been Royal yachtsmen – including Edward VII, George IV, George V, Prince Philip and Prince Edward – and during Cowes Week in August the little town is alive with the great and the good of the yachting fraternity.

Cowes has a good Maritime Museum, a military history museum, as well as the Sir Max Aitken Museum, which has nautical instruments and paintings.

FRESHWATER MAP REF 400 E7

The southwest tip of the Isle of Wight which ends in the jagged sea-girt chalk pinnacles of The Needles is known as the Freshwater Peninsula. The village of Freshwater itself is large and bustling, and was made famous by poet Alfred, Lord Tennyson who came to reside at Farringford – now a hotel – in 1853, soon after he was proclaimed Poet Laureate. The famous portrait photographer Julia Margaret Cameron settled here also, in the 1860s, and her home, Dimbola Lodge, on Terrace Lane, is now a museum.

THE NEEDLES & ALUM BAY
MAP REF 400 D7

The soaring, spiky chalk outcrops of The Needles are the Isle of Wight's most famous landmark. They sport a red-and-white striped lighthouse, topped by a small helicopter landing platform, which is best seen via boat trips from Alum Bay.

Set at right angles to the chalk, the cliffs at Alum Bay produce the island's most unusual souvenirs: clear glass novelty items that display the distinctive 12 shades of sand. The colours range from pink and gold to orange and brown, and are all found naturally in the cliffs here.

The sandstone strata of the cliffs are vertical, and were formed some 50 million years ago. You can view them from a spectacular chairlift ride down the cliffs to the beach at the bottom.

On the cliff edge is a monument to the Italian physicist and inventor, Marconi, who set up a wireless and telegraph station here at the end of the 19th century.

■ THE NEEDLES

The Needles Old Battery at Totland is a gun battery and fort with wonderful views over the Needles. It was built in 1863 as part of the defences for the large naval base at Portsmouth. Exhibitions tell the story of the fort during the world wars.

NEWPORT MAP REF 400 E7

Newport, the capital of the Isle of Wight, is a venerable old market town on the River Medina. Its squares and narrow, twisting streets may hide the river from view, but boats still ply their trade at the rejuvenated quay. Here, too, is the arts centre in a large converted warehouse. The pleasant High Street has many attractive buildings, and is dominated by the Guildhall, with its fine Ionic portico market designed by John Nash, now home to the Museum of Island History. St Thomas' Church has a beautiful marble monument designed by Marochetti to Princess Elizabeth, the youngest daughter of Charles I, who died of a fever aged 14 while she was a prisoner in Carisbrooke Castle.

A Roman villa, dating from the 3rd century AD, was discovered here in 1926. The villa has been excavated and is open to the public. Three of the public rooms have tessellated floors, and the largest also has a fireplace – this was an unusual feature in a Roman house. There is also a reconstructed Roman herb garden.

Northwest of the town is Parkhurst Prison, beyond which is Parkhurst Forest, the remaining glades and woodlands of a former royal hunting forest. This ancient woodland has been threaded by waymarked paths and is now one of the last remaining refuges of the red squirrel.

RYDE MAP REF 400 E7

When island visitors disembark at Ryde from the ferry, ex-London Transport underground trains take them down the 0.5-mile (800m) long pier, necessary because the coast shelves so gently that vessels can get no closer.

Ryde was developed in the late 18th century and is the largest town on the island, with some 24,000 residents. It has the usual seaside amusements as well as a 5-mile (8km) sandy beach. Ryde's summer carnival is a spectacular event.

Southwest of Ryde is Brickfields Horse Country, with horses of all sizes, wagon rides and pig-racing. At Ashey, Rosemary Vineyard, the largest of the island's three, offers tours, tastings and a shop. At Fishbourne, to the west, is Quarr Abbey, a modern foundation (1907–14) of Benedictine monks near the ruins of the earlier Cistercian Abbey. The Isle of Wight Steam Railway puffs out of Smallbrook Junction, just south of Ryde on its journey past Havenstreet to Wootton.

SANDOWN & SHANKLIN

MAP REF 400 E7 & 400 E8

The honky-tonk seaside neighbour of more sedate Shanklin, Sandown was founded as a resort in about 1800 and faces southeastwards out to sea across Sandown Bay. It is built at beach level, with the huge chalk walls of Culver Cliff to the north and the cliffed coast of Shanklin and Luccombe to the south. Sandown is a popular venue for family holidays, with its 6 miles (9.6km) of sandy beach and an esplanade and amusement park, a pier of 1878, cinema, zoo specialising in tigers and lemurs, and the fascinating Dinosaur Isle, a museum displaying life-size dinosaurs and offering guided fossil walks. At the Garlic Farm, near Newchurch, you can buy and learn more.

Shanklin, Sandown's quieter southern neighbour, is a resort that developed with the coming of the railway in 1891, and now has the best collection of beach huts on the island. You reach the beach by a lift from the clifftop, which has a superb view around Sandown Bay to the gleaming white heights of Culver Cliff. Inland is Shanklin Old Village, a former fishing village close to the winding glen of Shanklin Chine. This 300-feet (91.5m) deep, wooded and ferny fissure was much beloved of earlier tourists, including the poet, John Keats, who stayed at the Old Village in 1819 and composed part of 'Endymion' here. The Victorians flocked to tread its winding path past the 40-foot (12m) waterfall to the beach. Today, Shanklin Chine still pulls the crowds – its rare flora is of great interest – and the resort also has two theatres and seaside amusements.

VENTNOR MAP REF 400 E8

This south coast resort climbs the sheer cliff beneath flat St Boniface Down (the highest point on the island), as a series of terraces behind the sandy beach, so that the mainly Victorian buildings are built-up in layers and are joined by steep zig-zagging roads with corkscrew turns. There is something Mediterranean in this arrangement, and Ventnor has been dubbed 'the English Madeira'. Also the climate, too, is very good. Protected by the bulk of St Boniface Down, it basks in subtropical conditions.

Ventnor was a small fishing village up until 1841 – albeit much involved in smuggling – but in that year, a famous doctor, Sir James Clarke, publicly sang its praises and visitors started to come. The railway arrived in 1866, meaning Ventnor's development as a health resort was assured, attracting, among others, authors Macaulay, Dickens and Thackeray. Later it was the site of the Royal National Hospital for Consumption and Diseases of the Chest. The town's history is explained in Ventnor's Heritage Museum which has an extensive archive.

Ventnor divides into two parts, the elegant 'town' on the cliff face, where Ventnor ales are still brewed, and the seaside resort at the foot of the cliff.

The extraordinary climate is manifest in the Ventnor Botanic Gardens, which were planted in the 1970s, where some 3,500 species include palms and cork trees. The interesting Smuggling Museum, hidden in subterranean caverns beneath the Botanic Garden, has a large collection of fascinating relics, vividly illustrating the days when Ventnor was the unofficial 'headquarters' of illicit trade. Near byis the ancient village of St Lawrence with the Rare Breeds and Waterfowl Park. Isle of Wight Glass produces an exciting range of award-winning glassware.

The southern coast between Ventnor and St Catherine's Point is a region of landslides, where great masses of sandstone rock have been, and continue to be, carried down into the sea on a lubricating layer of blue clay. In fact, Ventnor has the biggest urban landslide problem in Britain. The Undercliff, a ledge which extends along the cliffs, is actually the top of an ancient landslide block. To appreciate the coast to the full, walk along part of the coastal path between Shanklin and Blackgang. From Shanklin the path first lies close to, and then on, the shore until you reach Ventnor and beyond. At St Lawrence, the path climbs up beyond the road and affords good views to the south before you reach Blackgang.

Nearby Blackgang Chine is an extraordinary theme park that combines static displays with fast fairground rides and lovely gardens. In fact the gardens were the initial inspiration for the park, created to attract Victorian vacationers.

WROXALL MAP REF 400 E8

The village of Wroxall was once no more than a small hamlet but the construction of the railway through a 0.75mile (1.2km) tunnel changed that and many of the old cottages in the main street were built to house the railway workmen. The village nestles in the downs and has a handsome Victorian church built from stone excavated in the tunnel workings. From Wroxall there are lovely walks to Ventnor, Shanklin, Whitwell and Godshill. The most notable attraction in Wroxall is Appuldurcombe House, once the most imposing house on the Isle of Wight and home to the Worsley family for 300 years. It then had a chequered history and the majority of the house was left as an impressive shell surrounded by 'Capability' Brown landscape. Now managed by English Heritage the front section of the building has been re-roofed and glazed and a portion of the interior has been recreated in all its 18th century baroque glory. This is open to the public from April to September. Appuldurcombe House also has an Owl and Falconry Centre.

YARMOUTH MAP REF 400 E7

The Lymington–Yarmouth ferry is the picturesque way of entry to the Isle of Wight, for Yarmouth is a compact little town with narrow streets and attractive houses, and a small harbour busy with yachts and a flourishing boatbuilder's yard. During the Middle Ages it was the most important Isle of Wight town, but decline set in and by 1800 it had only a few hundred inhabitants.

Yarmouth's sturdy castle was built against the French in 1547 by Henry VIII, and it remained in use until the 1870s.

It is hidden down an alley by the ferry, on King's Land, and is easy to miss. The pier near the lifeboat station was built in 1876 and was originally the landing stage for the Lymington ferry, but now it is a pleasant walkway.

Yarmouth's church, rebuilt 1614–26, contains an intriguing monument to Sir Robert Holmes, Governor of the Isle of Wight during the reign of Charles II. The figure was originally intended as a statue of the French 'Sun King', Louis XIV. The statue was being transported by sea so that the sculptor would be able to complete the head from life, but Holmes captured the ship carrying it, took the statue and had his own likeness attached to it instead. Holmes entertained Charles II at his house on the quay in Yarmouth, now the George Hotel.

West of Yarmouth is the 50-acre (20ha), wooded, Fort Victoria Country Park, based around the remains of a fort which was built in 1855. The many parts of the park afford superb views of the River Solent, and there are guided walks, a maritime heritage exhibition, a marine aquarium, a planetarium and a little model railway.

VENTNOR

FROM YARMOUTH TO FRESHWATER

This ramble encapsulates the contrasting landscapes, from the wildlife-rich tidal estuary of the River Yar and the wetland habitat of freshwater marshes housing wild birds, to farmland and the magnificent chalk headlands.

DISTANCE/TIME 9.5 miles (15.3km) 4h30 **MAP** OS Outdoor Leisure 29 Isle of Wight **START** Ferry terminal or pay-and-display car park opposite, Yarmouth, grid ref: SZ 354897 **TRACKS** Disused railway, woodland and downland paths, some road walking, 4 stiles **THE PUB** The Red Lion, Church Place, Freshwater. Tel: 01983 754925; www.redlion-wight.co.uk

1 From the square, head for church and along St James' Street. Cross Tennyson Road into Mill Road, past old Tide Mill. Go through gate and follow the railway line to The Causeway.

2 To return to Yarmouth, turn right, cross The Causeway to The Red Lion and Point 9. For the second stage, turn left at Point 2 and follow the lane to the B3399. Now turn left and cross into the Manor Road. Soon bear left ('Freshwater Way') towards Afton Down.

3 Go ahead at a junction beside the golf course. Follow the track to the clubhouse. Go through a gate and walk down the access track. Go right down into Freshwater Bay.

4 For the second loop option, walk past the Albion Hotel and turn right at Blackbridge Road, at Point 8. For the third section of the long walk, turn left by the bus shelter, along the 'Coastal Footpath'. As it bears left, keep ahead through kissing gates and climb a path on to Tennyson Down. Keep to the well trodden path to in order to reach the cross that stands at the top.

5 Cross the grass to the replica of Old Nodes Beacon. Here, turn very sharp right down a chalk track. Turn right into a car park and almost immediately climb sharp left.

6 The path drops to a gate, past woodland to an open area, and forks left at excavations. Cross a stile, keep left and shortly turn sharp left to a stile. Cross the field to a stile, and then turn right along field edge to a stile.

7 After a stile, cross a track, through a gate, follow the track, then go under a footbridge to a gate and the road. Turn right, pass the church, and go left down Blackbridge Road.

8 Before Black Bridge, turn left into Afton Marshes Nature Reserve. Walk along the nature trail, cross the footbridge and turn left on the path beside the stream to the A3055. Turn left and cross to join footpath F61 along the old railway to reach The Causeway.

9 Turn left to All Saints Church. Take path F1 between the churchyard and cottage. Cross two stiles. Continue on the farm road. At the farm entrance cross the stile on the left and bear right on the field edge to a stile.

10 At a track and the entrance to Kings Manor Farm, cross the stile and go on to a gate and a junction. Climb the stile on the right, go via a copse, over another stile and bear left, uphill along the field edge. Cross two stiles. Drop to woodland, emerging onto a metalled track. Turn left to the A3054 and right to the bridge, back into Yarmouth.

WALK 34

BLACKGANG CHINE & THE PEEPING PEPPERPOT

This intriguing ramble is around an area steeped in tales about shipwrecks, smuggling and three lighthouses. Before you lies the broad sweep of Chale Bay and high upon St Catherine's Hill to your right is a curious octagonal tower, known locally as the 'Pepper Pot', all that remains of a medieval lighthouse or beacon.

DISTANCE/TIME 5.5 miles (8.8km) 2h **MAP** OS Outdoor Leisure 29 Isle of Wight **START** Viewpoint car park above Blackgang Chine; grid ref: SZ 490767 **TRACKS** Field paths, downland tracks, coast path, 12 stiles **THE PUB** The White Lion, Niton. Tel: 01983 528479

1 From the car park, cross the road and climb the steps to a stile. Bear left around the field edge signed ('St Catherine's Oratory'). Cross the stile and steadily climb grassy downland to another stile. Ascend to the old lighthouse (Pepper Pot), ignore the stile by the trig point just beyond, and, keeping the fence on the right, continue downhill to reach a gate.

2 Go through the gate and proceed over a broad grassy swathe to Hoy's Monument. Return 55yds (50m) and take a bridleway left. Drop steeply through trees and bear left with the main path to a gate. Follow a bridleway left then bear right on the driveway.

3 Proceed at crossing of tracks (Downcourt Farm drive is to the right), heading downhill to a gate by a house. Walk along the right-hand field edge to a gate. Head down on a hedged path. At the T-junction, turn tight. Go through the gate soon emerging into field.

4 Keep to the left-hand field edge, beside an overgrown gully. Go through the first gate on the left. In a few paces, turn right. Take the path left just before a gate. Go through trees, cross a bridge and keep right. Gradually ascend a stony path (wet in winter), which bears left then steepens to reach a stile.

5 Walk straight ahead, following the defined path uphill beside a hedge to two stiles in field corner. Cross the right-hand stile and immediately turn right, down on to the path that heads diagonally uphill across the face of Head Down to a stile. Turn left along to a stile and a track.

6 Turn left, and then almost immediately right along a hedged bridleway. Head downhill, the path becoming metalled as it enters Niton. Just before a lane, bear right into the churchyard. Keep left, exiting the churchyard by a small gate and turn right alongside the A3055.

7 Take the footpath beside the last house on the left and ascend steeply through the trees to a stile. Keep ahead over grassland to another stile. Follow the left-hand field edge to the next stile.

8 Turn right along the coastal path, cross two stiles. You will soon emerge on to the open cliff top. Stay on the narrow path close to the cliff edge for nearly 1 mile (1.6km) to return to the car park.

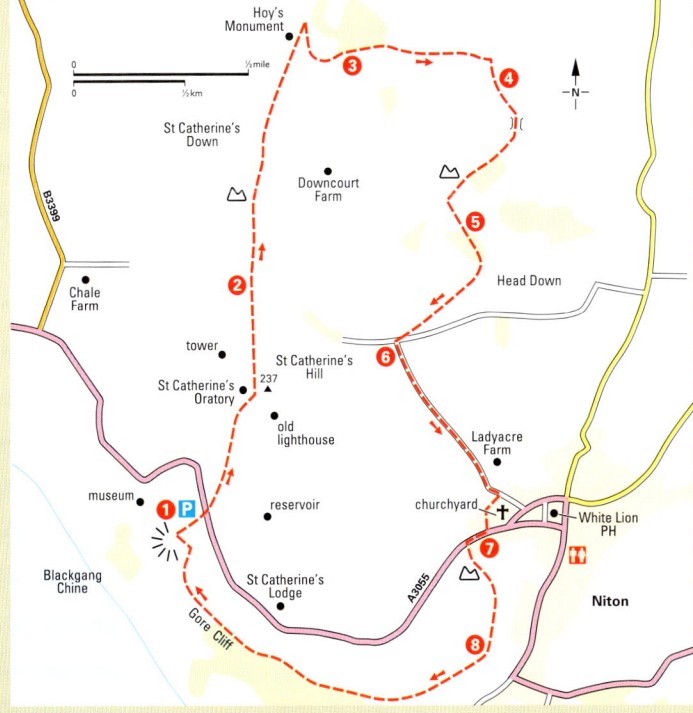

Cowes Week

More than a century old, and part of our heritage, Cowes Week is the premier sailing event in Britain. But then Cowes Week is all about boats: big boats, little boats, fast boats, slow boats, expensive boats, and some very, very expensive boats.

So successful has the event become that today it is the longest-running regatta in the world, the first official regatta taking place in 1812, on the Isle of Wight, accompanied by a review of the Trinity House Pilots. That first race was not for money, but for a gold cup with a value of just £100.

Many believe that Cowes owes its name as the yachting capital of the world to the building of a small boat for Elizabeth I. Royal patronage was sure to start a trend, but it took a while for sailing as a leisure pastime to catch on. In fact, although the Dutch developed leisure yachting in the meantime, 260 years and nine monarchs were to go by before the interest of the then Prince of Wales was to flourish into organised yachting after his succession to the throne. In 1826 the Royal Yacht Squadron formally organised three whole days of racing in the waters of the Solent.

Cowes Regatta itself had been going before The Yacht Club (as the Squadron was first known) was founded in 1815, and was based around the local Pilot Cutters receiving their licences. The event we know today has been held during the first week in August continuously every year except during the world wars. Now, Cowes Week hosts more than 1,000 competing boats.

Until 1914 big cutters raced, but the inter-war years saw the introduction of cruiser handicap classes, although the 6–8 and 12 metre boats attracted the most racing interest. After 1946, when for a few years there was a revival of big yacht racing, ocean racing classes started to predominate, especially after the first competitive race for the Admiral's Cup in 1957. The two ocean races that start and finish the week – the Channel and Fastnet races – began to gain in popularity. Because the Fastnet Race is held in odd-numbered years only, another offshore course is sailed in even years to attract ocean racers to the regatta.

After World War II yachting changed from being solely the province of the rich to a sport for the enthusiast. Today it is, arguably, a sport mainly for rich enthusiasts. But it remains no less exciting to see the Solent crowded, sometimes perilously, with hundreds of tiny spectator boats.

Despite being a regatta for thousands of sailors, Cowes Week is a huge moment in the British social calendar, taking place after the Goodwood and Ascot horse-racing festivals. The event maintains the same traditions of glittery yacht club balls, dinners, cocktail parties and concerts throughout the week, almost 200 years on.

The Solent is a unique stretch of water characterised by its tides and challenges, and during Cowes Week this busy waterway is filled with hundreds of racing boats and up to 300 bobbing spectator boats. All the races take place on the Solent, the sheltered waters and irregular tides of which invariably produce challenging, unusual and unpredictable conditions for the competitors. It gives even the most experienced helmsman and crew plenty of 'moments' and a non-stop sequence of problems to solve.

TOP LEFT The ABN AMRO ONE crew are seen concentrating and hard at work on the gruelling seventh day of racing.

TOP MIDDLE Competing is the name of the game at Cowes Week, whether it be in the races or the Timberland Tug of War.

TOP RIGHT Perhaps the most famous yachtswoman, Dame Ellen MacArthur, assisted on this occasion by her sailing partner Giles Chichester, sails in to Cowes at the helm of the legendary and newly restored *Gipsy Moth* IV.

LEFT The Class 1 fleet makes an awe-inspiring spectacle as it gets underway on sparkling water and under blue skies.

BELOW An exciting moment as the fleet of racers assembles on the start line off the Royal Squadron.

OPPOSITE A Sigma 33 broaches dangerously as she goes all out to reach the finish line on a blustery day at Skandia Cowes Week.

Despite the name, Cowes 'Week' actually runs for eight days, with at least 35 starts each day from the Royal Yacht Squadron, and around 1,000 racing boats taking part in the same number of classes. Each class is made up using the International Rating System which ranks the yachts' individual measurements. Traditionally, Class Zero has the largest boats (which are up to 98ft/30m long) and Class Seven, the smallest. The creation of a Super-Zero class in 2007 with its own race series, is a shrewd move intended to entice the owners and skippers of the world's largest and fastest ocean-racing yachts to compete.

This very British regatta is open to seasoned sailors and amateurs alike. More than 8,000 people are on the water each day, competing in dozens of different classes. To help further pack the overcrowded Solent, Cowes Week also hosts visiting foreign warships, sail training vessels and celebrated high profile maxi and round-the-world yachts.

For landlubbers, the highlight of the week's evening activities is the famous fireworks display held on the final Friday, and attracting a crowd of over 170,000 people. Princes Green is the place to be, if watching rather than messing about on boats is your preference. Claim a space early, take refreshments, a blanket, warm clothing, a woolly bobble hat, a cuddly toy or a loved one, and watch the yachts battle it out to the finish line. Don't go home too early: there will often be events on the water after the main racing has finished late in the afternoons.

For the non-expert, Cowes Week is a magical mystery mélange of rigging, canting keels, multihulls, monohulls, success, failure and champagne. But like most spectator sports, you don't have to fully understand what's going on to have fun.

DISTANCE/TIME 8 miles (12.9km) 1h45 **MAP** OS Explorer OL29 Isle of Wight **START** Medina Road pay-and-display car park, West Cowes; grid ref: SZ 499956 **TRACKS** Back streets of Cowes, tarred and level cycle track **THE PUB** The Bargeman's Rest, Newport. Tel: 01983 525828; www.bargemansrest.com

A LINEAR RIDE FROM COWES TO NEWPORT

This ride makes a relaxed day out, with easy access from the mainland. There is a lot to see from the safe, level trail, which follows the National Cycle Network route along the former Cowes-to-Newport railway line. You'll enjoy lovely views across the River Medina, with plenty of birdwatching on the way.

1 From Medina Road turn into Bridge Road, signposted 'Newport via cycleway'. Follow the road to the mini-roundabout at the top of the hill and turn left into Arctic Road, still following the signposted cycle route. Pass the UK Sailing Academy on your left and continue to the very end of the road.

2 Zigzag right and left as the cycle route joins the old railway line, which edges its way clear of industrial Cowes through a tunnel of trees. Pass the signposted footpath to Northwood on your right and, a little further on, look for the remains of an old bridge.

3 Beyond the bridge, look for a tall spire and pinnacles above the trees across the river. Around 0.5 mile (0.8km) from the gates of Osborne House, St Mildred's church was remodelled in the mid-18th century for use by the royal family. Continue on the track.

4 Now the views really open up, and between Pinkmead and Stag Lane you'll spot the old Ryde paddle steamer slowly rusting at Island Harbour Marina on the opposite bank. The hedges are thick with blackthorn, dog rose and crab apple, and in summer you'll see red admiral butterflies and dragonflies. Listen for the plaintive call of curlews.

5 The trail crosses the old trestle viaduct that once carried the railway line over Dodnor Creek. This area of open water, marshland and woodland was created in the 1790s when the creek was dammed to provide power for a proposed tide mill. Today the creek is a local nature reserve and you may see reed warblers, coots, moorhens and grey herons. Beyond the creek the cycleway climbs across Dodnor Lane and approaches industrial buildings on the edge of Newport. Look for a pair of concrete tracks that cross the trail and lead to a pair of slim concrete jetties built out into the river. A rolling gantry loads industrial products on to waiting barges. The facility was specially designed to minimise disturbance to the birds feeding on the mudflats of this protected wildlife site. Soon, reach the white gate at the end of the traffic-free route. Continue straight ahead as far as the post-box on the corner of Hurstake Road. Turn left to The Bargeman's Rest, and bear right at the bottom of the hill for the final 300yds (274m) to the pub.

6 Take a break before retracing your route to Cowes.

DISTANCE/TIME 16 miles (25.7km) 1h45 **MAP** OS Explorer OL29 Isle of Wight **START** Shalfleet village car park; grid ref: SZ 415895 **CYCLE HIRE** Wavells Cycle Hire, Yarmouth. Tel: 01983 813813 **TRACKS** Country lanes, old railway tracks, bridleways **THE PUB** New Inn, Shalfleet. Tel: 01983 531314

EXPLORING WEST WIGHT

The countryside between the high chalk hills of Compton and Brighstone Downs and Newtown Creek on the north coast is a joy to explore by bike.

1 Turn right out of the car park and return down the lane to the pub and road junction. Bear right, then left along Church Street, following the lane to a T-junction. Turn left, pass the post office and follow the lane for just under 1 mile (1.6km) to a second T-junction. Turn left, then right along Wellow Road, signposted Wellow and Thorley, and remain on this road for 2 miles (3.2km) to a T-junction beyond Thorley.

2 Turn right towards Yarmouth and near the outskirts, take the waymaked bridleway left, signposted Freshwater, and join the old railway track. Just past the former railway station, take the tarmac path right to visit Yarmouth, soon to turn left along Station Road, then right along Mill Road into the town. Retrace the route back to the old railway track. Follow this delightful trail beside the River Yar for 1.5 miles (2km) to the Causeway. Turn right to visit Freshwater church, otherwise turn left to reach the B3399.

3 Turn left and follow this open and wide road, which can be busy (great care to be taken), for 3 miles (4.8km) below Compton Down. Descend to a crossroads and turn left, signed to Newbridge. After a short climb the road levels and look out for a waymarked bridleway along the concrete drive to Eades Farm. (For the shorter route – keep on the lane to a T-junction and cross straight over to follow a bridleway for 0.5 mile (0.8km) to a road. Turn right and retrace your route back to Shalfleet and the New Inn).

4 For the longer route, turn right for Eades Farm, pass barns, keep left along a track and soon follow the narrow tarmac lane past houses to a T-junction on the edge of Newbridge. Turn right, then left for Lower Mill and Five Houses. Keep straight on at a T-junction, signed 'Five Houses', soon to follow the narrow lane left to the A3054.

5 Turn right, then left just beyond the bus park to follow a narrow unsigned lane. At the staggered crossroads, go across, signed 'Newtown'. Pass Waiter's Copse and soon turn sharp left to enter Newtown. Keep ahead past a distinctive house (Noah's Ark) and the Old Town Hall and drop downhill to cross a bridge. At the T-junction turn right, then take the first turning right, a lane, signed 'Coastal Path'. Bear right at the end. Follow the path across a footbridge and past a mill to reach a lane. Turn left to the car park.

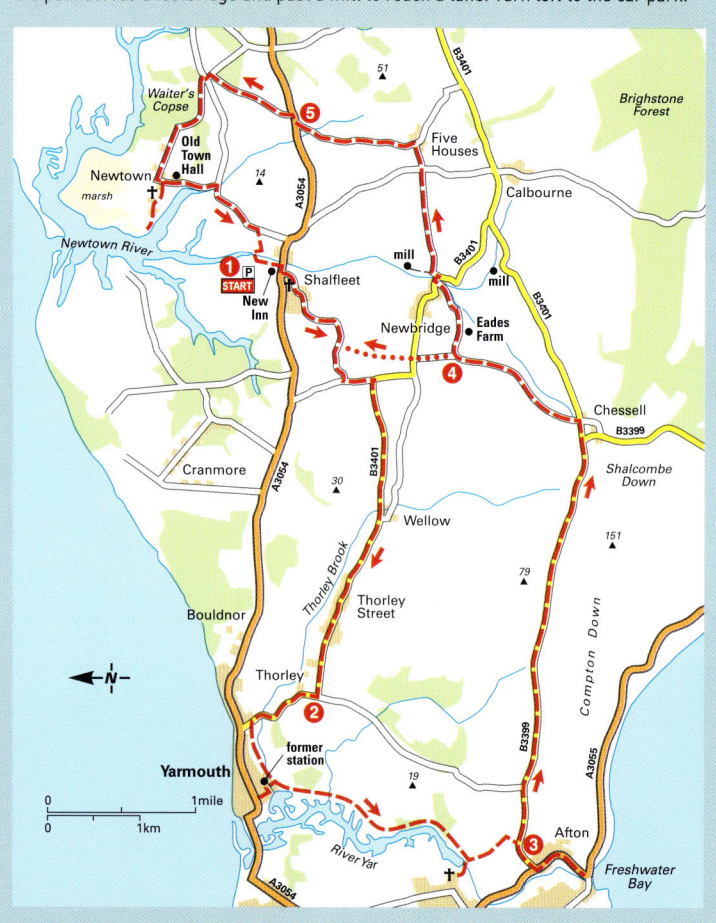

Winchester
& North Downs

CLOCKWISE FROM TOP LEFT: ALRESFORD STATION; SHOP SIGN, WINCHESTER; BOOKSHOP IN BROAD STREET, ALRESFORD; THE 13TH CENTURY FULLING MILL IN ALRESFORD; CEILING OF WINCHESTER CATHEDRAL

ALRESFORD MAP REF 400 E6

Lovely Alresford, with its wide streets of Georgian houses of brick and stucco, lies in the broad valley of the River Alre, hence the name (pronounced 'Allsford'). It is really two places – Old Alresford to the north of the river, which is now no more than a village with an adjoining park, and New Alresford, the attractive busy market town to the south which was 'new' in about 1200. Sitting between the two is Alresford Pond, created by Godfrey de Lucy, Bishop of Winchester, in the 13th century. Its dam, the Great Weir, is the largest non-military medieval earthwork in England and the only one that still serves this original dual purpose of dam and road

causeway. Today its 30 acres (12ha) are a haven for wildlife and also feed the famous ancient local watercress beds.

New Alresford retains its medieval street plan, with a T-shape formed by the spacious elegant Broad Street and West and East Streets, the old Winchester–London road. A borough by 1294, New Alresford was one of England's greatest wool markets. Two mills survive: the Town Mill and the old Fulling Mill. Fires devastated the town between the early 15th century and 1689, which accounts for its mainly Georgian appearance.

Approach from Old Alresford or from Bishop's Sutton for the most attractive introduction to the town – the south

approach from Cheriton leads through less inviting modern suburbs. Strolling through New Alresford is a delight. The town has a variety of interesting shops and some excellent craft workshops, and Broad Street, with its line of lime trees and pretty old fashioned lamps, is one of Hampshire's finest streets.

Mary Russell Mitford, author of the classic *Our Village*, was born at 27 Broad Street in 1787 and lived there until she was ten, when she moved with her father to Three Mile Cross near Reading – the village of her book. She later wrote, 'Alresford is or will be celebrated in history for two things: the first, to speak modestly, is my birth, the second is cricket'. Few

today would associate Alresford with cricket, but Taylor of Alresford, a member of the famous Hambledon Club was born here, and cricket writer and commentator John Arlott once lived at the Old Sun. Today Alresford is better known for its watercress beds and its steam railway, the Watercress Line.

North of Alresford, Northington Grange is the dramatic empty shell of a neoclassical mansion, where the 1999 movie *Onegin* was filmed.

CHAWTON MAP REF 400 F6

Jane Austen's house at Chawton has become an international literary shrine, helped by popular TV and feature-film adaptations of her novels. Once on a busy road junction between Guildford, Winchester and Portsmouth, the unspoiled village of Chawton today is even quieter than it was in Jane Austen's time, but you can easily imagine her walking out along the lanes to visit neighbours.

Jane's brother Edward installed his widowed mother and Jane and sister Cassandra at Chawton in 1809; his improvements for the house included the sash window with its Gothic arches on the right of the entrance. The women settled into a domestic routine whereby Cassandra kept house and her mother looked after the garden. This left Jane, whose main duty was preparing breakfast, free to write at her tiny 12-sided table, alerted to visitors by a creaking door that was deliberately left un-oiled. It was here that Jane revised *Sense and Sensibility* and the much-loved *Pride and Prejudice*, published in 1811 and 1813, and wrote *Mansfield Park*, *Emma* and *Persuasion*.

The rooms and gardens are as they would have been in Regency times, with a 'square piano' that visitors are very welcome to play and numerous family mementoes: the family teapot, the patchwork quilt made by the three ladies with tiny lozenge-shaped patches, family letters and portraits, and the donkey carriage that took them shopping in the nearby market town of Alton. Perhaps most evocative for devotees of the novels are Jane and Cassandra's topaz crosses, presents from their sailor brother Charles. Fanny Price, heroine of *Mansfield Park*, also receives an amber cross from her seafaring brother, and suffers much social embarrassment about the choice of gold chains to wear with it.

SELBORNE MAP REF 400 F6

Gilbert White's House takes up a long section of Selborne's characterful High Street, as befits the home of its most celebrated resident. White (1720–93) is best known for his *Natural History and*

WATERCRESS LINE, ALRESFORD

WINCHESTER CATHEDRAL CRYPT

Antiquities of Selborne, observations of the natural world recorded in the form of a series of letters. It has never been out of print since 1789. At the same time readable and ground-breaking, White's works inspired both the scientific observations of Darwin and the more poetic traditions of English nature writing. He was the first to describe the importance of earthworms in what we now call the ecosystem, and he helped to prove the phenomenon of bird migrations where previously people had speculated that birds hibernated in holes in the ground.

As was still possible in the 18th century, White managed to be in the forefront of knowledge in more than one field. He was an antiquarian, as well as an active clergyman and an innovative gardener, doing the best he could on a modest clergy income to follow the horticultural and landscaping advances of his day.

His garden, now restored to the form he created, is a delight, with walks meandering round the different areas, right up to the woods. The house re-creates the rooms as they would have been in the 18th century: the study has a dissected bird, grasses, a mouse nest and a deer skull alongside leather-bound volumes, drafts of sermons and a seed catalogue. Downstairs, you can see the original manuscript of the *Natural History*.

Also on the site, the Oates Museum commemorates Captain Lawrence Oates a member of Captain Scott's ill-fated Antarctic Expedition, and his uncle Frank Oates, a naturalist who died young in Africa. Robert Washington Oates, their descendant, helped with the purchase of the Gilbert White House in 1954.

Selborne offers some easy walks into the complicated countryside of woods and valleys that White observed so closely, such as the stroll through the churchyard to the enticing grassy valleys of Short Lythe and Long Lythe (National Trust), surrounded by beech woods.

The remains of the Selborne Yew, thought to be around 1,400 years old, stand covered by honeysuckle in the churchyard. Felled by a gale in 1990, this much-loved landmark was replanted but sadly failed to survive. A highly polished section from its largest branch is on display in the church porch, with dates back to 1509 marked on the tree rings. The church door with its ironwork scrolls is even older, dating from the 13th century. Inside, the church is wide and plain, dating from about 1180. The black slab in front of the altar commemorates the life of Gilbert White's grandfather; White himself is buried in the northeast corner of the churchyard, where his simple headstone is almost sunk into the ground.

Selborne has a pottery, an exotic woodcraft business, and a unique gallery showing the work of mouth and foot artists who have attained high artistic standards.

SHIRRELL HEATH MAP REF 400 E6
Shirrell Heath is an outlying spur of the extensive North Downs, 250 feet (75m) above sea-level. It is well wooded on the north and east slopes, and on the summit are several houses, including a convalescent home. From its isolated position, Shirrell Heath commands a magnificent view of the Hamble and Meon valleys, with the blue hills of the Isle of Wight on the horizon.

WINCHESTER MAP REF 400 E6
Physically, Winchester is relatively small. Spiritually, emotionally and historically it is large indeed. It was founded shortly before the Romans arrived in Britain, at an important crossing point on the River Itchen. A glance at a map shows how Roman roads radiate from the city like the spokes of a wheel, and certainly Roman Winchester – Venta Belgarum – was as important as this road pattern suggests.

Winchester's influence declined when the Romans left, so that when the shires were created in the 8th century, it did not give its name to the new county. Within a century the situation had been reversed and 'Vintanceastir', as Bede called it, was again ascendant. Alfred the Great made it capital of the West Saxons in AD 871 – Hamo Thorneycroft's statue of him stands at the foot of the High Street – and Winchester remained the capital of Wessex and, in a sense, of England, well into Norman times.

The city's prestige began to dwindle again once the Treasury moved to London, but the aura of past greatness still lingers and it has been said that Winchester's fine High Street has 'a greater wealth of historical associations than any other street in England'. Here you will find the glorious Buttercross, the Guildhall of 1713 (now a bank) with its overhanging City Clock, the arcaded, timbered row known as the Pentice, and the imposing 14th-century Westgate, a small fortified gateway that once served as a debtors' prison. Explore the little alleyways off here for a feel of the old medieval city – Abbey Passage, just below the Victorian Guildhall, is one of the best.

Activity
WALK TO WHITE'S ZIGZAG PATH
Walk from the village car park (behind the Selborne Arms) past White's house and down Gracious Street with its thatched cottages. Where the lane bends right, go left through a gate, follow the path over a stile then turn left along the bottom of the woods where there are views across White's garden to the village. At a National Trust sign take White's Zigzag path (cut by him and his brother in 1753) up to Selborne Common with views to the Surrey Heaths; return down the Zigzag path and go on through a kissing gate back to the car park.

Activity
WAYFARERS' WALK
This waymarked long-distance path (look for the WW markers), running 71 miles (114km) from Emsworth in Hampshire to Inkpen Beacon in Berkshire, is a good route out into some lovely chalkland countryside. On the way it passes through Hambledon and Droxford in the Meon Valley, Hinton Ampner estate (look for the signpost by the gate over the road near the estate church), Cheriton (where you can walk around a Civil War battlefield), New Alresford and over Watership Down.

Visit
JANE AUSTEN'S TOMB
A mystifying illness took Jane Austen to Winchester in search of medical attention in 1817. She died there that year aged 41 and is commemorated by a grave slab in the north aisle of Winchester Cathedral. The marker makes no mention of her writing – she was published anonymously in her lifetime – but waxes lyrical about her personal qualities as follows: '... The benevolence of her heart, the sweetness of her composure, the extraordinary endowments of her mind, obtained the regard of all who knew her, and the warmest love of her intimate connections...'

Visit
THE TIN CHURCH IN THE WOODS
At Bramdean Common, not far from Hinton Ampner, is the so-called Church in the Woods, a corrugated iron church erected in just five days in 1883 by a Romany gypsy community. It's no grand work of architecture, but worth seeing for its touching simplicity. There's still a local Romany community, and the graves in the tiny churchyard are neatly kept.

WINCHESTER CATHEDRAL

Winchester Castle, where both kings Henry III and Henry VIII's elder brother, Arthur, were born, was destroyed during the Civil War and only the Great Hall remains. The great painted round table-top which hangs on the west wall has been linked to King Arthur, but it was probably made in Tudor times.

The mighty cathedral does not dominate the city, but sits long and low among the trees and lawns of its lovely close. The present solid, squat Norman building was begun in 1097 by Bishop Wakelin on a floating foundation of logs, for the site was half swamp. In the 14th century Bishop William of Wykeham transformed it into the cathedral we see today, replacing the flat roof with great ribs and detailed mouldings, adding tall clustered columns around the original piers, and he introduced vast, spacious, elegant fan vaulting.

Winchester Cathedral is dedicated to St Swithun (died AD 862), who was bishop here, and his tomb lies in the cathedral. Also here is the tomb of William II (Rufus) and a plain slab to the novelist, Jane Austen, who died near by in College Street in 1817. Look out for delights such as the richly patterned medieval floor tiles, and a stained-glass window in memory of Izaak Walton, the famous angler. During school term time, evensong is sung by the cathedral choir at 5.30pm, Monday to Saturday, and 3.30pm Sunday. Parts of Winchester cathedral doubled as the Vatican for the 2006 blockbuster movie based on Dan Brown's *The Da Vinci Code*.

The cathedral close contains part of the priory destroyed by Henry VIII's officers, and the City Museum, while near by lie the ruins of the enormous Bishops' Palace, Wolvesey, largely demolished in 1800. The buildings of Winchester College, England's oldest public school, founded in 1387, lie at the end of College Street, and may be toured. A mile away to the south, and overlooking the River Itchen, you'll find the beautiful Hospital of St Cross – fine almshouses that date from the 12th century, with a superb Norman church and an ancient tradition of providing beer and bread for wayfarers, still given today on request.

Winchester is not all history, but is a living city, with excellent shopping, including interesting smaller shops, many good museums including a restored water mill, and a lively arts scene.

South of Winchester, Marwell Zoo is a family favourite, with lemurs, monkeys, giraffes, penguins, tigers and more. Free road trains make getting around the vast 100-acre (40.5ha) park easy, and there are animal shows and 'meet the keeper' sessions in the summer months.

90 MILES (144KM)

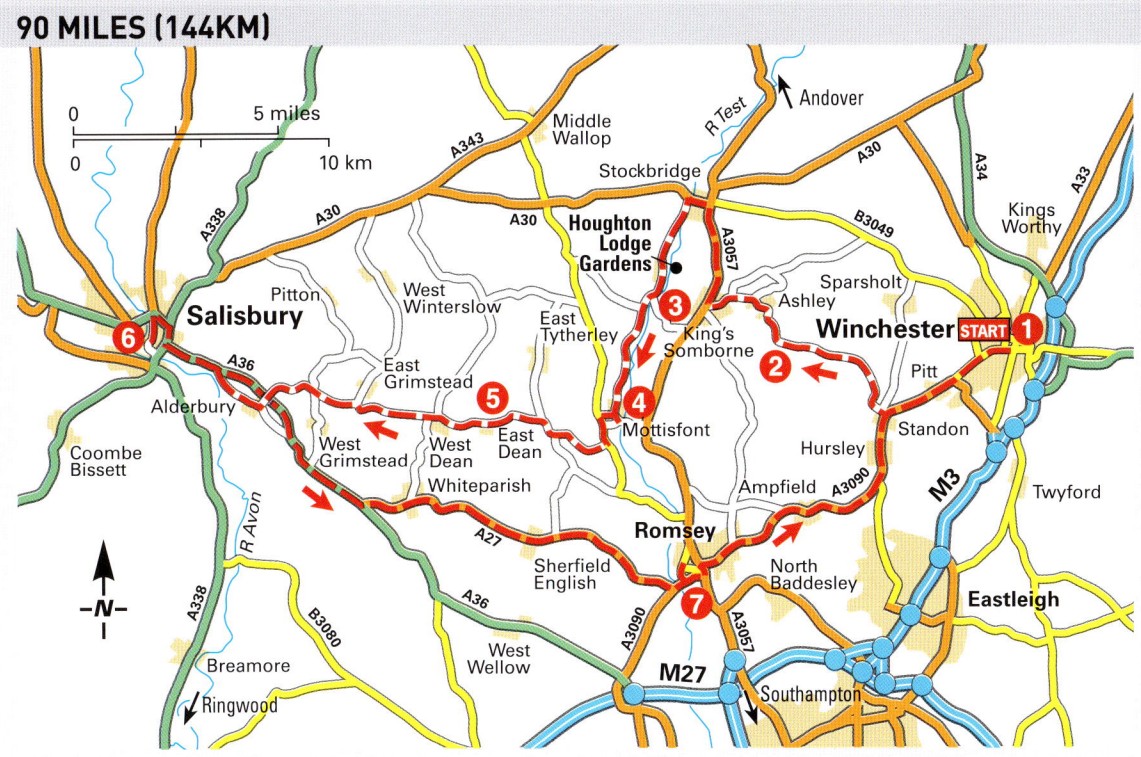

ALONG THE ROMANTIC ROAD

This circular route links the historic centres of Winchester and Salisbury, with their fine cathedrals, and the market towns of Stockbridge and Romsey, set deep in the beautiful Test Valley. The drive takes you through rolling countryside and passes many pretty villages. Along the way you will pass some of the area's most attractive houses and gardens and, if you have time, it's worth stopping at one or two places along the way to stretch your legs and appreciate all that these magnificent homes and their attractive gardens have to offer.

Route Directions

1 Leave the centre of Winchester, following signs for Romsey and the A3090. Pass the hospital, go straight on at a roundabout, and bear right at the next, signed to Romsey. Pass a golf course, left, go through Pitt and down a long hill, to turn right just before the village of Standon, signed to Farley Mount and Sparsholt. Very soon turn left, signed Farley Mount, and follow this narrow country lane through trees to the open hilltops for 2 miles (3km) to reach Farley Mount Country Park. Keep heading left.

There are several car parks on your right where you can stop and visit the country park. The folly monument is up to your left.

2 The road descends steadily through beautiful chalky landscape. Drive through the pretty village of Ashley with its white-painted church and old well. Bear left at the end of the village for Kings Somborne and Romsey. At the next junction bear left, and pass through the village of Kings Somborne with its pretty thatched houses. Turn right at the end, and right again in front of the Crown Inn on to the A3057. Follow this for 3 miles (4.8km) to a junction on the edge of Stockbridge and turn left at the roundabout, signed Salisbury. Drive through Stockbridge, cross the River Test and immediately turn

left on to a minor road, signed 'Houghton'. This road now runs along largely parallel with the river.

The village of Houghton is long and spread out. Look out for Houghton Lodge, on your left, with its glorious gardens and lawns sweeping down to the peaceful River Test.

3 Continue past the black-and-white timbered Boot Inn. After 2.5 miles (4km) reach a junction. Turn right for Dunbridge, and keep going straight ahead for Mottisfont. Continue on this narrow road through rolling farmland into Mottisfont village. Stop in the village to see the Grade 1 listed St Andrew's Church. Then go on through to visit the famous Abbey and gardens.

Mottisfont Abbey (NT) is adapted from a 12th-century priory. In the gardens are the National Collection of old-fashioned roses.

4 Retrace your route through the village and turn left on Bengers Lane, signed to Dunbridge and Broughton. At the junction with the B3084 turn left down Hatt Hill and go downhill into Dunbridge. Cross over the river and railway line and then turn right, signed to Lockerley. At the junction in Lockerley turn right, signed 'East Tytherley', pass under the railway and then turn left

after the church, for East and West Dean. Pass through Lockerley Green. The hamlet of Lockerley Green is built around a large village green.

5 Cross the railway, pass through East Dean village, and West Dean with its lumber yard and thatched cottages. Turn left by the old brick bridge, signed East Grimstead and Salisbury. Go straight ahead at the junction for East Grimstead, then go under the railway and soon you enter East Grimstead, with its neat little flint church. Turn left, signed to West Grimstead and Salisbury, and keep straight on this road, proceeding through wooded Alderbury. At the junction turn right for Salisbury, and continue downhill to meet the A36. Turn left and follow this into the middle of Salisbury, following signs round the ring road to the Central Car Park.

Explore the medieval city on foot (it is quite compact) taking in the cathedral and the museums that are housed in some of the historic buildings in Cathedral Close.

6 Leave Salisbury on the A36, signed to Southampton. Once you get to the end of the dual carriageway, look out for the viewpoint of Pepperbox Hill to your left. Descend to traffic lights and turn left on the A27, signed to Romsey and Whiteparish. Pass through Whiteparish, with its handsome old houses, and a string of hamlets that follow including Sherfield English. Look out for the bulky Abbey on your left as you descend further towards Romsey. At the junction turn left, signed Romsey and Winchester. Cross the River Test and, when you reach the roundabout by Broadlands, make a left turn to Romsey town centre.

In Romsey, visit King John's Hunting Lodge, now a heritage centre, and pick up a copy of a town trail to assist your exploration.

7 Return to the Broadlands roundabout and turn left for Winchester. Stay on the A3090, passing a turning on the left for Hillier Gardens. Continue through Ampfield and Hursley, a blend of real and mock-Tudor, to Standon. Now retrace your outward route back into the centre of Winchester.

A WALK AROUND THE ALRESFORDS

New Alresford is one of Hampshire's most picturesque small towns. Much of the architecture is Georgian, and a stroll around the three principal streets reveals traditional country-town shops plus outlets selling specialist clothes, antiquarian books and crafts. Close to both Old and New Alresford you will find a network of crystal-clear chalk streams, rivulets and channels that form the rivers Arle and Itchen and the Candover Stream. Since Victorian times these springs and rivers have played a vital role in making Alresford the 'Watercress Capital' of England, and the steam railway once transported watercress across the country.

DISTANCE/TIME 4 miles (6.4km) 1h45 **MAP** OS Explorer 132 Winchester **START** Pay car park off Station Road, New Alresford; grid ref: SU 588325 **TRACKS** Riverside paths, tracks, field, woodland paths and roads **THE PUB** The Globe on the Lake, The Soke, Broad Street, Alresford. Tel: 01962 732294; www.globeonthelake.co.uk

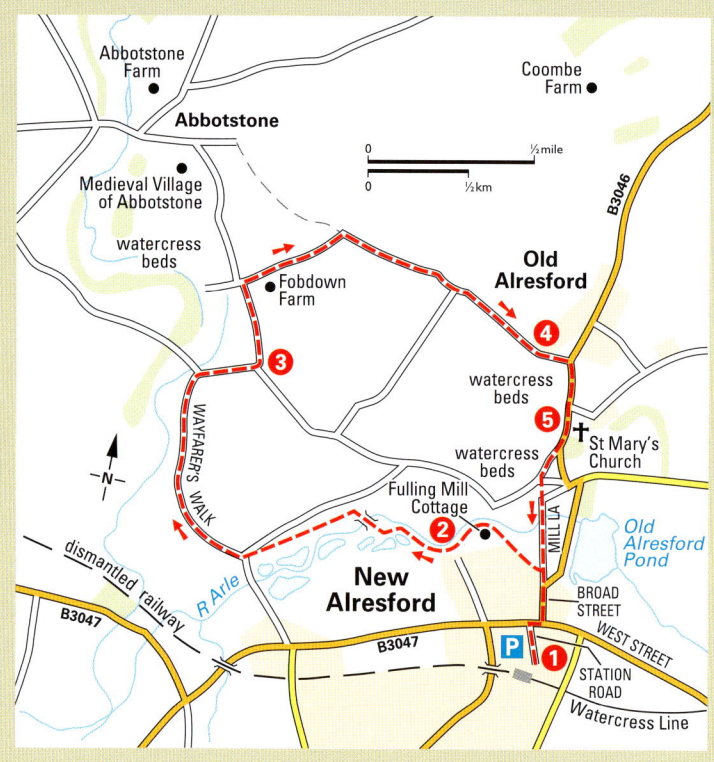

1 From the car park walk down Station Road to the T-junction with West Street. Turn right, then left down Broad Street and keep left at the bottom along Mill Hill. Half-way down follow the Wayfarer's Walk marker left, down Ladywell Lane, and soon join the river bank and pass the timbered and thatched Fulling Mill Cottage which straddles the River Arle. At the bottom of Broad Street is The Globe on the Lake pub where you can stop for a drink or a meal before you continue on your walk. If the weather is good, sit in the garden and enjoy the birds on the lake.

2 Continue to the bottom of Dean Lane and turn right, keeping to the riverside path. Cross a footbridge over the river, and ascend to pass by some cottages. Soon after, follow the footpath that skirts a private drive, bearing off to the left and following it along the field edge. Join a minor road and shortly bear right to walk up a stony track, signed Wayfarer's Walk. At a junction of tracks turn right (the Wayfarer's Walk goes left) and ascend to a minor road.

3 Turn left and then walk down until you get to Fobdown Farm and then take the lane on the right beside the farm buildings, signposted 'Right of Way'. Continue along the stony track, then on reaching a T-junction of tracks, turn to the right and follow the worn track for just over 0.5 mile (0.8km), gently descending into Old Alresford.

4 Pass the watercress beds on your right, and follow the now metalled lane left, past some houses. Turn right beside the green to reach the B3046. Cross over the road and walk up to the metalled path, turning right to reach a lane opposite.

5 After visiting the fine 18th-century St Mary's Church, cross over the road and turn left along a pavement to get to the small grass triangle by a junction. Bear right along the lane and take the footpath ahead over a stream and beside watercress beds, back down the stony lane to reach Mill Lane and the Georgian houses and shopfronts of Broad Street.

WINCHESTER

Explore the ancient town of Winchester with its historic streets and shops, attractive and restful Cathedral Close and Winchester College. Then venture into the countryside along the River Itchen and enjoy the tranquillity of river walks contrasting with the bustle of the city centre.

DISTANCE/TIME 3.5 miles (5.7km) 1h30 **MAP** OS Explorer 132 Winchester **START** Pay-and-display car parks in city centre; grid ref: SU 486294 **TRACKS** Established riverside paths through water meadows, 3 stiles **THE PUB** The Westgate Hotel, Winchester. Tel: 01962 820222

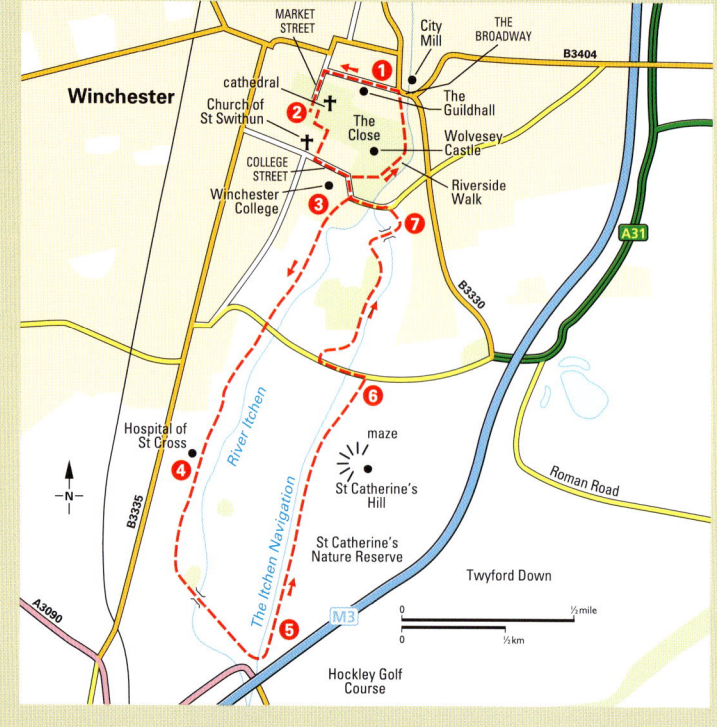

1 From King Alfred's statue on Broadway, walk towards the city centre, passing the Guildhall (tourist information centre) on the left. Join the High Street, then after 100yds (91m), turn left along Market Street. Continue ahead into Cathedral Close to pass the cathedral main door.

2 Turn left down the cloister, then right through the Close (signed 'Wolvesey Castle'), to Cheyney Court and exit via Prior's Gate. Turn left though Kingsgate, with the tiny Church of St Swithun above, then bear left down College Street and shortly you will pass an entrance to Winchester College. Beyond the road barrier, bear right along College Walk then turn right at end of wall, to continue along a track.

3 Go left through the gate by a private entrance to the College. Follow the path beside the River Itchen for 0.5 mile (0.8km) to reach a gate and road. Cross over the road and follow the gravel path, alongside the tributary, to reach another gate and then cross the open meadow towards the Hospital of St Cross.

4 Keep left alongside the wall and walk through the avenue of trees to a stile.

Continue along the gravel path to reach two further stiles and soon join a farm track leading to a road. Turn left and walk the length of a now gated road (traffic-free), crossing the River Itchen to reach a junction of paths by the M3.

5 Turn left along the path. Pass a gate on your right giving access to St Catherine's Hill. Keep left at the fork and drop down to follow the narrow path by the Itchen Navigation. Go through a car park to the road.

6 Turn left across a bridge and take the footpath immediately on the right. Keep to the path beside the water, disregarding the path to the left (this path leads to the College nature reserve). Soon cross a bridge by a collection of rowing sheds to join the metalled track.

7 Turn left, then turn left again on reaching the road. Follow the road left along College Walk then bear right at the end (signed 'Riverside Walk'). Pass the Old Bishops Palace (Wolvesey Castle) and follow the metalled path beside the River Itchen and then walk up the steps to Bridge Street, opposite City Mill (NT). Turn left to go back to King Alfred's statue.

Surrey Heaths

CLOCKWISE FROM TOP: VIEW FROM BOX HILL; GUILDFORD HIGH STREET; FLY AGARIC MUSHROOM, DEVIL'S PUNCHBOWL; GIBBET HILL, DEVIL'S PUNCHBOWL

BOX HILL MAP REF 401 G5

Box Hill, an outstanding area of woodland and chalk downland now in the care of the National Trust, has been a popular and renowned beauty spot for more than 200 years, attracting such literary notables as Jane Austen, Robert Louis Stevenson and John Keats. Its height may be modest at 400 feet (121m) but the views are magnificent. It is the best known summit of the North Downlands, and a rare, natural open space in such close proximity to London, and in summer has a good spread of orchid species to compliment the fine old oaks and beeches. The hill is an extremely good place for walkers, with routes of varying lengths shooting off from the information centre on the summit.

FARNHAM MAP REF 400 F6

A planned settlement, Farnham streets were laid out on a grid pattern in the 12th century, the attractive brick-built town of Farnham nevertheless has a strong Georgian air about it, having been virtually rebuilt on the back of the immense wealth generated by its 18th-century corn market, the largest in England.

Remains of Roman and Saxon dwellings have been found around Farnham, clearly pointing to a community here before the Norman arrivals. And there is evidence that men of the Old Stone or Palaeolithic Age (400,000 years BP) followed the gravel ridge above the present town. In time, Farnham found itself at a crossroads with ancient trails arriving from all directions, and as a result settlement continued and spread during the Bronze and Iron Ages.

In more recent centuries, it became a notable market town and a place that successfully combines the old with the new. Behind the Georgian fronts of some buildings, structures of Tudor and even earlier times are frequently found. The original core of the town has grown and spread over the centuries, and as you walk through its streets today there is a palpable sense of antiquity tastefully blended with modernity.

Farnham Castle, a Norman motte and bailey, first built in 1138 by the Bishop of Winchester, is a fine backdrop to the town and can be seen on the town's approaches. Now in the care of English Heritage, little is known of the first castle other than it had a tower. This was demolished in 1155 on the orders of Henry II, but recent archaeological excavations have revealed the large basement and foundations of the original tower at the centre of the motte. Major rebuilding work took place in the 12th and 13th centuries, with the earlier motte entirely surrounded by a keep. The castle remained a residence of the Bishops of Winchester through to the early 20th century, and much of what is seen today dates from the 15th to 17th centuries. Mary Tudor in fact stayed at the castle on her way to marry Philip of Spain at Winchester Cathedral, and Elizabeth I came to the castle on several occasions.

GODALMING MAP REF 400 F6

Godalming has existed since Saxon times and is even mentioned in the will of Alfred the Great. The name clearly has Saxon origins, 'Godhelms Ingus' roughly meaning 'the family of Godhelm', probably a reference to one of the first lords of the manor. By the time of the Domesday survey, Godalming had a population of 400 people. Then, the manor belonged to the King, but later, ownership was granted to the Bishop of Salisbury by Edward I.

The considerable history of Godalming can be traced in its architecture, from its parish church, which combines a Saxon chancel and Norman tower, to its 19th century town hall, an odd construction nicknamed the Pepperpot, for obvious reason when you see it. The town has more than 200 listed buildings, providing an architectural legacy that embraces everything from Tudor timbers to 17th century brickwork. Other noteworthy buildings are Edwin Lutyens 'Red House', and a significant English public school, Charterhouse, around a mile (1.6km) from the town on Charterhouse Hill. George Mallory, the British mountaineer who took part in the first three British Expeditions to Everest in the early 1920s, was a teacher at Charterhouse.

Godalming came to world attention in 1881, when it became the first town in the United Kingdom to have a public electricity supply installed. All was not well, however, and for a time the town reverted to gas lighting, before returning to the new system in 1904.

In 1887 Godalming was the birthplace of Chad 'Jack' Demaray, the Senior Wireless Officer on board the maiden voyage of the *Titanic*, and in 1894, of the writer Aldous Huxley, author of *Brave New World*. Television personality of the 1950s and actor, Terry-Thomas, byname of Thomas Terry Hoar Stevens, the mustachioed, gap-toothed comic noted for his film roles as a pretentious, scheming twit, died in Godalming in 1990.

GUILDFORD MAP REF 400 F5

The ancient capital of Surrey, busy Guildford is beautifully located at an ancient ford where the River Wey pushes its way through the North Downs. The town is believed to have been founded by Saxons following the departure of the Romans in 410. Just like Godalming, Guildford town was mentioned in the will of Alfred the Great, but grew to prominence with the rebuilding of its castle during the reign of King Henry II.

The modern town is bright and bustling, and has an intriguing menu of architectural styles. Dominated by the 17th-century Guildhall, the town also boasts Abbot's Hospital (1619), Guildford House (1660), and the Royal Grammar School, one of only a few places in Britain with a chained library. As well as a Norman castle there are several other historic buildings of note in Guildford, especially along its axial High Street. On Stag Hill is the modern cathedral (1936–68) designed by Sir Edward Maufe, the second newly sited Anglican cathedral built in England since the Reformation.

Genesis, the British progressive rock group noted for their atmospheric sound in the 1970s and extremely popular albums and singles of the 1980s and '90s, was founded in Guildford in 1967 by boyhood schoolmates at the Charterhouse public school in Godalming. Genesis were first known for their songwriting talents and lead singer, Peter Gabriel's uniquely theatrical onstage performances. After their lineup stabilised with the addition of drummer Phil Collins and guitarist Steve Hackett in 1970, the group developed a style that featured heavy synthesisers and musical arrangements emphasising intricate group performance over the individual pyrotechnics favoured by many of the progressive rock groups.

Charles Dodgson (better known as Lewis Carroll) (1832-1898), author of *Alice's Adventures in Wonderland* and *Through the Looking-Glass*, used to live in Guildford and is buried in the Mount Cemetery. Other authors from the town include P.G. Wodehouse (1881), comic novelist, short-story writer, lyricist, and playwright, best known as the creator of Jeeves, the supreme 'Gentleman's gentleman', and Gerald Seymour, who wrote *Harry's Game*.

HASLEMERE MAP REF 400 F6

The small market town of Haslemere lies in a lovely location in a wooded valley near the uplands of Blackdown and Hindhead. Surrey has many charming small towns and villages, but Haslemere has a unique flavour. Situated on the borders of Hampshire and West Sussex, this historic town with its brick and timber, tile-hung houses and cottages, is one of the highlights of the Surrey Hills Area of Outstanding Natural Beauty.

Haslemere is an isolated town. In 1394, Richard II granted the town a charter to hold a weekly market; apart from agriculture, Haslemere had important glass, leather and iron smelting industries. Elizabeth I declared the town a borough with the right to send two Members to Parliament. Elisabeth also issued a new charter in 1596 confirming the right to hold a weekly market, and granted the right to hold two annual fairs. The town commemorates the charter by holding a biennial Charter Fair in the High Street.

The Dolmetsch family, under the direction of Arnold Dolmetsch, originally from Le Mans in France, were internationally known as performers of early music on authentic instruments, and came to settle in Haslemere in 1916 where they subsequently founded a centre for the study of early music, and an annual summer festival in 1925.

HINDHEAD MAP REF 400 F6

At 800 feet (243m), Hindhead is Surrey's highest village, and enjoys fabulous views. In particular, it is well known for its famous beauty spot the 'Devil's Punch Bowl'. Now a site of special scientific interest, it was once the haunt of highwaymen and robbers who, not infrequently, met an ignominious end above the Devils Punch Bowl on Gibbet Hill where their remains were hung in chains as a warning to other would-be robbers. Surrounded by National Trust managed land and with Hindhead Common stretching to the east this is a beautiful and diverse landscape of rolling chalk downs, flower rich grasslands, acid heaths and ancient woodlands that provides some of the best walking in southern England.

John Tyndall (1820-1893), physicist and mountaineer, and an avid promoter of science, died in Hindhead. Tyndall discovered that water vapour absorbs much more radiant heat than the gases of the atmosphere and argued the consequent importance of atmospheric water vapour in moderating the Earth's climate – that is, in the natural greenhouse effect. A man who had climbed Mont Blanc three times, Tyndall claimed that the air around Hindhead was as pure as in Switzerland. Whether for that reason or not is unrecorded, but both Sir Arthur Conan Doyle and George Bernard Shaw lived in Hindhead. Improved roads and the railway made Hindhead a popular residential choice for a number of eminent Victorians and there are many splendid villas as well as imposing Arts and Crafts houses.

GUILDFORD

BOX HILL

This country park is worth visiting year-round and it is spectacular in the autumn when its trees put on a fine display of fiery colours. As well as its famous box trees which cling to the steep cliff-face, it was where John Logie Baird, inventor of television, conducted some of his experiments.

DISTANCE/TIME 4 miles (6.4km) 2h15 **MAP** OS Explorer 146 Dorking, Box Hill & Reigate
START National Trust car park, Fort Cottages, Box Hill Country Park; grid ref: TQ 178513
TRACKS Woodland tracks, with two sections on minor roads **THE PUB** The Running Horses, Mickleham. Tel: 01372 372279

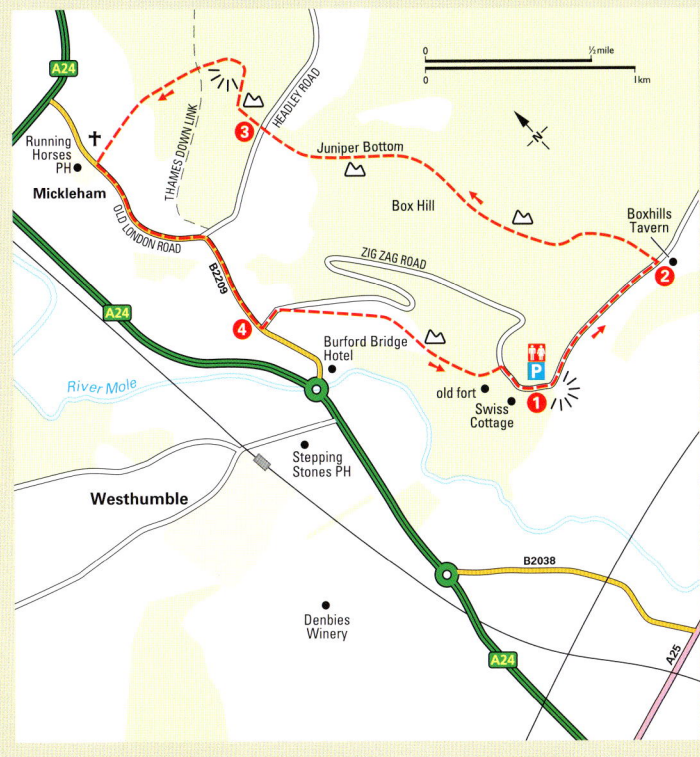

1 Turn left out of the car park. Swiss Cottage on the right (now a private house) was home to John Logie Baird during the 1920s and 30s. Cross over, and follow the roadside path for 0.5 mile (800m). Shortly after you set out, you'll see a path leading down to a viewpoint, built in memory of Leopold Salomons of Norbury Park. The commanding views here of Dorking and the Mole Valley are well worth the short diversion.

2 Just before Boxhills Tavern, recross the road and turn off to the left on the signposted public bridleway. Ignore all the turnings you pass, but follow the signposted route as it drops down through Juniper Bottom to Headley Road.

3 The next few hundred paces are very steep indeed. Alternatively, turn left on to Headley Road, and rejoin the route by turning left on to Old London Road. This will cut out Mickleham village, and shorten the walk by 0.75 mile (1.2km). Otherwise, cross straight over on to the public footpath and steel yourself for a seemingly interminable climb up the long flight of rustic steps. Just beyond the top of the steps the path bears right and here the gradient eases slightly. Soon you

come to a bench seat offering splendid views and a good excuse for a rest. Now follow the National Trust's 'long walk' waymarks as you bear left and drop down over the footpath crossroads with Thames Down Link. Clamber over a stile at the foot of the hill, and continue past the church into the village of Mickleham. Turn left and follow the Old London Road. Keep to the pavement on the right-hand side, which at times transforms into pleasant rural path running just a few paces away from the road. By the time you reach the junction with Zig Zag Road, it has returned to pavement again.

4 Cross over the junction with Zig Zag Road, and join the signposted bridleway that climbs steadily all the way back uphill to the National Trust centre. Near the top, you'll see an old Victorian fort on the right. Turn right at the top of the hill for the last 60yds (55m) stretch back to the car park.

WALK 38

GUILDFORD THROUGH THE LOOKING GLASS

Lewis Carroll, real name Charles Dodgson, author of *Alice's Adventures in Wonderland* and *Through the Looking-Glass*, rented The Chestnuts in Guildford as a family home for his six sisters. Although Dodgson didn't live in in the town himself, he visited his sisters regularly and knew Guildford well.

DISTANCE/TIME 4.25 miles (6.8km) 2h **MAP** OS Explorer 145 Guildford & Farnham
START Farnham Road car park, next to Guildford railway station; grid ref: SU 991494
TRACKS Paved streets, downland tracks and riverside towpath **THE PUB** The Red Lion, Shamley Green, Guildford. Tel: 01483 892202

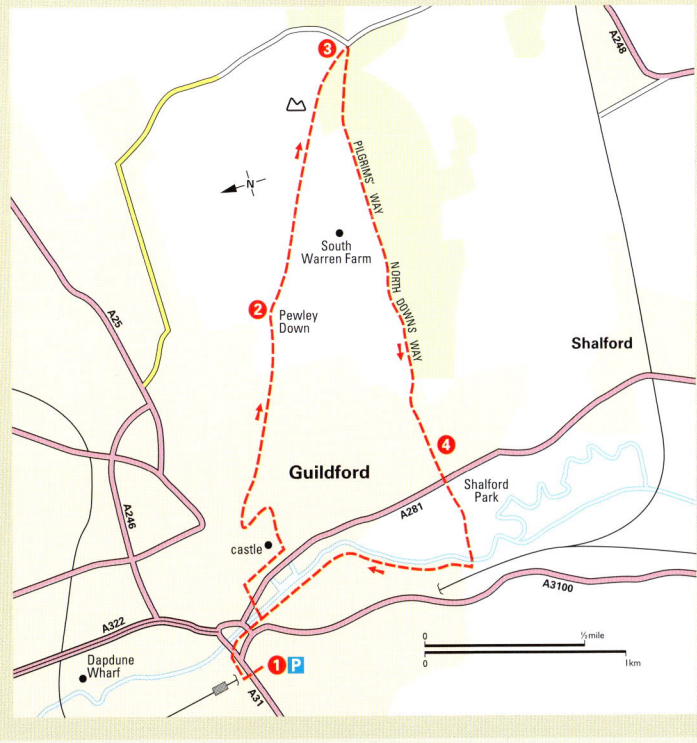

1 Leave the car park via a footbridge at Level 5. Cross Farnham Road and turn right. Just beyond the railway bridge drop into the subway on the left, and follow the signposts ('Town Centre via Riverside Walk'). Follow the riverside walk to the White House pub. Turn left over the bridge, continue into the High Street, and turn first right into Quarry Street. Pass Guildford Museum and turn immediately left through Castle Arch. Your route forks right here, into Castle Hill, but a quick diversion up the pedestrian path straight ahead brings you to Looking Glass statue in a small garden through an iron gateway on the right. Retrace your steps and follow Castle Hill past The Chestnuts. Turn left at the top, walk down South Hill, and turn right into Pewley Hill. Climb steadily past Semaphore House on the corner of Semaphore Road. At the end of the road, continue along the bridleway and follow it to the striking viewpoint pillar on the summit of Pewley Down.

2 Fork right at the viewpoint and then follow the path off the ridge, keeping the hedge on your left. Soon you'll enter a tunnel of trees, and emerge between hedges. Keep straight on at the crossroads by the Pewley Down information board, and continue for another

300yds (274m) until the path bears right and meets the North Downs Way National Trail at an acorn waymark post.

3 Turn right here and follow the waymarked North Downs Way past South Warren Farm to a residential street called Pilgrims Way. Turn left and follow the road past its junction with Clifford Manor Road.

4 Continue along Pilgrims Way to the A281. Cross over and walk across Shalford Park, signposted towards Godalming and Shalford. Beyond the trees you'll reach the River Wey; cross the footbridge, and follow the towpath towards Guildford, with the river on your right. Cross the lattice girder footbridge at Millmead Lock, and continue past the Alice statue on a little green near the White House pub. Now, follow the river bank until you reach the prominent 1913 Electricity Works on the opposite bank. Turn left, climb the steps, and retrace your outward route through the subway to the car park.

South Downs

CLOCKWISE FROM TOP: BUTSER HILL; DITCHLING; SOUTH DOWNS WAY; AMBERLEY CHURCH

ALFRISTON MAP REF 401 H7

With its worn market cross and a flint church on a spreading village green, known as the Tye, Alfriston looks like the ideal English village. The High Street with its narrow pavements has a selection of speciality shops, pubs and tea rooms.

The thatched, half-timbered Clergy House that lies by the green near the churchyard survived thanks to a far-sighted act of conservation in 1896, when it became the very first building bought by the National Trust.

The light chalky soils and dry, sunny slopes of the South Downs make for excellent wine-growing conditions. The English Wine Centre, just off the A27 near Alfriston, stocks a good selection alongside local preserves, fruit wines, beers and ciders. There are tutored wine tastings and the centre hosts the annual English Wine & Regional Food Festival on the first weekend of September.

AMBERLEY MAP REF 401 G7

With its many thatched houses and idyllic position by water meadows, this village presents a picture of rare perfection. A 10-minute walk from the rail station, it has plenty to fill a day, with walks on to the downs and along the River Arun, and an outstanding industrial museum. In the village centre, the Black Horse pub offers a pleasant way of idling away an afternoon. There's a view of the extremely imposing curtain wall of the medieval castle (now a smart hotel) from its north side if you walk down to the edge of the village from

where the great wetland of Amberley Wild Brooks spreads. This is an area of water meadows that's now managed as a nature reserve by the Sussex Wildlife Trust and is a prized habitat for dragonflies and, during winter flooding, various wildfowl such as Bewick's swans. A footpath from the village penetrates the reserve and offers a good walk, floods allowing, to Greatham Bridge – a multi-arched stone bridge dating from the 16th century and joined to a metal span over the River Arun.

Amberley Working Museum, just outside the village and next to Amberley station, is an open-air industrial museum in a disused chalk pit, with a series of buildings that include a foundry and an old fire station, a collection of vintage Southdown buses, resident craftspeople (such as a printer, a potter and a clay-pipe maker), and outdoor displays celebrating the industrial heritage and crafts skills of the southeast. Run by volunteers, it succeeds admirably in bringing the region's working past to life, and there's a lively calendar of events too.

ARUNDEL MAP REF 401 G7

The massive castle towers over Arundel. It was restored and is still occupied by the Dukes of Norfolk, whose ancestors have owned it since 1138. The castle's grounds take up half the hill on which the compact town sits, and you might feel almost on your knees yourself as you approach up steepening pathways. Today, however, you can visit the castle and explore Arundel's other attractions – enjoyable small shops

in the historic centre, a spectacular Victorian cathedral in the French Gothic style and more echoes of France in the shady avenue of Mill Road, popular for parking and picnicking and close to the starting point for river trips to Amberley and the Black Rabbit pub. Beyond here is the Arundel Wetland Centre with its remarkable birdlife and wild flowers.

Arundel's sloping, tapered square with its attractive cobbles and simple war memorial is surrounded by a smart group of individual-looking businesses. Tarrant Street, running off the High Street, has artisan and specialist shops, some in converted Victorian industrial buildings, such as the Old Print Works. Further uphill, Maltravers Street is an elegant mix of 18th-century town houses, with the road running on two levels. On the High Street are the Tourist Information Centre (offering a town audio tour) plus the volunteer-run Arundel Museum and Heritage Centre with eight rooms devoted to the history of the town. Nearby Arundel Ghost Experience, in the Old Town Hall, is likely to chill spines of all ages with its ghost stories and sinister prison cells.

Clustered at the top of town is a remarkable collection of religious buildings that could be said to embody Arundel's extraordinary religious history. St Nicholas', Arundel's 14th-century Church of England parish church, backs on to the Fitzalan Chapel (access via the castle grounds), bought by the castle when Henry VIII dissolved its religious foundation and to this day still Catholic.

Arundel Cathedral soars almost opposite. Completed in 1873 by the 15th Duke of Norfolk to celebrate Britain's mid-Victorian Catholic revival, it is an almost perfect-looking re-creation of the French Gothic style of about 1400, with strong vertical lines in honey-coloured Bath stone, flying buttresses and a great rose window. Inside a stained-glass window depicts the Earl of Arundel, Philip Howard, who was made a saint in 1970, alongside his faithful wife and dog.

Arundel Castle succeeds in giving a good impression of what entering the castle gates of the country's most powerful Duke might have felt like. The oldest part of the building is the keep, reached by many narrow steps, which has tableaux bringing the Civil War siege to life. Portcullis mechanisms are on view, and there are tremendous panoramas over the town, cathedral, coastal plain and Downs beyond. Of the occupied rooms on show, the Regency Gothic library is perhaps the finest, with its exuberant gilt balconies and plush red velvet sofas. Elsewhere, paintings by Canaletto, Constable, Turner and Van Dyck hang almost casually among hundreds of other works of art, and photographs of the ducal family meeting VIPs, such as popes and royalty, decorate the tabletops.

Outside, near the Fitzalan Chapel, a tea terrace set in beautiful gardens looks across to the cathedral. There's free access to the network of footpaths in the extensive park, which spreads over the Downs and features a large lake.

ARUNDEL CASTLE

BIGNOR MAP REF 400 F7

Tucked in deep countryside beneath a lushly wooded stretch of downs, Bignor village's square of streets boasts some marvellously unchanged old houses, including the Yeoman's House (or Old Shop), a thatched and half-timbered 15th-century cottage with an attractive overhanging upper storey.

Bignor is best known for its Roman villa. At first sight, what you see is a set of thatched buildings. These are shelters, which themselves have become historic structures, put up to protect the Roman remains in the early 19th century by John Hawkins, the landowner. He had the site excavated and transformed it into an early tourist attraction. Inside you can view some of the finest Roman mosaics in Britain, depicting glorious scenes from the lives of gladiators and mythical subjects, and in places you can even walk on the still-durable surface of a Roman floor.

What survives above ground is mainly from the 4th century AD. There's a full-scale bath suite with a cold plunge pool and a heated changing room, warm and hot rooms and a hot bath.

The discovery of Bignor was among the earliest evidence for Roman-style 'civilised' living in the countryside. Many other villas have since been discovered across southern England, usually in the same kind of position with a fine view.

CUCKMERE VALLEY MAP REF 401 H6

Winding its way slowly through the verdant South Downs to finally flow into the sea off the East Sussex coast, the River Cuckmere lies in a valley of beautiful countryside and threads through an area of great ecological importance.

However, there are plans to allow the natural flooding of this entire valley as the costs of preventing soil erosion has become prohibitive. This would mean the loss of an area of outstanding natural beauty, but could be beneficial to the biosphere in the long run.

DITCHLING MAP REF 401 G7

The photogenic old village of Ditchling looks out to one of the most frequented parts of the South Downs. The Bull and a couple of tea rooms make good stopping points in the village, and the Ditchling Museum, near the chuch, remembers the work of pioneer calligraphers Eric Gill and Edward Johnston (who devised the distinctive sans serif script used by London Transport), who worked here; there's also a local collection and changing exhibitions. From the village, a road climbs up to Ditchling Beacon, at 813 feet (252m) the highest point on the Sussex Downs. It's a great place to come for a picnic, to fly a kite, paraglide, walk the South Downs Way, or just drink in big views over the Weald and across to

the Surrey hills. A 1.25-mile (2km) stroll west from here brings you to the Clayton Windmills, nicknamed Jack and Jill; Jack is a private house, but Jill is a working corn mill open to visitors most summer Sundays and bank holidays.

GLYNDE MAP REF 401 H7

This is still very much an estate village, owned by Glynde Place, the Elizabethan manor house just north. As well as a tea room and pub with a large garden (the Trevor Arms), the village also has its own smithy. Bearing the date of 1907 by its horseshoe-shaped doorway, this has an assortment of tools hanging over a pair of brick-built hearths; the smith makes long bows as well as ironwork.

A signposted path leading off from a stile roughly opposite the Little Cottage Tea Room on Ranscombe Lane takes visitors up Mount Caburn. You will often see paragliders hovering over this summit, which looks down the Ouse valley towards the sea. Here. chalk-loving wild flowers carpet the slopes, and the site is encircled with Saxon and Iron Age ramparts.

Glynde Place is screened from the road by the stable block situated next to a Palladian-style church. The flint gables and brick chimneys at the front are from Tudor times, the back section was added in 1760. Knowledgeable guides introduce visitors to the family history, and with a

welcome absence of roping-off you can get up close to all the details, including miniatures and embroidery. The walls are hung with old masters brought back from an Italian Grand Tour – the efforts of 300 years of collecting by the (related) Morley, Trevor and Brand families. Stone wyverns crown the gates beyond the Coach House, where the Tea Room has a cobbled courtyard shaded by fruit trees.

North of the village is Glyndebourne Opera House, home to Britain's top country house opera company.

HERSTMONCEUX MAP REF 401 H7

The science of astronomy provides the link between here, Greenwich and the Canary Islands. The Royal Observatory, established in the reign of Charles II to record the position of the stars to aid navigation for sailors, moved out from Greenwich, London, in 1946, because the light and air pollution was making it too difficult to observe the night sky. For more than 30 years the Herstmonceux Castle estate was the home of British astronomical observations, but it moved its main telescope to the island of La Palma in 1984. The former complex, with its striking domes, is now home to the Observatory Science Centre – a place full of appeal to all ages. It's best to visit on a dry day, as the large-scale interactive exhibits in the adventure playground-like

Discovery Park outside are part of the fun, but there's also plenty indoors, with exhibits on optics, medieval machines, time, force and gravity, and more.

The romantic-looking 15th-century Herstmonceux Castle stands in a wide moat, and is the oldest brick building on such a scale in England. Henry VI's Treasurer, Sir Roger Fiennes, modelled it on French chateau designs and it was completed in 1446. Abandoned in the 1700s when the owners stripped it out to build a new mansion, Herstmonceux Place, nearby, it became a picturesque ruin and was restored from 1910. It is now the International Study Centre for Queen's University, Ontario: you can take guided tours inside to see the beautiful courtyard and some of the very modern lecture rooms – these overlook the moat, and have Jacobean panelling, a dungeon with a stone toilet and a resident ghost.

The Elizabethan gardens and grounds move from the formal to the wild, rising gently up from the castle. Within a high brick wall, robust yew hedges enclose rhododendron, rose and herb gardens and a giant tilted steel sundial. Outside the wall, paths lead over rough meadows to a folly, a lily-filled lake and woods known for their carpets of bluebells.

KINGLEY VALE NATIONAL NATURE RESERVE MAP REF 400 F7

Yew forests are extremely rare, and this one, found on the South Downs between Stoughton and West Stoke – is Europe's largest, although tests involving pollen analysis suggest there were yew forests elsewhere in the area during prehistoric times, as at Mount Caburn near Lewes. It's a marvellously eerie place, like some Tolkienesque fantasy, which is at its most spectacularly creepy and magical in the yew grove. Follow the path from the car park near West Stoke, keep forward at the next path junction, then go through a gate, to join the circular nature trail. Gnarled tree trunks have fallen over or twisted and continued to grow, creating a dark, gloomy canopy under which little else thrives. The luscious-looking berries are poisonous to us, but not to the hungry birds such as nuthatches, goldcrests and thrushes which feed on them. As you reach the top, the view opens out dramatically across Chichester Harbour – with the tall spire of Chichester Cathedral in view. The tall grassy hillocks up here are burial mounds consisting of a mound and ditch (or 'bell barrows') erected in the Bronze Age, doubtless for the view.

MEON VALLEY MAP REF 400 E6

Izaak Walton, known as the father of angling, loved to fish in the clear waters of the River Meon, still regarded today as one of Britain's best trout rivers. He famously penned his appreciation of the pastoral pastime in *The Compleat Angler*, published in 1653. Travelling between the attractive villages, from Wickham in the south to East Meon, you'll see the signs for trout fisheries where you can try your hand at the sport and get the idea of what it was that enthused Walton so much.

With some notable exceptions, the scenery here is pleasantly mild rather than dramatic. The valley's disused railway line, running from West Meon to Wickham, is now the particularly attractive Meon Valley Trail, a level route for walkers, horse-riders and cyclists. You can enjoy pottering around on a bike along the narrow lanes that connect the villages on the east side of the valley.

Further south, the Forest of Bere, a 865-acre (350ha) fragment of an ancient royal hunting forest, has numerous fine waymarked trails and picnic areas; there are also three designated car parks (West Walk, Woodend and Upperford Copse), and an exciting mountain bike trail that begins from West Walk.

One of Hampshire's most photogenic villages, East Meon has the infant river running along the middle of its quaint main street, lined with attractive brick and half-timbered houses, some thatched, and there's still a village smithy here – in operation for over a century. On a rise, the Church of All Saints dates from the mid-12th century and has mighty rounded Norman arches at the crossing of the chancel and the nave, and a wonderful Tournai font. Just across the road you can glimpse the medieval Court House, where the Bishops of Winchester once held court. Today the building is occasionally used for theatrical performances.

Old Winchester Hill National Nature Reserve is a dramatic stretch of chalk downland, where the steep slope has managed to escape modern farming, enabling a great range of wildlife to flourish. There are badgers, roe deer and dormice in the woodland, while more than 30 species of butterfly (including silver spotted skippers and speckled wood) can be found, and chalk-loving wild flowers such as orchids grow in profusion on the grasslands. From the main car park, an easy level track leads towards the fascinating Iron Age hill fort of Winchester Hill, within the ramparts of which are Bronze Age burial mounds, or barrows, which have never been excavated. There's also a very pleasant waymarked circular walk (it takes up to 2 hours) that leads downhill and along the hillside through woodland. For more detailed information, pick up a leaflet at the car park and consult the interpretative boards. The nature reserve is signposted from the A32 at Warnford; the road gets more scenic as you travel towards the Royal Navy communications school at HMS *Mercury*.

PETWORTH MAP REF 400 F6

The town of Petworth is dominated by the 17th-century Petworth House – its upper windows peering over near the church, and its great wall squeezing the A272 traffic uncomfortably close to the town's fine stone, half-timbered and tile-hung buildings. A spiky lamp standard acts as a road island near the curiously restored church. Petworth's shops are scattered around the streets near the square, where a Baroque bust of William III gazes at the cars from Leconfield Hall. Petworth Museum at 346 High Street, takes you to 1910 when Mary Cummings, seamstress of Petworth House, lived there.

Petworth House (National Trust) can be reached on foot via an entrance near to the church, or from a car park north of the town. Another car park located a mile (1.6km) or so to the north gives free access to the grounds, where cyclists are welcomed. The hilly parkland here represents 18th-century landscaping by the great 'Capability' Brown on an enormous scale, set against which the house itself can seem oddly restrained. Its flat classical frontage in creamy grey stone seems a little sunken into the ground and the pasture goes right up to the windows.

Inside, the main rooms of the house have immensely different characters, from the gilt mirrors and oil paintings in the Square Drawing Room to the Marble Hall with its black-and-white floor, cool sage-green paint and authentic Roman statuary. One highlight is the Carved Room, decorated in c1692 by Grinling Gibbons and the Petworth carpenter John Selden, with its astonishing carvings in limewood. The festoons of flowers, beads, birds, musical instruments, cherubs and lace have been created in three dimensions, and tend to rather upstage the four Turner landscapes which hang beneath Tudor family and royal portraits.

As you leave the house you are treated to a fascinating glimpse of the medieval manor around which the house was constructed. Opposite are found the servants' quarters, which now display the late Victorian kitchens and house the high-ceilinged tea room.

Visit
DEVIL'S DYKE

West of Ditchling Beacon at Devil's Dyke on the top of the Downs is a popular place to enjoy the far-reaching views or fly a kite. You can easily reach this area by bus from Brighton (open-topped bus No 77 from the seafront or rail station or No 79 from the rail station). Not everyone who comes here finds the Devil's Dyke itself – an impressively deep dry valley just behind the Devil's Dyke Hotel.

QUEEN ELIZABETH COUNTRY PARK
MAP REF **400 F6**

Butser Hill, now bisected by the A3 south of Petersfield, is the highest point on the South Downs. The Country Park gives open access to 1,400 acres (560ha) of woodland and downland within the East Hampshire Area of Outstanding Natural Beauty, with 20 miles (32km) of trails for walkers, cyclists and horse-riders, a demonstration Iron Age farm, an adventure playground and a varied programme of events.

Most of Butser Hill is designated a Site of Special Scientific Interest and since 1998 has been recognised as a National Nature Reserve. It's one of the largest areas of chalky grassland in Hampshire, with yew, beech and conifers providing additional habitats to a rich population of wild flowers, butterflies and lichens.

UPPARK MAP REF **400 F6**

On a hilltop site and the first great house in England to be built without an on-site water supply, Uppark found its geography worked against it in 1989 when the roof caught fire. The wind fanned the flames and water had to be pumped from over a mile (1.6km) away. Over the six-year restoration period builders and craftspeople rediscovered long-lost skills and revived old traditions – such as recording the events of the day on chimney pots. The entrance exhibition tells the story of the fire and restoration, the rescue of many artworks, how nearly 4,000 dustbins of fragments were salvaged, and the controversy over whether and how to rebuild. The National Trust decided to re-create Uppark as it had been the day before the fire, a seamless join, complete with all the marks of age.

The house itself is built of brick in a Dutch style, and was designed in about 1690 by William Talman. It seems to sit high up on a plateau and is surrounded by landscaped pasture. Children can play ball games on the pleasant South Lawn. Inside, thanks to an extraordinary family history, the restored interiors are almost unchanged since Sir Matthew Fetherstonhaugh and his wife furnished it so lavishly with rich fabrics and exotic mementoes from their honeymoon Grand Tour of Europe in the mid-18th century. Their son, Sir Harry, aged 71, married his 20-year-old dairymaid Mary Ann in 1825 and died 21 years later. Mary Ann lived on with her sister, keeping things as they had been in Sir Harry's heyday. H G Wells, whose mother was housekeeper here, remembers them as old ladies in velvet dresses. By the 1900s the next owners had already started work on conserving the fragile textiles, and Uppark passed into the care of the National Trust in 1954.

The reconstructions are completely convincing; only a look at the photographs in each room will show you where the joins are. Many stewards can relate personal stories of the day of the fire. The basement of spacious kitchens and servants' quarters, which was abandoned in the 1900s, escaped with least damage and seems stranded in time; the butler's room has a water gauge to show when the rooftop tanks need topping up. Also in the basement is the gigantic Uppark Doll's House, with Georgian furniture, glass and silverware. The stable block is more elaborate than the servants' dining hall, and the dairy is positively elegant.

WEST DEAN MAP REF **400 F7**

Nothing like a conventional museum, the Weald and Downland Open Air Museum is more like a spread-out village consisting of relocated historic buildings rescued from town centre redevelopment, road and reservoir schemes in Sussex, Kent and Surrey – complete with a watermill, ploughed fields and farm animals. It aims to promote public awareness and interest in old buildings and their surroundings, and does this brilliantly.

There's something for everyone, from children who will be fascinated by the low doorways and open fires to the professional builder or craftsperson. The buildings look as though they have always been there. Most look as they would have been when first built, perhaps as medieval halls, with reproduction furnishings and usually a steward on hand to answer questions. There's a village school from 1895, a carpenter's shop and even an animal pound rescued from the route of the M25.

Up in the woods, the pod-like modern gridshell building shows timber framing at its most innovative, and there are tours of the collection of building parts and rural tools kept in store underneath. Special events such as the Heavy Horse Spectacular (June) and Rare Breeds Show (July) are popular and there are demonstrations of flour milling and medieval cooking most days.

The open-air museum is part of the West Dean estate: you can glimpse the battlemented flint mansion (now West Dean College). Once a playground of King Edward VII, West Dean Gardens run along one side of the seasonal stream of the River Lavant, with walks across downland pasture leading up to an arboretum. The summer-houses and bridges of the Spring Garden are Regency style, while the great pergola with vines, clematis, climbing hydrangea and roses, and the immense walled kitchen garden and glasshouses are from West Dean's Edwardian heyday.

DISTANCE/TIME 11 miles (17.7km) 3h **MAP** OS Explorer 122 South Downs Way: Steyning to Newhaven **START** Free car park by Jack and Jill windmills; grid ref: TQ 304134. Alternative: Ditchling Beacon car park; grid ref: TQ 333131 **TRACKS** Quite bumpy chalk and grass tracks, some sections on clay **THE PUB** The Bull, Ditchling. Tel: 01273 843147

DITCHLING BEACON & THE CHATTRI WAR MEMORIAL

Cycle along one of the most spectacular sections of the South Downs: the route passes two windmills (Jack and Jill), and the Chattri War Memorial.

1 Turn left out of the car park, signed 'public bridleway to Ditchling Beacon'. Ignore a driveway, left, to Jack Windmill and another left track. Fork left uphill at a junction, to the South Downs Way. Follow the blue-arrow markers for most of the ride.

2 From Ditchling Beacon car park cross the road and take the South Downs Way opposite. The route climbs up two grassy rises and drops to cross a narrow farm road. Here the clay surface can be sticky after rain.

3 After the next left, a descending fork (which you avoid), look for a track on the right, marked with a blue arrow which leads to the site of Plumpton Plain, a Bronze Age settlement. Carry on along the South Downs Way.

4 Beyond a gate is a National Trust sign for Blackcap. Walk up to the summit by forking left to the trig point.

5 Unless you want to return along the South Downs Way, turn left at the summit after Ditchling Beacon (where Jack Windmill comes into view). It's marked with a blue arrow and a sign for 'Chattri and the windmills'. Descend at the second gate (waymarked 'Chattri and the windmills' No 13), detour to the Chattri War Memorial.

6 After the next gate, walk to the war memorial. Return to the junction at the previous gate, turn left: the route bends right (No 44) on a path, left (No 45), then downhill and right leaving the route to 'Chattri and the windmills' (at No 46), which continues ahead. The track crosses the South Downs Way via a farm to the windmills and the car park.

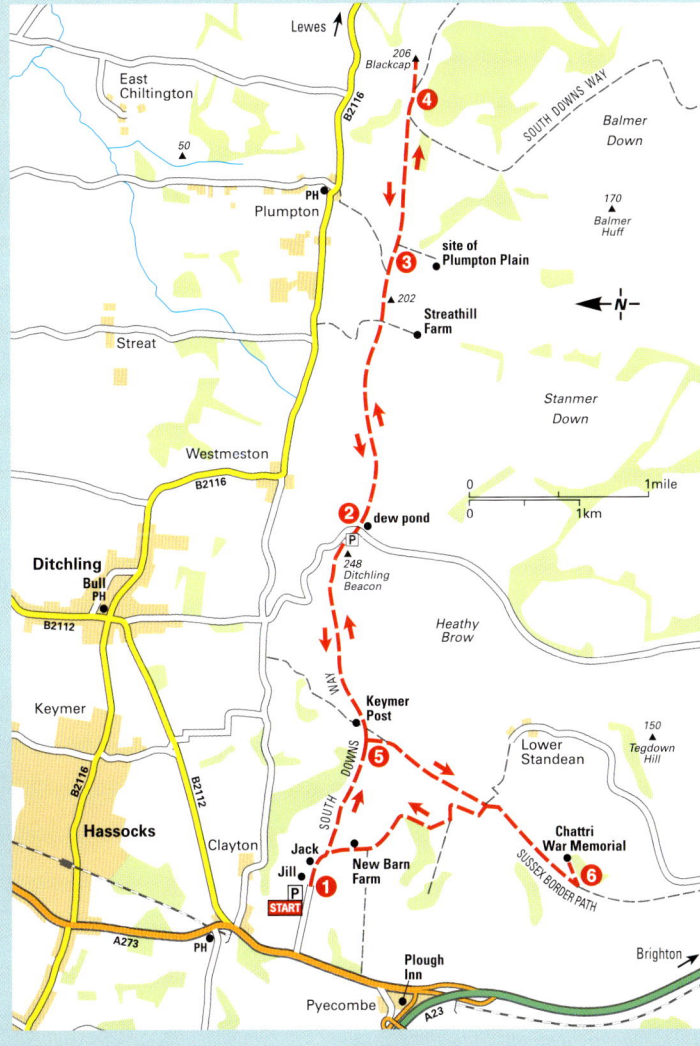

DISTANCE/TIME 12 miles (19.3km) 3h; alternative route 4 miles (6.4km) 1h **MAP** OS Explorer 122 South Downs Way: Steyning to Newhaven **START** Barcombe village centre, roadside parking; grid ref: TQ 418157 **TRACKS** Back lanes, hard stony track; extension on a track and fields **THE PUB** The Anchor Inn, Barcombe. Tel: 01273 400414

HAMSEY & BARCOMBE MILLS

Along this route of quiet lanes you'll find everything from Roman sites to wartime defences, and a mill pond and weirs. Off-road sections follow a disused railway track and an ancient 'green lane' that crosses fields and leads to the Lavender Line preserved steam railway.

1 With the Royal Oak pub on your right, go along the main street in Barcombe and turn left in front of the village sign for The Anchor Inn and Newick. At the bottom of the hill turn right on Boast Lane, signposted 'Anchor Inn'. After passing Delves Farm, and just before a house on the right, look for a track beyond a gate on the left, into a triangular field. At the next triangular area, look to your left for a gate with a yellow arrow on it: at the far end of the field a line of hedgerow trees rising up to the top right skyline actually marks the line of a Roman road that ran from London to Lewes. Continue along the track, which later follows the left side of a field and passes a wartime brick pillbox. The route drops to a footbridge. Continue across a meadow to the gate ahead, up over another footbridge and along a track; ignore driveways to the right. At the road T-junction turn right into Isfield. Continue along past the Laughing Fish pub on your left to visit the Lavender Line preserved railway.

2 From Isfield retrace your route across the meadows and back past the pillbox. Turn left on the road to continue to The Anchor Inn.

3 Retrace your route a short distance from The Anchor Inn and, just before Keeper's Cottage on the left, turn left on the old railway track, signposted 'licensed bridleway to Barcombe Mills'.

4 On reaching a road that is opposite the old Barcombe Mills station, take a detour left and then take the first road on the left. Turn right at the junction in front of the driveway to Barcombe House in order to reach the millpond and weirs of Barcombe Mills. Return the same way to the road, cycling past Barcombe Mills station. At the next junction go straight ahead for a short-cut back into Barcombe. For the main route, turn left here, and pass Barcombe church. Carry on along the road, keeping left at the next two junctions towards Hamsey.

5 Just after Hamsey Manor turn left down Whitfeld Lane to Hamsey. Here, there is a lovely half-timbered house called Yeoman's dated 1584; just after the house, turn left at a T-junction. From here the road crosses a former canal via a bridge. After the bridge, you can pick up the keys to Hamsey church from Pine Barn, the first house on the left to look around the church. The road then rises over the old railway to reach Hamsey church, a wonderful example of what medieval country churches used to look like. From this point, return to Hamsey, keeping left at the road junction that is by the canal bridge, and just past a pillbox.

6 Turn right at the T-junction. After Whitfeld Lane joins from the right follow signs for Barcombe to return to start.

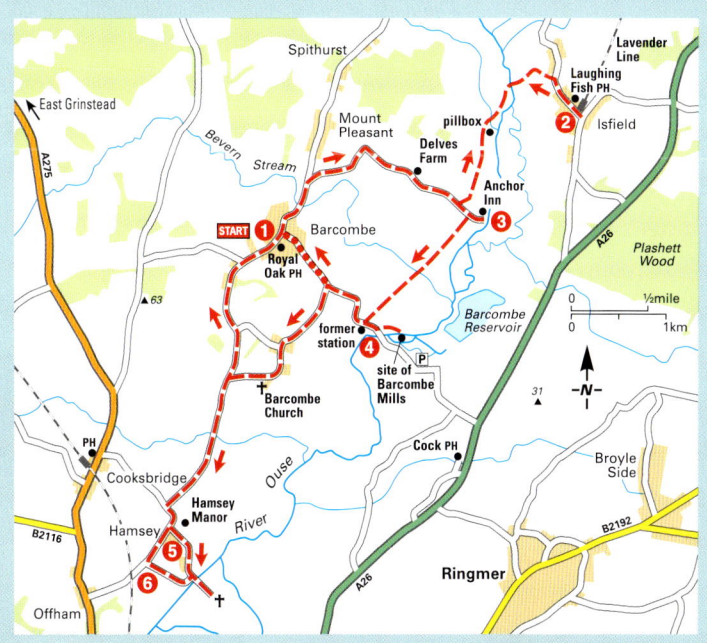

WILMINGTON

Visit the legendary chalk figure, which still puzzles archaeologists and historians. Theories abound about the origin of the Long Man and what he originally looked like. Did he carry a scythe and rake? Was he a fertility figure? How long has he been etched in the hillside? It is possible we will never know for sure.

DISTANCE/TIME 6.25 miles (10.1km) 2h30 **MAP** OS Explorer 123 South Downs Way: Newhaven to Eastbourne **START** Long-stay car park at Wilmington; grid ref: TQ 543041 **TRACKS** Downland paths and tracks, stretch of country road, 1 stile **THE PUB** The Giants Rest, The Street, Wilmington. Tel: 01323 870207

1 Head to the car park exit and then follow the path that runs parallel to the road, heading towards the Long Man. Bear left at the next gate and take the Wealdway to the chalk figure. You will climb quite steeply, the path curving to the right. Go through the gate. Avoid the Wealdway arrow and keep ahead towards the escarpment, veering right just below the Long Man.

2 Go through the next gate and cross the track. Bear left at the fence. After a few paces, you will reach a gate and sign for South Downs Way. Pass a small reservoir; follow the track to the road.

3 Turn left and then walk to the signpost ('Lullington church'), following the path beside cottages. After visiting the church, retrace your steps to the road. Turn right. Head down the lane, looking for Alfriston church on your right. Pass the turning to the village on the right and continue ahead towards Seaford. Look out for a post box and swing left (signed 'Jevington').

4 Follow the bridleway as it climbs steadily between tracts of remote downland. Keep left at the next main junction and there is a moderate climb. Avoid the bridle track branching off to the left and proceed towards Jevington. Lullington Heath National Nature Reserve is on the right now. Pass the bridleway to Charleston Bottom on the right and keep on the track as it climbs quite steeply. Pass a second sign and a map for the nature reserve and make for the junction with the South Downs Way.

5 Turn left and then follow the enclosed path to a gate. Go straight ahead alongside woodland and pass through a second gate. The path begins a gradual curve to the left and eventually passes along the rim of a dry valley, Tenantry Ground. Keep the fence on your left and look for gate ahead. Swing right as you approach the gate to reach a stile and then follow the path alongside the fence, crossing the top of the Long Man.

6 To your right, you can just make out the chalk figure down below. Continue ahead keeping the fence on your right and descend to a gate. Turn right here and retrace your steps to the car park at Wilmington.

QUEEN ELIZABETH COUNTRY PARK

Follow woodland and downland trails to a unique archaeological farmstead, continue through two of Hampshire's oldest and prettiest villages, Chalton and Buriton, and then climb Butser Hill for all-round views.

DISTANCE/TIME 6.75 miles (10.9km) 3h **MAP** OS Explorer 120 Chichester **START** Pay-and-display car park, Queen Elizabeth Country Park; grid ref: SU 718185 **TRACKS** Woodland paths, bridleways and forest track, 4 stiles **THE PUB** The Five Bells, Buriton. Tel: 01730 263584

1 From the car park follow the Woodland Trail (marked by the green striped posts) to the right. On reaching the road, turn left then right on the gravel path.

2 Ascend and fork right by a 'no-cycling' sign, taking the track at the wood edge. As the track swings left around the corner, turn sharp right over a stile. Leave the country park and turn left on to a bridleway. The path undulates but soon levels and then gradually descends to a road.

3 At the road, turn right to visit Butser Ancient Farm (the footpath in 50yds/46m avoids the road), otherwise turn left to follow the road for 0.5 miles (0.8km) into the village of Chalton. Turn left at the junction, signed 'Ditcham'.

4 In 250yds (229m) turn left along a byway. Continue between fields and soon descend between trees to a road. Turn left, going parallel to the railway for 0.25 miles (0.4km). Cross a stile on the right. Bear half left across a field and enter woodland.

5 At a junction of paths continue ahead and climb a wide forest track. Descend and fork left, then almost immediately right, down a signposted footpath to a road.

6 Turn right, then in 100yds (91m) take the footpath left and head steeply down through the trees to a stile. Now, bear half right across a field to a stile by a gate then follow the path around to the left, passing a pond into Buriton.

7 Turn left along the High Street. Beyond house No. 29, take the footpath left (or go straight on for The Five Bells pub). Go round the village hall and ascend alongside playing fields to a gate. Cross the railway line, go through a gate and follow the path to a junction with a bridleway. Turn right and steeply ascend to the road. Cross over into Hall's Hill car park.

8 Go through a gate and up a wide track (South Downs Way) back into the country park. Gradually ascend. Just after a track merges from the right, fork right and descend. Go through a gate and Benhams Bushes car park, walk down a metalled road, and then bear left, following the South Downs Way. Rejoin the road at Gravel Hill car park and retrace your route to the car park.

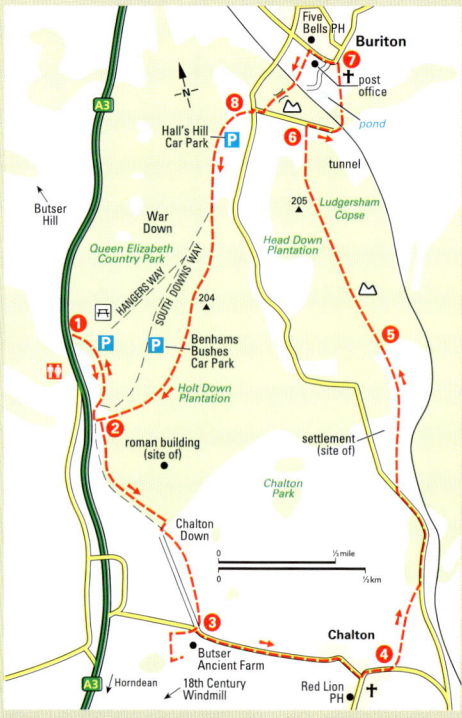

AROUND THE ARUN VALLEY FROM ARUNDEL

Follow the River Arun to Arundel Park and then tour this handsome Sussex town, dominated by its massive castle. The walk starts down by the River Arun and from here there are teasing glimpses of the castle, but it is not until you have almost finished the walk that you reach its main entrance. Following the river bank through the tranquil Arun valley, the walk reaches Arundel Park. Swanbourne Lake, a great attraction for young children, is located by the entrance to the park, but beyond here the park assumes a rather different character. You may start to feel slightly isolated at this point but don't worry; resume the walk and you will soon be back in the hustle and bustle of Arundel's busy streets.

DISTANCE/TIME 3.25 miles (5.3km) 2h **MAP** OS Explorer 121 Arundel & Pulborough **START** Fee-paying car park, Mill Road, Arundel; grid ref: TQ 020071 **TRACKS** Riverside and parkland paths, some road walking, 2 stiles **THE PUB** Black Rabbit, Offham. Tel: 01903 882828

1 From the car park in Mill Road, turn right and then walk along the handsome tree-lined pavement. Once you are past the bowling green a glance to your left will reveal a dramatic view of Arundel Castle with its imposing battlements.

2 Follow the road to the elegant stone bridge, cross over via a footbridge and turn right. Ignore the path left, and follow the riverside path, partly shaded by overhanging trees. Emerging from the cover, the path cuts across lush, low-lying ground to reach the western bank of the Arun. Turn left and walk beside the reed-fringed river to the Black Rabbit pub, which can be seen standing out against a curtain of trees.

3 From the Black Rabbit, follow the minor road in a roughly westerly direction back towards Arundel, passing the entrance to the Wildfowl and Wetlands Trust. Make for the gate leading into Arundel Park and follow the path beside Swanbourne Lake. Eventually the lake fades from view as the

walk reaches deeper into the park. Ignore a turning branching off to the left, just before a gate and stile, and follow the path as it curves gently to the right.

4 Turn sharply to the left at the next waymarked junction and begin a fairly steep ascent, with the footpath through the park seen curving away down to the left, back towards the lake. From this stretch of the walk there are fine views over Arundel Park. Pass through a gate with a stile on the left, then bear immediately right up the bank. Cross the grass, following the waymarks and keeping to the left of Hiorne Tower. On reaching a driveway, turn left and walk down to Park Lodge. Keep to the right by the private drive and make for the road.

5 Turn left, pass Arundel Cathedral and bear left at the road junction by the entrance to Arundel Castle. From here, walk down the hill into the bustling town centre. You'll find Mill Road and the car park at the bottom of the High Street.

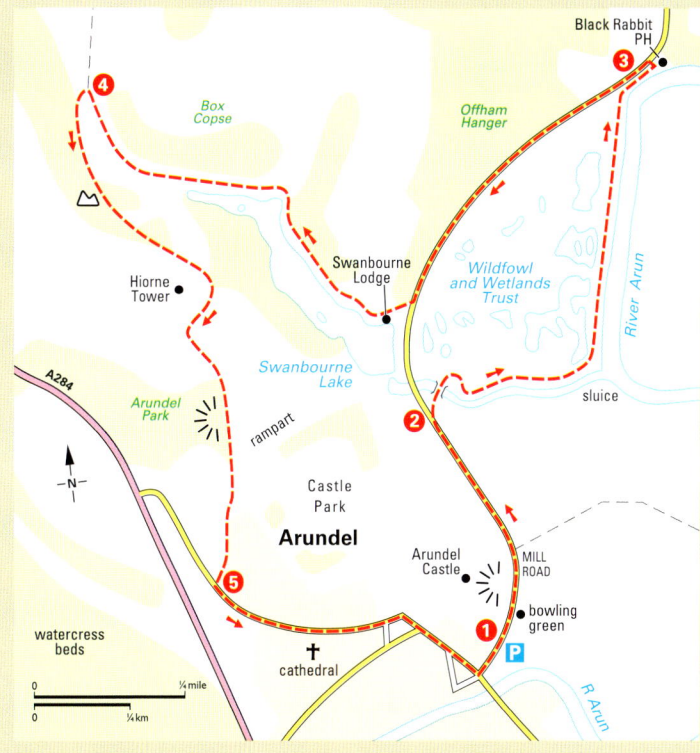

WALK 42

A CIRCUIT OF DEVIL'S DYKE BY POYNINGS

This is a fine walk with glimpses over the most famous of all the dry chalk valleys. Devil's Dyke is a geological quirk – a spectacular, steep-sided downland combe or cleft. It was probably cut by glacial meltwaters millions of years ago in the Ice Age. Views from this beauty spot stretch for miles in all directions. In good weather the slopes are busy with visitors, while in the skies hang-gliders swoop over the grassy downland. However, away from the car park and chalk slopes the walk heads for more peaceful surroundings.

DISTANCE/TIME 3 miles (4.8km) 1h30 **MAP** OS Explorer 122 South Downs Way: Steyning to Newhaven **START** Free car park, Summer Down; grid ref: TQ 268112 **TRACKS** Field and woodland paths, 6 stiles **THE PUB** Royal Oak, Poynings. Tel: 01273 857389

1 From the car park go through the kissing gate and veer right. Join the South Downs Way and follow it by trees. Soon the path curves left and drops down to the road. Leave the South Downs Way here, as the path crosses over to join the private road leading to Saddlescombe, and follow the verge for 75yds (69m). Bear left at the footpath sign and drop down the bank to reach a stile.

2 Follow the line of the tarmac lane as it curves right to reach a waymark. Leave the lane and walk ahead alongside power lines, keeping the line of trees and bushes on the right. Look for a narrow path disappearing into the vegetation and make for a stile. Drop down some steps into the woods and turn right at a junction with a bridleway. Take the path running off half left and follow it between fields and a wooded dell. Pass over a stile and continue to a stile in the left boundary. Cross a footbridge to a stile and now turn right towards Poynings.

3 Head for a gate and footpath sign and turn left at the road. Follow the parallel path along to the Royal Oak public house and then

continue to Dyke Lane on the left. There is a memorial stone here to George Stephen Cave Cuttress, a resident of Poynings for over 50 years, erected by his widow. Follow the tarmac bridleway; it soon narrows to a path. On reaching the fork, by a National Trust sign for Devil's Dyke, veer right and climb the steps.

4 Follow the path up to a gate and continue up the stairs. From the higher ground there are stunning views to the north and west. Make for a kissing gate and head up the slope towards the inn. Keep the Devil's Dyke pub on your left and take the road round to the left, passing a bridleway on the left. Follow the path that runs parallel to the road and look over to the left for a definitive view of Devil's Dyke.

5 Now head for the South Downs Way and shortly turn left close by a National Trust sign for Summer Down to a stile and gate. Follow the trail, keeping Devil's Dyke down to your left, and eventually you will reach a stile that will lead you back into Summer Down car park and your car.

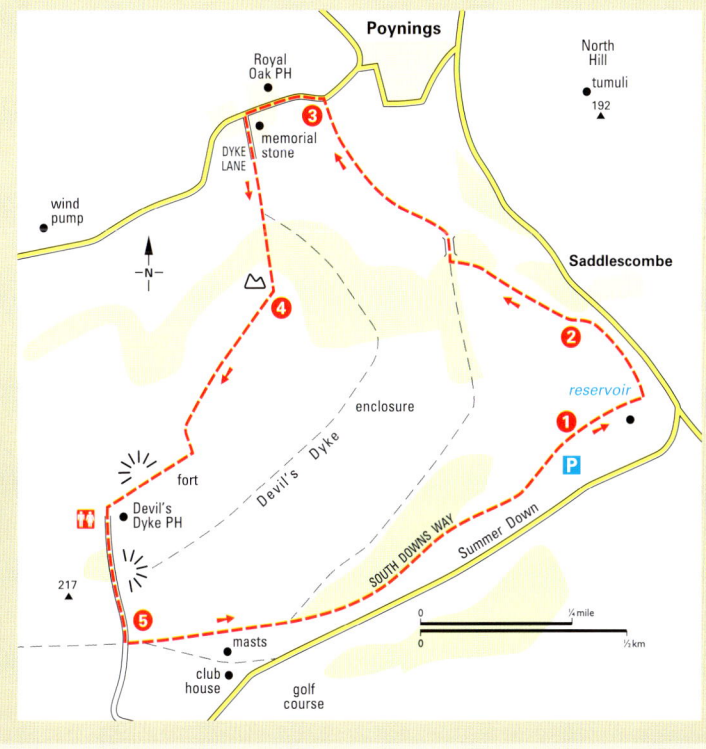

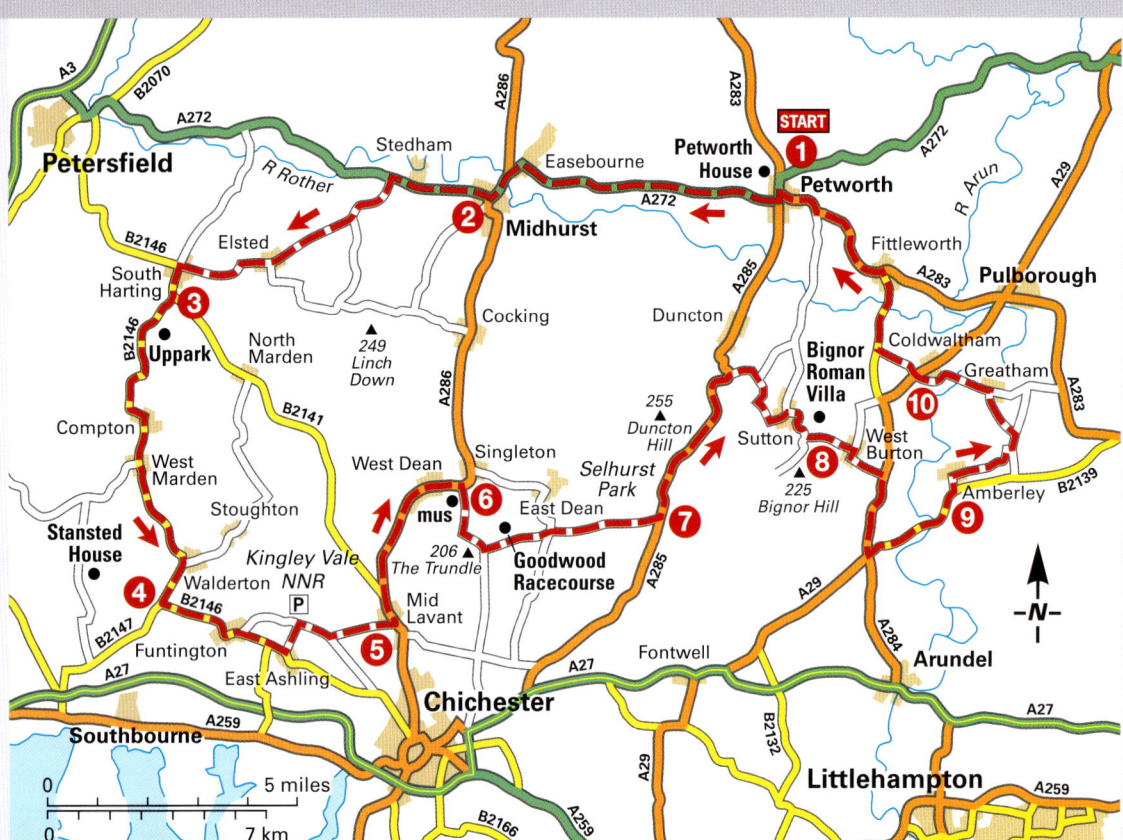

PETWORTH & AMBERLEY

This tour makes the most of the bewitching scenery of the West Sussex Downs, with glimpses of the distant sea. You can visit Petworth House and Uppark (both National Trust properties), or venture into Europe's largest yew forest at Kingley Vale, and see some of England's finest Roman mosaics at Bignor Roman Villa, discovered in the early 19th century. Learn about the region's traditional building styles at the Weald and Downland Open Air Museum, and find out about the working life of yesteryear in Amberley Working Museum.

Route Directions

Start the drive at Petworth, where the estate walls of Petworth House extend to the town centre. The house has the finest art collection of any National Trust property, and in addition to its stately rooms, has a huge deer park.

1 From Petworth, take the A272 west and drive through the village of Easebourne to reach the town of Midhurst.

Midhurst's beautifully preserved town centre, especially the section around the church, is well worth exploring.

2 Leave Midhurst by the A272 towards Petersfield. Leave the A272 near Stedham, turning left on a minor road through Elsted (where the delightfully placed Three Horseshoes makes a very pleasant stop) to turn left through South Harting.

South Harting was once the home of the prolific Victorian novelist Anthony Trollope, author of the Barsetshire novels as well as many more, and has an attractive sloping village street.

3 Fork right on to the B2146. Continue along this road. You will soon pass the entrance to the stately home of Uppark.

This supremely elegant Classical mansion suffered a huge fire in 1989 and the National Trust painstakingly restored it to what it was before the disaster. At West Marden you can divert right to Stansted House, a Georgian mansion in a great park, while at Walderton you can detour left to Stoughton.

4 Beyond Walderton, turn left to stay on the B2146, then take the B2178 towards Chichester, and at East Ashling turn left and continue following the National Nature Reserve signposts.

At North Stoke, a car park gives access to Kingley Vale National Nature Reserve. Follow the path from the car park, and at a path junction go ahead through a gate to follow the circular nature trail through the magical yew grove of Kingley Vale and up to the crest of the Downs, where Bronze Age burial mounds look across Chichester Harbour.

5 From this point, continue heading east and shortly turn left onto the A286 at Mid Lavant.

At West Dean are West Dean Gardens, in the grounds of a prestigious arts college, beautifully set along the River Lavant and looking up to the Downs. Very close by is the Weald and Downland Museum, where traditionally constructed buildings from all over southeast England have been re-erected. You can eat at the museum's café, or seek out the Fox & Hounds, a friendly 16th-century pub in Singleton village.

6 Turn right off the A286, beyond West Dean, following the road up to Goodwood racecourse, and fork left towards Petworth.

Beyond 'Glorious Goodwood' you will be able to see the sea at Bognor Regis. Selhurst Park, by the road on the left, is a forest area offering some fine views.

7 Turn left on the A285 towards Petworth. After 3.6 miles (5.8km), just where the road drops from the Downs, turn right at the bottom of the hill on a lane through Sutton to Bignor Roman Villa.

The villa contains magnificent mosaics and has been a tourist attraction since its chance discovery by a ploughman in 1811. You can also divert up on to the South Downs on a little lane ending on Bignor Hill, and explore

Stane Street, a dead straight Roman road now demoted to a track, but well preserved with its agger (ditch) still visible alongside.

8 Carry on through West Burton to Bury. Turn right on the A29, then take the B2139 at the roundabout.

You pass the Amberley Working Museum, in a chalk pit, and home to a community of craftspeople with re-erected buildings recalling earlier working life in the southeast of England. This is a good place to take a break and stretch your legs as you explore the museum.

9 Turn left into the beautiful village of Amberley, with its many thatched houses and the castle overlooking the water meadows. Follow the road that bends right by the Black Horse in Amberley village, and keep left at two junctions to the village of Greatham.

Greatham Bridge is an idyllic place to sit and relax beside the River Arun.

10 Cross the A29 at Coldwaltham, and turn right on to the B2138 to Fittleworth, where the unusual pub sign for the Swan spans the road. Turn left on the A283 and continue to Petworth where you can visit the 17th-century Petworth House (NT).

64 MILES (103.5KM)

LEWES, WAKEHURST PLACE & ASHDOWN FOREST

This route celebrates Sussex in all its diversity: starting from Lewes, beautifully set in the South Downs, it heads into the Weald. You encounter the primaeval-feeling heathlands and woods of the Ashdown Forest – the landscape of the immortal Winnie-the-Pooh stories – and pass some of the world's greatest gardens and the terminus of the Bluebell Railway, one of Britain's most engaging steam railways. Near the end you can finish in high style by driving up on to the Downs for a view far across southern England. There's no shortage of good pubs and tea rooms along the route where you can stop and take a break and have a bite to eat.

Route Directions

1 Leave the historic county town of Lewes on the A275. Cross the A272 at North Chailey and continue on the A275. You will pass Sheffield Park Station, the southern terminus of the Bluebell Railway on the left. A short distance on is the entrance to Sheffield Park Gardens.

You can detour ahead a short distance to Heaven Farm, on the left of the A275, which is a delightfully informal spot for lunch or tea.

2 Just after the entrance to Sheffield Park Gardens, turn right on a minor road to Fletching, where the Griffin Inn also makes an excellent lunch spot. Carry on to the A272, turn left to Maresfield, left at the A22, and at the next roundabout turn off to the B2026. This climbs over Ashdown Forest, keeping left at a fork with the B2188.

The sandy tracks, rolling heaths and clumps of pine trees make for a remote landscape. It was here that A A Milne set his Winnie-the-Pooh stories, and the scene is instantly familiar from E H Shepard's illustrations. This is vintage territory for picnics (with plentiful car parks), kite flying and bracing walks.

3 At Chuck Hatch you can detour left along a lane for the Poohsticks Bridge, which featured in Milne's stories. Soon you see the entrance to Pooh car park on the right.

The path from the car park goes through the woods, and at a corner of the road, turns right on a bridleway leading to the bridge. Though rebuilt since Milne's time, the bridge looks exactly like the original where Pooh and his friends enjoyed a game of poohsticks.

4 Return to the B2026 and continue to Hartfield. A shop here called Pooh Corner has a wide array of Pooh-related gifts. Take the B2110 west from Hartfield towards Forest Row, then take the second left turn past Coleman's Hatch, keeping forward by the weatherboarded Hatch pub (with a very pretty garden for good weather relaxing).

You will pass the Ashdown Forest Centre on your right. There is a display and also information about the forest.

5 Cross the A22 and take the minor road opposite, turning left at the next crossroads towards West Hoathly. At the next crossroads detour right past the end of Weirwood Reservoir to Standen house (NT).

This unusual Arts and Crafts house was designed by Philip Webb, a friend and associate of William Morris; the gardens have views over the Weald.

6 Carry on to the B2028, turn left along it, past the entrance to Wakehurst Place, which is maintained by the Royal Botanic Gardens at Kew, and home to the Millennium Seed Bank. Turn right at Ardingly, towards Balcombe, past Ardingly church and over one arm of Ardingly Reservoir.

This body of water looks almost natural, and provides scope for waterside strolls, as well as fishing and watersports such as canoeing, windsurfing and sailing.

7 Turn left on reaching the edge of Balcombe, and continue on this road towards Haywards Heath.

On the left you see the huge Ouse Valley Viaduct, which carries the London–Brighton railway. A footpath leads from the road and disappears underneath the structure, from which point you can appreciate an extraordinary view through all the oval spaces in the piers.

8 Further along the same road you will find Borde Hill gardens comprising superb parkland and woods.

There is always a spectacular show of blooms at these gardens during the early summer when the colourful rhododendrons and azaleas are out.

9 After Borde Hill gardens, turn left onto a minor road and then take the A272 to Haywards Heath, then the B2112 to Ditchling. The old village of Ditchling nestles at the foot of the South Downs (the Bull makes a welcoming stopping place, or there are a couple of tea rooms). From there head south to Ditchling Beacon.

From the car park at the top you can take a short stroll along the South Downs Way, enjoying the sweeping views over the Weald.

10 Return to Ditchling and then go east along the B2116 to join the A275 just outside Lewes town centre.

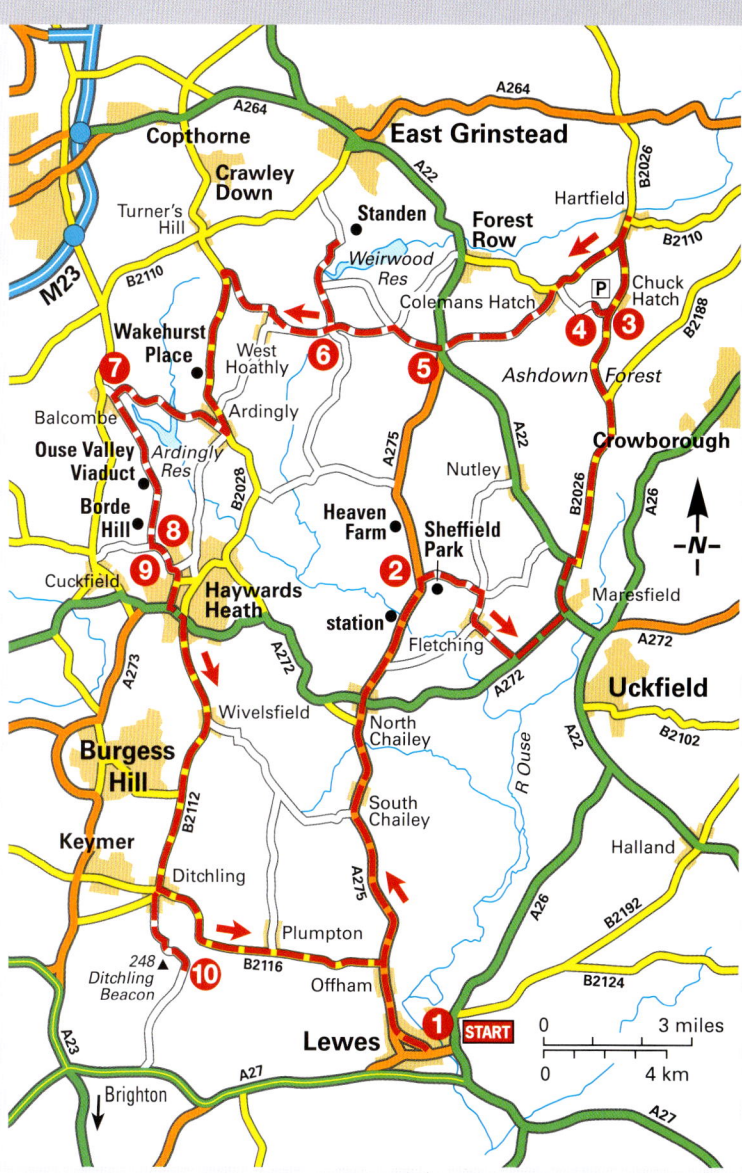

South Coast

CLOCKWISE FROM TOP LEFT: EASTBOURNE; SPINNAKER TOWER, PORTSMOUTH; EASTBOURNE; BEACHY HEAD

BEACHY HEAD & SEVEN SISTERS
MAP REF 401 H7

A high rollercoaster of turf-capped white cliffs undulates between Seaford and Eastbourne, rising to seven mini-peaks known as the Seven Sisters. The Channel continues to erode the sheer, crumbling chalk heights. From Seaford Head to Beachy Head to the east, this makes up the longest and most scenic stretch of undeveloped coast in southeast England.

The Seven Sisters Country Park encompasses the western part of the cliffs. Two large car parks either side of the A259 at Exceat give access into Friston Forest to the north and also Cuckmere Haven. This is the only undeveloped estuary in Sussex, with wildlife thriving in the meadows, reed beds and ponds.

Further east is Beachy Head, the highest point on the Sussex coast. This sheer chalk cliff plummets a full 534 feet (201m), with a lighthouse on the shore far below. The views up here are dizzying in the extreme (on a clear day you can see Dungeness to the east and the Isle of Wight to the west), but do be careful as the cliff edge is not stable. From Eastbourne, the South Downs Way leads up – or you can continue along the undercliff closer to the shore before a steep final ascent. From Terminus Road or from the pier in the town centre hop on an open-topped City Sightseeing bus that will take you up the zigzagging road (not in winter).

BRIGHTON & HOVE
MAP REF 401 G7

Brighton is unmistakably cosmopolitan, fun-loving and sophisticated. The cliché that it's a place for romantic frolics has been overtaken by its newer image as a gay capital, an arty vibrant place that keeps going until the small hours.

The beachfront changes in character from one moment to the next. Ornate Victorian lamp-posts, attractive coloured railings and the creamy white stucco frontages characterise one of the finest seaside townscapes in Britain, with bow-windowed Regency and grand Victorian façades. At the middle, ornate Palace Pier has a funfair. Near its entrance, the Brighton Sea Life Centre has displays including a walk-through glass tunnel.

To the east, Brighton Marina is a huge modern complex with outlet shopping, bowling alley, an eight-screen cinema, prestigious apartment complexes and a raft of waterfront restaurants and cafés. West of Palace Pier is the liveliest part of the beachfront. The booths under the esplanade are home to an artistic quarter, with little galleries alongside palmists, cockles and jellied eel stalls, bucket and spade shops, bars, henna tattooists and hair-braiders. Look out for the tiny Mechanical Memories Museum.

At night, the action revolves around the beachfront clubs, plus there are free performances at the Ellipse area, open-air cinema and music on the beach. The Brighton Centre has shows and gigs, with many big-name bands. By the beach near the ornate bandstand is a free paddling pool and playground. Major plans are afoot to transform the seafront.

Just behind the seafront from the west side of the Palace Pier is The Lanes, an intricate knot of little streets and alleys packed with restaurants, boutiques, and jewellery and clothes shops, with tempting cooking smells wafting from doorways.

Between the railway station and the Royal Pavilion is the North Laine – radically different from The Lanes. Here small streets have evolved into an alternative shopping and promenading area.

Just inland from The Lanes is the heart of Regency Brighton and the astonishing Royal Pavilion. Originally a simple farmhouse, it became a classical 'Marine Pavilion' before John Nash transformed it between 1815 and 1823 for the Prince Regent, later George IV, into an Indian fantasy of domes and minarets. Across the Pavilion Gardens, within the former Pavilion stables and riding school, the Brighton Museum and Art Gallery is one of Brighton's best free sights.

There are delightful hilly streets to the north, rising up to the Montpellier area – some of Brighton and Hove's most elegant Regency villas and terraces – and there's more of the same along the seafront. Preston Street, off Western Road, has a concentration of ethnic restaurants.

CHICHESTER HARBOUR
MAP REF 400 F7

Flat farmlands, saltmarshes and mudflats surround this vast natural harbour, where thousands of bobbing masts attest to its status as one of the major yachting havens of the south coast. There are footpaths, but the best way to see this natural wonder is from the water itself.

With West Itchenor as the starting point, Chichester Harbour Water Tours give 1.5-hour cruises on the harbour up to five times a day – with the chance to spot birds such as shelducks, teals and mergansers, as well as seals. Surfers head towards East Wittering and Bracklesham Bay when the conditions are right. On warm summer days it gets very busy at West Wittering, but the crowds soon thin out as you venture on to East Head.

On the western fringes of Chichester are the remains of the largest Roman building yet discovered north of the Alps. It is a huge complex with some 100 rooms and 60 mosaics, believed to be unique in Britain. Fishbourne Roman Palace has become one of the most celebrated archaeological excavations of its time.

Outside, the box hedges are planted in the same intricate patterns as the excavated Roman bedding trenches, and there's an exhibit on Roman gardening. In the impressive Collections Discovery Centre you can look into the foyer exhibition and see the experts at work.

EASTBOURNE MAP REF 401 H7

Though less obviously trendy than nearby Brighton, Eastbourne scores particularly strongly for its very appealing 4 miles (6.5km) of unspoiled seafront. It retains a gracious atmosphere, with rows of stucco-fronted hotels and guesthouses overlooking the beach. Central to the seafront is the ornate Victorian pier, with its fairy lights strung between lamp-posts and some of the best surviving ironwork and little kiosks of the era, picked out in blue and white paint. The Dome at the end houses a fully restored camera obscura, built in 1901. Near by is the turquoise flattened onion dome of the bandstand.

West from here you can stroll, join the skaters, or take the bus or seasonal hourly Dotto Train past the Wish Tower and the Lifeboat Museum. The promenade ends at the Holywell Tea Chalet. In the other direction, the Dotto Train runs along to Britain's largest man-made marina at Sovereign Harbour. There's a good range of waterfront restaurants and cafés, and harbour boat trips. On the way you'll pass Princes Park, with mini golf, bowls, putting and a model boating lake, and Royal Parade. Here the Redoubt Fortress, a 19th-century circular fort, now houses the Military Museum of Sussex.

The town's quirkiest attraction has to be How We Lived Then: the Museum of Shops, in Cornfield Terrace, a collection of some 100,000 items of bygone random merchandise set in rooms re-created to mirror times gone by.

NETLEY MAP REF 400 E7

At Netley, a Victorian town on the shores of the Solent, the Royal Victoria Country Park covers more than 100 acres (40ha) of woods, marshes and beach. There is a nature trail, miniature railway and walks.

The ruins of Netley Abbey stand brooding in woodland next to the Solent shore. Netley Castle, on the shore near the abbey and formerly the gatehouse, was one of Henry VIII's gun stations – its tall tower is Victorian, and it has been transformed into a wonderful folly with all the panoply of Gothic device.

PEVENSEY MAP REF 401 H7

The outer walls of Pevensey Castle enclose a huge oval of grassland. These full-sized walls are late Roman, with some medieval repairs, built to protect the busy port.

The medieval castle is set within a moat at the centre of the enclosure – William the Conqueror put a fort here in 1066, but what you see today is 13th century. Then the castle would still have been on the coast, surrounded by marshes. The castle was abandoned around 1500 after the harbour had silted up. But more than

400 years later it would have been a first defence against a shore invasion in World War II: you can see the rooms used by Canadian soldiers inside the towers, and a gun emplacement looks out over the tea rooms. Pevensey's other historic buildings include Old Mint House Antiques (1342) and the Court House museum.

The extensive shingle beach is at Pevensey Bay, about a mile (1.6km) away. To the north are the Pevensey Levels, a reclaimed marsh with reed-fringed ditches, tiny lanes and isolated farms.

PORTCHESTER CASTLE
MAP REF 400 E7

This is one of the most fascinating historical sites in Britain. The massive, 20-foot (6m) high walls of a 3rd-century Roman fort sit on a little promontory on the northern shore of Portsmouth harbour, facing directly across it and out to sea. It is the most complete Roman fort remains in northern Europe.

PORTSMOUTH MAP REF 400 E7

Portsmouth has been Britain's foremost naval base since the late 15th century, when it had the first ever dry dock. For a great view over the city, take the lift to the top of the elegant 600-foot (170m) high Spinnaker Tower, opened in 2005.

The town's biggest attraction is the collection of historic ships that can be visited in the Naval Dockyard. HMS *Victory*, launched in 1765, was Nelson's flagship at the Battle of Trafalgar in 1805 and is probably the most famous British warship; she is also the oldest commissioned warship in the world. The remains of *Mary Rose*, which sank off Southsea in July 1545, are housed in a specially designed and constructed building. 'Permanent conservation' is under way, and there is an exhibition of the artefacts found during salvage. HMS *Warrior*, the first 'ironclad', was launched at Blackwall in 1860, the largest, fastest and most formidable warship the world had ever seen. The Dockyard also houses the Royal Naval Museum and 'Action Stations', a thrilling high-tech Royal Naval experience using film and interactive technology.

During World War II Portsmouth was bombed heavily, and it is unfortunate that much of the rebuilding has been particularly uninspired. This being so, hurry through to the historic dockyard and follow the Millennium Promenade (Renaissance Trail) on foot through the bustling Gunwharf Quays shopping complex to The Point. Here is the oldest and most picturesque quarter of Old Portsmouth, where surviving attractive old streets have been restored, and face out on to a pretty little harbour.

The city has more than a dozen museums, including Charles Dickens' Birthplace in Old Commercial Road, but the City Museum and Art Gallery found in Museum Road is probably the best place to start. It features 'The Story of Portsmouth' and will point you in the direction of the other remaining historic buildings around the city, including the Landport Gate of 1760, the Square Tower of 1494 and the Royal Garrison Church. Beyond the tangle of Old Portsmouth's streets to the east, you emerge on to Southsea Common, faced by imposing terraces of 19th-century stucco.

SOUTHAMPTON MAP REF 400 E7

Modern Southampton has been made by its docks. Its famous double tides give prolonged high water, and there's a grand view of the comings and goings of cruise ships and the pleasure craft from Town Quay and Western Esplanade.

This is a sprawling, thriving, working city, with attractions that include some of the best shopping along the south coast, the fine City Art Gallery, a string of leafy green parks, and a little Maritime Museum set in a 15th-century warehouse near the shore, which tells of the great liners built here, and the last, fateful voyage of the RMS *Titanic*. The Solent Sky Aviation Museum, which offers hands-on experience of many of the exhibits, was founded in honour of R J Mitchell, designer of the Spitfire fighter plane which was constructed at Southampton's Supermarine Works.

The most interesting area lies south of the gleaming West Quay shopping centre, and it is worth parking there to explore on foot. The mall leads out on to Above Bar Street, a pedestrianised shopping street and one of several last surviving fragments of the medieval walled city. Stroll down here, passing the Dolphin Hotel where novelist Jane Austen celebrated her 18th birthday in 1793. Next door is the bombed-out Church of the Holy Rood, dedicated to the merchant seamen of the city, and including a memorial to the 500 local crew who died aboard RMS *Titanic* in 1912. Beyond nearby St Michael's, the oldest church in the city, dating to 1070, and the only one undamaged in the war, lie Bugle Street and French Street, with the Medieval Merchant's House of 1290 and the striking timbered Tudor House Museum and Garden. Another little interesting corner to explore is Oxford Street, its mellow old houses now filled with trendy restaurants, and with an Edwardian pub, the London Hotel, at one corner.

On the shore, ferries leave for the Isle of Wight and Hythe, and Ocean Village is a modern marina from where you can take a pleasant cruise of the harbour.

Visit
DRUSILLAS PARK

One of the top children's attractions in Sussex, Drusillas is an imaginative small zoo with lots of add-ons. There are cave-like interiors with child-friendly viewing of the smallest creatures, alternating with outside areas holding the larger animals like otters, meerkats and penguins. The route ends up in a huge adventure playground. Along the way there are plenty of hands-on activities that aim to blend the fun with the educational, such as the Zoolympics Challenge where children can rate their running and shouting performance against various animals. As you emerge into the playground and paddling area (extra charges for some activities) you get some idea of the origins of Drusillas as a pre-war tea rooms: the original cottage is still there. Birthday parties and animal adoption can be arranged, and there are special events such as summer visits from cartoon characters and weekends centred on reptiles or creepy-crawlies.

Activity
WINDSURFING

You can see Britain's top windsurfers in action at Eastbourne during Eastbourne Extreme, a festival of sport held in July. This seaside resort is regarded as one of Britain's best venues for windsurfing. If you'd like to have a go, the Watersports Centre (RYA accredited) in Royal Parade runs taster sessions and weekly courses. For the initial lesson, if you're a total beginner, you'll spend the day on Princes Park Lake before heading into the sea. Hove Lagoon in Brighton and Hove is another good place to learn.

Activity
FRISTON FOREST

The Seven Sisters Country Park at Exceat adjoins Friston Forest, laced with paths and mountain bike routes (from easy to challenging). Although it's relatively new, with a plantation of mainly beech, Scots and Corsican pine – created from 1926 and planted on an underground reservoir that serves Eastbourne – it does harbour a variety of wildlife. Tread quietly and you might spot adders, badgers, roe deer or foxes, and there are rare butterflies like fritillaries and clouded yellows. Surrounded by the forest is the village of Westdean. There's no parking in the village, so walk up the signposted route from the Seven Sisters Country Park car park.

DISTANCE/TIME 13 miles (20.9km) 2h30; shorter route 5.5 miles (8.8km) 1h **MAP** OS Explorer 124 Hastings and Bexhill **START** Pevensey car park (by castle; pay-and-display); grid ref: TQ 646048

TRACKS All on minor roads, except for bridleway at Herstmonceux; the short ride is on roads

THE PUB The Lamb Inn, Wartling. Tel: 01323 832116; www.lambwartling.co.uk

A LOOP FROM PEVENSEY TO HERSTMONCEUX

This is a journey between two castles that takes you through the Pevensey Levels in '1066 Country'. Although flat, the Pevensey Levels are full of colour, character and wildlife, while the South Downs rise dramatically in the background. The ride connects the castles at Pevensey and Herstmonceux.

1 From the car park, go to the main street in Pevensey and turn left along it, passing the outer wall of the castle (you can walk in through the gateway, where there is free access, if you don't intend to visit the castle fully later). Just after the Pevensey Castle pub turn right along Peelings Lane, ignoring a minor turn soon on the left. Turn right at a crossroads and follow signs to Hankham.

2 Turn right at a T-junction in Hankham, signposted 'Rickney'. Keep right at the next junction for Rickney (National Cycle Route 2). For a short loop back, at the next junction (in Rickney itself) turn right, then right after 1.5 miles (2.4km). Cross the roundabout and take the road back into Pevensey. To take the main cycle ride, turn left at the junction in Rickney (signposted 'Hailsham'), then take the first right, signposted 'Herstmonceux'. Both the short and full rides afford lovely views across the Pevensey Levels.

3 After 3 miles (4.8km) turn right at the next junction, and then keep right at the next two junctions to reach Herstmonceux Church. Have a look inside for the tomb of Thomas Lord Dacre (died 1553) and his son Sir Thomas Fiennes.

4 Past the church, where the public road ends, go forward, veering left on the bridleway, and follow blue arrows and waymarkers for the 1066 Country Walk. This leads over a surfaced area near college outbuildings and a car park, and through woodland (it can be muddy). It then crosses a field, with a view of Herstmonceux Castle to the left; it is not always open to the public. Ahead is one of the telescope buildings of the former Royal Greenwich Observatory. Push your bike up some steps and later you will see the other domes of the Herstmonceux Science Centre.

5 Turn right on the road (just to the left is the entrance to the Science Centre and Herstmonceux Castle and grounds) and cycle down to Wartling, keeping right in front of the Lamb Inn. Continue for 2.5 miles (4km) back to the edge of Pevensey.

6 Cross the roundabout carefully, using the cycle crossing points, and take the road into Pevensey to return to the start point.

DISTANCE/TIME 12 miles (19.3km) 4h; shorter route 7 miles (11.3km) 2h **MAP** OS Explorer 123 South Downs Way: Newhaven to Eastbourne **START** Seven Sisters Country Park pay car park; grid ref: TV 518995 **TRACKS** Compacted and forest tracks, road, rough tracks, stony descents

THE PUB The Plough and Harrow, Litlington. Tel: 01323 870632

FRISTON FOREST & CUCKMERE HAVEN

The ride takes you past three wonderful contrasts: the Cuckmere river as it meanders its way to the sea; the tranquil greenery of Friston Forest, planted in the early 20th century over an underground reservoir; and the sweeping views inland and towards the sea from the top of the Downs.

1 From the car park go towards the vehicular entrance, and just before the road turn right on a track signposted 'public bridleway to West Dean'. Look for the bicycle symbols in green, which denote the bike trail you will be following for the first part of the ride.

2 At the first house at West Dean keep heading forward on the track (signposted 'Exceat Hill'), following the green bike symbols. After 1 mile (1.6km) you will reach a junction marked with five tall red-and-white posts.

3 For a short return to West Dean, fork left almost immediatley after, and continue following the green bike symbols, turning right at the hard forest road (to the left you can see the tall red-and-white posts), then soon turn left at another bike symbol. The track rises (at the top a short path leads up right to a viewpoint and then falls). Leave the waymarked trail at a three-way fork, keeping right downhill, past a barrier and houses, then turn right at a road junction into West Dean. Pass the church and rectory and drop to a T-junction by Pond Cottage, then go ahead towards the flight of steps, where you turn right along the track you were following earlier and retrace to the start. For the main route, continue ahead at Point 3 and fork left near some power lines. Go past a barrier, and forward again on joining a metalled road, which becomes less surfaced (ignore side turns). On reaching a road, turn left along it to Jevington.

4 Turn left at Jevington and take the track signposted 'South Downs Way and church'. Continue uphill on the track, which steepens through the woods. Ignore side turns.

5 At the top emerge from the woodland, ignore the South Downs Way to the right and keep forward. There are wonderful views from this track and just to left is Lullington Heath Nature Reserve. The track later drops steeply and then rises to a junction by a small flint pillar on the left. Carry on downhill, forking left later to Litlington, where the track twists left and then right by farm buildings.

6 At the road turn left through Litlington. The road leads back to the turning to West Dean and the car park at Exceat. To extend the ride, carefully cross the main road through the gate by the bus stop, follow the bike route to the sea and then return.

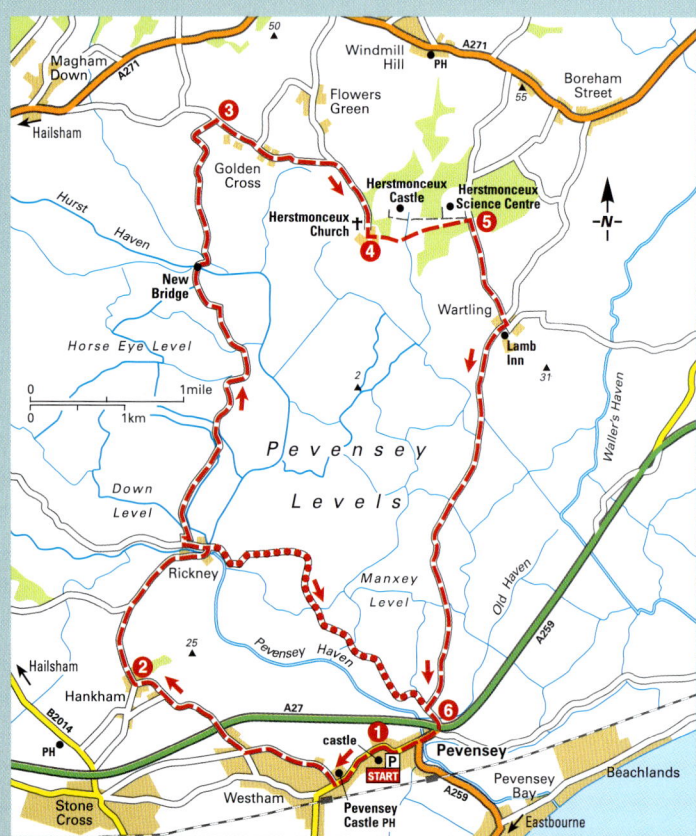

Windsor & the Thames

CLOCKWISE FROM TOP; WINDSOR CASTLE; FERNS IN KEW GARDENS; RICHMOND PARK DEER; NARROW BOAT ON THE THAMES, HENLEY

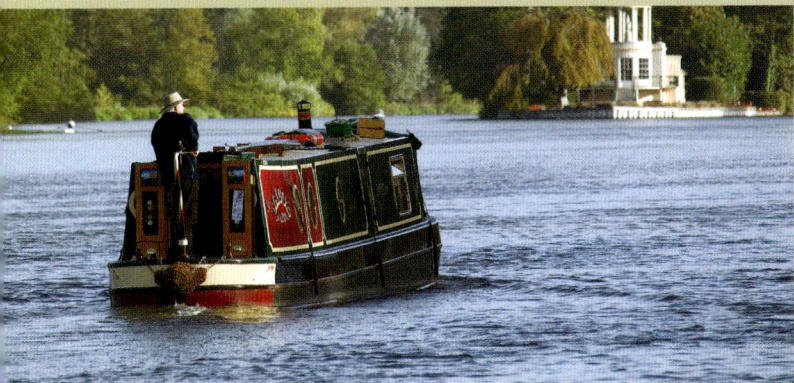

ASCOT MAP REF 400 F5

This rather small town is a Goliath in the horse-racing world, and the Fashion Stakes – not so much a race as a parade of glamorous hats. The first horse-racing on Ascot Heath, not far from Windsor, was endorsed by Queen Anne in 1711, and members of the Royal family have continued to attend the June meeting ever since. The Royal Ascot meeting lasts four days and has lent its name to the 'Ascot', a type of broad neck scarf. The principal event is the Ascot Gold Cup, established in 1807 and run over 2.5 miles (4km) by horses over three years old.

A number of notable people have lived in Ascot, Sir Edward Richard Henry (1850–1931), Commissioner of Police of the Metropolis, lived in Windsor Road, Ascot. He was responsible for the establishment of the central fingerprint bureau, followed by the development of the habitual criminals register to incorporate fingerprints and the criminal records office. Field Marshall Lord Roberts (1832-1914), soldier and statesman, known as Lord Roberts of Kandahar, lived at Englemere, on Kings Ride.

CLAREMONT & PAINSHILL
MAP REF 401 G5

These two early examples of 18th century picturesque landscapes, manmade but naturalistic, are recognised as important survivors of the English style of landscape gardening. Gardens such as these, Stowe and Stourhead led the movement away from the formal landscape style found thoughout Europe.

Conveniently located close to the A307, and not far from Esher, the house and garden at Claremont was designed as a pleasure garden and created over a number of years by Vanbrugh, Bridgeman, Kent and 'Capability' Brown, the most significant landscape gardeners of their day. By 1727 it was described as 'the noblest of any in Europe'.

The Claremont estate was sold to Lord Clive of India in 1769 and he demolished the existing house and replaced it with the mansion that is there today. Claremont became home to many royals during the 19th century, Queen Victoria spent much of her girlhood here but in 1922 the estate was divided and sold. The house and park were bought by Claremont School and the landscape garden was given to the National Trust. After many years of neglect the gardens underwent a full programme of restoration in the 1970's to return the landscaped park to its former glory.

Painshill was created a little later than Claremont but is no less important. Such was the drama of the original design that it is best described as a landscape theatre. The landscape was designed by the Hon Charles Hamilton and included a vast serpentine lake with idyllic scenes and romantic buildings at every turn. These included a Ruined Abbey, a Gothic Temple and Tower, Waterwheel, Grotto and glorious views. During the course of successive ownership the grounds became derelict and overgrown but in 1981 Elmbridge Borough Council bought 158 acres (64ha), almost all of the original acreage, formed the Painshill Trust, and began an ambitious restoration programme that has resulted in a splendid re-creation of the original 18th century landscape. Painshill is open all year, except Christmas and Boxing Day and has an excellent range of facilities.

COOKHAM & CLIVEDEN
MAP REF 400 F4

Cookham village has an identity crisis; it comprises three villages: Cookham Village, the centre of the original village, with an attractive High Street and a good mix of buildings, little changed over the centuries; Cookham Dean, a desirable and rather expensive area in which to live, and the bit in the middle, Cookham Rise, that has evolved around the village's railway station.

Author Kenneth Grahame who, as a child, lived at 'The Mount' (Herries School) in Cookham Dean, is said to have been inspired by the Thames at Cookham to write *The Wind in the Willows*. Quarry Wood in Bisham, adjoining, is thought to have inspired the original 'Wild Wood'. The famous English painter, Sir Stanley Spencer was born here and many of his works depict villagers and village life. Much of his artwork is in the Stanley Spencer Gallery in the centre of the village, close to where he lived. He is buried in the village churchyard.

East of Cookham, Cliveden, now a private hotel, is a masterpiece, a three-storey Italianate palace built by Sir Charles Barry for the Duke and Duchess of Sutherland. With stunning views across the Thames, Cliveden was the glittering hub of society as the home of Waldorf and Nancy Astor in the early part of the 20th century, and later infamously associated with the 'Profumo Affair'; Henry James, Rudyard Kipling and Winston Churchill were no strangers to Cliveden. The lovely estate with a celebrated parterre, has splendid formal gardens, each with its own character, an outstanding collection of sculpture and statues from the ancient and modern worlds, as well as extensive woodland and riverside walks.

ETON MAP REF 400 F5

The town of Eton, across the Thames from its sibling, Windsor, has an interesting high street, an eclectic mix of the traditional and the contemporary, bringing together antiques and modern art, an attractive town dotted with fine historic buildings.

But the town is known primarily for its College, the most famous public school in England. The school was founded in 1440

and still occupies the original buildings. Eton College was founded by King Henry VI to provide scholars for King's College, Cambridge which was opened the following year. The original name of the school was 'The King's College of Our Lady of Eton beside Windsor'. At the time of the schools endowment it provided free education for poor boys who lived at the school although it also admitted some fee-paying boys who lived elsewhere in the town. The total number of scholars was 70. To fund the school Henry gave it several holy relics and, perhaps more practically, large grants of land.

Life at school for the 15th-century schoolboy was a far cry from today. They were required to study for long hours and comforts were few and far between with only very basic facilities; the boys would have had to wash outside in all weathers using only cold water. From these 70 scholars, the school has expanded to nearly 1,300 boys aged from 13 to 18. No longer the sons of families unable to afford to teach them to read and write, Etons scholars must now pass an entrance examination and Eton College has become one of the most exclusive schools in the world. Not surprisingly, such a long history brings with it much tradition and the School uniform is much as it was in the 1850s. The boys stilll wear a black tailcoat and necktie, a waistcoat and pin-striped trousers. During its long career as an educational institution Eton has educated 18 former British Prime Ministers including the Duke of Wellington, Walpole, Pitt the Elder, MacMillan and Douglas-Home.

The original school buildings are a wonderful example of the Perpendicular Gothic style with additional buildings added over the next few centuries, notably Lupton's Chapel, finished in 1515. There are guided tours of the College available throughout the summer which offer a fascinating insight into life at the school over the last 600 years. These take you round the Cloisters, the College Chapel, the oldest classroom in the College and the Museum of Eton Life.

HAMPTON COURT PALACE
MAP REF **401 G5**

Get set for an action-packed day at one of the grandest royal palaces. Red-brick Hampton Court was built in 1514 by Thomas Wolsey, then Archbishop of York but soon to become Henry VIII's chief minister. By 1528, Henry had relieved Wolsey of ownership. Until 1737 it was the centre of royal and political life in England and associated with many important events in history. In 1533 Henry VIII honeymooned here with Anne Boleyn

and married his sixth wife Catherine Parr in 1543, whilst in 1647 Charles I was held prisoner in the palace by Oliver Cromwell, who lived there in 1653.

The palace has been the scene for many dramas and intrigues throughout history. The palace was opened to the public in 1838 by Queen Victoria and it has been a popular attraction ever since. This is partly because of its range of family-friendly events and exhibitions. There are horse-drawn carriage rides in the summer, ghost-hunting tours, Tudor cookery demonstrations and daily tours of the palace with costumed guides. In the winter an ice rink is formed in the west courtyard (book in advance).

It's worth exploring the palace and its gardens regardless of special events. Henry VIII's State Apartments are the centrepiece of the interior, decorated by woodcarver Grinling Gibbons, painter Antonio Verrio and blacksmith Jean Tijou.

Outside, try to navigate the famous maze or wander along Chestnut Avenue to admire the Diana Fountain.

The Maze is probably the most famous hedge maze in the world. It was planted as part of the gardens laid out for William of Orange between 1689 and 1695 by George London and Henry Wise. It was described with great wit in Jerome K. Jerome's novel *Three Men in a Boat*. Hampton Court Maze continues to attract hundreds of thousands of visitors each year.

HENLEY-ON-THAMES MAP REF 400 F4

A select upper-class town, and home of arguably the world's best-known annual rowing regatta, an event bizarrely emulated in the dry riverbed conditions of the Todd River in Alice Springs in central Australia, Henley lies along a beautiful stretch of the Thames. The town centre is richly endowed with curiosity and antiques shops, and fine buildings from the 15th to 18th centuries. You'll find exceptional examples of architecture along Bell Street, New Street and Hart Street. The Catherine Wheel Hotel in Hart Street (once the St Kathrine of Henley, whom the hotel is named after) is one of the oldest in the town. Charles I stayed at the Red Lion Hotel on New Street during his journey from London to Oxford in 1632.

St Mary's Church is worth a visit; the churchyard contains several interesting tombs, including that of Richard Jennings, a local of Henley, who was renowned as the 'Master Builder' of St Paul's Cathedral under Sir Christopher Wren. In relatively more recent years, the 1960s popular singer Dusty Springfield has a gravesite marker in St Mary's churchyard; her ashes were scattered here, and in Ireland on land at the Moher Mountains.

Beatrice Lilly (Lady Peel), the famous actress, lived at Peelfold, Mill End on Mill Lane, and spent many years at Henley. She was born in Toronto in 1894, and was one of the funniest and most spontaneous women of her generation. Her next door neighbour was a famous camp cabaret act – none other than Danny La Rue.

Henley Bridge, a pretty five arched bridge across the Thames which was built in 1786, sits on the river and joins the town to the village of Remenham where the Royal Regatta is actually held. The Henley Royal Regatta is firmly on some social calendars and lasts for four days in late June to early July, and annually rejuvenates a town that probably doesn't need any rejuvenating. The Regatta culminates with a fireworks display, which heralds a degree of partying that can run into the Henley Festival a week later.

Insight
GRINLING GIBBONS

Dutchman and master carver, Grinling Gibbons (1648–1721), was responsible for the beautiful detailed carvings of animals and flowers that can be admired in the King's Apartments at Hampton Court Palace.

Insight
PRINCESS SOPHIA DULEEP SINGH

Princess Sophia Duleep Singh (1838–93) was the youngest daughter of the then Sikh Maharaja Duleep Singh, a favourite of Queen Victoria. Queen Victoria, the Princess's godmother, granted her and her sister, Bamba, a grace-and-favour apartment within Hampton Court Palace in 1898. Although the Princess carried an air of refinement, Sophia and Bamba became involved in the Suffragette movement and Sophia was seen selling the published papers of the movement near the palace gates. Sophia later accompanied Emmeline Pankhurst on the suffragettes' march to Parliament in 1910.

KEW GARDENS MAP REF 401 G5

Even if you're not green-fingered, the Royal Botanic Gardens of Kew, to the west of London, are a magical place to spend a day. The gardens were given World Heritage Status in 2003 and have world-class collections of plants displayed in amazing greenhouses, stars themselves.

The Botanic Gardens began as two royal estates. They were combined in 1772 and became a horticultural centre at the time when exotic specimens were brought back from all over the world by sailors, explorers and botanists. That was the science; but there was an art to displaying these plants, for which gardener Lancelot 'Capability' Brown was responsible. In the Western Zone you can see his original design for the Rhododendron Dell.

Be warned: Kew Botanic Gardens cover 300 acres (120ha) so don't expect to see everything in one visit. Highlights include the unmissable Palm House, a multi-layered greenhouse designed by Decimus Burton that took four years to construct. On the opposite side of the Palm House lake, Museum No 1 houses the interactive Plants+People exhibition. In the Pagoda Vista Zone, Burton's Temperate House is the world's largest surviving Victorian greenhouse, home to a Chilean Wine Palm, which is the biggest greenhouse plant in existence, and to the rarest plant at Kew, a cycad from South Africa. There are plenty of inspiring spots to discover, such as Queen Charlotte's Cottage and Gardens, dedicated to British wild flowers. In winter, the largest ice rink in London is established at the gardens.

RICHMOND PARK MAP REF 401 G5

Richmond Park is the largest royal park and the most expansive green space in the capital. In the 17th century it was King Charles I's hunting ground, but the 650 deer that roam the park today have little to worry about. As well as 350 fallow deer, there are 300 majestic red deer. The deer herds, which are free to wander the grassland and the rare oak woodlands, are not difficult to spot. Other mammals living in this National Nature Reserve include nine species of bat and there are 144 species of bird, including a growing group of parakeets.

Although the park's landscape has changed very little over the past three centuries, it has a variety of modern uses. Cyclists and runners do laps of the perimeter; you can hire bicycles in the car park at the Roehampton Gate. There are two golf courses and three rugby pitches, which are sometimes used for polo matches. Fishing in the Pen Ponds requires a permit, while power-kiting needs just a good breeze and nerve.

THE THAMES PATH

Meandering gently from its source in the Cotswolds through several rural counties and on through the bustle of the City of London, the Thames Path follows England's best-known river for 184 miles (294km). On its way, the Path, a National Trail, passes peaceful water meadows rich in wildlife, historic towns and many lovely villages, finishing at the Thames Barrier near Greenwich.

The Thames Valley was first settled by prehistoric people of the New Stone Age, 6,000 years ago, in the region of Runnymede and Staines. Not surprisingly, the valley became an extremely important trading route for hundreds of years and only relatively recently, in the latter half of the 20th century, did the carriage of goods finally come to an end.

The towpath between Lechlade and Putney, along which much of the Thames Path now travels, was established towards the end of the 18th century.

A path along the Thames was among the original list of long-distance routes proposed by the Hobhouse Committee in 1948 and was subsequently supported by the Ramblers' Association, who published the first guide to the route in 1981. It was finally opened as a National Trail in 1996. Of all the National Trails in Britain, the Thames Path especially lends itself to piecemeal consumption, known by some walkers as 'Staggering from one pub to the next', but by others as the perfect way to experience a delightful and historic walk in different seasons.

WINDSOR MAP REF 400 F5

A handsome market town, Windsor sits on the south bank of the River Thames, to the west of London. The town is dominated by Windsor Castle, standing on the outcrop of chalk on which William I (the Conqueror: 1066–87) built the original fortress. Still in regular occupation as a royal residence the Castle is a conspicuous landmark for travellers approaching Heathrow Airport.

KEW GARDENS

AROUND HAMPTON COURT

In just ten years Henry VIII spent more than £62,000 (equivalent to £18 million today) rebuilding and extending the palace. Hampton Court dates back to the early 1200s, when the site was occupied by the Knights Hospitallers of St John of Jerusalem. The world-famous maze and the Great Vine (planted in 1768) continue to delight visitors. Real tennis has been played at Hampton Court by members of the royal family for more than five centuries.

DISTANCE/TIME 4.75 miles (7.7km) 1h45 **MAP** OS Explorer 161 London South **START** Car park in Hampton Court Road; grid ref: TQ 174697 **TRACKS** Gravel, tarmac and riverside tracks

THE PUB The King's Arms, Hampton Court. Tel: 020 8977 1729

1 Start by crossing Hampton Court Bridge, and then turn right through the main gates to Hampton Court Palace and walk along the wide drive. Just before the palace take a turn to the left through the gatehouse and then pass under the arch.

2 Turn right just before the tea room, heading through a gateway along a path through the gardens. At the end, on your right, is the Real Tennis Court building. Pass through another gateway and turn sharp right to walk alongside the Real Tennis Court and past the entrance to it. Henry VIII played real tennis here as did Charles I. Today Prince Edward and his wife Sophie are members of the 700-strong members-only club.

3 Take the central gravel path in front of the palace, past the fountain to railings overlooking the Long Water, an artificial lake nearly 0.75 mile (1.2km) in length. Head towards the footbridge on your right and go through the wrought-iron gates.

4 After 220yds (201m) the footpath bears left and joins a tarmac track. Follow this, turning left by several farm buildings, after

which the path runs parallel to the Long Water. Where the lake ends continue straight ahead at a crossing of tracks and bear right to skirt the left side of Rick Pond. Turn left through the metal gate, and walk along the enclosed footpath and through the gate to reach the River Thames.

5 Turn left along this lovely riverside path and follow it for around 0.75 mile (1.2km) until you arrive at Kingston Bridge. Here, you will join the road leading to a roundabout.

6 At the end of a row of houses turn left through a gateway. Immediately after the cattle grid bear right along the grassy path running along the left-hand side of the boomerang-shaped Hampton Wick Pond. Follow the straight path for about 0.75 mile (1.2km) back to Hampton Court Palace.

7 Bear right to cross the footbridge and follow the footpath back to the Real Tennis Court. From this point you can retrace your steps back to the start of the walk over Hampton Court Bridge and back into Hampton Court Road.

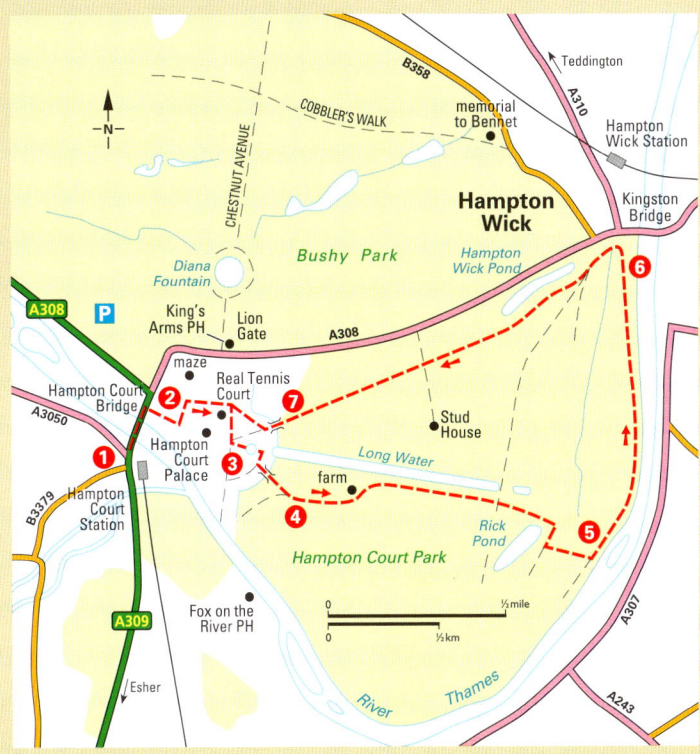

WALK 44

A CIRCUIT OF RICHMOND PARK

Discover London's largest open space at a leisurely pace. At 2,500 acres (1,012ha) Richmond Park has an abundance of wildlife in its hills, woodland gardens and grasslands. Although you will see only a fraction of the park on this walk, you will want to return again and again. The Isabella Plantation was created from an existing woodland and is organically run, resulting in a rich flora and fauna. More than 1,000 species of beetle have been recorded in the park, a National Nature Reserve and a Site of Special Scientific Interest.

DISTANCE/TIME 6.75 miles (10.9km) 2h30 **MAP** OS Explorer 161 London South **START** Car park at Pembroke Lodge in Richmond Park, grid ref: TQ189728 **TRACKS** Mainly tarmac paths

THE PUB The White Cross, Richmond. Tel: 020 8940 6844

1 From the car park at Pembroke Lodge turn right to follow the Tamsin Trail in the general direction of Ham Gate. The path veers to the right and later close to the road.

2 At the crossroads leading to Ham Gate turn left past Hamcross Plantation. At the next crossroads turn right to visit Isabella Plantation (rare trees and some magnificent azaleas), otherwise continue and turn left at the next main junction, before another plantation, and circle the wood clockwise along a track. Turn right, at the next junction, and follow the path to the end of the pond.

3 Turn right along the path between two ponds and continue ahead, ignoring the paths branching off that would lead you to a car park. After this, turn right and follow the road that swings to the left towards Robin Hood Gate. Deer are often spotted here but their coats give them good camouflage, especially against the bracken.

4 Turn left at Robin Hood Gate. Follow the path of the Tamsin Trail past Richmond Park Golf Course and on to Roehampton Gate.

5 Continue over the footbridge and, after a further 500yds (457m), the path winds to the right of Adam's Pond, which is one of the watering holes used by the deer. Follow the path across the upper end of the park, past Sheen Gate, to Richmond Gate.

6 Turn left at Richmond Gate. If you have time, look for the Henry VIII mound, which is at the highest point of the park in the formal garden of Pembroke Lodge. This prehistoric burial ground is not easy to find (take the higher path past cottage) but well worth the effort, for here is a view of the dome of St Paul's Cathedral 10 miles (16.1km) away. Henry VIII was said to have stood here while his second wife, Anne Boleyn, was being beheaded at the Tower of London. Retrace your steps and continue along the path to reach Pembroke Lodge and the start.

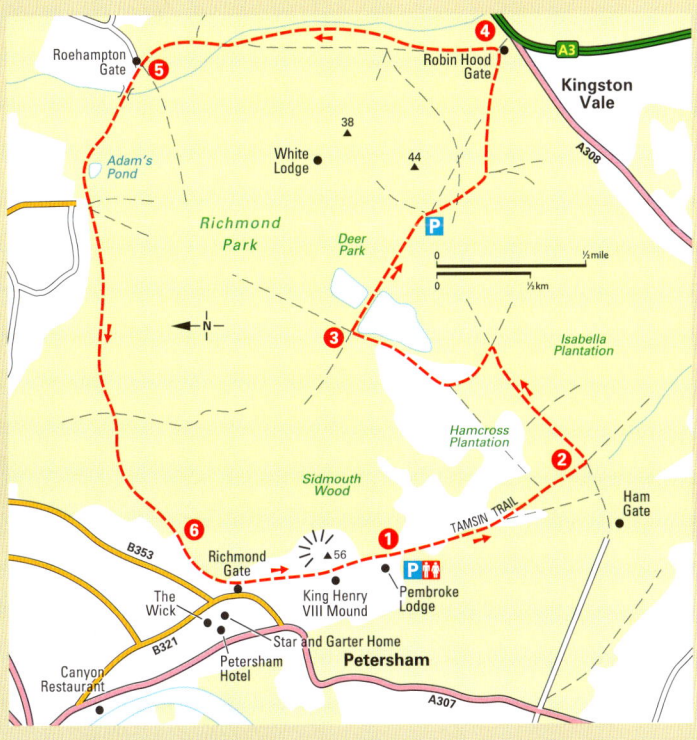

London

CLOCKWISE FROM TOP: CHANGING OF THE GUARD, BUCKINGHAM PALACE; KENSINGTON GARDENS

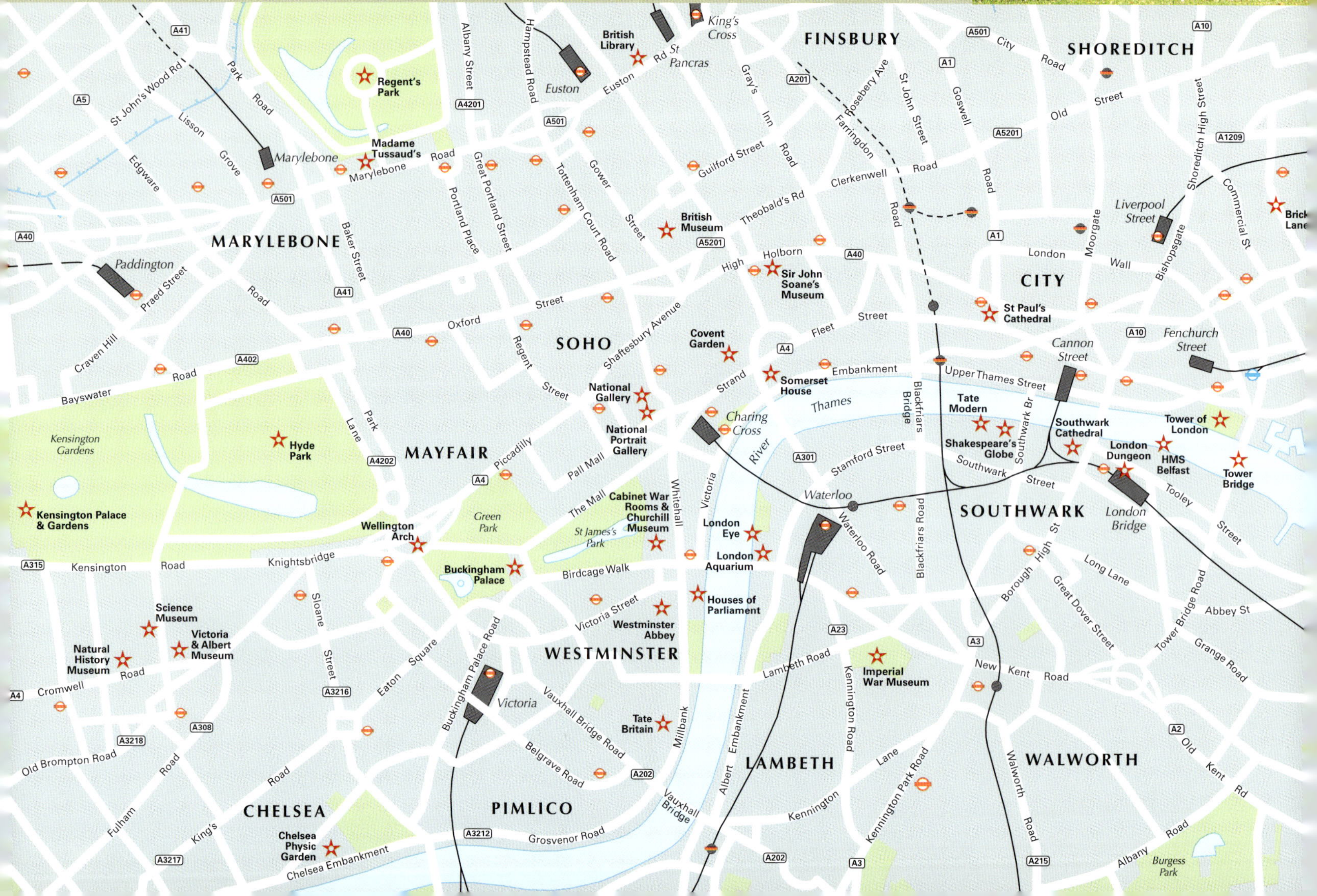

Central

BRITISH LIBRARY

The British Library's new home was completed in 1997 and while the block-like, red-brick exterior (by architect Colin St John Wilson) dismayed some observers, there's no doubting the value of the treasures within. Among them are documents and books that have defined Britain: the Lindisfarne Gospels, the Magna Carta and Shakespeare's First Folio. Editions of global significance include Sultan Baybars' Qur'an, the Gutenberg Bible and the Indian legend the Ramayana. What's more, the British Library is open seven days a week and entry to the galleries is free.

The variety of different exhibits is also surprising: although the library gets a copy of every new book published in the United Kingdom, you might not expect to see so many ancient maps on display or the detailed stamp collection. Musicians can read original music scores written by Bach, Mozart, Beethoven and Handel – and song lyrics by The Beatles. Or you can return to your childhood with the original version of *Alice's Adventures in Wonderland* by Lewis Carroll and first editions of Rudyard Kipling's *Jungle Book*. Special exhibitions are regularly scheduled and renowned writers often give talks.

BRITISH MUSEUM

The British Museum is arguably the finest museum of its kind in the world. It has unparalleled collections of art and antiquities that together document human civilisation across a number of cultures. There is far too much here to see in one day; the best idea is to choose just a handful of galleries at a time.

Most visitors head first for the museum's highlights, which include several Egyptian mummies, kept in a dimly lit room that adds to the eerie atmosphere. Also from Egypt is the Rosetta Stone, a slab of black basalt with text in three different languages that enabled experts to translate Egyptian hieroglyphics. As you might expect, ancient British history is especially well served by the museum. Must-see exhibits include the Mildenhall Treasure, Roman silverware unearthed in a Suffolk field; the Sutton Hoo Anglo-Saxon burial ship, also found in Suffolk; and Lindow Man, the prehistoric corpse of a man preserved in a peat bog.

Visiting the museum is not a dry experience and the curators try hard to interest children. A series of six family trails introduces youngsters to British history, ancient Greece and Egypt, and fantastical creatures. And during the school holidays there are activities, workshops and storytelling sessions, all geared to bring the past alive again.

One attraction at the British Museum that would be impossible to overlook is architect Norman Foster's Great Court, an airy, uplifting central courtyard.

BUCKINGHAM PALACE

Although Buckingham Palace is not the most aesthetically pleasing of the royal properties – it's the result of a botched job by architects Edward Blore and John Nash, who began the conversion of the original 1703 house into a royal palace in 1825 – it remains at the heart of London. Today, it is not only the royal family who can enjoy the palace, because during August and September the State Rooms and gardens are opened to the public.

It is fascinating to see not only the extravagant interiors but also how the rooms are organised. The Green Drawing Room is the place where guests gather before they are presented to the Queen, while grand State banquets are held in either the State Dining Room or the vast Ballroom. It is best to book a ticket to see these particular rooms in advance.

The Queen's Gallery, on Buckingham Gate, is open year-round. On display are old masters as well as jewellery, Fabergé eggs and Sèvres porcelain.

CABINET WAR ROOMS & CHURCHILL MUSEUM

It was in this bunker under Whitehall that crucial phases of World War II were planned by Winston Churchill. The rooms are functional yet sparsely furnished. They remain much as they were in 1945, with a map room for plotting troop movements with coloured pins, the Transatlantic Telephone Room for conversations with the President of the United States and a bedroom where Churchill took naps.

You can learn much more about the man himself, including the brand of cigar he smoked, in the Churchill Museum. The interactive Lifeline display allows you to discover what happened on some of the most important dates in his life.

BRITISH MUSEUM

COVENT GARDEN

London's first formal square was designed by the architect Inigo Jones in the 1630s. Bordered on one side by St Paul's Church and by the Royal Opera House on the other, Covent Garden Piazza is no more the quiet residential square that the 17th-century landowner John Russell intended. Instead, it is a tourist nexus, attracting thousands to the arcaded marketplace and the street performers outside. The result is that the lifts at Covent Garden tube station can be very congested: instead arrive at Leicester Square and walk up Long Acre – the distance between Covent Garden and Leicester Square stations is the shortest in the underground network.

The shops within the piazza are carefully selected – no chain stores here. There is still a daily market in the North Hall, with arts and crafts stalls on Tuesday through to Sunday. On Mondays antiques dealers set up their stalls. Jubilee Market, on the corner of Southampton Street, mainly sells cheap and cheerful souvenirs. The surrounding area has also attracted some more prestigious retailers: Floral Street, Henrietta Street and King Street are lined with boutiques, and Southampton Street has a number of stores selling equipment for outdoor activities. Back on the square, St Paul's Church, also by Inigo Jones, is known as the Actors' Church. Inside there are plaques dedicated to Charlie Chaplin and Vivien Leigh, amongst others. Art historians may be interested to know that woodcarver par excellence Grinling Gibbons was buried here in 1721.

HOUSES OF PARLIAMENT

British political power is concentrated in this majestic Gothic Revival building on the banks of the Thames. The Houses of Parliament, one of the world's earliest parliamentary democracies, are divided into the House of Lords and the House of Commons. The MPs of constituencies across Britain sit and deliberate in the Commons. Legislative proposals are then passed to the Lords for consideration.

During the summer recess, from early August to late September, British citizens can tour the House of Commons. The ticket office is adjacent to the Jewel Tower and is open from late July and tickets are available online. Security has been tightened, so note what you can and cannot take inside. The 75-minute tour begins at the Norman Porch and enters the Queen's Robing Room, where she prepares for the annual State Opening of Parliament in November. From here, visitors pass through the Royal Gallery, the Prince's Chamber, the House of Lords Chamber and into the central Lobby, where MPs congregate for TV interviews. The tour concludes in St Stephen's Hall and the 11th-century Westminster Hall.

The medieval Westminster Hall and the Jewel Tower are the only parts of the original Palace of Westminster which survived the fire of 1834. The Jewel Tower, or King's Privy Wardrobe, was built in 1365 to house Edward III's treasures. It is managed by English Heritage and is open to visitors all year round.

NATIONAL GALLERY

You would need to set aside several days, or weeks even, to do justice to the National Gallery's collection of art. Instead of trying to see everything and exhausting yourself, home in on what interests you.

There is such a treasure trove to choose from, with Italian Renaissance art in the Sainsbury Wing a particular strength: there are works by Botticelli, Leonardo and Raphael. Dutch masters, such as Vermeer and Van Dyck, occupy the North Wing, while the French Impressionists, including Monet, are a big draw for the East Wing. Reynolds, Constable, Turner and Gainsborough are just some of the home-grown artists on show, but as well as drinking in the art, also keep an eye on your surroundings: the building itself is of immense importance, a fact that is confirmed by its Grade I status.

The National Gallery, as befits the country's leading art gallery, also has events, talks, film seasons and performances. Every month there is a full and changing programme of workshops, brunches and evening lectures. Children can create personalised tours of the building in the Micro Gallery or sign up for trails, audio tours and art workshops.

NATIONAL PORTRAIT GALLERY

The National Portrait Gallery owns the world's largest collection of portraits. This surprisingly small space holds a collection of incredible quality and depth, making it a fascinating place for anyone interested in people, art or society. Royalty is represented by the stunning and varied portraits of the royal family in Room 33 and there are paintings of powerbrokers from Elizabethan, Stuart and Victorian times in subsequent rooms. These portraits

HOUSES OF PARLIAMENT

SOMERSET HOUSE

tell the story of art, science, industry and politics through the ages, with the most contemporary characters appearing in the ground-floor galleries. Famous faces here range from modern icon and football player David Beckham (in a video by Sam Taylor-Wood) to one of the most recent additions, a portrait of J K Rowling, author of the phenomenally successful Harry Potter series of novels.

Like the National Gallery, there are frequent talks, films and events at the National Portrait Gallery, which celebrated its 150th year in 2006; visit the gallery's website for more details.

SOMERSET HOUSE

Somerset House is the collective name for three art galleries held in this 18th-century riverside mansion: the Courtauld Gallery, the Gilbert Collection and the Hermitage Rooms. The house was built on the site of the Duke of Somerset's Tudor Palace and changed hands between various government departments and institutions several times during the 20th century. It has certainly embraced its current role with great enthusiasm.

Although the galleries are rather rarefied, Somerset House is a versatile venue for live music (think rock concerts rather than classical recitals) and even ice skating in the winter.

The Courtauld contains examples of art and sculpture from the early Italian Renaissance to 20th-century British pieces. The Gilbert Collection was donated to Somerset House five years before the death of collector Sir Arthur Gilbert in 2001. It is notable for focusing mainly on mosaics and includes some stunning pieces of pietre dure inlay work, but there are also vases, plates and candelabra. The Hermitage, by contrast, is dedicated to biannually changing exhibits from the Winter Palace in St Petersburg.

TATE BRITAIN

With the arrival of its sister gallery Tate Modern, Tate Britain has had much more exhibition space for its collection of 3,500 paintings. But even though it can now focus on British art from 1500 to the present day, the Victorian gallery still shows only a fraction of its vast collection. Rooms 1 to 17 are dedicated to British art from 1500 to 1900 – sporting scenes by Stubbs, Turner's moody landscapes and illustrations by Blake. Turner also appears in several rooms in the Clore Galleries, added in 1987. Rooms 18 to 31 cover British art from 1900 to the present, with one room featuring work by Lucian Freud, Francis Bacon and Reg Butler, and another covering 1960s Pop Art. Talks by art experts and short courses can shed

light on particular artists or periods. Whatever your taste, you should find something to entertain you at Tate Britain; if not, take the Tate boat down the Thames to the newer Tate Modern.

WESTMINSTER ABBEY

The setting for many a royal story, Westminster Abbey dates from 1066, when Edward the Confessor was the first of many monarchs to be buried here. Under the Normans the abbey and its abbot became wealthy and powerful forces. During the Dissolution of the Monasteries in the 16th century the abbey's royal connections spared it the dreadful fate of many of the country's other abbeys. Elizabeth I returned Westminster Abbey to royal control in 1579; her effigy is in the Lady Chapel. The abbey has hosted all but two coronations. The monarch sits on St Edward's Chair during the ceremony.

Burial here is an honour accorded not just to royalty and it is interesting to see the range of people commemorated here, including scientists (Darwin, Newton), actors, politicians and composers. Poets and writers occupy the south transept (Poets' Corner) and include Chaucer, Dickens and Kipling. The busts of the 17th-century poets Dryden, Jonson and Milton are worth seeking out. There are recitals and concerts throughout the year.

Activity
OUTDOOR ICE RINK

Don't forget your ice skates! In the depths of winter Somerset House hosts some of the most popular nights out in the capital with its open-air ice rink. The courtyard is frozen over and skaters take to the ice. The ice rink is in operation from late November to late January and you need to book tickets in advance. It's not London's only open-air ice rink: there are also skating rinks at Hampton Court, the Tower of London, Kew Gardens and even the Natural History Museum.

Visit
ST JAMES'S PARK

The smallest and most central of London's parks is also one of its most appealing. Flanked by the Mall and Horse Guards, St James's Park has no shortage of visitors passing through or relaxing on the grass, making it fine territory for people-watching. You can also spot unusual waterfowl on the lake. From the excellent Inn on the Park, visitors can enjoy the views of Buckingham Palace and the grand old buildings of Whitehall. If you feel the need for more space for a game of Frisbee or cricket, simply head across into neighbouring Green Park.

ST PAUL'S CATHEDRAL

North, Northwest & City

BRICK LANE

Brick Lane is one of the most cosmopolitan streets in London, a pulsating mélange of market stalls, shops, bars and many of London's cheapest (but perhaps not best) curry restaurants, which are mostly run by members from the area's Bangladeshi community. It takes its name from the brick and tile manufacturing workshops that sprang up in the Middle Ages; more recently it lent its name to Monica Ali's novel, *Brick Lane*, about life in London's Asian communities. Brick Lane is best visited on either Sunday morning, for the street market, or in the evening, when it throngs with Londoners hopping from one nightspot to another. Off to the side are some interesting courtyards, such as the Old Truman Brewery, now populated by young artists and designer boutiques.

HAMPSTEAD HEATH

Hampstead Heath is the largest green space in north London. It is now one of London's most welcoming habitats for wildlife and there are birdwatching and bat-spotting walks. Parts of the Heath have been designated Sites of Special Scientific Interest (SSSI).

But the majority of people associate Hampstead Heath with its ponds. There are 25 of them, but the Highgate Ponds for bathing are on the east side, off Millfield Lane. Towards the south of the Heath, Parliament Hill Lido offers more facilities. Close to the Lido there is an athletics track, though most recreational runners will prefer to jog on the Heath itself, among the families, horse-riders, cyclists, walkers and kite-flyers.

However, for many the real highlight of Hampstead Heath is its elevated vantage point – from Parliament Hill you can look out across London landmarks.

MADAME TUSSAUDS

Madame Tussauds waxworks collection is still one of London's most popular attractions, drawing in more than 2 million vistors, despite a high entry fee. Famous people know they have made it when their waxwork appears here and, conversely, that their star is shining less brightly when their likeness is melted down to be turned into a more recognisable celebrity.

Strasbourg born Madame Marie Tussaud cannot have envisaged how hugely popular her waxworks would become when she started the collection some 200 years ago. Modern techniques and technology mean that some of the newer exhibits are more interactive than others and it may be your only chance to actually touch stars such as J-Lo, Brad Pitt and Robbie Williams. Set pieces include the Garden Party, the Chamber of Horrors and the Spirit of London, which is a ride through 400 years of the city's history in a black cab.

REGENT'S PARK

Regent's Park, part of Henry VIII's hunting grounds, is perhaps London's most attractive park. It was landscaped by John Nash in the early 19th century and claims London's finest rose gardens, with 400 varieties and 30,000 plants.

The remainder of the 410 acres (166ha) contain 100 acres (40.5ha) of sports pitches and space for activities, including the Regent's Park Tennis Centre, which has courts available for non-members. There is also a Golf and Tennis School, again with practice facilities available to non-members. Netball players can chose from three courts, while runners have a cinder track on the north side of the park.

For a more leisurely time, how about rowing in a hired boat on the lake, dodging the wildfowl? There are several cafés, including the excellent Garden Café in Queen Mary's Garden. If that is too much effort, just sink into a deckchair (summer only) and enjoy the surroundings.

ST PAUL'S CATHEDRAL

St Paul's dome, 354 feet (108m) high – the only cathedral dome in Britain – rises unmistakably above the buildings of the north bank of the River Thames. The cathedral was commissioned after the Great Fire destroyed the original in 1666. Sir Christopher Wren mixed classical and Gothic architecture in its design, although it is the sense of scale that impresses most visitors: the dome is second in size only to St Peter's in Rome; inside, the dome and galleries appear even larger. The interior is a mass of soaring arches, intricate carving and gilding. To the right of the nave, steps lead up to the Whispering

Gallery; if you're here early enough and the cathedral is quiet you can hear a whisper from the opposite side of the nave.

Although it is a bit of a hike up the 530 steps to the dome's Golden Gallery, the climb is worth it for the panoramic views across London – they rival those from the London Eye, but are much cheaper! The tombs of the Duke of Wellington (with four lion's heads carved into the block of granite that it sits on), Admiral Nelson and Sir Christopher Wren are in the crypt, as is the cathedral's treasury. The cathedral celebrates its 300th anniversary in 2008.

SIR JOHN SOANE'S MUSEUM

Described as London's best-kept secret, this museum contains the fruit of decades of collecting by Sir John Soane, Professor of Architecture at the Royal Academy. He would open his house to visitors on the day before and the day after one of his lectures, and here they could see a crowded yet fascinating mix of sculpture, paintings, carvings, furniture and curios spread across the floorspace of three town houses. Today the rooms are organised according to Soane's original design.

Highlights include the Picture Room, which has hinged screens to extend hanging space; three Canalettos take pride of place in the New Picture Room. Given the variety of Soane's tastes, it isn't so surprising to come across the 3,000-year-old sarcophagus of Pharaoh Seti I and important Roman marbles and statues. Soane also built up an internationally acknowledged collection of Chinese tiles. It is worth noting that due to the limited space inside and the museum's popularity, there may be queues on Saturdays.

TOWER OF LONDON

The Tower originally came to national prominence in the 13th century, but the oldest building on the site dates from the 11th century. It was initially used as an armoury, fortress and royal residence and only later became a prison. The buildings around Tower Green include the Bloody Tower, where many of the most famous and important prisoners were kept. Traitors' Gate was the place where those accused of treason arrived by boat.

Hourly tours led by Beefeaters are recommended if you have children – the scarlet-clad Beefeaters are experts at bringing the stories to life. The armouries exhibition in the White Tower is an enthralling series of weapons and armour, but the highlight of a visit is seeing the Crown Jewels, on display in the Waterloo Barracks. Although you're herded through on a moving travelator, it's hard to miss the world's largest cut diamond, the Star of Africa, or the Imperial State Crown.

Southeast

CANARY WHARF

When Canary Wharf tower was under construction sceptics suggested that the shiny new offices there would remain forever unfilled. Who, they asked, would relocate their business to the deprived Isle of Dogs, especially since the Jubilee Line tube connecting Canary Wharf to central London had not been finished? The property crash of the early 1990s seemed to confirm the predictions, but step out of Norman Foster's cavernous Canary Wharf tube station today and you'll be confronted by the 800-foot (244m) Canary Wharf tower, and other sparkling skyscrapers.

The docks have been landscaped and surrounded by bars, restaurants and shops. Up to 80,000 people now work at Canary Wharf and thousands shop in the underground mall. You can learn to sail in the docks further down the Isle of Dogs, and the London Triathlon takes place on the roads and waterways.

The skyline, while not as awe-inspiring as that of Dubai or many American cities, is a good indication that Canary Wharf is well established as London's centre of business, and the home of many banks and media groups. There are restaurants, health clubs, department stores, bars and cinemas. Development has also spread south and east along the Docklands Light Railway, which runs between central London and Greenwich. Take this railway instead of the tube if you want to see the Docklands in all its glory.

HMS BELFAST

The heavily armoured battle cruiser HMS *Belfast* is now tied up alongside City Hall, but in World War II she was patrolling the seas and sinking German warships such as the *Scharnhorst*. Life-size models illustrate what daily life was like for sailors on board and visitors can have a go at targeting the huge six-inch guns. There are also guides on hand to add a little background to the exhibits. Children will seem better suited to the narrow gangways and hatches and they especially enjoy exploring the Belfast: weekend activities for families introduce children to other aspects of life at sea.

LONDON DUNGEON

For a gruesome, involving and extremely entertaining journey into the depths of London's dungeons just follow the signs from London Bridge station. This top attraction brings death and misery to life with vivid tableaux, hammy acting from guides in period costume with plenty of fake blood. It's not only London's dungeons and the associated torture and executions that are depicted; other low points in the

capital's history, including the Great Plague and the Fire of London, are covered. Children and the squeamish should approach this with caution.

ROYAL OBSERVATORY & PLANETARIUM

Greenwich is at the centre of the world – or at least the world's time zones. At the Royal Observatory you can step from one hemisphere to another before exploring the history of both time, space and the scientists who attempted to understand them. It's a fascinating place and well

worth visiting, not least for the largest refracting telescope in the country. The Observatory's recent Time galleries explore the roles time and timekeeping play in our daily lives.

TOWER BRIDGE

Tower Bridge, which connects the north bank of the Thames at the Tower of London with the south side of the river at the Design Museum, offers those with a good head for heights some excellent views along the Thames. The bridge's history – it was completed in 1894 after

eight years of construction – and workings are well described in the Tower Bridge Exhibition, but the highlight for many is the trip along the upper walkways. Those who make it up there get a great view of Norman Foster's environmentally friendly City Hall, the glassy, helmet-shaped home for London's Mayor. The mechanically minded will also enjoy the engine room, although the Victorian cogs and wheels no longer operate the bridge. If possible, try to time your visit for one of the 900 occasions during the year when the bridge is lifted to allow river traffic to pass below.

TOWER BRIDGE

South Bank & South

IMPERIAL WAR MUSEUM

The Imperial War Museum succeeds in covering conflicts involving Britain or the Commonwealth without sentimentality or jingoism. It presents the apparatus, art and aftermath of war with a combination of scholarly gravity and an instinct for what will interest and intrigue visitors.

In the soaring Large Exhibits Gallery, which opens the collection, World War II fighter planes, including a Spitfire, are suspended above tanks, boats and submarines. Many of the exhibits have stories of heroism attached to them, while others impress through the sheer sense of scale: how did World War II pilots squeeze into those tiny cockpits?

The behind-the-scenes exhibits in the ground-floor galleries are engaging. There are re-creations of the Blitz and trench warfare, while on the second floor you can enter the world of the spy. The next floor offers works from well-known war artists, such as John Singer Sargent, Paul Nash and Stanley Spencer.

But it is the permanent Holocaust Exhibition that provides the numbing counterpoint to the martial display below. The minutiae of death are chilling, while the filmed testimony of Holocaust survivors is very moving. The exhibition is not thought suitable for under-14s.

LONDON AQUARIUM

Learn to tell a conger eel from a moray eel at the London Aquarium, one of Europe's largest aquariums. The 50 displays are arranged according to 14 of the world's watery habitats, with the Atlantic Ocean exhibit forming the centrepiece. Sharks and stingrays patrol the inside of this three-storey tank and are hand-fed by divers daily.

There are 350 species in total at the aquarium and many visitors, children especially, develop a soft spot for the rays, which seem to enjoy being petted at the Touch Pool. However, the tanks with the most eye-catching residents are the Coral Reef and Indian Ocean displays, which contain species seriously endangered by overfishing and global warming.

Other habitats now include tropical freshwater, rivers, ponds, mangroves and rainforest waterways, where you will find catfish, pufferfish and – to the relief of the tank's other inhabitants – a species of piranha (vegetarian!) called pacu. Other species include starfish and jellyfish.

LONDON EYE

It was a publicity coup without equal. In the millennial flurry of new projects and buildings, the London Eye, to the surprise of most observers, stole the show from the Millennium Dome. Its popularity with Londoners and visitors alike has ensured that the wheel will continue turning on its central site opposite the Houses of Parliament for the foreseeable future.

So, what's the appeal of a 450-foot (137m) big wheel? It's not just the breathtaking views across the capital; views that even on a cloudy day stretch along the Thames to Canary Wharf and on a clear day can extend up to 25 miles (40km). And it's more than admiration for a feat of engineering that keeps 32 space-age glass pods suspended on a giant bicycle wheel of cables, girders and tubes for your half-hour revolution. No, it is perhaps the novelty of seeing some of the world's most recognisable landmarks, such as Buckingham Palace, and the Houses of Parliament from the air.

The genesis of the British Airways London Eye took seven years and was guided by experts from five European countries. Finally, after the wheel had been pieced together in a horizontal position, it was hoisted upright, using a technique that had been previously employed to erect oil rigs.

Be warned: the Eye is extremely popular during the summer and booking ahead is advised, especially if you're confident of picking a fine day. In the winter months there are night-time 'flights', which offer a different perspective.

SHAKESPEARE'S GLOBE

This is the brainchild of American actor Sam Wanamaker and was completed in 1997. It is a reconstruction of the theatre where William Shakespeare debuted many of his plays and is a must-see attraction. It is a work of great craft, thanks in large part to Wanamaker's insistence on building the new Globe Theatre only with tools, materials and techniques available in Elizabethan times (displays explain the construction process in detail). The original Globe was opened in 1599, but the circular, wooden playhouse burned down shortly afterwards.

Now, not only does the new Globe Theatre look fantastic but, during the busy summer performance season, you can see Shakespeare's work in as authentic a setting as possible. The season normally runs from May to October and the open-air stage means favourable weather is an advantage. It's standing room only in the pit in front of the stage but there are seats for those with less stamina. There are also family events through the year.

It was a popular Elizabethan custom for the 'groundlings' in the pit to heckle the actors, and today the audience is still essential to performances. The Globe provides drama without elaborate sets or props: Shakespeare's words and the building create their own magic.

LONDON EYE

SOUTHWARK CATHEDRAL

Glowing with the brightness of its recently cleaned and restored stonework, Southwark Cathedral may not look like one of London's oldest Gothic buildings, but it is. The cathedral was a simple priory church (dating from the 13th century) until 1905, when the diocese of Southwark was formed and the church became upgraded to a cathedral. You'll find a monument and window dedicated to William Shakespeare in the south aisle and the tombs of Bishop Lancelot Andrews, translator of the King James version of the Bible, and John Gower, an English poet who died in 1408.

On the north side of the beautiful nave, a finely detailed stained-glass window depicts people associated with Southwark and the cathedral, including preacher John Bunyan and Geoffrey Chaucer, who started his pilgrimage to Canterbury in *The Canterbury Tales* from the Tabard Inn, just off nearby Borough High Street. The Long View of London museum, a garden and a refectory are recent additions.

TATE MODERN

Tate Modern is simply the most important gallery of modern art in Britain. But despite a vast collection that includes some of the biggest names of the 20th century – Henri Matisse, Pablo Picasso, Andy Warhol and Francis Bacon – the art can be dwarfed by the towering architecture of the converted Bankside power station.

The building that the Tate Modern is house in (unmistakable at the south end of the Millennium Bridge), began life in the 1950s as a power station, designed by the man who also came up with Britain's distinctive red telephone boxes, Giles Gilbert Scott. After the power station was decommissioned, the Swiss architectural firm Herzog & de Meuron was charged with transforming the giant brick-and-steel frame building into a home fit for the Tate Gallery's ever-increasing collection of modern art.

There are two entrances to Tate Modern, at the west and north sides. Both lead into the awe-inspiring Turbine Hall, a vast space that lends itself to whatever monumental sculptures or installations are placed in it. The galleries are spread around the spacious upper levels.

In 2006, Tate Modern rehung its entire fabulous collection around the diverse art themes of Abstract Expressionism, Cubism, and Minimalism and Surrealism, following much criticism that the original organisation according to themes of landscape or history was too subjective and vague. Artists Anish Kapoor and Roy Lichtenstein now have works displayed for the first time at Tate Modern. Other artists, including Juan Muñoz, Thomas Schütte

and Mark Rothko now have rooms all to themselves. There are still seasonal exhibitions at the gallery.

One experience you shouldn't miss is a well-earned break in either the café on level two or the more expensive top-floor restaurant – both serve good food and offer excellent views over the Thames.

West & Southwest

CHELSEA PHYSIC GARDEN

You'll have to time your visit to Chelsea Physic Garden carefully: it is open only on Wednesdays and Sundays from April through to October. But the wait is worth it because the garden is not only of interest from a scientific and medical point of view, it is also a surprisingly serene place to catch your breath and relax.

The Physic Garden dates from 1673, when it was established to teach students about plants. This, of course, was a time when new plants and cuttings were being brought back to London on ships that had travelled the globe searching for new lands and new peoples to trade with. Its south-facing site on the bank of the Thames was chosen for its temperate climate, in the hope that many of the exotic specimens would survive – one such attraction is Britain's largest outdoor fruiting olive tree. By the 18th century, the garden had set up an international botanic seed exchange system, which continues today.

Most of the garden's plants, numbering some 5,000 species, have medicinal properties. Within the Physic Garden, the Garden of World Medicine is Britain's first garden of ethnobotany and there is also a Pharmaceutical Garden. Other corners are devoted to perfume, aromatherapy and even vegetables.

For more of an insight into the garden's history, guides are on hand to show visitors around, but it is just as rewarding to wander among the unusual shrubs, trees and plants before venturing back into the maelstrom of King's Road.

HYDE PARK

Hyde Park, which adjoins Kensington Gardens, is central London's largest royal park. Although the flat landscape verges on the featureless, there are interesting sights to find. Since Henry VIII bought the park in 1536 it has been the setting for some of London's dramas. Refugees from the slums camped in the park in 1655 in the hope of escaping from the Great Plague. The park was at the heart of disturbances in 1866 between the police and the Reform League, and since 1872 people have been permitted to speak freely at Speakers' Corner to the northwest. The park has become a convenient venue for large-scale open-air concerts.

TATE MODERN

Hyde Park is also a much-appreciated green space for Londoners to get out in the fresh air and get some exercise on bicycles and rollerblades. Both skaters and bladers congregate at Hyde Park Corner for a regular Friday-night skate, while cyclists are allowed on the park's roads but not its paths. Other sporting activities include impromptu games of football and softball, while the Tennis Centre allows non-members to turn up and play. Runners are a common sight and summer sees swimmers take to the water of the Serpentine at the Lido.

KENSINGTON PALACE & GARDENS

Kensington Palace, where she lived, will forever be closely associated with Diana, Princess of Wales. Flowers are still left tied to the black-painted gates to the Gardens on the anniversary of her death, while inside a collection of her dresses

forms a permanent exhibition. But there's more to Kensington Palace and Gardens than its most famous resident.

The Royal Ceremonial Dress Collection spans three centuries of regal finery, with the whole process of designing and fitting a dress explained. Upstairs the his-and-hers State Apartments include the understated Queen's Apartment and the over-the-top King's Apartment, where Queen Victoria was baptised. In the gardens, the Orangery is an elegant space in which to have lunch before exploring the gardens. The Sunken Garden is a highlight. However, it won't take you long to find the Serpentine Gallery to the south and the garden's two sculptures: *Physical Energy* and *Peter Pan*.

This just leaves the Albert Memorial on the southern edge of the gardens, a magnificent tribute to Queen Victoria's beloved husband who died in 1861.

(regarded as the forerunner of the computer), Stephenson's Rocket and Arkwright's Spinning Jenny. The full-size replica of the Apollo 10 command module is a highlight. On the first floor the Who Am I? area investigates the human brain and psychology, while the exhibition on power in the East Hall explores the past and future of energy.

As well as all the interactive computers and exhibits, there's a daily programme of IMAX film screenings and events, including the Science Night Sleepover.

VICTORIA & ALBERT MUSEUM

The third in South Kensington's trio of world-class museums will mesmerise anyone interested in art, culture or society. The V&A's field is the decorative arts, but through this subject it manages to traverse continents and centuries of human history and creativity.

There is too much to take in in one visit, so the best plan of action is to savour just one or two collections at a time. Highlights include the Fashion, Jewellery and Accessories collection, which displays fashionable dress from the 17th century to the present day. The Furniture and Furnishings collection consists of 14,000 items from the Middle Ages onwards, while the Ceramics collection is central to the museum. It includes everything from Egyptian relics to modern industrial ceramics via porcelain, such as the Meissen vulture acquired in 2006.

During school holidays and on most weekends there are events for families. There are also several trails around the museum for children aged 7 to 12 to follow. Best of all, the museum's Back-Packs scheme allows children to borrow one of a series of themed backpacks and use the contents to explore different subjects in a fun and informative way. You don't need to book and the themes include The Emperor's Party and Chinese Treasures as well as Fancy Furnishings.

WELLINGTON ARCH

Decimus Burton's arch was built in 1830 to celebrate the Duke of Wellington's victories over Napoleon's armies. It was relocated to its present site in 1882.

The statue of the Duke on horseback that topped the arch was replaced before World War I with a 38-ton bronze sculpture, the heaviest in Europe, called *Peace Descending on the Quadriga of War*, depicting four magnificent war horses and the Angel of Peace. There are three floors of displays explaining its use over the years, including as a police station; carry on to the top of the arch and take in the spectacular views of Buckingham Palace from the balcony.

NATURAL HISTORY MUSEUM

Where else can you see frighteningly realistic animatronic dinosaurs, as well as Britain's largest collection of actual fossil remains? Or experience the realistically scary tremors of an earthquake, then witness the eruption of a volcano?

The museum does an excellent job of engaging with younger visitors via the use of interactive or multimedia displays such as the Ant Colony, an army of leafcutter ants, or the Power Within room, in which the effects of the 1995 Kobe earthquake are replicated. Mostly, however, the exhibits don't need any help to enthrall: the creepy crawlies are a perennial favourite and the dinosaur skeleton takes pride of place in the cavernous central hall of the Life Galleries.

The Natural History Museum holds special exhibitions and regular talks and events, including activities for children.

SCIENCE MUSEUM

The Science Museum is practically right next door to the Natural History Museum and is similarly successful at stimulating children – thanks to its broad and liberal interpretation of the word science, which manages to include classic computer games and 3D films in its IMAX cinema.

The collections cover the stories behind many of the world's most important inventions: Charles Babbage's Calculator

THE RIVER THAMES, FOLLOWING ITS BRIDGES

Westminster Bridge was built in the 1740s. More than 100 years later, Hungerford Bridge extended the railway into Charing Cross. Work to replace Waterloo Bridge in 1939 took six years. Blackfriars Bridge has five cast-iron arches. Millennium Bridge is the newest crossing and London Bridge is a 20th-century structure.

DISTANCE/TIME 4.5 miles (7.2km) 2h30 **MAP** AA Street by Street London **START** Westminster tube station; grid ref: TQ 302797 **PATHS** Paved streets and riverside walk **THE PUB** The Anchor, 34 Park Street, Bankside. Tel: 020 7407 1577

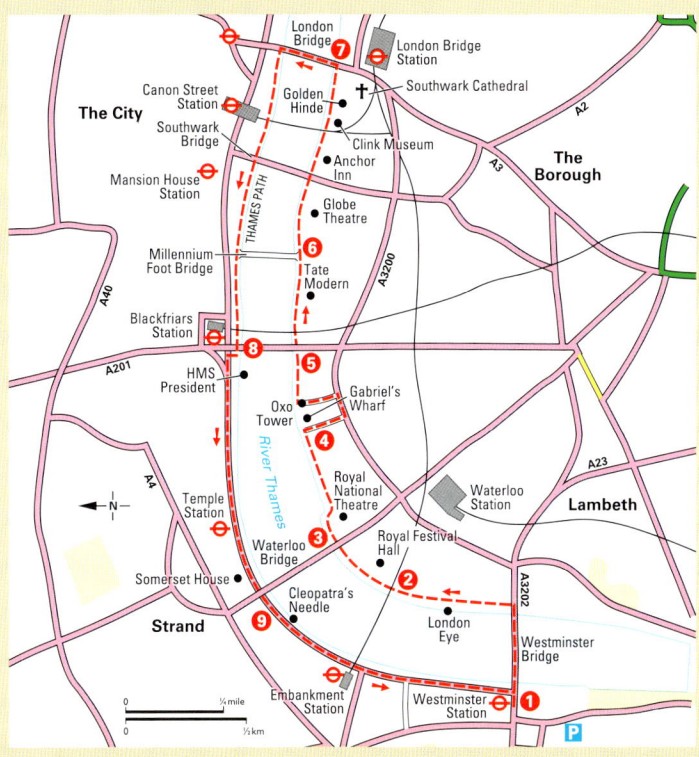

1 Leave Westminster tube station by Exit 1, following signs to Westminster Pier. Walk up the steps to your right and cross Westminster Bridge. Turn left along the riverfront. Ahead are the 32 transparent pods of the London Eye. Just past Jubilee Gardens, on the right, is the next bridge, Hungerford.

2 Continue past the Royal Festival Hall. Beyond the Hayward Gallery, under Waterloo Bridge is the National Film Theatre.

3 The path bends to the right, after the National Theatre, before the craft shops and restaurants of Gabriel's Wharf. Turn right at the Riviera restaurant and walk through the centre, lined on either side with small shops. Turn left at the end into Upper Ground and 100yds (91m) further on take another left turn into Barge House Street.

4 Ahead, an archway leads to the back of Oxo Tower Wharf. Enter the glass doors in the middle to catch the lift to the eighth floor for a better view of the skyline, or continue along the ground floor to the riverside exit.

5 Pass under Blackfriars Bridge. The former Bankside power station on your right was made with 4 million bricks. It is now home to the popular Tate Modern.

6 Continue along past the Millennium Foot Bridge and Shakespeare's Globe. Beyond this is Southwark Bridge and, 200 yds (183m) further on, Cannon Street Rail Bridge. A few paces on and you will pass the Clink Museum and the remains of Winchester Palace. Ahead is a full-size replica of Sir Francis Drake's ship, the *Golden Hinde*. Round the corner is stunning Gothic Southwark Cathedral.

7 Cross London Bridge, descend the steps, following signs for the Thames Path (West).

8 At Blackfriars Bridge the Thames Path joins the pavement next to the river. The first boat you pass on your left is HMS *President*. The next set of buildings to your right after Temple tube station belong to King's College, London. Further along is Somerset House where you can ice skate in winter.

9 After 200yds (183m) the path passes Cleopatra's Needle before arriving at Embankment tube station. Northumberland Avenue is the next road on your right. About 200yds (183m) further on is Horse Guards Avenue, sandwiched between the buildings of the Ministry of Defence and the Old War Office. When you reach Westminster Bridge turn right into Bridge Street, to reach Westminster tube station where you started.

WALK 46

CHELSEA

Chelsea is home to the most famous pensioners in Britain. They live in The Royal Hospital, founded by Charles II in 1692 for veteran soldiers. The minimum age is 65 and there is still accommodation for 500. They are easily recognised by their unusual three-cornered hats and their scarlet coats.

DISTANCE/TIME 3.25 miles (5.3km) 2h **MAP** AA Street by Street London **START** Sloane Square tube station; grid ref: TQ 281787 **PATHS** Paved streets and tarmac paths **THE PUB** The Coopers Arms, 87 Flood Street. Tel: 020 7376 3120

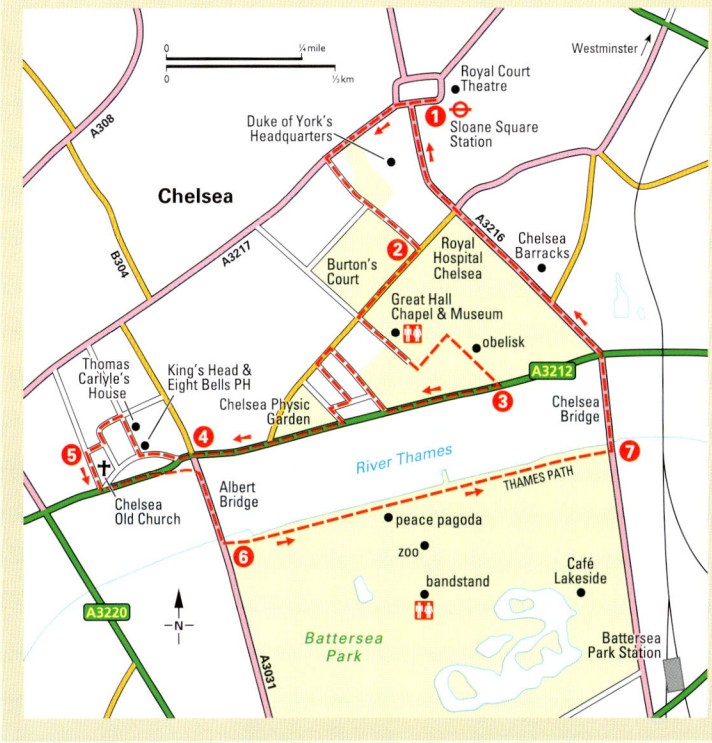

1 From Sloane Square tube station, cross the road ahead, then go across Lower Sloane Street. Walk past the Peter Jones store on the right and a few paces on your left is the Duke of York's Headquarters. Beyond this, you should turn left to go into Cheltenham Terrace, then bear left into Franklin's Row.

2 At the bottom of Franklin's Row turn right along Royal Hospital Road. Just beyond the lawns on the right turn left into the hospital grounds at Chelsea Gate. Continue to the end of the road and turn left on to open grass. Now walk around the obelisk, to the gates on the far side of the grass. Leave through the gates to the Chelsea Embankment.

3 Turn right along the Embankment and right into Tite Street. At the junction with Royal Hospital Road turn first left into Paradise Walk. Turn right and then sharp left towards the Embankment (turn right to the Chelsea Physic Garden entrance). Turn right into the Embankment.

4 At the traffic lights cross Oakley Street and bear right by the beautiful Boy with Dolphin statue into narrow Cheyne Walk. Turn first right into Cheyne Row, where Thomas Carlyle lived. At the end turn left into Upper Cheyne

Row, then left again into Lawrence Street marks the Chelsea Porcelain Works – then turn right into Justice Walk. (Don't be fooled into thinking the sign of a red-robed judge is that of a pub, it merely identifies where the old courthouse used to be!)

5 Turn left into Old Church Street and continue to the bottom of the street with Chelsea Old Church on the left. Turn left past the church and the statue of Thomas More. Walk through Chelsea Embankment Gardens, past the statue of Thomas Carlyle and, at the junction with Oakley Street, cross the road to Albert Bridge.

6 Cross Albert Bridge and turn left at the 'Riverside Walk' sign, through the gate into Battersea Park. Bear left and follow the riverside Thames Path, past the Peace Pagoda in the park, to Chelsea Bridge.

7 Just before Chelsea Bridge, turn right and then left at the road to leave the park. Turn left again at the gates to cross Chelsea Bridge. Continue ahead, over the Embankment, passing Chelsea Barracks on the right before joining Lower Sloane Street. Turn right at Sloane Square to retrace your footsteps to Sloane Square tube station.

Notting Hill Carnival

Notting Hill's annual summer carnival assaults all of the senses. The spicy aroma of jerk chicken sizzling on a grill gets the mouth watering. The bass from a dub reggae sound system makes your knees wobble and your stomach churn. All around people are jostling, shouting, laughing, drinking Red Stripe beer and dancing, and a gyrating dancer dressed as a 12-foot (3.7m) tall silver butterfly is swaying towards you.

If you don't like large crowds or boisterous parties, then Notting Hill carnival is certainly not for you. But if you do, then block out the last weekend of August (Saturday to Monday) in your diary and get ready to let your hair down.

The carnival was started in the late 1950s by members of the Caribbean community of the west London neighbourhood. The Notting Hill area had seen large-scale immigration from the Caribbean islands during the 1950s – many young Caribbean men and women were recruited to drive buses and do other jobs in a Britain with a decimated post-war population. The newcomers formed communities in the streets around Notting Hill, which was then a considerably more affordable place to live than it is today. Tensions existed between the incoming Caribbean population and indigenous Londoners and a Caribbean-style carnival was proposed as a way of making the Caribbean population feel at home and introduce their culture to curious Londoners.

Surprisingly, the first Notting Hill Carnival took place in 1959 indoors at the St Pancras Town Hall. It wasn't until 1965 that the party took its first steps outside when a parade route was devised around the main Notting Hill streets of Ladbroke Grove, Westbourne Grove and Chepstow Road. Rhuane Laslett and Claudia Jones were seen as the driving forces behind the carnival in its early years, and it remained very much a local event. But from the mid-1960s to the mid-1970s attendance at the carnival, which would become Europe's largest street party by the end of the century, had rocketed from a few thousand to 150,000. Over the years the carnival had to survive riots and a series of crime waves but, by 2000, 1.5 million people turned up to dance, drink and revel in the residential streets of Notting Hill. This temporary influx of vast numbers of people in party mode, obviously, had the potential to cause problems.

While the police usually attend in force, they take a 'live and let live' attitude; it's traditional for at least one photo of an awkward-looking policeman dancing with a gyrating sequined dancer to be published in the weekend's newspapers. But one group of people who really don't enjoy the carnival are Notting Hill's wealthy new residents. Since the 1990s the neighbourhood has changed dramatically, evolving into one of the most sought-after London addresses. The white stuccoed Georgian houses on the narrow streets are inhabited by celebrities and London's movers and shakers, while the Caribbean community which once lived here has moved to the north and west of the city over the years. Residents are not overly enthusiastic about a million people pitching up on their doorsteps every August Bank Holiday. Most opt to escape from the city and spend the weekend in the country or at least away from the packed streets of North London, watching the party unfold on television and perhaps keeping their fingers crossed that their house doesn't feature on the evening news.

While the carnival began as a specifically Caribbean-flavoured event for local residents in the 1960s, it has assumed a broader cultural mantle over the years and many varied communities play a role in planning and staging the event. Caribbean music, such as soca and calypso, is still the heart and soul of the carnival, but it faces loud competition from rap, house music, drum and bass, and reggae. However, despite the forty or so sound systems – mobile music stages staffed by a DJ and sometimes an MC and dancers – the roots of carnival lie in steelpan music. Many of the steelpan drummers who hammered out a tune in the carnivals of the 1960s still continue to play at the parade. Steelpan music itself developed in Trinidad in the West Indies during the 1940s when instruments were fashioned from dustbin lids, paint pots, old oil drums and a rhythm hammered out with sticks of bamboo. The sound became more sophisticated over the years until the sonorous, upbeat steelpan sound of today. At the carnival the steelpan bands compete in the Saturday evening Panorama competition, with the old tunes being as well received as ever. Carnival itself also began in Trinidad in 1833, as a celebration of the end of slavery – many of the stirring songs and tunes of carnival have been as much associated with protest and sorrow as they have with joy.

The weekend gets into full swing on the Saturday evening with the steel band competition – the winning band can call themselves the UK Champions of Steel - and a parade of extravagantly decorated floats and (some) outrageously costumed dancers around the 4-mile (7km) circuit of Notting Hill. This is the warm-up for the busiest day of the festival weekend, the Bank Holiday Monday. Sunday is children's day dedicated to youngsters, when up to 70 multi-coloured and beautifully adorned floats and steel bands, all featuring under-21 year olds, parade along the route from mid-morning onwards. Monday, a national holiday in the UK, is the climax of the carnival with all-day action on the route and surrounding streets. The most popular sound systems tend to be the ones that have a long history with the carnival, such as Good Times, manned by veteran DJ Norman Jay or Sancho Panza, which has staked out a space at the carnival since 1994 with a party-pleasing blend of house music.

With thousands of people milling around and many closed streets in west London, expect a certain degree of travel chaos on this weekend. Tube stations are often closed to minimise crowding and it may be quicker to walk to and from the carnival. However, moves are afoot to take the carnival to Hyde Park, where there will be more space and less disruption for visitors and residents alike. A future parade route would be plotted to wind its way from west London and to finish in the park, but this plan would face fierce resistance from some traditionalists. For the thousands of people that attend the revelry each year, the appeal of carnival lies as much in the ear-ringing sideshows and food stalls that pop up in Notting Hill's streets as the parade itself. Whatever happens to the carnival in years to come, people will always come together on the long, hot August weekend to eat, drink and dance.

TOP Energetic dancers moving to the passionate rhythms that flood the city streets help to create a party atmosphere on this festival weekend in August.

RIGHT The colourful parade winds its way past the crowds - the carnival is now believed to be one of Europe's biggest street parties.

LEFT Spectacular costumes are a much-loved feature of the carnival parade.

DISTANCE/TIME 2.5 miles (4km) 1h **MAP** OS Explorer 173 London North **START** West Carriage Drive car park; grid ref: TQ 269800 **TRACKS** Well-surfaced paths **THE PUB** The Wilton Arms, 71 Kinnerton Street. Tel: 020 7235 4854

DISTANCE/TIME 6 miles (9.7km) 1h45 **MAP** OS Explorer 162 Greenwich & Gravesend **START** Cutty Sark pub, Ballast Quay; grid ref: TQ 389782 **TRACKS** Largely surfaced cycle lanes, some cobbled streets **THE PUB** The Cutty Sark, 4–7 Ballast Quay. Tel: 020 8858 3146

AROUND HYDE PARK

Henry VIII and his court hunted in Hyde Park and Charles I opened the park fully to the public in 1637. The Serpentine, the vast ornamental lake dominating the park, was created in the 1730s by Caroline, wife of George II. The latest royal connection is the Diana, Princess of Wales Memorial Fountain.

1 From the West Carriage Drive car park, opposite the Serpentine Gallery, cross the road and join the cycle track on the pavement on the west side of West Carriage Drive. The Diana, Princess of Wales Memorial Fountain is on your right.

2 The track drops down on to the road to cross the Serpentine bridge. Once across be sure to look out for the point where the path resumes on the pavement, as the cycle lane on the road surface stops abruptly.

3 At Victoria Gate cross the road and follow the cycle path along The Ring. The path here is on the road but it is often traffic-free.

4 As you approach Cumberland Gate and Marble Arch, look for the cycle route sign for Chelsea Bridge and cross the road to pick up the cycle path on Broad Walk. You may need to reduce speed here as the cycle lane can be obstructed by crowds around Speakers' Corner. It then heads south on Broad Walk, a pleasant tree-lined boulevard.

5 On the approach to Queen Elizabeth Gate at Hyde Park Corner, follow signs to the right for Rotten Row to return to the car park at West Carriage Drive. On Rotten Row keep to the left on the fairly narrow path shared with pedestrians and rollerbladers. At West Carriage Drive, use the pedestrian crossing and pick up on the cycle track again on the west side in front of the Serpentine Gallery. (This simple circular ride can be extended eastwards with a foray along Constitution Hill's excellent parallel cycle track to see Buckingham Palace, or to the west to explore Kensington Gardens. Notices at the park entrances show where cycling is currently permitted.)

EAST FROM GREENWICH ALONG THE THAMES

In the space of just 3 miles (4.8km) of riverside there is at least a millennium's worth of London's industrial, military and seafaring heritage, from maritime Greenwich, which became the site of the prime meridian in 1884, to the Royal Arsenal at Woolwich, via the Thames Barrier and the Millennium Dome.

1 From Cutty Sark Gardens wheel your bike along the riverside walk to the Cutty Sark pub and turn right along Ballast Quay, then bear right into Pelton Road. At the Royal Standard pub turn left into Christchurch Way. As you approach the Alcatel complex, turn right into Mauritius Road. When you reach Blackwall Lane turn left into the bus lane. Just before the traffic lights take the cycle path on the left along the pavement of Tunnel Avenue. At the footbridge look for the green-surfaced track on the left.

2 Cross the footbridge and turn left into Boord Street. At Millennium Way, join the cycle path directly ahead. At West Parkside continue straight on and when you reach the riverside, turn right. Just past the colourful buildings of Greenwich Millennium Village you'll reach the Greenwich Peninsula Ecology Park.

3 The outer boardwalk is always open and considerate cyclists are welcome. Go on along the riverside path, which turns inland to skirt the Greenwich Yacht Club's fenced enclosure. Remain on the riverside past the aggregate recycling works. At the end of that section, stay on the street called Riverside, with the large Sainsbury's depot to your right. Look out for the remains of old dockside railway tracks on your left. At Anchor and Hope Lane take the off-road path to go straight ahead.

4 On reaching the Thames Barrier, the green-surfaced route around the complex is well-signed and quite easy to follow. At the former Thames Barrier Arms pub, go straight ahead along the path which is slightly overgrown and quite narrow. There is a steep slope up to the crossing at Woolwich Church Street. Turn left along the road here and when you reach the roundabout, take the second exit (Ruston Road). Look for the left turn where Ruston Road heads towards the river. Turn left here and turn left again at Harlinger Road. When you reach the T-junction turn right, then right once again.

5 A sign asks cyclists to dismount for the 40yd (37m) section between the road and the riverside. When you rejoin the riverside opposite the Tate & Lyle works on the north bank, turn right. When the pedestrian route uses steps to cross a wall, the cycle path heads inland, where you will find a ramp, and returns to the riverside.

6 At the cannons on the riverside turn inland past the Clockhouse Community Centre. At Leda Road make your way up the slope to join Woolwich Church Street. You may prefer to dismount and push your bike along the pavement to reach the Woolwich free ferry. At the Ferry Approach look for the cycle signs by the ambulance station. Pass the Waterfront Leisure Centre and the entrance to the Woolwich Foot Tunnel. Continue along the riverside to Royal Arsenal Pier, where a large piazza provides access to the revitalised Royal Arsenal complex, including the Firepower Museum. From here it is possible to cycle inland to explore the shops, pubs and restaurants of Woolwich centre before you cycle back to Greenwich.

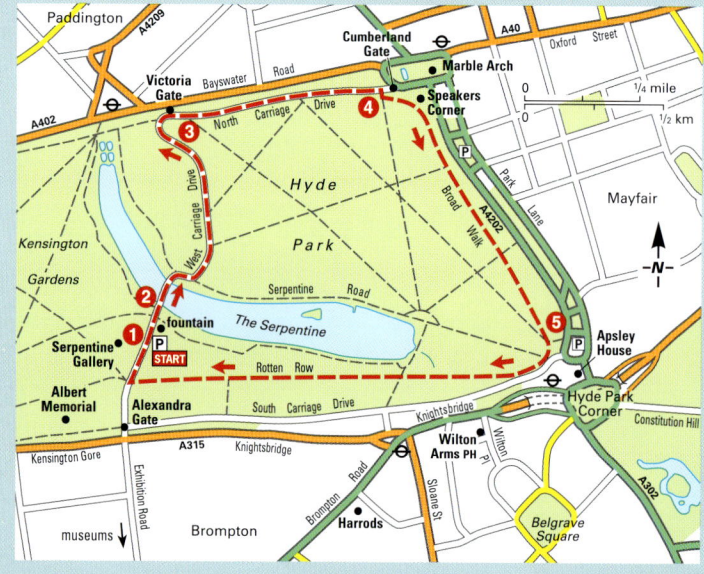

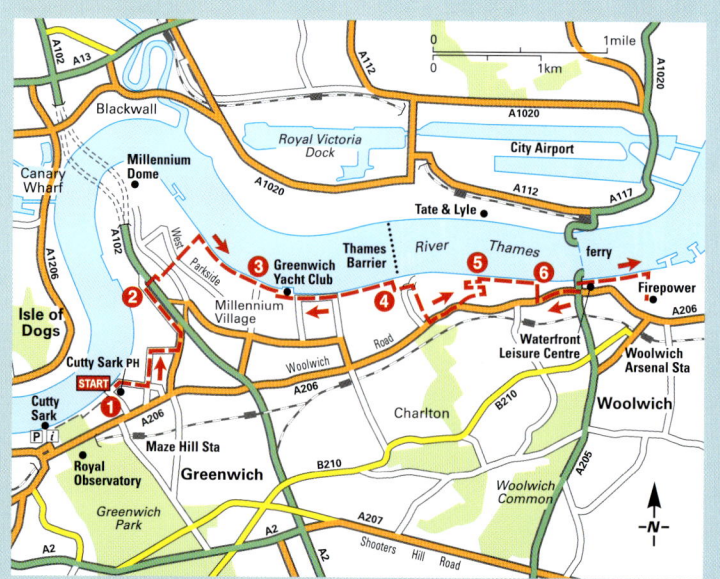

Canterbury & Kent Downs

CLOCKWISE FROM TOP LEFT: CANTERBURY CATHEDRAL; TIMBER-FRAMED CONQUEST HOUSE, CANTERBURY; HEVER CASTLE

CANTERBURY MAP REF 401 K5

Successfully combining modernity with venerable old age, Canterbury may be a place of pilgrimage for those of an historical bent, but it remains a bustling and very much a 21st-century destination of appeal to everyone.

The city stands on the site of Cantii, the capital of an Iron Age kingdom, and from 'Cantii' comes Kent. The city was also an important Roman stronghold, but after the Romans left Britain at the start of the 5th century, the city was left to the local populace until, in the year 602, St Augustine imposed Christianity on the site of a Roman church and so created Christchurch Cathedral. It was an important act that heralded Canterbury's future as the seat of the Archbishop of Canterbury, the spiritual capital of the Church of England and the Mother Church of the Anglican Communion.

Inevitably, the Normans focused their attention on Canterbury, and built a castle here around the year 1100. Within the next 70 years, the greater part of the magnificent cathedral we see today was rebuilt, and then rebuilt again in 1380, and added to around 1500. The cathedral is a truly breathtaking fusion of Romanesque and Perpendicular Gothic styles, and was the infamous place where Archbishop Thomas à Becket was murdered in 1170, if not quite by 'friendly fire' then certainly due to a misunderstanding. This historic

incident inspired author Geoffrey Chaucer to write his now well-known literary masterpiece *The Canterbury Tales* in 1387.

So important is Canterbury Cathedral in the scheme of things that along with the modest Church of St Martin, the oldest church in England, and the ruins of the Abbey of St Augustine, a reminder of the saint's evangelising role in the Heptarchy from 597, since 1988 they have collectively enjoyed World Heritage Status.

As you approach Canterbury, the cathedral still dominates the skyline, presenting 21st-century visitors the same awe-inspiring vision as their medieval counterparts. Making a pilgrimage was an important part of medieval life and thousands of pilgrims flocked to the city to visit the shrine of Thomas à Becket. For some 200 years this was actually the most popular shrine in Europe (outside Rome), and a most sumptuous affair, until it received the unwanted attentions of King Henry VIII's officer during the Dissolution of the Monasteries.

Today, Canterbury still welcomes visitors from around the world and has successfully blended its many ancient buildings with modern shops, bars and restaurants to retain both an old world elegance and a cosmopolitan vitality. The compact city centre is closed to traffic during the daytime to enable the narrow streets to be more easily and safely accessed by visitors.

HEVER MAP REF 401 H6

Tucked away between the villages of Penshurst and Edenbridge, Hever village is most famous for its castle. The castle was begun in 1272, when Edward I allowed a large manor house to be converted by Sir Stephen de Penchester. In the 15th century the then castle was acquired by the Bullen family – later to change their family name to Boleyn.

Hever Castle was home to Anne Boleyn, Henry VIII's wife from 1533 until her execution in 1536. The Boleyn family died out, leaving the castle to Henry VIII who promptly gave it to another of his wives, Anne of Cleeves. The fabric of the castle gave way until it was bought by the Astor family in 1903 and an ambitious programme of restoration was begun. After years of dedicated work, the castle was finally restored to its former glory with the addition of the beautiful grounds and gardens that you see today, and Lord Astor became Viscount of Hever, after being granted naturalisation as a Briton.

IGHTHAM & IGHTHAM MOTE
MAP REF 401 H5

Ightham is most famous for the nearby medieval moated manor house of Ightham Mote, although the village itself is of even greater antiquity, and an eye-catching place of half-timbered cottages and houses. Ightham is not mentioned in the Domesday Book, although place-name

evidence implies derivation from the Saxon 'Ehtaham', 'Ehta' being a personal name, while '-ham' signifies a settlement.

Ightham Mote is a 14th-century manor house, extensively restored by the National Trust in 1989-2004. While still taking in the fact that the dog kennel is a Grade I listed building in its own right, visitors can follow a tour route that includes the Great Hall, Old Chapel, Crypt, Tudor chapel with painted ceiling, drawing room with Jacobean fireplace, frieze and 18th-century wallpaper, and billiards room. There is an extensive garden and interesting walks in the surrounding woodland. Manor houses were the centre of secular village life, and the Great Hall often the scene of the manorial court and the place of assembly of the tenantry.

The House was home to the Selby family from the late 16th century to the middle of the 19th century, and there is a story that Dame Dorothy Selby warned Lord Monteagle not to attend Parliament on 5th November 1605, so leading to the discovery of the Gunpowder Plot. Some supporters of Guy Fawkes blamed Dorothy Selby for its failure, and walled her up in a secret room and left her to die. This may account for the occasional chill you experience on your tour of the house, and it doesn't matter if history prefers to identify Francis Tresham, brother-in-law of Lord Monteagle, as the person who warned him not to attend Parliament.

CANTERBURY

PENSHURST MAP REF 401 H6

This beautiful, quintessentially English village is situated in stunning countryside and falls either side of the River Medway.

The village is famous for its 16th-century grand house, Penshurst Place and its fantastic gardens. The house has some interesting features including an octagonal hearth.

Seat of the Sidney family since 1552, the house owes its current restorative state mainly to the 1st Viscount De L'Isle, William Sidney, who inherited the house at the end of World War II. Penshurst is still in the beloved hands of the Sidney family and has been the home of heir Viscount De L'Isle since 1991.

TUNBRIDGE WELLS MAP REF 401 H6

The cheerful and attractive town of Royal Tunbridge Wells, now included in the borough of Tunbridge Wells, flourished as a spa amid the Wealden forests after a medicinal spring (containing mild chalybeate waters) was discovered by Lord North, a courtier to James I, at the site in 1606. Before the discovery of the waters, the iron content of which was believed to have healing properties, the settlement was little more than a hamlet consisting of a few scattered cottages and farmhouses, with the result that there is nothing of the Tudor period here.

The healthy spa drew added popularity from its location on several hills of The Weald, one of the most scenic stretches of countryside in southern England. The springs, or 'wells', lie at one end of the colonnaded promenade known as Pantiles Parade, first paved in 1700, and, in effect, an 18th-century shopping precinct shaded by lime trees. From then until the early Regency period, Tunbridge Wells was one of the chief resorts of fashionable London society. It reached its height under the dandy and leader of fashion, Richard 'Beau' Nash, and was patronised by novelist William Makepeace Thackeray (who died there), Samuel Johnson and Sir Joshua Reynolds, among others. The Pantiles Parade, with other 17th-century features, is preserved beside the Church of St Charles the Martyr (1684).

Tunbridge Wells added 'Royal' to its name in 1909, after Edward VII officially recognised the popularity of the town amongst royalty and aristocracy by bestowing the official 'Royal' title. Royal Tunbridge Wells is one of only two towns in England to be granted this title, the other is Royal Leamington Spa. Today the town is every bit as charming, a quality it derives from its surfeit of 18th- and 19th-century elegance, most notably seen in Calverley Park and the beautiful buildings you see on Mount Sion.

CANTERBURY

This ancient cathedral city is now a vibrant, cosmopolitan settlement, close enough to the Channel ports and Eurotunnel to reflect a certain continental flavour. The cathedral is forever associated with Thomas à Becket who was murdered there in 1170. He was later canonised. Canterbury's streets have attracted pilgrims for centuries and was the destination of Chaucer's colourful travellers in *The Canterbury Tales*.

DISTANCE/TIME 3.5 miles (5.7km) 1h45 **MAP** OS Explorer 150 Canterbury & the Isle of Thanet **START** Castle Street (or one of several car parks in Canterbury); grid ref: TR 145574 **TRACKS** City streets and firm footpaths **THE PUB** Simple Simon's, Canterbury. Tel: 01227 762355

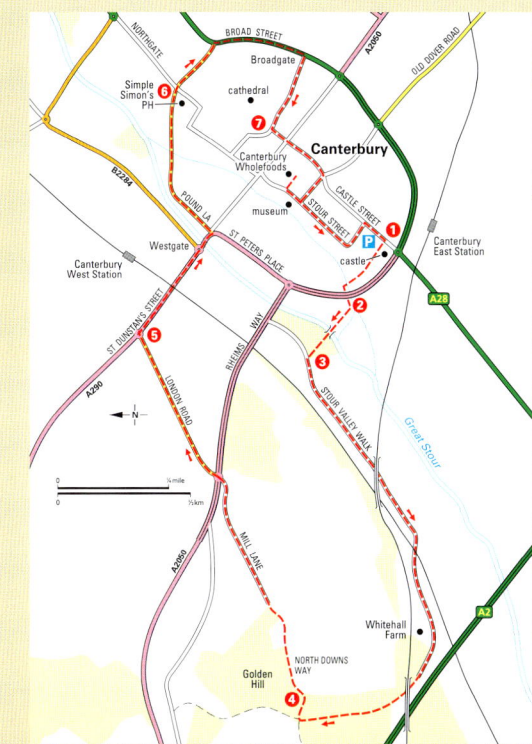

1 Go right from Castle Street car park then right again past the castle. At the end turn left on Centenary Walk. Where this finishes go right and walk beside the road. Cross the bridge, turn left, pass under another bridge and along the river to cross the road.

2 Cross some grassland, go over the bridge and through the children's play area. Walk across the car park and turn left up the road to join the Stour Valley Walk.

3 Go under the bridge and continue to the level crossing. Cross the railway, then stroll up past Whitehall Farm. Walk under an arch, through the gate and over a stream. The path bends round and the main road is on your left. At the junction turn right along the North Downs Way.

4 Go over the bridge and up the lane. To your left is Golden Hill – the point from which pilgrims traditionally had their first view of the city. When you come to a track, turn left and follow it round. Go right along Mill Lane to the main road. Take the underpass to cross Rheims Way, walk down London Road, then turn right into St Dunstan's Street.

5 Walk down into Canterbury to Westgate, then turn left along Pound Lane and carry on into St Radigund Street, where you will then find Simple Simon's pub situated on your right-hand side.

6 Continue into Northgate, go left then make a right turn down Broad Street. You are now walking around the outside of the city walls. From here, turn right along Burgate, and walk past the tiny 16th-century building called Pilgrim's Shop. Soon you will come to a pedestrianised area that brings you out at the Butter Market and the war memorial. At this point, on your right-hand side is the cathedral entrance.

7 From here turn left and walk down the road, go past the tourist information centre and then turn right to Stour Street. On the right here, is the city museum, set in ancient Poor Priests' Hospital. Almost opposite to the hospital, just down Jewry Lane, is Canterbury Wholefoods where you can stop and finish your walk with a refreshing cup of tea and a selection of delicious cakes. To return to Castle Street, turn left on Rosemary Lane and then right.

WALK 48

HEVER

Hever was in the ownership of the Bullen family when Anne Boleyn, Henry VIII's short-lived wife and mother to Elizabeth I, was born. Anne spent her childhood at this lovely moated castle. After Anne's father died, Henry VIII seized the castle and it became the property of Anne of Cleves after her divorce from Henry. In the early 20th century the buildings and gardens were restored.

DISTANCE/TIME 3.5 miles (5.7km) 2h00 **MAP** OS Explorer 147 Sevenoaks & Tonbridge **START** Car park by Hever Castle; grid ref: TQ 476448 **TRACKS** Paths, grassy tracks and field edges, some roads, 6 stiles **THE PUB** King Henry VIII, Edenbridge, Hever. Tel: 01732 862457

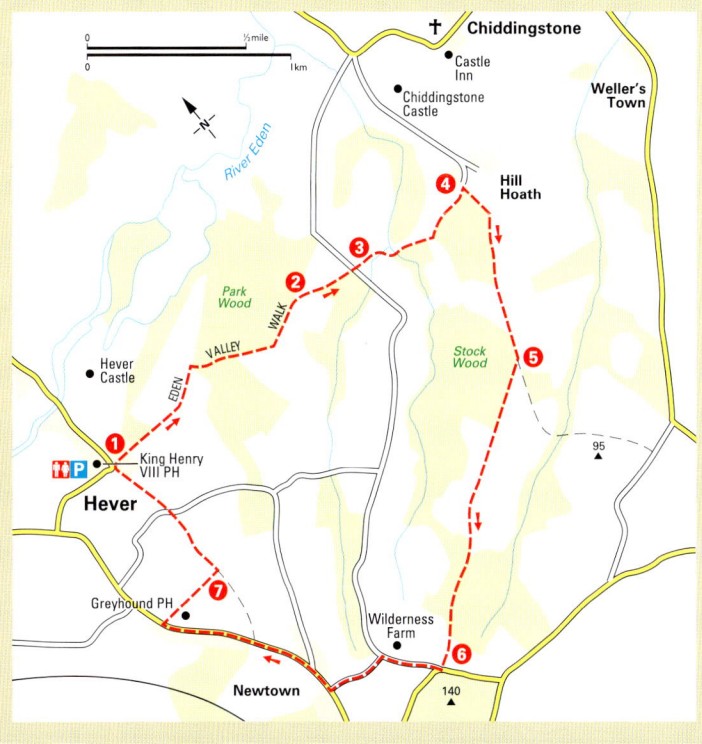

1 Walk under the lychgate and go through the churchyard following the Eden Valley Walk. The path goes downhill, across a bridge and soon becomes a narrow lane parallel to a road, offering occasional glimpses of the lake at Hever Castle. The lake looks natural but was actually created by William Waldorf Astor when he bought the castle in 1903. The path now bends round, goes through woodland, across another bridge and finally opens out.

2 When you come to the house, climb to the gate following the Eden Valley Walk (follow it all the way to Point 4). Pass another house and then take the track on the right-hand side, which winds round the edge of the meadow to woodland. When you reach the tarmac road, cross it and pop over the stile.

3 Continue along an enclosed track, which can get very muddy, crossing two more stiles and gradually heading uphill. Another stile leads you past deer fencing and through a gate on to the tarmac road at Hill Hoath.

4 Now turn back to the right and go through a large gate, so that you seem to be doubling back on yourself. This leads to a broad, grassy track. Walk ahead (don't be tempted into crossing the stile on your left) and walk between trees, passing a lake on your left-hand side. Soon enter much thicker woodland and the track becomes narrower, but is still clear to follow.

5 At a branching of several footpaths, bear to the right. Be warned, this part of the walk can be very muddy. Continue down the track, passing another two areas of woodland until you eventually reach the road.

6 Turn right here and continue on to Wilderness Farm. Once you arrive at the farm, take the road that leads to the left tracking in the opposite direction to the farm. When you reach another road take a right turn and walk up, past the road that leads away to the right. Continue ahead to take ther footpath on the right that runs alongside the Greyhound pub.

7 When you come to a fork in the path by two stiles turn left, then walk around the edge of the field and on past a pond. Continue walking ahead to a lane, where you turn left then take the footpath on the right. Follow this back into Hever.

PENSHURST

Overlooking the village, Penshurst Place has been in the ownership of the Sydney family since the 16th century. The property was revived after World War II following years of neglect in wartime. It is now the home of the present Viscount De L'Isle and his family. The gardens are simply stunning.

DISTANCE/TIME 3.5 miles (5.7km) 1h45 **MAP** OS Explorer 147 Sevenoaks & Tonbridge **START** On-street parking in village, also car park for Penshurst Place; grid ref: TQ 527438 **TRACKS** Broad tracks, short section on busy road, one badly signposted section by river, 2 stiles **THE PUB** Leicester Arms, Penshurst. Tel: 01892 870551

1 Walk up the main street of the village, then turn up the road opposite Quaintways tea room. Once you reach this point, turn right at the public footpath sign and cross the stile. From here, there are some superb views of Penshurst Place almost immediately in front of you. The house dates back to 1341 and the Great Hall is a fabulous example of medieval architecture. It has a timber roof, a beautiful musicians' gallery and a striking octagonal open hearth at its centre. There have been some notable visitors to the house over the years: Elizabeth I danced here with the very much favoured Robert Edward Dudley; the Black Prince ate a Christmas dinner here, and the children of Charles I were brought here after their father was executed. Now walk to a squeeze gate, cross the road, then go through another squeeze gate. Bear to the right in the direction of the lake. Go through a third squeeze gate and, keeping the lake to your right, walk around it then head towards trees.

2 The path now veers to the left and goes uphill. Go through two more squeeze gates then follow signs for Eden Valley Walk, which leads to the right. This is a 15-mile (24km) linear walk that traces the route of the Eden Valley from Edenbridge to Tonbridge.

3 Cross a stile and keep walking straight ahead along a wide, grassy track lined with trees. At the end of the track cut down to the right and continue along the busy road until you reach a sign for Eden Valley Walk on the right-hand side, just before bridge.

4 Go through a squeeze gate and walk through pastureland, tracking alongside the River Medway that flows on the left. Continue to walk by the river for about 0.25 mile (0.4km), then turn right, away from the water, and head across the pasture to a little bridge. Follow the footpath uphill until you get to a stile that then leads on to a concrete track. Turn right at this point and then take a left turn at the junction.

5 Continue walking ahead, go through a gate, then down to a stile. Bear left and walk down a track. Walk under an archway, then turn right and walk back to the village

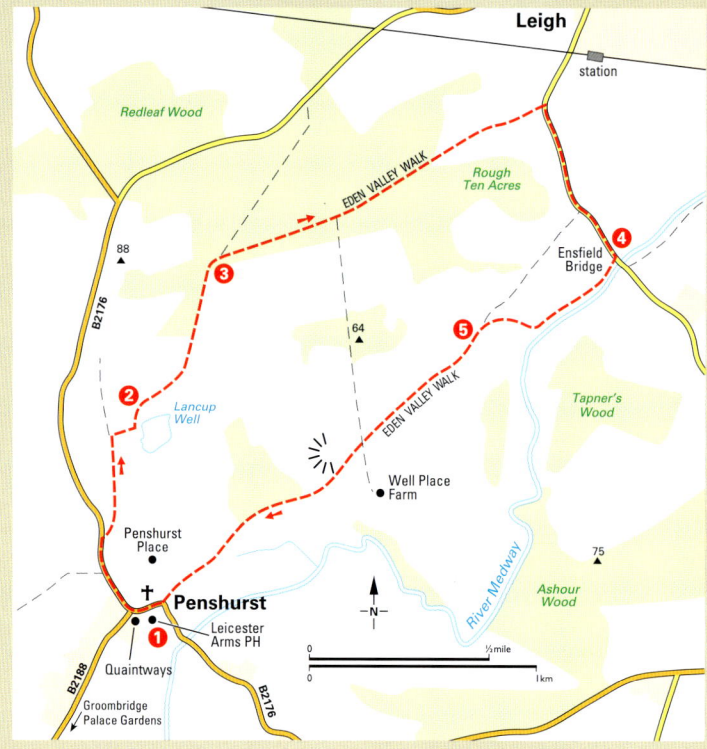

TUNBRIDGE WELLS

Follow the simple trail through this elegant spa town, discovering the origins of its famous Pantiles and royal patronage. Edward VII conferred the 'Royal' prefix since the town was so popular as a spa with the aristocracy. The Pantiles were originally paved with pantiles and the name has been retained.

DISTANCE/TIME 3 miles (4.8km) 1h30 **MAP** OS Explorer 147 Sevenoaks & Tonbridge **START** Car park behind The Pantiles; grid ref: TQ 582388 **TRACKS** Paved streets and tarmac paths **THE PUB** Beau Nash Tavern, Mount Ephraim. Tel: 01892 539350

1 From the car park behind The Pantiles, turn right and walk up to the main road. Cross over then walk up Major York's Road. Just after the car park take the footpath to the left and walk across the common, keeping straight ahead until you reach Hungershall Park. Turn left and continue following the road until you reach a footpath that leads up to the right.

2 Follow the path through trees, which eventually leads on to a private road. Keep ahead and when you reach the top take the track ahead through trees. After a horse barrier, bear right, pass a churchyard, then turn right and walk around the church and on to the busy main road.

3 Turn right and then cross the road to walk to a turning on the left (signed 'Toad Rock'). The path winds uphill to the rock. Now return to the main road. Turn left and continue until you pass Fir Tree Road. On the common, hidden by the trees, are Wellington Rocks.

4 Continue along Mount Ephraim to the cottages on the right, which are built into rock. Turn right to walk across grass to the picturesque old house that was once home to author William Makepeace Thackeray.

5 Walk along the path that runs by the left of the house and then walk along Mount Ephraim Road. This brings you out in front of a pedestrianised shopping area. Turn to the right and walk down, past the museum and library and the war memorial. From here, turn left to walk up Crescent Road and continue until you reach Calverley Park, a 19th-century housing development designed by Decimus Burton. As you enter the park you'll see a magnificent oak tree planted in honour of Air Chief Marshall Lord Dowding, who once lived here.

6 After admiring the tree, walk across Calverley Grounds to go down The Mews, then go right into Grove Hill Road. This brings you out to a roundabout; turn left and walk along the High Street. At the end go down Chapel Place and then pass Church of King Charles the Martyr. Once you reach here, cross the road then walk along the famous Pantiles and back to the car park.

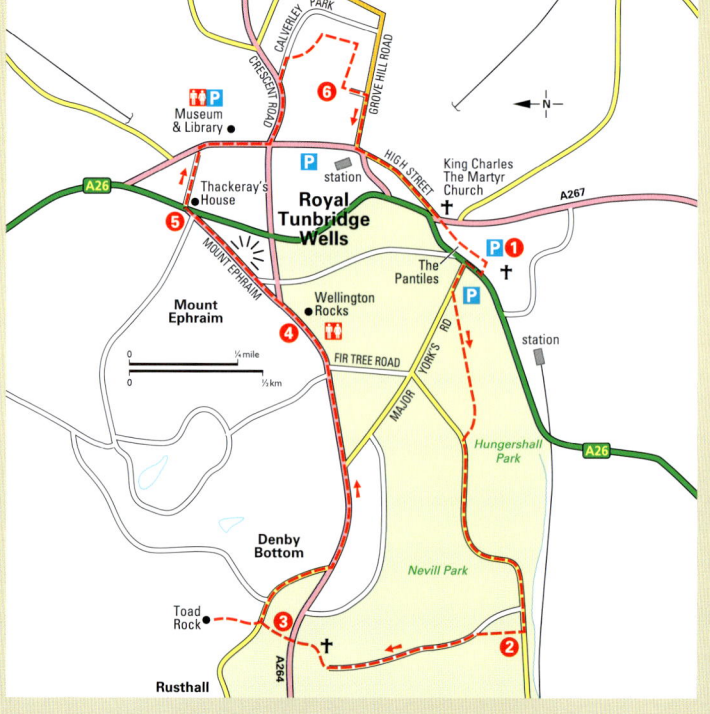

Oxford & the Chilterns

CLOCKWISE FROM TOP: THE RIDGEWAY; THE BRIDGE OF SIGHS, OXFORD; CHAUCER'S COTTAGE DOOR, WOODSTOCK

BLENHEIM & WOODSTOCK

MAP REF 400 E3

Most visitors to Woodstock come to visit Blenheim Palace, birthplace of Winston Churchill, and while the palace is undoubtedly a magnificent edifice and a stunning part of England's heritage, Woodstock has its own billing, and rightly so. This small town is a happy blend of mellow stone buildings dating from the 17th and 18th centuries, all of which jostle cosily for space alongside shops, pubs, restaurants and hotels.

The palace, built between 1705 and 1722, is one of England's greatest houses. It was intended as a gift to John Churchill, the 1st Duke of Marlborough, from a 'grateful nation' in return for military triumph against the French. But the gratitude was short-lived, and political infighting soon led to Marlborough's exile, and irreparable damage to the reputation of the architect Vanbrugh. Students of architecture will find in Blenheim one of the few buildings designed in the English baroque style, although architectural appreciation of the palace is as subjective today as in the 1720s.

The palace, still home to the Dukes of Marlborough, is open to the public, and contains tourist attractions in the grounds, which in themselves are a delight to explore, not least the avenue of small-leaved limes, but the overall atmosphere is that of a large country house.

Blenheim is a popular choice for film makers and it appears in a number of hits including *Harry Potter and the Order of the Phoenix* (2007), *History of the World Part 1* (1981) and *The Avengers* (1998).

MINSTER LOVELL MAP REF 400 D4

A long, thatched cottage-flanked street beside the River Windrush leads to an attractive 15th-century bridge in the Oxfordshire village of Minster Lovell. Situated along the lovely river bank, Minster Lovell Hall, built in the 1430s, was the home of Viscount Francis Lovell who supported Richard III, the last of the Plantagenet dynasty, against the Lancastrian contender for the crown, Henry Tudor, 2nd Earl of Richmond (later Henry VII). Although Lovell is said by some to have died with King Richard at Bosworth Field, there is a tale that following the battle, Lovell fled to Minster Lovell Hall, where he hid in a secret room. With unfortunate lack of foresight, only Lovell's manservant knew his concealed location. Unfortunately for Lovell, his manservant fell ill and died, taking his location to the grave. Years later, in 1708, Lovell's skeleton was discovered as repairs where being made to the hall.

Now in the care of English Heritage, the ruins of Minster Lovell consist of the great hall, entrance porch and the tower from the south wing. Of the rest of the building only foundations remain.

OXFORD MAP REF 400 E4

Lying just under 60 miles (96.6km) north of London, Oxford is a typical market town situated amid low hills at the meeting point of the River Thames and the River Cherwell. What distinguishes this town form many others like it in England, is its ancient university, with some 39 colleges spread throughout the city itself. Places at Oxford University are much sought-after by English students as well as those from abroad. And who can blame them? Apart from its excellent academic reputation and the feeling of following in many famous footsteps along its hallowed halls, the buildings themselves are so beautiful that many students feel it is a priviledge and a pleasure to study here.

There is a mellow ambience of past gentility about Oxford that feeds on the homely blend of amazing architecture and the sprawl of riverside meadows and parkland with their cyclists, punters and rowers. Of course, it's the architecture of the colleges that impresses first; masterpieces that range from the early Gothic of Merton College to the modernism of St Catherine's.

Oxford probably didn't need TV programme and personality, Inspector Morse, to bring it national acclaim. Although its origins are lost in time, Oxford has been an established town since the 9th century, with a significant educational influence in the city since 1167, when students who had been expelled from Paris settled here under the patronage of Henry II. But the university's colleges, of which there are 36, exert palpable influence but without entirely dominating city life. Beneath the mantle of education, the city of Oxford still lives and breathes, although, if you stay long enough, you gradually detect a frisson of tension between 'gown' and 'town'.

Within this city of 'dreaming spires' many beautiful, honey-coloured buildings exist, among them the Museum of History and Science, the Pitts River Museum, and the Ashmolean, England's oldest public museum, founded in 1683, and housing a huge collection of art and antiquity. The Bodleian Library and the nearby Sheldonian Theatre nestle in an area of mainly 17th-century buildings and seem to serve simply to satisfy every new visitor's vision of the city.

Time in Oxford is well spent, and, for the visiting tourist, there is much to detain you; the essence of England seeps from the walls, heritage, pomp and circumstance mingle with student Rag Weeks and the minutiae of daily life in a cosmopolitan setting. The lively covered market is one of Britain's oldest, having been going since 1773.

Oxford was also a place of great automobile manufacturing, and is where the Morris Oxford and the T-series MG sports car were created.

OXFORD

Oxford's university population and townspeople exhibit a fascinating contrast of lifestyles. In medieval times this duality led to occasional bloody battles, but although today's students are noted for their often boisterous post-exam antics, Oxford is an eminently civilized place where the traditions of "town and gown" rest easily side by side. On the one hand Oxford is mildly bizarre and eccentric, on the other it is a modern city in modern times. The best way to explore is undoubtedly on foot, with serendipity as a guide and frequent stops at coffee shops for on-going refreshment; but there is a range of organised tours by bus or with qualified tourism guides who deftly deduct aimless wandering from free-range exploration, and substitute knowledge and enthusiasm for one of the finest and most attractive cities in England.

THE RIDGEWAY MAP REF 400 E4

Linking the Chilterns and the North Wessex Downs, the Ridgeway is arguably one of the oldest 'roads' in Britain. Saturated in beauty, it weaves a way for 87 miles (139km) across open chalk downland through secluded valleys and woodlands, ancient sites, and passes within strides of the burial mound at Wayland's Smithy beyond which lies the White Horse of Uffington, largely following the same chalk ridge route used since prehistoric times by travellers, herdsmen and soldiers. The Ridgeway is a superb way of getting to know the chalk downlands and the Chiltern Hills.

The grasslands which occur on the downs provide some of the most interesting habitats in England, among the richest in terms of plant species that include several types of orchid. Butterflies, especially the many types of blue butterfly, which require particular chalk grassland plants for food, are a key part of the downland natural history. In the Chilterns, red kites, magnificent birds of prey reintroduced from Spain in the 1980s, are now so well established they far outnumber the buzzard. Fairly commonplace birds such as warblers and finches are found all along the Ridgeway, but skylarks, yellowhammers and corn buntings are especially characteristic of downland. Woodpeckers and nuthatches may well be spotted in the woodlands.

Apart from hundreds of rabbits, numbers of the much larger hare are sometimes found in open countryside, generally solitary animals most active at night. Two species of deer are found on the Ridgeway, roe and fallow, both of which are nocturnal and shy, making early mornings and late afternoons the best time to be out walking the Ridgeway.

OXFORD: CITY STROLL

This famous university city is renowned as the 'city of the dreaming spires'. Its architecture is wonderful, the venerable colleges spread across a large part of the central city. The Thames flows through Oxford where for part of its route it is known as the Isis. The city has long been associated with motor car production, although this has declined from its heyday in the 1960s and 1970s. From unique individual shops and central cafés and restaurants to ethnic outlets and eateries, this is a vibrant, lively place with excellent cultural offerings and happening nightlife.

DISTANCE/TIME 2.25 miles (3.6km) 1h15 **MAP** OS Explorer 180 Oxford **START** Parking in city centre, or use park-and-ride, or travel by train; grid ref: SP 513062 **TRACKS** Pavements, field and riverside paths, 2 stiles **THE PUB** Turf Tavern, 7 Bath Place, Oxford. Tel: 01865 243235; www.theturftavern.co.uk

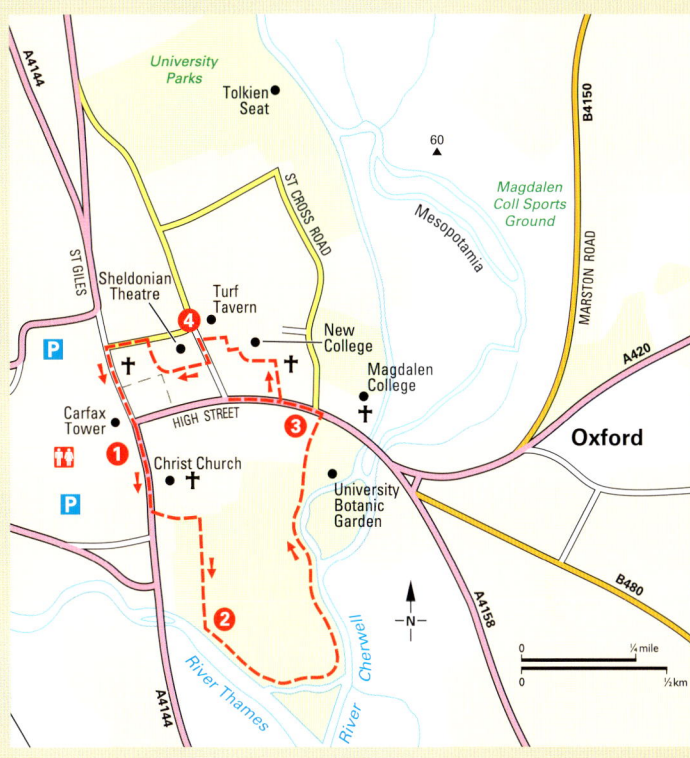

1 Begin the walk at Carfax, at the point where four of the city's main streets converge. Charles II was proclaimed King at Carfax Tower in 1660. Walk straight ahead into St Aldates and then head for the entrance to Christ Church, Oxford's largest college, founded in 1525 by Cardinal Wolsey. When he was disgraced it was refounded as King Henry VIII's College. Later it became known as Christ Church when the college and the cathedral became one. Leave by the south exit and walk ahead down tree-lined New Walk. On your left is Christ Church Meadow.

2 On reaching the Thames towpath, swing left and follow the river bank. Keep straight ahead until you reach the confluence of the Thames and River Cherwell. Avoid the steeply arched footbridge and keep alongside the Cherwell. The river meanders between meadows and sports fields. Leave the river bank and pass through the wrought-iron gates to walk up Rose Lane.

3 With Magdalen Bridge and the fine Magdalen College bell tower on your right, turn left at the High Street or 'the High',

as it is more commonly known in Oxford. From here, cross Longwall Street and turn right into Queen's Lane. Continue into New College Lane and if you look to the right, beyond an arch, is the entrance to New College. Keep walking along New College Lane to the Bridge of Sighs, a 1913 replica of its Venice namesake, and ahead of you now is the 1669 Sheldonian Theatre, designed by Sir Christopher Wren.

4 Turn left here for Radcliffe Camera and cross Radcliffe Square towards Brasenose College, which some people like to believe took its name from a door-knocker made in the shape of a nose. Turn right into Brasenose Lane, then turn right again into Turl Street, cutting in between Jesus College and Exeter College. Carry on for Broad Street and on the right is St Giles, where Charles I drilled his men during the Civil War. From this point turn left into Cornmarket Street, passing the Church of St Michael at the North Gate. The church's Saxon tower is the oldest building in Oxford. From here it is just a short walk to return to Carfax and the car park at the beginning of the walk.

WALK 52

MINSTER LOVELL: RIVERSIDE RAMBLE

A short distance from Minster Lovell, and a pleasant walk along the river, is the pretty village of Crawley with a river bridge and an old blanket mill. Just to the south of Minster Lovell lie the Charterville Allotments, the subject of a 19th-century social experiment. The 300 acres (121ha) were purchased by an early socialist and offered as smallholdings to poor families, along with £30 and a pig. The experiment failed but some of the cottages remain.

DISTANCE/TIME 4 miles (6.4km) 1h30 **MAP** OS Explorer 180 Oxford, Witney & Woodstock **START** Car park (free) at eastern end of Minster Lovell, above church and hall; grid ref: SP 321114 **TRACKS** Meadows, tracks, pavement and lane, woodland, 17 stiles **THE PUB** The Mill and Old Swan Inn, Minster Lovell. Tel: 0870 609 1152

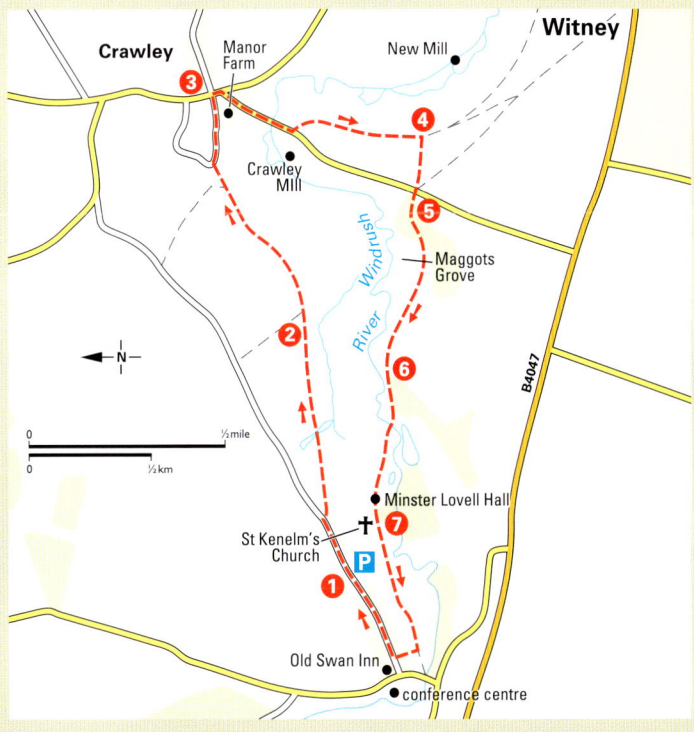

1 Walk up the lane (signed 'Crawley'). At the end of village cross a stile and turn right. Take the footpath diagonally left across the field (signed 'Crawley'). Cross a stile and keep straight ahead along the path, with a stone wall to your left. The mill chimney on the horizon belongs to Crawley Mill.

2 Cross a stile and continue ahead up a slight incline. Cross another stile, go through a gate and continue on a path, walking up the green tunnel of a lane. Pass above Crawley Mill. At the road turn right. Follow this down into Crawley. At the bottom, the Lamb Inn on the left is a good place for lunch.

3 Turn right and then follow the pavement past Manor Farm, with its huge pond. Cross the humpback bridge over the River Windrush. At the other side of the bridge cross the road. Turn left through the gate (signed 'Witney'). Follow a bridleway beside the stream, marked by a line of willows.

4 At a junction of paths by a gate look ahead and left to see New Mill. Turn right through a gate and walk up the field edge. Pass a gate

and cross the road. Climb over a stile, go straight on to a second stile, and follow the path down through woods.

5 At the bottom cross a stile and follow the path by a fence. The wild flower meadows of Maggots Grove lie to the right. Continue over three more stiles and bear left beside trees. Cross a stile by the meander of the river.

6 Cross another stile and enter woods. At a gate bear right, following arrows, and cross two footbridges. After a short distance cross a bridge over the river. Go through a squeeze gate towards Minster Lovell Hall. Climb a stile and go through a gate to the ruins.

7 Leave by the top entrance and walk through the churchyard. Cross a slab stile, and continue along a grassy path with the village up to your right. Cross the footbridge and stile and veer to the right. Cross one stile then another into Wash Meadow recreation ground. Keep right and go through a gate on to the high street, with the Old Swan Inn to the left. Turn right, then walk through the village to the car park.

NEW FOREST
■ TOURIST INFORMATION
Christchurch
49 High Street. Tel: 01202 471780;
www.christchurchtourism.info
Lyndhurst
New Forest Visitor Information
Centre. Main Car Park.
Tel: 023 8028 2269;
www.thenewforest.co.uk

■ PLACES OF INTEREST
Beaulieu: National Motor Museum
Palace House, Beaulieu Abbey.
Tel: 01590 612123; www.beaulieu.co.uk
Bolderwood Deer Platform
Signed from Bolderwood car park.
Fallow deer are fed here.
www.forestry.gov.uk/newforest
Breamore Manor House & Countryside Museum
Tel: 01725 512468;
www.breamorehouse.com
Bucklers Hard
Tel: 01590 616203;
www.buckhlershard.co.uk
Christchurch Priory Church
Quay Road, Christchurch.
Tel: 01202 485804;
www.christchurchpriory.org
Eling Tide Mill
The Toll Bridge, Eling, Totton.
Tel: 023 8086 9575;
www.elingtidemill.org.uk
Exbury Gardens & Steam Railway
Near Beaulieu. Tel: 023 8089 1203;
www.exbury.co.uk
A favourite with steam engine fans.
Hurst Castle
Hurst Point, by Keyhaven.
Tel: 01590 642344;
www.hurst-castle.co.uk
New Forest Cider
Littlemead, Pound Lane, Burley.
Tel: 01425 403589;
www.newforestcider.co.uk
New Forest Museum
Main car park, High Street, Lyndhurst.
Tel: 023 8028 3444;
www.newforestmuseum.org.uk
New Forest Reptile Centre
Emery Down. Tel: 023 8028 3141;
www.forestry.gov.uk/newforest
Place Mill
Quay Road, Christchurch.
Tel: 01202 487626;
www.visitchristchurch.info
Red House Museum
Quay Road, Christchurch.
Tel: 01202 482860
St Barbe Museum & Art Gallery
New Street, Lymington.
Tel: 01590 676969;
www.stbarbe-museum.org.uk
Spinners Garden & Nursery
Boldre, by Lymington.

■ SPORTS & ACTIVITIES
BOATING
Beaulieu River cruises
From Bucklers Hard, 3 miles (4.5km)
south of Beaulieu.
CANOEING & KAYAKING
Mudeford Ferry Adventure Voyages
Mudeford Quay.
CYCLE HIRE
AA Bike Hire
Fernglen, Gosport Lane, Lyndhurst.
Tel: 023 8028 3349;
www.aabikehirenewforest.co.uk
Country Lanes Cycle Centre
The Railway Station, Brockenhurst.
Tel: 01590 622627;
www.countrylanes.co.uk
Cycle Xperience Bike Hire
Island Shop, 2-4 Brookly Road,
Brockenhurst. Tel: 01590 624204;
www.cyclex.co.uk
Forest Leisure Cycling (FLC)
Burley. Tel: 01425 403584;
www.forestleisurecycling.co.uk
WALKING
Avon Valley Path
Christchurch to Salisbury Cathedral.

■ ANNUAL EVENTS & CUSTOMS
Beaulieu
Boat Jumble, Apr.
Auto Jumble, Sep.
Fireworks, end Oct.
Brockenhurst
New Forest Show, last week Jul
at New Park.
www.newforestshow.co.uk

ISLE OF WIGHT
■ TOURIST INFORMATION
Cowes
The Arcade, Fountain Quay.
Tel: 01983 813818
Newport
The Guildhall, High Street.
Tel: 01983 813818
Ryde
Western Esplanade. Tel: 01983 813818
Sandown
8 High Street. Tel: 01983 813818
Shanklin
67 High Street. Tel: 01983 813818
Yarmouth
The Quay. Tel: 01983 813818

■ PLACES OF INTEREST
Brading Roman Villa
Brading. Tel: 01983 406223;
www.bradingromanvilla.org.uk
Carisbrooke Castle & Isle of Wight Museum (EH)
1.5 miles (2km) southeast of Newport.
Tel: 01983 522107
Fort Victoria Country Park
Near Yarmouth. Tel: 01983 823893;
www.fortvictoria.co.uk

Heritage Museum
11 Spring Hill, Ventnor. Tel: 01983 855407;
www.ventnorheritage.org.uk
Isle of Wight Steam Railway
Tel: 01983 884343;
www.iwsteamrailway.co.uk
Maritime Museum
Beckford Road, Cowes. Tel: 01983 823433
Morton Manor
Brading. Tel: 01983 406168
Museum of Island History
Guildhall, Newport. Tel: 01983 823366;
www.iwight.com
The Needles Old Battery (NT)
West Highdown, Totland.
Tel: 01983 754772
The Needles Park
Tel: 0870 458 0022;
www.theneedles.co.uk
Newport Roman Villa
Cypress Road, Newport.
Tel: 01983 529720;
www.romans-in-britain.org.uk
Osborne House and Gardens (EH)
East Cowes. Tel: 01983 200022
Rosemary Vineyard
Ashey, Ryde. Tel: 01983 811084;
www.rosemaryvineyard.co.uk
Shanklin Chine
Shanklin. Tel: 01983 866432;
www.shanklinchine.co.uk
Smuggling Museum
Botanic Garden, Ventnor.
Tel: 01983 853677
Yarmouth Castle (EH)
Yarmouth. Tel: 01983 760678

■ FOR CHILDREN
Blackgang Chine
Chale, near Ventnor. Tel: 01983 730052;
www.blackgangchine.com
Isle of Wight Zoo
Yaverland Seafront, Sandown.
Tel: 01983 403883;
www.isleofwightzoo.com

■ PERFORMING ARTS
Medina Theatre
Fairlee Road, Newport. Tel: 01983 527020
Ryde Theatre
Lind Street, Ryde. Tel: 01983 568 099
Shanklin Theatre
Prospect Road, Shanklin.
Tel: 01983 862739

■ SPORTS & ACTIVITIES
ADRENALIN SPORTS
Wight Water Adventure Watersports
Tel: 01983 404987; www.wightwaters.com
High Adventure
Yarmouth. Tel: 07774 614883;
www.islandactivities.co.uk
Paragliding and fast boats.
BOAT TRIPS
Needles Pleasure Cruises
Tel: 01983 761567

CYCLE HIRE
Battersby Cycles
Ryde. Tel: 01983 562039
Extreme Cycles
Ventnor. Tel: 01983 852232
FISHING
Scotties Fishing Tackle
11 Lugley Street, Newport.
Tel: 01983 522115;
www.scotties-tackle.co.uk

■ ANNUAL EVENTS & CUSTOMS
Cowes
Cowes Week; late Jul-early Aug.
Tel: 01983 295744; www.cowesweek.co.uk
Isle of Wight County Show
Newport
Isle of Wight Festival; music festival,
mid-Jun. Tel: 08705 321321;
www.isleofwightfestival.org
Ryde
Carnival, end Aug/early Sep.
Yarmouth
Old Gaffers Festival, gaff-rigged yachts;
early Jun. Tel: 01983 760541;
www.yarmoutholdgaffersfestival.co.uk
Round the Island Race
Early Jun. Tel: 01983 296911;
www.roundtheisland.org.uk

WINCHESTER & NORTH DOWNS
■ TOURIST INFORMATION
Winchester
The Guildhall, High Street.
Tel: 01962 840500;
www.visitwinchester.co.uk

■ PLACES OF INTEREST
Gilbert White's House
The Wakes, High Street, Selborne.
Tel: 01420 511275;
www.gilbertwhiteshouse.org.uk
The Grange (EH)
Northington, near Alresford.
Tel: 02392 581059
Hospital of St Cross
St Cross Road, Winchester.
Tel: 01962 851375;
www.stcrosshospital.co.uk
Jane Austen's House
Chawton. Tel: 01420 83262;
www.jane-austens-house-museum.
org.uk
The Watercress Line
The Railway Station, Station Road,
Alresford. Tel: 01962 734866;
www.watercressline.co.uk
Winchester Castle & Great Hall
Castle Avenue. Tel: 01962 846476
Winchester Cathedral
The Close. Tel: 01962 857200;
www.winchester-cathedral.org.uk
Winchester City Mill (NT)
Bridge Street, Winchester.
Tel: 01962 870057

Winchester City Museum
The Square, Winchester.
Tel: 01962 848269;
www.winchester.gov.uk
Winchester College Tours
College Street, Winchester.
Tel: 01962 621209

■ **FOR CHILDREN**
Marwell Zoological Park
Colden Common, Winchester.
Tel: 01962 777407; www.marwell.org.uk
Family-friendly zoo.

■ **PERFORMING ARTS**
Chesil Theatre
Chesil Street, Winchester.
Tel: 01962 867086;
www.chesiltheatre.org.uk
Grange Park Opera
Grange Park, near New Alresford.
Tel: 01962 868888;
www.grangeparkopera.co.uk
Theatre Royal
21–23 Jewry Street, Winchester.
Tel: 01962 840440;
www.theatre-royal-winchester.co.uk
Tower Arts Centre
Romsey Road, Winchester.
Tel: 01962 867986; www.towerarts.co.uk
Off-the-wall acts.

■ **SPORTS & ACTIVITIES**
WALKING
The Clarendon Way
A 26-mile (42km) trail from Winchester
to Salisbury.

■ **ANNUAL EVENTS & CUSTOMS**
New Alresford
Watercress Festival
www.watercress.co.uk
2nd Sun in May. Children's activities,
farmers market, celebrity chefs.
Winchester
MayFest. www.winmayfest.co.uk
Folk festival with music and storytelling,
second weekend in May.
Hampshire Food Festival
www.hampshirefare.co.uk
Jun–Jul. Culinary events.
Hat Fair www.hatfair.co.uk
1st weekend of Jul, Thu–Sun. The
UK's longest-running festival of street
theatre. You'll find lots of audience
participation – be warned.
Winchester Festival
www.winchesterfestival.co.uk
Arts festival. Guided walks, Jul.

SURREY HEATHS
■ **TOURIST INFORMATION**
Guildford
14 Tunsgate, Guildford, Surrey GU1 3QT.
Tel: 01483 444333;
www.surreyheath.gov.uk

■ **PLACES OF INTEREST**
Guildford Cathedral
Stag Hill, Guildford, Surrey, GU2 7UP.
Tel: 01483 547860;
www.guildford-cathedral.org
Devil's Punch Bowl
www.nationaltrust.org.uk
Hindhead Common
Beside A3, at Hindhead, near crossroads
with A287; www.nationaltrust.org.uk

SOUTH DOWNS
■ **TOURIST INFORMATION**
Arundel
61 High Street. Tel: 01903 882268 or
01243 823140
Petworth
The Old Bakery. Tel: 01798 343523

■ **PLACES OF INTEREST**
Amberley Working Museum
Tel: 01798 831370;
www.amberleymuseum.co.uk
Arundel Castle
Tel: 01903 882173;
www.arundelcastle.org.uk
Arundel Museum & Heritage Centre
61 High Street. Tel: 01903 885708;
www.arundelmuseum.org.uk
Bignor Roman Villa
Bignor. Tel: 01798 869259
Butser Ancient Farm
Petersfield. Tel: 023 9259 8838;
www.butser.org.uk
Ditchling Museum
Church Lane, Ditchling.
Tel: 01273 844744;
www.ditchling-museum.com
Nymans Garden
Handcross, near Haywards Heath.
Tel: 01444 400321;
www.nationaltrust.org.uk
Petworth House & Park
Petworth. Tel: 01798 342207;
www.nationaltrust.org.uk/petworth
Queen Elizabeth Country Park
Petersfield. Tel: 023 9259 5040;
www.hantsweb.org.uk/qecp
Uppark House & Garden
South Harting. Tel: 01730 825415;
www.nationaltrust.org.uk/uppark
Weald & Downland Open Air Museum
Singleton. Tel: 01243 811348;
www.wealddown.co.uk
West Dean Gardens
West Dean. Tel: 01243 818210/811301;
www.westdean.org.uk

■ **FOR CHILDREN**
Arundel Ghost Experience
Old Town Hall, Duke's Path Entrance,
High Street. Tel: 01903 889821;
www.arundelghostexperience.com
Arundel Wetland Centre
Mill Road, Arundel.
Tel: 01903 883355; www.wwt.org.uk

■ **PERFORMING ARTS**
Glyndebourne Opera House
Tel: 01273 813813

■ **SPORTS & ACTIVITIES**
BOAT TRIPS
Arundel Boatyard
Mill Road, Arundel. Tel: 01903 882609
HORSE-RACING
Fontwell Park Racecourse
Arundel. Tel: 01243 543335;
www.fontwellpark.co.uk

■ **ANNUAL EVENTS & CUSTOMS**
Arundel
Corpus Christi
May/Jun. Tel: 01903 882297
Arundel Festival
Late Aug–early Sep;
www.arundelfestival.co.uk
Petworth
Petworth Festival
Jul–Aug. Tel: 01798 344068;
www.petworthfestival.org.uk

SOUTH COAST
■ **TOURIST INFORMATION**
Brighton
10 Bartholomew Square.
Tel: 0906 711 2255;
www.visitbrighton.com
Chichester
29a South Street. Tel: 01243 775888 or
01243 539435; www.visitchichester.org
Eastbourne
Cornfield Road. Tel: 01323 415450;
www.visiteastbourne.org
Portsmouth
Clarence Esplanade, Southsea.
Tel: 023 9282 6722
Southampton
9 Civic Centre Road. Tel: 023 8083 3333;
www.visit-southampton.co.uk

■ **PLACES OF INTEREST**
Beachy Head Countryside Centre
Tel: 01323 737273;
www.beachyhead.org.uk
Brighton Museum & Art Gallery
Royal Pavilion Gardens.
Tel: 01273 292882;
www.virtualmuseum.info
Charles Dickens' Birthplace
393 Old Commercial Road, Portsmouth.
Tel: 023 9282 7261;
www.charlesdickensbirthplace.co.uk
City Museum & Art Gallery
Museum Road, Portsmouth.
Tel: 023 9282 7261;
www.portsmouthcitymuseums.co.uk
Explosion! Museum of Naval Firepower
Priddy's Hard, Gosport.
Tel: 023 9250 5600; www.explosion.org.uk
Fishbourne Roman Palace
Fishbourne, Chichester.
Tel: 01243 785859; www.sussexpast.co.uk

Maritime Museum
Town Quay, Southampton.
Tel: 023 8063 5904
Netley Abbey (EH)
Tel: 023 8045 5157
Portsmouth Historic Dockyard
Victory Gate, HM Naval Base.
Tel: 023 9286 1512/9766;
www.historicdockyard.co.uk
Redoubt Fortress & Military Museum
Royal Parade, Eastbourne.
Tel: 01323 410300
Royal Navy Submarine Museum
Haslar Jetty Road, Gosport.
Tel: 023 9252 9217; www.rnsubmus.co.uk
Royal Pavilion
Church Street, Brighton.
Tel: 01273 290900;
www.royalpavilion.org.uk
Seven Sisters Country Park
Exceat. Tel: 01323 870310;
www.sevensisters.org.uk

■ **FOR CHILDREN**
Brighton Sea Life Centre
Marine Parade. Tel: 01273 604234;
www.sealifeeurope.com
Brighton Toy & Model Museum
Trafalgar Street (underneath railway
station). Tel: 01273 749494;
www.brightontoymuseum.co.uk
Fort Fun
Royal Parade, Eastbourne.
Tel: 01323 642833
Rides, go-karts – under 13s.
Hove Museum & Art Gallery
19 New Church Road, Hove.
Tel: 01273 290200;
www.hove.virtualmuseum.info

■ **PERFORMING ARTS**
Bandstand
Grand Parade, Eastbourne.
Tel: 01323 641984
Brighton Centre
Kings Road. Tel: 01273 290131;
www.brightoncentre.co.uk
Gigs, ice shows and more, with
top performers.
Brighton Dome
Church Street. Tel: 01273 700747;
www.brightondome.org
Opera, ballet, orchestral and
world music.
Chichester Festival Theatre
Oaklands Park. Tel: 01243 786650;
www.cft.org.uk
Congress Theatre
Compton Street, Eastbourne.
Tel: 01323 412000
Musicals, comedy, opera, ballet
and concerts.
The Cultural Centre
Eastbourne. This major new performing
arts venue is due to open near the
Congress Theatre in 2007.

Devonshire Park Theatre
Compton Street, Eastbourne.
Tel: 01323 412000

Joogleberry Playhouse
14–17 Manchester Street, Brighton.
Tel: 01273 687171; www.joogleberry.com
Jazz, comedy, cabaret.

Komedia
44–47 Gardner Street, North Lane,
Brighton. Tel: 01273 647100;
www.komedia.co.uk
Top comedy/cabaret venue.

The Mayflower
Commercial Road, Southampton.
Tel: 023 8071 1811;
www.the-mayflower.com

New Theatre Royal
20–24 Guildhall Walk, Portsmouth.
Tel: 023 9264 9000;
www.newtheatreroyal.com

Nuffield Theatre
University Road, Southampton.
Tel: 023 8067 1771

Royal Hippodrome
112 Seaside Road, Eastbourne.
Tel: 01323 412000

Theatre Royal
New Road, Brighton. Tel: 08700 606650;
www.theambassadors.com/theatreroyal

■ **SPORTS & ACTIVITIES**
BOAT TRIPS
Allchorn Pleasure Boats
The Promenade, Eastbourne.
Tel: 01323 410606

Blue Funnel Cruises
Ocean Village, Southampton.
Tel: 023 8022 3278; www.bluefunnel.co.uk

Chichester Harbour Water Tours
Tel: 01243 679504;
www.chichesterharbourwatertours.co.uk

SS Shieldhall
47 Berth, Eastern Dock, Southampton,
Dock Gate 4. Tel: 023 8022 5853;
www.ss-shieldhall.co.uk
GUIDED WALKS
Brighton Walks
Tel: 01273 888596;
www.brightonwalks.com
HORSE-RACING
Brighton Racecourse
Freshfield Road, Brighton.
Tel: 01273 603580;
www.brighton-racecourse.co.uk
HORSE-RIDING
Gleneagles Equestrian Centre
Allington Lane, West End, Southampton.
Tel: 023 8047 3370
WATER & BEACH SPORTS
The Brighton Watersports Company
West of Palace Pier. Tel: 01273 323160;
www.thebrightonwatersports.co.uk
Kayak hire and lessons, doughnut rides,
wakeboarding, waterskiing, parasailing,
surf lessons, watersports equipment.
Fast rib rides.

Chichester Watersports
Coach Road, Chichester.
Tel: 01243 776439

Lagoon Watersports Centre
Hove Lagoon, The Kingsway, Hove.
Tel: 01273 424842; www.hovelagoon.co.uk
Powerboat driving, windsurfing, sailing
and water skiing.

Ross Boat Trips
Pontoon 4, Brighton Marina.
Tel: 07836 262717;
www.rossboattrips.co.uk
Boat trips around the harbour.

SailnetUK
Pontoon 19, West Jetty, Brighton Marina.
Tel: 0870 850 5351; www.sailnetuk.com
Sailing for beginners.

■ **ANNUAL EVENTS & CUSTOMS**
Brighton
Brighton Festival, May.
Brighton Pride. Britain's biggest
gay and lesbian event, Aug;
www.realbrighton.com
Brighton & Hove Food & Drink Lovers
Festival, Sep.
Market and other gastronomic delights.
Brunswick Festival. Celebration of all
things Regency, Aug.
Kite Flyers Festival, Jul.
London to Brighton Bike Ride, Jun.
London to Brighton Veteran Car Run,
Early Nov. Vintage vehicles attempt the
journey from London, with them all finally
gathering together up on the Kemp
Town seafront.
Paramount Brighton. Popular comedy
Festival, Oct.
Chichester
Chichester Festivities, Jul.
Tel: 01243 785718;
www.chifest.org.uk
Eastbourne
Airbourne. Four-day air festival, Mid-Aug.
Beachy Head is a good vantage point.
Eastbourne Extreme, Jul; windsurfing,
parasailing, land yachting, inline skating.
Feastbourne, Oct; food festival
incorporating the Eastbourne Beer
Festival.
Festival of Fire and Magnificent Motors,
May Bank Holiday.
Netley
Fireworks Spectacular, Royal Victoria
Country Park, around 5 Nov.
Tel: 023 8045 5157
Netley Marsh Steam & Craft Show
Mid-Jul. Meadow Mead Farm.
Tel: 023 8086 7882;
www.netleymarshsteamandcraft
show.org
Southampton
Annual Kite Festival, mid-Jun
at Lordshill.
The Big Southampton Boat Show
Mid-Sep. Tel: 0870 060 0246

WINDSOR & THAMES
■ **TOURIST INFORMATION**
Windsor Information
PO Box 3086, Windsor, Berkshire,
SL4 6ZS
www.windsor-information.co.uk

■ **PLACES OF INTEREST**
Ascot Race Course
Ascot, Berkshire, SL5 7JX
Ticket Booking Line: 0870 727 1234;
www.ascot.co.uk
Cliveden
Taplow, Maidenhead, Buckinghamshire
SL6 0JA. Tel: 01628 605069;
www.nationaltrust.org.uk
Eton College
www.etoncollege.com
Hampton Court Palace
www.hrp.org.uk
Henley Royal Regatta
Regatta Headquarters, Henley-on-
Thames, Oxfordshire, RG9 2LY
Tel: 01491 572153; www.hrr.co.uk
Royal Botanic Gardens
Kew, Richmond, Surrey, TW9 3AB
Tel: 020 8332 5655; www.rbgkew.org
Richmond Park
www.royalparks.gov.uk/parks/richmond_
park/
Thames Path
www.thames-path.co.uk
Windsor Castle
Ticket Sales and Information Office,
The Official Residences of The Queen,
London SW1A 1AA. Tel: 020 7766 7304;
www.royalcollection.org.uk

■ **PERFORMING ARTS**
Theatre Royal
32 Thames Street, Windsor, Berkshire,
SL4 1PS. Tel: 09068 323366;
www.theatreroyalwindsor.co.uk/

LONDON
Central
■ **PLACES OF INTEREST**
British Library
96 Euston Road, NW1 2DB
Tel: 020 7412 7332;
www.bl.uk. Tube: King's Cross
British Museum
Great Russell Street, WC1B 3DG
Tel: 020 7323 8000;
www.thebritishmuseum.ac.uk
Tube: Russell Square, Tottenham
Court Road
Buckingham Palace
Buckingham Gate, SW1A 1AA
Tel: 020 7766 7301; www.royal.gov.uk
Tube: Green Park, Victoria
Cabinet War Rooms &
Churchill Museum
King Charles Street, SW1A 2AQ
Tel: 020 7930 6961; www.iwm.org.uk
Tube: Westminster

Covent Garden
Tube: Covent Garden
Houses of Parliament
Parliament Square, SW1A 0AA
Tel: 0870 906 3773; www.parliament.uk
Tube: Westminster
National Gallery
Trafalgar Square, WC2N 5DN
Tel: 020 7747 2885;
www.nationalgallery.org.uk
Tube: Charing Cross
National Portrait Gallery
2 St Martin's Place, WC2H 0HE
Tel: 020 7306 0055; www.npg.org.uk
Tube: Charing Cross, Leicester Square
Somerset House
The Strand, WC2R 0RN
Tel: 020 7845 4600;
www.somerset-house.org.uk
Tube: Holborn
Tate Britain
Millbank, SW1P 4RG. Tel: 020 7887 8000;
www.tate.org.uk
Tube: Pimlico
Westminster Abbey
Parliament Square, SW1P 3PA
Tel: 020 7222 5152;
www.westminster-abbey.org
Tube: St James Park, Westminster

■ **PERFORMING ARTS**
Adelphi Theatre
Strand, WC2E 7NA. Tel: 020 7344 0055;
Tube: Charing Cross
Blockbuster musicals and shows.
Aldwych Theatre
Aldwych, WC2B 4DF. Tel: 020 7379 3367;
www.aldwychtheatre.com
Tube: Covent Garden
Donmar Warehouse
41 Earlham Street, WC2H 9LX
Tel: 0870 060 6624;
www.donmarwarehouse.com
Tube: Covent Garden
Small-scale theatre that often stages
interesting left-field productions.
Odeon Leicester Square
22–24 Leicester Square, WC2H 7LQ
Tel: 0870 505 0007;
www.odeon.co.uk
Tube: Leicester Square
Multiplex cinema often used for
film premieres.
Ronnie Scott's Jazz Club
47 Frith Street, W1D 4HT
Tel: 020 7439 0747;
www.ronniescotts.co.uk
Tube: Leicester Square, Tottenham
Court Road
Jazz gigs that live up to the club's
formidable reputation. Late shows
on Fri and Sat nights.
Royal Opera House
Bow Street, WC2E 9DD
Tel: 020 7304 4000;
www.royaloperahouse.org

Tube: Covent Garden
The main venue for opera and ballet.

St Martin-in-the-Fields Church
Trafalgar Square, WC2N 4JJ
Tel: 020 7766 1100;
www.stmartin-in-the-fields.org
Tube: Charing Cross, Leicester Square.
Free lunchtime (and some evening)
concerts focus on baroque music.

Wigmore Hall
36 Wigmore Street, W1U 2BP
Tel: 020 7935 2141;
www.wigmore-hall.org.uk
Tube: Bond Street
Amazing acoustics in an attractive and
intimate classical music venue.

North, Northwest & City
■ **PLACES OF INTEREST**

Brick Lane
Tube: Aldgate East, Liverpool Street

Christ Church
Fournier Street, Spitalfields,
E1 6QE. Tel: 020 7859 3035;
www.christchurchspitalfields.org
Tube: Aldgate East, Liverpool Street

Hampstead Heath
Hampstead Heath Information Centre,
Parliament Hill Lido, NW5 1QR
Tel: 020 7485 3873 (recorded information).
Tube: Hampstead
Rail: Hampstead Heath

Madame Tussauds
Marylebone Road, NW1 5LR
Tel: 0870 400 3000;
www.madame-tussauds.com
Tube: Baker Street

Regent's Park
Regent's Park, NW1 4RY
Tel: 020 7722 3333;
www.londonzoo.co.uk. Tube: Baker
Street, Marylebone, Regent's Park

St Paul's Cathedral
EC4M 8AD. Tel: 020 7248 2762;
www.stpauls.co.uk. Tube: St Paul's

Sir John Soane's Museum
13 Lincoln's Inn Fields, WC2A 3BP
Tel: 020 7405 2107; www.soane.org
Tube: Holborn

Tower of London
EC3N 4AB. Tel: 0870 756 6060;
www.hrp.org.uk
Tube: Tower Hill

■ **PERFORMING ARTS**

The Barbican
Silk Street, EC2Y 8DS. Tel: 0845 120 7553;
www.barbican.org.uk
Tube: Barbican
Europe's largest arts centre.

Camden Arts Centre
Arkwright Road, NW3 6DG
Tel: 020 7472 5500;
www.camdenartscentre.org
Tube: Finchley Road, Hampstead
Exhibitions and performances.

Canal Café Theatre
Bridge House, Delamere Terrace,
Little Venice, W2 6ND
Tel: 020 7289 6054;
www.canalcafetheatre.com
Tube: Warwick Avenue
Award-winning comedy and theatre.

Electric Ballroom
184 Camden High Street, NW1 8QP
Tel: 020 7485 9006;
www.electricballroom.co.uk
Tube: Camden Town
Camden's rock showcase.

Electric Cinema
191 Portobello Road,
W11 2ED. Tel: 020 7908 9696;
www.the-electric.co.uk
Tube: Notting Hill Gate
Luxuriously refurbished with a
varied programme.

Gate Cinema
87 Notting Hill Gate,
W11 3JZ. Tel: 020 7727 4043;
www.gatecinema.co.uk
Tube: Notting Hill Gate
Leading art-house cinema.

Hackney Empire
291 Mare Street, E8 1EJ
Tel: 020 8985 2424;
www.hackneyempire.co.uk
Train: Hackney Central
This extravagantly decorated Edwardian
theatre is the vital venue for shows,
concerts, musicals and pantomimes in
the East End of London.

Open-air Theatre
Regent's Park, NW1 4NR
Tel: 020 7935 5756;
www.openairtheatre.org
Tube: Baker Street, Marylebone,
Regent's Park
Shakespeare on a summer evening.
Book in advance.

Sadler's Wells
Rosebery Avenue, EC1R 4TN
Tel: 0870 737 7737;
www.sadlerswells.com
Tube: Angel

Southeast
■ **PLACES OF INTEREST**

Canary Wharf
Docklands, E14. Tube: Canary Wharf

HMS Belfast
Morgan's Lane, Tooley Street, SE1 7JH
Tel: 020 7940 6300;
www.hmsbelfast.iwm.org.uk
Tube: London Bridge, Tower Hill

London Dungeon
28–34 Tooley Street, SE1 2SZ
Tel: 020 7403 7221;
www.thedungeons.co.uk
Tube: London Bridge

Royal Observatory & Planetarium
Greenwich Park, SE10 9NF
Tel: 020 8312 6565;

www.rog.nmm.ac.uk
Tube: Cutty Sark DLR, Greenwich DLR

Tower Bridge
SE1 2UP. Tel: 020 7403 3761;
www.towerbridge.org.uk
Tube: Tower Hill

■ **PERFORMING ARTS**

East Wintergarden
43 Bank Street, Canary Wharf, E14 5AB
Tel: 020 7418 2725;
www.eastwintergarden.com
Tube: Canary Wharf
This sparkling venue hosts events
including screenings of classic films.

Up the Creek
302 Creek Road, SE10 9SW
Tel: 020 8858 4581;
www.up-the-creek.com
Train: Greenwich
This comedy club confronts stand-up
comedians, experienced or fresh-faced,
with a raucous crowd.

South Bank & South
■ **PLACES OF INTEREST**

Imperial War Museum
Lambeth Road, SE1 9HZ
Tel: 020 7416 5000; www.iwm.org.uk
Tube: Lambeth North

London Aquarium
County Hall, Westminster Bridge Road,
SE1 7PB. Tel: 020 7967 8000;
www.londonaquarium.co.uk
Tube: Waterloo, Westminster

London Eye
County Hall, Riverside Building,
Westminster Bridge Road, SE1 7PB
Tel: 0870 500 0600;
www.ba-londoneye.com
Tube: Waterloo, Westminster

Shakespeare's Globe
21 New Globe Walk, SE1 9DT
Tel: 020 7902 1500;
www.shakespeares-globe.org
Tube: London Bridge, Southwark

Southwark Cathedral
London Bridge, SE1 9DA
Tel: 020 7367 6700;
www.southwark.anglican.org/cathedral
Tube: London Bridge

Tate Modern
Bankside, SE1 9TG
Tel: 020 7887 8000; www.tate.org.uk
Tube: St Paul's, Southwark

■ **PERFORMING ARTS
& GALLERIES**

Hayward Gallery
Belvedere Road, SE1 8XZ
Tel: 020 7921 0813;
www.hayward.org.uk
Tube: Waterloo
The gallery holds some of the most
exciting exhibitions of contemporary
art in London.

IMAX Cinema
1 Charlie Chaplin Walk, SE1 8XR
Tel: 08700 787 2525;
www.bfi.org.uk/imax
Tube: Waterloo
The cinema is accessed by underground
walkways. The screen is the UK's largest,
at more than 20m high by 26m wide.

National Film Theatre
South Bank, SE1 8XT
Tel: 020 7928 3535;
www.bfi.org.uk/nft
Tube: Embankment, Waterloo
This is the best venue in the city for
art-house movies.

National Theatre
South Bank Centre, SE1 9PX
Tel: 020 7452 3400;
www.nationaltheatre.org.uk
Tube: Embankment, Waterloo,
or Southwark
The National offers fresh takes on old
classics, as well as putting on new plays
and various exhibitions of photography.

Old Vic
Waterloo Road, SE1 8NB
Tel: 0870 060 6628;
www.oldvictheatre.com
Tube: Waterloo
One of London's finest theatres. The Old
Vic's artistic director is American actor
Kevin Spacey.

Purcell Room
South Bank Centre, SE1 8XX
Tel: 0870 380 0400;
www.rfh.org.uk
Tube: Embankment, Waterloo
The Purcell Room is used for solo
performances, chamber music and
contemporary music recitals.

Queen Elizabeth Hall
South Bank Centre, SE1 8XX
Tel: 0870 380 0400;
www.rfh.org.uk
Tube: Embankment, Waterloo
Small orchestral concerts, operas and
piano recitals are the Queen Elizabeth
Hall's mainstay.

Royal Festival Hall
South Bank Centre, SE1 8XX
Tel: 0870 380 0400;
www.rfh.org.uk
Tube: Embankment, Waterloo
This is the permanent base for the
London Philharmonic Orchestra, as
well as the Philharmonia and the
London Sinfonietta. Frequent classical
performances are held in the Festival
Hall's 3,000-seat auditorium.

Young Vic
66 The Cut, SE1 8LZ
Tel: 020 7928 6363;
www.youngvic.org
Tube: Southwark, Waterloo
Leading stage for younger directors
and artists – for audiences of all ages.

West & Southwest
■ PLACES OF INTEREST

Chelsea Physic Garden
66 Royal Hospital Road, SW3 4HS
Tel: 020 7352 5646;
www.chelseaphysicgarden.co.uk
Tube: Sloane Square, Hyde Park
W2 2UH. Tel: 020 7298 2100;
www.royalparks.gov.uk
Tube: Hyde Park Corner, Knightsbridge

Kensington Palace & Gardens
Kensington Gardens, W8 4PX
Tel: 020 7937 9561; www.hrp.org.uk
Tube: Bayswater, High Street Kensington

Natural History Museum
Cromwell Road, SW7 5BD
Tel: 020 7942 5000;
www.nhm.ac.uk
Tube: South Kensington

Science Museum
Exhibition Road, SW7 2DD
Tel: 0870 870 4868;
www.sciencemuseum.org.uk
Tube: South Kensington

Serpentine Gallery
Kensington Gardens, W2 3XA
Tel: 020 7402 6075;
www.serpentinegallery.org
Tube: Lancaster Gate

Victoria & Albert Museum
Cromwell Road, SW7 2RL
Tel: 020 7942 2000;
www.vam.ac.uk
Tube: South Kensington

Wellington Arch
Hyde Park Corner, W1J 7JZ
Tel: 020 7930 2726;
www.english-heritage.org.uk
Tube: Hyde Park Corner

■ PERFORMING ARTS

Bush Hall
310 Uxbridge Road, W12 7LJ
Tel: 020 8222 6955;
www.bushhallmusic.co.uk
Tube: Shepherd's Bush
Classical and acoustic concerts.

Royal Albert Hall
Kensington Gore, SW7 2AP
Tel: 020 7589 3203;
www.royalalberthall.com
Tube: South Kensington
Classical concerts and other events.

Shepherd's Bush Empire
Shepherd's Bush Green,
W12 8TT. Tel: 020 8354 3300;
www.shepherds-bush-empire.co.uk
Tube: Shepherd's Bush

CANTERBURY & KENT DOWNS
■ TOURIST INFORMATION

Canterbury Tourist Information Centre
12/13 Sun Street, Canterbury.
Tel: 01227 378 108;
www.visitcanterbury.co.uk

■ PLACES OF INTEREST

Canterbury Cathedral
www.canterbury-cathedral.org

Hever Castle & Gardens
Hever, Nr Edenbridge, Kent, TN8 7NG
Tel: 01732865224;
www.hever-castle.co.uk

Ightham Mote
Mote Road, Ivy Hatch, Sevenoaks, Kent
TN15 0NT. Tel: 01732 810378
www.nationaltrust.org.uk

■ PERFORMING ARTS

Gulbenkian Theatre
University Campus, University of Kent,
Canterbury, Kent, CT2 7NB
Tel: 01227 769075;
www.ukc.ac.uk/gulbenkian/

Marlowe Theatre
The Friars, Canterbury, Kent, CT1 2AS
Tel: 01227 787787;
www.marlowetheatre.com

OXFORD & CHILTERNS
■ TOURIST INFORMATION

Oxford Information Centre
15-16 Broad Street, Oxford, OX1 3AS
Tel: 01865 726871;
www.oxford.gov.uk

Wendover Community & Tourist Information Office
The Clock Tower, High Street,
Wendover, Buckinghamshire
HP22 6DU. Tel: 01296 696759;
www.chilternweb.co.uk

■ PLACES OF INTEREST

Ashmolean Museum
Beaumont Street, Oxford
www.ashmolean.org

Blenheim Palace
Woodstock, Oxfordshire, OX20 1PX
Tel: 01993 811091, (08700 60 20 80,
24 hour recorded information service);
www.blenheimpalace.com

Bodleian Library
Broad Street, Oxford, OX1 3BG
Tel: 01865 277180; www.bodley.ox.ac.uk

Pitts River Museum
South Parks Road, Oxford
Tel: 01865 270927; www.prm.ox.ac.uk

■ PERFORMING ARTS

New Theatre (Apollo Theatre)
George Street, Oxford, OX1 2AG
Tel: 0870 606 3500

Playhouse Theatre
8-12 Beaumont Street, Oxford
OX1 2LW
Tel: 01865 305305;
www.oxfordplayhouse.co.uk

Sheldonian Theatre
University of Oxford, Sheldonian
Theatre, Broad Street, Oxford
OX1 3AZ. Tel: 01865 277299;
www.sheldon.ox.ac.uk

PUBS
NEW FOREST

The East End Arms
Main Road, East End, near Lymington
SO41 5SY. Tel: 01590 626223;
www.eastendarms.co.uk
A traditional and comfortable New Forest pub serving brasserie-style food in the lounge bar, with options on the menu such as Toulouse sausages and toasted goats' cheese baguettes. However, no food is served on Monday, or Sunday evening, or during early March and throughout October.

The Filly Inn
Lymington Road, Setley, Brockenhurst
SO42 7UF. Tel: 01590 623449;
www.fillyinn.co.uk
The bar snacks at this cosy, traditional pub include baguettes and jacket potatoes, and there is a wider menu offering home-baked pies and perhaps roast ribs in barbecue sauce. There is also an extensive Hindi vegetarian menu, and cream teas are offered in summer. Children are welcome and dogs are permitted too.

The Master Builders House Hotel
Bucklers Hard SO42 7XB
Tel: 01590 616297;
www.themasterbuilders.co.uk
Large grassy areas in front of the pub run gently down to the Beaulieu River, making it a popular spot, especially on summer days. Fish pie and beef bourguignon may appear on the menu, with a good range of light snacks. Beers include Greene King IPA.

ISLE OF WIGHT
The Folly
Folly Lane, Cowes
Tel: 01983 297171
Easy access by both land and water makes this unusual Cowes pub a very popular venue in summer. It was constructed in part from the timbers out of the hull of an old barge, and makes good use of its nautical theme, offering a blackboard menu that includes spicy sausage 'Crewpot' casserole, or maybe fresh fish.

The Red Lion
Church Place, Freshwater
Tel: 01983 754925
The pub has a pleasant setting on the River Yar. Everything here is freshly made. Favourites might include gammon with parsley sauce, smoked haddock pâté, and apple pie and custard. The garden includes a herb garden – the perfect place to sup a pint of local Goddards ale – and dogs are also permitted here.

WINCHESTER & NORTH DOWNS
The Bell Hotel
12 West Street, New Alresford
SO24 9AT. Tel: 01962 732429;
www.bellalresford.com
An elegant revamp of an old inn with pine tables and a carpeted bar area. Try the baguettes, bar food or the watercress specialities, washed down with a local brew such as Itchen's Watercress Line.

Hotel du Vin
Southgate Street, Winchester SO23 9EF
Tel: 01962 841414; www.hotelduvin.com
The bistro of this Georgian hotel in the city centre makes an excellent if pricey stop for lunch or coffee. There's a stylish champagne bar and a pretty walled courtyard. Food has a French leaning, and dishes might include local trout.

The Wykeham Arms
75 Kingsgate Street, Winchester
SO23 9PE. Tel: 01962 853834
The 'Wyk', in an old back street near to Winchester College, is a local institution. It is furnished in part with old desks and ephemera from the school. The food is excellent, ranging from the Wyk cottage pie, to grilled sea bass with new potatoes. There is a choice of around 20 wines by the glass, and 60 more by the bottle.

SURREY HEATHS
The Bat & Ball Freehouse
15 Bat & Ball Lane, Boundstone
GU10 4SA. Tel: 01252 794564
Nestling at the bottom of the Bourne Valley, this 150-year-old inn is worth making the effort to find. The decor mixes old and new, with oak beams and terracotta floor tiles creating a rustic look. The home-made desserts are especially good here.

Red Lion
Shamley Green, Guildford GU5 0UB
Tel: 01483 892202
Situated opposite the village cricket green, this attractive old pub is the perfect place to sit in the pretty gardens and have a relaxing drink whilst listening to the crack of leather on willow on a summer afternoon.

SOUTH DOWNS
Black Horse
High Street, Amberley BN18 9NL
Tel: 01798 831552
A convivial place for a drink, lunch or dinner, with a good choice of vegetarian options, this 17th-century tavern has lovely open fires and original flagstones, and a set of sheep bells given to the landlord by the last local shepherd.

The Bull
Ditchling BN6 8TA. Tel: 01273 843147
This inn in the centre of the village was revamped a few years ago, but has kept its character-laden bar much the same and there's usually a large fire blazing. The nicely mellow side rooms (used mainly by diners, though you can eat the tasty food in the bar, too) are decorated with contemporary art. It's within striking distance of Ditchling Beacon and the view from the garden might inspire you to venture up there.

SOUTH COAST
Basketmakers Arms
12 Gloucester Road, Brighton BN1 4AD
Tel: 01273 689006
A wide array of malt whiskies, several real ales and inexpensive bar food are hallmarks of this friendly back-street pub. The two bare-boarded rooms harbour a fascinating stash of old tins, advertisements, posters and cigarette cards. Not far from the Theatre Royal, this place is open all day.

The Cowherds
The Common, Southampton SO15 7NN
Tel: 023 8051 6921
On the A33, at the heart of Southampton Common, this pub was once the haunt of cattle drovers on their way to London. Now it's the perfect spot for lunch or dinner – try the ham hock with mustard sauce, or perhaps the pork, apple and cider sausages with Cheddar mash. There's a patio outside and inside it's cosy with open fires, oak beams and wood panelling.

The Greys
105 Southover Street, Brighton
BN2 9UA. Tel: 01273 680734;
www.greyspub.com
The bar at this blue-painted street-corner pub is nicely straightforward, with basic furnishings, and a couple of real ales as well as an impressive Belgian beer selection. The shortish menu features very well-presented food, partly French in style, and served in generous quantities. Live music one or two days a week; children are not allowed inside.

The Still & West
2 Bath Square, Old Portsmouth
PO1 2JL. Tel: 023 9282 1567
At the top of Broad Street, and close to HMS *Victory*, this nautically themed 1504 pub has great views over the harbour and further out to the Isle of Wight. As you might expect, there's a good range of fish on the menu, including a trademark grill of fresh fish and mussels, and a wonderful seafood paella.

WINDSOR & THAMES
The Thatched Tavern
Cheapside Road SL5 7QG
Tel: 01344 623043
Just over a mile from the famous racecourse, this attractive 17th-century building features oak beams, flagstone floors and low ceilings. Traditional fare as well as international cuisine is offered here, and there is a lovely garden.

LONDON
The Bleeding Heart Tavern
19 Greville Street EC1N 8SQ
Tel: 0207 2428238
There's been a tavern here since 1746, and, although the promise of 'drunk for a penny, dead drunk for twopence' no longer holds true, plenty of old London spirit has been maintained in this scrubbed-up, contemporary version. Inside is a happy blend of smart and rustic, glass and stone decor that works really well. The menu is a delight for meat-lovers but there are some vegetarian options. The wine list is impressive, as is the choice of real ales.

The Jerusalem Tavern
55 Britton Street Clerkenwell
EC1M 5NA. Tel: 020 7490 4281
Named after the Priory of St John of Jerusalem, this historic tavern has been in four different locations since it was established in the 14th century. Now situated in one of London's most vibrant 'rediscovered' corners, the pub features rustic wooden tables, welcoming open fires and cosy nooks. Familiar pub fare and bottled beers from St Peter's Brewery complete the experience.

The Drapers Arms
44 Barnsbury Street N1 1ER
Tel: 020 7619 0348
Smart Islington gastro-pub offering one menu throughout. This place is a haunt of media types who prefer the upstairs dining room so if you want to so some celebrity spotting, you know where to book. Downstairs there are some lovely open fires and varnished wooden floors. The menu offers some interesting main courses and old favourites for dessert.

The Anchor & Hope
36 The Cut SE1 8LP. Tel: 020 7928 9898
Considering it is an award-winning gastro-pub, the Anchor & Hope is a remarkably down-to-earth place. The friendly atmosphere here attracts families and people with dogs are also made welcome. Quality British produce is used in the refreshingly unfussy menu and your meal could be complemented by a glass of good wine or a pint of real ale.

The Fire Station
150 Waterloo Road SE1 8SB
Tel: 020 7633 9161
Close to Waterloo Station and handy for the Old Vic Theatre and the Imperial War Museum, this remarkable conversion of an Edwardian fire station retains many of the building's original features. There is an imaginative menu and a set-price Sunday lunch is available.

North Pole Bar & Restaurant
131 Greenwich High Road, Greenwich
SE10 8JA. Tel: 020 8853 3020
This place gives you three choices in one building – an evening of piano playing in the Piano Restaurant, a cocktail bar, and a nightclub in the basement. Bar meals and European restaurant fare is available along with a good selection of wines and draught lagers. If you like live music, the entertainment here includes a regular list of tribute acts.

The Cross Keys
1 Lawrence Street, Chelsea SW3 5NB
Tel: 020 7349 9111
A Chelsea pub that has been a favourite haunt of the rich and famous for the past 40 years. Food is mainly modern European in style with more traditional dishes available on Sunday. The interior is quite quirky with a range of modern art on show on the first-floor gallery.

The Belle Vue
1 Clapham Common, Southside
SW4 7AA. Tel: 0207 498 9473
This is a great place to stop and relax, right opposite the green acres of Clapham Common. The lunch and dinner menus both feature fish and shellfish dishes, and the place is a favourite with locals for its Sunday lunches.

Swag & Tails
10/11 Fairholt Street SW7 1EG
Tel: 020 7584 6926;
www.swagandtails.com
A lovely Victorian pub, just a 5-minute walk from the hustle and bustle of busy Knightsbridge shopping streets. Tucked away down a little back street, this well-kept venue offers a sanctuary of stripped pine furniture, open fires and good wine. Meals are of a high standard with a Mediterranean bias.

The Freemasons
2 Northside, Wandsworth Common
SW18 2SS. Tel: 020 7326 8580
Although the interior is modern, the proprietors have managed to create the feel of a real local pub in the heart of Wandsworth – a local long sought after by the residents of the area.

The Seven Stars
53 Carey Street WC2A 2JB
Tel: 020 7242 8521
Built in 1602, the Seven Stars pub is one of the oldest ale houses in London. It is one of the few buildings that survived the Great Fire of London while many other buildings around it perished. Popular with the legal fraternity and journalist types because of its close proximity to the Inns of Court, the cosy little pub has a tiny Elizabethan staircase and is furnished in a traditional style. Good quality fare is offered here accompanied by a range of real ales.

CANTERBURY & KENT DOWNS
The Chapter Arms
New Town Street, Chartham Hatch
CT4 7LT. Tel: 01227 732536
The Chapter Arms is a pretty, flower-bedecked free house on the Pilgrim's Way, with a lovely leafy garden with fish ponds. The property was once three cottages owned by Canterbury Cathedral's Dean and Chapter – hence the name. Locally caught fresh fish major on the main menu and a choice of light snacks is also available.

The Dove Inn
Plum Pudding Lane, Dargate ME13 9HB
Tel: 01227 751360
Tucked away down a pleasant little lane, The Dove Inn is a picture-postcard village pub, complete with roses round the door outside and simple wooden floors and tables on the inside. The menu has some inspired dishes with a host of inventive main courses that features locally caught game. Bar meals are also served and there is a good range of wines.

OXFORD & CHILTERNS
The Anchor
2 Hayfield Road, Walton Manor
Tel: 01865 510282
This is a friendly pub with a relaxed atmosphere. The menu carries a good range of meals including all the favourites, such as fish and chips or sausage and mash. The pub was once patronised by local resident and author, T E Lawrence.

Turf Tavern
4 Bath Place, off Holywell Street, Oxford
OX1 3SU. Tel: 01865 243838
In the heart of Oxford, among the city's winding streets and little alleyways, the Turf Tavern is nestled next to the colleges. The sheltered courtyards provide a quiet haven for a drink in the summertime. You can choose from a selection of real ales and typical pub fare is offered on the menu.

TEA ROOMS
NEW FOREST

The Buttery
19–20 High Street, Lymington
SO41 9AD. Tel: 01590 672870;
www.thebuttery.org
A well-established and deservedly popular restaurant and tea room, the Buttery serves speciality coffees and teas, sumptuous clotted cream teas, and a great selection of tasty cakes – all hand-made on the premises. You can also get light lunches here, or if you are particularly hungry after walking in the Forest, even a full English breakfast.

The Buttery at the Brock & Bruin
25 Brookley Road, Brockenhurst
SO42 7RB. Tel: 01590 622958
Delicious homemade cakes and naughty-but-nice cream teas are top treats at this restaurant and tea room. Light lunches are also served daily, and breakfast too – handy if you're camping.

Montagu Arms Hotel
Palace Lane, Beaulieu, SO42 7ZL
Tel: 01590 612324;
www.montaguarmshotel.co.uk
An hospitable, 16th-century inn nestling in the pretty hamlet of Beaulieu, the Montagu Arms offers finger sandwiches, loaf cakes, scones, cream tea fancies, and shortbread. In season, you can enjoy locally grown strawberries served with your afternoon tea.

Tasty Pastries Bakery and Tea Room
16A High Street, Lyndhurst SO43 7BD
Tel: 023 8028 3448
The perfect place to pause for tea and cakes, or perhaps to buy freshly baked pasties, filled baguettes and sandwiches for a picnic.

ISLE OF WIGHT

God's Providence House
12 St Thomas Square, Newport
Tel: 01983 522085
This is the spot where, it is claimed, the Great Plague of the 1560s came to a halt – hence the name. Today it's a traditional tea room, serving coffee, teas and lunches.

Pearly Boise Ice Cream Parlour
57 High Street, Shanklin
Tel: 01983 864611
This wonderful emporium offers home-made ice cream in 27 flavours, including apple crumble, white chocolate and orange Cointreau. There are also sorbets to whet your appetite, and traditional milkshakes and sundaes. And for a retro treat, enjoy a knickerbocker glory! Coffee and pastries are also available.

Vineyard Café
Adgestone Vineyard, Upper Adgestone Road, Brading PO36 0ES
Tel: 01983 402503;
www.adgestonevineyard.co.uk
The oldest vineyard in Britain serves some of the best cream teas on the Isle of Wight, with freshly baked scones, and home-made cakes. Morning coffee and light lunches – including wine – are also available, and check ahead for special musical evenings.

WINCHESTER & NORTH DOWNS

Caracoli
15 Broad Street, Alresford
SO24 9AR. Tel: 01962 738730
With its fresh, modern décor and courtyard garden, this coffee shop and food store is a chic place for a light bite. Ingredients are carefully chosen: try their watercress scones. There's also an array of preserves, teas, coffees, chutneys and wines for sale.

Cassandra's Cup
Winchester Road, Chawton GU34 1SD
Tel: 01420 83144
On the corner of the street, opposite Jane Austen's house, and named after her sister, Cassandra's Cup has a cheerful interior with floral plates displayed on a dresser. Light lunches and tea and cakes are on offer.

Gilbert White's Tea Parlour
The Wakes, High Street, Selborne
GU34 3JH. Tel: 01420 511275;
www.gilbertwhiteshouse.org.uk
This tea room overlooking the busy village street is inside the house of the naturalist Gilbert White. Much of the food served here is made from 18th-century recipes. Try savoury homity pie or seed cake, accompanied by a good range of speciality teas.

Tiffin Tea Rooms
50 West Street, Alresford SO24 9AU
Tel: 01962 734394
This friendly, traditional tea room with its blue-and-white striped awning serves home-made cakes, cream teas and speciality teas and coffees.

The Wessex Hotel
Paternoster Row, Winchester
SO23 9LQ. Tel: 0870 400 8126;
www.wessexhotel.co.uk
From the relaxed lounge of this central hotel you look out on to Winchester Cathedral. They serve sumptuous traditional full afternoon teas, with home-made scones, jam, clotted cream, sandwiches and cakes.

SURREY HEATHS

Box Hill National Trust Tea Room
The Old Fort, Box Hill Road, Box Hill
Tadworth, Surrey KT20 7LB
Telephone: 01306 885502
Tea and cakes are served throughout the day at this well-run National Trust tea room where local produce and home-made goods are always on the menu.

SOUTH DOWNS

Belindas Tea Room
13 Tarrant Street, Arundel BN18 9DG
Tel: 01903 882977
A white-painted cottage in Tarrant Street. Go down the steps to an old English interior, with copper and brassware on the walls. Belindas serves cream teas, sandwiches and jacket potatoes, with a tempting list of traditional desserts.

Dolly's Pantry
West Street, Ditchling. Tel: 01273 842708
Dolly's is like a cake shop with an attached warren of low-ceilinged old rooms in traditional tea shop style. Alongside cream teas and coffees, Dolly's serves delicious all-day breakfasts, ploughman's and lunches such as quiche and salad. You can also have a glass of wine or beer with your meal.

Tiffins of Petworth
1 Leppards, High Street, Petworth
GU28 0AU. Tel: 01798 344560;
www.tiffinsofpetworth.co.uk
Tea rooms and restaurant with pastel-painted wooden tables and chairs, and words of wisdom on the walls. Tiffins serves breakfasts and lunches with the likes of lasagne and fisherman's pie alongside teas, coffees and home-made cakes. It also displays and sells a whole menagerie of ceramic and porcelain animals and other gifts.

SOUTH COAST

Cathedral Cloisters Café
Chichester Cathedral, Chichester
PO19 1PX. Tel: 01243 782595
Walk into the cathedral cloisters and you'll find this splendid self-service café. Airy and modern in style, it offers a range of afternoon teas and daily specials, as well as Sunday lunch.

Mock Turtle
4 Pool Valley, Brighton BN1 1NJ
Tel: 01273 327380
Devotees of cream teas have been tucking in here since 1972. All the food is home made, with tempting gateaux and meringues, and you can buy a pot of their jam to take home. Near The Lanes and the Royal Pavilion, and next to the National Express bus terminus.

Tower Café Bar
Spinnaker Tower, Gunwharf Quays
Portsmouth PO1 3TT. Tel: 02392 857520;
www.spinnakertower.co.uk
Take your morning coffee or afternoon tea in style (not at the top!) in Portsmouth's newest venue. Sandwiches and cakes give way to wine and beer in the evenings, as you sit and watch the sun go down over the harbour.

LONDON

The Ritz
150 Piccadilly, London W1J 9BR
Tel: 020 7493 8181;
www.theritzlondon.com
Part of the London experience, tea at the Ritz is an occasion to savour – and to dress for. Jeans are not welcome here. From the silver teapots to the finely cut sandwiches and delicate cakes and pastries, every detail has been considered. If tea is not your preferred beverage then maybe a glass of champagne will suffice. Make sure you reserve well in advance.

The Dorchester
Park Lane, London W1A 2HJ
Tel: 020 7629 8888;
www.dorchesterhotel.com
The Dorchester has its own blend of tea that is offered alongside others like China Oolong. Afternoon tea here is a relaxing affair, served by efficient staff and entertained by the tinkling of piano music. Beautifully laid tables are set with bone china groaning with sumptuous cakes and delicate sandwiches.

CANTERBURY & KENT DOWNS

The Moat Tea Rooms
67 Burgate, Canterbury CT1 2HJ
Tel: 01227 784514
These are lovely tea rooms just a short walk away from the centre of the city. In the 16th-century building you'll find rich, dark furniture and the fireplaces make it especially cosy in the winter. For chocolate lovers there is a delicious chocolate cake or you could try the Champagne cream tea.

OXFORD & CHILTERNS

Old Parsonage Hotel
1 Banbury Road, Oxford OX2 6NN
Tel: 01865 310210;
www.oldparsonage-hotel.co.uk
You can take tea in the lovely hotel restaurant or out on the terrace when the weather is good. Different blends of tea are available including the hotel's own blend, Old Parsonage Blend, which is served with a range of sandwiches and scones and crumpets.

Central England

Central England

The oft-called 'heart of England' is made up of two distinct landscapes – one of open fens and flatlands, ribbons of waterways and a coastline buffeted by the North Sea, the other rich with dramatic peaks and deep verdant gorges, and villages of stone cottages built using the power of its rivers.

History as well as nature has helped to sculpt these disparate areas, from the great battles of the Roundheads and the Royalists in the English Civil War, to the life-changing industrial processes and inventions that resulted from the Industrial Revolution.

Not just the cradle of industry, middle England was also the birthplace of its most famous bard, William Shakespeare, born in Stratford-upon-Avon. Other towns, such as the university town and educational mecca, Cambridge, fall within the fold of central England, and many of the towns themselves are blessed with fine architecture. Central England stretches to industrious Staffordshire, which reaches into the Peak District, and to the edge of England where Shropshire nudges into Wales. This really is a beautiful area, separately or as the sum of its parts.

Suffolk Coast

CLOCKWISE FROM TOP: RIVER BLYTH, BLYTHBURGH; ALDEBURGH MOOT HALL; LOBSTERS, ALDEBURGH

ALDEBURGH MAP REF 405 L6

People with an interest in British music will not need to be told about Aldeburgh; the annual Festival of Music and Arts, founded in 1948 by composer Benjamin Britten, singer Peter Pears and librettist Eric Crozier holds world renown, with many of the recitals given in Aldeburgh itself. Others are performed at the nearby Snape Maltings, a site reincarnated from disused malt houses into a concert venue of international acclaim that hosts a year-round programme of concerts.

Aldeburgh has always had an association with fishing and boat-building, one that continues to this day but in a time-honoured fashion, for fishermen still haul their boats onto the shingle beach and sell their catches daily from nearby huts. In fact, the seafront is remarkably little changed since Victorian times, a feature that gives Aldeburgh an infectious charm. For many it is this characteristic that is the attraction.

But things have changed: the early 16th-century Moot Hall, which houses an interesting museum, stands on the sea front, but was once at the centre of the town, such has been the serious amount of coastal erosion. And in the lovely 15th-century church there is a bust of local-born poet George Crabbe, although his birthplace at Slaughden has long been lost to the sea along with the remains of the village, originally built here by the Romans. The Suffolk-born scholar Edward Fitzgerald, translator of Omar Khayyám's works, was particularly taken with Alderburgh, while the English novelist Wilkie Collins holidayed here.

On the shingle bank at Slaughden stands England's most northerly Martello tower, one of 103 towers constructed along the south coast between 1805 and 1812 to defend against invasion by Napoleon.

BLYTHBURGH MAP REF 405 L6

Just inland from the Suffolk Heritage Coast, the Anglo-Saxon village of Blythburgh is set in an Area of Outstanding Natural Beauty and graced with a tidal river, marshes, heathland, small woodlands, pastures and arable fields. The tidal section of the River Blyth flows just to the north of the village reaching the sea at Southwold. Over the years the sea-walls have been breached and the land not reclaimed, creating a tidal lagoon, Blythburgh Water, which is immensely popular with coastal birdlife as a safe habitat.

In August 1577, a bolt of lightning hit and brought down the 15th-century church steeple, and the Devil was blamed. On the same day, Black Shuck, the legendary devil dog of the marshes is said to have run through the church, killing two parishioners. The damage to the roof meant that for a time congregations had to worship beneath umbrellas. The church is sometimes referred to by locals as the 'Cathedral of the Marshes', lending credence to the notion that Blythburgh was once much larger than today, but this is not so. Blythburgh has always been small, although it once had an important medieval priory, and attracted enough wealthy piety sufficient at least to build such a large church.

DEDHAM MAP REF 405 K7

The Dedham Vale and Stour Valley embraces one of England's most cherished landscapes, one of dignified villages, rolling farmland, rivers, meadows and ancient woodlands; it is what might be thought of as quintessential English lowland landscape. The Area of Outstanding Natural Beauty has a rich history, and has been an inspiration for many writers and artists, not least John Constable who immortalised the vale and the village church tower in his paintings more than 200 years ago. Indeed, this is very much 'Constable Country'. John Constable, born nearby in East Bergholt, attended the local school in Dedham, and Flatford Mill and Willy Lott's House on the River Stour are recognisable as featuring in many of Constable's paintings.

Pre-dating the Domesday Book, Dedham has prospered for around 1,000 years and in the 14th century was a major wool producer, attracting a colony of Flemish cloth workers seeking refuge from the turmoil on the Continent. As elsewhere, the town's fortunes varied with the wool trade, but revived in the 16th century with the manufacture of new high quality cloths. The wealth created by the wool trade financed the construction of the village church in 1492.

Because much of East Anglia's traditional grassland has been drained and ploughed, the hedgerows and wildflower meadows that remain are among some of England's most vulnerable pastoral landscapes, one enhanced by narrow lanes and characteristic timber-framed and thatched houses.

DUNWICH MAP REF 405 L6

A visit to the coastal village of Dunwich, surrounded by forest and marshland, serves only to demonstrate the destructive force of the sea. In the 7th century, Dunwich was a prosperous city, shipyard and fishing centre, where the first bishop of East Anglia established a Cathedral see, in so doing making Dunwich the capital of this part of England. At that time the coastline was a mile (1.6km) further east. Records from the 13th- and early 14th-century give an indication of the size of Dunwich with a shipping list comprising 11 warships, 36 trading ships and some 24 fishing smacks.

It was in the Middle Ages that the sea began to make significant encroachments into Dunwich, effectively destroying what was once a great port and in the process washing away nine medieval churches and two monasteries. In Dunwich Museum there is a small model showing how the town looked in the 12th century.

In spite of so much of Dunwich being missing, as it were, this remains a lovely place to visit, and the adjacent Dunwich Heath is popular with walkers. Local

VISIT
FLATFORD MILL

Flatford Mill flanks the River Stour in close proximity to the Suffolk-Essex border. The buildings here, particularly the Mill and Willy Lott's House, are instantly recognisable since they feature in numerous paintings by John Constable. Surrounded by lush lowland landscapes, wildlife habitats and places of historic interest, Flatford Mill is a graceful and moving place to visit, although there is no public access to the Mill or to the other buildings in the village. But the National Trust offers guided walks to the sites that Constable painted. There is a tiny 16th-century thatched cottage beside the river, also owned by the National Trust, which houses a permanent exhibition of Constable's work, including several showing the 'Bridge Cottage' and, of course, the famous Hay Wain (now in the National Gallery in London).

FLATFORD MILL

DUNWICH

legend has it that on a calm night the long-lost church bells can still be heard tolling deep beneath the waves. It's a starry-eyed story. Believe it or not; but listen, just in case.

FELIXSTOWE MAP REF 405 K7

In the days of press gangs, Felixstowe was not a place to drop your guard; if you did so you risked spending the next few months or years sailing the high seas. Before its development as a container port, Felixstowe was a traditional and truly genteel Edwardian seaside resort, the so-called 'Garden Resort of the East Coast'. Today, in spite of 'containerism', the town is still attractive; it has a long sand and shingle beach, and extensive and beautiful gardens line the promenade; some, like those by the Spa Pavilion and Town Hall, have been listed on the English Heritage Register of Parks and Gardens of National Importance.

A village has stood on the site since before the Norman Conquest, and eventually became a lynchpin in England's

defences. It's vital position was proved when, in 1667, Dutch soldiers landed and failed to capture Landguard Fort.

The town became a major port in 1886. In addition to shipping, tourism increased, and during the late Victorian era it became a fashionable resort, a trend initiated by the opening of Felixstowe railway station, and a visit by the German royal family.

The Landguard Peninsula is a nature reserve, with an historic fort and the Felixstowe Museum as well as a passenger ferry linking Felixstowe with Shotley and Harwich.

FRAMLINGHAM MAP REF 405 K6

Framlingham, with its attractive houses and shops all gathered around the triangular Market Hill, is a place steeped in history. The castle, built by the Earl of Norfolk, Roger Bigod, has an 800-year-old history. It was here, at Framlingham Castle, in 1553, that Mary Tudor gathered her supporters around her as she waited anxiously to learn whether she or Lady Jane Grey had been declared Queen.

The castle, one of the most important and beautiful medieval castles, is today in the care of English Heritage, and has one of the earliest curtain walls in England. Unlike other castles, it is possible to walk the full length of the 12th-century battlements. Little remains of the interior, other than a 17th-century poorhouse and medieval stone heads.

In a country surfeited with glorious church architecture, the parish church of St Michael in Framlingham is especially pleasing. The roof is particularly glorious with intricate fan tracery which conceals superb hammer beams. There is also a splendid collection of 16th-century tombs, belonging to members of the Howard family from the time when they owned the castle. The town also has numerous quaint buildings dating from the 17th, 18th and 19th centuries. You will find many of the best examples on Market Hill.

Framlingham, surrounded by country lanes that are ideal for walking and cycling, is an excellent base from which to explore an unspoiled part of Suffolk.

HADLEIGH MAP REF 405 K7

Hadleigh is a handsome market town at the very centre of the undulating Suffolk countryside. At the heart of Hadleigh, once a royal town for the 9th-century Danish King Guthrum, is a rich and important architectural legacy dating from Saxon times. There are not many towns of such character left in England today, and its medieval charm and architectural styles ranging from timber-framed to Georgian (with some fine examples of the ornamental plasterwork known as pargeting) are a great attraction for tourists, bolstered by a thriving business and community spirit. Once renowned for its woollen cloth, Hadleigh is an agreeable blend of old and new; 600 years ago Hadleigh was among the most important wool and market towns in England; by the 16th century only Ipswich and Bury St Edmunds were more prosperous. The elegant High Street is lined with those elegant timber-framed houses as well as a wide range of interesting shops, pubs and restaurants.

SUFFOLK COAST

ORFORD MAP REF 405 L7

To the south of Aldeburgh the isolated castle town of Orford has considerable charm. Its 800-year-old castle is open to the public, and the splendid church of St Bartholomew has hosted many performances over the years of works by Benjamin Britten, including *Noye's Fludde* in 1958 and *Curlew River* in 1964. At the time of the Domesday Book, Orford was little more than a hamlet. Less than 100 years later it had been transformed by Henry II into a busy port with a magnificent castle both to guard it and defend against unruly barons. Before the castle was built the area around Orford was dominated by the Bigod family from their castle at Framlingham. Hugh Bigod was the Earl of Norfolk and one of a group of dissenting barons in the reigns of Stephen and Henry II. Work began on the castle in 1165 and Henry also drained the marshes here making Orford a sheltered port.

When completed, Orford Castle consisted of a curtain wall with flanking towers, and a twin-towered gatehouse surrounding a polygonal keep. Alas, the curtain wall, gatehouse and towers have all decayed and nothing of them survives today. Standing alone and intact is the Great Tower of the original royal castle. It is a remarkable construction and resembles no other in Britain or Ireland, with its basic plan of a circular tower incorporating three great turrets.

Today, the town is sheltered from the penetrating North Sea by the great shingle bank of Orford Ness, the largest vegetated shingle spit in Europe. Not surprisingly, Orford Ness, wild, rugged and remote, is an important nature reserve containing, as it does, a variety of habitats including shingle, brackish lagoons, salt marsh, mud flats and grazing marsh. It provides an important habitat for breeding and passage birds as well as for delicate and unusual shingle flora, including a large number of nationally rare species.

SAXMUNDHAM MAP REF 405 L6

With such a delightful name the market town of Saxmundham is irresistible. It was once an important communication centre between London and Great Yarmouth, and developed with the coming of the railways in the 19th century. The better communication brought industry and attracted a prolonged period of Victorian building, from rows of small cottages to grand 19th-century statements of wealth that belie the much older roots of this ancient community. Saxmundham, or 'Sax', as it is known locally, is an historic market town at the centre of the unspoilt Suffolk Heritage Coast.

Not far from Saxmundham is Minsmere, one of the Royal Society for the Protection of Birds' most famous nature reserves, as it attracts thousands of varieties of migrant and wading birds.

For 'birders' Minsmere is a corner of heaven; is has been a reserve for over 50 years and pioneered the use of observation hides and management of wetland areas.

SUTTON HOO MAP REF 405 K7

A short distance from the town of Woodbridge, at Sutton Hoo, is the Anglo-Saxon royal burial site of King Raedwald where vast treasure was discovered in a huge ship grave. Sutton Hoo is arguably one of the most vital archaeological sites in Britain, looked on by many as the first chapter of English history. Lying on a low spur of land above the River Deben, one of several large mounds were excavated in 1939 to reveal a warrior's helmet, shield and a collection of gold ornaments in the remains of a burial chamber of a 90-foot (27m) ship. The significance of this important discovery is incalculable.

When, in the early 5th century, the Romans withdrew from Britain, it left the way open for people from Denmark, Germany and the lower Rhine to settle here, displacing and even enslaving the remnant Celtic and Roman people. These early settlers were the Anglo-Saxons, and their language formed the basis of the modern English spoken today. Two hundred years later, new kingdoms were formed: Suffolk and Norfolk becoming the Kingdom of the East Angles, and thereby setting the foundations of England as a country.

Anglo-Saxon custom decreed that important people were buried beneath mounds, often along with precious goods as a sign of their wealth and importance. The burial of an entire ship is unique to East Anglia and Scandinavia, and the burial mound at Sutton Hoo was a prominent and fitting memorial to a powerful leader.

The National Trust exhibition hall at Sutton Hoo houses a full-size reconstruction of the buried chamber and relates the history of how its treasures lay undisturbed for over 1,300 years. The burial mounds form part of a much larger estate, across which there are lovely walks with estuary views, across heathland and along woodland trails.

SOUTHWOLD MAP REF 405 L6

Once a Saxon port, the coastal town of Southwold has an ancient pedigree and is full of interest both for the casual visitor and for historians. The town became a prominent harbour in medieval times, but like so many towns on the east coast, faced the problem of silting, which brought about a decline in the importance of the harbour. In Victorian times it enjoyed a revival of fortunes as an understated seaside resort with none of the 'Kiss-me-quick' silliness of places like Great Yarmouth or Sheringham.

Surrounded by creeks, reed beds and marshes, and with the Blyth Estuary to the south, Southwold is a virtual island, and reminiscent of a typical seaside resort of the 1920s and 30s. It is an elegant town with some outstanding Georgian buildings dominated by a 100ft (30m) lighthouse, built in 1890. Southwold's pier was the first to be built in England since the 1950s and this, along with a cliff-top promenade above the beach dotted with brightly coloured beach huts, are all redolent of a bygone age. Elsewhere, pink- and blue-washed cottages and Georgian town houses border a number of greens intentionally left undeveloped to serve as firebreaks following a disastrous fire in 1659. William Denny's Buckingham House in the High Street is one of the most elegant and interesting; externally it seems to be a classic Georgian town house, but inside it reveals its 16th-century beginnings. Built by a wealthy Tudor merchant, the cellar is now a coffee house, and the ground and first floor an art gallery.

Southwold was granted a market charter in 1489, when it was a prosperous port with a good herring industry. But it was the herring trade that was partly instrumental in starting three vicious naval battles: the first in 1653 off Orfordness;

the second in 1664 just south-east of Lowestoft; and the Battle of Solebay in 1672, which was to be the first battle of the Third Anglo-Dutch War.

Southwold's maritime past, local archaeology, geology and natural history, as well as the history of the Southwold railway, are all portrayed in the museum in Victoria Street, set in a Dutch-style cottage. Incredibly, in 1839 there were 192 boats in Southwold catching herrings, sprats, smelts and shrimps as well as bigger fish for the London market.

For the literati, each November Southwold stages a literature festival, which has steadily become a popular attraction for artists and writers over the years. Like similar festivals elsewhere in Britain, that at Southwold makes an ideal escape from the bustle of the daily round, a time to engage with books and ideas in a most agreeable setting.

THORPENESS MAP REF 405 L6

The village was originally a small fishing hamlet in the late 19th century, with folklore stories of its role as a route for smugglers into East Anglia. Today,

Thorpeness is an agreeably bizarre and whimsical place, and shares an unspoilt beach with neighbouring Aldeburgh. Almost a century ago, the Scottish architect, barrister and playwright, Glencairn Stuart Ogilvie, who had made his money investing on the Russian Railways, created Thorpeness as a neo-Tudor seaside holiday village, among the heather and gorse of the Suffolk coast. His idea was to provide a safe and healthy holiday environment, where children could enjoy the magic and innocence of a traditional seaside holiday, a place for those who wanted to experience life as it was in Merrie England.

Oddly, perhaps, Thorpeness has been voted both as one of 'The Hundred Worst Places to Live in Britain' and as the 'Weirdest Village in England'. Close by, the Meare has islands named after characters in *Peter Pan* by J M Barrie, who was a close friend of the Ogilvies. Thorpeness Meare is an artificial lake used for fishing and boating, as well as a haven for wildfowl. At one end of the lake is a mock Norman castle, not surprising given the eccentricity of its surroundings.

WALBERSWICK MAP REF 405 L6

Just a short distance from the rather larger Southwold, Walberswick is a compact village with attractive houses; it is also a pleasant and popular river port. It was the home of the English Impressionist painter, Merseyside-born Philip Wilson Steer. Walberswick was also home to the Scottish designer, artist, architect and exponent of the art nouveau style in Scotland, Charles Rennie Mackintosh, after he left Scotland in 1914.

WOODBRIDGE MAP REF 405 K7

The market town of Woodbridge spreads across the banks of the River Deben, a short distance from Sutton Hoo, the most important Anglo-Saxon site in the Britain. With 1,400 years of recorded history, the town has diverse and interesting historical architecture, making it an fascinating town to explore on foot.

What Woodbridge does not have is a wooden bridge; the name derives from the Saxon 'Wode's town'. Its position on the Deben estuary made it a logical place for rope-making, sail- and ship-building industries since the Middle Ages.

WOODBRIDGE

SOUTHWOLD FROM THE PIER

This is a walk around an old-fashioned holiday resort on an island surrounded by the River Blyth, Buss Creek and the North Sea. There is just one road that leads in and out of this quintessentially English village, which prides itself on its lovely beach edged with colourful beach huts and its traditional seaside pier. An exhibition on the pier tells the history of the seaside holiday, complete with saucy postcards, kitsch teapots, palm-readers and old-style arcade machines.

DISTANCE/TIME 4 miles (6.4km) 1h30 Ascent: Negligible **MAP** Aqua3 OS Explorer 231 Southwold & Bungay **START** Grid ref: TM 511766 **PATHS** Riverside paths, seaside promenade, town streets, 2 stiles **THE PUB** The Crown, High Street, Southwold. Tel: 01502 722275

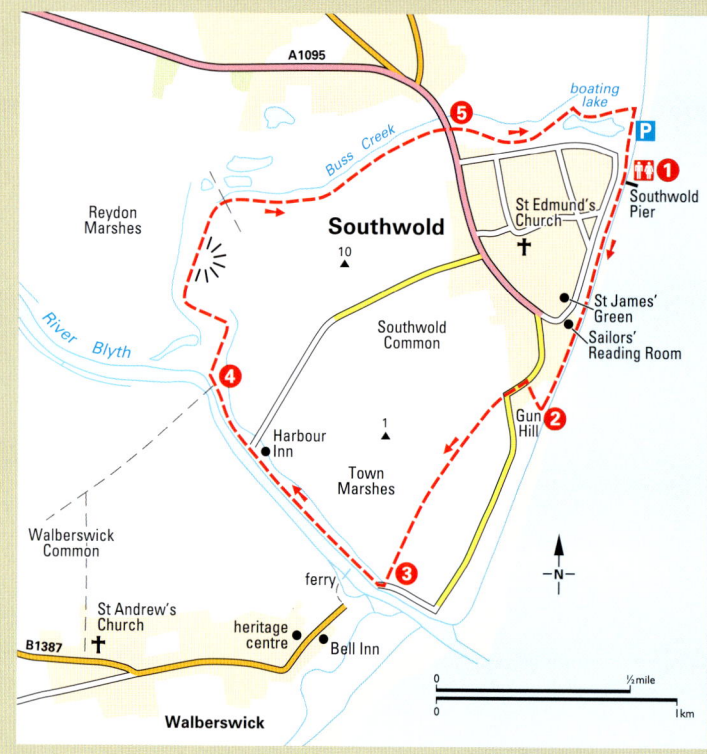

1 Leave Southwold Pier, recently rebuilt after years of storms and neglect and now providing a focus for good, old-fashioned fun, and turn left along the seafront. Follow either the promenade past a row of brightly coloured beach huts and climb some steps, or walk along a clifftop path with great views over the beach. After passing St James' Green, where a pair of impressive cannon stand either side of a mast, continue along the clifftop path to Gun Hill, where you can see six more cannon, captured at the Battle of Culloden near Inverness in 1746.

2 From the appropriately named Gun Hill, head inland alongside the large South Green. Turn left along Queen's Road to the junction with Gardner Road. Cross this road and look for the Ferry Path footpath, which follows the stream beside marshes as it heads towards the river. Alternatively, stay on the clifftop path and walk across the sand dunes to the mouth of the River Blyth.

3 Turn right and walk beside the river, passing Walberswick ferry, a group of fishing huts where fresh fish is sold, and the Harbour Inn. After about 0.75 miles (1.2km) you will reach an iron bridge on site of old Southwold-to-Halesworth railway line.

4 Keep straight ahead at the bridge, crossing a stile and following the path round to the right alongside Buss Creek to make a complete circuit of the island. There are good views across the common to Southwold, dominated by the lighthouse and tower of St Edmund's Church. Horses and cattle can often be seen grazing on the marshes. Keep straight ahead at a 4-finger signpost and continue walking along a raised path until you reach the white-painted bridge.

5 Climb up to the road and cross over the bridge, then continue on the path beside Buss Creek with views of the colourful beach huts away in the distance. The path then skirts a boating lake on its way down to the sea. Turn right and walk across the car park to return to the pier at the start of walk.

WALK 54

DUNWICH LOST CITY

Conjure up visions of a lost city as you stand on the cliffs gazing out to sea. Dunwich is a haunting place, where ghosts of the past assault your senses at every turn. High on the cliff near the start of the walk is the tombstone of Jacob Forster, all that remains of the churchyard of All Saints Church. The other graves have long since sunk without trace and Jacob Forster's bones lie all alone. Who was he, and what did he do to deserve such a fate? How long will it be until he goes too, to join his ancestors beneath the waves?

DISTANCE/TIME 8 miles (12.9km) 4h **MAP** Aqua3 OS Explorers 212 Woodbridge & Saxmundham; 231 Southwold & Bungay **START** Grid ref: TM 478706 (Explorer 231) **PATHS** Farm tracks, heathland paths, quiet roads, shingle beach **THE PUB** Ship Inn, St James Street, Dunwich. Tel: 01728 648219

1 Walk up the road from the beach car park and keep left at the junction. When the road bends, turn left on to the footpath that climbs through woods to the ruins of Greyfriars Friary. Turn left along the cliff top, go over a set of wooden steps and bear right through trees on the waymarked path. At end of the path, turn right along a track to a road.

2 Turn left off the road after 100yds (91m) on a track to Dairy House. Keep straight ahead as it enters Greyfriars Wood and continues to the road.

3 Turn left along the road for 0.5 miles (0.8km), passing two caravan sites on the left. As soon as you enter the National Trust land, turn left on to the path waymarked with white arrows.

4 Walk around the NT coastguard cottages and take the track beside Heath Barn field centre, then bear right onto the sandy path that climbs through heather. Keep on the path, bearing left and right at a crossing track to follow Sandlings Walk nightjar waymarks. At the bridleway, keep ahead on a farm track passing Mount Pleasant farm. Cross the road and keep ahead on a concrete lane to Sandy Lane Farm.

5 Turn right for 0.5 miles (0.8km) onto a shady lane to St James's Church, built in 19th century when Dunwich's other churches were falling into sea. For a short cut, keep straight ahead here to return to Dunwich.

6 Turn left at a road and, in 100yds (91m), go right at Bridge Nurseries. Keep to the right around farm buildings and stay on this track for 1.5 miles (2.4km) beside Dunwich Forest before turning seawards. Pass through a gate to enter a covert and fork right at a junction around Great Dingle Farm, then follow a path through reed beds towards the sea.

7 Turn right at a junction, with an old drainage mill to your left, and follow the flood bank across Dingle Marshes. Turn right to return to Dunwich along the beach or take the path behind the shingle bank.

A WARRIOR'S GRAVE AT SUTTON HOO

The discovery of an Anglo-Saxon ship burial at Sutton Hoo in 1939 shed new light on the 'Dark Ages' and opened up a whole new chapter of English history. It all came about when widow Edith May Pretty reported seeing visions of ghostly warriors dancing on the burial mound near her home. An archaeologist was called to investigate and in one of the mounds was found the remains of a wooden ship which contained a burial chamber. Gold and treasures were found within although the wood had rotted around it, the only thing missing was a body...

DISTANCE/TIME 7 miles (11.3km) 3h Ascent: 262ft (80m) **MAP** Aqua3 OS Explorer 197 Ipswich, Felixstowe & Harwich **START** Grid ref: TM 289492 **PATHS** Field-edge and riverside paths, farm lanes, short section of busy road, 3 stiles **THE PUB** Plough Inn, Sutton. Tel: 01394 411785

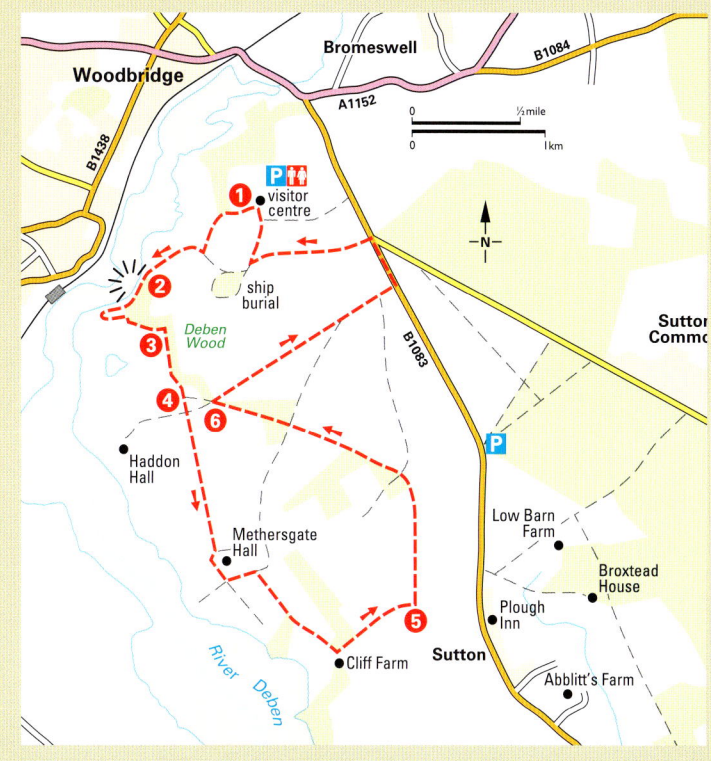

1 Take the signposted blue trail from the National Trust visitor centre, descending towards the river on a gravel track. Turn left opposite the entrance to Little Haugh and turn right by the map of Sutton Hoo Estate. The path narrows and turns left along a fence on its way to the river. Keep left around the meadow then cross the footbridge and climb some steps to the river bank with Woodbridge visible on the opposite bank.

2 Turn left then walk along the river bank (overgrown in places; the plank bridges can be slippery). After 400yds (366m), climb the steps to the left to leave the river and turn left around the turf field. Keep to the field edge as it swings right and climbs with woodland to the left and a reservoir to the right.

3 Turn right at the top of the rise to follow a bridleway along the field edge with Deben Wood to the left. At the end of the wood, the path swings half-left across a field then passes through a hedge on to a lane. Turn left here for short cut, picking up the walk in 300yds (274m) at Point 6.

4 Keep ahead for 0.75 miles (1.2km), crossing the drive to Haddon Hall. Bear right around farm buildings then left on the footpath beside a brick wall. Pass cannon on the lawn of Methersgate Hall. Continue with the River Deben opening out in front. Cross a stile and turn left across a field. Cross another stile and turn right along a lane. Continue for 1 mile (1.6km) as the lane bends left past Cliff Farm.

5 Turn left at the 3-finger signpost along the field-edge track, passing an embankment on the right. Keep to the public bridleway as it swings left around woodland. At the end, keep ahead between fields and continue as the path becomes a broad grass track, passing cottages to reach a minor lane.

6 Turn right and stay on the lane for 1 mile (1.6km) to the main road (B1083). Turn left and walk for 400yds (366m). Turn left opposite the road junction past a National Trust sign. When you see burial mounds on your left, turn right to the visitor centre on the National Trust permissive path.

WALK 56

FELIXSTOWE FERRY FISH & SHIPS

This walk shows you another side of Felixstowe, well away from the arcades and the sandcastles on the beach. It starts in the small hamlet of Felixstowe Ferry (a great place for excellent fish and chips) with its boatyard, fishing huts and ferry across the river. The walk then leads along the estuary of the River Debden and beside a peaceful stream called the King's Fleet, finally returning to the coast by way of two Martello towers.

DISTANCE/TIME 6.5 miles (10.4km) 3h Ascent: 164ft (50m) **MAP** Aqua3 OS Explorer 197 Ipswich, Felixstowe & Harwich **START** Grid ref: TM 328376 **PATHS** Field and riverside paths, country lanes, farm tracks, sea wall, 4 stiles **THE PUB** Ferry Boat Inn, The Ferry, Felixstowe. Tel: 01394 284203

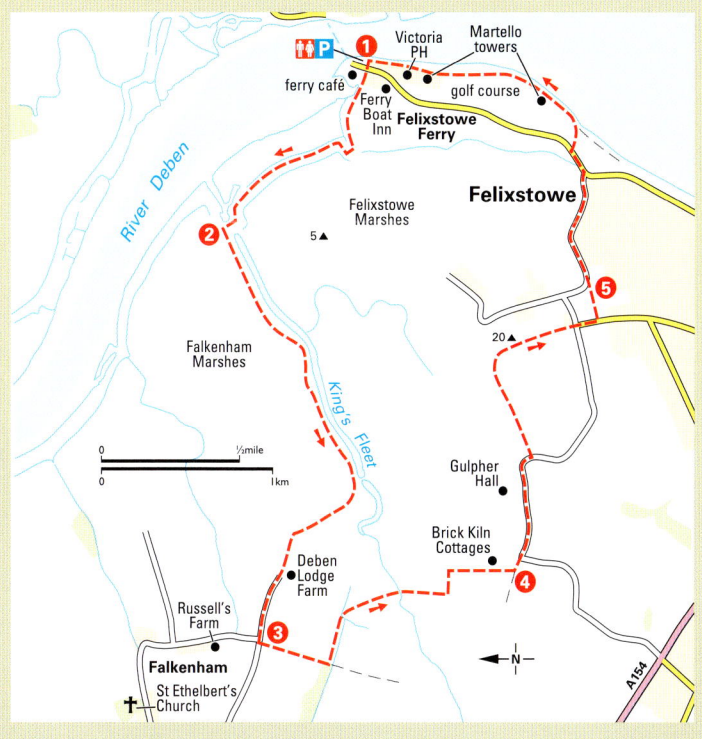

1 Take the tarmac path along the embankment behind the ferry café car park. The path passes a boatyard and follows the river wall as you look down on abandoned boats lying moored in muddy flats. Turn right across a stile to walk beside Deben Estuary. After 0.5 miles (0.8km) the path swings left and then right across an inlet at the entrance to King's Fleet.

2 Turn left to descend the embankment and walk along a broad track. Pass an old wind pump and stay on this track as it winds between farmland and King's Fleet. After 1 mile (1.6km) the track bends right and climbs to a farm where it becomes a tarmac lane. Continue to a T-junction.

3 Turn left across a field to climb to the ridge then drop down through the next field to The Wilderness (a belt of trees beside Falkenham Brook). Turn left through trees and follow a path alongside the stream, then bend right to cross a meadow. Make for a corner of the hedge opposite and bear right alongside a fence to cross a footbridge and continue on the grassy path between fields. At the end of the field, turn left

and continue to end of the hedge, then turn right to climb the track to Brick Kiln Cottages.

4 At the top of the track, turn left along the lane and stay on this lane past Gulpher Hall and the duck pond. As the road bends right, walk past the entrance to The Brook and turn left on a field-edge path. The path ascends then turns right around a field and cuts straight across the next field, unless it's diverted by crops. Pass through a gate and keep straight on along a lane, then turn left in 150yds (137m) on another path that runs between fields.

5 At a pill box, turn right on to Ferry Road down to the sea. Cross Cliff Road and turn left, walking past the clubhouse and turning half-right across the golf course on a signposted path to the sea wall. Turn left and walk along the wall, passing two Martello towers and a row of beach huts. Continue to the mouth of the estuary and turn left just before the jetty to return to the ferry café.

Cambridge & Fens

CLOCKWISE FROM TOP LEFT: RIVER CAM, CAMBRIDGE; ELY CATHEDRAL; KING'S COLLEGE, CAMBRIDGE

ANGLESEY ABBEY MAP REF 405 H6

This Jacobean-style house dates from 1600 and is built on the site of a 12th-century Augustinian priory. It contains an idiosyncratic collection of art depicting the tastes of Huttleston Broughton, 1st Lord Fairhaven (1896–1965).

Among the many paintings are works by Claude Lorraine, set alongside fine examples of furniture, silver and tapestries and one of the largest collections of clocks found in any of the properties of the National Trust. The priory is surrounded by a landscaped garden that provides year-round floral interest and an arboretum with more than 100 pieces of sculpture. The watermill has milling days on the first and third Saturday of each month, provided the water levels are adequate.

CAMBRIDGE MAP REF 405 H6

A wonderful and often bizarre synthesis of the everyday and the extraordinary, Cambridge is a pulsating city that has played a major role in the history of England, and reflects the very best of traditional and contemporary life.

Many who have yet to visit Cambridge may well have already experienced its allure; this, after all, is the place that inspired Darwin, Newton, Byron, Tennyson, Wordsworth and, more recently John Cleese, Graham Chapman, Eric Idle and Stephen Hawking. The university in Cambridge is one of the oldest in the world and one of the largest in Britain. It was formed in 1209 by students who fled here to escape hostile townspeople in Oxford, and built a university here; the two cities have been rivals ever since.

The centre of Cambridge is quite small and easily explored on foot; then at least you appreciate just how foremost the university is and the influence it has on the city. King's College Chapel literally dominates Cambridge and is famed for its Christmas carol concerts, a superb choir and its fine fan vaulting. Several of the college buildings are often open to visitors, but the view from the outside, especially the area across the river, is particularly agreeable. This area is known as 'The Backs' because it overlooks the backs of six of the riverside colleges. In the early morning, a thin mist often grazes the river and the college buildings, lending the landscape an eerie half-light. From here you can see the most famous view of Cambridge, embracing King's College and King's College Chapel, with Clare College on the left.

Lending its name to the city, the River Cam flows through the centre of Cambridge, and those in search of relaxation will find several ideal walks along its banks. But the best way to savour the atmosphere is to take a leisurely punt. You can hire a punt and do your own thing (but, be warned: it's far from easy), or you can let someone else do all the work, and hire a 'chauffeured' punt, leaving you free to admire the college buildings and intriguing bridges.

With such a large student population, there are plenty of pubs, wine bars, eateries and restaurants, perfect places for a coffee break or afternoon tea. And there is a wide range of shops, especially around the market square, which has been the market's location for centuries.

Music, theatre and live entertainment are popular in Cambridge. The Cambridge Corn Exchange and the Cambridge Arts Theatre promote the more traditional arts, the emphasis being on ballet, opera and orchestral concerts. More contemporary works are performed at the ADC Theatre and Drama Centre, the Junction, and the West Road Concert Hall.

ELY MAP REF 405 H6

Ely has its origins in the foundation of an abbey in 673 on the Isle of Ely, which was under the protection of Saint Ethelreda. Destroyed by Danish invaders in 870 and then not rebuilt for over a hundred years, the site was one of the last holdouts in England against the rule of William the Conqueror. Surrounded by treacherous marshlands, known as 'fens', the channels and overgrowing foliage made a labyrinth of the Ely countryside.

The stunning cathedral of Ely is known as the 'Ship of the Fens' for the distant views of its octagonal tower that dominates the surrounding low-lying wetlands. Oliver Cromwell lived in Ely for several years after inheriting the position of local tax collector. His former home dates from the 16th century and is now used as the Tourist Information Office and a museum with rooms displayed as they would have been in Cromwell's time. Today, Ely has some attractive Georgian buildings and a large park that together with the cathedral and its history make this an appealing place to visit.

GRANTCHESTER MAP REF 405 H6

Within walking distance of Cambridge, Grantchester is a lovely village of black-and-white half-timbered buildings, thatched cottages, a pretty church and flower-filled meadows. Its 'Englishness' was immortalised by the poet Rupert Brooke, who was a student at King's College before World War I, in his 1912 poem 'The Old Vicarage', Grantchester, in which he recalls happy days in the idyllic English surroundings of Cambridgeshire.

Grantchester is a favourite amongst both tourists and students travelling upstream from Cambridge by punt to eat a picnic in the meadows or at the tea gardens called The Orchard, as they have done since the 19th century.

WICKEN FEN

HEMINGFORD GREY MAP REF 405 G6

Spread along a bank of the River Great Ouse, Hemingford Grey is an attractive village that boasts timber-framed cottages and a church with an unusual spire. Also here is a Norman Manor House, once home to author Lucy Boston, which can be visited by appointment.

HOUGHTON MILL MAP REF 405 G6

Set on an island in the Great Ouse, the 18th-century five-storey, weather-boarded mill is the last working watermill on the river, and has intact machinery which is still operated today. Milling takes place on Sundays and Bank Holiday Mondays, with the resulting stone-ground flour for sale, and hands-on exhibits that appeal to all the family. The riverside meadows offer wonderful opportunities for walks, cycling and horse riding.

MADINGLEY MAP REF 405 H6

This unassuming village on the outskirts of Cambridge has two sites of particular interest: Madingley Hall, and the Cambridge American Cemetery and Memorial. Madingley is also mentioned in works by the poet Rupert Brooke.

WANDLEBURY MAP REF 405 H7

An area of beautiful grasslands, chalk slopes and hills that is heaven to walkers and nature lovers. Visitors also come here to see remnants of the Wandlebury Iron Age Hill Fort and the Wandlebury Ring, atop Gog Magog Hill.

WICKEN FEN MAP REF 405 H6

Britain's oldest nature reserve, Wicken Fen, has been managed traditionally for centuries by sedge-cutting and peat-digging to produce a unique fenland habitat rich in wildlife, particularly invertebrates. Wicken Fen is one of only four 'wild' fens which still survive in the Great Fen Basin.

The importance of the fen is demonstrated by the fact that it is not just a National Nature Reserve, but also a Site of Special Scientific Interest, a Special Area of Conservation and a RAMSAR site (an international wetland designation). Wicken is a top site nationally for molluscs, aquatic beetles, rove beetles, caddis flies, bees and spiders.

The nature of the wetland has played an important role in the social and economic life of the area, providing materials for thatch, bedding and animal feed, fish and fowl for food, and peat for fuel.

Today, Wicken Fen is a surviving fragment of the wilderness that once covered East Anglia, and can be explored along traditional wide droves and lush green paths, including a boardwalk nature trail, giving access to several hides.

WICKEN FEN THE LAST SURVIVOR

Step back in time through an authentic Cambridgeshire fen, virtually the last of its kind left in Britain. Wicken Fen is one of the oldest nature reserves in the country and is one of the most important, too. Over the last 400 years more than 99 per cent of East Anglia's ancient Great Fen has been drained and converted into farmland, richly productive for agriculture but largely sterile for wildlife. For generations Wicken peat has been cut for burning, and sedge (a grass-like plant) has been harvested for thatching.

1 From the nature reserve walk up Lode Lane towards Wicken. Before the main road turn right on to Back Lane. Follow the route, behind houses (including a windmill), which soon becomes track. At the far end of the lane, turn right on to a wide track through fields. (If you have parked in Wicken then take the signposted public footpath via Cross Green, just along from and opposite the pub, out to the fields.)

2 Follow the route to cross two footbridges. Don't take the path off to the left but continue straight ahead (beyond the green-painted second footbridge) along the bank of Monk's Lode, with St Edmund's Fen opposite.

3 After 550yds (503m) branch left by a new fence and gate for a long and straight track, out across fields to Priory Farm. Join the surfaced lane and continue to the end.

4 By the Environment Agency's private raised bridge turn right along the bank of Burwell Lode (ignore the footbridge). Continue on this path for 1.5 miles (2.4km) past Adventurer's Fen.

5 At a high-arched footbridge over the Wicken Lode turn right and, once over the stile, walk along this bank back towards Wicken Fen past a National Trust sign. If you continue across the footbridge and walk for 0.25 miles (0.4km) you come to Upware, with a pub and picnic area. Ignoring paths off into an open fen and fields on your right, continue along the bank until its junction with Monk's Lode.

6 Cross a short bridge by Goba Moorings and continue alongside Wicken Lode, not along Monk's Lode (to the right). The lush vegetation of Wicken Fen is now on either side, and across the water you will pass a lofty tower hide, one of several dotted around the reserve.

7 When you get to end turn left to explore the visitor centre (open Tuesday to Sunday). There is a small admission charge to the reserve itself, which is open daily from dawn to dusk. Near by is the restored Fen Cottage, and a thatched boathouse. To return to the car park and Wicken, simply walk back up the lane past houses.

DISTANCE/TIME 4.75 miles (7.7km) 2h Ascent: Negligible **MAP** Aqua3 OS Explorer 226 Ely & Newmarket **START** Grid ref: TL 564706 **PATHS** Mostly river banks and farm tracks, potentially slippery **THE PUB** Maid's Head, 12 High Street, Wicken. Tel: 01353 720727

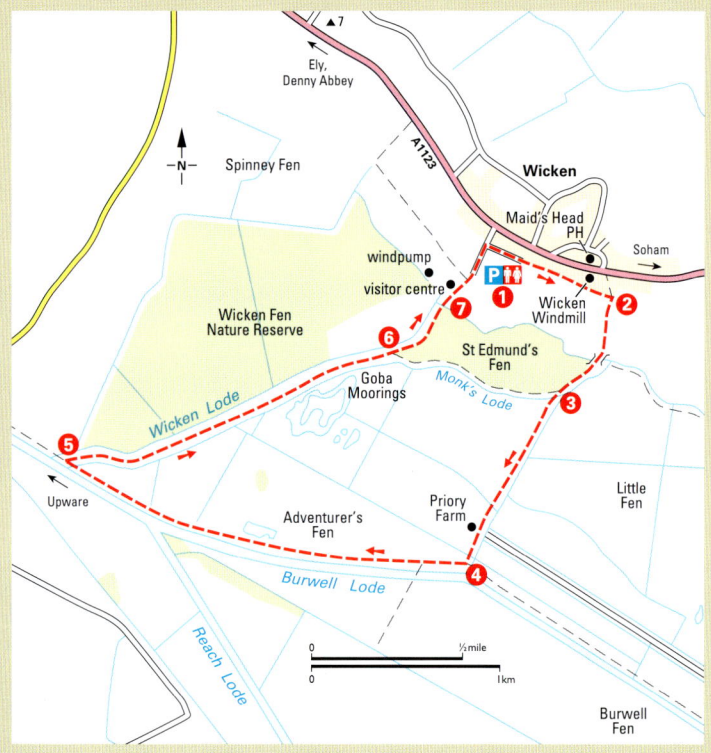

WALK 58

MANEA FENLAND'S BIG SKIES

An enigmatic landscape links remote Manea with an historic drainage cut. A landscape that is as flat and as bare as the fens may seem an uninteresting prospect for a walk but in fact there is much more to this unique place than first meets the eye, and what you see now isn't the way it looked in the distant past. Ancient tree trunks known as bog oaks are periodically uncovered from the peaty soil proving that this apparently tree-less country once presented a totally different scene.

1 Walk eastwards along the High Street (which becomes Station Road), past the post office and past the fish and chip shop, then turn right to join a public footpath that runs alongside the little primary school. When you reach a football pitch at the far end turn right and go past Manea Wood. Continue along the path as it bears right and approaches Bearts Farm.

2 Turn left by old barns and sheds for a wide track out into fields, with the farm on your right, to reach the attractive reedy lake known locally as 'The Pitt'. This was originally dug for clay, which was then transported across fields on a light railway to shore up the banks of nearby Old and New Bedford rivers. The Pitt is now a popular place for fishermen and wildlife.

3 At the end of the track turn right and go on to a lane, keeping the lake on your right, then when you reach the junction at the corner of the road turn left, which takes you on to Straight Road. Once here, follow this through the fields to the end.

4 Turn left on to Purl's Bridge Drove (signposted 'Welches Dam and RSPB reserve'). Follow this open lane to Purl's Bridge. Continue along the bank to reach Ouse Washes Nature Reserve (with a visitor centre and public toilets).

5 Return along the lane for 440yds (402m) and turn left for a signposted public bridleway by dark wooden sheds. Known as Old Mill Drove, this runs directly across open fields as far as the farm machinery and outbuildings of Boon's Farm. Turn right then walk along the dead-straight Barnes's Drove for 1.25 miles (2km) to a road at the far end.

6 Turn left and after 80yds (73m) turn off right over a stile for the public footpath across fields back into Manea (aim for the fire station tower). The route veers one way then the other as it skirts a series of pig enclosures – just follow the clear yellow waymarks past the enormous porkers. At the far side cross successive stiles and turn right, past the village stores, to follow the main road back to the centre.

DISTANCE/TIME 6.25 miles (10.1km) 3h Ascent: Negligible **MAP** aqua3 OS Explorer 228 March & Ely **START** Grid ref: TL 478893 **PATHS** Lanes and hard farm tracks **THE PUB** Rose & Crown, 30 High Street, Manea. Tel: 01354 680 454

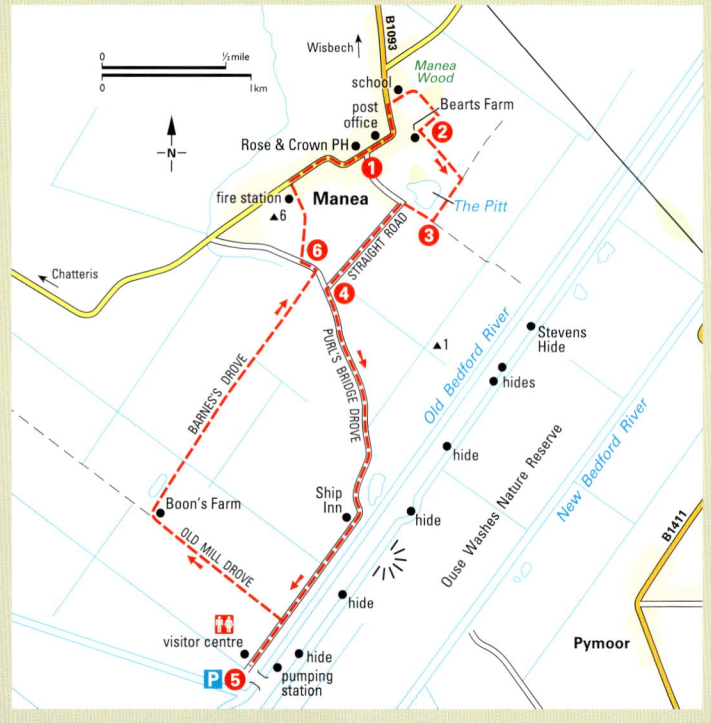

Norfolk Broads

CLOCKWISE FROM TOP LEFT: BULRUSH, BROADS WILDLIFE CENTRE; SUTTON MILL, NEAR STALHAM; GREAT YARMOUTH; BROADS WILDLIFE CENTRE

BECCLES MAP REF 405 L5

Some might argue that the heyday of Beccles was when this market town was a prosperous Saxon port, more than a 1,000 years ago. In fact, thinking of Beccles as a port at all is not so easy these days, as it is more than 6 miles (10km) from the sea. But there was a time when Beccles was on the very edge of the coast, and all that could be seen looking east was water. In time, land was reclaimed and wherries came to ply up and down the riverways, and today Beccles has a much to attract visitors. It lies at the southernmost extremity of the Broads, although the town itself is rooted across the county border in Suffolk. The name 'Beccles' is in fact a combination of two words: 'beck', a Scandinavian word meaning stream, and 'leas', meaning meadow. In fact, that's what medieval Beccles must have been for many years, largely a beautiful meadow by a stream.

The attractive little parish church of St Michael's has an interesting legend: the church tower has clock faces on only three sides, being blank on the side facing Norfolk, allegedly because the inhabitants of Beccles did not want to give the time for free to their neighbours!

GREAT YARMOUTH MAP REF 405 L5

Northwards along the coast, Great Yarmouth, the chief town and most popular resort on the Norfolk coast, is unashamedly bright, brash and breezy. It is unquestionably focused on seaside holidays and entertainment, the seafront offering a great sweep of arcades, fun fairs, bingo halls, crazy golf and attractions for children, not least 15 miles (24km) of wide, sandy beach from Winterton-on-Sea in the north to Hopton-on-Sea in the south.

The town stands on a peninsula formed by the combined influence of the rivers Bure, Yare and Waveney, and not surprisingly the town developed as a fishing port from which 'Yarmouth bloaters' earned it international renown. Much of the town's most fascinating architecture was destroyed during World War II, but enough remains, including parts of the original medieval town walls and several of its towers, to provide more than passing interest for visitors.

Great Yarmouth and the clutch of surrounding villages dotted along the edge of the Norfolk Broads blend easily with the beautiful countryside, in this interesting region which is steeped in coastal and maritime heritage.

LOWESTOFT MAP REF 405 L5

Britain's most easterly town, the first to catch the morning sun, is a delightfully busy holiday resort, significantly less tacky than Great Yarmouth to the north. Lowestoft originally was a small fishing and farming town perched on a cliff in the northern part of Suffolk. The main street consisted of merchants' houses, shops, schools and pubs, while away from the centre the town's streets were flanked by breweries, small industries and cottages, many occupied by farm labourers before the western part of the town began to be developed.

Since the 14th century, when that original fishing village began its expansion, Lowestoft evolved into a major fishing port and ship-building centre, and from Victorian times has benefited from its miles of golden beaches, increasing in popularity as a premier seaside resort. The inner harbour, known as Lake Lothing, plugs into Oulton Broad and the River Waveney, the most south-easterly point of the Broads.

There are some strong literary and artistic associations in Lowestoft: Thomas Nashe, the English dramatist was born here in 1567, as was composer Benjamin Britten (1913–76), probably best known for the *Young Person's Guide to the Orchestra* and his opera *Peter Grimes*. Oulton Broad is the place to which Norfolk author, George Borrow, returned following his travels, and where he wrote many of his books. He died here in 1881. Nearby Blundelston inspired Dickens' name for David Copperfield's childhood home, and was a place often visited by poet Thomas Gray, warmly remembered as one of the early writers about the English Lake District, after a visit in the late 18th century, and as the author of *An Elegy Written in a Country Churchyard*.

NORFOLK BROADS MAP REF 405 L5

The Norfolk and Suffolk Broads, a tangled network of flooded peat diggings, have transformed into an atmospheric

NORFOLK BROADS

landscape of enchantment and mystery, a place of woodland and fen, of grazing land and convoluted waterways. What is perhaps surprising is that this is a man-made environment, the product of Middle Age industry from the 9th to 14th centuries when peat was dug, almost on an industrial scale, to use as domestic fuel. Over the centuries, as if painstakingly embellished by the hand of some Renaissance artist, the land changed as water levels rose to create a patchwork of shallow lakes, or 'broads'. The result is a place of magic and special appeal. Amazingly, it was not until as recently as the 1960s that man's influence on the landscape was finally proven, so natural has the landscape become.

Some of the broads are flanked by fens, wet areas of reed and sedge that in former times were cut for thatch or to make the ridge along the top of thatched roofs. But as well as a source of building materials, the marshes also provided man with water and food – waterfowl, fish and eels. Then, as the necessity to keep cattle grew, so the fens were drained to provide grazing marshes, a series of open fields laced by a network of dykes, and dotted with wind pumps that provided the power to push the water along the dykes. In time, this became a unique landscape, threatened for a while in the 1970s as a move to develop arable land gained sway, but finally brought within the embrace of a National Park, which now holds the responsibility for the management and protection of this priceless landscape heritage. In the words of the Norfolk naturalist, the late Ted Ellis, the Broads are 'a breathing space for the cure of souls'. But they are more than that: these sometimes intimate nooks and crannies of reed-fringed pools, sometimes sky-laden expanses of open appeal, are a corner of heaven set aside for lovers of enchantment and the English countryside.

With over two million visitors each year, the Broads cannot compete with the Lake District, Yorkshire Dales or Peak National Parks, nor do they seek to. The Broads hold their own special appeal, and are no less deserving of the protection National Park status brings. Indeed, in some ways, the policies adopted for recreation, focused on promoting 'quiet enjoyment', are more critical than elsewhere because the Broads are also a profoundly important wildlife habitat; Nature's window on a grand scale. Today, wildlife-watching is a popular and inspirational experience best enjoyed by visiting one of the many nature reserves. With such a landscape diversity it is not surprising that other activities are also in demand here – fishing, sailing,

windsurfing, rowing, canoeing, boating and walking – and striking the right balance, one that is sympathetic to the needs of the Broads rather than to the needs of the people, is difficult and on-going.

There are few major centres of population within the National Park, but just beyond the boundaries lie the city of Norwich and the towns of Great Yarmouth and Lowestoft. Here you are on dry land, but the best way to explore the Broads themselves, given that they hug the courses of numerous rivers, is by boat, for then it is that the illusion of remoteness is heightened and the prospect of seeing something rare and wonderful is enhanced by an approach that is slow and quiet. Indeed, the Broads, with over 120 miles (200km) of navigable waterway, have been important for sailing and boating since Victorian times, offering a unique navigation system where special inland sailing craft – wherries – have evolved. Wherries have featured on the Broads for centuries and their use in river trade was instrumental in making Norwich England's second city. The earliest wherry-type vessel was square rigged, but by the early part of the 19th century the wherry had become single-sailed, and specifically designed for the shallow waters of the Broads.

NORWICH MAP REF 405 K5

The Broads, in the form of the River Wensum, tap a tentative finger at the very gates of Norwich, regarded by 17th-century traveller Celia Fiennes as 'a city walled full round of towers', while George Borrow, better known perhaps for his walk through 'Wild Wales' but who attended King Edwards School here, considered Norwich to be 'a fine old city, perhaps the most curious specimen [...] of the genuine old English Town'. Norwich is the county town of Norfolk, at the heart of East Anglia, and has held a regular market since Norman times.

For the curious traveller, Norwich has a wealth of historical architecture. The medieval period, a most prosperous time based on the wool trade, is represented by the 11th-century cathedral, 12th-century castle (now a museum) and a large number of parish churches. During the Middle Ages, founded on the wealth derived from wool, no less than 57 churches stood within the city walls; 31 still remain. This prompted the local saying that Norwich had a church for every week of the year, and a pub for every day. Certainly the over-riding impression on visiting Norwich is that of taking a step back in time, in the most agreeable sense. It is a modern city, but the scope for a little self-indulgent time travel is good.

NORWICH CATHEDRAL

Between 1650 and 1750, Norwich was considered to be second only to London in terms of its prosperity, with textiles still the mainstay of the economy. During the 1800s, newer industries appeared, notably printing and the production of leather.

Through the 20th century, Norwich never ceased to evolve. In the 1930s, the city saw the construction of the art deco City Hall, and in the 1960s, in common with cities across England, the University of East Anglia (UEA) admitted its first students. The university brought yet more innovative architecture to Norwich, in the pyramidal shape of Denys Lasdun's Ziggurats, followed in the 1970s by the striking structure of the Sainsbury Centre for Visual Arts, designed by Sir Norman Foster, designer of the famous Millau Viaduct in central France.

POTTER HEIGHAM MAP REF 405 L5

Gateway to the Upper Thurne, and focal point of the northerly Broads, Potter Heigham takes its name both from a pottery that once stood here and from the name of the Saxon lord, Heacham, who founded the settlement. This is a popular and busy water resort with a 14th-century bridge that is regarded by experienced boatmen to be the most difficult bridge to negotiate anywhere on the Broads.

Potter Heigham is the key to Hickling Broad, the largest and wildest of the Norfolk Broads, where there is an abundance of nature trails, boardwalks, sailing opportunities and wildlife. Birdwatchers will find equal pleasure in nearby Horsey Mere, a large triangular shaped broad with Horsey Mere Nature Reserve on the northern bank.

RANWORTH MAP REF 405 L5

Ranworth is a charming Broadlands village, located on Malthouse Broad (so called because of the old malt houses nearby). Ranworth Broad is a nature reserve and divided from Malthouse Broad by a thick bank. The village itself is dominated by the 14th-century church known as the Cathedral of the Broads. It has some splendid old woodwork, including one of the finest painted rood-screens in England. There is a glorious view from the top of the church tower which makes the climb more than worthwhile. But with ghostly monks and sightings of the Devil carrying the spirit of a local military man on horseback, Ranworth lays claim to being the most haunted village on the Broads. The ghost of a traitorous monk is also said to haunt St Benet's Abbey, a short way across the marshes and the River Bure. In the days immediately following the Norman Conquest, the monk betrayed his brethren to the soldiers of William the Conqueror in return for being made Abbot. True to their word, the Normans appointed him Abbot for life, and promptly nailed him to the abbey doors then skinned him alive as

reward for his treachery. The Normans had no love for traitors, even Saxon ones. Today, the abbey is in ruins, but is a distinctive sight with a windmill built into the walls of the gatehouse.

From Ranworth, the Broadlands Wildlife Centre can be reached along a nature trail through woods and marshes to an attractive thatched building, floating on pontoons. The upper gallery is an good place from which to observe the amazing diversity of wildlife on the Broads.

SOMERLEYTON MAP REF 405 L5

Somerleyton's pretty red-brick, thatched cottages grouped around a village green, and a gracious sense of calm and tranquility are not the only draw to this village on the Waveney. Nearby Somerleyton Hall is a lavish pile, built to announce Victorian wealth and grandeur. The Hall was originally a Jacobean manor, remodelled in 1844 into a stunning example of an early Victorian hall in the Anglo-Italian style. Beautiful architecture and antique furniture, trademark Crossley carpets, a distinct and pleasing 'lived-in' feel, and a yew maze of mind-boggling ingenuity gives Somerleyton huge appeal.

The village is named after a Viking, Sumarlithi, a non-aggressive invader who arrived in the 10th century and found the Norfolk countryside much to his liking.

STALHAM MAP REF 405 L4

The pleasant Broadlands market town of Stalham, perfectly placed for exploring Hickling and Barton Broads, still has its original name, derived from 'stal' (a pool of water) and 'ham' (a settlement or village). With its narrow high street and weekly market it retains a worldly 'otherness', a gentle and agreeable place where times gone by linger around every corner.

Stalham was on the Roman road to Caister, and would have been a popular staging post for the Romans heading to Caister and Great Yarmouth. The town is connected to the River Ant by a dyke, with its own staithe, where wherries and other trading vessels could moor.

Pre-dating the Domesday Book by many years, the town was originally divided into four manors. Much building took place over the years with the church of St Mary built in the 15th century and the Jacobean Manor house, Stalham Hall, in the 17th century.

Progress was steady rather than rapid, and by the 1880s the town, largely self-sufficient, still had a population of only 852. Its economy was mainly based on agriculture and was a base from which to export loads of grain and livestock by road and river.

As elsewhere throughout Britain, the coming of the railway brought new opportunities and prosperity, enabling the community to trade further afield. Today, Stalham, home to one of the principal holiday boat hirers, and with a weekly market and auction on a Tuesday, is a popular Norfolk town.

WROXHAM MAP REF 405 K5

Wroxham is looked on as the capital of the Norfolk Broads, and is the place where boating holidays started in the late 1800s. It has developed commercially over the years with numerous hotels, tea rooms and gift shops springing up near the river to attract visitors to the village.

Wroxham Bridge is a semi-circular road bridge and has only very low headroom at high water, of key concern for anyone wanting to continue upriver to the limit of navigation at Coltishall.

RANWORTH BROAD

WALK 59

LUDHAM & THE BROADS

Enjoy the windmill-studded skyline in this lovely stroll to the River Ant. No visit to Norfolk would be complete without a trip to the Broads. This is a patchwork of interlinked streams, lakes and channels that wind sluggishly over the flat land to the west of Norwich. Three major rivers – the Bure, Waveney and Yare – supply most of the water to the Broads' meres, ponds and marshes before entering the tidal basin at Breydon Water and flowing out into the sea at Great Yarmouth.

1 Leave the car park and busy marina and walk up Horsefen Road, going the same way that you came in.

2 Turn left at end of Horsefen Road, walking along the footpath that runs inside the hedge and parallel to the lane. When you see the King's Arms pub on your right and the 14th-century St Margaret's Church on your left, turn right up a road ('Catfield'). After a few paces turn left up School Road ('How Hill'). Houses soon give way to countryside and at a junction go straight across.

3 Turn right on the first road after the house called The Laurels, along the lane ('How Hill'). The lane winds and twists, and is fairly narrow. Soon you will reach How Hill House, a sail-less windmill and How Hill nature reserve. There are several marked trails through the reserve, if you feel like a pleasant diversion. When you have finished, continue down How Hill Road with River Ant and its reedy marshes to the left. Pass Grove Farm Gallery and Studio on your right, and look for the red-brick barn followed by a lane, also on the right.

4 Turn right down Wateringpiece Lane, where a sign warns you that this road is liable to flood. Pass the modern water tower on your left and walk past two large fields. At the end of the second field, look for the public footpath sign on your left. Take the path that runs along the edge of the field until it ends at a lane. This path can sometimes be overgrown, and nettles can be a problem.

5 Turn right on Catfield Road and walk along a footpath on the verge on the right. This road can be busy in summer, when visitors flock to Ludham and How Hill. Ignore the lane on your left, heading to Potter Heigham, and continue walking ahead to the crossroads by the chapel.

6 Go straight across, walking a few paces until you reach the next junction with Ludham church ahead of you. Turn left along Yarmouth Road, then turn right into Horsefen Road. This takes you back to the car park.

DISTANCE/TIME 5 miles (8km) 2h Ascent: 33ft (10m) **MAP** Aqua3 OS Explorer OL40 The Broads **START** Grid ref: TG 391180 **PATHS** Quiet country lanes and grassy footpaths

THE PUB King's Arms, High Street, Ludham. Tel: 01692 678386

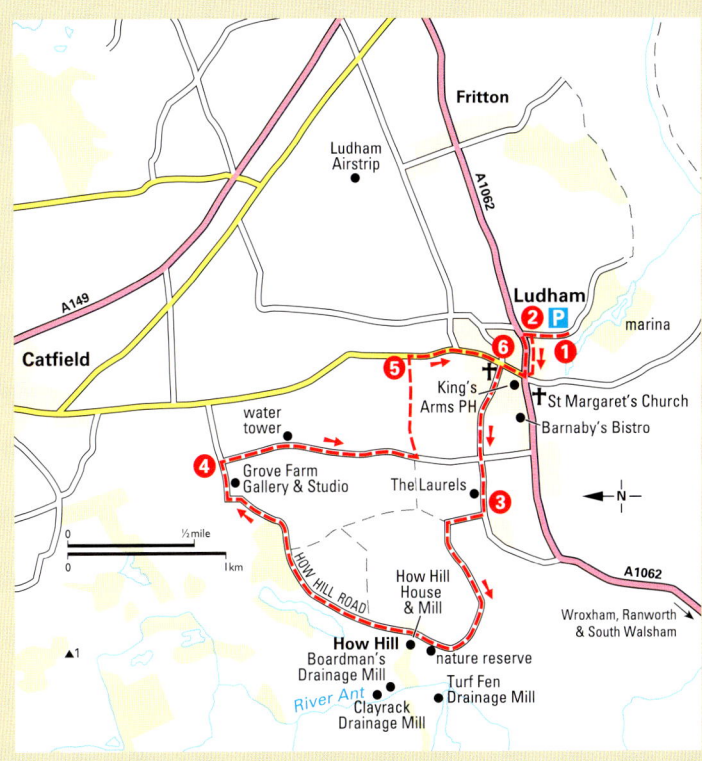

WALK 60

LODDON BOATS & BULRUSHES

This walk takes you through some of Norfolk's most attractive countryside, giving a taste of the silent and mysterious Broads and peaceful farmland, as well as sampling the delights of watching the boats jostle and jangle on their moorings along the banks of the busy River Chet. If you have time to spare then you can stop for a while at the picnic site where you can watch novice boatmen steering their crafts nervously towards the wider waterways of the Broads. Collisions are not unknown, and river-watching can be both a relaxing and an amusing pastime.

1 Turn right past the library on to Bridge Street and walk down the hill to cross the river into Chedgrave. At the White Horse pub go right, then look for the public footpath sign on the right just after a row of terraced houses. Meet a residential street and cross it to a footpath opposite, which runs between hedges, and continues to Chedgrave church.

2 Turn right at the end of the graveyard, passing a meadow on your left before going through a small gate at a public footpath sign on your right. Nettles can grow in abundance here. Go through a second small gate to a path along the north bank of the River Chet. Cross over two wooden footbridges, pass the Norfolk Wildlife Trust sign and continue to a stile.

3 Cross the stile and continue along the river path. Depending on the growth of reeds you may be able to see that you are on a causeway here, with the Chet on your right and the meres of Hardley Flood on your left. Cross a second stile, and see some tantalising glimpses of Hardley Flood and its

abundant birdlife. It is well worth pausing here if you are interested in birdwatching, since the Trust has erected nesting areas in the water. Continue along this path until the broad gives way to farmland and you can see Hardley Hall off to your left. The path then meets a wide farm track.

4 Turn left on the farm track. Go up a hill, passing Hill Cottage on your right-hand side. After 1 mile (1.6km) the farm track ends at a lane. Turn left towards woodland. Continue to a line of ancient oak trees and a sign to your left stating 'Loddon 1¼'. Don't take the left-hand footpath here, which heads to Chedgrave Common. Ignore the first turning on the left ('No Through Road'), and continue walking to the second.

5 Take this turning (signposted 'Church'). When you reach the church, look for a grassy footpath to the right which takes you back to Point 2, passed earlier in walk. Retrace your steps along the footpath, then go left on the main road, across the river and up the hill to the car park.

DISTANCE/TIME 5.25 miles (8.4km) 2h 15min Ascent: 98ft (30m) **MAP** Aqua3 OS Explorer OL40 The Broads **START** Grid ref: TM 362986 **PATHS** Footpaths along waterways, farm tracks and some paved roads, 2 stiles **THE PUB** Angel, High Street, Loddon. Tel: 01692 678386

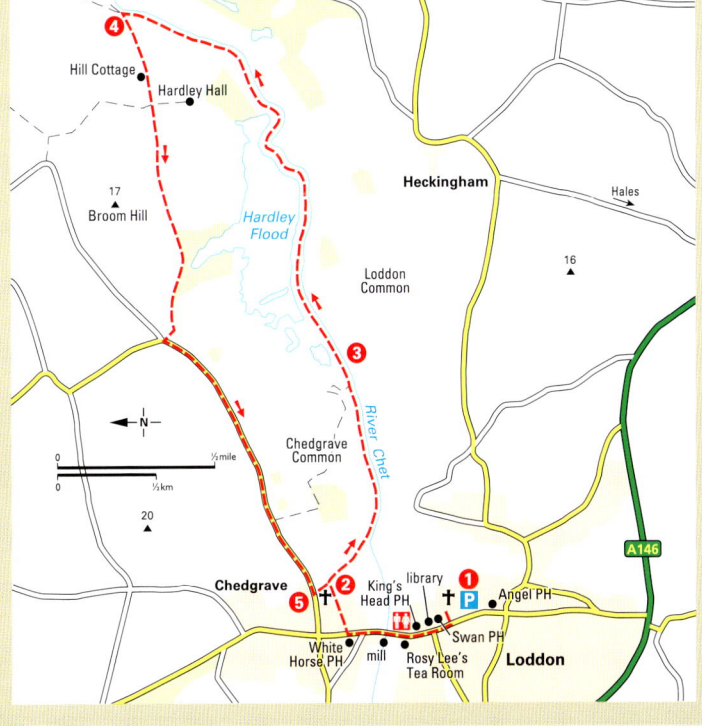

Lincoln & Rutland

CLOCKWISE FROM TOP: KNOT GARDEN MAZE, DODDINGTON HALL; STEEP HILL, LINCOLN

BELTON MAP REF 404 F4

A short distance north of Grantham, the hamlet of Belton is the location of honey-coloured Belton House. Built of limestone in 1685–88 for Sir John Brownlow, the house is a splendid example of Restoration country-house architecture. The interiors house fine Adam-style plasterwork and wood-carving, along with important collections of paintings, furniture, tapestries and silver. Outside, complementing the refined symmetry of the house, the grounds include elegant gardens, the Lakeside Walk, a remarkable landscaped park and the largest children's adventure playground in Lincolnshire.

BELVOIR MAP REF 404 F4

The Vale of Belvoir is rich, rolling, English countryside with wooded escarpments on which stands Belvoir Castle, ancestral home to the Duke of Rutland. It sits high above the village of Belvoir in a superb position on a hilltop and with a breathtaking view across the Vale of Belvoir. Built in a brilliant yellow ironstone with grey stone dressings the castle is very spectacular, with its towers, turrets, and crenellations, very much the 'beau' ideal of the romantic castle. The name (pronounced 'beever') derives from belvedere, and means 'beautiful view'. The castle houses a large collection of fine art, including a famous Holbein painting of Henry VIII. The Elizabeth Saloon is by far the most endearing room in the castle with rich gold decoration and a painted ceiling; the Grand Dining Room has a superbly decorated ceiling. The surrounding gardens, restored by the 10th Duchess of Rutland, and woodlands make a superb setting for the castle.

DODDINGTON MAP REF 404 F3

A short distance to the west of Lincoln, the hamlet of Doddington is all but dominated by its hall. Doddington Hall is a breathtaking Elizabethan mansion with walled courtyards and a gabled gatehouse, largely unchanged since it was completed in 1600. The Hall, still very much a family seat, has never been sold and its varied contents reflect 400 years of unbroken family occupation and eclectic collecting with fine textiles, porcelain and pictures.

GAINSBOROUGH MAP REF 407 K7

Once a strategic and important river port, Gainsborough is a busy market town, with some fine 17th-century red-brick architecture. Gainsborough Old Hall is one of the finest medieval manor houses in the country, built in the 1460s and today buckling inward beneath the weight of age bearing on its oak-framed skeleton.

Nearby Scampton is the home to the Dambusters Heritage Centre that commemorates the renowned 617 'Dambusters' Squadron who launched raids from the RAF base at Scampton on the Mohne, Eder and Sorpe dams in Germany in May 1943. The centre houses archive material showing how the squadron lived, trained and carried out their mission using the Barnes Wallis's revolutionary bouncing bomb.

LINCOLN MAP REF 404 F3

The triple towers of Lincoln Cathedral are visible for miles around. Closer inspection reveals a structure of bewildering design and complexity set amid an architectural history as good as anything in Britain. Roman ruins, Viking artefacts and cobbled medieval streets that date from Norman times are the elements that brought the makers of *The Da Vinci Code* here for filming, but which have served the local people and visitors for centuries.

The geological prominence of Lincoln invited settlement as far back as Bronze Age times. In fact, so important was this region strategically, that barely two years after the Battle of Hastings, William the Conqueror started work here on a castle, on a site occupied since Roman times, a structure that dominated the skyline until the cathedral was built.

Lincoln held power first as a Norman stronghold and then as a centre for the wool trade with Flanders, until the wool trade was relocated in neighbouring Boston. Five centuries were to pass before the town fully recovered from this shock to its economy, but gradually the town spread and divided into the 'Up Hill' area – one of middle class respectability – and 'Down Hill', where the grassroots people were based. Today, interest for visitors rests 'Up Hill', around the cathedral.

But while the cathedral and castle are at the heart of a city steeped in the history of England, the surrounding countryside is a perfect partner, dotted with stately homes, castles, hidden gardens, endearing villages and more Norman churches than any other part of Britain. Modern Lincoln is a vibrant and energetic city, a place where history comes to life and rubs shoulders with a very modern community.

LINCOLNSHIRE COAST
MAP REF 405 H3

The lovely, sandy coast of Lincolnshire offers opposing seaside experiences: on the one side there is the happy mayhem of the 'Fun Coast' from Skegness to Cleethorpes; on the other side, a region of unbroken tranquillity, the haunt of wildlife and a haven for birdwatchers and conservationists. Great stretches of natural country and coastline, such as The Boston Wash Banks, Gibraltar Point, Far Ings, Snipe Dales and Messingham are home to birds by the million.

LINCOLN CATHEDRAL

Insight
THE FAMOUS PEOPLE OF LINCOLNSHIRE

Lincolnshire has seen more than its fair share of celebrity:

Henry Bolingbroke, later King Henry IV, was born at Bolingbroke Castle.

John and Charles Wesley, fathers of Methodism, were born in Epworth.

Isaac Newton, scientist, was born at Woolsthorpe Manor.

Alfred Lord Tennyson, Poet Laureate is a son of Somersby.

Sir Joseph Banks, early botanist in Australia came from Revesby.

George Bass, explorer of Australia, was born in Aswarby.

Matthew Flinders, cartographer and man who named Australia, was born in Donington, near Spalding.

Lady Margaret Thatcher, first and only British woman Prime Minister, was born in Grantham.

Geoff Capes, Commonwealth Gold Medalist and twice strongest man in the world, was born in Holbeach.

Nicolas Parsons, broadcaster, like Mrs Thatcher, was born in Grantham.

Visit
LINCOLN CATHEDRAL: THE LINCOLN IMP

Visitors to Lincoln's magnificent cathedral may spend a long time hunting within its walls to find a legendary imp. Many stories surround this stone gargoyle tucked away in the cathedral, but all involve the fight between good and evil. According to one of the most told versions of the story, Satan sent an impish creature to Earth to cause trouble. In Lincoln Cathedral the imp caused much damage and was challenged by an angel who turned it to stone.

OAKHAM

Insight
GARDENS & GARDENING

In spite of its modest size, Rutland boasts many of England's most spectacular and inspirational garden settings, not least Barnsdale Gardens, designed and developed by the late Geoff Hamilton, which many BBC viewers will recognise as home to the TV programme *Gardeners' World*, and which comprises 37 individual smaller gardens and features, as well as a nursery.

Somewhat bizarrely the Clipsham Yew Tree Avenue is surely one of the most eye-catching sights in Rutland with over 150 tall yew trees clipped into an amazing variety of shapes including animals, a World War II Spitfire and even man landing on the moon. The avenue was once the main thoroughfare through the estate to Clipsham Hall. The topiary was begun in 1870 by Amos Alexander, the estate's Head Forester who lived in the gate lodge at the foot of the avenue. The clipping is carried out each autumn by the Forestry Commission's local craftsmen.

LITTLE CASTERTON MAP REF 405 G5

The village of Little Casterton is an unpretentious place, playing quiet host to the greatness of nearby Tolethorpe Hall, an early 17th-century manor house in Elizabethan style built by the Browne family of Stamford on the site of an early 15th-century manor house. The Hall was the birthplace of Robert Browne, who was one of the earliest non-conformist campaigners to split from the established Church of England of which Elizabeth was the head. The Queen called him 'Trouble-church Browne'. In 1620, Browne and other Separatists were among those who sailed on the Mayflower seeking religious freedom in the New World.

Today, Tolethorpe boasts one of the finest open-air theatres in Europe, the Rutland Open Air Theatre, established in 1977 and now attracting more than 30,000 people to an annual 13-week summer season of Shakespeare plays.

LOUTH MAP REF 407 L7

Nominally the 'capital' of the Wolds, it was in Louth that Alfred Tennyson went to school. Today, this is a bustling market town of fine 17th- and 19th-century buildings, and some unusual associations: St James' Church is an wonderful example of 16th-century architecture, its soaring spire at 295 feet (89m) makes it the tallest parish church spire in England. Equally unique, in Eastgate, a brass plaque marks the Greenwich Meridian of 0 degrees longitude which passes through the town, enabling visitors to stand simultaneously in the western and eastern hemispheres.

OAKHAM MAP REF 404 F5

The ancient county town of Oakham is a traditional market stronghold, bustling, vibrant and energetic, and with a pedigree that pre-dates the Domesday Book. The Market Place holds centre stage, although there seem to have been two market squares in Oakham at some time. Links with the past linger in the form of the stocks, the town pump and the ancient Butter Cross, where dairy produce was traditionally sold.

Nearby, Oakham Castle retains a strong link with Norman England, its Great Hall having been a court for over eight centuries, and is without doubt one of the finest examples of late 12th-century domestic architecture in England. It was built by Walkelin de Ferrers, a Norman baron, in about 1180-90. Over 200 horseshoes hang on the walls of the castle and reflect a unique custom that requires every peer of the realm, on their first visit to Oakham, to forfeit a horseshoe to the lord of the manor.

Past associations also find their way into the naming of different parts of the town: 'Deanshold' is a reminder of a time when part of the town was ruled by the Dean and Chapter of Westminster, while 'Lordshold' is the area ruled by the Lord of the Manor, housed in the castle.

In spite of strong links with the past, Oakham is very much a modern place of stylish boutiques and gift shops, designer outlets and markets, not least the traditional Farmers' Market which is held on the third Saturday of each month.

PICKWORTH MAP REF 404 F5

Devotees of poetry may be drawn to the Pickworth Lime Kiln, an odd destination, perhaps, but it was here that the 19th-century 'peasant' poet, John Clare, renowned for his *Poems Descriptive of Rural Life and Scenery*, worked as a lime burner. The small hamlet of Pickworth lies in a region characterised as the Clay Woodlands of the Rutland Plateau (a Jurassic limestone plateau). In the 13th century, Pickworth was a substantial village, but a hundred years later the it was nearly non-existent. It now comprises a small church and a chapel, which services a tiny population.

SEATON MAP REF 404 F5

At the southern edge of Rutland county, the tiny village of Seaton would be relatively unknown but for its spectacular viaduct, long renowned as Britain's longest brick-built railway viaduct, spanning the full width of the Welland Valley. Its 82 arches span the countryside for 0.75 miles (1km) and are a truly majestic sight.

STAMFORD MAP REF 405 G5

There is instant delight in simply wandering the streets of Stamford, not least because of the lovely 18th- and 19th-century Lincolnshire limestone buildings that lent themselves to the filming here of George Eliot's *Middlemarch*. The name Stamford derives from Old English and means 'stone ford', and refers to its crossing point of the River Welland.

The town straddles the Welland, although the main centre lies to the north of the river. That this was formerly a wealthy wool town is demonstrated by the large number of interesting churches, dating from the Middle Ages found here. Something of that antiquity lives on in St Martin's Antiques Centre where up to 60 antiques dealers vie for business selling a wide range of collectables.

Delighting in conservation status, Stamford retains much of its old world charm, and is commonly regarded as the finest stone town in England. Amongst its many historic buildings is the 15th-century Browne's Hospital, founded by one of the town's wool merchants, and more famously the grand Elizabethan Burghley House.

UPPINGHAM MAP REF 404 F5

Perched on a ridge in the south of Rutland, Uppingham is best known for its boarding school (where some of the Harry Potter sequences were filmed), but is home to a host of honey-coloured buildings that give the village a splendid and unique charm. This is an agreeable place of pubs, antique shops, second-hand book shops and tea rooms, a place to unwind and explore at a leisurely pace.

As with Oakham, in Uppingham the Market Place is the focal point, and dates from the 13th century. Uppingham grew to become an important local market town and a convenient coaching stop. There is, too, a history of medieval entertainment here, for Uppingham was a centre for bull baiting (in the Market Place), cock fighting (at the Falcon Hotel) and even dancing bears (off Orange Street). Unacceptable as those practices now are, they do nevertheless illustrate a part of the way of life as it was in medieval England, much like the famous Orange Fair that once met here, selling fruit both for marmalade and as a medicinal cure.

THE WOLDS MAP REF 407 L7

The chalkland area to the north-east of the city, known as the Lincolnshire Wolds, is an Area of Outstanding Natural Beauty. Although intensively farmed, the Wolds are a place of charm, attractive hamlets, villages and market towns. Here, people have lived and worked for centuries, and ancient packhorse trails and salt routes criss-cross the landscape in a telltale network of links that serve only to remind visitors how important this landscape was in the shaping of medieval England.

The notion that Lincolnshire is entirely flat is exploded amid this landscape of rolling hills and gentle valleys, meandering streams and secluded villages. In fact, this is the highest land in eastern England between Kent and Yorkshire and boasts fine views of the Pennines to the west and the North Sea coast to the east.

In spite of the Wolds being a working landscape with extensive woodland and grassland it is well suited to walking, cycling and the simple enjoyment of wildlife. The heavy incidence of farming invites the suggestion that the Wolds are not conducive to wildlife. But paradoxically there is an abundance of clear chalk streams here, and hedgerows and healthy copses that are rich in wildlife and actually benefit from man's constant tending of the landscape.

Neolithic man settled in this part of Lincolnshire more than 6,000 years ago, producing a landscape that by the arrival of the Romans had been extensively cleared and turned to cultivation, the key element in transforming prehistoric man from nomadic hunter-gatherer to settled farmer. In more recent times, the Wolds have become an inspirational landscape to those of the arts' world. Sheffield-born author and critic A S Byatt set her Booker Prize winning novel *Possession* in the Wolds, while many views of the Lincolnshire countryside were painted by the English watercolourist, Peter de Wint and can be seen, along with other artists' work, in Lincoln Art Gallery.

Master poet Lord Tennyson was born in the Wolds, at Somersby, and many of his poems are based on his life experiences here. Stockwith Mill stands on the River Lymn, in which authorities on Tennyson see *The Brook* (written in 1855), which sparkles 'out among the fern, To bicker down a valley'.

BURGHLEY HOUSE

DISTANCE/TIME 17 miles (27.4km) 3h **MAP** OS Explorer 234 Rutland Water **START** Whitwell car park; grid ref: SK 923082 **TRACKS** Largely smooth tarmac and compacted gravel and tarmac **THE PUB** White Horse, 2 Main Street, Empingham. Tel: 01780 460221; www.whitehorserutland.co.uk

DISTANCE/TIME 9.6 miles (15.5km) 2h **MAP** OS Explorer 223 Northampton & Market Harborough **START** Foxton Locks car park; grid ref: SP 692892 **TRACKS** Smooth gravel, narrow grassy track, road and rutted farm track **THE PUB** Bell Inn, 2 Main Street, Gumley. Tel: 01116 279 2476

AROUND RUTLAND WATER

This is a ride around Europe's largest man-made reservoir at the heart of England's smallest county. The nature reserve is one of the most important bird-watching centres in the UK. Depending on the time of year, Rutland Water is home to as many as 20,000 waterfowl. The dam itself is 1,312yds (1,200m) long and the maximim depth of the reservoir is 111 feet (34m). The reserve also boasts an environmental display, a viewing gallery, 22 hides and a nature trail.

1 From the car park exit opposite the bike shop and climbing tower, turn right and then immediately left into the marina. Follow the road round to the left away from the water's edge as it becomes a cycle track. Turn right at the tip of the inlet and continue around the water's edge until you reach another car park. Continue through this car park to reach the dam.

2 After crossing the dam, turn right at the end, through a pair of swing gates, and continue along the obvious tarmac track as far as Normanton Church. Beyond the church, cross a narrow tarmac road and continue straight through an uneven gravel parking area to reach the main Edith Weston car park, with public toilets, snack bar and bike shop. Proceed to the far end of the car park and turn right to continue around the water's edge, past the sailing club and marina.

3 A mile (1.6km) past the sailing club, the track delves into a small wood before dropping down a steep hill to a tight bend at the bottom; a sign near the top gives riders plenty of warning that this hill is coming up.

4 At the next road turn left up a steep hill to reach the B-road between Edith Weston and Manton. Cross the main road with care and then turn right towards Manton, following the cycle lane. At the first junction continue straight on into Manton. Soon after passing a phone box on your left, turn right, following a Rutland Water cycling sign. Bear left past the Horse and Jockey pub to reach a wide gravel track down to the A6003. Follow a narrow pavement at the bottom beneath the railway bridge (a sign advises riders to dismount for this bit) and stay on this pavement for a further 440yds (402m).

5 Turn right through a swing gate here, following the cycle track around the water's edge until it cuts across the Lax Hill peninsula. This track eventually leads to Egleton. Turn left into the village and then right again after around 200yds (182m). Continue past the church and stay on the road to the main road into Hambleton.

6 Turn left, and then right after 300yds (273m) along a short cycle track to reach the A606. From here, stay on the rolling pavement for 1.5 miles (2km), before heading right, back onto a gravel track and around the water's edge. At the bottom of the next tarmac road, turn left up the short sharp hill before turning right towards Barnsdale Wood car park. After going down and then steeply uphill to reach the car park, continue downhill again to the bottom, far right-hand corner of the car park; delve into Barnsdale Wood here and follow the track all the way back to the start point.

FOXTON LOCKS & THE GRAND UNION CANAL

Enjoy varied and challenging traffic-free riding along one of England's most famous canal systems. The Grand Union Canal actually started its life as lots of separate canals, which were joined to provide a navigable waterway from Birmingham to London. There are 10 locks at Foxton and it takes about 50 minutes for a boat to negotiate all of them.

1 From the car park exit, turn left along a gravel track to get to the bridge over the canal. Cross the bridge and turn right to reach the canal and, after about 330yds (300m), the locks themselves. Cycling isn't permitted on this section so you'll have to walk your bikes down this side of the locks (the Foxton Locks Museum is situated on the far side of the passing pond, and can be reached on foot). Stay to the left at the bottom to reach the shop and café.

2 Continue past the shop to cross a cobbled bridge. On the far side keep going in the same direction. The shingle track along this part of the canal is wide and smooth, although there are one or two places where the left hand edge has collapsed a little, so it's a good idea to stay right. After 1.5 miles (2km), you come to Debdale Wharf. Beyond Debdale Wharf, the path becomes narrow and grassy and in summer, this section may be overgrown bulrushes, but it should still be passable. At Gumley Road, the track becomes smoother and wider again, before continuing on to Saddington Road.

3 Just beyond Saddington Road, a short sharp climb takes you up to the right of Saddington Tunnel. A longer but more gentle rise, still on a wide gravel track, then takes you along the top of the tunnel, before an equally gentle descent carries you back down to Kibworth Road. From here it's possible to return the way you came, but what follows is an alternative for those who are still feeling energetic.

4 If the gate is locked here, you'll have to carry your bikes over the narrow stile, before crossing the road with care to reach another, wider stile. Another gradual downhill then takes you to a short, steep slope down to a fence above the canal. This can be ridden but you may prefer to walk it. At the fence turn left to continue along the canal. The path is quite narrow, and can be slippery in wet weather, so take great care here. At the next bridge, continue past it for about 30yds (30m) to reach a gate – go through this gate to reach the bridge.

5 Cross the bridge and continue to the top of the field ahead, where you'll find an enormous slab of granite welcoming you to Millfield Wood. Go through a gate and continue along a wide bridleway across a field. Follow the track as it bears left to reach Kibworth Road and then cross the road to continue in the same directiona along another gravel track.

6 After 1.5 miles (2km) of gentle downhill riding on a wide potholed track, turn right at the road to Smeeton, and then first left along Debdale Lane. This rough farm track rises gently and then more steeply to reach the canal. At the top of the track bear left towards Debdale Wharf Farm and then turn right at the farm to regain the towpath. From here, turn left to retrace your tracks back to the start.

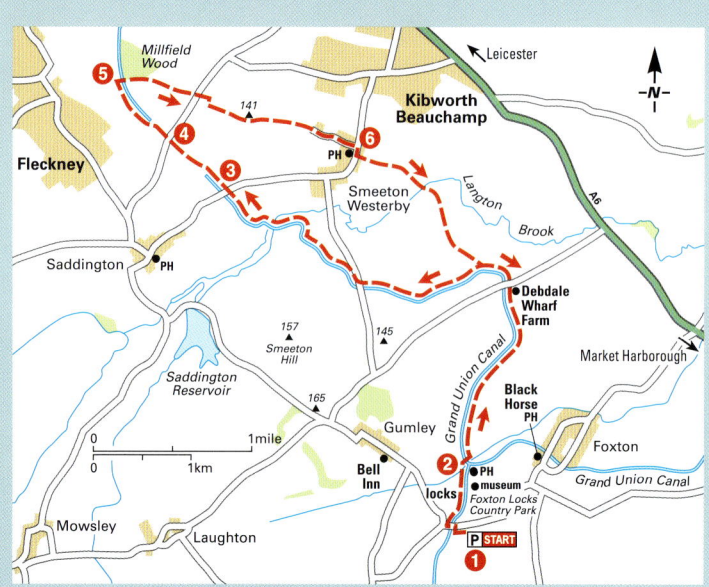

Worcester
& Malvern Hills

CLOCKWISE FROM TOP: LITTLE COMBERTON; APPLE TREES, LITTLE COMBERTON; GREAT MALVERN

GREAT & LITTLE COMBERTON

MAP REF 403 H6

Great Comberton is a small hamlet south of Pershore spread across the northern slope of Bredon Hill and the left bank of the River Avon. The village contains a large number of timber-framed 'black-and-white' cottages.

Little Comberton lies in one of the most fertile parts of the county, so it's no surprise that the main industry here is agriculture. The village is small, consisting of just one street of cottages, one of which has an attractive overhanging, timber-framed gable. Opposite the church is the Old Manor House, which dates from the early 17th-century. Near by Bredon Hill, rising conspicuously from the low-lying Severn Vale, once supported an Iron Age fort wherein excavation revealed a large number of mutilated bodies, presumably hacked to pieces in Roman times.

GREAT MALVERN MAP REF 403 H6

Water from the springs on the shapely Malvern Hills has been renowned for more than 300 years, but the village spa of Great Malvern grew only after the 'Water Cure', or hydropathy, was brought to the town from Austria in 1842 by a Dr Wilson. The first water cure establishment in Malvern was the Crown Hotel on Belle Vue Terrace, where one of Dr Wilson's patients made a miraculous recovery.

Today, Great Malvern is a particularly well-preserved Victorian spa town. From the 900-year-old Priory Church, tucked neatly into the hillside, the radiating roads are lined with an agreeable mix of architectural styles from elaborate Italianate and Dutch Gabled to Queen Anne Gothic and austere Scottish baronial.

But what makes the 'Malverns' – Great and Little, North, South, West, Wells and the Link, sometimes known as the 'Seven Sisters' – so appealing is the special relationship they have with the countryside that surrounds them, and in particular the Area of Outstanding Natural Beauty known as the Malvern Hills. More than 500 million years old, these are among the oldest hills in England (being of pre-Cambrian granite), and are embraced like a jewelled necklace by the townships which themselves are steeped in history.

For those 'in the know', Malvern is a byword for all that is good in performing arts, with festivals of the arts taking place throughout the year, attracting many leading actors, and audiences from across the world. George Bernard Shaw is thought to have founded the first theatre in Great Malvern. Famous British composer Edward Elgar, known to be fond of the Malvern Hills, also lived in Great Malvern and there is a statue in his honour at the centre of the town. For actors there can be no finer theatre in which to perform; nor one more paradoxical – so much is going on here, yet it is so refreshingly relaxing. Purity is in the air; and in the water, of course.

WORCESTER CATHEDRAL

PERSHORE MAP REF 403 H6

Positioned midway between Worcester and Evesham, in the lovely Vale of Evesham, an area important for fruit and vegetable production, the small market town of Pershore is a neat and idyllic gathering of mainly Georgian houses, a place of handsome architecture that contrasts rather abruptly with its rather compact and squat abbey, the remains of a significantly larger Benedictine building which was destroyed at the time of the Dissolution of the Monasteries.

Like most towns and villages in Worcestershire, Pershore is surrounded by beautiful countryside and is a haven for cyclists and ramblers.

WORCESTER MAP REF 403 H5

The city of Worcester clings to the left bank of the River Severn, and, given the propensity of the river to flood, it is not unusual to see large riparian areas, not least the racecourse and car parks, completely flooded. That aside, the city is a glorious mish-mash of architectural styles ranging from delightful timber Tudor buildings to elegant Georgian buildings, although modern developments have done nothing to enhance the historic heart of this ancient city.

Worcester's Norman cathedral is its crowning glory, a superb masterpiece of architectural design and craftsmanship. Among the numerous tombs within the cathedral, that of King John (1199–1216) is the most visited. Also in the cathedral is a memorial to Arthur Tudor who is buried here. Arthur Tudor was the older brother to the next in line, and subsequent heir to the throne, Henry VIII.

Worcester is a splendid shopping city, with seemingly endless streets of individual shops set against larger retail centres. Wandering the streets reveals a plethora of fascinating shops selling quality goods. The Hopmarket hosts a fascinating collection of small stores in an historic courtyard setting. The Shambles is the place to go for fine china, Royal Worcester, Royal Doulton, Wedgwood and Spode. Medieval Friar Street has a number of timbered buildings, and an especially fine example of the architecture of this time is The Greyfriars, a timber-framed merchant's house built in 1480. But perhaps the most intriguing place is tucked away behind the cathedral: the Museum of Worcester Porcelain relates the history of the city's principal industry since the mid-18th century. It adjoins the renowned Royal Worcester Porcelain Works where Dr John Wall and his associates formed the first Worcester Porcelain Factory.

Links between Worcester and the British Civil War are strong: the Battle of Worcester in 1651 was a key moment in the war, the final crushing defeat for the Royalist cause. The English Civil War ended at nearby Powick Bridge, where it had started nine years previously. Charles II, attempting to regain the throne, was lucky to escape the battlefield and eluded capture until he was able to slip away to France. (It was he who hid in an oak tree to evade his pursuers.) Oliver Cromwell described Worcester, his last battle as an active commander, as a 'crowning mercy'.

Just outside Worcester, at Lower Broadheath, is the birthplace of the child who was to become one of Britain's most renowned composers, Sir Edward Elgar, best known perhaps for his *Pomp and Circumstance* marches, one of which is commonly called *Land of Hope and Glory*. He also composed the *Enigma Variations*, evocative symphonies and a beautiful cello concerto.

At the height of his creativity, Elgar was often to be found walking the nearby Malvern Hills, indeed, near the end of his life he remarked 'If you are walking on the hills and hear music, don't be afraid, it's only me'. He died in 1934, and lies buried in St Wulstan's church in Little Malvern.

MARTLEY THROUGH THE CIDER ORCHARDS

As you walk through one of cider producer Bulmers' orchards, it's mind-boggling to think that the Bulmers Brothers began with just 1 acre (0.4ha) in 1888. In fact, nowadays Herefordshire and Worcestershire's orchards only provide a fraction of the Hereford plant's capacity. They now import a lot of concentrate from Europe.

DISTANCE/TIME 6.75 miles (10.9km) 3h Ascent: 720ft (219m) **MAP** Aqua3 OS Explorer 204 Worcester & Droitwich Spa **START** Grid ref: SO 766597 **PATHS** Field paths, lanes, orchard paths, tracks, river meadows, minor roads, 20 stiles **THE PUB** Crown, Martley. Tel: 01886 888265

1 Go through the churchyard to the B4204. Cross to the track. In 100yds (91m) enter the school's grounds briefly then walk in the trees that run parallel. Turn right at a stile, and then another, to re-enter the grounds. Briefly follow the left edge of the playing fields. Another stile gives on to a field. At the road turn left, then turn right (signposted 'Highfields'). Beside Lingen Farm go down the track. At a bend take the stile, and go across a field. Cross the stream and climb steadily taking the right-hand gates to reach a minor road.

2 Turn left and at Larkins go ahead. At The Peak walk behind Ross Green's gardens. Cross the fields to reach a road and go straight over, to a partially concealed stile, not diagonally to a fingerpost. Walk beside the barn, then onwards to another lane. Turn left to reach a fingerpost pointing into an apple orchard before Pear Tree Cottage.

3 Follow waymarkers through trees and emerge at a bridge over a ditch, beside apple-sorting equipment. Go 220yds (201m) up a track, to a gap in the evergreens. Turn left and walk down orchard ride. At a T-junction turn right and continue up to just before a gate beside a small house. Turn left, almost back on yourself. Go through the orchard, following faded yellow splodges about 1.5ft (45cm) up on tree trunks. Leave by a footbridge, crossing fields to the B4197.

4 Turn right and after 60yds (55m) take the track for 0.5 miles (0.8km) to Rodge Hill's top. Turn sharp left signed 'Worcs Way South'. Follow this for 1 mile (1.6km), then steps lead down to the road's hairpin bend.

5 Turn right and in 20yds (18m) turn left, but after 15yds (14m) turn right again into conifers. Emerge to drop down steeply. At the B4204 turn right for 200yds (182m). Turn left, skirt the barn to the left; go diagonally to the River Teme. Follow the riverside walk, into Kingswood Nature Reserve, for over 0.5 miles (0.8km). Leave the river when the wire fence requires it. Ascend a path, later a driveway, to the road.

6 Turn right going uphill; this soon bends left. Near the brow move right (waymarker) to walk in a field, not on the road. At the end turn left and in 275yds (251m), cross two stiles. Beside fields and allotments, emerge between the Crown and a garage. Pass the telephone box into the village. Turn right to the church and the start.

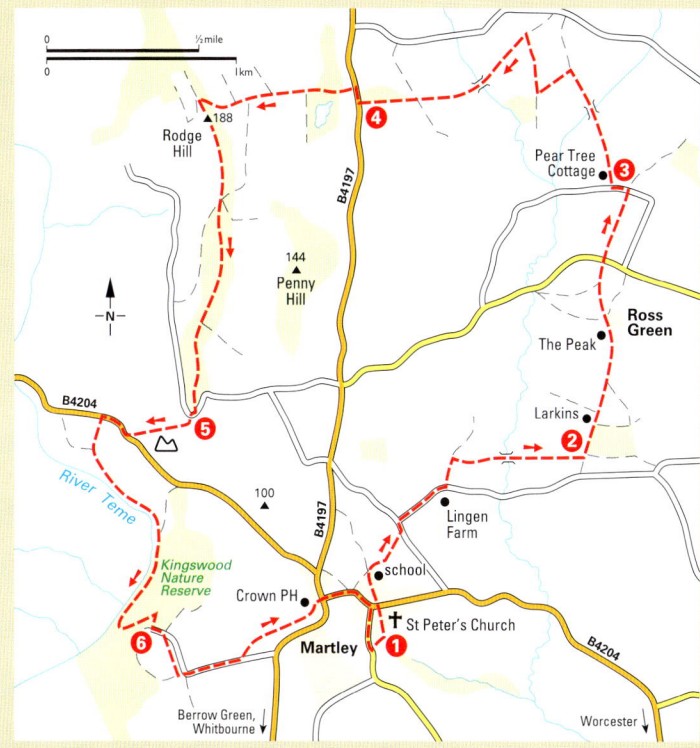

WALK 62

WORCESTER CITY SIGHTS & SMELLS

This is a town walk through Worcester, known for Sir Edward Elgar, its battle, its porcelain, its racecourse and, of course, its sauce. But what about its unsung hero? Sir Charles Hastings was a brilliant student who returned to Worcester Infirmary in order to begin a successful medical career. His dedication and medical observances led to the establishment of the British Medical Association, which still oversees the work of medical practitioners today. It is said that he attended every case during the three cholera outbreaks in 1832, 1849 and 1853.

DISTANCE/TIME 2.5 miles (4km) 1h30 Ascent: Negligible **MAP** Aqua3 OS Explorer 204 Worcester & Droitwich Spa **START** Grid ref: SO 846548 **PATHS** City streets and tarmac riverside path **THE PUB** Cardinal's Hat, 31, Friar St, Worcester WR1 2NA. Tel: 01905 22066

1 The described route begins at the city side of the road bridge, but you can pick it up anywhere – at The Commandery or the Guildhall, for example – depending on where you have left your car. Turn left, along North Parade, passing the Old Rectifying House (a wine bar). From here turn right up Dolday, then left, to pass in front of the bus station, heading along The Butts. Turn left along Farrier Street, then turn right into Castle Street, finally reaching the northern extremity of the route at its junction with Foregate Street.

2 Go right along Foregate Street, passing Shire Hall and the City Museum and Art Gallery, continuing along The Cross and into a pedestrianised area called High Street. From here, turn left into Pump Street. (Elgar's statue stands close to his father's piano shop, at the southern end of High Street.) Turn left again, into The Shambles. Once you reach a junction turn right into Mealcheapen Street. Take another right turn and you are in New Street (which later becomes Friar Street).

3 Head down this street (look out for King Charles' House; he stayed thre during the battle of Worcester in 1651). At the end of the street is a dual carriageway (College Street). Turn right then cross over if you wish to visit the cathedral.

4 Leave the cathedral along the College Precincts to a fortified gateway known as the Edgar Tower. (It is named after the 10th-century King Edgar, but was actually built in the 14th century. Go through this gateway to see College Green.) Continue along what is now Severn Street, which, unsurprisingly, leads to the River Severn. Turn right, to complete your circuit, by following Kleve Walk, a leafy waterside avenue; this section floods at some time most winters, and the cricket ground opposite was under several feet of water in 2000. For a more studied insight into the city's rich history, take a guided walk (on weekdays only) with a Green Badge Guide.

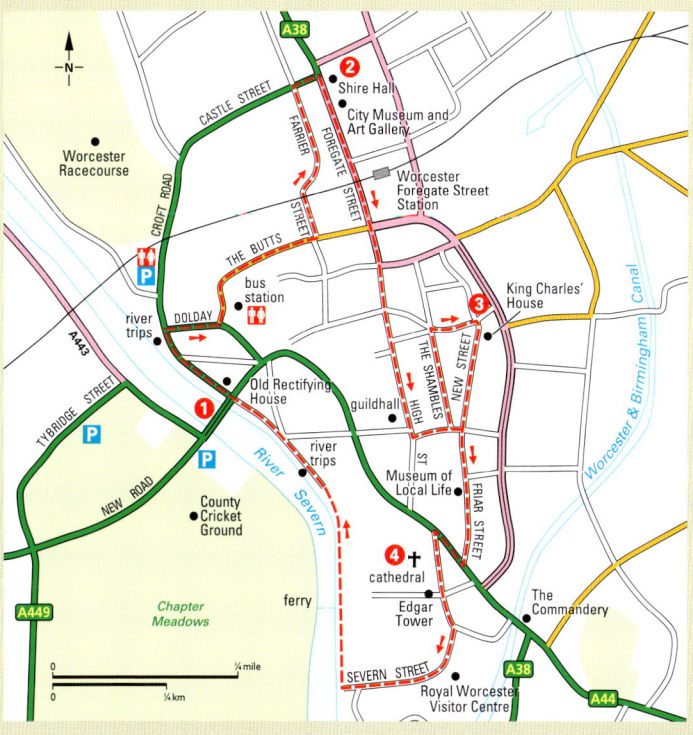

Stratford & Vale of Evesham

CLOCKWISE FROM TOP LEFT: STRATFORD-UPON-AVON; THE WATER GARDEN, KIFTSGATE COURT GARDENS; ROWING IN EVESHAM

ALCESTER MAP REF 403 J5

The ancient Roman town of Alcester stands at the confluence of two rivers, the Alne and the Arrow. The town owns some fine Tudor buildings and a church that is Gothic externally, but Classical inside, underpinning a fine architectural heritage that somehow works well with the host of independent, family-run shops found here. The town's medieval street pattern survives almost intact, along with ancient properties including the church of St Nicholas with its 14th-century tower, and the 17th-century town hall. Long the focus of attention of Roman scholars, the town is regarded as the best-understood Roman settlement in Britain.

CHARLECOTE PARK MAP REF 404 D6

The home of the Lucy family for over 700 years, the mellow brickwork of Charlecote Park perfectly highlights the essence of Tudor England. Queen Elizabeth and Shakespeare both knew the house well; in fact, the young Shakespeare is said to have been caught in the grounds poaching deer. Notwithstanding a hoard of memorabilia about the British Empire and a uniquely extensive portrait collection, it is the formal garden that is the real delight at Charlecote, opening onto a deer park skillfully landscaped by 'Capability' Brown that bestows a perfect excuse for a family picnic among the deer.

EVESHAM MAP REF 403 J6

Built in a protective loop on the banks of the River Avon, Evesham is an agricultural centre, a market town, situated in the middle of a fertile vale that has become Britain's foremost fruit-growing area. Abbeys like Evesham once dominated this region and were instrumental in developing orchards and gardens for the production of fruit and vegetables.

The medieval town grew up beside the 8th-century Benedictine abbey, one of the grandest abbeys ever built, but of which little survives today. Evesham bell tower is probably England's finest detached bell tower, and along with 14th- and 16th-century gateways and two medieval churches forms the principal remains of Evesham's once mighty abbey. The churches, were originally the abbey chapels and the bell tower was a combined gatehouse and campanile. The bell tower's peal of 12 bells certainly lives up to the grandeur of their setting, and are nationally acclaimed as a benchmark against which other English-hung rings are compared.

One of the abbey buildings houses the Almonry Museum and Heritage Centres which contains a mock-up Victorian kitchen and exhibits that commemorate the Battle of Evesham (1265) when Simon de Montfort, a thorn in the side of Henry III, was killed by the troops of Prince Edward, later King Edward I. Simon de Montfort, 6th Earl of Leicester, was the leader of the opposition to Henry III. After the rebellion of 1263-1264, de Montfort became de facto ruler of England and called the first directly-elected parliament, securing his place in history as one of the important founders of modern democracy.

ILMINGTON MAP REF 404 D7

Yellow-hued Cotswold limestone houses with pretty, well-tended gardens set amid a tangle of intersecting lanes on the Ilmington Downs, the highest point in Warwickshire, gives this agreeable village the mellow, rustic feel of a true Cotswold village. Less obviously, the village has a strong Morris dancing tradition, often performed in the grounds of the delightful manor house and especially on the annual Gardens Day.

During the summer months the Ilmington Morris Men dance on Wednesday evenings in the surrounding villages. The group was formed in 1974, and, among others, perform up to twenty traditional 'Ilmington' dances collected over the last hundred years. There is evidence of Morris dancing taking place in Ilmington since the 17th century, when dancers from Ilmington performed their sequences around a flag high up on Dovers Hill at Chipping Campden.

SHIPSTON ON STOUR MAP REF 404 D7

Shipston on Stour is a delightful, small market town on the edge of the Cotswolds, and very much a focal point for the surrounding rural communities with a variety of shops catering for both residents and tourists.

The town was formerly a vital centre for the trade of sheep and grain, and known as the 'Sheep-wash-Town' because in early summer the river was used for washing sheep. From the 14th to the 19th centuries Shipston lay along the route of the Welsh cattle drovers bound for London. In those days, droving was a thirsty business, so it is not surprising to find that Shipston has many pubs. The inns also served coaches as this was an important stop.

A three-day fair held in June dates back to the 13th century, while the annual Shipston Proms in June and July promotes a range of music from classical to rock.

A few miles to the south, and erected more than 4,000 years ago, the Rollright Stones on the Warwickshire-Oxfordshire border, are a sacred site on a hilltop high above the village of Long Compton. The site comprises some 77 chunks of weather-worn limestone: a principal stone circle known as 'The Kings Men', a prominent outlier called 'The King Stone', and the semi-recumbent remains of a megalithic tomb known as 'The Whispering Knights'.

STRATFORD-UPON-AVON

MAP REF 404 D6

There is little in this glorious market town, so steeped in the life and works of one of Britain's most eminent playwrights, to reveal much about William Shakespeare's early career. His birth and baptism are recorded, but other than the fact that 'he had been in his younger years a schoolmaster in the country' (John Aubrey, 1681), he remains a vague personage until he materialises virtually a fully fledged poet and playwright.

That he thereafter spent much of his life in Stratford is more than enough justification for the town to celebrate his presence in a way that, thankfully, is both tasteful and authoritative. For a sense of direction there is no better place to start than his birthplace, a fine 16th-century building on what was always a busy thoroughfare. Just on the edge of the town centre is Holy Trinity Church, itself an architectural delight, and here Shakespeare lies buried. Not far away, at Shottery on the town's outskirts, is the thatched farmhouse cottage where Anne Hathaway, Shakespeare's wife, grew up. The cottage remained in the possession of Anne Hathaway's descendants until the late 19th century, and still contains numerous items belonging to the family.

There is a world-class quality about Stratford, much of which would have prevailed without the bard as a marketing device, and it is quite a delight to stroll along the streets, inescapably imbued with Shakespeariana, taking in the splendours of medieval craftsmanship and the aura from 16th- and 17th-century England. Among the finest buildings, not least Shakespeare's birthplace, are Thomas Nash's House on Chapel Street owned by the first husband of Shakespeare's grand-daughter, Elizabeth; Hall's Croft in the Old Town, is named after Dr John Hall, who married one of Shakespeare's daughters. The most ornate house in Stratford is Harvard House, a splendid example of an Elizabethan town house. Rebuilt in 1596, Harvard House is the home of the Museum of British Pewter. Mary Arden's House and the Shakespeare Countryside Museum is at Wilmcote, 5 miles (8km) north of Stratford, a timbered farmhouse that was the home of Shakespeare's mother before she married John Shakespeare and then moved to Stratford.

Of course, Stratford is internationally renowned as the home of the Royal Shakespeare Company, long recognised as Europe's and indeed the world's leading classical theatre company. Its annual repertoire of productions features a mix of classical and modern drama and musicals with some of the best actors and directors in the world performing plays by Shakespeare, his contemporaries, other classical playwrights, as well as many new plays specially commissioned by the RSC.

More famous for its literary associations, Stratford bustles with culture and history, superb shops and restaurants, and a vibrant Friday market.

Besides Shakespeare there is much to enjoy from a day at Stratford. You could try your luck at the horses at exciting Stratford Races or take a tour of the city on an open-top bus, make a visit to a butterfly farm or spend the afternoon on a boat trip on the River Avon.

The medieval bridge spanning the Avon greatly contributed to the town's economic prosperity, and still provides a link between the town and the countryside of the Avon that awaits wider exploration.

Visit
STRATFORD'S THEATRES

The most famous theatrical company in the world, the Royal Shakespeare Company, has its home in Stratford-upon-Avon. It draws thespians from around the globe to take part in, and to watch, performances by the great and the good. The three theatres in town provide a variety of stage drama.

The Royal Shakespeare Theatre, or the Royal, has the largest space and was constructed in 1932.

The Swan was built to re-create the space and atmosphere of an Elizabethan theatre, and comes complete with galleries.

The Other Place, which opened for business in 1986, is the smallest and has a more intimate atmosphere.

A donation of land from Charles Flowers in 1875 was the beginning of a successful campaign to bring theatre here. Little did he know that one day Stratford would be so revered.

STRATFORD-UPON-AVON, IN THE BARD'S FOOTSTEPS

This is a tour of theatrical Stratford-upon-Avon, birthplace of William Shakespeare, to see its many sights. But there are other things to see in Stratford-upon-Avon, apart from the Shakespeare heritage. The medieval 14-arched Clopton Bridge forms a splendid gateway to the town. The town hall is a fine Palladian building and Harvard House, in the High Street, dates from 1596. The Falcon Hotel, the ancient guild hall and a row of timbered almshouses are also worth a visit.

DISTANCE/TIME 2.5 miles (4km) 1h Ascent: Negligible   **MAP** Aqua3 OS Explorer 205 Stratford-upon-Avon & Evesham   **START** Grid ref: SP 205547   **PATHS** Riverside paths and street pavements, no stiles   **THE PUB** Dirty Duck, Waterside, Stratford-upon-Avon CV37 6BA. Tel: 01789 297 312

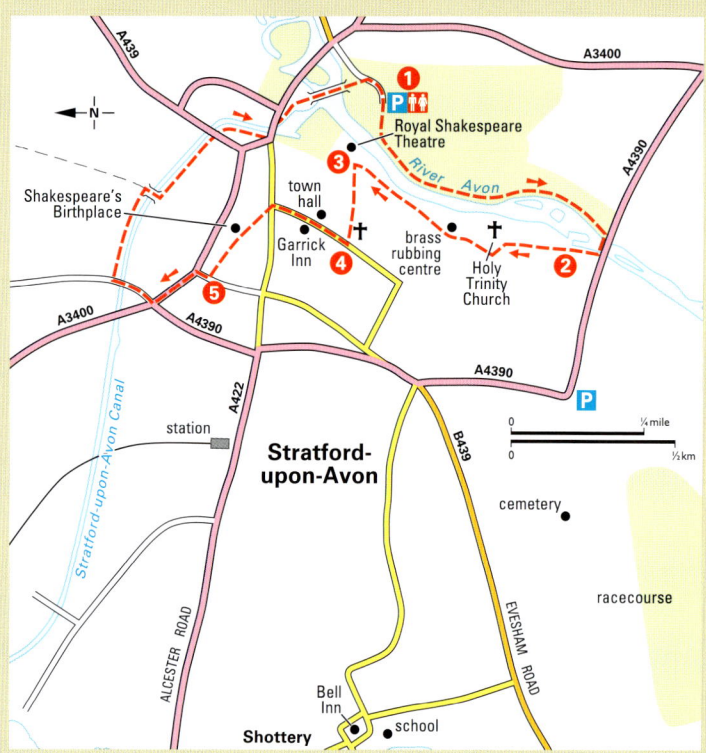

1 From the car park, walk along the banks of the River Avon opposite the famous Royal Shakespeare Theatre. Pass the weir until you come to the footbridge over river, just in front of the A4390 road bridge.

2 Go right over a footbridge and bear right past the old mill building into Mill Lane. Continue up Mill Lane and go through the churchyard of Holy Trinity Church, walking around the church to see the river view. Leave the churchyard through a main gate into Old Town and follow the pavement. Just before reaching the turning into Southern Lane, go right into New Place Gardens and walk up to the Brass Rubbing Centre. Continue past the ferry and stroll through attractive Theatre Gardens by the side of the Avon, exiting into Waterside and passing by the frontage of the old theatre building.

3 Go left up Chapel Lane, taking a little time to wander through Knot Gardens on your way up to Chapel Street. At top of the lane is the Guild Chapel to Shakespeare's Grammar School, and you'll have New Place Gardens to your right.

4 Go right along Chapel Street, passing the Shakespeare Hotel and the town hall into the High Street. Harvard House is on the left, near the black-and-white Garrick Inn. At the end of the High Street, bear left into Henley Street and walk along the pedestrianised area that takes you past Shakespeare's Birthplace and the Museum. At the top of Henley Street, bear right and then left into Birmingham Road. Cross the road at the pedestrian crossing and go left up to the traffic lights.

5 Head right up Clopton Road for 100yds (91m), go right up Clopton Road for 100yds (91m), then descend to the towpath of the Stratford-upon-Avon Canal. Follow this, going southeast. Cross over the canal at bridge No 68 and continue along the towpath into Bancroft Gardens by the canal basin where you will see an array of colourful narrowboats and the Royal Shakespeare Theatre. Cross old the Tram Bridge to the car park on the right.

CHARLECOTE PARK – AN ELIZABETHAN JEWEL

This is an easy walk into open countryside, starting at the delightful village of Charlecote, about 5 miles (8km) from Stratford-upon-Avon. There is an opportunity to visit the superb Charlecote Park (now cared for by the National Trust), which has been home to the Lucy family since 1247. The route passes along the banks of the River Dene to the edge of the village of Wellesbourne and then crosses farmland and lanes on its return to Charlecote, passing 19th-century Charlecote Mill.

DISTANCE/TIME 5 miles (8km) 1h30 Ascent: 33ft (10m)   **MAP** Aqua3 OS Explorer 205 Stratford-upon-Avon   **START** Grid ref: SP 262564   **PATHS** Field paths and farm tracks, 2 stiles   **THE PUB** Kings Head, Warwick Road, Wellesbourne CV35 9LX. Tel: 0870 1414799

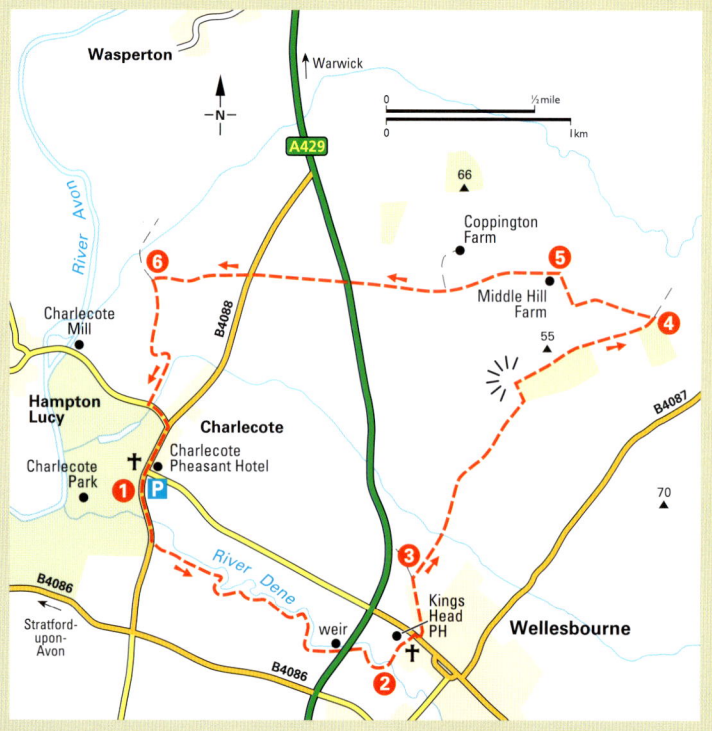

1 From Charlecote Park car park, go left along the grass verge and then cross over the River Dene. In about 100yds (91m), go left along the wide track that arcs left on to the clear fenced path by the side of the river and walk along for this 1.5 miles (2.4km) into Wellesbourne. You will pass a weir before you reach the footbridge near St Peter's Church.

2 Go left over the footbridge and up the fenced path to the left of the church until you reach the village. Continue up the road to the left of house No 21 – the Kings Head pub is on the left. Cross the main road in the village and walk up Warwick Road opposite.

3 In about 300yds (274m), just after passing Daniell Road, go right along the tarmac path at the back of houses. Cross the footbridge and continue over several fields. Take the footpath to the left of a copse of trees then go right into woodland. Turn left along a track at the top of the hedge of trees. You will emerge from the trees for short distance and then re-enter again. After you emerge for second time, look for a hedge gap to the left.

4 Carry on forward by passing through the gap and then continuing along footpaths until you get to Middle Hill Farm.

5 Continue left, between farm buildings then go to the right of the farmhouse and walk along the farm drive for about 0.75 miles (1.2km), passing the entrance to Coppington Farm on your way to the A429. Cross the road with care then the stile opposite on to a fenced footpath. After crossing a minor road continue along the driveway past a farm building.

6 In 100yds (91m), go left through a kissing gate into pastureland. A second gate leads into a large field that you walk around by the field hedge. Go right, through a further kissing gate, and continue to the right of the field hedge until you go through a final kissing gate on to Charlecote Road. Go left along the footway past a thatched cottage into centre of Charlecote, then turn right along the grass verge of the main street past half-timbered houses and Charlecote Pheasant Hotel, with St Leonard's Church opposite, to reach Charlecote Park car park.

DISTANCE/TIME 15.5 miles (25km) 3h30 **MAP** OS Explorer 205 Stratford-upon-Avon & Evesham **START** Stratford: Clopton Bridge, grid ref SP 203549 or Seven Meadows car park, grid ref: SP 195540 **TRACKS** Streets, disused railway line with good gravel surface, country lanes and farm track **THE PUB** Masons Arms, Welford Road, Long Marston. Tel: 01789 720586

STRATFORD GREENWAY

Explore the quiet countryside in which England's greatest bard grew up. Whilst Stratford was already a prosperous town before Shakespeare's day, it is probably due to his association that so many of the town's splendid 16th-century buildings have survived.

1 Leave Clopton Bridge along Waterside. Turn left at the end and then go left again into Mill Lane. It finishes in a narrow alley that leads to the river. The continuing path swings beneath a bridge to shadow the main road, shortly passing Seven Meadows car park.

2 If joining the railway track at Seven Meadows, turn right to Milcote picnic area. The way runs beside Stratford's racecourse then crosses the Avon by a picnic area and the River Stour. Go beyond Chambers Halt and Pearces Crossing to Milcote Station.

3 Through barriers and a parking area, cross a road to a picnic site. The track continues for 2 miles (3.2km), passing crossings at Knobbs Farm and the Airfield before reaching Wyre Lane Crossing. Leave right on Wyre Lane into Long Marston.

4 To return, either retrace your outward route, or keep ahead on the road to the village. There, turn off right to Dorsington. Carry on for 1.5 miles (2.4km) to a T-junction and go right to another junction in the middle of Dorsington. Take the lane on the right to Welford. Drop to a road and follow that right into modern Welford. Leave after just over 0.5 miles (0.8km) along Headland Road on the left, which is opposite St Peter's Church.

5 The onward route lies to the right along Church Street. At the end of Church Street by the Bell Inn, take the main road right through the village. Leaving Welford, turn off left to Weston and Clifford Chambers, going left again after 0.5 miles (0.8km) on a narrow lane to Weston-on-Avon.

6 At the bottom turn right past the church. Keep forward, later passing Milcote Manor Farm. The way disintegrates to dirt as it swings right to meet the disused railway at Chambers Crossing Halt. Follow it left back to Seven Meadows car park and Stratford.

7 If you began from the town, after passing Holy Trinity Church, carry on past Riverside and instead turn right at the next crossroads into Church Street. Go ahead along Chapel Street and High Street to a roundabout in the town centre, to return to your car park.

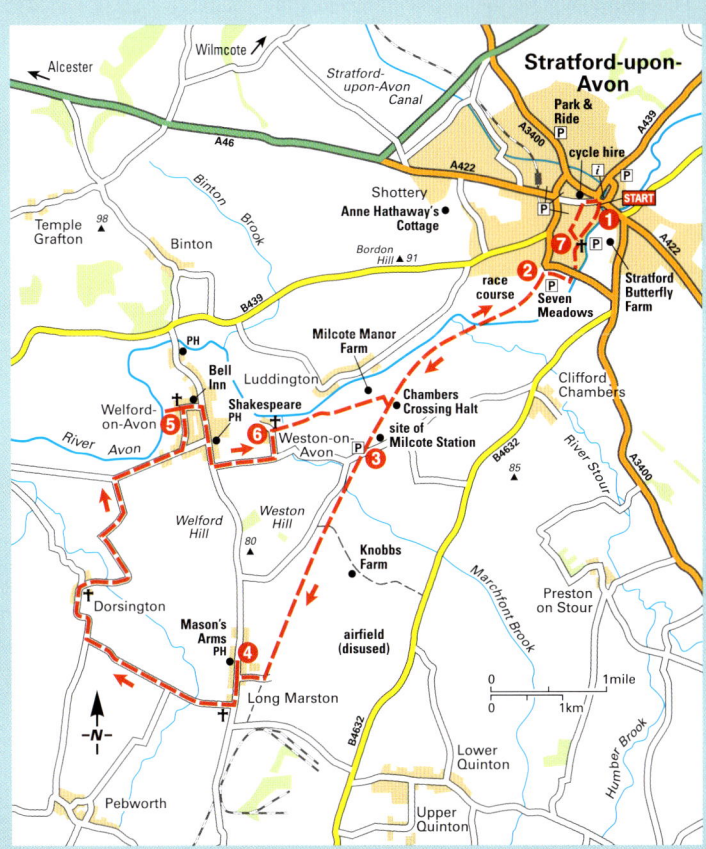

DISTANCE/TIME 9.75 miles (15.7km) 2h **MAP** OS Explorer 220 Birmingham & Explorer 221 Coventry & Warwick **START** Kingswood; car park in Brome Hall lane; grid ref: SP 185710 **TRACKS** Quiet lanes and canal towpaths; gravel surfaces **THE PUB** Boot Inn, Old Warwick Road, Lapworth. Tel: 01564 782464; www.thebootatlapworth.co.uk

BADDESLEY CLINTON & PACKWOOD HOUSE

A ride along towpaths that connect two old houses: Baddesley Clinton, in one of the most picturesque settings in the country, and former Benedictine priory, Packwood House.

1 Join the Stratford-upon-Avon Canal behind the car park, turn right past a lock to a bridge where the canal splits. Cross to the spur, which drops through a second lock to another bridge, there dismounting to descend four steps on the far side. Follow the towpath away from the junction, passing a picnic site and going beneath a railway bridge to meet the Grand Union Canal.

2 Cycle along the towpath to the right for some 0.75 miles (1.2km) to the second bridge (No. 63), leaving immediately beyond it for the lane above. Over the bridge, climb away past the Tom O' The Wood pub. At a 'Give Way' crossroads, keep ahead over the B4439, enjoying easy pedalling for a little over 0.5 miles (0.8km) to the end of the lane.

3 To the left, the way leads past Hay Wood, eventually meeting another junction. Go left again towards Lapworth and Baddesley Clinton, the lane shortly falling to pass the entrance of Baddesley Clinton, which lies opposite Netherwood Lane. Turn in beside the lodge and follow the winding drive to a car park at its end. The National Trust has provided separate facilities for cycles, enabling you to explore the house and nearby church on foot.

4 Returning to the main lane, turn left towards Hockley Heath, soon dropping to a blind humpback bridge spanning the Grand Union Canal. Beyond there, keep going over a railway bridge and, later, ahead at a crossroads beside the Punch Bowl. About 0.5 miles (0.8km) further on, the road turns sharply left. Exercising caution, turn off right onto a narrow lane leading past Packwood House, which stands beside the road only a short distance along.

5 Resuming your ride, carry on for almost another 0.75 mile (1.2km) to the second lane leaving on the left, Vicarage Road. It is signed to Packwood and Hockley Heath. Follow that for 0.5 miles (0.8km) and then turn left at an unsigned junction. Winding past Packwood's church, St Giles, the lane eventually ends at a main road, the B4439.

6 Turn left towards Lapworth and Warwick, but after 200yds (182m) and just before some white cottages, swing off right onto a gravel track, the entrance to Drawbridge Farm. Meeting the canal a few yards/metres along, follow the towpath left to the first of a long series of locks (No 2) heralding the canal's descent to Kingswood. Prudent cyclists will then dismount to negotiate the sharp dip and low ridge immediately beyond.

7 The path crosses to the opposite bank over a bridge below lock No 4, remaining on that side to pass beneath a road bridge and shortly reaching lock No 6. Beyond, locks then follow in quick succession, forming a staircase that drops the canal some 70ft (21m) in little over 0.5 miles (0.8km). The towpath reverts to the north bank below lock No 7, recrossing once more after lock No 14, where The Boot Inn lies, just along a track south of the canal. The final stretch continues along the towpath beneath a road bridge, bending past four more locks and under a final bridge to return you to the car park.

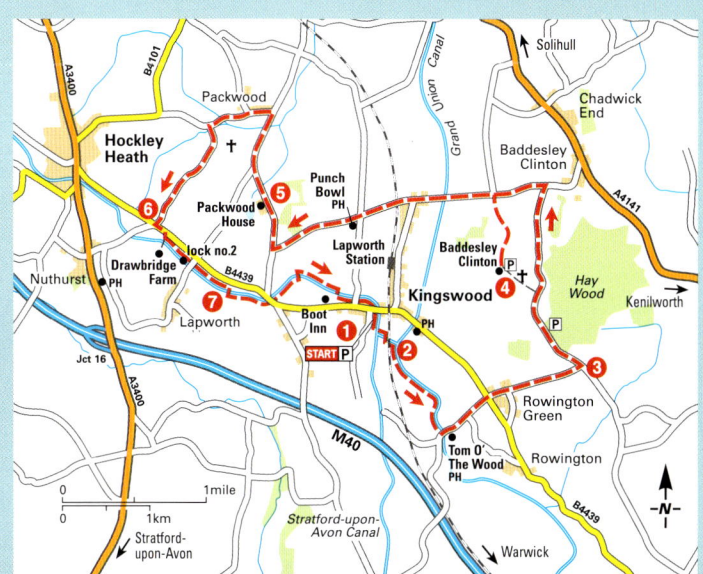

Shrewsbury & Ironbridge

CLOCKWISE FROM TOP LEFT: STATUE OF CHARLES DARWIN, SHREWSBURY LIBRARY; IRONBRIDGE; CHURCH OF ST CHAD, SHREWSBURY

ACTON BURNELL CASTLE

MAP REF 403 G4

Acton Burnell Castle is one of several semi-fortified manor houses located in Shropshire that would have been built for comfort, rather than battle, the most well known and best preserved of these being Stokesay Castle near Craven Arms (see Shropshire Hills and Stiperstones).

The village of Acton Burnell lies a few miles south of Shrewsbury, and it is puzzling to understand why a castle would be built in such a remote setting, until you realise that its position was very strategic, lying close to Watling Street, an old Roman road linking the city of Vironconium (Wroxeter) with Church Stretton.

What makes the red sandstone remains of Acton Burnell Castle, built in 1284–93 by Bishop Burnell, so historically significant is that the first parliament at which the Commons were formally represented was held here. Parliaments were held here twice, in 1283 and 1285.

ATTINGHAM PARK MAP REF 403 G4

Attingham Park was formerly the ancestral home of the Berwick family who lived here for more than 160 years. Each generation left its mark on the house which splendidly recalls the England of Jane Austen. This huge mansion is set in a magnificent deer park, landscaped by the renowned Humphrey Repton. Inside, collections include silver, Italian furniture and Grand Tour paintings collected by the 3rd Lord Berwick. Costumed guides bring Attingham's colourful history to life, including the story of the most corrupt election in the history of politics.

BUILDWAS ABBEY MAP REF 403 G4

Buildwas Abbey ruins overlook the River Severn, just as the 12th-centruy Cistercian Abbey did when it was home to a community of monks. It is they who initially built a stone bridge spanning the river at Buildwas.

COALBROOKDALE & IRONBRIDGE

MAP REF 403 H4

Nestled in a valley of the Ironbridge Gorge, Coalbrookdale was one of the places that the Industrial Revolution began. Coalbrookdale furnace produced the first cast iron for railway lines and went on to create the decorative gates for London's Hyde Park.

IRONBRIDGE GORGE

MAP REF 403 H4

Britain has 27 sites considered by UNESCO to have World Heritage Status. The Ironbridge Gorge and its museums were thus designated in 1986.

Ironbridge is renowned throughout the world as the cradle of the Industrial Revolution. Here you discover all the elements of progress that fuelled the rapid development of industry in the 18th century, from mines to railway lines. Nearby, in the Museum of Iron, the blast furnace from Coalbrookdale, built in 1708, is a reminder of the discovery of coke, while other elements of a burgeoning industry are found in award-winning attractions like Enginuity, the Jackfield Tile Museum, the Tar Tunnel, the Coalport China Museum and the Broseley Pipeworks, all contributing to an endlessly fascinating exposition of Britain's industrial heritage that will inspire young and old alike.

The amazing bridge at Ironbridge was the world's first bridge built entirely of iron, an event that had a profound influence on developments in the fields of technology and architecture.

SHREWSBURY MAP REF 403 G4

Shrewsbury looks to be on the brink of becoming an island, almost completely surrounded by the River Severn, or as A E Housman put it in *A Shropshire Lad*: 'High the vanes of Shrewsbury gleam, Islanded in Severn Stream'.

As the river is flowing from north to south, the town of Shrewsbury is entirely what the French would call on the Rive Gauche, the Left Bank, an allusion to Paris, where all things traditional and boring are on the right bank, and all things funky on the left. So, it is with Shrewsbury.

Famed for its array of steeples and towers, with the Severn forming a protective moat, Shrewsbury is among England's finest Tudor towns, boasting almost 700 listed buildings, including many stunning black-and-white timber-framed residences, a Norman abbey (home to Ellis Peters' fictional sleuth Brother Cadfael), a medieval castle, Georgian crescents and churches. The town is networked by 'Shuts' and 'Passages' – a unique maze of narrow alleys which crisscross the centre in bewildering fashion, and seem purposely designed to draw visitors into further exploration. Shrewsbury is also a floral extravaganza, a place that won the 'Britain in Bloom' Award in 2006, as might be expected from a town where the renowned gardener Percy Thrower was Parks Superintendent for 28 years – there's a massive horticultural legacy to live up to.

Shrewsbury Castle is a Norman red sandstone construction, first built in 1070 on the site of an original Anglo-Saxon fortification that would have guarded the approach to the town and the River Severn. Little of the castle survives today, as much of it was demolished under the reign of Edward I. The castle remained in private hands until 1924 when it was acquired by Shrewsbury Borough Council. Today the castle houses the informative Shropshire Regimental Museum including

spectacular collections of pictures, weapons, uniforms and memorabilia from the 1700s to present times.

In 2009, the town celebrates the birth of its most famous son, Charles Darwin, he of *The Origin of Species*. But rather than leave everything to the last minute, Shrewsbury has been holding a Darwin Festival since 2001, and will do so long after 2009 has passed.

Everywhere is Art in Shrewsbury, or so it seems. A contemporary arts scene thrives here, particularly in the visual arts featured mainly in the Shrewsbury Museum and Art Gallery – special exhibitions of Contemporary art; the Real Art Gallery – contemporary art is spread across two floors, and there is a relaxed coffee shop below, and the Bear Steps Gallery – a 15th-century timber hall has fortnightly changing exhibitions.

Complementing the visual arts is an invigorating cultural scene including the Music Hall, the Jazz and Roots Club, Shropshire Music Trust and The Gateway. Nor are shoppers neglected in Shrewsbury; as well as conventional High Street shops, there are a great many that simply aren't, but rather individual outlets for a whole plethora of crafts and goods. Of course, you don't need to shop; just chill out with a Chardonnay or a coffee at one of the many cafés and bars.

TELFORD & THE WREKIN
MAP REF **403 H4**

Built as a new town in the late 1960s and early 1970s, Telford absorbed many of the existing villages in this former coal producing area. It is the largest town in Shropshire partly due to its excellent transport links to the rest of the country. A few miles west of the town is The Wrekin, a hill that rises to 1,335 feet (407m) above the Shropshire Plain.

WROXETER   MAP REF **403 G4**

Wroxeter (or Viroconium) was the fourth largest Roman city in Britain. At first it was simply a legionary fortress but later acquired a thriving civilian city, peopled by retired soldiers and traders, many of whom decided to stay. Though much remains below ground, the most impressive features of the town today are the 2nd-century bath-houses.

The audio tour is especially revealing and tells how Wroxeter worked, and explains the health and beauty practices of its citizens, who came to number as many as 5,000. Important archaeological discoveries in recent years show what the city was like during the last years of Roman accommodation, and its subsequent adaptation to form the headquarters of a 5th-century British or Irish warlord.

Ironbridge

Did you know that tar is made from the remains of long-dead animals, and that it used to be used to treat rheumatism and skin complaints such as scurvy? Those are just two of the many fascinating answers to questions you never knew you wanted to ask that will be revealed by a visit to Ironbridge in the Severn Gorge and its award-winning museums in Shropshire.

The Severn Gorge has a long industrial history because of the ready availability of coal, iron ore, limestone and timber, and the proximity of the River Severn, which was used for transport. The monks at Buildwas Abbey were smelting iron in charcoal forges as early as 1200, and iron was made at Coalbrookdale from at least 1500. But, the smelting of iron was dependent on timber, and timber had to be made into charcoal first, and this was a long, slow process. But what changed all that was the discovery in 1709 by Abraham Darby that coke could be used for smelting, a discovery that literally changed the world. And it happened here, in the Ironbridge Gorge.

Suddenly, iron could be produced much less expensively, and in far bigger quantities. In 1779, the world's first iron bridge was cast; you can see it still spanning the Severn at Ironbridge. The building of the iron bridge led to an increased use of iron for many areas of engineering, and proved itself in 1795 when flooding damaged every local bridge except one – the iron bridge.

Many of the industrial scars are now healed, and the Severn Gorge is once again a lush and verdant area. But since the 1960s, the relics of such toil and industry that did remain have gradually been transformed into a stunning and award-winning collection of fascinating and innovative museums.

Today, Ironbridge is renowned throughout the world as the cradle of the Industrial Revolution. Here you discover all the elements of progress that fuelled the rapid development of industry in the 18th century, from mines to railway lines. In 1986, Ironbridge Gorge and its museums was awarded UNESCO World Heritage status, one of the first such sites in Britain: this is 'essential' England.

Ironbridge itself is built of warm, mellow brick, its attractive buildings clinging prettily in tiers to the north slopes of the gorge. Although Ironbridge has become a tourist centre, it has lost none of its charm, and it is a delight to explore the steep, narrow streets or walk into the woodlands above.

There are ten museums in the Ironbridge Gorge, and of these Blists Hill Victorian Museum is arguably the most popular. Here, Victorian life is re-enacted by townsfolk dressed in the clothing of the day. Many are ready to demonstrate exactly how tasks would have been done in a small industrial town towards the end of Queen Victoria's lengthy reign. The attractions at Blists Hill include a steam-operated pithead, a Victorian chemist, a squatter's cottage, a schoolhouse and a bank, where you can obtain Blists Hill's own form of money to spend in the town.

The newest museum, Enginuity, brings the story of Victorian industry right up to date. Here you get to play with a vast collection of interactive machinery and indulge in an intriguing array of activities including testing your speed and accuracy against a robot, generating power from water and looking at everyday objects through a powerful giant X-ray machine. The museum is divided into four zones: Materials, Energy, Design, and Systems and Control. Use the latest technology to move a simulated X-ray machine over everyday objects like a guitar, a mobile phone and a teddy bear, and experiment with gizmos used to design things we see and use everyday. This is a wonderful opportunity to give substance to a childhood dream by pulling a five-ton locomotive by hand – strange childhood, strange dream, maybe, but really good fun. If you're feeling especially generous, you can let the children try, too.

Other hands-on experiences can be found at the Coalport China Factory, which houses huge displays of china, produced over two centuries, and is home to nationally important collections of Caughley and Coalport porcelain. Here, in what was one of the country's largest manufacturers of fine china, you can make pottery yourself or watch live demonstrations. Likewise at the Jackfield Tile Museum across the river, a former world centre of the decorative tile industry.

And for a history of early iron-making and decorative castings, visit the Museum of Iron, which tells the story of iron-smelting up to the Great Exhibition of 1851. This is where the Coalbrookdale Company showed off its finest work. The Museum of Iron adjoins the original furnace used by Abraham Darby when he first smelted iron ore with coke. The iron produced was used in making cooking pots, rails, wheels and, of course, that rightly celebrated Iron Bridge. The story of the gorge itself is explained in the Museum of the Gorge, housed in a Gothic riverside warehouse where the fine porcelain goods from Coalbrookdale began their journey. The museum has a 40-foot (12m) scale model of Ironbridge as it was in 1796.

If that's not enough, there are the Darby Houses, which offer an insight into the life and times of the Darby family; Broseley Pipe Works, which saw over 350 years of traditional pipe-making crafts. Then there is the Tar Tunnel, dug from the hillside in 1787 when miners hit an underground spring of thick, treacle-like natural bitumen that became one of the great curiosities of the 18th century. In other parts of Britain such natural seepages are promoted as 'Treacle Mines'. The tar was mainly used to treat ropes and for caulking ships, but some small amounts were processed as 'Betton's British Oil', and peddled as a remedy for 'rheumatic and scorbutic affections'.

As well as Britain's best-known industrial monument, Ironbridge Gorge has also produced a few famous names: Billy Wright, the footballer who captained England in the 1950s, learned his skills on the streets of Ironbridge. On Church Hill, a house called The Orchard was once the home of Captain Matthew Webb, the first man to swim the English Channel. Also born nearby, like Captain Webb, in Dawley, was Edith Pargeter who, as Ellis Peters, became famous for her Cadfael novels, chronicling the adventures of a Welsh monk, set in and around Shrewsbury.

And the museums continue to develop; plans are afoot for the Blists Hill Victorian Town to be improved, adding to the excellence of these 'living' museums. The wonder of it all is that so much can be found in so small a space. You don't come to Ironbridge for just a few hours – think days.

CLOCKWISE FROM TOP LEFT Dressed in Victorian attire, the staff at Blists Hill Victorian Town recreate the day-to-day life of a 19th-century community.

Jackfield Tile Musuem features tiles from 1840 to 1960 by British designers. Here you can learn about the processes involved in making the various types of tile, including encaustic and embossed tiles.

The Victorian Cycle Rally is one of the many popular events held throughout the year at Blists Hill.

OPPOSITE The River Severn runs through the lush green of Ironbridge Gorge, called the Severn Gorge until the construction of Abraham Darby's wonderful feat of engineering.

DISTANCE/TIME 7.5 miles (12.1km) 1h30 **MAP** OS Explorer 242 Telford, Ironbridge & The Wreakin **START** Legge Road car park, Madeley; grid ref: SJ 700043 **TRACKS** Off-road tracks (can be muddy) and lanes, gentle descents and gradual climbs **THE PUB** The Swan, The Wharfage TF8 7NH. Tel: 01952 432306

THE SILKIN WAY TO IRONBRIDGE

Pedal back in time to discover what a 'Saggar-maker's Bottom Knocker' did. Although the gorge's natural resources had been exploited since medieval times, the industrial boom only began in 1709 with Abraham Darby's invention at Coalbrookdale, which used coke rather than charcoal to produce large quantities of cast iron cheaply. This pleasant cycle ride cuts through swathes of countryside once industrious in a different way.

1 Leaving the car park, cross the road and climb a set of shallow steps to a tarmac track, called the Silkin Way. Follow the track left, passing Station Road and dropping to curve beneath the main road. Swing right as you emerge and carry on at the edge of a park, later joining the pavement to reach Blists Hill Victorian Town. Keep going down the hill, the cycleway shortly diverging from the road on a gradual tree-lined descent following along the line of an old railway. Through a tunnel, the way courses enjoyably down, later passing beneath the ingenious Hay Inclined Plane. The track eventually ends in front of the Brewery Inn.

2 Cross the road to a gated track left of the pub, which descends past cottages to the riverbank. Bear right as it forks, rising to meet a road. Follow that over the Severn, and then leave immediately down steps on the right to reach a riverside path. It skirts a picnic area and climbs around to a gate, there joining the line of another disused railway. The track continues above the river for just over half a mile (0.8km) before passing Maws Craft Centre, once the site of a booming tile industry. A little further on as the track ends, keep ahead on the right-most of two roads, which leads past more tile works at Jackfield. These were built by Charles Lynam between 1871 and 1874 for Craven Dunnill & Co. and now house a fascinating museum.

3 Go forward at a junction, but as the road then bends to a reconstructed level crossing, turn off left to regain the line of the railway through Jackfield Sidings. Further on, beyond the Black Swan, pass beneath a skew bridge carrying the road to the Jackfield suspension bridge. It is then not far to the main car park at Ironbridge. Pedal through to the far side and dismount to cross the famous Iron Bridge into the town, where you will find the Malthouse a little way to the left.

4 The route from the bridge, however, is along the main street to the right. At a mini-roundabout, take the right fork ahead, the B4373 to Jackfield and Broseley, leaving the town past the ruins of the Bedlam Furnaces. Where the road later bends to Jackfield Bridge, keep ahead on a narrow, bumpy lane, which undulates along the valley to Coalport. Keep going forward at a later junction, a bridge that takes you over the Hay Inclined Plane, just beyond which, opposite the Shakespeare Inn, you will find the entrance to the Tar Museum. A little further on is the Coalport China Museum.

5 From the museum, go back along the lane a few yards/metres, turning off right onto a track that winds around Coalport Village Hall to an overflow car park. Pass through it right to find a track climbing to meet the Silkin Way. Turn left and retrace your outward route past Blists Hill to the car park from which you began. The way is steadily uphill, but the track is well-graded and the climb relatively easy.

DISTANCE/TIME 6.5 miles (10.6km) 1h30 **MAP** OS Explorer243 Market Drayton, Loggerheads & Eccleshall **START** Norbury Village Hall; grid ref: SJ 782235 **TRACKS** Canal towpath (one short grass section) and quiet lanes **THE PUB** Navigation Inn, Newport Road, Gnosall. Tel: 01785 822327

THE SHROPSHIRE CANAL

With more miles of canal than any other county, what better way to discover Staffordshire's countryside? The Shropshire Canal was built between 1830 and 1835 under the direction of Thomas Telford, creating a more direct link than hitherto between the industrial towns of England's heartland and the seaports along the Dee and Mersey rivers. The main Shropshire Canal survived and is today busy with leisure boats.

1 Out of the car park go right and then left to pedal through the village, signed to Oulton and Norbury Junction. Keep with the main lane as it bends right past a track leading to the striking village church, a large building, dedicated to St Peter, of much weathered sandstone that nestles below a massive brick tower. Leaving the village, go left at a fork signed to Norbury Junction and Gnosall.

2 You will be passing through Norbury Junction on the way back, so for the time being, carry on over the canal bridge and continue along the lane behind the old canal offices and workshops. Beside the lane is a millennium boulder, similar to one just beside the village hall, an erratic boulder stranded as the vast ice sheets that covered this part of the country melted at the end of the last ice age, some 10,000 years ago. Beyond cottages, the lane falls towards a wood, there bending sharply right to pass under a bridge (beware of traffic).

3 At the junction beyond, go left towards Gnosall, the lane rising gently along the base of a high wooded embankment upon which the canal runs. After a mile (1.6km), it twists beneath the canal once more (again watch out for traffic) and climbs to a bend beyond. Keep going with the undulating lane, eventually passing beneath a bridge that once carried the Stafford Newport Railway to a T-junction with the main road at the end.

4 Turn right, crossing the canal to find The Navigation on the right. If going to the pub, there are steps to the canal towpath from the car park, but an easier way lies down a ramp on the left-hand side of the road. Double back under the bridge and cycle away past the pub beside the canal, shortly going beneath the railway again. The bridge here is very wide, the passage almost tunnel-like, not due to carrying several tracks, but because it is skewed across the canal. Such bridges were disproportionately expensive if built in brick or stone, and it was only the invention of the skew arch that allowed the bridge to be preserved within the width of the upper passage. Shortly emerging from a cutting, there are pleasing views across the open countryside. The way continues to Shelmore Wood, where there is a stop lock, a device inserted periodically along the canal for isolating individual sections so that they could be drained for maintenance. Carry on in trees for another 1.25 miles (2km) to Norbury Junction, there crossing a bridge over the abandoned Wappenshall Branch to reach The Junction pub.

5 Leave the canal for the lane, and retrace your outward route left back to the car park by the village hall in Norbury.

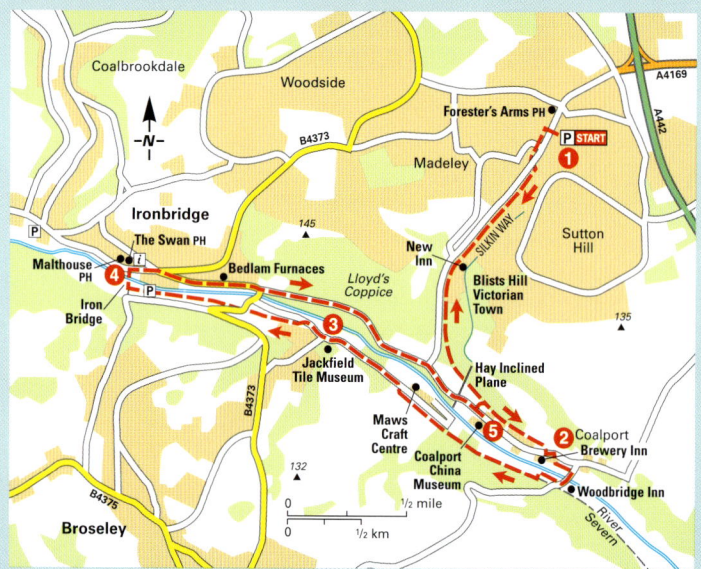

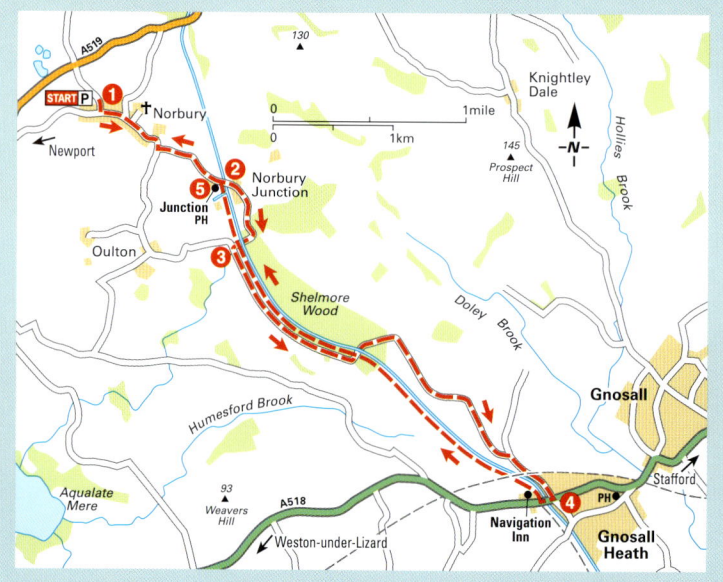

Shropshire Hills & Stiperstones

CLOCKWISE FROM TOP LEFT: MUCH WENLOCK PRIORY;
FEATHERS HOTEL, LUDLOW; CYCLING IN LONG MYND

BISHOP'S CASTLE MAP REF 403 G4

Bishop's Castle is a small and ancient town in an Area of Outstanding Natural Beauty to which it contributes admirably. This unassuming settlement is a unique base for the exploration of the South Shropshire uplands, but is fundamentally a medieval town with a fascinating architectural mélange of styles including a house built on crutches! Very much a rural market centre, the town sees regular cattle and sheep auctions, and a farmers' market. For almost a millennium, Welsh drovers brought herds of cattle and sheep and flocks of geese along the Kerry Ridgeway to the markets in Bishop's Castle. To cope with the thirst the drovers brought with them, the town has been brewing ale since 1642, and possibly longer.

The main street is disconcertingly steep but is flanked by curio and antique shops, as well as secondhand bookshops, a perfect place for collectors. And while at the top end of town it is worth visiting the old castle for a leisurely tour or picnic.

CHURCH STRETTON MAP REF 403 G4

Nestling into the flanks of Long Mynd and the towering Caer Caradoc, Church Stretton saw brief esteem between 1880 and 1900 as a spa town, a time of a rising passion for neo-half-timbering, which is the hallmark of the town. Today, more prosaically, Church Stretton is a convenient launch pad for the Stretton Hills and Long Mynd, especially Cardingmill Valley, a steep-sided ravine and an historic area of upland heath, where once sheeps' fleeces were combed. With over 30 walking routes and bridleways, this is an pleasant base for walkers and horse riders alike.

There are actually three 'Strettons' – Church Stretton, All Stretton and Little Stretton – all very much focused on those who enjoy outdoor pursuits, including gliding and paragliding, and who take to the skies from a base on Long Mynd.

Still happily and rightly clinging to its refined past with streets of individual shops, the lovely market town of Church Stretton has more to offer the visitor than the spa water treatments of old. The town has held a market charter since the reign of King John, and the tradition of the ancient market continues every Thursday, augmented by regular flea markets that draw in visitors from far afield. Many of Stretton's shops still have original frontages, dating from around 1600 when they were rebuilt following a major fire in the town. Church Stretton's church, dedicated to St Lawrence, is Norman and Early English in style and is famed for the sheila-na-gig, an ancient fertility symbol above the north door.

Calcium-rich water from the Stretton Hills is bottled and sold throughout England, and rises from natural aquifers deep in the fragile geological ground on which the whole of this region is based. Sustenance in another form emanates from Church Stretton, which each year hosts an apple fair and a food festival promoting delicious hand-raised pork pies and local-bred meats, as well as beer served, from the region's micro-breweries; in fact, in the 1970s, half the brew pubs in England were found in Shropshire.

Close by in Acton Scott is one of Britain's leading working farm museums. There are regular demonstrations of historic farming using traditional skills and period horse-drawn machines, milking by hand, butter-making in the dairy, visits from a wheelwright, farrier and blacksmith. In a woodsman's hut rakes and gate hurdles are made, all part of a setting designed to focus on rural life and the craft skills of estate life more than a century ago.

CLEOBURY MORTIMER
MAP REF 403 H5

Built on the banks of the River Rea, Cleobury Mortimer, the second smallest town in Shropshire, is the epitome of English rural village life. The town is close to the Clee Hills – Brown Clee and Titterstone Clee. Although not especially high, the Clee Hills of Shropshire are just one of only eight sites in England depicted on the 13th-century map of the world, the 'Mappa Mundi' found in Hereford Cathedral. Perhaps the significance is not evident, but without the quarries and mineral wealth of Titterstone Clee in particular, the towns and cities of Victorian England would have been all the poorer.

Cleobury's High Street was described by John Betjeman as a 'long airy curving street'. Nearby Ludlow tends to draw the visitors, but Cleobury Mortimer is every bit as worthwhile a destination, not least because of the church's twisted steeple and its distinctly unnerving state of imminent collapse, which, of course, it isn't about to do. The whole town is a lovely blend of age-old antiquity in the nicest possible sense.

CLUN MAP REF 403 G5

A E Housman considered that 'Clunton and Clunbury, Clungunford and Clun are the quietest places under the sun', and for much of the year that may well be true. But even the quietest places must occasionally go wild, and so each May Day Clun is a-bustle with celebrations, not least the Festival of the Green Man, who confronts Frostie, Queen of Cold, on the ancient bridge, and banishes her chilling ways as summer approaches. Clun's Green Man Day is a tradition that today embraces mummers' plays, wandering minstrels, medieval knights and Morris dancers, all performing in the shadow of the impressive Norman castle, although the town largely developed as a kind of staging post along a packhorse trail. The Clun Green Man, like all 'Green Men', personifies centuries of living in harmony with the land.

Clun is difficult to interpret; it is quite simply a comely, agreeable village, seemingly overlooked by the 21st century, but once a busy little place and hub of a radiating network of trails that brought Neolithic man, and, later, drovers of herds of cattle and flocks of geese en route to the English market towns and even London. Travellers still pass through Clun, for the village lies on the Shropshire Way.

LUDLOW MAP REF 403 G5

Ludlow, described by John Betjeman as 'England's finest town', is certainly one of Britain's best-preserved medieval and Georgian communities, one that grew in the shadow of its castle. Timber-framed buildings line the narrow streets of the old town centre, not least the stunning Feathers Hotel on Corve Street. Mill Street and Broad Street by contrast are lined with superb Georgian houses demonstrating a wide range of Georgian architectural styles. In fact, Ludlow boasts over 500 listed buildings, and the town centre is

a higgledy-piggledy jumble of building styles each leaning companionably on its neighbour for support.

The ancient Buttercross stands at the top of Broad Street which leads down one of the county's finest streets to the gatehouse. Behind the dominating Buttercross, St Lawrence's church is a dazzling example of the Perpendicular style. Inside are fine collections of medieval glass and skillfully crafted misericords in the choir that require no religious conviction to appreciate.

Ludlow has a less well-known distinction, too. This is the first town in the UK to be admitted to the Cittaslow network. Cittaslow, Italian for 'slow town', is an international network of towns, with the common aim of improving quality of life. It is about caring for the town and the people who live and work in it or visit it. It is about protecting the environment, about promoting local goods and produce, and about avoiding the 'sameness' that afflicts many towns in the modern world.

Ludlow's commercial heart revolves around the Market Square at the far end of which stands Ludlow Castle, built in the 11th century, and formerly a major centre of administration – the Court of

the Marches – for the vast tract of border land known as the Welsh Marches. In Tudor times Ludlow Castle was a popular resort patronised by members of the royal family, and it was here that Arthur, Prince of Wales, son of Henry VII, died. Nowadays, it is still a busy centre hosting numerous annual events including a popular vintage car rally, a Christmas Fayre, an annual food festival of international renown, and an excellent open-air Shakespeare production.

The town has grown up on the banks of the River Teme, and the river still plays an important part in the daily life of Ludlow. Linney Park is a lovely place for a picnic or to hire a rowing boat . Near the Millennium Green, the river widens and has a shingle 'beach' that has been a popular paddling spot for generations of Ludlow children. All around, the Shropshire countryside is perfect for walking and cycling, mountain biking, horse riding and canoeing, while the Marches are blessed with country houses, fine gardens and stately homes.

MUCH WENLOCK MAP REF 403 G4

Featured unmistakably in the John Cleese film *Clockwork*, Much Wenlock is a delightful mish-mash of timber-framed

houses, shops and pubs. Today, Much Wenlock's renown rests on the ruins of its fine 7th-century priory, still serenely set amid lush green lawns. The town grew around the priory, a local service industry meeting the daily needs of the nuns and monks. The ornate, timber-framed Guildhall is a 16th-century addition to the town, built over an open market area. Nearby, the church of the Holy Trinity is a Norman and medieval masterpiece, something that complements the town's rich legacy of homely architecture including the ancient, heavily timbered town house called Raynald's Mansion.

But Much Wenlock has another claim to fame, as the inspiration of the modern Olympic Games. Local-born doctor William Penny Brookes introduced a form of Olympic Games in 1850, 49 years before they were revived in Athens. The Much Wenlock Olympics, a mix of conventional athletic sports and events such as 5-a-side football, cricket and volleyball, are held annually in July.

SECRET HILLS MAP REF 403 G5

Unquestionably the finest place to begin an exploration of the Shropshire Hills, Secret Hills, the Discovery Centre, is at

STOKESAY CASTLE

Craven Arms, and a brilliant way of being transported back in time more than 4,500 million years, or you can just bob in for lunch and a chinwag.

The Shropshire Hills, Housman's 'blue remembered hills', form an Area of Outstanding Natural Beauty, and Secret Hills takes visitors on a balloon flight over the landscape, without ever actually leaving the ground. This is one of the most imaginative concepts, aimed at interpreting an ancient and vital landscape in a way everyone can understand and enjoy. This is a good place to start for another reason: the landscape and underlying geology of Shropshire is so complex and gives rise to so many different formations at surface level that it is a wise move to try to figure it out first. Here, a single step can cross more than 600 million years in time.

STOKESAY CASTLE MAP REF 403 G5

Stokesay Castle is a breathtaking sight, the best preserved 13th-century fortified manor house in England; the name is misleading as Stokesay is more domestic than military. Set amid the lovely Shropshire countryside, it seems a perfectly composed group of buildings with its timber-framed gatehouse and parish church intended to set the pulse of photographers racing. Lawrence of Ludlow, a man who made his fortune as

a wool merchant, bought the manor in 1281, and built a comfortable residence with defensive capabilities.

The castle has an open-hearthed great hall, with a superb cruck-framed roof, shuttered gable windows and precipitous staircase, little of which has changed since it was built. Across the courtyard stands the equally splendid gatehouse, with ornate timber-framing and elaborate carvings of Adam and Eve.

WENLOCK EDGE, LONG MYND & STIPERSTONES MAP REF 403 G4

Considered to be the finest geological escarpment in Britain, Wenlock Edge, was immortalised in literature by A E Housman, author of *A Shropshire Lad*, and by composer Ralph Vaughan Williams, who set Housman's poem to music.

What makes Wenlock Edge so remarkable is its limestone geology, composed of corals, fossilised crinoids, brachiopods, trilobites and shells, formed 425 million years ago. But not here, in what is today Shropshire, but thousands of miles away, south of Equator, roughly where the Seychelles are today. What makes a visit to this part of England all the more exciting is that the valley in which Craven Arms and Church Stretton to the north sit is directly above a crack in the earth's crust that once made this beautiful corner

of England one of the most geologically violent. Wenlock Edge is the proof of that; one of the sections of the Silurian Period is even called the Wenlock era. It's all so incredibly confused and confusing not least because Shropshire is built on rocks from 11 out of the 13 known periods of geology – the smallest area in the world to boast quite so many.

Across that fragile geological divide, the land to the west of Church Stretton rises into the formidable bulk of Long Mynd, a steep-sided uplift of heather moorland that flattens into a wide plateau, penetrated in places by in-cutting valleys formed by streams of which Cardingmill Valley is the best known.

The Long Mynd, or 'Long Mountain', is a ridge of high ground sandwiched between the Stiperstones to the west, and Wenlock Edge to the east. The highest point of the ridge is Pole Bank, 1,692 feet (516m) above sea level, across which runs an ancient track, the Portway. Most of Long Mynd was acquired by the National Trust in 1965.

While very attractive in fine conditions, the Long Mynd is treacherous in severe weather, and has claimed many lives. The Rev E D Carr's *A Night in the Snow* describes his experience in 1865 of surviving a winter's night on the Long Mynd when attempting to walk home

after visiting an isolated parishioner. The Long Mynd also features in the poetry of A E Housman, the novels of Mary Webb, and Malcolm Saville's Lone Pine series.

Further west lies Stiperstones, a name to conjure with, to dream up links with the Devil, indeed one of the rock formations is called 'The Devil's Chair'. Stiperstones, has far-reaching views and is crowned with a number of rocky tors said to have been placed there by the Devil in an endeavour to sink Stiperstones into the bowels of the earth so that all of the God-fearing people might perish. According to legend, the ghost of Wild Edric, a Saxon earl who defied the Normans, rides the hills whenever England is threatened by invasion.

Like so many places in Shropshire, Stiperstones features prominently in the works of writers like Mary Webb, who gave Stiperstones the name 'Diafol' in her novel *Golden Arrow*. D H Lawrence paid a fleeting visit, and used Stiperstones and the Devil's Chair as a key element in *St Mawr*. For Lawrence, Stiperstones was the place where 'aboriginal England' could still be felt; many would say it remains so to this day. Stiperstones is a National Nature Reserve and a haven for wildlife and birds normally associated with upland areas, including red grouse, curlew, peregrine falcon and ring ouzel.

WENLOCK EDGE: CLOSE TO THE EDGE

Take a walk along former drovers' roads that link the crest of Wenlock Edge to the fields and meadows of Corve Dale. This great tree-clad escarpment is one of Shropshire's most famous landscape features, partly because it plays a role in A E Housman's collections of poems entitled *A Shropshire Lad* and is also the subject of a choral poem by the composer Vaughan Williams.

DISTANCE/TIME 6.25 miles (10.1km) 3h Ascent: 689ft (210m) **MAP** Aqua3 OS Explorer 217 The Long Mynd & Wenlock Edge **START** Grid reference: SO 479875 **PATHS** Mostly good but ford on Dunstan's Lane can be deep after rain, 10 stiles **THE PUB** Sun Inn, Corfton SY7 9DF. Tel: 01584 861239

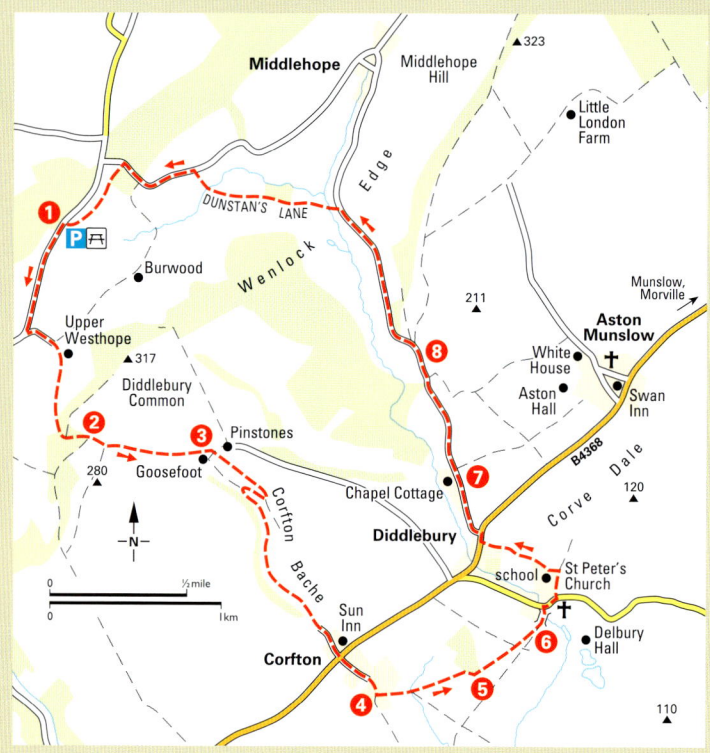

1 Turn left out of the car park that comes out along a lane. At a junction, turn left (signposted 'Middlehope'). Keep on at the next (signed 'Upper Westhope') where the road becomes a track and bends left towards a house. Go through a gate on the right instead and continue along the grassy bridleway that enters woodland. Keep straight on when you reach two cross paths.

2 The bridleway emerges into pasture; keep straight on along the left-hand edge to a corner. Go through a gate and then turn right on the field-edge path, which soon becomes a wide track.

3 Pass a cottage and, with barns ahead, look for blue arrows directing sharp right. Keep left above Corfton Bache, a deep valley, until the blue arrows send you down into the valley. Follow it to a road at Corfton and then cross to the lane opposite.

4 As the lane degenerates into a track, look on the left for the footpath starting at a kissing gate. Go diagonally left across pasture to a prominent stile at the far side. Cross the farm track and walk to the far right corner of arable field.

5 Go through a gate, then little way along the left-hand edge of another field until the gate accesses parkland. Follow the waymarker until St Peter's Church at Diddlebury comes into view, providing a guide.

6 Cross two stiles at the far side of the park; descend the slope, to the right of the fence. Cross the bridge to Diddlebury. Turn right, then left by the church. Join a footpath and pass right of the village hall, then diagonally right past the school, over two stiles and across fields to the road. Cross to the lane and fork right after a few paces.

7 The footpath leaves the lane on the right, almost opposite Chapel Cottage. Either turn right to visit the Swan Inn or continue.

8 At the junction with a bridle track by a sign ('Aston Top') keep left on a lane. After 0.75 miles (1.2km), branch left on a byway, Dunstan's Lane (no signpost or waymarker). Follow it to Middlehope road and turn left. Keep on at the Y-junction. When the footpath crosses a road, turn left into woodland. The path is signposted on the right, but not left – the left branch is few paces further on. Go through the woods to the picnic site.

MUCH WENLOCK PAYING HOMAGE TO ST MILBURGA

Visit the destination of medieval pilgrims in this peaceful walk in the countryside around Much Wenlock. Much Wenlock has been a market town for at least 700 years. It is a delightful little place, with charming old houses and a real working farm set back just off the High Street.

DISTANCE/TIME 6.25 miles (10.1km) 2h30 Ascent: 426ft (130m) **MAP** Aqua3 OS Explorers 217 The Long Mynd & Wenlock Edge; 242 Telford, Ironbridge & The Wrekin **START** Grid ref: SO 623998 (on Explorer 217) **PATHS** Field paths, couple of boggy patches, 16 stiles **THE PUB** Talbot, Much Wenlock TF13 6AA. Tel: 01952 727077

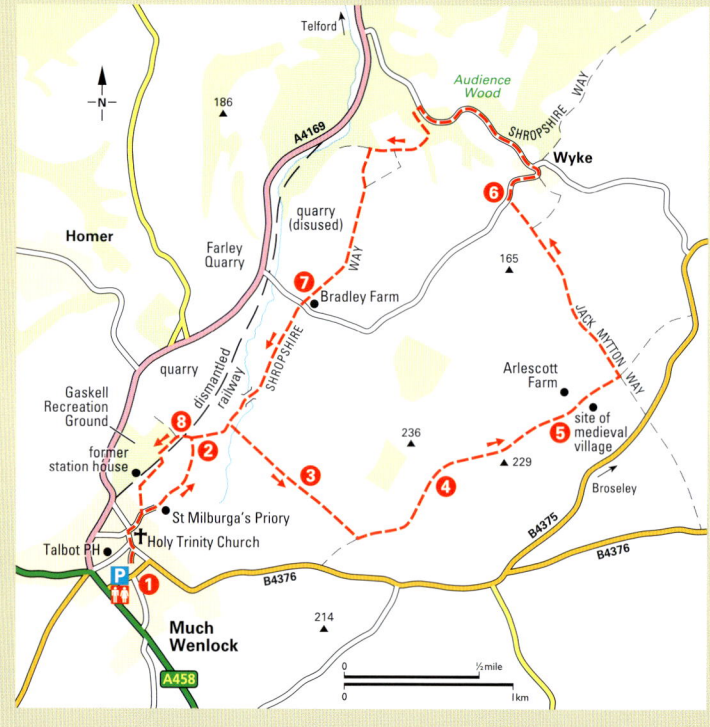

1 Go down Burgage Way, left on Mutton Shut to High Street, right to Barrow Street, then left. Pass the church, then turn first right on Bull Ring. Continue past the priory and along the lane (Shropshire Way).

2 Turn right along the track to a footpath junction. Leave the Shropshire Way here and follow the right-hand path. Cross the brook after crossing and you continue along the left-hand hedge to a waymarker directing you diagonally towards a stile.

3 Cross the stile and turn right along the field edge. Ignore the gate and stile in the corner; turn left, until another stile gives access to an adjacent field. Turn left to the far corner, climb over a low fence and along a narrow path.

4 Go through a gate at the end of the field and over a stile ahead, then on through a wood into a field. Keep by the left-hand hedge before joining a track to the left of a holly hedge. When the track bends right, keep ahead towards Arlescott Farm.

5 Two stiles give access to pasture to the right of the farm. Turn left, passing to the left of a pool and then to the right of Arlescott

Cottage to intercept Jack Mytton Way. Turn left to the pasture. Approaching the far side, veer away from the hedge to a gap in the lower hedge. Turn right, following a bridleway to a lane at Wyke.

6 Turn right, then left at a road junction. Back on the Shropshire Way, pass Audience Wood then turn left through woodland to reach fields. The path is waymarked along the field edges, then heads diagonally towards Bradley Farm.

7 Pass through the farmyard, turn left by the house, then right. Cross the lane to fields, going ahead to pastureland. Head for the far right corner, cross a footbridge and turn left to the path junction near Much Wenlock, encountered earlier. Turn right to rejoin the lane from Much Wenlock.

8 Turn right to a dismantled railway, go left for few paces, then right again at sign for Jack Mytton Way. Join the footpath on the left along the edge of Gaskell Recreation Ground. After passing a green shed, recross the old railway line and turn right on a fenced path. Pass the former station house, turn left and emerge near the priory. Finally, turn right to the start.

STIPERSTONES BACK TO PURPLE

Walk this route to take you from the mining village of Snailbeach to the dragon's crest of Stiperstones. At first sight it looks as though this walk will be all about industrial archaeology, for it begins at Snailbeach, formerly one of the most important lead mines in Britain. Mining ceased long ago and the derelict landscape has been transformed into one of the most fascinating post-industrial sites in the Midlands. But there's another transformation going on nearby. This is the Back to Purple project which aims to restore Stiperstones to its full glory.

DISTANCE/TIME 4.5 miles (7.2km) 2h Ascent: 951ft (290m) **MAP** aqua3 OS Explorer 216 Welshpool & Montgomery **START** Grid ref: SJ 373022 **PATHS** Good paths across pasture, moorland and woodland, 1 stile **THE PUB** Stiperstones Inn, Stiperstones, Snailbeach SY5 0LZ. Tel: 01743 791 327

1 Take Lordshill Lane opposite the car park, then join a parallel footpath on the left. Rejoining the lane, cross to the site of a locomotive shed, then continue up the lane, noticing the green arrows that are directing you to the main sites.

2 Turn right on a track between the crusher house and compressor house. A few paces past the compressor house, turn left up some steps. At the top, turn right, then soon left up more steps. Turn left to the Cornish engine house, then right and continue through woodland. A short detour leads to a smelter chimney, otherwise it's uphill all the way.

3 A sign indicates that you're entering Stiperstones National Nature Reserve (NNR). Woods give way to bracken, broom and bramble before you cross over a stile on to open hill. The path climbs a slope ahead to a stile/gate at top.

4 Two paths are waymarked. Take the left-hand one, which runs between a fence and the rim of a dingle on your right.

The path then climbs away from dingle and meets a rutted track. Turn right. Visible now is a rock tor, isolated from others near by. This rock is known as Shepherd's Rock.

5 Just beyond Shepherd's Rock is a junction marked by a cairn. Turn right here, then fork left to go round the other side of the rock. Leave NNR at a gate/stile. The path runs to the left, shortly bordered by hawthorn hedge. You'll soon see that this is an old green lane, lined at various points by either hedges/trees on both sides, one line of trees or tumbledown stone wall.

6 At the junction take the left-hand path back into the NNR. At the next junction, fork right to leave NNR at a gate by the plantation. Go diagonally across a field to a track; turn right, going back across the field, through the plantation, then cut across pasture on a bridleway.

7 Fork left at the bridleway junction and continue past Lordshill Chapel to a lane. Turn right and stay with it as it swings left to Snailbeach.

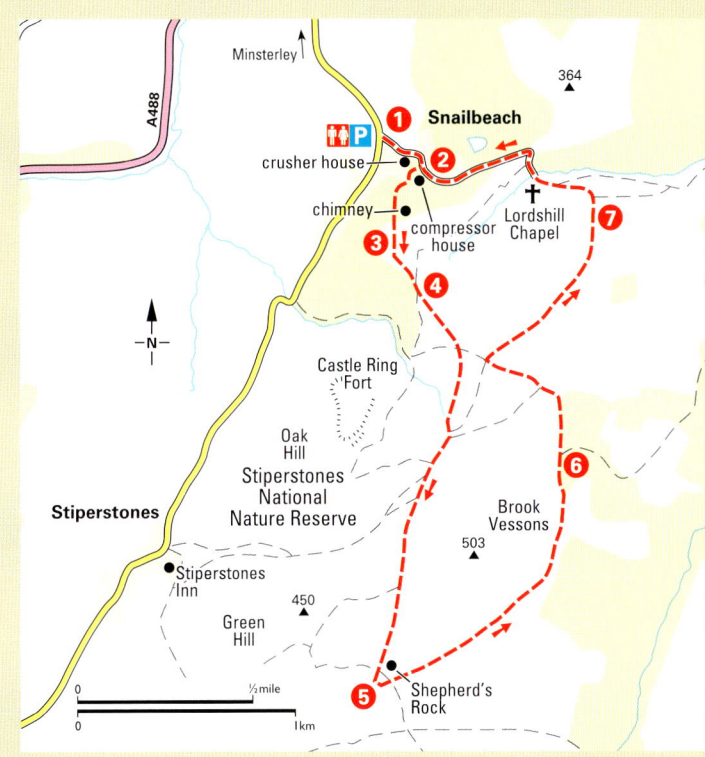

WALK 68

THE LONG MYND: AN ANCIENT SETTLEMENT

The Mynd is a wonderful place, which is sometimes referred to as the last wilderness in the Midlands. In truth, however, this is no wilderness. It has been subject to human use and, to some extent, human occupation, since the earliest times. It is liberally dotted with prehistoric remains, including Bronze Age tumuli and dykes, with an Iron Age fort on Bodbury Hill. An ancient road, the Port Way, runs along the top of the Long Mynd and has been in use for at least 4,000 years.

DISTANCE/TIME 7.5 miles (12.1km) 3h Ascent: 1,545ft (471m) **MAP** Aqua3 OS Explorer 217 The Long Mynd & Wenlock Edge **START** Grid ref: SO 453936 **PATHS** Mostly moorland paths and tracks, 3 stiles **THE PUB** Green Dragon, Ludlow Road, Little Stretton SY6 6RE. Tel: 01694 722925

1 Walk up Lion Meadow to the High Street and turn right. Turn left at The Square, go past the church and straight on into Rectory Field. Walk to the top left corner, turn right by the edge, soon entering Old Rectory Wood. The path descends to a junction. Turn left, soon crossing Town Brook, then climb again to a gate on to Long Mynd.

2 Go forward beside a brook to railings and continue with the brook on your left. After a slight height gain, the path begins to climb more steeply and heads away from the brook. Eventually the path and brook meet up again near the head of the latter.

3 The path crosses the brook. Go 50yds (46m) to a junction marked by the first in a succession of pink-banded posts. Follow these posts, gaining height gradually again. Ignore gthe branching paths and, after a slight rise, the summit is ahead on the left.

4 Meet an unfenced road about 100yds (91m) left of the junction. Turn left, ignore the path to Little Stretton and go straight on when the road bends left, joining a bridleway.

At the next junction, turn left to the summit, then keep straight on to Port Way. Turn right past the site of Pole Cottage.

5 Turn left on a footpath, signposted to Little Stretton. When the wide rutted track forks go left – you can see the path ahead, cutting a green swathe over the shoulder of Round Hill. Go straight on at the junction, then descend to Cross Dyke. After the dyke, the path ascends but soon levels out, then descends, to Little Stretton.

6 Cross at a footbridge by the ford and turn right on the lane for a few paces. Look for a footpath on the left. It climbs by the field edge to the top corner, then turns left, following the top of a steep slope to pasture. Follow the right-hand edge of this until the path enters woodland. Descend to Ludlow Road.

7 Join the bridleway next to the footpath. It climbs into woodland, emerging at a track, which becomes a road. As it bends right there's access left to Rectory Field. Descend to The Square, turn right on the High Street and left on Lion Meadow to the car park.

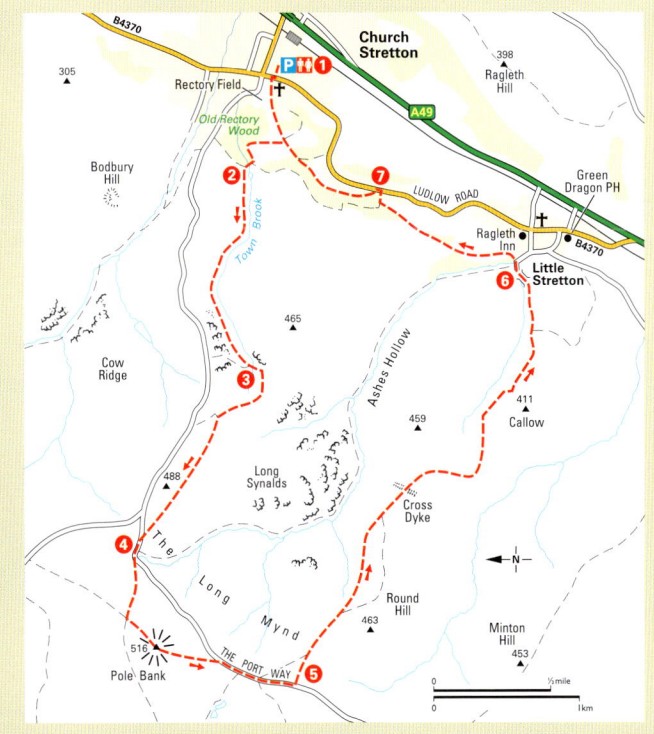

Offa's Dyke

CLOCKWISE FROM TOP LEFT: PONTEYSSYLTE AQUADUCT, LLANGOLLEN; CASTELL DINAS, LLANGOLLEN; DENBIGH CASTLE; OFFA'S DYKE FOOTPATH AT KNIGHTON

CEIRIOG VALLEY MAP REF 402 F3

'A piece of heaven that has fallen to earth' is how the last British Liberal Prime Minister, Lloyd George, described the Ceiriog Valley. The Ceiriog river, which has its birthplace deep in the heart of the Berwyn Mountains, is a tributary of the Dee. Here it flows through a pastoral countryside, dotted with farms, that wouldn't go amiss in a Constable landscape. Over the centuries, the valley has provided inspiration for three local bards: Huw Morus (1662–1709), the Reverend Robert Ellis (1812–75) and John Ceiriog Hughes (1832–87).

Glyn Ceiriog is the largest village. It expanded in the 19th century with the mining of slate and other minerals in the area. There are still remnants of a tramway that was built to convey the slate to the main line at Chirk.

Llanarmon Dyffryn Ceiriog is the most beautiful village in the valley, with a church, two old-world pubs and several whitewashed cottages clustering around a picture-postcard square. Lying by the confluence of the Ceiriog and a tributary, the Gwrachen, the village takes its name from the 5th-century missionary, St Garmon. A mound in the churchyard, Tomen Garmon, is a Bronze Age burial mound thought to be the place from where the missionary once stood to preach.

CHIRK MAP REF 402 F3

The border town of Chirk perches on a hillside separating the River Dee from the Ceiriog. It is a 'must' for canal enthusiasts who can marvel at Thomas Telford's magnificent ten-arched aqueduct, built in 1801 to convey the canal more than 70 feet (21m) above the valley bottom. Alongside there's an even taller viaduct, built by Henry Robertson in 1840 for the railway. Both were used to carry coal from the once-thriving Flintshire coalfields.

Chirk Castle, which overlooks the town and the Ceiriog Valley, was built in 1310 by Edward I's Justice of Wales, Roger Mortimer, to replace an older, 11th-century wooden motte-and-bailey castle south of the town. The walls have since been decorated by scores of glazed mullioned windows, hiding the stark repressive face those powerful circular towers would have issued.

DENBIGH MAP REF 402 F2

Denbighshire's medieval county town basks in the heart of the Vale of Clwyd, a wide and verdant valley dividing the rolling Clwydian Hills and the foothills of Mynydd Hiraethog's moorland.

Denbigh means 'little fortress', probably referring to the original hilltop castle belonging to the ancient Welsh princes, rather than the large Norman castle you see today. After defeating the Welsh in 1282, Edward I granted the town to Henry de Lacy, who became the first Lord of Denbigh. The castle and its town walls were completed not long afterwards. The fortress would see much action in the years that followed, culminating in a successful six-month siege of Royalist troops during the Civil War. Though the castle was to fall into decay not long afterwards, there's still much to see, including the gatehouse, fronted by two polygonal towers, and walls that give tremendous views of the town, valley and the Clwydian Hills. In the grounds is the 14th-century tower of the otherwise demolished St Hilary's Church, and an old statue believed to be Edward I. It takes very little imagination to conjure up images of how this powerful fortress would have looked.

Beneath the castle, Denbigh has many historical corners and buildings to explore. Narrow ginnels like Back Row thread quietly through the medieval part of the town, revealing buildings from the 15th century. The town also has the remains of a 14th-century Carmelite Friary, and the walls of an unfinished 'cathedral' dreamed up by Dudley, Earl of Leicester, lover of Elizabeth I, but abandoned on his death in 1588.

Denbigh is handily placed for an exploration of the Clwydian Hills, which have long been popular with walkers who delight in the heather ridges. Moel Famau, which means 'mother mountain', is at 1,818 feet (554m) the highest of the range. Its summit monument was built in 1810 to celebrate the jubilee of King George III.

KNIGHTON MAP REF 402 F5

Knighton, a country market town, rather affluent in its appearance, lies on the southern bank of the River Teme, surrounded by lovely low, rounded hills. The English border, including the town's hill, Panpunton, lies on the other side of the river. Tref y Clawdde, the Welsh name for Knighton, means town on the dyke, and a motte-and-bailey castle in the heart of town stands squarely on Offa's Dyke, an 18th-century earthwork – the only place where this happens.

The main street ascends gently to a fine Victorian clock tower and then on to Market Street, with Georgian houses and businesses with traditional shopfronts, rather than the brightly coloured plastic panels of the usual high street names.

Knighton has the scant remains of two castles, the open motte at Bryn-y-Castell to the east of town, and the remains of a Norman castle, sacked by Owain Glyn Dwr, which can just be seen at the back of the fire station. Both are now in private ownership. The town is an excellent base for walking, and the Offa's Dyke Centre can help with information and advice.

For centuries Welsh warlords had attacked their Anglo Saxon enemies in attempts to force them back across the Marches but, in the 8th century Offa, King of Mercia, decided to settle the disputes. He built a massive earthwork dyke running the full length of Wales, from Prestatyn to Chepstow, intended to mark out the political boundary of his kingdom, beyond which the Welsh were permitted only under strict control. The dyke in these parts is at its grandest, with clear earthwork lines straddling the moors. Today there is a well-established national trail along its length. The Glyndwr's Way, another national trail, also starts here.

LLANGOLLEN MAP REF 402 F3

The self-proclaimed gateway to Wales, Llangollen sits in the fertile and verdant Dee Valley, surrounded by the Llantysilio and Berwyn hills. The river is at the heart of the village and on any fair day you'll see scores of people congregating around the Elizabethan stone bridge, one of the Seven Wonders of Wales, watching the fast waters bursting over the riverbed rocks.

The bridge was extended in 1863 for the railway line, which linked Wrexham with Barmouth. Following the railway's closure in the 1960s, a preservation society was formed and today steam trains operate the 7.5 miles (12km) to Carrog. The society expects that it will eventually reopen the line to Corwen. Llangollen station is a reminder of days gone by, with its historic steam engines and rolling stock lined up on platforms that are spanned by the original Great Western region footbridge.

The Llangollen canal runs parallel to the railway and road. Pioneered by Thomas Telford, it provides another transport leisure link for attractive, horse-drawn narrowboats, which take visitors along the canal and over the Pontcysyllte Aqueduct, where a cast-iron trough carries the canal for 1,007 feet (300m), 120 feet (35m) above the River Dee.

Looking to the skies you can see the ruffled outlines of castle ruins perched on a limestone knoll above the town. Known as Dinas Bran, it was occupied by the Princes of Powys. A walk up the hill reveals that the ruins are quite extensive and the views up the Dee Valley are tremendous – they're far better than the famed Horseshoe Pass, a 4-mile (6km) drive away. Behind Dinas Bran are the long tiered limestone cliffs of Creigiau Eglwyseg. One of the most impressive sights of the region, they stretch to a place called World's End!

Just off the A542 Horseshoe Pass road in the deep, narrow Eglwyseg Valley, lies the ruined abbey of Valle Crucis, a name that means 'valley of the cross'. This was a reference to the cross that used to top the Pillar of Eliseg, a memorial to the 9th-century Prince of Powys. Established in 1201 by Cistercian monks from Strata Marcella near Welshpool, the abbey is sited in fertile pastures beneath a knoll delightfully named the Velvet Hill.

WELSHPOOL MAP REF 402 F4

Set amid Montgomeryshire's rolling verdant hills and wide valley of the River Severn, Welshpool, Y Trallwng to give it its Welsh name, has over the centuries become a prosperous and bustling market town. Until 1835 it was known as Pool; some of the old mileposts still refer to it in that way. 'Welsh' was added to the name to distinguish the place from Poole in Dorset. It was the Severn that brought trade to the town, for it was navigable by boat. The Montgomery Canal came to the town in 1797, part of a 33-mile (53km) system from Welsh Frankton in Shropshire to Newtown in Powys. Today's visitor can find out much more at the Powysland Museum and Montgomery Canal Centre, where there is a V-shaped basin used as a winding point and as a base for the Montgomery Canal Cruises.

The pride of Welshpool's town centre is its High Street, a thoroughfare of fine architecture, much dating from the Georgian era, but many much older half-timbered buildings belong to the 16th century. A building with a more dubious past is the Cockpit on New Street, which would have been the popular venue for cockfights until the ban of 1849.

Almost every tourist who comes to Welshpool comes to see Powis Castle, which was built for the warring Princes of Powys in around 1200. A long drive from Park Lane off the High Street leads through the fine estate's parklands, past mature oaks and grazing deer to reach the castle. Because of its continuous occupation since 1578, when the ownership passed to the Herbert family, the old fortress has become more of a mansion, with castellated ramparts, tall chimneys, rows of fine leaded windows and fine 17th-century balustraded terraces overlooking manicured lawns and neatly clipped yews. Lead statues of a shepherd and shepherdess keep watch over the many shrubs and perennial borders.

For those wanting to explore the Montgomeryshire hills even further, the Welshpool and Llanfair Light Railway can take you on an interesting journey through the picturesque and verdant Banwy Valley to Llanfair Caereinion.

HORSESHOE FALLS & THE VELVET HILL

This walk is probably one of the prettiest in North Wales. Though the Horseshoe Falls are an impressive piece of engineering, many visitors feel a bit let down that the falls are just a weir and not nature's own creation. But on Velvet Hill you should see wondrous landscapes in a hundred shades of green.

DISTANCE/TIME 4 miles (6.4km) 2h30 Ascent: 853ft (260m) **MAP** aqua3 OS Explorer 255 Llangollen & Berwyn **START** Grid ref: SJ 198433 **PATHS** Field paths in valley and on hillside, 7 stiles **THE PUB** Britannia Inn, Horseshoe Pass, Llangollen LL20 8DW. Tel: 01978 860144

1 From the car park walk down to the road, turn right for a few paces and then descend some steps to the back of Chain Bridge Hotel. From here, turn right to follow the path between the river and canal. Once through the kissing gate at the end of the canal you traverse riverside fields and go past Horseshoe Falls. The falls are in fact a weir created by Thomas Telford to harness the forceful waters of the Dee to feed and control the levels of the Llangollen and Ellesmere canals. From this point climb to Llantysilio church and on reaching the road, turn left through the pretty hamlet of Llantysilio to reach a junction.

2 Go though the five-bar gate and continue for a few paces along a side road, then climb along the rutted track, keeping the forest to your left. After a short while climb north on a high pastured hillside.

3 Through the gateway at the top of the field, the path swings right, keeping parallel to the top edge of another wood. The now narrow path descends to a complex of cottages at Pen-y-bryn. After squeezing through a ginnel to the right of the first cottage, the route follows the tarmac drive out to Horseshoe Pass road at the Britannia Inn.

4 Turn right along the road, then right again when you get to the first junction. Go over a stile on the left in order to head south across three fields. Turn right along the farm track and then left past a large stone-built house to eventually arrive at a narrow lane. Go left along this lane to meet Horseshoe Pass road again.

5 From here go over a stile on the right-hand side of the road ('Velvet Hill') and ascend by some quarry workings.

6 Turn right along the wide grassy track here, all the time climbing steeply through bracken to reach the ridge, where you turn left to make for the summit. The spectacular view from here takes in the meandering River Dee, the Afon Eglwyseg flowing beneath dramatic limestone terraces and Valle Crucis abbey.

7 Descend southwards on a narrow footpath to reach the fence which runs just above some woods. Do not be tempted to cross (as many have done in the past), but follow this fence downwards to the left to a stile. Once across the stile turn right and then continue along a path that leads back to the car park and picnic site.

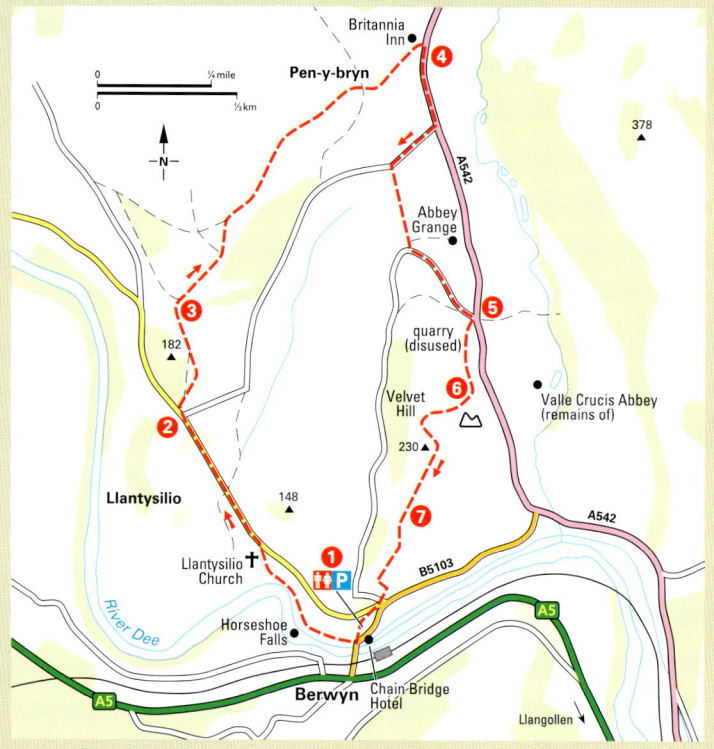

WALK 70

CEIRIOG VALLEY – IN THE BEAUTIFUL VALLEY

Discover an earthly heaven in one of ancient Clwyd's truly green and pleasant valleys. For 18 miles (29km), from its source on the slopes of Mount Ferna in the Berwyns to its meeting with the Dee, the beautiful Afon Ceiriog meanders through oakwoods, rocky hillsides and fertile cattle pastures.

DISTANCE/TIME 4.5 miles (7.2km) 2h30 Ascent: 575ft (175m) **MAP** Aqua3 OS Explorer 255 Llangollen & Berwyn **START** Grid ref: SJ 157328 **PATHS** Sketchy paths and farm tracks, 3 stiles **THE PUB** Hand Hotel, Llanarmon Dyffryn Ceiriog LL20 7LD. Tel: 01691 600666

1 From Hand Hotel, take the eastbound lane past the church and go uphill with the conifer plantation on your right. The pastures of Ceiriog will be below left.

2 At the far end of the plantation leave the road and take a farm track on the left. This track ends at a barn. Keep to the right of the barn and aim for the gate beyond it. Walk through the gate and maintain your direction, over the shoulder of a grassy knoll, then make your way to another stile in the fence ahead. Once beyond this, the route bends left ever so slightly, before going over yet another step stile.

3 After crossing two streamlets, keep to the field edge and track to the right of Ty'n-y-fedw farm. The track now enters woods. Take the lower left fork, staying parallel to river.

4 At the far end of the woods cross a field, keeping roughly parallel with the river, then aim for the gate at the top of the field. Pass through the gate and turn right to climb roughly southwest along an enclosed farm road, which crosses a country lane before continuing uphill through high pastures.

5 At a crossroads, turn right along a green track – part of the Upper Ceiriog Way. This heads southwest towards the green hill known as Cefn Hir-fynydd.

6 After about 300yds (274m) leave this track through a gate on the right. If you head west by the right edge of a rushy area and towards Pen y Glog's sparse crags, it will be easy to find the small stile in the next fence and then the wooden gate on the left soon afterwards. Go through the gate then descend past rocks that are on the left. Here, the sheep track levels out through some bracken to pass beneath more rocks.

7 A solitary wooden marker post acts as your guide to locate a wide grassy track, which runs through the valley of Nant y Glog and follows along the low slopes of the hill, Pen y Glog.

8 After swinging right, following the bend of a lively stream, the track terminates by a lane to the south of Llanarmon Dyffryn Ceiriog. Follow the lane past several attractive cottages and the village school to arrive by the Hand Hotel in the village square where you started.

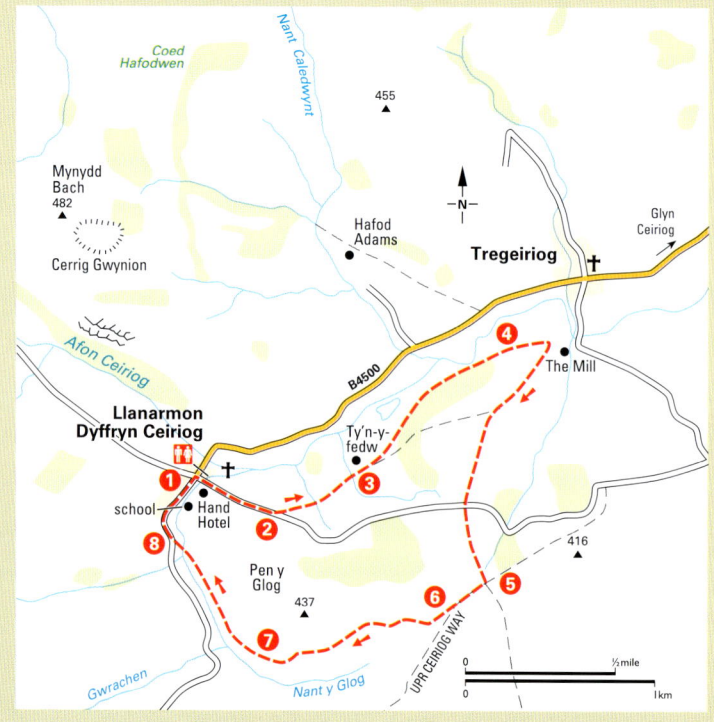

Peak District

CLOCKWISE FROM TOP LEFT: ASHFORD IN THE WATER; PAVILION GARDENS, BUXTON; THE OPERA HOUSE, BUXTON; DOVE DALE

Insight
THE RUDDY DUCK

One of Carsington Water's most controversial residents is the American ruddy duck. Just 50 years ago this little duck (it has a big blue bill, white cheeks, a reddish back and a stiff tail) was unknown outside the Wildfowl Trust, but it escaped and is now so widespread that it is threatening to overrun Europe, consequently diluting the genes of its close relative, the European white-headed duck, in the process.

Insight
NATURE RETURNED

Just north of Carsington and Hopton the landscape rises to a 1,000-foot (305m) contour, topped by a stone called King's Chair. This area is pockmarked by old lead mines and limestone quarries, but wild flowers abound on the open limestone and into the Via Gelliae, and in ash woodland there are patches of the rare herb *Paris quadrifolia*.

Visit
CHATSWORTH DEER

The deer at Chatsworth are fallow deer, which were introduced into Britain by the Normans to grace their hunting forests. Fallow differ from the native red and roe deer in having a spotted coat and broad antlers. A visit to Chatsworth's glorious parkland can give the impression of an English version of the African Serengeti, with cattle, sheep and deer instead of wildebeest and impala.

Insight
BILBERRY TIME

Purple bird droppings on moorland walls are a sign that it is bilberry time. Bilberry (blaeberry in Scotland and blueberry in America) grows on the slopes and along the road verges of Beeley Moor. The bell-shaped flowers give way to glorious dark purple berries in July; despite being rather inconspicuous, the fruit bushes are quickly stripped by grouse, foxes and other wild animals.

Activity
WILDLIFE OF THE MOORLAND

Of all the heather moorland in the Peaks the expanse above Beeley is probably the best place for wildlife. This has been due in part to its isolation and lack of access, but now it is possible to explore several of its finest areas without damaging the most sensitive ecological sites.

ASHFORD IN THE WATER
MAP REF 404 D3

Only 2 miles (3.2km) from Bakewell and just off the busy A6, it is a wonder that Ashford in the Water has kept any kind of dignity. In truth it is one of the most attractive and interesting of all the Peak villages, situated on a twist of the River Wye, on the ancient port but bypassed by the new road.

At the middle of Ashford is a green space, called Hall Orchard, once part of the grounds of Neville Hall, a medieval hunting lodge that stood on the eastern side. The space is now a playing field but there are some tall trees, notably limes, and around the rest of the village fine ash trees to offer shelter and shade. 'Oak won't grow in Ashford' goes the local saying, and this has proved true over the years.

The main attraction for visitors to Ashford is the river, crystal clear and full of trout. There is space to wander along the banks, and three bridges, of which two are old. Close to the cricket field the bridge on the closed road carries an inscription 'M. Hyde 1664'; the brief memorial refers to the Reverend Hyde, who was thrown from his horse and drowned in the river below. Upstream, on an old packhorse trail, is the attractive Sheepwash Bridge; a stone fold on one side shows where the sheep were held before being plunged into the river and made to swim across to clean their fleeces.

BAKEWELL MAP REF 404 D3

Bakewell is always busy with visitors and locals. Its streets are never free of traffic and bustle, but if you accept this from the outset there's every reason to enjoy this town; it is an exciting mixture of old and new, a tourist honeypot that is still serves as a working community.

There are a surprisingly few very old buildings considering the rich history of Bakewell (it was granted a market and 15-day fair in 1254), but there are a number of fine 17th-century structures, such as the Market Hall, which serves as the Peak District National Park Information Centre, and the Town Hall. Up the steep road on the west side of the town stands an airy grass-covered knoll on which sits the lovely parish church of All Saints. Like many of the churches in Derbyshire it is broad and low, but with a spire as sharp as a 3H pencil. Inside you will find there are some fascinating fragments of Saxon and Norman stonework, and the famous monument to Sir John Manners and his wife Dorothy, who are reputed to have eloped together from Haddon Hall in 1558. Outside the hall stands the shaft of a 9th-century stone cross, beautifully decorated with vine scrolls and figures.

BUXTON MAP REF 403 J2

Dropping down from the high moors into the elegant spa town of Buxton, on the River Wye, is enough to make anyone blink in disbelief as they find themselves emerging out of the bleak wilderness into a bower of parks and gardens and grand Palladian-style buildings.

Through the centuries health resorts have sprung up in all sorts of unlikely places, and none more so than Buxton. By the 18th century Buxton, in common with other spa towns, was set firmly on the fashion trail. The 5th Duke of Devonshire was responsible for the main wave of building innovation at Buxton. He had been impressed in the 1770s by the Royal Crescent at Bath and was awash with money from his Ecton copper mines. First he had the elegant semicircular Crescent built, complete with 42 pilasters and 378 windows, then the Great Stable with a central court and Tuscan columns, finally followed by Hall Bank and The Square, all built in a grand and imposing style.

In the 19th century the 6th and 7th Dukes carried on the work, so that by late Victorian times the spa in the valley had completely eclipsed the old market town on the upper slope. The Great Stable became the Devonshire Hospital, 'for the use of the sick poor', and was given a massive domed roof 156 feet (47.4m) across (it is now part of the University of Derby); terraces of hotels and guest houses sprang up to cater for the influx of affluent visitors to the Thermal and Natural Baths; the railways arrived, the beautiful Pavilion Gardens were laid out on the banks of the Wye, and in 1905 the magnificent Opera House was opened.

Surprisingly, the majority of Buxton's fine buildings are still functioning and thriving. The Edwardian Opera House has a full programme, taking advantage of the current renewed interest in opera. Outside is an immaculate square, complete with an ornate Victorian post box, and behind it run the Pavilion Gardens, complete with a Serpentine Walk.

CARSINGTON WATER MAP REF 404 D4

New reservoirs usually take years to blend with a landscape, and sometimes they never do. Carsington, opened by Her Majesty the Queen in 1992, already looks at home in the gently rolling hills southwest of Wirksworth.

Most of the Peak District's many reservoirs gather their water from acid moorland, so they are low in nutrients, and this in turn means they are poor for aquatic plants and animals. However, Carsington is quite different: it is filled largely by water pumped from rivers and so is excellent for wildlife. In the winter there are wildfowl by

the thousand, including widgeon, pochard and tufted duck; in the summer there are great crested grebes and dabchicks; and in the spring and autumn, at migration time, all sorts of waders and seabirds use the reservoir as an oasis on their way from coast to coast.

A third of the Carsington shore is set aside as a conservation area, but the rest is accessible by footpath, by bicycle and by horse. The main Visitor Centre is on the west shore, with an extensive car park (pay & display) off the B5035.

Hopton village is now dominated by the reservoir, though there is a bypass for the main road. Until 1989 Hopton Hall (not open) was the home of the Gell family, who made their fortune from the nearby limestone quarries, and made their name as scholars, politicians and travellers. Along the limestone rise towards the north runs the Hopton Incline, once the steepest gradient for any standard-gauge railway line in Britain, using fixed engines and cable-haulage to set the High Peak Railway on its journey from Cromford Wharf to Whaley Bridge. It is now the High Peak Trail. Further north again is the Via Gellia, a road created and named by one of the Gells, through flower-rich woodland along a valley west of Cromford.

CHAPEL-EN-LE-FRITH
MAP REF 403 J2

Unfortunately, a pretty name does not always guarantee a pretty, picture-postcard place. The frith, or forest, never really existed here except to formalise a vast tract of Norman hunting preserve; most of the Derbyshire countryside was open ground rather than woodland.

The most obvious feature of Chapel-en-le-Frith today is its rather dowdy main road, which sweeps south into a hollow and on towards Buxton. A bypass now carries A6 traffic around to the east, but it will take some years for this part of Chapel to brighten up. However, turning off the main road at the white-painted Kings Arms at the top of the town, brings you directly to the market place and a change of character. Lovely cobbled paths and a medieval cross and stocks stand at the heart of the little square, overlooked by a café called The Stocks. Except on market day (Thursday) this is a quiet and out of the way place, perfect for a cup of tea and a wander. Close by is the Roebuck Inn, and a little way further along the street, opposite the church, is what was once the Bull's Head Inn, of which only the sign, a wooden carved life-size shorthorn bull's head, still survives.

St Thomas à Becket Church stands on a grassy knoll overlooking a housing estate. The original chapel in the forest was built here around 1225, but was replaced in the early 14th century by a sturdier structure. Most of what is visible today is from the refurbishment of 1733, but there are hints of antiquity all around; the shaft of a Saxon cross, a weathered sundial, and a view across what must have been glorious hunting country to the scenic crag-fringed edges of Combs Moss.

CHATSWORTH MAP REF 404 D3

Towards the end of the 17th century, William Cavendish, the 4th Earl of Devonshire and soon to be made the 1st Duke for his part in putting William of Orange on the throne, decided his house needed a radical new look. For a while he tinkered with alterations, but finally knocked everything down and started again. Demolishing one great historic house to build another might seem an odd investment of a lifetime, but in those days great families were judged by their homes and gardens; fashion and taste was everything.

The Chatsworth House that rose from the rubble of the Elizabethan mansion was of a classical, Palladian style, to the duke's own design. It took about 30 years to complete and it set the seal on his new status – even some of the window frames were gilded on the outside. The irony is that he never saw it at its best. Great houses needed great gardens and grounds, and these took decades to

establish. In the middle of the 18th century 'Capability' Brown and James Paine laid the foundations of what we see today by altering the course of the river, building bridges and setting out woodland.

The house is bursting with great works of art in the most superb settings; the Painted Hall is a work of art in itself, with huge, swirling scenes from the life of Julius Caesar by Louis Laguerre on the ceiling and upper part of the walls. Splendour follows splendour as you progress through the house (a tour of about a third of a mile/0.5km), but one of the most engaging features is the wonderful painting of a violin on the inner door of the State Music Room.

None can deny the magnificence of the house itself; from any direction it looks majestic, and from the southwest, approaching Edensor on a sunny evening, it can be breathtaking. On the horizon to the east are the high gritstone moors; in the middle distance are tiers of woodland, melting into ribbons and stands of beech and oak and rolling parkland; and in the foreground winds the Derwent. The front of the house reflects the peach-glow of evening sunlight to perfection; around it are superb formal gardens and the fine Emperor fountain. This is a view that the 1st Duke could only have dreamed about.

The Chatsworth Estate stretches far and wide and includes grouse moors, working farmland and estate villages. Of

the villages Edensor catches the eye first. Until the 1830s the village stood a little closer to the river but the 6th Duke had it moved further back, out of sight. The new houses were a hotchpotch of styles; Italian, Swiss, almost anything but vernacular English. Only one house of the original village remains, called Park Cottage, but known at one time as Naboth's Vineyard. The biblical reference relates to the owner in 1838, who is supposed to have refused to sell or be relocated. Just 1 mile (1.6km) to the northwest lies Pilsley, more compact than Edensor, with the Chatsworth Farm Shop, a pub and a microbrewery.

Just outside the Chatsworth Estate to the south, but within its influence and historic ownership, lies Beeley. This old working village, tucked neatly away and with many of the elements of a much older settlement, has quite a refreshing character. A tannery once stood beside the brook, and there was an estate-built school and a barn to house the coal wagons that supplied the Chatsworth estate glasshouses with fuel.

DOVE DALE MAP REF 403 J2

Dove Dale's Stepping Stones appear on a thousand postcards and attract a million visitors. The Dove flows for 45 miles (72.4km), but only a short section of it is called Dove Dale; above the Viator Bridge it becomes Mill Dale, then Wolfscote Dale

and then Beresford Dale. But it is to the gorge of Dove Dale that the visitors flock, for within the space of a few miles of easy riverside walking, on a broad level path, there are superb craggy rocks and pillars (all named) rising out of dense ash woodland, sweeps of open pasture, banks of flowers, fine cascades of spring water and dark caves. There is no road, and only one main path, following the east (Derbyshire) bank. It is not even necessary to cross the stepping stones upstream from the car park on the Staffordshire side of the river, because there is a footbridge a few yards away.

EYAM MAP REF 404 D3

Disease was a fact of life in medieval England, and many of the Peak villages suffered the horrors of Black Death and plague. What made the weaving village of Eyam special was the attempt by the local rector, William Mompesson, to keep the outbreak in 1665–66 within the confines of the community. The whole village was put in quarantine, entire families tragically perished and Eyam became a byword for tragedy and self-sacrifice.

Eyam today is neither a sad place nor dwelling in the past. It stands on the hill brow between Middleton Dale and Eyam Moor. Visitors are impressed by the Saxon cross in St Lawrence's churchyard and come to enjoy the traditional well dressing and the sheep roast.

BAKEWELL

GLOSSOP MAP REF 407 G7

Textiles breathed life into Glossop; there was water power and coal a-plenty and a workforce who came from Stockport and Manchester. At the turn of the 19th century there were more than 56 mills in the eight townships of Glossopdale; most were cotton mills, but there were also paper mills, ropewalks and woollen mills. Not many thrived; those that did modernised with the times and took to power looms, which were steam-driven and needed more water and more coal.

Glossop suffered disastrously when the cotton industry collapsed in the 1920s, and it took decades to recover. Overspill housing from the 1960s has affected the character of the town too, but there are some fascinating nooks and crannies, hidden away in the fabric of the place.

Just beyond the housing estate of Gamesley lies the remains of the Agricolan Roman fort of Melandra Castle, whilst to the north of the town, near Howard Park, is Mouselow or Castle Hill, with important Bronze Age and Iron Age associations and the site of a motte-and-bailey built by William de Peverel. Glossop's roads to the east lead to Longdendale and the Snake Pass, whilst only a few miles to the west is the M67 and Manchester.

GOYT VALLEY MAP REF 403 J2

The River Goyt meets the River Tame in Stockport to form the famous River Mersey. Its upper and middle reaches cleave a deep, gorge-like valley through some of the most accessible moorland in the Peak District. This is an area that is threaded with byroads, pack-horse trails and old railway tracks, a place where Cheshire meets Derbyshire amidst a blaze of heather and bilberry-strewn uplands.

The Goyt River flows from south to north; it rises on the slopes of Cat and Fiddle Moor, a wild and windswept place with a reputation for having the worst weather. The moor is named after the Cat and Fiddle Inn; at 1,690ft (515m) it is the second-highest pub in England. Like other high-altitude hostelries, such as The Snake or Tan Hill, it was built in the turnpike era at the start of the 19th century and is still a welcome sight for traffic on the sinuous A537. There are few other buildings to be seen for miles around, but some facilities are available at Derbyshire Bridge, which is the usual starting point to explore the Goyt Valley.

HATHERSAGE MAP REF 404 D3

Stanage Edge divides featureless moorland from the verdant Derwent. Prehistoric pathways, Roman roads and packhorse trails criss-cross the moors and converge below the confluence of the Derwent and the Noe. On the raised south-facing shoulder of the valley lies Hathersage ('Heather's Edge'), a village built on passing trade and farming. Millstones were a speciality in the 18th century, hewn directly from quarry faces. Then came the Industrial Revolution and five mills were built, to make pins and needles. The mills had a short life, as did the men who ground the needle-points and had to breathe in the dust.

The most interesting buildings in Hathersage are along the main road and off School Lane. Past 15th-century Hathersage Hall and Farm, and up the narrow Church Bank, it is possible to walk around Bank Top, a green knoll overlooking the alder-lined Hood Brook and valley. The church crouches on the grassy brow. To the south stands Bell House and The Bell Room, once an inn and barn beside the village green and stocks; to the west stands the Vicarage, and to the east is Camp Green, the ramparts of a 9th-century stockade.

HAYFIELD MAP REF 407 G7

The picturesque name and rural setting disguise Hayfield's industrial past; the village once hummed and rattled to the sound of cotton and paper mills, calico printing and dye works. It has also resounded to marching feet and cries of protest – in 1830 a mob of 1,000 mill workers gathered to demand a living wage and were dispersed by hussars. Eleven men appeared at Derby Assizes as a result, but the cotton industry was in terminal decline and all the anger was in vain. A century later, on 24 April 1932, Hayfield was the starting point for the 'mass trespass' of ramblers onto Kinder Scout. This protest eventually resulted in 'the right to roam'.

Hayfield is a peaceful little village, catering for tourists of all kinds. It has plenty of little cafés and restaurants with quaint and inventive names. One of the most revealing places to while away a few minutes is by the bridge, next to the courtyard of the Royal Hotel, which looks out over the River Sett, from the war memorial to the jumble of cottages and sloping roofs at the back of Church Street. Nearby is St Matthew's Church, built on the foundations of an older church washed away in a flood.

Serious walkers head east out of the village, up and over the green foothills to the russet expanse of the Kinder plateau. Families and other easy-going ramblers head west along the Sett Valley Trail towards New Mills. The car park at the start of this 3-mile (4.8km) trail, separated from the main village by the A624, was once the railway station, and the trail follows the course of the single-track line. In its heyday thousands of visitors arrived here from Manchester via the New Mills branch line; Hayfield marked the end of the mill towns and therefore the start of the countryside.

HOLMFIRTH MAP REF 407 H7

Before the BBC television series *Last of the Summer Wine* became a national institution, the most famous comic characters to come out of Holmfirth were depicted on postcards published by Bamforths. Saucy seaside cartoons became a serious business for the family firm just after the World War I; they had already pioneered lantern slides and the motion picture industry but were outflanked in the end by Hollywood.

The town of Holmfirth is a gem, built at the confluence of the Holme and the Ribble, where the Norman Earl Warren built a corn mill. For several centuries the lower valley was left to the woods and the hilltop towns of Cartworth, Upperthong and Wooldale prospered, combining farming with weaving. There are fine stone farmhouses and cottages on the upper slopes of the valley, often absorbed into the outskirts of the newer town. With the expansion of the cotton mills in the mid-19th century tiers of three-storey terraced cottages sprang up lower and lower into the valley and eventually cotton mills crowded the riverside.

HOPE MAP REF 407 H7

The Hope Valley is the main access route from the Derwent Valley through to Castleton, Edale and the Dark Peak, so

HOPE

the road is often busy. The little village of Hope lies at the confluence of the Noe and the Peakshole Water, which emerges from the bowels of the earth 2 miles (3.2km) away at Castleton. Hope railway station lies half a mile (0.8km) out of the village, across the Noe to the east, and is a perfect starting point for a walk up Win Hill, one of the best bracing viewpoints in the whole Peak. Lose Hill, the dark twin of Win Hill and another fine viewpoint, lies due west on the opposite side of the Noe.

Hope Church is in the heart of the village and is a typically squat-spired affair, which dates back to the 14th century. Inside there are two stone coffin lids bearing hunting horns, the motif of royal forest huntsmen. Outside, next to the porch, is the shaft of a Saxon cross with weathered carvings on its face. Stone scrollwork on preaching crosses represents the height of Dark Age culture.

LANGSETT MAP REF 407 H7

The northeast corner of the Peaks is probably the least visited sweep of country for 50 miles (80.5km) around; driving south from Holmfirth or west from Penistone takes you across open moors and plateaux with the whole of Yorkshire spread out below in a cerulean haze. There are very few villages to catch your immediate attention, but the upper valleys of the Don and the Porter, which rise up to the same watershed as the Derwent on Howden Moor, are full of interest. The Porter has been dammed in several places above Stocksbridge and there are good access points to the reservoirs and riverside and high up onto the moors.

Heading out from the car park it is possible to explore the woodlands and shoreline of Langsett Reservoir or walk along the dam wall, past the crenellated valve tower (a miniature of a tower at Lancaster Castle), to the old stone-built hamlet of Upper Midhope.

Above Langsett Reservoir, the Brook House Bridge gives access to the ancient trackway of the Cut Gate, an old drovers' road which started at Derwent and leads all the way to Penistone. The track climbs south over Midhope Moor, which is uncompromising high ground inhabited mostly by mountain hares and short-eared owls, littered with ancient flints and overlooked by the burial mound of Pike Lowe. This is not a good place to get caught in bad weather.

LONGDENDALE MAP REF 407 G7

Above Glossop a cleft in the most desolate wilderness of Peak moorland runs north by northeast from the little town of Tintwistle to the Derbyshire-Yorkshire border, shielding the A628 as it climbs to Gallows Moss. Down the cleft runs the River Etherow, a tributary of the Mersey. Over a century ago the valley was dammed to create five reservoirs, and this has so altered the character of the place that it sometimes looks like an oasis in a desert; green woodland and pasture encircles pools of silver, over which white sailing dinghies pirouette and scud.

Longdendale is a favourite place for day trips out of Manchester, and the cultural roots of Tintwistle are entwined with the old Lancashire cotton mills. The waters of the Etherow were harnessed to power the mills and were dammed to provide water for the city. A wealth of railway lines were laid to link the great industrial cities of Manchester and Sheffield, following the valley up to Woodhead and the Prough, a 3-mile (4.8km) tunnel below the moors. But now all that is in the distant past; the weavers' cottages of Tintwistle are now picturesque and the course of the railway is a footpath. Nevertheless, the dale still serves the city in its own way and remains part of its heritage.

The graveyard of lonely Woodhead Chapel, set on a shoulder above the banks of the upper reservoir, contains the last resting place of navvies and their families who died of cholera while the second railway tunnel was being built in 1849. Crowden, above Torside Reservoir, is a famous youth hostel on the route of the Pennine Way and is a welcome sight for walkers after the rigours of Bleaklow to the south or Black Hill to the north. Apart from a few isolated farms and an Information Centre there are no other settlements in the valley.

LYME PARK MAP REF 404 C3

Lyme Park (National Trust) on the western edge of the Peak District is a modest mirror image of Chatsworth. The exterior, made grimy by the smoky air of Manchester, is Palladian in style, the work of the Italian architect Giacomo Leoni; it featured as 'Pemberley' in the BBC adaptation of *Pride and Prejudice*. The interior, housing family portraits and a collection of different clocks, is Elizabethan but with many additions and alterations.

Lyme was the home of the Legh family for 600 years and has sufficient style to make it one of the top visitor attractions in the area, set in a rural idyll of gardens, parkland and moorland, yet only a stone's throw from Stockport. Those who prefer outdoor attractions to the splendours of the stately home will enjoy the wildfowl on the lake and herds of red and fallow deer among the trees. The 1,300-acre (520ha) park also has excellent short walks and viewpoints: a modest alternative to the high hills if the weather is closing in.

MANIFOLD VALLEY MAP REF 403 J2

The Manifold and the Dove rise within a mile (1.6km) of each other below Axe Edge. As they head southeast together into limestone country, side-winding like pulled strands of wool, one is transmuted into a Staffordshire valley, the other into a Derbyshire dale.

The difference between the valley and the dale in landscape terms is quite minimal; they both cut a course through superb scenery, meeting finally at the village of Ilam, yet the Manifold Valley escaped all the Victorian hype and the more carnival atmosphere of Dovedale.

Wetton and Warslow villages, on the 1,000-foot (305m) contour on opposite sides of the valley, are the main access points for the most dramatic section of the Manifold. Neither makes very much concession to tourists, though both have good pubs (the Olde Royal Oak and the Greyhound). Warslow has a utilitarian look, as do its medieval iron stocks close to the school. It is an estate village of the Crewe family (of Calke Abbey, south of Derby) and lies at the very foot of the gritstone moors. Access to the moors can be reached by driving along the side road to the northwest. The village of Wetton is on the limestone, surrounded by dairy farms and barns, but its stout church and many of its cottages look as if they really belong amongst the heather.

A steep side road north of Warslow off the B5053 drops down to Ecton, and the most beautiful section of the valley begins. It runs southwards along a thin strip of level meadow, with steep, flower-studded, almost alpine-looking grassland on either side. The road, and what is now the Manifold Trail, follows the route of the Leek and Manifold Valley Light Railway, which opened in 1904 but only survived for 30 years; according to expert judgement it opened too late and closed too soon – if its odd Indian-style engines were still running today the line would make a fortune!

Close by to Wettonmill the Manifold usually disappears down swallow-holes, travelling all the rest of the way to Ilam underground. Meanwhile, the Manifold's tributary, the Hamps, heads southwards and the Manifold Trail stays with the old railway line, going along the Hamps to the large village of Waterhouses.

Once out of the depth of the valley, the steep limestone hill slopes are pockmarked with deep caves. The most famous and dramatic is Thor's Cave but Ossom's Cave and Elderbush have been explored or excavated and have produced items from the Stone and Bronze Ages, when this was good hunting country. All the domed hills, which are called Lows, are capped by cairns or barrows and it is very easy on the dry 'karst' hillsides to imagine yourself in another older world.

MATLOCK MAP REF 404 D3

Matlock is a tourist honeypot, but there is more to it than the fairy lights and family attractions. Old Matlock stands on the east bank of the Derwent, before it twists west, under the bridge. St Giles Church, the Rectory and Wheatsheaf House mark an original lead-mining settlement at the meeting of packhorse trails and turnpikes. Next door, Matlock Bath is the home of the Peak District Mining Museum, which incorporates Temple Mine, an old lead and restored fluorspar mine, with a self-guided tour that depicts its geology, mineralisation and mining techniques.

Matlock Bath started as a petrifying well and tufa quarry, but in 1696 a bath was cut into the encrusted limestone and a spa was born. In the 18th and early 19th century the cream of society took the waters, staying in fashionable hotels on the sides of the gorge. Then in 1849 the railway arrived and the place was swamped by day trippers.

MILLER'S DALE MAP REF 404 D3

The River Wye rises at Buxton but then flows east to dissect the limestone plateau. Each reach of the river has its own character, and each section of the narrow valley or dale has its own name. Thus Wye Dale turns into Chee Dale, which gives way to Miller's Dale, then Water-cum-Jolly Dale and Monsal Dale. In many respects

Miller's Dale, to either side of Litton Mill, is the most impressive and complete dale to visit. Not only does the Wye negotiate a barrage of natural obstacles here, side-stepping hills, twisting through gaps and gorges and rock faces, but also there are mill races and weirs where the power of the water has been diverted to drive 19th-century cotton mills (Litton and Cressbrook, a little way further downstream). A recreational footpath, the Monsal Trail, runs the length of the dale, allowing access to the old mill yards (some of the buildings are still in use, but not for weaving). There are footbridges at either end of Miller's Dale allowing access to convenient car parks.

THE ROACHES MAP REF 403 J2

There are few real peaks in the Peak District (the name is derived from the Old English *pecsaetan*, meaning hill-dwellers), but the most elegant and craggy-topped are in the far west: Hen Cloud, Ramshaw Rocks and The Roaches. They are gritstone outcrops, similar to those in the Dark Peak and Eastern Moors, but here they were more heavily contorted or squashed together, leading to a landscape of misfit valleys, steep slopes and rock faces rather than plateau moorland.

Ramshaw Rocks are probably the best-known outlier of the Roaches, because they tower above the roadside on the A53 north of Leek and have a face-like formation. The A53 and the quiet winding roads to the west of Axe Edge lead to some interesting places.

Axe Edge itself is too high to be anything but wild. One notable village tucked away just off the main road is Flash. It is claimed to be the highest village in England at 1,518 feet (462m). The River Dane rises nearby, jinking a course between hills and ridges and flowing southwest to Gradbach and Danebridge: this is thoroughly delightful countryside full of trees and meadows, old barns and cowslip banks.

The Roaches ridge lies a few miles to the southwest of Flash and runs northwest–southeast, its main rock-climbing exposures facing the setting sun. A footpath follows the crest of the ridge, linking with Back Forest, creating a 4-mile (6.4km) ridge walk.

SNAKE PASS MAP REF 407 G7

Weather warnings on television and radio have made Snake Pass famous; when the sun is shining across the rest of the Pennines, Snake Pass, the A57 between Sheffield and Manchester, may be closed because of severe blizzards.

The road from Ladybower and the Woodlands Valley strikes northwest, sheltered on a shoulder of the River

THE ROACHES

Ashop, but after Lady Clough it has nowhere to hide and crosses a windswept desert at 1,680 feet (512m). Bleaklow lies to the north, Kinder Scout to the south. In places the peat has been stripped away to reveal a surface of shattered stones, which is how the glaciers left the place after the last Ice Age. It is bleak; there are no trees, no barns and no walls.

Of course, the remote wildness of Snake Pass is irresistible and in fine weather it can be magical. The upper Woodlands Valley is pretty, dotted with old farms and birch-lined cloughs. There are two or three farms and cottages on the Snake Road before you reach the lonely Snake Pass Inn. At the top of Lady Clough, on the highest and most featureless ground, Snake Pass is crossed by the Pennine Way, close to the paved trackway of ancient Doctor's Gate. Travellers have been apprehensively venturing across these moors for thousands of years.

The Snake Inn was built in 1821 as Lady Clough House, when the original medieval track was turned into a turnpike road. If you should need to see how remote this hostelry is, there is a milestone outside the inn that records the 21 miles (33km) to Manchester and 17 miles (27km) to Sheffield. The low stone-built inn is an ideal place to stop for refreshment. Food is served most days of the week and accommodation is available.

STANTON IN PEAK MAP REF 404 D3

Stanton village is a ribbon of cottages on a steep and winding side road, built out of the limestone and below the brow of the gritstone, sheltered from the moor by old quarries and a swathe of tall sweet-chestnut trees. The initials WPT, carved into the lintels of many doorways, refer to William Thornhill, who built most of the village in the 1830s and whose family lived at Stanton Hall. The 18th-century Flying Childers Inn celebrates the greatest racehorse of its day, trained by Sir Hugh Childers for the 4th Duke of Devonshire. Opposite the inn is Holly House which still has half of its windows still blocked up to avoid the 1697 window tax.

Birchover Lane, running to the south of Stanton, follows along the western edge of the moor. Pathways trail through birch scrub and over carpets of heather and bilberry to the Bronze Age landscape. About 70 barrows or burial cairns have been identified on the small island of gritstone. The biggest, covering the site of twelve cremations, still stands 5 feet (1.5m) tall, inside a double ring of stones with an outer diameter of 54 feet (16.4m). There are three stone circles or monuments on Stanton Moor; the most famous is the Nine Ladies.

ARBOR LOW

Visit
ARBOR LOW'S ANCIENT STONES

Some 3 miles (4.8km) along the Long Rake west of Youlgreave, off the road to the left and easily accessible from a car park, is the famous henge of Arbor Low, probably built by the Beaker People in around 2000 BC. The whole monument, with a rock-cut ditch, a bank and a circle of 47 stones, measures 250 feet (76.2m) across. Although the massive stone blocks are all lying flat and some half buried, Arbor Low is still a powerfully atmospheric place, especially in winter sunlight.

Activity
TEGG'S NOSE & THE GRITSTONE TRAIL

The best introduction to the Cheshire slice of the Peak landscape is from Tegg's Nose Country Park, along Buxton Old Road to the east of Macclesfield. There are superb views from the Windy Way car park and walks along a network of tracks and pathways, by the old quarry or down through woodland to the reservoirs above Langley. It is possible at this point to join the Gritstone Trail, a pleasant waymarked footpath running the length of Cheshire from Lyme Park to Mow Cop.

WHALEY BRIDGE MAP REF 403 J2

This little town grew up with dust on its face and Goyt water in its veins. Coal and textiles provided the only gainful work – both have now gone. These days there is hardly a whisper of past industry and employment is more varied. Visitors call in on their way to the Goyt Valley or the Peak Forest Canal.

Just outside Whaley Bridge, above Bing Wood (a 'bing' is a slag heap) is the curious ridge known as Roosdyche. This ridge was once described as a Roman racecourse, on purely visual evidence – nobody could explain who or what else could have created such a flat-bottomed valley. The answer, of course, was ice.

South of the town is Toddbrook Reservoir, built to feed the Peak Forest Canal, and tiny Taxal village clustered around its church. Inside St James's are memorials to the Jodrell family, and a monument to Michael Heathcote, 'Gentleman of the Pantry and Yeoman of the Mouth to His Late Majesty King George the Second'. Heathcote lived to be 75 years old, so presumably nobody tried to poison the king during his time as official food-taster.

WILDBOARCLOUGH MAP REF 403 J2

Only a few outbuildings remain of the Crag mills that once made this valley have the hum of a minor industrial centre, which employed more than 600 people. The mills here specialised in the bleaching, printing and dyeing of cotton, then later carpets.

Along the valley today you'll find that most traces of the town's industrial heritage are camouflaged green. There are shrub-covered foundations, grassy trackways and mossy walls. The stream boasts pretty waterfalls and deep pools and is the territory of dippers and grey wagtails. The impression is of a rural backwater, at the foot of Shutlingsloe, the 'Cheshire Matterhorn'.

YOULGREAVE MAP REF 404 D3

A long, handsome village on the shoulder of Bradford Dale, Youlgreave (known as Pommie by most locals) has one of the most elaborate well-dressing ceremonies in the Peak District, taking place at Midsummer each year, when five wells are dressed (or decorated) with biblical scenes. The White Peak tradition has its roots in the days when wells were essential and were blessed to give thanks for water. However, in the case of Youlgreave the records only go back to 1829, coinciding with the provision of the village's own public water supply via a conduit from the Dale below. The water was gathered in a huge circular stone tank called The Fountain, which stands in the middle of the village. Nearby, on the opposite side of the street, is the Co-op

building, which once had a vital role in the social survival of the area but is now a youth hostel.

On the east side of Youlgreave, by the road which then sweeps down to Alport, stands All Saints Church. Essentially Norman and with an unusually broad nave, the most obvious feature of All Saints is its 14th-century tower, chunky and stylish in the best Perpendicular tradition. Inside are sturdy columns and a 13th-century font, unique in that it has two bowls, and the fine monuments include a tiny effigy of Thomas Cokayne, who died in 1488. The church was restored in 1870 and has some beautiful stained-glass windows by Burne-Jones and Kempe.

Three bridges cross the River Bradford below Youlgreave, including a clapper bridge of stone slabs and also a packhorse bridge, which is now used as a footbridge. The short walk to the confluence with the Lathkill is popular, but by turning southeast, over the main bridge and on to the Limestone Way, you can explore the fine countryside towards Birchover, past the Iron Age hill-fort of Castle Hill and the Nine Rings Stone Circle (four stones are still standing tall), to the rock tors of Robin Hood's Stride, Cratcliffe Rocks and Rowtor Rocks. Pagan myths, hermits' caves and a popular dining pub, the Druid Inn, are among the attractions of this magical corner of the Peak.

WALK 71

WOLFSCOTE & A RAILWAY TRAIL

The first part of this very enjoyable walk winds through the scenic Wolfscote Dale and Biggin Dale, and you'll be walking through the heart of the upland limestone country. The return route is an easy-paced one, using the Tissington Trail, which ambles quietly over the high pastures of Biggin and Alsop moors.

DISTANCE/TIME 7.5 miles (12.1km) 4h **MAP** OS Explorer OL24 White Peak **START** Tissington Trail pay car park at Alsop Old Station; grid ref: SK 156549 **TRACKS** Well-defined paths and trails, about 20 stiles and gates **THE PUB** Waterloo Inn, Biggin-by-Hartington. Tel: 01298 84284

1 From the car park at Alsop Old Station, cross over the busy A515 road (with care) and follow the Milldale Road, which is immediately opposite. Bear right at the junction and in about 200yds (183m) the option of a parallel footpath, left, keeps you safely away from traffic.

2 On reaching the bottom of the dale by Lode Mill, turn right to walk along the footpath, tracing the river's east bank through a winding and partially wooded valley.

3 Ignore the footpath on the right when you reach Coldeaton Bridge, but instead stay with Wolfscote Dale beneath the thickly wooded slopes on the right. Once you get beyond a stile the woods cease and the dale becomes bare and rock-fringed, with a cave on the right and the bold pinnacles of Peaseland Rocks up ahead. Here the valley sides open out into the dry valley of Biggin Dale, where this route continues on.

4 The unsigned path into Biggin Dale begins just beyond a stile in a cross-wall and climbs by that wall. It then continues through some scrub woodland and beneath limestone screes. Walk beyond a gate and enter into a nature reserve.

5 There's another gate at the far end of the nature reserve. Beyond it the dale curves left, then right, before dividing again beneath the hill pastures of Biggin Grange. We make a slight diversion left here, over a stile to follow the footpath, signposted to Hartington. On the other side of the wall there's a concrete dewpond.

6 After 200yds (183m) there's a junction of paths. This time ignore the path signposted to Hartington and keep walking ahead up the shallowing dale, and following the path to Biggin. It stays with the valley round to the right, passing a small sewage works (on the left) before climbing out of the dale to the road at Dale End.

7 Turn right along the road for a few paces then left, following a road past the Waterloo Inn and through Biggin village.

8 Turn right again approximately 500yds (457m) away from the village centre on a path that climbs to reach the Tissington Trail. Follow this lovely old trackbed south across the pastures of Biggin and Alsop moors. After walking for about 2 miles (3.2km) you reach the car park at Alsop Old Station and the start of the walk.

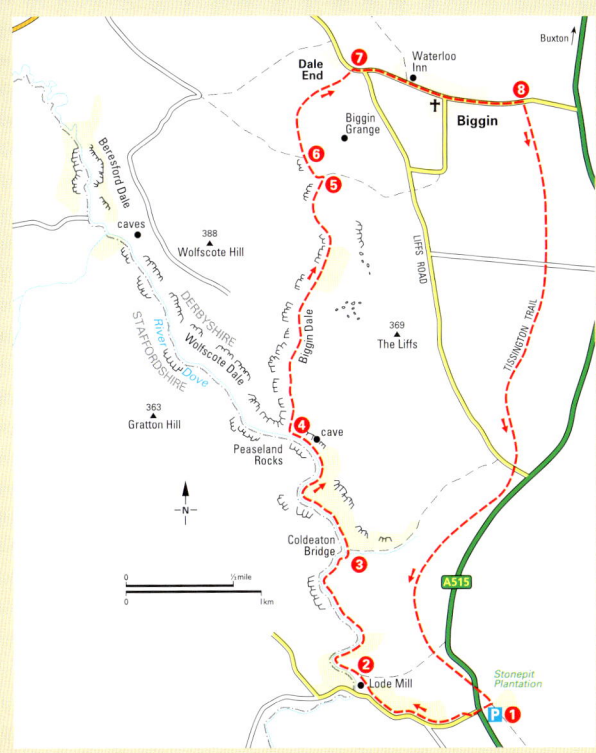

WALK 72

LONGNOR & HOLLINSCLOUGH

On this route you ramble over hills and dales in the footsteps of television's fictitious doctors. Longnor developed as a meeting place on the ancient trade routes.

DISTANCE/TIME 6 miles (9.7km) 3h30 **MAP** OS Explorer OL24 White Peak **START** Longnor market square; grid ref: SK 089649 **TRACKS** Some on road otherwise good footpaths, about 42 gates **THE PUB** Crewe and Harpur Arms, Longnor SK17 0NG. Tel: 01298 83205

1 From the market square take the Buxton road. Turn right into Church Street, then take the no-through road left. In 100yds (91m) look right for steps leading to a footpath. Follow the waymarkers, behind houses, over a stile and by a wall. Cross a stile, go downhill and turn left on to a farm road.

2 Keep left at the farm to a road. Turn right, past the traffic lights and before the bend fork left on a waymarked drive. At the end enter the gate to a path, through a gap stile, downhill, across a bridge and keep ahead, over a stile and left to a road.

3 Fork left on to a farm road, following the waymarked path. Cross a footbridge and turn left onto a field path by a stream to reach a road. Turn right (Hollinsclough), follow the road right and uphill. Turn right on to a bridlepath, through a gate and downhill.

4 In 50yds (45m) fork left by two stones and continue along the flank of the hill for 0.5 miles (0.8km). Where the path divides into three, fork left to pass by an old gatepost and go on a wide track. At the top turn left, through a farm to a lane. Turn right to a path on the left, opposite 'The Glen'.

5 Walk downhill and cross to the left of a ditch to find a stile leading to a bushy bank dropping steeply to a stream. Cross this and walk uphill to a stile. Trace the field road to a gateway right of Willshaw Farm. Turn back to the farm, through the farmyard and then fork right at a fingerpost. Walk ahead to another hillside path. Keep the hedge on the left to pass a waymark post. At the gully turn right on a path, cross two stiles to reach Hill Top Farm. Take the stile opposite and go around the field to a stile by a gate into a road.

6 Cross the road and take the farm road opposite. In 100yds (91m) go right steeply downhill, over a stile and follow the path. Just before the first footbridge, cross a stile on the left and head uphill left.

7 Continue walking uphill, through a gate in a stone wall to some ruined buildings. Follow the track right, below these ruins through to Ball Bank House Farm. Bear left after you pass two barns, then go left on to an indistinct footpath uphill, starting just behind the farmhouse.

8 At the top of the slope go through a stile, follow the wall uphill, then go over a further two stiles to the road. Turn left then right towards Longnor. Before the road bends left, cross a stile on the right, go downhill and over a slab bridge, then through a squeeze stile, up to a corner squeeze stile and then further stiles to lead on to a farm road. Turn right to return to the village.

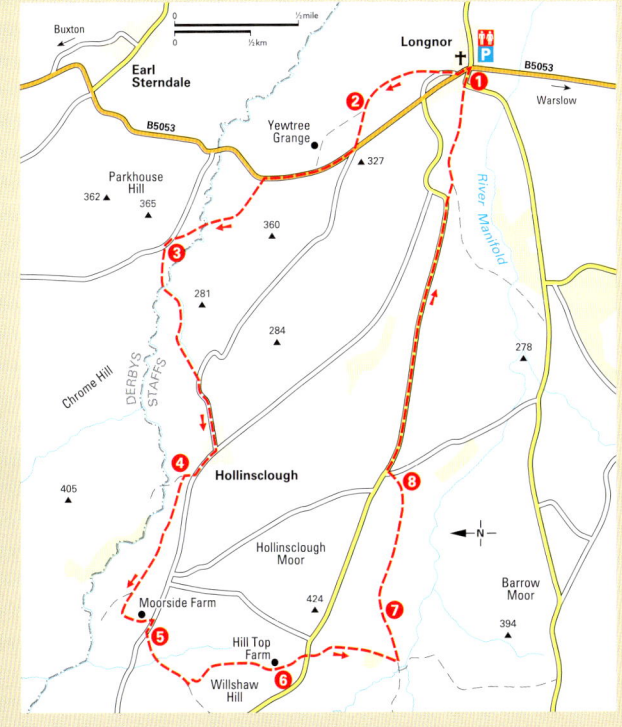

A BUXTON FIGURE OF EIGHT

An attraction in its own right, the town of Buxton lies at the heart of some outstanding countryside. There are high roads with magnificent views that radiate away from the town centre. This tour makes the most of the town's situation with a figure-of-eight route, out on the shoulder of the Goyt, back via Chapel-en-le-Frith and Dove Holes, then out again on the dramatic Axe Edge road and down towards Leek, before returning through quiet rolling farmland.

Route Directions

1 From Buxton, just above the Opera House, take the A5004 uphill towards Whaley Bridge, rising for a mile (1.6km) through woodland and then over moorland. After another half mile (0.8km) a cairn on the right marks the National Park boundary. Continue for 2.5 miles (4km) along the shoulder of the valley to the Upper Hall lay-by (wonderful views). Drive on for another 2 miles (3.2km), through Fernilee to the outskirts of Whaley Bridge, where you turn right along the B5470, signed Chapel-en-le-Frith. Pass by The Board pub and on for another 3 miles (4.8km) through Tunstead Milton to enter Chapel-en-le-Frith. Turn off at the Kings Arms, on the left, if you want to explore the centre of this old town.

2 Drive along the B5470 through Chapel-en-le-Frith for another mile (1.6km), past the Old Packhorse Inn on the left, then turn left following the sign for the A6 and Buxton. Go under the flyover and then turn right to join the A6, along a wooded valley for 2 miles (3.2km) to Dove Holes.

The workaday quarry village hides the site of a prehistoric henge. Despite the noise from the quarries and traffic from the A6, you'll doubtless find the remains impressive.

3 Continue on the A6 for 3 miles (4.8km) to Fairfield, a pretty village on the outskirts of Buxton. The road descends into the middle of Buxton; at the bottom, follow the signs for the A53 to Leek, via four roundabouts that are well signed, with the landmark dome of the former Devonshire Hospital to your right. Begin the second loop of the tour by following the A53 towards Leek, passing the Pavilion Gardens situated on your left. Continue uphill out of town for 2 miles (3.2km), through traffic lights and out on to open hilltops – the start of Axe Edge. The Dove and Manifold rivers rise here. The road gradually descends past a side road to Flash and out of Derbyshire into Staffordshire, then continues on for about 3 miles (4.8km) to Ramshaw Rocks on the right.

Ramshaw Rocks include a feature which looks like a face The Winking Man appears to wink at you if you drive north.

4 Continue on the A53 for another 1.5 miles (2.4km), down to Upper Hulme and Blackshaw Moor and off the high moorland.

In 2 miles (3.2km) pass the delightful Moss Rose Inn on the outskirts of Leek, then in less than half a mile (0.8km) turn left onto Springfield Road, signed for Ashbourne and Derby. Shortly you will reach a junction with the A523; turn right here to visit Leek or left to continue the tour.

Leek is a former market town, with a pretty Market Place. Built on a hill overlooking the River Churt, Leek is also called 'The Queen of the Moorlands' although it is somewhat overlooked now in favour of its much larger neighbouring town, Stoke.

5 Head uphill through rolling pastureland for 2.5 miles (4km) and pass a turn to the RSPB Nature Reserve of Coombes Valley, then on for 1.5 miles (2.4km) to Bottom House crossroads and the Green Man Inn. Turn left along the B5053 signed for Longnor and continue for 1.5 miles (2.4km) through Onecote. After 2.5 miles (4km) the road twists down to cross the pretty Warslow Brook, a tributary of the Manifold, then rises for a mile (1.6km) to the village of Warslow. Continue along the B5053 for 4 miles (6.4km), crossing the River Manifold before climbing sharply into Longnor.

Longnor is a compact and attractive village surrounded by farming country. Once an important centre for market trade, Longnor makes a pleasant stop in the Staffordshire Moorlands. It has some interesting buildings, constructed of stone mined locally, which include the Victorian market hall and the Norman church.

6 Bear left up out of the village (between the stores and The Horseshoe pub), cresting a ridge in 0.5 miles (0.8km) – beware of the traffic lights – before crossing the River Dove at Glutton Bridge, back into Derbyshire. The landscape changes quite abruptly as the road follows a limestone gorge (Glutton Dale) for half a mile (0.8km) up to a crossroads (Dalehead to the left, Earl Sterndale to the right). Keep driving ahead here; the road shortly curves to the left across a steep slope and rises to a crest before dropping past the quarries at Hind Low to a T-junction at Brierlow Bar. Turn left along the A515 and drive for just 3 miles (4.8km) to return to Buxton town centre and the start point of the drive.

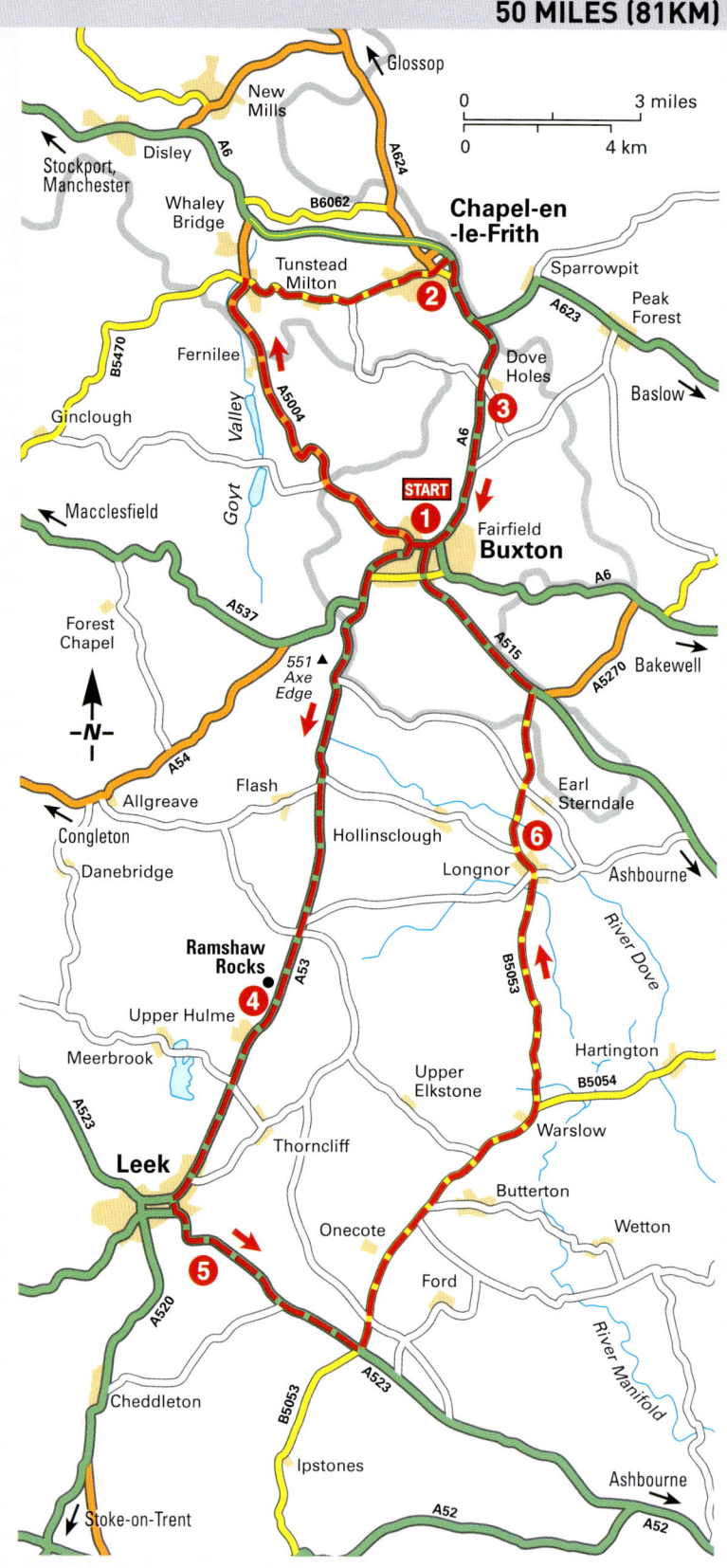

56 MILES (90KM)

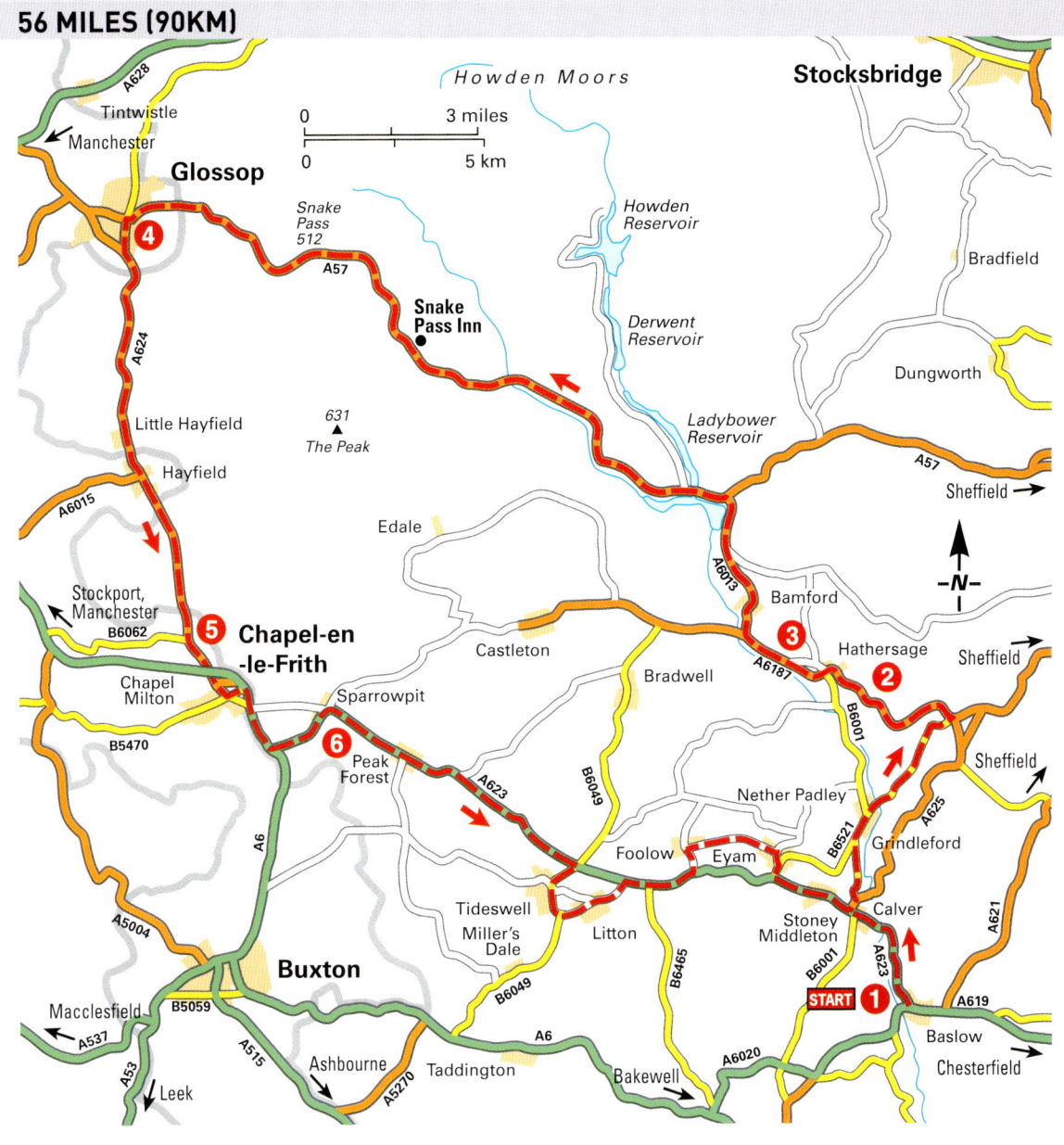

THE SNOW ROAD

This tour begins at Baslow, in the Derwent valley with gritstone cliffs to the east and the White Peak to the west. It heads north to Ladybower Reservoir and then climbs northwest to cross the Dark Peak by the infamous Snake Pass before dropping down to the little mill towns of Glossop and Chapel-en-le-Frith. The return route is over the limestone plateau of the White Peak and down-dale through Stoney Middleton. Check weather conditions before attempting the Snake Pass.

Route Directions

The tour starts in Baslow at the roundabout junction of the A619 and the A623. Baslow sits on the edge of Chatsworth Park.

1 Head north towards Manchester on the A623 for 2 miles (3.2km) until you reach the Calver traffic lights. Turn right on the A625, go ahead on the B6001, signed Grindleford, for 2 miles (3.2km) into the town. Here, keep ahead on the B6521 and cross the river bridge up into Nether Padley. Continue for 2 miles (3.2km). Pass Longshaw Lodge, right, and sweep up to a T-junction. Turn left onto the A6187 signed Hathersage. The road bears left and there are fine views of Hathersage Moor.

Discarded millstones lie among the birches, close to where they were cut – look for one in a car park on the right.

2 Drop down off the moor for approximately 3.5 miles (5.6km) and drive into the village of Hathersage, ever-popular with hikers.

Hathersage has historical links with the Robin Hood folklore and in the churchyard (on the right up School Lane and Church Bank) is Little John's grave.

3 Drive through Hathersage, then continue along the A6187 for a mile (1.6km) towards Castleton before turning right at traffic lights on to the A6013, signed for Bamford and Ladybower. Continue for 2 miles (3.2km), past the dam wall of Ladybower Reservoir, to a T-junction. Turn left on the A57, signed for Glossop. Continue for another 14 miles (22.5km); going up Woodlands Valley, along Ladybower, then past The Snake Pass Inn.

Snake Pass is one of the most exposed and lonely places in England, and the road really does snake its way over the dome of moorland before descending to Glossop.

4 Head into Glossop, turn left at traffic lights onto the A624, signed 'Chapel-en-le-Frith'. Continue for 4 miles (6.4km) to Little Hayfield, then on to Hayfield, with the village on the left and the start of the Sett Valley Trail on the right. Continue ahead for 2 miles (3.2km), past the Lamb Inn.

Here there is an imposing sweep of green hills and gritstone walls to the left and a hint of industry, New Mills, and the Derbyshire/

Cheshire border away to the right. New Mills was perfectly placed in the 18th century for the water-driven spinning and weaving factories that used the combined force of the River Goyt and the River Sett.

5 In a mile (1.6km) the road drops under a railway bridge to a junction. Turn left, signed 'Chapel-en-le-Frith'. Go under two viaducts and a flyover at Chapel Milton and into Chapel-en-le-Frith; go over a roundabout, still signed 'Chapel-en-le-Frith'. Turn left at a junction signed for the A6; turn left, pass beneath the flyover, turn right to join the A6 towards Buxton. Continue for a mile (1.6km), turn left at a roundabout on to the A623, signed 'Chesterfield and Sheffield'.

The landscape is different now; limestone country on a gently rolling plateau. Nestled between the hills of the southern pennines, Chapel-en-le-Frith was important in the early industrial years for it's association with the Peak Forest Tramway, which was essential for moving limestone from local quarries into the towns.

6 After 1.5 miles (2.4km) turn sharp right at The Wanted Inn and continue towards Chesterfield. In 4 miles (6.4km) turn right along the B6049 to Tideswell. Continue beyond the village for 500yds (457m) to a left turn signed (on the right) for Litton. Turn left here and drive through this peaceful little village, in 0.75 miles (1.2km) reaching a junction with the A623. Turn right, continue for a mile (1.6km), passing a garage. Turn left towards Foolow, then left again to reach the village. Turn right at The Bull's Head Inn and drive the 1.5 miles (2.4km) to Eyam.

At the square in the village centre, turn sharp right into The Dale, descending to rejoin the A623; turn left down Middleton Dale into Stoney Middleton. In just 0.75 miles (1.2km), cross over Calver traffic lights, driving 2 miles (3.2km) back to Baslow.

DISTANCE/TIME 15 miles (24.2km) 4h; shorter route 9 miles (14.5km) 2h30 **MAP** OS Explorer OL1 Dark Peak **START** Fairholmes Visitor Centre, Upper Derwent Valley; grid ref: SK176894 **TRACKS** Tarred lanes and rough mountain roads **CYCLE HIRE** Fairholmes. Tel: 01433 651261 **THE PUB** Yorkshire Bridge Inn, Bamford. Tel: 01433 651361; www.yorkshire-bridge.co.uk

DISTANCE/TIME 8 miles (12.9km) 3h30 **MAP** OS Explorer OL 24 White Peak **START** Carsington Reservoir Visitor Centre; grid ref: SK241515 **TRACKS** Compacted gravel, sand and earth tracks, with some back lanes **CYCLE HIRE** The Watersports Centre, Carsington Water. Tel: 01629 540478 **THE PUB** Red Lion Inn, Ashbourne DE6 1PR. Tel: 01335 370396

THE UPPER DERWENT VALLEY RESERVOIRS

This is a long and challenging cycle route around the stunning chain of reservoirs in the Upper Derwent Valley.

1 Head north from the Fairholmes Visitor Centre, rising to the level of the dam top of Derwent Reservoir. Easy cycling with great views takes you past the memorial to Tip, a sheepdog who kept vigil beside his master's body on Howden Moors.

2 Dipping in and out of Ouzelden Clough, the road passes close to the site of Birchinlee, or 'Tin Town'. Passing beside Howden Dam, the route circuits a long arm of Howden Reservoir to the turning circle at Kings Tree, the end of the tarred road. This is a good place to turn around (9 mile/14.5km round trip); the next section is more challenging.

3 Beyond the gate the route becomes a rough forest road that climbs gently through the woods above Howden Reservoir. At a fork keep right to drop to the old packhorse bridge at Slippery Stones. Just above the bridge swing sharp right to climb the roughening track along the eastern shore of the reservoir.

4 The going is pretty rough for a mile (1.6km) or so before a well-graded service road heralds the approach to Howden Dam. A steep, rougher descent follows before the route comes close to the reservoir edge where steep, grassy banks drop straight into the water, so take care here. The track improves considerably as the route nears Derwent Dam. Passing close to one of the towers, the way develops into a tarred lane and passes the first of some isolated houses.

5 You can cut short the ride by turning right to pass the foot of Derwent Dam to return to Fairholmes (9.5 miles/15.2km). The main route continues south past St Henry's Chapel, becoming rougher again as it rounds an inlet to an interpretation board describing the now-lost village of Derwent, which stood here until the 1940s.

6 Reaching a gateway, join the tarred lane and drop to the main road. Turn right along the wide cycle path across Ashopton Viaduct, and right again at the far end. Reaching a gateway, join the tarred lane and drop to the main road. Turn right along the wide cycle path across Ashopton Viaduct, and right again at the far end.

AROUND CARSINGTON WATER

Discover picturesque hamlets and abundant wildlife at one of England's largest reservoirs as you cycle this interesting route.

1 From the car park at the visitor centre look for the fingerposts pointing the way to the wildlife centre; this will bring you to the start of a compacted track just below the coach park. These initial stages are an easy settling-in section, with a few short hills and descents. The track is partly shared with walkers and partly designated as a horse and cycle route, so be prepared to stop and obey any instruction signs.

2 The track joins a tarred farm access road, shortly passing by the Sheepwash car park. Take extra care here as you join the car park access road before arriving at the main road. The way is diagonally across to the left and along the road for Carsington.

3 There's a steady climb before the lane descends into Carsington. The lane undulates gently through the village and the neighbouring hamlet of Hopton. Pass beside the wall surrounding the Hopton Hall Estate, a wavy barrier of bricks with square towers and rounded bays. At the far end of Hopton, pass by Henmore Grange before looking right for the waymarked, fenced path that drops steeply down to a gate on to the B5035.

4 Cross carefully here, go left signed for Millfields, and turn right along the track beyond a further safety gate. You're at the extremity of the reservoir here, with views down the length of the lake. The first of a long series of hills is soon encountered, leading to a gate into woodlands with a wealth of wild flowers, and many short descents and longer inclines. You rise high above the waterline here before cresting a final summit to reveal views towards the dam and valve tower, and a steep hill down, passing by a wooden carving, just one of the sculptures dotted around the reservoir. When you eventually reach a short section of tarred farm lane, turn up along this to a waymarked gate, right, back on to the track.

5 Further ups and downs bring you past a stone shelter; take a peek inside to find some inventive wooden carvings. Just past here turn up the old lane. Pass by the farmhouse before looking right for the waymarked gateway back on to the cycle track. From here you're once again on a dedicated cycle/horse track that brings you to a gateway on to a wide grass verge by the main road. Turn right down the verge and right again into Millfields.

6 The waymarking is confusing here. Take the marked cycle path past the entry barriers and then go sharp left along a track. Go round a bend and along a short straight section, then dogleg left then right along a sandy track to reach the dam. At the far end head back to the visitor centre.

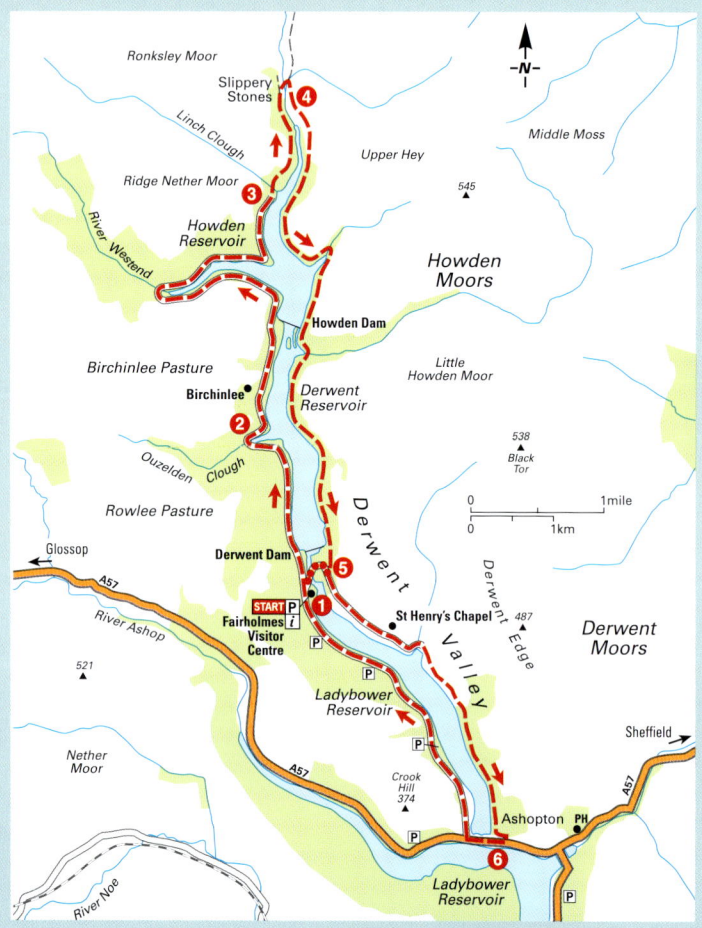

DISTANCE/TIME 8 miles (12.9km) 3h; shorter route 5.25 miles (8.4km) 1h15 **MAP** OS Explorer OL24 White Peak **START** Bakewell Old Station; grid ref: SK 223690 **TRACKS** Railway trackbed and lanes **CYCLE HIRE** None nearby **THE PUB** Monsal Head Hotel, Monsal Head. Tel: 01629 640250; www.monsalhead.com

DISTANCE/TIME 13 miles (21km) 3h30 **MAP** OS Explorer OL24 **START** The Manifold Inn; grid ref: SK 108593 **TRACKS** All on-road apart from a short section of the Manifold Trail at the end **CYCLE HIRE** Parsley Hay, 4 miles (6.4km) from Hulme End. Tel: 01298 84493 **THE PUB** Manifold Inn, Hulme End, HartingtonBuxton SK17 0EX. Tel: 01298 84537

BAKEWELL & THE MONSAL TRAIL

An easy ride from the town of Bakewell, with its railway heritage, which loops through a picturesque limestone village and riverside hay meadows.

1 Access to the trackbed is via the gap at the left side of the imposing structure. Turn left along the level track which, beyond some industrial units that occupy the former goods yard, runs initially through thin woods. After passing beneath the main road, Bakewell is soon left behind.

2 Beyond the warehouse here, the trees thin and become less constricting. The old trackbed passes under and over several roads before reaching the impressive buildings at Great Longstone's old station.

3 A sign warns you that there is no exit for cyclists beyond this point, however it is worth cycling 0.25 miles (0.4km) to the end of the useable track for great views across towards the River Wye in its deep valley. You can simply retrace your route back to Bakewell from here, a distance of 5.25 miles (8.4km) or return to Great Longstone Station and take the steep flight of steps, left, to a minor road. Turn left along this road for an easy, level ride to the village centre at Great Longstone.

4 At the market cross and village green, fork right along either of the lanes. Both wind down to the main street to reach the White Lion. Just beyond this, take Church Lane, left to the parish church. The road bends to the right here along Beggarway Lane, offering views up to Longstone Edge and odd glimpses back towards the buildings Bakewell.

5 In 0.75 miles (1.2km), turn right along the lane at a left-hand bend. Fork left here just before the bridge, up a gravelly ramp to regain the old railway. Turn left here to return to Bakewell. To extend the route you can now cycle across the car park and take Station Road downhill. On reaching the junction at the bottom of the road turn sharp left along Coombs Road, passing the car park entrance. This peaceful, level lane runs for about a mile (1.6km) to a high-arched viaduct crossing.

6 Immediately before the viaduct, look for the Monsal Trail board, left, indicating a short, sharp incline, up which you wheel your bicycle to the old railway. Turn left to return to Bakewell and enjoy the good views across the town.

THE STAFFORDSHIRE MOORLANDS

Cycle this lovely, undulating, on-road route through the countryside where the White Peak meets the Dark Peak.

1 Take the B5054 outside The Manifold Inn to a junction on the left signposted 'Sheen & Longnor'. This winding lane initially descends before starting a gradual climb between limestone walls. Sight-lines on this section are not good, but they improve after a slightly steeper pitch brings the route to the straggling village of Sheen.

2 Passing by the village inn, The Staffordshire Knot, then the church, the way again steepens slightly as it rises through a few bends to level out past Harris Close farm, with Sheen Hill's to the left. A long, easy ride follows, cresting to fall down a sharp hill with bad sight lines. At the junction keep ahead to reach Longnor.

3 At the heart of Longnor is the Market Square. This route crosses straight over the junction here, in front of the Horseshoe pub and along a lane signposted 'Royal Cottage and Leek'. Once out of the village there's a steep descent to a bridge over the River Manifold and the start of a climb up the valley side. In 0.5 miles (0.8km) the route levels to reach a left turn signposted 'Fawfieldhead and Newtown'. Follow this through to a T-junction and turn right along an undulating lane with pleasing views.

4 At a telephone box turn left along a lane signposted 'Warslow'. Soon you'll pass by the little chapel at Newtown (built 1837) off to your right. This is an airy, easy cruise along a high road, with the distinctive limestone hills at Ecton the main feature off to your left beyond Reaps Moor. Beyond a house called Hayshead the lane starts a long, gradual climb before levelling out beside Lum Edge and Warslow Moor.

5 Go straight across the crossroads, bear left at the junction, joining a road that rises gradually, soon crossing a cattle grid. Cresting another rise, there's a long descent into Warslow. Continue to pass the Greyhound Inn to a junction with the B5053.

6 Turn left along this road and remain on it for about 200yds (183m) to find a lane on the right, signposted 'Unsuitable for Heavy Goods Vehicles'. Carefully turn into this, which drops increasingly steeply as a narrow, winding lane. Keep right to descend to a bridge across the Manifold. Just beyond this turn left along the Manifold Way and follow this to Hulme End. Rejoin the main road and turn right to return to the nearby Manifold Inn and the start of the ride.

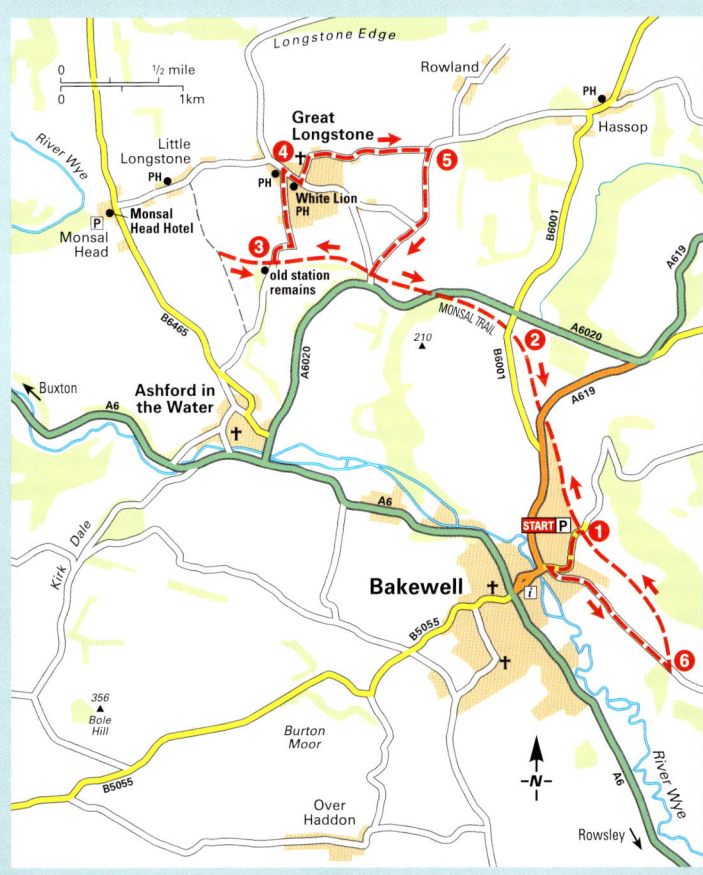

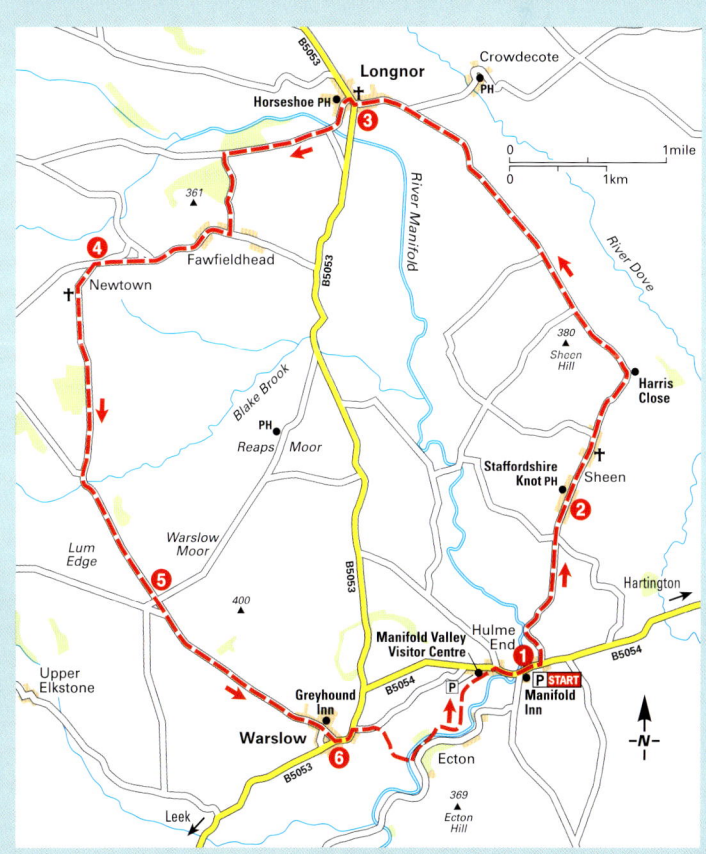

Sports in the Peaks

The mass trespass onto Kinder, the highest point in the Peak District, in 1932, is hailed as a landmark in a hard-fought campaign for access to moorland in Britain, at a time when open moorland, 'grouse' moorland, was keenly guarded to meet the demands of the game keeping interests of the landed gentry.

There is a tendency to celebrate the Kinder Trespass as the first demonstration against the closure of moorland walking areas. And while the Kinder episode was undoubtedly a major catalyst, there was an earlier mass trespass onto the West Pennine Moors around Bolton almost 40 years before, in 1896, which may well have fuelled the minds of the 20th-century protagonists. The moors of the West Pennines and the Peak District formed a natural rural escape for the workers in industrial towns and cities, and continue to do so. Some latter-day researchers attribute to the Peak District a sense of manliness, and the identification of masculine values with a certain type of landscape, especially during the inter-war years.

Today, the Peak District, the first designated national park in Britain, provides opportunities for a wide range of outdoor activities. A network of paths and long-distance trails, stretching for more then 1,800 miles (3,000km) in total, as well as large open-access areas, are available for hill-walking. Bridleways, intended originally for horse riding, are now also legally used by that new adrenalin-fuelled phenomenon, mountain-biking. Some of the longer trails, such as the Tissington Trail and the Monsal Trail, re-use former railway lines.

Although the ability to climb rocks was a key component of mountaineering in the French and Italian Alps, it is generally accepted that the 'sport' of rock-climbing, where the climbing took precedence over reaching summits, began in Britain in the Lake District. But it was only a short step before the many Peakland gritstone outcrops, such as Stanage and the Roaches, were recognised as some of the finest rock-climbing sites in the world. Climbing has been practised all over the Peak District since the late 19th century; James W. Puttrell is generally credited with starting the sport. Historically, gritstone crags – Laddow Rocks and Castle Naze – were the first to be explored, and others where access was not restricted by gamekeepers. This continued until the 1950s, when a post-war generation emerged and public access to crags became more widely available. The number of climbers increased, led by legendary figures such as Nat Allen, Joe Brown and Don Whillans.

Some of the Peak's large reservoirs, for example Carsington Water, with the relaxation of water catchment restrictions, have become centres for water sports, including sailing, fishing and canoeing. A variety of small sailboats is available for hire from sailing centres here, on production of the appropriate RYA level competence certificates. Powerboats are also evident on Carsington Water and centres around the lake run training courses for these vessels, in accordance with the RYA National Powerboat Scheme (for over 16s only). But one of the more peculiar sports in the Peak, and generally throughout the north of England and Scotland is that of fell-running, or mountain-racing. Although the sport is strongly competitive, it has a very introspective element; most fell runners compete against themselves or the clock, and the sport demands incredible running

strength and agility. The sport has much in common with cross-country running, but differs in its readiness to race over high mountains, not always on established paths, and often requiring navigational skills of the highest order. Moreover, the courses followed by fell-runners are considerably longer and vastly more demanding. Some routes over open moorland and rocky crags can be punishing both physically and mentally and it takes a certain strength and perseverance to endure the course.

The varied landscape of the Peak also lends itself to a sport pursued by that species of humanity that delights in throwing itself off high cliffs in the hope that a cat's cradle of thin cord and a pair of over-sized lady's undergarments will bring them safely back to earth, known to enthusiasts as paragliding. Soaring effortlessly and virtually soundlessly along the Peak ridges, suspended below a brightly coloured 'wing', making the most of up-currents, is a scintillating mix of hope, terror and avid, unabashed pleasure. Mam Tor to the west of Castleton is a hugely popular launch site. As a form of flying, paragliding is controlled by the Civil Aviation Authority who have accepted a self-regulatory system controlled by the British Hang Gliding and Paragliding Association. To become a hang-glider or paraglider pilot you must join an affiliated club and undergo training at a licensed school, of which there are several in the Peak.

Those people who like to drift across the skies paragliding have an equally adventurous cousin in the potholer. Potholing, the 'sport' of losing oneself underground in often damp, dangerous and flooded subterranean passageways, is a pursuit which has relatively fewer adherents compared to walking, or even rock-climbing. But the Peak is an ideal place to practice this minority sport. Unlike the limestone areas of Yorkshire, for example, there are few natural potholes in the Peak. However, the Peak abounds with natural caves of which Peak Cavern is the largest and most important. This and other 'showcase' caverns were a major tourist attraction in the 19th century when the 'Grand Tour' of Europe was less popular with the upper classes.

The proximity of the national park to major conurbations – and, with improved high-speed road networks, much further afield – means the number of visitors to the park has grown enormously in recent years. This poses unique challenges to those who manage the area. The Peak National Park Authority, the National Trust, and other landowners, work tirelessly to keep the upland landscape accessible to visitors for recreation, while at the same time protecting it from intensive farming, natural erosion and pressure from visitors themselves. An unavoidable strain exists between the needs of the residents of the Peak, the millions of people who visit annually, and the conservation needs of the area. The uneven distribution of visitors creates further stresses. Dove Dale alone receives 2 million visitors annually; other highly-visited areas include Bakewell, Castleton, Chatsworth, Hartington and the upper Derwent valley. Like many of the national parks, the Peak has become a victim of its own success.

With its sombre gritstone walls, rough-and-tumble heather moorlands and benign limestone dales the Peak District is one of Britain's best-loved landscapes. Fashioned by man over thousands of years, this is still a 'living landscape', one that supports a rich diversity of wildlife, culture and heritage. But that's quite another story.

OPPOSITE, CLOCKWISE FROM TOP LEFT Kinder Scout is a popular challenge for hikers. This large rocky outcrop, in the Peak District National Park, stands at around 1,970 feet (600m) above sea level.

The approach to Peak Cavern is dramatic but the cave itself is awesome. Once home to a community of rope-makers, the cave is beautifully lit to show off its geological splendours and the chambers also have superb acoustics.

The gritstone escarpment of the Roaches attracts rock-climbers of all abilities from around the world.

Hang-gliders hoping to catch that perfect thermal launch from the verdant hills in Staffordshire's Manifold Valley.

LEFT Spanning 85 acres (34ha), spring fed Errwood Reservoir in the Goyt Valley makes a great spot for fly fishermen keen to hook brown and rainbow trout.

MILLER'S DALE

The walk starts in Tideswell Dale, takes in Miller's Dale, passes Litton Mill and continues into Water-cum-Jolly Dale to follow the River Wye.

1 From the car park follow the path southwards from beside the car park's toilet block into Tideswell Dale, taking the right-hand fork to cross over the little bridge.

2 On leaving Tideswell Dale, go left on a tarmac lane to Litton Mill. Go through the gateposts to a concessionary path through the mill yard. Beyond the mill, the path follows the River Wye as it meanders through the tight, steep-sided dale.

3 The River Wye widens out in Water-cum-Jolly Dale and the path, which is liable to flooding here, traces a wall of limestone cliffs and then reaches Cressbrook. Do not cross over the bridge on the right, but instead turn left to pass behind Cressbrook Mill to reach the road.

4 Turn left along the road, and then take the right fork up to Cressbrook Dale. Where the road doubles back and heads take a track heading into the woods. At a major fork of tracks keep to the right; the track finally emerges in an airy clearing above the stream. Follow it to reach a footbridge crossing the stream and then take the right-hand fork path, which climbs to a stile in the top wall. (To avoid a steep climb to a viewpoint here, follow the valley-bottom path at the fork past the footbridge to rejoin the route at the stepping stones in Point 5.)

5 Do not cross the stile, but take the downhill path to the dale bottom, where there's a junction of paths. The one wanted here re-crosses the stream on stepping stones, and climbs into Tansley Dale.

6 At the top of the dale the path turns right and follows a tumbledown wall before crossing it on a step stile. Head for a wall corner in the next field, then veer right through a narrow enclosure to reach a walled track just south of Litton village.

7 Turn left along the track, to a country lane at the crown of a sharp bend. Keep straight on along the lane but leave it at the next bend for a cross-field path to Bottomhill Road. Across the road, a field path descends to the lane at Dale House Farm. Turn left, then right on a lane marked unsuitable for motors. Follow this road into Tideswell.

8 Go south down the main street, then right on to Gordon Road (in front of The Horse and Jockey pub), which then heads south.

9 Where this ends, continue down the stony track ahead, which runs parallel with the main road. At a gate keep left to a waymarked handgate; the path descends to a stile onto the road just above the treatment works. Turn right, in 150yds (137m) to take a path left, to join a path back to the car park.

DISTANCE/TIME 6 miles (9.7km) 3h **MAP** OS Explorer OL24 White Peak **START** Tideswell Dale pay car park; grid ref: SK 154743 **TRACKS** Well-defined paths and tracks, path in Water-cum-Jolly Dale liable to flooding, 12 stiles and gates **THE PUB** The George Hotel, Commercial Road, Tideswell. Tel: 01298 871382; www.george-hotel tideswell.co.uk

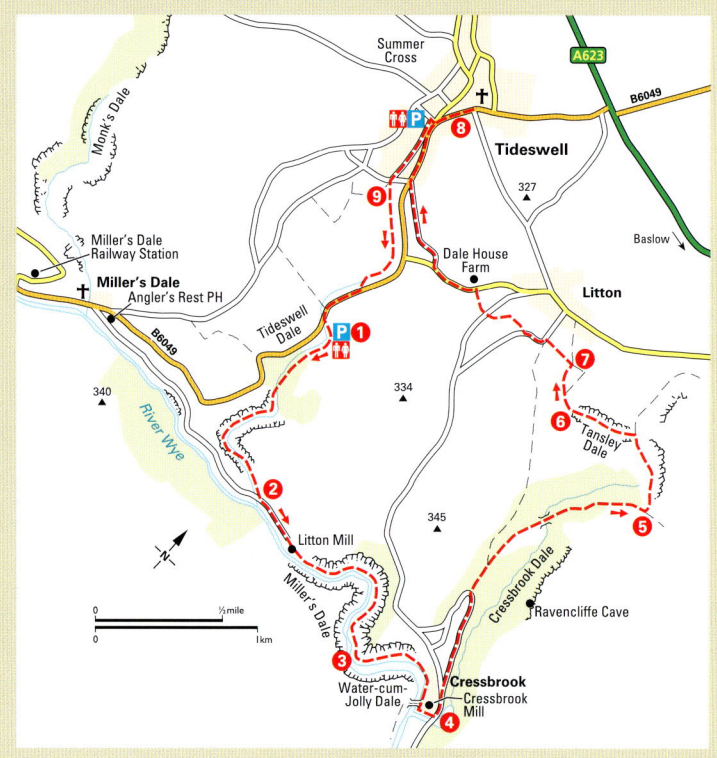

THROUGH MONSAL DALE

From Ashford's streets the route climbs to high pastures and continues over a viaduct, descends to Monsal Dale to the River Wye, and heads westwards through woodland to eventually return to Ashford.

1 From the car park turn right up Court Lane, then right again along Vicarage Lane. A footpath on the left doubles back left, then swings sharp right to continue along a ginnel behind a row of houses. Beyond a stile the path enters a field. Head for a stile in the top right corner to Pennyunk Lane. Turn left. This walled stony track winds among high pastures. Pass by a sign for Monsal Head, continuing to the end of the lane.

2 Turn left here past a stile and go up along a field edge. In 400yds (366m) turn right to go through two handgates to reach another track, heading north towards the rim of Monsal Dale. The path runs along the top edge of the deep wooded dale to eventually reach the car park at Monsal Head.

3 Here, take the path marked 'Access to Viaduct'. Descend steps and walk to a fingerpost pointing left for 'Viaduct & Monsal Trail'. Cross the viaduct; at the far end go through a stile on the left and take the middle of three paths down into the valley. (Not the steep path that plummets to the foot of the viaduct.)

4 From here, walk into the valley. The right of way is away from the river at first but you can trace the riverbank to emerge at Lees Bottom where there is a roadside stile.

5 Cross the A6 with care and go through the White Lodge car park where the path back to Ashford begins. Pass by the ticket machine and then go through the wide gap in the fence and along a surfaced path. Take a stile and remain on the compacted path. At a fork go left, and then shortly climb a stile at a waymark post for Ashford, Deepdale and Sheldon. A braided path climbs steeply ahead to reach another low-waymarked fork, here go left for Ashford and Sheldon. The path then continues on to rise to a small gateway and into Great Shacklow Wood.

6 The path climbs more easily now through the trees before levelling out as a ledged path along the steep wooded slopes. Ignore a path signed for Sheldon; eventually the path comes down to reach the river and then shortly passes behind a ruined mill, its wheels still in place. Remain on the path (ignore the bridge) to reach a minor road at the bottom of Kirkdale.

7 Turn left to walk along the road, down to the A6 and turn right making your way towards Ashford. Leave the road to cross Sheepwash Bridge. From here, turn right along Church Street and then make a left turn along Court Lane to reach the car park and the start point again.

DISTANCE/TIME 5.5 miles (8.8km) 3h **MAP** OS Explorer OL24 White Peak **START** Ashford-in-the-Water car park; grid ref: SK 194696 **TRACKS** Well-defined paths and tracks throughout, 17 stiles and gates **THE PUB** The Bull's Head, Ashford in the Water. Tel: 01629 812931

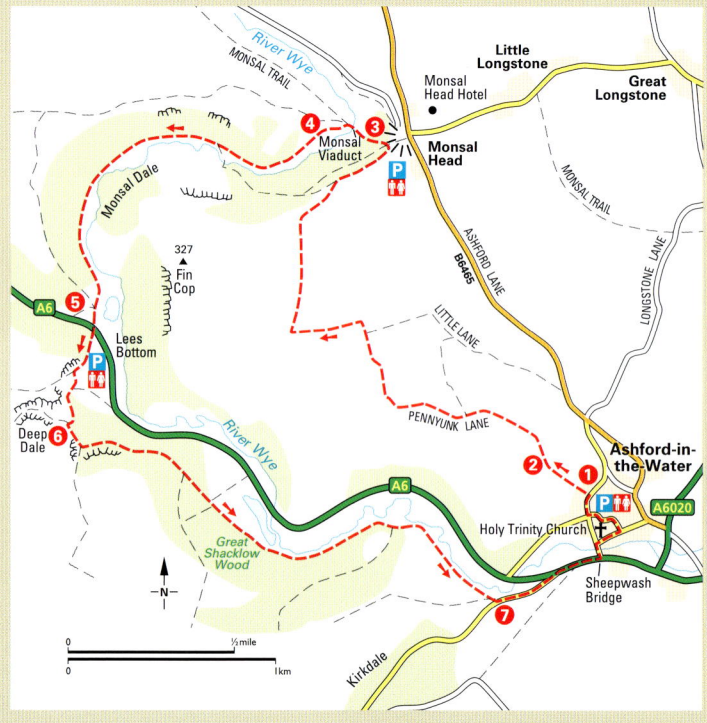

PENNINE WAYS ON KINDER SCOUT

One end of the Pennine long-distance trail ascends to the craggy outcrops of the Kinder Plateau. An edge walk goes round the chasm of Grindsbrook and passes the gritstone sculptures of Grindslow Knoll to the ravine of Crowden Brook. The route descends by the brook passing waterfalls then crosses the fields of Edale.

DISTANCE/TIME 5 miles (8km) 3h **MAP** OS Explorer OL1 Dark Peak **START** Edale pay car park; grid ref: SK 125853 **TRACKS** Rock and peat paths, about 16 stiles and gates **THE PUB** Old Nags Head, Hope Valley. Tel: 01433 670291

1 Turn right out of the car park pedestrian entrance by the toilets and head north into Edale, under the railway and past the Old Nags Head. Turn right by a path sign and follow the path across the footbridge over Grinds Brook.

2 Leave the main Grindsbrook Clough path by the side of a barn, taking the right fork that climbs up the lower hillslope to a gate on the edge of open country. Beyond the gate the path zig-zags above Fred Herdman's Plantation then climbs up the nose of the Nab to the skyline rocks. Where the path divides, take the right fork to the summit rocks of Ringing Roger (the echoing rocks).

3 Head towards the edge, to the left of a hut, climbing up a few steps to the path that runs along the rim of the plateau. For a long way it is paved. Follow this path above the cavernous hollow of Grindsbrook and past Nether Tor. Here, the old Pennine Way route is met on the east side by a large cairn.

4 Ignore the fork on the left and head for the outlier of the grey rocky peak of Grindslow Knoll. Follow the paved footpath to the right (west) to reach the head of another deep hollow, the clough of Crowden Brook.

5 Cross Crowden Brook, then immediately leave the edge to follow a narrow level path traversing slopes on the left beneath the imposing outcrop of Crowden Tower. This meets a rough path from the Tower before descending the steep grassy hillslopes to the banks of the brook. Take care, this is a very steep, rough descent and requires great care. The path now follows the brook, fording it several times.

6 Go through the stile at the edge of open country and then cross a footbridge over the brook, which is shaded by tall rowans, to change to the west bank. From here the path threads through woodland before descending in steps to the road at Upper Booth. From here, you now need to follow the Pennine Way path back to Edale.

7 Turn left along the lane and then left again into Upper Booth farmyard before crossing a stile tucked away at the top right corner, signposted for Edale. After following a track to a gateway, bear left uphill to a stile above an old barn. Here the way traverses fields at the foot of Broadlee Bank before joining a tree-lined track into the village at the Old Nags Head. Turn right down the road back to the car park.

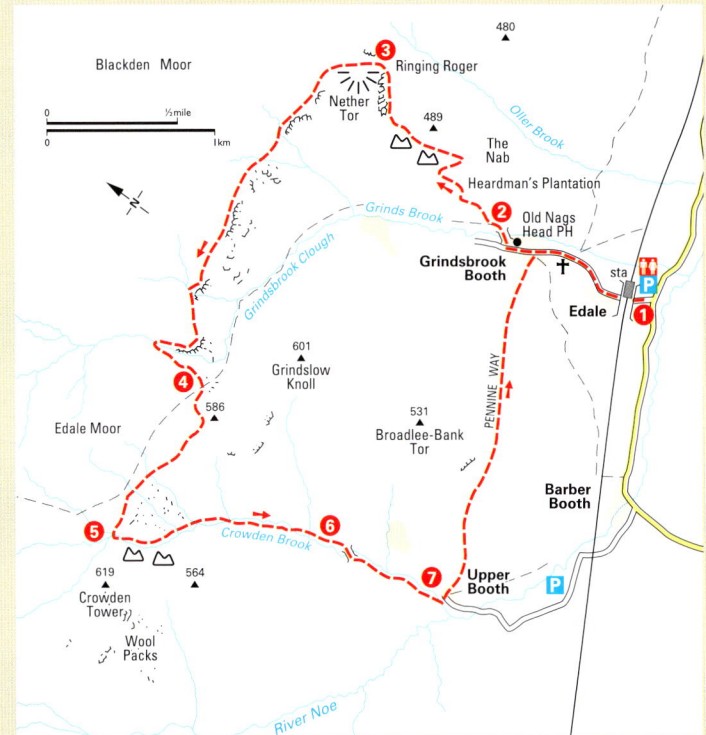

WALK 76

OVER WIN HILL

This walk from Hope to Win Hill threads through pastures above the River Noe passing Roman earthworks and there are views of Ladybower Reservoir, while the gritstone tors of Kinder Scout, the Derwent Edge, and Bleaklow fill the horizon.

DISTANCE/TIME 4.75 miles (7.7km) 3h **MAP** OS Explorer OL1 Dark Peak; grid ref: SK 172835 **START** Hope pay car park **TRACKS** Paths can be slippery after rain, around 23 gates and stiles **THE PUB** Cheshire Cheese, Edale Road, Hope. Tel: 01433 620381

1 Turn right out of the car park along Hope's main street. At the crossroads beside the church, turn right along Pindale Road. Cross the river bridge and continue along the lane to the next left turn, which is called Eccles Lane, and turn here.

2 After about 100yds (91m), go over a stile by a gate and follow the path, to the site of the Roman fort of Navio. Beyond the ancient earthworks go over a stile in a fence and bear half right across another field to reach the B6049 road at Brough.

3 Turn left to go through the village of Brough and then cross over the River Noe via the footbridge which is just past the agricultural merchant's mill. Go left over a stile and then head northwest to the A6187. Turn left along the road for 200yds (183m) to a gate just beyond a cottage. Follow the fence and brook on the right to pass to the right of houses.

4 Turn left along the lane towards the railway station and then go right along a narrow path which leads to a footbridge crossing the line. Cross the bridge and turn right at its far end, then left through a handgate to cross yet more fields, this time keeping the fence on your right and ignoring a stile footbridge that is on the right.

5 When you reach Aston turn left along the road and then almost immediately turn right to walk along a narrow, surfaced lane, signposted 'Win Hill & Hope Cross'.

6 In front of Edge Farm an unsurfaced track on the left takes the route along the top edge of some woods to a path junction above Twitchill Farm. You've a choice here. To avoid Win Hill turn left to Twitchill Farm and continue following the route directions in Point 7. To climb to the summit of Win Hill, turn right and then continue to follow a well-used path up the pasture and over the heathery slopes to the top of the hill. On a clear day there are superb views across this geologically turbulent area where the Dark Peak and White Peak meet, as well as across the Derbyshire Lake District of the Upper Derwent Valley.

7 From the summit retrace your steps back to the junction above Twitchill Farm. Go to the farm and walk the driveway to the railway.

8 Turn left under the railway tunnel, where the lane doubles back left and goes to Kilhill Bridge, then the Edale Road. The Cheshire Cheese Inn is 200yds (183m) to the right along here. To return to Hope, however, keep ahead to the village centre crossroads, and then turn right to return to the car park.

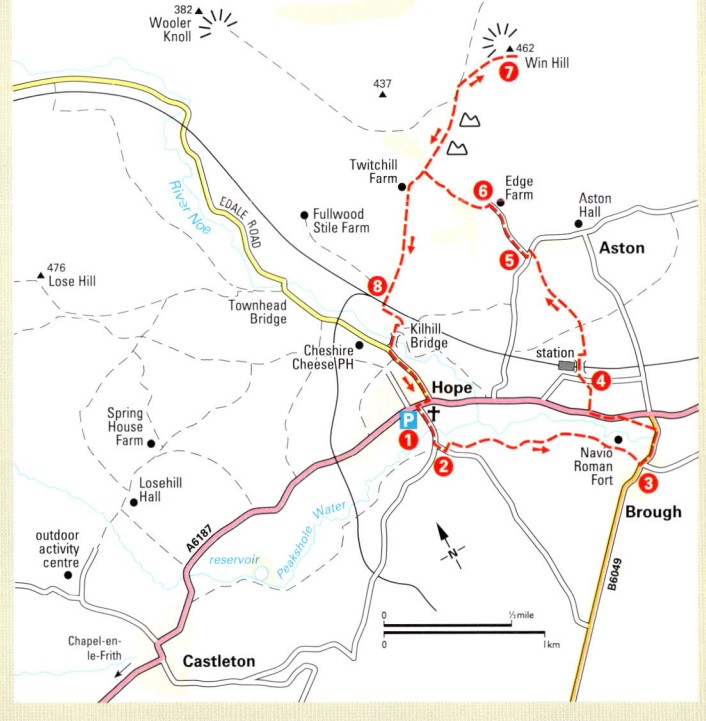

SUFFOLK COAST
■ TOURIST INFORMATION
Aldeburgh
High Street, Aldeburgh.
Tel: 01728 453637;
www.suffolkcoastal.gov.uk/tourism
Felixstowe
91 Undercliff Road West, Felixstowe.
Tel: 01394 276770;
www.suffolkcoastal.gov.uk/tourism
Woodbridge
Station Buildings, Woodbridge.
Tel: 01394 382240;
www.suffolkcoastal.gov.uk/tourism

■ PLACES OF INTEREST
Dunwich Museum
St James Street, Dunwich.
Tel: 01728 648796
Framlington Castle
Tel: 01728 724189; www.english-heritage.
org.uk/eastofengland
Landguard Fort
Viewpoint Road, Felixstowe.
Tel: 07749 695523; www.landguard.com
Orford Castle
Tel: 01394 450472; www.english-heritage.
org.uk/eastofengland
Sutton Hoo
Tel: 01394 389700;
www.nationaltrust.org.uk

■ PERFORMING ARTS
Snape Maltings Concert Hall
Snape, Saxmundham.
Tel: 01728 687110;
www.aldeburgh.co.uk

■ SPORTS & ACTIVITIES
NATURE RESERVES
Dunwich Heath
Tel: 01728 648505;
www.nationaltrust.org.uk
Orford Ness National
Nature Reserve
Tel: 01394 450900;
www.nationaltrust.org.uk
RSPB Minsmere Nature Reserve
Westelton, Saxmundham.
Tel: 01728 648281; www.rspb.org.uk

■ ANNUAL EVENTS & CUSTOMS
Aldeburgh
Aldeburgh Literary Festival, Mar.
Aldeburgh Easter Festival, Apr.
Alderburgh Festival, Jun.
Snape Proms, Aug.
Britten Festival, Snape Maltings, Oct.
Felixstowe
Easter Fair, Apr.
Historic Vehicle Rally, May.
Felixstowe Carnival and Fair, Aug.
Framlingham
Framlingham Gala, May.
Walberswick
Walberswick Crabbing Competition, Aug.

Woodbridge
Horse Show, May.
Suffolk Folk Festival, Jun.

CAMBRIDGE & FENS
■ TOURIST INFORMATION
Cambridge Visitor Information
Centre
The Old Library, Wheeler Street,
Cambridge. Tel: 0871 226 8006;
www.visitcambridge.org

■ PLACES OF INTEREST
Anglesey Abbey Gardens & Lode Mill
Lode CB5 9EJ.
Tel: 01223 810080;
www.nationaltrust.org.uk/angleseyabbey
Ely Cathedral
Chapter House, The College,
Ely. Tel: 01353 667735;
www.cathedral.ely.anglican.org
Houghton Mill
Houghton, near Huntingdon,
Cambridgeshire. Tel: 01480 301494;
www.nationaltrust.org.uk
This is the last working watermill that
exists on the River Ouse. A visit here is a
wonderful day out.
Oliver Cromwell's House
29 St Mary's Street, Ely.
Tel: 01353 662062;
www.eastcambs.gov.uk/tourism

■ FOR THE CHILDREN
Cambridge Uncovered
Live The City Ltd, The Old Crown Court,
Market Hill, Cambridge.
Tel: 0871 226 8006; www.livethecity.com
A self-guided tour with treasure hunt
clues to keep everyone entertained.

■ SPORTS & ACTIVITIES
GARDENS
Clare College Gardens
Trinity Lane, Cambridge.
Tel: 01223 333200; www.clare.cam.ac.uk
A beautiful example of a 20th-century
English garden.
The Orchard Tea Gardens
Mill Way, Grantchester CB3 9ND.
Tel: 01223 845788;
www.orchard-grantchester.com
NATURE RESERVES & COUNTRY PARKS
Wicken Fen National Nature Reserve
Lode Lane, Wicken, Ely,
Cambridgeshire.
Tel: 01353 720274;
www.wicken.org.uk

NORFOLK BROADS
■ TOURIST INFORMATION
Great Yarmouth
Maritime House, Marine Parade.
Tel: 01493 846345
Lowestoft
East Point Pavilion. Tel: 01502 533600

Norfolk Broads National Park
Tourist Information
Broads Authority, 18 Colegate,
Norwich. Tel: 01603 610734;
www.broads-authority.gov.uk
All information about the waterways.
Norwich
The Forum, Millennium Plain.
Tel: 01603 727927

■ PLACES OF INTEREST
St Benet's Abbey
Ludham
Derelict wind pump and Benedictine
monastery ruins on the edge of the
River Bure.
Somerleyton Hall
Tel: 01502 734901;
www.somerleyton.co.uk
Victorian extravaganza, with gardens,
garden trail, maze and miniature railway.

■ SPORTS & ACTIVITIES
ANGLING
Wroxham Angling Centre
Station Road. Tel: 01603 782453;
www.anglingdirect.co.uk
BOAT TOURS
Beccles
Waveney Stardust. Tel: 07817 920502
Hoveton/Wroxham
Broads Tours. Tel: 01603 782207;
www.broads.co.uk
Norwich, River Wensum
City Boats, Thorpe Saint Andrew,
Norwich. Tel: 01603 701701;
 www.cityboats.co.uk
Oulton Broad
Waveney River Tours. Tel: 01502 574903
CANOEING
Wroxham
Barnes Brinkcraft, Riverside Road.
Tel: 01603 782625
All levels of experience catered to on
the Broads and it's feeder rivers.
NATURE RESERVES
Hickling Broad
Reserve open daily 10–5; Centre open
Apr–Sep, daily 10–5.
Boarded walkway and visitor centre.
Ranworth Broads Wildlife Centre
Floating Broads Wildlife Centre open
Apr–Oct. Boardwalk.

LINCOLN & RUTLAND
■ TOURIST INFORMATION
Lincoln
9 Castle Hill, Lincoln. Tel: 01522 873213;
www.lincoln.gov.uk
21 The Cornhill, Lincoln.
Tel: 01522 541447;
www.lincoln.gov.uk
Lincolnshire Tourism, Beech House,
Waterside South, Lincoln.
Tel: 01522 526450;
www.visitlincolnshire.com

■ PLACES OF INTEREST
Barnsdale Gardens
The Avenue, Exton, Oakham, Rutland.
Tel: 01572 813 200
Belton House
Near Grantham. Tel: 01476 566116;
www.nationaltrust.org.uk
Belvoir Castle
Near Grantham. Tel: 01476 871002;
www.belvoircastle.com
Burghley House
Stamford. Tel: 01780 752451;
www.burghley.co.uk
Clipsham Yew Tree Avenue
Kesteven Forest, Rutland, Clipsham,
1 mile to the west, is the nearest town or
village. OS Grid Reference: SK 980 169.
Gainsborough Old Hall
Parnell Street, Gainsborough.
Tel: 01427 612669; www.lincolnshire.gov.
uk/gainsboroughholdhall
Lincoln Castle
Castle Hill, Lincoln.
Tel: 01522 511068;
www.lincolnshire.gov.uk/lincolncastle
Lincoln Cathedral
Tel: 01522 544544;
www.lincolncathedral.com
Oakham Castle
& Rutland County Museum
All enquiries to Rutland County Museum,
Catmose Street, Oakham, Rutland.
Tel: 01572 758440
Rutland Open Air Theatre
(Shakespeare)
Tolethorpe Hall.
www.stamfordshakespeare.co.uk

■ SHOPPING
Lincoln
St Mary's Shopping Park,
off High Street, Lincoln.

■ SPORTS & ACTIVITIES
BOAT TRIPS
Lincoln Boat Trips
Brayford Pool. Tel: 01522 881200;
www.lincolnboattrips.com
CYCLING
Rutland Water Cycling
Whitwell Car Park, Rutland Water
North Shore. Tel: 01780 460705;
www.rutlandcycling.co.uk
GOLF
Rutland Water Golf Course
Manton Road, Oakham.
Tel: 01572 737525
HORSE RIDING
Stretton Riding Centre
Stretton, Oakham.
Tel: 01780 410323
WATERSPORTS
Rutland Watersports
Whitwell Car Park, Rutland Water,
North Shore. Tel: 01780 460154;
www.anglianwaterleisure.co.uk

ANNUAL EVENTS & CUSTOMS
Burghley Horse Trials
Sep. Tel: 01780 752131 (not all year);
www.burghley-horse.co.uk
Oakham Festival
Jun–Jul.
Tel: 01572 756699;
www.oakhamfestival.co.uk
Oakham's annual art festival includes
poetry, music, comedy, theatre, dance
and film events.

WORCESTER & MALVERN HILLS
TOURIST INFORMATION
Malvern
21 Church Street, Malvern,
Worcestershire. Tel: 01684 892289
Pershore
Town Hall, 34 High Street, Pershore.
Tel: 01386 556591
Worcester
The Guildhall, High Street, Worcester.
Tel: 01905 726311
Heart of England Tourism, Woodside,
Larkhill Road, Worcester WR5 2EZ.
Tel: 01905 761100;
www.visitheartofengland.com

PLACES OF INTEREST
Elgar Birthplace Museum
Crown East Lane, Lower Broadheath,
Worcester. Tel: 01905 333224;
www.elgarmuseum.org
Great Malvern Priory
Tel: 01684 561020;
www.greatmalvernpriory.org.uk
The Greyfriars
Friar Street, Worcester.
Tel: 01905 23571;
www.nationaltrust.org.uk
15th-century timber-framed house.
Malvern Hills
Malvern Hills Conservators, Manor
House, Grange Road, Malvern.
Tel: 01684 892002;
www.malvernhills.org.uk
Pershore Abbey
Tel: 01386 552071;
www.pershoreabbey.org.uk
Royal Worcester Visitor Centre
Severn Street, Worcester.
Tel: 01905 746000;
www.royalworcesterfactoryshops.co.uk
Worcester Cathedral
Tel: 01905 21004;
www.worcestercathedral.org.uk
Worcester Porcelain Museum
Severn Street, Worcester.
Tel: 01905 746000;
www.worcesterporcelainmuseum.org
Decorate china in the 'Paint a Plate' area.

FOR CHILDREN
The Ghost Walk of Worcester
City Centre. Tel: 01905 759499

SHOPPING
Worcester Antiques Centre
Reindeer Court, Mealcheapen Street.
Tel: 01905 610680
Friar Street, New Street and Charles
Street have many shops and galleries.

SPORTS & ACTIVITIES
ANGLING
Leigh Sinton Farm Fishing Lake
Lower Interfields, Near Malvern.
Tel: 01886 832305;
www.fisheries.co.uk/leighsinton
BOAT CRUISES
Bickerline River Trips
South Quay, Worcester. Tel: 01905 831639
Worcester River Cruises
North Quay, Worcester.
Tel: 01905 611060;
www.worcesterrivercruises.co.uk
GOLF
Ravenmeadow Golf Club
Hindip Lane, Claines, Worcester.
Tel: 01905 757525
The Vale Golf Club
Hill Furze Road, Bishampton, Evesham.
Tel: 01386 462781

ANNUAL EVENTS & CUSTOMS
Autumn in Malvern Festival
Oct. Tel: 01684 569721
Worcester Christmas Fayre
Nov–Dec. Tel: 01905 726311

STRATFORD & VALE OF EVESHAM
TOURIST INFORMATION
Stratford-upon-Avon
Stratford Tourist Information Centre,
Bridgefoot, Stratford-upon-Avon.
Tel: 0870 160 7930;
www.shakespeare-country.co.uk

PLACES OF INTEREST
Anne Hathaway's Cottage
Cottage Lane, Shottery.
Tel: 01789 204016;
www.shakespeare.org.uk
Hall's Croft
Old Town, Stratford-upon-Avon.
Tel: 01789 292107;
www.shakespeare.org.uk
**Harvard House & the Museum of
British Pewter**
High Street, Stratford-upon-Avon.
Tel: 01789 204507;
www.shakespeare.org.uk
Nash's House & New Place
Chapel Street, Stratford-upon-Avon.
Tel: 01789 204016;
www.shakespeare.org.uk
**Shakespeare's Birthplace
& Exhibition**
Henley Street, Stratford-upon-Avon.
Tel: 01789 204016;
www.shakespeare.org.uk

FOR CHILDREN
Stomps
Stratford-upon-Avon. Tel: 01789 263334
Indoor softplay, pirate ship.
Stratford-upon-Avon Butterfly Farm
Swan's Nest Lane, Stratford-upon-Avon.
Tel: 01789 299288;
www.butterflyfarm.co.uk
Stratford-upon-Avon Mini Golf
The Recreation Ground, Swan's Nest
Lane, Stratford-upon-Avon.
Tel: 07703 883904
18-hole putting course by the River Avon.

SPORTS & ACTIVITIES
BALLOONING
Heart of England Balloons
Cross Lane Farm, Walcote, near Alcester.
Tel: 01789 488219
BOAT CRUISES
Avon Boating
Swans Nest Boathouse, Swans Nest
Lane, Stratford-upon-Avon.
Tel: 01789 267073
Bancroft Cruisers
Holiday Inn Stratford, Bridgefoot,
Stratford-upon-Avon.
Tel: 01789 269669;
www.bancroftcruisers.co.uk

SHREWSBURY & IRONBRIDGE
TOURIST INFORMATION
Ironbridge
The Visitor Information Centre, The Toll
House, Iron bridge, Telford.
Tel: 01952 884391
Shrewsbury
Shrewsbury Visitor Information Centre,
The Music Hall, The Square, Shrewsbury,
Shropshire. Tel: 01743 281200;
www.visitshrewsbury.com
Information and details of events in
Shrewsbury and surrounds.

PLACES OF INTEREST
Acton Burnell Castle
www.english-heritage.org.uk
Attingham Park
Shrewsbury, Shropshire.
Tel: 01743 708162;
www.nationaltrust.org.uk
Ironbridge Gorge Museums
The Ironbridge Gorge Museum Trust,
Coach Road, Coalbrookdale, Telford.
www.ironbridge.org.uk
Shrewsbury Abbey
Tel: 01743 232723;
www.shrewsburyabbey.com
Wroxeter Roman City
Tel: 01743 761330;
www.english-heritage.org.uk

SHOPPING
The Parade Shopping Centre
St Mary's Place, Shrewsbury;
www.paradeshops.co.uk

ANNUAL EVENTS & CUSTOMS
Darwin Festival
Feb. Tel: 01743 281281;
www.darwinshrewsbury.org
Shrewsbury Children's Bookfest
May. Tel: 01743 281200;
www.shrewsburybookfest.co.uk
A popular festival with little people in
mind, featuring all types of children's
books and publications.
Shrewsbury Folk Festival
Aug. Tel: 01746 281200;
www.shrewsburyfolkfestival.co.uk
**Shrewsbury International
Cartoon Festival**
Apr. Tel: 01743 281200
Shrewsbury Flower Show
Aug. Tel: 01743 234050;
www.shrewsburyflowershow.org.uk
Exhibits for all floral preferences.

SHROPSHIRE HILLS & STIPERSTONES
TOURIST INFORMATION
Church Stretton
Church Street, Church Stretton,
Tel: 01694 723133;
www.churchstretton.co.uk
Ludlow
Castle Street, Ludlow.
Tel: 01584 875053
Much Wenlock
The Museum, High Street,
Much Wenlock.
Tel: 01952 727679
Shropshire Tourism
Harlescott Barns, Harlescott,
Shrewsbury. Tel: 01743 462462;
www.shropshiretourism.info

PLACES OF INTEREST
Ludlow Castle
Tel: 01584 873355;
www.ludlowcastle.com
Stokesay Castle
Tel: 01588 672544;
www.english-heritage.org.uk

FOR CHILDREN
Acton Scott Historic Working Farm
Tel: 01694 781306
Traditional farming skills displays.

SHOPPING
Antique and Flea Markets
Ludlow – 1st & 3rd Sun of the month.
Bishop's Castle – 1st Sat of the month.
Farmers Markets
Ludlow – 2nd Thu of the month.
Bishop's Castle – 3rd Sat of the month.
Church Stretton – 2nd & 4th Fri of
the month.
Traditional markets
Ludlow – Mon, Wed, Fri, Sat.
Church Stretton – Thu.
Bishop's Castle – Fri.

■ SPORTS & ACTIVITIES

CYCLING
Wheely Wonderful
Petchfield Farm, Elton, Ludlow.
Tel: 01568 770755;
www.wheelywonderfulcycling.co.uk

GOLF
Elm Lodge Golf Course
Fishmore, Ludlow. Tel: 01584 872308;
www.elm-lodge.org.uk

HORSE RIDING
North Farm Riding Establishment
Whitcliffe, Ludlow. Tel: 01584 872026;
www.northfarmludlow.co.uk

QUAD TREKKING & MOUNTAIN BOARDING
The Edge
Walton Grange, Much Wenlock.
Tel: 07967 565266;
www.ridetheedge.co.uk

OFFA'S DYKE

■ TOURIST INFORMATION
The Offa's Dyke Centre
Knighton, Powys LD7 1EN.
Tel: 01547 528753;
www.offasdyke.demon.co.uk

PEAK DISTRICT

■ TOURIST INFORMATION
Bakewell
The Old Market Hall, Bridge Street.
Tel: 01629 813227
Buxton
The Crescent. Tel: 01298 25106;
www.visitbuxton.co.uk
Glossop
The Heritage Centre, Henry Street.
Tel: 01457 855920
Holmfirth
49–51 Huddersfield Road.
Tel: 01484 222444
Matlock
Crown Square. Tel: 01629 583388
Matlock Bath
The Pavilion. Tel: 01629 55082

■ PLACES OF INTEREST
Chatsworth House
Tel: 01246 565300; www.chatsworth.org
Home to the Duke and Duchess of
Devonshire. Child and adult audio tours
are available of both the house and
the grounds.
Eyam Museum
Tel: 01433 631371;
www. eyammuseum.demon.co.uk
The museum tells the story of the
bubonic plague, how it reached Eyam
and was contained there.
Glossop Heritage Centre
Henry Street, Glossop.
Tel: 01457 869176. Free.
Some 10,000 years of Glossop history and
development are explained by displays,
photographs and information sheets.

Haddon Hall
Bakewell. Tel: 01629 812855;
www.haddonhall.co.uk
A splendid house that has remained
virtually untouched by the passage of
time. Topiary gardens.
Heights of Abraham
Matlock Bath. Tel: 01629 582365;
www.heights-of-abraham.co.uk
Last of the Summer Wine Exhibition
Huddersfield Road, Holmfirth.
Tel: 01484 681408
Lyme Park
Disley. Tel: 01663 762023;
www.nationaltrust.org.uk
Nine Ladies Stone Circle
Stanton Moor.
Free.
Old House Museum
Bakewell. Tel: 01629 813642;
www. oldhousemuseum.org.uk
Peak District Mining Museum
The Pavilion, Matlock Bath.
Tel: 01629 583834; www.peakmines.co.uk

■ FOR CHILDREN
Chatsworth Farm & Adventure Playground
Tel: 01246 565300; www.chatsworth.org
Gulliver's Kingdom
Temple Walk, Matlock Bath.
Tel: 01629 580540;
www.gulliversfun.co.uk
Theme-park fun including rollercoasters.

■ SHOPPING
Bakewell
Market on Mon, includes cattle, except
Bank Holidays Mons when a general
market is held.
Buxton
Market Tue and Sat. Farmers markets
first Thu of month.
Chapel-en-le-Frith
Market Thu.
Matlock
General market, Tue and Fri.
Glossop
Indoor market Thu; indoor and outdoor
market Fri and Sat.
Holmfirth
Craft market, Sat and Bank Hols.
Farmers Market; 3rd Sun of the month.
General market, Thu.

LOCAL SPECIALITIES
Bakewell Puddings
Original Bakewell Pudding Shop, The
Square, Bakewell. Tel: 01629 812193;
www.bakewellpuddingshop.co.uk
Bloomers Original Bakewell Puddings,
Water Lane, Bakewell.
Tel: 01629 814844
Craft Workshops
Glossop Craft Centre, No 1 Smithy Fold,
off High Street East, Glossop.
Tel: 01457 863559

Pork Pies
Connoisseurs Deli, Water Street, Water
Lane, Bakewell. Tel: 01629 812044

■ PERFORMING ARTS
Buxton Opera House
Water Street, Buxton. Tel: 01298 72190;
www.buxton-opera.co.uk

■ SPORTS & ACTIVITIES

ANGLING
Fly
Carsington Water
Tel: 01629 540696; www.stwater.co.uk
Coarse
Combs Reservoir
Whaley Bridge. Tel: 01663 762393

BOAT HIRE
Carsington Water
Tel: 01629 540478;
www.carsingtonwater.com

CYCLE HIRE
Hayfield
Old Railway Station.
Tel: 01663 746222; www.peakdistrict.org
Manifold Valley Bike Hire
Earls Way, Old Station Car Park.
Tel: 01538 308609;
www.manifoldvalleybikes.com
Peak District National Park Centre
Waterhouses. Tel: 01298 84493
Whaley Bridge
The Bike Factory, 3 Market Street.
Tel: 01663 735020

GUIDED WALKS
Buxton
From Tourist Information Centre.
Tel: 01298 25106
Derbyshire Dales Countryside Service
Planning and Development Services,
Town Hall, Matlock.
Tel: 01629 761326
Full guided walks service.
Glossop
The walks (charge) last approximately
1.5 hours. They start from Glossop
Tourist Information Centre. For details
contact Glossop Tourist Information
Centre. Tel: 01457 855920
National Park Walks with a Ranger
Peak District National Park.
Tel: 01629 816200;
www.peakdistrict.org.uk
Professional Blue Badge Guides
Tel: 01629 534284

HORSE-RIDING
Buxton Riding Centre
Fern Farm, Buxton.
Tel: 01298 72319
Haddon House Riding Stables
Over Haddon, Bakewell.
Tel: 01629 813723;
www.haddonhousestables.co.uk

LONG-DISTANCE FOOTPATHS & TRAILS
The High Peak Trail
Follows the former High Peak Railway
from High Peak Junction (Cromford) to

Dowlow (south of Buxton). Derbyshire
Countryside Centre.
Tel: 01629 823204
Manifold Trail
Traces a former narrow-gauge railway
from Hulme End to Waterhouses,
8.25 miles (13km) of walking or cycling.
Visitor Centre at Hulme End.

ROCK-CLIMBING
Hathersage
Rock Lea Activity Centre, Peak Activities
Ltd, Station Road.Tel: 01433 650345;
www.iain.co.uk
Outdoor activity specialists.

WATERSPORTS
Carsington Water
Near Ashbourne. Tel: 01629 540478;
www.carsingtonwater.com

■ ANNUAL EVENTS & CUSTOMS
For the full programme visit
www.visitpeakdistrict.com
Well dressing in Chapel-en-le-Frith,
Buxworth and Buxton, Jul.
Ashford in the Water
Well dressing, late May–early Jun.
Blessing of the Wells Trinity Sunday, May.
Bakewell
Well dressing, late Jun/early Jul.
Carnival, early Jul.
Bakewell Show, early Aug.
Buxton
Antiques Fair, May.
Buxton Festival, Jul.
Buxton Fringe Festival, Jul.
International Gilbert & Sullivan Festival,
Jul/Aug.
Country Music Festival, Sep.
Chatsworth
Angling Fair, late May.
Horse Trials, mid/late May. Horticultural
Show, late Aug.
Country Fair, early Sep.
Music events, spring–autumn.
Dovedale
The Dovedale Dash, a 4.25-mile (6.8km)
cross-country run which starts on Thorpe
Pastures, early Nov.
Eyam
Well dressing and demonstration late
Aug. Plague Commemoration Service,
last Sunday in Aug.
Carnival, Aug/Sep.
Glossop
Jazz Festival, mid-Jun. Carnival and
Country Fair, early Jul.
Victorian weekend, early Sep.
Well dressing and Padfield Plum
Fair, Sep.
Hayfield
Well dressing, mid July.
Sheepdog Trials, Sep.
Holmfirth
Folk Festival, early May.
Youlgreave
Well-dressing, late Jun.

PUBS
SUFFOLK
Crown
High Street, Southwold, Suffolk
Tel: 01502 722275

This is a smart, no smoking old hotel with the emphasis on good food and good beer. The elegant beamed bar has a relaxed atmosphere with high-backed settles, kitchen chairs and bar stools. The smaller oak-panelled 'locals' bar has more of a traditional pubby atmosphere.

CAMBRIDGE & FENS
The Cock
Hemingford Grey, Cambridgeshire
Tel: 01480 463609

In spite of the emphasis on what is very good food at this attractive little hostelry, the public bar is very much a traditional drinking room, with an open wood burning stove. Plenty of special ales and beers on handpump, and a good choice of wines by the glass. The stylish restaurant serves lunches at sensible prices.

Dyke's End
8 Fair Green, Reach, Cambridgeshire
Tel: 01638 743816

The pub takes its name from the nearby Devil's Dyke, and attracts visitors from Cambridge and Newmarket. But the inn is very much a destination in its own right, with a reputation for fine food, well-kept real ales and excellent wines.

The Pheasant
Keyston, Cambridgeshire
Tel: 01832 710241

In the same family for 40 years, the Pheasant has an immaculate oak-beamed bar with a cosy atmosphere, open fires, simple wooden tables and chairs, guns on walls, and country paintings. They have a fine wine list, fresh or locally pressed juices. The food here has a high reputation, too.

Live and Let Live
40 Mawson Road, Cambridge
Tel: 01223 460261

This down-to-earth old local is a real ale enthusiast's find, with an interesting selection of well kept local beers plus around 20 Belgian beers, and a dozen malt whiskies. The atmosphere is relaxed and friendly, with pine tables, wooden chairs, and real gas lighting.

NORFOLK BROADS
The Buckinghamshire Arms
Blickling, Norfolk
Tel: 01263 732133

This 17th century former coaching inn serves good food, has a pretty garden and attractions of the Blickling Hall estate on the doorstep. The pub oozes character, and is a delight to visit, serving food at both lunch and in the evening.

The Fat Cat
West End Street, Norfolk
Tel: 01603 624364

Although the bar food is fairly basic, the range of beers at the Fat Cat is anything but, with as many as 30 real ales, this a classic town pub well worth seeking out. As well as their own beers and a fantastic choice of handpump or tapped from the cask ales there are six draught Belgian beers, draught lagers from Germany and the Czech Republic, bottled Belgian beers, country wines, and local cider.

King's Arms
West Gate Street, Blakeney, Norfolk
Tel: 01263 740341

This attractive old inn just a stroll from the harbour gets crowded at times. The simply furnished rooms have low ceilings, photographs, and work by local artists. Excellent range of inexpensive food, and a good range of speciality beers.

The Old Ram
Ipswich Road, Tivetshall St Mary, Norfolk. Tel: 01379 676794

The Old Ram, a former coaching inn has a long tradition of tending to the needs of man and beast. In those former days the inn was a-buzz with visitors, and nothing seems to have changed, except the replacement of coach and four with the modern motor car. This is still a great attraction for discerning diners and those who know a good pint when they see one.

Walpole Arms
Itteringham, Norfolk. Tel: 01263 587258

The large open-plan bar in this dining pub has exposed beams, stripped brick walls, little windows, a mix of dining tables, and quietly chatty atmosphere. Well kept beers on handpump, wines by the glass, cider, and local apple juice. Service can be a bit slow at busy times. There is a two-acre landscaped garden and vine-covered terrace to sit and relax on warm days, and a good choice of meals is offered.

LINCOLN & RUTLAND
The Blue Pig
9 Vine Street, Grantham, Lincolnshire
Tel: 01476 563704

This is an attractive, jettied Tudor pub, with open fire, low beams, panelling, stripped stone and flagstones, and lots of pig ornaments, prints and bric-a-brac. They serve a good range of interesting changing ales, simple lunchtime food. No children or dogs.

WORCESTER & MALVERN HILLS
The Bear & Ragged Staff
Station Road, Bransford, Worcester
Tel: 01886 833399

Laden with accolades, this was Worcestershire Dining Pub of the Year in 2007, 2006 and 2004. Real ales and a comprehensive wine list complement local produce like Herefordshire beef and fresh fish. There is a lovely patio and garden for those warm summer days.

The Nag's Head
Bank Street, Malvern, Worcestershire
Tel: 01684 574373

Along with bar meals served almost all day, the Nag's Head keeps an astonishing range of real ales on handpump. They also keep a fine range of wines by the glass, malt whiskies and Belgian beers.

The Swan
Whittington, Worcester
Tel: 01905 351361

Lovers of quality pub food have been dining here for years, during which the Swan has built an enviable reputation at the 'Pub with Food'. This popular country pub serves food with a Mediterranean tang, enhanced by a sun patio.

STRATFORD & VALE OF EVESHAM
The Bell
Alderminster, Stratford-upon-Avon, Warwickshire. Tel: 01789 450414

With an enviable reputation for fine dining, perfect for Sunday lunch with the kids, it is easy to forget that The Bell is also an excellent pub, and 18th-century coaching inn.

The Four Alls
Binton Bridges, Welford-on-Avon, Stratford-upon-Avon. Tel: 01789 750228

Open daily and offering inexpensive, quality bar meals, The Four Alls has a riverside pub garden and eating area, and a light, spacious interior.

SHROPSHIRE
The Armoury
Victoria Quay, Victoria Avenue, Shrewsbury, Shropshire
Tel: 01743 340525

Superb bar food is a hallmark here. The open plan interior, with arched windows, is housed in a former 18th-century warehouse. The pub is bright and light, with eclectic décor, and a lively buzz. There is a great stone fireplace at one end, lots of old prints on brick walls, and Colonial-style ceiling fans whirring away. The bar is stocked with up to eight real ales, a great wine list, 50 malt whiskies, dozens of gins, rums, vodkas, brandies, and a selection of liqueurs.

Three Fishes
Fish Street, Shrewsbury, Shropshire
Tel: 01743 344793

A chance to enjoy a pint of real ale in a smoke-free pub. Cask Marque and Camra 2007 Good Beer Guide recommended. This lovely pub serves home-cooked food daily.

PEAK DISTRICT
The Barrel Inn
Bretton, Eyam, Derbyshire S32 5QD
Tel: 01433 630856

Derbyshire's highest pub, The Barrel Inn stands right on the lip of Eyam Edge. Expect beers from Hardys and Hansons brewery and good-size portions of tasty, but unpretentious pub food, served in comfortable surroundings of antique seats, age-smoothed flagged floors, low beams, country prints and brass plates.

Cheshire Cheese Inn
Edale Road, Hope, Derbyshire S33 6ZF
Tel: 01433 620381;
www.cheshire-cheese.net

A compact, cheerful local with a warm welcome guaranteed. They stock beers from Peak District microbreweries and offers an ever-changing menu using local produce whenever possible.

The Lathkil Hotel
Over Haddon, Bakewell, Derbyshire DE45 1JE. Tel: 01629 812501;
www.lathkil.co.uk

This long-established inn's guests tuck into a mix of simple bar meals, inventive, top-notch dishes, and beers from Peak District breweries.

The Pack Horse Inn
Crowdecote, near Buxton, Derbyshire SK17 0DB. Tel: 01298 83618

Small rooms, simply furnished, beneath a higgledy-piggledy roof. Enjoy the fine food menu and beers from local microbreweries in the beer-garden.

Quiet Woman
Earl Sterndale, Buxton, Derbyshire SK17 9SL. Tel: 01298 83211

Home-made pork pies are washed down with Marstons or guest beers.

The Swan Inn
Macclesfield Road, Kettleshulme, Whaley Bridge, Cheshire SK23 7QU
Tel: 01663 732943;
www.the-swan-inn-kettleshulme.co.uk

Rescued from closure by a consortium of passionate and loyal villagers, this tiny pub is a champion of local brewery beers, complementing the range of largely locally sourced food. It's the perfect place to unwind after a good walk.

TEA ROOMS

CAMBRIDGE & FENS

The Botanic Garden Café
Cambridge University. Tel: 01223 336265
The café is to the rear of the Gilmour Building and serves a wide range of Fairtrade teas and coffees, soft drinks, sandwiches, toasted sandwiches and panini, cakes and snacks.

Café Eleven
11 Burleigh Street, Cambridge
Tel: 01223 369157
In the centre of Cambridge, this café is unpretentious and serves inexpensive sandwiches, coffee and tea.

Peacocks
65 Waterside, Ely, Cambridgeshire
Tel: 01353 661100
Light meals include Norfolk ham salad and home-made cakes, available all day, including scones served with Cornish clotted cream. The choice of teas is remarkable, with forty listed, from the usual suspects to many more unusual varieties. The Special Afternoon Tea includes finger sandwiches, scones with a choice of jam and cake.

NORFOLK BROADS

Mary Janes Fish and Chips Restaurant
Garden Street, Cromer, Norfolk
Tel: 01263 5112
It is unthinkable to visit Norfolk and not to head for the seafood delights of Cromer. In Cromer they pride themselves on serving only the best and freshest fish and chips. Mary Jones is both a take-away and an eat-in place, and isn't restricted to fish.

LINCOLN & RUTLAND

Sam's Place
11–12 St Mary's Street, Stamford,
Lincolnshire. Tel: 01780 766511
This traditional, friendly tea room is located above an antiques shop, and offers a good range of teas and coffees, and freshly baked scones.

Uncle Henry's Farm Shop & Coffee Stop
Grayingham Grange, Grayingham,
Gainsborough, Lincolnshire
Tel: 01652 640308
Of course, Uncle Henry's is a farm shop selling farm produce, but set in a converted 19th-century barn in a picturesque farmyard complete with duck pond and grazing animals. This local food hub is well worth visiting if you have children. As a bonus, the farm shop has the freshest fruit and vegetables, home-produced pork and meat from local suppliers.

Mount Pleasant Windmill Tearooms
North Cliff Road, Kirton in Lindsey,
Gainsborough, Northern Lincolnshire
Tel: 01652 640177
A chance for a quiet bite in a windmill. Mount Pleasant offers welcoming tea rooms serving light lunches, scones, cream teas and a delicious range of home-baked cakes made with the organic flour from the windmill. There is also a wholefood shop with quality chutneys, pickles and jams.

Stokes High Bridge
High Bridge, 207 High Street, Lincoln
Lincolnshire. Tel: 01522 513825
In a fine 16th-century half-timbered building on the medieval High Bridge, which spans the river Witham in Lincoln. Sit at the leaded windows in the restaurant, enjoy morning coffee, lunch or afternoon or high tea, while watching people, boats and swans below.

Tealby Tearooms
12 Front Street, Tealby, Market Rasen
Lincolnshire. Tel: 01673 838261
Savour a friendly atmosphere while enjoying delicious cream teas with home-made cakes and Lincolnshire Plum Loaf with either butter or cheese. Salads, sandwiches and snacks are also available or you can pick up a poacher pastie, a combination of prime pheasant and venison meat. Calorific home-made desserts include fruit pie with cream.

The Rutland Coffee House
10 Crown Walk, Rutland
Tel: 01572 722216
This traditional tea room and restaurant in a small arcade, just off the High Street offers a good range of all things calorific in the centre of this bustling little town.

WORCESTER & MALVERN HILLS

Assembly Room
The Guildhall, High Street, Worcester
Tel: 01905 722033
You could walk past the ornate and historical Assembly Rooms without ever popping in for tea or coffee. But amid such historical splendour and beneath the gaze of nobles you can enjoy tea, coffee, light snacks or a carvery lunch.

Cathedral Café
7 Severn Street, Worcester
Tel: 01905 745680
After a visit to this masterpiece of British architecture, the Cathedral Café is perfect for light meals (including vegetarian dishes), snacks, tea, coffee, and wine and beer. Children are welcome and high chairs are available.

Hodson's Coffee House and Restaurant
100 High Street, Worcester
Tel: 01905 21036
This air-conditioned eatery is renowned for its 'clean' food, which has earned it a National Heartbeat Award. Serving a wide variety of traditional meals, snacks and vegetarian dishes, Hodson's is a treasure.

STRATFORD & VALE OF EVESHAM

The Café Within
All Saints Parish Church, Bath Street,
Royal Leamington Spa, Warwickshire
Tel: 01926 429169
Open lunchtimes from Wednesday to Saturday, this is a friendly eatery serving home-made soup, light lunches, snacks, home-made cakes, tea and coffee. Children are welcome.

Bensons
4 Bard's Walk, Stratford upon Avon,
Warwickshire. Tel: 01789 261116
At Bensons you can pamper yourself with a Champagne breakfast or merely enjoy a pot of Earl Grey. To be recommended are the freshly baked croissants, Danish pastries, smoked salmon and lightly scrambled eggs or eggs Benedict.

Hathaway Tea Rooms and Bakery
19 High Street, Stratford upon Avon,
Warwickshire. Tel: 01789 292404
The building dates back to 1610, but has been used for this family business only since 1971. On entrance to the tea rooms you are greeted with a quaint bakery with delicious-looking cakes, all of which are baked on the premises. The tea rooms are on two floors.

Henley Ice Cream
152 High Street, Henley-in-Arden,
Warwickshire. Tel: 01564 795172
Although this famous 16th-century establishment has been producing traditional Premium Dairy Ice-Cream for over 65 years, it also does a good line in morning coffee and homemade cakes, hot or cold light lunches and afternoon cream teas, and is worth tracking down.
.

SHROPSHIRE

The Bird on the Rock
Abcott, Clungunford, Shropshire
Tel 01588 660631
The Bird on the Rock Café was the winner of The Tea Guild's 'Top Tea Place 2004' and is one of the world's Top 50 according to *The Independent*. People come from far and wide for its 1930s interior, English cottage garden, tea and coffees, and home-made cakes. The 'Complete Jeeves', is as noble as it sounds: a tiered cake stand arrives, piled high with sandwiches, scones and cakes.

De Grey's
5–6 Broad Street, Ludlow, Shropshire
Tel: 01584 872764
De Grey's is behind an attractive beamed bakery. Afternoon tea includes a sandwich, fancy cake, and fruit scone with jam and cream. Also available are teacakes, pastries, scones and buns. Meals are served throughout the day.

PEAK DISTRICT NATIONAL PARK

The Coffee Shop
Lyme Park, Disley, Cheshire SK12 2NX
Tel: 01663 762023
In the shadow of Lyme Hall, this unpretentious and welcoming place offers simple, filling fare.

Eyam Tea Rooms
The Square, Eyam, Derbyshire S32 5RB
Tel: 01433 631274
Overlooking the pretty square this tea room has a reputation for fine home-made cakes, gateaux and scones. There's also a good choice of vegetarian meals.

Grumbley's
Church Street, Hayfield, Derbyshire
SK22 2JE. Tel: 01663 741444;
www.grumbleys.com
This modern café-bar and bistro is popular with walkers to Kinder. Renowned for its inventive cooking, there's also a good range of snacks, pastries, cakes and more substantial meals; in the evenings it is a restaurant.

The Original Bakewell Pudding Shop
The Square, Bakewell, Derbyshire
DE45 1BT. Tel: 01629 812193;
www. bakewellpuddingshop.co.uk
Above the shop where Bakewell's famed recipe was recreated, this comfortable tea room has exposed beams reminiscent of a medieval barn. Don't miss out on a generous helping of Bakewell Pudding.

Woodbine Café
Castleton Road, Hope, Derbyshire
S33 6AA. Tel: 01433 621407
A welcoming, homely stone terraced cottage, with a sheltered tea garden, not far from Hope's distinctive church. The café offers an interior that is cosy and tranquil. They offer B&B.

The Wrinkled Stocking Tea Room
Huddersfield Road, Holmfirth, West
Yorkshire HD9 2JS. Tel: 01484 681408;
www.wrinkledstocking.co.uk
Cool pastel walls and crisp tablecloths – just what Nora Batty would expect! Indulge in home-baked speciality pastries and cakes and good Yorkshire tea. Sid's Café (Tel: 01484 689610), also a good pit-stop is a short stroll away.

Wales

Wales

Wales has always been, and remains today, a country within a country, which has for centuries passionately defended its identity and still proudly uses its Celtic mother tongue as a first language in some remote parts of the interior.

Blessed with some of natures finest gifts, Wales can boast dramatic mountain ranges, verdant pastureland, beautiful lakes and some of the most stunning coastline in Britain. Wales' western edges reach out into the Gulf Stream and consequently benefit from the balmy influence of the warm waters.

The people of this ancient land fought many long and bloody battles to keep their individuality and despite it becoming part of the Union in 1536, once you cross the border from England to Wales, it is apparent that you are entering a proud and different country.

Cardiff

CLOCKWISE FROM RIGHT: THE MILLENNIUM STADIUM;
BUTE PARK, FROM CARDIFF CASTLE

Glamorgan CCC
(Sophia Gardens)

Welsh Institute
of Sport

Cathays
Park

University
of Wales

National
Museum &
Gallery Cardiff

Welsh College
of Music
& Drama

City Hall

Cardiff
Crown
Court

Gorsedd
Gardens

Bute Park

Boulevard de Nantes

New Theatre

Greyfriars   Road

Cathedral Road

Sophia
Gardens

River Taff

Bute Park
Arboretum

Cardiff
Castle

Queens
West
Shopping
Centre

Cowbridge   Road

Castle   Street

High Street

Queen   Street

Queens
Arcade
Shopping
Centre

St Davids
Shopping
Centre

Working   Street

St David's
Cathedral

Centre for
Visual Arts

St
David's
Hall

Lower Cathedral Road

Cardiff RFC
(Cardiff Arms
Park)

Westgate

Despenser   Street

Clare
Street

Gloucester
Street

Tudor   Street

Clare   Street

Millennium
Stadium

Cardiff
County
Court

Fitzhamon   Embankment

Park   Street

Wood   Street

St   Mary   Street

The Hayes

Mill Lane

Bridge   Street

Central
Bus Station

Pendyris Street

Cardiff Central
Station

Penarth   Road

Crichton Street

UGC

Wales National
Ice Rink

Cardiff
International
Arena

Bute   Terrace

Adam   Street

Windsor

Central   Road

Tyndall   Street

Schooner   Way

E Tyndall   Street

Ocean   Way

Link

Sanquahar   Street

Richmond   Road

City   Road

The   Parade

West   Grove

Newport   Road

Fitzalan   Place

Station Terrace

Charles   Street

Churchill   Way

Guildford Street

Queen Street
Station

Cardiff
University

Capitol
Shopping
Centre

Stuttgarter Strasse

Park   Place

Park   Lane

North   Road

Museum   Avenue

Dumfries Place

Cardiff Royal
Infirmary

Glossop   Road

Piercefield   Place

Planet   Street

Metal Street

Moira   Place

Moira   Terrace

Constellation   Street

Meteor   Street

Magistrates
Court

CARDIFF CITY CENTRE
MAP REF **399 H3**

Much of Cardiff's history is encompassed within its castle, which stands proudly in the heart of the city. The moated Norman castle was built on the site of the Roman fort – some of the Roman foundation walls can still be seen. The castle was left ruinous by Owain Glyn Dwr, but eventually it was rebuilt by Richard Beauchamp, the Earl of Warwick and continued as a residence for several centuries.

The powerful Bute family, who were descendants of the royal Stuarts, took possession of the castle by marriage in 1797. It was the 3rd Marquis of Bute who commissioned William Burges to redevelop the living quarters into the gothic Victorian style you see today. No expense was spared: the interiors were opulent, using marble, gold leaf and fine hardwoods from around the world. Many of the rooms have amazing decorated ceilings, stained glass windows, murals of historical and mythological figures and fine works of art on the walls.

The city centre buildings are a mix of modern, Victorian and Edwardian. The Venetian style Morgan Arcade with its glass gable roofs and elegant balustrades is a particularly fine example of the

Victorian shopping arcades to be found in the city. The Butes were responsible for most of the 19th-century civic buildings, including the majestic City Hall, the Law Courts, and the National Museum, which are divided by long tree-lined avenues and the lawned gardens of Cathays Park. Built from gleaming Portland stone, the City Hall has a 200ft/60m high clock tower and a large dome topped by a Welsh dragon. Its fine Marble Hall with stained-glass windows provides a magnificent setting for the series of Serraveza marble statues of the 'Heroes of Wales'.

The buildings look across to the broad open spaces of Bute Park, once part of the grounds of Cardiff Castle, which you can see peeping through the trees. The 130-acre (52ha) park with its ornamental trees extends to the banks of the River Taff, where you look across to Sophia Gardens and the Glamorgan County Cricket ground. Also on the banks of the Taff are the two stadiums of Cardiff Arms Park. One is the home of Cardiff rugby club: the other, the gigantic Millennium Stadium. Seen from the river the gleaming stadium resembles the bridge of an ocean liner. You'll get the best view if you catch a waterbus from the Bute Park jetty and cruise to the waterfront of Cardiff Bay.

CARDIFF BAY MAP REF **399 H3**

Cardiff's prosperity and rise to importance came with the Industrial Revolution. The discovery of coking coal allowed the iron smelting industry to boom in the valleys to the north and Cardiff became the obvious choice for a port. The Bute family enlarged the docks and made Cardiff into one of the world's largest coal - and iron - exporting ports. Tiger Bay, the area between dock and city became one of the roughest but most lively multicultural centres in the world. Pubs with names like the Bucket of Blood and the House of Blazes were patronised by sailors from all corners of the globe.

By the 1970s, when the coal industry had been decimated, Cardiff's waterfront had become an industrial wasteland, an area of deprivation and decay. Tiger Bay had lost its soul. With this in mind the presiding Welsh Secretary, Nicholas Edwards announced the establishment of the Cardiff Bay Development Corporation. Its mission was to put Cardiff back on the international map and to create a thriving maritime city. The harbour at Cardiff had one of the world's most expansive tidal ranges: up to 46 feet (14m) – low tide rendered it inaccessible for up to 14 hours a day. The idea of a barrage that created

a 494-acre (200ha) freshwater lake out of the bay solved the problem but brought out vehement opposition from Friends of the Earth, the RSPB and local residents, who believed this would be an ecological disaster for the thousands of birds whose wetland and mud-flat habitat would be submerged beneath the lake. The Welsh Office believed that the scheme would be the catalyst for a complete dockside development and persisted with the plans. In 1993 the Cardiff Barrage Act was passed. The £220-million project included three locks for ships to pass through, sluice gates to control the water level in the lake, and a fish pass to allow the sea trout and salmon to access their spawning area in the Taff and Ely rivers. To compensate for the loss of wildlife habitat 1,000 acres (40ha) of farmland were flooded in the Gwent Levels 15 miles (24km) to the east to create a freshwater marsh.

The 0.75-mile (1.1km) long barrage, completed in 1997, and the 0.5-mile (800m) long sand and stone embankment provided an 8-mile (13km) waterfront in the bay. Besides picnic spots there's a sail-like structure with a wooden viewing platform where visitors can gaze out across the Bristol Channel to the distant West Country coastline. The bay is still

CARDIFF BAY WATERFRONT

PENARTH

Visit
CASTELL COCH – THE RED CASTLE
This fairytale castle a few miles north of Cardiff echoes those found in Bavaria, with its circular red sandstone towers and conical roofs. Built on a limestone outcrop on wooded hillslopes, the original Norman castle had fallen into disrepair, but the 3rd Marquis of Bute commissioned William Burges to refurbish the structure to the same extravagant standards that he lavished on Cardiff Castle.

Visit
THE NATIONAL MUSEUM WALES, CATHAYS PARK
Housed in one of the magnificent Portland-stone buildings of the Civic Centre A fascinating 'Evolution of Wales' discovery tour of Wales from the dawn of time, through the Iron Age and the Industrial Revolution to the present day. The collection of dinosaurs, both big and small, and a 'moving' woolly mammoth that roars are particularly memorable. The museum also exhibits one of the finest Impressionist art collections in Europe and includes work by Cezanne, Renoir and Monet.

good for bird watching. Long-legged waders like the grey heron, the egret, a small white heron-like bird, and the cormorant, another heron-like bird with a black coat, can be seen waiting patiently and silently for their fish suppers to swim by. The wetland reserve by the Taff Estuary hosts great crested grebe and snipe.

Cardiff's regeneration continued with Tiger Bay and the dock area. The pristine waters of the new lake were far easier on the eye than the tidal mud flats and it wasn't hard to sell the idea of luxury apartments in the bay. A newly formed National Assembly of Wales decided that they would build their Senedd Building in the heart of the development. Designed by Richard Rogers, the revolutionary building was constructed with energy conservation in mind – its renewable energy systems aim to cut running costs by nearly a half. Not far from the Senedd building is the Millennium Centre, which showcases the performing arts. Built from local slate it has a bilingual inscription in huge letters: 'In these stones horizons sing' and *Creu gwir fel gwydr o ffwrnais awen*, which in English means 'creating truth like glass from the furnace of inspiration'.

Old and modern mingle on the waterfront with the terracotta Pierhead Building lying right next to the Millennium Centre. Built by the Bute family in Gothic style, the Grade 1 listed old port headquarters now houses a permanent interactive exhibition that gives an insight into the workings of the National Assembly for Wales. Not far away, the Norwegian Church, which was built in 1869 as a place of worship for the large number of Scandinavian sailors, had fallen into disrepair by the 1960s. A trust set up by the author Roald Dahl, who was baptised here, financed the rebuilding of the church on the present site. The attractive spired timber building painted gleaming white is now a coffee shop and art gallery.

LLANDAFF MAP REF 399 H3
Although it's just a couple of miles from Cardiff's centre and officially part of the city these days, the ancient city of Llandaff has a long history of its own. Here, by the banks of the Taff, the 6th century Celtic saint, Dyfrig, founded one of Britain's earliest Christian communities. All that remains of the original church is an old stone cross, which can be seen by the Chapter House. Early in the 12th century the building of a much larger Norman cathedral was instigated by Bishop Urban, and during the next couple of centuries the proud building took shape in a mix of Norman and Early English styles. The Reformation saw the cathedral fall into neglect and it is said that it was used at various times as a beer house and a cattle shed. Later two towers collapsed and the roof of the nave caved in. Llandaff was described as 'a miserable village of mean cottages'. In 1734, however, the restoration began, first under John Wood who envisaged an Italian temple, then under J F Seddon and John Pritchard. The cathedral suffered more devastation during World War II when it was wrecked by a German bomb. Once again it was rebuilt. Under the guidance of architect George Pace it became an intriguing mix of ancient and modern. A huge arch bearing Sir Jacob Epstein's aluminium statue, *Christ in Majesty*, dominates the interior.

PENARTH MAP REF 399 H3
Sited on high headland overlooking the south bank of the Ely Estuary and Cardiff Bay, Penarth was for centuries a small fishing village that grew to prominence as a coal shipping port. However, the cliff-lined shingle beach, the fine outlook across the Bristol Channel and the clean sea air attracted wealthy coal and iron merchants, who built fine villas. Tourism was introduced by the Victorians, who constructed a long esplanade on the south shore, then added a pier and acres of flower-decked gardens and parkland. Penarth became known as The Gardens by the Sea. The town's fortunes flourished with the regeneration of Cardiff Bay and it can easily be reached by waterbus, car or train. The old coal harbour has been replaced by an attractive yacht marina, and the modern architect-designed waterfront contrasts with the classic Victorian buildings and leafy parks.

One of the town's skyline landmarks on Penarth Head, the Victorian parish church of St Augustine's, has a splendid 90-foot (27m) saddle-back tower.

ST FAGANS MAP REF 399 H3
Very much at the heart of St Fagans is the National History Museum. Sited in the grounds of St Fagans Castle, an Elizabethan manor house given over to the people of Wales by the Earl of Plymouth. Since its opening in 1948, more than 40 original buildings from different ages have been re-erected in the 100-acre (40ha) parkland, including a woollen mill from Brecknockshire, a pretty timber-framed Montgomery cottage (c1600), an 18th-century Unitarian chapel of the Teifi Valley and a longhouse from Radnorshire. Craftsmen demonstrate their skills in the mill and workshops, giving visitors a real taste of Welsh folklore and bygone days.

South Wales & Pembrokeshire

CLOCKWISE FROM TOP LEFT: OFF FISHGUARD; A LIFEGUARD STATION AT TENBY; A SEAL ON THE ROCKS; RED-AND-WHITE DECKCHAIRS ON TENBY'S SOUTH BEACH

FISHGUARD MAP REF 402 C6

Built in 1906 as a rival to the great shipping ports of Liverpool and Southampton, Fishguard never did fulfill that potential but remains a busy port and is the main sailing place in North Pembrokeshire.

Lower Fishguard was used as a location for the film adaptation of Dylan Thomas' *Under Milk Wood* in 1971 starring Richard Burton and Elizabeth Taylor. This area of the village makes up a third of the place, with Upper Fishguard and Goodwick completing the rest. All parts, however, cling to the shores of Fishguard Bay and have attractive fishermen's cottages sprinkled through the village streets.

Apart from its movie fame, Fishguard is also known for being the target of a failed and quite hopeless invasion attempt by the French in the late 18th century. In 1797 four vessels carrying French convicts and mercenaries, actually led by William Tate, an American, attempted to land at Fishguard Bay but were driven on by the cannon fire from Fishguard Fort. They went further around the coast to Carregwastad and came ashore only to get drunk on the local brew and to try to steal poultry. They were efficiently gathered up by the local farmers' wives and made to surrender in the local hostelry, the Royal Oak Inn, where evidence of this ridiculous saga can still be seen today.

The Royal Oak still plays an important part in village life today and is one of the venues for the Fishguard Folk Festival held each year. During the day, performances at this excellent event are perfect for families, while the more raucous performances take place at the pub in the evenings. The festival atmosphere is great and people can take part in music masterclasses.

HAVERFORDWEST & ST BRIDES BAY MAP REF 402 B7

Sited on the Western Cleddau, one of the two wide rivers that flow into the Milford Haven, Haverfordwest was, before the arrival of the railways, a thriving port with barges, small steamships and coasting vessels regularly docking on the quayside. The castle, which was built by the 1st Earl of Pembroke, Gilbert de Clare in the 12th century, dominates the village from its position atop a lofty crag above the river. Being a Norman stronghold, Haverfordwest was attacked and burned to the ground by Llewelyn the Great, but the castle survived, as it did when besieged in 1405 by another Prince of Wales, Owain Glyn Dwr. However, Oliver Cromwell ordered its destruction during the Civil War. The substantial walls and keep remain today and are still an impressive sight – second only to Pembroke in this region.

ST BRIDES BAY

Today Haverfordwest is a thriving market town, the principle shopping centre for the area, with many stores by the quayside. It's worth a visit to the town museum, which is housed in the castle off Church Street. Also worth seeing are the recently excavated ruins of the Augustinian Priory of St Mary and St Thomas the Martyr, a short walk from the centre.

Haverfordwest is an excellent base from which to explore Pembrokeshire's West Coast and St Brides Bay. Facing west to the Atlantic, most of the St Brides beaches are exposed to the prevailing winds. These whip up the surf and makes the coast here extremely popular for watersports such as surfing, windsurfing and, the new phenomenon, kite-surfing. The most northerly of the beaches is Newgale Sands, where golden sands stretch 2 miles (3km) from Newgale village in the north to the rocks of Rickets Head. A shingle bank separates the beach from the village. Patrolling lifeguards designate the safe swimming areas.

There's another long sandy beach at Broadhaven, a lively resort with a good range of facilities. It's worth exploring the northern end to see natural rock arches and stacks. To the south lies Little Haven. This pretty village with a slipway, used by the lifeboat, and a beach, is a popular place with sea-anglers.

Most spectacular is Marloes Sands where violent earth movements thrust up the rock strata to form steeply angled rocky cliffs that resemble yacht sails caught in a great gust of wind. Marloes village is a 0.6-mile (1km) walk from the isolated sandy beach.

INLAND GOWER MAP REF 398 F3

Back in 1956 the Gower Peninsula was designated Britain's first Area of Outstanding Natural Beauty, and it certainly lives up to that description. As well as this, a third of the area is a Site of Special Scientific Interest, not forgetting that a large stretch of the Gower coastline has been recognised as a Heritage Coast.

The Gower Peninsula's landscape is diverse and encompasses wooded valleys and soaring limestone cliffs on its southern coast, in complete contrast to the salt marshes and mud flats near to the northern coastline. Inland, you'll find heath, grazing land and farmland that is broken up into tiny parcels of fields. Each terrain is important to wildlife and the mud flats are especially vital to a great variety of wild birds (consequently the area is also very popular with twitchers).

Inland also, there is a smattering of little villages, such as Reynoldston, situated on the Cefn Bryn ridge from where there are far-reaching views of the peninsula. Also of interest on inland Gower are the ruins of the 14th-century Weobley Castle. It's fortifications are indicative of its defensive position, and there were modifications made to strengthen them in the 15th and 16th centuries. However, the castle was used in later years as a farmhouse and there is an exhibition on site tracing its history within the building.

SOUTH WALES & PEMBROKESHIRE

Visit
SKOMER

There's a summer ferry (not Mondays) to Skomer Island from Martin's Haven on the headland west of Marloes. On the short voyage you may see porpoises and dolphins, or even a basking shark. You'll almost certainly see some puffins peeping from their burrows. Like much of the mainland Skomer Island is girt with dark volcanic cliffs, which accommodate southern Britain's largest colony of nesting seabirds. On the pink thrift and sea campion-decked clifftops are the remnants of an Iron Age settlement – a standing stone, burial cairns, ancient field boundaries and the earthworks of hut circles. Footpaths criss-cross the island. Do not stray off the paths.

Visit
BURIAL CROMLECH

Pentre Ifan is probably the finest example of a Neolithic burial cromlech in Wales. It dates back to around 3500 BC and its huge capstone measures over 16 feet (5m), poised on three 8-foot (2.5m) uprights, which seem to frame and capture Carn Ingli's mystical outlines to perfection, especially when the sun is low in the sky. The cromlech can be accessed free of charge and is well signposted from the A487 east of Newport and the B4329 Preseli road at Brynberian.

Visit
THE GUN TOWER MUSEUM

Built in 1851 to protect the Royal Naval Dockyard at Pembroke, the Gun Tower houses a museum illustrating Pembroke's military heritage. You can learn about life as experienced by one of Queen Victoria's soldiers who waited for an invasion that never came, see models of the old navy dockyard where more than 200 ships were built, and learn about the World War II flying boats – Pembroke was the world's largest flying boat base.

Activity
RAMSAY ISLAND

You can take the regular Ramsay Island boat from the slipway at St Justinian's, 3 miles (5km) west of St David's and you will be transported across the fast-flowing Sound and infamous reef known as the Bitches to a haven for wildlife. Ramsay Island's rugged coastline, with its 300-foot (91m) cliffs and isolated rock coves, is home to the largest colony of grey seals in southwest Britain.

PEMBROKE CASTLE

MANORBIER MAP REF 398 E2

Overlooking the South Pembrokeshire Heritage Coast, Manorbier draws visitors for its beautiful sandy beach or to marvel at its magnificent castle.

Manorbier Castle was begun in the 12th century and managed to evade attack from both the Welsh and Cornwell's armies, surviving intact. The castle is still the baronial home of the Barri family.

MILFORD HAVEN MAP REF 398 D2

'It's one of the world's finest harbours,' Admiral Lord Nelson claimed as he gazed admiringly across the vast blue waters of Milford Haven. And this lovely sheltered estuary has provided one of Britain's most important maritime strongholds since the days of the Tudor kings. And yet Milford Haven the town is a more recent affair, built and planned in the late 18th century by Sir William Hamilton, the husband of Nelson's mistress, Emma. In the 1960s the big ships arrived – carrying crude oil for processing in new refineries. Of these, only the Texaco plant now survives. Today Milford boasts a pleasant harbour front and marina, overlooked by the Georgian buildings of Hamilton Terrace. In 1991 memories were rekindled when the Tall Ships Race came to town.

MYNYDD PRESELI

MAP REF 402 C6

The Mynydd Preseli rise from Cardigan Bay at Fishguard and Newport. They reach their peak at Foel Cwmcerwyn, 1,760 feet (536m) above sea level. They're not that high by Welsh standards but these peaks have always been synonymous with all things spiritual.

Buried beneath your feet are the settlers from pre-history: the Neolithic tribes who were here before the 'true Welsh', the Celts, came from across the sea. Cromlechs, the earthwork and stone remains of fortress walls and hut circles, are liberally scattered across the map for you to discover. Stonehenge in Wiltshire was built from rocks hewn from the Preselis. The rock that the monoliths were carved from, an igneous spotted dolerite, is exclusive to Carnmenyn on the eastern side of the range.

If you've first visited the county's English-speaking south coast you may be surprised when you arrive at Rosebush, a tiny village that lies to the south of Foel Cwmcerwyn, for this friendly place is Welsh-speaking. The little village, which is the starting point for the best Preseli walks, has a campsite and one of the best inns in Wales, Tafarn y Sinc.

NEWPORT MAP REF 399 H3

While its neighbour Fishguard is bustling with cars and lorries rushing to make the ferry to Ireland, life in little Newport, tucked away in the far northwest corner of Pembrokeshire, chugs along at a more relaxed pace. Here the distinctive crag-topped Carn Ingli ('Angel Mountain') rises from the back gardens of the villagers' cottages, while small boats bobble from their moorings or lean against the sandbars of the Nevern Estuary. Although only 1,138-feet (347m) high, Carn Ingli is distinctively rugged and its cloak of heather and gorse is capped by jagged outcrops of dolerite. The ramparts that remain from an Iron Age fort ring the summit of the hill, which is scattered with the foundations of many of those early settlers' circular huts.

Newport Castle is part fortress, part manor house – it has been inhabited as a private dwelling for the past 150 years. Built in the 13th century by Norman baron William Fitzmartin, the castle was held for centuries by the powerful lords of Cemaes. As can be seen from its ruined battlements, the fortress was involved in bloody conflict, first in 1215 when captured and sacked by Llewelyn the Great, Prince of Wales, then by Owain Glyn Dwr. Fitzmartin also established St Mary's Church, whose impressive Norman square tower vies for dominance with the castle.

The River Nevern divides Newport's two beaches. On the north side there's an excellent sandy beach with safe bathing away from the currents of the river mouth. Parrog beach on the south side is for walkers who can stroll along the clifftops, past thickets of colourful gorse.

PEMBROKE MAP REF 398 D2

Pembroke is an attractive walled town with a 900-year history dating back to its Norman castle, which overlooks the town from its perch on a limestone crag. Surrounded by water on three sides, the castle, built by the Earls of Pembroke, was one of the biggest and most powerful in Wales. The walls of the keep are 7 feet (2m) thick and 75 feet (23m) high. A secret underground passage burrows beneath the Great Hall to the harbour. Harry Tudor, the grandson of John of Gaunt and a descendant of Llewelyn the Great, was born in the castle. On returning from exile he advanced with an army that defeated Richard III at Bosworth Field, after which he was crowned King Henry VII.

In 1977 Pembroke was designated an Outstanding Conservation Area. In the bustling main street, lined with both Georgian and Tudor buildings there are some fascinating shops, and good cafés and restaurants. If it's peace you're after, a stroll by the river and Mill Pond will take you around the castle walls.

RHOSSILI MAP REF 398 F3

This delightful town enjoys an enviable position at the end of Rhossili Bay, a beautiful golden beach, and the village backs on to open downland of Rhossili Down, complete with many archaeological wonders. The downs rise up to The Beacon which climbs to 632 feet (193m) and from which there are great views. This hill is also popular with avid hang-gliders and is now under the ownership of the National Trust.

Of historical note are the Bronze Age burial mounds on the downs and the Neolithic burial chambers. The chambers can be found just north of the Beacon at Sweyne's Howes.

Just past Rhossili to the west is Worm's Head, the most westerly point on the Gower Peninsula. A set of rocks takes you to the outer point, but take care.

ST DAVID'S MAP REF 402 B6

Set on a windswept plateau, St David's, Britain's smallest city, is as isolated from urban life as is possible. Flanked by the dolerite crests of Carn Llidi and Carnedd-lleithr, this looks and feels as if it is an inhospitable corner of the world. And so it was when Dewi, a 6th-century Celtic preacher who was later to become St David, patron saint of Wales, sailed from Ireland to set up his monastery here.

When you arrive in St David's and walk up the High Street past the gift shops, cottages, the boat-trip vendors' offices and the cafés, there are no signs of the grand ecclesiastical buildings. They're hidden in the hollow of the Alun Valley behind Cross Square, and it's only when you descend down the Pebbles to the Bell Tower that they appear. At first glance the cathedral appears as austere as the surrounding landscape, yet the purple-hued sandstone and perfect proportions give it quite an impressive presence. Inside, the cathedral is light and airy, with striking ornamental Norman arches and the slightly leaning piers of the nave lead your gaze to a splendid roof constructed of Irish oak.

The oldest part of the current cathedral, the nave, dates back to 1180 – the original tower collapsed in 1220. In the early 14th century Bishop Henry de Gower raised the walls of the aisles, inserted much grander windows and built the south porch, transept chapels and Lady Chapel. A century later Bishop Vaughan built the tower up to its present height and added the splendid roof.

In 1862 George Gilbert Scott renovated the cathedral. While doing so he discovered two skeletons, believed to be St David and his friend St Justinian, now kept in an oak chest in the Holy Trinity Chapel.

For around nine days in May and June each year, St David's Cathedral holds a festival of classical music. St David's three cathedral choirs attend, as well as many top musicians from around the world.

Across the Alun stream the large and magnificent ruins of the Bishop's Palace, today make a good venue for concerts and plays. There are permanent exhibtions.

SAUNDERSFOOT MAP REF 398 E2

Once a small fishing village, which flourished with finds of high-quality anthracite coal, Saundersfoot has since been caught up in near-neighbour Tenby's popularity. It's not hard to see why. Set at the foot of a pleasant wooded valley, the village has an attractive harbour alongside wonderful golden sands. The village is a popular centre for fishing, sailing and all manner of water sports.

From Saundersfoot you can easily get to Amroth and the start of the lengthy Pembrokeshire Coastal Path.

RHOSSILI

■ TENBY

There's another National Trust car park (toll) at Stackpole Quay near to the site of Stackpole Court. The mansion was demolished in 1963 when punitive taxes forced the Cawdors to dispose of their Welsh assets. The quay, a tiny inlet with a stone-built harbour pier, marks a clearly visible transition between the old red sandstone cliffs of Manorbier and the limestone of southwest Pembrokeshire. A short walk across fields and clifftops leads to some steps down into Barafundle Bay, a traffic-free golden sandy beach ideal for swimming or a spot of sunbathing. Further sojourns through the pines and sycamores at the far end of the bay take you to the cliffs, arches and stacks of Stackpole Head.

If you time your visit for when the military are not training, you can take the minor road leading south from Bosherton to St Govan's car park. Steps lead down to the 13th-century St Govan's Chapel, a tiny building wedged into a fissure at the base of the cliffs on the site of a Celtic hermit's cell. St Govan, an 11th-century saint, is believed to be buried beneath the altar.

TENBY MAP REF 398 E2

Tenby, by far the biggest and most successful of Pembrokeshire's resorts, is surrounded by caravan sites and it's often buzzing with coach parties and holiday-makers from all backgrounds. On Bank Holidays the town feels like it's going to burst with the weight of its own popularity. But Tenby has undeniable beauty. Brightly colour-washed cottages wrap themselves around a small sandy beach, framed by the pier of the lifeboat station, the harbour and the small boats in the bay. Take an after-dinner stroll along the promenade with those cottages and the old castle floodlit against the night sky.

Tenby has two distinct parts. Within the largely intact medieval town walls many of its ancient narrow streets have been cobbled to re-create their authenticity, but outside these walls, overlooking the large South Beach, the Victorian influence is there in the traditional seaside terraces.

Castle Hill looks down on both the old and new towns, but little remained of the castle after its destruction in the Civil War. Much of the town's history from the Stone Age to present times can be traced by visiting the Tenby Museum and Art Gallery on Castle Hill. This includes charters and privileges granted by the Tudors and the Earls of Pembroke.

A devised town trail visits the walls and many of the historic buildings, including the Tudor Merchant's House (National Trust), which is fitted out with authentic furnishings and has three walls with the remains of early frescoes.

SOLVA MAP REF 402 B6

Three miles (5km) east of St David's is Solva, a village of two parts. The more modern upper village lines the A487 coast road, while in the lower, more attractive part, cottages, small shops and restaurants cluster around the harbour at the sheltered head of a long, winding tidal inlet. These days Solva is a busy little tourist trap but it was founded on maritime traditions. A thriving port until the arrival of the railways, it had warehouses and a dozen or so limekilns. Solva once boasted a passenger service to New York. Unusually, the passengers would have to bring their own food for the voyage!

Though it's a fine place for pottering about and having a spot of lunch, Solva is one of the best bases for a coastal walk, maybe to St David's (get the bus back), or just a stroll along the Gribin, where there's an Iron Age settlement and a perfect view back to the village.

STACKPOLE MAP REF 398 D2

The 2,000-acre (810ha) Stackpol estate, which was once owned by the powerful Scottish Cawdor family but now managed by the National Trust, is situated between Bosherton, Stackpole and St Govan's Head. It encompasses some of Pembrokeshire's finest coastal scenery.

Bosherton, a tiny village at the western end of the estate, is well placed for a visit to the Bosherton Lily Ponds. These were created by flooding three limestone valleys. It has been claimed that this was the home of the Lady of the Lake and from where King Arthur gained his sword, Excalibur. It's certainly a magical place for nature lovers, who can wander through the woodland at the waters' edge to reach the seashore at Broad Haven beach. A June visit will reveal water lilies on the waters of the Western Arm. Visitors include the cormorant, grey heron, kingfisher, coot and moorhen, and you're likely to see dragonfly on the lakes.

STRUMBLE HEAD – AN INVIGORATING TRUNDLE

The headland cliffs tower above the pounding Atlantic surf, the path cuts an airy, at times precarious, line across their tops and the sky is alive with the sound of seabirds. Atlantic grey seals, porpoises and even dolphins are regularly spotted in the turbulent waters.

DISTANCE/TIME 8 miles (12.9km) 3h30 Ascent: 920ft (280m) **MAP** Aqua3 OS Explorer OL35 North Pembrokeshire **START** Grid ref: SM 894411 **PATHS** Coast path, grassy, sometimes muddy tracks, rocky paths, 21 stiles **PARKING** Car park by Strumble Head **THE PUB** Lighthouse Ferryboat Inn & Restaurant, Goodwick. Tel: 01348 874747

1 Walk back up the road and cross a stile on the left on to the coast path. Pass above the bays of Pwll Bach and Pwlluog then drop steeply to a footbridge behind the pebble beach of Porthsychan.

2 Follow the coast path waymarkers around Cnwc Degan and on down to the bridge, where two footpaths lead away from the coast. Continue along the coast, past a cottage on the right then climb and drop a couple of times, before you reach the obelisk at Carregwastad Point.

3 Follow the track inland and cross a stile on to a track; turn right, away from the coast path. Continue with the path up through a gorse wall; turn right on to a good track. Take this track through a succession of gates and around a left-hand bend.

4 Ignore the track to the right and continue up a cattle track to a farmyard where you swing right then left, after farm buildings, to the road. Turn right and follow the road past a large house to a waymarked bridleway on the left. Pass Trenewydd and go through a gate on to a green lane. Follow this up to another gate and on to open ground.

5 Turn right here and follow the wall along until you get to a gate opening to the walled track; follow the track to a road. Turn left and climb up to the car park beneath Garn Fawr. Turn right, on to a hedged track. Follow this up, through a gap in the wall, and over rocks to a trig point.

6 Climb down and cross the saddle between this tor and another, which is slightly lower, to go south. From here head west towards an even lower outcrop and pass it on the left. This becomes a clear path that leads down to stile. Cross this and then turn left then right on to a drive to a road.

7 Walk straight across and then on to the coast path where you can enjoy lovely sea views. Bear right from this point, cross a stile to drop down towards Ynys y Ddinas, a small island ahead. Navigation is easy as you continue on a coastal path north, over Porth Maenmelyn and up to a cairn.

8 Continue along the coast, towards the lighthouse, until you drop to a footbridge above Carreg Onnen Bay. Cross the stile into a field, then another back on to a coast path and return to the car park.

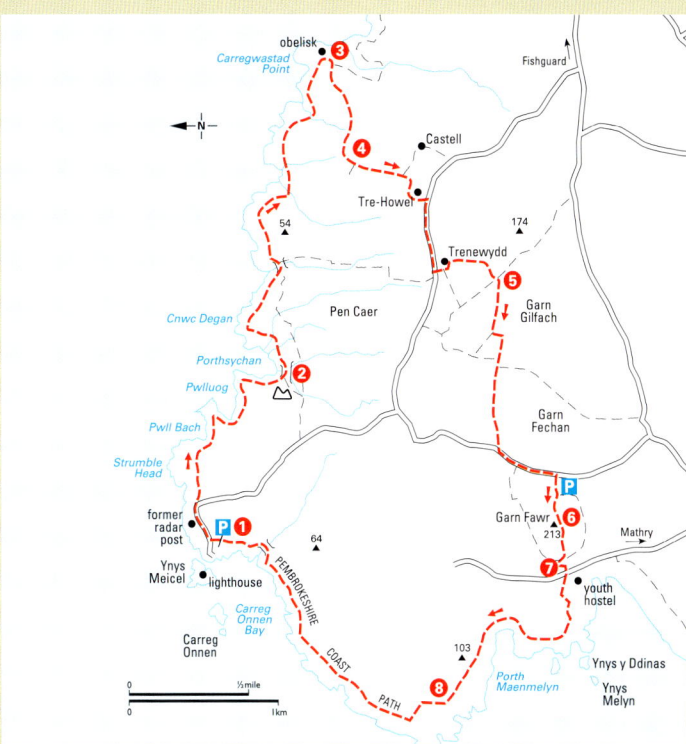

WALK 78

MARLOES ISLAND VIEWS

The Marloes Peninsula forms the westernmost tip of the southern shores of St Brides Bay. The paddle-shaped headland is a popular place to walk, due to the narrow neck that affords minimum inland walking for maximum time spent on the coast. It is famous for its stunning scenery, which includes two of the Pembrokeshire Coast National Park's finest and least-crowded beaches, some secluded coves that are often inhabited by seals, and wonderfully rugged coastline.

DISTANCE/TIME 6 miles (9.7km) 2h30 Ascent: 420ft (128m) **MAP** Aqua3 OS Explorer OL36 South Pembrokeshire **START** Grid ref: SM 761089 **PATHS** Coast path and clear footpaths, short section on tarmac, 10 stiles **PARKING** National Trust car park above Martin's Haven, near Marloes village **THE PUB** Lobster Pot, Marloes. Tel: 01646 636233

1 From the car park turn left on to the road and make your way down to the bottom of the hill. Bear round to the left and then proceed through the gate ahead into Deer Park. Turn left and then follow the path to a stile and on to the coast.

2 Keeping the sea to your right, continue easily along over Deadman's Bay to another stile. The next section cruises along easily too, passing the earthworks of an Iron Age fort on the left. The route then crosses another stile as you begin to approach Gateholm Island.

3 It is possible to get across to the island at low tide, but care is needed to scramble over the slippery rocks. To continue the walk, follow the coast path above the western end of beautiful Marloes Sands until you drop down easily back to the main beach access path. If you are taking this walk in the spring or summer you'll be impressed by the pretty small flowers that carpet the cliff tops. These are sea campion (white) and thrift (pink) and both are common along the Pembrokeshire coast.

4 Turn left and climb up to the road; turn right here. Follow the road along for around 0.75 miles (1.2km) to the bridleway on the left. Follow this down and turn left into Marloes village.

5 Pass the Lobster Pot on the left and continue ahead to leave the village. Ignore the few tracks on the right, as the road bends around to the left, and continue out into open countryside where you will finally meet a footpath on the right.

6 Walk down to the edge of the field and bear around to the left to drop back down on to the coast path above Musselwick Sands. Turn left and follow the path west for over 1.5 miles (2.4km) to Martin's Haven. The *Dale Princess*, a 50-seat passenger boat, departs from Martin's Haven to Skomer Island regularly every morning during the summer and returns during the afternoon. As well as the wildlife and relics of ancient civilisations, there's also some fine walking. Please note that dogs are not allowed on the island. Meet the road and climb past an information centre back to the car park.

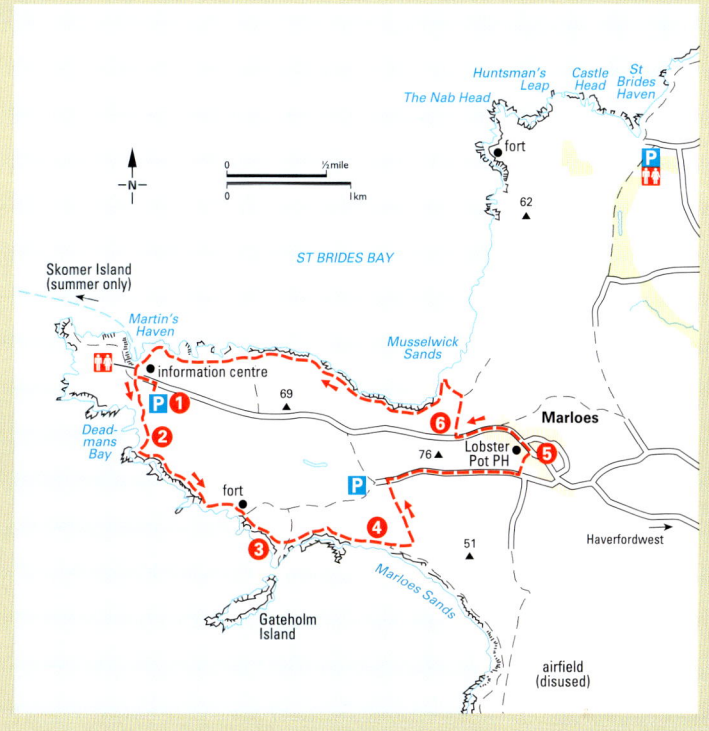

GOWER PENINSULA: THE ROCKY ROAD

This route takes you on a linear trek along the most scenic stretch of the Gower Coast – and you get to make your return journey by bus. The limestone cliffs of the Gower coast are justly popular with rock climbers. Along this section are a number of well-known routes that span from easy beginners' climbs to high-grade test pieces. If it's fine, you're almost bound to spot some climbing activity as you follow the coastline along to Rhossili.

DISTANCE/TIME 6.5 miles (10.4km) 3h Ascent: 850ft (260m)   **MAP** aqua3 OS Explorer 164 Gower   **START** Grid ref: SS 467851   **PATHS** Coast path for the whole distance, 8 stiles   **PARKING** Large car park in Port-Eynon (buses provide logistical links on this linear route)   **THE PUB** The Ship, Port Eynon. Tel: 01792 390204

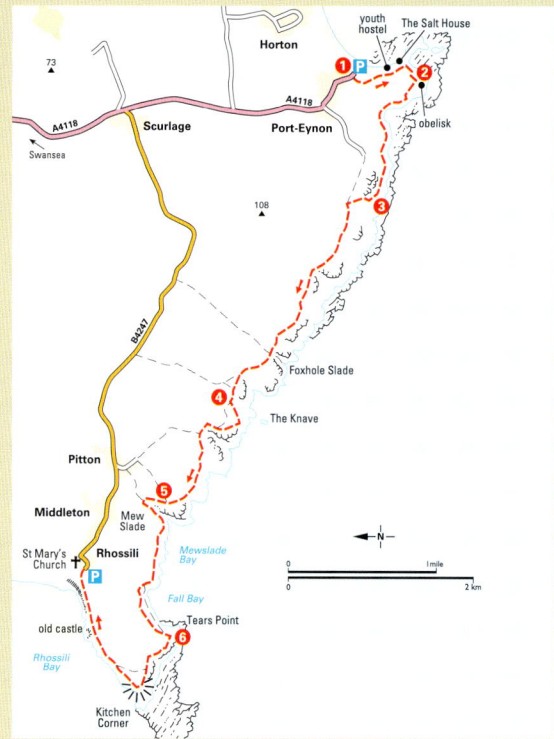

1 From the car park head out towards the sea, following the sandy track that leads past the youth hostel and continues on to the ruins of the Salt House, where an information board gives plenty of history on the area. Continue behind the beach then fork right to climb steeply past a quarry to an obelisk at the top.

2 Follow the cliff tops along and drop to a stile. Cross this to walk behind the rocky beach. Keep right at a fork to climb slightly, then drop left down some steps to a second stile. Cross this and follow the path as it squeezes between impressive limestone cliffs and steep scree. You'll hurdle the rocky terrace and drop beneath more crags before heading down to reach a broken wall.

3 Cross the wall and turn right to climb steeply to a good path. Turn left on to this and follow the wall to Foxhole Slade. Cross the iron stile in a dip and climb back up. (This area is owned by the National Trust.) After 200 yards (183m), next to a gate on the right, fork left. Don't be drawn out on to the coast, instead continue in the same direction until you join the wall again and drop to a stile.

4 When you reach this point cross over the stile and bear left which will take you back out on to the cliff top. Cross another stile and continue walking to a fence, which you then follow to the head of a huge hollow. Cross behind this hollow and proceed along the line of the wall to Mew Slade. As the wall bears right, keep walking straight ahead keeping to the steep path that drops awkwardly into the valley.

5 Turn left at the bottom, and drop over to a stile on the right. Cross the stile to reach a small cove and then follow the narrow path that contours around the hillside eventually to rejoin the main coast path above. Bear left on to this and continue along to another dip. Keep high to round the head of the valley and then proceed down again, keeping the wall on your right.

6 Leave the wall to head back up a grassy down to the cliff tops where you veer around to the right to follow the cliffs along. To continue on to Rhossili, keep walking past the car park to a bus stop on the left by St Mary's Church, from where you can catch a bus to the start point.

WALK 80

ST DAVID'S HEAD: A ROCKY RAMBLE

St David's Head is steeped in legend and peppered with the evidence of ancient civilisations. It would be difficult to imagine a more atmospheric place but for its full effect visit at sunset and watch the sky turn red over the scattered islets of the Bishops and the Clerks, located on the west of the headland. St David's Head itself is magnificent and if you spend some time exploring here you will find a series of rocky terraces where you can shelter from the wind and again enjoy the fine views out to sea and to Ramsay Island.

DISTANCE/TIME 3.5 miles (5.7km) 2h Ascent: 425ft (130m)   **MAP** Aqua3 OS Explorer OL35 North Pembrokeshire   **START** Grid ref: SM 734271   **PATHS** Coast path, clear paths across heathland, 2 stiles   **PARKING** Whitesands Beach   **THE PUB** 14–16 Goat Street, St David's Tel: 01437 721666

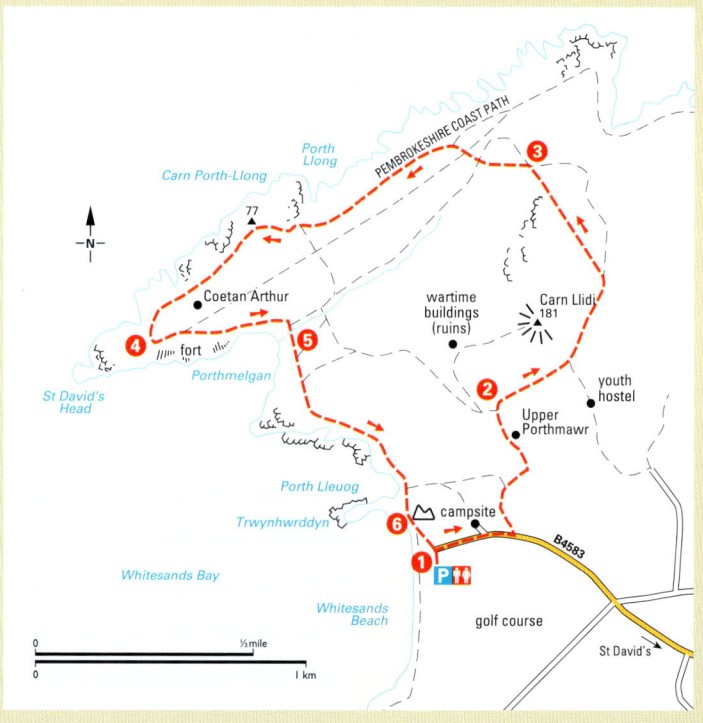

1 From the start point at Whitesands Beach head back up the road, pass the campsite and take the track on the left, and then take the second track on the left. From here, bear right where the track splits and continue around the left-hand bend to walk up to some buildings. Keep to the left to walk between the houses and then continue on until you reach a gate.

2 From the gate, turn right on to open heathland and follow the footpath along a wall beneath Carn Llidi (take time out to enjoy the lovely views from this hill, especially if you are out at sunset). Pass along the track that drops down to the youth hostel on the right and continue around to where the path splits. Take the higher track and keep going in the same direction until, at a corner of the wall, a clear track runs diagonally left towards the coast.

3 Follow this track to the coast path and turn left to stay close to the cliff tops. At Porth Llong, the path bears right to climb to a cairn. You'll find that the headland

is a labyrinth of paths and tracks, but for maximum enjoyment try to remain as close to the cliff tops as possible. The official coast path doesn't go as far as the tip of the peninsula, but plenty of other tracks do, so follow one as far as you wish especially if you want to enjoy great sea views.

4 From the tip, turn left and make your way through rocky outcrops on the southern side of the headland. As you approach Porthmelgan you'll be able to pick up the obvious path that traverses the steep hillside back down into the valley, which shelters a small stream.

5 Cross the stream and climb up some steps on other side. Continue to a kissing gate where the National Trust land ends and maintain your direction. Pass above Porth Lleuog and the distinctive rocky promontory of Trwynhwrddyn, which is worth a visit.

6 The path then drops steeply down to the road from where you can easily walk to an entrance back to Whitesands Beach.

MILFORD HAVEN: ITS TWO FACES

The peninsula offers some challenging walks including this interesting circular route. The outward leg, as far as the sands of Freshwater West, is about as tough as coast-path walking gets, dipping and climbing on narrow, often exposed, paths. The return leg is a little more civilised, tracking around Angle Bay and following field edges out on to the headland.

DISTANCE/TIME 8 miles (12.9km) 3h30 Ascent: 1,017ft (310m) **MAP** Aqua3 OS Explorer OL36 South Pembrokeshire **START** Grid ref: SM 854031 **PATHS** Coast path and easy tracks over agricultural land, short road section, 37 stiles **PARKING** Car park at West Angle Bay **THE PUB** Old Point House Inn, Angle. Tel: 01646 641205

1 Facing the sea, walk left out of the car park and pass between the café and the public toilets in order to reach a waymarked stile. From here follow the field edge along, crossing several further stiles to get to a narrow, hedged track that leads to a set of stone steps.

2 Follow the good track for a few paces and then take the fork right to drop towards a ruined tower stood on the headland. Continue back up, cross some more stiles and then make your way down to the footbridge. Climb up from this and eventually pass Sheep Island on your right.

3 Continue along the coast, dropping steeply into a succession of valleys, climbing back up each time. As you reach the northern end of Freshwater West, keep your eye open for a footpath waymarker to the left.

4 Cross a stile and walk up the floor of valley, swinging left to a stile at the top. Cross the next field, and stile, and continue to a road, the B4320. Turn left on to the road and walk past a cluster of houses to a right-hand turn. Follow this down to the coast, turn left on to the coast path and merge on to a drive.

5 Take the drive to a footpath sign on the right. If you time your walk so that the tide is low when you get to this point, you can cross the estuary here and continue along the bank of pebbles to a road on the other side. If the tide is in, carry on along the road into Angle village and bear right when you get to the church in order to follow a dirt track along the other side.

6 Continue around, pass Old Point House Inn on your left and follow the field edges to a gravel turning point above the lifeboat station on your right. Keep walking straight ahead, over a stile, and follow the bottom of the field system into a wooded area.

7 Here, you'll join a broad track that runs around Chapel Bay cottages and fort. Keep to the right to cross a stile and then follow a narrow path back above the coast. This rounds the headland by Thorn Island.

8 As you descend into West Angle Bay, the path diverts briefly into a field to avoid an area of landslide. Continue to walk downwards and eventually bear right on to a drive that will finally take you back into the car park.

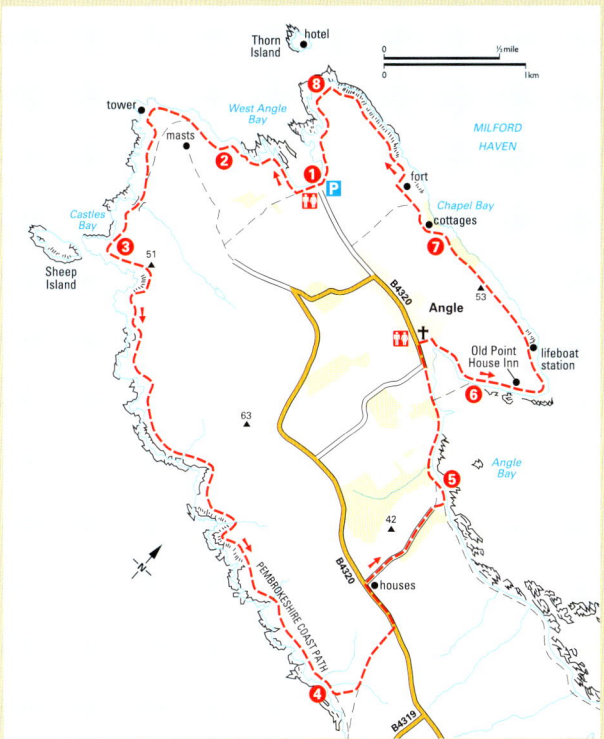

WALK 82

MYNYDD PRESELI: ROMANCING THE STONES

This walk forms a contorted, narrow figure-of-eight that scales the most spectacular hill on the ridge, traces the line of the famous dolerite outcrops, or cairns, and then makes an out-and-back sortie to an impressive stone circle. Convoluted it may be, but it's packed with interest. When you reach Foeldrygarn (which means 'bare hill of three cairns'), you will see the remains of three Bronze Age burial cairns as well as the ruins of an Iron Age fort.

DISTANCE/TIME 5.5 miles (8.8km) 2h30 Ascent: 560ft (170m) **MAP** Aqua3 OS Explorer OL35 North Pembrokeshire **START** Grid ref: SO 165331 **PATHS** Mainly clear paths across open moorland, no stiles **PARKING** Small lay-by on lane beneath Foeldrygarn **THE PUB** Pendre Inn, Cilgerran. Tel: 01239 614223

1 Walk to the right out of the lay-by along the lane from Crymych, then turn right up a stony track. When you come to a gate, keep going straight ahead for another 100yds (91m) or so, and then fork left on to a grassy track, which soon becomes clearer as it winds its way up the hillside. Follow this all the way to some rocky cairns and a trig point on Foeldrygarn.

2 Bear left at the summit and look for the grassy track that drops down to the south. Cross over the heather-clad plateau beneath, aiming to reach the left-hand corner of the wood. When you meet the main track, make a right turn to walk keeping the edge of the wood on your left.

3 Leaving the wood here, the path then climbs slightly up to eventually reach some rocky tors. The second of the tors, the one that's closest to track, has a sheepfold at its base. Shortly after this, the path forks and at this point you follow a left-hand track. This will take you down to the nearest of a group of outcrops to your left, Carn Gyfrwy.

4 Continue on quite faint paths to a clutch of larger outcrops ahead, then curve right and drop slightly to Carn Menyn, the lowest of the bunch, perched precariously on the escarpment edge. It was from here, in Wales, that the bluestones that form the mysterious inner circle of Stonehenge were believed to have been transported – incredibly – more than 200 miles (320km) to Wiltshire. The path becomes clearer here and drops slightly into the marshy saddle that can be seen ahead.

5 In the saddle you'll meet the main track. Turn left and follow it steadily up towards Carn Bica, which is visible on the hillside ahead of you. Just before this, you'll cross over a circle made by stones of Beddarthur.

6 Turn around and retrace your steps back to the saddle. Climb slightly to pass the tor with a sheepfold and stay on this main path to walk beside the plantation once more, now on your right. At the end of this path, drop on to a grassy track, down to a gate. Turn right on to the lane and continue back to the car park.

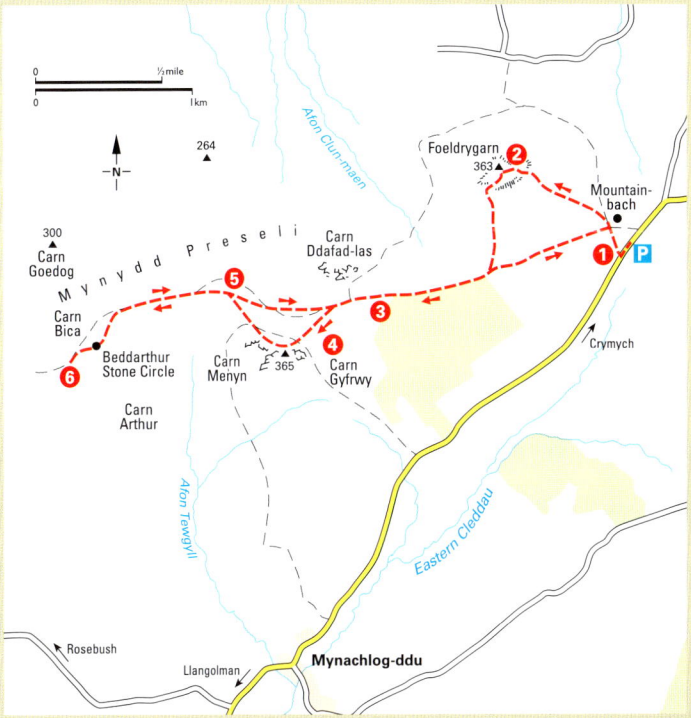

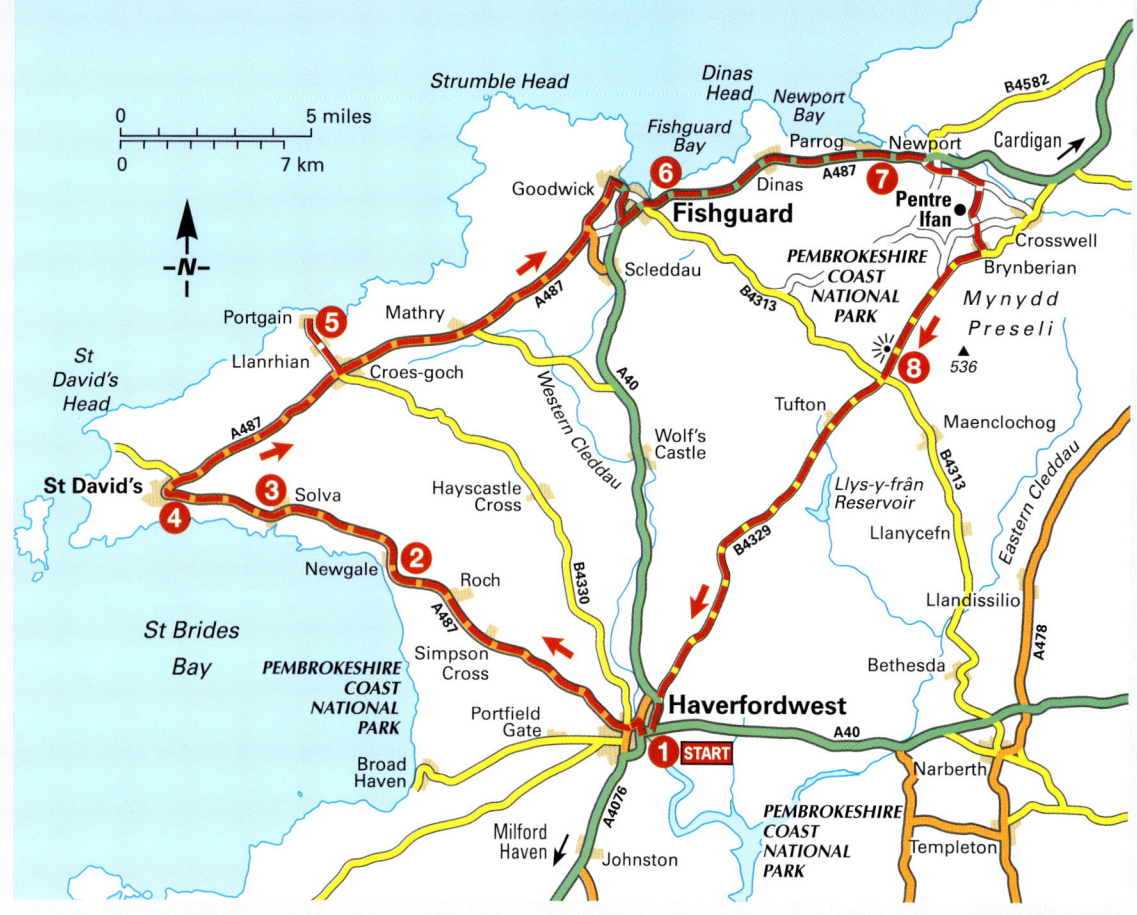

A TOUR OF NORTHERN PEMBROKESHIRE

From Norman Haverfordwest we cross the Landsker into the land of the Celts and Neolithic tribesmen. This tour follows the ancient pilgrims to St David's Cathedral, visits Pembrokeshire's most picturesque coastal village, and seeks out one of Britain's largest and best preserved burial chambers at Pentre Ifan before climbing onto the mysterious Mynydd Preseli, where the blue obelisks of Stonehenge were hewn out of the mountains.

Route Directions

1 From Haverfordwest quayside, head north past Castle Square to reach a roundabout. Take the A487 signed St David's. Across rolling pastureland you'll see Roch Castle perched on a rocky outcrop.

Built by the Normans in the 13th century, Roch Castle is one of the Landsker castles used to repress the Welsh-speaking people and keep them contained in the hills. Nowadays, it offers self-catering holidays.

2 The road drops to the sands at Newgale, where there are often surfers or windsurfers enjoying the waves. After climbing around the headland, the road descends into the wooded valley sheltering Solva, one of Pembrokeshire's prettiest coastal resorts.

Detour left to see the older lower village and harbour, where there's a good-sized car park. There are plenty of cafés here for morning coffee and a bite to eat, or you could take a short walk over the Gribin to reach the sea cliffs on the headland.

3 Return to the main road, which climbs past the upper village and across more pastures to reach St David's.

The pay car park lies at the entrance to the attractive village. The cathedral and the extensive ruins of the Bishop's Palace are unmissable sights.

4 Veer right in the village centre, still following the A487, now signed to Fishguard. After 6 miles (10km), once you are in the hamlet of Croes-goch ('the red cross'), take the second turning on the left, a minor road passing through Llanrhian where you go straight ahead at the crossroads to return to the coast at Portgain.

Once a busy port exporting slate and granite around the world, Portgain's harbour is now the domain of small fishing craft and pleasure boats. If you've worked up an appetite, then stop off at the historic Sloop Inn for lunch – relics and old photos lining the walls give an insight into the history of the village.

5 Return to the A487 and turn left for Fishguard. The road first drops to the coast at Goodwick, where a left turn brings the route on to a new road detouring first right, then doubling back left at the large roundabout to enter Fishguard. On reaching the bustling town centre stay with the A487, signposted Cardigan, and descend to the more attractive lower town.

You can park here and walk along the quayside, taking in all the water-borne activity of the harbour.

6 Beyond Lower Fishguard the A487 climbs from the harbour and heads for Newport, a small seaside resort, which is dominated by the ruffle topped Mynydd Carn Ingli.

If a spot of sunbathing would fit the bill, the best beach lies across the Nevern Estuary and is reached using narrow and circuitous lanes. Closer at hand is Parrog, where you could stretch your legs along the clifftops. There's also the rather good Morawelon Café Bar if you want more relaxation.

7 Continue along the A487 signed Cardigan, until you see signs for Pentre Ifan on the right. These lead up country lanes to the Iron Age burial cromlech (free). Continue on the lane going straight over at the crossroads to Brynberion. Once through the village

turn right on the B4329, which climbs the northern slopes of the Preseli Hills to a high pass (1,330ft/405m) along the main ridge.

It's only a short walk up the hill to the right (west), Cerrig Lladron, where there's a view indicator to highlight the superb western panoramas of the Pembrokeshire and Cardigan Bay coastlines.

8 The B road descends all the way back to return to Haverfordwest, but if you're looking for somewhere for supper, turn left at the first crossroads, then left again through the little hamlet of Rosebush to the Tafarn Sinc, a wonderful old-fashioned pub.

Snowdonia National Park

CLOCKWISE FROM TOP LEFT: OGWEN VALLEY; TRYFAN, OGWEN VALLEY; A CAMPSITE AT THE BASE OF TRYFAN; CONWY CASTLE

ABERDYFI MAP REF 402 D4

In the most southwestern corner of the Snowdonia National Park, Aberdyfi is the finest of Merionydd's coastal resorts. Rows of picturesque, pastel colour-washed cottages, shops and inns, and the small harbour are tucked beneath the steep grassy slopes of the Tarren Hills and the sands of the Dyfi Estuary and Cardigan Bay. Those beaches extend northwards for almost 4 miles (6km) to Tywyn. Besides swimming, sunbathing and sandcastle building, Aberdyfi is popular for many watersports, including sailing. On most weekends hundreds of yachts with a multitude of colourful sails can be seen gliding across the waves.

Inland from Aberdyfi, the Happy Valley delves into the Tarren Hills. Its river, the Afon Dyffryn-gwyn, flows from Llyn Barfog, which means the Bearded Lake. Some say that the name Barfog could relate to Barfog, the colleague of King Arthur. Tales abound about Arthur slaying the mythical beast, Afanc, here, and there's even a nearby summit rock named Carn March Arthur, 'the cairn of Arthur's horse'. Could it be more simple, and that the rushes that infest the lake's edge form the beard?

On the other side of the Happy Valley Lane the Tarrens proper begin. These superb, grassy whalebacks span some 10 miles (16km) to the Dysynni Valley and offer some of the best wilderness ridge-walking in this part of Wales. Although blighted by conifer forests in places, there are many Neolithic cairns and stunning views of mountain coast and estuary, especially at sunset.

BALA MAP REF 402 E3

Bala's jewel is its lake, Llyn Tegid, the largest natural lake in Wales. This beautiful lake, surrounded by the Aran and Arenig Mountains, is popular for watersports, and with anglers too; pikeperch, trout, salmon and roach are plentiful.

The village is dominated by the wide main street, whose austere architecture is camouflaged by the brightly coloured signs of cafés, gift shops and inns. Bala has notable religious roots, a fact reinforced by the number of chapels and the statue of Dr Lewis Edwards, founder of the Methodist College, and, opposite the White Lion, a statue of the Reverend Thomas Charles, one the founders of the British and Foreign Bible Society.

BARMOUTH MAP REF 402 D4

The Snowdonia National Park borders bypass Barmouth on the side of the Rhinog Mountain. The largely Victorian resort built into the rocks is quite touristy. When walking the promenade past the funfair and the fish-and-chip cafés visitors could be forgiven for thinking they were on the Fylde Coast, and Barmouth has been blessed with the same wonderful sands. Those who look for more than a beach holiday and who choose to explore a little further, will find true beauty and majesty in the surrounding mountains and the Mawddach Estuary. The Rhinogydd range, which rises from the backyards of the resort, features some of the finest mountains in Wales.

A fascinating web of stairs and alleyways leads from the High Street up to Hen Bermo, the old town, built almost vertically and haphazardly up the cliffs. Eventually you will come to Dinas Oleu ('the Fortress of light'), donated to the National Trust by the local Talbot family.

As there wasn't enough room to squeeze the main road from Harlech between the foothills and the sea, all roads climbed inland, over the Rhinog mountain passes. However, in the mid-19th century a coast road was built borrowing ground from the beach area. In 1867 the railways followed, crossing over the Mawddach Estuary on a half-mile (800m) new bridge which had a swing section to allow shipping to pass. The new breed of Victorian tourist flocked here for the sea air, the beaches and the bathing. One of those visitors was William Wordsworth, who described the view across the estuary towards Cadair Idris as sublime and equal to any in Scotland.

BEDDGELERT MAP REF 402 D3

Beddgelert has a location to die for, tucked away near the confluence of the Glaslyn and Colwyn valleys, and beneath the lusciously wooded lower crags and bluffs of Snowdon. The centrepiece of the village is a pretty twin-arched stone bridge over the lively Glaslyn. Huddled around the bridge are the stone-built cottages, inns, and cafés. Beddgelert and the area around it once made it to Hollywood, for scenes from Ingrid Bergman's film, *The Inn of the Sixth Happiness*, were shot here.

Beddgelert, which means 'Gelert's grave', takes its name from the Celtic saint, Kelert. Some tourist literature would have you believe that Gelert was Llewelyn the Great's faithful dog, killed by his master, who mistakenly believed it had butchered his child. The myth and subsequently the building of the grave were ploys by David Pritchard, the first landlord of the Royal Goat Hotel, built in 1803, to bring more visitors to his hotel.

The Sygun Copper Mines to the north of Beddgelert are well worth seeing. You'll go on foot on a self-guided audio-visual tour through winding tunnels to see the veins of copper ore in chambers that are coloured by a fascinating array of stalactites and stalagmites.

Looking downwards onto the copper mine from Snowdon's slopes is Dinas Emrys, a rocky wooded knoll capped with the ruins of an old fort, possibly from the Iron Age and probably used in the time of Llewelyn the Great. Legends tell that it was the refuge of Arthurian magician Merlin, and of Vortigern, a 5th-century British king who was fleeing from the Danes. Access to the area is difficult, sometimes even dangerous, and is not advised.

To the south of the village the A498 Porthmadog road enters the Aberglaslyn Pass, where the flanks of Moel Hebog and the 700-foot (213m) splintered cliffs form a cavernous rocky gorge, through which the waters of the River Glaslyn transform into white torrents as they pound the boulders of the riverbed. In the next few years the Welsh Highland Railway will recommence its journey through the pass.

BALA LAKE

Visit
UNDERGROUND TOURS

At the award-winning Llechwedd Slate Caverns at Blaenau Ffestiniog, visitors can take a miners' tramway into the heart of the slate mountain, where a miner guides them around spectacular 19th-century caverns of cathedral-like proportions. There's also a Deep Mine tour starting with Britain's steepest railway (1:1.8), where a 25-minute underground walk reveals the social condition in which the miners lived as told by 'the ghost of a Victorian miner'. Re-created Victorian shops plus a licensed restaurant and a pub complete this interesting experience.

Visit
CAER LLEION FORT

Conwy Mountain forms the backdrop to the town and its castle. High on the hillside are the remains of a much older civilisation, for here lies Caer Lleion fort. Evidence shows that boundary walls surround more than 50 Iron Age hut circles. The walls have almost, but not quite, crumbled into the hillside from which they came. Sadly, the huts, with their roofs thatched with rushes and reeds, have not survived.

BETWS-Y-COED

BETWS-Y-COED MAP REF 402 E2

Betws-y-Coed, pronounced 'betoose ee koyd', is the most popular of all the Snowdonian resorts and on most days, especially during the busy summer months, its main street, the A5, will be choc-a-bloc with traffic. Sheltered by enormous hillside forests and sited near to the confluences of the Conwy and two of its tributaries, the Lledr and the Llugwy, Betws-y-Coed is renowned for its waterfalls. One flows beneath the Pont-y-Pair ('the bridge of the cauldron'), which was built in 1468 at the heart of the village. This is always popular with sunbathers who lounge on the crags that line the banks. The Swallow Falls, best viewed from the north bank of the Llugwy, is a spectacular torrent, lying some two miles (3km) west up the road, while the Conwy Falls can be found on the Penmachno end of the village, accessed from the car park of the Otter Restaurant and Café.

Every day walkers and climbers gather before and after their mountain adventures. There are more gear shops for them to browse than food stores. Nightlife tends to centre on the Royal Oak's Stables Bar – those wanting a seat have to get there early most weekends.

One of the popular visitor attractions is the motor museum. Created from the private collection of the Houghton family, it includes several exotic and rare cars such as Bugatti, Aston Martin, Bentley and the Model T Ford.

Lead played a big part in the popular town's early development and if you take one of the forest walks up to Llyn Parc you'll see many of the relics from the old mines. Further east is Llyn Crafnant, a beautiful mountain lake reached by narrow winding lanes from Betws or on foot along a bridleway from the next village west, Capel Curig.

Capel Curig is the true gateway to the big mountains of Snowdonia and as such is considered to be the best-placed resort for weekend mountain walkers and climbers who want an early start.

BLAENAU FFESTINIOG
MAP REF 402 E3

Arrive at Blaenau Ffestiniog on a rainy day and you'll see nothing but slate. The houses are built from it, they're roofed with it and their gardens and backyards are piled up with it – great slag heaps that disappear into the low slate-grey clouds. Slate is Blaenau's heritage and they're proud of it. The slate has been mined and quarried from the Moelwyn and Manod mountains that lie either side of the 900 foot-high (275m) valley head where the town stands. When the cloud lifts, the mountains reveal themselves to be finely sculpted with distinctive shapes.

This slate town has its ghostly relics. Take a look at the valley of Cwmorthin, just beyond the suburb of Tanygrisiau. A slatey track climbs beneath the Moelwyn crags past a forlorn-looking lake into a valley that has been devastated by quarries and mines. Beyond the high-chimneyed shell of the old barracks, you can also see the rusting pulley wheels and the bogies of the old slate carts.

Blaenau lies at the end of the narrow-gauge Ffestiniog Railway from Porthmadog, a splendid journey around the Moelwyn and through the beautiful oak woods and pastures of the Ffestiniog Valley. The journey takes you past Tanygrisiau's lake and power station. These form part of a hydroelectric scheme where cheap-rate power is used to pump water up to the higher tarn, Llyn Stwlan, whose head of water is then stored until needed at peak periods.

Blaenau's smaller neighbour, Llan Ffestiniog, is a typical Welsh village with a small square and a large chapel, surrounded by verdant scenery. Roaring deep in the valley, below the village church, are the waterfalls known as Rhaeadr Cynfal, plunging into a 200-foot (60m) craggy ravine. The large, dominant rock pillar that stands at the top of the falls, Huw Llwyd's Pulpit, was named after a 17th-century warrior and poet who lived in the village.

CONWY MAP REF 402 E2

Few rivers can match the Conwy for true beauty. Its source, Llyn Conwy, lies high in moorland known as the Migneint but soon it is tumbling down the mountainsides to Betws-y-Coed. Here, it calms, passing through pastures before meandering across sandbars and mudflats out into the estuary between Conwy and the headland of Llandudno's Great Orme.

Conwy, the town, is one of the great treasures of Wales; a place where history parades itself around every corner. Three fine bridges, including Thomas Telford's magnificent suspension bridge of 1822 and Stephenson's tubular railway bridge, cross the estuary beneath the castle, allowing both road and the railway into this medieval World Heritage Site.

Conwy's castle has the shape we expect in our fairy-tale castles. It dates back to 1287 when the powerful English king, Edward I, built it as part of his 'iron ring' to repress the rebellious troops of Llewelyn the Great, who had given him a great deal of trouble in his conquest of Wales. A statue of the revered Welsh prince dominates Lancaster Square.

Great town walls 6-feet (2m) thick and 35-feet (10.7m) high with three original gates and numerous towers still encircle the old town. The walkway along the top of these walls offers splendid views of the castle, the Conwy Estuary and the rocky knolls of Deganwy. At the wall's end, steps descend to the quayside where fishermen sort their nets and squawking seagulls watch out for the scraps. In summer there is a good selection of boat trips, some just around the estuary; others further afield to Anglesey.

Conwy has many fine old buildings. The half-timbered Aberconwy House (National Trust) has origins in the 14th century, although most of its structure belongs to around 1500. The equally impressive Plas Mawr is a large mansion, built for the Wynne family in 1576. Now in the hands of CADW, the building has fine interior plasterwork.

St Mary's Church occupies a central but quiet position in the town, on the site of a Cistercian Abbey of which it was once a part; the abbey was moved to this location by Edward I in order to acquire its former setting for his castle.

DINAS MAWDDWY MAP REF 402 E4

Dinas Mawddwy, a small village just off the main highway (A470), lies sheltered from the westerly winds by the high pass, Bwlch Oerddrws, in a sylvan hollow close to the valleys of the Cerist and the Dyfi rivers. It's a centre for walkers and climbers who flock to Cwm Cywarch where gigantic crags soar to the Aran ridges. The Dyfi valley is simply delectable in these parts. The sleek profiled velvety hills with a patchwork of heather, bracken and moor grass, are mellowed by hedgerow, oak woods and whitewashed farm cottages – this is truly God's country. Indeed it used to be the stamping ground of St Tydecho, cousin of St Cadfan and one of three saints sent from Brittany in the 6th century to introduce Christianity to Wales.

DOLGELLAU MAP REF 402 E4

Dolgellau sits snugly among pastureland that rises from the banks of the Mawddach and Wnion to the great cliffs of Cadair Idris. An impressive seven-arched bridge, Y Bont Fawr, built in 1638 but heavily modified in subsequent centuries, crosses the Wnion and leads into the market town. Narrow, austere streets of stone and slate buildings lead into a large central square.

Dolgellau's origins as a village lie in the 12th century when it was attached to the Cistercian monastery at Cymer Abbey. Very little remains in the town from that period – even the old Parliament building, Cwrt Plas yn Dre, where Owain Glyn Dwr plotted the downfall of the English in 1398, was pulled down in 1881. The town grew during the 18th and 19th centuries from the proceeds of a large wool industry – celebrated every year in the local Wool Race – and a gold rush of the same era. At its peak more than 500 men were employed in the gold and copper mines in the hills around Dolgellau.

Come to Dolgellau early on a Sunday morning and you'll see scores of walkers, stocking up with bread, cakes and soft drinks in readiness for a trip up Cadair Idris. Steeped in Celtic legends and myths, Cadair Idris, The Seat of Idris, is the most romantic of Welsh peaks. Though not quite reaching the heights of central Snowdonia, Cadair has all the grandeur of Snowdon and a little bit more – fine crag-bound tarns, sheer rockfaces and wide-sweeping views across what seems like the whole of Wales. It is set in a green, fertile landscape of oak woods, dashing streams and pretty stone cottages dotted across pastoral foothills. The main starting points for Cadair are Minffordd, which lies just north of Tal-y-llyn, and Pont Dyffrydan car park on the Old Cader Road, the start of the well-worn route known as the Pony Path.

SNOWDONIA NATIONAL PARK

HARLECH MAP REF 402 D3

Harlech Castle stands on a great 200-foot (61m) crag defiantly watching out over Tremadog Bay. It's one of the most dramatic castles in the United Kindgom. Although the outer walls are badly damaged, the majestic inner curtain wall and their great round corner towers are well preserved. Built for Edward I around 1280, the castle would have been protected by what were then sea cliffs (the sea has since receded to reveal coastal plain and sand dunes), while a deep moat protected the rear landward side. The castle kept the Welsh at bay until 1404 when it was taken by the Welsh leader Owain Glyn Dwr, who then had himself crowned here as Prince of Wales, witnessed by noblemen from Scotland, France and Spain. A long siege here during the Wars of the Roses inspired the famous Welsh marching song 'Men of Harlech'.

Harlech village is quite small. The old quarter lies on the hillside by the castle, while the holiday quarter, including a hotel, campsites, apartments and the railway, spreads across the plains. Visitors come here for the magnificent beaches whose position, with the mountains of Snowdonia spanning the skyline across Tremadog Bay, is quite spectacular.

Behind the village, narrow country lanes wind through the impressive Rhinog Mountains, a range that consists of thick beds of gritstone and shale formed in

the Cambrian era – some of the world's oldest surface rocks. The gnarled and faulted crags are riven by deep transverse canyons that create repeated obstacles to those wanting to walk along the 'ridge'. Boulders and scree from the eroded gritstone slabs are frequently covered with knee-deep heather. Early roads, paths and tracks all ran east–west, following the natural lie of the land.

LLANBERIS & SNOWDON
MAP REF 402 D2

The successes and failures of Llanberis have always been linked to its mountains. From the moment in the late 18th century that they decided to quarry the slate from Elidir Fawr, Llanberis was transformed from a tiny village into a bustling lakeside town, as it is today. In its prime the Dinorwig Quarry employed 3,000 men, many of whom travelled from far afield. When the slate quarry finally closed without warning in August 1969, mountain tourism was ready to take its place.

The Snowdon Mountain Railway, Britain's only rack-and-pinion railroad, opened in 1896. Unfortunately, the first day proved disastrous, for an out-of-control descending train derailed itself before tumbling down steep slopes. One passenger who had jumped from a falling carriage was killed. Today many thousands of passengers listen to the running commentary as their steam

engine travels through woodland and over a viaduct before puffing up the mountain. In 2007 a new summit hotel with wide, picture windows replaced the much-maligned old 'hovel'.

The slate industry lives on through the town's Welsh Slate Museum, which occupies the same Dinorwig site on the northeast shore of Llyn Padarn. At the museum you can get an insight into a miner's life and his work, watch a craftsman split the rock into fine tiles and see the largest waterwheel on mainland Britain. The enormous wheel, some 50 feet (15.4m) in diameter, was built by the De Winton company in 1870 and harnessed the power of the water that had been piped from the slopes of Mount Snowdon to turn the slate machinery in towns below.

LLANRWST MAP REF 402 E2

Llanrwst has always flirted with tourism but has never stepped out of the shadow of its neighbour Betws-y-Coed. It is claimed that the three-arched bridge over the Conwy was designed by Inigo Jones, and although there's little evidence of this, it certainly is elegant. But the 16th-century bridge is extremely narrow and allows single-file traffic only. The 15th-century ivy and Virginia creeper-clad cottage of Ty Hwnt i'r Bont next to the bridge is a National Trust tea house.

A few miles north down the Conwy Valley at Caerhun, is the site of a Roman

fort, Canovium, established soon after the invasion of Wales under Cnaeus Julius Agricola between AD 75 and 77. The Roman cohorts marched into the hills, tamed the Ordovices tribesmen who farmed the high Carneddau slopes, and constructed a surfaced road over Bwlch y Ddeufaen, which would link with their fort at Segontium (Caernarfon).

RHINOG MTS (ROMAN STEPS)
MAP REF 402 E3

From the Mawddach Estuary in the south, the Rhinog range, the Rhinogydd, pushes its way northwards to the Vale of Ffestiniog across 24km (15 miles) of the most unrelenting and roughest country in Wales. The hard Cambrian gritstone favours the growth of heather above all else and, with the profusion of huge boulders buried in peat, give the whole area an appealing rugged splendour.

SWALLOW FALLS MAP REF 402 E2

Swallow Falls, near Betws-y-Coed, is the most renowned and popular display of water power in Snowdonia, and is easy to access from the adjacent A5. Here, the beautiful Afon Llugwy rages and roars down from the mountains through tree-girt, granite chasms, until it smashes itself against the jagged rocks and crags that divide its flow into foaming cascades which tumble downwards between thickly wooded banks to a pool below.

59 MILES (95KM)

5 Drive through Llanberis, passing the scenic lake of Llyn Padarn on your right, before leaving the mountains for the fantastic coast and castle at Caernarfon.

Here a visit to the royal Caernarfon Castle is a must. Also worth seeing are the ruins of the Roman fort Segontium, which is situated on the outskirts of the town.

6 Follow the coast road (A487) east towards Bangor, just before which you join the A55 dual carriageway signed to Conwy and Betws-y-Coed. If it's fine, and there's a spare hour or so, take the turning signed Abergwyngregyn. Take this minor road south to a forestry car park, which lies just beyond the bridge over the Afon Rhaeadr-fawr. A very gentle but superbly scenic there-and-back walk takes you through a verdant upland glen to the spectacular Aber Falls.

At the Aber Falls, the fantastic Afon Goch tumbles hundreds of feet down impressive cliffs of quartz-streaked Cambrian granophyre. The glen is now part of the Coedydd Aber National Nature Reserve, which was set up in 1975 by the Nature Conservancy Council (now English Nature) as an important ecological site and example of a broad-leaved woodland habitat.

7 Return to the A55 and head back to Conwy tracking the coastline that runs to your left until you turn inland for Conwy.

THROUGH THE MOUNTAINS OF SNOWDONIA

The first part of the route skirts the edge of the Snowdonia National Park, passing through small villages in the fertile Vale of Conwy, before reaching Betws-y-Coed and Capel Curig nestling in the foothills of Moel Siabod. The route climbs to the high Pass of Llanberis and passes a couple of lakes before reaching the coast. There is an opportunity to visit the Aber Falls, before returning to Conwy.

If you want a huge all-day breakfast or a good mug of tea, you'll find the Pinnacle Café, popular with both walkers and climbers, is a good choice. But if you prefer a bar meal, then try Cobdens.

Route Directions

This tour starts and ends at the historic town of Conwy. The castle here is one of the finest of Edward I's 'iron ring' and walking along the town walls offers splendid views over the rooftops, the pretty Conwy Estuary and Great Orme. The harbour always echoes to the sound of the seagulls that follow the fishermen at work.

1 From Castle Square, right in the centre of Conwy, take the B5106 road south through a narrow gate in the town wall, and under the railway. Once through the outskirts of town, the road winds through very pleasant countryside with tidal waters of the Afon Conwy in the wide pastoral valley on your left and the sprawling Carneddau mountains, right. Continue to Trefriw.

Those interested in textiles and fabrics might want to visit the Trefriw Woollen Mills, established in 1859 alongside Afon Crafnant.

2 Continue south along the B5106 and turn right a couple of miles south of Trefriw. Pass the manor-house Gwydir Castle, and continue ahead to reach Betws-y-Coed. Turn right along the A5 in Betws, following the signs to Capel Curig. Soon you will reach Swallow Falls.

In Betws there's a picturesque waterfall right in the village centre, and a very good range of shops for tourists. It's worth stopping at the falls, which can be seen from near the roadside, though a walk along the north bank offers a more spectacular view.

3 The next village on the A5, Capel Curig, is the gateway to the mountains of Snowdonia. Take the left fork (A4086) by the Pinnacle Café to pass Llynnau Mymbyr, two lovely windswept lakes set amid wild surroundings beneath the barren slopes of Moel Siabod. The Snowdon massif soon appears ahead.

4 At a junction take the right fork (A4086) at the Pen-y-Gwryd Hotel and follow the road through the rugged Pass of Llanberis, which squeezes between Snowdon the highest mountain in Wales, and the rocky Glyderau range. At the bottom of the pass lies Nant Peris, a village shoehorned into narrow pastures between the mountainsides. At the entrance to the larger village of Llanberis is the massive round tower of 13th-century Dolbadarn Castle, overlooking Llyn Peris. Llanberis has a wealth of tourist attractions and time demands that you will have to choose. If there's at least 2.5 hours to spare, you could take the scenic Snowdon Mountain Railway to the highest summit in Wales.

The fascinating Welsh Slate Museum is situated in Padarn Country Park. Alternatively, you might enjoy a visit to Electric Mountain and take a tour bus to the hydroelectric pump-storage power station built into the heart of the mountain of Elidir Fawr.

WALK 83

LLYN CRAFNANT, THE TWIN LAKES

Llyn Crafnant is serenely beautiful, and it's only 5 minutes from the car to its northern tip. Here, at the head of the 'valley of garlic', is a lake surrounded by woodland, lush pasture and craggy hills. The walk is easy too, on an undulating forestry track that gives a slightly elevated view of the lake. The lower pastures are dotted with pretty, whitewashed cottages and the hill slopes at the head of the valley are tinged with heather and the golden grey of the crags on the ridge.

1 Turn right out of the car park and follow the lane to the north end of Llyn Crafnant, a beautiful lake surrounded by thick woodland, verdant pasture and gentle hills. Turn right and follow the forestry track along the northwest shores of the lake, then make your way along the lower left fork.

2 Ignore the first stile on the left, and instead climb with the forestry track. Keep a watch for the waymarked footpath on which you should descend left to pass beneath the cottage of Hendre. Go over a footbridge on the right, then turn left down the track past modern chalets.

3 Turn left along the road that heads back towards the lake. Leave this at the telephone box for the path (signed 'Llyn Geirionydd') and waymarked with blue-capped posts. This climbs through conifer forests and over shoulder of Mynydd Deulyn.

4 Descend on the winding forestry track, still following the obvious blue-capped posts. Ignore the track forking to the right – that leads to Llyn Bychan.

5 On reaching the valley floor, leave the track to go over the step stile that stands on the left. The path crosses a field beneath Ty-newydd cottage before tracing Llyn Geirionydd's shoreline. At the northern end of the lake, the path keeps to the right of a wall and meets a far track.

6 Turn left along this, then right to Taliesin Monument erected in 1850 to commemorate the 6th-century bard who is known to have lived here at the northern end of Geirionydd. Many of Taliesin's poems recall tales of magic and mystery, and they often relate to the heroics of King Arthur, who some believe was his one-time master. Descend to green path heading northwest, then north, descending towards Crafnant Valley.

7 Veer left to cross a ladder stile and follow an undulating path that leads over rock and heather knolls.

8 The path eventually swings left to reach an old mine. Here, take the lower track on the right which descends back to the valley road and the forest car park.

DISTANCE/TIME 5 miles (8km) 3h Ascent: 656ft (200m) **MAP** Aqua3 OS Explorer OL17 Snowdon **START** Grid ref: SH 756618 **PATHS** Clear paths and forestry tracks, 7 stiles **PARKING** Forestry car park, north of Llyn Crafnant **THE PUB** The Old Ship, Trefriw. Tel: 01492 640013

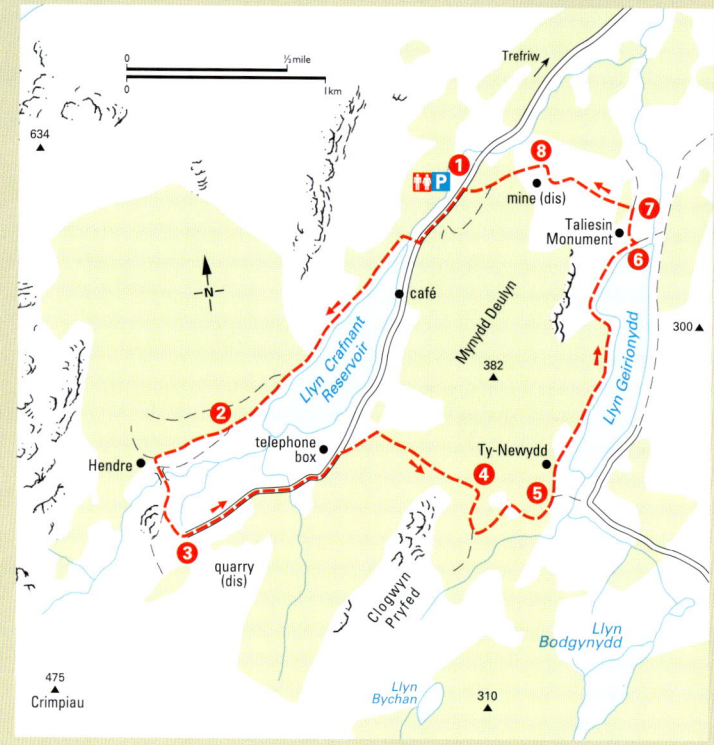

WALK 84

OGWEN – THE DEVIL'S KITCHEN

If you come to here when the damp mountain mists swirl in and out of the blackened mossy crags, and waterfalls drop from those mists like plumes of steam, you will experience the atmospheric menace, and perhaps understand the legend and the shepherds' folklore that says Idwal is the haunt of demons and damned water. However, sunshine can paint a very different picture, with golden rocks and small mountain birds flitting through the grasses.

1 The Cwm Idwal nature trail starts to the left of the toilet block at Ogwen and climbs up the hillside to pass some impressive waterfalls before turning right and continuing up the hill.

2 Go through a gate in a fence, which marks the boundary of National Nature Reserve, and turn left along the side of Llyn Idwal's eastern shores. The clear footpath climbs into the dark shadows of Cwm Idwal.

3 Now leave the nature trail, which turns right to complete the circuit around the lake. Instead ascend beneath the rock-climbing grounds of Idwal Slabs and across the stream of Nant Ifan, beyond which a footpath zig-zags up rough boulder ground to the foot of Twll Du – Devil's Kitchen. If the weather, and preferably the forecast too, are fine, climb to Llyn y Cwn at top of this impressive defile. If not, skip this bit and turn right. The rich soils on the crags around Twll Du allow many species of Arctic plants to flourish free from animal grazing. Collectively the foliage seems to flow down the rocks and you can see why it is called the Hanging Gardens.

4 To ascend Twll Du climb the engineered path as it angles left up the rock face, which will now be on your right-hand side, above an extensive area of scree and boulder. At the top you come to a relatively gentle (by comparison) grassy hollow between rising to the summits of Y Garn, to the right, and Glyder Fawr, to the left.

5 Just beyond the first grassy mounds, you come across the small tarn of Llyn y Cwn, which makes a great rest and picnic spot. Now retrace your steps carefully to the bottom of Twll Du.

6 From here descend over rocky ground down to the western side of Llyn Idwal. The path eventually reaches, and then rounds, the northern shoreline to meet the outward route at a gate near the outflow stream. From here, you simply follow the same route of your outward journey back to the car park at Ogwen.

DISTANCE/TIME 3 miles (4.8km) 2h30 Ascent: 1,706ft (520m) **MAP** Aqua3 OS Explorer OL17 Snowdon **START** Grid ref: SH 649603 **PATHS** Well-defined paths, 2 stiles **PARKING** Small car park at Ogwen **THE PUB** Cobdens Hotel, Capel Curig. Tel: 01690 720243

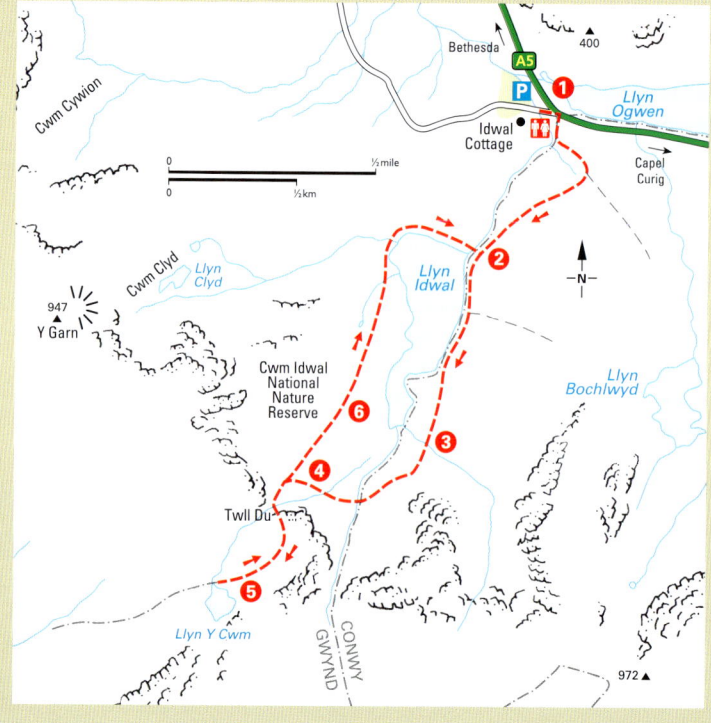

DOLGELLAU – THE KING'S FOREST

If ever there's a case for walking in the rain this is it. There are trees for shelter, two bounding rivers and two waterfalls which look their best when in spate. Just settle for that as long as there's a dry spell when you reach the top of the small hill at the end of the valley.

DISTANCE/TIME 4 miles (6.4km) 2h Ascent: 660ft (200m) **MAP** Aqua3 OS Explorer OL18 Harlech, Porthmadog & Bala **START** Grid ref: SH 735263 **PATHS** Forest tracks and paths, 2 stiles **PARKING** Tyddyn Gwladys forest Car Park near Ganllwyd **THE PUB** Cross Foxes Inn, Dolgellau. Tel: 01341 422487

1 Turn right out of the car park and follow the flinted forestry track with Afon Mawddach below to the right. The track passes beneath the terraced Mostyn cottages.

2 Take a higher track to the left of Ferndale holiday cottages – once gold-mine workshops and a blasting plant. Gold has been mined throughout Wales for centuries, but there were large finds of good quality gold in the 19th century, when Dolgellau became another Klondyke. The track eventually swings right to cross Afon Gain, close to its confluence with Mawddach.

3 On reaching the other side, detour left along a rough path to take a closer look at Pistyll Cain waterfalls. The impressive cascades splash 150ft (45m) against dark rocks into a deep pool below. Return to the main track, and turn left to the old mine's mill buildings.

4 Just beyond the mill are Rhaeadr Mawddach falls. Spend 5 minutes admiring the natural phenomena. Ignore the footbridges here and double back left on the slaty path climbing through a conifer plantation – ignore the cycle route on the right, near the beginning of this path.

5 After winding your way up the hillside, the path finally gets to a junction. Ignore the signed footpath that leads straight ahead, but instead turn right on to a track that has a white-topped post (No 30) next to it. This track soon becomes a grassy path that emerges from the forest at a small gate, and continues as an enclosed track through high pastures in an area that was once the main Gwynfynydd Mine. The track then passes above Ty Mawr farm, and eventually becomes a tarred lane.

6 Turn right on meeting the country lane and follow it almost to Bedd y Coedwr farm. Just here a footpath signpost points the way downhill on a field path that then continues to the right of some attractive birch woods. From here, the path then veers right through some heather-cloaked scrub and eventually becomes rough and overgrown in some places until it reaches an old mine track down by the banks of Mawddach.

7 Keep following the track past the shafts of the gold mines to reach the outward route by Rhaeadr Mawddach. From this point, retrace your steps back along to the car park where you began.

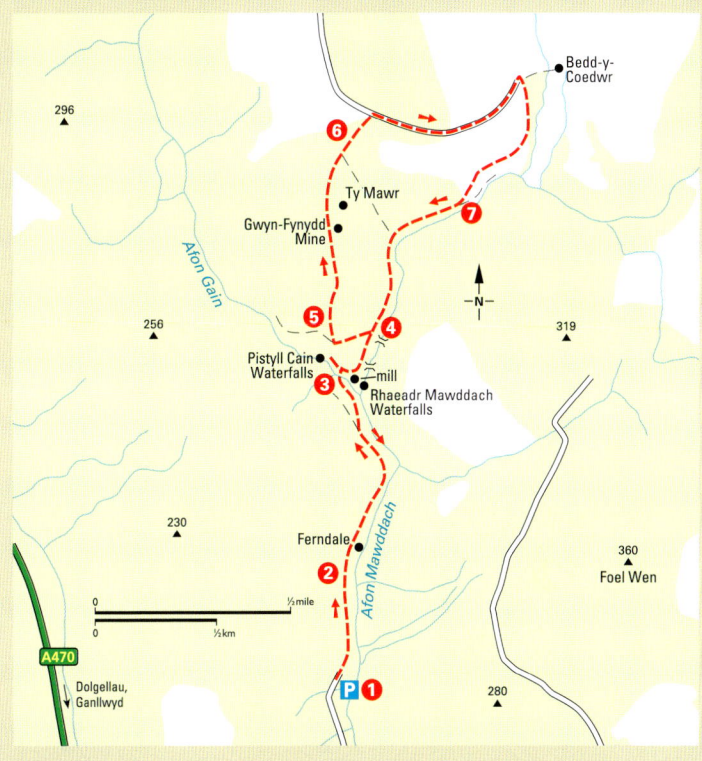

WALK 86

ROMAN STEPS WITH THE DROVERS

Cwm Bychan is one of the treasures of Snowdonia and the Roman Steps one of its oldest highways. The road from Llanbedr into Cwm Bychan is a joy, passing through oak woods, by the banks of a bubbling stream and beneath the small rocky castles of the Rhinog foothills. Drovers used this track too on their way to market with their cattle.

DISTANCE/TIME 7 miles (11.3km) 4h Ascent: 1,575ft (480m) **MAP** Aqua3 OS Explorer OL18 Harlech, Porthmadog & Bala **START** Grid ref: SH 646314 **PATHS** Peaty paths through heather and farm tracks, 11 stiles **THE PUB** Castle Cottage Restaurant, Y Llech, Harlech. Tel: 01766 780479

1 Go through the gate at the back of the car park at Llyn Cwm Bychan, and over a paved causeway across a stream. Beyond the stile the path climbs up through woodland.

2 Climb over a stile to leave the woodland and cross a stream on a small bridge. The path nicks right to go through a gap in the wall, then left again, heading towards Rhinog rocks. It slowly veers left and, now slabbed with 'steps', climbs through a heather-clad rocky ravine to enter a nature reserve. The steps continue the climb to the cairn marking the highest point along the rocky pass of Bwlch Tyddiad.

3 Over the col, continue along a path that descends into a grassy moorland basin beneath Rhinog Fawr then, beyond a stile, enter the conifers of Coed y Brenin plantation. A well-defined footpath tucks away under trees and eventually comes to a wide flinted forestry road, along which you turn left.

4 After about 1 mile (1.6km) the road swings right to head east, watch out for a waymarked path on the left which will eventually take you out of forest. After a short way along this path, a waymark guides the route left, then another waymark points to the right to pass the ruins of Hafod-Gynfal. Beyond this place head north to go over a ladder stile and out of the forest.

5 There's no path across the grassy moor of Moel y Gwartheg. Just head north here, with the cliffs of Craig Wion well to your left and bridge across the huge expanse of Llyn Trawsfynydd at five minutes past the hour.

6 Further downhill a fence on the left-hand side guides you down towards the isolated cottage of Wern Fach. Cross over a stile just short of the cottage, then turn left uphill, following the clear waymarks which guide you over the first of many ladder stiles.

7 A wet moorland footpath climbs up to the lonely col of Bwlch Gwylim, a narrow pass between Clip and Craig Wion. At this point Cwm Bychan and the start of the walk come into view. The footpath then descends to the southwest, through banks of heather, before turning right to continue down the slopes to the car park and the start point.

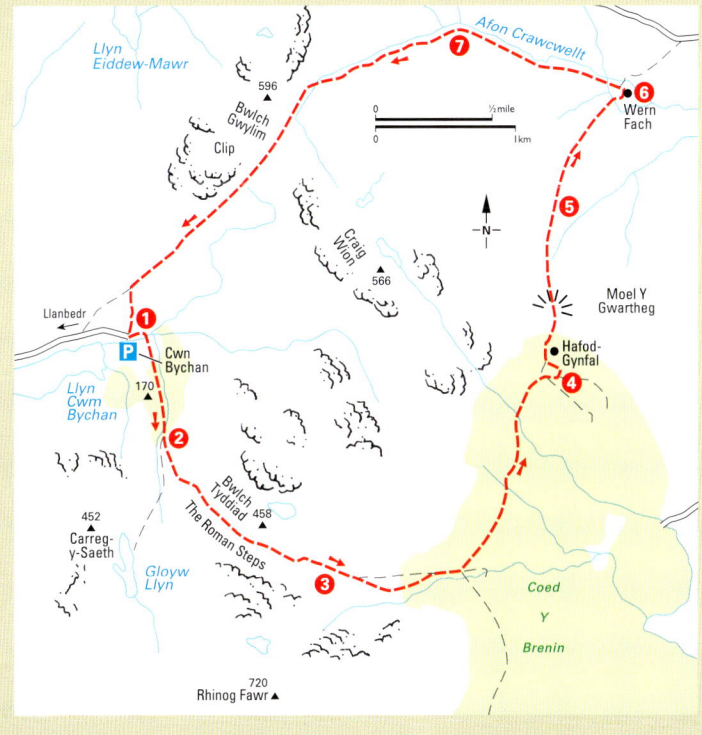

DISTANCE/TIME 13.5 miles (22km) 3h30 **MAP** OS Explorer OL13/14; OS Landranger Sheet 161 **START** Skenfrith Castle, Nr Monmouth; grid ref: SO 457202 **TRACKS** Quiet B-road and country lanes **CYCLE HIRE** Monmouth Cycle Hire, 7 St Vincents Drive, Monmouth, Gwent NP25 5DS. Tel: 07782 270114 **THE PUB** The Angel Inn, Grosmont. Tel: 01981 240646

A TRAIL OF TWO CASTLES – SKENFRITH & GROSMONT

This cycle tour passes through lovely countryside, passing two forgotten fortresses, and country pubs and cafés which are dotted along the route.

1 Skenfrith is a delightful place in summer. The low-lying castle ruins include a keep surrounded by a four-towered curtain wall. Beautifully sited between the village green and the banks of the Monnow, sunny summer days see the castle surrounded by picnickers, many eating ice creams from the shop opposite. Leave Skenfrith on the narrow northbound lane, passing St Brigit's church, where the road winds past the last of the cottages. The very narrow road lined by hedgerow wends it way through streamside farm pastures, before coming to a T-junction with the B4347.

2 Turn left here, then right at the next junction along the B4521 signed Abergavenny. Beyond the scattered hamlet of Walson the road climbs steadily uphill. Stay with the B-road at the next crossroads, ignoring the right turn to 'Dawn of the Day'. Beyond this there's a winding downhill section into the hamlet of Cross Ash.

3 At Cross Ash leave the B-road by a bus shelter on a sharp left-hand bend and turn right for Grosmont. Take the wider left fork at the next junction, heading steadily uphill with the partially wooded hill of Graig Syfyrddin up on the right.

4 Take the left fork, dropping past Grosmont Wood Farm. Views have opened out to show the distinctive craggy outlines of Ysgyryd Fawr (the Skirrid), then sweeping panoramas of the long ridges of the Black Mountains across the fields of the Monnow Valley. A lane joins in from the left, then you keep straight ahead at the next junction.

5 The road passes an old chapel and a cluster of houses at the junction with the Llanfihangel Crucorney road. Turn right by the phone kiosk and continue, now following the undulating lane signed for Grosmont. After 2.5 miles (4km) turn right along a narrow lane, again signed to Grosmont, to descend into the village.

6 Turn right along the B4347 through the attractive award-winning village, whose cottages have lovely gardens. The whitewashed Angel Inn, which is set back from an unusual sandstone village hall, offers a choice of tasty bar meals and West Country ales and has a pleasant beer garden to the rear. Gentle Jane's Tearoom is just down the road near the spired church. The castle, which is off to the left at the end of a short narrow lane overlooking the River Monnow, is surrounded by a deep moat – dry these days – and the skeletons of its ruined curtain walls, three towers and a gatehouse look rather gaunt against their verdant backdrop.

7 Returning to the B-road, continue past the campsite, ignoring the minor right fork lane. The route has now entered the Monnow Valley. If you want a food stop, the Part y Seal tea room is a well-signposted short detour on the left. Beyond the tea room the lane climbs right on the north side of Graig Syfyrddin. Ignore the minor right fork and leave the Monnow Valley behind. The road meets the outward route at Point 2, where you turn left and continue on the narrow lane back to Skenfrith.

DISTANCE/TIME 16 miles (26km) 2/3h **MAP** OS Explorer 200; OS Landranger Sheet 147 **START** Car park at Cwmdauddwr off B4518 west of Rhayader; grid ref: SN 966677 **TRACKS** Railway track and country lane **CYCLE HIRE** Clive Powell Mountain Bikes, Cwmdauddwr Arms, West St, Rhayader. Tel: 01597 811343 **THE PUB** The Elan Valley Hotel, Elan Village. Tel: 01597 810448

THE ELAN VALLEY TRAIL

An easy reservoir railway route with a little bit extra. It's a pleasant ride on well-surfaced paths and railway tracks through stunning scenery. The superb Victorian dams on the route are a bonus, especially when the headwaters are thundering down them. Benches near the dams offer a place to rest.

1 The trail starts on the opposite side of the road to the car park, you can't miss the sculptured wooden gate and gateposts by the artist Reece Ingram. Note the carved red kite on the gate. The tarred course of the old railway leads across fields. After about 500yds (450m) the track bypasses the old railway tunnel, now part of the Radnorshire Wildlife Trust Reserve. The tunnel has been modified as a habitat for hibernating bats.

2 Beyond the tunnel the route comes to the former junction with the Mid Wales Valley line, part of the Cambrian Railway (and later the Moat Lane and Brecon section of the GWR). Beyond this the track draws closer to the roadside again.

3 Around 2.5 miles (4km) from the start, the trail joins the road for a short distance turning left at a T-junction. From here you can either follow the road downhill to the visitor centre, which has a café, or cross the road to continue along the trail, which soon comes to the Caban-y-Coch dam.

4 If you need a rest there's the first of many sculptural benches just beyond the dam – they're at 0.6 miles (1km) intervals and were the work of artist Dominic Clare. The track now runs beside the reservoir with the rock-fringed slopes of Craig y Foel soaring above you on your right-hand side.

5 After curving, the track approaches the viaduct and submerged dam between the reservoirs of Garreg-Ddu and Caban-y-Coch. On the upstream side of the dam is the Foel Tower, where water is drawn and conveyed by tunnel to the filter beds, to eventually reach Birmingham which is 75 miles (120km) away. The submerged dam helps maintain a level sufficient to keep the Foel Tunnel charged with water, whilst the lower Caban-y-Coch lake would be used to discharge into the Afon Elan the mandatory 29,000 gallons (131,837 litres) a day required to keep the ecological status quo. The track continues past the Foel Tower along one of the most scenic parts of the route – lined by birch trees, and with the cliffs and screes of Craig Dolofau ahead.

6 The trackbed climbs to the road, which should be crossed (with care) before continuing on an incline through trees. It soon swings left to the top of the Pennygarreg dam, one of Elan's most spectacular sights when the foaming overspill waters are tumbling to the river below. You're on the level again now as the track passes beneath woods and through a section exploded through huge crags.

7 The trail ends at the fine 13-arched Craig Goch Reservoir dam where you can stop before retracing your route. A better option is to cross to the other side of the dam and then turn left along the road as it winds high above Pen-y-Garreg Reservoir, before descending through the woods beneath its dam. You now join the outward route at the bottom of the incline (Point 6) and then follow the track all the way back to Rhayader.

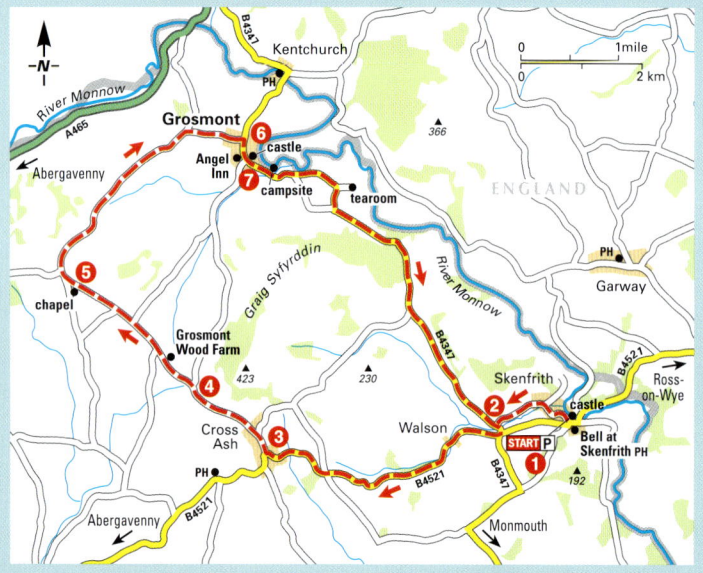

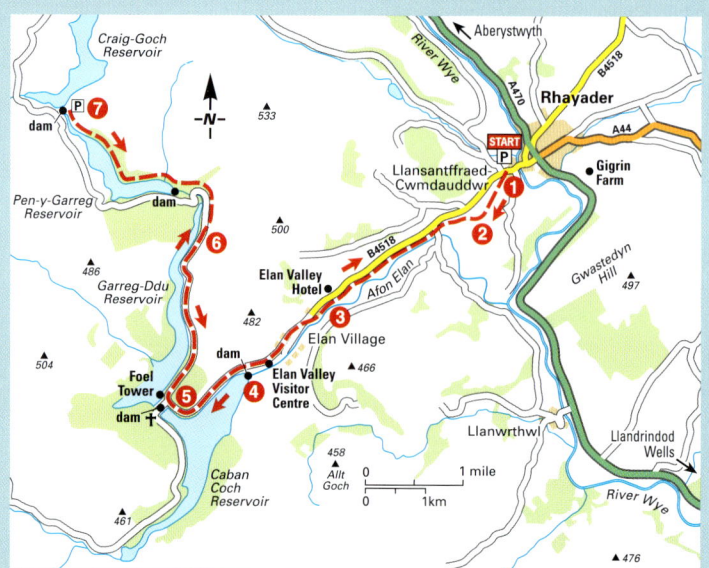

DISTANCE/TIME 6 miles (9.7km) 2h30 **MAP** OS Explorer: either 255 or 256; OS Landranger Sheet 117 **START** Llangollen Wharf; grid ref: SJ 215423 **TRACKS** Canal towpath, hilly country lanes **CYCLE HIRE** Llangollen Bike Hire. Tel: 01978 860605 **THE PUB** The Britannia Inn, Llangollen. Tel: 01978 860144

DISTANCE/TIME 14 miles (22.8km) 2h30 **MAP** OS Explorer17 Snowdonia, Snowdon & Conwy Valley **START** Slate quarry car park, Caernarfon; grid ref: SH477627 **TRACKS** Gravel cycle trail, quiet country lanes **CYCLE HIRE** Beics Menai Cycles, Slate Quay, Caernarfon. Tel: 01286 676804 **THE PUB** The Harp Inn, Tyn'llan, Llandwrog. Tel: 01286 831071

ACROSS THE LLANGOLLEN SKYLINE

Enjoy Llangollen's beautiful valley on a lofty skyline ride. The Dee Valley is one of Wales' most beautiful places. Verdant hills and a still-lively meandering river contrast with the extensive crags and screes of the Trefor Rocks. Although the ride is strenuous on the climbs, the route offers exquisite lofty views of the landscapes.

1 Fed by the waters of the River Dee, diverted at the Horseshoe Falls east of Llangollen, Thomas Telford's 43-mile (69km) narrowboat canal was completed in 1805. For many years barges carried slate and lime from the town and brought in coal from the nearby Ruabon coalfields. Today it is one of the best loved and most scenic of leisure canals. From Llangollen Wharf take the eastbound towpath past the narrowboat moorings. Through the trees there will be lovely views of the Dee Valley on the right and the castle-topped hill of Dinas Bran on the left. The canal passes under the Llangollen road.

2 Watch out for the whitewashed Sun Trevor pub on the left. When you see it, follow the exit track just preceding the canal bridge. Through a kissing gate the track climbs away from the towpath, before turning left over the bridge to the main road. Cross the road with care before following the lane opposite behind the inn. The climb is steep at first but it steadies as height is gained. Soon the lane is raking over the hillslopes high above the Dee and beneath limestone crags. A lane joins in from the right as you pass beneath Trevor Rocks. You are now following Offa's Dyke. The road descends for a while, with the domed knoll of Dinas Bran, which dominates the view ahead.

3 There's a footpath to the summit of Dinas Bran starting from a narrow lane on the left, and if there's time it would be a good idea to secure the bikes and detour on foot to the extensive castle ruins. When you get to the top, the ruins are large and impressive. The castle was almost certainly built for the Princes of Powys, but you can still see the embankment of a much earlier Iron Age fort. The Welsh castle's demise isn't known for certain, but it was probably laid waste by Edward I. Back on the cycle route, the high lane, which is lined by twisted hawthorn trees, climbs steadily beneath the tiered limestone cliffs with the rocks of Creigiau Eglwyseg ahead.

4 The views are so wide-sweeping and magnificent that it seems a shame to come down, but to avoid using busy main roads the route turns left on a lane signed to Llangollen. After passing Garth Wood the narrow lane descends steeply (take care).

5 Turn left at the next T-junction, Dinbren Road and then right at a crossroads by Tower Farm Campsite (Tower Road). This brings you down to the A542 after crossing the Llangollen canal.

6 Don't cross the road but turn left along the pavement, then go left through the smaller of two gates on to the canal towpath. This route leads back to Llangollen Wharf, where the café awaits to offer refreshments.

BETWEEN THE MOUNTAINS & THE MENAI STRAITS - CAERNARFON

This ride is a delight for cyclists looking for a gentle ride with just a few hills. The route takes you through an old railway trail and quiet country lanes as you peddle through through the countryside, enjoying views of majestic Snowdonia to the east and across to Anglesey to the west.

1 From Slate Quay car park, pass the Harbour Offices to join a road between the railway line and warehouses. In 300 yards (274m) join the old trackbed on the left and pass beneath the impressive Lon Eifion cycle route sign. With the Welsh Highland railway to your left, gradually climb above the harbour and leave the town. Cross a lane by a house , signposted 'Hendy', continue to cross another road and keep to the trail to reach Bontnewydd, where you cross the Afon Gwyrfai. Gently ascend through a cuttting, pass Dinas station to reach a road at Llanwnda, with the village church to your left.

2 If you wish to continue south on the traffic-free trail (returning to Llanwnda), go round the gate opposite. Otherwise, go right along the narrow lane for 2 miles (3.2km) ignoring a turning on the right and soon drop down to the waters of the Afon Carrog. Climb to a junction. go right and then left at the next junction to reach Llandwrog. Turn right by the Harp Inn; the road descends to a junction in 0.5 mile (0.8km). Go right for Dinas Dinlle and soon reach the seafront.

3 Retrace your route to Llandwrog and turn left before the Harp Inn, still on your outward bound route. Keep to this lane for 0.75 mile (1.2km) to cross the Afon Carrog and pass a small cluster of buildings (telephone box). Continue to a sharp right bend and bear off left along a quiet narrow road leading to Foryd Bay. The lane bears right close to the water's edge, eventually reaching a crossroads. Go left here through the hamlet of Saron.

4 The road descends to a bridge at Pont Faen, crossing the Afon Gwyrfai, and rises to a junction, just before the Llanfaglan village sign. Turn left and continue for less than 0.5 mile (0.8km) to the water's edge at Foryd Bay, with excellent views across the Isle of Anglesey. This delightful lane hugs the coast and passes the small windswept Llanfaglan church, isolated in a field to your right. The road bears right and runs along the front of the harbour at Caernarfon. Wheel your cycle across the Aber footbridge and retun to the castle and the start point of the ride.

Brecon Beacons & Central Wales

CLOCKWISE FROM TOP: RIVER USK AND BLACK MOUNTAINS; PENNYWORT, LLYN BRIANNE RESERVOIR; LLANGORSE LAKE; MAEN LLIA (LLIA'S STONE), FOREST FAWR

ABERGAVENNY MAP REF 402 F7

Abergavenny, which is by far the largest town in the upper Usk Valley, occupies a large basin surrounded by three very distinctly shaped mountains: the cone-shaped Sugar Loaf Mountain and the craggy Ysgyryd Fawr in the north; Blorenge in the south. It's also well situated as a base to explore the Black Mountains and the Brecon Beacons.

Although it took a pounding after the Civil War, Abergavenny's Norman castle is still worth seeing, as is the museum next door. There's no shortage of castles in the surrounding area too. Raglan lies 10 miles (16km) east along the A40, while the lesser-known 'three castles' of Grosmont, Skenfrith and White Castle are hidden away in low, rolling hills a few miles to the east. Along some of the narrowest country lanes imaginable in the beautiful Vale of Ewyas, lie the romantic ruins of Llanthony Priory founded by Augustinian canons early in the 12th century.

For visitors who find Abergavenny a little too busy – they do get traffic jams here – Crickhowell, up the Usk Valley, is a picturesque village that is well sited for many of the attractions in the area.

BRECON & PEN Y FAN

MAP REF 402 F6

Although the Romans made their home here, Brecon's roots date back to the 5th century when it was governed by the Celtic chieftain, Brychan, who gave his name to the town. Situated at the confluences of three rivers, the Usk, Honddu and Tarell, the town grew in importance during Norman times when a Benedictine monastery, a castle and formidable town walls were built. In the Act of Union of 1536 Brecon was listed as one of four local capitals and in 1542 Henry VIII set up a chancery here, installing the exchequer in the castle.

In modern Brecon the once-important castle's remains are no more than a battlemented wall set in the gardens of the Castle of Brecon Hotel, while only fragments of the town wall still stand near Captains Walk.

St John's Church, part of the monastery, survived Henry VIII's Dissolution and in 1923 it was elevated to cathedral status. The impressive old, red sandstone building was extensively refurbished in 1872 by Sir Gilbert Scott, whose finest work is the chancel's vaulted ceiling.

The town centre's buildings are a mix of Georgian, Jacobean and Tudor, with a network of narrow streets leading off the Bulwark. The 19th-century Shire Hall with its Athenian-style columns, houses the lively and fascinating Brecknock Museum and Art Gallery, while Brecon's military history is well-recorded and celebrated at the Museums of the Royal Regiment of Wales in the Barracks.

Each August, Brecon swings to its own jazz festival – one of Britain's premier jazz events. For those who like old steam railways, the Brecon Mountain Railway puffs 7 miles (11km) from Pant just north of Merthyr Tydfil, into the foothills of the Brecon Beacons. You can see the repair workshop for the locomotives at Pant.

Seemingly always in view from the town and riverbanks, the Beacons' twin peaks, Pen y Fan (2,907feet/886m) and Corn Du (2,863feet/873m) display their angular outlines, finely sculpted northern cliffs and shadowy cwms to perfection. The proliferation of walking gear shops in the town shows that many visitors come to walk and there's no finer place than Brecon to explore southern Britain's highest mountains, the Black Mountains.

Visit
DEVIL'S BRIDGE

The Vale of Rheidol narrow-gauge railway takes passengers on an hour-long journey to Devil's Bridge. At Devil's Bridge coin-operated turnstiles allow access to paths into a spectacular wooded gorge where you'll see three bridges, one on top of another (legend has it that the lowest one was built with the help of the Devil) and the Mynach Falls.

Visit
PLYNLIMON

Plynlimon Fawr (Pumlumon in Welsh) is one of the country's three principle mountains – the other two are Snowdon and Cadair Idris. George Borrow, a 19th-century writer, loved the mountain, and sipped the water from the sources of its rivers, the Severn, the Wye and the Rheidol. Two corners of this wild mountain that are worth visiting are Llyn Llygad Rheidol to the north of the main summit, and Glaslyn, a high windswept lake reached by car from the Machynlleth–Llanidloes mountain road.

PEN Y FAN

Visit
WATERFALL COUNTRY

Four streams, the Nedd, Pyrddin, Mellte and Hepste, tumble from the moors of Fforest Fawr to cut deep gorges through the more permeable limestone rocks. They create a series of spectacular waterfalls in the woods north of Pontneddfechan. All are approachable by footpath from car parks south of Ystradfellte.

Visit
LLANTHONY PRIORY

A little road climbs south from Hay over the Gospel Pass before descending into the beautiful Vale of Ewyas, where the romantic ruins of Llanthony Priory bask in the beauty of its surroundings and the backdrop of the Black Mountains. The Priory was established in 1103. After an attack by Owain Glyn Dwr the priory was left ruinous, but there are still substantial arches, walls and towers to explore. Unusually, you can enjoy the view over a pie and a pint, as there's a pub in the grounds.

Visit
CENTRE FOR ALTERNATIVE TECHNOLOGY

The Centre for Alternative Technology was founded in 1973 and utilised the disused Llwyngwern slate quarry, 2 miles (3.2km) north of Machynlleth. The centre now has a workforce of 90 permanent staff and volunteers on the 7-acre (2.8ha) site. Visitors can get up the hill on an amazing water-powered cliff railway. They will see exciting interactive displays along with some practical ideas for their own homes.

Insight
HAY-ON-WYE LITERARY FESTIVAL

The Hay Festival was likened to a cult music event, which took place in the 1960s, by former American President Bill Clinton in2001, when he referred to the festival as 'The Woodstock of the mind'. Renowned throughout the world as 'the' place to be at the end of each May by bibliophiles, the festival draws speakers from the worlds of publishing and politics as well as people from the performing arts. The festival is open to everyone and attracts families with small children. The event is the brainchild of Richard Booth, who opened a secondhand bookshop in the little town in 1961 and the idea of a festival began. Today, Hay-on-Wye is also known as Booktown.

GLYNTAWE & UPPER SWANSEA VALLEY MAP REF 402 E7

The transition from stark industrial landscapes to rural ones happens very suddenly in the Swansea Valley. One minute you're in Ystradgynlais on the edge of the old coalfields, the next you've turned the corner past Abercraf into the magical garden-like landscapes of Glyntawe and you're staring across the River Tawe up to the limestone crags of Cribarth, a southern outlier of the Black Mountain. Glyntawe, a sprawling village, is one of the best starting points for a climb on the Fan Hir escarpment to the highest Black Mountain summit, Fan Brycheiniog.

The limestone geology of the valley has left it with its major attraction, the Dan yr Ogof Caves, discovered in 1912. This is Wales' largest subterranean cavern system extending to 10 miles (16km), where visitors can enter a weird world of impressive stalactites, stalagmites and underground waterfalls brought to life with lighting and music.

The south side of the valley is dominated by Craig y Nos Castle, once home to world-famous Victorian opera singer Adelina Patti. This Gothic mansion, now a grand hotel, is surrounded by superb riverside gardens with mature woodland fringing meres and meadows, which now form a valuable part of the Craig y Nos Country Park.

HAY-ON-WYE MAP REF 402 F6

Hay-on-Wye lies in the northeast corner of the Brecon Beacons National Park by the sleepy banks of the River Wye, and sheltered by the sweeping slopes of the Black Mountains. With the flower-decked meadows and rolling green hills of Radnorshire in the north, spring and summer in Hay are delightful times.

The name 'hay' comes from the Norman word *haie* meaning 'enclosed place'. It's known that there was a settlement here when King Offa of Mercia built his dyke here in the 8th century. There are only fragmented remains of the old Norman town walls in the Newport Street area, but this would have been a heavily fortified border town since the 13th century when William de Breos built his castle. The baron soon fell out with King John and was forced to flee to France, where he died in poverty; it's believed that after sacking the castle King John's men starved the baron's wife and child to death. Further attacks and destruction came at the hands of Llewelyn the Great and Owain Glyn Dwr, and by fire as late as 1977.

Today Hay is a vibrant market town known for its 30-plus secondhand and antiquarian bookshops, and tourists come from all over the world to visit the annual literary festival. Among a maze of narrow streets you'll discover many fascinating old buildings, including a colonnaded

19th-century butter market, the attractive 16th-century Three Tuns pub, which still has its horse-mounting block outside, and the Victorian clock tower.

LLANDOVERY & TYWI VALLEY
MAP REF 402 E6

Llandovery, known here as Llanymyddfri – 'the church amongst the waters' – was described by the 19th-century writer, George Borrow, as 'the pleasantest little town in which I have halted in the course of my wanderings'.

The area was once occupied by the Romans, whose fort, Alabum, was sited near to St Mary's Church by the Afon Bran to the north of the town. The castle, which was built for the Norman baron Richard Fitz Pons in the 12th century, was captured by the Welsh in the Glyn Dwr Revolts. It changed hands several times over the centuries. In 1532 its owner, Rhys-ap-Gruffydd, was executed at the behest of Henry VIII for treason and, in an act of revenge by the Welsh, the castle was destroyed, never to be rebuilt. A recently erected statue of Llewelyn ap Grufydd stands guard on the grassy mound beneath the remains of the castle keep.

Across the car park from the statue you'll find the Heritage Centre where you can get information about the many walks in the area, and discover the myths and history of the region.

YSTRADFELLTE

LLANGORS

Llandovery's history is intertwined with the fortunes of the cattle drovers. When thieves made travelling on Wales' rugged roads a hazardous exercise, the local farmers hired the drovers to drive cattle to the more lucrative markets of England and to settle accounts for them with non-local people. This meant that drovers needed to handle large sums of money and led to the introduction of banking systems, some of them even issuing bank notes. One of the most successful of these was David Jones' Black Ox Bank, which was taken over at the turn of the 20th century by Lloyds.

To the south of Llandovery, the Black Mountain (or Mynydd Du as it is known in Wales) lies at the western end of the Brecon Beacon Range, rising in grand escarpments of old red sandstone. Glacial action has formed magnificent cliffs on the northern and eastern faces of the group and also provided two lovely tarns: Llyn y Fan Fawr and Llyn y Fan Fach. Myddfai, which is sheltered in the northern foothills of the Black Mountain, is a particularly picturesque village with a fine 13th-century church and splendid country pub, the Plough, which is well worth a visit for a pint.

LLANGORS MAP REF 402 F6

The little village of Llangors is delightful in itself but what makes it a real gem are the magnificent views of the Brecon Beacons that can be had from its superb location. Not only is the village blessed with such a grand vista, but is also a only couple of miles away from the largest natural lake in South Wales.

Llangors lake stretches for a mile (1.6km) in length and half a mile (0.8km) in width, and covers an area of 327 acres (132 ha), although to walk around its circumference would be a 5-mile (8km) trek. The lake has drawn settlers since ancient Celtic times and was mentioned in the 12th century by Gerald of Wales, who commented that the beautiful lake had plenty of waterfowl.

A striking feature of the lake is the crannog, or man-made defensive island, at its centre. The island is thought to date back to 889–893 AD. It is also thought to have been one of the royal sites of medieval Brycheiniog, one of the kingdoms of medieval Wales.

Today, Llangors draws people still and every year the village is full of enthusiastic musicians who come to take part and enjoy its popular music festival, which features folk-rock, jazz and even an experienced ceilidh band. There are also children's entertainments laid on and the atmosphere is relaxed and welcoming.

The lake draws a different crowd and is the perfect place for watersports lovers and anglers (coarse fishing). All types of boating fun takes place here including sailing, canoeing and water-skiing, and the surrounding countryside and mountains are delightful for walking and hiking. Those with equine interests can horse ride in the area or you can get a birds-eye-view of the dramatic landscape if you go up in a glider from the Black Mountains Gliding Club. The excellent Llangorse Rope Centre is the place to go to practice your climbing skills for later adventures in bouldering or pot-holing.

Llangors lake is a site of Special Scientific Interest mainly because it is naturally eutrophic. This means that the water is naturally high in nutrients which tends to make it appear slightly murky. It also means, however, that the habitat is highly productive which goes a long way to explain why this expanse of water is so popular with waterfowl.

Visit
THE DINAS NATURE RESERVE

This RSPB reserve, which lies 10 miles (16km) north of Llandover, has a footpath over wetlands and through oak woodland to the steep slopes of Dinas. There's a cave in the crags here, where Twm Sion Catti, the Welsh Robin Hood, hid from his enemies. Red kites can often be seen soaring above the trees and in summer, you can also see dippers, pied flycatchers, common sandpipers and grey wagtails.

Visit
GIGRIN FARM RED KITE FEEDING STATION

Gigrin Farm, an upland sheep farm on the A470, 0.6 mile (1km) south of Rhayader, is an official RSPB feeding station for red kites. It's fascinating to see first the noisy crows arriving on the scene, then the red kites and buzzards swooping down to foil the smaller birds. The number of kites visiting here can vary from a dozen to around 400 or so. Feeding the birds takes place every afternoon.

Machynlleth Alternative Technologies

Home to a proud nation of people, a place of verdant valleys and numerous rugged and rather splendid mountains, Wales, the central part of the country in particular, is also home to the interesting Centre for Alternative Technology (CAT), an award-winning eco-centre, and a living example of what we each can do to make the world a cleaner, much more pleasant place and to help our environment to last longer. Quite early on in your visit to CAT you are told that the 'earth is one big creature working together; if we don't interfere, it should last forever'. Wishful thinking, perhaps, but this is what the Centre is all about: making you think.

CAT is dedicated to exploring and demonstrating 'globally sustainable, whole and ecologically sound technologies and ways of life'. It explains and teaches sustainable development, but despite its name does not give undue attention to alternative technology, focusing instead on general environmentalism. The Centre is open to visitors throughout the year, holds residential courses, and publishes information on organic farming, gardening, and ecologically friendly living. Rather than the doom and gloom, or off-beat view of things normally associated with 'alternative' anything, the Centre takes a constructive and elevating approach, demonstrating all kinds of environmental technologies in an interesting and informative way.

Without actually going there you might be forgiven for thinking that the Centre is some time-warp hippie and idealist-populated drop-out manifestation. In fact it's a hugely pleasurable and thought-provoking visitor attraction – and there's no sign of sackcloth, ashes, incense or sandals, or even doing without meat. The Centre is based on realism and embraces all forms of positive change.

CAT was the brainchild of and was founded by old Etonian businessman-turned-environmentalist Gerard Morgan-Grenville. It was opened in 1974. The centre utilises the disused Llwyngwern slate quarry near Machynlleth, where it occupies a 7-acre (2.5ha) site. When the quarry was operational, the slate was sent via the narrow gauge Corris railway to Machynlleth where it was then transferred for onward shipment via the mainline railways to help supply the building trade throughout the country.

Some 12 people live permanently at CAT, and they and all the facilities are largely self-sustaining. This is achieved with a good supply of solar-and hydro-power, productive fruit and vegetable gardens, a reed-bed sewerage system and free-range hens for fresh eggs. The on-site restaurant is, as you might expect, notoriously but wholesomely vegetarian. Facilities include a water-balanced funicular railway, solar-, hydro- and wind-power, a low-energy house, a site-wide electricity grid powered by renewable energy (any excess is sold to the national grid), displays of organic gardening methods, a hydraulic ram pump and straw-bale and rammed-earth buildings.

This is not some ramshackle ghetto of tents, lean-to's and life-style protesters, but an in-depth, well-researched, thoughtful and highly sophisticated illustration of green technology at work. The funicular railway that greets your arrival is powered by water; you climb into the bottom car, making it heavier, and water is released into tanks in the top car to balance it out. When there is sufficient weight above, the top car descends, hauling the bottom one up. The site, now occupied by the water-operated funicular was formerly the quarry incline with two parallel tracks. The weight of the loaded wagons coming down was used to haul up the returning empties with a wood and cast-iron winding drum at the top controlled by a braking system to prevent runaways.

Water-balanced funicular technology was very widespread in the 19th century, but most of the funiculars were progressively replaced by electrically operated systems. The CAT railway is the only modern, water-operated funicular.

There are around 20 buildings in all, with different examples of low impact eco-buildings like the straw bale theatre. But they are all practical visions of ecologically benign living, showing, in this world-climate-conscious era, how heat, power, water, food and waste can be handled with a minimal eco-footprint.

On the face of it, you might think that CAT would be all too sophisticated for children. But quite the contrary. Specifically catering for children there are activities that explain solar wind and wave power, an adventure playground, a maze, and a smallholding with farm animals – but there is an important message too. The Centre has its own reservoir and water supply in an old slate quarry, and its own sewage systems. In fact the treatment of sewage is one of the Centre's most famous pioneering achievements, using composting toilets and reed beds, although you may not want to investigate this splendid achievement too closely.

Adults will find the Centre immensely edifying, intentionally so, with illustrations of sustainable architecture in cut-away houses that explain how much more environmentally friendly our lifestyles might be. The Centre is also a reliable source on almost any aspect of organic gardening and sustainable living. There's lots of information available on energy conservation, compost-making and other important aspects of gardening organically. Equally important are the way we do things – like avoiding chemicals when gardening, achieving more with less, and not excluding nature from our living and working spaces.

In the final analysis, CAT expounds a belief in valuing communities, and their right to control their immediate environments. The Centre for Alternative Technologies is one of the very few places in the UK where you can get holistic advice covering every aspect of energy use and environmental impact. They can help with everything from changing light bulbs to building a new house. In this way, the knowledge and experience gleaned from the Centre's 30 years of existence and research can be passed on in simple, practical ways so that everyone can feel that they are contributing in some small way to avoiding the slow pollution and destruction of the environment.

For those who want to consider these topics to a higher degree, the Centre is also home to a successful MSc course in Advanced Environmental and Energy Studies. Run by the University of East London, the course is based entirely at CAT and covers many aspects of environmental science and its business applications.

There is also a regular programme of short- and long-term volunteer placements for those who wish to get involved with the work of The Centre for Alternative Technologies, covering specific tasks and buidling work as well as administrative duties. Contact CAT or visit www.cat.org.uk for information and details.

LEFT FROM TOP Solar panels fitted to the Information Centre roof play a vital part in the self-sustaining power supply here.

Rich, nutrient loaded compost is used throughout the gardens at CAT.

This innocent-looking hut contains the Rocket Composter – an innovative device that turns kitchen and restaurant waste into nutrient-rich soil ready to use for vegetable growing, all in a couple of weeks. The clever design features a well-insulated chamber in which the vegetable matter is turned over by a screw every day, so accelerating the decomposing process.

RIGHT FROM TOP The eco-cabins blend easily into the environment and are powered by their own renewable energy system. Cabins also have monitoring systems so that residents can monitor their input and output of energy.

Wind-power is a vital 'clean' energy source and this community turbine in the Dyfi Valley is thought to save some 70 tonnes of carbon dioxide emissions each year.

Insight

THE PHYSICIANS OF MYDDFAI

Llyn y Fan Fach at the northern foot of the Black Mountain is an eerie place to be when the mists swirl around the gullies, and it's not surprising that there's some mystery and legend lurking beneath its waters. From its depths a flaxen-haired fairy appeared and enchanted a local farmer's boy, Rhiwallon. After altercations with her husband the fairy returned to the waters. However, the couple sired three sons, who would learn from their mother about medicine. The boys became the first in a line of Physicians of Myddfai, the last was Dr C Rice Williams of Aberystwyth, who died in 1842.

Visit

FOREST FAWR GEOPARK

The area in the Brecon Beacons known as Forest Fawr was designated a Geopark in October 2005 by UNESCO. Forest Fawr is the Welsh translation for 'Great Forest' and it is within this great forest that you will find some of the great natural wonders of Wales. The Geopark encompasses the Welsh National Snow Caves and the Brecon Beacons' mighty reservoirs.

MACHYNLLETH MAP REF 402 E4

Machynlleth shelters on high ground to the south of the wide valley of the Dyfi, where the mountains of Snowdonia give way to the rolling foothills of Plynlimon. A fine 17th-century four-arched stone bridge spans the river on the road leading into this small market town. An 80-foot (24m) Victorian clock tower of an extremely ornate design forms the hub of this town centre and looks down on a wide Maengwyn Street, where the weekly Wednesday markets are held. Here you'll also find Parliament House, a medieval town house standing on the site of the building where Owain Glyn Dwr held the last independent Welsh Parliament in 1404. It now hosts an Owain Glyn Dwr interpretative centre. The 14th-century Royal House at the junction of Garsiwn Lane and Penrallt Street is so called because Charles I stayed here in 1644.

Plas Machynlleth and its parklands, which lie between Maengwyn Street and the hills to the south, is a mansion built between the 17th and 19th centuries for the Marquis of Londonderry. The property was left to the town on the 7th Marquess' death in 1948 and now houses the fascinating Celtica heritage centre.

Today Machynlleth has an appealing mix of all things Welsh, Celtic mysticism, and green idealism. The unusual shops and the wholefood café are a testament to this, as is the Centre for Alternative Technology. The townsfolk were a bit dubious when the 'hippies' first set up the alternative living centre, but their fortunes are now intertwined.

RHANDIRMWYN MAP REF 402 E6

Once an important old lead-mining village, Rhandirmwyn lies in the valley of the Upper Tywi, 9 miles (14km) north of Llandovery. This is a real haven for those who like riverside walks, angling and bird-spotting. Two fine bird reserves are set among the riverside crags, where the boisterous Tywi and Doethie rivers twist between rocky, oak-clad peaks. Beneath the conical hill called Dinas, the rivers converge in a violent cauldron of foam.

A short way upstream, where the Doethie meets the Pysgotwr, is one of the wildest gorges in Mid Wales. A few miles north of Rhandirmwyn along winding lanes, Llyn Brianne Reservoir is among plantations of spruce and larch in the narrow valleys of the Tywi and Camddwr.

RHAYADER MAP REF 402 F5

Rhayader's full Welsh name is Rhaeadr Gwy, meaning 'waterfall on the Wye'. The waterfall to which it refers was actually blown up in 1780 to make way for the bridge over the river.

Dominated by its opulent Victorian clock tower, which lies at the crossroads in the centre of the village, Rhayader is a very pleasant town set among some of the finest river scenery in Mid Wales. The poet Percy Shelley was drawn to these parts in 1809. He lived in the cottage of Nantgwyllt in the Elan Valley, then a famed beauty spot. However, the planned flooding of the Elan Valley was to change the nature of the scenery forever.

In the first part of the scheme, four reservoirs, the Craig Goch, Penygarreg, Carreg-ddu and Caban-coch were created. Nantgwyllt was among the dwellings submerged by the reservoirs. A church, chapel, school and numerous farms were submerged when the scheme was completed in 1904. A fifth reservoir, the Claerwen, was completed in 1952. Some one hundred years later the reservoirs have blended almost seamlessly with their surroundings and the power of the dams, and the white waters thundering down them, adds great character to the landscape. The visitor centre gives an intriguing insight into the construction of the dams, the railway built to supply them and the lives of the construction workers involved in the project. The old railway trackbed now forms the Elan Valley Trail, which is a marvellous facility for waterside walking or cycling.

RHANDIRMWYN

WALK 87

PORTH YR OGOF, ALONG THE WATERFALLS

You could start or end this walk with a visit to the Porth yr Ogof caves. The route takes in lovely riverside scenery and four waterfalls created as the inland rivers rush through the mountainous area. At Sgwd yr Eira you can walk behind the waterfall (take care as the path here can be slippery).

DISTANCE/TIME 4 miles (6.4km) 2h Ascent: 360ft (110m) **MAP** Aqua3 OS Explorer OL12 Brecon Beacons National Park Western & Central areas **START** Grid ref: SN 928124 **PATHS** Riverside paths, some rough sections and steps, no stiles **THE PUB** The New Inn, Ystradfellte, Aberdare. Tel: 01639 720211

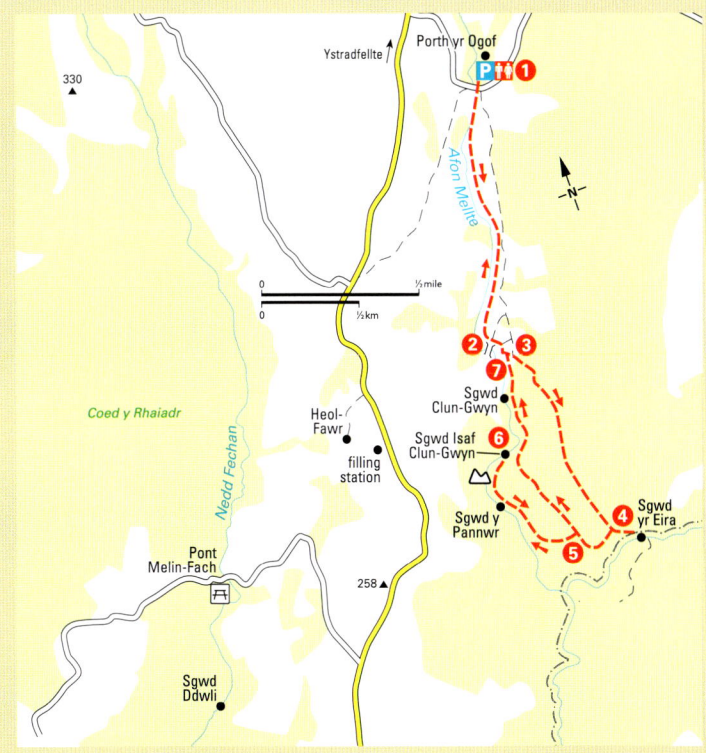

1 Cross the road at the entrance to the car park and head down towards the left of two paths, clearly waymarked with a yellow arrow. Follow this left-hand path on to the river bank, then keep the river to your right and follow a rough footpath eventually through two kissing gates to reach a footbridge.

2 Continue straight ahead, and then drop into a dip and afterwards climb steeply out. Keep left to climb to a broken wall where the path forks. Take the left fork here (the bottom right-hand path has a fence along it) and follow close to the edge of the wood. When you see some odd green-banded marker posts, follow them to the waymarked crossroads where you turn right, now following red-banded posts.

3 Continue through a dark tunnel of trees and emerge into more evenly spaced deciduous woodland. Continue to follow the waymarked trail until you get to a post directing you on a downhill track. Follow this track and then bear around to the right when you reach the edge of the forest. This leads to the top of a set of wooden steps, on the left.

4 Go down the steps to Sgwd yr Eira (Waterfall of the Snow) and then, having edged along the bank and walked behind the falls (waterproofs are recommended), retrace your steps back to the edge of the wood. Turn left and continue, still following the red-banded posts, to a fork marked with a green-banded post.

5 Turn left and descend to the riverside. Turn left again here to Sgwd y Pannwr (Fullers Falls) and then turn around to walk upstream to Sgwd Isaf Clun-Gwyn (Lower Waterfall of the White Meadow). Take extra care here, as the ground is very steep and rough around the best viewpoint place.

6 Retrace your steps downstream to your descent path and then turn left to climb back up to the fork at the top. Turn left here and follow the red-banded waymarkers along to Sgwd Clun-gwyn, where there's a fenced-off viewing area. From this point on the walk, continue along the main trail to the place where you split off earlier on.

7 Keep to the left-hand side to drop into a dip and retrace your steps past the footbridge and back to Porth yr Ogof.

WALK 88

PEN Y FAN – THE BEACONS HORSESHOE

This is the connoisseur's way up to the high ground of Pen y Fan, the highest summit in the Brecons. Pen y Fan, with its twin summit of Corn Du, and Cribyn and Fan y Big, form a 'horseshoe' around the head of a river. The going is steep from the car park on to the head of the remote Cwm Gwdi where the path then follows rocky old quarry tracks before it passes on to the grassy spur that leads on to Cefn Cwm Llwch, a good walk where you will be rewarded with magnificent views.

DISTANCE/TIME 7 miles (11.3km) 4h Ascent: 2,100ft (640m) **MAP** Aqua3 OS Explorer OL12 Brecon Beacons National Park Western & Central **START** Grid ref: SO 025248 **PATHS** Well-defined paths and tracks, some quiet lanes, 4 stiles **PARKING** Car park at end of small lane, 3 miles (4.8km) south of Brecon **THE PUB** Markets Tavern Hotel, Brecon. 01874 623595

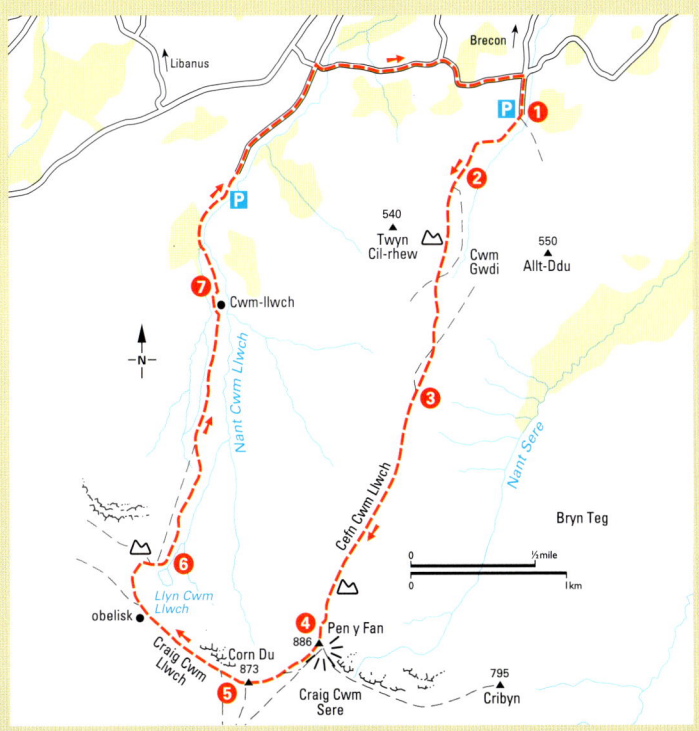

1 Walk uphill from the car park and pass an information plinth before crossing a stile. Walk along the right-hand side of a field to the top right-hand corner and then bear left to continue along a fence to another stile.

2 Follow a broad but faint grassy track straight on. It gradually becomes a better-defined stony track that swings slightly left and climbs up the hillside. Continue ahead, up towards the head of Cwm Gwdi, and keep ahead, ignoring a few right forks, until the path levels out on Cefn Cwm Llwch.

3 Continue along the ridge towards the summit ahead. As you reach the foot of the peak, the track steepens considerably, offering views over a perilous gully that drops into Cwm Sere on the left. Continue to climb steeply over a few rocky steps to reach the summit cairn on Pen y Fan.

4 Bear right to follow the escarpment edge along and drop into the shallow saddle beneath the rising crest of Corn Du. Continue up on to this summit, then bear left to drop down through rocky outcrops on to

easier ground below. Bear sharp right once you reach the grassy hillside to walk north beneath the peak.

5 Continue down the hill and pass Tommy Jones obelisk with the steep crags of Craig Cwm Llwch on your right. Above the lake, the path forks; take the right-hand option and drop steeply, around a dog-leg and over moraine banks to the lake shore.

6 A clear track leads north from the lake; follow it over easy ground to cross a wall that leads on to a broad farm track. Take this down to the gate in front of a building and climb the stile on the left. Cross the compound and climb another stile to follow the waymarker posts around to the right on to another track, beyond the building.

7 Bear left on to this track and follow it down, over a footbridge, to a parking area. Keep ahead, through a gate to a T-junction, where you turn right. Cross the bridge and continue for over 1 mile (1.6km) to another T-junction. Turn right and walk uphill back to the car park.

RHAYADER ELAN VALLEY EXPLORER

This simple circuit explores some of the remote hillsides above the Elan Valley – a beautiful area around a chain of lakes. Note that navigating this route is difficult in poor light. The Elan Valley is an area of outstanding beauty and it is a haven for plant and wildlife, although its dams were created with the more practical intention of supplying the people of Birmingham with water.

DISTANCE/TIME 5.5 miles (8.8km) 2h30 Ascent: 1,050ft (320m) **MAP** Aqua3 OS Explorer 200 Llandrindod Wells & Elan Valley **START** Grid ref: SN 899720 **PATHS** A mix of good tracks and faint paths over moorland that can be boggy, 1 stile **PARKING** Small car park by the bridge at the start **THE PUB** Triangle Inn, Rhayader. Tel: 01597 810537

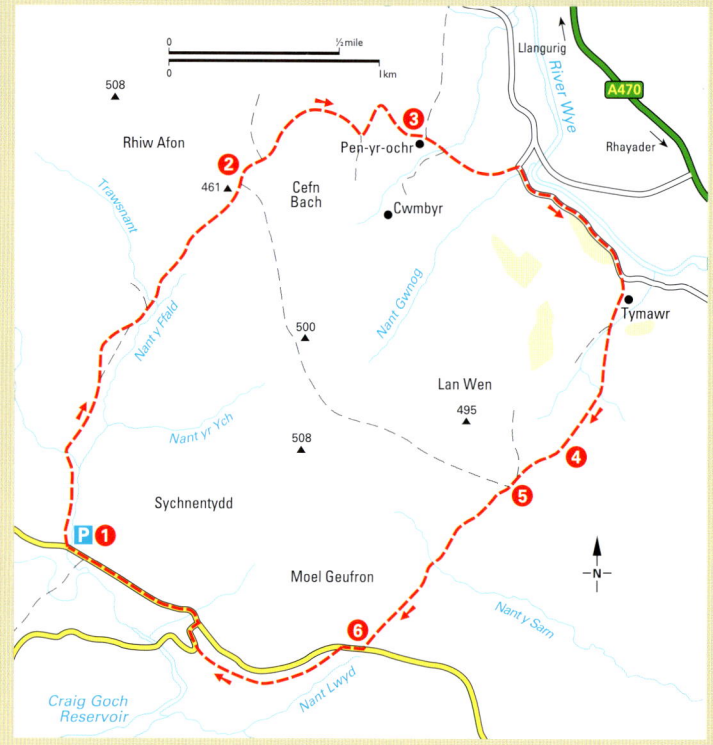

1 To begin the walk, turn right out of the car park and cross over a bridge. Turn right on to a stony track and then follow it easily up into the valley. As the main track bears sharp left, keep straight ahead on very faint path that continues up the valley. As you reach a shallow pass at the top, cross over to the other side of the valley.

2 Here you'll find a good track that contours around to the east and drops down into the Wye Valley. When you get to the junction with another track, turn left and go through a gate to drop into the bottom left-hand corner of a field. Turn right here and continue forward into a farmyard.

3 Bear left and then right and continue along a drive to a second turning on the right, waymarked 'Wye Valley Walk'. Turn right and continue to the drive of Tymawr on the right. Walk up the drive and pass by the house until you get to a fork where you keep left. Continue along this clear track, above a plantation, to a stile.

4 Go across this and keep left to climb up towards the plateau at the head of the valley. Don't follow the more obvious track, which

clearly contours around the head of the valley. When you reach the top, keep heading in same direction until you meet a faint track and a bank that run across hilltops.

5 Turn right for a few yards and then bear diagonally left, down the open hillside, aiming for the lowest point of the road that you can see on the opposite hillside. Contour around slightly and cross a small stream. Continue in the same direction, keeping to the grassy hillside just above the boggy hollow that is on your lefthand side.

6 Turn right on to road and then fork left on to the narrow path runing parallel to the road but below it. Follow this to Elan Valley Road and turn right, to climb up to a junction, and then left to continue back to the car park.

CENTRAL BRECON BEACONS – CWMCYNWYN

This walks follows airy ridges to some of the lesser-visited peaks of the Brecon Beacons. One such peak is that of Cribyn, which stands at an altitude of 2,608 feet (795m) and is a particularly great place for taking photographs of the magnificent and dramatic scenery all around.

DISTANCE/TIME 9.5 miles (15.3km) 5h30 Ascent: 2,360ft (719m) **MAP** Aqua3 OS Outdoor Leisure 12 Brecon Beacons National Park **START** Grid ref: SH 039244 **PATHS** Mostly clear paths along broad grassy ridges, 3 stiles **THE PUB** Clarence Inn, 25 Watton, Brecon. Tel: 01874 622810

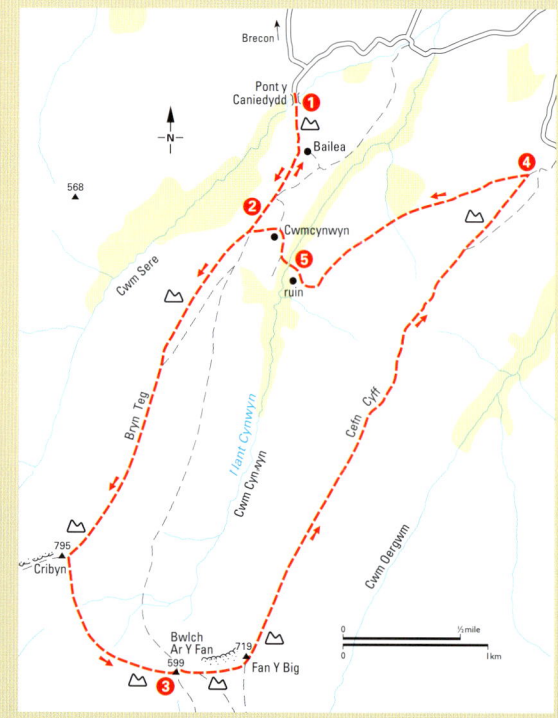

1 Cross the bridge and climb steeply up the road past Bailea on your left. Keep walking straight ahead when you eventually reach a junction where the road levels. From this point, follow a stony track up to the gate that leads further on to an area of open ground by a National Trust sign.

2 Continue walking straight up the track and then fork right, climb over a stile, to then again climb, but more steeply, on to the crest of a grassy ridge. Follow the ridge along and then climb steeply again up the sharp snout of Cribyn. (A good spot to stop and take photos.) Bear left at the summit and follow the escarpment edge along, eventually dropping steeply down into Bwlch ar y Fan.

3 Cross the track in the saddle and then proceed to climb steeply up the hillside opposite. Bear around to the left at the top of the hill and continue up the summit of Fan y Big. Keep going ahead in the same direction to drop steeply down the broad grassy ridge. The going then eases for a while, steepens again for a short distance but then eases once again. Continue until the path drops steeply once more, to the edge of open ground.

4 At this point of the walk, bear left, towards the bottom, and follow the path along as it contours around the hillside above a wall. After a short spell of walking alongside the wall, it drops away to your right. Continue traversing until you see a ruined building away down to your right. Cross the stile here and follow a track down around a bend by the ruined building. Continue to follow this track to a stream, which you can ford.

5 Climb up the other side of the stream's banks and turn right now, on to a good track. Follow this into a farmyard and then turn left, proceed through a gate, and on to a grassy track. Continue upward until you reach another gate, which then leads out on to open ground at the foot of Cwmcynwyn. Turn right here and follow the track back down to the start and your car.

NEUADD RESERVOIRS IN THE BRECON BEACONS

This is a fine way to visit the area's highest ground as any, or all, of the big peaks can be bypassed if required. It's also an easy way to gain the tops, as it starts at an altitude over 1,300ft (396m) and, with the exception of two short but stiff sections, the climbing remains gentle to the point of being almost undetectable. Walkers can also glimpse the seldom-visited valley of Cwm Crew.

DISTANCE/TIME 7.5 miles (12.1km) 4h Ascent: 2,000ft (610m) **MAP** Aqua3 OS Explorer OL12 Brecon Beacons National Park Western & Central **START** Grid ref: SO 032179 **PATHS** Clear well-trodden paths, small boggy patches, rocky track; 1 stile **PARKING** Small lane leading north from Pontsticill **THE PUB** Crown Inn, Merthyr Tydfil. Tel: 01685 388198

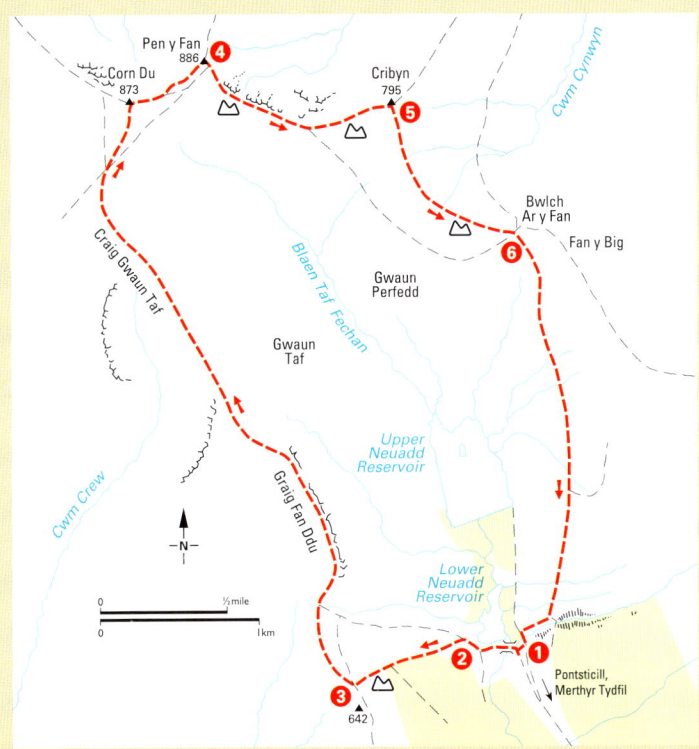

1 Continue up the small lane to a little gate, which leads into the grounds of a reservoir. Keep walking ahead to drop down on a narrow path to the concrete bridge across the outflow. Cross the bridge and climb up on to the bank opposite where you then bear left to walk along the top of the bank. This will take you to a gate that leads out on to open moorland.

2 Go through this gate and keep ahead, taking the left-hand of two tracks, which leads easily uphill towards the edge of a mainly felled forest. Follow the clearly defined track upwards, with the forest to your left, and then climb steeply up the stony gully to the top of the escarpment.

3 At the top, turn right on to the obvious path and follow the escarpment for over 2.5 miles (4km). You'll drop into a distinct saddle area with the flat-topped summit of Corn Du directly ahead of you. Carry on and, where the path forks, keep ahead and climb easily up on to the summit. Follow the escarpment edge along then drop down into another saddle, where you take the path up on to the next peak, Pen y Fan.

4 Again, from the summit cairn, follow the escarpment around and then drop down steeply, on to a rocky path, that will take you down into the deep col beneath Cribyn. Keep ahead to climb steeply up to the cairn on the narrow summit. Note: this climb can be avoided by forking right and following another clear path that contours right around the southern flanks of the mountain and eventually brings you out at Point 6.

5 From the top, bear slightly right and follow the escarpment around to the southeast. After a long flat stretch, drop steeply down into the deep col, Bwlch ar y Fan.

6 Cross a stile and turn right on to a well-made track that leads easily down the mountain. Follow this for over 1.5 miles (2.4km), until it starts to swing slightly to the left and drops steeply into a rocky ravine. Turn right here on to a track and take it down to a gate. Go through this, turn left and follow the track to its end. Turn right on to another track that leads back to the head of the lane. Go through a gate and continue to follow the lane back to your car.

WALK 92

CRAIG CERRIG-GLEISIAD, BACK TO NATURE

This is one of many possible walks in the 156-acre (63ha) National Nature Reserve but it is the closest to the National Park Visitor Centre on Mynydd Illtud Common, near Libanus. It is a great source of information about the National Park and hosts some great displays and has a programme of guided walks.

DISTANCE/TIME 4 miles (6.4km) 2h Ascent: 1,050ft (320m) **MAP** Aqua3 OS Explorer OL12 Brecon Beacons National Park Western & Central areas **START** Grid ref: SN 972221 **PATHS** Clear footpaths and broad stony tracks, 4 stiles **PARKING** Pull-in by picnic area on A470, 2 miles (3.2km) north of Storey Arms **THE PUB** Tai'r Bull Inn, Libanus. Tel: 01874 625849

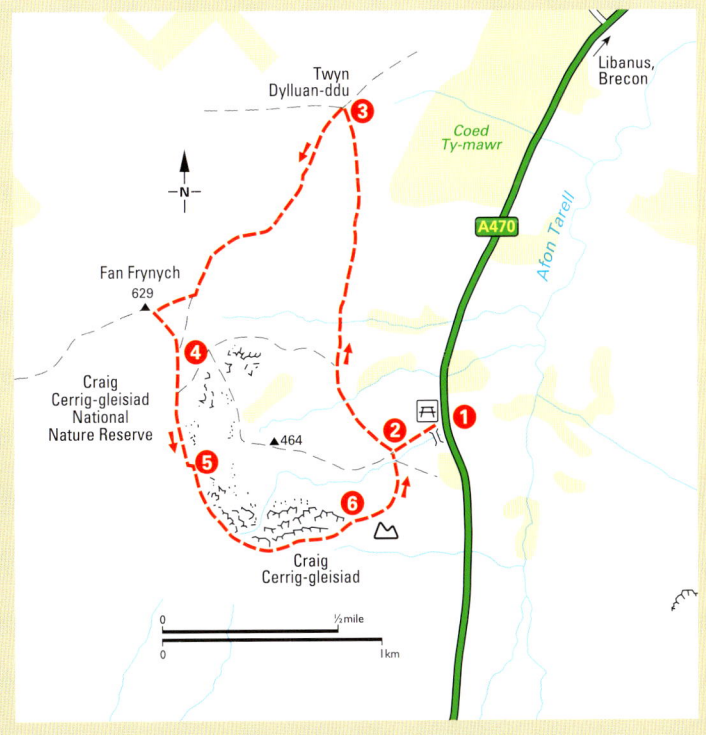

1 There is a bridge and a small picnic area at the southern end of the lay-by. Walk towards this and go through the adjacent signposted kissing gate ('Twyn Dylluan-ddu and Forest Lodge'). Head towards the crags, following the clear footpath, until you come to a gap in the next wall.

2 Pass through this and turn right to follow the drystone wall north. Head down into a small valley, cross the stream, then the stile to continue in the same direction. Drop into another, steeper, valley and climb out, still following the track. Continue through bracken to a stile.

3 Cross the stile and turn left on to a stony track. Follow this up to a gate and a stile and continue through rough ground, churned up by mining, until it levels out on the dished-shape plateau. Bear right here to the whitewashed trig point of Fan Frynych, then turn sharp left to return to the main track above the escarpment.

4 Turn right on to the main track again and continue past another area of rough ground before dropping slightly down into the broad but shallow valley. At the bottom, go over a stile that is just by a gate.

5 Cross another stile on your left and turn right to continue in the same direction, this time with a fence to your right. Climb up to the highest point, then follow the obvious path around the top of the cliffs. The path starts to drop, easily at first but getting steeper as you go.

6 Continue carefully down the steep section and follow the path around to the left when you reach easier ground. This leads you to a stream, which you can ford or jump (it's narrower a few paces downstream). Turn right, through a gap in the wall, and follow the outward path back to the car park.

CARDIFF
■ TOURIST INFORMATION
Cardiff Visitor Centre
The Old Library, The Hayes.
Tel: 02920 227281
Penarth
The Esplanade.
Tel: 02920 708849

■ PLACES OF INTEREST
Cardiff Castle
Castle Street, Cardiff.
Tel: 029 2087 8100;
www.cardiffcastle.com
Castell Coch
Castle Street, Cardiff.
Tel: 029 20878100/20810101
Llandaff Cathedral
The Cathedral Green, Llandaff, Cardiff.
Free.
National History Museum
St Fagans, Cardiff.
Tel: 02920 573500;
www.museumwales.ac.uk/en/stfagans
Free.
National Museum
Cathays Park, Cardiff.
Tel: 029 20397951;
www.museumwales.ac.uk/en/cardiff
Free.

■ SHOPPING
Extensive shopping in a traffic-free environment. Several Victorian arcades full of small independent shops and many of the larger chain stores selling a wide range of Welsh-made crafts and goods including jewellery.

■ PERFORMING ARTS
Chapter Arts Centre
Market Road, Canton Cardiff.
Tel: 029 2031 1050; www.chapter.org/
Millennium Centre
Bute Place, Cardiff. Tel: 0870 402000;
www.wmc.org.uk
St David's Hall
The Hayes, Cardiff. Tel: 029 2087 8444;
www.stdavidshallcardiff.co.uk

■ SPORTS & ACTIVITIES
BOAT TRIPS
Bay Island Voyages
Lock Keeper's Cottage, Britannia Park
Cardiff. Tel: 01446 420692;
www.bayisland.co.uk
Cruises around Cardiff Bay and the coast.

■ ANNUAL EVENTS & CUSTOMS
Cardiff Worldport Festival
Jun–Jul. www.worldport-festivals.com
Live music at various venues in the city.
Part of the Cardiff Summer Festival.
Cardiff Summer Festival
Jul–Aug. www.cardiff-festival.com
Local, national and international events.

SOUTH WALES & PEMBROKESHIRE
■ TOURIST INFORMATION
Fishguard
Town Hall, The Square.
Tel: 01348 873484
Haverfordwest
19 Old Bridge Street.
Tel: 01437 763110
Milford Haven
94 Charles Street.
Tel: 01646 690866
Newport
2 Bank Cottages, Long Street.
Tel: 01239 820912
Pembroke
Commons Road.
Tel: 01646 622388
St David's
National Park Visitor Centre, The Grove.
Tel: 01437 720392
Saundersfoot
Harbour Car Park.
Tel: 01834 813672
Tenby
The Croft.
Tel: 01834 842404

■ PLACES OF INTEREST
Caldey Island
Off Tenby. Tel: 01834 844453;
www.caldey-island.co.uk
Take a boat trip from Tenby to see the Benedictine monastery, enjoy quiet walks and fine beaches.
Castell Henllys
Off the A487 between Newport (Pembrokeshire) and Cardigan.
Tel: 01239 891319;
www.castellhenllys.com
One of many prehistoric Iron-Age promontry hill forts in Pembrokeshire National Park, now an award-winning interpretative archaeological site.
Dinosaur Park
Gumfreston, Tenby.
Tel: 01834 45272;
www.thedinosaurpark.co.uk
A 1-mile (1.6km) long walk complete with prehistoric monsters and woodland trail.
Folly Farm
Begelly, Kilgetty.
Tel: 01834 812731; www.follyfarm.co.uk
A family adventure park with a fun fair, theatre, play barn, exotic animals, restaurant and coffee shop.
The Gun Tower Museum
Pembroke Dock.
Tel: 01646 622246; www.pembroke-dock.co.uk/Guntower.htm
Pembrokeshire's naval heritage.
Pembroke Castle
Tel: 01646 684585;
www.pembrokecastle.co.uk
Impressive ruins with well-preserved remains of the 14th-century town walls.

St David's Bishop's Palace
St David's, Pembrokeshire.
Tel: 01437 720517;
www.cadw.wales.gov
Extensive and impressive ruins next to cathedral. The entry fee includes 'Lords of the Palace' exhibition.
St David's Cathedral
St David's.
Tel: 01437 721760;
www.stdavidscathedral.org.uk
Built on the site of St David's 6th-century monastery.
Tenby Museum & Art Gallery
Castle Hill, Tenby.
Tel: 01834 842809;
www.tenbymuseum.org.uk
The interesting and informative displays here include the archaeology, geology and martime and social history of the town, plus various exhibits of the work of local artists.
Tudor Merchant's House
Quay Hill, Tenby.
Tel: 01834 842279
Re-creates the atmosphere of family life in Tudor times, including a small garden fills with herbs and plants used during Tudor times.

■ FOR CHILDREN
Oakwood Theme Park
Narberth.
Tel: 01834 891376;
www.oakwoodthemepark.co.uk
Roller coasters and more.
Teifi Valley Narrow Gauge Railway
Nr Newcastle Emlyn.
Tel: 01559 371077;
www.teifivalleyrailway.co.uk
Pleasant scenic train journeys through stunningly wooded countryside, where there is also a choice of delightful woodland walks.

■ SHOPPING
Markets
Fishguard, Thu. Farmers market fortnightly, Sat.
Haverfordwest, fortnightly.
Pembroke Dock, Fri.
St David's, weekly Women's Institute market, Thu.
Tenby, indoor market, Mon, Tue, Thu–Sat.
Narberth
The town has become a popular centre for antiques shops.

■ PERFORMING ARTS
Theatr Gwaun
West Street, Fishguard.
Tel: 01348 873421;
www.theatrgwaun.ukart.com.
Torch Theatre
Milford Haven.
Tel: 01646 695267; www.torchtheatre.org

Queens Hall
Narberth.
Tel: 01834 861212;
www.thequeenshall.org.uk

■ SPORTS & OUTDOOR ACTIVITIES
ANGLING
Coastal Fishing
Amroth for bass, flounder and mackerel (boat hire).
Haken Point, Milford Haven for dogfish, bass and pollack.
Whitesand Bay for bass and flatfish.
Coarse Fishing
Peterstone Coarse Lakes, Wentloog, Newport for huge carp, bream and tench.
Tel: 01633 680905
Yet-y-Gors Fishery, Manorowen, Fishguard.
Tel: 01348 873497;
www.yet-y-gors.co.uk
Lakes for carp bream, roach, rudd, perch and tench. Fly fishing for trout also available.
River Fishing
The Nevern, which rises from the Preseli Hills and flows out to sea at Newport, is very good for sea trout.

BEACHES
Barafundel Bay
Popular with sun seekers, walkers and swimmers. Accessed from the Stackpole Quay car park.
Broadhaven, St Brides Bay
Another long sandy beach popular for watersports.
Dale
A shingle beach well known for yachting, diving and windsurfing.
Freshwater West
Big Atlantic waves make this sand and shingle beach ideal for surfers.
Little Haven, St Brides Bay
Small sheltered cove next to the village of Little Haven.
Manorbier
A busy beach, popular with surfers, swimmers and families.
Marloes Sands
This crescent-shaped sandy beach has interesting rocky outcrops.
Newgale Sands, St Brides Bay
Exposed beach especially popular for surfing and kite surfing.
Saundersfoot
Popular sandy beach beyond the harbour.
Tenby North
The little sandy beach is overlooked by the harbour and town's old quarters.
Tenby South
A good expanse of sandy beach, very popular with bathers.
Whitesands, St Davids
Fine long sandy beach with safe swimming and surfing areas designated by the summer lifeguards.

BOAT TRIPS

Tenby Harbour to Caldy Island
Tel: 01834 844453

Brunel Quay, Neyland to Grassholm, Skokholm & Skomer Dale Sailing
Tel: 01646 603124;
www. dale-sailing.co.uk
St Justinian to Ramsey Island
Several companies operate boat trips from St Justinian near St David's to Ramsey Island. Their booking offices are all in St David's.
Useful websites:
www.ramseyisland.co.uk
www.thousandislands.co.uk

CYCLING

Llys-y-fran
An 8-mile (12.8km) circuit of the broad reservoir situated 8 miles (12.8km) northeast of Haverfordwest.
www.cyclepembrokeshire.com/cycleroutes/other_routes.asp

Neyland to Johnston railway path
This pleasant cycle route takes you on a path for 5 miles (8km) each way.

HORSE RIDING

Dunes Riding Centre
Cotts Lane, Martlewy, Narberth.
Tel: 01834 891398;
www.dunes-riding.co.uk

East Nolton Riding Stables
East Nolton Farm, Nolton Haven, Haverfordwest.
Tel: 01437 710360;
www.noltonstables.com

Havard Stables
Trewiddyg Fawr, Dinas Cross, Newport.
Tel: 01348 811452

Llanwnda Riding & Trecking
Penrhiw Fach, Llanwnda, Goodwick.
Tel: 01348 873595;
www.pembrokeshireonline.co.uk/riding_fishguard/index.htm

WALKING

Pembrokeshire Coast Path
www.pembrokeshirecoastpath.com
A good bus service for walkers operates along the whole length of the path.

Pembrokeshire Coastal Bus
Tel: 01437 776313;
www.pembrokeshire.gov.uk/coastbus
Regular bus services run up and down the coastline.

■ ANNUAL EVENTS & CUSTOMS

Fishguard
Fishguard Folk Festival, May.
Fishguard International Music Festival, Jun.
Fishguard Jazz Festival, Sep.

Narberth
Winter Carnival, Dec.

St David's
Cathedral Festival, May/Jun.

Tenby
Arts Festival, late Sep.

SNOWDONIA NATIONAL PARK

■ TOURIST INFORMATION

Aberdyfi
The Wharf Gardens.
Tel: 01654 767321

Bala
Pensarn Road.
Tel: 01678 521021

Barmouth
The Station, Station Road.
Tel: 01341 280787

Beddgelert
Canolfan Hebog.
Tel: 01766 890615

Betws-y-Coed
Royal Oak Stables.
Tel: 01690 710426

Blaenau Ffestiniog
Unit 3, High Street.
Tel: 01766 830360

Conwy
Conwy Castle.
Tel: 01492 592248

Dolgellau
Eldon Square.
Tel: 01341 422888

Harlech
Llys y Graig.
Tel: 01766 780658

Llanberis
1b High Street.
Tel: 01286 870765

■ PLACES OF INTEREST

Aberconwy House
Castle Street, Conwy.
Tel: 01492 592246;
www.aberconwyhouse.co.uk
Fourteenth-century merchant's house – one of the finest examples of its kind you will find in Wales.

Alice in Wonderland Centre
3 & 4 Trinity Square, Llandudno.
Tel: 01492 860082;
www.wonderland.co.uk
Life-size displays of Lewis Carroll's Alice in Wonderland story.

Chirk Castle
Chirk, near Wrexham.
Tel: 01691 777701;
www.chirk.com/castle.html
Magnificent medieval fortress on the Welsh Marches.

Conwy Castle
Castle Street, Conwy.
Tel: 01492 592246; www.greatcastles ofwales.co.uk/conwy.htm
A masterpiece of fascinating medieval military architecture.

Conwy Valley Railway Museum
Betws-y-Coed Station Yard.
Tel: 01690 710568;
www.conwyrailwaymuseum.co.uk
Miniature steam train railway rides in picturesque countryside.

Denbigh Castle
Tel: 01745 813385;
www.denbigh.com/castle.html
Striking ruins crowning a steep hill above the town. Free.

Electric Mountain
Llanberis Tel: 01286 870636;
www.wales-underground.org.uk/electric/information.shtml.
Guided tours around an underground hydro-electric power station.

Great Orme Mines
Great Orme, Llandudno.
Tel: 01492 870447;
www.greatormemines.info
Fascinating Bronze Age copper mines to explore.

Llechwedd Slate Caverns
Blaenau Ffestiniog.
Tel: 01766 830306;
www.llechwedd-slate-caverns.co.uk
A tour of the underground world of the slate miner.

Motor Museum
Betws-y-Coed.
Tel: 01690 710760;
www.betys-y-coed.co.uk/attra/motor.htm
Exhibits include Bugatti, Aston Martin, Bentley, Bullnose Morris, Ford T and British motorbikes.

Plas Mawr
High Street, Conwy.
Tel: 01492 580167
Built between 1576 and 1585, this is possibly the best-preserved Elizabethan townhouse in Britain.

Quaker Heritage Centre
Ty Meirion, Sgwar Elson, Dolgellau.
Tel: 01341 424442
Tells the story of the local Quaker community that lived here, of their persecution and finally, their emigration to Pennsylvannia. Free.

Rhuddlan Castle
Near Rhyl.
Tel: 01745 590777;
www.rhyl.com/rhuddlan.html
Rhuddlan's massive twin-towered gatehouse immediately catches the eye.

Rhyl Sky Tower
Rhyl Promenade.
www.rhylsuncentre.co.uk/sktower.html
A 240-foot (73m) modern tower whose observationcar rotates to give birds-eye views of the North Wales Coast.

Snowdon Mountain Railway
Llanberis.
Tel: 0870 4580033;
www.snowdonrailway.co.uk
Travel up Snowdon, highest mountain in England and Wales on Britain's only rack-and-pinion railway.

Trefriw Woollen Mills
Trefriw.
Tel: 01492 640462;
www.t-w-m.co.uk

The mill specialises in the manufacture of magnificent Welsh double weave (tapestry) bedspreads (carthenni) and beautiful tweeds. Visitors can tour the mill and see goods being made or buy from the shop. Free.

Welsh Slate Museum
Dinorwig Quarry, Llanberis.
Tel: 01286 870630;
www.museumwales.ac.uk/en/slate
The museum, housed in old Victorian buildings, gives an insight into the day-to-day goings on of a miner's life. Free.

■ FOR CHILDREN

Harlequin Puppet Theatre
Rhos on Sea Promenade, Colwyn Bay.
Tel: 01492 548166
Opened in 1958, this is Britain's only remaining puppet theatre devoted solely to marionettes.

Rhyl Sun Centre
East Parade, Rhyl.
Tel: 01745 344433;
www.rhylsuncentre.co.uk
An indoor tropical water park, with 'white rollers' to surf and daredevil waterslides to thrill and to scare.

SeaQuarium
Promenade, Rhyl.
Tel: 01745 344660;
www.seaquarium.co.uk
Come face to face with sea creatures.

■ SHOPPING

MARKETS

Bangor, Sun Farmers' Market.
Blaenau Ffestiniog, Tue.
Barmouth, Thu and Sun in summer.
Colwyn Bay, Tue and Sat – farmers' market, Thu.
Conwy, Tue.
Llanrwst, Tue.
Prestatyn, Tue, Fri, Sat.
Ruthin, Thu.
Trefriw Woollen Mill (see above) and Meirion Mill at Dinas Mawddwy have lovely Welsh fabrics and tapestries.
Wrexham, Mon.

■ PERFORMING ARTS

Clwyd Theatre
Mold.
Tel: 0845 330 3565;
www.clwyd-theatr-cymru.co.uk

The Dragon Theatre
Jubilee Road, Barmouth.
Tel: 01341 281697

Theatre Ardudwy
Harlech.
Tel: 01766 780667;
www.theatrardudwy.co.uk

Theatr Colwyn
Abergele Rd, Colwyn Bay.
Tel: 01492 532668;
www.theatrcolwyn.co.uk

Venue Cymru
Promenade, Llandudno.
Tel: 01492 872000;
www.venuecymru.co.uk

■ **SPORTS & OUTDOOR ACTIVITIES**
ANGLING
Bala Lake
Llyn Tegid (Bala Lake), Wales's largest natural lake, stocks large pike, also perch, roach, trout, eel and grayling.
Crafnant Fishery
Llyn Crafnant, above Conwy Valley near Trefriw. Tel: 01492 640818
Lake with brown and rainbow trout.
Llandudno, Colwyn Bay, Rhos, Deganwy, Rhyl, Mostyn Docks
Shore fishing.
Llyn Brenig
Fly fishing lake filled with rainbow trout. Permits from The Visitor Centre, Brenig Reservoir, Cerrigydrudion.
Tel: 01490 420463
Day permits from machines.
BEACHES
Aberdyfi
A sandy beach, ideal for families.
Abergele
A good beach popular with windsurfers and canoeists. Good car parking.
Barmouth
Long sandy beach away from the estuary, ideal for sunning or beach games.
Colwyn Bay
A lively pier and a good arcing sandy beach sheltered by the Little Orme.
Conwy
Good beach with sand dunes a mile (1.6km) west of the town, just beyond the marina.
Fairbourne
Good sandy beach, ideal for swimming and playing beach sports.
Harlech
A straight beach with miles of golden sand, ideal for swimming.
Llandudno
Two excellent sandy beaches either side of the Great Orme. The West Beach has a pier and many activities like Punch and Judy shows.
Prestatyn
A 4-mile (6.5km) bar of sand, very popular with families.
Rhyl
3 miles (5km) of sand, good for families.
Tywyn
Cobbles with good sand at low tide, popular beach for families.
CYCLING
Excellent for mountain biking. There are many routes in Coed y Brenin (forest) where there's a visitor centre, café and bike shop.
Enquiries: Tel: 01341 440728;
www.beicsbrenin.co.uk

There's a traffic-free ride along the promenade from Rhos-on-Sea (near Colwyn Bay) to Prestatyn (16 miles/26km – one way), and a 9-mile (14.5km) circuit at Llyn Brenig Reservoir near Denbigh.
GOLF
Chirk Golf Club
Chirk, near Wrexham.
Tel: 01691 774407;
www.chirk.com/golf.
18 holes.
Ffestiniog Golf Club
Y Cefn, Festiniog.
Tel: 01766 762637;
www.ffestinioggolf.org
9 holes.
Llanymynech Golf Club
Pant, near Oswestry.
Tel: 01691 830983;
www.llanymynechgolfclub.co.uk
18 holes.
Old Colwyn Golf Club
Woodland Avenue, Old Colwyn.
Tel: 01492 515581;
www.oldcolyngolfclub.co.uk
9 holes.
Rhos-on-Sea Golf Club
Glan-y-mor Road, Penrhyn Bay, Llandudno.
Tel: 01492 549641; www.rhosgolf.co.uk
18 holes.
Tyddyn Mawr Golf Club
Crawia Road, Llanrug, Caernarfon.
Tel: 01286 674919;
www.welshgolfcourses.com/north/tyddynmawr.php
9 holes.
HORSE RIDING
E Prichard Pony Trekking
Felen Rhyd Fach,
Maentwrog.
Tel: 01766 590231
Gwydyr Stables
Penmachno,
Near Betws-y-Coed.
Tel: 01690 760248;
www.horse-riding-wales.co.uk
Ruthin Riding Centre
Ruthin.
Tel: 01824 703470
Sychdyn Riding Centre
Tai Cochion, Greenbank Lane, Sychdyn, Mold.
Tel: 01352 840284
The Trekking Centre
Abergwynant Farm, Penmaenpool, Dolgellau.
Tel: 01341 422377
Tynllwyn Riding Stables
Tynllwyn Farm, Brynmaen, Colwyn Bay.
Tel: 01492 580224;
www.walesdirectory.co.uk/tl/stables.htm
SAILING CENTRES
Aberdyfi
Harbourmaster, The Quay.
Tel: 01654 767626

Barmouth
Harbourmaster, The Quay.
Tel: 01341 280671
Conwy
Harbourmaster, Harbour Office, Conwy Quay.
Tel: 01492 596253
SKIING
Llandudno Ski and Snowboard Centre
Wyddfyd, Great Orme, Llandudno.
Tel: 01492 874707;
www.llandudnoskislope.co.uk
WALKING
The area is the best in Wales. Snowdon, the Glyderau and the Carneddau ranges are the most popular for walking.
WHITE WATER RAFTING
Canolfan Tryweryn
Frongoch, Bala.
Tel: 01678 521083; www.ukrafting.co.uk

■ **ANNUAL EVENTS & CUSTOMS**
Conwy River Festival
Early Aug. Tel: 01492 596253;
www.conwyriverfestival.org
Llanberis Film Festival
Tel: 01286 685503; www.llamff.co.uk
Early Mar, various venues.
Ruthin Festival
Tel: 01824 703832; ruthinfestival.co.uk
Music festival, Jun/Jul.
Sesiwn Fawr
Dolgellau.
Tel: 08712 301314; www.sesiwnfawr.co.uk
Folk and rock festival. Eldon Square, Jul.

BRECON BEACONS & CENTRAL WALES
■ **TOURIST INFORMATION**
Abergavenny
Swan Meadow, Monmouth Road.
Tel: 01873 857588
Aberystwyth
Terrace Road.
Tel: 01970 612125
Brecon
Cattle Market Car Park.
Tel: 01874 622485
Hay-on-Wye
Oxford Road.
Tel: 01497 820144
Llandovery
Kings Road.
Tel: 01550 720693
Llandrindod Wells
Old Town Hall, Memorial Gardens.
Tel: 01597 822600
Llanidloes
54 Longbridge Street.
Tel: 01686 412605
Machynlleth
Canolfan Owain Glyndwr.
Tel: 01654 702401
Rhayader
The Leisure Centre, North Street.
Tel: 01597 810591

■ **PLACES OF INTEREST**
Brecon Cathedral
Cathedral Close, Brecon, Powys.
Tel: 01874 623857;
www.breconcathedral.org.uk
Magnificent 11th-century cathedral.
Carreg Cennen Castle
Trapp, near Llandeilo.
Tel: 01558 822291; www.brecon-beacons.com/Carreg-Cennen-Castle.htm
Thought by many to be Wales' most spectacularly sited castle on high cliffs overlooking the Tywi Valley.
Centre for Alternative Technology
Machynlleth.
Tel: 01654 705950;
www.cat.org.uk
See some of the solutions to the challenges facing Earth.
Ceredigion Museum & Coliseum Gallery
Coliseum, Terrace Road, Aberystwyth.
Tel: 01970 633088; www.aboutbritain.com/CeredigionMuseum.htm
A fine collection of historic objects including the furniture, archaeological finds, agriculture, seafaring and lead mining industries of the people of Ceredigion.
Dan-yr-Ogof Showcaves
Brecon Road, Penycae.
Tel: 01639 730284;
www.dan-yr-ogof-showcaves.co.uk
Visit the underground world of stalagmites, stalactites, waterfalls, a museum and the dinosaur park.
Dinas Nature Reserve
Rhandirmwyn.
RSPB reserve with beautiful walk and shop/information centre. Charge for car park.
Dolaucothi Gold Mines
Pumpsaint, Llanwrda Carmarthenshire.
(Site off A482 between Lampeter and Llanwrda.)
Tel: 01558 650177; www.wales-underground.org.uk/dolaucothi
Free for National Trust members only (excludes underground tour). The only known Roman gold mine in the UK.
Gigrin Farm Kite Feeding Station
South St, Rhayader.
Tel: 01597 810243
See the rare bird of prey, the red kite.
National Cycle Collection
The Automobile Palace, Temple Street, Llandrindod Wells.
Tel: 01597 825531;
www.cyclemuseum.org.uk
Boneshakers, penny farthings and modern bikes.
National Library of Wales
Penglais, Aberystwyth.
Tel: 01970 623816; www.llgc.org.uk.
Entry here includes exhibitions (some free of charge), there is also a cinema and a restaurant.

■ FOR CHILDREN

Brecon Mountain Railway
Pant Station, Merthyr Tydfil.
Tel: 01685 722988;
www.breconmountainrailway.co.uk
A narrow-gauge steam line.

Vale of Rheidol Railway
Park Avenue, Aberystwyth.
Tel: 01970 625819;
www.rheidolrailway.co.uk
One of the Great Little Trains of Wales.

■ SHOPPING

Markets
Abergavenny, Tue. Farmers market,
4th Thu of month.
Aberaeron, Farmers Market – Sat.
Aberystwyth, 3rd Sat of the month;
Brecon, Tue and Fri.
Cardigan, Farmers market first Thu
of month, Apr–Dec.
Hay-on-Wye, Thu.
Lampeter, alternate Tue.
Llandrindod Wells, Fri. Farmers market
last Thu am of the month].
Llanidloes, Sat; Machynlleth, Wed.

■ PERFORMING ARTS

Aberystwyth Arts Centre
The University of Wales, Aberystwyth,
Penglais Campus, Aberystwyth.
Tel: 01970 622882;
www.aberystwythartscentre.co.uk

The Tabernacle
Penrallt Street, Machynlleth, Powys.
Tel: 01654 703355

Theatr Brycheiniog
Canal Wharf, Brecon.
Tel: 01874 611622

Theatr Hafren
Llanidloes Road, Newtown.
Tel: 01686 625007;
www.theatrhafren.co.uk

■ SPORTS & OUTDOOR ACTIVITIES

ANGLING
Freshwater
There are numerous opportunities
for fishing on farms, lakes and rivers,
including the Clwydog Reservoir near
Llanidloes, the Beacons Reservoir at
the head of the Taff Valley and the River
Tawe in Carmarthenshire. Permits and
licences are available from tackle shops
and Tourist Information Centres.

BOAT TRIPS
New Quay Boat Company
Newquay.
Tel: 07989 175124;
www.newquayboattrips.co.uk
Pleasure and fishing trips.

CYCLING
Cycle Routes
Taff Trail (from Cardiff to the Brecon
Beacons through a variety of landscapes
– urban and open moorland).

The shore of Lake Llangors is a very
important habitat for water-based bird
and wildlife.
Elan Valley Trail.

GOLF
Borth & Ynys Golf Club
Aer y Mor, Borth.
Tel: 01970 871202
18 holes.

Cradoc Golf Club
Penoyre Park, Cradoc, Brecon.
Tel: 01874 623658;
www.cradoc.co.uk
18 holes.

Machynlleth Golf Club
Newtown Road, Machynlleth.
Tel: 01654 702000; www.welshgolf
courses.com/mid/machynlleth.php
9 holes.

Rhosgoch Golf & Leisure Club
Rhosgoch, Builth Wells.
Tel: 01544 370286;
www.rhosgoch-golf.co.uk
18 holes.

St Idloes Golf Club
Trefeglwys Road, Llanidloes.
Tel: 01686 412559;
www. llanidloes.com/golf_club
9 holes.

HORSE RIDING
Cantref Riding Centre
Cantref, Brecon.
Tel: 01874 665223; www.cantref.com

Mills Bros
New Court, Felindre, Three Cocks,
Brecon.
Tel: 01497 847285

Taliesin Riding Centre
Erglodd, Taliesin, Machynlleth.
Tel: 01970 832215

Underhill Riding Stables
Underhill Farm, Dolau, Llandrindod
Wells.
Tel: 01597 851890

WALKING
Long Distance Routes
The Beacons Way – 100 miles (160km)
through the beautiful Brecon Beacons.
Glyndwr's Way – 132 miles (212km)
between Knighton and Welshpool,
via Machynlleth.

■ ANNUAL EVENTS & CUSTOMS

Brecon Jazz Festival
Tel: 01874 625557;
www.breconjazz.co.uk, mid-Aug.

Hay Festival
Tel: 01497 821217l;
www.hayfestival.co.uk
Literary festival, end May to early Jun.

Musicfest Aberystwyth
www.aberfest.com, end Jul.

Royal Welsh Show
Builth Wells.
Tel: 01982 553683
Agricultural show, mid to end Jul.

PUBS
CARDIFF

Caesars Arms
Cardiff Road, Cardiff CF15 9NN
Tel: 02920 890486
The Caesars Arms attracts a well-heeled
clientele to its heated patio and terrace
looking out over the lovely gardens and
surrounding countryside. The inn prides
itself on its vast selection of fresh fish,
seafood, meat and game, and its friendly,
relaxed atmosphere. Draught ales are
somewhat overshadowed by a massive
wine list, which has many selections
available by the glass.

SOUTH WALES & PEMBROKESHIRE

Cambrian Inn
6 Main Street, Solva SA62 6UU
Tel: 01437 721210
The Grade II-listed 17th-century inn
at the entrance to Lower Solva offers
both restaurant and bar meals in cosy
surroundings. Expect to see pasta dishes,
steaks and vegetarian dishes with real
ales such as Brains Reverend James.
No children under 10 or dogs in the bar.

Ferry Inn
Pembroke Ferry, Pembroke Dock
SA72 6UD. Tel: 01646 682947
Once the haunt of smugglers, this fine
16th-century inn is set on the banks of
the Cleddau River, with good views across
the estuary from the nautical-themed
bar and waterside terrace. The menu
offers a range of fresh local fish such as
turbot, Dover sole and sardines. Other
gastonomic options include steak and
ale pie, and vegetable korma.

The Georges Restaurant/Café Bar
24 Market Street, Haverfordwest
SA61 1NH. Tel: 01437 766683
This remarkable 18th-century building
incorporates many original features in
its restored vaulted cellar and eating
areas. Its delightful walled garden, which
enjoys spectacular views over the ruins
of 12th-century Haverfordwest Castle,
has outdoor heating for those chillier
evenings. An extensive range of good
home-cooked food is served all day, and
given the close proximity of the sea, there
are plenty of fish dishes on the menu.

The Stackpole Inn
Jasons Corner, Stackpole SA71 5DF
Tel: 01646 672324;
www.stackpoleinn.co.uk
The 17th-century Stackpole Inn is popular
with walkers and locals.The extensive,
award-winning bar and restaurant menu
includes fresh locally caught fish that
appear on the 'just in' specials board and
old favourites such as Welsh black beef.

SNOWDONIA NATIONAL PARK

The Castle Hotel
High Street, Conwy LL32 8DB
Tel: 01492 582800;
www.castlewales.co.uk
A rather grand 16th-century coaching inn
adorned with many antiques and some
fine paintings by Victorian artist John
Dawson-Watson, who it is said painted to
pay for his lodgings here. You can dine in
Shakespeare's brasserie-type restaurant
or there's a popular bar serving excellent
meals, but be early to grab a table.

Dovey Inn
Seaview Terrace, Aberdyfi LL35 0EF
Tel: 01654 767332; www.doveyinn.com
This historic inn, on the estuary of the
River Dovey, is only 20 yards from the
sea and the fine sandy beach. The village
clings to the hills above the estuary,
once a major slate port and now a sailing
centre. An extensive seafood menu
includes Thai spiced shark steak, fish
pie, Bantry Bay mussels, chargrilled
swordfish and tuna steak with red wine
fish gravy. There are plenty of other
delicious options on offer, including
sandwiches, light bites, vegetarian
dishes, meat dishes, pasta and pizza.

The Groes Inn
Tyn y Groes, Conwy LL32 8TN
Tel: 01492 650545; www.groesinn.com
Dating back to 1573, the Groes Inn,
overlooking the scenic Conwy Valley,
became the first licensed inn in Wales.
A traditional but luxurious inn, garlanded
with delightful flowerboxes in summer,
it retains beamed ceilings and log fires.
Anything from a light snack to gourmet
meals (with seafood specials) can be
enjoyed in the bar or restaurant. Not an
ideal place for kids.

Stables Bar, Royal Oak
Betws-y-Coed LL24 0AY
Tel: 01690 710219
In an extension to Betws-y-Coed's largest
hotel, the Stables Bar efficiently produces
tasty bar meals time after time, even
though the bar is usually extremely busy.
On summer evenings there's a large
outside dining area where you can eat
under the trees and the stars.

White Horse Inn
Capel Garmon, Betws-y-Coed LL26 0RW
Tel: 01690 710271
A cosy 400-year-old inn in the village
of Capel Garmon: one with beamed
ceilings, log fires and a panoramic view
of the Conwy Valley and the mountains of
Snowdonia. The inn is well known for its
fine food. It also serves a wide selection
of fine wines and real ales.

BRECON BEACONS & CENTRAL WALES

Clytha Arms
Clytha, Abergavenny NP3 9BW
Tel: 01873 840206

This family-run free house has an outstanding reputation for its food and real ales. Bass, Felinfoel and Hook Norton ales are joined by an ever-changing selection of guest beers, and there's also a good choice of wines by the glass. Bar snacks include a range of delicious sandwiches and ploughmans, as well as hot dishes like hake fish cakes with tomato salsa. Raglan's famous 15th-century castle is near by, while Cardiff, with its historical attractions and superb shopping, is a 40-minute drive.

The Felin Fach Griffin
Felin Fach LD3 0UB
Tel: 01874 620111

Felin Fach Griffin is a country inn in a quiet valley on the edge of the Brecon Beacons National Park. At the pub's heart are comfortable, deep leather sofas surrounding a large newspaper-strewn farmhouse table, and a warming open fire, (nearly always alight). The food is simple but delicious and you can usually get delicacies such as tuna steak with aubergine caviar, artichoke and sauce vièrge; grey mullet with crushed potatoes, spinach and chive butter; and local venison with autumn fruits and dauphinoise potato.

Kilvert's Hotel
The Bull Ring, Hay-on-Wye HR3 5AG
Tel: 01497 821042

This attractive ivy-clad Georgian free house is popular with the local community and tourists alike, and has a small flagged outdoor terrace area in the front, a charming rustic oak-beamed bar serving real ales such as Brains Reverend James, alongside a range of favourite bar meals like braised Welsh lamb, pizzas and pastas. The elegant restaurant specialises in lamb, such as North African lamb with ginger, chickpeas and chilli, and a large range of fish and seafood, in cluding calamari andd whitebait.

Kings Head Inn
1 Market Square, Llandovery SA20 0AB
Tel: 01550 720393

A comfortable 16th-century former coaching inn and drovers' bank situated in the centre of town. The exposed stone walls, wood beams and cosy welcoming fires combine to give the inn a warm and convivial atmosphere. The excellent food is based on fresh and wholesome Welsh produce.

TEA ROOMS
CARDIFF

Crema Coffee Shop
Millennium Centre, Cardiff CF10 5AL
Tel: 02920 484884

This is a stylish modern venue in the buzzing heart of the arts centre serving mouth-watering cakes, including a wicked chocolate fudge cake, with a wide range of coffees and teas.

Gwalia Tea Rooms
The Museum of Welsh Life, St Fagans, Cardiff CF5 6XB. Tel: 02920 566985

Many of the buildings which form part of the museum have been moved stone by stone from various parts of Wales, and one of them is the old general store which houses the Gwalia. Bentwood chairs, an etched glass screen and old photographs set the scene for the traditional tea menu, with its home-made cakes and local specialities like Welsh rarebit, Teisen Lap (light and spicy fruit cake), Gwalia rock cake and an excellent selection of speciality teas.

Norwegian Church
Harbour Drive, Cardiff Bay, Cardiff CF10 4PA. Tel: 02920 2049 3331

Built in 1869 as a place of worship for Scandinavian sailors in Cardiff, this attractive white wooden building has a popular tea room where you can indulge yourself with excellent calorific cakes and a range of snacks.

SOUTH WALES & PEMBROKESHIRE

The Boathouse Tea Room
Stable Yard, Stackpole SA71 5DE
Tel: 01646 672058

Close to the old stone jetty, this popular licensed café has a large outdoor area for alfresco dining. The quiches are delicious while tasty sandwiche fillings include fresh crab, and the reviving cream teas have tempting cakes.

Morawelon Café Bar & Restaurant
Parrog, Newport, Pembrokeshire SA42 0RW. Tel: 01239 820565

Set on the Parrog beachfront, you can indulge yourself here with many varieties of tea or coffee and delicious cakes, or you can tuck into a mouth-watering meal that might include freshly caught local crab, washed down with a glass of wine.

The Old Printing House
20 Main Street, Solva SA62 6UU
Tel: 01437 721603

The award-winning tea room/restaurant is located at the heart of the village of Solva in an 18th-century house and paper mill with beamed ceilings and stripped stone walls. The tea room is noted for its freshly baked bread and cakes, home-made soups and chutneys and traditional cream teas. It's an ideal place to stop after a walk on the coastal path.

Tudor Lodge Restaurant
Jameston, Manorbier SA70 7SS
Tel: 01834 871978;
www.tudorlodgerestaurant.co.uk

This restaurant has a clean, modern style with walls hung with contemporary paintings and a good atmosphere, but with traditional, blazing log fires for when the sun cools. The food is excellent and prepared using fresh local produce wherever possible, whether it is for light lunches or evening meals.

SNOWDONIA NATIONAL PARK

Cemlyn Restaurant and Tea Shop
High Street, Harlech LL46 2YA
Tel: 01766 780425

An award-winning tea shop and restaurant serving over 20 varieties of teas, along with coffees, delicious home-made cakes and sandwiches. Try local specialities such as bara brith or fruit cake, perhaps on a sun terrace with its spectacular views of Harlech Castle, Royal St david's Golf Course, Cardigan Bay and the Snowdonian mountains. There's a patio for outdoor seating in fine weather, and bed-and-breakfast accommodation is also available.

Lyn's Café and Teagarden
Liverpool House, Church Street, Beddgelert LL55 4YA
Tel: 01766 890374

Sited by the River Colwyn in Beddgelert, the cosy café has a splendid riverside garden where you can relax with a coffee or tea. Alternatively, choose from a menu of breakfast items, snacks, light meals, clotted cream teas and evening meals. The café is licensed in the evening.

Pete's Eats
40 High Street, Llanberis LL55 4EU
Tel: 01286 870 117

This is (perhaps) one of the best chippys in the world, and, if you're in a mood to be self-indulgent, look no further. It's lively and popular among the climbers and hillwalkers who mix with the locals.

The Plas
High Street, Harlech LL46 2YA
Tel: 01766 780204

After clambering over the castle or a bracing walk along the sands, set aside a long, languid afternoon for savouring the atmosphere of this lovely house and its delicious afternoon tea, where you can enjoy the view while you tuck into the sandwiches, cakes and scones.

BRECON BEACONS & CENTRAL WALES

The Angel Hotel
15 Cross Street, Abergavenny NP7 5EN
Tel: 01873 857121

Enjoy afternoon tea in comfort and style, in this refurbished hotel. There is an interesting selection of artisan speciality teas to choose from. Cakes and pastries from specialist baker, Sally Lane, are served, and whether you choose to take tea in the restaurant, sitting room or outdoors in the courtyard, the service is friendly and welcoming. There are also many specialty teas to try from the Mighty Leaf Tea Company, which are perfect with which to accompany a slice of cake.

Giglios Coffee Shop
10 Bethel Square, Brecon LD3 7JP
Tel: 01874 625062

A modern licensed coffee shop and restaurant in the heart of Brecon. Excellent cream teas, gateaux and sandwiches, such as smoked salmon and cream cheese, Thai green chicken, or salmon with dill mayonnaise. A wide variety of teas and coffees is on offer.

The Granary
20 Broad Street, Hay-on-Wye HR3 5DB
Tel: 01497 820790

The splendid licensed café has a cosy bistro style interior with outside tables looking across to the town's Victorian clocktower. Food includes sandwiches, jacket potatoes and warming soups as well as full main meals.

Nant y Bai Mill
Rhandirmwyn, Llandovery SA20 0PB
Tel: 01550 760211

A wonderfully situated country café/restaurant/B&B in the beautiful Tywi Valley, the old mill serves light lunches (sandwiches, jacket potatoes, Welsh rarebit), afternoon teas and excellent evening meals in a cosy atmosphere.

Pilgrims Tea Rooms & Restaurant
Cathedral Close, Brecon LD3 9DP
Tel: 01874 610610

This charming tea room and restaurant can be found in Cathedral Close, next to Brecon's magnificent cathedral. The tea room still has the look and feel of the 15th-century barn next to it. In good weather, customers can sit outside and enjoy the delightful aroma from the beautifully laid out herb garden, and spend the afternoon relaxing in the cloisters while they sip their tea. Meals are created using locally grown produce and the premises is fully licensed so, if you wish, you can have a glass of wine with your lunch instead of a cup of tea.

Northern England

Northern England

The northern reach of England is famous for its diverse landscape that is home to many of the country's beautiful National Parks.

The rolling green of the Yorkshire Dales is in stark contrast to the craggy mountains of the Lake District or the broad sandy beaches of the west coast, and a myriad hills and dales in between, all with their individual sense of drama and beauty. Even the climate seems to change from the rugged and wild west coast to the calmer and milder eastern shores, both providing a home to many important species of birds and plants.

The influence of the Industrial Revolution is evident still on the land in this beautiful region and in its cities. Great tracts of land once used for heavy manufacturing and engineering plants have been redeveloped and there are many excellent museums here to celebrate the area's industrial heritage.

Lake District

CLOCKWISE FROM TOP: LAKE CONISTON; WAST WATER; LANGDALE

AMBLESIDE MAP REF 406 E4

At the northern tip of lake Windermere, Ambleside is a convenient base for touring the central Lakes, with Grasmere and the Langdale valleys a short drive away. The town has adopted this role with gusto; it seems that every other shop sells walking boots and outdoor clothing.

The Romans first saw the strategic potential of this site, and built a fort they called Galava close to where the rivers Brathay and Rothay flow into Windermere. Centuries later, during Queen Victoria's reign, the town gained fame and prosperity through the growth of tourism.

Ambleside won its market charter in 1650, and a few buildings, including a watermill, survive from this time. However, the best-known building in Ambleside is also the smallest: Bridge House is built on a little bridge that spans the beck of Stock Ghyll. It now serves as a diminutive National Trust information centre.

It is just a short walk from the centre of Ambleside to the lake at Waterhead. Like a Bowness Bay in miniature It has a short stretch of beach, dinghies for hire and ever-hungry ducks. The steamers *Swan*, *Tern* and *Teal* call in at Waterhead on their round-the-lake cruises.

BARROW-IN-FURNESS
MAP REF 406 E5

Even the most loyal locals would hesitate to describe Barrow as beautiful. Until the mid-19th century there was just a tiny fishing village here. What made it grow at an astonishing rate were the iron- and steel-making industries, closely followed, logically, by the construction of ships.

The shipbuilding company of Vickers became almost synonymous with Barrow, and even today the docks and shipyards are an impressive sight. For a fascinating overview head for the popular Dock Museum on North Road. The museum tells how, within a generation, Barrow had become a major force in maritime engineering. Other exhibits focus on older shipbuilding traditions and its pioneers.

A surprise awaits visitors who drive past the museum – a road bridge links Barrow with the Isle of Walney. A glance at the map shows this to be a geographic oddity shielding the tip of the Furness peninsula, and Barrow itself, from the ravages of the sea. The southern tip of the Isle of Walney is a haven for wildlife.

Between Barrow and Dalton, in the 'Vale of Deadly Nightshade', is Furness Abbey. Now an evocative ruin of weathered, salmon-coloured sandstone, it was, in its heyday, second in importance only to Fountains Abbey in North Yorkshire. Parts of the abbey (now in the hands of English Heritage) still stand to their full height, in a romantic wooded setting.

BORROWDALE MAP REF 406 E3

This glorious wooded valley, which runs south from Derwent Water, contains two of the Lake District's most dramatic natural features – the Bowder Stone and the Jaws of Borrowdale. The Stone is signposted along a path east of the B5289 Borrowdale road, south of the village of Grange. Why stop to look at a stone? Well this one weighs about 2,000 tons and appears to be balanced, ready to topple over. A set of steps leads up to the top of its 36 feet (11m), and despite the attempts of almost everyone who visits to give it a push, it hasn't fallen yet. It was put into place by a glacier, which later melted around it.

Here, too, are the so-called Jaws of Borrowdale, where the high crags on either side of the valley almost meet, squeezing the road and the river (the B5289 and the River Derwent) together as they both try to get through. Both do, and the road then swings round to the west, through the village of Seatoller, to climb through the equally dramatic Honister Pass, which links Borrowdale with Buttermere.

BUTTERMERE & CRUMMOCK WATER MAP REF 406 E3

These two lakes in the Buttermere valley, separated only by a half-mile (0.8km) strip of meadowland, were probably one lake originally. Buttermere is perhaps the more beautiful, although Crummock Water is twice its size and claims one of the most impressive waterfalls in the Lakes. Scale Force, on its western side, plunges 172 feet (52m) on its way to the lake. The path to Scale Force, however, begins in tiny Buttermere village, and is a rough walk to the tree-lined gorge through which Scale Beck plummets.

Buttermere is also surrounded by high hills, such as the 2,126-foot (648m) Fleetwith Pike which guards the Honister Pass and the 1,959-foot (597m) Hay Stacks. The easy two-hour walk around Buttermere is an impressive one, with superb views in all directions. To the northwest are the Derwent Fells, with Derwent Water beyond, while to the west above Burtness Wood stands a range of dramatic crags and fells.

Visit
THE ARMITT COLLECTION

Ambleside's museum was founded as a library in 1909 by the Armitt sisters. This fine small museum illustrates the life and work of writers and artists such as John Ruskin and Beatrix Potter. The collection includes most of Beatrix Potter's scientific illustrations as well as pictures by artists such as William Green and J B Pyne.

Visit
TRADITIONAL SPORTS

At Ambleside Lakeland sports are held on the Thursday before the first Monday in August, including fell racing, hound trails, and Cumberland and Westmorland wrestling.

Activity
W2W CYCLE ROUTE

The Walney to Wear Cycle Route was inspired by the success of the Coast to Coast route, which runs from St Bees. The W2W, Sustrans regional route 20, crosses the Lake District peninsulas in easy stages to Kendal before heading up the Lune Gorge, then over the Eden Valley and across the Pennines. Its total route is 151 miles (241km) from Walney Island to Wearmouth, near Sunderland.

BOWDER STONE

CONISTON

CARLISLE MAP REF 406 E2

If you want to begin with the history of Carlisle, the award-winning Tullie House Museum and Art Gallery in Castle Street with its interactive displays is the place to start. It traces the history of Carlisle from before the Romans to the railways and beyond, via the reivers, Robert the Bruce and the Roundheads. It also has very good natural history displays.

Linked to the museum by the Millennium Gallery, Carlisle Castle dates from 1092. The keep dates from the same time, but many of the distinctive rounded battlements were added by Henry VIII to house artillery. Rooms in the gatehouse are decorated in medieval style, while a warren of chambers and tiny passageways in the castle can be explored. Also here is the Museum of the Border Regiment. Its collection of weaponry, uniforms, medals and other items reveal many tragic and heroic stories from the wars in which the regiment has been involved.

Carlisle Cathedral was founded in 1122. It was first a priory but became a cathedral in 1132 and can claim to have held a daily service for almost 900 years. Inside, the first thing to strike the eye is the magnificent high ceiling. Its stained glass dates from the 14th to the 20th centuries. Do not miss seeing the buildings opposite the main entrance.

The Fratry was a monastic common room in the 13th century and now contains the cathedral library and the Prior's Kitchen Restaurant. Across from the Fratry, the 13th-century Prior's Tower was used, among other things, as a place of refuge. Inside the tower, which can be seen by arrangement, is a ceiling with 45 panels, hand-painted in 1510.

Slightly overshadowed by the cathedral, but worth a visit, is St Cuthbert's Church, which was also built in the 12th century, although the present buildings date from the 1700s. Its most unusual feature is a moveable pulpit, mounted on rail tracks.

The city walls give some idea of the extent of the place in Roman times, as they were built around the remains of the Roman town and fort. The West Walls which were completed in 1200 and run behind St Cuthbert's and around the cathedral, are the best surviving examples.

CARTMEL MAP REF 406 E5

First-time visitors will wonder why a village as small as Cartmel should have such a large and magnificent church. In the 12th century when Cartmel (along with Carlisle and Lanercost) was chosen as the site for an Augustinian priory, the original endowment stipulated that local people should always have the right to worship in the priory church.

Much of the stone from the priory was re-used to build what is now the village of Cartmel, and the only other tangible relic of monastic times is the gatehouse (in the care of the National Trust, now a heritage centre). The stepped market cross stands near by, but the markets themselves are long gone. The Cartmel of today is a pretty little village, worth exploring in its own right as well as for its gem of a church.

To the south of the village is Holker Hall, the home of the Cavendish family and the Hall itself retains the feel of a family home. The 25 acres (10ha) of gardens and woodland are justifiably renowned. Extensive outbuildings now house the Lakeland Motor Museum, where devotees of the internal combustion engine will find a fascinating collection of historic cars and other vehicles, dating from the early days of motoring to the present.

CONISTON MAP REF 406 E4

Overlooked by the huge bulk of the Old Man of Coniston and near to the northern tip of Coniston Water, the village enjoys a superb setting. A little off the beaten track, Coniston caters best for those who want to explore the magnificent range of peaks that rise up behind the little grey town.

It was these mountains, and the mineral wealth they yielded, that created the village of Coniston. While copper had been mined in this area since the Roman occupation, the industry grew most rapidly during the 18th and 19th centuries. The story of copper mining, slate quarrying and farming, as well as the lives of celebrities such as John Ruskin, Arthur Ransome and Donald Campbell, are told in the Ruskin Museum.

A short stroll from the centre of Coniston brings you to the shore of the lake where a public slipway allows the launching of boats (no powered craft).

Few houses enjoy a more beautiful setting than Brantwood, in an estate on the eastern shore of the lake. From 1872 to 1900 this was the home of John Ruskin, artist, poet and social reformer, who became the most influential and controversial art critic of his time. The grounds are an attraction in their own right, and the house is filled with many of Ruskin's drawings, watercolours and other items recalling the man whose ideas influenced such intellectual giants as Mahatma Gandhi and Leo Tolstoy. Ruskin is buried in Coniston churchyard.

Tarn Hows is a short drive from Coniston off the B5285 Hawkshead road. Just yards from the National Trust car park, you can gaze across the tarn, studded with islands, surrounded by gorgeous conifer woodland and the most beautiful backdrop of rolling hills.

DERWENT WATER MAP REF 406 E3

South from Keswick spreads Derwent Water. It is the lakeland's widest lake at 1.25 miles (2km) and is attractively dotted with islands. These include, in the very centre, St Herbert's Island, named for the saint who lived here as a hermit in the 7th century. Derwent Isle was once home to German miners who came to work around Keswick and the Newlands Valley in the 16th century. With Borrowdale closing in to the south, and crags on either side of the lake's southern half, Derwent Water is a popular favourite. Popular too is the way in which it can be explored by using the ferries that run between the seven landing stages around the lake, allowing visitors to get off and walk the many footpaths through the surrounding woods and up to the various viewpoints.

The eastern side is rich in waterfalls, such as the spectacular Lodore Falls in the southeastern corner, which is one of the ferry stops. Much of the land here is owned by the National Trust. This is largely due to the efforts of Canon Hardwicke Rawnsley, vicar of Crosthwaite, the parish church of Keswick. He was Secretary of the National Trust from its formation until his death in 1920. The beautiful Friar's

Crag, on the northern shore of Derwent Water close to the Keswick boat landings, was given to the National Trust (along with Lords Island and Calf Close Bay) to be his memorial. The view from here was deemed by Ruskin 'to be one of the finest in Europe'.

ESKDALE MAP REF 406 E4

Here is another beautiful valley that remains relatively quiet when so many other places are busy with tourists. The reason is inaccessibility; to explore Eskdale most people will have to negotiate the twists, turns and hairpin bends of the Hardknott and Wrynose passes, or else take the long way round, meandering through south lakeland. All the better, then, for those who venture this far west, for Eskdale is well worth the effort.

Hardknott Pass, rising 1,000 feet (305m) out of Eskdale in little more than a mile (1.6km), is one of the most spectacular roads in the country; a few of the hairpin bends are as steep as 1-in-3 (33%). The steep ascent holds few terrors for car drivers these days; most problems arise at peak holiday times. And if the road is icy, or you are towing a caravan, you shouldn't even consider it!

However, when you gaze down from the remains of the fort at the western end of the Hardknott Pass it is easy to see why the Romans chose this site. Hardknott Castle Roman Fort (owned by English Heritage) enjoys a commanding position down into the green valley of Eskdale.

This is excellent walking country, with plentiful rights of way and room to roam. For more than 30 years the Ravenglass and Eskdale Railway has enabled sightseers and hikers to venture into the heart of Eskdale without blocking up the narrow road with their cars. This delightful narrow-gauge railway used to carry iron ore from the Eskdale mines to the coast; now the engines carry passengers up the valley. There are seven stations along the line, all offering opportunities for scenic walks with the option of taking a later train back down to Ravenglass.

The terminus, at Dalegarth, is just a short walk from Boot, a tiny village with a friendly pub, the Boot Inn. Just up the valley, the Woolpack recalls a time when this was a watering hole for the men who drove packponies heavily laden with fleeces down to the coast. Beyond a packhorse bridge spanning Whillan Beck is the delectable grouping of tiny buildings

that comprise Eskdale Mill. Cereals have been ground here since 1578, but milling ended during the 1920s. The overshot waterwheel was adapted to supply electricity to upper Eskdale; the valley was connected to the mains in 1955.

GRANGE-OVER-SANDS
MAP REF 406 E5

Looking out over Morecambe Bay is the charming resort of Grange-over-Sands, with its ornamental gardens, promenade and relaxed ambience.

Thanks to the Gulf Stream, Grange enjoys a mild climate, a factor which helps to explain why so many people find this a pleasant place for their retirement years. Springtime is reckoned to be warmer in Grange than anywhere else in the north. Gardeners with green fingers are encouraged by the climate, and plants grow here that would be unlikely to survive elsewhere on the west coast.

GRASMERE MAP REF 406 E4

The village of Grasmere is central, geographically and historically, to the Lake District. Set in a valley surrounded by hills, and a short stroll from Grasmere lake, the village is a gem.

Literary pilgrims have flocked to Grasmere since the days when William Wordsworth's 'plain living and high thinking' produced some of the finest romantic poetry. It was during a walking tour of the Lake District, with his lifelong friend Samuel Taylor Coleridge, that Wordsworth first spied the little house that would become his home for eight of his most productive years.

Despite its size, the house was filled with the artistic luminaries of the day, and it was here, between 1799 and 1808, that Wordsworth composed some of his best-known poems. He knew the house as Town End. It was years later, after the poet's death, that it was christened Dove Cottage. The house is open to the public, and an adjacent coach house has been converted into the Wordsworth Museum with a collection of manuscripts and books. The attached Jerwood Centre is used for academic studies.

By the time Wordsworth's wife, Mary, was expecting their fourth child, Dove Cottage was too small to house them adequately. The family moved first to Allan Bank and the Rectory (both in Grasmere, and now private homes), before making one last move to Rydal Mount.

GRIZEDALE FOREST MAP REF 406 E4

The Grizedale estate, between the lakes of Coniston Water and Windermere, was the first forest owned by the Forestry Commission, and was used to encourage recreational activities. The forest was opened to the public in the 1960s, and Grizedale is now the largest forest in the Lake District. The Grizedale Forest combines two roles: woodland recreation and the commercial production of timber.

Your first stop should be the visitor centre and the adjacent gallery, where you can get a guide to the many waymarked trails.

An imaginitive move brought art into the forest. Sculptors were sponsored to create works in woodland settings; more than 80 original sculptures nestle among the trees or stand on hilltops.

KENDAL MAP REF 406 F4

For motorists coming from the M6, the first sight of Kendal, in the valley below, means that the Lakes are 'only just round the corner'. Though some motorists drive on the bypass, impatient to reach Bowness or Windermere, others prefer to see what Kendal has to offer. The one-way traffic system can be frustrating so it's better to explore on foot and investigate Kendal's numerous 'yards' or alleyways.

Catherine Parr, sixth wife of Henry VIII, was born in Kendal Castle, whose splendid view over the town repays the climb, though the castle is in ruins.

Near the parish church is Abbot Hall. This elegant Georgian house is now an equally elegant art gallery, showing works by the many artists – including Ruskin and Constable – who were inspired by the Lakeland landscape. The Museum of Lakeland Life and Industry, also at Abbot Hall, brings recent history to life, with reconstructed shops, room settings and a farming display. The study of Arthur Ransome, author of *Swallows and Amazons* and many other children's books, has been painstakingly recreated.

At the opposite end of town, close to the railway station, the Kendal Museum has fascinating displays of geology, archaeology and natural and social history, based on the collection of 'curiosities' first

exhibited by William Todhunter in 1796. He charged 'one shilling per person; children and servants 6d each'. There are displays of wildlife, both local and global (though the case full of iridescent humming birds seems gross by today's standards).

One of Kendal's best-known sons was Alfred Wainwright (1907–91), whose seven handwritten guides to the Lakeland hills became classics in his own lifetime. You can see Wainwright's little office in Kendal Museum, where he held the post of honorary curator for many years. A hand-drawn map reveals that his interests were already in place at the tender age of ten. However, it wasn't until he was 45 that he began the mammoth task of writing his Pictorial Guides, which were indispensable reading for many years to come. Other books about his beloved North Country followed, until his death in 1991.

KESWICK MAP REF 406 E3

Keswick is a natural centre for mountain climbers, country walkers and more leisurely tourists alike. It is small, with a population of under 5,000, but is said, for its size, to have more beds for guests than anywhere else in the country. This gives an idea of how busy it can get here.

If now reliant on tourism, in the past mining kept it alive. The industry flourished in the 16th century with the formation of the Company of Mines Royal. Expert miners came from Germany and settled on Derwent Isle. But as mining declined by the second half of the 19th century, so in 1865 the Cockermouth–Penrith railway line was built, bringing mass tourism.

Graphite is the reason the Cumberland Pencil Museum exists here today. A delightfully quirky specialist collection,

it shows that even the humble pencil has a fascinating history. The first was made locally in the 1550s, though you can see modern production methods too, and the largest pencil in the world!

Even if you are not mad on cars, you'll find that the Cars of the Stars Motor Museum is a fascinating collection. Some are merely interesting vehicles, such as a Fiat from 1972 painted to look like the Noddy Car. The 'Star Cars' range from one of the Reliant Robins used in *Only Fools and Horses*, to a Morris 8 Tourer driven in *All Creatures Great and Small*, and a selection of cars used in the James Bond films, including several Aston Martins.

One of the oldest museums in the county, the Keswick Museum and Art Gallery has a good display on Lakeland's literary connections. This covers the poet Robert Southey in particular, who moved to Greta Hall in Keswick (now part of a school) to join his brother-in-law, Coleridge, and remained there for over 40 years until his death in 1843. He became Poet Laureate in 1813. There is also a fine period scale model of the Lake District as it was in the early 19th century. The geology collection is of national importance and contains mineral examples from the Caldbeck Fells. Geology is also the key to the Keswick Mining Museum. As well as mineral collections, there is an excellent bookshop of industrial archaeology.

On the northern edge of Keswick at Crosthwaite is the Church of St Kentigern, whose best-known incumbent, Canon Rawnsley, was the first Secretary of the National Trust. He was also an author, journalist, educationalist and orator, and his influence pervades almost every corner of Keswick and Cumbria.

Visit
CASTLERIGG STONE CIRCLE

Just 2 miles (3.2km) east of Keswick is one of the most dramatic and atmospheric stone circles in Britain. It dates from about 2000 BC, but its purpose remains unknown, adding to its enigmatic qualities. The 38 stones in the circle itself, with a further 10 set in the centre, are surrounded by high fells, with Helvellyn to the southeast. The stones are made of volcanic Borrowdale rock, brought here by the glaciers of the Ice Age. The construction is actually oval in shape, 107 feet (33m) across at its widest point, and the name means 'the fort on the ridge', though no evidence of any fort exists here. Castlerigg Stone Circle is in the hands of the National Trust.

THE LANGDALES

MAP REF 406 E4

The Langdales are considered to be two of the most beautiful valleys in the Lake District. They are no secret, as you will find if you try to make the circular drive around Great Langdale and Little Langdale on a weekend in summer. The road is very narrow so it's best to park at Skelwith Bridge or Elterwater, and then you can tackle the area on foot. There are climbs and scrambles here to challenge the sure-footed, as well as lowland rambles if you just want to enjoy the view.

At Skelwith Bridge, where the B5343 Langdale road branches off from the A593, is Skelwith Force. The path to the waterfall continues to Elter Water, where you can enjoy one of the many views that seems to typify the Lake District – the distinctive silhouette of the Langdale Pikes, popular with walkers. The twin humps of Harrison Stickle (2,415 feet/736m) and Pike of Stickle (2,323 feet/708m) can be glimpsed from many different points.

Beyond the village of Chapel Stile, the Great Langdale valley opens up. The valley floor is divided by stone walls, dotted with farmsteads and surrounded by a frieze of mountain peaks. The valley road meanders past the Old Dungeon Ghyll Hotel. After a steep climb the road drops, with views of Blea Tarn, into the Little Langdale valley. Though not as stunning as the main valley, it is delightful and has good footpaths. From Little Langdale a minor road branches west, to become first Wrynose Pass and then Hardknott Pass – exciting driving if your brakes are in good order!

LOWESWATER MAP REF 406 E3

One of the smaller lakes but is no less delightful for that, Loweswater (National Trust) is often less crowded than those lakes with an easier access. To reach it involves a short drive on the B5289 down Lorton Vale from Cockermouth, but many motorists simply continue down the main road that leads to nearby Crummock Water and Buttermere. If you plan to explore Loweswater, take a turning through Brackenthwaite, leading along the north shore of the lake with parking at either end. Swimming is not allowed.

Loweswater village is little more than a church, a village hall and a pub, with a scattering of whitewashed farm buildings surrounded by woodland and meadows. The woods offer many leafy footpaths and are cared for by the National Trust.

NEAR SAWREY MAP REF 406 E4

Beatrix Potter first came here on holiday in 1896, fell in love with the place and used the royalties from her first book, *The Tale of Peter Rabbit* (1901), to buy Hill Top. It was in this unpretentious little 17th-century farmhouse that she wrote many of the books that have delighted readers throughout the world.

The success of the books allowed Beatrix Potter to buy up farms and land: all her properties were bequeathed, on her death in 1943, to the National Trust. Her will decreed that Hill Top should remain exactly as she had known it. Visitors will recognise details from the pictures in her books and even the adjacent inn, the Tower Bank Arms, will be familiar to readers of *The Tale of Jemima Puddleduck* (1908). Despite its unprepossessing exterior, Hill Top is chock full of Beatrix Potter memorabilia, including original drawings. Hill Top is so popular that it is best avoided at peak holiday times. The Beatrix Potter Gallery at Hawkshead and The World of Beatrix Potter at Bowness also hold lots of interest for 'Potterphiles'.

THE LANGDALES

ULLSWATER MAP REF 406 E3

On the western shores of Ullswater, a series of splendid waterfalls tumbles down through the wooded gorge of Aira Beck, which flows into the region's second largest lake, some 7.5 miles (12km) long. The falls are known by the name of the largest, the 70-foot (21.3m) drop of Aira Force, on land owned by the National Trust. There's also an arboretum, a café and a landscaped Victorian park.

Back in 1802, the falls didn't just feed the waters of Ullswater, they fed the imagination of William and Dorothy Wordsworth. The poet and his sister were walking near by, when Dorothy observed the 'daffodils so beautiful...they tossed and reeled and danced.' Her words were transformed into one of the best-loved of English poems, William Wordsworth's 'Daffodils'. Aira Force itself is also the setting for another of William Wordsworth's poems, 'The Somnambulist'.

It is appropriate that the poet was inspired by what, for many people, is the lake among lakes, indisputably beautiful. The southern tip of its slim shape falls below the shoulders of Helvellyn to the west, and is reached through the dramatic Kirkstone Pass, which rises to 1,489 feet (454m). Near here is the Kirkstone Pass Inn, third highest pub in the country.

At Pooley Bridge on the lake's northern tip, a fish market used to be held in the main square, and this area is still rich in trout and salmon. A short walk up to Dunmallard Hill reveals Iron Age remains and lovely views. Below, at the pier near the 16th-century bridge, two 19th-century steamers, *Lady of the Lake* and *Raven*, leave to take visitors down the lake. They call at Howtown, roughly halfway along Ullswater's eastern shore, then travel on to Glenridding at the southern end. A popular option is to combine a cruise with a walk, and no finer walk is reputed to exist in the Lakes than that between Howtown and Glenridding.

There is no road through this steep-cliffed southeastern shore of the lake. The cruise boat could be rejoined at Glenridding. The lake's length may be only 7.5 miles (12km), but that is also roughly the distance by foot from Howtown to Glenridding. The curve of its crescent shape accounts for the rest, with an extra stretch round the bottom loop of the lake.

ULVERSTON MAP REF 406 E5

Ulverston, on the fringe of Morecambe Bay, is sufficiently off the beaten track to maintain an unhurried air, though Thursdays and Saturdays find the market square thronged with stalls. On top of Hoad Hill, overlooking the town, is a 90-foot (27.4m) copy of the Eddystone Lighthouse.

ULLSWATER

It is no help to ships, however, being a monument to Sir John Barrow, Ulverston-born in 1764. A founder member of the Royal Geographical Society, his story is told in the town's heritage centre.

In Upper Brook Street the Laurel and Hardy Museum is an attraction for those who still can't hear the 'Cuckoo Waltz' without thinking of the much-loved bowler-hatted buffoons of the silver screen. It is not so much a museum as a haphazard collection of Laurel and Hardy memorabilia, assembled here because Stan Laurel (the shorter one) was born in Ulverston in 1890. No souvenir is deemed too trivial for inclusion in the displays and visitors can watch clips from some of the pair's 105 films in a tiny cinema shoehorned into a corner of the museum.

WASDALE & WAST WATER
MAP REF 406 E4

The bleakly beautiful valley of Wasdale must be approached from the west, and for most visitors that involves a lengthy drive. The reward is that Wasdale will be spectacularly empty when the Lakeland honeypots are thronged with visitors.

If the view up to the head of the valley seems familiar, it's because the National Park Authority created their logo from this view of Wast Water and the three peaks, Yewbarrow, Great Gable and Lingmell, whose symmetry frames the view. Scafell Pike, near the valley head is, at 3,210 feet (978m), the highest peak in England.

Although it is just 3 miles (4.8km) long, Wast Water is the deepest lake in England. The screes that dominate the southern shore continue their descent fully 250 feet (76m) into the cool clear waters.

The road hugs the water's edge until you reach Wasdale Head; communities don't come much smaller or more welcoming than this. At the Wasdale Head Hotel walkers and climbers congregate. Ensconced in a comfortable chair you can forget that you are miles from anywhere...

Activity
CONSERVING CUMBRIA

Visitors can do a lot to help the environment simply by parking their cars and using the waymarked walks or seeing the beautiful countryside by cycling along some of the marked cycle routes. Other environmentally friendly modes of transport include taking the local trains, buses, minibus tours, or one of the launches on the lakes. During the summer an open-top bus service operates between Bowness, Windermere, Ambleside and Grasmere. The Coniston Rambler links Windermere, Ambleside, Hawkshead and Coniston, and a service from Keswick leaves for Borrowdale and Buttermere. Minibus tours are a popular way of seeing the high passes; their main centres are Windermere and Keswick.

WINDERMERE

WHITEHAVEN MAP REF 406 D3

In the middle of the 18th century Whitehaven was the third largest port in Britain, after London and Bristol, thanks to the local industries. Today, Whitehaven has a small fishing fleet, and its harbour is a conservation area, with several monuments to its mining industry, which finally died out in 1986. Your first stop in Whitehaven should be The Beacon, on West Strand, which offers an insight into the history of the town and harbour through audio-visual presentations and exciting displays. On the top floor is the Weather Gallery, full of high-tech equipment. On the headland above The Beacon is the winding gear and engine house of the Haig Colliery Mining Museum. Haig was the town's last deep pit. Now it records the often tragic stories of the town's mining past, in which more than 1,200 men, women and children died.

The town boasts many handsome Georgian buildings and has two churches that are worth seeking out. St Begh's, from around 1868, is striking as it was built from white stone with a red stone dressing. St James' is slightly older, from 1753, with Italian ceiling designs and a very moving Memorial Chapel. It was dedicated first to those who lost their lives in the two world wars, and later also to local people who were killed in mining accidents. A miner's lamp serves as the Sanctuary lamp.

Book lovers should note that Whitehaven has the largest antiquarian bookshop in Cumbria, and one of the largest in the north of England. Michael Moon's Antiquarian Bookshop in Roper Street claims to have 100,000 books on its mile (1.6km) of shelving, with room for at least a hundred book browsers.

WINDERMERE & BOWNESS-ON-WINDERMERE MAP REF 406 E4

To many visitors, a visit to the Lakes implies nothing more strenuous than mooching around the shops of Windermere and Bowness, and a relaxing boat trip on the lake. It cannot be denied that these twin towns (almost joined into one these days) attract a disproportionate number of holiday-makers. Though traffic congestion is a problem around the area, walkers can escape the crowds surprisingly quickly, even on the busiest bank holidays.

The popularity of Windermere and Bowness is largely historical. Windermere is as far into the heart of the Lake District as the railway was ever driven. William Wordsworth lamented the coming of the railway; he foresaw that his beloved Lakeland would be spoiled irretrievably by an influx of visitors. Certainly the railway opened up the area to working people.

It may seem a bit odd that it is Windermere, rather than Bowness at the water's edge, that takes its name from the lake. This was to provide the railway station with a more appealing name; until the branch line opened in 1847, Windermere was known as Birthwaite.

Bowness offers its visitors a warm welcome, and is continually developing new enterprises for their pleasure. A few years ago it was hard to find a decent place to eat; now you can take your pick from a wide array of good bistros, cafés, Indian restaurants, pizza parlours and the ever-popular fish and chip take-aways.

The water of England's longest lake laps on the beach at Bowness Bay. Swans and ducks, fed by visitors, enjoy an indolent lifestyle. Sleek clinker-built dinghies can be hired by the hour. The less energetic can enjoy a lake-long cruise, via Waterhead and Lakeside (linking to the steam trains of the restored Lakeside–Haverthwaite Railway), on the cruise ships *Tern*, *Teal* and *Swan*. Since 2005, when the National Park Authority's contested 10mph water speed limit took effect, Windermere has become a more peaceful lake.

Opposite Bowness Bay is Belle Isle. In 1774, when notions of the 'romantic' and 'picturesque' were at their height, a Mr English built an eccentric residence. Its round design brought so much ridicule on his head that Mr English was prompted to sell his unusual home.

The island site was earlier occupied by a manor house, which was besieged by troops of Roundheads while the Royalist owner was busy fighting in Carlisle. Archaeological finds reveal Belle Isle was also occupied during Roman times. It was bought in 1781 as a present for Mrs Isabella Curwen, and renamed in her honour. While most of Windermere's little islands are now owned by the National Trust, Belle Isle is still privately owned.

At the bottom of Bowness Hill is The Old Laundry, which caters for visitors and locals alike. As well as a theatre, there is a regular programme of exhibitions and events. Here, too, you'll find the World of Beatrix Potter, which uses the latest technology to bring to life the stories of Peter Rabbit, Jemima Puddleduck and many other much-loved characters.

On the A592 Bowness to Ambleside road, at the Windermere Steamboat Museum, you will find a fascinating collection of craft mostly steam-powered launches from the Victorian and Edwardian eras. They are moored afloat in a wet dock and some are taken out on to Windermere; their peaceful progress across the water is somehow entirely in keeping with the grandeur of their surroundings.

Here, happily restored, is *Esperance*, the conveyance of shipping magnate Henry William Schneider when he travelled to his office in Barrow. The steam launch *Dolly*, built in 1850, is acknowledged to be the oldest mechanically propelled boat in the world. Lovers of Arthur Ransome's children's books, such as *Swallows and Amazons*, will be happy to find the author's own rowing boat on display.

A further 2.5 miles (4km) north along the Ambleside road brings you to Brockhole, a fine house with gardens that shelve down to the lake shore. The house has, since the late 1960s, been the National Park Visitor Centre, with gardens, displays, exhibitions, an adventure playground and a range of events.

The eastern shore of Windermere is, for much of its length, in private hands. Mill owners bought up plots of land to create tranquil oases with stunning views of the lake. Thus it is that the drive along the lake (on the A592) can be disappointing; there are few public access points to the water's edge. However, the less-populated western shore, much of it managed by the National Trust, offers lakeside walks.

For an elevated view of the lake, take a path to the left of the Windermere Hotel. Within a few minutes you will have a glorious view of the lake and the southern Lakeland fells from Orrest Head. Another excellent viewpoint is the rounded hill called Gummer's How, which can be approached via a minor road just north of Newby Bridge. From the top (half an hour's walk from the car park) you will be able to see almost the length of Windermere.

OVER HAMPSFELL FROM GRANGE-OVER-SANDS

A walk through woods, gardens and over open fell above a charming seaside resort which retains a refined air of quiet dignity. The town has many fine and interesting buildings and its ornamental gardens, complete with ponds, provide suitable solitude in which to relax and enjoy a picnic.

DISTANCE/TIME 4 miles (6.4km) 2h **MAP** OS Explorer OL7 The English Lakes (SE) **START** Car park below road and tourist office, central Grange; grid ref: SD 410780 **TRACKS** Paths and tracks, can be muddy in places, 7 stiles **THE PUB** The Lancastrian, Grange-over-Sands. Tel: 01539 532455

1 From the north end of the car park walk through the ornamental gardens. Spend some time exploring the gardens but the most direct route keeps left, close to the main road. Exit to the mini-roundabout and take the road signed to Newby Bridge, Ulverston and Windermere. Go up and round the bend, and find steps up to reach a squeeze stile on the left, signed 'Routen Well/Hampsfield'.

2 Take the path up through Eggerslack Wood. Cross over a track and continue ahead, past a house on the left. Steps lead on to a track. Cross this diagonally to follow a track, signed 'Hampsfell', which makes one zig-zag and then climbs through the woods, passing old reservoirs. At the top is a wall and stile.

3 Cross the stile and follow the signposted path up the open hillside, passing sections of limestone pavement and little craggy outcrops. Cross another stile and go right along the wall. Where it veers away, continue in the same direction, following a grassy track past ancient stone cairns to the tower landmark of the Hospice of Hampsfell.

4 Turn left at the tower and follow the path over the edge of a little limestone escarpment (take care on the slippery rock). Continue over another escarpment and then gently down to a stile. Keep ahead through a dip and up the green hill beyond. Cross over the top and descend again to a gate and stile. Although the path bears left here, it is usual to continue directly to the little cairn on Fell End, with fine views over Morecambe Bay. Go sharp left to rejoin the main path, which skirts to the left of a little valley of thorn bushes and descends to a gate and a road.

5 Cross the road, take the squeeze stile and descend diagonally across the field to a gate on to a road by the front door of Springbank Cottage. Descend the surfaced track to enter a farmyard and bear right to a stone stile. Go over the hill, following the path parallel to the wall and cross a stile into a narrow path. Follow this round the corner and down to a road junction. Go left on a private road/public footpath, and then bear right at the fork. At the next junction turn right to descend the track and at the following junction go left down Charney Well Lane. At another junction, bear left below the woods of Eden Mount. Keep descending to reach a T-junction and go right. At the junction with a larger road go left and past the church and clock tower to a junction with the B5277. Go left, then right to the car park.

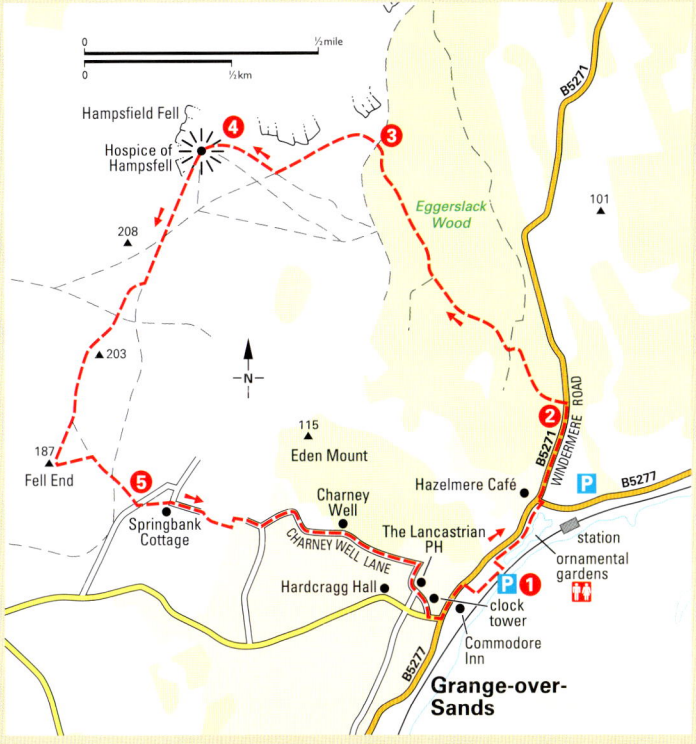

WALK 94

FROM ELTERWATER TO LOUGHRIGG TARN

Elter Water and Loughrigg Tarn are amongst the prettiest stretches of water in the region, with bluebell woods, swans and a waterfall. Each season delights, with daffodils by Langdale Beck in spring, bluebells in Rob Rash woods in May, yellow maple in Elterwater in October and shades of green, everywhere, all summer.

DISTANCE/TIME 4 miles (6.4km) 2h **MAP** OS Explorer OL7 The English Lakes (SE) **START** National Trust pay-and-display car park, Elterwater; grid ref: NY 328048 **TRACKS** Grassy and stony paths and tracks, surfaced lane, 4 stiles **THE PUB** The Britannia Inn, Elterwater. Tel: 01539 437210; www.britinn.net

1 Go through a gate and walk downstream beside Great Langdale Beck and through the mixed woodlands of Rob Rash. A little gate leads through a stone wall, and the open foot of Elter Water lies to the right. Continue ahead along the path through the meadows by the river. This section can be wet and is prone to flooding. (If the meadow is flooded, then a detour to the road will bypass it.) Pass through a gate and enter mixed woods. Keep along the path to pass Skelwith Force waterfall down to the right. A bridge crosses a channel to a viewing point. Keep along the path to pass through industrial buildings belonging to Kirkstone Quarry.

2 Kirkstone Gallery (now called Touchstone Interiors) is on the right, as the path becomes a small surfaced road. Continue to meet the A593 by the bridge, where there are picnic benches. Turn left to pass the Skelwith Bridge hotel. At the road junction, cross directly over the Great Langdale road to reach a lane just left of the phone box and bus shelter. Follow the lane, steeply at first, to a T-junction. Turn right over the bridge, then bear left up a narrow path. Go left on a track and then fork right, in front of a row of cottages. Where the track splits, bear left, through a gate with a sign for Loughrigg Tarn and Grasmere. Follow the track to overlook the tarn. Half-way along the tarn cross the stile over the iron railings on the left.

3 Follow the footpath down the meadow to traverse right, just above the tarn. The path bears right to climb a ladder stile over a stone wall. Follow the grassy track up the hill to a gate and stile on to the road. Turn left along the road, until a surfaced drive leads up to the right, signposted 'Public Footpath Skelwith Bridge'. Pass a small cottage. The track becomes much rougher as it passes a higher cottage, Crag Head. By a holly tree about 50yds (46m) further on, a narrow path goes sharply back right, up the hillside, to gain a level shoulder between the craggy outcrops of Little Loughrigg.

4 Follow the path over the shoulder and past a little tarn on the right, then descend to meet a stone wall with railings on top. Follow the wall down, under power lines, and soon find a ladder stile leading over the wall into the upper woods of Rob Rash. A clear path descends steeply to the road. Cross over diagonally right to a gap in the wall next to the large double gates. Descend a track to meet up with the outward route. Bear right to return to Elterwater village.

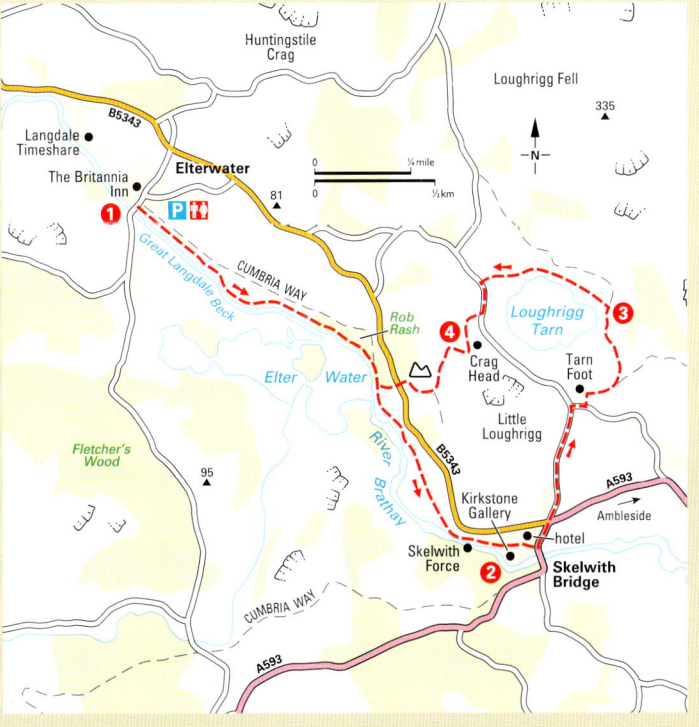

DISTANCE/TIME 12 miles (19.3km) 2h **MAP** OS Explorer OL4 The English Lakes (NW) **START** Bowness Knott car park; grid ref: NY 109153 **TRACKS** Good forest roads, occasionally bumpy **THE PUB** Shepherd's Arms Hotel, Ennerdale Bridge. Tel: 01946 861249; www.shepherdsarmshotel.co.uk

WILD ENNERDALE

A superb ride through the forest beyond Ennerdale Water. This route, entering the heart of the high fells, joins the world of the mountaineer, the fell-runner and the long-distance walker. The Forestry Commission and National Trust own large tracts of woodland and the lakeshore. There is no road alongside Ennerdale Water, but this route gives you some wonderful views of clear water, which is a reservoir for some Cumbrian towns.

1 Turn left from the car park, rolling down to the shores of Ennerdale Water. The track runs beside the lake for about 1 mile (1.6km), then continues through the forest above the river, here called Char Dub. 'Dub' is a common dialect word for a pool, while 'char' refers to a species of fish. Continue past Low Gillerthwaite Field Centre and then the youth hostel at High Gillerthwaite.

2 Just past the youth hostel the track forks. Keep right (really straight ahead). The track goes up and down more than you might expect. Take care on fast downhill bends where the surface is loose. Above all, don't grab the brakes. At the next fork 1 mile (1.6km) further on, a sign to the right points to Pillar. Save the Pillar road for the return and keep straight on – in fact, this track straight ahead gives the best views of the Pillar Rock. The way climbs gradually to a more level stretch with open views across the valley to Pillar directly opposite. Pillar Rock is the centrepiece of a mass of crags strewn across the north face of the mountain. At this point you could turn back.

3 As Pillar falls behind, the valley head opens up. There's a space where you may find vehicles and then the main track curves down right.

4 Straight ahead through a gate is a much rougher track leading 400yds (366m) to Black Sail Hut – many people may prefer to walk for some or all of it. You can make yourself tea or coffee (leave a suitable donation). Return to the gate. The bridleway going up right climbs to Scarth Gap Pass and then descends to Buttermere. Ignore it, and go back through the gate and down left to the River Liza.

5 Splash through the ford and swing round right. Now keep straight ahead along the track, mostly downhill, ignoring branches off the track up and left until it swings down to the river.

6 Cross the bridge and go up to the 'Pillar' signpost. Rejoin the main track of the outward route to return to your car at the car park.

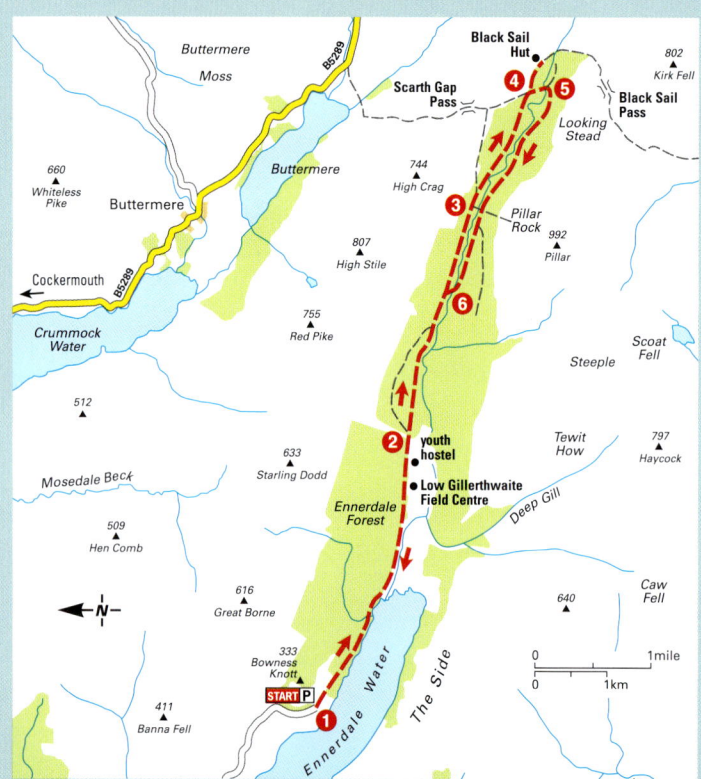

DISTANCE/TIME 7 miles (11.3 km) 1h15 **MAP** OS Explorer OL4 The English Lakes (NW) **START** Near Little Town, south of Skelgill; grid ref: NY 232194 **TRACKS** Lanes, mostly quiet **THE PUB** Swinside Inn, Newlands. Tel: 01768 778253; www.theswinsideinn.com

MEANDERING IN NEWLANDS

This classic Lakeland cycle route, west of Derwent Water, is surrounded by scenery that, even by Lakeland standards, is stunning, although you will catch glimpses of only one lake – Bassenthwaite.

1 From the parking place head up the steep hill to Little Town. Once through Little Town, relax and enjoy a fine winding, mostly downhill, run through the valley to Stair and a junction at the bottom of a hill.

2 Turn sharp right on to a narrow lane. The sign says 'Skelgill – Narrow Gated Road'. Climb again, with the hill of Cat Bells ahead. The lane steepens as it twists through Skelgill, reaching a gate just above. To the left of the isolated Swinside Hill, to the north, the stretch of water you can see is Bassenthwaite Lake. The lane passes a small parking area before reaching a T-junction on a bend. Turn left, downhill, over a cattle grid and round another sharp bend. The road levels out, then climbs to a junction.

3 Go left; the junction proves to be triangular. Go left again. As the road swings round to the right there are fantastic views up the valley and to the surrounding fells: Dale Head, Hindscarth, Maiden Moor and Robinson. Just beyond is the Swinside Inn. Turn right beside the pub on a narrow lane signed to Ullock and Braithwaite. Keep left where a road branches right to Ullock.

4 Cross a stone-arched bridge over Newlands Beck and begin a short climb, steep at the start. As it levels out there's another fleeting glimpse of Bassenthwaite Lake. At a T-junction turn sharp left. The road runs south, generally level along the base of the steep slopes, and just high enough above the valley floor to give open views. Dip down to a small bridge. Just beyond is the start of the principal walkers' path up Causey Pike; you may well see figures struggling up the initial steep slope of Rowling End. A little further on, keep straight on past a sharp left turn (for Stair, Portinscale and Grange). There are wonderful views of the beautiful Dales from here.

5 Very shortly, a steep stony track drops off to the left to a ford. Those seeking a moment's mountain-bike excitement can choose this track – it merely cuts off a short corner of the road. Alternatively, continue more sedately, round over a bridge to a wooden house. Turn left (signed to Newlands Church, Little Town) and drop down, then swing round, heading straight up the valley with its glorious range of fells ahead.

6 As you come right down into the valley bottom, turn right on the no-through-road to Newlands Church – closer even than the advertised 0.25 mile (0.4km). Retrace your route to the last junction and turn right, where it's only a few more pedal strokes to the bridge and the car park just beyond.

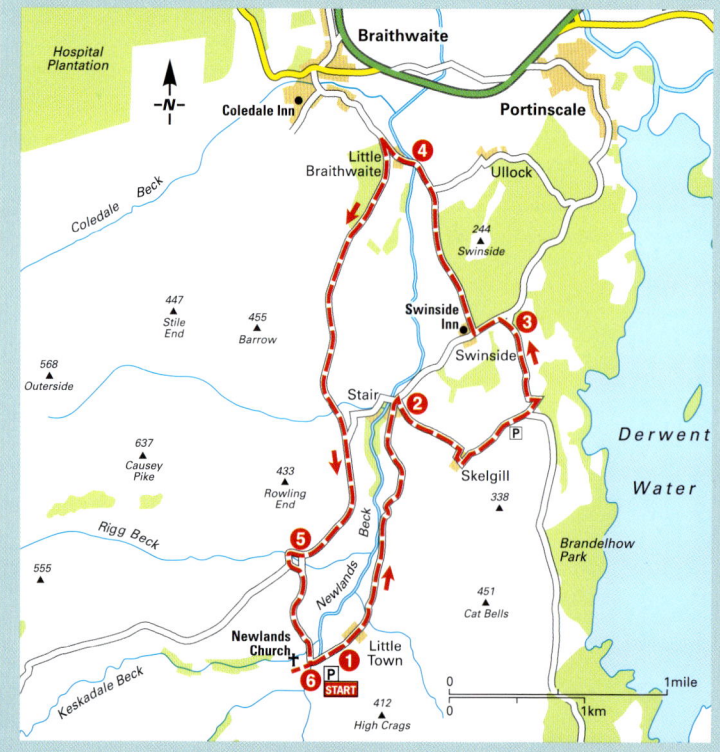

DISTANCE/TIME 8.75 miles (14.2km) 1h **MAP** OS Explorer OL5 The English Lakes (NE) **START** Village car park, Askham; grid ref: NY 513237 **TRACKS** Quiet lanes **THE PUB** The Queens Head, Askham. Tel: 01931 712225

DISTANCE/TIME 11 miles (17.7km) 2h longer route (off road); shorter route 6.5 miles (10.4km) 1h **MAP** OS Explorer OL5 The English Lakes (NE) and OL315 Carlisle **START/FINISH** Armathwaite village; grid ref: NY 504461 **TRAILS/TRACKS** Lanes with two optional off-road sections **THE PUB** The Duke's Head, Armathwaite. Tel: 016974 72226

AROUND ASKHAM & BAMPTON

This pleasant road circuit has few steep gradients and is away from the main tourist routes and begins and ends in Askham.

1 From the car park follow the main road south through the village past greens left and right. Keep on along this road, enjoying the generally easy gradients and views down the valley to the Shap Fells. Across the valley on the left is the sharp profile of Knipe Scar.

2 After just over 1 mile (1.6km), on the boundary of Helton, branch off right on a loop road to go through the village. The extra climb is worth it for the pretty cottages and flowery verges. Ease back to rejoin the valley road and continue, with limestone walls and small fields flanking the road on the right. As the road starts to descend, two lanes branch off to the right from a shared junction.

3 Follow the left-hand lane for 400yds (366m) to a cattle grid. Continue until the lane reaches open fell. There are good views here and you may find fell ponies grazing. Retrace to the road at the start of Point 3 and turn right to continue, now descending. At the bottom go right over Beckfoot Bridge and continue along the valley floor, passing pretty cottages at Butterwick. Climb to the edge of Bampton, and go into the village.

4 The post office and village shop has a café attached. Over the bridge opposite the shop, it's just a short way up the lane to the pretty Mardale Inn. (For a longer ride continue up this lane for 2 miles/3.2km to Naddle Bridge and Haweswater.) Continue along the main valley road towards Bampton Grange, swinging left into the village over a bridge crossing the River Lowther, and past the Crown and Mitre pub.

5 On the edge of the village, turn left, signposted 'Knipe, Whale'. Cross a cattle grid on to open fell. Look up to the right to the low crags of Knipe Scar. The lane climbs gently, with great views of the valley and the fells to the west. Descend to a junction by a phone box and turn right through a gate. Climb steeply to another gate, beyond which the road continues to climb gradually. The going levels off for a stretch before beginning to descend. Whizz back down into the valley, keeping straight on at a junction, and down to the river at Crookwath Bridge.

6 The climb away from the river is gentle but quite sustained. It then levels off just before a T-junction. Emerge with care as some traffic moves quite fast here, and almost immediately go right, back into Askham.

THE EDEN VALLEY FROM ARMATHWAITE

Discover an unsung but lovely corner, with two exciting off-road options. Armathwaite is a pretty settlement, with a small pele tower on the shore of the River Eden, now a country house.

1 Head north through the village and past the church. Continue along this lane, before a dip alongside a railway viaduct. Now climb, in two stages, to the level crossing at Lowhouse Crossing. Bump across the line and continue less steeply to a junction near Froddle Crook. The old, rusty signpost has lost one arm.

2 For the shorter ride, turn left here and follow the lane beside the High Stand Plantation, with fine views, to the crossroads at Blackmoss Pool. Go straight across to rejoin the longer route. For the longer route, go straight ahead at Froddle Crook for 1.5 miles (2.4km) to a turning on the left signed to Cotehill.

3 To stay on tarmac turn left here and follow the road for 1 mile (1.6km) to the crossroads in Cotehill village, then turn left. For the off-road alternative, continue ahead to a bridge over the railway and then pass a small wood on the left. At the end of the wood follow a bridleway sign left through a gate and down a short track. Where this bends left into a farmyard continue ahead, through an awkward gate, and follow field edges. At the bottom of the second field, just below the railway line, bear right on a short track to a gate and out on to the tracks. Cross with care. Go through the gate on the other side and straight out along the green track, rounding a bend to reach a clearer track. Follow this more easily, to emerge on to a road. Turn left for a short climb into Cotehill. At a crossroads, go straight across to rejoin the road alternative.

4 Carry straight on, signed to Armathwaite. Climb to Stand End, then on beside High Stand Plantation to the crossroads at Blackmoss Pool (more marsh than open water).

5 Turn right, signed to Aiketgate and Low Hesket. The tree-lined lane runs dead straight, first down, then up. A view of the fells opens up as the road dips to a T-junction. Turn left, signed to Nunclose and Armathwaite, and make a short climb into the hamlet of Aiketgate. A fork in the road, opposite the phone box, offers another off-road option.

6 To stay on the tarmac, keep right, and then bear left at the next fork. The lane begins a descent and the off-road alternative rejoins half-way down, at Windy Nook. For the off-road adventure, take the left fork at Point 6. The tarmac lane leads into a stonier track, climbing steeply. The gradient eases, but the track continues stony up to the crest. The descent ahead is on a much greener track. Go through the gate and on downhill, curving right. The final 100yds (91m) before the road are steep and tricky: consider walking. Rejoin the road at Windy Nook and turn left (pass the turning for Nunclose). The road goes towards a railway viaduct. Go left at a junction and into Armathwaite.

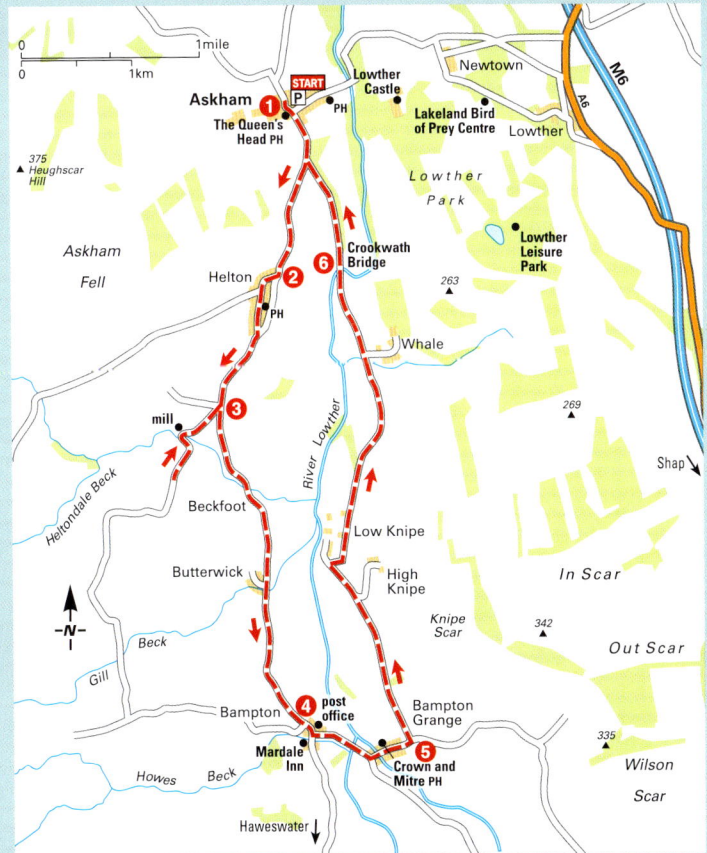

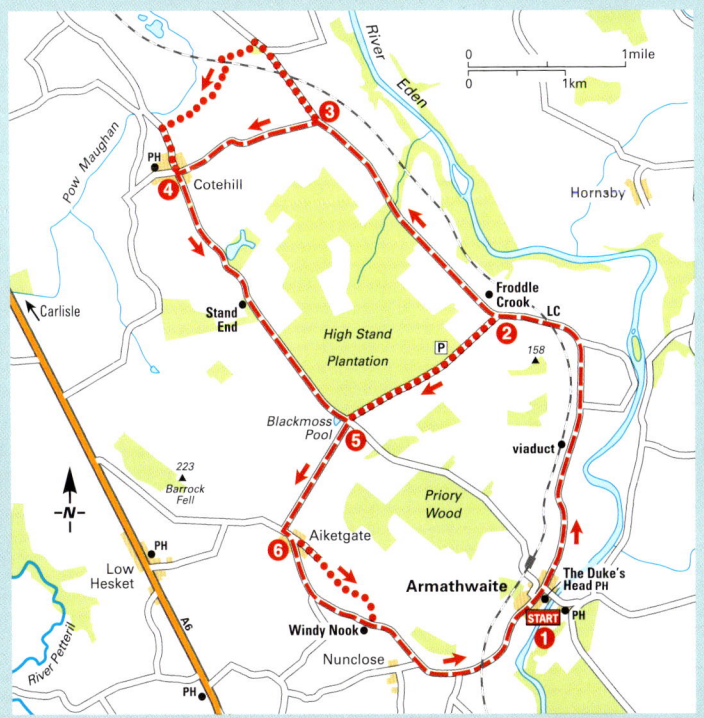

OVER MUNCASTER FELL

Muncaster Fell is a long and knobbly fell of no great height. The summit rises to 758 feet (231m), but is a little off the route described. A winding path negotiates the fell from end to end and this lovely linear walk takes you from Ravenglass to Eskdale Green, returning on Laal Ratty, a narrow-gauge train.

DISTANCE/TIME 6 miles (9.7km) 2h30 **MAP** OS Explorer OL6 The English Lakes (SW) **START** Car park at Ravenglass, close to station; grid ref: SD 085964 **FINISH** Eskdale Green Station; grid ref: SD 145998 **TRACKS** Clear tracks and paths, muddy after rain, 1 stile **THE PUB** King George IV Inn, Eskdale Green. Tel: 01946 723262; www.kinggeorge-iv.co.uk

1 Cross footbridges over the mainline and miniature railway lines, and continue along a narrow path. Turn right along a tree-lined lane signed to Walls Castle. The bathhouse is about 500yds (457m) along.

2 Continue along the footpath/cycle track, which swings left (signed 'Muncaster') away from the tarmac road. Follow the track to an open view of dunes and the sea. Continue up a short way, then turn left before some buildings. Follow the track up a little wooded valley and past a small lake, then across fields and into another wood. Keep straight ahead (signed 'Esk TR') to the visitors' entrance to Muncaster Castle grounds. Turn left, under a gateway, to the main road.

3 Turn right. Cross the road just beyond Muncaster Guest House. The road then leads to a bend, where Fell Lane is signposted uphill. Climb steadily for 0.75 mile (1.2km). Reach a little wooded dip, fork right, then left, passing secluded Muncaster Tarn on the left. Go through the gate at the top of the track to open fellside.

4 The path roughly follows the edge of a coniferous plantation, at the end of which the summit of Muncaster Fell is visible above. The main path continues just to the right.

5 Keep right again at the next fork. The path meanders to avoid bogs and remain roughly level, with good views over Eskdale. Eventually a panorama of fells opens up at the curious structure known as Ross's Camp, a large stone slab which was turned into a picnic table for a shooting party in 1883.

6 Continue along the footpath, looping round a broad boggy area to reach a corner of a dry-stone wall. Go down through a gateway. The houses of Eskdale Green appear through a gap in the ridge, with Scafell rising behind. Descend (it's nearly always wet), keeping fairly close to the wall, until a drier path bears right across the dip through bracken and scattered trees. Make a short ascent on a well-buttressed stretch, then descend sparsely wooded slopes, through a gate, ending on a track near another gate.

7 Go through the gate and turn left, to a prominent boulder, then bear right to the end of a wall under some trees. A clear path follows the wall, then bears slightly right and down to a stream. Follow the narrow track beyond, joining a wider track just below the railway. Follow the track almost to the road, then turn sharp left to reach Eskdale Green Station. Or, to find the King George IV Inn, turn right along the road for 300yds (274m).

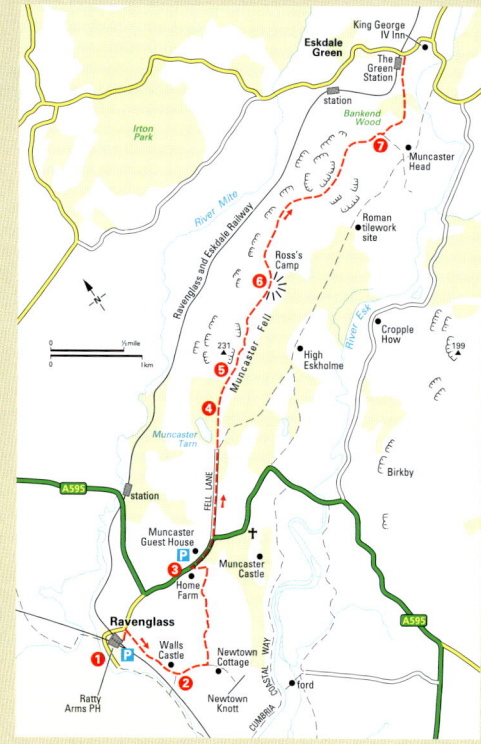

WALK 96

SEATHWAITE & THE DUDDON VALLEY

William Wordsworth loved the Duddon Valley so much that he wrote many sonnets about it. Follow in his footsteps by a chattering beck and through a gorge, where little has changed since his day. There's tarmac on those winding, walled lanes, but the byres and woods and lively stream are still untouched.

DISTANCE/TIME 5 miles (8km) 3h **MAP** OS Explorer OL6 The English Lakes (SW) **START** Seathwaite: roadside pull-off, grid ref: SD 231975; limited roadside parking near pub; grid ref: SD 228960 **TRACKS** Paths, tracks, can be muddy below Seathwaite Tarn, 9 stiles **THE PUB** The Newfield Inn, Seathwaite. Tel: 01229 716208; www.newfieldinn.co.uk

1 From The Newfield Inn car park at Seathwaite, follow the road past the little church. After about 400yds (366m) turn right on to the tarmac lane towards Turner Hall Farm, then take a track on the left signposted 'High Moss'. Keep left at a junction and follow the track to the isolated houses of High Moss. Skirt the houses on the left, then go through the gate behind them and follow the field path, ahead and then bearing left, out to the Walna Scar Road.

2 Turn right up the road. Where the tarmac ends, turn left on to the utility company's access road to Seathwaite Tarn. This pleasant green track climbs steadily up the fellsides to reach the reservoir dam.

3 Retrace your steps for 400yds (366m) to a waymarked post that highlights a downhill path. The path, though faint at first, weaves through rock and rough pasture and then steeply downwards beside a mountain stream. Cross a gate/stile, and then continue on to another gate, and then cross a ladder stile to the banks of Tarn Beck.

4 Cross the footbridge and turn left and then follow a footpath along the lower edge of a wood. Pass behind a cottage and continue

along to a ladder stile. Skirt a very wet area, then go through a gap in the wall and climb up to the Duddon Valley road.

5 Cross the road and follow the signed bridleway to the Fickle Steps, boulders which allow you to cross the River Duddon. Caution: if the river is high and the steps are awash, do not cross. The steps are too far apart for younger children to negotiate, but it may be possible to paddle if the river is low. If there is any doubt, return by the road. (A footpath from opposite the church takes you to Wallowbarrow Gorge from the other end.)

6 Assuming you have crossed over safely, turn left on the riverside path. Cross a footbridge over Grassguards Gill. The path gradually pulls away from the river, then traverses steep slopes above the tight wooded Wallowbarrow Gorge, before descending again to cross boulder-strewn terrain on the bank of the River Duddon, eventually reaching an arched stone footbridge.

7 Cross over the bridge and then turn right, following the east bank of the Duddon, to meet a tributary, Tarn Beck. Go up to a footbridge and cross to a short track out on to the road. Turn left to return to Seathwaite.

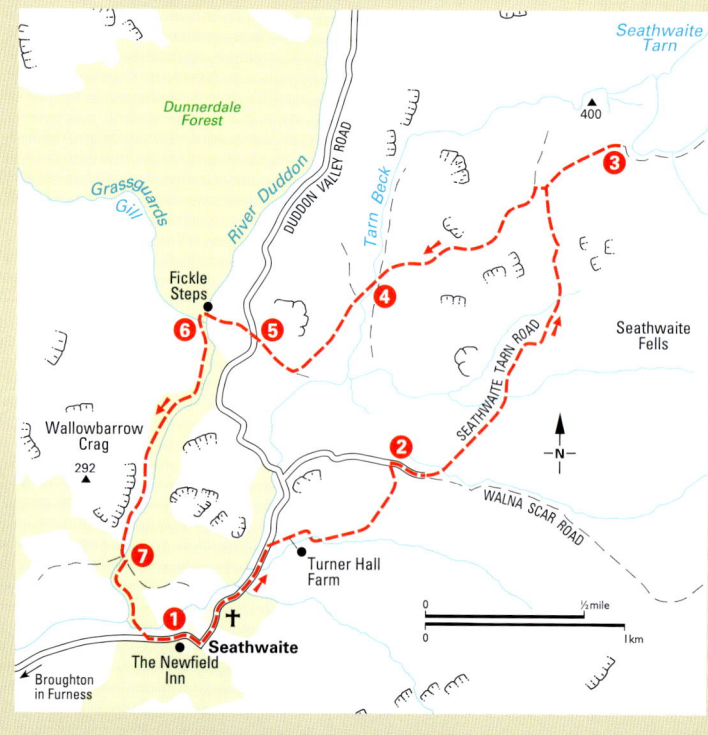

KESWICK'S WALLA CRAG ABOVE DERWENT WATER

At the foot of Borrowdale – often referred to as the most beautiful valley in England – the northern head of Derwent Water opens to Keswick and the northern fells with dramatic effect. The highlight of this walk is undeniably the panoramic views from the heights of Walla Crag to the surrounding fells.

DISTANCE/TIME 5.25 miles (8.4km) 3h **MAP** OS Explorer OL4 The English Lakes (NW) **START** Lakeside car park, Keswick; grid ref: NY 265229 **TRACKS** Good paths and tracks, steep ascent and descent, 3 stiles **THE PUB** Lake Road Inn, Keswick. Tel: 01768 772404

1 Proceed down the road to Derwent Bay. Go left opposite the landing stages, past a toilet block, on the track through Cockshot Wood. At a fork take the higher left-hand path. Exit the wood on to a fenced path, across a field to the Borrowdale Road. Cross, and climb stone steps into Castlehead Wood. Turn left, then bear right and climb steeply, levelling off at a shoulder. In a little way a steeper path climbs to the right, to Castle Head's rocky summit – a great viewpoint.

2 Return to the shoulder, and then turn right, heading downhill, curving right but keeping left at a fork, until rough steps lead down to a kissing gate. Take the path between fields to a road and houses. Go right and follow the road to its end at Springs Farm. Bear left on a track climbing through Springs Wood. Bear right at the fork, then as you follow the edge of the wood you pass a TV mast. At a kissing gate, dip back into the wood, cross a footbridge and go up rough steps to a lane. Turn right and then follow the lane to its end below Rakefoot.

3 Cross the footbridge and ascend the rough track by the stone wall. Go through a gate to open fell and follow the wall up right. At a dip the main path cuts off the corner of the wall and rises to a kissing gate. The path beyond this runs close to steep, unfenced drops in places. (To avoid these simply follow the wall left to a stile near the summit cairn.) Follow the path, crossing the head of a gully (Lady's Rake), and climb to the polished rock cap of Walla Crag and superb views.

4 Continue in the same line to reach a stile and then cross back over the wall. A grassy path descends parallel to the wall, becoming steeper as it drops down towards Cat Gill. You now keep descending steeply, taking care as you meet stone steps and slippery rock, until a track bears right near a footbridge, then you will descend more easily through Great Wood. At a junction of tracks, drop down left to a tarmac track and go straight across down a path to a gap in the wall by Borrowdale Road. Pass through another gap in the wall opposite and a take the short path that leads to the lake shore.

5 Go right, following the shore around Calfclose Bay. Leave the shore to skirt round Stable Hills, following its drive until a gate on the left leads to a path through damp Ings Wood. The path continues round Strandshag Bay to Friar's Crag. Go right and easily back via Derwent Bay to the car park.

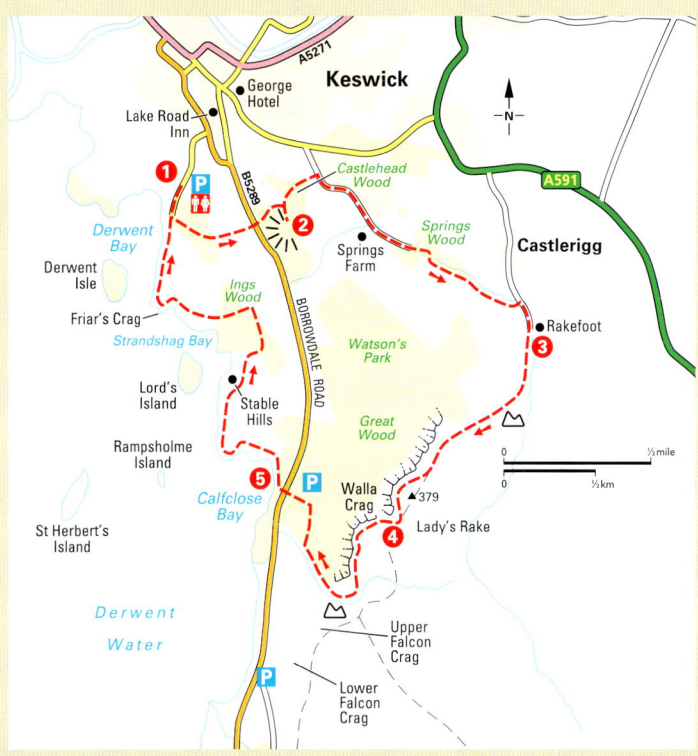

WALK 98

FROM GARRIGILL TO ASHGILL FORCE

This walk passes through a broad valley to discover exciting waterfalls and ravines. The hills here are big and bare with simple outlines, and Ashgill Force waterfall has a dramatic overhang that allows you to walk behind the falls, although the rocks can be slippery, so you should wear suitable shoes, and take care.

DISTANCE/TIME 3 miles (4.8km) 1h30 **MAP** OS Explorer OL31 North Pennines **START** Parking on green in front of post office, Garrigill; grid ref: NY 7444150 **TRACKS** Field paths, tracks and a quiet lane, 17 stiles **THE PUB** George & Dragon Inn, Garrigill. Tel: 01434 381293; www.garrigill-pub.com

1 From your parking place, walk down the road in front of the post office and the George & Dragon Inn (signposted 'Alston, Nenthead') to a bridge high above the River South Tyne. The road bends to the left but then a track continues straight ahead. Follow this, but note that it's very steep at first, to reach a tarmac lane at a bend.

2 Turn right immediately, signed to Pasture Houses, go through a gate and straight across a field. Cross a stile and continue to a gate below some new and restored buildings, then on to a stile. Bear right towards a farm and trees. Go through a gate in the field corner and then along the left (upper) side of the barn. Cross the yard diagonally to a track that leads out to a road.

3 Cross directly to a stile. Follow the wall below gardens on the left, then continue ahead to a stile. Keep straight ahead and level to another stile, then aim for another farm ahead. Go left of the first building and into the yard, then go left and right between the houses to a stile where the lane bends left again. Cross a short field and emerge on to a track. Cross this, and the paddock beyond, to a stile. Turn right, along the back of a house and through a gate into a field.

4 Turn left and then follow a green track, parallel to the wall and then descending to a footbridge and a four-way fingerpost.

5 Don't cross the bridge but turn left and follow a path left of Ashgill Beck. Continue to a footbridge with the main falls visible ahead. Cross the bridge and head to the falls, passing old mine workings on the right. If you walk behind the falls, be careful as the surface is loose, wet and slippery.

6 Retrace your steps, crossing the first footbridge, to the lower footbridge by the four-way fingerpost. Now continue downhill, still following Ashgill Beck.

7 Where Ashgill Beck meets the River South Tyne, cross a stile on to the riverside path. Follow the path, paved with flagstones in places, above a wooded gorge-like section. Where the river curves away to the left, it's possible to continue straight ahead across a rushy field. Go past a bridge (to Mid Crossgill) and continue along the river, under tall pines, to reach another four-way fingerpost.

8 Turn left across the bridge; walk up to a gate opposite Low Crossgill farm. Turn right along the road that leads back into Garrigill.

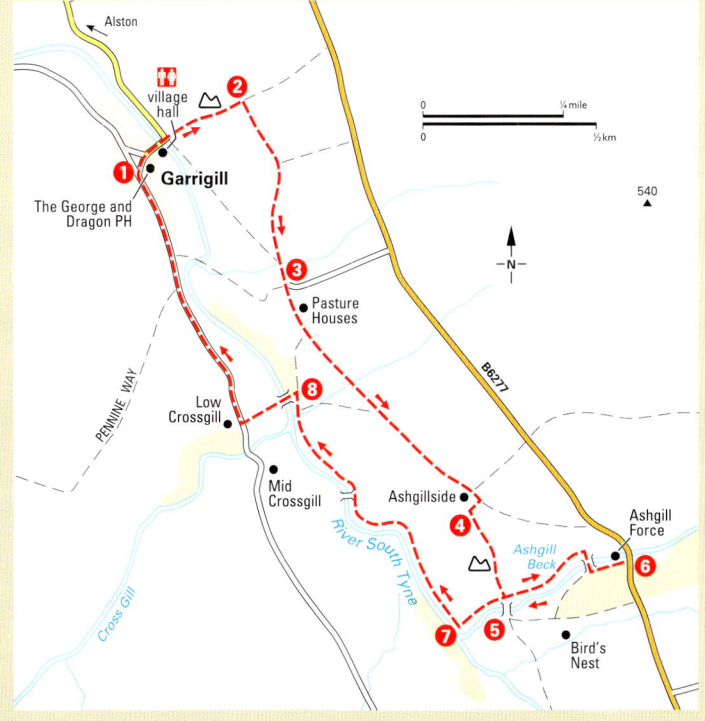

FROM PATTERDALE BY ULLSWATER

Ullswater is undoubtedly one of the loveliest lakes. It was the sight of golden daffodils amongst the trees and beside the shore that inspired Wordsworth's most widely known poem, 'I wandered lonely as a cloud' (1807). This walk takes you along the shores of Ullswater to Silver Point, a spectacular viewpoint.

DISTANCE/TIME 4 miles (6.4km) 1h45 **MAP** OS Explorer OL5 The English Lakes [NE] **START** Pay-and-display car park, Patterdale; grid ref: NY 396159 **TRACKS** Stony tracks and paths, no stiles **THE PUB** Patterdale Hotel, Patterdale. Tel: 01768 482231; www.patterdalehotel.co.uk

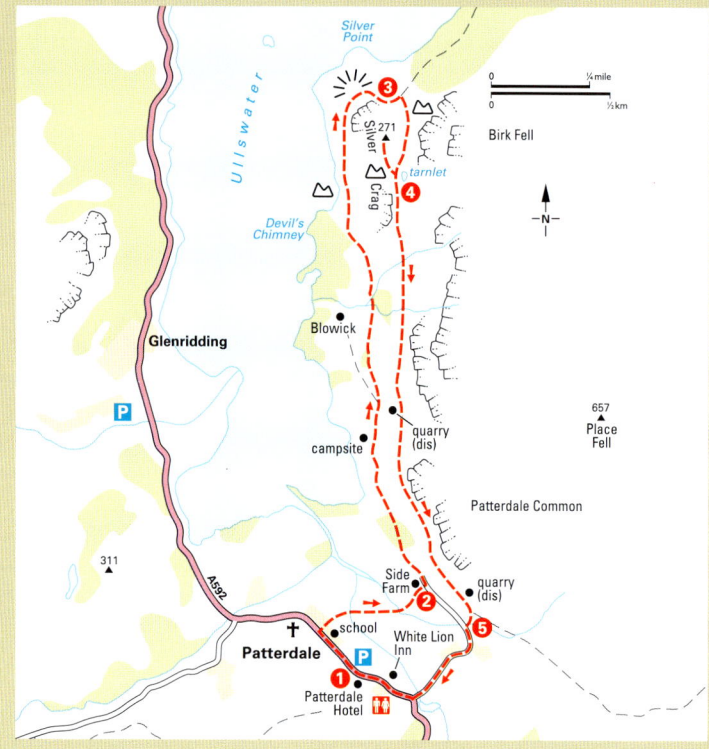

1 Walk out to the main road. Cross over to gain the pavement and turn right. Opposite a sign for Side Farm cross back to a stony track, signed 'Howtown and Boardale'. Follow the track over a bridge and up between the buildings of Side Farm. Turn left on to another roughly surfaced track.

2 Follow the undulating track, with a stone wall on your left. The lake and Glenridding appear away to the left, with the lead mine remains visibly prominent in the valley beyond. Keep ahead on above the campsite and through further undulations before the path ascends again to crest a craggy knoll above the woods of Devil's Chimney. Make a steep rocky descent (care is required) before the path levels to traverse beneath the craggy heights of Silver Crag. In places the steep ground falls directly to the lake below. A slight ascent, passing some holly trees, gains the shoulder of Silver Point and a superb view of Ullswater.

3 Continue on the path, which now sweeps round beneath the end of Silver Crag, until a steep stony path, which is eroded in places, breaks off to the right. Ascend this path, climbing steeply through the juniper bushes, into the narrow gap that separates Silver

Crag to the right from the main hillside of Birk Fell to the left. This little valley is quite boggy and holds a small tarn.

4 The path ahead soon begins a gradual descent back towards Patterdale. (If you have energy to spare, a short steep ascent leads to the top of Silver Crag – the view is not that much better than from Silver Point, but you are more likely to enjoy it in solitude. Where the main path levels out, climb steeply through a grassy gap between the crags. Bear right at the top on a narrow path through the prickly juniper, to the top. Descend by the same route to the main path.) The path traversing the open fell is easy, though it may be boggy in places. Pass above an old quarry, tree-filled and unfenced, and then descend across the slate spoil from another quarry. An artificial cave here usually has a waterfall spilling over its lip. Continue along the hillside above Side Farm, passing through more quarry workings. Descend to meet a wider track and follow it down to the right to a gate.

5 Go through the gate and bear left on a lane. Bear right at the next junction and through the meadows back to the main road. Turn right back into Patterdale.

KIRKBY LONSDALE TO WHITTINGTON

From the old market town to Whittington village, on the Cumbria/Lancashire border, this circular walk goes over rolling hills, through farmland and woods, returning to the village of Whittington along the banks of the lovely Lune. The walk passes close to Sellet Mill, reputedly the second largest waterwheel in Britain.

DISTANCE/TIME 4.75 miles (7.7km) 2h30 **MAP** OS Explorer OL2 Yorkshire Dales – Southern & Western **START** Devil's Bridge car park, Kirkby Lonsdale; grid ref: SD 615782 **TRACKS** Overgrown and indistinct in patches, quiet lanes and tracks, 17 stiles **THE PUB** Dragon's Head, Whittington. Tel: 015242 72383

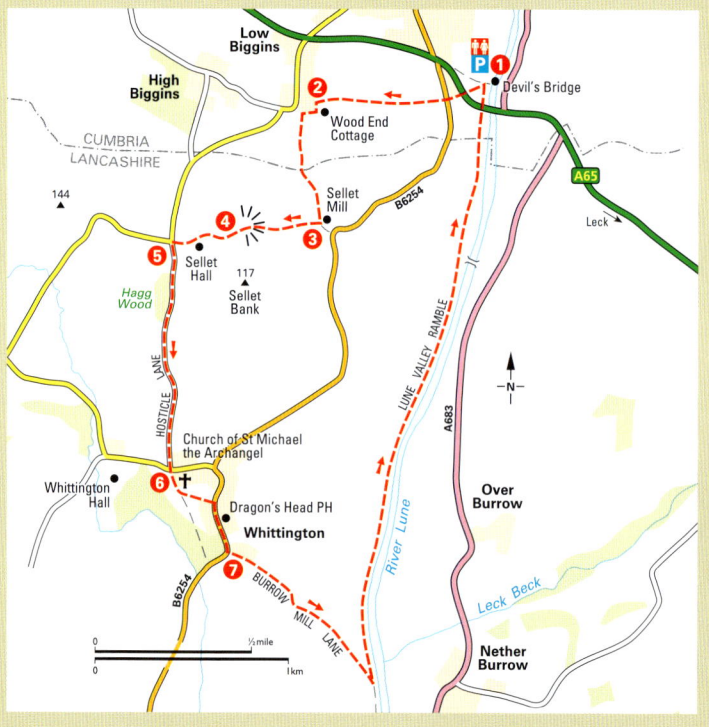

1 From the west bank of the river, a few paces downstream from Devil's Bridge, head across a park to a kissing gate on to the A65. Cross, and walk through a meadow and between houses to cross the B6254. Enter another meadow and go uphill, with the walled wooded area on your left. Go over the hill and through two stiles. Turn left at a gap stile to the farmyard at Wood End Farm.

2 Turn right on the farm track to reach Wood End Cottage. Go left in front of the cottage along a walled path, which is rough in places (please take care). A stream comes in from the left and tries to take over the path, but drier ground is ahead. Stay on this path until it opens out by Sellet Mill's millpond.

3 Turn right by the farm buildings and walk up the field, with the fence to your left, until just past the end of a garden. Go left through a yellow marked gate and walk across a small field to another marked gate, followed by a shallow stream. Bear right to skirt Sellet Bank, aiming for the corner of a hedge under pylons. Keep the hedge to your right.

4 Go through a yellow marked stile on your right, then skirt round a wooded area to reach Sellet Hall. Turn right and follow the

wooden fence, with marker arrows, then keep on over the corner of the field to cross a stile and drop down a couple of steps to the road at a T-junction. Turn left along Hosticle Lane towards Whittington village.

5 The tall trees of Hagg Wood are on your right as you follow the lane.

6 Go a few paces left at the T-junction, cross over the road and turn right over a pebbled mosaic to the Church of St Michael the Archangel. Keep the bell tower on your left before taking steps to reach a stile and the graveyard. Go through a gate in the lefthand corner and keep straight ahead across two small fields to a stone stile leading to a narrow, walled lane. Emerging on to Main Street, turn right and follow the road past the Dragon's Head.

7 At a sharp right bend on the village's edge go left on a gritty track. Follow the track between fields to a pair of gates. Go through the left-hand gate. Bear left to pick up the Lune Valley Ramble and follow it to the A65 bridge at Kirkby Lonsdale. Go through a gate and up steps to the left of the parapet. Cross over the road, and drop down the other side to cross the park at the start of the walk.

58 MILES (93KM)

The town was the site of Holme Cultram Abbey. Some of its buildings survived to become the splendid parish church. Robert the Bruce's father was buried here in 1294, 25 years before his son sacked the abbey.

7 Leave Abbey Town on the B5302, then just beyond Waverbridge turn left on to an unclassified road, signed to Aikhead and Station Hill. On reaching the A596, turn left, then right into Wigton and then right again into the town centre.

A feature of this town is the gilded granite fountain, erected in the 19th century. it shows four fine bronze reliefs of the Acts of Mercy.

8 Leave Wigton by going left in the town centre signed B5305 and then soon B5304. After about a mile (1.6km) cross the A595 and the continue ahead for 7 miles (11.2km) on an unclassified road, to arrive in Caldbeck on the B5299.

To visit the village, park in the car park by the bridge and walk beside the river to a little bridge giving access to the Church of St Kentigern.

9 Leave Caldbeck in the same direction by which you entered the town, but bear left on to the B5299 (to the left of the Oddfellow's Arms). After driving for about 3 miles (5km), at a fork keep to the B5299 and then continue for another mile (1.6km) to a sign for Ireby. Turn left and then descend into the village where you should turn left again and follow the signs for Bassenthwaite.

Here you enter the Lake District National Park, where there are 14 'lakes' and it is one of the remaining places in Britain that the red squirrel still inhabits.

10 Continue to a junction where a road from Uldale comes in on the left. Continue down to meet the A5291. Turn right, then left in front of the Castle Inn Hotel on to the B591. Keep ahead on the B5291, cross Ouse Bridge and turn left to a parking area.

This is a good place to stop and take a stroll.

11 Keep on the B5291 for about half a mile (0.8km) to meet the A66, turn right and drive back along it to reach Cockermouth.

FROM THE MOUTH OF THE CROOKED RIVER

This tour starts at Cockermouth, famous as the town where William Wordsworth was born. The route continues to the coast at Maryport, before heading north, hugging the coastline and passing through small fishing villages and an Area of Outstanding Natural Beauty. It then turns inland, taking in small villages and pretty market towns, crossing the boundary of the Lake District National Park and finally returning to Cockermouth.

Route Directions

In Cockermouth explore and breathe in some of its character – visit Wordsworth House (the poet's birthplace) in Main Street. The 13th-century Norman castle is partially ruined but a section is still occupied by the Egremont family; however, the castle is rarely open.

1 Take the A594 out of Cockermouth and drive for approximately 7 miles (11.2km) until you get to Maryport.

A port in Roman times, Maryport was developed in the 18th century by Humphrey Senhouse. Visit the interesting harbour, pretty marina, excellent Maritime Museum and Aquarium, then go up the hill to the Roman Museum and enjoy the superb view over the town.

2 Continue on the main route, passing King Doniert's Stone on the left (where there is parking). At the next junction, turn right, signed 'Draynes, Golitha Falls'. After 300 yards (274m), a left turn over a bridge leads to a car park with toilets.

From here, it is a short walk to the spectacular Golitha Falls, a favourite beauty spot and National Nature Reserve that lies alongside the River Fowey. The reserve covers an area of 18 hectares of woodland with the River Fowey running through it and creating several pretty cascades along its way.

3 From here, head towards the right, with the coastline to your left, and continue along the main route to Allonby.

Allonby retains much of its appeal from its days as a Georgian and Victorian bathing resort. Just across the Solway lies Scotland, and the Galloway hills.

4 From Allonby continue to drive north for 6 miles (9.6km) on the B5300 to Silloth, keeping the coast on your left.

Until 1857 Silloth was a fishing village; it expanded as a port when linked by rail with Carlisle; the town still preserves its charming Victorian spa atmosphere.

5 Continue straight on past the green and drive for about 1.5 miles (2.4km) to the village of Skinburness.

This is a designated Area of Outstanding Natural Beauty, with a wonderful coastline and stunning views across the sea to Dumfries and Galloway.

6 Drive on a narrow road from Skinburness for another 2 miles (3.2km). Turn left on to the B5302 and go through Calvo to reach Abbey Town.

THE REIVERS' TOUR

From the 4th to the late 17th centuries, the land around Carlisle, on the hazy border between England and Scotland, was one of the most lawless places in Britain. Reivers were the villainous families who lived on either side of the border and who plundered each other's property and cattle, killing each other into the bargain. There was even a reiving thieving season, beginning in August and lasting for three months, until the law courts reconvened. Today the quiet, countryside gives no indication of how awful this area must have been for its inhabitants. Reiving has left its dreadful mark on the English language with the word 'bereaved'.

Route Directions

The length of this tour is 68 miles (109km). It begins at Carlisle, the county town of Cumbria and the largest city in the area. There has been a settlement here since Celtic times, followed by the Romans, the Romano-Celts, Anglo-Saxons, Danes, Normans, Scots and English. Carlisle's imposing castle, which now houses a Regimental Museum, is a reminder of this constant conflict. The cathedral, built by the Normans, is also an indication of their search for peace after creating mayhem in the district, as they did in the rest of Britain. Visit the Reivers Exhibition at Tullie House to gain an accurate picture of the wild time and events, before starting out on your journey into the past.

1 Leave Carlisle on the A7. Drive round Hardwicke Circus roundabout and cross the River Eden. Shortly go right along the B6264 towards Hexham and Newcastle.

This is the area through which cattle, sheep and vegetables were brought to Carlisle. As Carlisle had been the traditional market centre for miles around and as roads were practically non-existent, the people had very little choice in where they could go to get the best prices.

2 Cross the M6 and meet a roundabout, where you take the 2nd exit on to the A689. Pass the airport runway and then turn left with the sign to the airport and Irthington. Continue through Irthington.

Here in Irthington village only a grassy mound indicates the probable remains of the Norman castle that once stood here.

3 About a mile (1.6km) after Irthington, turn right on to the A6071 and keep ahead. After crossing the bridge, turn left to Walton.

The course of Hadrian's Wall passes through the village. There was once a fort at Castlesteads, in the trees up to your left as you enter. There is little to see in the way of remains here, but the Wall's National Trail passes through.

4 Keep forward through Walton and at the junction with the B6318 turn right, signposted 'Gilsland and Greenhead'. Just after a mile (1.6km) turn left for Askerton Castle and Bewcastle church. At Bewcastle turn right up to the church and the cross.

Bewcastle is very close to the Scottish border and this proximity was one of the reasons that made it the focus for reiving activity – consequently there were many tracks leading through the area. In 1582 Thomas Musgrave, Captain of Bewcastle, and his tenants lost 700 cattle, 300 sheep, and crops and buildings were burnt. The history of Bewcastle goes back much further – to Celtic and Roman times. During the 2nd and 3rd centuries AD there were around 1,000 Roman soldiers stationed here. In the churchyard the Bewcastle Cross is an excellent example of Anglo-Saxon sculpture and a very early Christian memorial, as the majority of Anglo-Saxons were still pagans at this time. During the time of the reivers, it was said that only women were buried in the churchyard, because all the men were hanged in Carlisle.

5 At Bewcastle, turn left, and then at the junction take the right fork. Go right at the T-junction on to the B6318, which bears left. Continue for 4 miles (6.4km) to where the B6318 turns left. Do not take this left turn but continue straight ahead on a minor road, then bear right at the next junction, heading for Newcastleton. You are now in Scotland.

In Newcastleton take the opportunity to visit the Liddesdale Heritage Centre and Museum. This history museum and genealogical research facility houses a large collection of artefacts. A commemorative bicentenary tapestry created by local needleworkers is a unique exhibit. The museum also includes a superb collection of railway memorabilia in connection with the Waverley line, which had a station here.

6 Return south on the B6357 and after Canonbie join the A7 to return to England through Longtown and Carlisle.

On the edge of Longtown, Arthuret church overlooks the site of an important battle in the 6th century AD. According to Welsh poems, 30,000 were slain on the field and the wizard Merlin (Myrddin) was driven to madness by the death of his lord Gwenddoleu here.

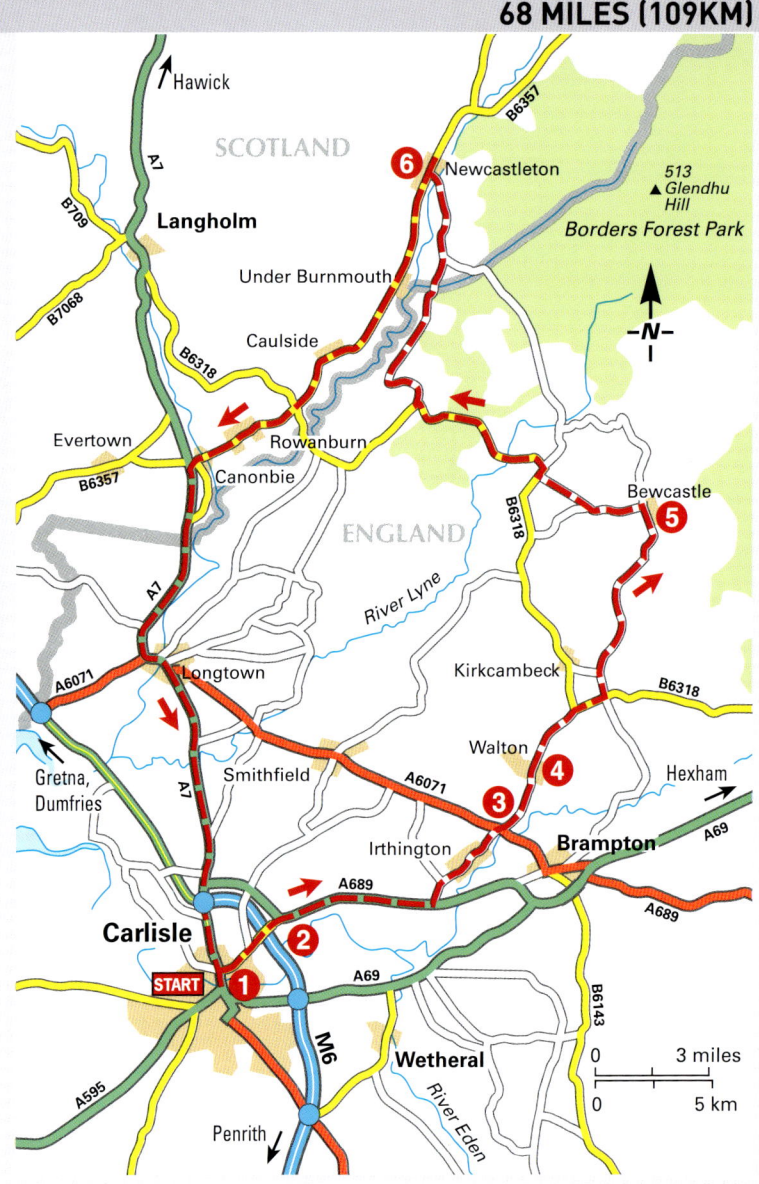

Yorkshire Moors

CLOCKWISE FROM BELOW LEFT: ROBIN HOOD'S BAY; ROSEBERRY TOPPING; ST HILDA'S ABBEY, WHITBY; STANDING STONE, FRYUPDALE

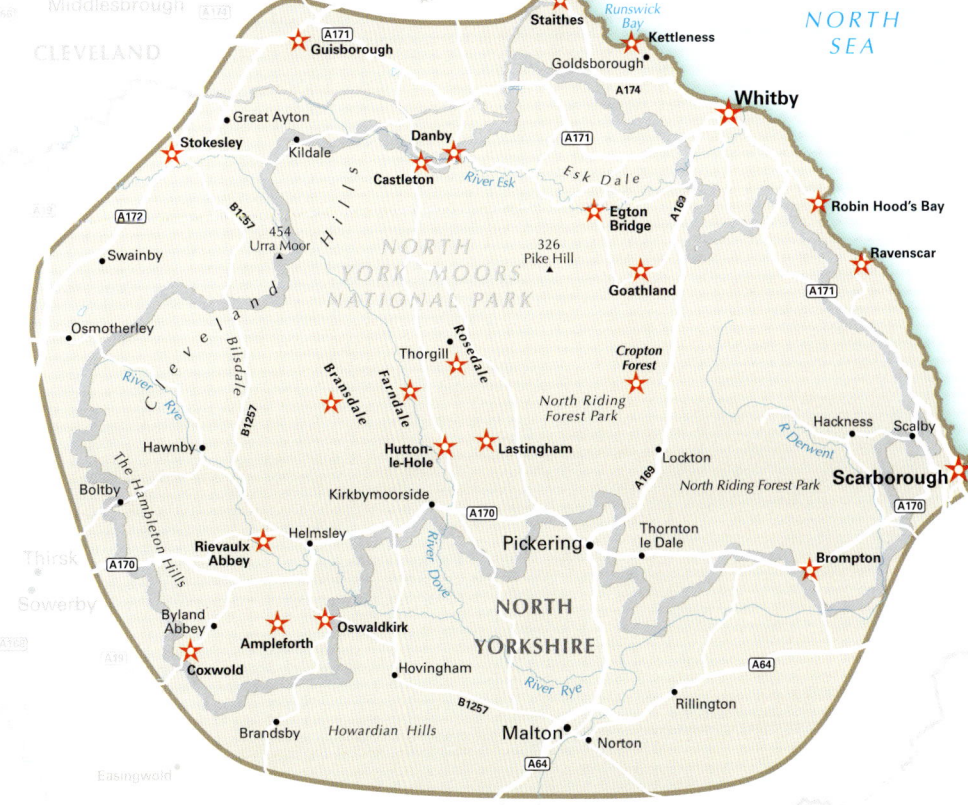

AMPLEFORTH MAP REF 407 J5

Best known for its public school and Benedictine monastery, Ampleforth is a linear village of handsome houses that overlooks the Howardian Hills. French monks, fleeing religious persecution in their homeland in 1793, found sanctuary in England and patronage from the Fairfax family, settling at Ampleforth in 1802. As theirs had been a teaching order, they built a school within the monastery. The oldest school buildings date from 1861, while the monastery dates from 1894–98. But both establishments have been extended up to the present day.

Just after the end of World War I, headmaster Father Paul Nevill, who was also the parish priest, commissioned Robert Thompson of Kilburn to make a wooden cross for the churchyard in the village. Father Nevill was so impressed by the woodcarver's craftsmanship that Thompson was asked to make furniture for the school. The library remains one of Robert Thompson's most ambitious commissions. The present abbey church

is a new addition, built between 1922 and 1961 to a design by Sir Giles Gilbert Scott; it too contains fine examples of woodwork and carvings by Robert Thompson.

BRANSDALE MAP REF 407 J4

The unspoiled valley of Bransdale drives deep into the moors, but most visitors pass by. For a delightful drive, leave Helmsley along the A170 towards Kirkbymoorside looking out on the left for a signpost to Carlton (and Helmsley Youth Hostel). The road loops around Bransdale and then returns to the A170 about 5 miles (8km) further east at Kirkbymoorside.

Beyond the houses that comprise the village of Carlton, the views open up dramatically. To the left is unenclosed heather moorland; to the right the valley bottom is divided up by neat drystone walls either side of Hodge Beck. This pattern is punctuated by a handful of farmsteads. The moors, with barely a tree to be seen, echo to the evocative calls of the curlew, red grouse and lapwing; sheep graze the grassy verges and wander across the

road. Unenclosed for the majority of the way, the road heads north; look out left for examples of inscribed milestones.

Flour was ground for centuries at Bransdale Mill (National Trust, but not open to the public), accessible, on foot only, from either side of the valley head. The present building, dating from 1811, was built by William Strickland and his son, Emmanuel, the vicar of Ingleby Greenhow. Stones inset into the mill walls are inscribed with 'improving' texts in Hebrew, Latin and Greek.

The road then makes a broad sweep to the right, before continuing the circuit of Bransdale. Here sturdy farmsteads with fanciful names – Cow Sike, Toad Hole and Spout House – gaze down into the bottom of the valley. Before arriving in Kirkbymoorside, you can visit Gillamoor and Fadmoor, a pair of typical moorland villages barely half a mile (800m) apart.

BROMPTON MAP REF 407 K4

Motorists on the A170 tend to drive straight through Brompton in their haste to get to the Yorkshire coast. The pretty little village is set around a small lake, into which the church doors were thrown during the Civil War; they were later recovered and re-hung. The poet William Wordsworth took the time to get to know the village, for he courted Mary Hutchinson, a local girl who lived at Gallows Hill Farm. They were married, in 1802, in Brompton's church.

The village has a unique (though sadly little-known) place in the history of aeronautics. Everybody knows it was Wilbur and Orville Wright who made the first manned flight, in their flimsy craft, *Kittyhawk*. Yet a remarkable 50 years before that memorable occasion, an unsung squire of Brompton Hall quietly set about building a flying machine.

Brompton Hall (now a school and not open to the public) had been the home of the Cayley family since Stuart times, and Sir George Cayley (1771–1857) developed an unquenchable scientific curiosity. His inventions included caterpillar tracks and a new form of artificial limb, prompted by an accident to one of his estate workers.

But the prospect of flight remained Sir George's passion. Even before the 18th century was out he was designing gliders – continuing to refine the craft's aerodynamics until he had a controllable machine that could carry a man. His various experiments proved that a contoured wing could provide much greater lift than a wing with a flat profile.

Though an inscription in the church porch acknowledges Sir George as the 'Father of Aeronautics', his pioneering efforts are largely overlooked. Facing the main road through the village is the

six-sided building, the summerhouse, now boarded up, unfortunately, where Sir George worked on his flying machines.

CASTLETON MAP REF 407 J4

The castle is long gone from Castleton; only the name and a mound to the north of the village remain – a lot of the stone from the ruined castle was probably used to build Danby Castle. Castleton used to have regular markets and a goods yard on the railway; the markets have long gone, but the village still has its passenger station on the Esk Valley railway line.

The River Esk, which rises at Esklets in Westerdale to the south, is joined at Castleton by a tributary, Commondale Beck. To the north of the village is an expanse of moorland, but the landscape is very different from that of the south, with a selection of minor roads, tracks and footpaths exploring a landscape of great variety. Two routes 'take the high road' over Castleton Rigg, enjoying panoramic views down into Westerdale and Danby Dale, and on to Ralph Cross (used as the National Park emblem) and the head of beautiful Rosedale. This is moorland scenery at its best; valley bottoms divided up into neat fields by drystone walls, the pattern interrupted by little copses.

COXWOLD MAP REF 407 J5

Coxwold, about 3 miles (5km) south of Kilburn, has a 15th-century village church, with an eight-sided tower, overlooking the handsome houses lining the broad main street, which include almshouses dating back to the reign of Charles II.

Shandy Hall opposite the church was once the home of Laurence Sterne (1713–68). As a writer Sterne was a relatively late developer, not picking up his quill until the ripe age of 46. The publication of his picaresque novel, *The Life and Opinions of Tristram Shandy, Gentleman*, happened as he became the vicar of Coxwold. Literary success was immediate, and Sterne was able to indulge his taste for high living. He contracted pleurisy and died in 1768. His skull is buried in Coxwold churchyard. Dilapidated Shandy Hall was renovated in the 1960s and filled with manuscripts and first editions and opened to the public.

To the south of Coxwold is Newburgh Priory, which was designed and built as an Augustinian house in 1145. After the Dissolution of Monasteries, Henry VIII rewarded his chaplain, Anthony Bellasis, by giving him the building. He, and the owners who followed him, transformed the priory into a fine country house.

The beautiful setting of Byland Abbey (English Heritage) wasn't the first site chosen by the band of Cistercian monks who came here from France. They had

BROMPTON FOREST

DANBY

settled briefly near Old Byland, but it was reckoned to be unsuitable because the monks were confused by hearing the bells of nearby Rievaulx Abbey. Finally, in 1177, work began on Byland Abbey. The dramatic west façade, with its 26-foot (8m) diameter window, still stands to its full height, and gives an impression of just how huge the nave used to be.

CROPTON FOREST MAP REF 407 J4
The extensive moors are continually evolving, and one of the most dramatic changes of the 20th century was the creation of large-scale conifer plantations. The Forestry Commission began this in the 1920s; now the area comprises one of the most extensive man-made forests in the country. Cropton Forest occupies a large area of the North Riding Forest Park between Rosedale in the west and Newtondale to the east.

The woodlands are now reaching maturity, and upwards of 120,000 tons of timber are felled every year to meet consumer demand. More recently, care has been taken to ensure that plantings harmonise with their surroundings. Areas of broadleaved and mixed woods provide a more varied habitat for wildlife.

Cropton Forest provides plenty of outdoor activities – there is a campsite, forest cabins and educational outdoor

activity centres set out amid the trees, and opportunities for walking and biking. The North Yorkshire Moors Railway, from Pickering to Grosmont, passes through the eastern edge of the forest, and stations at Levisham and Newtondale provide easy access for visitors to the woodland.

Roman roads are not hard to find, on the map at least. The Roman road, commonly known as Wade's Causeway, across Wheeldale Moor and immediately to the north of Cropton Forest, is still that rare thing – a Roman road which is still visible on the ground.

There are Roman remains at Cawthorn Camp, believed to have been used as a training camp, which is signposted from the minor road between the villages of Cropton and Newton-on-Rawcliffe. From the purpose-built car park the waymarked path, no more than a mile (1.6km) long, guides you around them. The well-preserved earthworks reveal a camp, two forts and an annexe wedged side by side on a plateau, which enjoys panoramic views to the north across to the moors.

DANBY MAP REF 407 J4
The lovely village of Danby lies on a crossroads; blink and you've missed it. But it was to this little village that John Atkinson came, at the age of 36, as minister of the parish. He was Essex-born

and until the end of his long life retained the natural curiosity of the newcomer. One of his major passions was prehistory, and the moors, with their burial mounds, standing stones and wayside crosses, provided much to excite his mind.

There are a number of interesting features in the immediate vicinity, and the easiest way to see them is to park up at the National Park's Visitor Centre, just half a mile (0.8km) from the village on the road to Lealholm. The Moors Centre represents the public face of the National Park. Here you can discover what makes the North York Moors so special and the unique habitats that the moors support. The Moors Centre hosts exhibitions and events, including guided walks. The evolution of the moorland landscape is explained, and those whose needs extend no further than tea and a slice of cake are equally well catered for. The Moors Centre sits in 13 acres (5.2ha) of land, close to the Esk, a lovely spot to enjoy a picnic or a stroll along the riverside on a gloriously sunny day. There are waymarked walks to help you explore the area; longer walks start from the car park.

EGTON BRIDGE MAP REF 407 J4
Egton and Egton Bridge are two villages separated by both the River Esk and a steep descent. Egton appeared in the

Domesday Book as Egetune, meaning 'the town of the oak trees'. The oaks are gone, as are the annual hiring fairs, when farmers would look to employ farm labourers. The village is important as the venue, every August, for one of the area's largest agricultural shows.

A new bridge, built in 1993, spans the River Esk at Egton Bridge. The stone arch replaces an ugly metal structure that was itself merely a replacement for the original bridge, which was swept away in floods in the 1930s.

Egton Bridge was the birthplace in 1599 of Father Nicholas Postgate, who ministered to his Catholic flock at much danger to himself. In 1678 he was sentenced – in his 80s – to be hanged, drawn and quartered. In remaining staunchly Roman Catholic, Egton Bridge became known as 'the village missed by the Reformation'. The impressive Catholic Church of St Hedda contains relics of Father Postgate's ministry. Half-way up the hill to Egton is a house with a tiny chapel hidden in the roof, reached by a secret passage. The room was rediscovered 150 years after Postgate's death, since when it has been known as the Mass House.

Ramblers alight at Egton Bridge, a stop on the Middlesbrough to Whitby line, and walk along the Esk Valley to Lealholm to catch the next train home.

Activity
CLEVELAND WAY

When it was inaugurated in 1969 the Cleveland Way was only the second national trail in the country. The name of the walk derives from the Cleveland Hills and is a little ambiguous, since for most of its 110-mile (176km) length it lies inside the North York Moors National Park. The roughly horseshoe-shaped route breaks into two distinct sections. From the start at Helmsley, you pass through the moorland scenery of the Hambleton and Cleveland Hills. The highest point is within the National Park when the walk traverses Urra Moor. Once the North Sea is sighted, at Saltburn, walkers follow the coastal path down to the finishing point at Filey Brigg. An extra section of the Cleveland Way, known as the Missing Link, has been developed to take walkers in a complete loop from Scarborough back to Helmsley. This circular walk is about 180 miles (288km) long.

Activity
THE CROSSES WALK

The Crosses Walk is a challenge walk of about 53 miles (84.8km), created to be undertaken in a single day. Starting and finishing at the village of Goathland, it uses 13 prominent crosses as waymarkers.

FARNDALE MAP REF 407 J4

Farndale is a delightful valley at any time of the year, but every Eastertime it blooms with a profusion of golden wild daffodils. The daffodil walk accompanies the River Dove between Low Mill and Church Houses. This is an undeniably pleasant stroll, and suitable for wheelchairs, but try to pick a weekday, if possible, to make your visit; or venture a little further afield, for wild daffodils can be found throughout the valley. The traffic has become so heavy in recent years that a field in the village of Low Mill becomes a car park while the daffodils are in bloom. There is a park-and-ride bus service operating from Kirkbymoorside and Hutton-le-Hole.

The greatest threat to the daffodils has been the numbers of visitors, who were once unable to admire the spectacular springtime displays without gathering armfuls of the flowers. Once market traders found this free source of daffodils the flowers were in danger, and in 1953 about 2,000 acres (810ha) of Farndale were designated as a nature reserve. Resist the temptation to pick any.

At other times of the year Farndale reverts to a peaceful farming community. Both sides of the valley are accessible: from either Kirkbymoorside and Hutton-le-Hole on the A170 to the south, or, most dramatically, from the north down a steep road which descends from Blakey Ridge just to the south of the Lion Inn.

GOATHLAND MAP REF 407 K4

This pleasant village has achieved fame by proxy as the location for the popular television series *Heartbeat*. On the small screen Goathland is transformed into fictional Aidensfield. Episodes were filmed throughout the moors, but the village of Goathland will be especially familiar to viewers; there is no need to search for locations the cameras have blessed.

Goathland was a popular destination for visitors long before the television series began, and though by no means the prettiest village on the moors, it is certainly well worth visiting in its own right. The broad grass verges, closely cropped by sheep, lead directly on to the heather and bracken of the moors. The village also makes an excellent centre for exploring the surrounding moorland and the stretch of Roman road known as Wade's Causeway. Fame brings its own problems, however, and Goathland does get very busy on bank holidays.

Black-faced moorland sheep are everywhere, local farmers enjoy grazing rights throughout the village, so the sheep roam where they will. They have only the most rudimentary road sense, though.

A brief investigation of the village and its surroundings will reveal a number of delightful waterfalls. The best known is the 70-foot (21m) Mallyan Spout, easily reached via a footpath adjacent to the Mallyan Spout Hotel. The hotel's Victorian architecture is a reminder that the first influx of visitors came with the building of the railway in the 1830s. Before that, the village's moorland setting kept it in relative isolation. Goathland's church, just a century old, but on a site of Christian worship for a thousand years, was furnished by Robert Thompson of Kilburn. Look for the little carved mice that were the craftsman's trademark.

Goathland was one of the stations on the main Whitby–Pickering line, a status it retains now that the once-defunct line has a new lease of life as the North Yorkshire Moors Railway. The steepest section of the line was known as the Beck Hole Incline, and it was so steep that the earliest carriages had to be hauled up and down by using a system of counter-balanced weights: a very hazardous procedure.

GUISBOROUGH MAP REF 407 J3

Guisborough's broad main street and cobbled verges indicate that markets have been held here for centuries. The old market cross is topped by a sundial. Today the market traders put up their stalls on Thursdays and Saturdays.

Beyond the main street and the market cross is the largely 15th-century Church of St Nicholas, where a cenotaph reinforces the links between the local de Bruce family and the Bruces of Scotland. Robert the Bruce's grandfather is buried near by at Guisborough Priory.

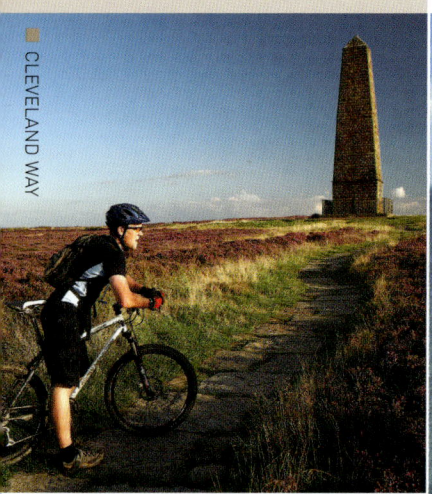

CLEVELAND WAY

KETTLENESS

The huge east window of the ruined Augustinian priory still stands to its full height of nearly 71 feet (20m), gazing out across farmland. To wander around the evocative ruins is to escape the bustle of Guisborough's busy streets. The priory was built in the early 14th century by Robert de Bruce, who was related to the Scottish king, Robert the Bruce. In the monks' contemplation of the life to come, the monks did not neglect to lay up their treasures on earth, and by the time of the Dissolution they had become one of the richest communities in the north.

Guisborough Hall, now a luxury hotel, sits in beautiful wooded surroundings. The original hall was built by Sir Thomas Challoner, whose son began mining alum on the moors in about 1600. The industry proved to be vital to the local economy during the next three centuries. Challoner stole the secrets of alum mining and processing from the Pope, who had enjoyed a near-monopoly in the industry. He even persuaded some of the Pope's miners to accompany him to England. For this, the Challoner family was excommunicated from the Catholic Church.

Just a mile (1.6km) out of town, on the A173 in the direction of Skelton, is Tocketts Mill. The water of Tocketts Beck still turns the waterwheel of this fine old flour-mill, and on certain milling days the building is open to the public.

HUTTON-LE-HOLE MAP REF 407 J4

It is to Hutton-le-Hole's benefit that it lies just off the main A170 between Thirsk and Scarborough, for it has managed to maintain its distinct personality instead of selling its soul to the tourist trade. One of Yorkshire's 'picture postcard' villages, its houses are set back from Hutton Beck, a little watercourse spanned by a succession of pretty little bridges. The village green is the size of a meadow, but the grass is cropped short by grazing sheep, which wander wherever they choose.

The houses of discreet grey stone, with the red-tiled roofs so typical of the moors, lend a timeless air to the village. The tiny church has some very fine oak furniture made by Robert Thompson of Kilburn, carrying his trademark carved mouse.

Don't neglect to visit Ryedale Folk Museum. This open-air collection is based on the displays of bygones built up by two local collectors. For nearly 500 years a thatched, cruck-framed cottage stood here in Danby village. In 1967 this typical farmer's house was moved to the museum's 2.5-acre (1ha) site. The tall, 16th-century manor house, also thatched and cruck-framed, is a huge hall open to the roof beams. Other museum buildings house a primitive 16th-century glass furnace, a photographer's studio, and a row of shops recreated as they would have looked more than a hundred years ago. Throughout these buildings, exhibits in their own right, are informal displays on past life in such moorland villages. Events are held here throughout the year.

KETTLENESS MAP REF 407 K3

The handful of houses clustered together in Kettleness look as if they could fall off the cliff top at any minute. That's precisely what happened in 1829, when a landslip devastated the entire community. Fortunately, the villagers had enough warning of the impending disaster to vacate their homes and businesses and were rescued by a ship waiting for them offshore. But you may wonder, why bother to rebuild the village on such an exposed site? The answer can be found by taking a path down on to Kettleness Point, a barren and rocky promontory. Here are the remains of productive alum mines where alum was shovelled out of the cliffs.

How precarious a living alum mining provided can be appreciated by the fact that the foundations of a large number of the mining buildings end at the cliff edge. The folk of Kettleness lost their livelihood, and their village, in the landslide of 1829; however, mining and processing of alum was fully operational again within five years.

Today, Kettleness Point is a dramatic moonscape, offering nesting sites for seabirds and, to the north, a view of Runswick Bay. The promontory forms part of the Heritage Coast, a sort of linear national park, which aims to preserve undeveloped coastlines with some of the most spectacular scenery along the east coast. Protection is now given to the 36-mile (57.6km) stretch of coastline that lies between Saltburn and Scalby Ness, on the outskirts of Scarborough.

Goldsborough, half a mile (0.8km) inland, was the site of a 4th-century Roman signal station. All that remains to be seen on the site are some grassy earthworks, 220 yards (200m) from the road linking Kettleness and Goldsborough. Excavations early in the 20th century produced a number of very interesting Roman finds, which suggested that the signal station might have ended its days by being suddenly ransacked. Near by you'll find a modern coastguard station.

LASTINGHAM MAP REF 407 J4

The casual visitor to the small village of Lastingham will see a collection of good-looking houses, a few wellheads and a welcoming inn, but Lastingham has something more to offer – a unique place in the history of Christianity.

GUISBOROUGH

St Cedd left the island of Lindisfarne (Holy Island) in AD 655 and chose this site for a monastery. St Cedd was buried in his monastery, close to the altar. In 1078 Abbot Stephen of Whitby moved his own community to Lastingham. He built a crypt dedicated to St Cedd, in which the saint's remains were re-interred. Apart from a few minor changes the crypt looks the way it did almost a thousand years ago.

The present church, planned merely as the abbey's chancel, was eventually consolidated to meet local needs.

OSWALDKIRK MAP REF 407 J4

The village of Oswaldkirk is strung out along the road beneath the steep and well-wooded Oswaldkirk Bank, and looks out across the Ampleforth Valley. The community takes its name from St Oswald's parish church. St Oswald became King of Northumbria in AD 634, and has a special place in the history of the Christian Church. The Venerable Bede wrote about St Oswald in his *Ecclesiastical History of the English People* in AD 731.

Oswald was deeply impressed by the monastic community on Iona, founded by St Columba. Once a Christian convert, he grafted the new faith on to familiar customs, for example, building Christian churches on pagan sites. It was Oswald who gave Lindisfarne to St Aidan and the monks of Iona as another sanctuary from which to spread Christianity.

One Easter, while Oswald and Aidan were about to share a meal, Oswald learned that there was not enough food to feed the poor at the gate. The king gave them his own food, still on its silver platter. Aidan was so moved by this act that he took the king's right hand and said, 'May this hand never perish'.

Oswald died in AD 642 while fighting the heathen King Penda of Mercia. Penda had Oswald's body dismembered and stuck on stakes. But Oswald's right hand did not wither, and it was taken to Lindisfarne as a venerated relic. Oswald was elevated to sainthood, and many tales of miraculous cures were associated with his bones.

The nave of St Oswald's church is largely Norman; cross fragments confirm that Oswaldkirk was already settled in Anglo-Saxon times. A couple of 'mother and child' sculptures in the porch offer an evocative contrast – one is modern, the other is Anglo-Saxon.

RIEVAULX ABBEY

RAVENSCAR MAP REF 407 K4

Great things were planned for Ravenscar. A developer named John Septimus Bland decided to build a holiday resort that he thought would rival Whitby and Scarborough. A station was built, Bland laid out the town's network of roads and began to build shops and houses. But Bland's company went bankrupt, and work stopped. Despite the panoramic sea views, this exposed site was clearly unsuitable for such a development. It is geologically unstable, and visitors would have been faced with an awkward descent to the stony beach far below.

You can see Ravenscar's street layout today, though grass is growing through where the buildings ought to have been. When the Raven Hall Hotel was built in 1774, it was simply Raven Hall. The hotel was to have been the centrepiece of the resort; now it stands alone, its mock battlements a landmark for miles around.

The Romans built a signal station here; its foundations and an inscribed stone (on display in Whitby's Pannett Park Museum) were found when Raven Hall's own foundations were being laid. The signal station relayed warnings of Anglo-Saxon invaders to military bases.

This part of the coastline (in the care of the National Trust, visit their Coastal Centre in Ravenscar) was exploited for alum, used in dyeing to fix colours permanently. Remains of the quarries and buildings can be found near the town.

RIEVAULX ABBEY MAP REF 407 J4

A short drive (or pleasant stroll) from Helmsley is one of Yorkshire's finest treasures. Today the setting of Rievaulx Abbey (English Heritage) is sheltered and inviting, but when Walter l'Espec dispatched a group of French monks to find a suitable site on which to build a new community it was reported to be fit only for 'wild beasts and robbers'.

In 1131, the monks began to build the mother church of the Cistercian Order in England. Many people today consider Rievaulx to be the pre-eminent Cistercian abbey in the country. The nave is Norman, while the rest of the abbey was built in the Early English style.

The monks may have started out with a strictly ascetic attitude towards wealth and lifestyle, but the 140 monks and nearly 600 lay brothers of Rievaulx Abbey succeeded in creating great influence. By 1538, at the Dissoution of Monasteries, the monks had become very wealthy indeed.

Cut into the hillside above the abbey is Rievaulx Terrace (National Trust), a curved grassy promenade that is more than a match for the landscaped terrace at nearby Duncombe Park. The terrace at Rievaulx offers strollers tantalising glimpses of the abbey between groups of trees, with fantastic views of the Rye Valley and Hambleton Hills. There are temples, one in the Ionic style, with a fine sumptuous interior, the other Tuscan, to mark both ends of the terrace.

ROBIN HOOD'S BAY MAP REF 407 K4

Robin Hood's Bay vies with Staithes for the title of the prettiest fishing village on Yorkshire's coastline. Both communities have to juggle the demands of tourism with the needs of local people. To visit Robin Hood's Bay leave your car at the top of the hill, where there are two large car parks. The road down to the beach is a cul-de-sac and visitors' cars are barred.

Apart from the access road, the houses, clinging precariously to the side of the cliff, are reached by narrow alleyways and steps. A jumble of whitewashed cottages and red-tiled roofs lead down the main street and almost into the sea. A story tells of a ship which at high tide came so close to shore that its bowsprit knocked out the window of a pub!

There is no harbour. Where once there were more than a hundred fishing boats, there are now just a handful, and they are launched down a slipway. Many of the old fishermen's cottages are now holiday homes. There is a good stretch of sandy beach and a rocky foreshore; children love to investigate the little rock pools left in these scars by the receding tide. Take care; it is easy to get cut off by the tide when it starts coming in again.

Robin Hood's Bay has had its share of wild storms, their effects exacerbated by the softness of the rock that forms the cliffs. A sea wall helps to blunt the worst of the buffeting, though every winter still brings memorable storms.

ROSEDALE MAP REF 407 K4

Rosedale is a lovely tranquil valley. City visitors will feel a long way from the noise and grime of Yorkshire's industrial heartlands. But just one hundred years ago the scene was very different: Rosedale was a veritable moorland 'Klondike'.

Ironstone had been mined here, sporadically, since the Iron Age. During the 13th century mining added to the wealth of the monks of Byland Abbey; but it was only in the middle of the 19th century that the extent of Rosedale's subterranean wealth was realised, with the discovery of massive quantities of top-grade iron ore. The Industrial Revolution brought a huge demand for iron and the blast furnaces on the rivers Tees and Tyne needed a constant supply for building ships, railways and general engineering.

The transport of ore was difficult from isolated Rosedale. In 1861 the North Eastern Railway Company built a line from Battersby Junction on the Stockton–Whitby line, over the bleak moorland to Rosedale West. In 1865 a branch was built around the head of Rosedale to the east mines, joining the original line at Blakey Junction, just below the Lion Inn on Blakey Ridge. To reach Teesside the wagons, now laden with ore, were winched down the descent of the Ingleby Incline.

The Rosedale railway was closed in 1929, by which time the valley's mining boom was over. The route of this line is used today by walkers, cyclists and horse riders. The valley is quietly 'going back to nature', but the massive calcining kilns (where ironstone was roasted to reduce its weight) have been preserved in memory of Rosedale's mining past.

SCARBOROUGH MAP REF 407 K4

The resort of Scarborough can claim to be one of the oldest in the country. Its prosperity goes back to the occasion in the year 1620, when a visitor, Mrs Elizabeth Farrow, was drinking a glass of spring water. Finding the water acidic in taste, she came to the natural conclusion that something that tasted so unpleasant must surely have medicinal qualities too.

Promises of miraculous cures have always had willing ears. Scarborough's spring water was said to cure many ills, even hypochondria. Scarborough's spring water certainly contains Epsom salts and a cocktail of minerals. The taking of the waters was soon put on a more commercial footing. Scarborough became known as a spa town; a name borrowed from the Belgian resort. Scarborough was put firmly on the map as a place where the well-heeled might come to recuperate. A local doctor also started to extol the health-giving properties of sea bathing.

Scarborough Castle has dominated the town with an air of fortress-like impregnability for the best part of a millennium. On its headland, between the North and South Bays, it enjoys an uninterrupted view over the town and out to sea. Remains of earlier defences have been unearthed, including an Iron Age settlement and a Roman signal station.

Scarborough has enough attractions to keep visitors coming back for more. Cricket lovers eagerly anticipate the Scarborough Festival, traditionally held towards the end of the season. Playwright Sir Alan Ayckbourn keeps faith with local theatre-goers by premiering most of his plays here in his Stephen Joseph Theatre. The miniature North Bay Railway runs for just under a mile (1.6km) between Peasholme Park and the Sealife Centre at Scalby Mills where you can see a colourful Caribbean-style coral reef.

STAITHES MAP REF 407 J3

It is easy to miss the Staithes turning off the main A174 coast road. Nor is the first sight of the village very promising. You have to drive half a mile (0.8km), park in the pay-and-display car park and proceed on foot if you want to see the place.

This perfectly preserved Yorkshire fishing village is divided into two by Cowbar Beck and the steep-sided gorge through which it runs. For centuries the people of Staithes coped with the twin problems of an inhospitable site and the ravages of the North Sea. The Staithes we see today is a village that would be immediately familiar to the young James Cook, who spent an impatient 18 months working at the counter of a draper's shop in the village before realising his ambition to go to sea. The whitewashed houses, pantiled roofs, fishing cobles and lobster pots would make him feel at home.

STOKESLEY MAP REF 407 J4

Stokesley maintains the unhurried character of a market town. The broad verges of West Green create a little space between the Georgian façades of the houses and the main street that winds through the town. Stokesley still has markets every Friday on the cobbled edges of the main street. Each September, the market town is the site of one of the largest agricultural shows in the area.

The big open spaces include College Square and the market square. Behind them is Levenside, where the River Leven, little more than a stream at this point, follows its tranquil winding course between grassy banks and underneath a succession of little bridges. The oldest of these is the handsome arch of a fine old packhorse bridge; near by is a ford.

WHITBY MAP REF 407 K4

Those who take a leisurely stroll along the pleasant harbour front may be forgiven for thinking of Whitby as just another resort. But Whitby has a long, illustrious and genuine history as one of the country's most important seaports.

Whitby's setting itself is dramatic, with houses clinging on to the steep slopes on either side of the River Esk. Whitby has always gazed out to sea. By the 18th century it was a major port, with shipbuilding, fishing and whaling. The fine Georgian houses at the west end of the town, built by wealthy shipbuilders and fleet owners, attest to this success.

Elsewhere, more traditional cottages, whitewashed and with red-tiled roofs, housed the fishermen. Space was at a premium, so their houses were built in close proximity, mostly up the steep inclines on the eastern side of the Esk. They are linked by ginnels and steps. Leave your car in one of the long-stay car parks near the marina; Whitby's narrow streets were not built for cars.

The town was prosperous during the 17th and 18th centuries with the mining and refining of alum. Coal was brought here to fire the cauldrons that separated alum from rock, and stone was needed for building; this increase in trade required the building of a better harbour. In 1753 a company was set up in the town to undertake whaling expeditions, using the sturdy ships already being built here.

Smaller boats sailed out of Whitby to net herring, and the fish market was one of the busiest. The men still fish, but on a much reduced scale.

In AD 655 King Oswy of Northumbria celebrated a victory in battle by promising his daughter as a bride of Christ. He founded a monastery on Whitby's eastern cliff, much where the later abbey's ruins stand today. The first abbess was Hilda and for her goodness and piety she was recognised as a saint. St Hilda's abbey was destroyed by Viking raiders. The abbey that replaced it was begun in the 11th century; this is what we see today.

Sharing the abbey's site is St Mary's Church. St Mary's parishioners have to tackle the 199 steps up to the church. At the bottom of Church Steps is the oldest part of town. If those 199 steps have taken their toll enjoy a drink in one of the harbour-side pubs.

On Grape Lane, by the harbour, you will find the home of ship owner and Quaker, Captain John Walker, to whom the young James Cook was apprenticed in 1746, before enlisting in the Royal Navy. Today the building houses the Captain Cook Memorial Museum, with fascinating room sets and exhibits about his life.

the crossroads, signposted 'Castleton'. In Castleton village, turn right half-way up the hill, signed 'Guisborough'. Cross the River Esk once again, to climb up on to lovely open moorland. At the first junction by the White Cross base go left on a road signed 'Commondale and Stokesley'. Pass through Commondale, as fine moorland views open up. Continue through Kildale and then take two right turns following the signposts back to Great Ayton and the start of the tour.

AROUND THE CLEVELAND HILLS & ESK DALE

This route skirts the Cleveland Hills, passes high cliffs and fishing villages, before exploring the more intimate landscape of the delightful Esk Valley. Staithes, Whitby and the string of villages along the Esk Valley are well worth exploring, and Lealholm, towards the end of the drive, makes an ideal place to stop for a picnic.

Route Directions

The drive starts and ends at Great Ayton, a handsome town where Captain James Cook spent much of his boyhood. Houses overlook the River Leven, and rearing up behind them is Roseberry Topping.

1 Leave Great Ayton along the A173, signposted 'Whitby and Guisborough'. Roseberry Topping is the hill with a 'bite' taken out of its summit due to ironstone mining. Turn right at a roundabout heading towards Whitby on the A171. Keep straight ahead at the roundabout, on the outskirts of Guisborough, but turn left at the next roundabout, on to the A173, signposted 'Redcar and Saltburn'. Go across another roundabout, almost immediately, and then pass restored Tocketts Mill. Turn left at traffic lights in Skelton (signposted 'Whitby'), soon to go right at a roundabout on the A174, signed 'Brotton & Whitby'. Cross over four more roundabouts, bear right at the fifth, signposted 'Whitby', and go through Carlin How, to get your first sight of the sea. Follow Whitby signs (A174), down hairpin bends near Skinningrove, where the Cleveland Ironstone Mining Museum can be found.

The mining museum at Skinningrove, located on the site of the Loftus Mine, is based on the collections of enthusiast Tom Leonard who was a great collector of mining artefacts. The mine opened in 1983 and has many dedicated volunteers who conbtribute to its success.

2 Go through Loftus, still following the A174. Sea views open out as the fishing village of Staithes appears on the horizon. Pass the unsightly bulk of Boulby Potash Mine, and then Staithes.

To visit the delights of the old part of the village leave your car at the top of the village, and explore the village and harbour on foot.

3 Continue on the A174 through rolling farmland past Lythe and its church. Whitby Abbey can be seen on the horizon as you drop down steeply into Sandsend. Take great care on Lythe Bank; there have been a number of runaways here. After passing Whitby golf club you approach the town itself.

4 At a mini-roundabout, turn right, following signs for the A171 'Scarborough and Pickering'. Turn right again at a T-junction near a garage. Take the left-hand fork soon after, turn left at another roundabout to reach traffic lights. Turn right, still following signs for the A171 'Scarborough and Robin Hood's Bay'. Over the bridge there is a road to your left. Take this if you want to see the church and abbey at close quarters. Otherwise your road is to the right, opposite, and signed, rather unpromisingly, to 'Larpool Lane Industrial Estate'. This unclassified road takes you to Ruswarp village and the River Esk. From here, keep close to the river for most of the way back to Great Ayton.

5 Turn right to cross over Ruswarp's river bridge and adjacent railway line, then turn immediately left on the B1410 to Sleights. Follow the River Esk and then go left at a T-junction on to the A169, signposted 'Pickering'. When you are almost through the village of Sleights, look out for a road on the right, signed 'Grosmont and Egton'.

There are fine views into the delightful Esk Dale before dropping down into Grosmont, where the North Yorkshire Moors Railway connects with the Middlesbrough–Whitby branch-line services.

6 Carry on to Egton, where you follow the signs left to 'Egton Bridge', turning left again at a T-junction. Turn right just after the church, signposted 'Glaisdale'. Climb steeply to a T-junction; turn left here and negotiate the precipitous 1-in-3 (33%) Limber Hill.

The hill heads down to the ancient stone arch of Beggar's Bridge that once carried trains of packhorse ponies over the River Esk.

7 Climb through the straggle of houses in Glaisdale; the signs are now for Lealholm. Keep ahead on the main road, eventually to turn right at a T-junction to descend into Lealholm village.

With its fine arched Beggar's Bridge, stepping stones and grassy river banks, this is one of the prettiest villages along the Esk Valley.

8 Cross the bridge over the River Esk, and then turn left immediately, signposted 'Danby'. Pass graceful Duck Bridge and the National Park's Moors Centre, where it's worth stopping if you have time, but otherwise bear left to Danby village. Keep ahead at

60 MILES (96.5KM)

DISCOVER THE WESTERN MOORS

Starting from Helmsley, this tour takes you through the western moors and dales, around the superb Cleveland and Hambleton Hills, taking in Rievaulx Abbey, Byland Abbey, Coxwold and Helmsley along the way. The best walking is around Chop Gate in Bilsdale, and Sutton Bank. A section of the tour is on narrow roads; please drive with care.

Route Directions

1 Begin the tour in Helmsley along the B1257, taking a left turning from the top of the square and a right turning by the church, signposted to Stokesley. After 1.5 miles (2.4km), turn left down an unclassified road, signed 'Old Byland'. Immediately before a little bridge, turn right over the River Rye, to see the impressive ruins of Rievaulx Abbey ahead, in its delightful setting. Drive past the abbey, through the village and uphill to rejoin the B1257. Turn left, signed 'Stokesley'.

As you pass a conifer forest on your right, beautiful views open up of Bilsdale ahead. After the scattered houses of Chop Gate climb Hasty Bank with its viewpoint; look out on the right for the distinctive profile of Roseberry Topping.

2 At a mini-roundabout in Great Broughton turn left, signed 'Kirkby' and 'Carlton', with the escarpment of the Cleveland Hills rearing up on your left. Go through Kirkby and Rusby, right at the T-junction, then left, on to the main A172 in the direction of Thirsk. After 2.5 miles (3.4km) turn left, signed 'Swainby'. Turn right over the bridge in the middle of Swainby, a pleasant village sitting astride a beck, and immediately left. Climb gradually uphill on to Scarth Wood Moor. Pass Cod Beck Reservoir and continue on into Osmotherley. Bear right, in the centre of the village, by the market cross, 'Northallerton and Thirsk'.

Next to the stepped market cross is a curious stone table; market wares were probably displayed here. John Wesley certainly put it to good use as an open-air pulpit on the many occasions he preached in the town.

3 Turn right at the T-junction and on to the A19, signposted to 'Thirsk,' to join the dual carriageway southbound. Leave at the second turning on the left, signed 'Over Silton'. For the next few miles you are on very narrow roads, so please drive with care. Drive through Over Silton. At a T-junction a mile (1.6km) beyond, go left, signed 'Kepwick and Cowesby'. Drive uphill to a T-junction, which is adjacent to the gatehouse of Kepwick Hall; go right here, through the pleasant little village of Kepwick. Take the next turning on the left, signed 'Cowesby'. Drive through Cowesby (there is a sharp right bend in the village centre) to Kirby Knowle. Pass the parish church and turn left towards Felixkirk. Take the next two left turnings, both signed 'Boltby'. Descend into

Boltby, a pretty arrangement of cottages in the honey-coloured stone that is so typical of this area.

4 Climb steeply out of the village and continue steeply again through Boltby Forest; at the top, turn right, signed 'Old Byland and Cold Kirby'. Follow this ruler-straight section of the route, part of the old Hambleton Drove Road – as you turn right you can see the old, unmetalled track continuing to the left. At the end of the road turn right at a T-junction, signed to 'Thirsk and Sutton Bank'. Pass the car park at the top of Sutton Bank.

If you need to take a break and stretch your legs, this is the ideal spot – a waymarked path along the top of the bank offers easy walking and breathtaking views across the Vale of York.

5 Go left at a T-junction by the car park, on to the A170, signed 'Scarborough'. Take the first turning on the right, signed 'Yorkshire Flying Club, White Horse'. Drive downhill through woodland until you get to the White Horse car park.

A short walk from here allows a closer investigation of the white horse, carved into the steep hillside in 1857 – though this is one landmark that looks better from a distance.

6 Continue on down to a T-junction. At this point, turn right and take a slow drive into the village of Kilburn.

Look out for a half-timbered building: this is the furniture-making workshops and showroom founded by craftsman Robert Thompson, whose work carries a carved mouse.

7 Drive through the village; after 2 miles (3.2km) go left at a T-junction to arrive in the main street of Coxwold. Turn left at the crossroads at the bottom of the village, signed 'Byland Abbey Ampleforth and Helmsley'. Laurence Sterne (author of *Tristram Shandy*) was once the vicar of Coxwold.

Opposite the church is Shandy Hall, his home, which is now a museum devoted to Sterne's life and work.

8 Pass the evocative ruins of Byland Abbey, drive through Wass and on to Ampleforth, then pass Ampleforth Abbey with its famous Catholic public school. Oswaldkirk is next;

once at the end of the village bear left, going steeply uphill, signed 'Helmsley'. At the top of the hill turn left, along the B1257 and right at the Trafalgar Arch at Sproxton, and you will soon return to Helmsley.

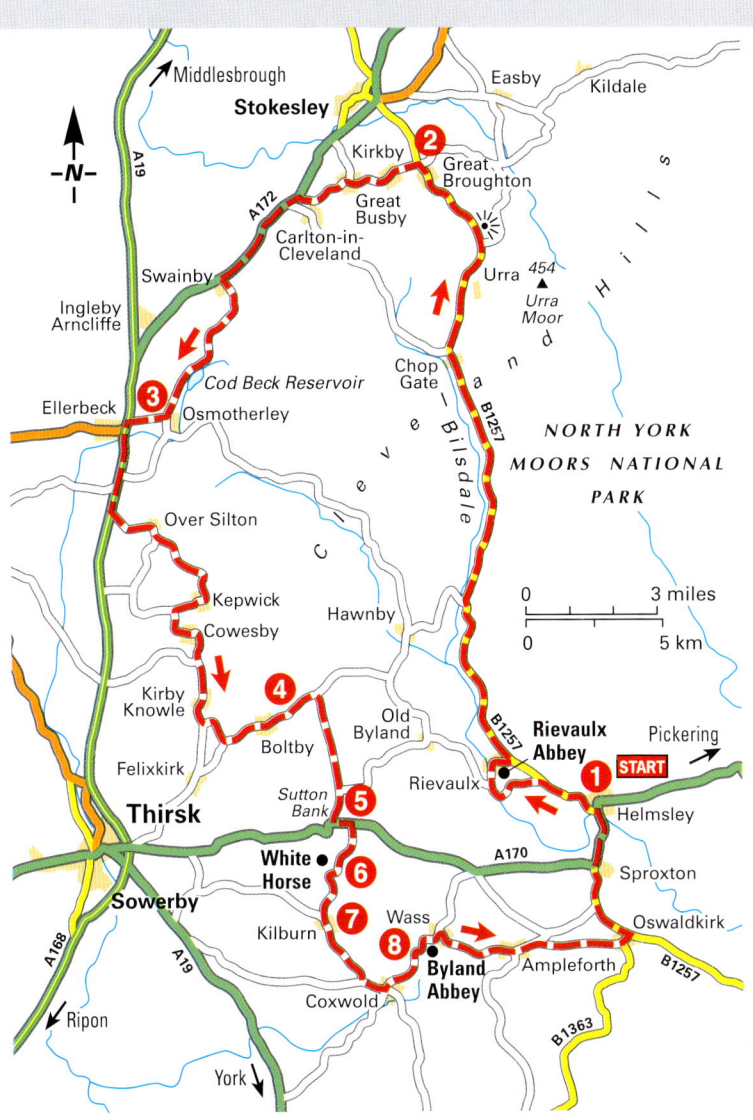

ROSEBERRY TOPPING & CAPTAIN COOK COUNTRY

Climb Roseberry Topping, once mined for ironstone, for views of the countryside. After the descent from the summit, and the climb again to the woodland, the track descends over Great Ayton Moor. Ahead, the Captain Cook Monument, a stone obelisk 52ft (15.5m) high, dominates the view. The explorer was born in 1728 within sight of Roseberry Topping at Marton (then a village, but now a suburb of Middlesbrough) and went to school at nearby Great Ayton. After you have gone through the gate after Point 5, the dips and hollows in the ground to the left are the remains of an ironstone mine, Ayton Banks. Further on you'll pass by Gribdale Terrace, a row of cottages built to house the iron miners and their families.

DISTANCE/TIME 5.5 miles (9km) 2h30 **MAP** OS Explorer OL26 North York Moors – Western **START** Car park at Newton under Roseberry; grid ref: NZ 570128 **TRACKS** Hillside climb, then tracks and field paths, 3 stiles **THE PUB** The Royal Oak Hotel, Great Ayton. Tel: 01642 724047

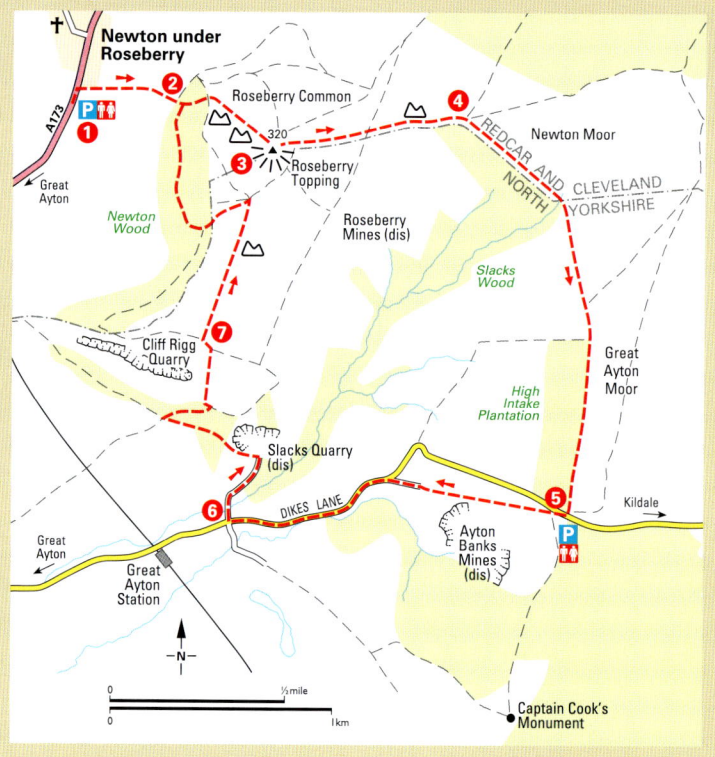

1 Take the rough lane beside the car park that leads in the direction of Roseberry Topping. The path goes through a gateway then rises to a second gate when you are at the beginning of the woodland.

2 Go through the gate into National Trust land and turn left. There is a well-worn path to the summit, with several variations to the route. Some paths are easier than others but whichever you take, it is a stiff climb to the trig point on the top of the hill.

3 From the summit, you take the Cleveland Way path on the opposite side from the ascent, going down a track that rises through a gate to the corner of woodland. Pass through another gate and turn right to walk alongside the wood.

4 Along this track as it follows the edge of the wood. It passes through another gate and goes past a second area of wood, descending the hillside to reach a road.

5 Turn right, cross the cattle grid and bear left past a bench to reach a gate. Then turn right to go over a stile, down the field, over another stile and out into a lane. Walk past the cottages and you will reach a road, where you go straight ahead.

6 At a crossroads go right, down Aireyholme Lane. Follow the lane as it winds past houses, then take a signed footpath left through woodland. After 0.5 miles (0.8km) go right up a path ascending through the woods, turning left at a crossing path and continuing along the edge of the woodland. Continue bearing right to reach a track to farm buildings, which goes left then right to a gate.

7 Walk across two fields to reach a stile, then continue uphill to the tower. Beyond the tower, take a grassy path left down a gully, to reach a gate into woodland. Follow the path downhill, walking through the woods to return to the gate at the top of the lane, leading back to the car park.

WALK 102

A LOOP FROM SWAINBY TO WHORLTON

From the once-industrial village of Swainby, this walk takes in fine views from the northern edge of the North York Moors plateau. The route then passes through Whorlton village, deserted since it was devastated by the plague in the 14th century and the survivors moved away.

DISTANCE/TIME 6 miles (9.7km) 2h30 **MAP** OS Explorer OL26 North York Moors – Western **START** Roadside parking in Swainby village; grid ref: NZ 477020 **TRACKS** Tracks and moorland paths, lots of bracken, 11 stiles **THE PUB** The Black Horse, Swainby. Tel: 01642 700436; www.blackhorseswainby.co.uk

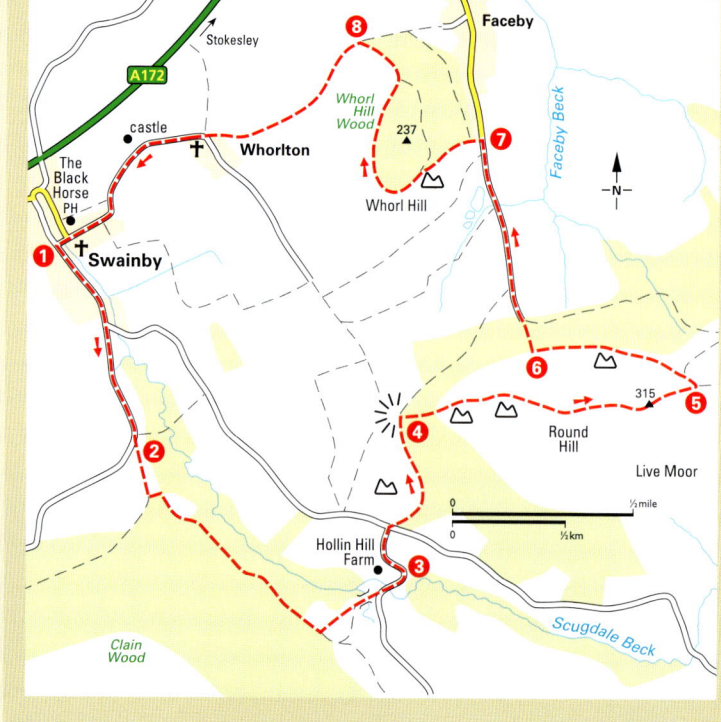

1 With the church on your left, walk to the right of the stream. Continue past a sign 'Unsuitable for Coaches' and head uphill. As the road bends to the right, follow the bridleway sign to Scugdale, up the track.

2 Go through two gates, turning left after the second into woods to join the waymarks for the Cleveland Way National Trail. Walk through the woods and turn left, at an opening, down to a stile. The footpath goes across the fields to another gate. Cross the footbridge then turn left along a lane, with another footbridge, over Scugdale Beck.

3 Follow the lane past Hollin Hill Farm to a T-junction. Cross the lane and go through a Cleveland Way signed gate. Walk up the path beside woodland to a gate.

4 The path turns right to a gate and goes on to a paved track. Go ahead at a crossing to another gate, and continue to the heather moorland. After the first summit, the path drops into a dip. After the paved path ends, take a very narrow path to the left.

5 After about 100yds (90m) you reach a concrete post. Take the left fork in the path and then follow it down the gully to a fence

beside a wall. Turn left here, forking left down another gully to reach a signpost by a wall and fence. Follow the sign left and then go over a spoil heap to a gate on your right.

6 Once through the gate, go straight down the hill through woodland. At the bottom cross a track to a stile by a gate and go down the lane. Just past some houses, where Whorl Hill Wood begins, take a footpath over two stiles and climb alongside the inside edge of the wood.

7 The track bends right with the perimeter of the wood and levels out. When you reach a T-junction, turn left and follow the track downhill to a stile and out of the woods. Go straight ahead through a gateway and follow a grassy track beside the farmhouse.

8 Go over a stile beside a gate and follow the track along the hillside. Go over a stile with steps beyond, turn left at the bottom and follow the field edge. Go over a waymarked stile by a gate and along the field. Walk to a gate at the end and then follow the metalled lane passing Whorlton church and castle to return to Swainby village. To get to the Black Horse pub, turn right along the lane that traces the nearside bank of the stream.

WALK 103

BYLAND ABBEY & OLSTEAD OBSERVATORY

This is a gentle walk from the romantic ruins of Byland Abbey through some lovely woodland to an old observatory at the highest point of the walk. The lumps and bumps of the final field you cross are the remains of the monks' ponds, some used for breeding fish.

DISTANCE/TIME 5 miles (8km) 2h30 **MAP** OS Explorer OL26 North York Moors – Western **START** Car park behind Abbey Inn in Byland Abbey; grid ref: SE 548789 **TRACKS** Woodland tracks, field paths, 11 stiles **THE PUB** The Abbey Inn, Byland Abbey. Tel: 01347 868678; www.bylandabbeyinn.com

1 Walk towards the abbey ruins and turn left along the lane at the abbey's north side. At a public footpath sign, go left and walk up the drive of Abbey House. Go right through a waymarked gate just before the house. After going through a second gateway bear left, skirting a bank towards the field's top left-hand corner. Go though a waymarked gate and walk behind a bench seat. Go through two more gates and on to a tarred lane just to the left of the buildings of Wass village.

2 Turn left. At a T-junction go through a gate signed 'Cam Farm, Observatory'. The path climbs then leaves the wood edge to rise to a terrace. After a stile take the left-hand path, signed 'Cam Farm', to join a track going uphill to the forestry vehicle turning circle.

3 Turn right and, before a waymarked metal gate at the edge of the forest, go left along the inside wood edge. Follow the path, which bends left to Oldstead Observatory. Stay left of the observatory and go down a slope to a track going steeply downhill.

4 Turn right along a track, signed 'Oldstead', then take a left turn at the next junction, over a stream where the path is joined by another track and becomes a tarred country

lane. Then turn left at the T-junction to pass through the village of Olstead. Just before you reach the 'road narrows' sign, turn left.

5 Go through gateposts and over a cattle grid. As the avenue of trees ends, take a waymarked path to the right, and go uphill to a stile, before climbing a steep grassy bank. The path can become overgrown.

6 On reaching a tarred lane turn right, then take a track to the left by the Oldstead Grange sign. As you near the house, turn left towards barns and wind your way through the farmyard to a stile by a metal gate. Bear half-right downhill on the track, then bend slightly right to a waymarked stile.

7 Just 10 yds (9m) after the stile turn left and go through a wood to a Byland Abbey signpost. Follow the path out of the woods bending left beyond Cams Head Farm. Follow the hedge on the left, go through a large gap, now with the hedge to the right.

8 The path crosses more fields with the abbey ahead. In the last field veer left to follow the fence to a roadside stile. Turn left along the lane, then left again past The Abbey Inn to return to the car park.

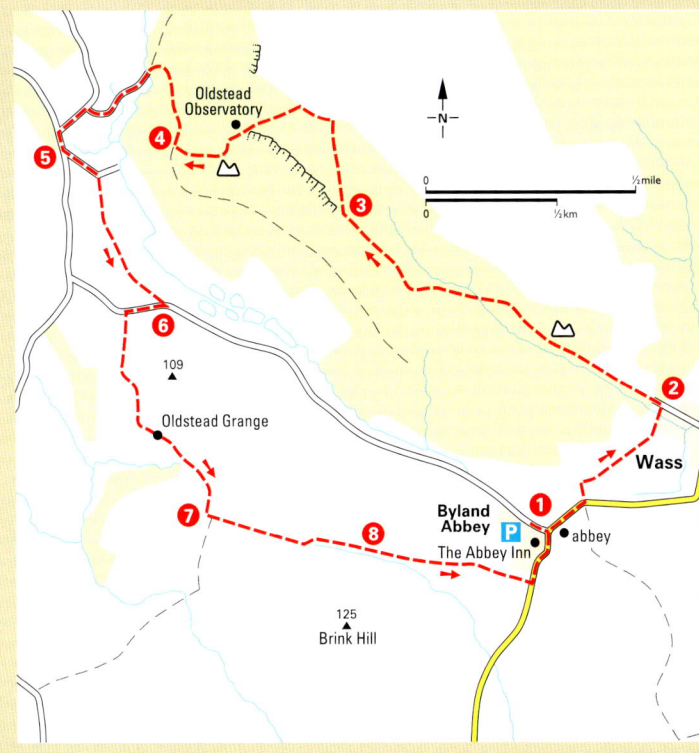

WALK 104

OUT ON THE TILES AT BOLTBY & THIRLBY BANK

The western boundary of the North York Moors National Park passes just outside Boltby. It is a delightful place, with a tiny 19th-century chapel and stone-built houses. Our route passes Tang Hall and Southwoods Hall before going through Midge Holme Gate and into woodland. On the top of Boltby Scar, as you begin the descent from the Cleveland Way you pass the remains of a Bronze Age hill fort.

DISTANCE/TIME 5.25 miles (8.4km) 2h **MAP** OS Explorer OL26 North York – Western **START** Boltby village. Roadside parking in the village; grid ref: SE 490866 **TRACKS** Mostly easy field and woodland paths; one steep, muddy climb; 10 stiles **THE PUB** The Carpenter's Arms, Felixkirk (southwest of Boltby). Tel: 01845 537369; www.carpentersarmsfelixkirk.co.uk

1 From the humped-back bridge in the centre of Boltby, follow the signposted public footpath along the stream to a gate, and go through three more gates to pass over a small footbridge to a stile. Continue ahead, following the stream, going over another three stiles, to cross over a stone footbridge.

2 Continue to go across two stiles and then turn right to reach another stile beside a gateway. Continue ahead, crossing a plank across a drainage ditch. Cross the field to a stile and a stone bridge. At another stile in a crossing fence, go ahead through the next field to reach a waymarked gate. Continue along the side of the field to a wooden stile, then through a gate on to a metalled track.

3 Turn left and, at the end of the farm buildings, go right by a sign to Southwoods and through a gate to go diagonally across the field. Bend left at a waymarked gate to continue with a wire fence on your right. The path veers left and down to another gate.

4 Continue through another gateway and past a house. Continue along the metalled track, and across a crossing track to a gate.

Confusingly this old track is named Midge Holm Gate. Follow the track to reach another gate beside a cottage, Southwoods Lodge, and go on to a metalled lane.

5 Turn left here, following the track, then turn left up a public footpath, which is signposted to Thirlby Bank. This is a steep and often muddy track that ascends the ridge, past another public bridleway sign to reach a Cleveland Way sign at the top.

6 Turn left and then follow the long-distance footpath for about a mile (1.6km) along the ridge, until you reach a public bridleway sign to the left, to Boltby. Descend to a gate then follow the woodland ride, crossing a track to a gate. Continue ahead down the field, go through a gate, and continue following the track round to the right.

7 At a signpost, turn right towards Boltby, to reach a gate. Pass a tree stump with a mosaic of a toadstool and then continue down to a gate on to a lane. Cross a footbridge and continue up the metalled lane. At the T-junction in the village, turn left to the hump-backed bridge.

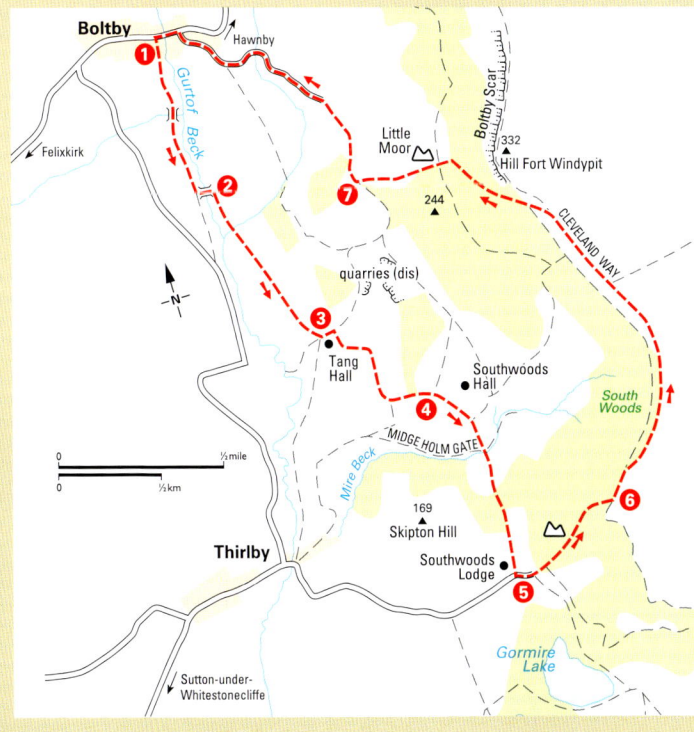

WALK 105

LASTINGHAM & HUTTON-LE-HOLE

From Lastingham and St Cedd's monastery the walk reaches Spaunton before leading on to Hutton-le-Hole clustered around an irregular green and along the banks of a beck. The route passes through fields and woodland on the return leg.

DISTANCE/TIME 4.5 miles (7.2km) 2h **MAP** OS Explorer OL26 North York Moors – Western **START** Village street in Lastingham; grid ref: SE 729905 **TRACKS** Farm tracks and field paths, 8 stiles **THE PUB** The Blacksmiths Arms, Lastingham. Tel: 01751 417247

1 From The Blacksmiths Arms walk back down to the village green and turn left, following signposts for Cropton, Pickering and Rosedale. Where the road swings left, go right along a lane to wind over a small bridge and beside a stream. Climb to a footpath sign, and go right, uphill, through a gate and woodland on to a handgate on to a road. Take the upper right fork lane, signed 'Spaunton'.

2 Follow the road through Spaunton, and bend right at the end of the village, then turn left by the public footpath sign over the cattle grid into the farmyard. The waymarked track curves through the farm to reach another footpath sign, where the track bends left. At an outbuilding the track bends left again.

3 After about 200yds (185m), follow a public footpath sign right and walk on to another sign as the track bends left. After 100yds (91m) take a footpath to the right, down the hill into woodland. Where the path divides, take the left fork down to a stile on your right, going off the track and down a steep grassy path into the valley. Descend beside a stream to a stile by a gate, which takes you on to the road in Hutton-le-Hole.

4 From here, turn right up the main street. After passing the Barn Hotel and the Wychwood Gifts shop turn right again,

following a route signed to Lastingham. Once you go beyond a gate, pass through a garden and to the right of some sheds until you reach a stile, which gives entry to a large field that is sometimes used as a campsite. Turn left and follow the edge of the field and go over two more stiles to a kissing gate before a footbridge. Follow the path now through woodland to a gate and take the grassy track to the road.

5 Turn right and follow the road for 0.5 mile (0.8km) and then turn left when you reach a footpath sign just before the road descends to a stone bridge. A rutted track bends to the right, running between farmland on the right and Spaunton Moor.

6 Just before Camomile Farm, leave the track on the left and follow the footpath sign and waymarker posts to round a copse of sycamore trees, beyond which you descend into a valley. Cross over the stream to a stile and a kissing gate. Continue walking with the wall on your right-hand side to another kissing gate and another stile, which will lead you to a carved stone with a cross and a three-pointed sign.

7 Turn right, downhill, through a gate and on to the metalled road that descends to the village of Lastingham.

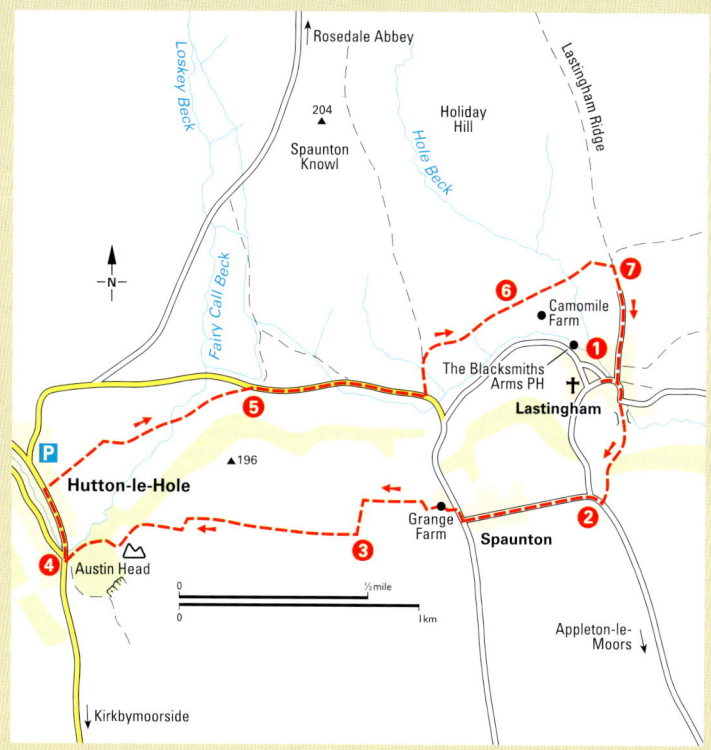

WALK 106

THE IRON VALLEY OF ROSEDALE

Rosedale is a peaceful valley that pushes northwest into the heart of the North York Moors. Yet little more than 100 years ago the village of Rosedale Abbey had a population ten times its present size. The reason was the discovery of ironstone in the 1850s. The remains of the Rosedale East Mines can be seen during the walk.

DISTANCE/TIME 3.5 miles (5.7km) 1h30 **MAP** OS Explorer OL26 North York Moors – Western **START** Roadside parking in Thorgill – please be considerate; grid ref: SE 708964. **TRACKS** Mostly field paths and tracks, 11 stiles **THE PUB** The Milburn Arms Hotel, Rosedale Abbey. Tel: 01751 417541

1 From your parking place in the hamlet of Thorgill, continue up the lane, pass a public bridleway sign and go through a metal gate to a track. Follow the track, going through a wooden gate and beginning to rise. Almost opposite to a farmhouse on the left, go right to cross over a wooden stile beside a gate.

2 Walk down the slope to pass over the stream on a gated footbridge, then turn slightly left to go uphill on the opposite bank beside the trees. Continue walking through a gate into the field and then continue ahead, going over a stile then through a metal gate into the yard of Craven Garth Farm. Go through another gateway and pass between the buildings to reach Daleside Road, a metalled country lane.

3 Turn right; just before reaching the cottage, turn left up a track by the parish notice board. A little way up the track look for a stile beside the gate to Clough House.

4 Go over the stile and follow the track downhill towards the wood, passing around the garden of Clough House. Continue to reach a stile, where you turn right and follow the waymarked path through the wood to reach a stile on to a road.

5 Turn right and then go left through a gate at a bridleway sign. Go down the grassy path to meet a level track. Turn left. Just before a gate, turn right, following the bridleway sign. Continue downhill to reach a ladder stile, and go straight ahead across the field to reach a gateway on to a road by a bridleway sign.

6 Cross the road and continue ahead. After passing through a gateway, turn right at the footpath sign before the bridge. The track climbs steeply to a road. Turn left along the road to a T-junction.

7 Turn left. Opposite the Bell End Farm sign turn right through a gate, and head down the field to a stile. The path bends and descends steeply. On reaching a fence, turn sharp right to go over a boardwalk and through a waymarked gate. Follow the path over two stiles. Turn left down the track, which passes though a gateway, and go straight on.

8 Just beyond a gate, go left, following the stream, to cross over a footbridge with stiles at each end. Follow the footpath uphill heading towards farm buildings. Follow waymarks through the buildings and up the farm track to reach a lane. Turn right here and go back to your car-parking place.

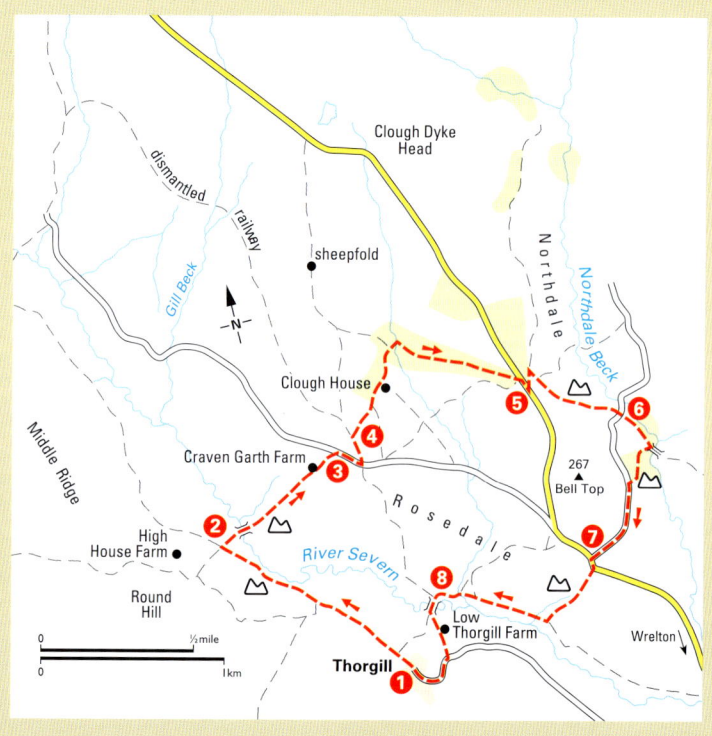

DISTANCE/TIME 7.4 miles (12km) 2h **MAP** OS Explorer OL26 North York Moors – Western **START** Sutton Bank Visitor Centre; grid ref: SE 516831 **TRACKS** Good level lanes followed by undulating bridleways on the edge of the escarpment **THE PUB** The Hambleton Inn, Sutton Bank. Tel: 01845 597202; www.hambletoninn.co.uk

DISTANCE/TIME 6miles (9.7km) 2h **MAP** OS Explorer OL27 North York Moors **START** Car park at Addlestone Field, Dalby Forest; grid ref: SE 883897 **TRACKS** Forestry roads and several narrow paths, mostly well graded **THE PUB** New Inn, Thornton le Dale. Tel: 01751 474226

THE HAMBLETON HILLS

Enjoy some of northern England's best views and experience a bit of adventure with a ride along the edge of the escarpment. The long tarred lane that takes you north from Sutton Bank seems unremarkable, but there's a history dating back to the Iron Age tribes who settle here around 400 BC. They would have used the route long before the Romans followed in their footsteps.

1 Before you leave Sutton Bank Visitor Centre, take a look at the panoramas to the south and west. From here you can see for miles across the flat fields of the Vales of Mowbray and York. Alf Wight, alias the fictional vet James Herriot, believed this view to be the finest in England. Apparently, both York Minster and Lincoln Cathedral are discernible on a clear day. From the visitor centre car park, turn left up the lane signed to Cold Kirby and Old Byland. Then take the left fork past Dialstone Farm and its tall communications mast, before heading north on an ever-so-straight lane through cornfields and pastures.

2 The lane comes to a T-junction by a triangular wood, called the Snack Yate Plantation. This is a popular starting point for serious mountain bikers who will swoop down on rough tracks through Boltby Forest. Your route turns left down the lane. It's a gentle downhill for a short distance. Just before the road dives off the edge, turn left through a gate on to a grassy bridleway to cycle along the escarpment's edge. You are now riding on the Hambleton Hills. The first stretch is slightly uphill, but the track is firm and the views wide-sweeping. You'll see a small reservoir surrounded by forestry and the little village of Boltby huddled beneath a pastured hill.

3 The bridleway climbs to the top of the hill at High Barn, an old stone ruin shaded by a fine stand of sycamore. The going eases at this point and the cliffs of an old quarry appear up ahead. Here the bridleway goes through a gate on to a walled track for a short way. Ignore the bridleway on the left (it goes back to the Hambleton Road), and stay with the edge path to the hill above the rocks of Boltby Scar. This is the highest point of the ride. Note the wind-warped larch trees here – they add to the views across the Vale of Mowbray.

4 The trees of the Boltby Forest now cover the west slopes, almost right up to the summit. Beyond the next offshoot bridleway, which you should ignore, the path becomes much narrower with a few embedded rocks in some places. The difficulties are short-lived, but the younger and less experienced riders might prefer to dismount and walk for a bit here. The riding gets easier again as the bridleway arcs right above South Wood. At the end of this arc you turn left to a sign that tells you that the continuing edge path is for walkers only. This is a fine spot to linger and admire the views. To the south the half-moon-shaped Gormire Lake lies in a nest of broad-leaved woodland and beneath the sandy-coloured Whitestone Cliff.

5 When you've rested for a while, turn left on a bridleway to Dialstone Farm. This heads east across large prairie-like fields. Beyond a wood, the High Quarry Plantation, you will see the hurdles of the equestrian centre. Past the large farm, turn right along the tarred lane, then right again, back to the visitor centre car park.

DALBY FOREST

This is a short ride through the forest to seek the wildlife – if you stay quiet and look hard enough, you'll see it in abundance. Roe deer happily inhabit the forest and you may be very lucky and see a badger if it is late in the day. Besides the common blue tits, you're quite likely to see a wading heron, or a tiny warbler. The forest is made up of a variety of trees including the many broad-leaf species such as oak, alder and hazel, but is mostly pine and spruce.

1 The green cycle route begins beyond the trees at the southeast end of the large Adderstone Field (the furthest from the visitor centre). Here you turn left along a narrow slightly downhill track. Ignore the two lesser, unsigned left fork tracks.

2 Turn right along a much wider forestry track which takes a winding course round the afforested valley of Worry Gill. Where the more demanding red route goes off on a rough track to the right, your green route goes straight on, still using a well-graded track.

3 Where a track doubles back, go straight on up a steady hill before meeting up with the forest drive again. Cross this with care – it can be busy – before turning right along it for 200yds (183m). Turn left along a narrow path signed with red and green waymarkers and just before a 30mph speed limit sign.

4 The path reaches a flinted road at the southeast edge of the forest. Turn right along this, then turn left at the next junction. To your left the rougher high pastures of Ebberston Low Moor decline to the greener, more fertile fields of the Vale of Pickering.

5 Turn right just before Givendale Head Farm along a rutted farm track which has a disitinctive grassy island in the middle of it. Turn right at the next junction (Post B) continuing on a downhill section, followed by an uphill one where you're joined by a farm track coming in from the left.

6 A long hill follows to a wide junction where you go straight on along a tarred lane. A sign tells you that you're now at the head of Flax Dale. Stay with the tarred lane at the next bend and junction. Turn right at the crossroads along a long sandy track (Post A), then turn right again at the next junction. Note the linear earthwork to both left and right – nobody seems to know the exact origins of these.

7 After going straight on at the next junction past a fine stand of Scots pines, you get fine views over the farm pastures of High Rigg to reach Levisham Moor. Here, there's another downhill section followed by an uphill one. Take a right fork at Newclose Rigg. Where the red route goes straight on, your green route veers right along the main track. There's a downhill left curve beyond which you take the upper right fork, which brings the route back to the forest drive opposite Adderstone Field.

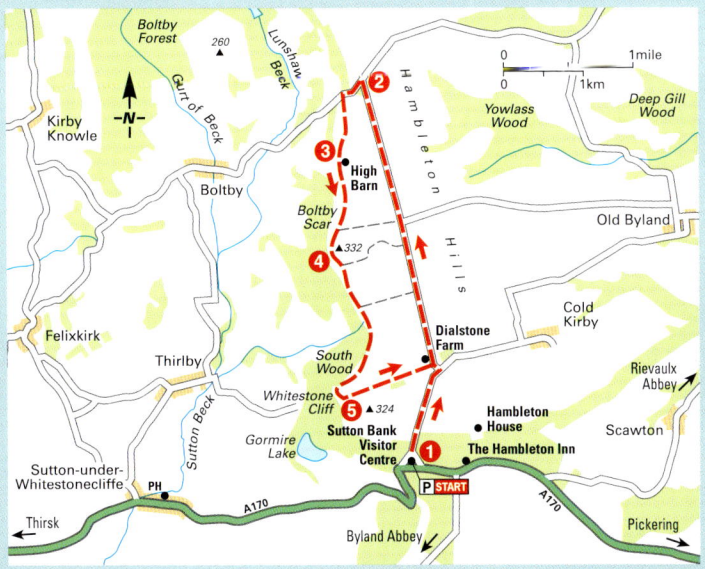

DISTANCE/TIME 11.25 miles (18.1km) 2h **MAP** OS Explorer OL27 North York Moors – Eastern **START** Roadside parking on way into Ravenscar; grid ref: NZ 980015 **TRACKS** Almost entirely on well-surfaced old railway track; short street sections at Ravenscar and Robin Hood's Bay **THE PUB** The Laurel Inn, Robin Hood's Bay. Tel: 01947 880400

DISTANCE/TIME 9.3 miles (15km) 2h **MAP** OS Explorer 300 Howardian Hills and Malton **START/FINISH** Roadside parking in the main street, Terrington; grid ref: SE 670706 **TRACKS** Country lanes with some hills **THE PUB** Bay Horse Inn, Terrington. Tel: 01653 648416

FROM RAVENSCAR TO ROBIN HOOD'S BAY

The former railway line between Whitby and Scarborough can now be followed, in its entirety, on two wheels. The full distance is 20 miles (32.2km) one way, so this ride picks out probably the finest section, looping around Robin Hood's Bay. It is a little confusing that the name of the bay and the much-photographed village are exactly the same, but the ride gives great views of the former and a chance to visit the latter.

1 Descend the road until it bends sharply right. Turn left, past the National Trust Coastal Centre, and continue on an obvious descending concrete track. A rougher section needs more care, but lasts less than 100yds (91m). Now swing left and go through a gate on to the old railway trackbed and a much easier surface.

2 The track now runs below the scarred face of the alum workings, with some ups and downs that clearly don't match the original rail contours exactly. After this section, take care crossing a steep concrete track that runs down to a farm.

3 Pass under an arched bridge. Note more quarried cliffs up on the left, while looking down to the right – if the tide is not too high – there are extensive rocky platforms in the bay, with conspicuous parallel strata. There's a short cutting and the sea views are hidden by tall gorse and broom, then it becomes more open again as the track swings gradually inland. A tall embankment crosses a steep wooded valley. Go under a bridge and then make a sharp left turn on to a lane.

4 Go up 20yds (18m), then sharp right to continue on the track. Keep right at a fork and the track resumes its steady gentle descent, then starts to turn uphill for the first time on the ride. As you come out into the open after a tunnel of trees, the direct way ahead is again blocked (unless you're Evel Knievel!). Here slant down left, cross a lane, and then climb back up on to the continuing trackbed.

5 Pass a cricket ground, next the back of a caravan site, then a farm. Cross the rough farm track and keep straight on ahead, through a gate where the surface changes to tarmac, on the outskirts of Robin Hood's Bay. Go through another gate and drop down to a road. Turn right down this road for 100yds (91m) then go left on a lane signposted to the Station Workshops. At the top of the rise is the old station building and just beyond it is a large car park. (It is, of course, possible to descend the road all the way into the village of Robin Hood's Bay, but it's a very steep climb back. An alternative is to lock the bikes at the car park and head down on foot.)

6 Continue alongside the car park, drop down to a road, turn left and almost instantly go right right (very nearly straight across) on to Mount Pleasant. Follow this to its end then bear left up a short gravelled ride to regain the railway path. Continue for about 0.5 mile (0.8km). You will have some good views back now over Robin Hood's Bay to the cliffs near Ravenscar. Look for a National Trust sign for Ness Bay. There is open access on foot so you could leave your bikes and walk down to the headland, a great spot for a picnic, especially on a fine day. This makes as good a turnaround point as any, though the track continues into Hawsker and on to Whitby.

TERRINGTON & CASTLE HOWARD

This is a ride through Yorkshire's most magnificent estate. The house was severely damaged by fire in the middle of the 20th century but was rebuilt to its former glory and is now one of England's most popular houses to visit. It has collections of paintings, sculpture, ceramics and more. The grounds include a range of gardens and the estate comprises farms and woodland.

1 Terrington is a peaceful little village with fine sloping greens either side of the main street, giving the place a spacious feel. The cottages, which are largely Victorian, are built with local limestone. Above them, just off the main street, stands the church, a square-towered building that dates back to Saxon times – there's an interesting Anglo-Saxon window in the south aisle. Much of the church's structure is 13th-century but it was modernised around 1860. Heading east past the ivy-clad Bay Horse Inn towards Castle Howard is a slightly downhill stretch, a nice start – although the tea rooms tempt you straight away. If it's hot, a splendid avenue of trees on the way out of the village will offer some welcome shade.

2 Take the right fork, signed 'Ganthorpe, York', 0.5 miles (0.8km) out of the village. Now you pay for your downhill as the road climbs to the top of Cross Hill, where there's a good view back to Terrington. The lane levels out as it passes through the stone cottages and farms of Ganthorpe. This hamlet was the birthplace of the historian Arthur Toynbee (1886–1975) and the botanist Richard Spruce (1817–93), who travelled to places like the Andes and the Amazon in search of specimens for scientific research. There's another short downhill section as the lane bends right by Sata Wood, then it's uphill again.

3 Turn left at the T-junction, where you get glimpses of a couple of the Castle Howard domes, then left at the crossroads following the directions to Slingsby and Castle Howard. The road, known as the Stray, is straight ahead and madly undulating like a Roman road, with wide verges and avenues of trees lining the way. Some of the traffic is speedy so take care! Soon you pass beneath the extremely narrow stone arch of the Castle Howard estate's Carmire Gate, which is flanked by castellated walls, then you come upon the gate house with its pyramidal roof. There's a roundabout next to a 100ft (30.5m) obelisk of 1714 dedicated to Lady Cecilia Howard. Here you need to decide whether or not to visit the palace (highly recommended).

4 Continuing down the Stray you'll pass the Obelisk Ponds, which are enshrouded by woodland, then the Great Lake, across which you can get a great view of the magnificent palace and its many domes.

5 Turn left for 'Terrington' at the crossroads just beyond the lake. The lane soon swings right and climbs through the trees of Shaw Wood. If you have mountain bikes and are experienced riders you could take the bridleway at the next bend (South Bell Bottom) then double back on the track over Husket and Ling Hills to meet the lane further west. If not, continue along the lane, which winds downhill across Ganthorpe Moor to meet the outward route by the first T-junction east of Terrington. Though you've still got the trees for shade, the downhill is now an uphill so you'll probably deserve that refreshment at the Bay Tree Inn.

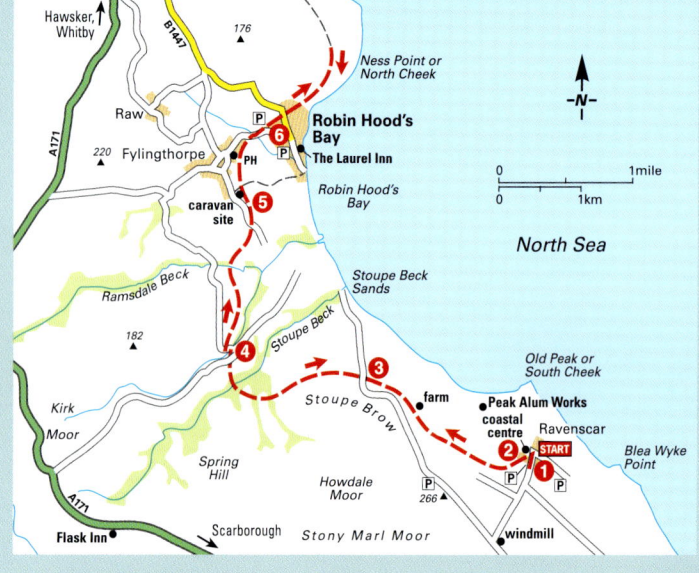

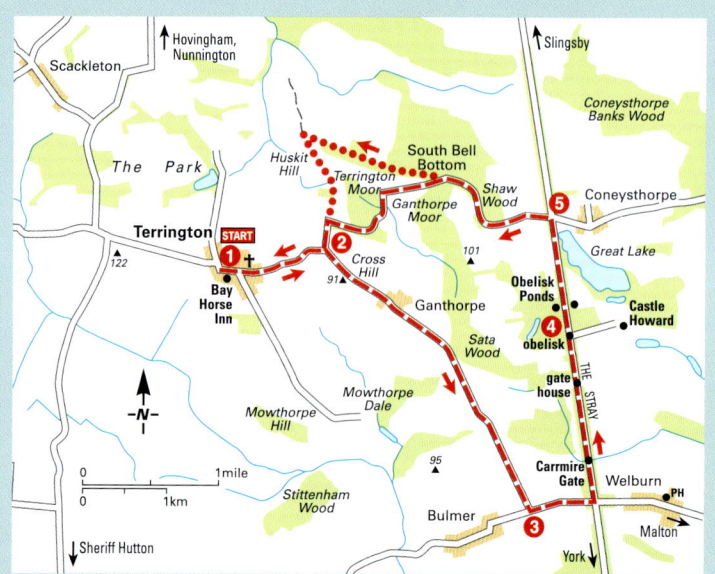

WALK 107

THROUGH SCARBOROUGH'S RAINCLIFFE WOODS

Just outside Scarborough, a walk through woodland to the rare remains of a glacial lake. The steep hillside of Raincliffe Woods overlooks a deep valley carved out in the Ice Ages. Although mostly replanted in the 1950s and 60s, the woods in places retain remnants of ancient oak and heather woodland – look out for the heather and bilberry bushes beneath oak trees that will show you where. Throughout the walk you will come upon humps and banks, depressions and pits that show that this hillside has been a hive of human activity in the past.

DISTANCE/TIME 5 miles (8km) 2h **MAP** OS Explorer OL27 North York Moors – Eastern **START** Hazelhead picnic site on Mowthorpe Road, near road junction; grid ref: SE 984875 **TRACKS** field tracks, woodland paths, some steep, 2 stiles **THE PUB** Ox Pasture Hall Country Hotel, Throxenby. Tel: 01723 365295

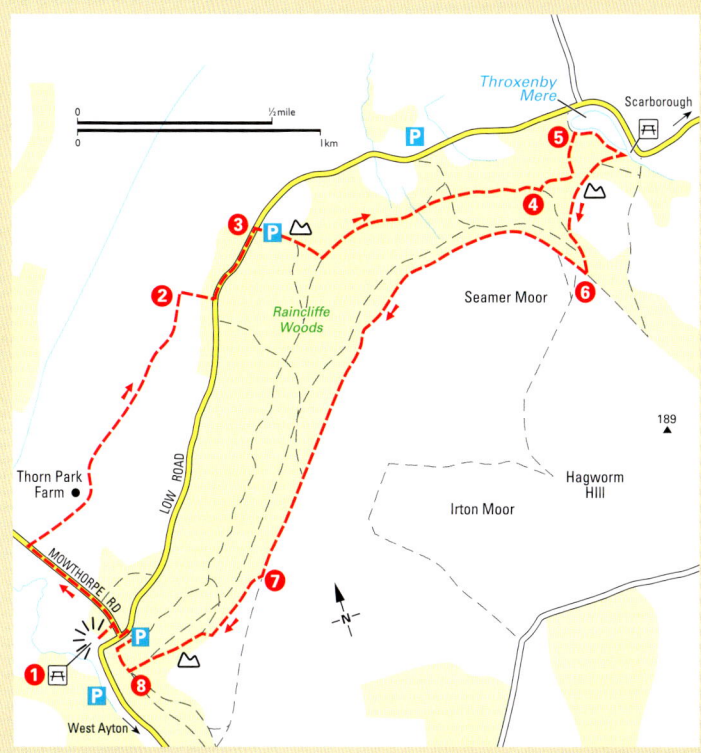

1 From the start, walk on to the road and turn left, downhill. After the woodland ends, pass houses on the right, then opposite a bungalow, No 5, turn right down a track to Thorn Park Farm. Follow the track as it bends left by the farm buildings, then right past a cottage to a metal gate. Continue to follow the track as it bends left then right, then passes through two gateways.

2 Just before the next gateway turn right and walk up the field side to a stile beside a gateway, which takes you on a short path to the road. Turn left. Follow the road to the next car park on the right.

3 Go through the car park towards the gate and uphill on the path ahead. Where the main path bends right, go ahead, more steeply, to reach a crossing, grassy track. Turn left through a gate and follow the path. Where it forks, take the right-hand path.

4 Look out for a path on the left, which immediately bends right over a drainage runnel. The path goes down into a small valley. Turn left, heading downhill, then follow the path as it bends right again, going past an old quarry. The path then descends to Throxenby Mere.

5 Turn right along the edge of the Mere. Just before you reach a picnic place, turn right through an area bare of undergrowth to take a path that goes up steeply until it reaches a grassy track at the top of the hill.

6 Turn right and go through a metal gate, then follow the path for a mile (1.6km), parallel with the wall. It passes through a gateway with a stile by it and finally reaches a gate with a public bridleway sign.

7 Don't go through the gate into fields, but turn right and continue into woodland. Where the main path swings left and another goes right, go ahead, steeply downhill. When the path joins another go left, go down steps and along a boardwalk to meet a crossing path.

8 Turn right and descend to a gate into a car park. Turn left on to the road, and left again to a road junction. Turn right, following the Harwood Dale sign, for the picnic site.

WALK 108

EARLY WARNINGS AT FYLINGDALES & LILLA CROSS

The past and the future come together on this walk on the North Yorkshire coast. Unlike in most of upland Britain, the most important roads and tracks in the North York Moors follow the ridges between the valleys. The tracks are often marked by standing stones or crosses. The most impressive and ancient of the Moor's crosses is Lilla, commemorating an act of bravery in AD 626, when Lilla died protecting King Edward of Northumbria. Dominating the middle section of the walk is the improbably large sandcastle that houses the Fylingdales early warning system.

DISTANCE/TIME 7.5 miles (12km) 2h30 **MAP** OS Explorer OL27 North York Moors – Eastern **START** May Beck car park; grid ref: SE 893025 **TRACKS** Forest tracks and moorland paths, 3 stiles **THE PUB** The Birch Hall Inn, Goathland. Tel: 01947 896245

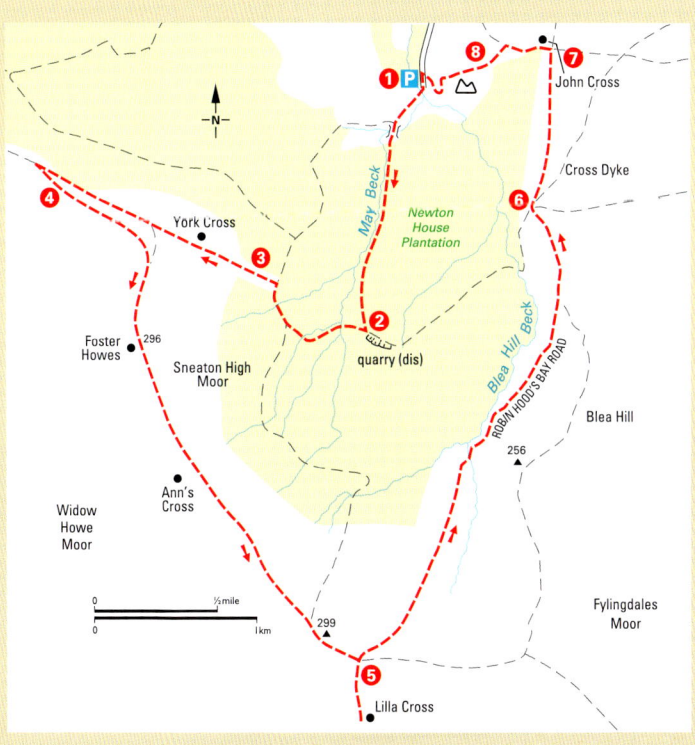

1 Walk up the wide track opposite the approach road. Where the track bends round to the right, go left down a signed footpath and descend to cross over a bridge and continue along the green track. Go through a kissing gate and continue up the side of the valley, finally swinging away from the stream and continuing into the forest.

2 On reaching a forest road turn right, passing a flooded quarry on your right. At the next junction of forest roads bear right. After about 0.5 miles (0.8km), look for a broad ride to the left, with a white cycle waymark by it.

3 Go up the ride, leaving the forest, and out on to moorland. Continue past the base and shaft of York Cross. Pass a track going left and continue until you reach a waymarked (bridleway) post, where you turn sharp left.

4 Walk along the track and continue with the fence on your right. Pass Ann's Cross to your right and 0.5 miles (0.8km) beyond this you'll reach a T-junction, where you turn right and continue along the bridleway.

5 When you reach a crossroads with a signpost, turn right along the track to visit Lilla Cross, which can be seen a little way away. After visiting the cross, return to the crossroads, and then go straight ahead, following the Robin Hood's Bay sign. The path goes parallel with the forest edge.

6 Go right when you reach a post with the number 9 on it. Carry on to pass by posts 8 and 7, and then veer left when you eventually reach a trail sign.

7 Pass post 6 (by the remains of John Cross) and go through a gate, to continue walking downhill on a track. When you reach a yellow waymarker leave the track and walk down to the left until you get to a waymarked stile near the ruins of a building.

8 Go to the left of the ruined building and make for another stile. Follow the obvious footpath downhill through the bracken, passing two public footpath signs, and climb over another wooden stile to reach the road. Turn left to return to the start.

Yorkshire Dales

CLOCKWISE FROM TOP: KNARESBOROUGH; THORNTON FORCE;
PEN-Y-GHENT; COW AT SWALEDALE

BOLTON ABBEY MAP REF 407 G5

Bolton Abbey Estate is owned by the Duke of Devonshire and is an enjoyable amalgamation of recreational, historical and geographical, with guests at the Devonshire Arms enjoying the comforts of one of the best hotels in the country, as well as being one of the region's best restaurants. For most people, though, Bolton Abbey is a day out in the car, within easy reach of Bradford and Leeds, with ample parking and plenty to see and do.

The first people to enjoy the site were the Augustinian monks who moved here from Embsay in 1154 to found a new priory. It was finished by the next century and now lies in evocative ruins by the banks of the River Wharfe. The adjoining priory church of St Mary and St Cuthbert is far from ruined, however, and is one of the finest churches in the Dales. Built in 1220, it escaped the Dissolution of the Monasteries, only to fall victim to a dwindling congregation. Now restored, Bolton Abbey has breathtaking stained-glass windows.

If you drive along the B6160 to one of the car parks (day tickets allow you to move between several car parks) you will pass under a narrow stone archway, part of an aqueduct that once carried water to the mill, of which little now remains.

There are many good walks to be had around the estate, including marked nature trails near the river and through Strid Wood, which is a Site of Special Scientific Interest. A leaflet showing the colour-coded walks is handed to visitors at the car park entrance.

DENT MAP REF 406 F4

If there were ever a vote for the most attractive village in the Dales, it would hardly be surprising if Dent won first prize. It is a beautiful cluster of pretty whitewashed cottages and cobbled streets nestling in the lush green valley that is Dentdale. As a result it is extremely busy in the holiday season, and is perhaps best visited at other times if possible.

Dent is on the Settle–Carlisle Railway line and is the highest mainline station in Britain, at 1,150 feet (351m), but if you are planning to travel by train, be warned that the station is 5 miles (8km) from the village itself. There is only a connecting bus service on Saturdays (a Wednesday service goes once a day from Cowgill, about half a mile/0.8km down the valley).

Dent boasts a flourishing artistic community, from practitioners of Dent's knitting tradition to painter John Cooke, musician Mike Harding and photographers John and Eliza Forder, whose books on life in the Dales are sold in the local shops. On the road to Sedbergh you will find the

DENT HEAD VIADUCT

Dent Crafts Centre, a display of local and not-so-local arts and crafts, which also has a café and opens as a restaurant on weekend evenings. In Dent there are cafés and pubs and a good choice of accommodation and souvenir shops.

Adam Sedgwick was born in Dent in the Old Parsonage in 1785, attended the local grammar school and went on to become the Woodwardian Professor of Geology at Cambridge. The pink Shap granite memorial fountain in the main street marks his career as a geologist. This was not always merely a memorial, as it also provided the town's main water supply until the 1920s. In 1985, to commemorate the 200th anniversary of his birth, the National Park Authority created the Adam Sedgwick Geology Trail, near Sedbergh. Leaflets are available at National Park Centres and tourist information centres.

Near the Sedgwick Stone stands St Andrew's Church, which has a Norman doorway, although most of the church was rebuilt in the late 19th century. Inside are some unusual Jacobean box-pews and flooring of Dent marble. Both black and grey marble were quarried near here. The Stone House Marble Works flourished in the 18th and 19th centuries at Arten Gill, southeast of Dent Station, where you will also find the Dent Head Viaduct, yet another of the marvellous constructions on the Settle–Carlisle Railway line.

FOUNTAINS ABBEY MAP REF 407 H5

To describe Fountains Abbey as a ruin does it a disservice, and even the term 'remains' does not prepare the visitor for the awesome and graceful sight of the best-preserved Cistercian abbey in Britain. It looks as if it may have been only a few years ago that the monks finally moved out. Fountains Abbey was designated a World Heritage Site in 1986, and is one of the largest monastic ruins in Europe.

Fountains Abbey was founded in 1132 by a group of monks who left a Benedictine abbey in York because the order was not strict enough for them. The buildings you see today were mostly constructed in the years from 1150 to 1250, though the North Tower, which looms up into the sky, is a 16th-century addition.

A visitor centre caters for the 300,000 people who visit the site each year. It incorporates an auditorium, a restaurant and kiosk and the largest National Trust shop in Britain. You can also see the restored monastic mill, and some rooms in Fountains Hall, the 17th-century home of the subsequent owners of the abbey.

The adjoining grounds of Studley Royal were created in the 18th century and then merged with Fountains Abbey in 1768. They were the work of John Aislabie, and his son, William. The landscaping took 14 years and another decade for the the buildings. There are several paths around the gardens, through which the River Skell flows, and acquiring a map is probably a good idea as there is a great deal to see including fine temples and water cascades.

GRASSINGTON MAP REF 407 G5

Grassington may look as if it has always been a small, sleepy Dales town, but this is not the case. With the discovery of large lead deposits on the surrounding moors, it was a thriving industrial town from the 17th to the 19th centuries.

Modern Grassington is the major tourist centre in Upper Wharfedale, with guesthouses, shops and eating places radiating out from its cobbled square. It also has a National Park Centre, near the village centre, and the Upper Wharfedale Folk Museum, a tiny, enjoyable collection which explores the history of mining here.

Five miles (8km) southeast, off the B6160 road, is Appletreewick village, where the hillside Parcevall Hall Gardens, which were laid out from 1927, are planted with specimen trees and shrubs from western China and the Himalayas. The gardens have formal terraces, a glorious rose garden, rock garden, woodland walks, orchards, a 15th-century farmhouse and wonderful views of Wharfedale.

Six miles (9.6km) to the southeast of Grassington on the B6160, is Barden Tower, a medieval hunting lodge that was renovated and used by Lady Anne Clifford in the mid-17th century. Lady Anne was an admirable woman whose name you will encounter throughout the Yorkshire Dales. She built charitable institutions and renovated buildings, including Barden Tower. She also restored Brougham Castle at Penrith in Cumbria, where she died.

The Lady Anne Clifford Trail, which was established in 1990, commemorates the 400th anniversary of her birth in Skipton Castle, where the trail begins. This 100-mile (161km) long-distance path leads through the Yorkshire Dales and the Upper Eden Valley to Brougham Castle.

Visit
THE STRID

As the River Wharfe flows through the Bolton Abbey Estate, in one place it thunders through a narrow ravine just a few feet across – little more than a stride, or strid. If you feel a desire to jump across, bear in mind that several people have been killed doing just this, as they slipped on the rocks and fell into the fast-flowing river, which is up to 30 feet (9m) deep in places. One of the leaflets handed to visitors asks them to 'remember that anything that goes into the Strid rarely surfaces for several days'.

You have been warned!

Activity
ROLL OUT THE EGGS

Parents of young children might like to know that an earlier Easter Monday egg-rolling tradition was revived at Fountains Abbey in the 1980s, at the suggestion of an estate worker who recalled the tradition from his own childhood there. Hard-boiled eggs are thrown or rolled down a hill, a prize being given to the one that goes the furthest before finally disintegrating completely. In some areas, children would decorate their eggs and put them on display, before rolling them down the nearest slope and finally eating any eggs that remained edible.

Activity
TAKE THE HIGH ROAD

Drive south out of Hawes through Gayle, heading for Kettlewell, and you will cross Wether Fell and Fleet Moss Pass, reaching a height of 1,857 feet (566m). This is the highest road in the Yorkshire Dales, and one of the highest in all England.

Visit
THE NORBER BOULDERS

Follow the bridleway between Clapham and Austwick and you will see a signpost to the Norber Boulders. This scattering of boulders, each on its own little pedestal of rock, at first glance looks as if it ought to be of some human significance, but in fact is a natural occurrence. The boulders, also called the Norber Erratics, are several hundred million years old and were deposited in their present location by the actions of a glacier about 25,000 years ago during the last Ice Age. They are made of Silurian gritstone, the type of rock found in Crummack Dale about half a mile (0.8km) to the north.

HARDRAW MAP REF 407 G4

Hardraw is a hamlet that would probably be visited only by those passing through on the Pennine Way if it was not for the existence of Hardraw Force. At 96 feet (29m) it has the longest free drop of any waterfall in England – above ground, at least – and was painted by Turner on his travels through the Yorkshire Dales. Another unusual feature is that to reach it you must pass through the Green Dragon pub, paying a small entrance fee as you do so. The volume of water from the fall is not great, and it is therefore best visited after heavy rain. Those who do not mind a slight splashing can walk round behind the fall, although care must be taken on the wet rocks as they are slippery. In 1739 and 1881, the falls froze completely to produce an impressive 100-foot (30.5m) icicle.

The Force falls into a pool in a natural amphitheatre, and the acoustics here are such that an annual brass band contest takes place every September, a tradition that goes back to 1885. Past winners include famous names such as the Black Dyke Mills Band and Besses o' the Barn.

HARROGATE MAP REF 407 H5

Although not within the Yorkshire Dales as such, Harrogate is by far the largest town on their fringes, and a magnet for anyone with serious shopping – or just window-shopping – to be done. It is an attractive and lively place with theatres, cinemas and good restaurants, and a plethora of new hotels and conference centres created by the hospitality industry. But Harrogate has not lost its charm, and the spa town that developed after the discovery of a spring in 1571 is still plainly visible.

An important feature of Harrogate is its lush greenery, especially the wide swathes of grass and flower beds, known as the Stray, that sweeps right through the town. These 200 acres (81ha) are protected under an ancient law, which ensures that residents and visitors alike are entitled to enjoy these facilities. There are more pretty flowers as well as a boating pond, playground, crazy golf and plenty of other activities in the Valley Gardens, Harrogate's main park. Its entrance is close to the Royal Pump Room Museum.

Flower lovers will not want to miss a visit to the Royal Horticultural Society Garden at Harlow Carr on the outskirts of Harrogate off the B6162. This was the HQ of the Northern Horticultural Society (until its merger with the RHS in 2001) and is set in 68 impressive acres (28ha), a lovely mix of the formal and informal, with a gardening museum, plant and gift shops, and places for refreshments. Several courses, demonstrations and practical workshops are held in the Study Centre.

Harrogate's origins can be traced in the octagonal Royal Pump Room Museum, which was built in 1842 in order to enclose the old sulphur well on this site. In addition to serving up local history, the museum serves up cups of the pungent spa water that first made the town so famous. It claims to be the strongest sulphur water in Europe, so some visitors may prefer Perrier, or to refresh the palate with a visit to Betty's tea rooms, a real Yorkshire institution, which offers delicious cream cakes and Yorkshire fat rascals.

Not quite a Yorkshire institution is a visit to a Turkish baths. Harrogate is one of the few places where you can enjoy a Turkish bath in all its original 19th-century splendour at the Turkish Baths and Health Spa in the Royal Baths Assembly Rooms. Its Victorian exterior masks a beautifully renovated tiled interior, which includes a cold plunge bath, hot rooms, a steam room, massage room and a relaxing rest room for when the ordeal is over. There are both male and female sessions, so check first if you are thinking of going.

Harrogate Volunteer Guided Walks Group conduct tours of the town. Low Harrogate tours begin outside the Royal Pump Room Museum, while tours of High Harrogate start at the main entrance to Christ Church on the Stray; both tours last for one hour. The dates and times of these free and fascinating tours are available from the local tourist information centre.

HAWES MAP REF 407 G4

Family businesses make up the shops in the main street in Hawes, and it is certainly the place to stock up on good local produce, especially on the busy Tuesday market day when stalls line the streets and farmers conduct their business at the livestock market along the Leyburn road.

For a taste of Wensleydale cheese, and the chance to watch it being made, head for the Wensleydale Creamery. This factory has a flourishing visitor centre which includes a museum, video display, licensed restaurant, shop, free cheese-tasting and viewing platforms.

A more conventional museum is the fascinating Dales Countryside Museum, in the Station Yard. The arrival of a railway link in 1877 boosted Hawes' fortunes. The trains no longer run but Hawes is now well established as the main town of Upper Wensleydale. The museum (which also contains a Tourist Information Centre and a National Park Centre) has first-class displays on life in the Dales, particularly on small local industries such as knitting and peat-cutting. Its collection is enhanced by the inclusion of material donated by the local authors and historians, Marie Hartley and Joan Ingilby.

HUBBERHOLME MAP REF 407 G5

With its riverside setting, surrounded by trees in the valley floor, there are fewer more picturesque villages to be found than Hubberholme. It is not surprising, then, to discover that it was the favourite place of J B Priestley. This Bradford author, who wrote *The Good Companions* and many other books and stage plays, loved Hubberholme and visited it often. He drank in the village pub, and a plaque in the local church commemorates his great affection for the tiny village where he chose his ashes to be scattered.

The Church of St Michael and All Angels, one of the delights of the Dales, was originally a chapel in the Norman hunting forest of Langstrothdale Chase. A major attraction is its rood loft from 1558, which only survives thanks to Hubberholme's isolation. In 1571 an edict was issued in the York Diocese to destroy all rood lofts in the region, but Hubberholme's was one of only two in Yorkshire to escape destruction. Look also for the wooden mouse symbol of Robert Thompson, who made much of the church's more recent woodwork.

INGLEBOROUGH MAP REF 406 F5

There are several ways of approaching Ingleborough on foot, from Clapham, Ingleton, Horton in Ribblesdale and Chapel-le-Dale, and each is an energetic but rewarding climb to the top of the peak's 2,373 feet (723m). Until accurate measurement of hills became possible, Ingleborough was long believed to be the highest point in Yorkshire. We now know that it is surpassed by both Whernside and Mickle Fell. At the top of Ingleborough is a wide plateau, with a triangulation point and a stone windbreak, and of course grand views. An Iron Age fort once stood here, and horse races have been run in more recent memory, with large bonfires still lit occasionally for special celebrations.

The path from Chapel-le-Dale is the shortest and the steepest approach, giving a daunting impression of the challenge to come as you look up at Ingleborough's heights. From Clapham the walk is about 4 miles (6.4km) one-way, passing Ingleborough Cave. Ingleborough's slopes have a lot of potholes, so you need to take care if you stray from the path.

South of the summit of Ingleborough you'll see the Gaping Gill pothole, though to describe it as a pothole is like calling Westminster Abbey a parish church. In fact you could probably fit the abbey inside Gaping Gill: some mathematician has certainly worked out that you can fit York Minster Cathedral inside the main cavern. This is about 120 feet (37m) high and 500 feet (152m) long, and the stream

INGLEBOROUGH

of Fell Beck plunges down into it from the surface, making it one of the highest waterfalls in Britain at 364 feet (111m). The breathtaking sight of the interior of Gaping Gill is normally reserved for experienced potholers, but twice a year, on spring and summer bank holidays, local caving clubs set up a winch and bosun's chair and allow members of the public to share the experience.

INGLETON MAP REF 406 F5

Ingleton has too much modern sprawl to be called a pretty village, but it has an attractive centre with steep winding streets going down to the gorge where its celebrated Waterfalls Walk starts. Before the arrival of the railway in the late 19th century, bringing the visitors and walkers who heralded much of the new development, Ingleton relied on its woollen and cotton spinning industries, and before that coal mining and stone quarrying. Now instead of mill-workers' cottages there are guesthouses, shops and several pubs, though the rock quarry is still one of the largest in the Dales.

The Church of St Mary the Virgin is in a dominating position, and has been rebuilt several times, though the 15th-century tower remains. Its oldest feature is a Norman font, which was rediscovered in 1830. It had been hidden in the river below during times of religious persecution. The church also has what is known as the 'Vinegar Bible', so-called because of a misprint in 1717 in what should have been the Parable of the Vineyards.

On the B6255 to the northeast of Ingleton is the White Scar Cave, the best show cave in the Dales. With rivers and waterfalls, these make for exhilarating subterranean guided tours.

JERVAULX MAP REF 407 H4

This superb Cistercian monastery, now mostly in ruins, is a truly evocative place, filled in summer with the scent of the glorious wild flowers that grow around the crumbling grey stones. The abbey was founded in 1156 and eventually owned much of Wensleydale. Sheep, cattle and horses were bred by the monks, who were the first to make Wensleydale cheese.

Despite the fact that the buildings are in a ruinous state there is still plenty to see, such as the staircase, which is known as the Night Stairs, which led from the monks' upstairs dormitory to night services in the church. Other abbey remains which can be identified include the cloister, the infirmary, the kitchen as well as the parlour. Jervaulx is on private land but open access is allowed, with an honesty box for admission money. There is a car park, a tea room and souvenir shop.

KNARESBOROUGH

KIRKBY LONSDALE MAP REF 406 F5

This tiny market town stands just over the border in Cumbria and marks the far western limit of the Yorkshire Dales. It is a delightfully unspoilt place, whose charms have been recognised by artists and authors, from Constable and Turner to Ruskin and Wordsworth, all of whom have sung its praises over the years.

A Roman fort has been excavated at Burrow, just 2 miles (3.2km) south of the town, and in 1227 King Henry III granted a market charter which allowed for a weekly market and an annual fair. The fair died out in the 19th century, but the market still thrives every Thursday in Market Place. Here the the lovely butter cross dates from the early 20th century.

The Church of St Mary the Virgin is a most impressive building. It is thought to date from the late 11th and early 12th centuries, and a Norman archway beneath the solid square tower is a beautiful construction. It has some fine stained glass and a carved pulpit. Outside, near the north entrance, is a tower which can be seen in J M W Turner's famous painting of 1822, *Kirkby Lonsdale Churchyard*, which serves as another reminder of the timeless nature of this attractive little town.

On the edge of town, the medieval Devil's Bridge spans the River Lune. It is one of the town's most notable features with three graceful arches striding over the water and is a very popular meeting place for bikers. Its date is not certain, though records from the late 14th century tell of repairs to a bridge in the town. The bridge is now open for pedestrians only. A short way down the river is a piece of limestone, known as the Devil's Neck Collar, through which a hole has been worn by the action of the water.

KNARESBOROUGH MAP REF 407 H5

Knaresborough is considered to be one of the most picturesque market towns in the Dales, much of it perched on ridges of rock rising above the River Nidd, on which rowing boats are usually bobbing about. A viaduct crosses high above the river, while old houses peek through the trees on one side, looking across at the parkland and woods that conceal Mother Shipton's Cave on the opposite bank.

In the time of Mother Shipton, the Yorkshire prophetess, this land was a large hunting forest, and Knaresborough must have looked even more beautiful. Mother Shipton, said to have been born in the cave in 1488, gained a reputation as a prophet. It is claimed that she foretold the attempted invasion and subsequent defeat of the Spanish Armada in 1588, and predicted the devastating Great Fire of London in 1666. You can visit the cave as part of a self-guided audio tour, along with the Petrifying Well – in which minerals in the water turn any object placed inside it to stone – and a small museum.

The town's official museum is up in the Old Courthouse in the grounds of Knaresborough Castle. It houses local items and a gallery devoted to the Civil War in Knaresborough, but is enjoyable not least because Knaresborough seems to have had more than its fair share of rather odd characters over the years, and their doings are well chronicled.

In addition to Mother Shipton there was Robert Flower, who lived in a cave on the riverside and was known locally as St Robert because of his alleged powers as a healer; Eugene Aram, a schoolmaster who murdered a shoemaker in St Robert's cave and escaped justice for 13 years; and John Metcalfe, who went blind at the age of six, but later went on to enjoy various careers including, quantity surveyor, road building pioneer, accomplished violinist and part-time smuggler!

These days, Knaresborough Castle is much reduced, but it has also seen its fair share of characters over the years. The murderers of Thomas á Becket sought refuge here for a time, and royal visitors included Edward III, King John and Richard II, who was imprisoned here in 1399. The dungeon remains just as it was. There are knowledgeable guides on hand to answer questions, and regular tours of the sallyport (a secret access to the moat). With a small park around the remains, this is a popular spot to sit and enjoy the lovely views over the river.

At the market place, as well as a bustling Wednesday market, you will find the oldest chemist's shop, or apothecary, in Britain, thought to have been here since the 13th century, but trading continuously since 1720. The market is first mentioned in 1206, but is known to have been held each and every Wednesday since 1310, the day fixed by Edward II's charter.

The Church of St John contains some Norman remains, and a Tudor font with a lockable cover to prevent witches stealing the holy water. By the church, a street named Water Bag Bank drops steeply down to the river. The name arose because the town's water supply was once brought up here on horseback in leather bags.

MALHAM MAP REF 407 G5

Malham is a magnet for visitors to the Dales. Malham Cove is one of Britain's most impressive natural features and consequently the area has become almost too popular for its own good. At busy times the National Park Centre car park overflows and the roadside verges disappear under the wheels of parked cars. There are a number of cafés, pubs, outdoor shops and guesthouses to accommodate the crowds.

The half-mile (0.8km) walk to Malham Cove is signed from the village centre. The limestone rock face seems to tumble down the 250-foot (76m) cliffs, and extends for about 1,000 feet (305m). Try to picture the water that once flowed over the cliff face, helping create today what has been aptly described as a 'dry waterfall'. This natural amphitheatre is simply the most visible part of the Craven Fault. It is a steep climb up man-made steps to the top, but your reward is a view over the moors around Malham, north to Malham Tarn and over the limestone pavements. It is in these pavements that some of the area's wide variety of unusual plants can be found.

Malham Tarn, north of the village, is in the care of the National Trust and the Field Studies Council. It is 1,229 feet (374m) above sea level, and the tarn and surrounding area have been declared a Site of Special Scientific Interest. A track leads down past Tarn House, where the Field Studies Council run regular courses on the natural history of the area. It is a particularly important area for plant life and as a breeding ground for many birds: a hide is open to the public to enable views of parts of the lake that can't be accessed on foot. Tarn House was also the home of Walter Morrison whose visitors included Charles Darwin, John Ruskin and Charles Kingsley, author of *The Water Babies*.

PATELEY BRIDGE MAP REF 407 H5

The main attraction at Pateley Bridge is the Nidderdale Museum, but the town is also a good base for visiting nearby places of interest. Many of the buildings date from the 18th and 19th centuries though as they are built with gritstone the town can appear to be a rather dour place in gloomy autumnal weather.

There is nothing dour, though, about the award-winning Nidderdale Museum, housed in the town's former workhouse. Founded in 1975, it grew from just a very small collection to one which today provides all the information you need about life in Nidderdale, from the spread of religion and the development of transport to collections of cameras and razors that have been owned by local people. Some of the most enjoyable exhibits are the reconstructed shops and offices. All have fascinating memorabilia, and the museum is much loved and well looked after.

To the north of Pateley Bridge, near Lofthouse, is How Stean Gorge, also known as Yorkshire's 'Little Switzerland'. The ravine of up to 80-foot (24m) deep was hacked out in the Ice Age. Pathways lead by the fast-flowing river through ferns and by lush, dank undergrowth; there are bridges on different levels and fenced galleries on rocky ledges. There are also a few caves, the best known being Tom Taylor's Cave, with a 530-foot (162m) walk underground (take a torch).

PEN-Y-GHENT MAP REF 407 G5

The lowest of this region's Three Peaks, Pen-y-ghent in profile looks like a face, thrusting its jaw out defiantly as if challenging anyone to climb to the top of its 2,277 feet (694m). In its capacity as the third highest of the Three Peaks, many people assume it is the third highest peak in the Yorkshire Dales. This honour, in fact, goes to Buckden Pike.

Unusually, for this most distinctive of Yorkshire's hills, Pen-y-ghent carries a Celtic name, meaning 'hill of the border', once marking the edge of one of the English tribes' kingdoms. For those who want to tackle its challenge, the most common route is a 3-mile (4.8km) hike from Horton in Ribblesdale, following the signs for the Pennine Way, which passes right over the top of the hill.

At the end of the track out of Horton, just beyond the point where the route turns sharp right towards the hill, there are two potholes. The larger is the huge gaping hole known as Hull Pot, into which Hull Pot Beck disappears. Treat these potholes with extreme caution.

The climb up to the summit of Pen-y-ghent is steep in places, with a little bit of scrambling. At the top, walkers can revel in views across to the other peaks, north across the fells of Langstrothdale Chase, and south over Ribblesdale and Lancashire's Forest of Bowland.

RICHMOND MAP REF 407 H4

To approach Richmond from Swaledale is to see the importance of the town to the dale. The road winds through lovely wooded valleys, eventually revealing Richmond Castle standing high on its hill high above the river. The castle, now cared for by English Heritage, dates from the Norman period and inside is Scolland's Hall, which dates from the 11th century and claims to be the oldest hall in England. The panoramic views down the river and over the surrounding area are splendid.

Behind the castle is Richmond's huge cobbled Market Place, with its Market Cross and the unusual sight of Holy Trinity Church: unusual because there are shops and a museum built into the base of the building, which was almost destroyed several times and then later restored, since its construction in around 1150. The curfew bell sounds from the church's clock tower, at 8am and 8pm every day.

The museum in the church is that of the Green Howards, one of Yorkshire's proudest regiments. Inside are smart modern displays, but this is actually only one of three museums in Richmond. The Richmondshire Museum itself is a typical collection of historical items.

Richmond's best museum, however, is the Georgian Theatre Museum. The theatre, built late in the 18th century, is the only one in the world that still survives in its original state. As well as attending a show in the evenings, visitors should take one of the guided tours to have a glimpse behind the stage, into the dressing rooms and inside the original box office. Volunteer guides make the place come alive.

A mile (1.6km) southeast of the town centre, via a walk along the banks of the Swale, is Easby Abbey (English Heritage). The ruins of this medieval monastery are impressive. They certainly make a fitting destination for a pleasant walk, though, where Swaledale comes to an end.

RIPON MAP REF 407 H5

In AD 672 St Wilfrid built a church on the site of what is now Ripon Cathedral, and the crypt of that church can still be visited, making it the oldest complete Saxon crypt in any English cathedral. The west front of this cathedral dates from 1220, the east front from 1290, and inside there are 500-year-old woodcarvings, a 16th-century nave and some exceptional stained-glass work. A building not to be missed.

Close by, in St Mary's Gate, visitors move from God to the godless, in the Ripon Prison and Police Museum. Housed in the cell block of what was first the Ripon Liberty Prison and later its Police Station, the museum tells the vivid story of Yorkshire law and disorder. It has some chilling but never gruesome displays. It's one of a series of sites making up the Yorkshire Law and Order Museums. The city's Law and Order Trail will also take you to the Old Workhouse Museum and the Courthouse Museum.

All around Ripon attractions vie for attention. The Lightwater Valley Theme Park, with its enormous rollercoasters and other rides, is high on the list for families. There are lots of eating places and gift shops, and the Lightwater Village, with factory, fashion and food shops.

Just 2 miles (3.2km) east of Lightwater Valley is Norton Conyers, a lovely country house which dates back to the mid-14th century. Visitors will hear the legend of the Mad Woman, a story also heard by Charlotte Brontë when she visited the house in 1839. The character possibly inspired the mad Mrs Rochester in *Jane Eyre*, written eight years later, but there are other claimants to this honour.

FROM ADDINGHAM TO ILKLEY

This walk takes you from the extended village of Addingham, which grew as the textile trades expanded, through rolling country and along a stretch of the lovely River Wharfe to the spa town of Ilkley. During the reign of Queen Victoria, the great and the good came to Ilkley to take the medicinal waters.

DISTANCE/TIME 5.5 miles (8.8km) 2h30 **MAP** OS Explorer 297 Lower Wharfedale **START** Lay-by at eastern end of Addingham, on bend where North Street becomes Bark Lane by information panel; grid ref: SE 084498 **TRACKS** Riverside path and field paths, some road walking, 7 stiles **THE PUB** The Fleece Inn, Addingham. Tel: 01943 830491

1 Walk 50yds (46m) up the road, and descend steps down to the right, signed 'Dales Way'. Bear right and then cross over the River Wharfe on a suspension bridge. Follow a tarred path along a field edge. Cross a stream and join a metalled track between walls to emerge at a minor road by a sharp bend. Go right, then after 0.5 mile (0.8km) of road walking reach Nesfield.

2 About 200yds (183m) beyond the last house, and after the road crosses a stream, bear left up a stony track (signed to High Austby). Where the track turns left, take a stile between two gates and cross the field, keeping parallel to the road. Go through the top gate and follow the fence on the right to go through another gate next to a stone stile. Follow the wall on your right-hand side. Beyond a small conifer plantation, take a ladder stile in the fence ahead to keep left of Low Austby Farm.

3 Across the field cross a footbridge over a stream, and then beyond a stile enter a wood. Descend a path, leaving the wood by another stile. Follow a fence uphill, and then cross the middle of a field to a stile at the far end and enter a wood. Follow a path through trees, to a road, via a wall stile. Go right, downhill, to a junction. Go right, over

Nesfield Road, and take a path to the left of an electricity sub-station. Follow the river to Ilkley's old stone bridge.

4 Cross the bridge. Turn right on to a riverside path (from here to Addingham you are following the well-signed Dales Way). Soon continue along a lane, passing Ilkley Lawn Tennis Club. Opposite to the clubhouse, take the footpath, turn left, through a kissing gate, and then across pasture. Negotiate a further seven kissing gates to return to the River Wharfe. Cross a stream on a footbridge, and enter woodland. Go across another stream to meet a stony track. Go right and descend to the river. Go through another kissing gate and then follow a grassy path (woodland and fence to your left) before joining the old A65 road.

5 Follow the road by the river for 0.5 mile (0.8km). Go right, before houses, to Old Lane. Pass between the houses of Low Mill Village to a riverside path. Pass the rectory (left), and the old rectory (right), and look for a kissing gate. Take the steps and follow the path to a bridge crossing Town Beck. Take a grassy path across pasture in front of the church. Join a tarred path, then go across a bridge, between houses, to re-emerge on North Street. Turn right to the lay-by.

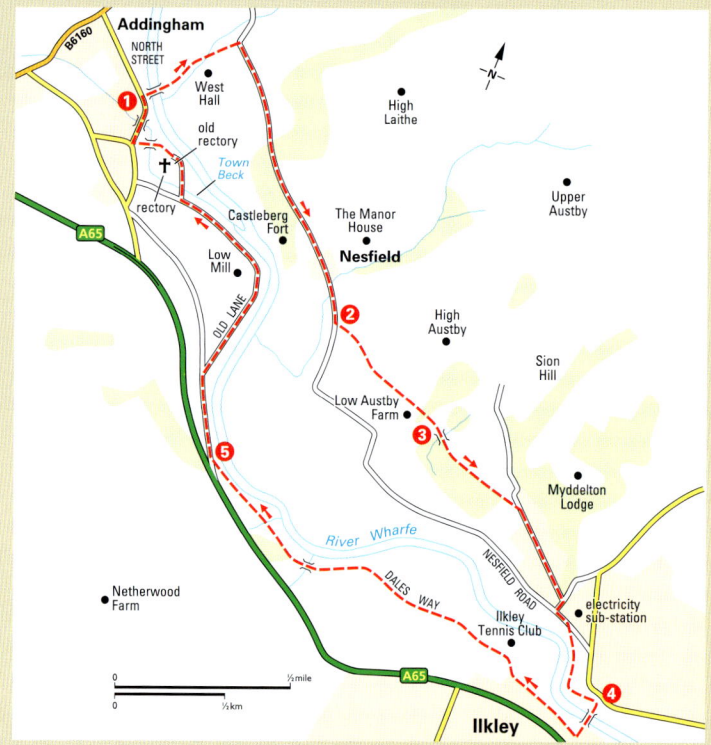

RIVER & WOODLAND AT BOLTON ABBEY

This walk takes you over moorland and alongside the Strid to the romantic Bolton Abbey. The route also passes through woodland where information boards explain the birds and plants, including sessile oak. Characteristic of the area, sessile oak is distinguished from the pedunculate oak by its acorns that have no stalks.

DISTANCE/TIME 6.75 miles (10.9km) 2h30 **MAP** OS Explorer OL2 Yorkshire Dales – Southern & Western **START** Main pay car park at Bolton Abbey; grid ref: SE 071539. **TRACKS** Field and moorland paths, then riverside paths, 4 stiles **THE PUB** Devonshire Arms Hotel (Brasserie), Bolton Abbey. Tel: 01756 710441; www.thedevonshirearms.co.uk

1 Leave the car park at its north end, past the village store and the telephone box. Turn right, walk down the left side of the green, then turn left. Pass under an archway. Opposite the battlemented Bolton Hall, turn left on to a track through a signed gate. Where the track bends left, go through a gate on the right with a bridleway sign. Cross the next field, aiming slightly to the left for a fingerpost to the right of some trees, then pass to the right of some pools. Continue through the gate beyond, then turn right towards a gate into the wood.

2 Go through the gate and follow a clear track through woodland to reach the top gate which leads out into a field. A signpost highlights the direction of the faint grass path that crosses fields and goes towards some rounded grassy hills. In the second large field the path crosses over a well-defined track to reach a gate in the wall corner. Beyond this turn right to follow a wall then climb a small hill, with wide views to the Lower Barden Reservoir and the lovely heather hills of Barden Moor. Next take a green path which descends to the road below.

3 Turn right along the road. After about 0.75 mile (1.2km) go right through a gate by a sign 'FP to B6160'. Follow the path across

sodden fields. The path meets and follows a wall on the left, and then a footpath diversion sign points the way left over a stone stile. Descend by a wall on the left to a roadside stile directly opposite to the Strid car park.

4 Cross over the road and go through the car park and pass beside the Strid Wood Nature Trails Kiosk. Follow the most prominent path, signed 'The Strid'. Turn left just before Lady Harriot's Seat and drop to the river bank where you turn right to reach the narrowest part of the river at the Strid.

5 From the Strid, continue to walk along the riverside path to an information board and gateway. Ignore the path signed 'Lud Stream' and continue along the main track slanting away from the river to reach the Cavendish Pavilion. Go through a gate, turn left by the café and then cross the footbridge.

6 Immediately at the end of the bridge turn right signed 'Bolton Abbey'. Follow the path parallel with the river, descending to a bridge beside stepping-stones and the priory.

7 Cross the bridge, then walk up the slope and the steps to a gateway – known as the Hole in the Wall. Go through the gateway then ahead by the green to the car park.

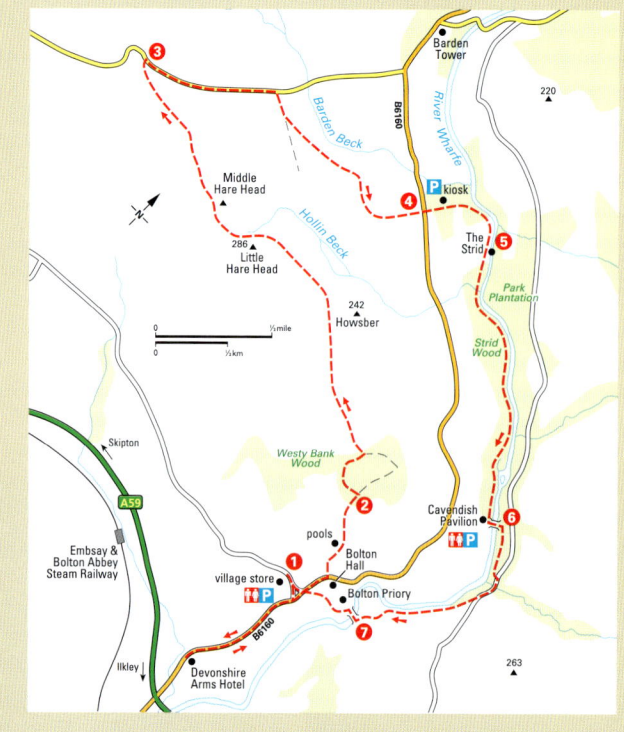

WALK 111

A CIRCULAR WALK TAKING IN MALHAM COVE

The noble Malham Cove is the majestic highlight of this limestone Dales walk. As you begin the walk, the stream from Malham Tarn suddenly disappears in a tumble of rocks. This is the aptly named Water Sinks. The now-dry valley of Watlowes, just beyond Water Sinks, was formed by water action. It was this stream in fact that produced Malham Cove, and once fell over its spectacular cliff in a waterfall 230feet (70m) high. It is 200 years since water reached the cove.

DISTANCE/TIME 6.25 miles (10.1km) 3h **MAP** OS Explorer OL30 Yorkshire Dales – Northern & Central **START** At Water Sinks, Malham Tarn, near gateway across road; grid ref: SD 894658. **TRACKS** Well-marked field and moorland paths, more than 400 steps in descent from Malham Cove, 5 stiles **THE PUB** The Buck Inn, Malham. Tel: 01729 830317; www.buckinnmalham.co.uk

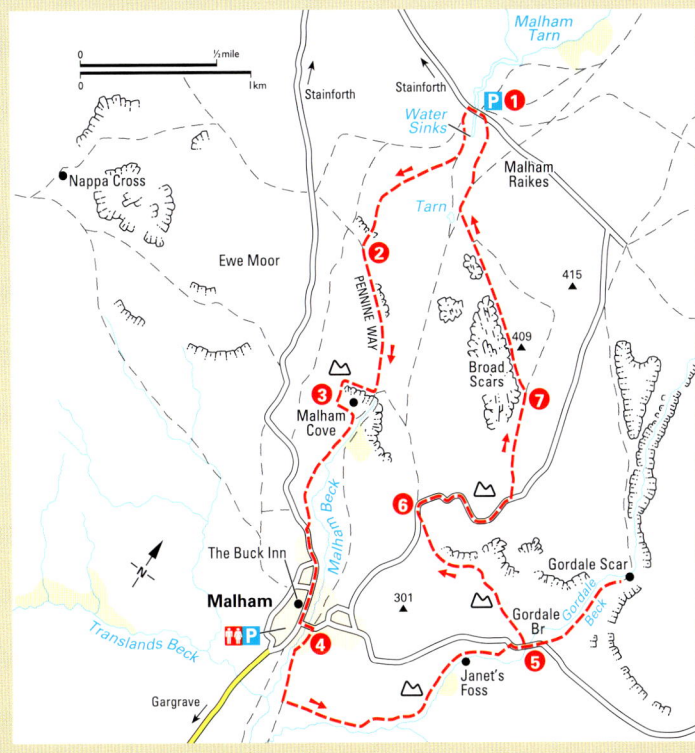

1 From the car park, walk right along the lane and through the gate, before turning left through a kissing gate at the Malham Raikes, Langscar Gate sign. Walk down to a drystone wall on your left and then follow a deepening dry valley. Beyond a cave in crags to the left, an engineered path doubles back right into a second dry valley.

2 Turn left and follow the footpath down the valley to reach a limestone pavement which is at the top of Malham Cove. Turn right and walk along the pavement to reach steps, which begin by an opening in a wall. Over 400 steps descend in zigzags to the bottom.

3 When you reach the bottom, turn right along the path beside the river to reach the road. Turn left and now follow the road into the centre of Malham village.

4 The Buck Inn lies on the right side of the road, just beyond the little bridge. Go over the bridge, then turn right along an unsurfaced lane between the river and a row of cottages. At the end a gravelled footpath signed 'Janet's Foss' heads south across fields. At a junction with the Pennine

Way, turn left across more fields, then into woodland. At Janet's Foss the path climbs left to reach the Gordale road. Turn right along the road, towards Gordale Scar.

5 At the bridge go through a gate to the left. (To visit Gordale Scar, continue to walk ahead here. Next, take a signed gate to the left and follow the path up through a field into the gorge. Keep going on the obvious route as far as the waterfall and then follow the same route back to the previously mentioned bridge.) On the main route, follow the signed public footpath uphill through two stiles and out on to a lane.

6 Turn right and then walk uphill on the winding lane for just 0.25 mile (0.4km), to a ladder stile over the wall on your left. Follow the track, going left at a fork to reach another footpath fingerpost.

7 Turn left to walk along the edge of the limestone clints of Broad Scars to reach some small pools. Turn right at the sign for Malham Tarn, go over a ladder stile in a cross-wall and then take the left fork of the path and follow it to return to the car park.

WALK 112

A CIRCUIT FROM LOFTHOUSE

This is a pleasant walk from Lofthouse to Ramsgill and Middlesmoor in the valley of the River Nidd, across the rich farmland and moorland landscape. Nidderdale is a designated Area of Outstanding Natural Beauty. In the 19th and 20th centuries parts of the dale were dammed for reservoirs to supply water to Bradford.

DISTANCE/TIME 7 miles (11.3km) 3h **MAP** OS Explorer OL30 Yorkshire Dales – Northern & Central **START** Car park by Memorial Hall in Lofthouse; grid ref: SE 101734. **TRACKS** Mostly field paths and tracks, may be muddy, 20 stiles **THE PUB** Crown Hotel, Middlesmoor. Tel: 01423 755204

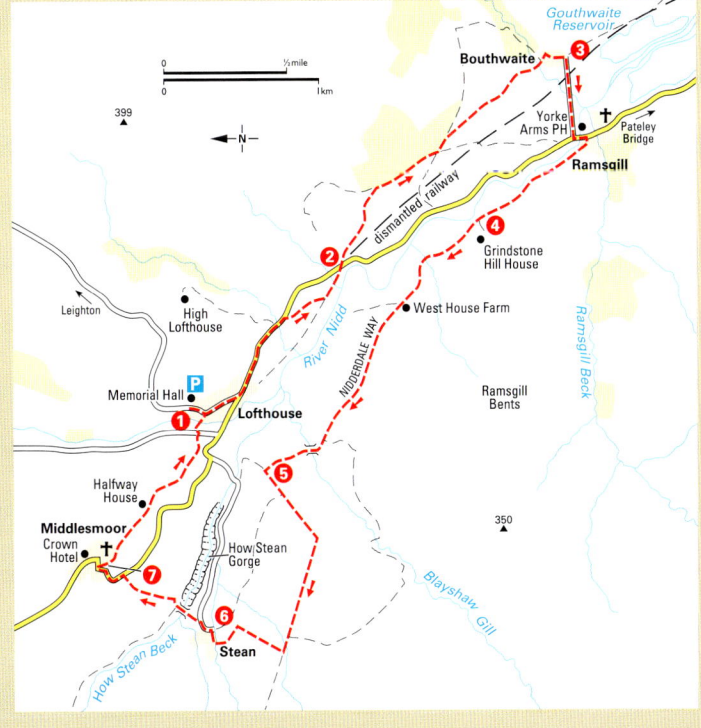

1 Walk downhill past the Memorial Hall to the main road. Turn left. When you are past the drive for the Old Vicarage, go right, through a stile, signed Nidderdale Way. The path joins a track to a gate. Don't go through but turn left, follow a wall, then maintain direction across a field. Over a stile at the far end turn half right to join the causeway of an old railway, out to a roadside stile.

2 Go across the road, then through a gate. Follow the wire fence to a stile, then cross the field ahead. Before the next gateway, go left over a stile, avoiding the railway trackbed. Bear left and climb to a gate where a Nidderdale Way signpost points towards the woods on the skyline. Through a kissing gate the path follows the lower edge of the woods. The narrow path passes above Longsight House. Take the right-hand fork towards Longsight Farm to go to the left of a farmhouse. Now, follow the waymarkers to a gate and ladder stile. Over the stile descend by a hedge on the left and go over a wooden bridge, where a gravel track leads past the buildings of Bouthwaite and to the road.

3 Turn right down the road to reach a T-junction. Turn left, over the bridge. Take the next track right, bear right signed 'Stean'.

4 At West House Farm cross a stile between the farm and a bungalow, cross the road and follow the waymark posts, heading left to join a track by outbuildings. Go up the valley before dropping to a barn. Descend on a track into a wooded valley and over a bridge.

5 At a T-junction, go left, and follow the walled track as it bends right. At a T-junction go right. At the bottom, bend left above houses and drop to the road at Stean.

6 Beyond the phone box, take a stile on the left signed 'Middlesmoor'. Drop to cross a bridge over the Gorge then climb the far banks to a gate. Then go diagonally across the field and over a stile. Follow the wall up to the road. Turn left towards Middlesmoor. Retrace your steps and turn left beside the Wesleyan chapel to the gate of the church.

7 Turn right before the gate, through a stile signposted 'Lofthouse'. Go down steps then through a stile and two gateways by Halfway House. Continue through a small gate then go diagonally left to a gate in the corner. In the lay-by go left on the nearside of the cricket ground to reach a gate. Cross the lane and a bridge, then bear right to the centre of Lofthouse. Turn right to the car park.

DISTANCE/TIME 8 miles (12.9km) 2h **MAP** OS Explorer 289 Leeds **START** Sicklinghall Road, Wetherby; grid ref: SE 397483 **TRACKS** Well-compacted gravel railway trackbed lanes and smooth bridleways **THE PUB** The Castle, Spofforth. Tel: 01937 590200

DISTANCE/TIME 9.75 miles (15.7km) 1h30; extension 12.5 miles (20.1km) 2h **MAP** OS Explorer OL30 Yorkshire Dales – Northern & Central **START** Small car park on A684, Aysgarth; grid ref: SD 995889 **TRACKS** Grassy tracks; short rough sections; return can be muddy **THE PUB** The Wheatsheaf Hotel, Carperby. Tel: 01969 663216; www.wheatsheafinwensleydale.co.uk

THE HARLAND WAY

The meandering Harland Way forms the basis of a delightful rural ride following in the tracks of the old steam trains and visiting one of Yorkshire's most fascinating Norman castles situated at Spofforth. Lying among the peaceful pastures of the Crimple Valley, Spofforth is an idyllic backwater for a Sunday afternoon ride.

1 With your back to the car park entrance, turn right along the railway trackbed, highlighted by a Harland Way fingerpost. The old line has been exploded through the bedrock to reveal limestone crags, and is now hung with lovely woodland that offers plenty of welcome shade on hot sunny summer days.

2 Take the left fork at the road junction that used to be known as the Wetherby Triangle. You are soon joined from the right by another branch of the line and then together the routes head west towards Spofforth. Half-way along the track you have to dismount to get through a metal gateway and almost immediately again at another gate. The trackbed forges ahead through an avenue of beech, hawthorn, ash and rowan before coming out into the open. Now you'll see thickets of wild roses and bramble, with scabious and purple vetch among the numerous wild flowers of the verges. Here there are wide views across cornfields, and soon the tower of Spofforth church comes into view ahead.

3 The Harland Way ends beyond a gate just short of the village. Take a gravel path which veers right across a green on to East Park Road. This threads through some modern housing to come to the main road where you should turn right. If you have young children it might be better to dismount here to cross over the road, and use the pavements to get to The Castle inn.

4 Just beyond the pub, where the road bends to the right, take the lane on the left, leading to the castle. When you've explored the 14th- and 15th-century remains of Spofforth Castle retrace your route past the pub then turn right along Park Road. Beyond the houses this becomes a stony bridleway, which rises gently across the fields.

5 Ignore all turn-offs until you come to Fox Heads Farm. Turn left along the track here, passing left of the farmhouse. The dirt and stone track descends to a bridge over a stream, then climbs again past an old quarry. Though there are a few climbs the track is still quite easy, being smooth-surfaced and reasonably well drained. Often it's lined with bramble, ferns and foxgloves, and the odd tree. Just beyond the summit of a hill the track bends to the right. After being joined from the right by a second farm track it comes to the road, just to the west of Sicklinghall village.

6 Turn left along the road into the village. On the right there's a pond with lilies and coots, then on the left there's another pub, the Scott Arms. The winding road makes a long but gradual descent towards Wetherby, passing the upmarket Linton Springs Hotel on your right. Beyond the hotel, ignore the right turn 'to Linton'. After passing through some housing in the Wetherby suburbs watch out for the blue cyclists' sign. This marks the access road back to the car park.

GREEN WAYS OF WENSLEYDALE

This route follows a magical green ribbon of a bridleway along a broad terrace high above the valley. You start in Aysgarth, best known for the Aysgarth Falls and can stop and visit Castle Bolton.

1 Cross the footbridge and follow a tarmac path out to a wider lane. Bear right, up to a road and turn right. After 2 miles (3.2km) Carperby is a left turn signed for Castle Bolton. Pass under the corner of one of the towers and at the top turn left.

2 Where the lane swings up into the car park, go ahead through a gate and along a track. Follow this through several gates and go to the left of some farm sheds. After going through the next gate, the track winds left through another gate and then right again. The track beyond is distinctly rougher; dismount and walk here.

3 At the next gate bear left above the wall. After some lawn-like grass, dip to a ford to more grassy going. At the next gate bear half left on to a smooth green track, following signposts to Askrigg and Carperby. After 0.5 mile (0.8km) you will reach Low Gate.

4 At Low Gate go up the hill on a green track, signed for Askrigg. Level out and descend to a gate where Peatmoor Lane crosses. Follow the green track ahead, across a level grassy plateau, until it descends to Oxclose Gate. From here the track skirts left of conspicuous bare ground and the spoil heaps on the site of a former lead mine.

5 Opposite this area the track has a gritty surface, and descends to a gate, with a ford beyond. Dismount and wheel the bikes across this ford and beware of the drop just below. Follow the stony track through another gate. Go up to another gate, swing left through it and down 50yds (45.7m) to a signpost.

6 For the shorter of the two loops, descend the steep track to Woodhall. The surface is loose in places, and inexperienced riders should dismount and walk down. Turn left on the wider road for an easy run, back to the start. For the extension, turn right and then climb the steep track. After two gates the gradient eases. Go through a gate alongside a small plantation. Beyond is the final climb, very tricky in places with bare rock and large loose stones. Over the top there's smooth grass, then a final section of rutted track leads to a gate by a barn. The track beyond soon descends, getting steeper and rougher. At a junction turn sharp left, almost immediately meeting tarmac. Follow the steep lane, down into the hamlet of Nappa Scar and turn left on to the wider road.

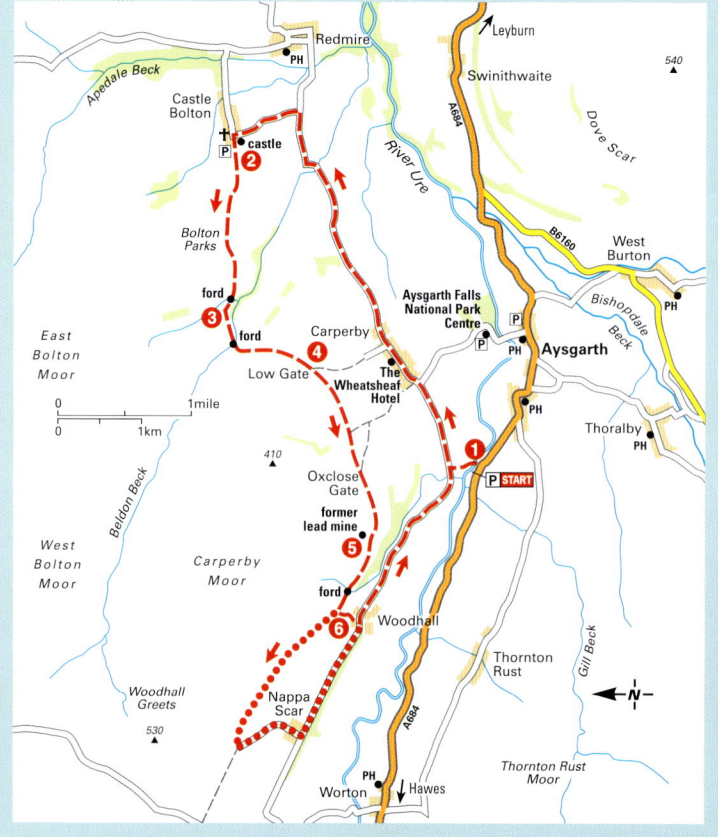

WALK 113

FROM ARNCLIFFE TO KETTLEWELL

You'll need good boots for this walk through rocky hillside, moorland and meadows from Arncliffe to Kettlewell, returning alongside the River Skirfare. Arncliffe sits on a spit of gravel above the river's floodplain. Before the bridge was built, a ford allowed travellers an easy crossing for the many ancient tracks that meet here.

DISTANCE/TIME 6.5 miles (10.4km) 3h30 **MAP** OS Explorer OL30 Yorkshire Dales – Northern & Central **START** Arncliffe, near church; grid ref: SD 932719. **TRACKS** Mostly clear, some rocky sections, may be muddy, 23 stiles **THE PUB** Blue Bell Inn, Kettlewell. Tel: 01756 760230; www.bluebellinn.co.uk

1 With your back to the Falcon Inn, turn right past the green, then left by the church. Cross the bridge and turn right over a gated stile. Walk parallel with the river and go up steps to cross the road via two stiles. Turn half right and follow a steep path across pastureland and limestone (slippery after rain) through woods up Park Scar to a stile.

2 Follow the path across hillside to a ladder stile. Pass a signpost and go through a gap in a tumbled wall to another signpost. Continue to a ladder stile, then cross the corner of the field to a ladder stile at the ridge top.

3 Descend to join a wall on your right. Ignore the track through a gate, instead cross the wall lower down on a ladder stile. Continue towards Kettlewell, descending to a signpost. Cross over a track to a limestone scar. Descend through a narrow cleft (The Slit), descend to a stile and, beyond it, a footpath sign. Turn right, go through a gate on to the road. To pay a visit to the pub, turn left over the bridge and into the village centre; the Blue Bell Inn is on the right. Return here.

4 At the far side of the main bridge, go south for 300yds (274m), then go right through a gate signposted 'Hawkswick'. Climb through woodland, go through a waymarked gate, then turn half right through a gap in the wall, passing a ruined building. Continue winding steeply to a gap in a wall beside a ladder stile. Bear left to another stile and ascend the path beneath limestone crags to cross a stile in the ridge wall. With Littondale in view, continue downhill, bending right by a cairn.

5 A sunken track goes down from the right to join the path. Follow it with a wall on your left. Go through the stile into Hawkswick. Turn left at the junction to take an unsurfaced lane, which bends right between buildings before reaching the main valley road.

6 Cross and then follow the road, bending to the right. Before farm buildings, on the left, turn right to the footbridge; do not cross, but turn left at the 'Arncliffe' sign to follow the riverside path. The path leaves the river to a gate. It all but disappears in a field, but the river bank returns to lead to a footbridge.

7 Walk to the right of a barn and through a gate, then left to a wall stile. Cross a track, go through three stiles, walk beside the river, to go through a gate near a house. Follow the waymarkers to a kissing gate and walk past the church to your car.

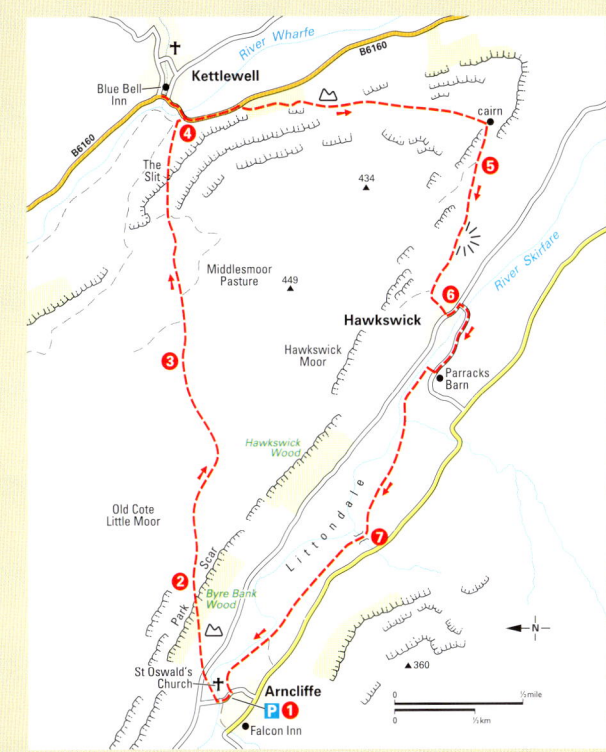

WALK 114

ALONG LANGSTROTHDALE FROM HUBBERHOLME

This lovely walk takes you from J B Priestly's favourite Dales village, along Langstrothdale and back via a limestone terrace. The popular literary figure enjoyed supping the local ale at the George, in Hubberholme, and the churchyard there is the resting place for his ashes. The church itself has a wonderful wooden rood loft and the pews bear the 'mouse' trademark of craftsman Robert Thompson.

DISTANCE/TIME 5 miles (8km) 2h **MAP** OS Explorer OL30 Yorkshire Dales – Northern & Central **START** Beside river in Hubberholme, opposite church (not church parking; grid ref: SD 927782. **TRACKS** Field paths and tracks, steep after Yockenthwaite, 11 stiles **THE PUB** The George Inn, Hubberholme. Tel: 01756 760223; www.thegeorge-inn.co.uk

1 Go through a Dales Way signed gate near the east end of the church, bend to the left and then take the lower path, signed 'Yockenthwaite'. Walk beside the river for 1.75 miles (2.8km) through three stiles, a gate and two further stiles. The path eventually rises and reaches another stone stile into Yockenthwaite.

2 Go through the stile and bend left to a wooden gate. Walk ahead through a farm gate by a signpost to Deepdale and Beckermonds. Before the track reaches a bridge, go right and swing round to a sign to Cray.

3 Go up the hill and, as the track curves right, continue to follow a slightly higher grass track highlighted by a Cray and Hubberholme sign. Part-way up the hill go right at a footpath sign through a wooden gate in a fence.

4 Go through a second gate to a footpath sign and ascend the hillside. Go through a gap in a wall by another signpost and then follow the obvious path through several gaps in crossing walls. Now the path climbs left to reach a stile at the edge of woodland.

5 Cross the bridge beyond and continue to walk through the woodland, back on to high pasture. The high path follows a line of limestone crags with Buckden in the valley below, before arcing left into the hollow of Crook Gill. Continue over a footbridge spanning the gill, then climb up the far banks to pass to the right of a large barn. The footpath then winds its way down the valley. From here, go through a gate and carry on ahead across meadowland to a gateway on to a track, and on to a stone barn.

6 Bend round to the right once you get beyond the barn, and head down to a public footpath sign to Stubbing Bridge. Go down the path between some stone walls, then pass through a wooden gate and on to a grassy hillside. Continue downhill to meet the stream by a waterfall.

7 Continue to walk along the streamside path through shady woodland. Cross over a wooden stile and then continue on past a barn to a stone stile out on to the road. Turn right along the road and it will take you back to where you left your car at the parking place in Hubberholme.

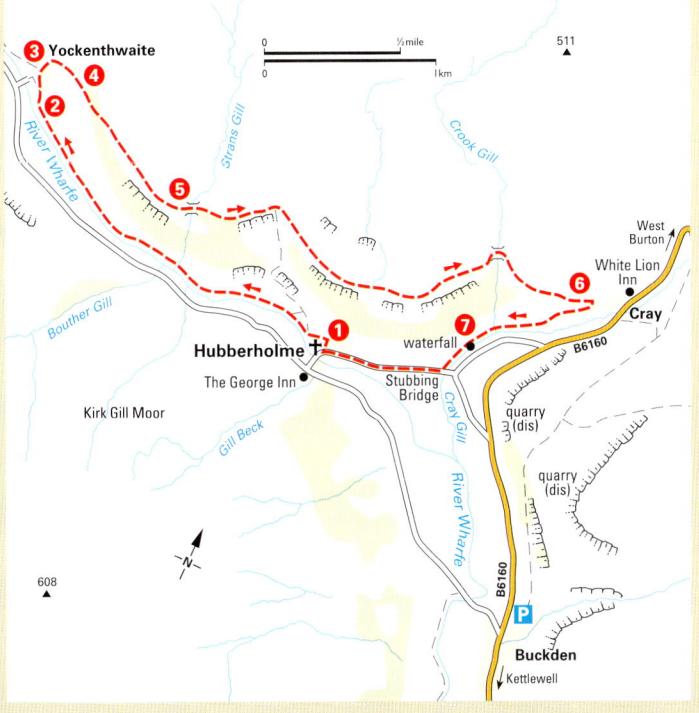

Tea Room Traditions

One of the great British pleasures, one that few other nations quite understand and even fewer adequately replicate, is the ritual of taking tea. The popularity of a 'cuppa' was a strong economic incentive throughout Britain, and prompted the evolution of often quaint and intimate salons everywhere – the National Trust alone boasts tea rooms at almost 200 of its sites, and few public attractions these days survive without the almost obligatory tea room.

Yet tea, that most vital of English beverages, is a latecomer to Britain. The custom of drinking tea originated in China 5,000 years ago, and it was not until the mid-17th century that the beverage first appeared in England.

A tea room is a form of café or tea house peculiar to Britain, but these days also present in other Commonwealth countries. They tend to be small establishments, sometimes occurring in the most improbable places to serve visitor needs, but in their heyday tea rooms played a widespread and significant role in British social life.

With an observance bordering on ritual, tea rooms provide a delightful core service, offering customers cream tea, or Devonshire tea, in some cases served from silver teapots and poured into china cups, and a scone with jam and clotted cream. However, this pleasant experience is far more widely available these days than Devonshire clotted cream might suggest – you can even get Devonshire Teas in Australia, presumably a touch of nostalgia for many expats living there. In Scotland, teas are usually served with a variety of scones, pancakes, crumpets and other cakes. And almost every part of Britain serves its own regional specialities – Yorkshire parkin, Lancashire Eccles and Chorley cake, the ubiquitous carrot cake and muffins, Bakewell puddings (they don't call them 'tarts'), Banbury cakes, Dundee cake – there are just so many of them.

In the 18th century, tea was expensive and heavily taxed, a luxury only the well-to-do could afford, and the rich were not for sharing the pleasure. Doubts arose about the suitability of tea for 'persons of an inferior rank', but the increasing concern within the Temperance movement over the habitual drunkenness of the working classes led to the promotion of tea as an alternative. From the 1830s, many new cafés and coffee houses opened up as a temperance alternative to pubs and inns.

The tea room itself was developed towards the end of the 19th century, when Catherine Cranston opened the first of what became a chain of Miss Cranston's Tea Rooms in Glasgow, providing elegant, well-designed social venues that enabled well-to-do and unchaperoned women to socialise without male company. They were an instant success. The 'birth' of the seemingly very English tradition of the tea room in Glasgow may surprise people, but Miss Cranston was keen to engage a new breed of talented designers, and became a patron of the distinctly unique Charles Rennie Mackintosh who designed the complete building of The Willow Tearooms in Glasgow, contrasting a strikingly modern exterior with intriguing interior designs.

From the 1880s, fine hotels began to offer tea service in tea rooms and tea courts, and by 1910 they had begun to host afternoon tea dances as the dance craze swept the country. By the 1950s, tea rooms of all kinds were widespread in Britain, but in the years to come, cafés became more fashionable, and tea rooms, as such, less common, though the distinction is often blurred. Country tea rooms offering cream teas, such as are found throughout Yorkshire especially, are a hearty tourist attraction in many areas, and many book publishers produce books of 'Tea Shop Walks' so that walkers can conclude their day out in a time-honoured British manner.

Because tea was highly valued, it was kept by the lady of the house and not entrusted to the care of the housekeeper, and it was always the lady of the house also who would serve the tea. But eventually, the beverage tea became generally affordable and the growing middle class imitated the affluent and privileged and found that the meal 'tea' was an economical way of entertaining friends. Thus afternoon tea quickly became the norm in many households.

Traditionally, 'afternoon tea' is a light meal taken around four o'clock, and although few these days actually take afternoon tea, as such, it is still available in high quality hotels, and follows a long-established template: loose tea is to be served in a previously warmed teapot, with milk and sugar to be added according to taste. This is accompanied by various sandwiches (customarily cucumber, egg and cress, fish paste, ham or smoked salmon), scones (with butter, clotted cream and jam), and often with cakes and pastries (such as Battenberg or Victoria sponge), all served on a tiered stand.

TOP LEFT The Bakewell Pudding Shop, in the Peak District National Park, Derbyshire. Here you can buy cakes, preserves and Bakewell puddings – also erroneously called Bakewell 'tarts' in other parts of England.

BELOW LEFT Traditional scones - best served warm with strawberry jam and clotted cream accompanied by a refreshing cup of tea.

BELOW Light, fluffy Victoria sponge layered with strawberries and cream often appears on afternoon tea menus.

OPPOSITE Silver cutlery, delicate bone china crockery and opulent surroundings create the perfect setting for this most English of traditions.

The story is probably apocryphal, but afternoon tea is said to have originated with the 7th Duchess of Bedford, who in the early 1800s hit on the idea of having tea in the late afternoon to bridge the gap between luncheon and dinner, which in such lofty social circles would not be served until well into the evening.

'High tea' is an early evening meal, taken usually between five and six o'clock as a substitute for both afternoon tea and the main evening meal. The actual term 'high tea' comes from the meal being eaten at the 'high' or table of the house. High tea would typically provide cold meats, eggs or fish, cakes and sandwiches, and is an informal meal served in many families. For agricultural workers however, high tea was traditionally a meal that combined both daily meals and was eaten just after nightfall.

In the north of England, 'tea' is the main evening meal, even if no-one is actually drinking tea. It is traditionally eaten at five o'clock or later, sometimes as late as 9pm. Tea as a meal is synonymous with supper in the south of England, and the midday meal is sometimes termed dinner, rather than lunch. It's all a little confusing, but part of the on-going and agreeable idiosyncrasy of the North-South divide so ably described in Stuart Maconie's best-selling book *Pies and Prejudice*.

To ensure that the highest standards are observed in British rural tea shops, there is now a Tea Council, dedicated to maintaining traditions and quality, and each year it distinguishes a worthy tea room with an award. And while the attendant cakes and sandwiches, although no doubt delicious, may not always be as healthy as we might like, latest research has shown that your daily cuppa provides you with antioxidants, and contributes successfully to your daily fluid target.

SEMER WATER MAP REF 407 G4

Yorkshire's largest natural lake was formed in Raydale during the Ice Age when a retreating glacier left behind a huge clay dam, and another was blocked in by a glacier in Wensleydale. The resultant melt water formed Semer Water, which is now a very popular place. It is usually busy at all times with anglers, boaters, watersports enthusiasts, nature lovers, swimmers, walkers and those who simply want to stop and admire the splendid views.

It's possible to walk all the way round the lake, which is ringed by three pretty little villages – Countersett, Marsett and Stalling Busk – with a fourth settlement said to be lying on the bed of the lake! Another explanation for the lake's origins claims that a beautiful city once stood here. An angel, disguised as a beggar, went round the city asking for food and drink, but was turned away at every home. The angel left the city and finally found food and shelter in the home of a poor man and his wife. On leaving the next morning, the angel turned to the city and said:

Semerwater rise – Semerwater sink,
And cover all save this lile house
that gave me meat and drink.

The waters did rise to create the lake, and beneath its surface you may just hear the occasional sound of bells from the long-drowned city. The poor man's cottage survived, and is said to be at Low Blean, on the eastern edge of Semer Water.

SETTLE MAP REF 407 G5

The day to visit Settle is Tuesday – market day – when busy stalls are crammed into Market Square and visitors jostle with locals from the surrounding farms and villages. Settle is quite a lot smaller than nearby Skipton, but it is still a great place for shopping, with some old-fashioned family-run stores adding to the appeal of its 18th- and 19th-century buildings.

The composer, Edward Elgar, had a very good friend in Settle, a Dr Buck. Elgar stayed with him often, in his house overlooking the Market Square, where a plaque commemorates the connection. Also overlooking the square is a two-storey row of shops known as the Shambles. In the 17th century this was an open market hall, which later became a butcher's shop. Arches and cottages were added in the 18th century, and the second storey was built above the cottages in 1898. In front of the Shambles is a fountain pillar erected in 1863 to replace the former market cross, and in front of this is a café with one of the most unusual names: Ye Olde Naked Man Café. Take a look behind Ye Olde Naked Man and you will see Bishopdale Court, typical of the many old yards and alleyways in Settle's streets.

One of the important natives of Settle is Benjamin Waugh, who founded the National Society for the Prevention of Cruelty to Children (NSPCC). He was born in a saddler's shop in what is now Lloyds TSB Bank, off the Market Square. Perhaps Settle's most unusual building is Richard's Folly, on School Hill, close to the Market Square. The house was built in 1675 for a local tanner, Richard Preston. He called it Tanner Hall, but it earned its 'folly' nickname because it stood empty long after Richard's death. It has since been restored and houses a museum.

West of Settle you'll find the rather oddly named Giggleswick. The village is renowned for its public school founded in 1553, and a much quieter place than Settle for visitors to wander around. Russell Harty, broadcaster and author, once worked as a teacher at the school.

To the west of Giggleswick, on the A65, is the Yorkshire Dales Falconry and Conservation Centre, with a collection of birds of prey from around the world. The outdoor aviaries are built from local limestone and are very attractive.

SKIPTON MAP REF 407 G5

Skipton buzzes with life, a bustling market filling its main street with stalls four days out of seven. It has modern shops, ancient inns, churches, a museum, restaurants and hotels, as well as a Norman Castle, over 900 years old but still in a superb state of preservation.

Skipton Castle is one of the most complete and well-preserved medieval castles in England. It was the birthplace of the indomitable Lady Anne Clifford and bears the Clifford family motto of 'Desormais' (Henceforth) in large lettering above the splendid main entrance gate. The castle's huge appeal to visitors is indicated by the fact that there are tour sheets in several languages. Take one to find your own way around its warren of rooms. Some of the original Norman building remains, but most dates from the 13th century, later damaged during the Civil War but renovated by Lady Anne Clifford in the mid-17th century.

Beside the castle is the Holy Trinity Church, which dates mainly from the 14th and 15th centuries, although there was a church here in the 12th century. It contains the tombs of many members of the Clifford family (though not Lady Anne), and a fine Tudor roof and screen.

Castle and church stand at the top of the High Street; half-way down is the Craven Museum, housed in Skipton's Town Hall. There is a small exhibition relating to one of Skipton's most famous sons, Thomas Spencer, of Marks and Spencer, who co-founded the company; other more conventional exhibits depict life ancient and modern in Skipton and the surrounding Craven area. One of the exhibits is a simple piece of cloth that was discovered in one of the Bronze Age graves near by. It is believed to be the oldest piece of cloth to be discovered in Britain. The museum is a good place to browse, wet or fine.

SEMER WATER

Visit
BRITAIN'S WILD WEST
Situated close to the Ribblehead Viaduct are just a few trenches, which are all that remain of Batty Green. This was the name that was given to the village of wooden huts that housed up to 2,000 workmen in the 1870s, when they were working on the Settle–Carlisle Railway line. There are interpretative panels near to the site and a further display inside the station. Batty Green and other shanty-towns were Britain's own Wild West in Victorian times, with saloons, religious missions, good-time girls and fearsome reputations.

Activity
THE YORKSHIRE DALES CYCLE WAY
This almost circular route of 130 miles (209.2km) was devised by John Keavey of the Cyclists' Touring Club, at the request of the National Park Authority, to give cyclists an enjoyable and safe way of seeing the best that the Dales has to offer. The route begins and ends in Skipton, and is mostly on back roads that are waymarked with blue signs that carry a white cycle and a large direction arrow. It is suggested that the average cyclist could tackle the route in six days, each day's stage being between 18 and 25 miles (28.9 and 40.2km). A folder containing full details and laminated maps for each section is available from National Park Centres and other outlets.

Visit
THE 'CORPSE WAY' TO GRINTON
The parish church of St Andrew in Grinton was for centuries the church for the whole of Swaledale. People who died in the upper reaches of the Dale would have to be brought to Grinton on what became known as the 'Corpse Way'. There are a number of Norman remains at the church, although most of it dates from the 13th to 15th centuries.

Visit
THE TURNER TRAIL
J M W Turner visited Wensleydale and Swaledale in 1816, and produced a great number of paintings as a result of his trips. At 16 of the sites he painted, or is known to have visited, seats have been erected to enable visitors to enjoy the same stirring views. A leaflet from tourist information centres entitled 'The Turner Trail' lists these places.

The oldest building in Skipton's High Street is the Red Lion Inn. It was built in the late 14th or early 15th century and was once partly a farm. It is said to have been owned by Richard III. Still visible in the forecourt is a bear-baiting stone.

But the town of Skipton, like Settle, is a place whose back streets need to be explored. There are also pleasant walks to be enjoyed along the canal-side towpaths. The Leeds and Liverpool Canal passes through town joining the Ellerbeck and Springs Canal, adding to the atmosphere that Skipton, for centuries, really has been the 'Gateway to the Dales'.

SWALEDALE VILLAGES
MAP REF 407 G4
Swaledale names are mostly short and sharp, from their Norse origins: Muker, Keld, Thwaite, Reeth, Angram. Even the longer ones are spat out with those same short Norse vowels: Gunnerside, Arkengarthdale. Most of the villages in this area are short and sharp too, strung out along the B6270, but they welcome tourists and offer lots of places to shop, stay and eat, and a range of local craft studios. Beyond Keld, the 'knots' end, the lonely road crosses the fells to Nateby and Kirkby Stephen at the northern end of the valley of Mallerstang, as it opens out into the lovely Vale of Eden.

Travelling from Reeth, Gunnerside is the first sizeable community you reach. It is an appealing place with grey stone cottages, which were once the homes of lead miners, looking down on the River Swale with high-rising moors. Norse settlers were attracted by its sheltered location at the confluence of Gunnerside Gill and the larger river. Later, lead mining brought prosperity, and the remains of mines can be found just a short distance from the centre of the village. Another walk is to the unusual Ivelet Bridge.

Beyond Ivelet is Muker, a collection of stone cottages clustered in jigsaw streets that zigzag steeply up from the main road. Plaques on the church wall commemorate Richard (1862–1928) and Cherry (1871–1940) Kearton, brothers who were born in Thwaite and went to school in Muker. They devoted their lives to watching wildlife and became early pioneers of wildlife photography. There is also a Literary Institute, an echo of the Norse origins of its unusual name, for Muker means 'a cultivated plot'.

Scarcely a mile (1.6km) west of Muker is Thwaite, where the cottage in which the Kearton brothers were born still stands. This idyllic place hides the tragedy of the flood of 1899 when the waters of Thwaite Beck swept down and almost wiped out the community. It is said that flowers washed from Thwaite's cottage gardens were later found growing in Muker.

The last Swaledale village is Keld, quietly going about its business, set back from the main road in a dead end that leads down to the River Swale and some of Swaledale's most impressive falls. The Pennine Way passes the edge of Keld before heading northwards up Stonesdale to the lonely outpost of Tan Hill. The Swaledale road goes west through some of the most dramatic scenery in the Yorkshire Dales before arriving at Nateby, just outside the boundary of the National Park, in the valley of Mallerstang.

WENSLEY MAP REF 407 G4
Wensley is one of the small villages that many people pass through on their way to the dale that took the village's name. It is hard to imagine that this was once the main settlement in Wensleydale, the first place to receive a market charter, in 1202, with the only market in the dale for the following 100 years. Wensley flourished until plague struck in 1563, when the focus of Wensleydale life shifted a mile (1.6km) to the east, to Leyburn, and later westward to Askrigg and then Hawes.

The Church of the Holy Trinity remains as a reminder of that former importance, with parts of the building dating from 1240. Its attractive pale stone tower was built in 1719, and inside you will find an 18th-century pulpit and a 17th-century font. There's also a memorial to the Scrope family, from Castle Bolton who had close connections with the church. When the Scropes built Bolton Hall in 1678 Wensley began its regrowth as an estate village.

Near the church is the gate that leads to Bolton Hall, and also near here is the river on which there is a small waterfall and also Wensley Mill. Today the mill houses the White Rose Candles Workshop.

WALK 115

HAWES & HARDRAW

These popular settlements both have something to offer visitors and walkers – Hawes is famous for Wensleydale cheese and motorcyclists, who gather here on summer weekends, and Hardraw for its spectacular waterfall. The walk in-between takes in farmland and moorland scenery.

DISTANCE/TIME 6 miles (9.7km) 2h30 **MAP** OS Explorer OL30 Yorkshire Dales – Northern & Central **START** Pay car park off Gayle Lane at west side of Hawes; grid ref: SD 870898 **TRACKS** Field and moorland paths, may be muddy, 44 stiles **THE PUB** Green Dragon Inn, Hardraw. Tel: 01969 667392; www.greendragonhardraw.co.uk

1 From the top end of the car park turn left and then right over a stile signed 'Youth Hostel'. The path flirts with a track, which ends by a stone outbuilding and then rises to a stile. Continue west across several fields passing a barn and crossing a lane, to reach the B road. Turn left and then right through a gate signed 'Thorney Mire House'. Continue 0.5 mile (0.8km) to a gate that leads to a lane. Turn right. Follow this for 0.75 mile (1.2km), under the viaduct to the road at Appersett.

2 Turn left across the bridge. Follow the road and cross the next bridge, then bend left to reach the junction. Now go through a stile, signposted 'Bluebell Hill'. Cross the field, go through a gate and cross over a bridge, then bear half left uphill. Go through a gate and continue to reach a crossroads signpost.

3 Turn right and follow the valley to a stile (Bob's Stile). Cross the field beyond, go over a stile and then turn left to reach a ladder stile across a wall into a field. Go across the field towards Hardraw, across a stile and then over a ladder stile on to a lane.

4 Turn right and then left at the main road and cross over the bridge. Hardraw Force entrance is through the Green Dragon Inn.

Immediately beyond the pub, turn left and go right through a signed gate in the wall, through a courtyard and over a stile. Follow the flagged path over another stile, steeply uphill, over a stile and up steps. By the house, go through a stile and to the right of the stables, then through two more stiles on to a lane by the Simonstone Hall Hotel.

5 Turn right, then left. Quickly turn right through a stile ('Sedbusk'). Continue through a gate, over two ladder stiles and a gateway, then through 14 stiles into Sedbusk.

6 Turn right along the road, bend left near the post-box to go downhill. Go right, over a stile ('Haylands Bridge'). Cross the field, bend right to a stile in a crossing wall, then down to a stile on to a road. Cross to another stile and continue, cross a stream, go over a stile, then bear right over a humpback bridge. Go through a gated stile on to a road.

7 Turn left. Cross over Haylands Bridge and go right through a kissing gate ('Hawes'). Follow the path, cross a stile, turn left, then right to the main road. At the junction cross the road and turn right past the post office. Follow the main road. Turn left after the school for the car park.

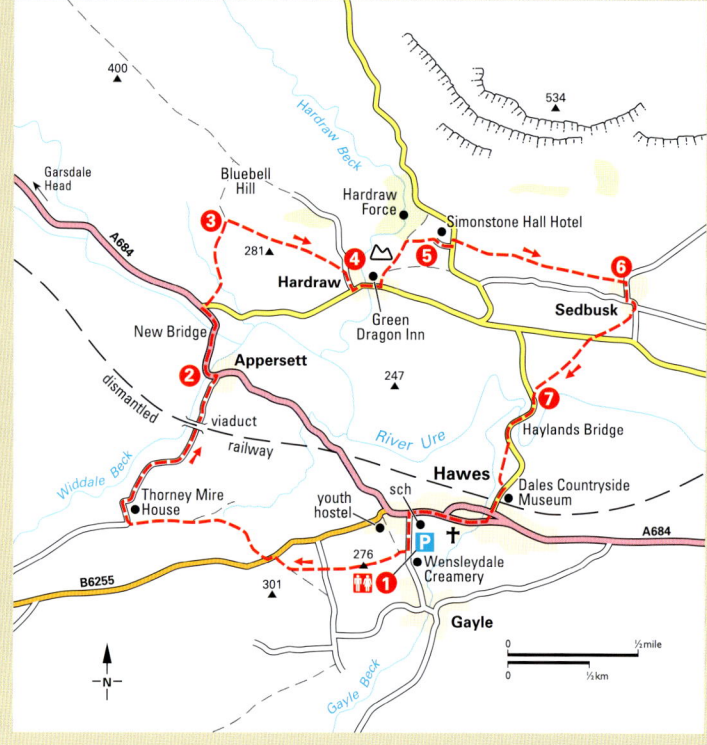

WALK 116

FROM WEST BURTON TO AYSGARTH

This pleasant walk travels between two typical Dales villages, and back, via the famous Aysgarth Falls on the River Ure and some unusual farm buildings.

DISTANCE/TIME 4.25 miles (6.8km) 2h **MAP** OS Explorer OL30 Yorkshire Dales – Northern & Central **START** Centre of West Burton, by (but not on) the Green; grid ref: SE 017867 **TRACKS** Field and riverside paths and tracks, 35 stiles **THE PUB** The George & Dragon, Aysgarth. Tel: 01969 663358; www.georgeanddragonaysgarth.co.uk

1 With your back to the Fox and Hounds pub turn left along the lane, past the village shop. When you are opposite Meadowcroft go left through a ginnel, signed 'Eshington Bridge'. Cross the road, turn right then left, go through a gate and down steps. Pass a barn, go through a gateway and across the field. Go through a gap in the wall with a stile beyond. Bend right to a stile on to the road.

2 Turn left, go over the bridge and up the narrow lane. As it bends left go through a stile, signed 'Aysgarth', then on through a gated stile. Continue to a gap in the fence near a barn, then through a gate. Bend left to a gate in the field corner, go through and on to a stile with a footpath signpost. Turn right and drop to another signpost, pointing half right into a grassy hollow.

3 Continue ahead to a stile in the field corner. Now, follow the signpost direction 'to Aysgarth' uphill to a gateway and go through a stile on the right. Cross the field half left to go through a gated stile on to a lane. Turn left and then almost immediately turn right through a stile that is signed 'Aysgarth'. Go through three more stiles to a road.

4 Turn right into the village, past The George & Dragon. At the left bend, go ahead toward the Methodist church, then go right at the

green, and follow the lane. Go through a gate by Field House and continue to another stile, turning left along the track. Follow the path through eight stiles to reach the road.

5 Go ahead into the churchyard, pass right of the church, go through two stiles, through trees, then over another stile. Follow the path towards the river, down steps to a gate and then a stile. When the footpath reaches the river bank, take a signed stile right.

6 Follow the path over two more stiles to a signpost, bending right across the field to a road. Turn left to cross over the bridge, turning right into woodland a few paces beyond, signed 'Edgley'. Go over a stile and cross the field to a gate on to the road.

7 Turn right. After 150yds (137m), go left over a stile, signed 'Flanders Hall'. Walk below the follies to a footpath sign. The route then crosses two tracks from the farming complex of Sorrellsykes Park. Past the last house, waymarking posts highlight the route across a dyke, then above a copse of trees.

8 Opposite a stone barn on the hillside to the left, go right, through a gate, and down through two more gates. Go over three stiles to a lane, turn right and over a bridge to join the village road. Turn left, back to the Green.

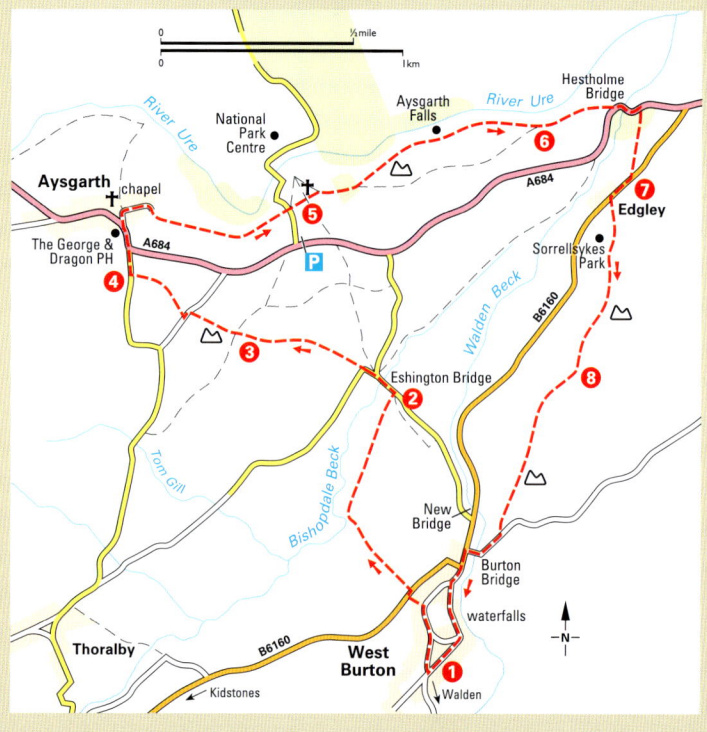

FROM KELD TO MUKER

This is a classic walk in Upper Swaledale from Keld to Muker along Kisdon Side and backed by the River Swale. Keld – its name is the Old Norse word for a spring – is one of the most remote of the Dales villages. Set at the head of Swaledale, its small cluster of grey stone cottages is a centre for some of the most spectacular walks in North Yorkshire. It is worth taking some time to explore the village of Muker when you get there. Like many of the Swaledale settlements, it rapidly expanded during the 18th and 19th centuries because of the lead-mining industry.

1 Walk back down the car park entrance road, and straight ahead down the gravel track, signed 'Muker'. Continue along at the upper level, ignoring a path downhill to the left. Go through a gate, ignoring the left fork path signed to Kisdon Upper Force.

2 At another signpost take the right fork – the Pennine Way route. The narrow path traverses rough stony hillsides high above the River Swale before easing down bracken-covered sheep pastures towards Muker.

3 Where the Pennine Way goes right, leave it to follow a walled path signed 'Muker'. This joins a stony farm track, which winds down to the north end of the village.

4 Those who wish to take a break at The Farmers Arms should follow the lane all the way to reach the main Swaledale road. Otherwise, to continue the walk, turn left and left again by a sign to Gunnerside and Keld. Follow the paved path across hay fields to reach the river. Turn right and then go over a stile to the footbridge.

5 Ascend the steps beyond the footbridge and turn left to join a stony track, signed 'Keld'. Keep ahead on the track, which follows the course of the River Swale before crossing a tributary, Swinner Gill, on a footbridge by the remains of some old lead mine workings.

6 The track climbs the hill and leads into woodland before being joined by the track on 'Wainwright's Coast-to-Coast Walk' beneath Crackpot Hall.

7 Go left by a wooden seat, at a sign to Keld. Follow the stream beside East Gill Force waterfalls all the way down to a footbridge. Go through the gate and turn right, uphill, to a T-junction, where you turn right and follow the path back to the car park.

DISTANCE/TIME 6 miles (9.7km) 2h30 **MAP** OS Explorer OL30 Yorkshire Dales – Northern & Central **START** Signed car park at west end of Keld near Park Lodge; grid ref: NY 892012. **TRACKS** Field and riverside paths and tracks, 10 stiles **THE PUB** The Farmers Arms, Muker. Tel: 01748 886297

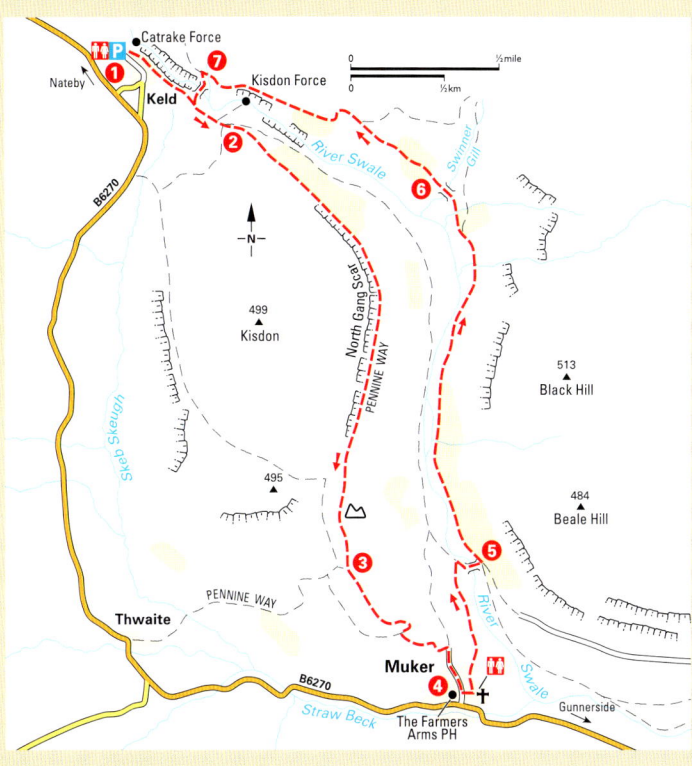

WALK 118

LANGTHWAITE IN ARKENGARTHDALE

Follow a route around an austere valley where lead workers once toiled leaving a mine-scarred moorland landscape with evocative remains of industry. One of the most northerly of the dales, Arkengarthdale runs northwards from Swaledale into dark moorland, with the battle-scarred Stainmore beyond its head.

1 Leave the car park, turn right, then right again into Langthwaite. Go over the bridge and continue ahead between cottages. Climb up the hill and follow the lane to the hamlet of Booze. Pass the farmhouse and a stone barn and follow the track to a gate.

2 After the gate, where the track bends to the left, go straight on next to a broken wall. Bear right to go past a ruined cottage, then follow the path to the stream. Walk upstream, go through a gate and then cross the stream on stepping stones. Go left on a faint path over the moorland.

3 Turn left along a gravel track beyond a wooden hut, then straight on along the grass track where the gravel track bends right. Turn left at a T-junction. Where the wall on your right ends, leave the track, bending right to a gate in the wall corner.

4 Follow the small gully downhill and go through a gate. Turn right along a track, continue through a gateway and on to another track by a barn. Follow this track as it bends left by a stone wall and then passes farm buildings. Go through a small gate down a greasy track to a second gate, followed immediately by a gate into the Scar

House grounds. Follow the drive as it bears right, downhill and over a bridge. Turn right along the track to a road.

5 The CB Inn is to the left down the road. If you want to cut the route short, it's 0.5 mile (0.8km) to the start of the walk. Otherwise turn left, back uphill, to a T-junction. Turn right and climb along the road. Where the road begins to level out (opposite an old barn) turn left along a signed track.

6 At a gravelled area go right to a sunken track that goes up above Moor Intake Farm. The track meets a stony track above a metal shed, then doubles back uphill with it before zigzagging to cairns next to a spoil heap. Turn left along the track over an area of spoil heaps. The track eventually follows the ridge top. It is joined from the right by a shooters track from Bleaberry Gill. More cairns direct the track down Turf Moor to the road.

7 Turn left then right at a sign by Bouldershaw House, then left just before the buildings. When half-way down the hill, go through a gate in the wall on the right and continue the descent. Beyond Gill House turn left across fields to the road. Turn left for the car park.

DISTANCE/TIME 8 miles (12.9km) 3h15; shorter route 4.5 miles (7.2km) 2h **MAP** OS Explorer OL30 Yorkshire Dales – Northern & Central **START** Pay-and-display car park in Langthwaite; grid ref: NZ 005024 **TRACKS** Mostly clear tracks, some heather moor, 4 stiles **THE PUB** The CB Inn, Arkengarthdale. Tel: 01748 884567; www.cbinn.co.uk

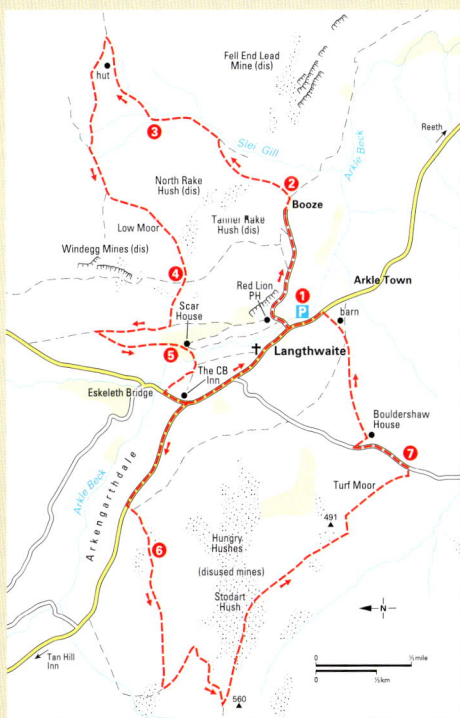

MAJOR PEAKS & MINOR DALES

This drive takes you through some of the minor but most beautiful dales such as Ribblesdale, Dentdale, Mallerstang, Deepdale and Kingsdale, and passes on the way the Three Peaks: Whernside, Ingleborough and Pen-y-ghent. You'll also be able to see the marginally smaller but equally dramatic hills of Wild Boar Fell and High Seat, on the northern boundary of the National Park.

Route Directions

1 From Settle take the B6480 north to its junction with the A65. Turn right on to the A65 travelling towards Kirkby Lonsdale. Turn right on to the B6255 to reach Ingleton, and its unique Waterfalls Walk.

Ingleton is a small but friendly place with some steep streets, tourist shops and a fine parish church. Follow the signs for 'Village Centre' and then the 'Waterfalls Walk'.

2 At the start of the Waterfalls Walk, which is marked by a large sign, the road swings sharply left and then right again. Watch for the right turn along here signposted 'Dent'. Follow this road through Thornton in Lonsdale and turn sharp right by the church, still following signs for Dent. This is a narrow, gated, but glorious road through Kingsdale, following Kingsdale Beck and then climbing, with the summit of Whernside at 2,415ft (736m) on your right-hand side before descending steeply into Deepdale. Turn left at the next junction going towards Sedbergh. Continue left through the cobbled streets of Dent, which are delightful but not designed for drivers looking in vain for signposts, until you emerge on the other side. Continue towards Sedbergh, passing through the very green Dentdale and following the road round to the right. Bear left over the bridge at Millthrop and follow the road signed 'Town Centre'. Go straight on at the roundabout and turn right on to the main street in front of the Reading Room.

Sedbergh has a Wednesday market and there is also a monthly farmers' market, where you can buy locally produced goods and crafts.

3 At the far end turn left, following the signs for Hawes, Kirkby Stephen and Brough. Follow the A683 alongside the River Rawthey all the way out of the National Park with the Cautley Spout and the Howgill Fells to your left. From the moors the road descends towards Kirkby Stephen. Turn right on to the A685 into this unspoiled town between the Yorkshire Dales and the Lake District.

One attraction is its parish church of St Stephen, with 18th-century bread shelves and a 10th-century Norse stone cross.

4 In Kirkby Stephen turn right on to the B6259 for Nateby, staying on the road through Nateby and down through the valley

of Mallerstang, with Wild Boar Fell on your right and Mallerstang Edge and High Seat, left. Wild Boar Fell rises to 2,323ft (708m) (higher than Pen-y-ghent at 2,274ft/693m), and gets its name because the last wild boar in England was said to have been killed here. Its ruggedness remains.

5 At the T-junction by the Moorcock Inn, turn left on to the A684 towards Hawes but before you reach the centre of Hawes; turn right on to the B6255 heading towards Horton in Ribblesdale and Ingleton.

This lovely winding road passes through Widdale and up and over Gayle Moor, bringing into view the magnificent sight of the Ribblehead Viaduct, carrying the Settle–Carlisle Railway line. The railway was built in the late 19th century, and is one of the most impressive feats of engineering. It is the most beautiful route in England, driving both under and over the Dales. Overlooking the railway line is Whernside, the largest of the Three Peaks, followed by Ingleborough and finally Pen-y-ghent. Though the smallest of the peaks, the brooding face of Pen-y-ghent has a special appeal.

6 Just before the viaduct, turn left on to the B6479 to pass through Horton in Ribblesdale, Stainforth and on to Settle. This road runs through Ribblesdale with Ingleborough, right. Next, you'll see the unmistakable looming shape of Pen-y-ghent on your left. The road then runs along the banks of the River Ribble and back down into Settle.

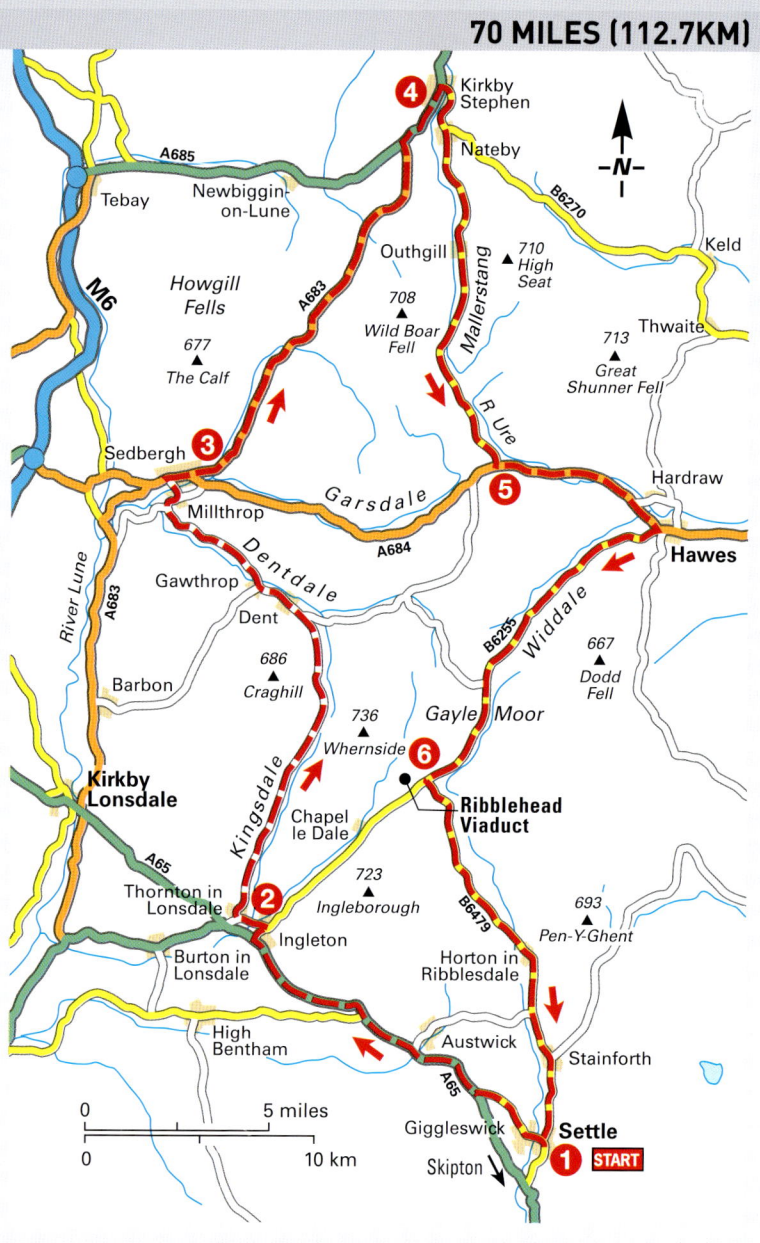

TO SMALL TOWNS & LARGE VILLAGES

Middleham, with its market, splendid Norman castle and horse-racing stables, is the smallest town in the Yorkshire Dales – much smaller than many villages. This drive takes in some of the attractive places that hover between town and village, such as Kettlewell, Grassington, Leyburn and Pateley Bridge, where the tour starts, and some of the finest scenery the Dales have to offer.

Route Directions

The drive starts in Pateley Bridge, a lively market town in the heart of Nidderdale with its own fascinating local museum, good shopping and a tourist information centre.

1 From the centre of Pateley Bridge take the minor road that leads north from near the bridge itself, towards Ramsgill and Lofthouse. Pass Gouthwaite Reservoir on your right. In Lofthouse turn right and take the steep road out of the village, over the moors towards Masham. Continue for about 6 miles (9.7km), passing two more reservoirs on your right. Take the third left turning, as you approach Healey, heading towards Ellingstring. Turn left at the crossroads, continue to the junction with the A6108 and turn left to Leyburn passing the remains of Jervaulx Abbey, right.

Founded in 1156, the abbey is in complete contrast to grand and busy Fountains Abbey, yet in its day Jervaulx was one of the most important Cistercian abbeys in Yorkshire.

2 Continue on the A6108 and drive through Middleham, with its quaint cobbled market squares, its cottages built of grey stone and its racing connections.

Middleham is considered to be 'the Newmarket of the north', with its 16 or so racing stables. The impressive castle ruins was the much-favoured home of King Richard III, whose son Edward was born here in 1473.

3 Continue to Leyburn, a busy Wensleydale town with many tea shops for visitors as well as a wealth of everyday shops. In Leyburn turn left, then right following the signs 'A6108 Richmond'. Drive through Bellerby, turn right then left, still with the A6108. The road first takes you over upland pasture then along the wooded Alpine-like slopes of Swaledale towards Richmond. At this point you can choose to take a detour and continue into Richmond, which stands at the foot of Swaledale, for a leisurely visit.

Richmond's castle commands an impressive position above the river. The town has a large cobbled square, a church with shops in its side, riverside walks and three good museums.

4 If you are not taking the detour, continue as before and as you reach Richmond pass a right turn to Catterick, turn immediately left up Hurgill Road, past a car park on the left. This road takes you back along the Swale but climbs high above the river, before dropping steeply down to Marske. Cross the bridge and turn right towards Reeth, then turn left on to the B6270 to Grinton. In Grinton turn right on to a minor road and take the right fork following the signs for Redmire. You are now on an impressive high moorland road passing disused lead mines. When the road finally descends, take the first turning on the right for the village of Castle Bolton then turn right for Carperby. Take a left turn to visit Aysgarth Falls – a very popular beauty spot. Although they consist of three different sections, only the Upper Falls are visible from the road. Near by are a mill, a carriage museum and tea rooms, while Aysgarth village itself is another half-mile (0.8km) away, on the main Wensleydale road.

5 Beyond Aysgarth Falls turn left on to the A684 signposted 'Leyburn' and then take the second turning on the right on to the B6160 following the signs into West Burton.

This has been described as the prettiest village in the Dales. It has a large village green, on which horses graze and children play. There is a pub and a pottery, but no church or market. Burton Force waterfall is a short stroll away.

6 Rejoin the B6160 to drive along the lovely Bishopdale, and over Kidstones Pass to Buckden in Wharfedale. Pass the small town of Kettlewell on the left.

Kettlewell is a centre for walkers tackling nearby Great Whernside. It is also on the Dales Way long-distance footpath, and was once a centre of the lead-mining industry.

7 Continue ahead and look out for Kilnsey Crag on your right, easily identified as it juts out dramatically towards the main road. Kilnsey Crag is popular with climbers, filmmakers and peregrine falcons.

8 Continue on the B6160 then turn left to reach the centre of Grassington, a popular village for people who appreciate stalactites and stalagmites amongst other things.

This is an attractive, large village with cobbled streets, 17th- and 18th-century houses, pubs and a museum of Upper Wharfedale life.

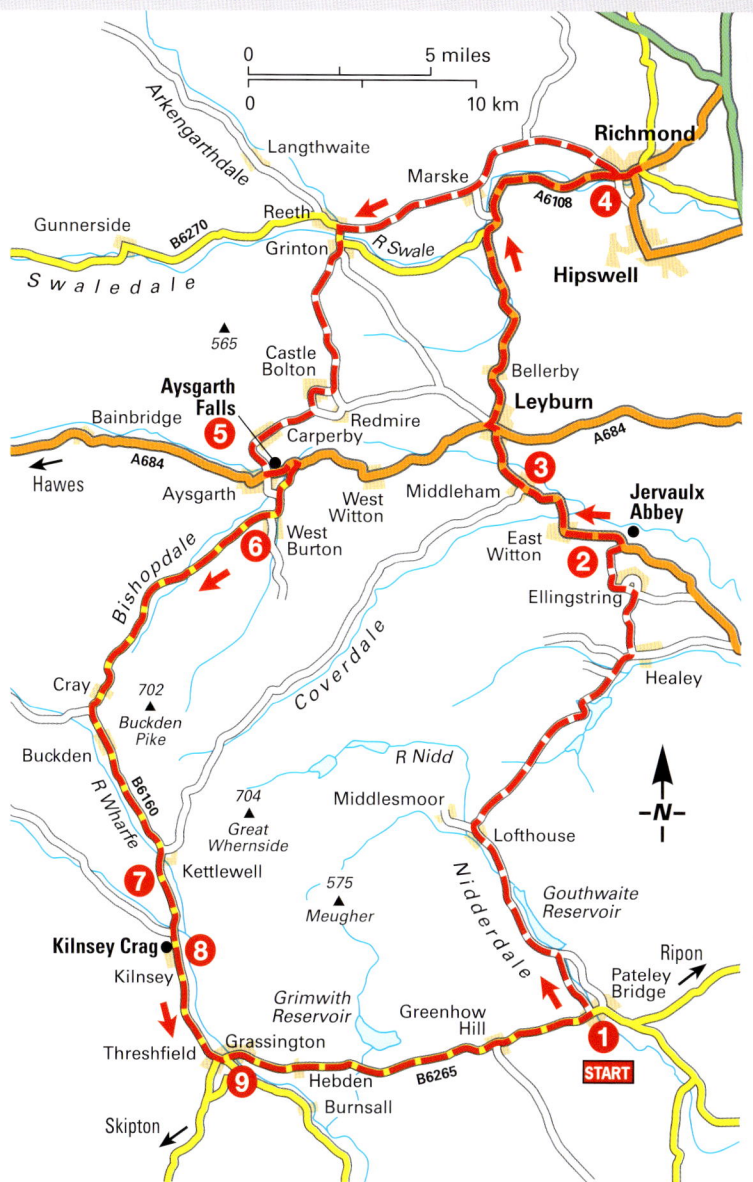

9 Drive around the centre of Grassington, and leave on the B6265 and then make the return journey to your starting point at Nidderdale and Pateley Bridge.

Northumbria & Coast

CLOCKWISE FROM TOP: A PUFFIN, FARNE ISLANDS; HOUSESTEADS FORT, HADRIAN'S WALL; DUNSTANBURGH CASTLE

FOUNTAINS AT ALNWICK

Visit
MEDIEVAL FUN

Visit Alnwick at the end of June for a taste of medieval life at Alnwick Fair Week. The Fair begins with a costumed street procession held on the last Sunday in the month. Festivities continue through the week, with people in medieval garb mingling with the visitors. Alnwick also hosts an International Music Festival in August, with musicians and dancers from all over Europe.

Visit
AYDON CASTLE

Aydon Castle is really a very early fortified manor house, built at the end of the 13th century and given its battlements in 1305. Where it was most vulnerable, to the north, it has an irregular outer bailey, and behind that a small, open courtyard, with the living quarters to one side. Instead of a keep there was a hall and a solar with a fine fireplace and beautifully detailed windows – don't miss the bearded face staring out from above the northern one.

ALNWICK MAP REF 409 L6

Alnwick (pronounced 'Annick') has been the stronghold of the Percy family since 1309. They went on to become the Earls of Northumberland, then in the 18th century, the Dukes of Northumberland. Alnwick Castle's strong walls and round towers, although altered over the centuries, owe their outline to the Normans. Its barbican, the best surviving in Britain, and the impressive gateway, with stone figures mimicking an ever-watchful garrison, were added when the Percys arrived.

The medieval interior was transformed into a Renaissance palace by the 4th Duke in the 19th century. It glows with fine woodwork and marble and is filled with treasures, including paintings by Titian, Canaletto, Van Dyck and Andrea del Sarto. There are two stunning cabinets made for Louis XIV, and two Meissen dinner services. The castle grounds are famous as Hogwarts in the Harry Potter films.

The park was landscaped by the renowned designer 'Capability' Brown, a Northumberland man. It is now home to the spectacular new gardens created by the Duchess, complete with a restored great cascade, hundreds of fountains and the world's biggest tree house.

Alnwick Castle does not dominate the attractive stone-built town, but its influence is apparent. The 15th-century parish church lies near the castle, while at the other end of town is a survivor of the town walls begun in 1434, the narrow Hotspur Gate, named after the most famous member of the Percy family, Shakespeare's Harry Hotspur. Alnwick's cobbled market place bustles with life, and there are shops selling local produce, crafts and antiques.

The pastures below the castle are the scene for a mammoth Shrove Tuesday football match, which uses the Lion and Denwick bridges as goals.

ALWINTON MAP REF 409 K6

This small village lies in the Upper Coquet Valley and is set between the Cheviots and the more rugged Harbottle Hills, making it a good base. Sir Walter Scott stayed at the popular Rose and Thistle while researching his heroic tale, *Rob Roy*.

Alwinton church is on the hillside south of the river, and from its large churchyard there are wonderful views. Each October the village hosts the last of the season's traditional country shows – the Border Shepherds' Show – with sheep, fell racing and sheepdog trials.

At Chew Green, 8 miles (12.8km) west of Alwinton, is one of Britain's best Roman earthworks. The remains of a fort and camp are visible among the hills. Drive to the site from Redesdale when the army firing ranges are not in use – with superb views along the Roman Dere Street.

BAMBURGH MAP REF 409 L5

Bamburgh for many means the castle, dominating both the village and the coast. It looks so medieval that film crews use it as a backdrop. Yet the castle is both more and less historical than it looks. The great Whin Sill crag has been defended since the Iron Age and became the site of a fort for the Anglians in AD 547 and was given by King Ethelfrith to his wife Bebba; Bebba's burgh became Bamburgh.

An eventful progress through the centuries ensued until the castle fell to the Normans, who began the stone castle we now see. Additions were made in later centuries, creating a castle that was virtually impregnable until its defeat in 1464 during the Wars of the Roses.

The shattered remains passed to the local Forster family and they held it – but largely left it in a derelict state – until the early 18th century, when Lord Crewe, the Bishop of Durham, undertook repairs and left the castle as a charitable trust.

The castle was sold in 1894 to Lord Armstrong, an eminent inventor and industrialist. He restored the castle to its present appearance. The State Rooms now appear late Victorian, and they are palatial, particularly the Great Hall with its impressive roof and musicians' gallery.

Bamburgh village can be extremely busy at the height of the tourist season, but it is a pleasant place for a stroll. Its parish church stands on the site of the chapel used by St Aidan and has a beautiful early 13th-century chancel and Forster family monuments, as well as the much-visited grave of the Victorian heroine Grace Darling in the churchyard. Bamburgh also has an attractive sandy beach. Budle Bay, an area of wetland west of Bamburgh, is a nature reserve visited by many wildfowl – information boards will help you to identify them.

BELLINGHAM MAP REF 409 K7

St Cuthbert's Church, a fascinating early 13th-century building, was rebuilt in the early 17th century, when it was given its stone-vaulted roof, probably to protect it from the frequent Scots' raids.

Outside Bellingham's Town Hall is more evidence of fierce warfare – a gun captured at the Boxer Rebellion in China in 1900 – and the presence of army training areas is felt here today. For ten years from 1838 the town was a thriving iron and coal centre, but the industry was killed by competition from foundries nearer Newcastle upon Tyne and on Teesside.

Bellingham hosts an agricultural show in August and is a good base for exploring the Kielder area and the Northumberland National Park. Some 7 miles (11.3km) northwest of Bellingham, in the Tarset Burn valley, is Black Middens Bastle, one of very few which are open to the public.

BERWICK-UPON-TWEED

MAP REF 409 K4

Berwick-upon-Tweed was a Royal Burgh of Scotland until William the Lion surrendered it to the English in 1174. Over the next 300 years it changed hands 11 times, became a free town in 1482 and an independent state in 1502. It became part of Northumberland only in 1974.

Such a turbulent past gives Berwick its own gritty individuality. A fascinating town, it holds a unique place in both British and military history. In the Middle Ages it was protected at its north end by the castle, first mentioned in 1160 and rebuilt at the end of the 13th century. Its White Wall plunges from the castle to the river, protecting precipitous steps known locally as 'The Breakynecks'. The Constable's Tower is impressive, and you can see part of the northwest wall from the station platform – much more was demolished when the railway arrived.

Berwick had medieval town walls – the best remaining stretch lies alongside the cliffs between Meg's Mount and the railway bridge – but more important are its Elizabethan ramparts. Built between 1558 and 1569, when the Scots and the French were threatening England, they are unique in Britain. The walk along them should not be missed, to see the 22-foot high (6.7m) stone-faced walls, 12 feet (3.6m) thick at the base and topped with grassed mounds. They were never properly finished. In 1568 Mary, Queen of Scots, fled to England, thus removing some of the Scottish threat – and when Scottish King James VI became James I of England in 1603 they were redundant.

Berwick remained a military town, however, and Britain's earliest barracks, dating from the early 17th century, held nearly 600 men. They now house the King's Own Scottish Borderers Museum and the town Museum and Art Gallery, which, alongside exhibits of local history, has something of a surprise – outstanding works of art, including paintings by Degas and Daubigny, medieval carvings and Chinese ceramics. Modern art is displayed at the Gymnasium Gallery, on the Parade.

Opposite the Barracks is Berwick parish church – built in the 1650s, during the Commonwealth. Oliver Cromwell, a friend of the benefactor, hated bells, so there is no tower. Bells did arrive here, but were hung in the mid-18th century Guildhall, Berwick's most prominent building, with its tall tower and spire.

Among Berwick's landmarks are its bridges. Early wooden bridges were swept away. Without one for 200 years, Berwick put up another wooden bridge in Tudor times, but it was King James VI, going to London in 1603, who demanded, and eventually paid for, the magnificent 1,164-foot long (355m) Old Bridge. It remained the only road bridge in the town until the Royal Tweed Bridge was built in 1928, but the most spectacular bridge, Robert Stephenson's Royal Border Bridge, 2,152 feet (656m) long on 28 high arches, was built for the railway in 1846.

CHILLINGHAM MAP REF 409 K5

Chillingham village, with its Tudor-style houses, was built by the Earls of Tankerville, related by marriage to the Grey family. In the church the tomb of 15th-century Sir Ralph Grey has some rare figures of saints that escaped later religious destruction. The Greys fought against the Scots and, often, the Percys of Alnwick. Their fortress, Chillingham Castle, was started in 1245, but much of its present appearance dates from 1344.

All was nearly lost when the castle was left empty after the contents were sold in 1933. There was a fire during the time that soldiers were billeted here in the 1940s and rot ravaged the rest, until Sir Humphrey Wakefield, related to the Greys, bought the castle in the 1980s and began its triumphant restoration.

Visitors can see the splendid Great Hall, with banners and armour, as well as antique furniture, tapestries and restored plaster- and metalwork, carving and masonry. There is even a torture chamber, suitable for a place reputed to be 'the most haunted castle in England'. The gardens, revived after years of neglect, include woodland walks and a topiary garden on the site of the tournament ground.

CORBRIDGE MAP REF 407 G2

The first Roman fort to stand at Corbridge – Corstopitum – was built around AD 90, more than 30 years before Hadrian's Wall, to guard the bridge where Dere Street crossed the Tyne. The Stanegate, built earlier by Agricola's troops, also crosses the fort on its way into Carlisle. As a vastly important junction, Corstopitum had a succession of forts – the one we see today is the fourth, built about AD 140 as the Romans occupied Scotland. It was an important military headquarters, depot and supply base, even after the Romans finally gave up on Scotland towards the end of the 2nd century. By degrees it changed into a town, much of which is still buried, though its stones are found in many Corbridge and Hexham buildings.

The excellent museum is full of finds from the site, including inscriptions and some small, often personal objects. The tour takes you past the granaries, perhaps the most memorable part of the fort, and the best preserved in Britain, with floors of stone slabs on low walls.

The square courtyard to the north of the main street (part of Stanegate) was never finished and no one is quite sure what it was. Opposite are the military compounds, where you can trace the workshops and officers' houses before descending into the former strongroom to see where soldiers and locals worshipped both Roman and local gods.

The town suffered from invasion by Danes and Scots. Not surprisingly, there are two defensive pele towers in Corbridge. One, at the end of Main Street, dating from the 13th century was converted into a house in about 1675. The other, the Vicar's Pele, is made from Roman stones and was probably put up in the 14th century.

St Andrew's Church, too, uses some Roman stones – between the tower and the nave is a whole Roman archway. The tower's lower parts were probably built before AD 786, and there is more Saxon work in the walls, as well as a Norman doorway and a 13th-century chancel.

CRASTER MAP REF 409 L5

A picturesque village that seems almost to tumble into the sea, Craster became a haven for fishing in the 17th century, although its harbour, today used by pleasure craft and traditional cobles, was given its present form in the 1900s. It was built by the local landowners, the Crasters. The trade it was involved in then was the export of whinstone (used for roads and kerbs), and you can still see the concrete arch that once supported the chipping silos. The quarry is now the National Trust car park, a good starting point for walks to Dunstanburgh Castle.

CHILLINGHAM CASTLE

DUNSTANBURGH CASTLE

DURHAM MAP REF 407 H3

Even without the great cathedral and castle that dominate its skyline the city of Durham would be spectacular. The River Wear does a huge loop, in a deep ravine, coming almost to meet itself. From this superb defensive position the city developed, down the hill and outwards, but from whichever side you approach – and especially if you arrive at the station by rail – Durham is a magnificent sight.

The city is a place for visiting on foot. Gently climbing from the market place up Saddler Street you will see elegant Georgian houses from one of Durham's most prosperous times, interspersed with small specialist shops and university departments. Owengate leads into Palace Green, dominated by the cathedral's north side and surrounded by fine university buildings, with the castle to your right.

It was in Durham that St Cuthbert's bones finally ended their century-long journey from Holy Island in AD 995, but the present cathedral building, with its three massive towers, dates from 1093. Enter by the north door with its replica sanctuary ring (a 12th-century door-knocker). The original is in the Treasury.

The main effect of the interior is of enormous strength. Huge columns, alternate ones patterned with bold geometric incisions hold up the earliest Gothic roof anywhere. The east wall is dominated by a rose window, and below it is the Neville Screen, made from creamy stone. Beyond this is the 13th-century Chapel of the Nine Altars, with its tall lancet windows, overlooked by St Cuthbert's tomb which has just a simple stone slab. In the choir, the Bishop's throne is the highest in Britain.

In about 1170, the monks built a Galilee Chapel at the west end, perched precariously over the ravine. The tomb of the Venerable Bede is here. Off the cloisters, try not to miss the Monks' Dormitory, with its huge wooden roof, and the Treasury, full of silver, pre-Conquest embroidery and manuscripts, and relics of St Cuthbert. To get the classic cathedral view, go to Prebends' Bridge, reached from South Bailey.

The castle, begun in 1072, now houses University College, and its 18th-century gatehouse has a Norman core, as does the massive keep, which was rebuilt in 1840. The highlight of a tour around the castle is a visit to the splendid Norman gallery and the Norman chapel.

College buildings cluster in the streets around the castle and cathedral. The churches – particularly St Oswald's, near the elegant Kingsgate Bridge – are worth exploring. The Heritage Centre at St Mary-le-Bow, North Bailey, vividly tells the history of Durham, while Durham University Oriental Museum, off Elvet Hill Road, is full of wonderful Chinese porcelain and jade. The Durham Light Infantry Museum reflects the military past of the regiment and the city.

A good way to see the best the city has to offer is to take this 2.5-mile (4km) walk. Start in the Market Place, and from the statue of Lord Londonderry on his horse, walk along Silver Street to descend to Framwellgate Bridge. Immediately at the end of the bridge turn left down the steps by the Coach and Eight pub to reach the river bank, going straight ahead with the castle and cathedral across the river. Now walk behind the riverside buildings to Prebends' Bridge, begun in 1772 with funds from the Canons (Prebendaries) of the cathedral. Do not cross the bridge, but continue alongside the river. On the opposite bank you will see the charming Grecian-style Count's House.

Walk along the riverside path until it ascends into St Oswald's churchyard. Turn left into Church Street and at the end of the buildings, go left over Kingsgate Bridge, then up the steps at the end and into Bow Lane. At the top, turn left along North Bailey (if the cathedral is closed, turn right here and then take the first left on to Palace Green). After about 100 yards (91m) go right through the 16th-century archway leading to the informal little square called The College. Follow the wall on the right and turn right again at its end to go through a tunnel that leads into the cathedral cloister. Go left and right, around the cloister and then into the cathedral.

Leave the cathedral by the south door and walk towards the castle. At the end of the first building go left, signed Museum of Archaeology, past the house where J M Falkner, the author of *Moonfleet*, lived. Continue down to a crossing path, turn left and follow the main path downhill to the east end of Prebends' Bridge.

Turn sharp right along the river bank, past the Museum of Archaeology and up the steps on to Silver Street. Turn right here and after a few yards take another right turn to go through a narrow opening into Moatside Lane. Follow the passage to emerge in Saddler Street and then turn left into the Market Place.

ELSDON MAP REF 409 K6

Elsdon by the River Rede was the capital of the remote Middle March – one of three protective areas set up in 1249 along the Scottish border. The attractive triangular green is surrounded by mainly 18th- and 19th-century houses. From early in the 12th century the village was guarded by Elsdon Castle; its motte-and-bailey earthworks are very well preserved.

The 14th-century Elsdon Tower, once a defensive pele for the vicars of Elsdon, stands near the church. The church, another St Cuthbert's, said to be one of the places where his body rested during its wanderings, is isolated on the green. Its bell-turret dates from 1720, but most of the building is from the 14th century. Inside are narrow aisles and thick walls. More than 1,000 skulls, and bones, were found here – bodies of soldiers who fell at the Battle of Otterburn in 1388.

HADRIAN'S WALL

Insight
ROMAN STOPS ON HADRIAN'S WALL

CARVORAN Magnis fort at Carvoran was built before Hadrian's Wall, to guard the junction of the Stanegate and the Maiden Way. The only stones still visible are part of the northwest tower. Adjoining the fort is the exciting Roman Army Museum, with finds from Magnis and other sites along the Wall, and a large-scale model of the fort. To the west, there is a fine stretch of the *vallum*, and further beyond this lies 14th-century Thirlwall Castle, beside Tipalt Burn.

HOUSESTEADS Housesteads – Roman Vercovicium – is the most visited fort on Hadrian's Wall due to its spectacular site, impressive remains and access to one of the best parts of the wall. Visit the museum first, then climb to the remains of town buildings by the South Gate. The gate itself was rebuilt as a bastle in the Middle Ages. Through it, to the right, you can visit the communal latrines, where 12 soldiers could sit. Walk along the wall westwards to Milecastle 37 – the views are wonderful – and on, if you can, to Steel Rigg, to see how the military structures of Rome have been absorbed into the landscape.

CARRAWBURGH Brocolitia, the fort here at Carrawburgh, remains largely unexcavated, though it is known to have been added in around AD 130. Near by are the remains of the most complete Mithraic temple to be found in Britain. The uninitiated gathered in a small ante-room. Beyond this was the temple, with three altars (those you see today are replicas) and statues of Mithras' attendants, Cautes, with his torch raised to represent light, and Cautopates, torch down for darkness.

CHESTERS Where Hadrian's Wall crossed the North Tyne, the Romans built a wooden bridge guarded by Cilurnum fort, now called Chesters. Near by are remains of the bridge, but they are better preserved over on the opposite bank, reached by a footpath from the bridge at Chollerford. In the river you can see an original pier, which carried the wooden pedestrians' bridge, as well as a later stone bridge built in about AD 206 to carry vehicles; two of its three piers can still be seen when the river is low.

HADRIAN'S WALL MAP REF 409 K7

Around AD 80 the Romans constructed a road – Stanegate – south of the Great Whin Sill. It went from Corbridge, where Dere Street crossed the River Tyne, to Carlisle. Guarded by forts, it was not originally a frontier, for Roman troops were active far into Scotland. But in about AD 100 Emperor Trajan withdrew to the Stanegate, building new forts and watchtowers on the Whin Sill. Trajan's successor, Hadrian, visiting in AD 122, ordered the construction of a wall which would be the limit of the empire and would offer protection from the tribes in the north that resisted Roman invasion.

Running 80 Roman miles – 73 modern miles (117.5km) – the Wall was built of local sandstone and ran between the Tyne and the Irthing; further west turf was used, later replaced by stone. It began 10 Roman feet – 9.5 feet (3m) – wide, later reduced to 8 feet (2.4m), or sometimes 6 feet (1.8m). The *vallum*, a high-banked ditch south of the Wall to control civilians at the frontier, was another modification.

The Wall was probably around 21 feet (6.4m) high. Regular crossing points gave the Romans control: the barbarians could pass through into the Empire, but only to approved markets, unarmed and with a military escort. Later, in more troubled times, some of the gates were blocked.

When Hadrian died, the new emperor, Antoninus Pius, abandoned the Wall, pushed into Scotland and built the Antonine Wall (of turf) from the Forth to the Clyde. But the troops retreated to the Whin Sill in AD 160, when a new route – the Military Way – was built between the Wall and the *vallum* to improve access.

By around AD 407 the empire was breaking up; at this time the British army chose its own emperor, Constantine III, who went off to win Rome, leaving Britain undefended. The auxiliaries at the Wall drifted away, and it became a quarry for local farmers. Hadrian's part in the Wall's construction was forgotten until 1840, and it has only been in the 20th century that the site has gained legal protection.

HALTWHISTLE MAP REF 406 F2

Haltwhistle Burn flows into the South Tyne east of the town of Haltwhistle, and there are pleasant walks alongside the burn up to Hadrian's Wall. Haltwhistle is also a good place from which to explore the north Pennines. But don't neglect the attractive town centre, its stone streets radiating from the market place giving it a slightly stern, Scottish air. Some of its Victorian station buildings, including the stationmaster's house, waiting room and ticket office, date from as early as 1838.

The Red Lion Inn is based on a defensive tower, probably of the 17th century, when Haltwhistle was still at the mercy of Scottish raiders. It was under the protection of the powerful Ridley family.

The church is one of the best in Northumberland, at least on the inside – its exterior is rather unprepossessing. It is mostly Early English in style, with long, thin lancet windows, and was carefully restored in 1870, when the wonderful stained glass, made by William Morris's company, was put in the east windows. Haltwhistle was once a thriving centre of industry (there are still manufacturing plants in and around the town), and by the burn you can see the remains of woollen mills, collieries and brickworks.

HEXHAM MAP REF 407 G2

St Etheldreda made a gift of Hexham manor to her spiritual adviser, Wilfrid, for supporting her against her husband King Egfrith. Wilfrid built the priory – it was never an abbey – in about AD 674. Wilfrid's crypt, reached from the new nave built in 1907, was built of Roman stones from Corstopitum (Corbridge), many still with carvings or inscriptions.

The rest of the priory is impressive, too, especially the early 13th-century choir, the north transept with fine lancet windows and, in the south transept, the Night Stair for the Augustinian canons to descend from their dormitory for night prayers. Look out for the nearby Roman tombstone of standard-bearer Flavius.

The priory was kept apart from the town by a row of houses set towards the market place, with its stone-columned Shambles, still used by traders. Be sure to visit 14th-century Moot Hall, a miniature castle with an archway tunnelling through it, which now houses the Border Library and Gallery. Through the arch, in Hallgate, is another fearsome tower, the Archbishops' Gaol. Built about 1330, it houses the Border History Museum.

HOLY ISLAND MAP REF 409 K5

Holy Island has been known by this name since the 11th century, although its Celtic name, Lindisfarne, is just as familiar. The island was given to St Aidan in AD 635 by the King of Northumbria, and it became respected throughout Europe. Even more famous and influential was St Cuthbert, whose life and teaching drew pilgrims. He died in AD 687 and was buried in the church. When it was sacked during Danish raids in AD 875 the monks fled with his bones, searching for a safe and permanent home for them. The remains arrived in Durham more than 100 years later.

Lindisfarne seems an ideal setting for the monastic life – bare, windswept and flat, surrounded by sands covered by the sea twice daily. Before crossing to the island via the causeway, check the tides and note any warnings. A refuge is provided for the foolhardy who don't.

South of the square is St Mary's Church. Near by in the Heritage Centre there is an electronic copy of the famous Lindisfarne Gospels (with 'turnable' pages) – the original is in the British Museum. It was illuminated here in AD 698. Just offshore St Cuthbert's Island was used by the saint when he needed total solitude.

Next to the church are the remains of Lindisfarne Priory, built of beautiful red sandstone. It was founded by the Bishop of Durham in 1083, and finished by 1140. Its columns are patterned with zigzags and chequers. The remaining rib of the crossing, known as the rainbow arch, shows that it once had a strong tower. Part of the cloister remains – in contrasting grey stone – but there is not much more, except a gatehouse and defensive walls against the Scots. The nearby museum tells the story of the island.

Stones from the Priory were used in the 1540s to build a fort on Beblowe, a rocky crag on the south shore. The fort's purpose was to defend the harbour, where part of Henry VIII's fleet had taken shelter in 1543 and where today the boats of the lobster and crab fishermen mingle with the pleasure craft. These defences were never tested before peace with the Scots came 60 years later. It was neglected until Edward Hudson, founder of *Country Life* magazine, bought it in 1902 and commissioned architect Edwin Lutyens to adapt it for use as a home. Lutyens' gardening collaborator Gertrude Jekyll designed the tiny walled garden 500 yards (457m) north of the castle.

OTTERBURN MAP REF 409 K6

Otterburn has had a place in military history since the Battle of Otterburn, on 19 August 1388, brought together the son of the Earl of Northumberland, Harry Hotspur, and Earl Douglas, who commanded a Scots raiding party. Versions of the battle vary, but most people agree that the Scots raiders beat Hotspur, that Douglas was killed and Hotspur was captured and later ransomed. The Percy Cross, in a plantation northwest of the village, is traditionally where Douglas died. Today's soldiers practise live firing on the Otterburn Training Area: on some days there is public access along rights of way and roads – check locally.

At Otterburn Mill, originally built in the 18th century, you can buy fine tweeds and woollens, while Otterburn Hall, a YMCA hostel, has forest walks, nature trails, and activities such as archery and canoeing.

ROTHBURY MAP REF 409 K6

One of the main tourist centres of Northumberland, Rothbury, the capital of Coquetdale, is an attractive town, with stone buildings spreading outwards from an irregularly shaped green and a medieval bridge over the River Coquet.

The town was harried by William Wallace's army in the 13th century, and proclaimed the Old Pretender as James III in the 18th, but since the 19th century it has developed as a holiday centre.

The parish church underwent a Victorian restoration, which destroyed a Saxon tower and left little of the rest, but it is worth visiting for a glimpse of the font whose bowl dates from 1664, but stands on part of the 9th-century Rothbury Cross, decorated with Celtic-inspired designs.

East of Rothbury the Coquet rushes through a narrow gorge at The Thrum – you can reach it by a footpath from the bridge. In places no more than 5 feet (1.5m) wide, the river has scoured the sandstone here into contorted shapes.

Cragside (National Trust), east of Rothbury, is a major tourist attraction, but with a country park and gardens, it is usually easy to find a quiet corner. Built for the 1st Lord Armstrong by the architect Norman Shaw, it is a fantastic creation, a cross between an English manor house and a Bavarian *schloss*. It hangs over the wooded gorge of Debdon Burn in a sea of trees and its interior is full of heavy, late-Victorian atmosphere, though parts are dark and cramped. Spectacular exceptions include the fine library and the drawing room, with its huge alabaster fireplace.

HOLY ISLAND

Kielder Water

Tucked away at the top of Northumberland, close by Hadrian's Wall and the Scottish Border, Kielder Water, with a 27-mile (43km) shoreline, is by far the largest man-made lake in Europe, and sits at the heart of the equally impressive Kielder Forest, Britain's largest forest, covering an area of over 153,140 acres (62,000ha). The lake is the reason why water shortages are unheard of in Northumberland, except on the national news, even though the county is one of the driest in Britain.

Kielder Forest, is also one of Britain's biggest nature reserves, where the hills, rivers and open areas add to the rich diversity of the forest making it an ideal habitat for some 6,000 roe deer, and one of the few places in England still home to native red squirrels, rather than the American grey variety. There is a tranquil beauty here, enhanced by activities such as sailing and other watersports, fishing and ferry cruises. The lake fringes and forest glades are best explored on foot, on a bicycle or on horseback.

Sitka spruce is the main species at Kielder, a tree that thrives best in the hostile upland environment, accounting for around three-quarters of the forest area: 12 per cent is Norway spruce, 9 per cent lodgepole pine plus a small percentage of larch, broadleaf and the once-ubiquitous Scots pine. And if the sometimes sombre aspect of a dense pine plantation is not your thing, then the on-going planting of natural broad-leaved trees, taking the percentage of hardwoods from just 1 per cent in the original forest to 8 per cent by 2020, will eventually make a real difference.

At the end of the day, Kielder's main purpose is commercial timber production. Half the timber produced here is taken straight to the saw mills in the north of England and southern Scotland for construction timber, fencing and packaging. The remaining half,

consisting of small round wood cut from smaller trees and the tops of much bigger trees, goes to a paper mill at Workington in Cumbria, and is turned into carton board, cereal packets and boxes.

Central to the area stands Kielder Castle. Built in 1775 as a hunting lodge for the Duke of Northumberland, the Castle is dressed with mock fortifications and is now the focal point for visitors to the forest. The Castle itself houses a series of exhibitions about birds, wildlife, history and the daily working of the Forest. The grounds include picnic sites, a children's playground, walking trails, cycling routes (cycle hire on site), a mountain bike skills loop, and orienteering routes. Within the grounds of the Castle is a work of art, one of a few at Kielder, called Minotaur, which is a maze built of basalt stone and glass. The Castle, now one of Kielder Forests visitor centres, houses a Forest Enterprise exhibition.

Kielder Water Birds of Prey Centre at Leaplish Waterside Park, offers a direct 'hands on' experience during which you meet all the northern indigenous owls, as well as birds of prey and other owls from around the world. It is one of the largest and most fascinating collections of birds of prey in the north of England, boasting over 60 birds and 28 species. Weather permitting, flying demonstrations take place three times a day.

Free-range birdwatching at Kielder can be difficult because of the density of trees. But birds of prey are the star attractions, and Forest Enterprise have created a raptor viewpoint at Bakethin, about a mile (1.6km) from Kielder Village. Kestrels are seen regularly, and there is always a chance of seeing merlin, peregrine or goshawk. Nor are sparrowhawks uncommon; indeed the Forest Information Centre at Kielder Castle has

seasonal video footage of a nearby sparrowhawk nesting site. Bakethin Reservoir has been declared a nature reserve, and attracts ospreys as well as sizeable numbers of wildfowl and gulls at all times of the year. In the main conifer forest, the elusive crossbill flits through the tree canopy, whilst the more deciduous areas of the North Tyne Valley attract pied flycatcher and redstart especially during the breeding season.

With over 372 miles (600km) of waterways in the forest, and the reservoir at its centre, otters are increasingly a common (if secretive) inhabitant, but there are now signs that otters are using all the major waterways in the area. The European otter is part of the same family as badgers, weasels, stoats, pine marten and mink, and is listed in the International Union for the Conservation of Nature (IUCN) Red Book as 'vulnerable to extinction'. The number of otters in Britain is not known, but they are on the increase in some areas, and the steps being taken at Kielder to maintain and improve their habitat are vital to the future well being of this amphibious and charismatic creature. Being at the top of the food chain, otters are predators, hunters rather than being hunted, and have a diet mainly of fish, small mammals and birds. The main threat to otters is from humans through the destruction of their habitat and from pesticides running off farmland and polluting watercourses.

The remarkable diversity of Kielder is shown in the fact that here there are no fewer than nine Sites of Special Scientific Interest. Embracing some 7,500 hectares, this represents 4 per cent of the total SSSI area in England alone, and sites include ancient woodland, fossil trees, geological sites, moorlands and the extensive Border Mire peat bogs. Access to part of the mires has been improved by the completion of a boardwalk, which just happens to surround one of the best ponds for dragonflies in Northumberland.

Cycling, walking, sailing, birdwatching and simple relaxation and enjoyment with the family are all major attractions at Kielder, and are enjoyed by many through the balmy days of summer. But above all else, away from the main centres of sports and activities, there is a serenity and tranquility that belies the man-made nature of this stunning place, where herds of silent deer slip through the serried ranks of spruce like shadows in springtime, and the wind seems forever tangled in the trees.

TOP LEFT Budding mountainbikers get ready to test their brakes on a skills coaching course in Hamsterley Forest.

TOP RIGHT *Skyspace* at Cat Cairn in Kielder Forest, is an underground chamber that is accessed by a tunnel. The 3m circular opening in the top allows natural light to shine in and create a changing pattern of light on the inside throughout the day.

ABOVE LEFT A Ruppell's Griffon vulture at the Kielder Water Birds of Prey Centre.

ABOVE RIGHT Husky racing has been taking place at Kielder for many years. The rigs use wheels for most of the year and skis during snowy weather conditions.

OPPOSITE Kielder Water, surrounded by Kielder Forest. The Forestry Commission owns all of the forest land on this side of the border, excluding Kielder Reservoir and a 50 metre strip of trees that surrounds it. This strip of land is largely unplanted and owned privately.

SEAHOUSES & FARNE ISLANDS

MAP REFS 409 L5

Seahouses has a prosperous air, geared to the tourist industry. In the town there are some pleasant fishermen's cottages around Craster Square and a busy harbour, built in the 18th century but much enlarged in the 19th. At the harbour you can get boat trips to the Farne Islands, and there are fine sands to the north and south of the sheltering Snook Point.

St Aidan spent each Lent on Inner Farne, one of the 28 Farne Islands (or 15, if you count at high tide), and St Cuthbert lived here from AD 676 to AD 685. His cell on Inner Farne was surrounded by an embankment so that all he could see was heaven. St Cuthbert's Church on Inner Farne, near the site of his hermitage, dates mostly from about 1370 and has 17th-century woodwork, brought here from Durham Cathedral.

To the west, Prior Castell's Tower may have held a lighthouse from the days when there were Benedictine monks on the island. Today's white-painted lighthouse, which is open to visitors, was built in 1809. Further out, beyond Staple, is Longstone, a rather uninviting, low, bare rock with a red-and-white striped lighthouse, built in 1826. This was where the Darling family lived, and from where Grace and her father set out on their rescue mission.

For many visitors the attraction of the Farne Islands is their wildlife, especially the birds and the seals. Egg collectors caused unprecedented damage in the 19th century, and the Farne Islands Association, set up in 1880, employed watchers to protect the breeding birds. The National Trust has owned the islands since 1925, and permits to land on Inner Farne and Staple Island must be bought from the Wardens. Check, too, that your boatman is licensed to land his passengers. During the breeding season, from May to July, landing is restricted – and if the weather is bad you may not be able to land at all. There are nature walks on both these islands.

The delightful little puffins are always favourites with visitors, but you may also see fulmars, petrels, razorbills, ring plover, rock pipits, eiders (known locally as St Cuthbert's – or Cuddy's – Chicks), kittiwakes, cormorants, terns, guillemots, shags, oystercatchers and, of course, gulls. The boat trips usually pass near enough to see their nesting sites, and on Staple and Inner Farne you can walk, with care, among their nests.

VINDOLANDA MAP REF 409 J7

Agricola had a turf fort at Vindolanda in the AD 80s to guard the Stanegate, and part of the paved road, as well as a Roman milestone, can still be seen here. Another fort was built before Hadrian's time, and when the wall was put up, the fort was rebuilt in stone, then almost totally rebuilt 100 years later, with its usual rectangular shape. The layout of the headquarters and parts of the gates are clearly visible.

Vindolanda also has the biggest civilian settlement that can be seen on the wall. Visit the mansion (an inn for travellers) with its bathhouse, and the large 'corridor' house, part of which was a butcher's shop. At the town bathhouse hairpins and a child's sandal were found in the drains. You can see some of the pink waterproof plaster that lined the walls and floors.

Children visiting Vindolanda usually make for the reconstructions of parts of Hadrian's Wall. The Turf Wall shows what the original part of the wall was like before it was rebuilt in stone. More impressive is the Stone Wall, nearly 23 feet (7m) high, with battlements, turret and ditch.

Vindolanda's waterlogged soil has helped to preserve many details of daily life – the museum shows some of them, including leather shoes, textiles and ornaments. There is also a replica of a Roman kitchen. Most important are the wooden writing tablets, with gossip, invitations, letters asking for new underwear, and accounts of food stores, bringing the people vividly to life.

WARKWORTH MAP REF 409 L6

Shakespeare, who set three dramatic scenes of *Henry IV* here, called the ruins of Warkworth Castle 'this worm-eaten hold of ragged stone'. Actually, the huge keep is one of the most spectacular in Britain. Set in a loop of the River Coquet on the site of the original motte, its plan is a cross superimposed on a square, and it stands to its full height, partly restored in the 19th century for the Duke of Northumberland. The original 11th-century structure was replaced by a stone castle before 1158 and was sacked by the Scots in 1174. The Percys lived at Warkworth rather than Alnwick until the 16th century and the Lion Tower carries their crest.

The Percy Lion is also carved on the keep wall that dominates the little town, where the medieval street plan is still evident. Georgian and Victorian houses lead down the hill to the church and the fortified bridge. The Old Pretender was proclaimed here in 1715, his army dined at the Masons' Arms and in the church his Catholic chaplain said prayers.

The church has a 14th-century spire but inside is almost all Norman, with a stone-vaulted chancel, its roof ribs decorated with zigzags. This church was the scene of a massacre in 1174, when the Scottish army killed most of the population of Warkworth, seeking refuge inside.

VINDOLANDA

AROUND DRURIDGE BAY

This walk takes in a nature reserve, country park and beach. The biggest attractions here are the birds. Resident species are joined by those migrating between the summer feeding and breeding grounds in the north and Africa, where many over-winter. Wimbrel, dunlin and sanderling are among the migrating species, whilst redshank, plover and bar-tailed godwit winter here. You will also see whooper and Bewick swans plus favourites such as tits, finches, blackbirds and robins.

1 A waymarked footpath beside the car park entrance winds between the nature reserve and a caravan site towards the coast. Through a gate at the bottom, turn right on to a track, which soon passes two gates giving access to bird hides overlooking the lake.

2 Leaving the reserve, now continue a little further along a tarmac track to reach an informal parking area on the left, where there is easy access on to the beach. Now, follow the shore past Togston Links, across a stream and on below Hadston Links.

3 After 1.25 miles (2km), wooden steps take the path off the sands on to the dunes. Cross a tarmac track and continue over a marshy area into pinewood. Beyond the trees, emerge by a car park and walk across to the Druridge Bay Country Park visitor centre, where there is a café and toilets.

4 A footway to the left winds around Ladyburn Lake, soon passing a boat launching area. Keep to the lower path, which soon leads to stepping stones across the upper neck of the lake. If you prefer not to cross there, continue around the upper edge of a wooded nature sanctuary above the water to a higher footbridge. Over the bridge and through a gate, turn right by the field edge, soon dropping around an internal corner to reach a kissing gate. Now descend through trees to regain the lake by the stepping stones.

5 This side of the lake has a more natural feel to it, the path winding through trees to emerge beside a lushly vegetated shoreline where swans like to feed. After crossing a bridge over the lake's outflow, carry on back to the visitor centre.

6 Retrace your steps to the beach and turn back towards Hauxley, but when you reach the point where you originally dropped on to the sands, remain walking along the shore towards Bondi Carrs. Seaweed can make the rocks slippery, so be careful clambering over them as you round the point. Coquet Island then comes into view ahead. Not far beyond there, after passing a look-out post and approaching large rocks placed as a storm defence, leave across the dunes, retracing your outward path along the short distance back to the car park.

DISTANCE/TIME 5.5 miles (8.8km) 1h45 **MAP** OS Explorers 325 Morpeth & Blyth; 332 Alnwick & Amble **START** Car park at Hauxley Nature Reserve; grid ref: NU282024 (on Explorer 332)

TRACKS Paths and tracks, with good walk on beach **THE PUB** Widdrington Inn, Morpeth. Tel: 01670 760260 (beside a roundabout on the A1068, about 4 miles/6.4km to the south)

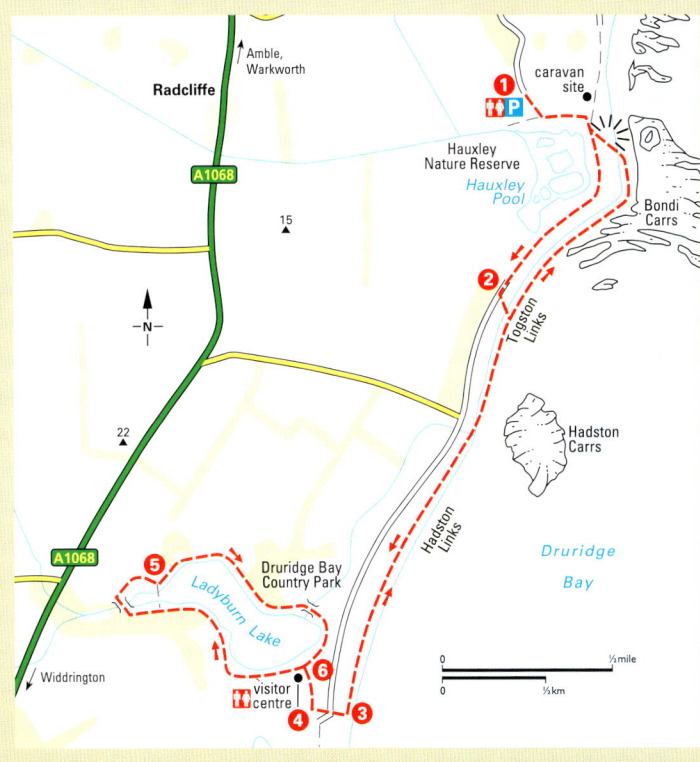

WALK 120

THE ANCIENT SPIRIT OF THE SIMONSIDES

This walk visits a hill that had religious significance to early settlers and is now a rock climbers' playground. Many sites show evidence of human activity that dates back 5,000 years to the Iron Age. Conifer forests now cover the lower reaches of the hills, but the summit crags remain clear. As a sport, rock climbing began in Northumberland in the late 19th century and the crags of Simonside were among the first to be developed.

1 From the notice board in the picnic area, walk through the gate on to the broad forest road. Follow this road gently uphill, swinging to the right round the long hairpin bend, then back left at the top of the hill. When the road splits, take the right-hand fork, past the communications mast and go gently down the hill. When you get to the next junction, take the left-hand fork and follow the road past the sign that indicates a detour to Little Church Rock.

2 When you come to the marker post, where a narrow track leads to the left, ignore this and continue to walk along the broad track, which by now is becoming grassy. After passing an enormous, heavily overgrown boulder, continue to walk to the small cairn that marks the start of a subsidiary track on the left. Continue to follow this path uphill through the forest and then emerge out on to the heather-covered hillside. At this point you will see Simonside's crags 0.5 mile (0.8km) away to your left.

3 Continue up the narrow track to join the broader one at the edge of the upper forest and follow this for about 275yds (251m) to the

corner of the trees. A rough track, sometimes quite muddy in places, picks its way through boulders up the hillside. Follow this, keeping the crags on your left-hand side, on to the plateau and then walk along the top of the crags to the large cairn, probably a burial mound, on the summit.

4 Away from the summit, the track splits into two. Follow the right-hand fork across some boggy ground for 580yds (530m). Climb the short rise, always keeping the wonderfully wind-sculpted Old Stell Crag to your left and move round on to the summit and another large cairn.

5 Take the narrow path that leads down to join the lower track. This leads, in about 0.5 mile (0.8km), to the cairn on Dove Crag. At the Y-junction, 0.25 mile (0.4km) further on, follow the right fork gently uphill to reach The Beacon cairn, and continue downhill for 0.5 mile (0.8km) to join the road at Lordenshaws car park.

6 Turn left and follow the road for 1 mile (1.6km) until you arrive back at the forest picnic area you left at the start of the walk.

DISTANCE/TIME 5.5 miles (8.8km) 3h **MAP** OS Explorer OL42 Kielder Water & Forest **START** Large car park at forest picnic area; grid ref: NZ037997 **TRACKS** Generally good, but steep and muddy in places **THE PUB** The Queen's Head Hotel, Townfoot, Rothbury. Tel: 01669 620470; www.queensheadrothbury.com

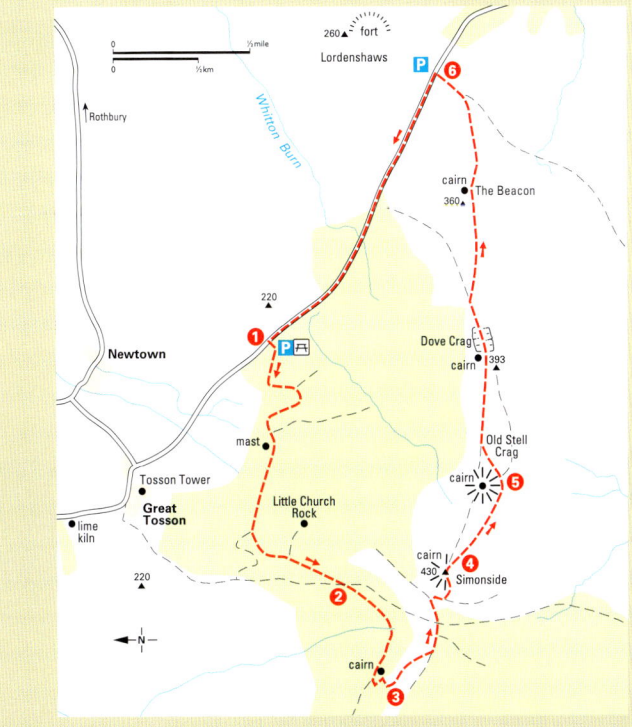

The gated narrow road needs care as it winds for 7 miles (11.5km) – wide verges allow passing. The road drops into North Charlton. At the A1 turn left and after a mile (1.6km), turn right, signed 'Preston Tower, Ellingham'. After about 2 miles (3.2km) you will see the 1392 Preston Tower.

This has a medieval Border life display. With its robust 7-feet (xxm) thick walls, this original Pele tower has retained two of its fine turrets.

6 At the T-junction just beyond, turn left to 'Beadnell, Seahouses'. Go over the level crossing at Chathill, continue for 3.5 miles (5.6km) past Beadnell and along the coast on the B1340, into Seahouses. At the first roundabout turn right, at the next roundabout turn left, following the 'Coast' signs to ancient Bamburgh with its wonderful coastline.

Bamburgh has a huge, square Norman castle, visible for miles around atop a 180ft (xxm) basalt crag. The castle walls were impregnable until thet War of the Roses when cannon fire proved too much for its fortifications.

7 Go round Budle Bay and at the T-junction in Waren Mill turn left to 'Belford, Wooler'. In 2.5 miles (4km) turn right on the A1 and left to Belford. Just before the church go left on the B6349 to 'Wooler'. In 2.5 miles (4km), turn right on a narrow unclassified road signed 'Hazelrigg, Lowick'.

There are spectacular views of the Cheviots to be had from here. For environmental scientists, Hazelrigg has a significant weather station.

8 Turn right at a T-junction after 2 miles (3.2km), to 'Holburn, Berwick'. A little way along here is the track to St Cuthbert's Cave. After 5 miles (8km) cross the B6353, then after 0.5 mile (0.8km) turn right to 'Kentstone, Beal'. At the A1 go straight over to visit Holy Island, checking the tides for your return journey first.

Lindisfarne has a ruined priory, a Tudor castle and a heritage centre. As well as the Holy Island scriptures to see, the heritage centre pays tribute to the bravery of its seafaring islanders.

9 Otherwise, turn left towards Berwick, passing Haggerston Castle. In 4.5 miles (7.2km) go right at the roundabout along the A1167 to 'Scremerston, Berwick'. At the next roundabout go straight on, over the bridge and into the town centre.

NORTHUMBERLAND'S COAST & HILLS

Castles, spectacular views of the Cheviots, wild moorland and the coastal islands are among the highlights of this circular drive from England's most northerly town. Extend the drive by 10 miles (16km) if you visit Holy Island, but before you set out be sure to check on the tides.

Route Directions

Start at the historic town of Berwick-on-Tweed. Fought over by the Scottish and the English for centuries, Berwick is England's most northerly situated town and lies almost equidistant between Newcastle and Edinburgh.

1 From the centre go over the Royal Tweed Bridge, signed 'Newcastle, A1' and go right, signed 'Coldstream A698'. Head right at the first roundabout and then straight on at the second, following Coldstream signs. After 3 miles (4.8km), turn right along an unclassified road signed 'Horncliffe, Norham Castle'. In 2 miles (3.2km) pass the ruins of Norham Castle to enter Norham.

Norham Castle was one of the strongest border castles and saw much fighting until the union of the Scottish and English crowns removed the need for defence here.

2 Follow the road past the cross and at the T-junction turn left, signed 'Berwick', on the B6470. After 0.5 miles (0.8km) turn right along an unclassified road. At the T-junction turn left on the A698, to Berwick, then fast right on to an unclassified road, signed 'Felkington'. Follow this winding road for 4 miles (6.4km), following signs for Etal and Ford, to reach the B6354, where you turn right. Follow the road for 3 miles (4.8km) through Etal to Ford.

In Ford, visit Lady Waterford Hall, with murals depicting locals in biblical scenes. The pretty building, with its two front gables, was originally used as the village school.

3 Just before Ford church go right, signed 'Kimmerston'. After 1.5 miles (2.4km) turn right at the T-junction, signed 'Milfield'. Go over Redscar Bridge and straight on to meet the A697, where you turn left towards Wooler and Morpeth. Follow the main road through Akeld and at a junction a mile beyond turn right (signed 'Wooler light traffic only') then continue into the centre of Wooler.

This bustling market town is popular with walkers heading to the Cheviots. Once made prosperous by the wool trade from the Cheviot sheep, Wooler is a popular stop along the long-distance path St Cuthbert's Way.

4 At the end of the main street turn left by the church then cross the main road on to the B6348, signed 'Chatton', 'Belford' and 'Chillingham Castle, Wild Cattle'. After 2.5 miles (4km) there is a sharp right-hand bend at the top of a hill. Beyond this, follow the main road for 2.5 miles (4km) to Chatton. Turn right at the 'Chillingham, Alnwick' sign. Follow the road past the entrance to the Wild Cattle Park and the castle.

5 At the brow of the hill turn left to 'Hepburn Wood Walks'. Follow the road through Hepburn and then uphill, past Ros Castle.

CAR TOUR 22

70 MILES (112.7KM)

THREE DALES

This is a spectacular drive that takes you to the valleys of the Tyne, Wear and Tees and across some of England's wildest and most remote moorland. Much of the route is within the officially designated North Pennines Area of Outstanding Natural Beauty. Note: Some of the route passes over unfenced, high moorland. You should not attempt this drive in bad weather or when visibility is low.

Route Directions

Hexham is a good town to explore on foot, with its attractive Victorian shop-fronts, fine medieval buildings and 7th-century abbey.

1 From the centre of Hexham take the B6305 west towards Allendale turning left at the traffic lights by the Fox Inn. Follow the main road, signed 'Allendale', to Catton. Go through Allendale town.

Allendale's centre has an attractive square surrounded by stone houses. The market town became prosperous in the 17th century due to the success of its lead mines.

2 Continue down the valley of the River East Allen for 7.5 miles (12.1km) through spread-out Sinderhope and on into Allenheads, once an important lead-mining centre. After driving 1.5 miles (2.4km) beyond the village, cross the County Durham border and then descend into Weardale. The B6295 joins the A689 as you reach Cowshill. At the junction you can divert from the main route by turning right for 2.5 miles (4km) to visit Killhope Wheel & the Lead Mining Centre.

A discovery trail leads visitors through the site, devoted to the local lead-mining industry, or you can take a guided tour and go underground.

3 On the main route, turn left to go through Cowshill and Ireshopeburn and into the centre of St John's Chapel, with its 18th-century church and the only Town Hall in a Durham village. Turn right up a narrow entry, Harthope Road, signed 'Langdon Beck'. The unclassified road eventually goes over a cattle grid and climbs steeply on to Harthope Moor. This is one of the highest public roads in England, attaining an altitude of 2,057ft (627m).

Do not attempt this route in bad weather or limited visibility. The road is marked by tall, narrow poles, indicating the route when the road itself is covered by snow.

4 Follow the road for 5 miles (8km), to descend, with wide views of the valley, into Teesdale. At the junction with the B6277 turn left, signed 'Langdon Beck, Middleton'. After half a mile (0.8km) of driving a road to the right leads to Cow Green Reservoir and Cauldron Snout. Continue along the B6277 for 3 miles (4.8km) to reach the spectacular High Force waterfall.

One of the highest single-drop waterfalls in England, this is where the Tees plunges over Great Whin Sill.

5 In 1.5 miles (2.4km) is Bowlees Visitor Centre, and then the road enters the former lead-mining centre of Middleton-in-Teesdale. Immediately after crossing the bridge into Middleton turn sharp left, up a steep hill signed 'Stanhope'. After half a mile (0.8km) turn right, again signed 'Stanhope'. After 4.5 miles (7.2km) pass over a cattle grid, go round a sharp right-hand bend and turn left immediately, then left again on to the B6278. The road goes over moorland with spectacular views.

6 After 8.5 miles (13.7km), descend into Weardale. Just before the river the road bends left and then right over a bridge to join the A689. Turn right into the centre of Stanhope and turn left, signed 'B6278 Edmundbyers', just beside the Grey Bull pub. Go up the steep hill through Crawleyside and after 2.5 miles (4km), where the main road goes slightly right, continue ahead on an unclassified road, signed 'Blanchland'. Follow this road for 5.5 miles (8.8km) across open moorland and descend into the valley of Beldon Burn at Baybridge. Go over the bridge, crossing back into Northumberland, and follow the road into Blanchland.

The honey-coloured, mainly 18th-century houses in the centre of Blanchland are set around two informal squares separated by an archway of the monastic gatehouse.

7 In the village take the road straight ahead beside the abbey tower, signposted 'Corbridge, Hexham'. As the road ascends there are views over Derwent Reservoir. The road then passes through Slaley Forest and descends to the very narrow Linnels Bridge over Devil's Water, and 2 miles (3.2km) further on takes you back into the centre of Hexham town.

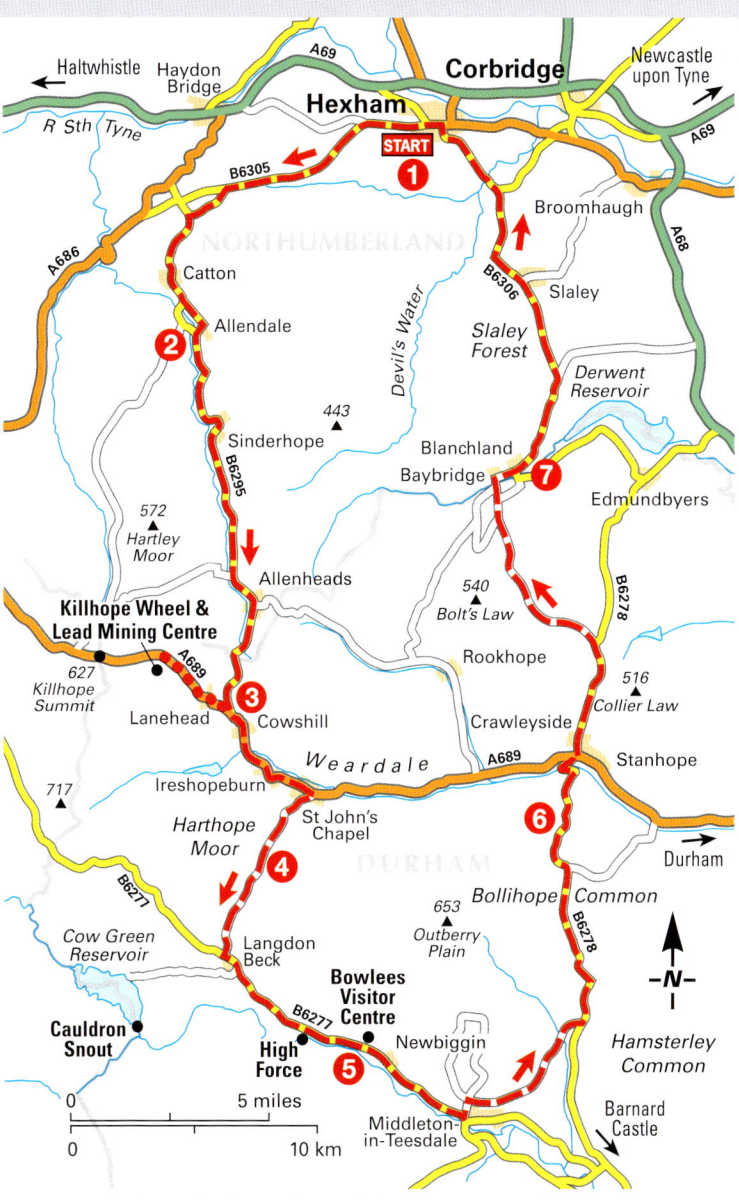

WALK 121

THROUGH THE GORGE OF THE RIVER COQUET

This is a fairly demanding but spectacular walk through some of Northumberland's geological history. Nowhere is this geology better laid out to view than it is around the gorge of the River Coquet, west of the village of Alwinton. To the north are the volcanic Cheviot Hills, while to the south are the fell sandstones. And in the gorge itself, at Barrow Scar, the layers of the cementstones lie fully exposed.

DISTANCE/TIME 4.5 miles (7.2km) 3h **MAP** OS Explorer OL16 The Cheviot Hills **START** Car park at Alwinton; grid ref: NT 919063 **TRACKS** Mostly hill footpaths, 8 stiles **THE PUB** The Rose and Thistle, Alwinton. Tel: 01669 650226; www.roseandthistlealwinton.com ❶ Close to MoD artillery range over Barrow Scar. When red flags flying, walk may be inadvisable

1 Turn right, out of the car park, and follow the road for 700yds (0.6km) to a gate on the left leading to Barrow Mill. Go through the gate and down to the farm, passing the remains of a corn-drying kiln dating from 1812. Go through another gate into a field, cross this and pass through a gate to the river bank. Ford the river. After a period of rain, this will involve getting your feet wet.

2 Enter the field and follow the fence to the right to a gate. Go through this or over the stile about 20yds (18m) away to the left and continue to the derelict farm buildings. Follow the track up the hillside to the right-hand corner of the conifer forest.

3 About 50yds (46m) before reaching a signpost marking the edge of a military firing range, you need to follow a less well-defined track across the heather-covered hillside to the right, rising slightly, until you come to a wire fence. Follow this fence over the top of Barrow Scar, always keeping the fence on your right. When you meet a second fence, follow this to a stile. Cross the stile and go down to an obvious loop in the river. In late summer, the bracken here may be deep and the track can be partially obscured.

4 At the river bend, cross a stile, then over another one after 100yds (91m). Cross the field and a stile into the farmyard at Linshiels. Go through the farmyard, across two bridges and join the road. Turn left and follow the road just past the farm buildings, to a signpost pointing to Shillmoor.

5 Go up the hillside, over a stile and follow the track overlooking the gorge and its waterfalls. This is the most spectacular part of the walk. For a short distance, the slopes below are quite precipitous and care is needed, though the track is good. When the track splits, keep to the higher branch and go round the hillside to join a more prominent track leading up from the left. Turn right and follow the track uphill.

6 At the top of the slope continue across level ground, then descend to a stile. Cross this and follow the track, over another stile and down to the road. Follow the road for a mile (1.6km) back to the village of Alwinton.

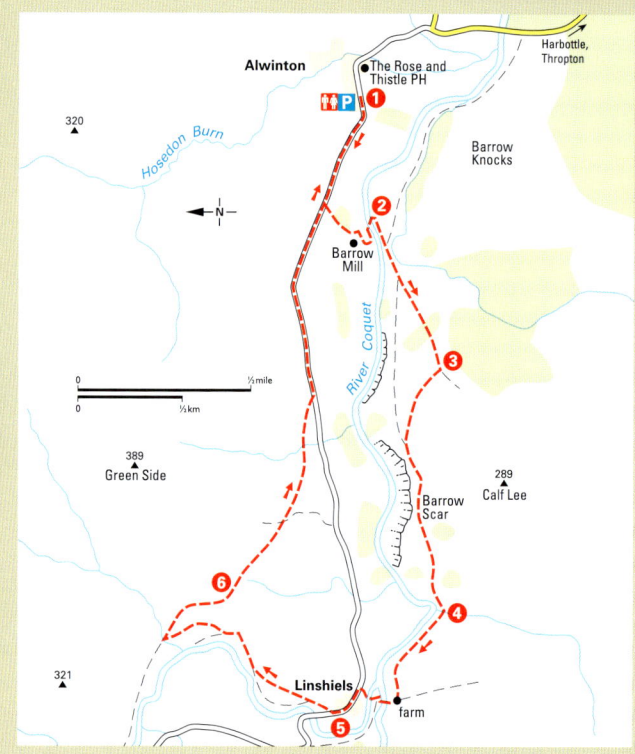

WALK 122

TARSET BURN & NORTH TYNE

The area around Lanehead is called Tarset but there is no Tarset village – only the burn in its valley, a name and the scant remains of a castle. The walks leads to the hamlet of Thorneyburn, which consists mainly of the church and the former rectory. The farmhouse at Redheugh probably began as a fortified bastle house.

DISTANCE/TIME 7.5 miles (12.1km) 3h **MAP** OS Explorer OL42 Kielder Water & Forest **START** Tarset Village Hall car park; grid ref: NY793858 **TRACKS** Burnside and moorland paths and tracks, some wet areas **THE PUB** The Hollybush Inn, Greenhaugh, Hexham. Tel: 01434 240391

1 Walk to the staggered crossroads in the middle of Lanehead and turn right, signed 'Donkleywood'. At the Redmire cottages turn right. Go through a gate, over two stiles and through a hand gate. Bear left to a stile in the field corner. Bend right, following the river bank and go over five stiles. The path rises, goes through a gate and to a footbridge. Go through a gate at the end, then ahead to meet a track. Turn left to farm buildings.

2 Go through two gates between the buildings, then ascend the lane. As it bears left, go ahead, walking past a waymarker and downhill to cross the stream. Pass by another waymarked post and go through a gateway. Bend right after it, go through a hand gate and turn left along the fence. Go over a stile on the right, then turn half left towards the house and church. Keep left of a ruined wall, and bear left to follow a wall down to a stream.

3 Cross the stream, go over the stile beyond and climb the hill. Bear left past the church to a gate. Turn right along the lane and at the T-junction turn left. Follow the lane past Redheugh farm and the 'Forestry Commission Sidwood' sign to the Sidwood Picnic Area, near to the white buildings.

4 Turn left, signed 'Slaty Ford'. Follow the path through the wood a little way, then go right. Go over a crossing track and continue uphill. After the track levels out, it goes beside woodland to a gate. Continue through the field, through plantations, to cross a ford then past a sign to a crossing track.

5 Turn left and go over another ford. Continue up to a gate. After 0.25 mile (0.4km) look for a stile in the wall on your right. Go over and bear half right down the field. Cross a stream, up to a wire fence and follow it left. Go right, through a gate, and cross the field, through a gate into the farmyard.

6 Take the right-hand gate to your left. Go through another gate and bear left to follow the track. At the bottom turn left along the road. As it rises, take a footpath over a stile. Follow the riverside path and pass through a kissing gate, to the suspension bridge.

7 After a hut, bear left. Cross the railway embankment and go through a gate. Bear half right to a large tree in the field corner and join the road. Turn right, then bear left on the road. Go over a cattle grid. Cross the bridge and walk to Lanehead, turning left at the junction to the parking place.

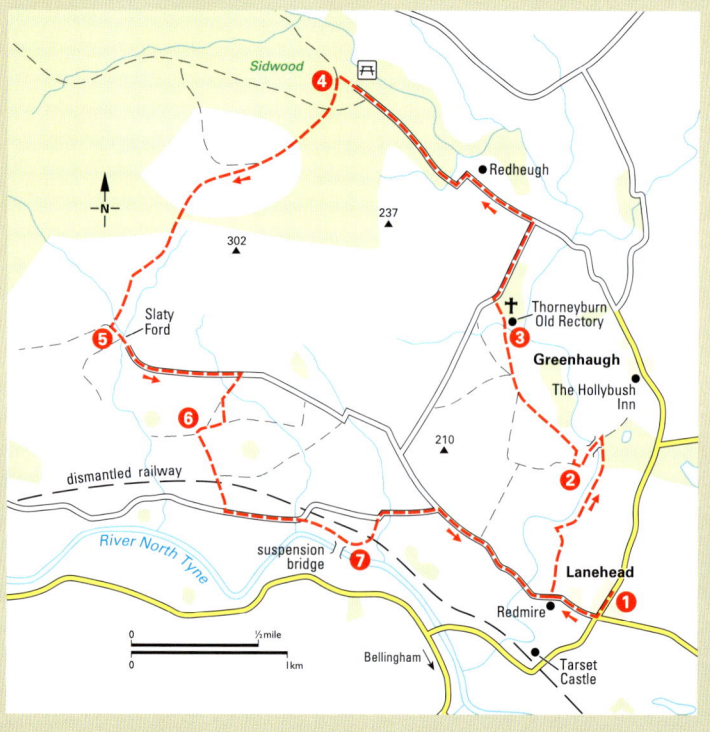

WALK 123

SMUGGLERS & THE LIGHT OF MARSDEN BAY

You will walk along the coast near South Shields, and inland to the Cleadon Hills, passing two windmills. The first, in Marsden, retains its sails; the other was built in the 1820s, but was later damaged in a storm. In World War II it housed Royal Observer Corps members who scanned the North Sea for enemy aircraft. The 1871 Souter Lighthouse protected ships from the rocks called Whitburn Steel.

DISTANCE/TIME 5.5 miles (8.8km) 2h **MAP** OS Explorer 316 Newcastle upon Tyne **START** Whitburn Coastal Park car park; grid ref: NZ412635 **TRACKS** Roads, tracks, field and coastal paths **THE PUB** The Marsden Grotto, Coast Road, Marsden. Tel: 0191 455 6060

1 Leave the car park at its southern end, following the gravel track towards the houses. The path winds and goes past a sign for Whitburn Point Nature Reserve. Follow the track ahead to go through a gap in a wall and turn right. The path bends right, left and right again to join a road into houses. Go straight ahead to join the main road.

2 Cross the road and turn left. Walk down the road until you reach the windmill. Turn right to enter the grounds of the windmill. Next, go up the slope on the path and then between houses. Bear left then turn right to reach a T-junction.

3 Go straight ahead on a path that goes to the right of house No 99. When you reach another road turn left. Just after the first bungalow on the right, turn right along a signed track. Follow the track towards the farm. Go through the farmyard, cross over two stiles and follow the lane beyond, with a hedge to your right. Where it ends, turn right and climb over a stile.

4 Follow the path along the field edge. Go over another stile, after which you are gradually ascending. The path bends left

then right, still following the field edge. Go over another two stiles. The path will bring you to Cleadon Windmill.

5 Go right of the windmill, following the wall on your right. Go right through a kissing gate, then bear slightly right (a brick tower to your left). Go parallel with the wall on your right. Go across a track and through a wire fence at right angles to the wall. Follow the path across scrub to emerge by a yellow post by the golf course.

6 Cross the course, following the yellow posts and watching for golfers. Cross a stone stile and turn right along a signed footpath, with the wall on your right. The path descends by houses to a road.

7 Cross and take the footpath almost opposite, to the right of a caravan site, towards the sea. Cross the busy A183 carefully and then turn right, following along the sea edge. Marsden Rock is near by, and the Marsden Grotto is to your left as you cross the road. Follow the coast as it bends left to Lizard Point. After a visit to the lighthouse, continue on a path slightly inland from the coast to return to the car park.

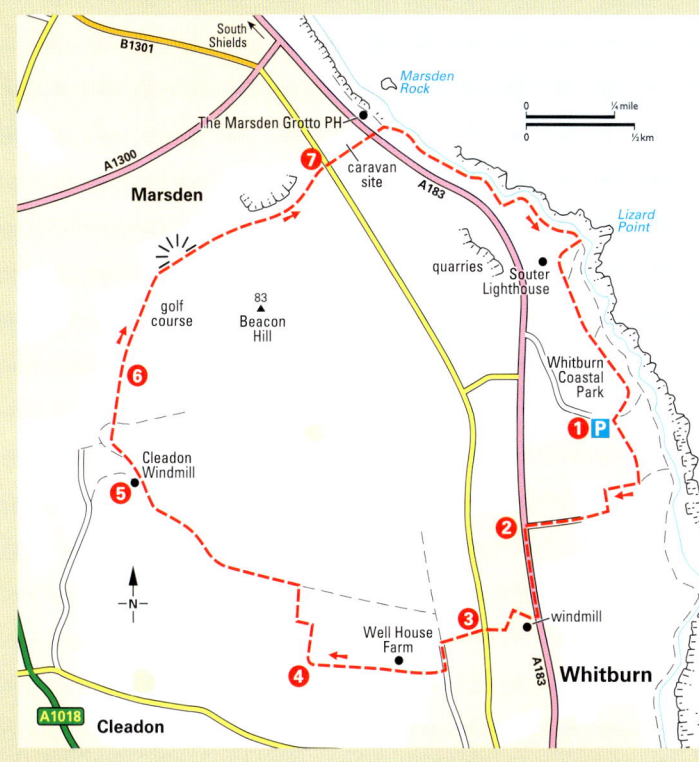

WALK 124

ALONG HADRIAN'S WALL

The Romans built the Wall to repel the Picts and Britons. It was planned to span the land between the River Irthing at Thirlwall and Newcastle, but added a turf wall that would extend to the west coast at Bowness on the Solway Firth. After the Romans left Britain the Wall decayed and its masonry was re-used.

DISTANCE/TIME 8 miles (12.9km) 4h **MAP** OS Explorer OL43 Hadrian's Wall **START** Steel Rigg (pay) car park; grid ref: NY750677 **TRACKS** Mainly well-walked National Trails, 16 stiles **THE PUB** The Milecastle Inn, Military Road, nr Haltwhistle. Tel: 01434 321372; www.milecastle-inn.co.uk

1 From the car park descend into a grassy depression beneath Peel Crags. The path here arcs left and climbs back to the ridge in a series of steps before following the cliff tops past Turret 39a and Milecastle 39.

2 There's another dip, then a climb to Highshield Crags. Beyond the lake the footpath climbs past Hotbank farm.

3 At the next dip, Rapishaw Gap, turn left over the ladder stile and follow the waymarked Pennine Way across undulating moorland. The first stile lies in the far right corner of a large rushy enclosure. A clear cart track develops beyond a dyke and climbs to a ridge on Ridley Common where you turn half left to descend a grassy ramp.

4 The path slowly arcs right to meet and cross a fenced cart track at Cragend. Here a grass track zigzags down to reach a moorland depression with Greenlee Lough in full view to your left. At the bottom the ground can be marshy and the path becomes indistinct in places. A waymark points a sharp right turn but the path loses itself on the bank above it. Head north here, keeping the farmhouse of East Stonefolds at ten minutes to the hour. The next stile lies in a kink in the cross wall.

5 Beyond this, turn half left to cross a field, cross a ladder stile and turn left along the farm track, passing through East Stonefolds. The track ends at West Stonefolds. Right of way should pass through the farm and over a stile on the right past the farmhouse. They encourage you to take the route in a field at the back of the farm (on the right) by leaving a 'dogs running free' sign.

6 Past the house continue, with a wall to the left, along a grassy ride, and go over a step stile to reach a junction of routes. Go straight ahead on the permissive path, signposted to the Greenlee Lough Birdhide. The path follows a fence to the lake. Ignore the stile unless you want to go to the hide, but instead continue walking alongside the fence.

7 Go over the next stile and cross wetlands north of the lake on a duckboard path, which swings right to a gate. Beyond this continue on the path, northwest, guided by waymarker posts to the farm track by the healthy-looking conifers of the Greenlee Plantation.

8 Turn left and follow the track past Gibbs Hill farm. Past the farmhouse a tarmac lane leads back towards the Wall. Turn left at the T-junction to return to the car park.

DISTANCE/TIME 13 miles (20.9km) 2h30 **MAP** OS Explorer OL42 Kielder Water & Forest **START** Falstone car park; grid ref: NY723874 **TRACKS** Minor roads, lanes and tracks **CYCLE HIRE** Kielder Castle Visitor Centre, Kielder. Tel: 01434 250392 **THE PUB** The Pheasant Inn, Stannersburn, Falstone. Tel: 01434 240382

DISTANCE/TIME 12 miles (19.3km) 2h **MAP** OS Explorer OL43 Hadrian's Wall **START** National Park Visitor Centre pay car park at Once Brewed; grid ref: NY752668 **TRACKS** Roads and country lanes **CYCLE HIRE** Eden's Lawn Cycle Hire, Haltwhistle. Tel: 01434 320443 **THE PUB** Twice Brewed Inn, Once Brewed, Bardon Mill. Tel: 01434 344534

BOTH SIDES OF THE TYNE

This cycle ride takes you along both banks of the River North Tyne which has its source on Deadwater Fell in the nearby Cheviot Hills. It then flows into Europe's largest artificial lake at Kielder Water before emerging at Falstone then flowing south to join the River South Tyne at the 'meeting of waters' near Hexham. From here it continues as the River Tyne into the city of Newcastle. This is a very peaceful route through some splendid scenery. At Kielder Water there is a range of family-friendly activities including watersports and walking trails and at this point there is the opportunity to extend this route to include some of the many cycle trails through Kielder Forest. It is also worth spending some time exploring Falstone village. The Victorian schoolroom is part of the Tynedale Renewable Energy Trail and has been converted into an excellent tea room, while the village churchyard has several interesting gravestones from the early 18th century. Look out for one depicting a girl holding hands with a skeleton. Part of the run out from Falstone takes you along the disused line of the old Borders County Railway that once ran from Riccarton Junction to Hexham. It now forms part of the Reivers Cycle Route before disappearing under water at Kielder Dam.

1 Exit the car park at the start and turn right on to a lane. Continue along it to cross a bridge by a church. The lane turns right and away from the river then forks at Mouseyhaugh. Keep left here, crossing a cattle grid, then go through a gate.

2 Cross another bridge and go through another gate then continue along the track to High Hawkhope Farm. Go through a gate and circle the right of the farmstead to reach a crossroads. Turn left on to Regional Cycle Route 10, The Reivers Route.

3 Head uphill on this broad track passing through a forestry plantation. Just before the top of the hill the trees stop and you can see along Kielder Water. On the left is a memorial erected to commemorate the opening of the reservoir by Her Majesty the Queen on 26 May 1982.

4 Continue cycling to the top of the hill and then turn left to head down to and along the road across the dam. At a T-junction with the road turn left and keep on this route, passing the Pheasant Inn to reach the Tyne Bridge after 4.5 miles (7.2km).

5 Cross the bridge and head uphill to the hamlet of Lanehead. At a junction turn left on to a narrow lane signposted to Donkleywood. This is The Reivers Route, which meanders along the edge of the Tyne valley going through several gates.

6 At one point you will cross over the old railway line at what was a level crossing, still with well-preserved gates. Beyond Donkleywood, climb to the highest point of the route before descending into Falstone. Go under a railway bridge then turn right opposite the Blackcock Inn to return to where you started.

AROUND HADRIAN'S WALL & THE STANEGATE

This cycle route takes you along the finest section of Hadrian's Wall, past two Roman forts and along an ancient Roman road. Hadrian's Wall became a World Heritage Site in 1987 and in 2005 the name was changed to the Frontiers of the Roman Empire WHS. The site was extended to include some remains of the Roman frontier between the rivers Rhine and Danube. The Roman Empire had conquered as far as Mons Graupius in Northern Scotland by AD 83 but unable to hold their gains the Romans gradually withdrew to a line stretching from the Solway Firth to the Tyne. There they built a chain of forts along the road known since medieval times as the Stanegate. Emperor Hadrian decided to consolidate the frontiers of his empire and in AD 122 had a wall built close to the line of Stanegate to 'separate the Romans from the barbarians' in the north who refused to accept Roman dominion. The ride takes in Housesteads fort, the most visited on the Wall, so in order to avoid the crowds try not to plan your ride for a weekend falling in high summer. Along the route the views of the Wall and the surrounding countryside are spectacular and the temptation to dismount and explore will be strong.

1 Exit the car park and turn left. At a T-junction turn right on to the B6318. (A turn almost immediately to the left heads uphill to reach a car park at Steel Rigg, where a footpath leads walkers along one of the finest sections of Hadrian's Wall.)

2 Continue along the B6318. This is a straight, undulating road with a superb view of the Wall. After cycling approximately 2 miles (3.2km) pass a turn-off signed for Bardon Mill on your right and in another 0.5 mile (0.8km) pass the car park for Housesteads fort.

3 Housesteads is the most complete Roman fort in Britain and you may want to spend some time exploring here. Afterwards continue along the road for another 1.7 miles (2.7km) then turn right at a sign for Haydon Bridge. The building on the corner here has a tea room and is built on the site of a Roman signal station.

4 Head along this narrow lane cycling downhill at first, followed by a short, energetic pull up to the top of the next hill. Just past Grindon Hill Farm take a right turn at the crossroads on to Cycle Route 72, heading towards Bardon Mill. This is the line of the Stanegate, an important Roman road that ran from Corbridge to Carlisle.

5 Keep ahead on 'Cycle Route 72' with a grand view of the Wall on your right and over Thorngrafton Common on your left. There is a great view of Housesteads and, further on, Vindolanda. After a downhill section make a right turn, still continuing on Cycle Route 72, following signs for Vindolanda.

6 Head downhill to reach the museum entrance. Pass by the entrance then continue uphill, passing the top car park and a thatched cottage before reaching a T-junction. Turn right on to Pennine Cycle Route 68 and keep on it to reach the start.

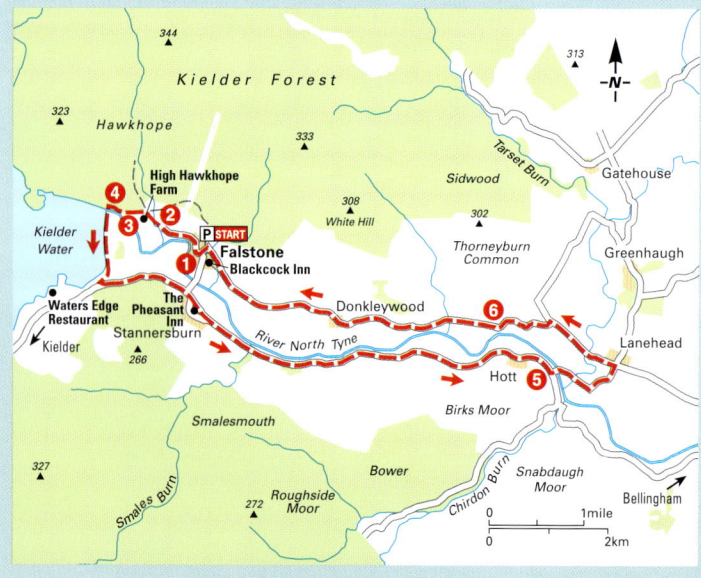

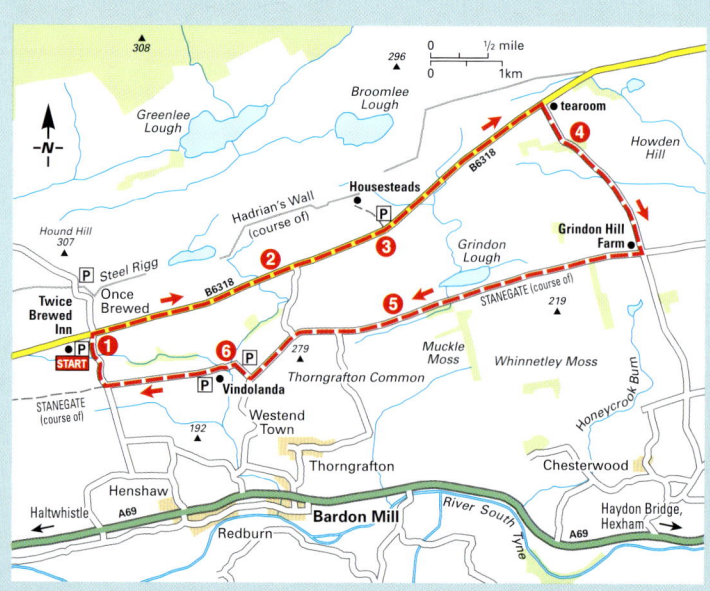

LAKE DISTRICT

■ TOURIST INFORMATION

Ambleside
Central Buildings, Market Cross.
Tel: 01539 432582

Barrow-in-Furness
Forum 28, Duke Street.
Tel: 01229 894784

Bowness-on-Windermere
Glebe Road, Bowness Bay.
Tel: 01539 442895

Coniston
Main car park. Tel: 01539 441533

Grange-over-Sands
Victoria Hall, Main Street.
Tel: 01539 534026

Kendal
Town Hall, Highgate. Tel: 01539 725758

Keswick
Moot Hall, Market Square.
Tel: 01768 772645

Ullswater
Main car park, Glenridding.
Tel: 01768 482414

Ulverston
Coronation Hall, County Square.
Tel: 01229 587120

Whitehaven
Market Hall, Market Place.
Tel: 01946 852939

Windermere
Victoria Street. Tel: 01539 446499

■ PLACES OF INTEREST

Abbot Hall Art Gallery
Kirkland, Kendal. Tel: 01539 722464

Abbot Hall Museum of Lakeland Life & Industry
Kirkland, Kendal. Tel: 01539 722464

The Beacon
West Strand, Whitehaven.
Tel: 01946 592302

Beatrix Potter Gallery
Main Street, Hawkshead.
Tel: 01539 436355

Brantwood
Coniston. Tel: 01539 441396

Brockhole
On the A591, Windermere.
Tel: 01539 446601

Cars of the Stars Motor Museum
Standish Street, Keswick.
Tel: 01768 773757. Cars from TV and film.

Cartmel Priory
Cartmel, Grange-over-Sands.
Tel: 01539 536261

Castlerigg Stone Circle
2 miles (3.2km) east of Keswick.

Cumberland Pencil Museum
Southey Works, Carding Mill Lane,
Keswick. Tel: 01768 773626
Displays of the history of the pencil and
details of modern production methods.

Dock Museum
North Road, Barrow-in-Furness.
Tel: 01229 894444

Dove Cottage
Grasmere. Tel: 01539 435544

Eskdale Mill
Boot. Tel: 01946 723335

Furness Abbey
Barrow-in-Furness. Tel: 01229 823420
Extensive remains of the Cistercian abbey
built in 1147.

Haig Colliery Mining Museum
Kells, Whitehaven. Tel: 01946 599949;
www.haig1.freeserve.co.uk

Hardknott Castle Roman Fort
Hardknott Pass. Remains of the Roman
fort can be seen at the western end of
Hardknott Pass.

Hill Top
Near Sawrey. Tel: 01539 436269

Holker Hall and Gardens
Cark-in-Cartmel, Grange-over-Sands.
Tel: 01539 558328. Includes the Lakeland
Motor Museum.

Kendal Museum of Natural History & Archaeology
Station Road, Kendal.
Tel: 01539 721374

Keswick Mining Museum
Otley Road, Keswick. Tel: 017687 80055
Mining memorabilia and an exceptional
bookshop devoted to geology and
industrial archaeology.

Keswick Museum and Art Gallery
Fitz Park, Station Road, Keswick.
Tel: 01768 773263. Displays of letters
and manuscripts; also local geology and
natural history.

The Lakes Discovery Museum @ the Armitt
Rydal Road, Ambleside. Tel: 01539 431212

Laurel & Hardy Museum
4c Upper Brook Street, Ulverston.
Tel: 01229 582292

Ravenglass & Eskdale Railway
Ravenglass. Tel: 01229 717171
Steam and diesel trains run along a
7-mile (11.2km) track from Ravenglass
to Dalegarth.

Ruskin Museum
The Institute, Coniston. Tel: 01539 441164

Windermere Steamboat Museum
Rayrigg Road, Windermere.
Tel: 01539 445565

The World of Beatrix Potter
The Old Laundry, Bowness-on-
Windermere. Tel: 01539 488444

■ FOR CHILDREN

Trotters World of Animals
Coalbeck Farm, Bassenthwaite, Keswick.
Tel: 01768 776239;
www.trottersworld.com
A small, conservation-oriented zoo, with
feeding displays and a soft play area.

■ PERFORMING ARTS

The Brewery Arts Centre
Kendal. Tel: 01539 725133

Civic Hall
Whitehaven. Tel: 01946 852821

Coronation Hall
Ulverston. Tel: 01229 582610

Forum 28 Theatre & Arts Centre
28 Duke Street, Barrow-in-Furness.
Tel: 01229 894489

The Old Laundry
Crag Brow, Bowness-on-Windermere.
Tel: 01539 488444

Rosehill Theatre
Moresby, Whitehaven. Tel: 01946 692422

Theatre by the Lake
Lakeside, Keswick. Tel: 01768 774411

■ SPORTS & ACTIVITIES

ANGLING

Bassenthwaite Lake
Permits from Keswick TIC or
Pheasant Inn. Tel: 01768 776234

Derwent Water
Permits from Keswick TIC.

BOAT HIRE

Derwent Water
Derwent Water Marina, Portinscale.
Tel: 01768 772912

Keswick Launch
Tel: 01768 772263

BOAT TRIPS

Coniston
Coniston Ferry Services, Castle Buildings,
Near Sawrey, Ambleside.
Tel: 01539 436216
Steam Yacht Gondola, Gondola Pier,
Coniston. Tel: 01539 441288

Derwent Water
Regular passenger service. Keswick
Launch. Tel: 01768 772263

Ullswater
Ullswater Navigation & Transit Co. Ltd.
Tel: 01768 482229

Windermere
Windermere Lake Cruises, Newby
Bridge, Ulverston. Tel: 01539 531188

CYCLE HIRE

Ambleside
Biketreks, Rydal Road. Tel: 01539 431505
Country Lanes, Windermere Railway
Station. Tel: 01539 444544

Keswick
Keswick Motor Co, Lake Road.
Tel: 01768 772064
Keswick Mountain Bike Centre, Southey
Hill Estate. Tel: 01768 775202

Whitehaven
Haven Cycles, Preston Street.
Tel: 01946 63263

CYCLING

Coast-to-Coast (C2C) Cycle Route
A 140-mile (224km) route linking
Whitehaven and Workington to
Sunderland.

The Eskdale Trail
The Ravenglass and Eskdale Railway is
a virtually traffic-free route. Details from
stations at Ravenglass or Dalegarth.

The Reivers Cycle Route
A 190-mile (306km) cycling route
which runs from Tynemouth as far
as Whitehaven.

Wear to Wear (W2W) Cycle Route
This superb trans-Pennine route
(Sustrans Regional Route 20) begins
on Walney Island and traverses the
southern lakes on its 151-mile
(243km) path northeast.

GOLF COURSES

Barrow-in-Furness
Barrow Golf Club, Rakesmoor Lane,
Hawcoat. Tel: 01229 825444
Furness Golf Club, Central Drive,
Isle of Walney.
Tel: 01229 471232

Keswick
Keswick Golf Club, Threlkeld Hall.
Tel: 01768 779324

Whitehaven
Whitehaven Golf Club, Red Lonning.
Tel: 01946 591144

HORSE-RIDING

Kendal
Holmescales Riding Centre, Holmescales
Farm, Old Hutton. Tel: 01539 729388

Windermere
Lakeland Pony Trekking, Limefitt
Park, Troutbeck, Windermere.
Tel: 01539 431999
www.lakelandponytrekking.co.uk

LONG-DISTANCE FOOTPATHS & TRAILS

The Cistercian Way
This 33-mile (52.8km) walking route goes
from Grange-over-Sands to Roa Island,
near Barrow-in-Furness.

Coast-to-Coast Walk
A 190-mile (304km) walk from
St Bees Head to Robin Hood's Bay
in North Yorkshire.

The Cumberland Way
An 82-mile (131.2km) crossing of the
Lake District from Ravenglass to Appleby.

The Furness Way
A 71-mile (114km) walk from Arnside
to Ravenglass and crossing the
Furness Peninsula.

The Pennine Way
The country's premier National Trail (all
268 miles of it) crosses the high Pennine
ridge between Dufton and Alston;
www.nationaltrail.co.uk/PennineWay/

The West Lakes Way
A 70-mile (112km) walking route from
Whitehaven to Millom taking in Scafell
and Black Combe.

SAILING

Bassenthwaite
Bassenthwaite Sailing Club.
Tel: 01768 776341

Crummock Water
Woodhouse, Buttermere
Permits and boats for hire.
Tel: 01768 770208

■ ANNUAL EVENTS & CUSTOMS

Ambleside
Rushbearing Ceremony, first Sat in Jul.
Ambleside Sports, late Jul.
Lake District Summer Music Festival,
early to mid-Aug.

Barrow-in-Furness
Barrow Horticultural Society Show,
early Sep.

Bassenthwaite
Sailing Week, early Aug.

Borrowdale
Borrowdale Shepherds' Meet and Show,
mid-Sep.

Buttermere
Shepherds' Meet, mid-Sep.
Buttermere Show, early Oct.

Cartmel
Cartmel Steeplechases, Spring
Bank Holiday.
Agricultural Show, early Aug.
Cartmel Races, Aug Bank Holiday.

Coniston
Coniston Water Festival, late May to
early Jun.

Eskdale
Eskdale Tup (ram) Show, late Sep.
Eskdale Show, late Sep.

Grange-over-Sands
Edwardian Festival, mid-Jun.
Lakeland Rose Show, Jul.

Kendal
Kendal Torchlight Procession, early Sep.
Westmorland County Show, early Sep.

Keswick
Keswick Literature Festival, Mar.
Keswick Jazz Festival, mid-May.
Keswick Mountain Festival, May.
Carnival, mid-Jun.
Keswick Convention, mid to late Jul.
Keswick Victorian Fair, early Dec.

Loweswater
Loweswater and Brackenthwaite
Agricultural Show, mid-Sep.

Ulverston
North Lonsdale Agricultural Show,
late Jul.
Lantern Procession, Sep.

Whitehaven
Copeland Carnival, early Jul.

YORKSHIRE MOORS
■ TOURIST INFORMATION

Danby
The Moors Centre. Tel: 01287 660654

Guisborough
Priory Grounds, Church Street.
Tel: 01287 633801

Hutton-le-Hole
Ryedale Folk Museum.
Tel: 01751 417367

Scarborough
Brunswick Shopping Centre,
Westborough. Tel: 01723 383636
Harbourside, Sandside.
Tel: 01723 383636

Whitby
Langborne Road. Tel: 01723 383636

■ PLACES OF INTEREST

Byland Abbey
Coxwold. Tel: 01347 868614

Captain Cook Memorial Museum
Grape Lane, Whitby. Tel: 01947 601900;
www.cookmuseumwhitby.co.uk

Guisborough Priory
Guisborough. Tel: 01287 633801

National Trust Centre
Ravenscar. Tel: 01723 870138 or 870423

The Moors Centre
Lodge Lane, Danby. Tel: 01439 772737
or 01287 660792;
www.nationalparks.gov.uk/nym_core

Rievaulx Abbey
Rievaulx. Tel: 01439 798228

Rievaulx Terrace
Rievaulx. Tel: 01439 798340

Robin Hood's Bay Museum
Fisherhead.

Ryedale Folk Museum
Hutton-le-Hole. Tel: 01751 417367;
www.ryedalefolkmuseum.co.uk

Scarborough Castle
Tel: 01723 372451

Shandy Hall
Coxwold. Tel: 01347 868465

Tocketts Watermill
On A173, 1 mile (1.6km) east
of Guisborough.

Whitby Abbey
East Cliff, Whitby. Tel: 01947 603568

■ PERFORMING ARTS

Futurist Theatre & Cinema
Foreshore Road, Scarborough.
Tel: 01723 365789;
www.futuristtheatre.co.uk

Spa Entertainment Complex
South Bay, Scarborough.
Tel: 01723 376774
www.scarboroughspa.co.uk

Spa Theatre
South Bay, Scarborough.
Tel: 01723 357869

Stephen Joseph Theatre
Westborough, Scarborough.
Tel: 01723 370541; www.sjt.uk.com

Whitby Pavilion Theatre
West Cliff, Whitby. Tel: 01947 604855
or 820625; www.whitbypavilion.co.uk

■ SPORTS & ACTIVITIES
ANGLING
Fly fishing
The Mere, Scarborough. Tickets on site.
Sea fishing
Staithes & Whitby.
Ask at the harbour, or the TIC.
CYCLE HIRE
Oswaldkirk
Golden Square Campsite, Oswaldkirk.
Tel: 01439 788269

BOAT TRIPS
Whitby
Trips round the bay leave from the
West Pier.
GOLF COURSES
Scarborough
North Cliff Golf Club, North Cliff Avenue.
Tel: 01723 360786
South Cliff Golf Club, Deepdale Avenue.
Tel: 01723 365150
HORSE-RIDING
Farsyde Stud and Riding Centre.
Tel: 01947 880249;
www.farsydefarmcottages.co.uk
LONG-DISTANCE FOOTPATHS & TRAILS
The Cleveland Way
A 110-mile (176km) walk from Helmsley
to Filey Brigg; www.clevelandway.gov.uk
The Esk Valley Walk
Scarborough to Whitby Railway Trail
Route for walkers and cyclists follows the
old railway line. (Cycle hire at Hawsker.)

■ ANNUAL EVENTS & CUSTOMS

Castleton
Castleton Show, Sep.

Coxwold
Coxwold Fair, Jun.
Agricultural Show, mid-Aug.

Egton
Egton Show, late Aug.

Egton Bridge
Gooseberry Show, early Aug.

Helmsley
Ryedale Festival, Jul/Aug.

Hutton-le-Hole
World Merrills Championships, (board
game) Sep.

Robin Hood's Bay
Folk Festival, Jun.

Rosedale
Rosedale Show, Aug.

Scarborough
Scarborough Fayre, Jun.
International Music Festival, Jun.
Scarborough Cricket Festival, end
Aug/Sep.

Stokesley
Stokesley Show, Sep.

Whitby
Planting of the Penny Hedge,
Ascension Eve, May.
Morris Dance Festival, Jun.
Blessing of Boats, mid-Jul.
Whitby Angling Festival, Jul.
Whitby Folk Festival, Aug.
Whitby Regatta, mid-Aug.

YORKSHIRE DALES
■ TOURIST INFORMATION

Grassington
National Park Centre, Colvend, Hebden
Road. Tel: 01756 752774

Harrogate
Royal Baths, Crescent Road.
Tel: 01423 537300

Ingleton
Community Centre Car Park.
Tel: 015242 41049

Kirkby Lonsdale
24 Main Street. Tel: 015242 71437

Knaresborough
9 Castle Courtyard. Tel: 0845 3890 177

Pateley Bridge
18 High Street. Tel: 0845 3890 179

Richmond
Friary Gardens, Victoria Road.
Tel: 01748 850252/825994

Ripon
Minster Road. Tel: 0845 3890 178

Settle
Town Hall, Cheapside. Tel: 01729 825192

Skipton
38 Coach Street. Tel: 01756 792809

■ PLACES OF INTEREST

Bolton Abbey Estate
Visitor centres and gift shops.
Tel: 01756 718009. Fee for the car parks.

Craven Museum & Gallery
Town Hall, High Street, Skipton.
Tel: 01756 706407

Dales Countryside Museum
Station Yard, Hawes. Tel: 01969 666210

Dent Village Heritage Centre
Dent. Tel: 015396 25800;
www.dentvillageheritagecentre.co.uk

Easby Abbey
Richmond. Medieval abbey remains
(English Heritage) set beside the
River Swale.

**Fountains Abbey & Studley Royal
Water Garden**
Ripon. Tel: 01765 608888
World Heritage Site managed by the
National Trust. Parliament Street,
Harrogate.Tel: 01423 556746

Georgian Theatre Royal
Victoria Road, Richmond.
Tel: 01748 823710
www.georgiantheatreroyal.co.uk
Dating from 1788, the theatre closed in
1848, but was restored and reopened in
1962. It is still used for live productions
and it has a museum with old playbills,
photographs and the oldest complete set
of painted scenery in England.

Green Howards Regimental Museum
Trinity Church Square, Market Place,
Richmond. Tel: 01748 826561
The military history of the Green
Howards, going back to the 17th century,
is illustrated here, together with displays
of uniforms, weapons and medals.

How Stean Gorge
Near Lofthouse, Pateley Bridge.
Tel: 01423 755666

Ingleborough Cave
Clapham. Tel: 015242 51242
Tours of cave formations and streams.

Ingleton Waterfalls Trail
The Falls, Ingleton. Tel: 015242 41617

A 4.5 mile (7.2km) circular trail on boardwalks in the gorge and through meadows and woodland.

Jervaulx Abbey
Jervaulx. Tel: 01677 460226; www.jervaulxabbey.com.

Knaresborough Castle
Knaresborough. Tel: 01423 556188

Mother Shipton's Cave
Knaresborough. Tel: 01423 864600

Nidderdale Museum
Millfield Street, Pateley Bridge.
Tel: 01423 711225

Norton Conyers
Ripon. Tel: 01765 640333

Old Courthouse Museum
Castle Yard, Knaresborough.
Tel: 01423 869274

Parcevall Hall Gardens
Off B625 between Grassington and Pateley Bridge. Tel: 01756 720311

RHS Garden Harlow Carr
Crag Lane, Otley Road, Harrogate.
Tel: 01423 565418; www.rhs.org.uk

Richmond Castle
Richmond. Tel: 01748 822493
Occupying a stunning position overlooking the River Swale, the castle is now in ruins, but visitors can see the keep, two towers and Scolland's Hall.

Richmondshire Museum
Ryder's Wynd, Richmond.
Tel: 01748 825611
Museum of local history.

Swaledale Folk Museum
Ripon Museum Trust, The Workhouse Museum, Allhallowgate.
Tel: 01765 690799;
www.riponmuseums.co.uk

Royal Pump Room Museum
Royal Parade, Harrogate.
Tel: 01423 556188

Skipton Castle
Tel: 01756 792442
Very well-preserved medieval castle.

Stump Cross Caverns
Between Pateley Bridge and Grassington. On B6265 west of Pateley Bridge.
Tel: 01756 752780

Upper Wharfedale Folk Museum
Grassington Square, Grassington. Exhibits relating to Upper Wharfedale all housed in 18th-century former lead-miners' cottages.

Wensleydale Creamery Visitor Centre
Gayle Lane, Hawes. Tel: 01969 667664

Wensleydale Railway
Leeming Bar Station. Tel: 08454 505474

White Scar Cave
On B6255 north of Ingleton.
Tel: 015242 41244
Britain's largest show caves, with tours to falls and rivers.

Yorkshire Dales National Park Centre
Malham. Tel: 01729 830363
Local literature, displays on the natural

history, the local community and the work of conservation bodies. 24-hour information screen.

■ FOR CHILDREN
Lightwater Valley Theme Park & Village
North Stainley. Tel: 0870 458 0040

■ SPORTS & ACTIVITIES
ANGLING
Fly fishing
Ingleton
Trout fishing on local rivers. Permits available from Village News, Main Street, Ingleton. Tel: 015242 41683

Kirkby Lonsdale
River Lune. Weekly and daily permits available from Kirkby Lonsdale Tourist Information Centre.
Tel: 015242 71437

Pateley Bridge Scar House Dam
Day tickets from Lofthouse Post Office.
Tel: 01423 755203
Also check 'Where to fish' on www.harrogate.gov.uk

Skipton
River Aire in and around Skipton. Contact Tourist Information Centre in Skipton.

BALLOON FLIGHTS
Skipton
Airborne Adventures, Old Burton Croft, Rylstone. Tel: 0870 7554447;
www.airborne.co.uk

BOAT HIRE
Knaresborough
Blenkhorns Boat Hire, 2 Waterside, High Bridge. Tel: 01423 862105
Rowing boats, punts and canoes for hire.

Skipton
For information about boat hire contact Skipton Tourist Information Centre.
Tel: 01756 792809

BOAT TRIPS
Skipton
Various companies in the area operate boat trips along the Leeds and Liverpool Canal including Pennine Boat Trips of Skipton, Waterside Court, Coach Street.
Tel: 01756 790829
Details of other operators are available from Skipton Tourist Information Centre.
Tel: 01756 792809

CYCLE HIRE
Ingleton
Howson's. 13 Main Street.
Tel: 01524 241422

Skipton
Dave Ferguson Cycles, 1 Brook Street.
Tel: 01756 795367

CYCLING
The Yorkshire Dales
Cycle Way
This is a 130-mile (209.2km) circular cycling route that starts and finishes in Skipton.

GUIDED WALKS
Several guided walks in the area are organised by the National Park Authority, Friends of Dalesrail and Dalesbus Ramblers. For more information contact the Tourist Information Centre in Settle. Week-long as well as other short break holidays for walkers in the Yorkshire Dales are organised by H. F. Holidays Limited, Imperial House, Edgware Road, London.
Tel: 020 8905 9558;www.hfholidays.co.uk

HORSE-RACING
Ripon
2 miles (3.2km) southeast of Ripon on B6265. Tel: 01765 602156;
www.ripon-races.co.uk

HORSE-RIDING
Pateley Bridge
Bewerley School of Horsemanship, Bewerley Old Hall. Tel: 01423 712249

Malham
Yorkshire Dales Trekking Centre, Holme Farm. Tel: 01729 830352; www.ydtc.net

LONG-DISTANCE FOOTPATHS & TRAILS
The Dales Way
A fantastic 81-mile (130km) lowland walk through the heart of the Yorkshire Dales connecting Ilkley in the south with Bowness-on-Windermere in the north.

The Nidderdale Way
This 53-mile (85km) walk tours the moors and gritstone outcrops of the lovely valley of Nidderdale, starting and finishing in Pateley Bridge.

The Pennine Way
The mother of all long-distance walks enters the area west of Skipton, before heading off over the fells from Malham.

The Six Dales Hike
A 42-mile (67.6km) walk through North Yorkshire from Settle to Skipton.

The Yorkshire Water Way
The first 41-mile (66km) section of this reservoir-themed walk enters Upper Nidderdale from Kettlewell, before crossing over to the Washburn Valley on its way to Ilkley.

■ ANNUAL EVENTS & CUSTOMS
Dent
Dent Gala, late Aug.
Fountains Abbey
Egg-rolling, Easter Mon.
Grassington
Grassington Festival,
mid-Jun to early Jul.
Grassington Festival,
mid-Jun to early Jul.
Hardraw
Hardraw Brass Band Festival, contact The Green Dragon, Hardraw.
Tel: 01969 667392
Harrogate
Harrogate International Youth Music Festival, held every Easter, with

performances throughout the region including at Ripon Cathedral.
Spring Flower Show, late Apr.
The Great Yorkshire Show, mid-Jul.
Harrogate International Festival, late Jul to early Aug.
Trans-Pennine Run for vintage vehicles, from Manchester to Harrogate, early Aug.
Autumn Flower Show, mid-Sep.
Hawes
Hawes Gala, late Jun.
Hubberholme
On New Year's Day the 'Hubberholme Parliament' sits in the George Inn after a church service.
Ingleton
Annual Fellsman Hike, Ingleton to Threshfield, early May.
Gala and mountain race, mid-Jul.
Horticultural Show, early Sep.
Northern Antiques Show, late Sep.
Jervaulx
Jervaulx Horse Trials, early Jun.
Malham
Malham Show, late Aug.
Pateley Bridge
Nidderdale Show, late Sep, held in Bewerley Park.
Reeth
Reeth Show, late Aug.
Richmond
The Richmond Meet, Spring Bank Holiday weekend.
The 'Poor Old Horse' Mummers' Play takes place around Christmas.
Ripon
Setting the Watch by the Ripon Hornblower every evening in the market place by the Obelisk at 9pm.
Every Thurs at 11am the Ripon Bellringer declares the market open.
International Festival, mid-Sep.
Ripon Charter Festival, late May to early Jun.
St Wilfrid's Feast Procession, Sat before the first Mon in Aug.
Settle
Maypole celebrations at Long Preston, Sat after May Day.
Skipton
Skipton Gala, early Jun.
Game Fair, held at Broughton Hall, late Jun.
Medieval Festival, early Dec.

NORTHUMBRIA & COAST
■ TOURIST INFORMATION
Alnwick
The Shambles. Tel: 01665 510665;
www.alnwick.gov.uk
Bellingham
Fountain Cottage, Main Street.
Tel: 01434 220616
Berwick-upon-Tweed
106 Marygate. Tel: 01289 330733;
www.berwickonline.org.uk

Corbridge
Hill Street (seasonal). Tel: 01434 632815
Durham
2 Millennium Place. Tel: 0191 384 3720
Haltwhistle
Railway Station. Tel: 01434 322002
Hexham
Wentworth Car Park. Tel: 01434 652220
Northumberland National Park Headquarters
Eastburn, South Park, Hexham.
Tel: 01434 605555; www.northumberland-national-park.org.uk

■ **PLACES OF INTEREST**
Allenheads Heritage Centre
Tel: 01434 685568
Alnwick Castle
Tel: 01665 510777;
www.alnwickcastle.com
Aydon Castle
Corbridge.
Tel: 01434 632450;
www.english-heritage.org.uk
Bamburgh Castle
Tel: 01668 214515;
www.bamburghcastle.com
Barnard Castle
Tel: 01833 638212;
www.english-heritage.org.uk
Bellingham Heritage Centre
Station Yard, Woodburn Road.
Tel: 01434 220050
Berwick Castle
Berwick-upon-Tweed.
www.english-heritage.org.uk
Border History Museum
The Old Gaol, Hallgate, Hexham.
Tel: 01434 652349;
www.tynedaleheritage.org
Bowes Castle
Tel: 0191 269 1200;
www.english-heritage.org.uk
Brinkburn Priory
Longframlington.
Tel: 01665 570628;
www.english-heritage.org.uk
Chillingham Castle
Tel: 01668 215359;
www.chillingham-castle.com
Coquet Island, RSPB Reserve
Tel: 01665 712313
Durham Dales Centre
Castle Gardens, Stanhope.
Tel: 01388 527650;
www.durhamdalescentre.co.uk
Farne Islands & Longstone Lighthouse
Inner Farne and Staple Island.
Tel: 01665 721099;
www.nationaltrust.org.uk
Grace Darling Museum
Radcliffe Road, Bamburgh.
Tel: 01668 214465
Heatherslaw Corn Mill
Ford. Tel: 01890 820488;
www.ford-and-etal.co.uk

High Force
Near Middleton-in-Teesdale. England's highest waterfall.
Tel: 01833 640209; www.rabycastle.com
Killhope Lead Mining Centre
Tel: 01388 537505;
www.durham.gov.uk/killhope
Lady Waterford Hall
Ford. Tel: 01890 820503;
www.ford-and-etal.co.uk
Lindisfarne Centre
Marygate, Holy Island.
Tel: 01289 389004;
www.lindisfarne-heritage-centre.org
Lindisfarne Priory
Holy Island. Tel: 01289 389200;
www.english-heritage.org.uk
Moot Hall & Gallery
Market Place, Hexham.
Tel: 01434 652351
Paxton House
Paxton. Tel: 01289 386291;
www.paxtonhouse.co.uk
Rokeby Park
Rokeby, Barnard Castle.
Tel: 01833 637334
Vindolanda (Chesterholm)
Bardon Mill. Tel: 01434 344277;
www.english-heritage.org.uk

■ **FOR CHILDREN**
Durham Dales Centre
Castle Gardens, Stanhope.
Tel: 01388 527650;
www.durhamdalescentre.co.uk
Fenton Centre
Tel: 01668 216216;
www.fentoncentre.com
Farming and birds of prey.
Kielder Water Bird of Prey Centre
Tel: 01434 250400;
www. discoverit.co.uk/falconry
Marine Life Centre & Fishing Museum
Main Street, Seahouses.
Tel: 01665 721257
Otterburn Hall (YMCA)
Tel: 01830 520663;
www.otterburnhall.com
Forest walks and rare breeds.

■ **PERFORMING ARTS**
Alnwick
Playhouse. Tel: 01665 510785;
www.alnwickplayhouse.co.uk
Berwick-upon-Tweed
The Maltings Theatre and Arts Centre, Eastern Lane. Tel: 01289 330999;
www.maltingsberwick.co.uk
Hexham
The Queen's Hall Arts Centre, Beaumont Street, Hexham. Tel: 01434 652477

■ **SPORTS & ACTIVITIES**
ANGLING
Sea angling
Alnmouth: enquire at harbour.

Berwick-upon-Tweed: Shore fishing is restricted because of seals. For boat fishing, enquire at Berwick harbour.
Fly fishing
Kielder Water Visitor Centre.
Tel: 0870 240 3549. Permits from the machines at the lodge by the dam, at Leaplish Waterside Park and Bakethin Weir car park.
Coarse fishing
North Tyne River: Permits from the Black Cock Inn, Falstone.
Tel: 01434 240200
Also ask at TICs and tackle shops.
ABSEILING, CAVING & CLIMBING
Kingsway Adventure Centre, Alston Road, Middleton-in-Teesdale. Tel: 01833 640881; www.kingswaycentre.co.uk
ARCHERY
Kingsway Adventure Centre, Alston Road, Middleton-in-Teesdale.
Tel: 01833 640881
www.kingswaycentre.co.uk
CANOEING
Teesdale Canoe Club, Barnard Castle.
Tel: 01833 650691
Kingsway Adventure Centre, Alston Road, Middleton-in-Teesdale.
Tel: 01833 640881
www.kingswaycentre.co.uk
CYCLE HIRE
Alnwick
Alnwick Cycles, 24 Narrowgate.
Tel: 01665 606738;
www.alnwickcycles.co.uk
Bamburgh
Mountain Bike Hire. Tel: 01668 214535
Haltwhistle
Eden's Lawn Cycle Hire.
Tel: 01434 320443
Kielder
Kielder Bikes, Kielder Castle.
Tel: 01434 250392
Wooler
Haugh Head Garage. Tel: 01668 281316
CYCLE ROUTES & LONG-DISTANCE FOOTPATHS
Coast & Castles Cycle Route
A 200-mile (320km) ride, from Newcastle to Edinburgh.
The Northumberland Coast Walk
A 25-mile (40.2km) walk, from Alnmouth to Budle.
The Northumbrian Coastline
A 61-mile (98.2km) walk, from Berwick to North Shields.
Pennine Cycleway
A 355-mile (571km) ride from Derbyshire to Berwick.
Pennine Way
A 270-mile (434km) path from Kirk Yetholm in the Scottish Borders to Edale in Derbyshire.
Reivers Cycle Route
A 187-mile (300km) ride from Tynemouth to the Scottish borders and Whitehaven.

St Cuthbert's Way
A challenging 62-mile (100km) path that runs all the way from Melrose to pretty Lindisfarne.
Coast to Coast the Roman Way
This 150-mile (240km) cycle ride takes you from the Cumbrian coast to the North Sea.
Hadrian's Wall Path
An 84-mile (134km) walk from Wallsend to Bowness-on-Solway.

■ **ANNUAL EVENTS & CUSTOMS**
Alnwick
Shrove Tuesday Football.
Fair, late Jun–early Jul.
International Music Festival, late Jul–early Aug.
Northumbrian Gathering, Nov.
Alwinton
Border Shepherds' Show, mid-Oct.
Barnard Castle
Meet Weekend, late May.
Steam Fair, late May.
Tractor Pull, Apr, late Dec.
Truck Show, late Aug.
Bellingham
Bellingham Show, late Aug.
Berwick-upon-Tweed
Border Marches, May.
Riding the Bounds, early May.
May Fair, last Fri in May.
Northumbrian Gathering, weekend after Easter.
Bowes
Agricultural Show, early Sep.
Corbridge
Northumberland County Show, Spring Bank Holiday Mon.
Durham
Durham Miners' Gala, early Jul.
Durham County Show, mid-Jul.
Egg Rolling at Penshaw Monument, Easter weekend.
Kite Festival, early Jul.
Children's kites to competition types.
Eggleston
Eggleston Agricultural Show, mid-Sep.
Haltwhistle
Walking Festival, Spring and Autumn.
Hexham
Abbey Festival, mid-Sep.
Folkworks Hexham Gathering, late May.
Kielder Castle
Kielder Forest Festival, early Aug.
Otterburn
Otterburn Festival, Jul.
Rothbury
Traditional Music Festival, mid-Jul.
Stanhope
Agricultural Show, early Sep.
Whittingham
Whittingham Show, Aug.
Wooler
Glendale Show, late Aug.

PUBS
LAKE DISTRICT

Black Bull
1 Yewdale Road, Coniston LA21 8DU
Tel: 015394 41335;
www.conistonbrewery.com
Built around 400 years ago, this coaching inn is supplied by the excellent brewery to its rear. Bar meals are pretty standard, but the restaurant offers superb meals.

Boot Inn
Boot, Eskdale CA19 1TG
Tel: 0845 130 6224;
www.bootinn.co.uk
Formerly known as the Burnmoor, this friendly pub is good for families. The new conservatory dining area has enviable views of the surrounding fells and the garden in the summer.

Drunken Duck
Barngates, Ambleside LA22 0NG
Tel: 015394 36247;
www.drunkenduckinn.co.uk
This pub is a popular place to stop with walkers and cyclists. Here you can get excellent beer and food, and enjoy the fine views.

Golden Rule
Smithy Brow, Ambleside LA22 9AS
Tel: 015394 32257
Considered by many to be one of the few true pubs, this is a haven of good craic in front of real log fires. Beers are from Robinsons, and the food is rather limited, but the welcome is warm.

NORTH YORK MOORS

The Black Swan Inn
Oldstead, Coxwold YO61 4BL
Tel: 01347 868387;
www.theblackswaninn.com
This is a proper, traditional country pub with a relaxed and welcoming atmosphere. As you'd expect there is real ale available in the Drovers Bar, with its flagged floor, comfy chairs and a bar made by Robert Thompson's craftsmen in nearby Kilburn. There's a pretty garden, and views of woodland and hills. The food is freshly prepared from local ingredients and includes a particularly impressive choice for vegetarian diners.

Duke of Wellington Inn
Danby YO21 2LY
Tel: 01287 660351;
www.danby-dukeofwellington.co.uk
An attractive inn, in the scattered village of Danby with wide views of the village in its moorland setting. Inside, the décor is warm, welcoming and traditional, and there is a good selection of whiskies and local beers. The evening menu tends to be slightly more adventurous than the list of dishes offered at lunchtimes.

Laurel Inn
New Road, Robin Hood's Bay YO22 4SE
Tel: 01947 880400
Situated near to the bottom of the winding main street, this pub has a cosy, traditional atmosphere, with a welcoming open fire. It offers real ales and simple but wholesome food – including tasty thick soups in the winter.

The Mallyan Spout Hotel
The Common, Goathland YO22 5AN
Tel: 01947 896486;
www.mallyanspout.co.uk
You could bump into the stars of television's popular series *Heartbeat* (which is filmed near here), while you have afternoon tea at the Mallyan Spout. Choose from scones, delicious cakes and sandwiches, or a more substantial meal from the selection that's served all day. Relax in the lounge or enjoy the garden.

Moorcock Inn
Langdale End, Scarborough YO13 0BN
Tel: 01723 882268
This remote Moors pub has a tiled floor and an odd assortment of benches set out in two small rooms. However, you're guaranteed a decent drink, with a changing selection of beer from local, regional and microbreweries. Home-cooked food is available and in the summer, you can sit outside in the garden and enjoy the view.

YORKSHIRE DALES

The Angel
Hetton, Skipton BD23 6LT
Tel: 01765 730263
The reputation of this fine pub stretches far. A string of awards, including some from the AA, reflect its prominence as one of the best dining pubs in the north of England. The emphasis is on modern British food, freshly cooked and using local beef, lamb, pork and cheese. The fish is delivered fresh daily.

George Inn
Kirk Gill, Hubberholme, Skipton
BD23 5JE. Tel: 01756 760223;
www.thegeorge-inn.co.uk
The George Inn was a favourite of the writer J. B. Priestley. The 'Hubberholme Parliament' still sits here at New Year, but year round it is popular with visitors who come for the locally sourced lamb, pork and beef dishes. Typical dishes might include home-made soup, Yorkshire Pudding filled with mince or Black Sheep casserole (lamb cooked in the ubiquitous Black Sheep beer).

Green Dragon Inn
Hardraw, Hawes DL8 3LZ
Tel: 01969 667392;
www.greendragonhardraw.co.uk
Even without the access to Hardraw Force behind the pub, you would still want to visit the Green Dragon for its hand-pulled ales and traditional game casserole and home-made steak pie.

King's Head
Bridge Inn, Low Wath Road, Pateley Bridge, Harrogate HG3 5HL
Tel: 01423 711484
The Bridge may look like a traditional Dales pub, but it has only been open since 2003. In that short time it has established a reputation for excellent, locally sourced food and reliable beers.

Lister Arms
Malham, Skipton BD23 4DB
Tel: 01756 830330
An old coaching inn that caters well for the summer hordes while retaining a villagey feel inside. Diners will find a mix of Tex-Mex and traditional food, and there's a children's menu. Beer lovers may be tempted by the dazzling array of Belgian beers as well as the reliable stock of British cask and bottled ales.

Royal Oak
36 Kirkgate, Ripon HG4 1PB
Tel: 01765 602284
The Royal Oak is just a few steps away from Ripon's Market Square. Expect tasty, freshly cooked food to be served every lunchtime, from a 'salad or chips' style menu, and the beer is from Timothy Taylor's of Keighley.

Sun Inn
Main Street, Dent, Sedbergh LA10 5QL
Tel: 01539 92520
Dent may feel like a village in which time has stopped, but the Sun Inn was a pioneer in the revolution that revitalised many country pubs. The Dent brewery was established behind the pub in 1990, and though the brewery has now moved up the road to larger premises, you can still enjoy its output at the Sun, particularly when accompanied by flavoursome, no-nonsense food – the sausages and pies are truly excellent.

The Woolly Sheep Inn
38 Sheep Street, Skipton BD23 1HY
Tel: 01756 700966
At the foot of Skipton's main shopping street, this is a Taylor's pub, which serves excellent beer and 'hearty food for healthy appetites', by which they mean the usual mix of steak, chicken, Cumberland sausage and scampi.

NORTHUMBRIA & COAST

The Cheviot Hotel
Bellingham NE48 2AU
Tel: 01434 220696;
www.thecheviothotel.co.uk
The Cheviot Hotel is a great place to relax, either in the bar or the restaurant. Using locally sourced ingredients, the hotel's menu includes traditional dishes as well as sandwiches and snacks.

Victoria Inn
86 Hallgarth Street, Durham DH1 3AS
Tel: 0191 386 5269;
www.victoriainn-durhamcity.co.uk
The Victoria Inn opened its doors in 1899 and the interior has changed very little since then. In this Victorian gem there are real ales – an ever changing selection – and more than 70 types of whisky (and whiskey). However, the Victoria does not serve food.

Milecastle Inn
Military Road, Cawfields, Nr Haltwhistle NE49 9NN. Tel: 01434 321372;
www.milecastle-inn.co.uk
Only a few hundred yards from one of the best bits of Hadrian's Wall, the stone-built Milecastle Inn has a beamed bar – you can eat here or in the restaurant. Local game is a strong suit of the menu, and people travel miles just to sample one of the speciality pies – try the Poacher's Pie, with beef and venison, or the wild boar and duckling pie.

Dipton Mill Inn
Dipton Mill Road, Hexham NE46 1YA
Tel: 01434 606577
Dipton Mill Inn is a country pub standing a few miles from Hexham, beside a trickling stream. In the summer you can sit outside in the garden. The pub offers good bar meals, but its secret is that round the back there is the Hexhamshire microbrewery that produces its own real ale including tipples with such interesting names as Devil's Water, Whapweasel and Old Humbug.

Twice Brewed Inn
Bardon Mill, Hexham NE47 7AN
Tel: 01434 344534;
www.twicebrewedinn.co.uk
The Twice Brewed Inn is not far from both the Roman sites at Vindolanda and Housesteads, this inn is a wonderful place to relax from the rigours of marching up and down Hadrian's Wall. In the bar there is always a great selection of real ales, and you can eat well in the bar and in the restaurant. Local produce is to the fore. Don't forget to check out the varieties of cheese offered on the local cheeseboard.

TEA ROOMS
LAKE DISTRICT
The Apple Pie Eating House and Bakery
Rydal Road, Ambleside LA22 9AN
Tel: 015394 33679

Lakeland gingerbread is just one of the favourites here. With views over Bridge House and the hills, it's the ideal spot to enjoy the delicious treats, baked dishes or just a cappuccino.

Fellbites
Dalegarth Station, Boot, Eskdale
Tel: 01229 717171;
www.ravenglass-railway.co.uk

At the valley terminus of 'laal Ratty' the Fellbites café can serve a trainload of hungry and thirsty passengers at a time with freshly cooked food and hot tea and coffee. They use locally sourced ingredients in the preparation of their inviting food wherever possible.

Grange Bridge Cottage Tea Shop
Grange in Borrowdale, Borrowdale
CA12 5UQ. Tel: 017687 77201

Just a few yards from the famous double bridges, this 400-year-old cottage is home to a favourite on the Borrowdale tea shop trail. Home-baked cakes, cream teas and light lunches are served in the beautiful Riverside Tea Garden.

Harbour Gallery & Café
The Beacon, West Strand,
Whitehaven CA28 7LY
Tel: 01946 592302;
www.thebeaconwhitehaven.co.uk

Unwind in the peaceful Harbour Gallery Café, surrounded by the individual artwork of local and community groups. Freshly made sandwiches and snacks are available as well as excellent cream teas. Admission to the adjacent Harbour Gallery is free.

Hazlemere Café & Bakery
1 Yewbarrow Terrace,
Grange-over-Sands LA11 6ED
Tel: 015395 32972

Taste more than 25 types of cuppa at this traditional Victorian tea room. Local specialities include Cumberland Rum Nicky and pheasant burgers.

Low Sizergh Barn
Farm Shop and Tea Room,
Kendal LA8 8AE. Tel: 015395 60426;
www.lowsizerghbarn.co.uk

Low Sizergh Barn, on an organic dairy farm near the Lake District National Park, has everything from a tea room and farm shop to a craft gallery and farm trail. Enoy a cup of tea and then head out to watch the cows being milked!

Yew Tree Farm
Walkers' Tea Room, Coniston LA21 8DP
Tel: 015394 41433;
www.yewtree-farm.com

In a cosy farmhouse room furnished by Beatrix Potter herself, the Yew Tree continues a fine tradition of Cumbrian tea shops, where all of the food is made from scratch. The farm runs the tea shop and B&B and sells its own heritage meats.

NORTH YORK MOORS
Abbey Tea Rooms & Store
Rosedale Abbey YO18 8SA
Tel: 01751 417475

As well as plain, fruit and cheese scones, the tea rooms also serve cherry scones, scones made with treacle, scones made with blueberries and ginger...and you can spread them with blueberry and lavender jam. If you're more peckish, try the Yorkshire Ham afternoon tea.

Coxwold Tea Rooms
School House, Coxwold YO61 4AD
Tel: 01347 868077;
www.coxwoldschoolhouse.co.uk

You can eat in either of the two rooms, one very cosy and the other airy, or outside in the tea garden. You can treat yourself to afternoon tea with home-baking, or sample the delights of Yorkshire ham and eggs.

Elizabeth Botham & Sons
35/39 Skinner Street, Whitby YO21 3AH
Tel: 01947 602823; www.botham.co.uk

The tradition of fine baking, begun in 1865, is still going strong in this superior first-floor café. Your big problem will be what to choose from the menu – gingerbread with Wensleydale cheese, lemon buns, Yorkshire tea brack loaf, a cream tea, or salads, sandwiches or baked potatoes.

The Old Bakery Tea Rooms
Chapel Street, Robin Hood's Bay
YO22 4SQ. Tel: 01947 880709

A lovely, traditional tea room in the heart of the village. The bread and cakes are produced in the attached bakery. Scones with home-made preserves are a favourite, along with the chocolate and coffee cakes.

Stonehouse Bakery & Tea Shop
3 Briar Hill Avenue, Danby YO21 2LZ
Tel: 01287 660006

This traditional bakery in the centre of Danby bakes fabulous breads. They also make the range of delicious sandwiches for the adjoining tea shop. Cakes, too, come from the bakery's ovens, and their scones are perfect with jam and cream in a traditional cream tea.

YORKSHIRE DALES
Abbey Tea Rooms
Jervaulx, Ripon HG4 4PH
Tel: 01677 460226;
www.jervaulxabbey.com

Just across the road from the abbey ruins, the Abbey Tea Rooms do swift trade with visitors using the car park. Sit in the garden and enjoy the delicious home-made honeycakes, or scones, or sit inside for something more substantial.

Betty's
1 Parliament Street, Harrogate
HG1 2QU. Tel: 01423 877300;
www.bettys.co.uk

The story of this noble Yorkshire institution began here in 1919, and you can still choose from more than 50 varieties of tea and coffee and more than 300 breads, cakes and chocolates if you visit even now. The glorious art nouveau interior was designed by Charles Spindler's studio in Alsace in the 1930s.

Cavendish Pavilion
Bolton Abbey, Skipton BD23 6AN
Tel: 01756 710245;
www.cavendishpavilion.co.uk

Bolton Abbey has a number of tea rooms but this one has the best setting, between the priory ruins and The Strid.

Country Harvest
Ingleton, Carnforth LA6 3PE
Tel: 015242 42223;
www.country-harvest.co.uk

This is a great place to linger on your way home, or to take stock as you enter the Dales proper. The shop offers locally produced food and crafts. You can sample many of the items, including breads baked fresh on the premises.

Hazel Brow Farm
Low Row, Richmond DL11 6NE
Tel: 01748 886224;
www.hazelbrow.co.uk

With tray bakes, fresh scones, carrot cake and perhaps a 'Hazelbrowman's lunch', the Organic Café at Hazel Brow strives hard to ensure as much of its produce as possible is certified organic.

The Old Granary
17 High Street, Pateley Bridge,
Harrogate HG3 5AP
Tel: 01423 711852

You'll find The Old Granary in the centre of delightful Pateley Bridge. It's the perfect place for a quick bite or a light lunch. As well as various teas and coffees, the tasty home-made apple crumble is always popular. They are also sometimes open in the evenings for dinner.

Pen-y-ghent Café
Horton-in-Ribblesdale, Settle
BD24 0HE
Tel: 01729 860333

An institution amongst walkers, cyclists and runners who take up the Three Peaks Challenge, this is more than just a place for a mug of tea and a piece of home-made cake (although it is excellent for both). The weekend safety service ensures walkers can log in and log out.

Ye Olde Naked Man
Market Place, Settle BD24 9ED
Tel: 01729 823230

This busy tea shop and bakery in the Market Place takes its name from a peculiar relief carved above the doorway dated 1663. Inside sample tempting cakes or pastries or try a savoury pie. The shop sells the café's produce including delicious breads.

NORTHUMBRIA & COAST
Copper Kettle Tea Rooms
21 Front Street, Bamburgh NE69 7BW
Tel: 01668 214315;
www.bamburghcastle.com/business/copper-kettle.htm

On the main street which runs from the church to the castle, the Copper Kettle Tea Rooms is a delightful, cosy building, with panelled walls, arched windows and a pretty garden. As well as its famous cream teas, the café offers light meals and snacks, including excellent home-made soup.

Café Beangoose
Selby House, Holy Island,
Berwick-upon-Tweed TD15 2RX
Tel: 01289 389083

You'll find the Café Beangoose near to the Heritage Centre and the Priory, and it is a real treasure. Take tea either inside the pretty white building or in the attractive garden. There is a wide range of specialist teas and a choice of cakes.

The Almshouses
Palace Green, Durham DH1 3RL
Tel: 0191 386 1054

The Almshouses, a tea room with a fine view, hobnobs with Durham Castle on one side and the cathedral on the other. It's a handy place for an afternoon tea or for a choice of something more substantial at lunchtime.

Harley's Tea Rooms
Bridge Street, Rothbury NE65 7SE
Tel: 01669 620240

In the heart of Rothbury, this is a family-run café housed inside an old stone building. Harley's can provide you with a full afternoon tea or just a light snack.

Scotland

GLEN COE

Scotland

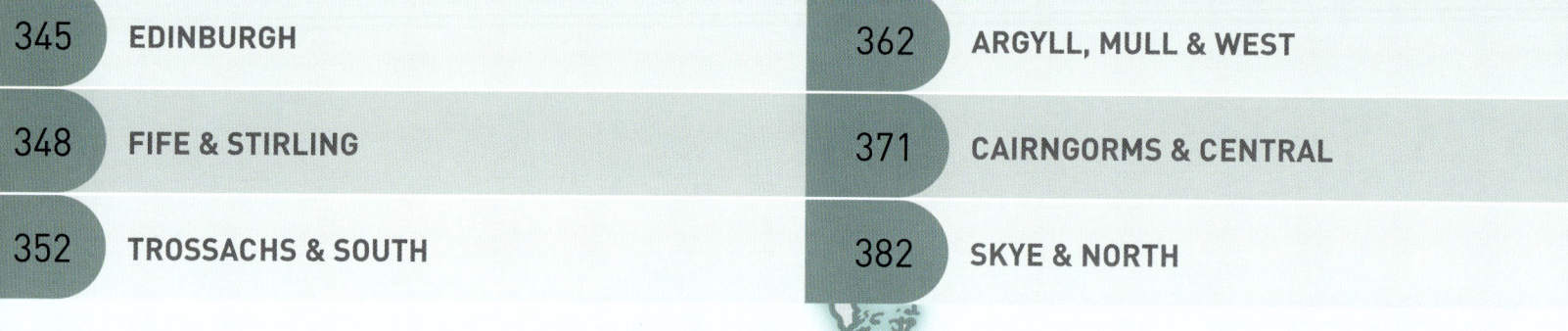
As the ideal destination for active holidays, the Scottish Highlands were first 'discovered' at the end of the 18th century, when fear of wilderness and mountains gave way to the Romantic movement that celebrated the majesty and wonder of the natural landscape. Visitors came first to gaze in awe, and thrill to major events of recent history that included a doomed Jacobite monarchy and the last gasps of the feudal clan system. By the time Queen Victoria fell in love with it all in the mid-19th century, sporting estates were taking hold, and the country was perceived by some as a limitless playground for the pursuits of hunting, shooting and fishing.

Today, those traditional, monied sports still play an important part in the economy of the Highlands, but most visitors are drawn here for other activities. These include walking, mountain biking, birdwatching and adventure sports and watersports such as quad biking, sea-kayaking, mountaineering and white-water rafting. The opportunities for getting out there and enjoying the landscape are boundless.

Edinburgh

LISTINGS 391

CLOCKWISE FROM TOP LEFT: PRINCES STREET; HOLYROOD PALACE;
FORTH RAIL BRIDGE, SOUTH QUEENSFERRY; SALISBURY CRAGS

India Place
India Street
Gloucester Lane
Moray Place
Heriot Row
Howe Street
Abercromby Place
Queen Street
York Place
St Mary's RC Cathedral
Playhouse Theatre
Cinema
Greenside Row
Calton Hill
Royal Terrace
Montrose Terrace
NEW TOWN
ABBEYHILL

Georgian House
Charlotte Square
Glenfinlas Street
Young Street
George Street
Hanover Street
Frederick Street
Hill Street
Thistle Street
Rose Street
Queen Street
George Street
Lane
St Andrew Square
Scottish National Portrait Gallery
St James Shopping Centre
Leith Street
Waterloo Place
Regent Road
National Monument
Regent Gardens
Calton Road
Regent Terrace
Regent
Abbeyhill
Abbeyhill
Milton Street

Shandwick Place
Princes Street
Princes Street Gardens
Royal Scottish Acadamy
The Mound
National Gallery of Scotland
Princes Mall
Waverley Bridge
North Bridge
Waverley Station
East Market Street
Calton Road
Calton Road
Scottish Parliament Building
Palace of Holyroodhouse
Parliament Visitor's Centre
Dynamic Earth
Drive

King's Stable Road
Camera Obscura & World of Illusion
Edinburgh Castle
Esplanade
Johnston Terrace
Terrace
Scotch Whisky Heritage Centre
Grassmarket
The Real Mary King's Close
The Writer's Museum
Edinburgh Dungeon
City Art Centre
Cockburn St
High Street
St Giles Cathedral
Parliament House
JK House
The People's Story
Cannongate Kirk
Canongate
Museum of Edinburgh
Holyrood Road
Queen's Drive

West Approach Road
Lothian Road
Castle Terrace
Grassmarket
West Port
Greyfriars Kirk
Edinburgh College of Art
Bread Street
Lauriston Place
Cowgate
University of Edinburgh
National Museum of Scotland
South Bridge
Chambers Street
University of Edinburgh
Drummond Street
University of Edinburgh
Pleasance
Pleasance Festival Theatre
Dumbiedykes Road
OLD TOWN
Holyrood Park

Morrison Street
Gardner's Street
Semple St East
Grey Street
Ponton St
Lauriston Place
Chalmers Street
Lauriston Gardens
Lauriston Street
Lauriston Place
George IV Bridge
Lothian Street
Potterrow
Nicolson Street
Chapel Street
Buccleuch Street
Clerk Street
St Leonard's Street
Salisbury Crags

Fountainbridge
Gilmore Place
George Sq
Meadow Lane
Meadow Park
Queen's Drive

Visit
ROYAL BOTANIC GARDEN
The largest collection of Chinese plants to be found outside China grows in the Royal Botanic Garden in Edinburgh. The Chinese Hillside is just one of the many delights to be explored in this beautiful, green oasis, which has 5,000 plants in the rockery garden alone. The gardens cover 70 acres (28ha) of landscaped and wooded grounds in the north of the city and hide an art gallery, a café and shop.

Visit
UNDERGROUND EDINBURGH
Edinburgh's Old Town is thickly piled – upon itself. For an atmospheric and rather creepy insight into the living conditions here in the mid-18th century, you can visit Mary King's Close, a narrow alleyway opposite St Giles Cathedral, preserved when the City Chambers were built straight over the top. More of these buried streets riddle the foundations of the Old Town, and can be seen in the Tron Kirk, on the Royal Mile.

Visit
GREYFRIAR'S BOBBY
Edinburgh's favourite statue is much less imposing than the Scott Monument on Princes Street, and stands at the top of Candlemaker Row, opposite the Museum of Scotland. It depicts a Skye terrier, and was raised in 1873 in memory of a loyal little dog who slept faithfully on his master's grave in the nearby Greyfriars Kirkyard for 14 years after the man's death. Local people fed him on scraps each day as he kept his lonely vigil.

SCOTT MONUMENT

GREYFRIAR'S BOBBY

EDINBURGH MAP REF 409 H4

Edinburgh grew up in medieval times as a warren of narrow streets around the ancient castle. Wealth led to expansion in the 18th century and the gracious development of the New Town. Today it is the grand home of the new Scottish Parliament, and is the financial, legal and tourism hub of Scotland. Its annual arts festivals are world renowned, and in 2005 the city was declared the first ever literary capital of Europe because of its numerous connections with esteemed writers over the centuries, from Walter Scott, Robert Louis Stevenson and Arthur Conan Doyle to today's writers, J K Rowling and Alexander McCall Smith.

Central Edinburgh is relatively compact, and divides into two halves: the narrow, steep, curving streets of the Old Town to the south of Princes Street Gardens, and the neat grid-patterned, broad boulevards and crescents of the New Town to the north of Princes Street. The Old Town is built along a ridge of rock that stretches from the castle for around a mile eastwards to Holyrood Palace, which lies in the shadow of the tilted volcanic hill of Arthur's Seat. All the main streets run parallel to this line – Queen Street, George Street (great for designer shopping) and Princes Street

(good high street shopping) to the north; Castle Street, Lawnmarket, High Street and Canongate (which together form the famous 'Royal Mile') run along the top of the ridge; and Grassmarket, Cowgate and Chambers Street (home to the Royal Museum and Museum of Scotland) less regularly to the south.

The best places to get your bearings are from the top of Calton Hill, at the east end of Princes Street, or standing at the castle esplanade. Views extend north to the Firth of Forth, the Forth bridges and the hills of central Scotland, south to the Pentland Hills, and east to the conical mound of Berwick Law.

The main highlight of the Old Town is magnificent Edinburgh Castle, a solid symbol of the Scottish nation which has withstood centuries of battering. It was mostly destroyed during the Lang Siege of 1567–1573, but was rebuilt by James Douglas, Earl of Morton, regent to the young James VI. Edinburgh's role in modern times as a garrison fortress is celebrated each summer with a military tattoo, with regimental displays and pipe bands from places around the world. The greatest treasures on display here are the royal crown and sceptre, with the Stone of Destiny, on which loyal Scottish kings were once crowned.

The Museum of Scotland is housed in a strikingly modern building in the Old Town. This is where you can see Scottish treasures including the famous Lewis chess pieces, the exquisite 1st-century Hunterston brooch and the beautiful 8th-century Monymusk Reliquary. The comprehensive collections at this fine museum help to explain Scottish history from its earliest times to the present.

Edinburgh's still-named New Town covers an area of about 1 square mile (318ha) to the north of Princes Street, and is characterised by broad streets of spacious terraced houses with large windows and finely detailed ornamental door arches. Until the mid-18th century, Edinburgh had been neatly contained on the ridge between Arthur's Seat and the castle. Conditions became overcrowded and insanitary and, as a new age of scientific advance and intellectual enlightenment dawned, so the need for expansion became clear. A competition was held in 1766 to design a new city to the north. The winner was unknown architect James Craig (1744–1795), and within three years the first house was ready. The first New Town was so successful that a second one was laid out in 1802, extending north towards Leith. While Princes Street has lost its shine in the glare of modern

commerce, the broad Charlotte Square, with its fine preserved Georgian House, is the epitome of the planners' intentions.

The North Bridge was needed to enable pedestrians to reach the new city without foundering in the (then) muddy valley. A second link, the Mound, came about by accident, when 'Geordie' Boyd, a clothier in the Old Town, started to dump earth rubble in the marsh. Soon the builders from the New Town joined in, as they dug out foundations for the new buildings and dumped the residue. It took 2 million cartloads of rubble to complete the job, and the causeway became the Mound, later home to the National Gallery. This superb collection of paintings includes works by talented Scottish painters such as Henry Raeburn, Allen Ramsay, David Wilkie and William McTaggart, in addition to international masters including Vermeer, Van Dyke, Raphael and Monet. The tour buses that congregate on Waverley Bridge, by the main railway station, offer the easiest and most efficient introduction to the city, with a choice of four different routes taking in the main attractions and linking you to the sites outside the city centre such as the Botanical Gardens and the old port of Leith (good for shopping, trendy bars and the Royal Yacht Britannia).

EDINBURGH CASTLE

Fife & Stirling

CLOCKWISE FROM TOP: ST ANDREWS; STIRLING; CRAIL HARBOUR

EAST NEUK VILLAGES MAP REF 409 J3

A 'fringe of gold' is how James II described the coastal villages of this eastern corner (and 'neuk' is a Scots word for corner) of Fife, way back in the 15th century. However, he was referring to the area's many prosperous little fishing communities rather than golden beaches, although these can be found too, at Elie and around Largo Bay.

Most of this shoreline is rocky, and the villages that cluster around their diminutive harbours seem to be packed in as tightly as sardines huddled against the rising land. They are characterised by neat harbours piled with lobster pots and fishing nets, buildings with pantile roofs and whitewashed, crow step gables, thick stone walls and small windows to fend off the elements – little fisher houses clustered along winding narrow lanes that grew up long before motorised vehicles were dreamed of.

In fact, you could drive through Fife on the A917 and overlook these little gems completely, but approach from the sea or on foot along the route of the Fife Coastal Path and it is a different matter.

The East Neuk villages are strung out in line: Elie, St Monans, Pittenweem, Anstruther and Crail. Each has its own character. Picturesque Pittenweem, for instance, was once the main fisheries port for the area, and had a priory in the 13th century which was dedicated to Fillan, a 7th-century saint who lived in a cave and spent his life converting the local Picts to the Christian faith.

Anstruther was a herring port and has the feel of a resort town complete with fish and chip shops. It also has a darker side, as an historic centre for smuggling. A chief attraction today is the Scottish Fisheries Museum, an extensive and fascinating collection of fishing craft and stories down the ages. St Monan's, dominated by the squat tower of its 14th-century Auld Kirk, was noted for ship-building as well as fishing in the 19th century.

Elie, with its golden sands, became a popular seaside holiday resort in the 19th century. A causeway leads to a rocky islet, with panoramic views across the Firth of Forth, and a watersports centre. And Crail, the most easterly of the villages, had particularly strong trading links with the Low Countries, which is reflected in its architecture and in the tolbooth bell, which came from Holland in 1520.

ST ANDREWS & FIFE MAP REF 409 J2

The broad sweeps of golden sands that lie to the north of St Andrews attracted the attention of Adolf Hitler during World War II, who saw them as the perfect landing site for a planned invasion force. Although his plans came to nothing concrete anti-tank defences may still be seen along the tree line. The undulating turf between the beaches and the more fertile farmland is known in Scotland as the links, a term which has become almost synonymous with golf courses. St Andrews is where the game is said to have originated, and it has six of them, of which the Old Course of the fine Royal and Ancient Golf Club, founded in 1754, is the most famous.

The town itself received its royal charter in the mid-12th century, and the spectacular ruined cathedral set above the harbour dates from then. St Andrews retains its medieval street plan, with North Street, South Street and Market Street the main arteries spreading west from the cathedral. Before the building's destruction during the Reformation in the 16th century, this was known as the ecclesiastical heart of Scotland, and a major pilgrimage site. The castle in its present form dates from around 1390, but was originally constructed by the bishops as essential defence. Its most remarkable features lie underground: the chilling bottle dungeon, 24 feet (7.3m) deep and hewn from solid rock under a tower, from which no prisoner could escape. A mine and counter mine are legacies of an attempt to break a siege of 1546–1547 by the Duke of Argyll. His men tunnelled towards the castle but were thwarted when the defenders dug out a counter-mine and headed them off.

Today, what might have become simply an elegant and sleepy resort town is kept wide awake by its thriving and ever-growing in popularity, university – Scotland's most venerable – which dates from 1413, and where Prince William attended.

The National Trust for Scotland owns two properties on the eastern tip of Fife. Both show the hand of the Arts and Crafts restorer, Robert Lorimer (1864–1929).

In the rolling hills to the south of the bustling town of Cupar lies the Hill of Tarvit Mansionhouse, an Edwardian house filled with elegant furniture and fine paintings, and surrounded by formal gardens. In contrast, by a peaceful corner to the south, just inland from St Monans, lies beautiful Kellie Castle, dating from 1360, and restored with eccentric charm by the Lorimer family. The castle is set beside an interesting, rambling, walled Arts and Crafts garden.

St Andrews secretly also played a part in monitoring the security of Great Britain for many years, but evidence of this is now common knowledge. A hole, 131 feet (40m) deep, in the ground between St Andrews and Anstruther was the secret location of Scotland's Nuclear Command Centre, built in the 1950s as fear of the Cold War was growing. It is eerie to think that, in the event of nuclear attack, a self-supporting military community of around 300 people could have survived in the cramped conditions of this concrete-lined shelter. In 1994 the bunker opened its doors to the public as Scotland's Secret Bunker, a preserved time-capsule of a fearful age.

STIRLING MAP REF 408 F3

This ancient royal burgh grew up around a strategic crossing point of the River Forth before the waterway widens to the east and eventually becomes impassable. The Old Bridge, at the northern end of the town, once carried the only route north on this side of the country. Because of this Stirling remained the key to the north and was in a powerful geographical position up until the Kincardine Bridge opened to the southeast in 1936. Plans for a second bridge are underway.

However, the town's most spectacular landmark is its castle, set high above the once-marshy plain on a rocky crag, and fought over by Scots and English in the 13th and 14th centuries. It was later remodelled as a royal palace favoured by Stuart kings, becoming the birthplace of James II and James IV, temporary home to an infant Mary, Queen of Scots, and the chosen site of James VI's coronation. Visitors can tour the castle and see the exhibition in the Queen Anne casemates. In the Chapel Royal there are two tapestries that represent a modern reworking of the Hunt of the Unicorn series.

Fabulous views from the castle's Esplanade extend to the Campsie Fells in the west and the start of the brooding Highland hills to the north. Several magnificent 17th-century buildings can be seen in the old town, including Argyll's Lodging (once used as a military hospital), before Victorian developments take over at the bottom of the hill.

Stirling's other great landmark is the imposing National Wallace Monument, the tower which crowns Abbey Craig. It was constructed during a revival of nationalist sentiment in 1869, to commemorate the Battle of Stirling Bridge in 1297, when William Wallace won a profound victory against Edward I's English forces, killing thousands and hounding the wounded into the marshes to die. The structure now houses this patriotic hero's broadsword, and you can climb the 246 steps to the top for views to the distant Forth Bridges.

Just to the south of Stirling, the battlefield of Bannockburn was the site of a major Scots victory in their wars against English oppression in 1314. King Robert the Bruce took on the superior forces of Edward II and won decisively. Stirling was

the last English stronghold north of the River Forth, and while its fall was only a stage in the fight for independence (which would continue to rage on for another 14 years), this great victory consolidated the power of Robert I, effectively silencing any rival claimants to the Scottish throne. For the first time, the Scots were able to present a united front against their old enemy, the English and their Crown.

As well as monuments to bloody battles fought and won, or rebuilt strongholds showing the might of Scottish warlords, there are also peaceful structural tributes. Southeast of Stirling, near the village of Dunmore, sits a distinctive folly, a rare example of architecture inspired by fruit. It's the Pineapple, a garden retreat built to adorn Dunmore Park in 1761 by John Murray, the 4th Earl. The rendered stone foliage tops an octagonal Gothick tower. Nobody knows quite why it was built, but pineapples were considered a rare and exotic delicacy at the time. The attractive gardens and surrounding parkland are owned by the National Trust for Scotland, and the Landmark Trust lets out the folly as holiday accommodation.

Visit
THE ISLE OF MAY

The Isle of May is a rocky outcrop in the Firth of Forth, 6 miles (9.7km) offshore and clearly visible from the villages of the East Neuk. It is accessible in summer by boat from Anstruther. Now in the care of Scottish Natural Heritage, it is given over to wildlife, which includes breeding colonies of terns and puffins, eider ducks, and a small resident colony of grey seals.

Visit
FRUITFUL FOLLY

Southeast of Stirling, near the village of Dunmore, sits a distinctive folly, a rare example of architecture inspired by fruit. It's the Pineapple, a quirky garden retreat built to adorn Dunmore Park in 1761 by John Murray, the 4th Earl. Nobody knows quite why it was built, but pineapples were considered a rare and exotic delicacy at the time. The attractive gardens and surrounding parkland are owned by the National Trust for Scotland.

STIRLING

DISCOVER A ROMAN WALL & THE CANAL AT FALKIRK

A stroll along Scotland's old canal system to see the striking 21st-century Falkirk Wheel – the world's first rotating boat lift. It was designed in order to reconnect the Forth & Clyde canal with the Union canal and so restore a centuries-old link between Glasgow and Edinburgh.

DISTANCE/TIME 2 miles (3.2km); 4 miles (6.4km) with monument 1h **MAP** OS Explorer 349 Falkirk, Cumbernauld & Livingston **START** Lock 16, by The Union Inn, grid ref: NS 868800. Falkirk is on the A803 **TRACKS** Canal tow paths and town streets **THE PUB** The Union Inn, Lock 16, Falkirk. Tel: 01324 613839

1 Start at The Union Inn by Lock 16. This was once one of the best-known pubs in Scotland and catered for passengers on the canal. Turn right now, away from the canal, then go right along the road. Turn right along Tamfourhill Road and go through the kissing gate on the left-hand side of the road. Alternatively, don't turn up Tamfourhill Road yet, but continue walking uphill to go under the viaduct. Keep going until you reach a monument on the left (it commemorates the Battle of Falkirk, 1298, in which William Wallace was beaten by Edward I's troops). Retrace your steps, under the viaduct, then turn left into Tamfourhill Road, and left through the kissing gate on the left-hand side of the road.

2 This takes you to a section of the Roman Antonine Wall. Walk along here, parallel with Tamfourhill Road. When you reach the point where you can go no further, climb bank on the right-hand side and go down the steps to join the road by a kissing gate.

3 Go left to continue along the road – you'll soon see another kissing gate on the left to another, much shorter, section of the wall. Leave the wall, rejoin the road and maintain direction to reach a mini-roundabout. Turn left here, along Maryfield Place. When you reach the end, join the public footpath signed to the canal tow path and woodland walks.

4 Follow this track up and over the railway bridge, then on to reach the Union Canal. Don't cross the canal but turn right and walk along the towpath. This is a long straight stretch, and is popular with local joggers. Eventually you'll reach Roughcastle tunnel – but remember that it currently closes at 6pm to protect the Wheel from vandalism.

5 Walk through the tunnel to the new Falkirk Wheel and yet another section of the old Antonine Wall. You can walk on as far as the Wheel, then walk down to the visitors' centre at the bottom. Bear right to cross the bridge over the Forth and Clyde Canal.

6 Turn right now and walk along the tow path. Lots of dog walkers and cyclists come along here (so take care if you are walking with a dog), and people frequently go canoeing along the canal. Keep walking until you come back to Lock 16, then turn right and cross the canal again to return to the start of the walk at The Union Inn.

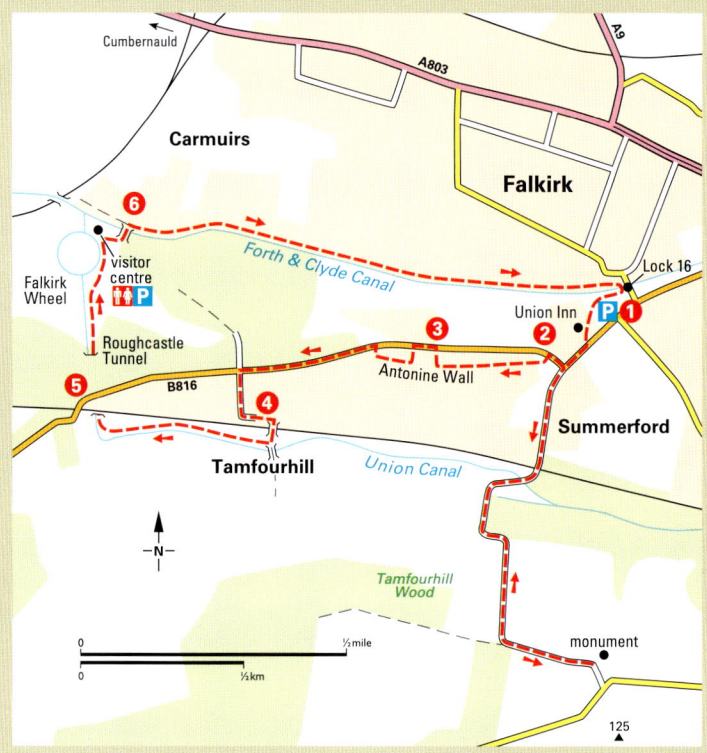

WALK 126

SOLDIERS & SAINTS ON THE PENTLANDS

A lovely bracing walk that takes you across the hills and past Edinburgh's huge reservoirs. Although this walk starts from Edinburgh's busy city bypass, you'll soon think you're miles from the city.

DISTANCE/TIME 7 miles (11.3) 3h **MAP** OS Explorer 344 Pentland Hills **START** Grid ref: NT 212679 **TRACKS** Wide firm tracks, short stretches can be muddy, 3 stiles **THE PUB** The Spylaw Tavern, Colinton. Tel: 0131 441 2783

1 From the car park by the bypass follow the signs pointing in the direction of Easter Kinleith and walk along the metalled track. You will reach the water treatment works on your left-hand side. Continue on past the works to reach the gate by the East of Scotland Water sign.

2 Pass through the kissing gate and continue walking ahead, keeping Torduff Reservoir on your left-hand side. When you reach the top of the reservoir, walk over the little bridge and follow the metalled track as it bends round to the right. Walk under a line of electricity pylons, and go over a small bridge, passing an artificial waterfall on your left-hand side, and continue past Clubbiedean Reservoir.

3 Your path now bears right, with fields on either side. Pass under another line of pylons and walk to Easter Kinleith farm. Now follow the path as it bends back to the left, sighposted 'Harlaw'. Pass a sign for Poet's Glen and continue ahead, over a bridge and on to a large white house on the left-hand side called Crossroads.

4 Turn left and follow the sign for Glencorse Reservoir. Follow this track, past a conifer plantation on your left-hand side, then cross a stile next to a metal gate. Continue ahead until you reach two more metal gates, where you cross a stile on the left-hand side signposted to Glencorse.

5 Follow the track, with the hills on either side, and cross an old stone stile. Continue in the same direction until you come to a copse of conifers on the right-hand side, with Glencorse Reservoir ahead. Turn left here, following the sign to Colinton by Bonaly.

6 Walk uphill and continue in the same direction to go through a gap in a wire fence. The track now narrows and takes you through the hills; until it eventually opens out. Continue in the same direction to reach the fence encircling conifers. Keep the fence on your left and walk further down to cross a stile on the left-hand side.

7 Walk past Bonaly Reservoir, then through the kissing gate and walk downhill, getting good views over Edinburgh as you descend. When you reach a wooden gate, go through and continue ahead, walking downhill, with trees on either side. Go through another kissing gate and then follow the tarmac path ahead, which shortly passes a Scout Centre on the right-hand side followed by Bonaly Tower. Turn left at the bridge which crosses over the bypass and return to the car park at the start of the walk.

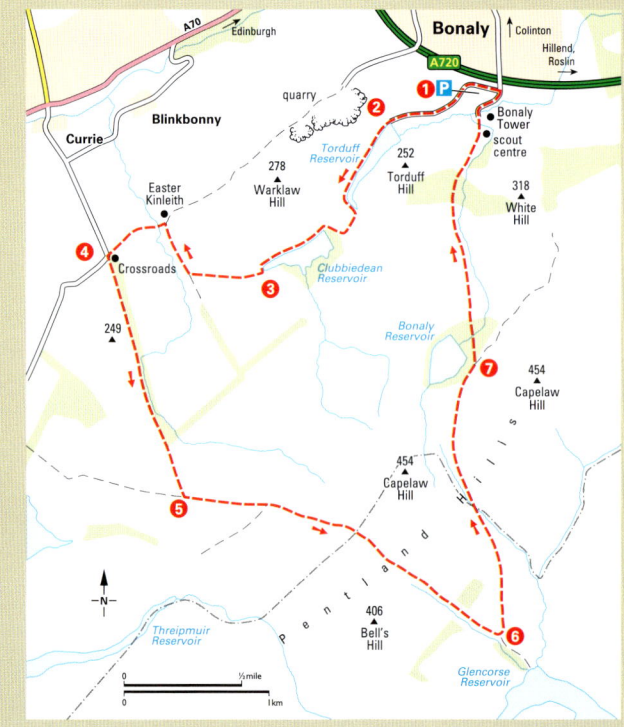

A FISHY TRAIL IN FIFE

Take a bracing linear coastal walk through the villages of Fife's East Neuk. This corner of the east coast is dotted with picturesque fishing villages, which nestle close together yet retain their own distinctive character.

DISTANCE/TIME 4.5 miles (7.2km) 2h **MAP** OS Explorer 371 St Andrews & East Fife **START** Grid ref: NO 506170 **TRACKS** Ancient streets and golden sands **THE PUB** The Golf Hotel, 4 High Street, Crail. Tel: 01333 450206

1 From the tourist information centre walk down Talbooth Wynd. At the end turn right and go to the garage, where you bear left. Walk by the old castle wall to a lookout point, for a view of the picturesque harbour. Bear right and walk on to the High Street.

2 Turn left and walk along the road, passing the two white beacons, which help guide boats into the harbour. Turn left and walk down West Braes, following the signs for the Coast Path. When you reach Osbourne Terrace bear slightly left, go down some steps, through the kissing gate and on to a grassy track by the shore.

3 From here you follow the path as it hugs the shoreline. You should soon see cormorants perched on rocks to your left and will also get views of the Isle of May. Go down some steps, over a slightly boggy area, and continue walking until you reach tow derelict cottages – an area known as The Pans.

4 Walk past the cottages and continue along the shore, then hop over a stone stile. You'll now pass flat rocks on the left, which are covered with interesting little rock pools. Cross the burn by the footbridge – you'll now be able to see the Bass Rock and Berwick Law on your left and the village of Anstruther ahead, and will soon reach some caves.

5 Pass the caves, then cross a little stone stile on the left-hand side and go over a footbridge. Your track is narrower now and takes you past fields on the right, then some maritime grasses on the left. Big stepping stones now take you to another stile, which you climb over to reach Caiplie.

6 Go through the kissing gate by the houses, follow the wide grassy track, then go through another kissing gate to walk past a field. The path now runs past a free-range pig farm and up to a caravan park.

7 You now continue along the shore, following the tarmac track to reach a play area and war memorial on the right. Maintain direction now as you enter the village of Cellardyke – often known as Anstruther Easter – and continue to reach the harbour. Pass the harbour and The Haven restaurant and continue walking along John Street and then James Street.

8 Once you reach the end of James Street maintain your direction, then follow the road as it bends down and round to the left. You will then walk past a guiding beacon and you will eventually come into Anstruther's busy little harbour. You can now either walk back to Crail or take the bus back, which leaves from the harbour.

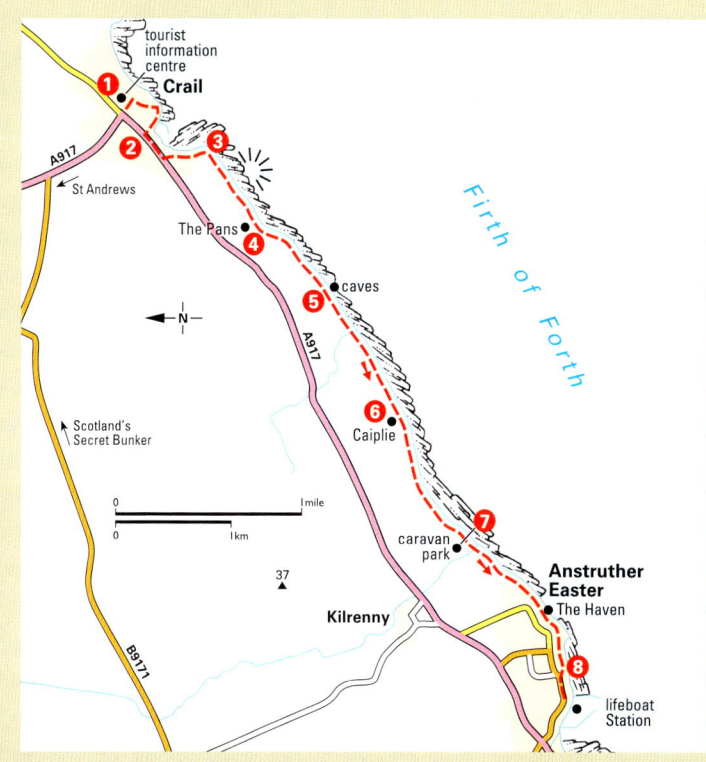

WALK 128

A LEISURELY CIRCUIT OF CULROSS

An easy walk that ends on the cobbled streets of an historic town, where a prosperous trading history is reflected in the stylish buildings.

DISTANCE/TIME 3 miles (4.8km) 1.5h **MAP** OS Explorer 367 Dunferline & Kirkcaldy **START** Grid ref: NS 983859 **TRACKS** Generally firm paths, some muddy woodland tracks **THE PUB** Dundonald Arms, 6 Mid Causeway, Culross. Tel: 0870 478 6321

1 Turn left out of the car park and walk along the road, with the bay to your left and housing on your right. Continue walking, past some cottages, until you reach the edge of the town. Take care of traffic as there is no pavement. Pass the entrance to Dunimarle Castle on your right and continue until you reach the entrance to Blair Castle, now a memorial home for miners.

2 Turn right and walk up the tarmac drive (signposted 'private'), which is lined with rhododendrons. Walk until you can see the castle on the left. Before you reach it, take the right-hand turning in the trees and follow it as it bears to the right. Continue until you reach Blair Mains farmhouse on the left.

3 Continue following the track, walking under a line of pylons with fields on either side. Walk ahead towards the trees and continue following this track until you reach a metal gate on the left-hand side. Look carefully and you should spot a wooden fence post on the right-hand side, with the words 'West Kirk' and 'grave' painted on it in white. Take the narrow right-hand path immediately before it, which runs through the trees.

4 Follow this path to go through a kissing gate and continue walking ahead, with trees on your left and fields on your right. Go through another kissing gate, and continue in the same direction as the path opens out to a wider, grassy track. When you reach a crossing of paths, continue ahead along the narrow path and walk under a line of pylons. You will soon pass the remains of a church on the left-hand side.

5 Continue ahead, past the old cemetery, and walk in the same direction until the track joins a tarmac road. Walk in the same direction until you reach a junction. Turn right here and head downhill – watch out for traffic at this part because the road can become very busy. You will soon reach Culross Abbey on the left-hand side.

6 It's worth stopping at this point to visit the abbey. You can then continue to walk on downhill, down Tanhouse Brae, and will soon reach the Mercat ('old Market') Cross, with The Study on the right-hand side. Continue walking in the same direction, down Back Causeway, until you reach the main road.

7 Turn right, walk past the tourist information centre, past the Tron (the old burgh weighing machine), then past the large ochre-coloured building on the right, which is Culross Palace. To reach the starting point, continue walking in the same direction – the car park is on the left-hand side, just past the children's play area.

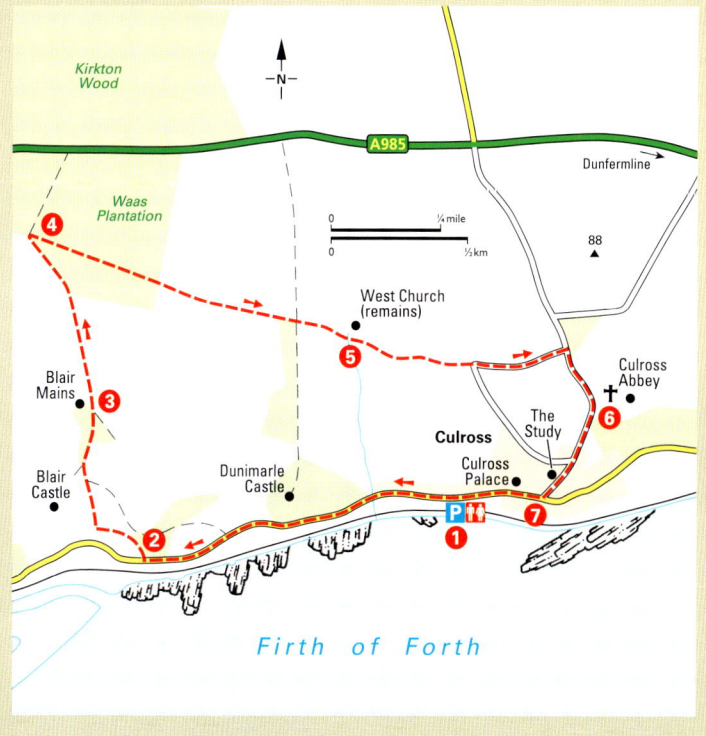

Trossachs & South

CLOCKWISE FROM TOP LEFT: SCOTT'S SHIP RRS *DISCOVERY*, DUNDEE; BLAIR CASTLE; CALLANDER

ABERFELDY MAP REF 409 G1

Born in Ireland, General George Wade (1673–1748) served as Commander-in-Chief of North Britain from 1724 to 1740, and left his long-lasting mark on the Scottish Highlands in the form of almost 250 miles (400km) of military roads and some 40 bridges to go with them. Today, one of his finest bridges still carries the traffic of the A827 over the River Tay at Aberfeldy, a pleasant stone-built town in the heart of Perthshire. The bridge's elegant structure, with its four obelisks and five graceful spans, was designed for Wade by the architect William Adam. On the bank nearby stands a monument to the Black Watch Regiment.

Signs in the town point the way to walking trails that lead to the Birks of Aberfeldy, birchwoods celebrated by the poet Robert Burns. On the edge of the town, the Dewar's distillery offers a visitor centre and tour, culminating in a tasting. Outside you might see native red squirrels. To the west, at Weem, is the 16th-century stronghold of Castle Menzies, a restored Z-plan tower house. One of the rooms used by Bonny Prince Charlie has been furnished and decorated in the style he would have known.

Loch Tay lies 5 miles (8km) to the west of Aberfeldy, with the picturesque village of Kenmore at its eastern end. A splendidly spired gateway marks an entrance to Taymouth Castle, now a golfing holiday resort. The town also has a great watersports centre, but its most unusual attraction has to be a replica round-house or crannog, set low over the waters of the loch.

This is part of the Scottish Crannog Centre, the visitor centre for an on-going project that is exploring and excavating the 18 or so similar Iron Age dwellings that once lined these shores. Crannogs were community dwellings built on wooden stilts. The cold, peaty water of the loch has helped to preserve timber, plant and food remains and even scraps of cloth, and the discoveries made here reveal much about the way of life of the crannog builders. Visitors are able to watch, and take part in, demonstrations of ancient crafts.

Shortly before it reaches Aberfeldy, the Tay is joined by the waters of the River Lyon. This river flows down from one of Scotland's most beautiful valleys, Glen Lyon, which lies sandwiched between Loch Tay and Loch Rannoch. Entry to the glen is through the dramatic and steep-sided pass at Fortingall, or over the mountain pass by Ben Lawers.

CALLANDER MAP REF 408 F3

Callander straddles the A84 northwest of Stirling, and is the eastern gateway to the Trossachs. During the 19th century it was a flourishing resort town, and the grandeur of the Victorian buildings along its main street bears this out.

On a summer's day the little town is packed out with visitors, keen to enjoy the varied shops and tea rooms, and to track down the history of Rob Roy, a folk hero. Rob Roy MacGregor (1671–1734) took refuge with his people in the local hills, and his story is told at the visitor centre in the former church on the main square. His grave is in the churchyard at Balquhidder. There are several good walks from the town centre, leading to Bracklinn Falls and the Callander Crags.

The Hamilton Toy Collection in Main Street has toys from the 19th century onwards, including dolls, teddy bears, model train sets, toy soldiers, books, jigsaws and games. It is as popular with adults eager to relive their childhood days, as with children.

To the west of the town, beyond the woollen weaving mill and display at Kilmahog, is the scenic spot of the Pass of Leny, with the Falls of Leny accessible from the roadside car park. Of interest to cycling enthusiasts, the Callander to Strathyre Cycleway runs past here too, following the route of the former railway line from Callander up the western shore of Loch Lubnaig towards Killin.

To the southwest of Callander lies the Lake of Menteith, where you can hire a boat and fishing tackle and try casting for rainbow trout. Alternatively, a ferry goes out to the lovely tree-covered island where the romantic ruins of Inchmahome Priory stand. Augustinian monks made it their home in 1238, and the infant Mary, Queen of Scots was hidden here for three weeks in 1547 after the Battle of Pinkie Cleugh before she was eventually smuggled to safety in France.

Southeast of Callander on the A84 lies the rural village of Doune, with a substantial ruined castle at its heart, hidden amid the trees on a curve of the River Teith. Built by the powerful regent of Scotland, Robert Stewart, Duke of Albany, in the late 14th century, it is comparatively simple in construction, with a main block of buildings set within a courtyard and contained by a mighty curtain wall. The fabric of the castle is maintained by Historic Scotland. You can climb to the top of this for panoramic views of the village and the surrounding countryside, and there are lots of little stairways as well as chambers to explore. Its medieval austerity and imposing stature gave the castle a starring role in the film *Monty Python and the Holy Grail*.

CRIEFF MAP REF 409 G2

The old spa town of Crieff lies above the meandering River Earn west of Perth, on the edge of the Highlands. For a time in the 17th century it took the alternative name of Drummond, in honour of local patrons, but the original name was restored in the 18th century, after the town was burned down by Jacobite rebels.

Crieff grew up as a centre for cattle drovers, who passed through here on their way south to England or north to the Highlands. The linen and tanning industries thrived for a while, but were overtaken by the growth of the Lowland factories. Today Crieff is an industrious service town, celebrated for the quality of its schools, and as a main hub for activities including fishing, cycling, and water sports on Loch Earn. There is good walking through the hills, too, with a signposted trail from the town centre north to Knock Hill offering great views.

The Drummonds had their castle 3 miles (4.8km) south of the town, and while the castle itself is still private, the fabulous formal 17th-century garden has been restored to its former state and is open on summer afternoons. The burial chapel of the Drummonds stands beside the Innerpeffray Library. Founded in 1691 it is the second oldest library in Scotland.

To the north of Crieff a narrow road leads up the remote Glen Turret to Loch Turret, passing the scenic beauty spot at the waterfalls of the same name. Begun in 1775, Glenturret Distillery is home to the Famous Grouse Experience, which is entertaining and offers a glimpse into the serious business of making whisky.

DUNDEE MAP REF 409 H2

Dundee was founded on a 19th-century industrial base which, over time, was famously reduced to the three 'J's: jam, jute and journalism. Today it is busy reinventing itself as a lively centre for the arts and hands-on science, and celebrating its maritime and industrial heritage. The main focus of rejuvenation has been along the waterfront, where the three-masted Royal Research Ship Discovery is now berthed; she was built here in 1900–1901, and her maiden voyage was to the Antarctic. In 1902 she became trapped in the pack ice, and survived two timber-crunching winters before breaking free and sailing home. The modern museum alongside tells her story. Nothing beats exploring the ship herself, however, and witnessing the cramped conditions of the brave men who crewed her.

Moored nearby, the frigate Unicorn was built in 1824 and is the oldest British warship afloat. In the same corner is Sensation: Dundee, a state-of-the-art celebration of science geared to children, centred on the five senses.

Wool and flax were both woven in Dundee, long before the important advent of jute in the early 19th century caused a boom in the town's growth. The plant fibre was imported from India and softened with whale oil before being spun and woven. By the 1870s most Indian mills were undercutting Dundee prices, and the industry had to scale down. It was hit hard again by the post-World War I recession. A fascinating survivor is the Verdant Works, which explains how Dundee developed so quickly, and why more women than men were employed by the jute industry.

D C Thomson (1861–1964), son of a Dundee shipping entrepreneur, founded the newspaper company that still bears his name in 1906. *The Sunday Post* and the *Weekly News* are still produced here, along with many local papers, but the company's best loved creations were its popular comics for children, the *Beano* and *Dandy*. Statues of the characters Minnie the Minx and Desperate Dan can be seen on the High Street.

Insight
PONTIUS PILATE
The pretty hamlet of Fortingall is claimed by some to be the birthplace of Pontius Pilate. It is said that he was born here, the son of a Roman soldier and a local girl, before rising to become the Roman prefect of Judea and Samaria. The Fortingall connection seems to have arisen from a headstone in the churchyard, marked simply 'PP'.

Insight
WHO PAYS THE FERRYMAN?
Until 1535, anybody wishing to cross the River Teith at Doune had to pay a ferryman to be rowed across. One day James Spittal was refused passage when he showed up without any money. Spittal was the wealthy tailor to James IV, and took the slight personally. It is said that, out of spiteful anger, he paid for the building of a bridge here to permanently deprive the ferryman of his living. The bridge is still standing, though it was modified in 1866.

CRIEFF

DUNKELD MAP REF 409 G2

A picturesque little 18th-century town with a tiny Gothic cathedral, Dunkeld lies surrounded by glorious woodland on the banks of the River Tay. Everything here, bar the cathedral, was destroyed by the Jacobites after their 1689 victory at Killiecrankie. When it was rebuilt, terraced cottages were squeezed into a compact centre of just two main streets: Cathedral Street and High Street, with a neat little square, called The Cross. The pleasing uniformity of Dunkeld owes much to this rebuilding by the Dukes of Atholl, and more to the carefully done restoration of around 20 houses by the National Trust for Scotland since the 1950s. The Trust has a shop in the main square, in a building distinctive for the iron 'ell' mounted on its exterior. The ell was a unit of measurement equivalent to 37 inches (92.5cm). The graceful stone bridge which links Dunkeld to Inver, much favoured as a subject by painters, was a masterpiece in 1809 of the great engineer Thomas Telford.

Dunkeld's ruined cathedral stands in a picturesque, shady setting on the banks of the river, and the crumbled building dates back to the 13th century, although its history as a monastic site goes back to the 6th century. Kenneth MacAlpin, the first king of Scotland, brought St Columba's bones here from Iona in around 850, thereby making it an important medieval ecclesiastical centre. The most substantial part left standing today is the choir, which still serves as the parish church. Close by the end of the cathedral furthest from the main entrance, look out for a sign indicating the 'Parent Larch'. This particular tree was imported from Austria in 1738, and became the source of many trees in and around nearby forests, planted up by the Dukes of Atholl between 1738 and 1830.

There are plenty of good circular signposted walks in the woods around here and along the river bank, with carpets of bluebells in late spring, and red squirrels to look out for – a leaflet from the tourist office gives full details. One walk leads through mixed woodland along the River Braan and up to the folly of the Hermitage, or Ossian's Hall, set above the Black Linn Falls.

Little Dunkeld is the last resting place of the great Scottish fiddler, Neil Gow (1727–1807), who composed many dance tunes and fine airs and was famous throughout Britain for his skill. His violin is on display at Blair Castle.

KILLIN MAP REF 408 F2

The village of Killin is set beneath the hills where the River Dochart tumbles over an extensive waterfall and into the western end of Loch Tay. Once home to the MacNabs, it is at the heart of the ancient district of Breadalbane, and has now become a popular walking, fishing and touring centre. The interesting Breadalbane Folklore Centre located in St Fillan's Mill shares its premises with the local tourist office, and offers an intriguing insight into Scottish legends of kelpies, brownies and other mythical creatures. The mill originally powered machines for the weaving of tweed. The ruins of 16th-century Finlarig Castle, a Campbell stronghold, stand at the head of the loch. It has what are said to be the only surviving remains in the country of a beheading pit, reserved especially for the execution of the gentry.

The National Trust for Scotland is noted for its preservation of some grand castles, but lists some more modest dwellings, too. One of the humblest is along the narrow Glen Lochay Road, just north of Killin. Moirlanich Longhouse is a long, low 19th-century farmhouse, built with a cruck frame. At least three generations of the Robertson family lived here, until the 1960s, and the house has been preserved, complete with a 'hingin' lum' (suspended chimney) and traditional wooden box beds.

The view from Killin up Loch Tay is dominated by the bulk of Ben Lawers, 1,214m (3,984ft), the highest mountain in the area. It is known for its delicate alpine flora, and with the neighbouring Tarmachan range, is a popular focus for walkers. The area is a national nature reserve, and information about walking here is available from the Mountain Visitor Centre on the southern flank.

KIRRIEMUIR MAP REF 409 H1

Kirriemuir is the gateway to the great Glens of Angus, the long valleys which stretch north into the open moorland of the Grampian Mountains, forming the southern edge of the mighty Cairngorms National Park. The range includes Glen Esk, Glen Clova and Glen Prosen, and they all offer superb hill-walking, with Glen Clova giving access to remote Glen Doll. The glens are all home to red and black grouse, golden eagles, ptarmigans and capercaillies, red and roe deer. Antarctic explorer Robert Falcon Scott and Edward Wilson, the expedition's doctor and artist, came to the area to plan their ill-fated voyage to the South Pole, and are commemorated by a fine memorial fountain in Glen Prosen.

Kirriemuir itself is an industrious red sandstone town, built on the revenues of weaving and farming. The town hosts an annual walking festival in June, and has a small aviation museum, but its main claim to fame is its associations with the playwright and novelist J M Barrie. The creator of Peter Pan was born here in 1860, the son of a weaver and one of ten children, and his birthplace is now an evocative museum. The wash-house round the back of the property served as Barrie's first theatre, and may have inspired the Wendy House in Peter Pan (1904). Although he lived for most of his life in London, Barrie wrote with great affection about the small-town life of Kirriemuir, disguised as 'Thrums' in his tales. In 1930 Barrie presented the community with a novel gift after they had honoured him with the freedom of the town: a camera obscura on nearby Kirrie Hill, for far-reaching views over the surrounding countryside (check back at the birthplace for opening times).

About 5 miles (8km) to the south of Kirriemuir lies Glamis Castle, family seat of the Earls of Strathmore and Kinghorne, and the childhood home of the late Queen Elizabeth, the Queen Mother. With its multiple turrets and fairytale battlements Glamis Castle (pronounced 'Glahms') is a vision of what a Scottish castle should look like, and the interior is equally fabulous too, with moulded plaster ceilings and fine panelling. At its core is a medieval tower house, dating back to around 1372. The surrounding parkland is well worth exploring, with its formal Italian garden and a pinetum. For a total contrast, six 18th-century cottages in the nearby village house the Angus Folk Museum, showing how the rural community lived.

DUNKELD

PERTH MAP REF 409 G2

The Roman settlement of Perth was founded on the banks of the River Tay in the 1st century; in the Middle Ages it became the capital of Scotland. Today it is a lively city at the centre of a thriving and established farming community, its compact core offering great shopping and bohemian cafés that spill out onto the pavements. With its theatre, City Hall, a concert hall and other venues, not to mention galleries and cinemas, Perth is an active centre for music and the arts, culminating in a lively festival in May.

Perth's extensive parks are headed by the North Inch and the South Inch, beside the river, and there are several gardens to explore in the area, including Branklyn, which is specially noted for its blue Himalayan poppies (Meconopsis). Scotland's National Heather Collection resides at Bells Cherrybank Gardens, to the west of the city centre, where there are around 900 varieties.

In recent years Perth has developed as the adventure capital of Scotland, with an ever-longer list of adventure sports and activities to take you out and about across the region. So if the more traditional sports of fishing, golf, pony trekking, mountain biking and hill-hiking seem tame, you can get your adrenalin rush by quad biking, off-road driving, abseiling, canoeing, waterskiing, cliff-jumping, white-water rafting or even paintballing. The tourist office has more details.

PITLOCHRY MAP REF 411 H8

This bustling town in the wooded valley of the River Tummel is based around one long main street, running parallel with the river, and lined with shops and eating places. The geographical heart of Scotland, it first appeared on the map when General Wade built a military road through here, and it has been a popular holiday resort since the 19th century.

A footbridge leads across the river to the Festival Theatre, with its Explorers' Garden, opened in 2003 to celebrate 300 years of botanical exploration and collection of artefacts from around the world by Scots. There is a view from the footbridge to the salmon ladder, which was installed as part of a hydroelectric dam system along the river and which also created Loch Faskally, a local beauty spot. Learn more at the Scottish Hydroelectric Visitor Centre, which gives access to an observation window where you can watch the wild salmon jumping (usually between April and October).

Just to the north of the town is the conservation village of Moulin, with its 17th-century church and ruined castle in the shadow of Ben Vrackie. The writer Robert Louis Stevenson stayed here in 1881, and described it as a 'sweet spot'.

Some three miles (4.8km) north of Pitlochry is the narrow, wooded gorge of Killiecrankie, on the River Garry. This was the site of a battle in 1689 when a Jacobite army defeated government troops. Continue north and you'll reach Blair Castle, a white-painted mansion in a majestic setting of trees and gardens, with hills behind. It's been the ancestral home of the Dukes and Earls of Atholl for more than 700 years, and can claim its own private army. Bonnie Prince Charlie slept in the now tartan-clad tower room in 1745. The exterior of the castle reflects a Victorian make-over in 1863 and inside are wonderful artefacts and paintings.

THE TROSSACHS MAP REF 408 F3

The Trossachs is an area of outstanding natural beauty in central Scotland, now with protected status as the main sector of the Loch Lomond and the Trossachs National Park. Scotland's first such designated park, its land stretches for 720 square miles (1,865 sq km) from the Argyll Forest Park in the west over to Callander in the east, and from Killin and Tyndrum up in the north to Balloch in the south, at the foot of Loch Lomond. The Trossachs is the region lying to the east of Loch Lomond which was first 'discovered' by travellers in the late 18th century, and was popularised for a wider audience as a thrilling backdrop to the novels of Sir Walter Scott (1771–1832). Scott's famous poem, 'The Lady of the Lake' (1810), was set in identifiable and accessible places across the Trossachs, and attracted many tourists to the area.

The village of Aberfoyle is the key to this region, giving easy access to the wooded hills of the Queen Elizabeth Forest Park and the peak of Ben Venue (729m/2,319ft), as well as Loch Katrine to the north. There are great opportunities for walking and cycling, including a pretty cycle route that runs through the Forest Park and along the shores of Loch Venachar and Loch Lubnaig to Balquhidder, Lochearnhead and Killin. The Trossachs Discovery visitor centre in Aberfoyle is a mine of information about activities in the area. The Scottish Wool Centre behind it offers an entertaining Sheepdog School Show, as well as a chance to see lambs and sheep shearing in season.

Reintroducing Species

What little remains of a once huge Caledonian Forest is today being eroded by the ever-increasing population of red and sika deer. The only way to restore the balance, many claim, is to reintroduce the deer's natural predator, the wolf, to the wilds of Scotland. Without such action the forest and its ecosystem is in increasing danger of disappearing forever.

For millions of years, Scotland was covered in trees – a pristine wilderness of birch, rowan, aspen, juniper and Scots pines. When the Romans arrived a mere two millennia ago, they called Scotland 'Caledonia', meaning 'wooded heights'. Today, only one per cent of that mighty Caledonian Forest remains, and attempts to revive the forests by restocking are thwarted by the very icon of Scotland, the red deer. With no natural predators except for man in the short hunting season, deer populations have simply grown out of hand. Ironically, of the six species of deer in Scotland, only two are native. But the red deer in particular is threatening the very existence of both the remaining forest and the animals that depend upon it.

When the forest was rich in flora, it was rich in wildlife too. Now, with the beaver, wild boar, lynx, moose, brown bear and wolf all gone, only a few birds – the capercaillie, crested tit and endemic Scottish crossbill – remain.

Thankfully, steps are now underway to reintroduce some of Scotland's native species of wildlife. Duncan Horwood's book *The Stonor Eagles* relates the passing of the last of the white-tailed eagles from Scotland. But these magnificent birds were reintroduced in the 1970s, and have now become locally widespread, notably on the islands of Mull, Rhum and Skye. In fact today, Mull is fast becoming one of the prime wildlife tourism destinations in Scotland, and the opportunity to see golden and sea eagles is one of the main attractions on offer.

Capercaillie are the largest and by far the most impressive of the grouse family. Sadly, it was their dependency on woodland which was in juxtaposition with man's intense forest felling, that led to their extinction in Britain in the 18th century. They were reintroduced in 1837, initially with considerable success, but the demands for timber during two world wars once more pushed this interesting creature into decline. They continue to struggle, but have limited strongholds in Scotland, and a poor breeding record is once again making them vulnerable.

Staying with birds, if you take the road from Castle Douglas down to Loch Ken in Dumfries and Galloway there is a better than average chance that there will be a red kite circling above, marked out by its distinctive reddish-brown colour and forked tail. This road is a favourite foraging ground for the 100 birds which have been released into the area since 2001 and have become a popular local attraction.

Until recently red kites were a rare site in Scotland. By 1879 they had been wiped out in Scotland, mainly as a result of poisoning and egg collecting. The birds were reintroduced in 1989 and releases continued to 2004 at three sites around the country, as part of a joint project between SNH and RSPB Scotland.

The story of the beaver is less happy. Due to hunting, European beaver became extinct in England and Wales in the 12th century, and only survived in Scotland until the 1600s. By the 18th century, beaver were close to extinction across most of Europe, but since the 1920s, successful reintroductions have taken place in twenty-three European countries, but sadly not Britain. For our prehistoric ancestors, the sight and sound of beavers along the rivers of Britain would have been familiar.

As an effort to reintroduce beaver into Scotland, in 1998, a public consultation was undertaken by Scottish Natural Heritage (SNH), to consider the trial reintroduction of European beaver. The results showed the Scottish people to be overwhelmingly in favour of the proposal. In February 2005, SNH, who wanted a licence to reintroduce beaver to Forestry Commission land at Knapdale in Argyll, wrote to the Scottish Executive asking for ministerial approval to proceed and to issue a licence for the trial. Seven months later, the Scottish Executive said no.

Wild boar is increasingly appearing in butchers' shops, supermarkets and restaurant menus, but sadly not in the wild. Unlike many extinct British species, wild boar existed in Britain long after the Roman occupation. Under Norman rule, punitive laws were passed forbidding anyone to kill them, but they nevertheless became extinct in Britain in 1683, as a result of hunting and absorption into domestic herds. The ultimate omnivore, eating anything and everything, wild boar have recently re-established themselves in southern England, largely as escapees from farms. Glen Affric is just one of a number of Scottish locations that have been the scene of an experiment with wild boar to help regenerate the Caledonia forest by eating invasive bracken shoots, and other estates in Scotland have small herds of wild boar in enclosed areas.

Throughout history, pine martens have been regarded as the most beautiful of British mammals, with a fur so soft only kings might wear it. These lithe, ferret-like animals have impressive speed and agility which, alas, allows them to chase down red squirrels. Their taste for game birds made them unpopular with game estates, and the marten has suffered widespread persecution. They are now a protected species, and their numbers are increasing rapidly in Scotland.

The iconic native species in Scotland, red squirrel, has suffered greatly from habitat loss, persecution and competition from the introduced grey squirrel. The red squirrel is most at home in the dense coniferous forests of Scottish plantations.

It is not all doom and gloom: plans exist to see the long-term introduction of rare species to the Alladale wilderness, forty miles north of Inverness. The plans are still plans, but within the confines of a 37-mile electric fence, packs of wolves, a dozen European brown bears, lynx, boar and European elk may well, one day, be roaming free.

LEFT FROM TOP Wild boar forage once again in the pine woodland of Glen Affric.

The windswept hills of Glen Falloch are home to the scant remains of the once-great Caledonian Forest, which at one time covered the area in thick woodland.

A fine red stag in the Glengoulandie Deer Park – the tips of its antlers are known as 'points'. In March and April the stags shed their antlers as new bone grows.

Pine martens have made a rapid come-back in the wild now that they are a protected species. The animals' bushy tails grow to half the length of their bodies.

RIGHT FROM TOP The large capercaillie is still fighting for survival as a breed due to its diminished natural woodland habitat.

Sightings of pretty crested tits are now more frequent in the Cairngorms.

Some 15 miles (24km) from Loch Ness, Glen Affric's lake and rivers create a romantic picture when the mists roll down from the surrounding hills.

ABOVE CALLANDER

Steep wooded paths lead you through the crags for superb views of the Trossachs. Known unofficially as the eastern gateway to the Highlands, Callander is a great place to strike out from and explore the breathtaking surrounding countryside with its snow-clad mountain backdrop.

DISTANCE/TIME 3 miles (4.8km) 2h15 **MAP** OS Explorer 365 The Trossachs **START** Riverside car park, grid ref: NN 625079 **TRACKS** Forest tracks and some rocky paths. **THE PUB** The Lade Inn, Kilmahog, just west of Callander. Tel: 01877 330152

1 From the Riverside car park, walk back to the main road, then turn left. Follow this, then turn right along Tulliepan Crescent. Just in front of the new housing estate, turn left and follow the wide track. Where the track splits, take the path on the left that is signposted 'The Crags'.

2 Your path now winds steeply uphill through the trees and can get slippery if there's been a lot of rain. Keep following the path and cross a footbridge. Climb to reach a wall on the left-hand side, after which your path narrows. Follow it to pass a large boulder.

3 Continue following the path, which eventually bears left, up some steps to a fence. Cross another footbridge, scramble over some rocks and go through a metal kissing gate. You eventually come to a memorial cairn, created in 1897 for Queen Victoria's Diamond Jubilee. On a clear day there are stunning, panoramic views of the surrounding countryside.

4 Leaving the cairn, your path now begins to wind downhill. It's rocky in places and you'll need to take some care as you descend. After a while you'll spot the road through the trees. Once you reach here, turn right into the trees and walk down to join it.

5 Turn right along the road – you'll see the Wallace Monument near Stirling in the far distance. You'll soon pass a sign on the right-hand side for the Red Well, where the water runs a reddish colour owing to the presence of iron traces in the local rock. Continue until to a car park on your left. You can make a detour here to see the Bracklyn Falls.

6 After the car park, stay on the road for about 100yds (91m), then turn right to climb some wooden steps (signposted 'The Crags Upper Wood Walk'), but the sign faces away from you. Walk past a small building, cross a little footbridge and then walk on to a crossing of several footpaths.

7 Turn left, then turn right. Continue walking through the woods, cross a footbridge and, when you reach a wider, slate-covered track, turn right and walk uphill. At the end of the track, turn left and proceed downhill until you finally get to a wooden seat and another narrow footbridge.

8 Take the path that runs to the right of the seat (don't cross the footbridge). Follow the path downhill and back to the place where you entered the woods. Turn right, then go left along the main road and walk back into Callander and the car park at the start.

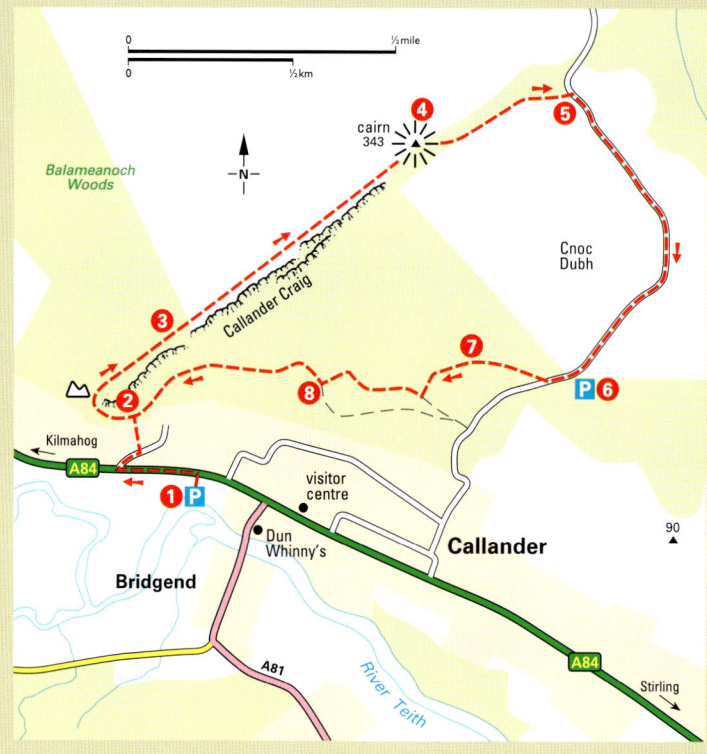

WALK 130

FROM BALQUHIDDER TO CREAG AN TUIRC

A forest walk to a cairn at the summit of a knoll and a bench where you can rest and enjoy the far reaching views of the River Balvag, Loch Voil and the atmospheric Braes of Balquhidder. This is Rob Roy country, where the 17th-century outlaw lived and died. Immortalised in the 19th century by Sir Walter Scott in his novel *Rob Roy* (1817), the romantic myth of Rob Roy MacGregor's turbulent life was retold in the 1995 film of the same name starring Liam Neeson and Jessica Lange. The Old Kirk at Balquhidder is the final resting place of Roy alongside his beloved wife Mary and two of his four sons. A surrounding bronze rail marks the grave.

DISTANCE/TIME 2.5 miles (4km) 2h **MAP** OS Explorer 365 The Trossachs **START** Balquhidder church, grid ref: NN 536209 **TRACKS** Forest roads and hillside, 2 stiles **THE PUB** Monachyle Mhor, Balquhidder. Tel: 01877 384305; www.monachylemhor.com

1 From the car park at Balquhidder church, walk along a dirt track, go past a shed and cross a stile on the right-hand side which gives access to the forest. Follow the direction arrows on the green signposts pointing to Creag an Tuirc along a forest track and heading up the hill.

2 Continue on this obvious trail for about 0.5 mile (800m) then turn right, once you reach a green building. From here carry on and again follow the clearly signposted route that takes you along a forest road.

3 After another 0.5 mile (800m) cross a gate which is on the right-hand side, go slightly downhill on some stone steps and across a small stream. The path then continues to go uphill on some stone steps, passes through an area of old pine trees and then on towards the summit of a knoll. Here there is a cairn erected by the Clan Maclaren Society in 1987 to commemorate their 25th anniversary. The plaque proclaims that this place is the ancient rallying point of their clan.

4 A seat below the cairn is a grand place to rest after the climb up here. Sit for a while and enjoy the superb views over the meandering line of the River Balvag and the length of Loch Voil with the Braes of Balquhidder rising steeply above it. You can see the route that Scottish hero Rob Roy's funeral procession would have taken from Inverlochlarig down to the village itself, and also the churchyard where his body lies. Now retrace your steps back down the hill but before the top of the stone steps, take path to the left signposted 'Forest Walk'. This continues downhill, down a set of steps, across a small bridge, through bracken, over a stream and across a stile. It then passes through a small wood of young native trees before finally emerging on to the forest road.

5 Turn left here and retrace your steps back downhill over the stile and turn left to return to the car park. From here enter the churchyard and turn left. You will find Rob Roy's grave on the left in front of the ruins of a pre-Reformation church.

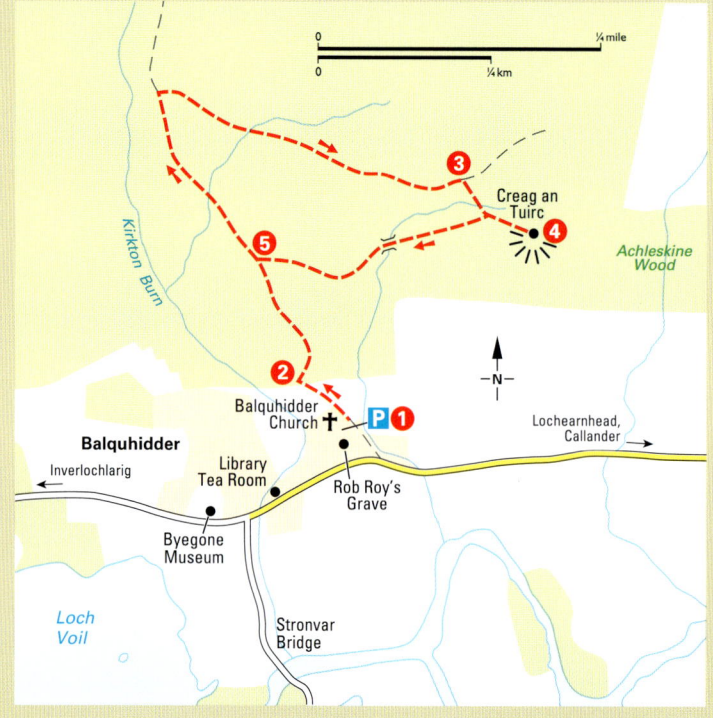

THE BRAES O' KILLIECRANKIE

A deeply wooded riverside walk leads from the famous battlefield to Loch Faskally. When James II was ousted from England in a bloodless coup in 1688, the Scots Parliament (the Estates) voted to replace him with William of Orange. The Stuarts had neglected and mismanaged Scotland, and had mounted a bloody persecution of the fundamentalist Protestant (Covenanters) of the Southern Uplands.

DISTANCE/TIME 8.75 miles (14.1km) 4h **MAP** OS Explorer 386 Pitlochry & Loch Tummel **START** Balquhidder church, grid ref: NN 536209 **TRACKS** Wide riverside paths, minor roads, no stiles **THE PUB** Old Mill Inn, Pitlochry. Tel: 01796 474020

1 Cross the front of the visitor centre to steps, signed 'Soldier's Leap', leading down into the wooded gorge. A footbridge crosses the waterfall of Troopers' Den. At the next junction, turn left ('Soldier's Leap'). Ten steps down, a spur path on the right leads to the viewpoint above the Soldier's Leap.

2 Return to the main path, signed 'Linn of Tummel', which leads down to join the River Garry below the railway viaduct. After a mile (1.6km) it reaches a footbridge.

3 Don't cross this footbridge, but continue ahead, signed 'Pitlochry', along the riverside under the tall South Garry road bridge. The path runs around a huge river pool on to a tarred lane; turn right here. The lane leaves the lochside, then passes a track on the right, blocked by a vehicle barrier. Ignore this; shortly turn right at a signpost, 'Pitlochry'.

4 Immediately bear left to pass along the right-hand side of Loch Dunmore, following red-top posts. A footbridge crosses the loch, but turn away from it, half right, on to a small path that becomes a dirt track. After 110yds (100m) it reaches a wider track. Turn left, with a white/yellow waymarker. After 220yds

(201m) the track climbs; white/yellow markers indicate a small path right, which follows the lochside. Where it rejoins the wider path, bear right at a green waymarker and cross a footbridge to the A9 road bridge.

5 Cross Loch Faskally on the Clunie footbridge below the road's bridge and turn right, on to a quiet road around the loch. In 1 mile (1.6km), at the top of the grass bank on the left, is the Priest Stone. After the Clunie power station, you reach a car park on the left. Here a sign indicates a steep little path down to the Linn of Tummel.

6 Return to the road above for 0.5 miles (800m), to cross a grey suspension bridge on the right. Turn right, downstream, to pass above the Linn. A spur path back right returns to the falls at a lower level, but the main path continues along the riverside (signed 'Killiecrankie'). It bends left and goes down wooden steps to the Garry, then runs upstream and under the high road bridge. Take the side-path up on to the bridge for the view, then return to follow the descending path signed 'Pitlochry via Faskally'. This runs down to the bridge, Point 3. Return upstream to the start.

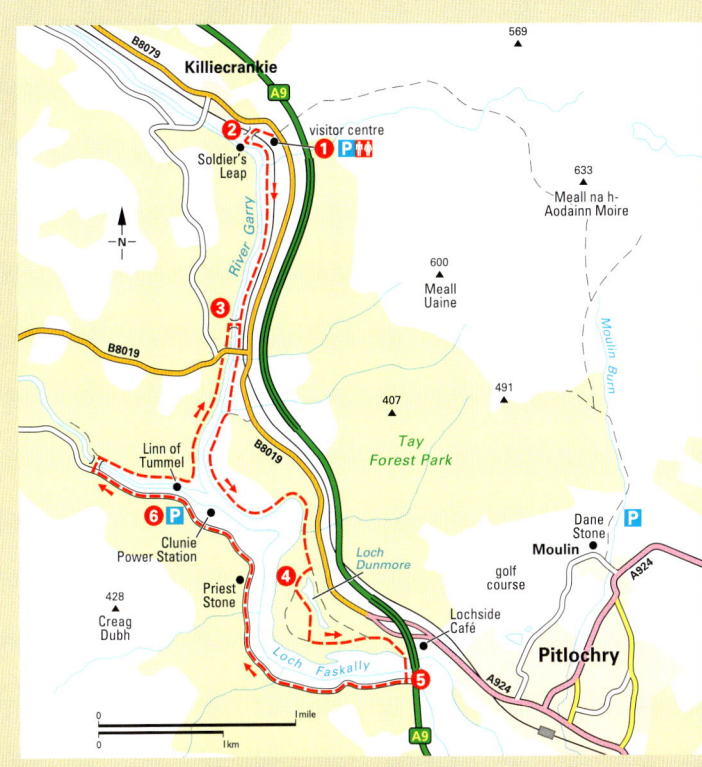

WALK 132

THE MYSTERIOUS STONES OF ABERLEMNO

This walk takes you through agricultural land once inhabited by the Picts, a fascinating ancient British tribe. Had history turned out differently you would have been doing this walk in Pictland, not Scotland. The Picts inhabited this northern part of Britain for thousands of years, yet we know little about them. Neither their language nor manuscripts have survived, and their culture remains a mystery.

DISTANCE/TIME 3 miles (4.8km) 1.45h **MAP** OS Explorer 389 Forfar, Brechin & Edzell **START** Grid ref: NO 522558 **TRACKS** Quiet agricultural land and ancient carved stones **THE PUB** Royal Hotel, Castle Street, Forfar. Tel: 01307 462691

1 From the car park turn right and walk along the road, then go first left, signed 'Aberlemno church and stone'. Continue past the church – the famous Pictish stone is in the churchyard – and follow the road as it bends round to the right. Follow the road until you reach a T-junction.

2 Turn right and follow this road, passing the entrance to Woodside on the left. At the corner, follow the road as it bends right. Walk down to join the B9134, turn right and follow this a short distance until you reach a turning on the left.

3 Turn left along this road, signed 'Finavon Hill'. The road winds uphill, passing by several outcrops, then tracks under a line of pylons. Carry on along this road as it follows the base of a hill.

4 Continue following the road and you will soon see a mast, followed by a pond on the left, and will pass a hill on the right, once topped with an ancient fort. Continue to reach a padlocked gate on the left. You can make a diversion here. Climb the gate and walk up the track, passing two ponds to eventually reach a house.

5 Turn right on the track and walk back on yourself, through a gate in a deer fence and past some pheasant feeders. Go through a gate at the bottom, turn left to the road.

6 If you've done the diversion, turn left, if not, continue following the road, which now winds downhill (you'll soon reach an electricity sub station and mobile phone mast). At some houses, turn right.

7 Walk past Bogardo house and follow the track as it swings left between fields. Turn right at the gap and cross the field, then go right again at the next field. At the top of the field go left and walk to the far end. You'll now have to scramble over an often watery, overgrown ditch and also climb a barbed-wire fence.

8 Maintain direction, walking on the pasture to the right of the fence (the track is overgrown). At the end, turn left through a gate and continue along the obvious track, to pass Woodrae. Continue to pass an old dovecote on the left, then turn right at the road. Walk uphill, past Balbinny and on to the junction. Finally, turn right in order to make your way back to Amberlemno.

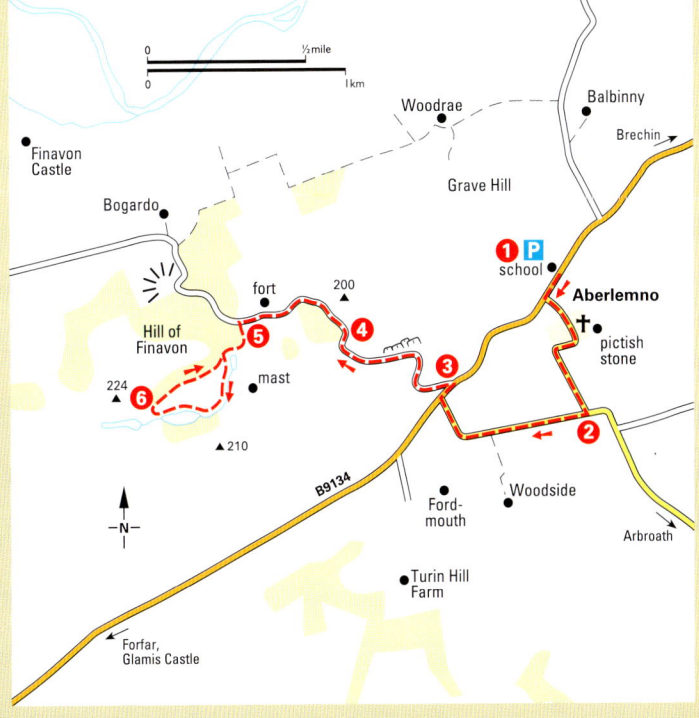

Aberfoyle is surrounded by the pine trees of the Queen Elizabeth Forest Park, and the visitor centre, situated a mile to the north has comprehensive information about the area's walking and cycling routes. The Scottish Wool Centre in Aberfoyle attracts many visitors.

6 Continue on the A821 and the A81. At the intersection with the A811, turn right to pass Drymen, and then go through Gartocharn.

Quiet little Gartocharn is best known for the wonderful view up Loch Lomond from the hill, Duncryne (142m/462ft), known fondly to locals as the 'Dumpling' behind the village.

7 Continue on the A811 through Balloch and turn right at the A82. Follow this main route north, and after about 9 miles (15km) pass the turning to the pretty village of Luss. Continue on by the west shore of the Loch as it narrows. Lying near the foot of Loch Lomond, Balloch has an ultra-modern shopping mall with fantastic views of the loch. Pass Inverbeg where you can catch a ferry across the loch to the isolated settlement of Rowardennan.

8 Rejoin the A82 and keep travelling up the west shore of the loch. After Ardlui, the mountains become more rugged as you continue up Glen Falloch to Crianlarich. Turn right here on to the A85. Go through Glen Dochart. Pass Loch Lubhair on the left, with Ben More (1,171m/3,842ft) on the right. Turn left at the A827 to return to Killin.

TROSSACHS TRAIL

Starting from attractive Killin village, with the Falls of Dochart on its doorstep, this drive explores the varied and magnificent scenery of Scotland's first designated national park of Loch Lomond and the Trossachs. The route takes in the Duke's Pass where there are spectacular views of the surrounding countryside.

Route Directions

1 Leave the hill-walking centre of Killin on the A827, and follow this northeast for 17 miles (27km) to Kenmore. As you pass Loch Tay on the right, the big, bare-looking mountain of Ben Lawers (3,984ft/1,214m) looms up to your left.

The area is now a National Nature Reserve and is celebrated for its variety of Arctic and alpine flora, which thrives on the lime-rich soils. Look for mountain hares on the high ground. The National Trust for Scotland has a visitor centre, signposted from the road. Kenmore supports a watersports centre and on the loch is the Scottish Crannog Centre.

2 Continue along the A827 for a further 6 miles (10km) until you get to Aberfeldy. Pass a stirring memorial of 1887 to the men of the Black Watch on the southern side of the bridge.

The Black Watch regiment was enrolled into the British Army in 1739, and took its name from the soldiers' dark tartan, which was carefully selected to differentiate them from the Guardsmen, or 'Red Soldiers'. The Black Watch served as a famous regiment from 1739 to 2006 when, due to military reorganisation, it became a battalion within the new Scottish Regiment.

3 Leave by the A826, and follow this wild road up over the high moors. Turn right at the A822, then right at the A85 and follow this into Crieff. Continue on the A85 for 19 miles (31km) through Comrie to Lochearnhead.

This small town at the tip of Lochearn grew when the railway was built through Glen Ogle, which lies to the north and links up with Killin, passing to a height of 289m (948ft). Edinample Castle, a castellated mansion of 1630, lies where the Burn of Ample runs into the loch.

4 Leave by the A84 and follow it for 14 miles (23km) southward to Callander, passing a turning right to Balquhidder, where outlaw Rob Roy MacGregor (1671–1734) is buried in the churchyard, alongside his wife, Helen, and his sons. Continue along the A84 and then turn left at the A821. After passing the Trossachs Hotel, follow signs (right) to Loch Katrine. Leave your car in the parking area at the end and take a walk or bicycle ride beside this loch, 9 miles (15km) long, whose island-studded beauty became legendary after Sir Walter Scott's description in 'The Lady of the Lake'.

While recreation is to the fore as visitors come in droves to enjoy the scene and take a ride on the steamer, the loch also has a serious practical function, supplying central Glasgow with fresh water via an underground pipeway some 35 miles (56km) long.

5 Return to the A821 and turn right. Follow the A821 for 7 miles (11km) over the hills on the Duke's Pass, and continue through the dense Achray Forest to the little town of Aberfoyle. The Achray Forest forms a quarter of Queen Elizabeth Country Park.

106 MILES (171KM)

EAST OF INVERNESS

Legend and history come to life in this scenic Highland tour which takes you to the east of Inverness. It's a reasonably long distance to drive so you may want to stay overnight en route and take a couple of days to complete the drive. The tour starts at Culloden, a name most people will be familiar with from history lessons on the great battle here. You continue on to two castles, Cawdor and Brodie, and on to the religious community and eco-village at Findhorn. This innovative village, opened in 1985, features 55 ecologically efficient buildings and four wind turbines.

Route Directions

1 From the Culloden Battlefield & Visitor Centre head west on the B9006 to reach the A9. Join the A9 and follow it to Inverness.

Inverness, 'the Capital of the Highlands' is a working city but also a tourist hub, and, for many, the gateway to Loch Ness.

2 Drive out of Inverness on the A96, travelling through the flatlands south of the Moray Firth. Turn left onto the B9039 to reach the small fishing village of Ardersier, then take the B9006 to Fort George, a distance of 12 miles (19km).

Fort George was constructed between 1748 and 1769 on a narrow spit of land which protrudes out into the Moray Firth, facing Chanonry Point on the Black Isle. With many landward defences, the site originally covered 12 acres (29.6ha), and was designed to accommodate a garrison of over 2,000 men. The fort, named after George II, was set here to protect Inverness from seaward attack, and as part of the violent backlash to subdue the Highlands after the bloody battle of Culloden. It is unaltered, a superb example of an artillery fort.

3 Drive the 12 miles (19km) back to Ardersier, then follow the B9006 and the B9090 to Cawdor Castle.

This 14th-century castle is associated with the play *Macbeth*. Kilravock Castle (private) stands to the west, the 15th-century family seat of the Roses and in the shadow of its more famous neighbour. It can number both Bonnie Prince Charlie and his nemesis, the Duke of Cumberland, among its visitors in the hours before Culloden (1746).

4 Leave Cawdor Castle and continue on the B9090. Stay on this road and follow it until you get to Nairn.

Silent-movie star and famous comic actor Charlie Chaplin (1889–1977) liked to take his holidays at this prosperous resort town, with its fine beach, good golf course and variety of activities for all the family. Villas and hotels spread back from old Fishertown by the shore, where the former little fishermen's cottages are so tightly packed together. The attractive little harbour dates from 1820, and was designed by engineering legend Thomas Telford.

5 Leave by the A96, passing Auldearn, site of a major battle between Covenanters and Royalists in 1645. Drive down this road through the shady plantation of Culbin Forest. Turn left for a visit to Brodie Castle.

A Z-plan tower house dating back to 1567, Brodie Castle is set in attractive parkland that is famous for its spring show of daffodils. Remodelled into a comfortable home in the 19th century, it remained in the private hands of the Brodie family until 1980, after which it passed to the National Trust for Scotland. The family's collection of fine art, books and furniture is outstanding, and includes many works from the 17th century, from that of the Dutch masters to the Scottish Colourists.

6 Regain the A96, and stay on this road into Forres. Continue on the A96, then turn left at the B9011 and follow this road to Findhorn.

Ever vulnerable from the sea and shifting sand dunes, this is the third village on the site to be called Findhorn – the first village was buried by sand in 1694, the second washed away in 1701. Once a major port, the harbour is now given over to pleasure craft. In 1962 the Findhorn Community was founded here by Peter and Eileen Caddy and Dorothy Maclean to create a more spiritual and sustainable way of living. This thriving community now has more than 400 permanent residents, and supports an extensive holistic education programme and also boasts an eco-village.

7 Return along the B9011 and A96 to Forres. Head south on the A940 and join the A939 for Grantown-on-Spey, a total distance here of 27 miles (43km).

Grantown-on-Spey lies at the edge of the Speyside whisky country, and makes a useful touring centre. The village was planned in the late 18th century by Sir James Grant, and the arrival of the railway in 1863 heralded its popularity as a health resort. The railway was lost in the 1960s, but the town is still popular with walkers and anglers, and in winter accommodates some of the overspill of skiers from nearby Aviemore.

8 Leave on the A95 towards Aviemore, and at Dulnain Bridge turn on to the A938 to Carrbridge, noted for its picturesque old bridge of 1717, and the Landmark Forest Heritage Park. Continue on the A938 and join the A9, heading towards Inverness. Just after Daviot, turn right onto the B851. Then turn left at the B9006 and follow it to the major battle site of Culloden Moor where the tour started.

Just east of Culloden, a minor road (B9091) passes Clava Cairns, three of the most important chambered cairns in the country, dating from the Bronze Age (free access). The two outer ones are passage graves, topped with a massive flat slab. The perimeters of all three cairns are marked by a ring of standing stones, often carved with 'cup' marks.

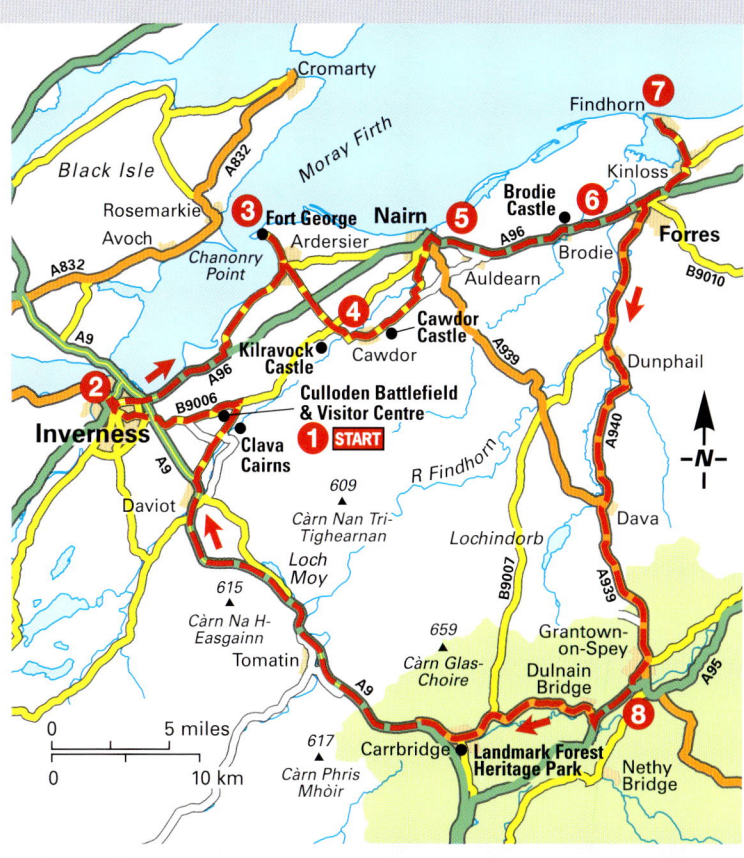

Argyll, Mull & West

CLOCKWISE FROM TOP LEFT: CHARLES RENNIE MACKINTOSH AT HOUSE FOR AN ART LOVER, GLASGOW; ABBEY CLOISTERS, IONA; TEMPLE WOOD STANDING STONES, KILMARTIN; BOATS MOORED AT CRINAN

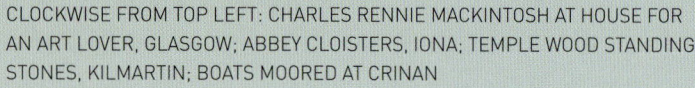

CRINAN CANAL

ARDNAMURCHAN & MORVERN

MAP REF 410 D7/408 C1

You can go no further west on mainland Britain than Ardnamurchan Point, with its spectacular views over to Mull, Coll and Tiree. The whole peninsula, with its rocky hills and desolate moorland, gale-blown trees and pretty heather-capped promontories, has an 'end-of-the-world' feeling. The main road mostly hugs the northern shore of Loch Sunart, rich in birdlife, and you can take a minor road to Ardnamurchan's north coast as the main road passes round Beinn nan Losgann, or continue to the little crofting village of Kilchoan, where a ferry goes to Tobermory on Mull. The 13th-century Mingary Castle, is the place where King James IV finally accepted the submission of the Lord of the Isles in 1495; Hanoverian troops built barracks inside it 350 years later.

Morvern, across Loch Sunart, is a rugged land with gentler green glens. Lochaline, a popular yachting haven, is reached either by road along Glen Gleann, or by ferry from the Isle of Mull. There are two castles to visit in the area – the remains of Ardtornish, east of the village, and well-preserved Kinlochaline at the head of Loch Aline. The silica sands at Lochaline have been quarried commercially for manufacturing optical glass. Fiunary, along the Sound of Mull, was the birthplace of George Macleod, founder of the Iona Community. Caisteal nan Con is a small fortress guarding the Sound of Mull. The road ends some 4 miles (6.4km) beyond, near Drimnin, with views towards Tobermory.

ARRAN, ISLE OF MAP REF 408 D5

Generations of Clydesiders have enjoyed holidays on this attractive island, caught between the Ayrshire coast and the Kintyre Peninsula, yet it remains unspoiled. The Highland Boundary Fault runs through the island, and while the mountain of Goat Fell (874m/2,867ft) dominates the skyline to the north, the south is much more level. This reflects the geology of the country as a whole, and Arran is often tagged 'Scotland in Miniature'. Glen Rosa offers fairly easy walking, while Goat Fell and Glen Sannox are more rugged, and there are plenty of opportunities for a range of other outdoor activities, including golf and pony trekking, around the island. Brodick is the biggest town, with villages catering for visitors scattered round the 56-mile (90km) coastline.

The red sandstone Brodick Castle is the island's biggest single attraction, with its extensive collection of porcelain and silver, some 19th-century sporting pictures and trophies, and a beautiful country park of meadows and woodland.

The gardens include a world-renowned collection of rhododendrons. The seat of the Dukes of Hamilton, the estate has a history that dates back 800 years.

The legacy of much earlier settlers may be seen in the chambered cairns at Clachaig, Whiting Bay and other sites, and also in the stone circles on Machrie Moor. These stones date from the Bronze Age but there is also evidence that the site was previously occupied in the Neolithic era.

In recent years the island has developed a name for its food produce, which includes cheese and smoked meats. Around the courtyard of Home Farm, just north of Brodick, you can see the cheese being made at the Island Cheese Company, and you can purchase delicately smoked fish, rich game and free-range poultry next door at Creelers Smokehouse. The fragrant soaps of Arran Aromatics share the same site. Arran Fine Foods, at Lamlash, sells a range of locally produced mustards and preserves.

Ferries sail to Arran from Ardrossan (year-round) and Claonaig, by Skipness (summer). The Ayrshire coast between here and Prestwick Airport is famous worldwide for the quality of its golf courses, centring on Troon.

CRINAN CANAL MAP REF 408 D3

In 1847 Queen Victoria and Prince Albert sailed the 9 miles (14.5km) of the Crinan Canal aboard the barge *Sunbeam* – a journey followed later in the century by MacBrayne's steamers in order to sell 'Royal Route' excursions from Glasgow to Oban. Today you are most likely to see pleasure craft negotiating the canal's 15 locks, but its original purpose was to enable merchant traffic to and from the Western Isles to avoid the hazardous voyage around the Mull of Kintyre. Two famous engineers worked on the Crinan Canal, which finally opened in 1801. John Rennie was responsible for the original engineering work, and Thomas Telford masterfully solved all of the problems with the water supply.

From the basin at Ardrishaig, where it leaves Loch Fyne, the canal hugs the wooded hillsides as it climbs up to its highest point of 64 feet (19.4m). On the hills above Cairnbaan are reservoirs that constantly replenish the water down in the canal as it descends underneath the unusual hand-wound rolling bridge at Dunadry. Beyond this the landscape then opens out into the flat marshland near to the River Add estuary. The canal ends at the picturesque haven of Crinan Harbour, with beautiful views over the Sound of Jura. With some luck you may find a 'puffer' in the harbour to remind you of the canal's past glories.

ARRAN

DUNOON MAP REF 408 E4

Paddle steamers used to bring huge crowds from Gourock to Dunoon, and there are still regular ferry services here. On the grassy headland between the town's two bays are the remains of the 13th-century royal castle, largely destroyed in 1685. Below is the 1896 statue of Burns's love, Highland Mary, erected to mark the centenary of the poet's death. Dunoon is busiest each year during late August for the Cowal Highland Gathering, when pipe bands gather from all over the world.

Morag's Fairy Glen, off the road south from Dunoon, has shaded walks along the Berry Burn, but for more expansive views, continue onward to Toward Point lighthouse (not open) at the southern end of the A815, where you can look out across the water to Bute and down to Largs. In the grounds of the 19th-century Castle Toward stands ruins of a 15th-century tower house. This is where the Campbells of Ardkinglas besieged the Lamonts, who were Stuart loyalists. Although guaranteed safety, 36 Lamont men were taken to Dunoon and hanged.

Just north of Dunoon at Lochan Wood is the attractive Cowal Bird Garden, and this area is rich in ancient sites. Near Sandbank, on the shore of Holy Loch, are the huge stones forming Adam's Grave, a remaining Neolithic burial chamber, and you can take a trail from near Ardnadam Farm to see the ancient field boundaries and the site of a prehistoric enclosure.

Bute has been the holiday playground for generations of Glaswegians, most of whom arrive at Rothesay on the ferry from Wemyss Bay. Stood on the Firth of Clyde, Rothesay has a late 19th-century atmosphere created by its solid, mostly Victorian houses and decorative Winter Gardens, but much more ancient are the ruins of the moated and circular 13th-century Rothesay Castle.

The island largely consists of green and fertile hills, with superb views across the narrow Kyles of Bute to the mainland and to mountainous Arran. Just off the east coast road is one of Bute's hidden gems, the extraordinary Victorian Gothic Mount Stewart House, surrounded by extensive gardens that lead down to the shore.

Insight
BRUCE & THE SPIDER

In 1307, on his way back from exile on Rathlin Island, off Northern Ireland, Robert the Bruce mustered his troops in Glen Cloy, on Arran, before heading to the Scottish mainland to try once more to oust the English and claim the throne. According to legend, he was roused from despair and inspired to fight once more – and succeed this time – by watching a spider, spinning its web and succeeding only on the seventh attempt to attach its thread. In another version of the story, he watched the spider in a cave near to Blackwaterfoot on Arran, known still as the King's Caves.

Activity
GOING DOWNHILL FAST

Glen Coe's skiing may not be as fashionable as Klosters, but it can be just as exciting. From White Corries at the top of the glen, where the fascinating Museum of Scottish Skiing and Mountaineering puts the sport into perspective, a chairlift takes skiers (and summer visitors) high into the mountains, where there are superb views to Rannoch Moor and beyond. There are 15 runs catering for all abilities, some with intriguing names – Fly Paper, for example, and Mug's Alley. Instruction is available. If hurtling downhill doesn't appeal, the Glen Coe area offers cross-country skiing, ski mountaineering, snowboarding, speed skating, and even paragliding.

Insight
SPANISH TREASURE

There is a fascinating old treasure map, now on display at Inveraray Castle, showing the location of the wreck of a Spanish galleon that sank in Tobermory Bay in 1588. After the defeat of the Armada, many Spaniards attempted to get home via the north of Scotland. The legend goes that one such vessel was given food and other supplies by the people of Mull, but the Spanish refused to pay, and even locked up Donald Maclean, who had come to collect the payment. He managed to escape, and blew up the ship, which sank in the bay. Confusion reigns as to whether the ship was a troop carrier, the *San Juan de Sicilia*, or a treasure ship, the *Florida*. Treasure hunters still dive here in search of a shower of golden ducats, yet so far only a few coins and cannon have been raised.

GLASGOW

GLASGOW MAP REF 408 F4

Scotland's second city, Glasgow grew on the back of the tobacco trade with the New World to become one of the major industrial and engineering centres of Britain in the 19th century. In the 20th century its fortunes changed, as ship-building and manufacturing slumped after World War II. In recent years, however, it has reinvented itself as a vibrant and stylish place to be, making the most of its Victorian heritage of buildings, celebrating the designs of its most famous son, Charles Rennie Mackintosh (1868–1928), and investing in daring new projects that include the 'Armadillo' Scottish Exhibition and Conference Centre and the titanium-clad Science Centre. The trendy bars, cafés and restaurants spill out onto the pavements, and the city is known across the world for its classy shopping, with malls selling everything from top quality modern furniture to luxury chocolate, and bold, cutting edge designer fashion, in addition to hand-crafted jewellery.

Glasgow is full of things to do and see. Highlights include the treasures on show in the newly reopened Kelvingrove Museum; the fabulous Science Centre, with around 500 interactive exhibits to explain everything from the structure of the Forth Bridge to the movement of an artificial limb; and the People's Palace – the red-brick museum of local life on

Glasgow Green which captures the wit, eccentricity and gritty character of the city, telling its history through familiar objects and quotes from real people. South of the city centre, in leafy Pollok Park, is Glasgow's outstanding art collection, made by shipping magnate William Burrell, and displaying a small range of exquisite pieces – from original paintings to Chinese porcelain to some medieval tapestries and stained glass – in a small, purpose-built gallery. Musts on the Mackintosh trail include Glasgow School of Art, the House for an Art Lover, the Mackintosh House at the university's Hunterian Museum, and the famous Willow Tea Rooms. The Kibble Palace, a vast Victorian glasshouse in the Botanic Gardens of the West End, is the perfect escape on a wet or chilly day.

GLEN COE & RANNOCH MOOR
MAP REF 410 F8/408 E1

On 13 February 1692 the Campbell clan defied the age-old traditions of Highland hospitality and massacred 38 members of the Macdonald clan in Glen Coe. Alastair Macdonald, like many clansmen reluctant to accept William and Mary as ruling monarchs, failed to get papers attesting his loyalty to a magistrate by the deadline, the end of 1691, though they did arrive in Edinburgh in the new year. However, the papers were secretly suppressed by

the Under Secretary of State, who then told Campbell of Glenlyon that the Macdonalds 'must all be slaughtered'. Campbell and his men, pretending to be delayed on a trip, were accommodated by the Macdonalds in Glen Coe for a fortnight, then cold-bloodedly slaughtered their hosts.

The atrocity took place in the lower glen by Glencoe village, where the now heather-roofed Folk Museum offers displays of real Highland life. The most dramatic part of Glen Coe is higher up. From the roof of the National Trust for Scotland Visitor Centre there is a fine view of outstanding mountain scenery of stark peaks and glittering waterfalls. You can get details about the many exhilarating walks from the Visitor Centre; there is challenging climbing here too.

Southeast of Glen Coe, Rannoch Moor is a vast expanse of peat bog, treacherous even in the driest season. Rannoch actually means 'watery' in Gaelic. The finest view is perhaps from the railway as it crosses on its way north to Fort William, but the best approach by car is along Loch Rannoch. On its south side is the Black Wood of Rannoch, native Caledonian forest of ancient pines and groves of alder, birch and juniper. Just beyond Bridge of Gaur is a house built as barracks for Hanoverian troops after Culloden – a bleak posting. Rannoch Station is the end of the road, but you can walk on from here on old tracks.

INVERARAY MAP REF 408 D3

Inveraray, on the shores of Loch Fyne, is as fine an example of town planning as you will find, created by the 3rd Duke of Argyll in the 1740s to sit at the gates of his grand new home. It seems a great deal of trouble to go to, just to move your ancestral home by 0.5 mile (0.8km), but this was, after all, the extravagant 18th century. The little town that the Duke created is stylish, with a wide main street of white-painted houses running up to the classical kirk. Down at the waterfront are brilliant white arches, one of which leads up to All Saints Episcopal Church – climb the bell-tower for a wonderful view of the town, the castle, the loch and the hills.

Inveraray Castle, now home to the current 12th Duke and his family, is a neo-Gothic building with pointed sash windows and battlements. Inside, its most spectacular feature is the Armoury Hall, the tallest room in Scotland, which is dramatically adorned with pikes, axes, swords and muskets.

Moored on the loch side is the three-masted vessel Arctic Penguin, upon which you can take a turn at steering, ring the ship's telegraph, visit the engine room and watch archive film of old sailing and steam ships. Inveraray Jail, near the kirk, is open to visitors, where you can be part of the crowd hearing a trial, and in the 19th-century cells you can try out canvas hammocks and turn the crank machine.

KILMARTIN MAP REF 408 D3

The waters of Loch Awe once flowed southwards through the glacier-formed Kilmartin Glen, depositing sediment on the valley floor. The area was occupied by farmers from early prehistoric times, and the concentration of monuments that they left behind makes this one of the richest archaeological areas in Scotland. At Achnabreck is the largest group of cup-and-ring marked rocks in Britain, but even more impressive remains are to be found further north.

The tall, flat-faced Ballymeanoch standing stones and a line of burial cairns stretch towards Kilmartin village. Ri Cruin is a crescent of boulders in a grove, and carvings of axeheads and, possibly, a boat's keel can be seen on the stones. The three Nether Largie cairns are higher – especially the most southerly, with its large chamber topped by huge stone slabs. Central to the site is Temple Wood Circle, begun around 3000 BC and modified several times up to 1200 BC. To get the most out of this fascinating area visit the superb interpretative museum in Kilmartin village. Carnasserie Castle, further up the valley, is a well-preserved fortified house from the 16th century.

KINTYRE MAP REF 408 C5

At the north end of Kintyre and 38 miles (61km) from Campbeltown, the pretty fishing port of Tarbert has rows of colour-washed houses as well as the remains of a 15th-century tower house built on the site of a former royal castle. The Campbeltown road follows the wind-swept west fringe of Kintyre, with wide views over to Jura and Islay, and then the hills give way to a gentler landscape towards the handsome harbour of Campbeltown. By the waterfront is the 15th-century Campbeltown Cross, and nearby is an unexpected delight – the 1913 art deco front of the 256-seat Picture House. Davaar Island, reached on foot at low tide, shelters the harbour, and on its south side is a restored cave-painting of the crucifixion, originally created by Archibald MacKinnon in 1887.

St Columba landed near Southend at the foot of the peninsula – a ruined chapel and two footprints carved in a nearby rock mark the spot. A winding road eastwards goes to the Mull of Kintyre, with its lighthouse – a stark, windswept place, only 12 miles (19.5km) from Ireland. A single-track, hairpin road with breathtaking views over Arran follows the western coast back to Campbeltown; alternatively retrace your route up the B842, diverting west to the sands of Machrihanish, where the golf course is on the bay's edge.

To the north of Campbeltown, the east coast route is slow and winding, with tree-lined glens and fertile valleys. Up the valley from the battlemented castle at Saddell (now let by the Landmark Trust) are the remains of Saddell Abbey, with its impressive collection of carved gravestones (open access). Carradale, further up the coast, is a small rural village beside a beautiful sandy bay. You can catch the summer ferry from Claonaig to Lochranza on Arran, and at Skipness you can explore the fine castle ruins or wander around the 13th-century Kilbrannan Chapel.

LOCHGILPHEAD MAP REF 408 D3

Lochgilphead was once the centre of herring fishing on Loch Gilp, with a wooden pier stretched across the bay, but the fish mysteriously vanished before World War I. Mills and dyeworks also disappeared, and, besides tourism centred around the Crinan Canal, the main employer is now Argyll and Bute Council, which has its headquarters at Kilmory Castle.

The castle gardens, which are now open to the public, were partly laid out by Mr Joseph Hooker, first director of Kew Gardens. A little further to the north is Auchindrain Township, a former crofting settlement which now gives visitors an experience of Highland life.

Glacial action reversed the waters of Loch Awe, to the north of Lochgilphead, to flow through the dramatic Pass of Brander instead of through Kilmartin Glen. The longest loch in Scotland – measuring nearly 25 miles in length – it is very narrow, and the north end is dominated by the peak of Ben Cruachan.

INVERARAY

LOCH LOMOND MAP REF 408 E3

Part of Scotland's first National Park (Loch Lomond and the Trossachs National Park was established in 2002), Loch Lomond has two very distinct characters – the narrow upper loch is hemmed in by mountains, and stretches up into the heart of the Highlands, while the broad, island-speckled southern end is bordered by fertile farmland. Here, within easy reach of Glasgow, are some of the loch's most popular attractions.

Balloch, with its modern castle, country park and opportunities for boat cruises, sits astride the only natural outlet from the loch, and is a popular centre. The Loch Lomond Shores Visitor Centre includes an information centre and shopping outlets. Along the west side, just off the well-used A82, is Luss, a smart estate village which was the setting for the television series, *Take the High Road*.

Lomond's east side is much quieter, offering walking and outdoor pursuits. From Balmaha there are some good views over several of the loch's 38 named islands – especially Inchcailloch, once the site of a nunnery, and now part of the Loch Lomond National Nature Reserve. Much of the eastern shore is within the 50,000-acre (20,000ha) Queen Elizabeth Forest Park.

The narrow road ends at Rowardennan, from where there is a stiff climb up the 3,192 feet (973m) of Ben Lomond. To visit the beautiful Inversnaid, approach from Aberfoyle or by ferry come from Inveruglas – unless you are energetic enough for the walk along the West Highland Way approach from Rowardennan.

It is on the shores of Loch Lomond that the 95-mile (153km) West Highland Way, Scotland's first long-distance footpath, makes the transition from easy lowland walking to the harder going rugged terrain of the Highlands. Starting from Milngavie (pronounced Mull-guy) on the outskirts of Glasgow, the route makes its way north to Fort William, often using ancient and historic routes. These include old drove roads that were once used by cattle dealers to get their animals to market (like the Devil's Staircase out of Glen Coe), military roads instituted by General Wade to aid in suppressing the clans, some old coaching roads and even discarded railway lines. Walk all the way if you wish – experts recommend going south to north, to build up stamina for the hills – or take a short walk along the route; there is no shortage of breathtaking sections, and you may see red deer and, just possibly, golden eagles on the way.

MULL & IONA MAP REF 408 C2 & 408 B2

Take the time to properly explore and discover Mull and you will find it full of interest and beauty. Craignure is the main arrival point, and from Old Pier Station the Mull and West Highland Narrow Gauge Railway runs the extremely scenic 1.25 miles (2km) to Torosay Castle. This line boasts a real rarity – a modern steam locomotive, built in Sheffield in 1993.

Torosay Castle is actually a Victorian mansion, set in 12 acres (5ha) of superb gardens. The house is full of character and is enthusiastically shared with all visitors by its resident owner – you are positively encouraged to sit on chairs, peer into cupboards and browse through the family scrapbooks. Nearby, on a craggy point with wonderful views along the Sound of Mull, is 13th-century Duart Castle, centre for the Clan Maclean.

Mountains give way to pretty pastoral scenery on the way to the little island's capital, Tobermory, with its houses painted in jolly colours around the bay – a familiar sight to fans of TV's *Balamory* for young children. Tobermory's tourist attractions – the Mull Museum and the distillery – are tiny. Calgary, further on, has an interesting sculpture trail and the best sandy beach on the island.

West of Ben More, Mull's highest mountain, is the Ardmeanach peninsula, the tip of which is only accessible by an arduous 5.5-mile (9km) path. Its main sight is MacCulloch's Tree, 50 feet (15m) high and engulfed in lava more than 50 million years ago. Boat trips round Mull sometimes give passengers a view of it. Mull's main road is mostly single track and traverses the moorland from the east coast to Loch Scridain, and on across the Ross of Mull to Fionnphort, for the Iona ferry. South of the road is fine walking country, with a coastline of basalt stacks and sea arches – wild and lonely, and full of fascinating wildlife.

Iona is a magical place. Most visitors make straight for the abbey, but you should spare time for the remains of the 13th-century priory, built for the use of Augustinian nuns. St Columba founded his monastery in AD 563 where the abbey now stands, and from it the teachings of Christianity radiated throughout Europe. The monks compiled a library of illuminated manuscripts including the *Book of Kells*, now on show in Dublin's Trinity College Library. Columba's foundation ended in AD 806 when Vikings slew 68 monks at Martyrs' Bay. Later a church and buildings erected there by

LOCH LOMOND

OBAN

Insight
FERRY CONVENIENT
You can't get far in Western Scotland without needing to catch a ferry at some point, especially if you want to visit any of its 130 or so inhabited islands. Many of the shorter routes are operated by local owners and provide an excellent service, but Caledonian MacBrayne – CalMac – is undoubtedly the name you will come across most. The company was formed in 1973 when MacBraynes, operators of shipping services mostly to the Western Isles since 1851, joined forces with the Clyde-based Caledonian Steam Packet Company, founded in 1889. CalMac sails to 22 islands and operates more than 29 ferries in a huge range of sizes, from the largest vessels working the Ullapool to Stornoway route, capable of taking 690 passengers and 123 cars, to the six-car ferries that ply from Oban to Lismore and from Ballycastle in Northern Ireland to Rathlin Island.

Insight
LANGUAGE OF THE LAND
In Scotland lakes are lochs, and 'ben' means mountain. Like many Highland place names, these are Gaelic words, and the words often give an idea of the kind of place they refer to – 'kin' (Gaelic ceann), for example, means head, so Kinloch means the top of a lake, while 'inver' (inbhir) denotes an outlet – Inverness is where the River Ness meets the sea. 'Tarbert' (or 'Tarbet') means isthmus or crossing place. Other pointers include 'ard', a height, 'ban' meaning white; 'beg', confusingly meaning little, and 'more', meaning great. It all adds another dimension to the landscape.

12th-century Benedictine monks were left in ruins after the Reformation, until restoration began in 1910. Currently the home of the Iona Community, founded in 1938, the abbey welcomes pilgrims from around the world. Right beside it is the ancient burial ground of the Scottish kings, among them notably Macbeth and Duncan. The abbey does get busy with visitors at times, but although the island is small, it is possible to escape the crowds quickly and enjoy the fine sands and rocky landscape, the wild flowers and birds, and far-reaching sea views.

Many visitors will know of Staffa because of composer Mendelssohn's 'Fingal's Cave' overture. He came to this extraordinary island in 1829, to visit the cavern on its south side. Here, the dark volcanic basalt has cooled and formed its characteristic six-sided columns, making it look like a massive cathedral organ. The enormous interior of Fingal's Cave is also like a cathedral; weather permitting, visitors can land from some of the boat trips in the area.

OBAN MAP REF 408 D2
To experience the true splendour of Oban, you should climb at dusk to MacCaig's improbable Gothic Coliseum and watch the glorious sunset over the Firth of Lorne and the mountains of Morvern and Mull. MacCaig engaged a group of unemployed stonemasons to work on his spectacular tower from around 1897, and though it was never finished, it is Oban's most notable landmark. At the foot of the tower, the pretty bay, sheltered by the nearby island of Kerrera, is alive with pleasure craft of all types, especially in summer.

Much of the broad harbour front is dominated by a bank of hotels. Ferries bound for the Hebrides depart from Railway Quay. Here, too, is famous Caithness Glass where you can see jewel-like paperweights being made, and there is a shop where you can purchase the glass. Oban Distillery, in the heart of the town, welcomes visitors, and near by you'll find Geoffrey (Tailor) weaving tartans.

Northwards, the soaring tower of St Columba's Cathedral dominates the bay, and beyond it are the haunting remains of Dunollie Castle. A few miles further on, Dunstaffnage Castle, a mostly ruined stronghold with gatehouse, two round towers and 10-foot (3m) thick walls, stands on a rocky outcrop, and was once the prison of Flora Macdonald.

Across the Connel Bridge in Barcaldine is the Scottish Sea Life Sanctuary, where you can see British marine life at close quarters. South of the town is the Oban Rare Breeds Farm Park with farm animals, woodland walks and a pets' area. From here, drive on to Arduaine Garden with its wonderful views to the Isle of Jura.

ALONG THE CRINAN CANAL & AROUND MÒINE MHÒR

A lengthy but easy stroll along the 19th-century Crinan Canal, the walk passes through Mòine Mhòr (managed by Scottish Natural Heritage), Scotland's last wild peat bog, a birdwatchers' paradise, echoing with the distinctive cry of the curlew as it returns each spring.

DISTANCE/TIME 8.25 miles (13.3km) 5h **MAP** OS Explorer 358 Lochgilphead & Knapdale North **START** Dunardry Forest car park, grid ref: NR 824908 **TRACKS** Canal tow-path, country roads and farm tracks **THE PUB** The Cairnbaan Hotel & Restaurant, Cairnbaan, by Lochgilphead. Tel: 01546 603668

1 From the car park go down some steps, cross the road and turn left. Keep going to a white cottage on your right. Turn right and on to a dirt track that runs behind the cottage then go through a gap between the fence and a wall. Cross the canal over Dunardry Lock and turn left on to the tow-path.

2 Head along the tow-path as far as Bellanoch Bridge then turn right bringing you to the road, cross Islandadd Bridge and on to the B8025. This narrow road runs right through the Mòine Mhòr. Keep going for approximately 2 miles (3.2km). From here turn right on to an unclassified road signposted for Drimvore.

3 Follow this for about 1.75 miles (2.8km) as it runs through the National Nature Reserve and passes the farms of Dalvore and Drimvore. Finally reach a T-junction with the A816 and turn right. Then, after 0.5 mile (800m), an Historic Scotland fingerpost will point you in the direction of Dunadd Fort.

4 Turn right here on to a long straight farm road, passing the farm of Dunadd, until you reach the Historic Scotland car park. Go towards the hill on a well-trodden path, past the house on the left and through a kissing gate. Continue along the pathway to emerge through a gap in some rocks within the outer ramparts.

5 Continue from here to the summit and after you have admired the views, seen the carvings and put your foot in the carved footprint, return by the same route to the car park. Leave it and turn right on to a farm track. Go through a gate then go left through another gate and follow it as it curves left.

6 There is a gate just before the road turns right. Continue to follow the road through another gate to the steading of Dunamuck Farm. Turn left through the steading, go through a gate and then downhill on a small farm road, continuing to reach a T-junction with the A816.

7 Turn right on to the road and follow it for about 0.5 mile (800m), then turn right on to an unclassified road which is clearly signposted to The Cairnbaan Hotel. After a short distance turn right on to the B841 towards Crinan. As the road turns left across the swing bridge keep going straight ahead and on to the canal tow-path. Follow this path back to Dunardry Lock and retrace your steps to the car park.

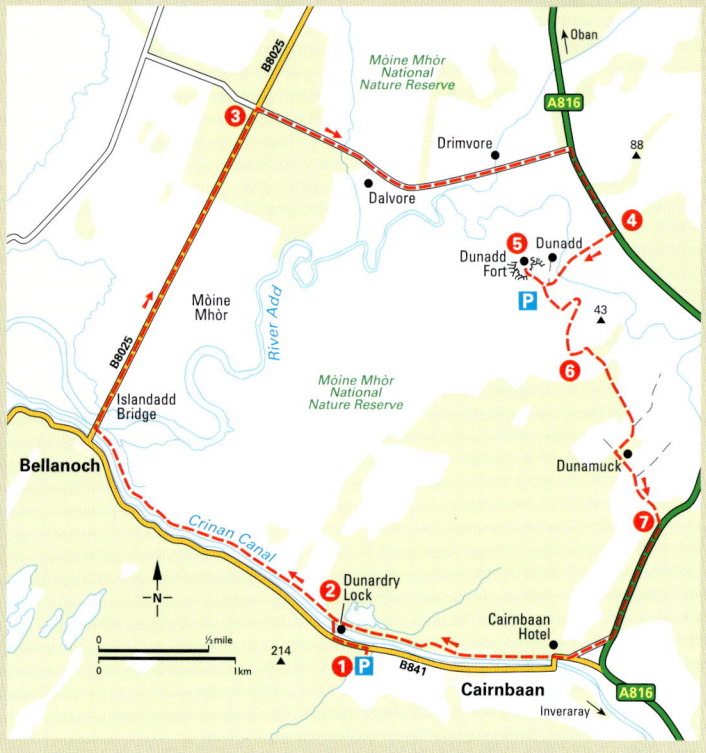

THE CARBETH HUT COMMUNITY

A short walk in the shadow of the Campsie Hills, to discover the Carbeth hut community established after World War I by the unemployed seeking an escape into the countryside. The first hut was built in 1919 and by the 1930s there were more than 30 dwellings, built from free or extremely low cost materials.

DISTANCE/TIME 3 miles (4.8km) 2h30 **MAP** OS Explorer 348 Campsie Fells **START** The Carbeth Inn (check beforehand with landlord if you wish to park here), grid ref: NX 524791 **TRACKS** Roads, access tracks and footpaths, 1 stile **THE PUB** The Carbeth Inn, Blanefield. Tel: 01360 770002

1 From the car park at The Carbeth Inn turn right on to the A809. After about 438yds (400m) take the first turning right on to the B821. Then, continue on this road for a mile (1.6km) passing next to a collection of huts on the left and ignoring a public footpath sign to the right.

2 Turn right at the signpost for the West Highland Way. There's also a Scottish Rights of Way Society signpost next to this pointing to the Khyber Pass Road to Mugdock Country Park, the favoured route of the early walkers heading out of Glasgow to the Campsie Fells and beyond.

3 Go through a gate and then continue along a surfaced access road. Ignoring the Kyber Pass turn-off, keep right and go over a stile to follow the West Highland Way along the access road to a few more huts. After passing some huts on the right and another hut on the left, look out for a partially hidden public path signpost on the right beside a West Highland Way marker post.

4 Turn right here on to a narrow but well-surfaced footpath and continue along it, passing Carbeth Loch on the right-hand side, to reach the junction with the drive leading to Carbeth House. This is a private house and is not open to the public. Turn left, pass a house on the right then take the next turning on the left.

5 Continue along this lane ignoring a public right of way sign pointing right, then head uphill to reach a further grouping of the Carbeth huts. At the first hut, a green one, the road forks with a narrow path branching to the right. Ignore this and take the wider road which passes to the left of the hut.

6 Keep on this road as it passes through the main part of the Carbeth huts, an extraordinary assortment of small dwellings, shanties and shacks. Ignore all of the smaller tracks branching off this road. They allow access to individual huts or other parts of the settlement.

7 Eventually pass a much larger hut on the right, then a smaller green one with a fenced garden on the left, and follow the road as it curves to the left. Continue downhill on this to reach the T-junction with the A809 beside The Carbeth Inn. Turn right and return finally to the car park.

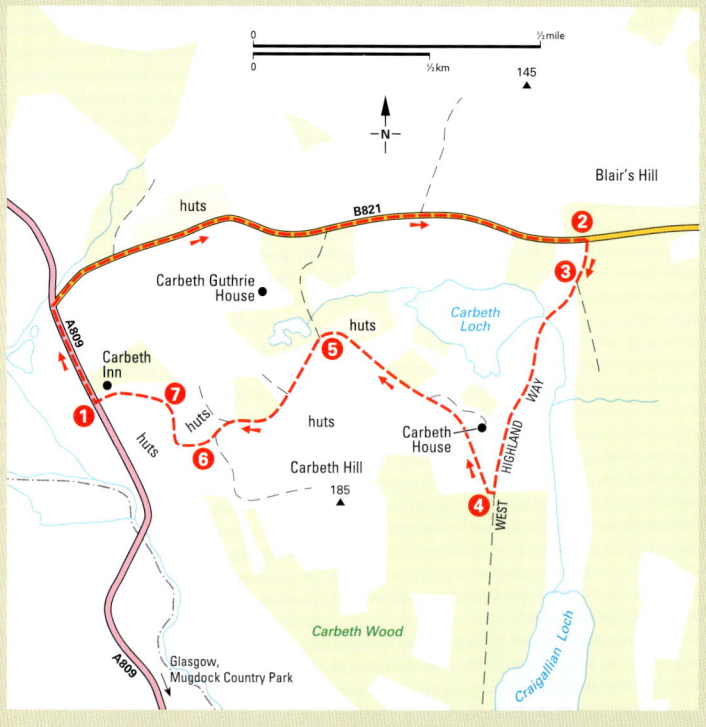

WALK 135

INTO THE LOST VALLEY

A rugged waterfall walk into the hidden hollow where the MacDonalds hid their stolen cows. Here, for centuries leading up to the massacre of 1692, the MacDonalds hid their stolen cattle when the rightful owners came storming in over the Moor of Rannach with torch and claymore.

DISTANCE/TIME 2.75 miles (4.4km) 2h15 **MAP** OS Explorer 384 Glen Coe & Glen Etive

START Grid ref: NN 168569 **TRACKS** Rugged and stony, stream to wade through, 1 stile

THE PUB The Clachaig Inn, Glencoe. Tel: 01855 811252

1 From the uphill corner of the car park, a faint path slants down to the old road, which is now a well-used track. Head up-valley for about 650yds (594m). With the old road continuing as a green track ahead, your path now bends down to the right. It had been rebuilt, with the bog problem solved by scraping down to the bedrock. The path reaches the gorge where the River Coe runs in a geological dyke of softer rock. Descend on a steep wooden step ladder, to cross a spectacular footbridge.

2 The ascent out of the gorge is on a bare rock staircase. Above, the path runs through regenerating birch wood, which can be very wet on the legs; sheep and deer have been excluded from the wood with a temporary fence. Emerge over this by a high ladder stile. The path, rebuilt in places, runs uphill for 60yds (55m). Here it bends left; an inconspicuous alternative path continues uphill, which can be used to bypass the narrow path of the main route.

3 The main route contours into the gorge of the Allt Coire Gabhail. It is narrow with steep drops below. Where there is an alternative of rock slabs and a narrow path just below, the slabs are more secure. You will hear waterfalls, then two fine ones come into view ahead. After passing these, continue between boulders to where the main path bends left to cross the stream below a boulder the size of a small house. (A small path runs on up to the right of the stream, but leads nowhere useful.) The river here is wide and fairly shallow. Five or six stepping stones usually allow dry crossing. If the water is above the stones, then it's safer to wade alongside them; if the water is more than knee-deep the crossing should not be attempted.

4 A well-built path continues, now with the stream on its right. After 100yds (91m) a lump of rock blocks the way. The path follows a slanting ramp up its right-hand side. It continues uphill passing above the boulder pile that blocks the valley. At the top of the rockpile the path levels, giving a good view into the Lost Valley.

5 Drop gently to the valley's gravel floor. The stream vanishes into the gravel, to reappear below the boulder pile on the other side. Note where the path arrives at the gravel, as it becomes invisible at that point. Wander up the valley to where the stream vanishes, 0.25 miles (400m) ahead. Stop here and return to the path and follow it right back to the start.

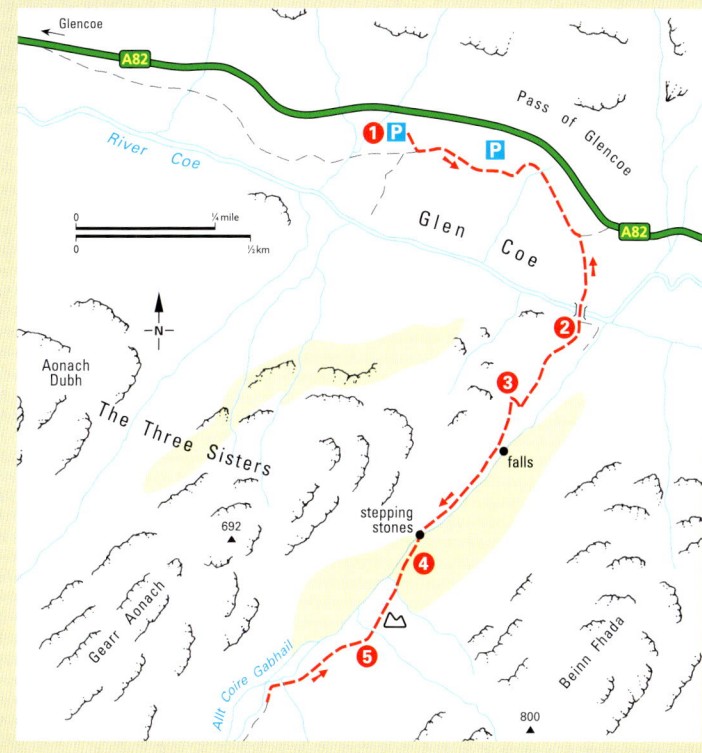

WALK 136

THE NEOLITHIC MONUMENTS OF KILMARTIN GLEN

A short walk back in time to the stones and monuments in the valley of the ghosts. In around 5000 BC, nomadic hunter gatherers frequented this area but left little evidence of their presence other than piles of bones and shells in caves. In the Iron Age, warring tribes ringed the glen with hill forts and it is one of these, at Dunadd, that the Scotti tribe from Ireland founded their capital in the 6th century AD. St Columba came to Kilmartin during this century and is believed to have established the first Christian church here.

DISTANCE/TIME 3.5 miles (5.7km) 3h **MAP** OS Explorer 358 Lochgilphead & Knapdale North

START Grid ref: NR 835988 **TRACKS** Boggy fields, old coach road and country lanes, 3 stiles

THE PUB Horseshoe Inn, Kilimichael Glassary, Lochgilphead. Tel: 01546 606369

1 From the car park visit Kilmartin church to view the stones and the Kilmartin Cross. Leave the church, turn left and walk along the road past Kilmartin House, exit the village and head downhill towards a garage on the left. Just before the garage turn left, go through a kissing gate and head across the fields to the Glebe Cairn.

2 From the cairn, head in a half right direction across the field to cross a stile. In wet weather this can be very boggy so stout footwear is advisable. Cross the stream by a bridge. Go through a gate and turn left by a bridge. Go through another gate and turn left on to the old coach road. Follow this to the next cairn. Go left over a stile and follow the path to visit the cairn.

3 Return to the road and turn left, continuing to the next cairn. After exploring this, follow the coach road to Kilmartin school to a metalled road. Go through a crossroads, past Nether Largie farm and, ignoring the cairn on the left, continue a short distance to Temple Wood ahead on the right.

4 Go through a gate on the right into Temple Wood, then return by the same route. Turn right on to the road and walk to a T-junction. Turn left and walk along the road until you reach a sign on the right for Ri Cruin Cairn. Cross the wall via a stile and go along the well-defined path to the ancient monument.

5 Return by the same route and turn right on to the road. Follow it to a T-junction then turn left and keep straight ahead until you reach the car park at Lady Glassary Wood. Opposite this take a path to the left signposted to Temple Wood. Cross a bridge, go through a gate, cross another bridge and head towards the standing stones.

6 Turn right and walk across the field away from the stones towards a wood. Go through a gate and follow the fenced path to Nether Largie Cairn. From here continue along the fenced path, go through another gate and turn right on to the road. Continue past Nether Largie farm and Kilmartin school and then retrace your steps backs to Kilmartin church and the car park.

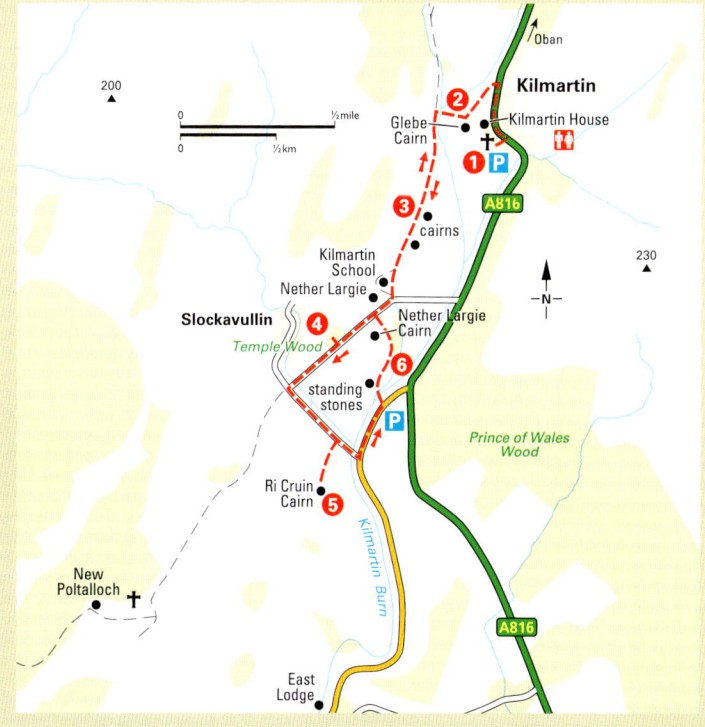

THE SHORES OF LOCH KATRINE

Glasgow's water supply in the heart of the Trossachs, Loch Katrine, takes its name from the Gaelic 'cateran', a Highland robber – a fitting place then for the birthplace of Rob Roy MacGregor, the bandit, who was born at Glengyle at the western end of the loch. This is the heart of MacGregor country and one of their clan graveyards lies near the head of the loch. Rob Roy's lasting fame is due to a novel of the same name written by Sir Walter Scott and the loch, too, owed its early popularity to one of Scott's poems, *The Lady of the Lake*. First published in 1810, Scott's description of the dramatic scenery encouraged tourists to visit the Trossachs.

DISTANCE/TIME 6.75 miles (10.9km) 4h30 **MAP** OS Explorer 364 Loch Lomond North; 365 The Trossachs **START** Grid ref: NN 404102 (on explorer 364) **TRACKS** Water board roads, hill tracks

THE PUB The Forth Inn, Aberfoyle. Tel: 01877 382372

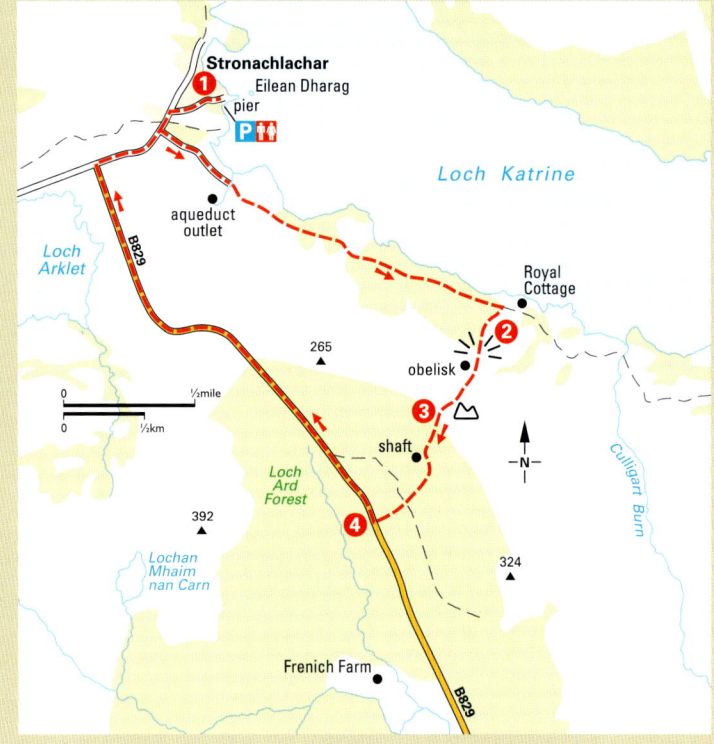

1 From the car park follow the road back towards the B829 and take the second turning on the left. This is an access road for Scottish Water vehicles only. Continue along the access road until you come to a cattle grid with green gate posts at the building known as Royal Cottage. Turn right just before this on to a rough gravel track that heads through some dense bracken.

2 As the path emerges on to open hillside you will see the first of several ventilation shafts and beyond it, on the hill, a strange obelisk. Follow the path along this line. When you reach the obelisk be sure to look back for a super view over Loch Katrine below and across to the hills with their narrow passes where Rob Roy and his men moved from Loch Katrine to Balquhidder and beyond, moving cattle or escaping from the forces of law and order. Continue following the line of the ventilation shafts towards a chimney-like structure on top of a hill. From here take a righthand direction taking you downhill. Take great care on this section as the path has severely eroded and has become very steep.

Once you reach the bottom, pass through the gap at the junction of two fences. At this point go towards the left.

3 Follow a well-defined track that goes through some pine trees and past another ventilation shaft. Keep left at the shaft. It can be very muddy on this short stretch. Continue on the path until it intersects a forest road by a stream. Cross the road and look for a faint track continuing downhill in the same direction. In summer this path may be difficult to find because it's hidden by bracken. In this case follow the line of the telephone poles. Eventually after working downhill through some more woodland the track emerges on to the B829.

4 Turn right here and follow the road (it emerges from Loch Ard Forest into open countryside). Loch Arklet can be seen on the left; it is now connected to Loch Katrine by an underground pipeline. When the road reaches a T-junction with the Inversnaid road, turn right. As the road forks, turn right again and return to Stronachlachar Pier.

WALK 138

ARIUNDLE OAKWOODS & THE ELEMENTS OF CHEMISTRY

On the way to the lead mine and waterfalls of Strontian Glen, the walk passes through the Ariundle National Nature Reserve. In the mountains, the native wild wood of Scotland was the Scots pine. Here on the warm, damp sea coast, the wild wood is of oak. The Ariundle oakwood owes its survival to human interference. The destructive livestock and deer of Scotland's forests were kept out so that the oaks could be coppiced – harvested on a seven-year cycle.

DISTANCE/TIME 7 miles (11.3km) 3h45 **MAP** OS Explorer 391 Ardgour & Strontian **START** Grid ref: NM 826633 **TRACKS** Good through woodland, sketchy on open hill, no stiles

THE PUB Ariundle Centre, Strontian. Tel: 01967 402279

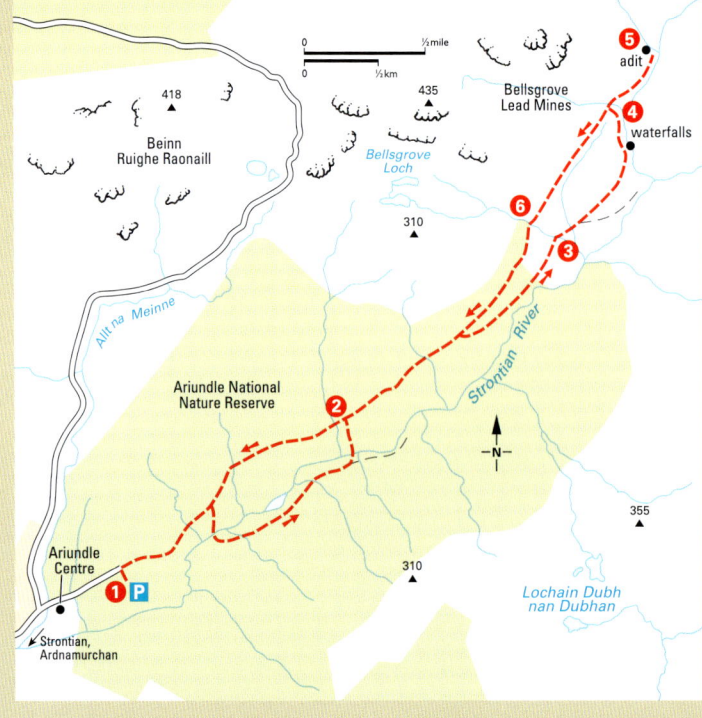

1 From the car park, continue along the track into the oakwoods. After 0.5 miles (800m), a path turns off at a waymarker on the right. It crosses the Strontian River and heads upstream. After 0.75 miles (1km) it recrosses the river, following a duckboard section to rejoin the oakwood track.

2 Turn right to reach a high gate in a deer fence. The track immediately forks. Take the downward branch on the right to emerge into open grazings at river level. The track ends at a gate and stream.

3 Ford the stream on to a rough path. This crosses three more small streams, then forks. The lower, right-hand branch continues alongside the Strontian River, but the path, which is quite faint, slants up to the left to a solitary holly tree. Here it turns straight uphill for 50yds (46m), then bends right to slant up as before, passing 200yds (183m) below a bare rock knoll. The remains of wooden steps are in the path and a few cairns stand beside it. It steepens slightly to pass below a small crag with three different trees growing out of it – rowan, hazel and oak.

With a large stream and waterfalls ahead, the path turns uphill and reaches the brink of the small gorge. Above the waterfalls, the slope eases and there is a footbridge down on the right (don't cross); it acts as a useful landmark. Just above, the path reaches the broken dam wall of a former reservoir.

4 A green path runs across the slope just above. You can turn right on this, heading up beside the stream for about a quarter mile (400m). Here you will find a spoil heap; a heather bank marks the entrance to an adit – a mine tunnel running into the hill.

5 Return along the green path past Point 4, with the remains of the Bellsgrove Lead Mines above and below. The path improves into a track, following a stream down a small and slantwise side valley. As this stream turns down to the left, the track contours forward, to cross a wooded stream valley by a high footbridge above a waterfall.

6 A wide, smooth track continues ahead though a gate. It shortly rejoins the outward route. Follow the track back to the car park.

Cairngorms
& Central

CLOCKWISE FROM TOP: PARTRIDGE IN THE CAIRNGORMS;
HEATHER, GLEN ESK; LOCH MORLICH, AVIEMORE; BOAT OF GARTEN

Visit
SANTA'S HELPERS

This area of ancient forest is associated with rare native creatures such as wildcats, red squirrels, pine martens and capercaillies. Since the 1950s, however, it has also been home to a herd of handsome, horned interlopers originating in Sweden: reindeer. Visit a herd of them at the Cairngorm Reindeer Centre in Glenmore Forest Park, where they graze on the hillside.

Insight
CLOOTIE DUMPLING

The Clootie Dumpling is a suet pudding, or dumpling, traditionally wrapped and boiled in a cloth – the word 'clout' is the broad Scots for a cloth. The puddings are usually sweetened, and contain some raisins and currants, orange peel and spices. They are particularly associated with Hogmanay, or New Year. The dumpling can be served hot after it has been boiled, or the cooled pudding can be sliced up and the wedges fried in butter.

AVIEMORE MAP REF 411 H6

The once-sleepy, remote railway station settlement of Aviemore was developed in the 1960s as a ski destination, and while it has never been able to rival the brash attractions of the Continental ski resorts, it manages to hold its own as an activities centre for the Cairngorms National Park. Its arcaded main street is a hang-over from an earlier time, but there is now a good range of outdoor shops and places to eat and relax.

The Rothiemurchus Estate, 1.5 miles (2.5km) to the south, has belonged to the Grant family since the 16th century. Elizabeth Grant's very readable account of her early life there, *Memoirs of a Highland Lady*, gives a captivating insight into the workings of the land here some 200 years ago, when timber was sawn by hand and floated down the Spey, and the idea of sustainable forestry was in barely its infancy. Today the estate offers an amazing variety of outdoor pursuits in the beautiful setting of mountains, lochs and Caledonian pine forest. This is the remains of the Old Wood of Caledon which once covered the whole country, harbouring wolves and bears, but long

since was cleared for timber, fuel and farmland. Try your hand at anything from clay pigeon shooting to off-road driving, or more peaceable activities of birdwatching, cycling, fishing and horse trekking. Don't miss the local cheeses and estate venison in the farm shop.

To the south, a good walk lasting about 1.5 hours leads around lovely Loch an Eilean, with its picturesque remains of a 15th-century castle.

Loch Morlich, 7 miles (12km) east of Aviemore, is perfect for water-based activities including sailing, windsurfing and canoeing. There is a very popular camping site, and Glenmore Lodge is a training centre for mountaineers.

Situated just to the north of Aviemore, at Carrbridge, the Landmark Highland Heritage theme park has displays on local history and wildlife as well as a treetop walk, adventure playgrounds, a maze and water slides. Another point of interest at Carrbridge is the old Packhorse Bridge, which straddles the fast-flowing River Spey. Following serious flooding in the area in 1829, the bridge was damaged and what remains is a perfect – yet fragile – stone arch to the west of town.

BOAT OF GARTEN MAP REF 411 H6

Boat of Garten is an attractive little Victorian village on the west bank of the River Spey, between Aviemore and Grantown, and gets its name from the ferry that once operated here (replaced by a more convenient bridge in 1898). It is a key stop on the now preserved and restored Strathspey Steam Railway, and its station was once the point where Highland and Great North of Scotland rail companies swapped trains. The railway currently runs from Aviemore all the way to the little country station at Broomhill, which found unlikely fame as 'Glenbogle' station in the TV series, *Monarch of the Glen*. The town also has a challenging golf course, which has been described by some in the golf fraternity as a miniature version of Gleneagles.

Two miles (3km) to the east lie the still waters of Loch Garten, in the Abernethy Forest, where ospreys have nested since 1959. The RSPB has a hide there, overlooking the distant nesting site, and from where you can watch the activities of the birds in intriguing close up via a video-link. There are walking trails all through the woods around the loch. Abernethy,

BRAEMAR

a national nature reserve, is the biggest Scots pine forest remaining in Britain and home to other interesting birds such as crested tits, crossbills and capercaillies.

Just to the north, the resort village of Nethy Bridge is set amid heather-clad hills and native woodland, with the ruins of 13th-century Castle Roy close by and visible from the road. The walls stand up to 25 feet (7.6m) high.

Northeast of Boat of Garten, off the A95, lies the pretty little village of Dulnain Bridge. Its chief attraction is the Speyside Heather Garden and Visitor Centre at Skye of Curr, where you can purchase display heathers. There is also a garden centre, an antique shop, an art gallery, and an interesting restaurant dedicated to the Clootie Dumpling.

BRAEMAR & DEESIDE
MAP REF 411 J7

When, in 1852, Queen Victoria and her consort Prince Albert picked an estate between Ballater and Braemar on which to build their holiday home, the entire Dee Valley acquired a cachet which it has never quite lost. Members of the royal family still spend their summer holidays at Balmoral Castle, enjoying country pursuits in the hills and forests. The Braemar Gathering in September is the most famous Highland games, predating Queen Victoria's arrival by some 20 years.

Braemar itself is a bustling place, spread over the banks of the Cluny Burn. Braemar Castle lies to the east, an L-plan tower house, converted to a star-fort and barracks in the mid-18th century to guard an important military road. It is privately owned, and currently closed to visitors.

To the west, a narrow road leads upstream to the Linn of Dee, where the river plunges down between polished rocks into foaming pools. This is part of the 72,598-acre (29,380ha) Mar Lodge Estate, managed by the National Trust for Scotland. There are signposted walks. The road ends near the Earl of Mar's Punchbowl, where, it is said, the Earl brewed punch in a natural bowl in the rocks before the Jacobite uprising of 1715. A long-distance walk from here heads into the Lairig Ghru pass to Speyside.

From Braemar the A93 follows the meandering of the river as it flows for 60 miles (96km) to the coast at Aberdeen. Ballater is a small granite-built spa town, once the terminus of a railway branch line. This is celebrated at the Old Royal Station, now an information centre which recalls the days when famous guests would alight here on their way to Balmoral. It also has some interesting little shops and an excellent tea room. To the east lies Glen Tanar, with birch woods at the Muir of Dinnet, and good walking over the Grampian hills to the Glens of Angus.

CAIRNGORMS NATIONAL PARK
MAP REF 411 J6

In 2003 the Cairngorms were designated Scotland's second national park, which covers a wide area of upland to the east of, and including, the Spey Valley. Over to the south the boundary continues from Dalwhinnie right across to the Glens of Angus, taking in Glen Esk before turning north to pass east of Ballater and up to Glenlivet. The centre of the national park is made up of the high granite plateaux of the Cairngorm mountains, riven by steep-sided glens and deep corries, creating a sub-Arctic environment that is unique in Britain. An estimated half the area of the national park has been cleared of trees over the centuries, and it is now open heather moorland, managed for grouse shooting. Around the margins, ancient areas of native woodland survive, the original forests have been felled and replanted for their timber many times.

The park takes in two great river valleys, the Spey and the Dee, and it is along these that most of its small population of about 14,000 live and work, their numbers swelled in summer by visitors looking for outdoor adventure, and in winter by snow-sports enthusiasts.

There's an extensive network of paths in the glens and forests around the Cairngorms, from starting points such as Nethy Bridge, Rothiemurchus,

Aviemore, Glenmore, Grantown-on Spey, Tomintoul, Ballater, Braemar and glens Tanar, Doll and Feshie. More experience is needed to tackle the heights such as Ben Macdhui (1,309m/ 4,295ft), Cairn Gorm (1,245m/4,085ft) and Cairn Toul (1,293m/4,242ft). There are plenty of great opportunities for cycling, fishing and golf, and watersports are focused on Loch Insh or Loch Morlich. There are ski centres at Cairngorm, the Lecht and Glenshee, and a funicular railway runs to the summit of Cairngorm for the views (for conservation reasons there is no access beyond the summit station during the summer).

Signs of the earliest settlers may be seen in the hummocks of hill forts such as Dun da lamh, near Laggan, and the mound of a crannog on Loch Kinnord. Queen Victoria was enchanted by this romantic landscape and built her holiday home, Balmoral Castle, at Braemar in 1853, popularising the region and also beginning a royal connection that still holds strong to this day. The castle sits amongst more than 50,000 acres of beautiful countryside, and was once described by Queen Victoria as a 'paradise in the Highlands'. In many of the local towns you will find royal paraphernalia, but one of the oddest memorials associated with her is the crown-shaped monument that was built over a spring in remote Glen Mark, known as the Queen's Well.

DISTANCE/TIME 14 miles (22.5km) 3h **MAP** OS Explorer 403 Cairn Gorm & Aviemore **START** Inverdruie Car Park, grid ref: NH902109 **TRACKS** Decent tracks and woodland trails, some sections of road **CYCLE HIRE** Rothiemurchus Visitor Centre, Inverdruie. Tel: 01479 812345 **THE PUB** The Old Bridge Inn, 23 Dalfaber Road, Aviemore. Tel: 01479 811137

DISTANCE/TIME 11 miles (17.5km) 2h **MAP** OS Explorer 365 The Trossachs **START** The Forth Inn (ask permission to park) Cycle Hire Trossachs Holiday Park, Aberfoyle. Tel: 01877 382614; grid ref: NN523010 **TRACKS** Road, forest tracks (good condition), some quite sleep rises **THE PUB** The Forth Inn, Main Street, Aberfoyle. Tel: 01877 382372

ROTHIEMURCHUS ESTATE

The Rothiemurchus Estate is set right on the edge of the remarkable Cairngorm Mountain massif, the vast mountain plateau that was recently designated the UK's largest national park. The estate lies just outside the resort town of Aviemore, the self-styled 'Adventure Capital of the Highlands'. Rothiemurchus is one of best places in Scotland to enjoy swathes of indigenous Caledonian woodland on a ride that steers through Scots pine, birch and juniper forest on an undulating trail that also scoops around a brace of wood-shrouded lochs. There is a real sense of being somewhere genuinely unspoilt and pristine here, with clear evidence of how the land was formed during the last ice age 10,000 years ago, such as rounded hillocks (known locally as 'drumlins'). Wildlife abounds on the route – look out for everything from red squirrels and crossbills, through to capercaillie and pine marten.

1 From the visitor centre car park make your way southwards on a route that quickly takes you into the lush Caledonian forests. En route to the first loch of this cycle ride you pass an old croft (small farm holding).

2 Loch an Eilein, one of Scotland's prettiest lochs, unfurls after you pass by the car park (the car route comes in further to the west). The 'Loch of the Island' is named after the small islet that nestles in the middle of the silvery blue water, which is topped off with a picturesque old abandoned castle. Cycle right around or just skirt the northern fringes if you are short on time.

3 Breaking east, the trail delves on into a thick forest that is alive with lots of little lochans. One of the most charming is Lochan Deo, which is set just south of the main forest track between the two main lochs. Hop off your bike for five minutes and take a peak at a lochan that is usually deserted.

4 The trail is now deep within the Caledonian forest. Take time to stop and listen to the singing of the birds and for rustles amongst the trees as this is deer country with myriad other wildlife also to be found in the woodland undergrowth.

5 Cross the Cairngorm Club Footbridge, the footbridge which sweeps you over Am Beanaidh. It is a pleasant spot with the water rushing below. The rocky banks make a good place to relax for a moment before pushing on to Loch Morlich.

6 Loch Morlich is a popular place for watersports and draws many waterskiing and boating enthusiasts. From here there are stunning views of the Cairngorm mountains on a clear day. There is a beach on the eastern shores of the loch by the watersports centre. From Loch Morlich turn left and the route breaks back west following the road to Inverdruie, with patches of cycling trail offering an alternative along the way.

QUEEN ELIZABETH FOREST PARK

The Loch Ard Forest in the hilly Trossachs region of Central Scotland is part of the Queen Elizabeth Forest Park. The route soon leaves the tourist-friendly village of Aberfoyle and rambles through thick forests and around the hills that pepper this area, known affectionately by many Scots as the 'foothills of the Highlands'. Look out for grazing red and roe deer, capercaillie, wood ants and stunning barn owls.

1 From The Forth Inn head towards Aberfoyle's main car park behind the inn and then turn right past the cars looking towards a small exit. Take a right turn here and head up the minor road to a junction where you make a left turn on to an even quieter road that meanders west in search of Loch Ard.

2 Before going into the hamlet of Milton leave the road to take the track to the left, which curls around towards the loch. You are now in the forest proper so take care on the looser woodland tracks as you head west, snatching tempting glimpses of the beautiful loch as you cycle along.

3 After a short section deep inside the forest, the track then drops back down to the loch at Couligarten. Keep a sharp look out for a left turn just past Couligarten – if you get all the way to the aqueduct you have come too far.

4 The path rises up through the forest cutting and tracks between a series of low wooded hills that lie to the left of Duchray Water. You cross over the waterway at the Duchray Bridge after a zigzag section. Continue on the trail as it starts to curve back towards Aberfoyle village.

5 After tracking a section that traverses some old mine shafts you then pick up the Bofrishlie Burn (burn is Scots for stream), which tumbles down towards Aberfoyle; avoid the smaller tracks that break off the main route as they lead deeper into the forest and you run the risk of getting lost.

6 As the route leaves the forest behind it becomes surfaced and passes to the west of Doon Hill (the 'hill of the fairies') just before The Covenanters Inn hotel comes into view on the left. The Forth Inn is only a short cycle away now across the River Forth, accessible via the right turn into the main village car park from where you set out.

FORRES

CULLODEN MAP REF 411 G5

The fierce Battle of Culloden finally marked the end of Stuart ambitions to reclaim the throne of Britain from the Hanoverians. On this bleak and desolate moorland east of Inverness, 5,000 Highlanders under the command of the Young Pretender – Bonnie Prince Charlie – faced 9,000 troops led by the Duke of Cumberland. It was 16th April 1746, a day of bitter cold, with snow flurries. The Highlanders, used to short skirmishes, were no match for the disciplined and well-armed soldiers, and despite courageous fighting were swiftly defeated. Cumberland ordered that no prisoners should be taken.

Although it can be very crowded in summer, Culloden remains a moving place. The 1,200 Highlanders who died were buried in clan graves, marked by small, weathered stones. The 76 English dead lie in the Field of the English. Coloured flags fly over the battlefield to mark the disposition of the armies. The focal point of the area is a 19th-century memorial cairn, built where the fighting was most ferocious. The excellent Visitor Centre has clear explanations of the battle, its causes and its aftermath.

FORRES MAP REF 411 H5

The ancient market town of Forres, lying on the River Findhorn, was once plagued by witches. William Shakespeare made full use of this in *Macbeth* (c1606), when he set scenes with the three 'weird sisters' in the area. Three more witches, burned to death, are commemorated with an iron-bound stone in the town. Sueno's Stone, on the eastern outskirts, is a Pictish cross-slab which stands 6m (20ft) tall and is believed to date from the 9th or 10th centuries. The sandstone is intricately carved in five sections with vivid scenes from an unidentified and bloody battle. Southeast of the town, Cluny Hill is the highest point, topped by an octagonal tower, raised in 1806 to commemorate Lord Nelson. It is believed to be the first such monument in Britain, and provides a magnificent viewpoint. To the south of Forres, the Dallas Dhu Historic Distillery is preserved by Historic Scotland.

Remarkably, Pluscarden Abbey is the only medieval foundation in Britain still used for its original purpose. Just east of Forres, the monastery is home to 27 Benedictine monks, and a haven of spiritual retreat for both men and women. The monastery was founded in 1230 by Alexander II, and during the Reformation in the 16th century was gradually abandoned. In 1943 restoration began and, in 1974, it was granted abbey status. Today the white-habited monks work here and care for the abbey buildings.

Insight
SHINTY

Kingussie is known as a stronghold of the Gaelic sport of shinty. It's a team game similar to hockey, and the highlight of the shinty players' year is the Camanachd Cup Final, held in mid-June in different venues across the country.

Visit
THE COOPER'S CRAFT

None of the distilleries of Strathspey could thrive without the wooden barrels or casks in which the spirit is left to mature. For an insight into the cooper's skill, you can visit the family-run, fully working Speyside Cooperage just south of Craigellachie. Nowadays, oak for the barrel staves is largely imported from the US, and the cooperage produces around 100,000 casks a year for shipping worldwide – oak is preferred for its qualities of 'breathing'.

Visit
EARLY CAIRNS

The fascinating Clava Cairns near Culloden open a window on our remote ancestors. They were probably built between 2000 and 1500 BC. Clava Cairns is part of a series of such historic monuments found only in the region of the Moray Firth.

KINGUSSIE MAP REF 411 H6

The little town of Kingussie lies in the beautiful Spey Valley, once the capital of the ancient area of Badenoch, and with a history that dates back to pre-Pictish times. Today it is best known as home to the Highland Folk Museum, a place with fascinating indoor and outdoor exhibits. In fact, the museum occupies two sites, the other being situated at Newtonmore, to the south. The main house here contains traditional furniture and bygones, and a representation of a Highland kitchen; in the grounds you will find a reconstructed Hebridean mill and a salmon smokehouse in addition to a primitive blackhouse from Lewis. There are regular craft demonstrations during the summer.

Southeast of Kingussie are the impressive Ruthven Barracks, dramatically set on a grassy mound, formerly the site of a castle, and built in 1718 in order to subdue the Highlands, following the 1715 rebellion. Despite being set on fire by the fleeing Jacobite army in 1746, there are still considerable remains. The garrison here guarded General Wade's military road, leading from Glen Truim.

The adjacent Insh Marshes Reserve (RSPB) has hides and nature trails. There is also a guided tour. You can walk from here to beautiful Glen Tromie.

Just to the north of Kingussie, off the B9152, is the noted Highland Wildlife Park, an extensive reserve and exhibition of themed habitats dedicated to Scottish wildlife, and part of the Royal Zoological Society of Scotland (the owners of Edinburgh Zoo). A driving tour takes in herds of red deer, as well as ancient breeds of bison and horse, before you explore the rest on foot. Look out for otters, owls, boars, Arctic foxes, wildcat and eagles. You can also follow, in your car, the vehicle that delivers a feed at 10am each day, or take a guided tour in the morning or afternoon. The centre is perhaps best known for its collection of wolves, and a raised walkway takes visitors safely into the heart of their (well-fenced) enclosure. The last wild wolf in Scotland was killed in 1743.

The nearby village of Kincraig is the access point for Loch Insh, popular for watersports, and its ski school has a dry ski slope (60m/200ft). A church on the loch shore reputedly stands on a site where worship has been continuous since the 6th century. Kingussie is just 12 miles (20km) from Aviemore ski resort and so is a popular stop for winter holidaymakers.

SPEYSIDE MAP REF 411 J5

The Spey is one of the foremost salmon rivers in Scotland, flowing northeast from its source on Craig a' Cleat, in the Monadhliath Mountains along a broad strath, or valley, finally reaching the sea at Spey Bay, to the west of Buckie. Although it starts in the mountainous Highlands, its lower reaches are more characteristic of lowland scenery. Along its course, it is fed by streams from high in the Cairngorms, including the Feshie and the Nethy.

The river itself is unnavigable, but the Speyside Way long-distance footpath follows its route for 84 miles (135km) from the police station at Aviemore to the coast, passing Grantown-on-Spey, Cromdale and the Craigellachie Forest, with spur paths joining from Tomintoul and Dufftown.

The Spey Valley is equally renowned for the quality of its malt whisky – you'll not have to travel far without spotting the distinctive pointed chimney-caps of a distillery, for there are more than 30 along the river and its tributaries. Pick up the official 75-mile Malt Whisky Trail for a tour of some of Scotland's finest. Some distilleries that welcome visitors include Glenfiddich, founded by William Grant in 1887 at Dufftown, and the Aberlour Distillery (Walkers Shortbread is also made in Aberlour).

Grantown-on-Spey is one of the largest settlements along the riverbank. The township was planned out in 1765, and has a spacious, genteel feel to it even nowadays. Its creator was James Grant, and the arrival of the railway here in 1863 heralded the town's popularity as a health resort. The railway folded in the 1960s, and the town is now much better known as a centre for anglers, and walkers keen to explore the Cairngorms. Its story is told in the local museum.

A WALK TO LOCHAN A' CHOIRE

A fairly challenging linear walk, which takes you sometimes over fairly rocky and rugged ground, through areas of regenerating clusters of woodlands leading to the outflow of Lochan a' Choire. From here there is a stunning view of the old crag walls of looming Coire Ardair.

DISTANCE/TIME 8 miles (12.9km) 4h15 **MAP** OS Explorer 401 Loch Laggan & Creag Meagaidh

START Nature reserve car park at Aberarder track end beside Loch Laggan, grid ref: NN 483872

TRACKS Mostly good, wet and stony in places, there are no stiles **THE PUB** Monadhliath Hotel, Laggan. Tel: 01528 544276; www.laggan.com/Monadhliath

1 A grey gravel track leads to Aberarder farm. Here there is an information area that includes an undercover picnic table. Pass to the right of the farm buildings, following a footprint waymarker on to a rebuilt path.

2 The path rises through an area of bracken, then crosses a boggy stretch on old railway sleepers. It heads up the valley of Allt Coire Ardair, keeping a little way up the right-hand side, becoming fairly rocky and rugged as it ascends through an area of regenerating birch trees. Now the splendid crags of Coire Ardair come into sight ahead. The path crosses many small streams then bends to the left, slightly downhill, to join the main river. Tiny rowan trees are attempting to regenerate through the blanket of heather, and among the wild flowers in the boggy ground are the pretty pink and white pyramids of the heath spotted orchid (the leaves have spots). A peaty area, crossed on railway sleepers, leads up suddenly to the outflow of Lochan a' Choire.

3 The outflow is a wonderful viewpoint for the crag walls of Coire Ardair. These walls are too loose and overgrown for rock climbing, but when they are covered in snow and hoarfrost they are perfect for winter mountaineers. This circuit around the lochan is considerably more rugged than the path up the glen, and could be avoided altogether if the outflow stream is too full, or if you prefer to stop for a picnic nearby. Cross the outflow stream near where it emerges from the lochan and then follow a small path round the shore to the notable clump of boulders marked by a stretcher box. (The stretcher is used for removing mountain casualties from the foot of the crags.) One of the boulders forms a small cave, with a spring running through it. A vigorous rowan tree, seeded where deer can't get at it, shows that without grazing pressure this glen would be wooded even at this altitude of 2,000ft (610m).

4 After the boulder cave you must cross rocks and scree. This short section is awkward. Once past the head of the lochan, slant up away from the shore. A path descends from high on the left, coming out of the notch called the Window. Join this and turn down to the loch's outflow (Point 3 again). Quite clearly there is no way out of this dead-end valley that doesn't involve serious mountain walking – or one of those winter climbs up the icy gullies. Return down the valley by the outward path.

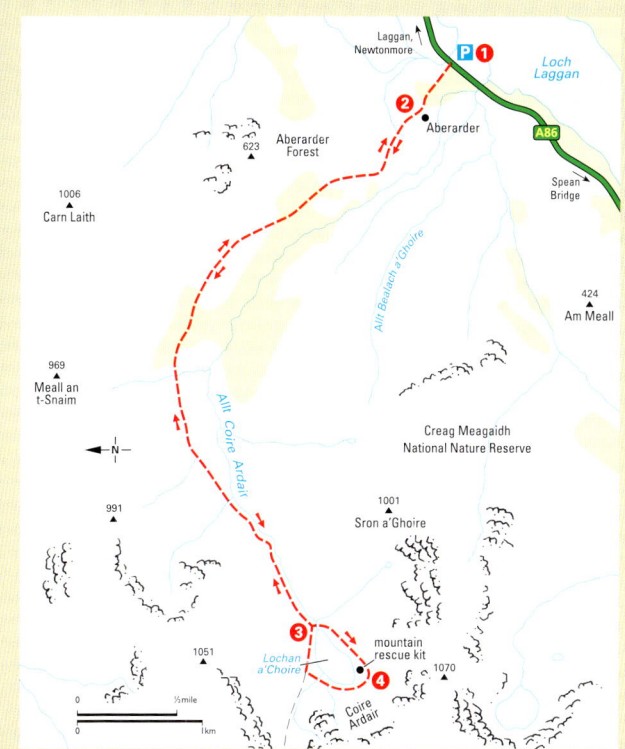

WALK 140

LOCH AN EILEIN'S CASTLE & ORD BAN

A relatively easy walk, around Loch an Eilein and its castle, surrounded by ancient pines and the mountains rising majestically behind. Walk quietly and you may see some of the unique birdlife that exists in the forest including the small crested tit and the stout Scottish crossbill.

DISTANCE/TIME 4.25 miles (6.8km) 1h45 **MAP** OS Explorer 403 Cairn Gorm & Aviemore

START Estate car park near Loch an Eilein, grid ref: NH 897084 **TRACKS** Wide smooth paths, optional steep hill with high ladder stile **THE PUB** The Old Bridge Inn, Dalfaber Road, Aviemore. Tel: 01479 811137; www.oldbridgeinn.co.uk

1 From the end of the car park at the beginning of the walk, a made-up path leads to the visitor centre. Turn left to cross the end of Loch an Eilein, then turn right on a smooth sandy track. The loch shore is nearby on the right. There are several small paths leading down to it if you wish to visit. As you cycle just past a red-roofed house, there is a deer fence that runs across, with a gate.

2 The track now becomes a wide, smooth path, which runs close to the loch side. After a bridge, the main track forks right to pass a bench backed by a flat boulder. The smaller path on the left leads into the hills and through the famous pass of the Lairig Ghru, eventually to Braemar. After crossing a stream at a low concrete footbridge, the path bends right for 120yds (110m) to reach a junction. Just beyond this point is a footbridge with wooden handrails.

3 To shorten the walk, cross this footbridge and continue along the main track, passing Point 4 in another 170yds (155m). For a longer walk, turn left before the footbridge on to a narrower path that will pass all around Loch Gamhna. This second loch soon appears on your right-hand side. Where the path forks, keep right to pass along the loch side, across its head (rather boggy) and back along its further side, to rejoin the wider path around Loch an Eilein. Turn left here.

4 Continue around Loch an Eilein, with the water on your right, to a reedy corner of the loch and a bench. About 55yds (51m) further on, the path turns sharply to the right, signposted 'footpath'. Continue for approx 500yds (418m) parallel to the loch. After a gate, turn right to the loch side and a memorial to Major General Brook Rice who drowned here while skating. Follow the shore to the point opposite the castle, then back up to the wide track above. A deer fence on the left leads back to the visitor centre.

5 From here, a stiff climb (around 500ft/152m) can be made on to the rocky little hill of Ord Ban, a superb viewpoint. Cross a ladder stile immediately to the right of the toilet block and follow the deer fence to the right for 150yds (137m), up to a point behind the car park. Just behind one of the last birches on the slope, a small path then zigzags up the steep slope. It slants to the left to avoid crags, then crosses a small rock slab (take care at this point of the walk if it is wet) and continues on to the summit. Descend by the same path back to the start.

Moray Firth Dolphins

Bottlenose dolphins (*Tursiops truncates*) have been living in and around the Moray Firth in the northeast of Scotland for years, and as a result they have become a major tourist attraction. Moray Firth dolphins are larger than other populations of bottlenose dolphins, a significance that is attributed to the cold water of the Firth.

Experts from the Whale and Dolphin Conservation Society (WDCS) near Inverness, however, fear that expansion of the off-shore drilling industry beyond the Moray Firth is threatening to drive the dolphins away. With fewer than 130 remaining, data collected from the Firth predicts an annual decline of almost 6 per cent in the dolphin population; in short that means extinction in a little less than 50 years.

Also known as grey porpoise, black porpoise and cowfish, bottlenose dolphins grow to between 10 and 12 feet (3–4m) and live for up to 30 years (although some females have been known to reach the grand old age of fifty!). They are highly sociable mammals, living together in groups or 'pods' and communicating through high-pitched clicks or whistles. It has been suggested by some experts that bottlenose dolphins can stun their prey by producing very loud noises.

Bottlenose dolphins are very active and often seen bow-riding, surfing, lobtailing – slapping its fluke up and down on the surface of the water – and breaching – leaping completely out of the water, often twisting and then falling sideways back into the water. They can easily leap several yards, and are sometimes seen playing 'games' with seaweed, coral or other animals. Bottlenose dolphins sometimes bow-ride in front of large whales like the humpbacks, as they are pushed along by the pressure wave. The easiest way of recognising a bottlenose dolphin is to look out for an obvious dark and curved-back dorsal fin.

When a calf is first born, a bottlenose dolphin mum whistles repeatedly so that her calf learns her particular call and is always able to find her, even among whole gatherings of mothers and calves. A bottlenose mother's milk contains 14 per cent fat which is over four times the amount of fat in human or cow's milk.

The Moray Firth (like Cardigan Bay in Wales) is one of the key sites in Britain for whales, dolphins and porpoises (cetaceans). The species most commonly spotted from the shore are bottlenose dolphins and harbour porpoises. There are several locations around the coastline of the firth that are perfect for dolphin and porpoise-watching.

But the Moray Firth is not just about dolphins. Minke whales are often seen in the outer Firth during late summer and autumn. Whereas dolphins and porpoises have teeth to catch their prey, the minke whale has plates of baleen in its mouth – what look like long, furry combs – and takes huge mouthfuls of water, straining it out through the baleen leaving the food behind in its mouth – ingenious, and a bit messy in restaurants, but it works for the whale.

Orcas (killer whales – *Orcinus orca*) also occasionally enter the Firth, travelling in small family pods. They are actually the largest member of the dolphin family. Easy to spot with their black and white markings and the distinctively tall dorsal fin of the males. The huge dorsal fin of the bull orca can reach a height of 6 feet (1.8m, as tall as a man, and taller than many). Adults can range from 18–25 feet (5.5–10m), and weigh anything from 2.5 to 9 tonnes. Orcas have a fearsome reputation as killers, and have a diet of fish, squid, seabirds, turtles, sea lions, seals and other cetaceans. A typical orca eats about 5 per cent of its body weight a day, as much as 880lbs (400kg) of food, or the same as 40 large supermarket bags of potatoes.

Whales and dolphins do not sleep in any commonly understood sense, but simply rest on the surface of the sea, or nap briefly while swimming. Remarkably, each side of the brain takes turns to 'switch off', while the other half remains alert and keeps the animal breathing. Two kinds of seal also live in the Moray Firth: common seals and grey seals. Grey seals have long, straight 'Roman' noses, while common seals have a face rather like a dog. Over 1,500 common seals live along the Firth and can often be seen lounging on sandbanks. In fact, the Moray Firth is the only place in Europe where seals can be watched from a main road: at low-tide from the A9 Cromarty Firth bridge. As many as 500 grey seals visit during the summer months.

The protection and conservation of whales and dolphins around the British coastline is vitally important, and no more so than along the beautiful waters of the Moray Firth. Here the Whale and Dolphin Conservation Society has a Wildlife Centre, based at the mouth of the River Spey on the south side of the Moray Firth. It is about an hour's drive from Inverness. Here, the River Spey, the second longest river in Scotland, flows rapidly into the Firth after a 100-mile journey from the Monadhliath Mountains all the way to the west of Laggan.

The Moray Firth Centre was converted from a former salmon fishing station that has existed on the site since 1768, but today houses an excellent visitor exhibition and a series of education and public awareness initiatives. Now managed by the WDCS the centre exists primarily to contribute to the protection and conservation of the Moray Firth dolphins and their habitat. But as well as being famed for the dolphins, the Centre's location is also within a wonderful wildlife haven, home to other fascinating species such as ospreys, grey and harbour seals, otters, wildfowl and waders, all part of a large nature reserve that forms part of the largest vegetated shingle habitat that now exists in Scotland.

That such a range of whale, dolphin and porpoise species naturally exists around the coastline of Britain is not widely known, and people need to realise that not all cetaceans are exotic species of warmer waters. And while you may want to travel to warmer countries every now and then you can't really use dolphins as an excuse: they are part of the natural heritage of Britain.

TOP Swimming in pods, dolphins can be seen leaping from the water in what appear to be spectacular performances laid-on for human entertainment, but are in fact natural behaviours for dolphins in the wild.

ABOVE Moray Firth's waters are home to many creatures including a large population of grey seals. Males can grow up to 6.5 feet (2m) long and can weigh up to 47 stone (300kg), while females develop to a maximum length of 6 feet (1.95m) and a maximum weight of 16 stone (100kg). Males are distinctly different to females and have darker coats while females have lighter coats with dark spots. Grey seal pups, of course, are easily distinguished by their white, soft downy fur that changes colour as the seal matures.

OPPOSITE Dolphin-watching boat trips are a must here on the 2000 square miles (518sq km) of the Moray Firth. However, not all the dolphin-watching boats sortie just for pleasure. Some of the boats, like the one operated by Aberdeen University, have been collecting data about the bottlenose dolphin population here since 1990, and many individual dolphins have been recorded.

MOORLAND ON MORRONE

The hill at the back of Braemar gives a taste of the Cairngorms. Coming down the back of Morrone Hill, descend through several different plant zones, and the home ground of two distinctive Grampian birds – the grouse and the ptarmigan. The ptarmigan turns white in the winter, but an easy way to recognise it is by where it lives – a grouse above the heather line is a ptarmigan.

DISTANCE/TIME 6.75 miles (10.9km) 4h15 **MAP** OS Explorer 387 Glen Shee & Braemar
START Grid ref: NO 143911 **TRACKS** Well-made but fairly steep path, track, 1 stile
THE PUB The Fife Arms, Braemar. Tel: 01339 741644

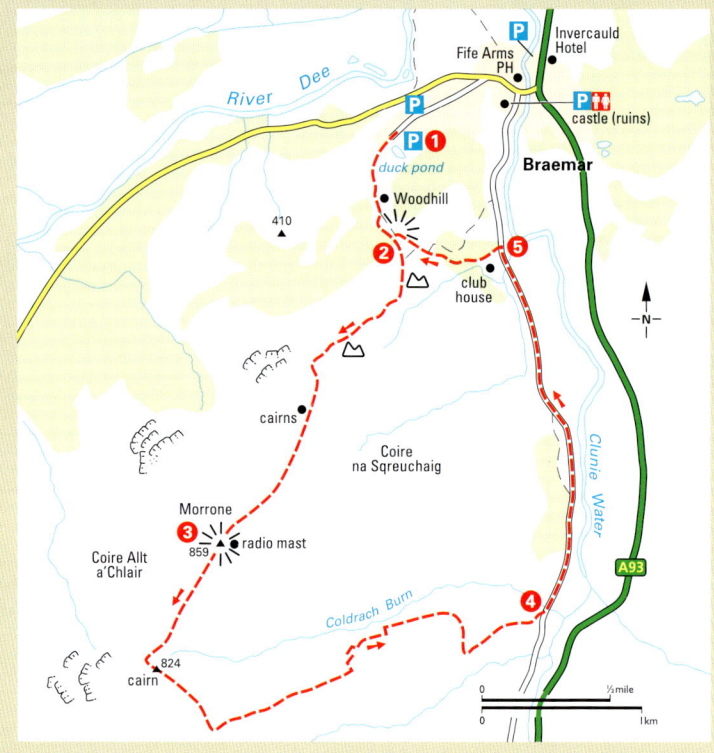

1 Take the wide track uphill, to the right of the duck pond at the top of Chapel Brae, bearing left twice to Woodhill house. The house can be bypassed by taking a small footpath on the right which rejoins the track just above. When the track forks again, bear left to a viewpoint indicator.

2 Cross a track diagonally to a hill path marked 'Morrone'. The path has been rebuilt with rough stone steps. Higher up, it slants to the right along a line of rocky outcrops, a geological dyke of harder rock. At the top of this it turns directly uphill, passing five sprawling cairns. These are the turning point in the Morrone Hill Race that is part of the Braemar Games. The wide, stony path runs up to the radio mast and other ugly constructions on the summit.

3 The summit, if you turn your back on the buildings, has fine views across Deeside to the high Cairngorms. On the main tops, Ben Macdui and Beinn a' Bhuird, snow may show right through the summer. To the east you will see Loch Callater and the White Mounth plateau. A notable hump is Caca Carn Beag, one of the summits of Lochnagar. Morrone's summit area is bare stones, but if you go past

the buildings you'll find the start of a wide track. It runs down to a shallow col and climbs to the cairn on the low summit beyond. Here it bends left towards a lower col, but before reaching it, turns left again down the side of the hill. A gentle zig-zagging descent leads to the road by the Clunie Water.

4 Turn left alongside the river, for 1.5 miles (2.4km). Ben Avon with its row of summit tors fills the skyline ahead. After a snow gate and golf clubhouse comes a road sign warning of a cattle grid (the grid itself is round the next bend). Here a track, back up to the left, has a blue-topped waymarker pole.

5 Go up between the caravans to a ladder stile with a dog flap. A faint path leads up under birches, bearing right and becoming clearer. After a gate in a fence the path becomes quite clear, leading to a Scottish Natural Heritage signboard and blue waymarker at the top of the birchwood. The path becomes a track with a fence on its right and, 220yds (210m), reaches the viewpoint indicator, Point 2. From here you can return to the duck pond at Point 1.

CROMBIE WATER & THE WHISKY HILLS

A walk through a green valley and bare heather moor in the smugglers' country of Glenlivet. Long before the coming of licensed distilleries, whisky was part of the economy of the Highlands. After the hard work of the barley harvest came the quieter occupation of mashing and distilling. The draff (dregs) from the mash-barrel went to feed the cows, while the spirit itself warmed the crofter through the harsh storms and bitterly cold snows of winter.

DISTANCE/TIME 6.25 miles (10.1km) 3h15 **MAP** OS Explorer 420 Correen Hills & Glenlivet
START Grid ref: NJ 218257 **TRACKS** Waymarked, muddy and indistinct in places, 11 stiles
THE PUB The Pole Inn, Knockandhu

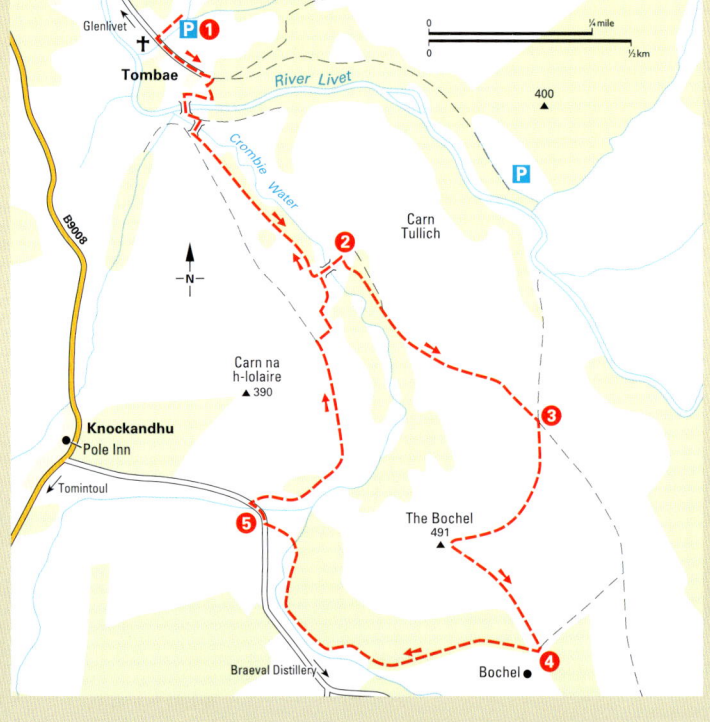

1 At Tombae church, turn left for 330yds (300m) to a stile on the right. A track leads down into birchwoods. Bear right at a waymarker and follow the main track to a bridge over the River Livet. After 60yds (55m), turn right to another bridge (over Crombie Water). Turn half left, up to a stile beside a field gate. Now follow the top of the low wooded bank above the Crombie Water to reach a footbridge (grid ref 226245).

2 Across the footbridge, a small path runs across a meadow into a wood, slanting up to the right to a green track. Turn right and follow this gently up through the wood, then bend left on to heather moorland. Below the abrupt hill of The Bochel the track forks. Keep ahead, with a waymarker. The way becomes a peaty path. At the top of the first rise is a stile with a gate alongside. There path, with a waymarker, leads to a gateway in another fence. Don't go through, but turn right, with the fence on your left, to a stile with a signpost.

3 For an easier alternative, follow the sign for Walk 10, ahead. Just before a house, turn right at another signpost and follow a

track towards Bochel farm. But the main route goes over The Bochel itself. Across a stile, turn uphill on small sheep paths to the summit cairn. Turn left, to descend towards the white Braeval distillery below the Ladder Hills. As the slope steepens, you'll see Bochel farm below. Head down the left-hand edge of the nearer pine wood to join the rough track leading into the farm.

4 At once a stile on the right leads to a faint path into the plantation. This soon becomes a green track running just above the bottom edge of the wood. It becomes slightly more worn and then runs out to a road.

5 Turn right, over a bridge to a waymarked stile again on the right. The track rises into open fields that sweep away above the river. At its highest point, a waymarker points down to the right. Follow this down to a fence, with a waymarked stile on the left, then carry on through an area thick with heather, with a fence on your left. Turn downhill to a stile at the bottom. Cross and turn left, ignoring another stile on the left, to reach the footbridge (Point 2). Retrace the first part of the walk to Tombae.

THE PASS OF RYVOAN & THE THIEVES' ROAD

Following cattle thieves and drovers to the lochan used by the fairies for their laundry. The Pass of Ryvoan has all the atmosphere of a classic Cairngorm through-route. It's a scaled down version of the famous and fearsome Lairig Fhru that cuts through the Cairngorm range southwards to Aviemore. You pass from the shelter of the forest to a green lochan, trapped between two high and stony mountainsides. Once through the narrow gap, you're in different country. Here you will find wide moors and a ring of peaks around the horizon.

DISTANCE/TIME 5 miles (8km) 2h15 **MAP** OS Explorer 403 Cairn Gorm & Aviemore **START** Grid ref: NH 980095 **TRACKS** Smooth tracks, one steep ascent, no stiles **THE PUB** The Winking Owl, Grampian Road, Aviemore. Tel: 01479 810646

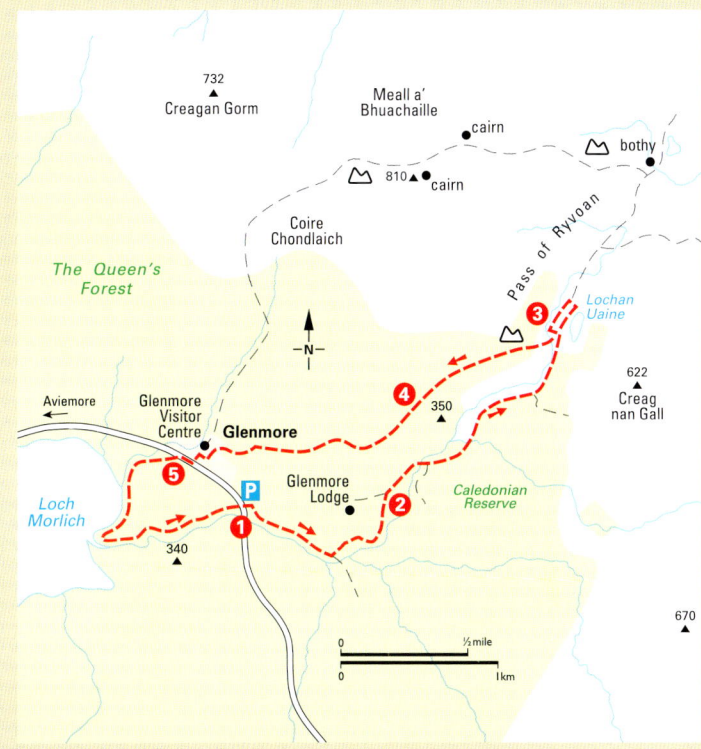

1 Head upstream on a sandy track to the left of the river. Interpretation signs explain the flowers of the forest you may come across, many of which are ferns and mosses. After 550yds (500m), turn left on a wide smooth path with blue/yellow waymarkers. Ahead is a gate into Glenmore Lodge rifle range; here the path bends right, to a wide gravel track.

2 Turn right, away from Glenmore Lodge, to cross a concrete bridge into the Caledonian Reserve. Immediately keep ahead on a smaller track (marked with a blue waymarker) as the main one bends right. The track narrows as it heads into the Pass of Ryvoan between steep wooded slopes of pine, birch and scree. At a sign that warns of the end of waymarking, a path turns left, with a blue waymarker, which you take in a moment. Just beyond this, steps up to the right lead down to Lochan Uaine. Walk round to the left of the water on the beach. At the head of the loch a small path leads back up to the track. Turn sharp left, and go back to the junction already visited; from here, turn off to the right on to the narrower path with the blue waymarker.

3 This small path crosses some duckboards and heads back down the valley. Very soon it starts to climb steeply to the right, up rough stone steps. When it levels off the going is easier, although it's still narrow with tree roots. The path reaches a forest road at a bench and a waymarker.

4 Continue to the left along the track. After a clear-felled area with views, the track re-enters trees and slopes downhill into Glenmore village. Just above the main road turns right, through a green barrier, to reach Glenmore Visitor Centre. Pass through its car park to the main road.

5 Cross to Glenmore shop. Behind a post-box, steps lead down to the campsite. Pass along its right-hand edge to a path into woods. Head left across a footbridge to the shore of Loch Morlich and follow the beaches until another river blocks the way. Turn left along the riverbank. Ignore a footbridge, but continue on the wide path with the river on your right. Where the path divides, the smaller branch continues beside the river through bushes to the car park.

WALK 144

SIR JAMES GRANT'S TOWN

In about 1750, young Mr James Grant decided that Speyside could do with some grand architecture as he'd seen in Edinburgh and persuaded his father, Sir Ludovic to help. The town was to be supported by a linen factory. Sadly, the linen factory floundered and it wasn't until Queen Victoria visited the town in 1860 that it was really admired, but the handsome town has been attracting tourists ever since.

DISTANCE/TIME 7 miles (11.3km) 3h **MAP** OS Explorer 419 Grantown-on-Spey **START** Grid ref: NJ 035280 **TRACKS** Tracks and smooth paths, 1 stile **THE PUB** Grant Arms Hotel, The Square, Grantown on Spey. Tel: 01479 872526

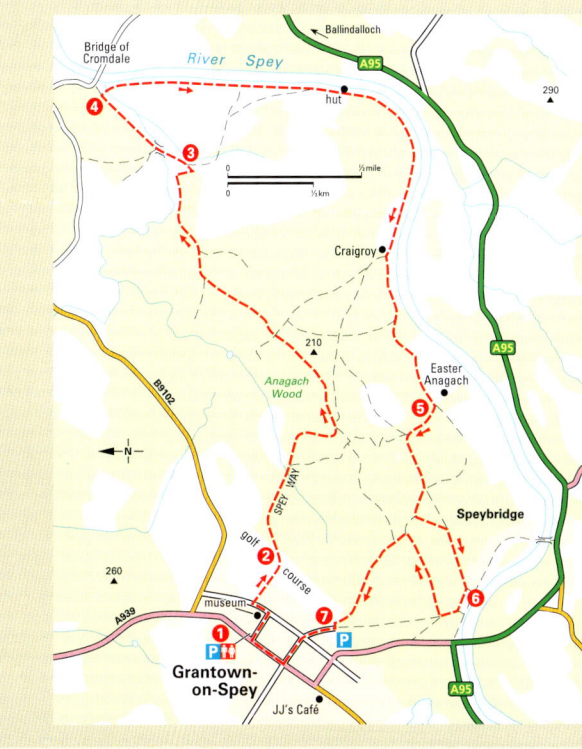

1 Go down past the museum. Turn left into South Street, then right into Golf Course Road. A tarred path takes you across the golf course to a small gate into Anagach Wood.

2 The wide path ahead has a blue/red waymarker. At a junction, the blue trail departs to the right; turn left, following a Spey Way marker and red-top poles. Keep following the red markers, turning left at the first junction and bearing left at the next. When the track joins a new fence, keep ahead, following a Spey Way marker.

3 Emerge into open fields and, after crossing a small bridge, turn to the right through a chained gap stile. A path with pines on its left leads to a track near the River Spey. (Bridge of Cromdale is just ahead here.)

4 Turn sharp right on this track alongside the river. At a fishers' hut it re-enters forest. About 0.75 miles (1km) later it diminishes to a green path and slants up past the cottage of Craigroy to join its entrance track.

5 At Easter Anagach, a grass track on the right has red waymarkers and runs into a birchwood. With a barrier ahead, follow

marker poles to the left, on to a broad path beside a falling fence. At the next junction, turn right, following the red poles, over a slight rise. Descending, turn left just before a blue-top post, on to a smaller path with blue and red posts. This runs along the top of a ridge, to reach a bench above a lane. To the left down the lane is the handsome stone bridge built by Major Caulfield as part of the military road system.

6 The path bends right, alongside the road, to meet a wide track which is the former military road. Turn right, to a path on the right with green-top posts. At a small pool, the main path bends left for 150yds (135m), with blue and green posts; take the path ahead, with green posts. A very old tree in the middle of the path was once used for public hangings. At a five-way junction bear left to find the next green post. At the edge of the golf course turn left to a small car park and information board.

7 Follow the tarred street uphill, past the end of the golf course, to Grantown's High Street. Turn right to The Square. Just past the Grant Arms Hotel, a sign points right, to the museum.

Skye & North

CLOCKWISE FROM TOP LEFT: CAVELL GARDENS, INVERNESS; ULLAPOOL; CUILLIN HILLS, ISLE OF SKYE

APPLECROSS MAP REF 410 D5

Looking north from the picture-postcard village of Plockton, the rugged hills of Applecross fill both the view and the imagination. Until the last century this peninsula was almost as isolated as Knoydart. Rough tracks linked the old settlements along the coast down to Toscaig, and access up from the south was via the breathtakingly spectacular Bealach-na-Ba pass, which rises to some 2,050 feet (624.8m). In 1965 a road was started around the northern margin from Shieldaig, making it a pleasant circular driving route around this remote and beautiful place.

An Irish saint established a religious community here in the 7th century, but it was destroyed in a Viking raid. Today it is hard to believe that 3,000 people once thrived with their cattle in the green, fertile valley around the quiet village of Applecross itself – cleared from the land when the Mackenzies sold it off for a sporting estate; only the outlines of their deserted cottages remain.

Applecross Bay is a welcoming curve of pinkish sand, with an excellent little inn noted for its fresh seafood.

BLACK ISLE MAP REF 411 H4

The Black Isle is the fertile spit of land between the Cromarty and Moray Firths. The central forested ridge carries the peninsula's older name of Ardmeanach, and was part of lands gifted by Mary, Queen of Scots to her husband (and cousin), Lord Darnley.

Cromarty, set on the northeastern tip of the peninsula, is a delightfully built 18th-century town, an important centre of fishing and commerce until the 19th century, when it was bypassed by the railways. The whitewashed Courthouse Museum tells the town's story, with the aid of computer-controlled, animated figures. Hugh Miller, a 19th-century geologist, social commentator and also writer, lived in the little thatched cottage next door. The cottage is now in the care of the National Trust for Scotland. The fossil beach where he worked is 2 miles (3.2 km) away at Eathie.

The Moray Firth is also the best place to go to spot dolphins. Bottlenose dolphins found around the Scottish mainland are some of the largest in the world, and in the Moray Firth area there is currently one of only two resident populations in Britain, with at least 88 individuals identified. Cromarty has become the best place in Britain to see bottlenose dolphins in the wild – boat trips run by Dolphin Ecosse are available throughout the year. There are also whale-watching trips in August and September.

Fortrose looks out across the Moray Firth. The cathedral was completed in the 15th century, but in the 16th was then unroofed, before Cromwell plundered its sandstone blocks to build the fortifications in Inverness. On the other side of the spit (once a popular spot for witch-burning but now dedicated to golf) lies Rosemarkie, notable for the fascinating Pictish remains displayed at the Groam House Museum and Pictish Centre.

The mudflats of the Beauly Firth attract a large number of birds – over-wintering greylag and pink-footed geese graze the fields around, and a variety of sea ducks, including goldeneye and scoter, may be spotted near the Kessock Bridge.

In the graveyard of the parish church of Avoch, near Rosemarkie, lie the remains of the great Scottish explorer Sir Alexander Mackenzie (1755–1820). Mackenzie travelled to Canada in 1779 and was soon trading furs for the North West Company. Based at Fort Chipewyan on Lake Athabasca, he set out with a team of native Canadian Indians in 1789 to discover a route across the continent, but found instead a long river, which would be named after him, leading up to the Arctic Ocean. In 1793 he became the first caucasian man to cross the Rockies and finally reach the Pacific.

CANNICH MAP REF 410 F5

The broad Strath Glass from the north leads to the modern village of Cannich where four valleys meet. Eastwards, down Glen Urquhart, is the prehistoric Corrimony Cairn, still with its stone roof and eleven standing stones. Dramatic Glen Cannich is entered by a winding road between bare mountain tops, with groves of birch and alder. It widens towards Loch Mullardoch and its dam, 9 miles (15km) west of Cannich, at 2,385 feet (726.5m), is the longest in Scotland.

The approach to Glen Affric, perhaps the most beautiful of Scottish valleys, passes the popular Dog Falls. Along this 6 mile (9.7km) stretch of Loch Beinn a'Mheadhoin are parking spots, many with fine walks starting from them. On the opposite side is one of the largest remnants of the ancient Caledonian Pine Forest, fenced to keep out deer and allow regeneration. Beyond the loch the road ends, but you can walk on to Loch Affric – a magical scene of clustered hills, birch and pine forest; during the autumn there is dazzling colour and a hint of snow on the peaks. You can also follow the old track up through the mountains to Sheil Bridge in Kintail.

Today, local employment in the town is provided by the many hydro-electricity plants in the area and the forestry industry, as well as conservation and tourism.

FORT WILLIAM MAP REF 410 F7

Fort William's greatest asset is its close proximity to Ben Nevis, Britain's highest mountain, which stands sentinel over the Nevis range about 7 miles (11.5km) to the north. The town, the biggest in the

THE GATE OF FORT WILLIAM

Western Highlands, is also at the southern entrance to the Great Glen and at the head of Loch Linnhe, with routes to Badenoch and Skye. But this is not just a place to venture from – it has its own delights too. The idiosyncratic West Highland Museum, famous for the Jacobite collections held there, lives up to its description as 'an old-fashioned museum – it is full of information and surprises' with an eclectic range of displays, including natural history, Highland clothing and crofting. Housed since 1926 in what was once the British Linen Bank, the museum is thought by many to be the best museum dedicated to the Highlands in the whole of Scotland. Treasures of the Earth, at Corpach to the west of town, is a fascinating and huge collection of rare gemstones, crystals and fossils, including Europe's largest uncut emerald – a thing of great beauty. Visitors can also discover how amethyst crystals take a quarter of a million years to grow just 1 inch (3cm).

Until recently the tops of Scotland's mountain ranges were the exclusive preserve of the athletic, but now everyone can experience breathtaking views without so much as getting out of breath. Panoramic vistas to the upper slopes of Aonach Mor (4,000 ft/1,219.2m) open up from enclosed gondola cable cars which cover about 1.5 miles (2.4km) in their climb to an altitude of 2,150 feet (655.3m). The ascent takes about 15 minutes and at the top, in addition to the views across Loch Lochy, the Great Glen, Loch Eil and the Inner Hebrides, you will find a restaurant, a sports shop, telescopes, interpretative plaques and slide presentations. There are a number of walks but do keep to the paths, both for your own safety and for conservation. Two recommended walks are to Sgurr Finnisg-aig (taking about 20 minutes each way) and to Meal Beag (taking about 30 minutes in each direction).

Until well into the 19th century everyone thought that soaring Ben Macdhui in the Cairngorms and, in fact, not Ben Nevis, was Britain's highest mountain. It was the peak everyone climbed, including Gladstone and even Queen Victoria. The then Queen wrote in her journal, 'Nothing could be grander or wilder; the rocks are so grand and precipitous, and the snow on Ben Macdhui has such fine effect.' Like Everest, only recognised as the world's highest mountain in the 19th century, Ben Nevis remained unrecognised until accurate measurement was finally made by the Ordnance Survey in 1846 and the issue was resolved – Ben Nevis is the highest at 4,406 feet (1,343m), and Ben Macdhui is a close runner-up at a height of 4,296 feet (1,309m).

Visit
THE PARALLEL ROADS

In a quiet valley 18 miles (29km) to the northeast of Fort William is a geological phenomenon that is unique in Britain. Glen Roy and its side valleys are marked by three strange parallel lines known as the 'Parallel Roads', not roads at all, but the shorelines of an ancient glacial loch. Towards the end of the last Ice Age, some 10,000 years ago, the valley was dammed with ice that melted in three stages, leaving these strange horizontal ridges along the valley slopes. Scottish Natural Heritage explains it all on an interpretative board above the car park. To get to Glen Roy from Fort William, go north on the A82, turn right on to the A86 at Spean Bridge, then left on an unclassified road at Roy Bridge.

Visit
EILEAN DONAN CASTLE

One of the most photographed and romantic castles in Scotland, Eilean Donan is perched on a rock just offshore in Loch Duich, linked to the mainland and a modern visitor centre by a stone bridge. There has been a fortification here since the 13th century and its 14-foot (4.26m) thick walls have withstood the onslaught of both men and the elements; in 1719 the castle came under fire from Government warships and was subsequently abandoned as a wreck after the attack. The castle owes its appearance today to restoration between 1912 and 1932, by Lt Col John MacRae-Gilstrap, who had a vision of how it should look.

Visit
CONCRETE BOB'S VIADUCT

The West Highland Railway gives wonderful views down Loch Shiel from the Glenfinnan Viaduct, and the viaduct itself is impressive. It was built when the line from Glasgow, which had struggled across Rannoch Moor to Fort William by 1894, was extended to Mallaig in 1902. Curving over 1,000 feet (308m) over the River Finnan, its 21 concrete arches are up to 100 feet (30.5m) high. The viaduct was designed for Robert MacAlpine (later Sir Robert, founder of the civil engineering firm) whose nickname was Concrete Bob. Legend has it that buried within the Glenfinnan Viaduct are a horse and cart that fell headlong into the concrete before it was set.

GAIRLOCH MAP REF 410 E4

This popular holiday village with its excellent Heritage Museum is spread around a sunny, sandy bay, with the heights of the delightfully named Flowerdale looming behind. There are superb views out to the islands, and Gairloch lies at the heart of a fine scenic area which takes in the incomparable Loch Maree. West from the village, the road winds around the bay and eventually turns into a track, leading to the former lighthouse at Rubha Reidh. Beyond sheltered Badachro the road passes sandy bays to end at Redpoint, but energetic walkers can take the long path to Diabaig on Loch Torridon.

Behind Gairloch the A832 leads to Loch Maree, famous for its fishing. It is surrounded by high mountains and scattered with islands. The highest peak on the northern shore is Slioch (3,219 feet/981m), while to the south Beinn Eighe, with its cap of white quartzite, lies at the heart of Britain's first National Nature Reserve. Find out about nature trails and picnic spots at the visitor centre at Aultroy, towards the eastern end of the loch.

Isle Maree, by Letterewe, was the site of a 7th-century hermitage, and may even have had much older, druidical connections. Queen Victoria fell in love with the whole area when she visited in 1877, giving her name to the waterfall that plunges down near Talladale.

GLENELG MAP REF 410 E6

The old military road that leads up to Glenelg rockets off the main Kyle of Lochalsh road, climbing rapidly up the Mam Ratagain pass to a fine viewpoint offering stunning views of the lovely Five Sisters of Kintail above Loch Duich. There follows a gentler descent into Glen More, where a side road goes to the six-car turntable ferry that is a romantic summer alternative to the modern bridge to Skye. The Glenelg road passes the gaunt remains of Bernera Barracks, built in 1722 for Hanoverian troops (ruins fenced off for safety reasons). Continue for 2.5 miles (4km) into Glen Beag for Glenelg's most famous sight – its two brochs. Close by at Sandaig, was the home of *Ring of Bright Water* author Gavin Maxwell.

GLENFINNAN MAP REF 410 E7

Glenfinnan will always have a special place in Scottish history, for it was here that the event which Winston Churchill called 'one of the most audacious and irresponsible enterprises in British history' began – the 1745 Jacobite Rising. The monument tower of 1815, with its 1834 figure of a Highlander, may not be on the exact spot where Bonnie Prince Charlie unfurled his father's white and red silk banner, yet it is most romantically set at the head of Loch Shiel, overlooking the wooded Eilean Glean Fhianin and the mountains of Sunart and Moidart. Climb the tower for the best views of the loch.

The clan chiefs were dismayed that the Prince had brought only seven followers, not the French troops they had expected. They were persuaded to join him only by the example of Cameron of Lochiel, who brought 700 men to Glenfinnan for the Prince. So on 19 August 1745 the banner was set flying, the Old Pretender was proclaimed King James III & VIII, with the Prince as his Regent, and the army – still only 1,200 strong – began its campaign. Capturing Edinburgh easily and defeating General Cope in the 15-minute battle at Prestonpans on 21 September, the determined men set out for London. But with little English support and no hope of French help, they turned back at Derby that December and met their doom at Culloden in April 1746.

GLENFINNAN VIADUCT

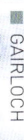

GAIRLOCH

The story is vividly told in the Visitor Centre nearby, which also traces the Prince's journeys through the Western Highlands and Islands after Culloden.

INVEREWE MAP REF 410 E4

Surrounded by barren peat bogs, rocks and water lies Inverewe, one of Britain's most remarkable gardens, and a must-see for plant-lovers from all over the world. Lying on the same line of latitude as Moscow and Hudson's Bay, the site must have seemed a daunting challenge when Osgood MacKenzie inherited the Inverewe Estate in 1862 from his step-father. Osgood possessed every skill and quality necessary in order to create this wonderful oasis – imagination, vision, perseverance and patience.

First he planted a shelter belt of pines and firs, carted out the rocks and replaced them with hundreds of tonnes of garden soil. Once protected against strong winds, Inverewe could benefit from the warming effects of the North Atlantic Drift. Rhododendrons were planted in profusion, and still provide one of the most spectacular attractions in the early summer. Paths meander between the blooms and beneath the pines, and pass an almost bewildering array of rare and exotic plants, collected from all over the world. Rock gardens are bright with alpines, including many species from New Zealand, and the area named 'Japan' is planted with a rich and unusual variety of tree ferns and palms.

There are wonderful views along the loch from the tip of the garden at Cuddy Rock, and also from the front of the house, built in 1937 after fire destroyed Osgood's original building. Mackenzie died in 1922, and his daughter Mairi, who had maintained and developed his vision, presented the garden to the National Trust for Scotland in 1952.

INVERNESS MAP REF 411 G5

Inverness is known as the 'Capital of the Highlands', Scotland's newest city (designated in 2000) and a popular holiday centre, set on the banks of the River Ness at the eastern extremity of the Great Glen. Commanding the east–west facing corridor to Moray and Aberdeen as well as the main north–south route through Scotland, its location has given the town a strategic importance that has resulted in a much-chequered history. Inverness was probably well established by the time of St Columba's visit in AD 565. Certainly King Duncan (c1010–1040), notably of Shakespeare's *Macbeth*, had his castle in the town, and various clan chiefs and disaffected Jacobites have stormed through the town over the centuries.

Today Inverness is a busy administrative centre for the Highlands and Islands and presents a mostly 19th-century face. Even the dominating red sandstone walls of Inverness Castle were rebuilt during Victoria's reign as a Sheriff Court and jail, with a monument to Flora Macdonald on the castle esplanade. On the opposite side of the river loom the two massive towers that top St Andrew's Episcopal Cathedral, which contains an interesting collection of Russian icons. The Inverness Museum and Art Gallery (due to reopen in 2007), has fine examples of Highland artefacts and displays on the archaeology, social as well as the natural history of the Highlands. The museum hosts various exhibitions, performances and talks.

From the museum you can see Craig Phadrig, a vitrified Iron Age fort on a wooded hill west of the River Ness, reached by a steep forest trail from Leachkin Brae. In Huntly Street next to the river you can visit the largest kilt-making workshop in Scotland – Hector Russell's Scottish Kiltmaker.

INVERPOLLY MAP REF 410 F3

North of Ullapool the habitation is sparse and the landscape becomes altogether bigger and wilder, with giant, bare mountains looming out of bleak, bitter moorland. The Inverpolly National Nature Reserve, managed by Scottish Natural Heritage, offers access to this fine, dramatic countryside in all its glory, and the visitor centre at Knockan is a good place to start. The diversity of habitats in the region is revealed, including bogs, lochs and patches of ancient woodland, with a corresponding diversity of flora. A geology trail here illuminates the formation of the Assynt area, and part of the 'Moine Thrust' can be seen in the rocks of Knockan Cliff. There are excellent views from the top of the mountains of Coigach. Of these, Stac Pollaidh (2,008 ft/ 612m) is the most popular, and a relatively easy walk leads up from the minor road by Loch Lurgainn. Look out for deer and birds of prey, and you may even see signs of wildcats in the area. To the north on a clear day you can see the familiar form of Suilven (2,402 ft/732m), but this peak is strictly for experienced mountaineers.

There is a further extensive nature reserve at Inchnadamph. From this point the road leads round the shores of Loch Assynt, past the rocky ruins of Ardvreck Castle. Beyond this place is the popular harbour of Lochinver (this links up with a narrow and very scenic road from Loch Lurgainn). Up the coast, just north of the hamlet of Clachtoll, the circular remains of a broch from the first century AD can be seen on the shoreline.

SKYE & NORTH

LOCH NESS MAP REF 411 G6

It would be difficult for anyone but the most hardened sceptic to gaze out over the waters of Loch Ness without just the small hope of seeing something which might be interpreted as a 'sighting'. Mentioned in writing as long ago as the 7th century, when St Adamnan's Life of St Columba tells of the saint calming the creature down after an apparent attack on a monk, the Loch Ness Monster – or, familiarly, Nessie – has become the focus of the tourist industry here. Drumnadrochit is the main centre for this, offering the Original Loch Ness Visitor Centre with a large-screen cinema, exhibition and sonar scanning cruises, and the Official Loch Ness Monster Exhibition with audio-visuals and a 'life-size' model of Nessie.

Monster or no, Loch Ness is beautiful and it contains more water than all the lakes and reservoirs in England and in Wales put together. The loch is 24 miles (38.6km) long, 1 mile (1.6km) wide and 750 feet (228.6m) deep, making it one of the largest bodies of fresh water in Europe. The loch forms a major part of the Caledonian Canal, which links the west coast with the Moray Firth, and follows the line of the dramatic Great Glen, cutting Scotland in two halves. This spectacular geological fault has provided a way through the mountains for centuries of travellers and is tracked today by the A82 between Fort William and Inverness.

MALLAIG MAP REF 410 D6

This small, busy fishing harbour, facing the Isle of Skye across the Sound of Sleat, stands at the end of the A830 from Fort William, more romantically known as the 'Road to the Isles'. The term comes from the cattle-droving days, before the railway arrived in 1901, but it holds the evocative promise of a special destination for today's travellers. It is also the last stop on the famous West Highland Line, and ferries from Mallaig can take you on to Skye, Rum, Eigg, Muck and Canna. The town has an aquarium dedicated to local species and the fishing industry of the town, and a heritage centre. The steam train *Jacobite* runs from Fort William to Mallaig, passing Morar on the way.

A couple of miles outside Mallaig, at Morar, the waters of Scotland's deepest freshwater loch tumble and cascade down a spectacular waterfall and into a beautiful sandy bay. One of the long, white-sand beaches along here provided the setting for the film *Local Hero*. A leisurely drive southwards is enchanting, passing through mixed woodland, with fine views to the islands. Allow yourself plenty of time – it's a slow, winding road and mainly single track until you reach the little church above Lochailort.

SHIELDAIG & TORRIDON
MAP REF 410 E5

The villages around Loch Torridon are picturesque, but cannot compete with the grandeur of some of the finest mountain scenery in Scotland. The road east from Shieldaig, a whitewashed, 18th-century planned village overlooking the pine-clad Shieldaig Island, gives views over Upper Loch Torridon to the huge mountain mass dominated by Ben Liathach.

Of red Torridonian sandstone, 750 million years old and 3,339 feet (1,024m) high, Liathach has a row of seven peaks topped with shining white quartzite from 150 million years later. It forms part of the National Trust for Scotland's 16, 100-acre (6,520ha) Torridon Estate. The Trust's Countryside Centre in Torridon village can advise on the best routes in the mountains, but guided walks are recommended for the 5-mile (8km) ridge between Liathach's peaks. The Deer Museum has a herd of wild deer, and information about their life on the hills.

Further on, Beinn Eighe presents a forbidding face to the traveller, but like the other mountains has impressive corries to the north. Britain's first National Nature Reserve was founded here in 1951 to protect the native Caledonian pine forest on its slopes.

The road north of Loch Torridon, with wonderful views over to the Applecross peninsula, passes through Fasag, built to house families displaced in the clearances, and through several crofting settlements to end at Lower Diabaig, from where you can walk to Redpoint, far out on the coast of Wester Ross.

SKYE, ISLE OF MAP REF 410 D5

Skye is the largest and most famous of the Inner Hebrides, dominated from every view by the high peaks of the Cuillins. The jagged gabbro (igneous rock, like basalt) of the Black Cuillins and the mystical-looking pink, scree-covered granite of the Red Cuillins have proved an irresistible challenge for mountaineers – the most inaccessible peaks were only conquered at the end of the 19th century. Located to the north, on the Trotternish peninsula, is an extraordinary broken ridge, jutting out from which are jagged peaks and pillars that loom eerily on misty days.

Road signs written in Gaelic as well as English quickly tell you that you're in a different culture, and Skye retains a strong Gaelic identity, encouraged at the college, Sabhal Mòr Ostaig, in Sleat. At the Aros Centre, just south of Portree, a forest walk illustrates the letters of the Gaelic alphabet. There are crofting museums at Colbost and Kilmuir, with several reconstructed homesteads.

Portree is the island's capital. This little town was named after a royal visit in 1540 by James V – *port righ* means king's harbour – and its formal square is a miniature delight. The town is the gateway to the Trotternish peninsula. Taking the road up the eastern side, look out for the column of the Old Man of Storr and other strange rock formations up on your left, and for the columnar formations and dramatic waterfall at the Kilt Rock on the coast to your right, just before Staffin. There are marvellous views from here across to the blue hills of the mainland.

Heading west from Portree brings you to the wilder side of the island, with the Waternish and Duinish peninsulas like two long fingers reaching out towards the Outer Hebrides. At Carbost, the Talisker Distillery produces a distinctive peaty, smoky malt whisky. Dunvegan is the family seat of another powerful Skye clan, the MacLeods, and claims to be Scotland's oldest inhabited castle, being occupied since the 13th century.

Broadford is the main centre for exploring the south of the island, and if the weather is clear, drive over to Elgol to experience some of Britain's most magnificent scenery. The road winds below the mighty Red Cuillins and beside Loch Slapin before descending an alarmingly steep road into Elgol (not suitable for caravans). You can see across to the island of Soay, with Canna, Rum and Eigg to the south.

After the barrenness of the mountains, Sleat seems a veritable Garden of Eden. Lovely Armadale Castle Gardens and the Museum of the Isles are well worth a visit. There are excellent exhibitions, genealogical research facilities, guided walks, a restaurant and much more.

Skye is an unlikely crossroads among the islands. You can reach it by ferry from Mallaig (about 40 minutes), or across the strong currents by Glenelg (summer only), or across the new bridge at Kyle of Lochalsh. The bridge provoked controversy when it was built, but is low enough to be unobtrusive. Ferries to the outer islands leave from the harbour at Uig, on the Trotternish peninsula, and sail over to Raasay from Sconser.

STRATHPEFFER MAP REF 411 G5

Once hailed as 'the Harrogate of the North', Strathpeffer is a curious phenomenon to find above the Highland line – a genteel, attractive little spa town, complete with Victorian architectural twirls such as verandahs and ornamental barge-boards.

Locals had known about the curative properties of the mineral springs here for centuries, but thanks to a serious scientific analysis of the water in 1819, Strathpeffer became a boom town. Inevitably, tastes change, and Strathpeffer's popularity declined after World War II. Many of the spa buildings have disappeared, and the old wooden railway station now houses a museum of childhood. There are several good places to walk here, including the ridge of Knock Farril to the south, and through the woods to the Falls of Rogie to the west. Salmon may be seen in the Blackwater River here, and there are pleasant picnic sites between the trees.

ULLAPOOL MAP REF 410 F3

As you approach on the A835, the pretty little whitewashed town of Ullapool is neatly laid out before you on a spit of land curving into Loch Broom. The tidy grid-plan of the streets reveals that this is a model town laid out to a plan developed by the British Fishery Society in 1788.

The site was chosen particularly to provide a good fishing harbour, and to squeeze out the Dutch herring vessels which had taken advantage of the lack of local boats. The herring did not last, however, and, without the lifeline of the railway, the settlement declined.

The Fishery Society had chosen their site well, however, and in the first half of the 20th century boats came from the east coast and fortunes revived. Until the mid-1990s, the local economy was given a boost by the 'Klondyker' factory ships from Eastern Europe, processing the catches of east coast trawlermen in the loch's sheltered waters. Sadly, the collapse of the Russian economy saw them disappear and now tourism is the main industry. Learn more about crofting, fishing and emigration at Ullapool's good, small museum, set in a former church.

Ullapool is the gateway to the remote northwestern tip of Scotland, as well as the main ferry port for Stornoway, in the Outer Hebrides. Around the coast at Achiltibuie is the Hydroponicum, a scientific delight, where bananas and other exotic plants thrive without soil – seeing is believing! At the head of Loch Broom, take time out to stop and see the dramatic Corrieshalloch Gorge, and the impressive suspension bridge just below the Falls of Measach.

SKYE

TO FLOWERDALE FALLS

On most summer days, either the harbour porpoise or common dolphin – or possibly both – can be seen, given a little patience, in Loch Gairloch. A loch cruise is the best way to see these creatures. After walking along the Gairloch shoreline, take the fairly easy route up a rocky valley to Flowerdale Waterfall.

1 Cross the road and head up to the right of the cemetery. Turn left at its corner, heading into a clump of trees to a track above. Turn right until a footbridge leads you on to a wide path that then runs downhill. With a wall corner just ahead, turn to the right (signed 'Flowerdale Waterfall'). A track runs down to a tarred driveway.

2 Turn left to pass Flowerdale House. The way is marked with red-topped poles. From here, the track passes to the left of an old barn and turns right at a sign for the waterfall to pass Flowerdale Mains. In 438yds (400m) pass a concrete bridge on the right.

3 Follow the main path ahead, keeping to the left of the stream to reach a footbridge built by the Royal Engineers, just before you get to lovely Flowerdale Waterfall.

4 The path leads up past the waterfall to cross a footbridge above. It runs into a pine clump, then turns back down the valley. After another footbridge it joins a rough track, which meets a forest road beside Point 3.

3. Turn left, away from the bridge, through felled forest that is regenerating with at least five different species (birch, alder, pine, willow and rowan).

5 Look out for a blue-topped pole marking a path on the right with a footbridge. It leads through meadowland and bracken with blue waymarker poles. The path bends right at an old fence cornerpost and goes down through bracken and birch to pass above and left of an enclosed field. Turn right to pass under two oak trees and cross a stream to get to an earth track.

6 Turn left for a few steps, until a bracken path runs up to the right past a waymarked power pole. The path bends left under oaks, then drops to rejoin the earth track. This soon meets a larger track, which is the old road from Loch Maree to Gairloch. Turn right along this, through a couple of gates, to reach The Old Inn at Charlestown.

7 Cross the old bridge, and the main road, to the pier. Turn right at a sign labelled Gairloch Chandlery, to find a tarmac path signposted for the beach. This passes to the left of a pinewood, then turns right into the trees. It bends left and emerges to run along the spine of a headland. Before heading out to sea it turns sharp right, and then crosses above a rocky bay to the fort (An Dun). Finally, a duckboard path runs along behind the beach, turning right to the car park.

DISTANCE/TIME 5.25 miles (8.4km) 2h45 **MAP** OS Explorer 433 Torridon – Beinn Eighe & Liathach or 434 Gairloch & Loch Ewe **START** Beach car park, southern end of Gairloch, grid ref: NG 807756 **TRACKS** Tracks and smooth paths, mostly waymarked, no stiles **THE PUB** The Old Inn, Gairloch. Tel: 01445 712006; www.theoldinn.net

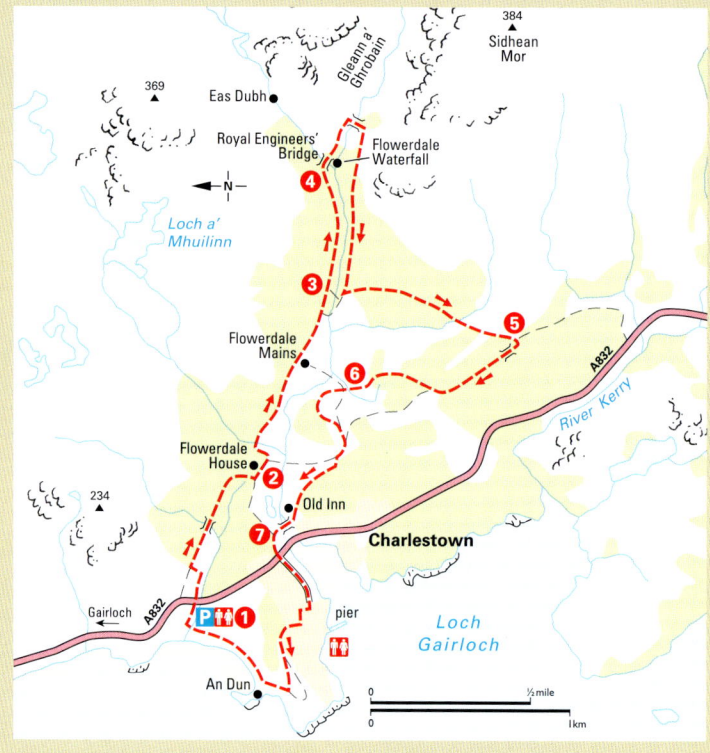

WALK 146

SEA EAGLES AT PORTREE BAY

While walking beside Portree Bay, keep at least one eye looking out to sea; you may spot the sea eagles that nest in the cliffs at Portree. The Aros Experience, just south of Portree, has the RSPB's closed-circuit TV link with the sea-eagle nest. Most nest action occurs between April and July (the young hatch in April), and the 'nest cams' give a magical insight into eagle chick behaviour and allows people to witness the moment when a chick tentatively takes to the air for the first time.

1 Walk north on A855 out of Portree for 200yds (167m). Turn off the main A855 on a lane signed 'Budh Mor', to the shoreline and to a small parking area. From here a tarred path continues along the shore. After a footbridge, the path passes underneath hazel bushes, which show the ground-branching habit of former coppicing, cut back every seven years for timber and firewood. The path rounds the headland to reach the edge of a level green field called The Bile.

2 A wall runs up the edge of The Bile. Ignore a small gate, but turn left with the wall on your right. Just before the field corner you pass a large fuchsia bush, spectacular in mid-summer. About 25yds (23m) later the path forks. Turn right, crossing a small stream and the wall, to head along the top edge of The Bile. Turn right, down a fence, to a field gate. Cross the top of the next field on an old green path, to cross a stile at its corner. You will see a track just beyond.

3 Turn sharp left, up the track. At the top it passes through two gates to reach a stony road just to the right of Torvaig. Turn left

past the house and cross the foot of a tarred road into a gently descending track. It runs down and passes between two large corrugated sheds and carries on through to a gate with a stile.

4 The grassy path ahead leads further down and takes you into Portree, but you can take a short, sometimes rough, diversion to Dun Torvaig (an ancient fortified hilltop) above. Return to the gravel path, passing by above Point 4 to join the wall that stands on the right. The path leads down under goat willows into a wood where it splits; stay on the path close to the wall.

5 At the first houses (called The Parks Bungalow 5), keep going downhill on a tarred street. On the left is the entrance to the Cuillin Hills Hotel. A few steps further on, fork right on to a stony path. When you get to the shore road, turn right across a stream and then turn immediately right again on a path that runs up for 60yds (55m) to a craggy little waterfall. Finally, return again to the shore road and turn right to get back to the walk start point.

DISTANCE/TIME 2.75 miles (4.4km) 1h15 **MAP** OS Explorer 409 Raasay, Rona & Scalpay or 410 Skye – Portree & Bracadale **START** Portree on main A855 above harbour, grid ref: NG 485436 **TRACKS** Smooth, well-made paths, farm track, 3 stiles **THE PUB** Well Plaid, The Royal Hotel, Portree. Tel: 01478 612525; www.royal-hotel.skye.com

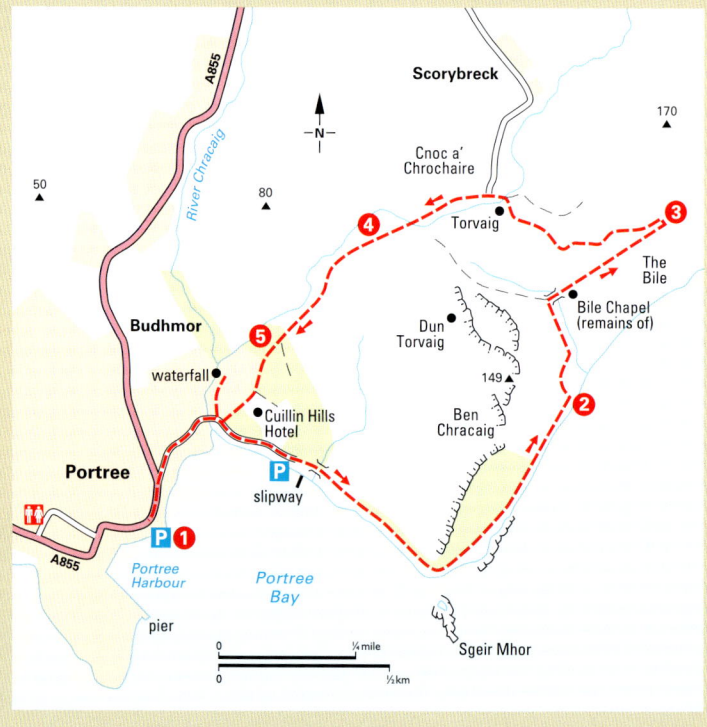

STRATHPEFFER & THE FALLS OF ROGIE

A fairly easy riverside and forest walk from the Victorian spa town of Strathpeffer to the Falls of Rogie. If you stand on the suspension bridge at the falls between July and September, when the river is fairly full, you might glimpse leaping salmon.

DISTANCE/TIME 10 miles (16.1km) 5h **MAP** OS Explorer 437 Ben Wyvis & Strathpeffer
START Strathpeffer, grid ref: NH 483582 **TRACKS** Waymarked paths and track, no stiles
THE PUB Achilty Hotel, Contin. Tel: 01997 421355; www.achiltyhotel.co.uk

1 Head along the main road towards Contin. At the edge of the town, turn right at a signpost for Garve then, at a bend in the lane, turn left, following another signpost.

2 Pass round to the left of Loch Kinellan, then keep ahead up a faint path through an area of gorse bushes to the corner of a plantation. Here you join a larger track leading into the forest. After another 438yds (400m) it reaches a signpost.

3 Turn left for View Rock on a good path with green waymarkers. At View Rock, a side-path diverts to the right for the viewpoint. After a steep descent, ignore a green path turning off to the left and follow green waymarkers downhill. At a forest road turn left, then back right for 60yds (55m) to a path on the left. It crosses another forest road to a car park.

4 At the end of the car park pick up a wide path signed 'River Walk'. After a stream culvert, the main path bends up to the right, past a waymarker with a roe deer head to a forest road. Turn left, signposted 'Garve', and after 80yds (73m) bear left, heading in a slightly downhill direction.

5 Continue on for 600yds (549m), where you will come across a small track on the left that is signed 'Falls of Rogie'. At its foot, cross a

footbridge below the falls and turn right, upstream. The path has green waymarkers and after 438yds (400m) it bends to the left away from the river. The path then crosses some rocky ground to a junction. Turn up right, to a car park.

6 Leave the car park through a wooden arch and follow green waymarkers back to the bridge. Retrace the outward route to Point 5 and turn sharp left up another forest road. It leads uphill to a four-way junction.

7 Turn right on a smaller track to pass between obstructing boulders, then left on a rutted path to rejoin the same track higher up. After 600yds (549m) it reaches the signpost at Point 3. Keep ahead and retrace the outward route to Point 2. Turn left on the tarred lane, which becomes a track. Keep ahead towards a house, but before it, turn left through a kissing gate, with a second one beyond leading into a plantation with a signpost for the town of Strathpeffer.

8 Follow the main track ahead until you see Strathpeffer on the right. At the next junction bear right down the wood edge and turn right into the town. The street on the left leads past a little church with a square steeple. Once you arrive here, turn down right to get to the main square.

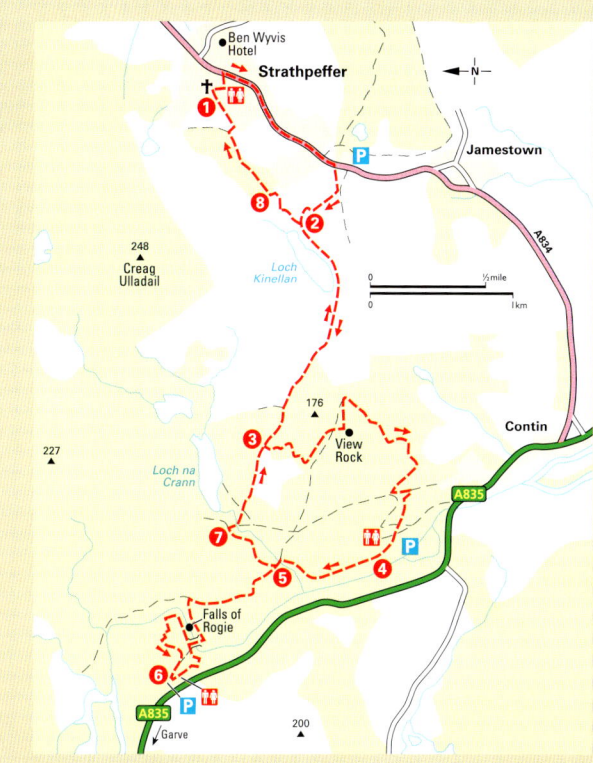

WALK 148

LOOKING OVER THE SEA TO SKYE

This is a bracing coastal walk along Loch Alsh, with stunning views of Skye, the sea and a fish farm. Fish farming is a tough life: mending a net that's 3ft (90cm) underwater is not comfortable when the water is still, but it invariably breaks on the day of a howling gale – hauling the cages out of the water for cleaning is the toughest job of all. Yet because of depleted fish stocks we are reliant on these farms for much of the salmon we consume.

DISTANCE/TIME 7.55 miles (11.7km) 3h30 **MAP** OS Explorer 413 Knoydart, Loch Hourn & Loch Duich **START** Grid ref: NG 795213 **TRACKS** Tracks, grassy shoreline, minor road, no stiles
THE PUB The Glenelg Inn, Glenelg. Tel: 01599 522273; www.glenelg-inn.com

1 A track runs out of the car park, signed for Ardintoul and Totaig. It ascends gently through two gates, then goes through a third into a plantation. With high power lines just above, the track forks. Take the left-hand one, downhill, passing an arrow painted on a rock. The track runs between the feet of a tall pylon and then climbs again to contour through a birch wood. It runs in and out of a tiny stream gorge, then gently descends towards the shore. On the other side of Loch Alsh, the white houses of Balmacara are directly ahead.

2 At the shoreline, the track disappears into an open field strip. Follow the short-cropped grass next to the shingle beach, passing a salmon farm that is situated just offshore. When the trees once more run down to the sea, look for a green track that follows along next to the shore. It passes below a small crag with birch trees to reach open flat ground near Ardintoul Farm. Keep along the shore, outside field walls, and sometimes taking to the stripy schist shingle, towards a square brick building on the point ahead. Before reaching it you come to a wall gap. Here a track that's simply a pair of green

ruts runs directly inland. It joins a gravel track, where you turn left to regain the shoreline at Ardintoul.

3 The track runs along the shoreline, then turns inland to climb the hill behind. The steeper uphill sections are tarred. Below on the left, the Allt na Dalach runs into Loch Alsh, with a clear example of a gravel spit where river debris runs into tidal water. The track enters plantations, crosses a stream and bends right to to the Bealach Luachrach. There are peat workings on the left.

4 The energetic can make a diversion here on to Glas Bheinn (the grading and timing given for this walk don't include this). From the road's high point, turn right up a wet trees gap to reach open hillside. Follow the remains of an old fence up the first rise. Where it bends right, continue straight uphill to the summit, returning by the same route. The old fence makes a useful guide back into the tree gap. Continue downhill from Point 4 on the unsurfaced road, which reaches the tarred public road a mile (1.6km) north of Glenelg village. A grassy verge between road and sea leads back to the ferry pier.

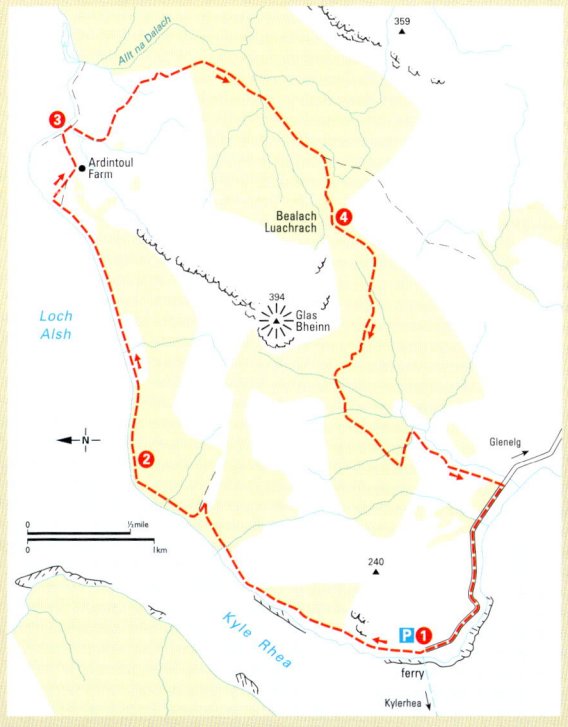

FARIGAIG FOREST & LOCH NESS

This is a delightful walk that has wonderful views overlooking Loch Ness and takes you past the home of a different monster, the Beast of Boleskine. With so many fine sights in Scotland, it's a shame that such large numbers of people still flock to try to see the one that doesn't actually exist.

DISTANCE/TIME 4.25 miles (6.8km) 2h15 **MAP** OS Explorer 416 Inverness, Loch Ness & Culloden **START** Grid ref: NH 522237 **TRACKS** Waymarked paths and tracks, no stiles **THE PUB** Craigdarroch House Hotel, Lower Foyers. Tel: 01456 486400

1 Leaving the car park, follow yellow waymarkers uphill near a stream. After 100yds (90m), a path on the right is signed 'Loch View'. After you pass by a bench, the path contours briefly then turns up left, to a higher viewpoint. It then turns back sharply right and descends on earth steps through a little crag to a forest road. Next, turn right and continue for 200yds (183m).

2 Turn up left on a footpath with more yellow waymarkers. The path has a low, heavily mossed wall alongside as it bends up to a higher forest road. Turn right and walk for about 150yds (135m) until you reach a sharp left-hand bend. Keep ahead here, on a small footpath through an area of cleared forestry, then go steeply up to the left under trees. At the top, bear left along a little ridge, dropping gently downhill to a viewpoint.

3 Return for 100yds (90m) and bear left down the other side of the ridge. The path descends steeply to a forest road. A sign indicates Lochan Torr an Tuill, nearby on the right, with a picnic table.

4 Return down the forest road, past where you joined it. It climbs gently, then descends to the sharp right bend where you turned off earlier – the waymarker says 'to Car Park'

on the side now facing you. After 150yds (135m), at another 'to Car Park' waymarker, turn left down the path with the low mossed wall on the side facing you. Turn left, past a red/green waymarker. The track kinks left past a quarry.

5 Where the main track bends right, downhill, keep ahead on a green track with a red/green waymarker. It emerges from trees at a signpost. Follow this all the way down to the right towards Easter Boleskine house. Green waymarkers here indicate a diversion to the left of the house, to join its driveway track below. Follow this down to the B852.

6 Turn right for 50yds (45m). Below the left edge of the road is a tarred track. Turn down past a red/green waymarker to cross this track, with two blue waymarkers leading into a path beyond. This passes down to the right of electricity transformers. At the foot of the slope, the main path bears right with a blue waymarker. It runs above the loch shore and joins a gravel track just below Lower Birchwood House. At a tarmac turning circle, an overgrown jetty on the left is great for monster-watchers. The tarred lane ahead leads up to the B852, with the car park just above it on the right.

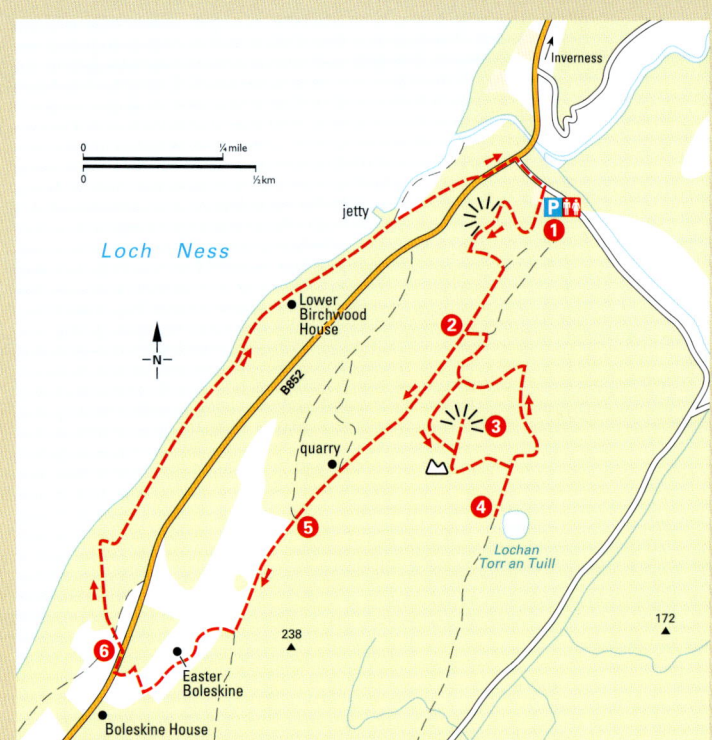

WALK 150

HEART OF THE CUILLINS

The Black Cuillin Hills, seen through Skye's moist Atlantic air, appear blue and under romantic sunset light almost purple. This land is like nowhere else, even in Scotland, for crag, boulder and jagged horizon. The special quality of Skye is obvious to the eye, but even more so to the foot. The black rock grips the foot like Velcro. This is gabbro, formed in the magma chamber of a massive volcano that stood here 50 million years ago.

DISTANCE/TIME 5.75 miles (9.2km) 4h **MAP** OS Explorer 411 Skye – Cuillin Hills **START** Grid ref: NG 409206 **TRACKS** Mountain paths, one boggy and tough, 2 stiles **THE PUB** Sligachan Hotel, Sligachan. Tel: 01478 650204

1 From the parking area, the track leads on through Glenbrittle campsite to a gate with a kissing gate. Pass left of the toilet block to cross a stile. Turn left along a stony track just above, which runs gently downhill above the campsite, to rejoin the Glenbrittle road.

2 Keep ahead to cross a bridge with the white Memorial Hut just ahead. On the right are some stone buchts (sheep-handling enclosures) and here a waymarked path heads uphill to reach a footbridge over the Allt Coire na Banachdich.

3 Cross the footbridge and head up to the right of the stream's deep ravine. Look out for a short side-path on the left for the best view of the waterfall at its head. Its Gaelic name, Eas Mor, means simply 'Big Waterfall'. Above, the path bears right, to slant up the hillside. This part of the path has never been built or repaired and is bog and scree. It passes above Loch an Fhir-bhallaich and forks, with the left-hand and higher branch being drier but with loose eroded scree. It rounds a shoulder into the lower part of the Coire Lagan and then meets a much larger and better path.

4 Turn uphill on this path, until you reach a belt of bare rock that blocks its way into the upper corrie. This rock has been smoothed by a glacier over thousands of years into gently rounded swells known as 'boiler-plates'. A scree field runs up into the boiler-plate rocks. The best way to proceed keeps going up the left edge, below a slab wall with a small waterslide, to the highest point of the scree. Head up left for a few steps on bare rock, then back right on ledges to an eroded scree above the boiler-plate obstruction. Look back down your upward route to note it for your return. The trodden way slants up to the right. With the main stream near by on the right, it goes up to the rim of the upper corrie.

5 The boiler-plate slabs at the lochan's outflow make an excellent place to stop for a picnic. Walking mainly on bare rock, it's easy to make a circuit of the lochan. For the return journey, retrace your steps all the way back to Point 4. Ignoring the right fork of the route that you came up by, keep going straight downhill on the main path. It runs straight down to the toilet block at Glenbrittle campsite.

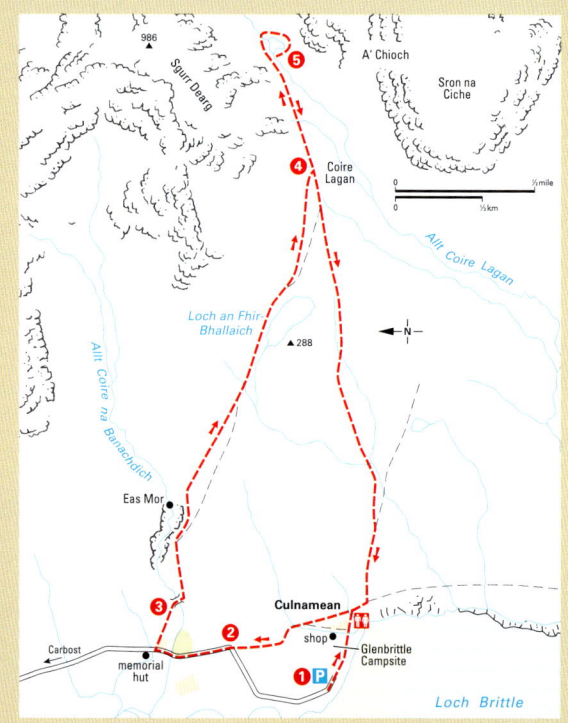

EDINBURGH
■ TOURIST INFORMATION
Edinburgh & Scotland Information Centre
3 Princes Street, Edinburgh.
Tel: 0845 2255 121
Forestry Commission Scotland
Silvan House, 231 Corstorphine Road, Edinburgh. Tel: 0845 367 3787;
www.forestry.gov.uk/scotland
Historic Scotland
Longmore House, Salisbury Place, Edinburgh. Tel: 0131 668 8800;
www.historic-scotland.gov.uk
Holyrood Palace
Canongate, The Royal Mile, Edinburgh.
Tel: 0131 556 5100;
www.royalcollection.org.uk
National Trust for Scotland
Wemyss House, 28 Charlotte Square, Edinburgh. Tel: 0131 243 9300;
www.scotlandforyou.co.uk
Royal Museum
Chambers Street, Edinburgh.
Tel: 0131 247 4422; www.nms.ac.uk
Scottish Natural Heritage
12 Hope Terrace, Edinburgh EH9 2AS.
Tel: 0131 447 4784; www.snh.org.uk
Scottish Wildlife Trust
Cramond House, 16 Cramond Glebe Road, Edinburgh.
Tel: 01131 312 7765; www.swt.org.uk

■ PLACES OF INTEREST
Edinburgh Castle
Tel: 0131 225 9846;
www.historic-scotland.gov/uk
Georgian House
Charlotte Square, Edinburgh.
Tel: 0131 226 3318
Museum of Scotland
Chambers Street, Edinburgh.
Tel: 0131 247 4422; www.nms.ac.uk
National Gallery of Scotland
The Mound, Edinburgh.
Tel: 0131 624 6200; www.nationalgalleries.org
Royal Botanic Garden
Inverleith Row, Edinburgh.
Tel: 0131 552 7171; www.rbge.org.uk

■ SHOPPING
In Edinburgh, there are plenty of shops on George Street as well as Victoria Street. A Harvey Nichols store has opened on St Andrew Square. As well as the national chains, Edinburgh has many speciality shops where you can buy all manner of Scottish paraphernalia, some more authentic than others.

■ SPORTS & ACTIVITIES
CYCLE HIRE
Biketrax
Tollcross, Edinburgh.
Tel: 0131 228 6633

■ ANNUAL EVENTS & CUSTOMS
Edinburgh
International Festival and Fringe Festival, Aug.
Military Tattoo, Aug.
Hogmanay, 31 Dec.

FIFE & STIRLING
■ TOURIST INFORMATION
Fife
Castle Esplanade, Fife.
Tel: 08707 200622
St Andrews
70 Market Street, St Andrews.
Tel: 01334 472021

■ PLACES OF INTEREST
Argyll's Lodging
Castle Wynd, Old Town, Stirling.
Tel: 01786 431319;
www.historicscotland.gov.uk
Bannockburn Visitor Centre
Glasgow Road, Stirling.
Tel: 01786 812664
Bannockburn Visitor Centre
Glasgow Road, Stirling. 2.5 miles (4km) southeast of Stirling.
Tel: 01786 812664; www.nts.org.uk
Hill of Tarvit Mansionhouse
2 miles/3.2km south of Cupar off A916.
Tel: 01334 653127
Kellie Castle (NTS)
Northwest of Pittenweem.
Tel: 01333 720271
National Wallace Monument, Stirling.
Tel: 01786 472140;
www.scottish.heartlands.org
Scottish Fisheries Museum
Harbourhead, Anstruther.
Tel: 01333 310628;
www.scotfishmuseum.org
St Andrews Cathedral and Castle
South Street, St Andrews.
Tel: 01334 477196
Stirling Castle
Upper Castle Hill, Stirling.
Tel: 01786 450000;
www.historic-scotland.gov/uk
The Pineapple
Dunmore Park, Dunmore.
Tel: 01324 831137

■ FOR CHILDREN
Scotland's Secret Bunker
Crown Buildings, Troywood, near St Andrews.
Tel: 01333 310301
A tunnel leads to the fascinating secret underground command rooms used by government Secret Service personnel during the Cold War.
Scottish Deer Centre
Bow-of-Fife, by Cupar.
Tel:01337 810391; www.tsdc.co.uk
More than 140 deer, bird of prey demonstrations, tree-top walk and more.

■ SPORTS & ACTIVITIES
ADVENTURE SPORTS
East Neuk Outdoors
Cellardyke Park, Anstruther.
Tel: 01333 311929
Cluny Clays
Cluny Mains Farm, by Kirkcaldy.
Tel: 01592 720374

TROSSACHS & SOUTH
■ TOURIST INFORMATION
Perth
West Mill Street, Perth.
Tel: 01738 450600
Trossachs Discovery Centre & Aberfoyle Tourist Information Centre
Main Street, Aberfoyle.
Tel: 08707 200604

■ PLACES OF INTEREST
Angus Folk Museum (NTS)
Kirkwynd, Glamis.
Tel: 01307 840288
Aviation Museum
Kirriemuir.
Tel: 01573 573233;
www.kamrafa.co.uk
J M Barrie's Birthplace (NTS)
9 Brechin Road, Kirriemuir.
Tel: 01575 572646
Bell's Blair Atholl Distillery
Pitlochry (at southern end of town).
Tel: 01796 482003
Bells Cherrybank Gardens
Perth. Tel: 01738 472800;
www.thecalyx.co.uk
Ben Lawers National Nature Reserve
Mountain Visitor Centre (NTS), off A827.
Tel: 01567 820397
Blair Castle
Blair Atholl, just off A9.
Tel: 01796 481207; www.blair-castle.co.uk
Branklyn Garden (NTS)
116 Dundee Road, Perth.
Tel: 01738 625535
Castle Menzies
Weem, by Aberfeldy.
Tel: 01887 820982
Dewar's World of Whisky
Aberfeldy Distillery, Aberfeldy.
Tel: 01887 822010; www.dewarswow.com
RRS *Discovery*
Dundee.
Tel: 01382 201245; www.rrsdiscovery.com
Doune Castle (HS)
Tel: 01786 841742
Drummond Castle Gardens
Muthill, Crieff.
Tel: 01764 681433;
www.drummoncastlegardens.co.uk
Earthquake House
Comrie.
Edradour Distillery
Pitlochry.
Tel: 01796 472095;
www.edradour.co.uk

Famous Grouse Experience
The Hosh, Crieff.
Tel: 01764 656565;
www.famousgrouse.com
Glamis Castle
Glamis.
Tel: 01307 840393;
www.glamis-castle.co.uk
Hamilton Toy Collection
Main Street, Callander.
Tel: 01877 330004
The Hermitage
Some 2 miles (3km) west of Dunkeld.
Tel: 01350 728641. Free.
Inchmahome Priory
Port of Menteith.
Tel: 01877 385294
Killiecrankie Visitor Centre
3 miles (5km) north of Pitlochry.
Tel: 01796 473233
Loch of the Lowes Visitor Centre
Off A923 northeast of Dunkeld.
Tel: 01350 727337; www.swt.org.uk
Moirlanich Longhouse
Near to Killin.
Tel: 01567 820988
Perth Museum & Art Gallery
78 George Street, Perth.
Tel: 01738 632488; www.perthshire.com. Free.
Rob Roy and Trossachs Visitor Centre
Callander.
Tel: 01877 330342
Scone Palace
Scone, by Perth.
Tel: 01738 552300;
www.scone-palace.co.uk
Scottish Crannog Centre
Loch Tay, Near Aberfeldy.
Tel: 01887 830583
Scottish Hydroelectric Visitor Centre
Pitlochry.
Tel: 01796 473152; www.aboutbritain.com/HydroElectricVisitorCentre.htm
Learn about the power of water here.
Scottish Wool Centre
Aberfoyle.
Tel: 01877 382850
Unicorn
Dundee.
Tel: 01382 200900;
www.frigateunicorn.org
Verdant Works
West Henderson's Wynd, Dundee.
Tel: 01382 225282;
www.verdantworks.com

■ FOR CHILDREN
Sensation: Dundee
Greenmarket, Dundee.
Tel: 01382 228800; www.sensation.org.uk
Hands-on science centre that puts the fun back in to physics. Six themed zones take you through the science behind the senses and there are interactive exhibitions galore.

■ SHOPPING

Perth Farmers' Market, First Sat each month.
Continental Market, regular markets featuring continental produce.
Gardener's Market, check online at www.perfectperth.com for info on market dedicated to all things for the garden.
Art on the River, art market with works of art displayed along Tay Street.
Craft Market, Scottish crafts at their best covering some 30 stalls.
For all markets check online at www.perfectperth.com for details.

■ PERFORMING ARTS

Dundee Contemporary Arts
152 Nethergate.
Tel: 01382 909900;
www.dca.org.uk
Dundee Rep Theatre
Tay Square, Dundee.
Tel: 01382 223530;
www.dundeereptheatre.co.uk

■ SPORTS & ACTIVITIES
ADVENTURE SPORTS
Highland Adventure Safari
Drumdewan, Aberfeldy.
Tel: 01887 820071;
www.highlandadventuresafaris.co.uk
BOAT TRIPS
SS *Sir Walter Scott*
Trossachs Pier Complex.
Tel: 01877 376316;
www.lochkatrine.co.org
CYCLING
Escape Route
3 Atholl Road, Pitlochry.
Tel: 01796 473859; www.escape-route.biz
GOLF
Crieff Golf Course
Ferntower, Perth Road.
Tel: 01764 652909; www.crieffgolf.co.uk
Gleneagles
Auchterarder.
Tel: 01764 662231; www.gleneagles.com
Pitlochry Golf Course
Golf Course Road, Pitlochry.
Tel: 01796 472792

■ ANNUAL EVENTS & CUSTOMS
Blair Castle
Glenfiddich Piping Championships, end Oct.
Atholl Gathering and Highland Games, end May.
Crieff
Highland Gathering, Aug.
Kirriemuir
Angus Glens Walking Festival, early Jun.
Perth
Festival of the Arts, May.
Highland Games, Aug.
Pitlochry
Highland Games, Sep.

ARGYLL, MULL & WEST
■ TOURIST INFORMATION
Inveraray
Front Street, Inveraray.
Tel: 08707 200616;
www.visitscotlandheartlands.com
Isle of Arran
By the pier, Brodick, Isle of Arran.
Tel: 01770 302140
Mull
Craignure Tourist Office, located down by the Pier.
Tel: 01680 812377
Oban
Argyll Square, Oban.
Tel: 01631 563122;
www.scotland-info.co.uk

■ PLACES OF INTEREST
Arduaine Garden
20 miles (32km) south of Oban, on A816.
Tel: 01852 200366
Ardnamurchan Lighthouse Visitor Centre
Ardnamurchan Point. Tel: 01972 510210
Botanic Gardens
Great Western Road, Glasgow.
Tel: 0141 334 2422
Brodick Castle, Garden & Country Park
Brodick, Isle of Arran.
Tel: 01770 302202
Burrell Collection
Pollok Country Park, Glasgow.
Tel: 0141 287 2550;
www.glasgowmuseums.com. Free.
Carnasserie Castle
2 miles (3km) north of Kilmartin, off A816. Free.
Duart Castle
1.5 miles (3km) from Craignure. Mull.
Tel: 01680 812309; www.duartcastle.com
Dunadd Fort
Kilmartin Glen. Free.
Dunstaffnage Castle
4 miles (6.5km) north of Oban, off A85.
Tel: 01631 562465
Glasgow School of Art
167 Renfrew Street, Glasgow.
Tel: 0141 353 4526; www.gsa.ac.uk
Glencoe & North Lorn Folk Museum
Glencoe, Ballaculish. Tel: 01855 811664
Glencoe Visitor Centre
Glencoe. Tel: 01855 811307
House for an Art Lover
Bellahouston Park, 10 Dumbreck Road, Glasgow.
Tel: 0141 353 4770;
www.houseforanartlover.co.uk
Inveraray Castle
Inverarary.
Tel: 01499 302203;
www.inveraray-castle.com
Island Cheese Company
Brodick, Arran.
Tel: 01770 302788;
www.islandcheese.co.uk

Isle of Arran Distillery Visitor Centre
Lochranza, Arran. Tel: 01770 830264;
www.arranwhisky.com.
Tours.
Kelvingrove Art Gallery & Museum
Argyle Street, Glasgow.
Tel: 0141 287 2699;
www. glasgowmuseums.com. Free.
Kilchurn Castle
Loch Awe.
Tel: 01866 833333
Kilmartin House Museum
Kilmartin.
Tel: 01546 510278; www.kilmartin.org
Kilmory Castle Gardens
Lochgilphead.
Tel: 01546 602127;
www.argyll-bute.gov.uk
Loch Lomond Shores Visitor Centre
Benlomond Way, Balloch.
Tel: 01389 722199
Mount Stewart House
Rothesay, Bute.
Tel: 01700 503877;
www.mountstewart.com
Mull Museum
Main Street, Tobermory, Mull.
Oban Distillery
Stafford Street, Oban.
Tel: 01540 672219; www.malts.com
People's Palace
Glasgow Green, Glasgow.
Tel: 0141 554 0223;
www.glasgowmuseums.com. Free.
Rothesay Castle
Castlehill Street, Rothesay, Bute.
Tel: 01700 502691
Scottish Sealife Sanctuary
Loch Creran, Barcaldine. Argyll.
Tel: 01631 720386;
www.sealsanctuary.co.uk
Torosay Castle and Gardens
Mull. One mile (1.6km) south of Craignure. Tel: 01680 812421

■ FOR CHILDREN
Arctic Penguin (Inveraray Maritime Experience)
The Pier, Inveraray.
Tel: 01499 302213;
www.inveraraypier.com
A three-masted schooner that has many items of maritime memorabilia including some touching mementoes from former seamen to their loved ones.
Cowal Bird Garden
Lochan Wood, Sandbank Road, Dunoon.
Tel: 01369 707999
With donkeys, goats, owls, pigs and rabbits, this small animal park is especially suited to families and those with small children.
Glasgow Science Centre
50 Pacific Quay, Glasgow.
Tel: 0141 420 5000;
www.gsc.org.uk

Set in its amazing space-age building, the museum inside does not disappoint. State-of-the-art technology is used to translate theory to reality in a fun way. The IMAX theatre adds to its appeal.
Inveraray Jail
Church Square, Inveraray.
Tel: 01499 302381;
www.inverarayjail.co.uk
Oban Rare Breeds Farm Park
Glencruitten, by Oban.
Tel: 01631 770608;
www.obanrarebreeds.com
Rare breeds of pigs, goats and sheep are kept here. Follow a path through woodland to get to all the animals.

■ SHOPPING
Arran Fine Foods
The Old Mill, Lamlash, Arran.
Tel: 01770 600606;
www.paterson-arran.com
Creelers Smokehouse
Home Farm, Brodick, Arran.
Tel: 01770 302797;
www.creelers.co.uk
Dunoon Ceramics
Pot Shop, 162 Argyll Street, Dunoon.
Tel: 01369 704360
Geoffrey (Tailor) Kiltmakers & Weavers
309 Sauchiehall Street, Glasgow.
Tel: 0141 331 2388;
www.geoffreykilts.co.uk
Island Cheese Company
Home Farm, Brodick, Arran.
Tel: 01770 302788;
www.islandcheese.co.uk
Loch Lomond Shores
Ben Lomond Way, Balloch.
Tel: 01389 721500;
www.lochlomondshores.com
Tiso Glasgow Outdoor Experience
50 Couper Street, Glasgow.
Tel: 0141 559 5450; www.tiso.com

■ SPORTS & ACTIVITIES
BOAT TRIPS
Cruise Loch Lomond Ltd
The Boat Yard, Tarbet, Loch Lomond.
Tel: 01301 702356;
www.cruiselochlomond.co.uk
Waverley Excursions Ltd
33 Landsfield Quay, Glasgow.
Tel: 0845 1304647;
www.waverleyexcursions.co.uk
GOLF
Cowal Golf Club
Dunoon, off A815 at Kirn.
Tel: 01369 705673;
www.cowalgolfclub.com
18-hole course.
Tobermory Golf Club
Erray Road, Tobermory, Mull.
Tel: 01688 302338;
www.tobermorygolfclub.com
9-hole course.

HORSE-RIDING
Argyll Riding
Dalchenna, Inveraray.
Tel: 01499 302611; www.horserides.com

LONG-DISTANCE FOOTPATHS
Isle of Arran Coastal Way
Circular route, 65 miles (104km).
www.coastalway.co.uk

Kintyre Way
New footpath developed to run from
Tarbet to Southend, 90 miles (60km).
www.kintyre.org

West Highland Way
This is Scotland's most famous long-
distance trail. The trek stretches from
Glasgow to Fort William, and is 95 miles
(150km) long.
www.west-highland-way.co.uk

WILDLIFE TOURS
Discover Mull
Ardrioch Farm, Dervaig, Mull.
Tel: 01688 400415;
www.discovermull.co.uk

Island Encounter
Arla Beag, Aros, Mull.
Tel: 01680 300441;
www.mullwildlife.co.uk
Wildlife tours of the island, including
eagles, owls, otters and more. Advance
booking essential.

Sea.fari
Easdale Harbour, Seil, by Oban.
Tel: 01852 300003; www.seafari.co.uk.
Wildlife safaris in rigid inflatables.

Turus Mara
Penmore Hill, Dervaig, Mull.
Tel: 01688 400242; www.turusmara.com.
Cruise tours from Ulva Ferry, Mull, or
Oban, to Treshnish Isles, Staffa and Iona;
times vary.

WINTER SPORTS
Glencoe Ski Centre
Kingshouse, Glencoe.
Tel: 0871 871 9929;
www.glencoemountain.com

■ ANNUAL EVENTS & CUSTOMS
Dunoon
Cowal Highland Gathering, late Aug.
Glasgow
Celtic Connections, folk music festival,
Jan.
International Jazz Festival, early Jul.
World Pipe Band Championships,
mid-Aug.
Inveraray
Highland Games, mid-Jul.
Oban
Kilmore and Kilbride Highland Games,
mid-Jun.
Argyllshire Highland Gathering, late Aug.
Taynuilt
Taynuilt Highland Games, late Jul.
Tobermory, Mull
Mull Music Fest, mid-Apr.
Tour of Mull Car Rally, mid-Oct.

CAIRNGORMS & CENTRAL
■ TOURIST INFORMATION
Aviemore
Grampian Road, Aviemore.
Tel: 01479 810363
Cairngorms National Park Authority
Tel: 01479 873535;
www.cairngorms.co.uk

■ PLACES OF INTEREST
Aberlour Distillery
High Street, Aberlour.
Tel: 01340 881249
Balmoral Castle
Ballater.
Tel: 013397 42534;
www.balmoralcastle.com
Cairngorm Mountain Railway
Cairngorm Ski Area, by Aviemore.
Tel: 01479 861261;
www.cairngormmountain.org
Dallas Dhu Historic Distillery
South of Forres.
Tel: 01309 676548
Glenfiddich Distillery
Dufftown.
Tel: 01340 820373; www.glenfiddich.com
Highland Folk Museum
Duke Street, Kingussie.
Tel: 01540 661307; www.highlandfolk.com
Loch Garten Osprey Centre
By Boat of Garten.
Tel: 01479 821894; www.rspb.org.uk
Mar Lodge Estate
Braemar. Tel: 013397 41433;
www.marlodgeestate.org.uk
Pluscarden Abbey
Pluscarden, Elgin.
Tel: 01343 890257;
www.pluscardenabbey.org
Speyside Cooperage
Dufftown Road, Craigellachie.
Tel: 01340 871108;
www. speysidecooperage.co.uk
**Speyside Heather Garden
& Visitor Centre**
Skye of Curr, Dulnain Bridge.
Tel: 01479 851359;
www.heathercentre.com
Strathspey Steam Railway
Aviemore, Boat of Garten.
Tel: 01479 810725;
www.strathspeyrailway.co.uk

■ FOR CHILDREN
Cairngorm Reindeer Centre
Reindeer House, Glenmore.
Tel: 01479 861228;
www.reindeercompany.demon.co.uk
See Britain's only herd of reindeer living
free in the Cairngorms.
Highland Wildlife Park
Kincraig, by Kingussie.
Tel: 01540 651270;
www.highlandwildlifepark.org
Breeds of naturally wild animals

including mouflon, elk and Highland
cattle can all be seen here. Interesting
and makes for a good day out.
Landmark Highland Heritage Park
Carrbridge.
Tel: 01479 841613;
www.landmark-centre.co.uk
A living museum with authentically
dressed 'Highlanders' showing how life
was in days gone by.

■ SHOPPING
Lamont Sporrans Ltd
8 Invercauld Road, Braemar.
Tel: 013397 41404;
www.lamontsporrans.co.uk
Full range of kilts and Highland dress.

■ SPORTS & ACTIVITIES
ADVENTURE SPORTS
Absolute Full On Adventure
24 Cairngorm Avenue, Aviemore.
Tel: 07885 835838;
www.fullonadventure.com
Glenmore Lodge
By Aviemore.
Tel: 01479 861256;
www.glenmorelodge.org.uk
Rothiemurchus Estate
By Aviemore.
Tel: 01479 812345;
www.rothiemurchus.net
GOLF
Grantown-on-Spey Golf Club
Golf Course Road.
Tel: 01479 872079;
www.grantownonspeygolfclub.co.uk
Kingussie Golf Club
Gynack Road, Kingussie.
Tel: 01540 661600;
www.kingussie-golf.co.uk
LONG-DISTANCE PATHS
Speyside Way
This trek takes you from Aviemore to
Buckie, 84 miles (135km).
www.speysideway.org
WATERSPORTS
Loch Morlich Watersports Centre
Glenmore Forest Park, near to Aviemore.
Tel: 01479 861221; www.lochmorlich.com
WILDLIFE TOURS
Speyside Wildlife
Rothiemurchus Visitor Centre, situated
by Aviemore.
Tel: 01479 812498;
www.speysidewildlife.co.uk
WINTER SPORTS
Aviemore Ski & Snowboard Hire
131 Grampian Road.
Tel: 01479 811711; www.osatravel.co.uk
Experienced winter sports outfitter for all
your skiing and snowboarding needs.
Glenshee Ski Centre
Cairnwell, by Braemar.
Tel: 013397 41320;
www.ski-glenshee.co.uk

■ ANNUAL EVENTS & CUSTOMS
Aviemore
Highland Feast – Scottish food and drink
festival, end Sep to Oct.
Speyside
Spirit of Speyside Whisky Festival, end
Apr to May.

SKYE & NORTH
■ TOURIST INFORMATION
Fort William
Cameron Centre, Cameron Square,
Fort William.
Tel: 01397 703781
Glenfinnan
National Trust of Scotland Information
Centre, Glenfinnan, A30, 18 miles (29km)
west of Fort William.
Tel: 01397 722250
Inverness
Castle Wynd, Inverness.
Tel: 01463 234353
Portree
Bayfield Road, Portree, Skye.
Tel: 01478 612137

■ PLACES OF INTEREST
Aonach Mòr Gondola Ride
Torlundy.
Tel: 01397 705825;
www.nevis-range.co.uk
**Armadale Castle Gardens and Museum
of the Isles**
Armadale, Sleat, Skye.
Tel: 01471 844305; www.clandonald.com
Aros
Viewfield Road, Portree, Skye.
Tel: 01478 613649; www.aros.co.uk
Beinn Eighe Visitor Centre
Aultroy. Tel: 01445 760254
Caledonian Canal Visitor Centre
Ardchattan House, Fort Augustus.
Tel: 01320 366493; www.waterscape.com
Colbost Croft Museum
Colbost, by Dunvegan, Skye.
Tel: 01470 521296
Dunvegan Castle
Skye.
Tel: 01470 521206;
www.dunvegancastle.com
Eilean Donan Castle
Loch Duich, Kintail.
Tel: 01599 555202;
www.eileandonancastle.com
Fortrose Cathedral
Cathedral Square, Fortrose.
Tel: 01667 460232. Open access.
Gairloch Heritage Museum
Achtercairn, Gairloch.
www.gairlochheritagemuseum.org.uk
Glenfinnan Monument
Glenfinnan.
Tel: 01397 722250
Groam House Museum
High Street, Rosemarkie.
Tel: 01381 620961

Highland Wineries
Moniack Castle, Kirkhill.
Tel: 01463 831283;
www.moniackcastle.co.uk
Wines, liqueurs, sauces and preserves
are all sold in this castle.

Hugh Miller's House
Church Street, Cromarty.
Tel: 01381 600245

Hydroponicum
Achiltibuie, north of Ullapool.
Tel: 01854 622202;
www.thehydroponicum.com

Inverewe Garden
Poolewe.
Tel: 01445 781200

Inverness Castle
Castle Hill, Inverness.
Tel: 1463 243363

Inverness Museum & Art Gallery
Castle Wynd, Inverness.
Tel:01463 237114;
www.invernessmuseum.com. Free.

Knockan Visitor Centre
Inverpolly National Nature Reserve, off
A835 north of Ullapool.
Tel: 01854 613418

**Loch Ness 2000: Official Loch Ness
Monster Exhibition Centre**
Drumnadrochit.
Tel: 01456 450573;
www.loch-ness-scotland.com

Mallaig Heritage Centre
Tel: 01687 462085;
www.mallaigheritage.org.uk

Original Loch Ness Visitor Centre
Drumnadrochit.
Tel: 01456 450342;
www.lochness-centre.com

St Andrews Cathedral
15 Ardross Street, Inverness.
Tel: 01463 233535

Skye Museum of Island Life
Kilmuir, north of Uig, Skye.
Tel: 01470 552206

Talisker Distillery
Carbost, Skye.
Tel: 01478 614308; www.malts.com

**Torridon Visitor Centre
& Deer Museum**
The Mains, Achnasheen.
Tel: 01445 791368

Treasures of the Earth
Corpach, by Fort William.
Tel: 01397 772283

Ullapool Museum
7–8 West Argyle Street, Ullapool.
Tel: 01854 612987;
www.ullapoolmuseum.co.uk

Urquhart Castle
Drumnadrochit, Loch Ness.
Tel: 01456 450551

West Highland Museum
Cameron Square, Fort William.
Tel: 01397 702169;
www. westhighlandmuseum.org.uk

■ **FOR CHILDREN**
Bright Water Visitor Centre
The Pier, Kyleakin, Skye.
Tel: 01599 530040; www.eileanban.org
This is an informative and fun centre
ostensibly to educate about the island
and conservation.

Jacobite Steam Train
Operates between Fort William and
Mallaig.
Tel: 01524 737751
Follow the West Highland Line on Harry
Potter's Hogwarts steam train. The full
84-mile (135km) journey starts from the
highest mountain in Scotland, passes
the deepest loch, goes near the most
westerly railway station and passes
the shortest river in Britain. It truly is a
journey of extremes and a great day out.

Kylerhea Otter Haven
Kylerhea, Skye.
The mixed conifer plantation here is
home to a colony of otters. If you look up
you may be lucky enough to see golden
eagles circling above.

Skye Serpentarium/Reptile World
The Old Mill, Harrapool, Broadford, Skye.
Tel: 01471 822209;
www. skyeserpentarium.org.uk
Snakes, lizards, frogs and other reptiles
are all here, and there are regular
handling sessions for those who like to
touch as well as look.

■ **SHOPPING**
Castle Gallery
43 Castle Street, Inverness.
Tel: 01463 729512;
www.castlegallery.co.uk
Modern art.

Hebridean Jewellery
95 High Street, Fort William.
Tel: 01397 702033;
www.hebridean-jewellery.co.uk.
Jewellery in Celtic designs.

**Hector Russell Scottish Kiltmaker
Visitor Centre**
4–9 Huntly Street, Inverness.
Tel: 0800 980 4010;
www.hector-russell.com

Highland Stoneware
North Road, Ullapool.
Tel: 01854 612980;
www.highlandstoneware.com

Holm Mills Shopping Village
Dores Road, Inverness.
Tel: 01463 223311
Weaving exhibitions.

Inverness Farmers' Market
Eastgate Precinct, Inverness.
Tel: 01309 651206

Nevisport
High Street, Fort William.
Tel:01397 704921; www.nevisport.com
Outdoor adventure sports equipment
and clothing.

Skye Batiks
The Green, Portree, Skye.
Tel: 01478 613331; www.skyebatiks.com
Colourful items crafted to island patterns
and styles.

Spean Bridge Mill
Spean Bridge, 10 miles (16km) north of
Fort William.
Tel: 01397 712260
Weaving mill.

■ **SPORTS & ACTIVITIES**
ADVENTURE SPORTS
Raasay Outdoor Centre
Raasay House, Raasay, off north Skye.
Tel: 01478 660266;
www. raasayoutdoorcentre.co.uk
Sailing, cycling, climbing, kayaking and
much more. This centre has an excellent
reputation worldwide and is staffed by
experienced instructors.

Whitewave: Skye's Outdoor Centre
Kilmuir, Skye.
Tel: 01470 542414; www.white-wave.co.uk
Rock climbing, kayaking, guided walks
and more. All activities are catered to and
there are instructors on hand to help.

BOAT TRIPS
Bella Jane Boat Trips
Elgol, Skye.
Tel: 0800 731 3089; www.bellajane.co.uk
Explore Loch Coruisk, the Small Isles and
Skye wildlife. Advance booking essential.

Calum's Seal Trips
Shore Front, Plockton.
Tel: 01599 544306;
www.calums-sealtrips.com
Boat trips out to see the local population
of grey seals in their native habitat.

Cruise Loch Ness
Knockburnie, Inchnacardoch, Fort
Augustus.
Tel: 01320 366277;
www.cruiselochness.com
Cruise the loch aboard the *Royal Scot*
which is fitted with a special 3D imaging
system to show you what's going on in
the deep.

Dolphin Ecosse
Cromarty.
Tel: 01381 600323

Inverness Dolphin Cruises
Shore Street Quy, Inverness.
Tel: 01463717900;
www.inverness-dolphin-cruises.co.uk
Boats leave Inverness harbour and sail
into the Moray Firth where there is the
best chance of seeing dolphins as well as
many types of birds.

Summer Isles cruises
From Ullapool: Tel: 01853 612472;
from Achiltibuie: Tel: 01854 622315
These day cruises take you to the outlying
islands and unusual rock formations off
the mainland. There is a one-hour stop
on an island featured on each cruise.

CYCLING
Barneys
35 Castle Street, Inverness.
Tel: 01463 232249;
www. eastgatebackpackers.com

Highland Cycles
16A Telford Street, Inverness.
Tel: 01463 234789;
www.highlandcycles.co.uk

Island Cycles
The Green, Portree, Skye.
Tel: 01478 613121; www.isbuc.co.uk
Cycle hire here as well as fishing tackle
hire for anglers.

GOLF
Inverness Golf Club
Culcabock Road, Inverness.
Tel: 01463 239882;
www.invernessgolfclub.co.uk
This par 69 course welcomes visitors
and has a variety of tee times available
throughout the week.

Isle of Skye Golf Club
Sconser, Skye.
Tel: 01478 650414;
www.isleofskyegolfclub.co.uk
9-hole course that is open year round.

Loch Ness Golf Course
Fairways, Castle Heather, Inverness.
Tel: 01463 713335;
9- and 18-hole courses; also large
leisure complex.

Strathpeffer Spa Golf Club
Golf Course Road, Strathpeffer.
Tel: 01997 421219; strathpeffergolf.co.uk
18-hole course established 1888.

HORSE-RIDING
Highland Riding Centre
Borlum Farm, Drumnadrochit.
Tel: 01456 450220; www.borlum.com

Skye Riding Centre
Suledale, by Portree, Skye.
Tel: 01470 582419;
www.skyeridingcentre.co.uk
Pony trekking for all abilities, plus
disabled facilities.

LONG DISTANCE PATH
Great Glen Way
73-mile (118km) trail from Fort William
to Inverness, then cycle trail.
www.greatglenway.com

WINTER SPORTS
Nevis Range
Torlundy, north of Fort William.
Tel: 01397 705825;
www.nevis-range.co.uk
Ski and snowboarding centre for all
abilities and experience levels.

■ **ANNUAL EVENTS & CUSTOMS**
Armadale
Skye Festival, late Jul, early Aug.

Inverness
Tattoo, Northern Meeting Park, late Jul.

Portree
Skye Highland Games, Aug.

PUBS
EDINBURGH
Doric Tavern
15–16 Market Street, Edinburgh
EH1 1DE. Tel: 0131 225 1084;
www.thedoric.co.uk
A good public bar, bistro and wine bar offer something for everybody in this comfortable and authentic popular Old Town hostelry, a short way from the castle. There is a full range of seafood, game, meat and vegetarian dishes on the bistro menu, including Scottish old favourites such as Cullen skink and haggis. More traditional pub food is on offer downstairs in the Doric Bar which oozes with atmosphere.

The Shore Bar & Restaurant
3 Shore, Leith EH6 6QW
Tel: 0131 553 5080
Overlooking the Water of Leith and close to the port, this is a great place to come for good Scottish seafood. There is a friendly bar for pre-dinner drinks and a cosy dining room to eat in. Not just an evening venue, the Shore Bar serves a good range of sandwiches at lunchtime.

FIFE & STIRLING
Clachan Inn
2 Main Street, Drymen, Loch Lomond
G63 OBG. Tel: 01360 660824
The Clachan Inn is reported by some to be the oldest alehouse in Scotland, with a license dating to 1734. Many walkers use this inn as a pit stop as they make their way along the West Highland Way.

Cross Keys Hotel
Main Street, Kippen FK8 3DN
Tel: 01786 870293
Kippen is a small village in the Fintry Hills, some ten miles (16km) west of Stirling and just off the A811. Close by, lovely Burnside Wood is managed by people from a local community group, and is perfect for walking and nature trails. This friendly pub, dating from 1703, on the high street offers excellent home-made food, including a creamy smoked haddock omelette, and steak and mushroom pie. Beers include Harviestoun Bitter & Twisted. Children are welcome, and dogs are allowed here too.

The Settle Inn
91 St Mary's Wynd, Stirling
Tel: 01786 474609
Licensed from the 1600s, this atmospheric inn is in a great position near to Stirling Castle and happens to be the oldest alehouse in Stirling. The Settle is a traditional Scottish inn serving a wide range of real ales.

The Ship Inn
The Toft, Elie KY9 1DT
Tel: 01333 330246
Elie is a perfect place to stop in the East Neuk villages. On the busy waterfront at Elie Bay, The Ship has been here since 1838. Activities such as beach cricket, live music and summer Sunday barbecues all add to the friendly, relaxed atmosphere. The full menu makes the most of good local suppliers, including fish from St Monans and traditionally made haggis from nearby Lundin Links. The wide range of beers served here include Bellhaven Best, and the wine list is also extensive if even a little eclectic. Children and dogs are both made welcome here.

TROSSACHS & SOUTH
Lade Inn
Kilmahog FK17 8HD
Tel: 01877 330152
Set in its own grounds on the Leny Estate west of Callander, this white-painted free house was built as a tea room in the 1930s and first licensed three decades later. The cosy bar has a welcoming open fire decorated by a collection of brasses, and the non-smoking restaurant offers real Scottish cooking. Expect Lade Inn sausages with Arran mustard; baked cod with herb and garlic curst; and baked field mushrooms with pine kernels and smoked Lochaber cheese.

Monachyle Mhor
FK19 8PQ. On A84, 11 miles (18km) north of Callander. Tel: 01877 384622; www.monachylemhorcom
This small, award-winning farmhouse hotel has dramatic loch and mountain views and Rob Roy's resting place is not far away. The interiors are resplendent with open fires, antique furniture and sporting prints mixed with original modern art. Excellent menus change daily and reflect the seaons, with ingredients coming from the hotel's own organic garden, as well as the rivers, lochs and hills of the Trossachs. There are several golf courses nearby, or you can just enjoy the views with tea and scones on the lawn.

Moulin Hotel
11–13 Kirkmead Road, Moulin,
Pitlochry PH16 5EW
Tel: 01796 472196
Moulin's summer courtyard and garden, and winter log fires and pub games make it popular with walkers, tourists and locals all year round. There is a choice of real ales from its own micro-brewery, and the Gaelic fare on a lengthy all-day menu are a big plus.

ARGYLL, MULL & WEST
Cairnbaan Hotel & Restaurant
Cairnbaan, by Lochgilphead PA31 8SJ
Tel: 01546 603668
At this former 18th-century coaching inn, lighter meals are served in the lounge bar and conservatory, with lots of seafood but other choices too, such as chicken stuffed with haggis. Situated at lock 5, almost half-way along the Crinan canal, the hotel was built in the late 18th century, when the canal itself was also being constructed.

Craignure Inn
Isle of Mull PA65 6AY
Tel: 01680 812305
The present bar makes good use of the original stables at this former drovers' inn. The inn has a great atmosphere and regularly features live music from folk bands to jigs and reels to blues. The bar menu has many traditional dishes and some special local delicacies such as Mull cheddar and smoked trout.

Crinan Hotel
Crinan, Argyll & Bute PA31 8SR
Tel: 01546 830261; www.crinanhotel.com
The hotel is set by the little harbour, basin and lock at the end of the Crinan Canal, and offers the choice of the bar or restaurant. In both the seafood is excellent, offering such delights as a warm tart of local scallops with smoked bacon and juicy sun-dried tomatoes, or perhaps West Coast mackerel.

CAIRNGORMS & CENTRAL
The Old Bridge Inn
Dalfaber Road, Aviemore, Highland
PH22 1PU. Tel: 01479 810270
A cosy, friendly Highland pub overlooking the River Spey, with an attractive riverside garden as a bonus for high summer. Bar meals include lamb chops with redcurrant jelly, Aberdeen Angus steaks, or perhaps chicken breast marinated in lime, yoghurt and coriander. There's also a large selection of malt whiskies to sample.

Tipsy Laird
68 High Street, Kingussie, Highland
PH21 1HZ. Tel: 01540 661334;
www.thetipsylaird.co.uk
If you want to try something really tasty then look out for the venison burgers. Other equally appetising choices include freshly prepared soup, and sandwiches or grilled panini on the light lunch menu. This is a popular walkers' and outdoor enthusiasts' pub so it can get quite busy at times. For those who want a rest as well as lunch and a pint there is hostel-style accommodation available.

SKYE & NORTH
Applecross Inn
Shore Street, Applecross, Highland
IV54 8LR. Tel: 01520 744262
Overlooking Skye and the Cuillins, this traditional white-painted inn standing on the shore of the remote and lovely Applecross peninsula is known for its imaginative menu. Local fish and game appear on the menu, but it's the seafood that is usually outstanding, from the simplest prawn tails with Marie-Rose dip, to king scallops cooked in garlic butter with lemon, herbs and crispy bacon. Puddings are tempting too, with fruit crumble or raspberry cranachan on the list.

Glenelg Inn
Glenelg IV40 8JR. From Shiel Bridge (A87) take unclassified road to Glenelg. Tel: 01599 5222273;
www.glenelg-inn.com
The inn is a conversion of the 200-year-old stables set in a large garden stretching down to the sea, with stunning views across the Sound of Sleat. Folk singers and musicians are frequent visitors to the bar. In addition to the cosy bar, there is a guests' private morning room and an atmospheric dining room. The menu offers traditional Scottish fare based on local produce, including plenty of fresh fish and seafood.

The Old Inn
Carbost, Isle of Skye IV47 8SR
Tel: 01478 640205
Stone walls and wooden floors characterise this former croft house, now a popular inn favoured by walkers and climbers. At one time rents from farming tenants were collected here. Nowadays the inn serves traditional and hearty Scottish food, such as sausage hotpot, haggis and neeps, and freshly caught baked salmon. The patio terrace overlooks Loch Hariport.

Moorings Hotel
Banavie, PH33 7LY. Tel: 01397 772797;
www.moorings-fortwilliam.co.uk
Situated right next to the tricky-to-navigate Neptunes Staircase set of locks on the Caledonian Canal, this is a modern hotel that serves excellent food and has a good selection of wine. Not only can you watch the comings and goings on the water, but you can enjoy views of Ben Nevis and also Aonach Mor from the upstairs rooms. Choices for dinner include Aberdeen Angus steak, but the specialities of the house are its fish dishes; Lochaber smoked and cured fish platter or seafood served in a paella style are just a few of the choices.

TEA ROOMS
EDINBURGH
Always Sunday

170 High Street, Edinburgh EH1 1QS

This lovely café offers a little bit of Sunday afternoon relaxation every day of the week. Sit and sip a fair-trade coffee or tuck into all-day deli dishes, share a pot of tea and munch on a slab of delicious home-made cake. A bright city place to have afternoon tea.

George Inter-Continental

19–21 George Street, Edinburgh EH2 2PB. Tel: 0131 225 1251

Afternoon tea is celebrated in refined elegance at this gracious New Town hotel, designed by Robert Adam. Pass through the marble-floored foyer and look up at the detailed plasterwork and fine chandeliers. The lobby lounge serves tea and snacks throughout the day. Choose from a traditional Highland tea, served from 3pm, with finger sandwiches and Dundee cake, or Georgian tea with champagne and millionaire's shortbread, or perhaps dip into gravadlax and Belgian waffles from the à la carte menu.

The Tea Room

158 Canongate, Royal Mile, Edinburgh EH8 8DD. Tel: 07771 501679; www.the-tea-room.info

This charming tea room is decorated with beautiful linen tablecloths and watercolours by local artists, and opens its doors daily for light lunches and delicious teas. Choose a traditional afternoon tea, or treat yourself to a cream tea, with home-baked scones and cakes. Come on a Thursday afternoon to have your tea leaves read.

FIFE & STIRLING
Kind Kyttock's Kitchen

Cross Wynd, Falkland KY15 7BE

If you're exploring in Fife, let the aroma of freshly baked scones and pancakes entice you to this comfortable, well-established tea room in the historic village of Falkland. The preserves and cakes are home-made, too, and a small selection is offered for sale. Soups, sandwiches, salads and sweets are also served at lunchtime.

TROSSACHS & SOUTH
The Gleneagles Hotel

Auchterarder, Perth & Kinross PH3 1NF Tel: 01764 662231; www.gleneagles.com

With an international reputation for high standards and its championship golf course, this grand hotel, close to the A9, is one of the finest in Scotland. It's main restaurant has a coveted four AA

rosettes, but if dining here seems a little over the top (or beyond your budget), why not treat yourself to an afternoon tea. Perhaps if the standard package with delicious cakes, sandwiches, pastries and scones isn't enough, try the champagne version or even sample a whisky-taster's tea! Reservations are essential if you want to come here at weekends.

Perthshire Visitor Centre

Bankfoot, Perth PH1 4EB

Tel: 01738 787696; www.macbeth.co.uk

Lying some 7 miles (11.3km) north of Perth on the A9, this busy centre is based around quality shopping. Stock up on Loch Fyne fresh salmon and oysters, Macsween's tasty, renowned haggis and locally made fruit wines before relaxing in the 120-seater restaurant, which serves a tempting combination of home baking and locally sourced produce.

The Watermill

Mill Street, Aberfeldy PH15 2BG

Tel: 01887 822896; www.aberfeldywatermill.com

This extensive complex now includes a bookshop, music shop and art gallery all in a converted watermill, infused with the aroma of freshly brewed coffee. Enjoy a fruit smoothie on the terrace, or a speciality coffee with your cake – all the products are locally sourced or organic where possible. And the old waterwheel is still used to power the lighting!

ARGYLL, MULL & WEST
The Coach House Coffee Shop

Loch Lomond Trading Co Ltd, Luss G83 8NN. Tel: 01436 860341; www.lochlomondtrading.com

Gaelic music, log fires and a kilted proprietor set the scene at this friendly coffee and gift shop in the pretty village of Luss, on Loch Lomond's western shore. The perfect spot for a light meal or tea stop, it offers home-made rolls and soup, and speciality fruit cake baked with ale and studded with crystallised ginger.

Kilcamb Lodge Hotel

Strontian, Highlands PH36 4HY

Tel: 01967 402257; www.kilcamblodge.co.uk

If you're looking for a place to stop on the Ardnamurchan Peninsula, then seek out this fabulous and friendly, 300 year-old stone-built hotel just outside the village of Strontian. Basic afternoon tea includes mouthwatering home-baked shortbread, possibly flavoured with hazelnuts or orange, while a full afternoon treat includes sandwiches, cake and scones with jam and cream. Here, the main restaurant has a great reputation, too.

Tchai-Ovna House of Tea

169 Deanston Drive, Glasgow G41 3LP

Tel: 0141 649 7258; www.tchaiovna.com

Tchai Ovna is an Eastern European inspired haven on a busy street in the bustling city of Glasgow. There are no cream cakes on offer here but the huge choice of teas range from realtively well-known tastes such as Darjeeling to unknown blends from Nepal. The emphasis is on the tea and the relaxing experience. As in Middle Eastern and European tea houses, you can buy healthy food snacks such as falafel and vegetarian delicacies to accompany your choice of brew.

The Willow Tea Rooms

217 Sauchiehall Street, Glasgow G2 3EX. Tel: 0141 332 0521; www.willowtearooms.co.uk

Above a jewellery shop, this is one of Kate Cranston's original tea rooms designed by famous Charles Rennie Mackintosh in 1903. Sip your tea or coffee and tuck into delicious cakes, sandwiches and scones in the elegant surroundings of the Room de Luxe, with its wall-panelling, stylish stained glass and distinctive silver chairs.

CAIRNGORMS & CENTRAL
Brodie Countryfare

Brodie, by Forres, Morayshire IV36 2TD

Tel: 01309 641555; www.brodiecountryfare.com

On the A96 close to Brodie Castle, this busy shopping complex offers a food hall and good delicatessen full of rich aromas. Only the best local ingredients are served up in the restaurant, whether it's freshly baked scones with your cup of tea or a more substantial meal.

The Clootie Dumpling

Speyside Heather Garden & Visitor Centre, Skye of Curr, Dulnain Bridge, Highland PH26 3PA

Tel: 01479 851359; www.heathercentre.com

Tea, coffee, sandwiches, speciality soups and other traditional home-made foods are available all day – but the highlight has got to be the Clootie Dumpling, which is served in 21 different ways.

Culloden Visitor Centre

Culloden Moor, Inverness, Highland IV2 5EU. Tel: 01463 790607

This is a great place to stop and refuel when you have been out on the moor, especially if the weather is inclement. The lovely café/restaurant here serves light lunches and snacks, including vegetable soups complimented by freshly baked cheese scones.

The Victorian Station Coffee Shop

Station Square, Ballater AB35 5QB

Tel: 07840 745313

Walk where Queen Victoria once walked and visit the special waiting room built especially for the Queen's use. Then complete your day's visit to the handsomely restored Old Royal Station by tucking into some home-baking at this excellent café, with its good Italian-style coffees. Freshly made food includes soups, toasties and paninis.

SKYE & NORTH
The Ceilidh Place

14 West Argyle Street, Ullapool, Highland IV26 2TY. Tel: 01854 612103

An Ullapool institution since it opened in 1970, this unique complex combines several different places to sit back and relax: an all-day coffee shop, a bar and a restaurant with a bookshop, art gallery and performance venue. For cake-lovers, freshly baked cakes are part of the appeal of the all-day menu, but for something more substantial you might try the fennel, courgette and tomato gratin, or perhaps a dish of locally caught fish. For good weather days you can eat outside and dogs are permitted in the garden.

Inverlochy Castle Hotel

Torlundy, by Fort William, Highland PH33 6SN. Tel: 01397 702177; www.inverlochycastlehotel.com

For a memorable Scottish afternoon tea with a stunning backdrop of a loch and high mountains, it would be hard to beat this luxurious castle hotel just north of Fort William. There's a wide variety of teas on offer to accompany the tempting array of scones, cakes, pastries and biscuits, served in the majestic Great Hall or the stunning drawing room which overlooks the loch.

Loch Torridon Country House Hotel

Torridon, Highland IV22 2EY

Tel: 01445 791242; www.lochtorridonhotel

How do you fancy a high tea in every sense of the word? Using all the polished silverware and the very best china, pots of tea or coffee freshly brewed to accompany the delicately cut cucumber sandwiches, fluffy light scones with scrumptious fruit jam and spoonfuls of thick cream and calorific home-made cakes – but all taken on the top of a mountain, and led by a mountain guide? This is one of the most unusual options available at this delightful Highland hotel situated on the shore of Loch Torridon. You can have all this at sea level too, or opt for coffee and fresh shortbread and enjoy the views.

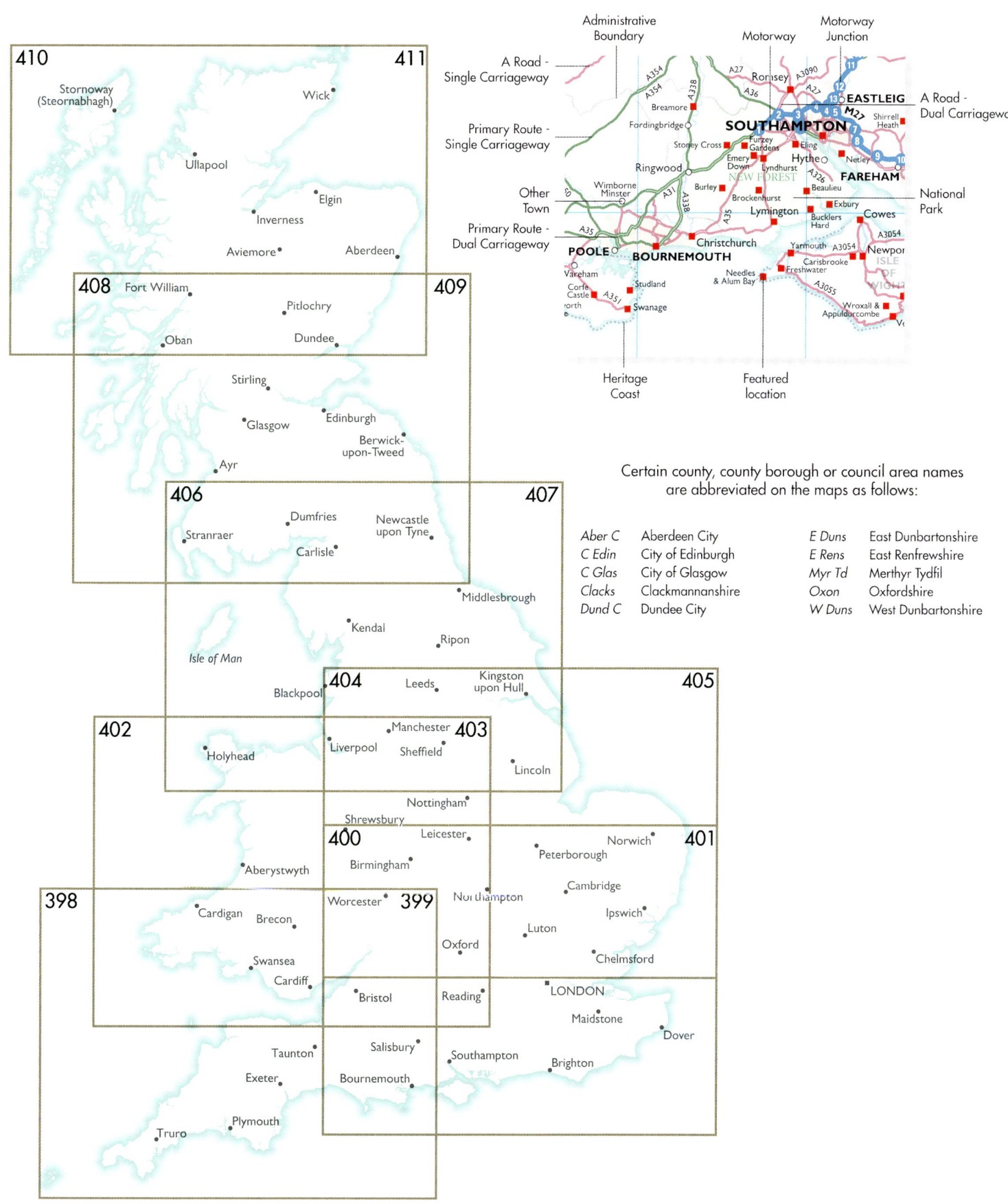

Administrative Boundary

Motorway

Motorway Junction

A Road - Single Carriageway

A Road - Dual Carriageway

Primary Route - Single Carriageway

Other Town

National Park

Primary Route - Dual Carriageway

Heritage Coast

Featured location

Certain county, county borough or council area names are abbreviated on the maps as follows:

Aber C	Aberdeen City	E Duns	East Dunbartonshire
C Edin	City of Edinburgh	E Rens	East Renfrewshire
C Glas	City of Glasgow	Myr Td	Merthyr Tydfil
Clacks	Clackmannanshire	Oxon	Oxfordshire
Dund C	Dundee City	W Duns	West Dunbartonshire

Scale of mapping pages 398 - 411   1:1,000,000

0   20   40   60   80   100 kilometres

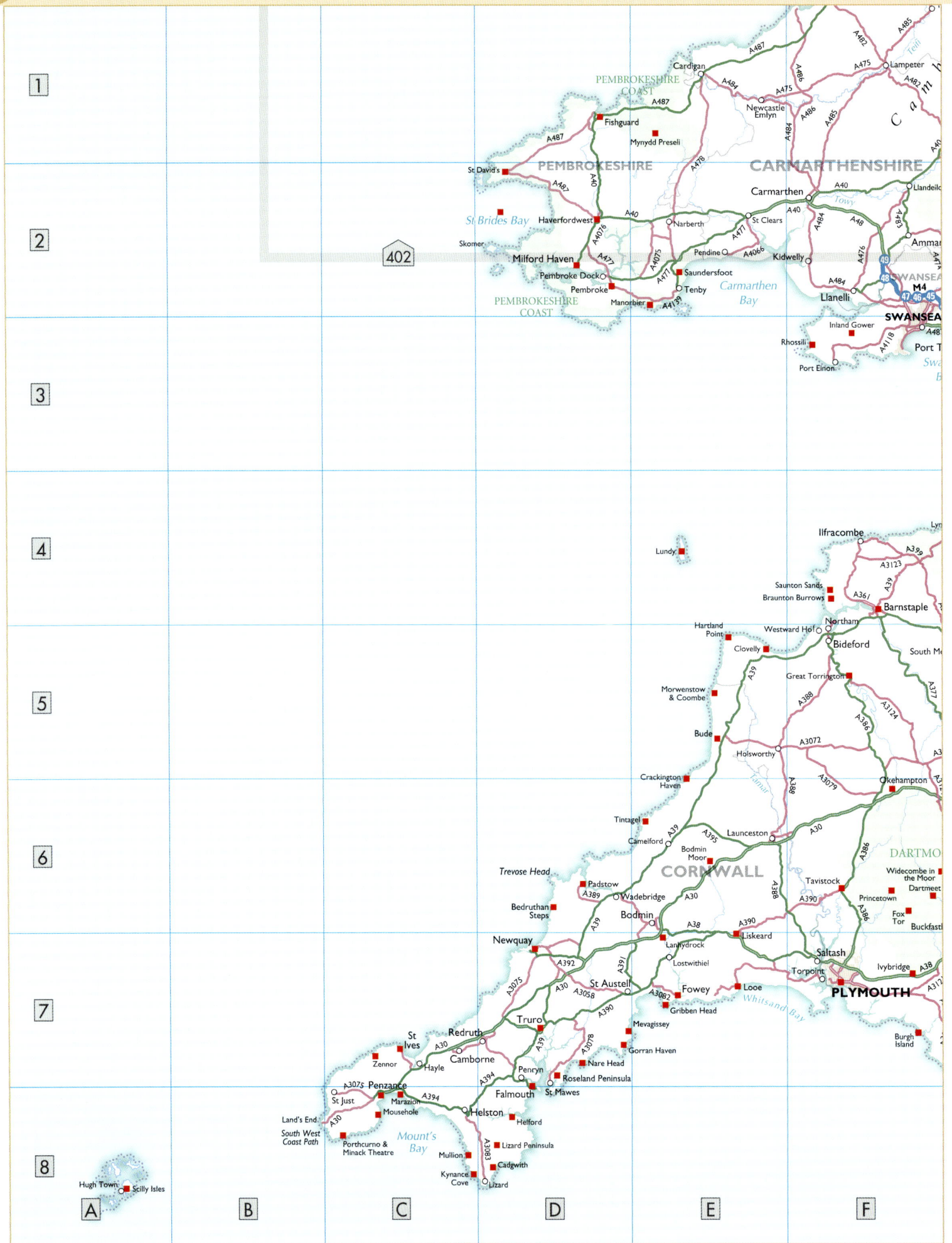

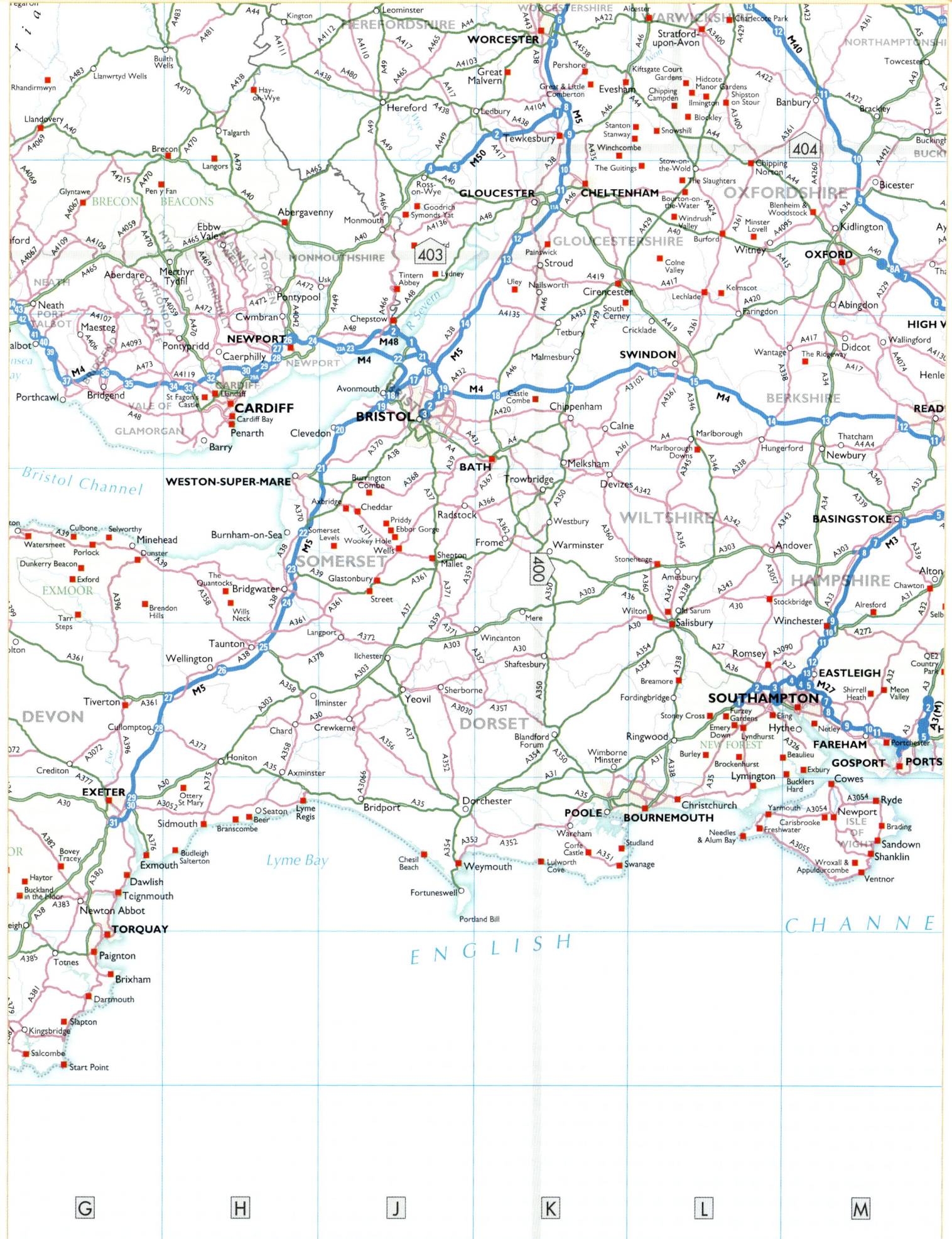

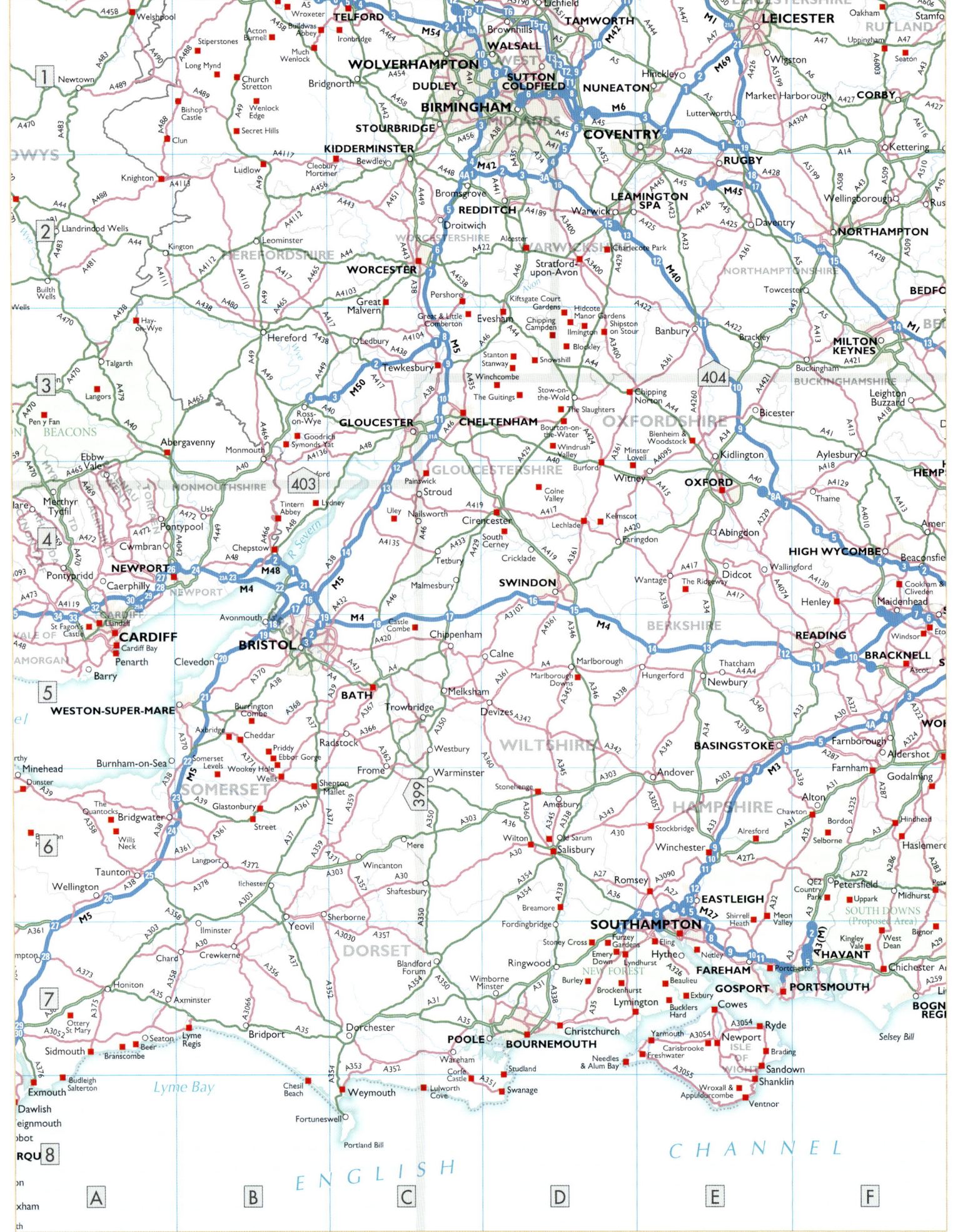

G H J K L M

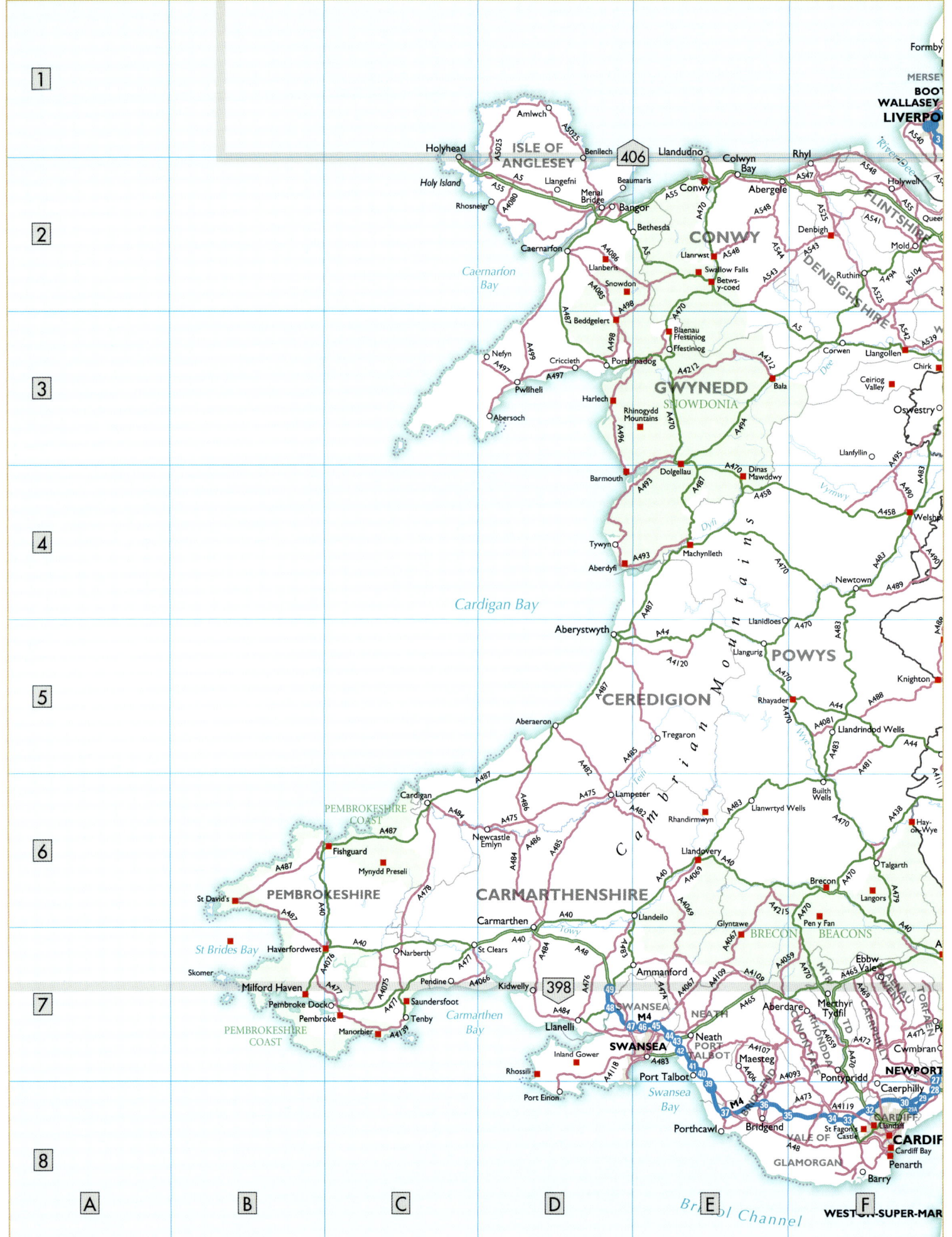

1

2

3

4

5

6

7

8

A   B   C   D   E   F

Formby

MERSEY

BOOT
WALLASEY
LIVERPOOL

River Dee

Holyhead
Amlwch
ISLE OF
ANGLESEY
Benllech
Llandudno
Colwyn
Bay
Rhyl
A5025
406
A548
A5048

Holy Island
Llangefni
Beaumaris
Menai
Bridge
Bangor
Conwy
Abergele
A55
A548
A544
A525
Holywell
Denbigh
Mold
FLINTSHIRE
Queen
Rhosneigr
A55
A5
A55
A5
A541
A5104

Bethesda
CONWY
A548
A543
Ruthin
DENBIGHSHIRE
A49A
A542
A539

Caernarfon
A4086
Llanrwst
Snowdon
Llanberis
Swallow Falls
Betws-
y-coed
A5
A543
A5
W
A4085
A498
A470
Corwen
Llangollen
Chirk
A5

Beddgelert
A487
A498
Blaenau
Ffestiniog
Ffestiniog
A4212
Bala
Ceiriog
Valley
Oswestry

Nefyn
Criccieth
Porthmadog
GWYNEDD
SNOWDONIA
A4212
Dee
A494
Llanfyllin
A495
A483
A499
A497
Pwllheli
A497
Harlech
Rhinogydd
Mountains
A496
Dolgellau
A470
Dinas
Mawddwy
Vyrnwy

Abersoch
A493
A487
A458
A458
A490
Welshp
Barmouth
Dyfi
A483
A470

Tywyn
A493
Machynlleth
A470
Newtown
A489
Aberdyfi

Cardigan Bay
A487
Llanidloes
A470
A483
POWYS
Aberystwyth
A44
Llangurig
Knighton
A4120
A470
A44
A488
CEREDIGION
Rhayader
A470
A4081
Llandrindod Wells
A44

Aberaeron
A482
Tregaron
Cambrian Mountains
A483
A481
Builth
Wells
A485
A487
Teifi
Wye
A470
A482
A483
A438
A487
Lampeter
A475
Llanwrtyd Wells
Hay-
on-Wye
Cardigan
PEMBROKESHIRE
COAST
A484
A475
A486
Rhandirmwyn
A487
Newcastle
Emlyn
A484
A486
A485
Llandovery
A40
Talgarth
A487
Fishguard
A478
CARMARTHENSHIRE
A40
A483
A470
A40
Brecon
A479
Mynydd Preseli
A40
A4069
Langors

St David's
A487
A40
Carmarthen
A40
Llandeilo
A4215
A470
BRECON
BEACONS
A483
Pen y Fan
A40
Glyntawe
A4067
A483
St Brides Bay
Haverfordwest
A4076
A40
St Clears
A484
A48
PEMBROKESHIRE
A477
Narberth
A477
Ebbw
Vale
A465
A469
Skomer
A4075
A4066
Pendine
Ammanford
A4109
A4109
A470
MYR
CAEN
Milford Haven
A477
Kidwelly
398
A476
49
A474
A4067
Aberdare
Merthyr
Tydfil
A472
Pembroke Dock
Saundersfoot
48
SWANSEA
NEATH
A465
TORFA
Pembroke
Tenby
47
46
45
Neath
PORT
TALBOT
A4107
RHONDDA
Cwmbran
Manorbier
A4139
Carmarthen
Bay
Llanelli
43
42
Maesteg
A4063
Pontypridd
NEWPORT
Inland Gower
A483
41
44
A406
A4093
Caerphilly
27
Rhossili
A4118
Port Talbot
40
39
M4
Bridgend
A473
A4119
CARDIFF
28
29
Swansea Bay
37
36
35
34
33
32
23A
Porthcawl
Bridgend
VALE OF
St Fagans
Castle
Llandaff
Cardiff Bay
Port Einon
38
GLAMORGAN
Penarth

Bristol Channel
Barry
WESTON-SUPER-MAR

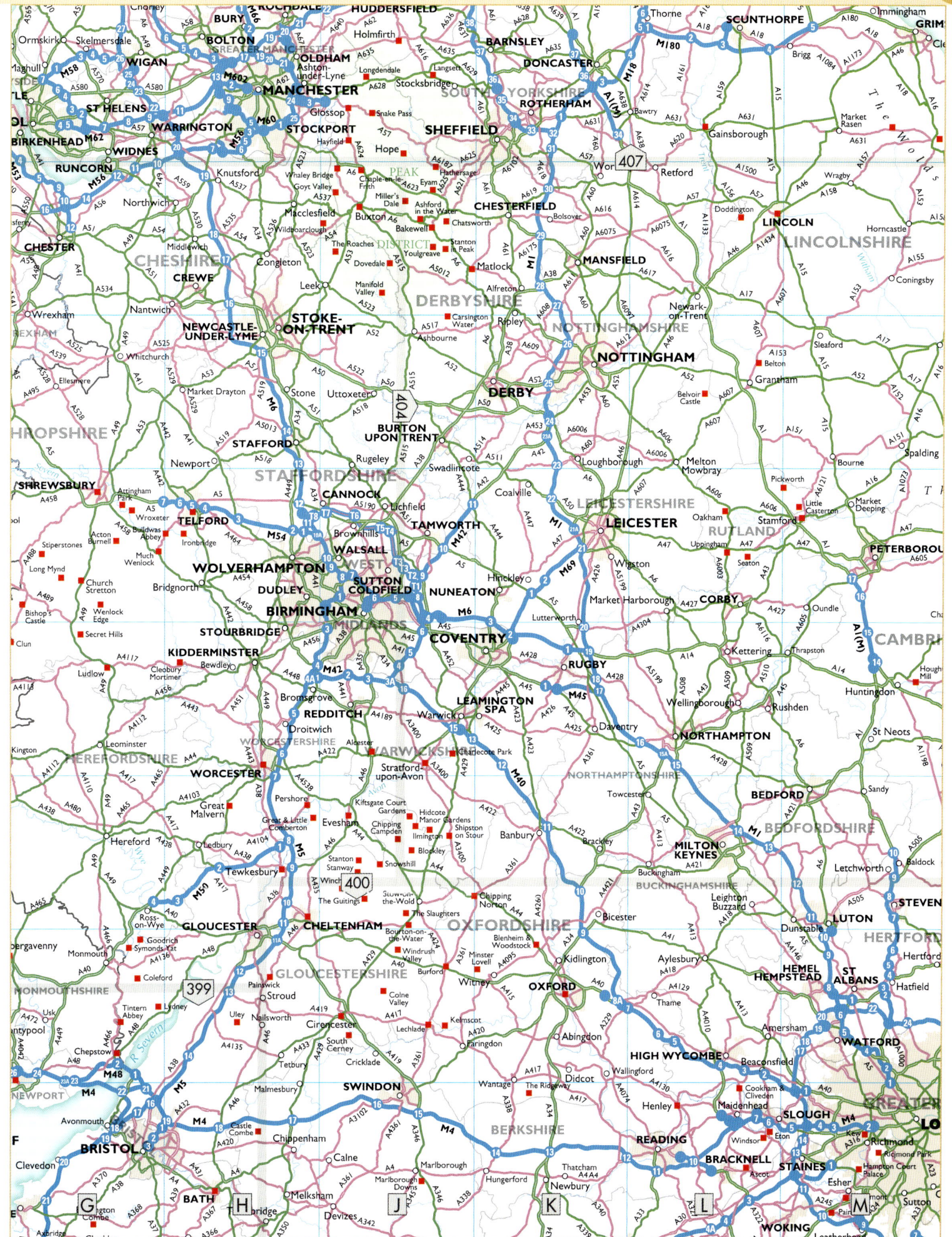

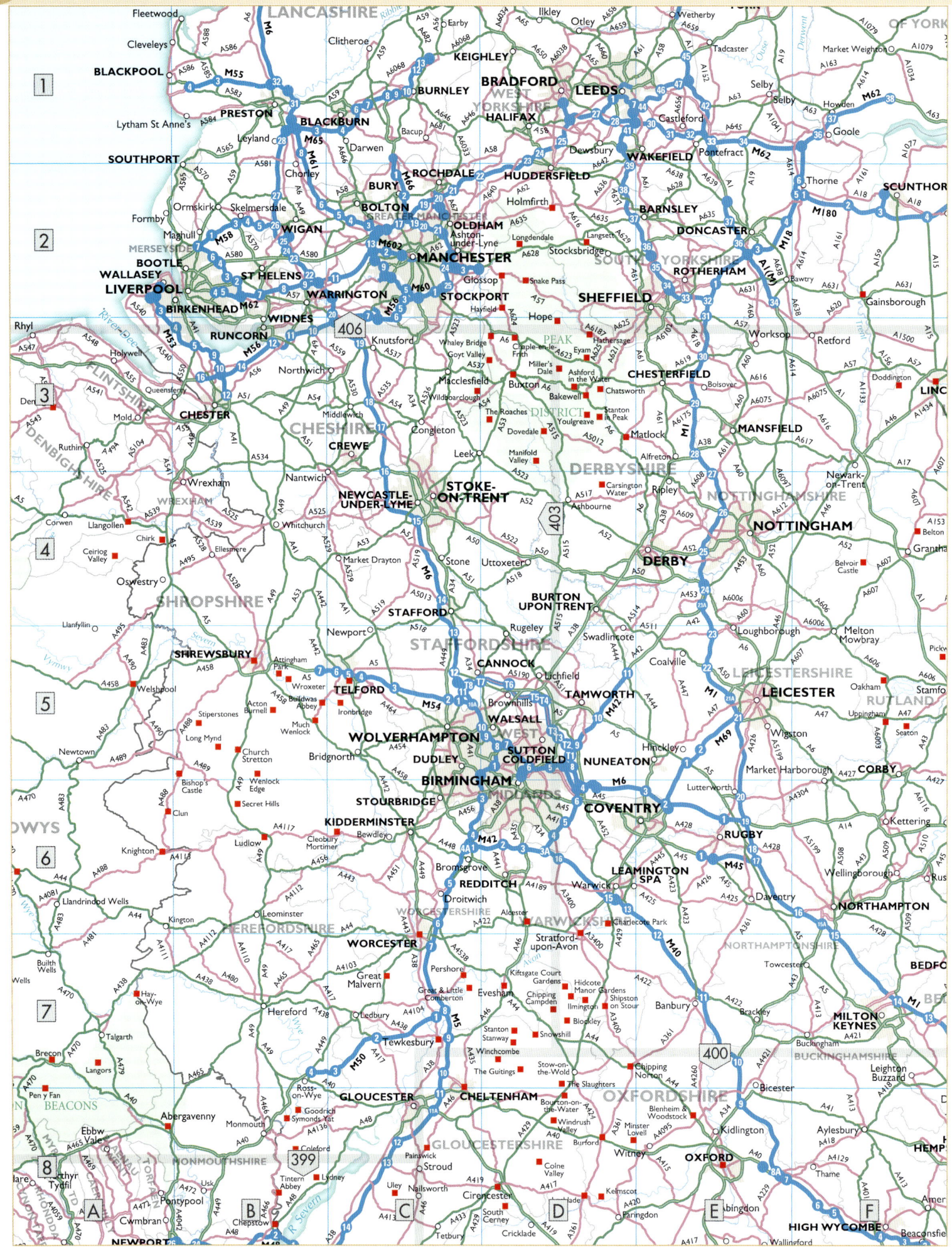

Hornsea
Beverley
KINGSTON UPON HULL
Withernsea
A1033
R Humber
Immingham
GRIMSBY
Cleethorpes
Brigg
Market Rasen
Louth
Mablethorpe
Wragby
LINCOLNSHIRE
Alford
Well
Horncastle
Skegness
Sleaford
Boston
Coningsby

The Wash
Hunstanton
Wells-next-the-sea
Sheringham
Cromer
Holt
North Walsham
Fakenham
Aylsham
Stalham
Potter Heigham
Holbeach
King's Lynn
Wroxham
Ranworth
Acle
Norfolk Broads
Caister-on-Sea
Spalding
Bourne
The Fens
Wisbech
Dereham
NORFOLK
NORWICH
GREAT YARMOUTH
Little Casterton
Market Deeping
Swaffham
Watton
Wymondham
THE BROADS
Somerleyton
LOWESTOFT
PETERBOROUGH
March
Downham Market
Attleborough
Bungay
Beccles
Oundle
Thrapston
Chatteris
Littleport
Thetford
Diss
Harleston
Halesworth
Southwold
Walberswick
CAMBRIDGESHIRE
Ely
Mildenhall
Eye
Blythburgh
Dunwich
Houghton Mill
Huntingdon
Wicken Fen
Saxmundham
Thorpeness
St Neots
Anglesey Abbey
Newmarket
Bury St Edmunds
Framlingham
Aldeburgh
Sandy
CAMBRIDGE
Grantchester
Wandlebury
Stowmarket
Wickham Market
Woodbridge
Orford
Sutton Hoo
SUFFOLK
IPSWICH
Haverhill
Sudbury
Hadleigh
Royston
Saffron Walden
Letchworth
Baldock
Halstead
Felixstowe
Harwich
STEVENAGE
Bishop's Stortford
Great Dunmow
Braintree
COLCHESTER
LUTON
HERTFORDSHIRE
Hertford
Witham
Maldon
ESSEX
CLACTON-ON-SEA
Frinton-on-Sea
HEMEL HEMSTEAD
ST ALBANS
Hatfield
HARLOW
CHELMSFORD
Epping
Chipping Ongar
Billericay
Burnham-on-Crouch
WATFORD
BRENTWOOD
Rayleigh

G   H   J   K   L   M

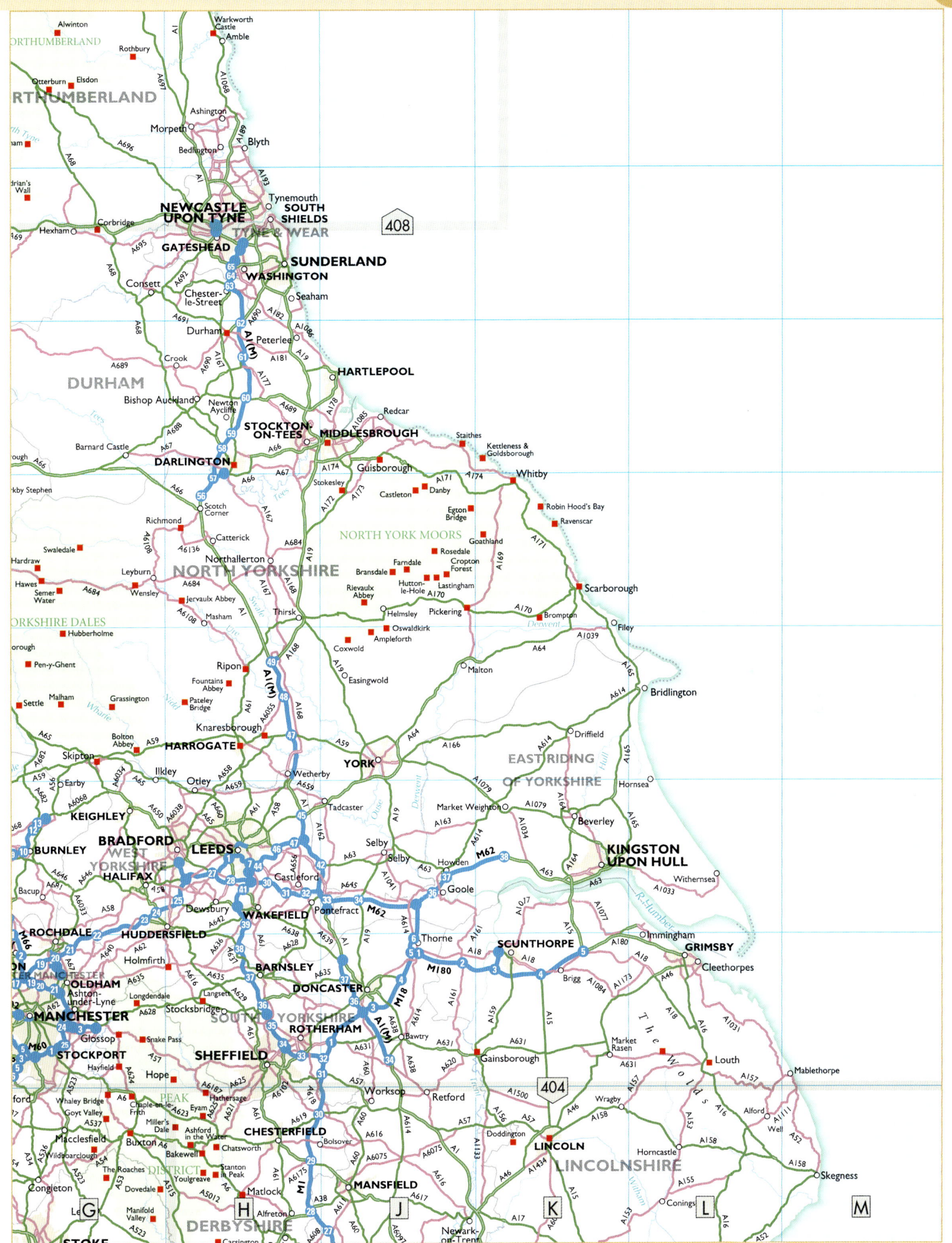

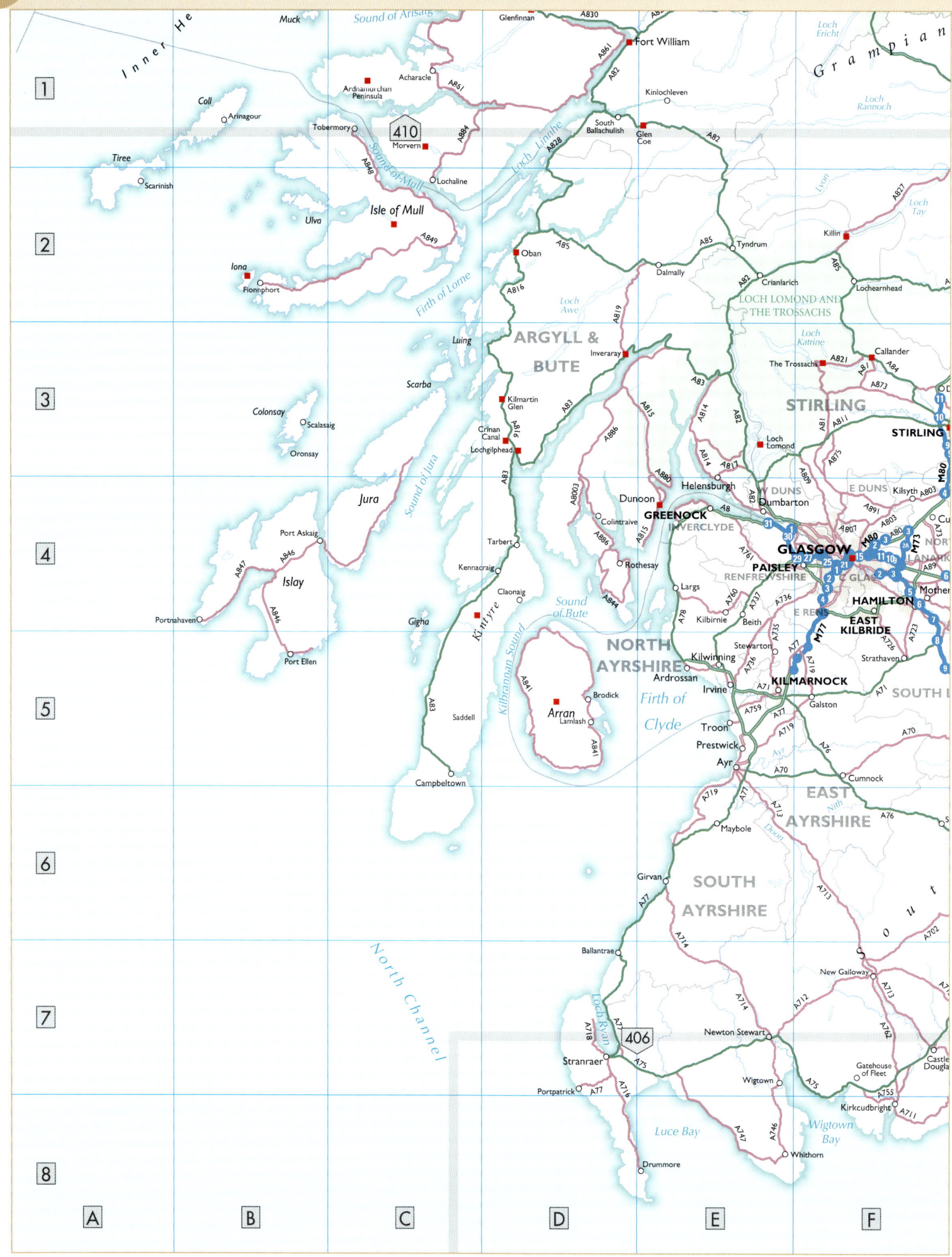

A   B   C   D   E   F

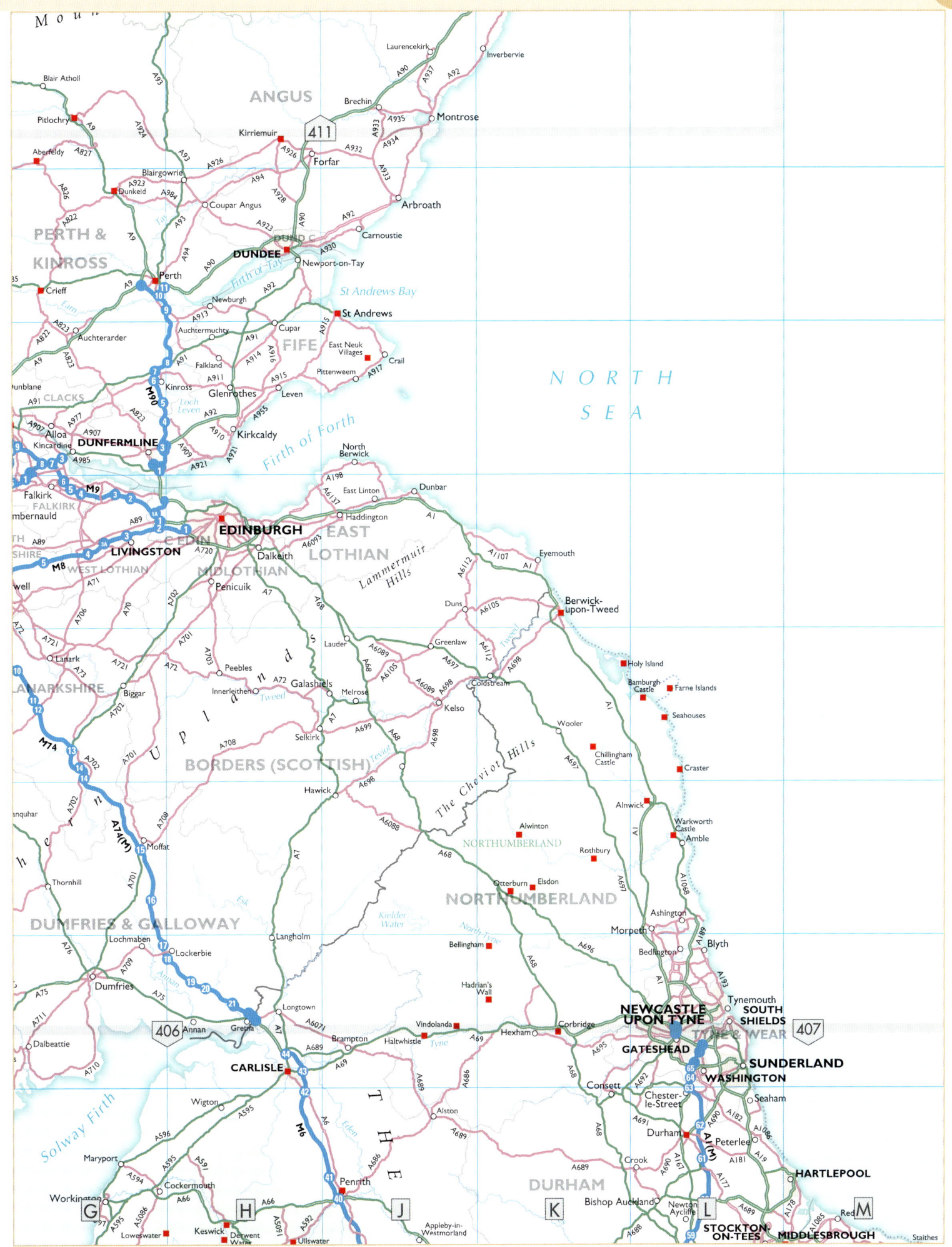

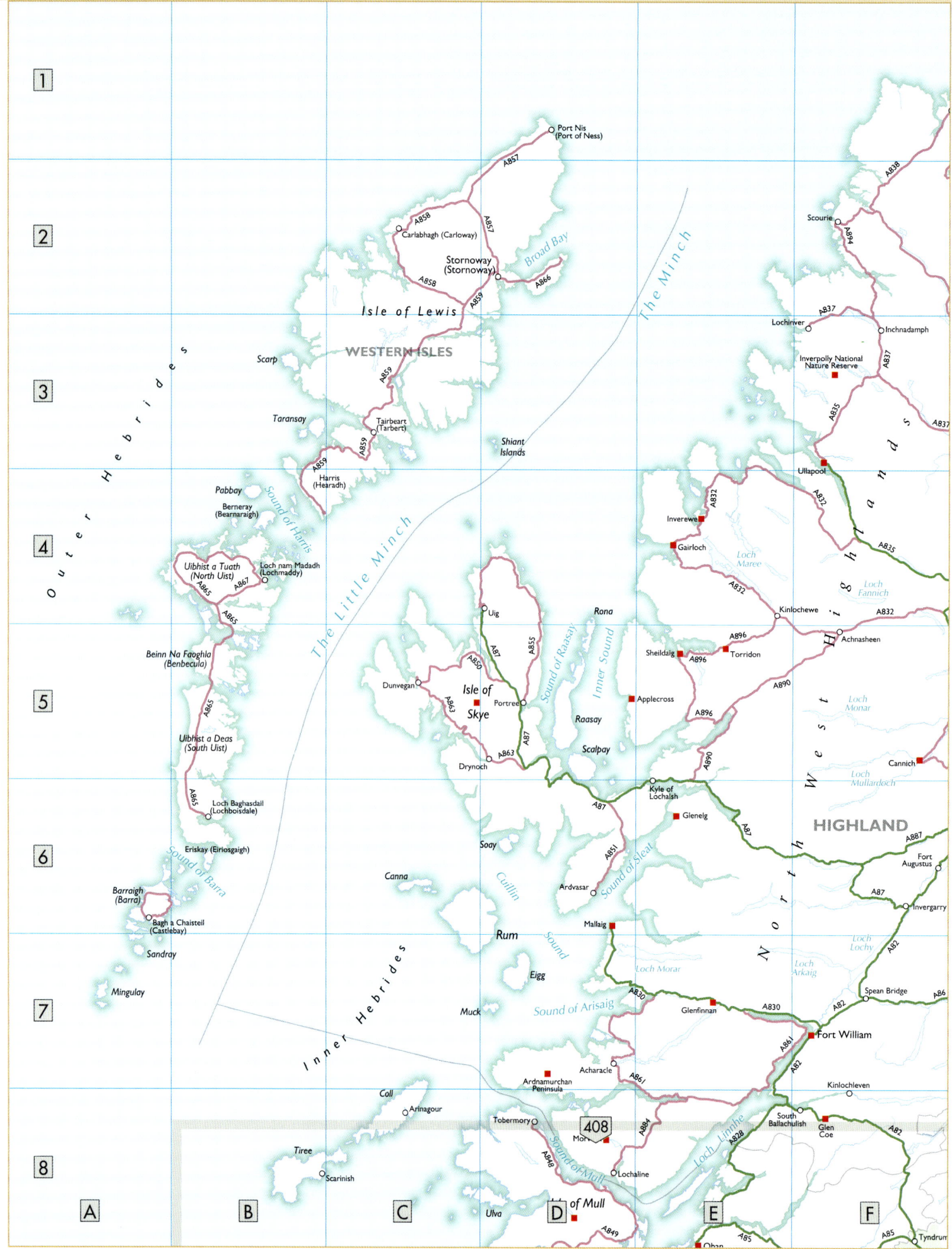

Port Nis
(Port of Ness)

A857

Scourie

A894

A838

Carlabhagh (Carloway)

A858

A857

Stornoway
(Stornoway)

Broad Bay

The Minch

Lochinver

Inchnadamph

A837

A858

A859

A866

A837

Isle of Lewis

Inverpolly National
Nature Reserve

WESTERN ISLES

Outer Hebrides

Scarp

A859

Taransay

*Shiant
Islands*

A835

A837

Tairbeart
(Tarbert)

A859

A859

Ullapool

*Harris
(Hearadh)*

A859

Inverewe

A832

Pabbay

*Berneray
(Bearnaraigh)*

Sound of Harris

Gairloch

*Loch
Maree*

H i g h l a n d s

A835

*Uibhist a Tuath
(North Uist)*

Loch nam Madadh
(Lochmaddy)

A832

*Loch
Fannich*

A867

A865

The Little Minch

Kinlochewe

A832

Uig

Rona

A896

Achnasheen

*Beinn Na Faoghla
(Benbecula)*

A865

A850

A87

A855

Sound of Raasay

Sheildaig

A896

Torridon

A896

Inner Sound

Dunvegan

A863

*Isle of
Skye*

Portree

Applecross

A890

*Loch
Monar*

A865

*Uibhist a Deas
(South Uist)*

A87

Raasay

Scalpay

A896

North   West

A865

A863

Drynoch

Cannich

Loch Baghasdail
(Lochboisdale)

A890

*Loch
Mullardoch*

Kyle of
Lochalsh

HIGHLAND

Eriskay (Eiriosgaigh)

Sound of Barra

A87

Glenelg

A87

A887

Soay

*Barraigh
(Barra)*

A851

Fort
Augustus

Bagh a Chaisteil
(Castlebay)

Cuillin

Ardvasar

Sound of Sleat

A87

Invergarry

Sandray

Mallaig

*Loch
Lochy*

A82

Mingulay

Inner Hebrides

Rum

Sound

Eigg

Loch Morar

*Loch
Arkaig*

Spean Bridge

A6

A830

Muck

Sound of Arisaig

Glenfinnan

A830

A82

A861

Fort William

Acharacle

A82

Kinlochleven

Coll

Ardnamurchan
Peninsula

A861

Arinagour

South
Ballachulish

Glen
Coe

A82

Tobermory

408

A884

Tiree

Scarinish

of Mull

Sound of Mull

Loch Linnhe

A828

Lochaline

A848

A849

Ulva

Oban

A85

Tyndrum

A85

Durness

A838 Bettyhill Melvich A836 Thurso Scrabster John o' Groats

Tongue

Loch Loyal

A836 A838

Altnaharra

Loch Naver

A897

A9

A836

A838

Loch Shin

Lairg

A839 A839

Bonar Bridge

A816

A836

A949

Dornoch

Golspie A9 Brora

Tain

A9

Cairron

Alness

Invergordon

Cromarty

Cromarty Firth

A862

A834 A832

Strathpeffer

Dingwall

Black Isle

Fortrose

Muir of Ord

A831

A862 A861

Culloden

Inverness

A831

Drumnadrochit

A833

A82

A82

Loch Ness

Invermoriston

Monadhliath Mountains

Pentland Firth

Island of Stroma

South Ronaldsay

A961

A836

A9

Thurso

A99

A882

Wick

A9

A9

A99

Lybster

Dunbeath

A9

Helmsdale

Moray Firth

Lossiemouth

Buckie A942 Cullen Portsoy

A941

Elgin A96

A98

Banff

Aberchirder

A95 A97

Turriff

Fraserburgh

A98

A981

A90

A981 A950

A952

Peterhead

Nairn

A96

A939

A940

Forres

A941

Rothes

Keith

A96

Spey

Aberlour

Speyside

A95

A939

Grantown-on-Spey

A938

Carrbridge A95

Boat of Garten

Aviemore

Kingussie

Newtonmore

A86

Spey

A889

A9

Loch Laggan

Loch Ericht

Dufftown A920 Huntly

A941

A95

A96

A944

Kildrummy Castle

A939

A97

A944

A97

A93

ABERDEENSHIRE

CAIRNGORMS

Braemar

River Dee

Grampian Mountains

Blair Atholl

Loch Rannoch

Pitlochry A9

Aberfeldy A827

Lyon

A827

Loch Tay

Killin

A97

A947

A920 Ellon

A95 A97

A97

Oldmeldrum

Inverurie

Alford

A980

A944

Kintore

A96

Dyce

ABE C

ABERDEEN

A93 A980

Aboyne

Ballater

Banchory

Muick

A93

A944

Don

Dee

A957

Stonehaven

Laurencekirk

A90 A937 A92

Inverbervie

ANGUS

Brechin

Kirriemuir

Forfar

A926

A938

A924

A9

A93

Blairgowrie

A923

Dunkeld

A984

A826

A822

Coupar Angus

PERTH &

DUND C

A926

A932

A933 A935

Montrose

A934

A933

A94

A928

A90

A923

K

A92

Carnoustie

A930

Arbroath

Kirriemuir

A75

A90

A981

A948

Ellon

A975

A90

Stonehaven

G H J K L M

The Automobile Association would like to thank the following photographers and companies for their assistance in the preparation of this book.
Abbreviations for the picture credits are as follows: (AA) AA World Travel Library; (t) top; (b) bottom; (c) centre; (l) left; (r) right

1 AA/J Miller; 3 AA/A Mockford & N Bonetti; 4 AA/J Smith; 6 AA/A Burton; 7 AA/A Burton; 8 AA/J Miller; 9 AA/J Wood; 11cl AA/J Wood; 11cc AA/J Wood; 11cr AA/J Wood; 11b AA/J Wood; 12 AA/J Wood; 13 AA/J Wood; 14 AA/J Wood; 15 AA/J Wood; 16 AA/C Jones; 19 AA/C Jones; 20 Ben Foster/Eden Project; 21cl AA/J Wood; 21c AA/J Wood; 21r Simon Burt/apexnewspix.com; 21b R Moltmaker/Eden Project; 22 AA/C Jones; 23 AA/J Wood; 24 AA/J Wood; 25 AA/J Wood; 31tc AA/N Hicks; 31tr AA/C Jones; 31cr AA/N Hicks; 31cl AA/N Hicks; 31cc AA/N Hicks; 31b AA/N Hicks; 32 AA/C Jones; 33 AA/N Hicks; 34 AA/N Hicks; 35tl AA/N Hicks; 35tr AA/N Hicks; 36 AA/C Jones; 37 AA/N Hicks; 38 AA/N Hicks; 43tc AA/N Hicks; 43tr AA/N Hicks; 43c AA/N Hicks; 43b AA; 44 AA/N Hicks; 45 AA/N Hicks; 46 AA/C Jones; 51tr AA/N Hicks; 51cl AA/J Tims; 51c AA/J Tims; 51cr AA/N Hicks; 51b AA/N Hicks; 52 AA/N Hicks; 53l AA/J Tims; 53tr AA/J Tims; 53cr AA/J Tims; 54 AA/N Hicks; 58tr AA/J Tims; 58cl AA/J Tims; 58cr AA/J Tims; 59 AA/J Tims; 60 AA/J Tims; 61 AA/J Tims; 63tr AA/M Jourdan; 63cl AA/N Hicks; 63cr AA/M Jourdan; 63b AA/A Burton; 64 AA/A Burton; 65 AA/M Jourdan; 66 AA/A Burton; 69tc AA/E Meacher; 69r AA/J Tims; 69cl AA/J Tims; 69cc AA/J Tims; 70t AA/J Tims; 70b AA/E Meacher; 71tr AA/D Hall; 71cr AA/D Hall; 71cl AA/H Palmer; 71cc AA/D Hall; 71b AA/D Hall; 72 AA/S Day; 73 AA/D Hall; 74 AA/H Palmer; 75 AA/D Hall; 76 AA/D Hall; 78 AA/D Hall; 85l AA/H Williams; 85r AA/A J Hopkins; 86 AA/I Burgum; 87l AA/S Day; 87r AA/C Jones; 88 AA/C Jones; 95 AA/J Tims; 97tr AA/D Forss; 97c AA/A Burton; 97b AA/A Burton; 98 AA/A Burton; 99 AA/A Burton; 100 AA/A Burton; 101 AA/A Burton; 105cl AA/W Voysey; 105cr AA/T Souter; 105cl AA/S & O Mathews; 105b AA/A Burton; 106 AA/A Burton; 107 AA/S McBride; 108 AA/A Burton; 110 onEdition; 111tl onEdition; 111tc onEdition; 111tr onEdition; 111c onEdition; 111br onEdition; 113tc AA/M Moody; 113tr AA/M Moody; 113cl AA/S Day; 113cr AA/M Moody; 113b AA/M Moody; 114 AA/M Moody; 115 AA/S Day; 116 AA/M Moody; 119tr AA/J Miller; 119cl AA/J Tims; 119c AA/J Tims; 119cr AA/J Tims; 120 AA/J Tims; 122tr AA/M Moody; 122cl AA/J Miller; 122cr AA/J Miller; 122b AA/J Miller; 123 AA/J Miller; 124 AA/J Miller; 125 AA/J Miller; 126 AA/J Miller; 132tc AA/J Miller; 132r AA/A Burton; 132cl AA/J Miller; 132cc AA/J Miller; 135t AA/J Tims; 135cl AA/J Tims; 135cc AA/N Setchfield; 135r AA/N Setchfield; 136 AA/J Tims; 137 AA/R Turpin; 138 AA/N Setchfield; 140t AA/M Jourdan; 140c AA/M Jourdan; 141 AA/N Setchfield; 142 AA/R Victor; 143 AA/M Jourdan; 144 AA/N Setchfield; 145 AA/S McBride; 146 AA/M Moody; 147 AA/N Setchfield; 148 AA/N Setchfield; 150 Jon Arnold Images/Alamy; 151t Getty Images; 151b Robert Harding Picture Library Ltd/Alamy; 153tc AA/M Birkitt; 153tr AA/P Baker; 153cr AA/M Busselle; 154 AA/M Birkitt; 157tr AA/Bob Johnson; 157c AA/D Hall; 157cr AA/C Jones; 158 AA/C Jones; 167 AA/T Mackie; 169tr AA/T Mackie; 169cl AA/T Mackie; 169bl AA/T Mackie; 170 AA/T Mackie; 171 AA/T Mackie; 172 AA/T Mackie; 173 AA/T Mackie; 176tc AA/C Coe; 176tr AA/T Mackie; 176c AA/C Coe; 177 AA/T Mackie; 179tc AA/T Mackie; 179tr AA/A Baker; 179c AA/T Mackie; 179b AA/T Mackie; 180 AA/C Coe; 181 AA/R Ireland; 182 AA/T Mackie; 184t AA/T Mackie; 184c AA/T Mackie; 185c AA/T Mackie; 185br AA/A J Hopkins; 186 AA/M Birkitt; 187 AA/M Birkitt; 189t AA/M Moody; 189c AA/M Moody; 189b AA/M Moody; 190 AA/M Moody; 193tc AA/M Moody; 193tr AA/D Hall; 193c AA/M Moody; 194 AA/M Moody; 196tc AA/C Jones; 196tr AA/M Hayward; 196c AA/C Jones; 197 AA/M Hayward; 198 AA/J Welsh; 199tl Ironbridge Gorge Museums; 199tr Ironbridge Gorge Museums; 199c Ironbridge Gorge Museums; 201tc AA/M Short; 201tr AA/R Surman; 201c AA/M Hayward; 202 AA/C Jones; 203 AA/M Hayward; 206tc AA/N Jenkins; 206tr AA/N Jenkins; 206c AA/I Burgum; 206b AA/C & A Molyneux; 209tc AA/T Mackie; 209tr AA/T Mackie; 209c AA/T Mackie; 209b AA/T Mackie; 211 AA/T Mackie; 212 AA/T Mackie; 213 AA/T Mackie; 214 AA/T Mackie; 215 AA/T Mackie; 216 AA/T Mackie; 222tl AA/T Mackie; 222tr AA/M Birkitt; 222bl AA/T Mackie; 222br AA/T Mackie; 223 AA/T Mackie; 231 AA/M Moody; 233cl AA/I Burgum; 233cr AA/N Jenkins; 234 Billy Stock/PhotolibraryWales; 235 Jeff Tucker/PhotolibraryWales; 236tcl AA/M Moody; 236cl AA/M Moody; 236b AA/M Moody; 236r AA/M Moody; 237 AA/R Ireland; 238 AA/N Jenkins; 239 AA/I Burgum; 240 AA/M Moody; 245 AA/W Voysey; 246tc AA/S Watkins; 246tr AA/S Watkins; 246cr AA/S Watkins; 246bl AA/G Munday; 247 AA/N Jenkins; 248 AA/C Jones; 249 AA/G Matthews; 250 AA/N Jenkins; 256tr AA/C & A Molyneux; 256cl AA/C & A Molyneux; 256c AA/N Jenkins; 256b AA/N Jenkins; 257 AA/N Jenkins; 258 AA/N Jenkins; 259 AA/N Jenkins; 260tl Centre for Alternative Technology; 260cl Nick Turner/Centre for Alternative Technology; 260bl Centre for Alternative Technology; 261tr Centre for Alternative Technology; 261br Centre for Alternative Technology; 262 AA; 271 AA/T Mackie; 273tr AA/A Mockford & N Bonetti; 273cr AA/A Mockford & N Bonetti; 273bl AA/A Mockford & N Bonetti; 274 AA/A Mockford & N Bonetti; 275 AA/A Mockford & N Bonetti; 276 AA/A Mockford & N Bonetti; 277 AA/T Mackie; 278 AA/T Mackie; 279 AA/A Mockford & N Bonetti; 280 AA/A Mockford & N Bonetti; 289cl AA/M Kipling; 289c AA/M Kipling; 289cr AA/M Kipling; 289bl AA/M Kipling; 290 AA/M Kipling; 291 AA/M Kipling; 292cl AA/M Kipling; 292bl AA/M Kipling; 292c/r AA/M Kipling; 293 AA/M Kipling; 294 AA/M Kipling; 295 AA/M Kipling; 304tc AA/T Mackie; 304tr AA/T Mackie; 304c AA/T Mackie; 304bl AA/T Mackie; 305 AA/T Mackie; 307 AA/T Mackie; 308 AA/T Mackie; 309 AA/T Mackie; 314 AA; 315tl AA/T Mackie; 315cl AA/J Freeman; 315br AA/J Freeman; 316 AA/T Mackie; 317 AA/T Mackie; 322tr AA/R Coulam; 322cr AA/R Coulam; 322bl AA/R Coulam; 323 AA/R Coulam; 324 AA/R Coulam; 325 AA/R Coulam; 326 AA/R Coulam; 327 AA/Cameron Lees; 328 AA/R Coulam; 329tl Forestry Commission; 329tr Forestry Commission; 329cl Kielder Water Birds of Prey Centre; 329cr Forestry Commission; 330 AA/R Coulam; 343 AA/Sue Anderson; 345tc AA/J Smith; 345tr AA/J Smith; 345cl AA/J Smith; 345cr AA/J Smith; 346bl AA/K Paterson; 346c/r AA/J Smith; 347 AA/R Elliot; 348tr AA/J Smith; 348cl AA/Michael Taylor; 348cr AA/S Day; 349 AA/S Whitehorne; 352tc AA/K Paterson; 352tr AA/J Smith; 352c AA/S Anderson; 353 AA/J Smith; 354 AA/J Smith; 355 AA/S Day; 356tl Pete Cairns/Nature Picture Library; 356cl AA/S Day; 356bl AA/H Williams; 356br Laurie Campbell; 357tr Laurie Campbell; 357tc Pete Cairns/Nature Picture Library; 357br AA/S Anderson; 362tc AA/S Whitehorne; 362tr AA/R Elliot; 362c AA/S Anderson; 362b AA/D Hardley; 363 AA/K Paterson; 364 AA/S Whitehorne; 365 AA/S Whitehorne; 366 AA/S Anderson; 367 AA/S Anderson; 371t AA/J Smith; 371c AA/J Smith; 371cr AA/J Smith; 371b AA/S Anderson; 372 AA/J Smith; 373 AA/J Smith; 375 AA/S Anderson; 376 AA/J Smith; 377 Scottish Viewpoint/Alamy; 378t Charlie Phillips; 378cr AA/M Moody; 382tc AA/S Anderson; 382tr AA/S Whitehorne; 382c AA/S Whitehorne; 383 AA/J Carnie; 384 AA/J Carnie; 385 AA/S Whitehorne; 386 AA/J Smith; 387 AA/S Whitehorne

Every effort has been made to trace the copyright holders, and we apologise in advance for any unintentional errors.
We would be pleased to apply any corrections in any future edition of this publication.